PROCEEDINGS OF
THE THIRD INTERNATIONAL CONFERENCE ON CREATIONISM
HELD JULY 18 - 23, 1994

PITTSBURGH, PENNSYLVANIA
USA

TECHNICAL SYMPOSIUM SESSIONS

Edited by
Robert E. Walsh

Sponsored by
CREATION SCIENCE FELLOWSHIP, INC.

362 ASHLAND AVENUE
PITTSBURGH, PA 15228
USA

Library of Congress Catalog Card Number: 95-069254

ISBN Cloth: 0-9617068-7-2

Printed in the U.S.A.

Library of Congress Publication Data

International Conference on Creationism (3rd: 1994: Pittsburgh, PA)
    Proceedings of the Third International Conference on Creationism:
Held July 18 - 23, 1994, Pittsburgh, Pennsylvania, U.S.A. / Robert E. Walsh, editor

    "Sponsored by Creation Science Fellowship, Inc."

    Includes bibliographies.

    1. Creationism--Congresses   I. Walsh, Robert E., 1954-.
    II. Creation Science Fellowship, Inc. (Pittsburgh, PA, USA)   V. Title

ISBN 0-9617068-7-2 (Cloth)

TABLE OF CONTENTS

PREFACE

The Third International Conference on Creationism (ICC) represents a departure from previous ICCs. Whereas the first two Conferences ('86 & '90) were devoted to the theme *The Age of the Earth*, the Third ICC was devoted to the *Developing and Systematizing of the Creation Model of Origins*. The ICC is the only gathering in Creationism today for the sole purpose of rigorously developing a Biblical/rational view of earth and universal history. It provides an arena for creation researchers to gather with the expressed purpose of furthering our understanding of the Creator's work. Because the ICCs present a rare opportunity for creation researchers to formally and informally discuss ideas, a wealth of excitement has been generated about this forum.

The peer review process for the Third ICC was distinct from past ICCs. As outlined in the ICC Call for Papers, the prospective authors were required to submit to the Technical Review Committee (TRC) a 500 word summary, detailing the intended paper and its topic. The responsibility of the TRC was to rigorously evaluate each summary and determine if that topic was appropriate for submission into the ICC peer review process. The preliminary evaluation was based on the specific category of the summary and the following criteria:

> (1) Is this topic important to the development of the creation model? (2) Does this topic provide an original contribution to the creation model? (3) Is this topic formulated within a young-earth, young-universe framework? (4) If #3 is not satisfied, does this topic offer a (positive and constructive)[1] criticism, with a possible young-earth, young-universe alternative? (5) If this topic is polemical in nature, does it deal with a new topic rarely discussed within the origins debate? (6) Does this summary provide evidence of faithfulness to the grammatico-historical/normative interpretation of Scripture?

Upon completion of this initial screening, each participant was notified as to the standing of their submission(s). Upon acceptance each summary was categorized into a specific area(s) of concern. The TRC designed these areas to provide a listing of categories most needing research within the creation model and offered prospective authors a mechanism for focus. Each area had a specific ICC Editor responsible for working with the prospective author to improve his/her paper for final approval into the ICC. These areas and their associated ICC Editors were:

(1)	Philosophy of Science	-	Paul A. Nelson, M.S.
(2)	Life Sciences	-	Wayne Frair, Ph.D.
(3)	Astro-Sciences	-	Donald B. DeYoung, Ph.D.
(4)	Social Sciences and The Humanities	-	Paul D. Ackerman, Ph.D.
(5)	Earth Sciences	-	Steven A. Austin, Ph.D.
		-	Kurt P. Wise, Ph.D.

These editors are to be congratulated for their untiring efforts in helping the prospective authors improve upon their initial submissions and provide the best possible development of the paper's theme. The Board of Directors of CSF and the ICC Technical Review Committee wish to thank these men for their hard work and burning of the midnight oil in bringing about the best in each author's work and the most productive ICC to date.

The Technical Review Committee provided the ICC Editors criteria by which to evaluate each paper. These criteria were:

> (1) Does this paper make an original contribution to the creation model? (2) Is this paper well-documented with respect to the relevant literature? (3) Does this paper consider alternative explanations? (4) Does this paper demonstrate an awareness of its own limitations? (5) Does this paper provide a basis for further research in its area? (6) Does this paper exhibit sound methodology? (7) Does this paper demonstrate proper use of materials and equipment? (8) Does this paper properly present sufficient data to address its stated aims? (9) Does this paper properly interpret its data? (10) Does this paper properly develop its mathematical models (if applicable)? (11) Does this paper appropriate apply mathematical models to its important examples? (12) Is this paper tightly and coherently reasoned? (13) Is this paper faithful to the grammatico-historical/normative interpretation of Scripture?

Upon the reception of the paper's first draft its ICC Editor and author worked together to formulate a coherent articulation of the paper's topic. If after this "working" period the paper was not finally accepted, the author was provided with additional positive criticism and encouraged to continue working on the paper, either to be submitted elsewhere, or continue working until the Fourth ICC to be held in 1998.

The ICC Technical Review Committee would like to thank everyone who submitted papers to the Third ICC, whether finally accepted or not; your work is crucial to the furtherance of the creation model and we encourage all to continue and strive for excellence in this endeavor!

THE IMPORTANCE OF THE ICCs

No greater evidence of the importance of having such technical meetings can be seen than in the accounts of American physicist Richard Feynman's attendance at the many physics conferences early in his career. During the late 1940's and early 1950's some of the greatest theoretical physicists periodically gathered to discuss the formulation of quantum electrodynamics (QED). These meetings contained discussions (formal and informal) that helped formulate ideas and theories, bringing about a systematic view of QED. One such conference was the Shelter Island Conference.

> "... there was generated the idea of organizing several small conferences on the foundations of quantum mechanics. The aim was to make an evaluation of the current status of the fundamental problems, and to have serious and critical discussions among the best experts on current specific topics of interest.

> The first of these conferences took place on 2-4 June 1947 at Ram's Head Inn on Shelter Island, at the tip of Long Island, and the general theme of the conference was 'Problems of quantum mechanics and the electron'. This conference turned out to be a cornerstone in the development of quantum electrodynamics. As Feynman himself recalled later on: 'There have been many conferences in the world since, but I've never felt any to be as important as this... The Shelter Island Conference was my first conference with the big men... I had never gone to one like this one in peacetime". [2,p.215]

Continuing,

> "At first, Feynman's fundamental article (RMP, 1948) [3], did not arouse much interest among theoretical physicists, who were not familiar with Feynman's new approach to doing quantum mechanics. As Feynman recalled: 'At the Shelter Island Conference, a lot of exciting things were discussed and talked about." [2,p.200]

The ICCs provide a unique opportunity for creation researchers to discuss and develop the latest ideas within the discipline of creation. Creationists in the future must take greater advantage of such opportunities if the scientific modeling of creation origins is to ultimately develop into a rigorous discipline.

To this end the Creation Science Fellowship, Inc. continues to sponsor these very important meetings and by God's grace they will provide a solution to a fundamental need among creation scientists -- the need of discussion and personal interaction among researchers.

It is to the rigorous development and systemization of the creation model of origins that the Creation Science Fellowship, Inc., sponsors of the ICCs, dedicate this Volume as the written record of the Third International Conference on Creationism.

Robert E. Walsh
Proceedings Editor
Pittsburgh, PA USA
February, 1995

REFERENCES

[1]   This grammatical construction is an intentional figure of speech called, *Hendiadys*. It is formed when one item is intended, but being described with two elements; whereupon the second item becomes a *superlative* adjective of the first. Hence, this construction is to be understood as **very constructively positive**.

[2]   Mehra, Jagdish, **The Beat of a Different Drum**, Oxford University Press, New York, NY, 1994.

        This is a wonderful book outlining the "life and science" of Richard Feynman, arguably America's greatest theoretical physicist of the 20th century and quite a "safe-cracker". Dr. Feynman died on February 15, 1988.

[3]   Feynman, Richard, P., **Space-time approach to non-relativistic quantum mechanics**, Review Modern Physics, 20(2), 1948.

        This paper was essentially derived from his Ph.D. thesis at Princeton.

ACKNOWLEDGMENTS

On behalf of the Board of Directors of the Creation Science Fellowship, Inc. (CSF), I would like to thank everyone involved in making the Third International Conference on Creationism (ICC) a great success, the largest creation conference ever held and perhaps the most successful.

Special thanks must go to several people intricately involved with the day-to-day administration of this ICC, starting long before the conference itself.

They are Russ Bixler and Cornerstone Television for their continual support of this conference and encouragement over the years.

Dennis Wert, CSF Chairman, and the Wert family, whose phone, organization, and writing skills were immensely utilized.

Steve Rodabaugh, Technical Review Committee (TRC) Chairman, whose professional experience and expertise with the technical review process was invaluable. The TRC consisted of Dennis Blackburn, Lionel Dahmer, Robert Harsh, Don Schell, William Stillman, Robert Walsh, and Dennis Wert.

The ICC Editors were indispensable to the quality of the conference by reviewing and aiding the authors in producing the best possible papers. They were:

> Philosophy of Science, Paul A. Nelson
> Life Sciences, Wayne Frair
> Astro-sciences, Donald B. DeYoung
> Social Sciences and the Humanities, Paul D. Ackerman
> Earth Sciences, Steven A. Austin and Kurt P. Wise

Dennis Blackburn, CSF Treasurer and the coordinator's right-hand man, seeing that no detail was overlooked.

Tony Piccirilli, ICC Bookstore manager, again brought about a remarkable display and collection of some of the finest creation materials available.

Aaron Wharton of Riverside Video whose expertise in the video arts made a large contribution in the quality of the taping of each session.

On-site coordination would have been impossible without the help and volunteerism of a host of people willing to sacrifice time and effort. They are (forgive my memory):

Ginny Allison, Nancy Bernheisel, Susan Brophy, Chris Brooks, Sue Ellen Butler, Bill Curtis, Lionel Dahmer, Paul Daly, Mark Elfstrand, Carol Harsh, Julie Harsh, Jim Hilston, Mat Hopsecher, Hank Jackson, Sheila Jackson, Jack Klingman, Pat Klingman, Harry Lieb, Jack McCartney, Glen McDougal, Ralph McKelvy, Reid Moon, George Plaks, Steve Rape, Cathy Rodabaugh, Rachel Rodabaugh, Don Schell, Marty Schell, Terry Skogen, Bill Stillman, Marcia Thompson, Brandon Vallorani, Ray Vallorani, Bethel Wert, Dennis Wert, Pat Wert, Steve Wert, Aaron Wharton, Carol Wharton, Amy Wilson, and John Wilson.

I can only hope no one has been left out who devoted time and energy to make the Third International Conference on Creationism a success.

Thanks to everyone involved!

See you all in 1998!

Special congratulations go to Dr. Andrew Snelling in recognition of his work entitled, **Regional Metamorphism within a Creationist Framework: Garnet Composition**, receiving the ICC Best Technical Paper Award and presented to him on the final evening of the Conference.

Robert E. Walsh
1994 ICC Coordinator
February 1995

A SEARCH FOR RADIOCARBON IN COAL

GERALD E. AARDSMA, Ph.D.
Institute for Creation Research
10946 Woodside Avenue N.
Santee, California 92071

KEYWORDS: radiocarbon, Flood, coal, fossil carbon

ABSTRACT

The discovery of any measurable quantity of radiocarbon in fossil carbon deposits, such as coal, would have profound significance for geo-chronometry since, according to the conventional geological time scale, radiocarbon in such deposits should have become extinct long ago. Reports of measurable radiocarbon levels in such deposits have appeared within the creationist technical literature from time to time. However, in every case the work being reported on was done by non-creationist scientists who felt their results implied the presence of contamination by modern radiocarbon, not residual indigenous radiocarbon. Clearly, a specially designed creationist research program is required to settle this question.

Such a program was instituted at ICR several years ago. A large-volume liquid scintillation detector has been constructed to search for radiocarbon in fossil carbon. In this paper I describe this apparatus and discuss the results of measurements to the present time.

INTRODUCTION

It is of interest to search for indigenous radiocarbon in coal and other fossil carbon reservoirs because such a discovery would falsify all old-earth models for the formation of these deposits, and demonstrate that something is seriously wrong with the old-earth time scale. The old-earth model places the ages of these deposits in the millions of years range. Since the half-life of radiocarbon is only 5730 years, it is immediately apparent that, if the old-earth time frame is correct, these deposits should contain no indigenous radiocarbon whatsoever.

The recent-creation model, on the other hand, predicts the probable presence of radiocarbon in these deposits, albeit at very low levels. Based upon our (admittedly limited) understanding of the pre-Flood environment, it has been suggested that less than about one ^{14}C atom per 3×10^{15} carbon atoms should be found in these reservoirs [1]. (That is, a ^{14}C concentration below about 3×10^{-16} ^{14}C atoms/C atom is expected in these reservoirs.) This low level requires specialized apparatus to detect; the normal equipment found in most radiocarbon laboratories today is typically only able to detect radiocarbon down to a level of about one ^{14}C atom per 1×10^{15} carbon atoms at best (i.e., their sensitivity limit for ^{14}C detection is less than about 1×10^{-15} $^{14}C/C$).

The construction of a radiocarbon detector to make such low-level measurements is by no means easy or routine. Nonetheless, the significance of the discovery of indigenous radiocarbon in these deposits seems sufficient to justify the necessary cost and effort.

SPURIOUS CLAIMS

It is possible to find claims within the creationist literature to the effect that ^{14}C has already been found in abundance in fossil carbon materials such as coal. These claims are invariably found to be unsubstantial when investigated carefully. Unfortunately, such claims continue to enjoy wide circulation among lay creationists.

Several typical specimens of this sort can be found, for example, in the chapter on ^{14}C dating in the widely circulated lay volume entitled "The Answers Book" [5]. It cites the following two cases:

1

"Coal from Russia from the "Pennsylvanian," supposedly 300 million years old, was dated at 1,680 years.

Natural gas from Alabama and Mississippi (Cretaceous and Eocene, respectively) should have been 50 million to 135 million years old, yet C^{14} gave dates of 30,000 to 34,000 years, respectively."

Obviously, if these cases are valid, further expenditure of time and effort to measure radiocarbon in coal is unnecessary -- it has already been done! But, unfortunately, they are not valid.

Both cases seem to be drawn from Table 4 of a paper by Whitelaw [12] which appeared in *CRSQ* several decades ago, and one must go to that paper to obtain a complete reference in both cases. A brief look at the original reference [10] in the first case (Pennsylvanian coal from Russia) immediately reveals that the sample was not Pennsylvanian coal at all. This is evident first of all by the fact that it is part of a date list which is broken into three parts: "geologic samples", "archaeological samples", and "fossil animals". Clearly, Pennsylvanian coal would be listed as a geologic sample, but this sample of "coal" is listed as an archaeological sample.

Furthermore, the archaeologists involved with this sample felt that its A.D. date confirmed their view of the peopling of the region. Now, to be sure, some archaeologists have had trouble catching on to some of the subtleties inherent in radiocarbon dating, but none that I know of would suppose for a minute that they could date an archaeological site by radiocarbon analysis of a piece of coal found on the site. Obviously, if a piece of coal were to yield a date, that date would reflect upon the formation of the seam from which the coal came, not the date of the site where the coal was found.

In the original reference the sample is described as "scattered coals in a loamy rock in deposits of a 26-m [river] terrace". This *Radiocarbon* reference must originally have been translated from Russian and it is not unreasonable to suppose that there was some loss of descriptive clarity as a result. But it seems pretty clear that what is being described here is certainly not "Pennsylvanian coal". There is, in fact, no indication anywhere in the original reference that these samples were from the "Pennsylvanian", nor is there any hint that they were expected to be "300 million years old"; these appear to be purely apocryphal embellishments to the original account. Surely, what the Russians intended to convey (and what nearly everybody would understand), is that these samples were *charcoal* from a not too ancient campfire.

The original reference [9] in the second case (natural gas) immediately reveals that both Whitelaw and *The Answers Book* have, unfortunately, neglected several very important ">" (strictly greater than) signs. The "dates" in this case are given in the original publication as ">30,000" and ">34,000". Thus, these natural gas samples were not dated to "30,000 to 34,000 years" at all. In fact, the original reference plainly notes "infinite age as expected". Clearly, 30,000 to 34,000 years was the sensitivity limit of the apparatus which was used to measure the ^{14}C content of these samples (this corresponds to one ^{14}C atom per about 6×10^{13} carbon atoms, or a sensitivity of about 1.7×10^{-14} -- not at all unreasonable for ^{14}C detection apparatus at this early date); these numbers do not reflect measured actual ages for these natural gas samples.

To the best of my knowledge, no serious effort has been made to measure the actual ^{14}C content of any fossil carbon reservoir. The present experiment is, therefore, unique and necessary.

PREVIOUS STUDIES

There have been a number of radiocarbon measurements on samples of interest to us, particularly anthracite, within the (non-creationist) radiocarbon community. Interestingly, the results of these experiments do not paint a uniform picture. Some techniques seem to show an absence of ^{14}C in anthracite to extremely low levels, while others seem to show the presence of ^{14}C at only moderately low levels.

The rationale behind the use of anthracite in these labs was that, since anthracite is "known" to be millions of years old, it should provide a suitable material for background determination in the radiocarbon detection apparatus. In some instances the measured "background" was higher than expected, indicating the presence of ^{14}C in the anthracite itself or introduction of modern ^{14}C somehow during chemical preparation of the anthracite sample for dating. The researchers involved have generally concluded that anthracite must be subject to some kind of "contamination" problem.

In 1958 Haring *et al.* [6] used an isotope enrichment technique to measure an anthracite sample and found an upper limit for the ^{14}C concentration of about 1×10^{-16} $^{14}C/C$. This same technique was again applied to anthracite in 1978 by Grootes [3] who found an upper limit of 7.4×10^{-17} $^{14}C/C$. To my knowledge, this is the most sensitive measurement of ^{14}C in anthracite (or any other carbon-rich material) to date.

These results seem to conflict with more recent measurements using the accelerator mass spectrometry (AMS) experimental technique. For example, Schmidt *et al.* [8] reported finding ^{14}C in anthracite at levels greater than 1.5×10^{-15} $^{14}C/C$, Vogel *et al.* [11] reported finding 4.8×10^{-15} $^{14}C/C$, and Gurfinkel [4] reported values greater than or equal to 3.6x10^{-15} ^{14}C/C. Finally, in a recent paper, Lowe [7] stated that it is fairly common for AMS labs to find ^{14}C present in coal in the range of 2.0x10^{-15} to 4.5x10^{-14} ^{14}C/C.

As mentioned above, the presence of ^{14}C in coal well above the sensitivity limit of the AMS measurement apparatus was not anticipated. Lowe [7] has suggested that this may be due to contamination of coal by modern ^{14}C through microbial and fungal action in the coal substrates. If this is the case, it is curious that similar levels of contamination were not found in the anthracite used in the earlier isotope enrichment measurements. The isotope enrichment results seem to imply that modern contamination is being introduced during sample preparation for the AMS technique. It is perhaps noteworthy, along this line, that the AMS sample preparation procedure does seem considerably more elaborate and involved than is the case for isotope enrichment.

This line of thinking leads to the expectation that anthracite, at least, will probably not be found to contain indigenous ^{14}C at concentrations in excess of the limit imposed by Grootes' [3] result mentioned above (i.e., 7.4 x 10^{-17} ^{14}C/C). If this is correct, then the really interesting results will not be forthcoming until measurements with greater sensitivity than Grootes' can be made. This tall order is the ultimate goal of the ICR Radiocarbon Lab; it will probably take a number of years to achieve.

This ultimate goal should not, however, be felt to diminish the importance of the measurements at lower sensitivity which will be made along the way, such as the first results from our lab reported below. The fact that AMS measurements have repeatedly given finite ages for anthracite *is* mystifying and intriguing, especially when the researchers who made the measurements claim these results are not due to contamination introduced during sample preparation, but must be due to contamination in the anthracite itself (e.g., [4] page 342]. One wonders whether there might be something defective about the isotope enrichment method which causes it to overlook some ^{14}C, but it is difficult to see how such an oversight could arise. Another possibility is that the anthracite used in the different experiments came from different coal mines which, in fact, contain different indigenous ^{14}C concentrations. But it is difficult to imagine how coal seams having such different ^{14}C concentrations could arise.

Clearly, the matter of the possible presence of ^{14}C in fossil carbon deposits is far from settled. Whatever experimental light can be shed on this matter is of interest to creationists. As R. H. Brown [2] has recently pointed out, "These findings are of particular interest to individuals who are looking for models that relate the historical data in the Bible to modern scientific observations."

APPARATUS

There are three principal techniques employed for the detection of ^{14}C today. These are gas counters, liquid scintillation counters, and AMS. Of these three, liquid scintillation offers the largest sample volume, and it has the added advantage of relatively low cost. For our purpose of measuring the lowest possible ^{14}C concentration, it is of paramount importance to work with as large a volume of carbon as possible to maximize the number of ^{14}C atoms for detection. Thus, liquid scintillation is the obvious choice for our work. However, it is necessary to build our own liquid scintillation spectrometer, as instruments with the large volume we require for this research program cannot be obtained commercially.

For this ^{14}C detection method, the carbon sample to be dated is first converted to a liquid aromatic hydrocarbon such as benzene, C_6H_6, or toluene, C_7H_8. The ^{14}C atoms of the original sample are incorporated along with the stable ^{12}C and ^{13}C atoms of the original sample into these new benzene or toluene molecules. In this resultant sample liquid a relatively small quantity of fluorescent chemicals is dissolved. These chemicals function to convert ^{14}C decay energy into light photons. The mixture of sample liquid and dissolved fluorescent chemicals is called the "scintillation cocktail".

The flash of light which is produced whenever a ^{14}C atom decays within the scintillation cocktail is detected by photomultiplier tubes (PMTs) and converted to an electrical pulse. Generally two PMTs are used together. This permits noise pulses in the individual tubes to be discriminated against through coincidence detection. That is, only pulses which appear simultaneously within both PMTs are counted as signal; pulses arising individually within only one PMT at a time are rejected as noise.

Other sources of noise, or background pulses, within the apparatus are due to external and internal radiations. Any radiation (e.g. x-ray or γ-ray) from any source can produce scintillation pulses within the sample liquid which look the same as the pulses produced by a ^{14}C decay. These are principally due to the decay of radioactive substances in the materials of which the detector is constructed and in the materials external to the detector (e.g., concrete floor, plaster walls, etc.). For this reason, the entire apparatus is normally surrounded by lead to shield it from the external component of this chronic background radiation, and the detector itself is constructed, as much as possible, of materials known to be relatively free of radioactive atoms.

Energetic cosmic radiation is another chronic source of background pulses. Because of their high energy, cosmic rays are able to penetrate the lead shield surrounding the spectrometer. This cosmic component can be reduced by incorporating anti-coincidence detection of some type into the detector or by operating the apparatus deep underground.

The ICR detector is a large-volume liquid scintillation spectrometer. It is constructed of a teflon tube approximately 57 cm long, with a 3.8 cm bore. A 2 inch (5 cm) diameter PMT is mounted at each end of the teflon tube via o-ring seals. The teflon and PMTs are held together by spring pressure inside a slightly larger diameter copper pipe. The entire assembly is surrounded by 10 cm of lead. At the present time this apparatus is operated in an above-ground lab at ICR; no effort to suppress the cosmic ray background has yet been made.

A gold-plated, thin-walled, quartz tube is installed inside the teflon tube to act as a light reflector. The scintillation cocktail is loaded into the teflon tube through two small ports in the teflon.

The electrical pulses from the PMTs are processed for coincidence within the triggering circuitry of an HP 54501A digitizing oscilloscope. Coincident pulses are digitized and passed to a 286 Vectra computer for storage on magnetic tape. The digitized pulses are then transferred to a 486 computer and individually analyzed for pulse height using a least-squares fitting procedure, and summed (i.e., two tube total) pulse height spectra are generated.

METHOD

For the initial phase of this experimental program it is adequate to use commercially available toluene as our sample. Toluene is produced commercially from light oils from coke-oven gas and coal tar, and from petroleum. Thus, it is derived from the fossil carbon reservoirs which are of interest to recent-creationists. It is, of course, a disadvantage that the provenance of the commercial product is unknown. (It seems most likely that it represents a mixture from a variety of different sources, in fact.) However, there is a very great cost advantage with the commercial product which highly recommends it for at least the initial phases of this project. The sample which has been used in the present experiment is a toluene-based scintillation cocktail available from Aldrich (catalog number 32,712-3).

An unusual feature of the current experiment is the lack of a known infinite age sample for use in measuring the spectrometer background. We are, in effect, seeking to measure the ^{14}C concentration within what is normally regarded as the background sample. Thus, it is necessary to adopt the following measurement procedure.

First, a pulse height spectrum of the sample (commercial cocktail) containing the unknown ^{14}C concentration, $\{^{14}C\}$, is taken. This is called the "sample" spectrum. This spectrum contains N pulses after a counting livetime of T, or an overall measured "sample" activity of $A = N / T$.

Next, a known, relatively large, quantity of ^{14}C (the ^{14}C "spike") is added to this sample, giving it a total ^{14}C concentration of $^t\{^{14}C\}$. A second, "total" pulse height spectrum is collected. This spectrum contains ^tN pulses after a counting livetime of ^tT, or an activity of $^tA = {}^tN / {}^tT$.

The spectral shape for ^{14}C decay for our spectrometer is then determined by an appropriate subtraction of the "sample" activity spectrum from the "total" activity spectrum. The resulting difference spectrum is called the "spike" activity spectrum, as it is due entirely to the ^{14}C added in the spike. It will have an overall activity of ^sA.

Finally, the fraction, f, of the "spike" activity spectrum which will fit under the graph of the "sample" activity spectrum is determined. This fraction of the "spike" activity represents the maximum activity in the "sample" spectrum which can be attributed to ^{14}C. It is used to place an upper limit on the ^{14}C concentration in the sample by means of the following simple derivation.

We begin with the proportionality relation:

$$\{^{14}C\} / {}^\cdot A = {}^s\{^{14}C\} / {}^sA \qquad (1)$$

where $^\cdot A$ is the activity due to ^{14}C in the sample, and the remaining symbols are as defined in the text above. The maximum value for $^\cdot A$ is:

$$^\cdot A \le f \times {}^sA \qquad (2)$$

Combining these two equations gives:

$$\{^{14}C\} \le f \times {}^s\{^{14}C\} \qquad (3)$$

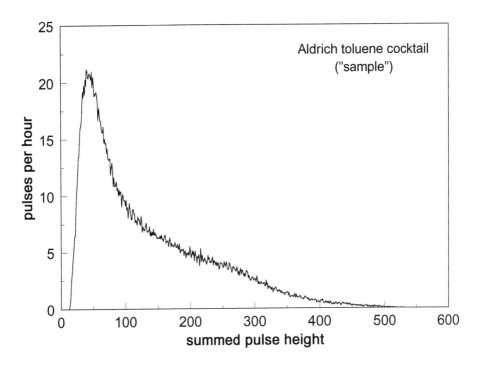

Figure 1: Pulse height spectrum from Aldrich toluene-based cocktail.

RESULTS

Figure 1 shows the activity spectrum for the Aldrich toluene-based cocktail; this is the "sample" spectrum. Figure 2 shows the ^{14}C spectral shape which was obtained for the "spike" by subtracting the figure 1 spectrum from the "total" spectrum (not shown). (Note that the spectral shape is appropriate for ^{14}C which is a β-emitter.) Finally, figure 3 shows the family of curves which result from subtraction of various fractions, f, of the figure 2 curve from the figure 1 curve.

It is apparent that the largest possible fraction which can be subtracted without leaving significant negative residuals is 0.06. This represents an absolute maximum for f. This can possibly be refined by observing that it seems reasonable, on theoretical grounds, to expect the spectral shape of the residual (true background) activity spectrum (figure 3) to decrease monotonically as one goes from smaller to larger pulse heights. Thus, a better upper limit for ^{14}C in this sample might be represented by the f = 0.03 curve.

The ^{14}C spike raised the ^{14}C concentration in the sample volume to $^{s}\{^{14}C\} = 5.3 \times 10^{-13}$ $^{14}C/C$. With this value for $^{s}\{^{14}C\}$, equation 3 above yields a maximum ^{14}C concentration in this sample (Aldrich cocktail) of 2.9×10^{-14} $^{14}C/C$ (for f = 0.06), and it seems probable that this concentration is, in fact, less than 1.5×10^{-14} $^{14}C/C$ (using f = 0.03).

CONCLUSION

The various claims and measurements of ^{14}C concentration in fossil carbon deposits which have been discussed in this paper, together with the present measurement, are summarized in figure 4. It must be stressed that our measured value is an upper limit only and does not yet represent proof of the existence of indigenous radiocarbon in fossil carbon deposits. It does, however, demonstrate the complete absence of ^{14}C in this sample in the 10^{-13} $^{14}C/C$ or higher range, in concert with the AMS and isotope enrichment results. Claims such as that found in Whitelaw/*The Answers Book* for "Pennsylvanian coal" are, as expected, not supported.

While it is evident that considerable work will need to be done before the sensitivity evidenced by Grootes' results can be attained, it is nonetheless pleasing that our sensitivity already permits measurements within the

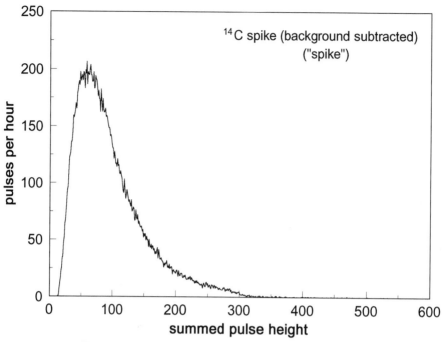

Figure 2: Pulse height spectrum from ^{14}C spike; background has been subtracted using the figure 1 spectrum.

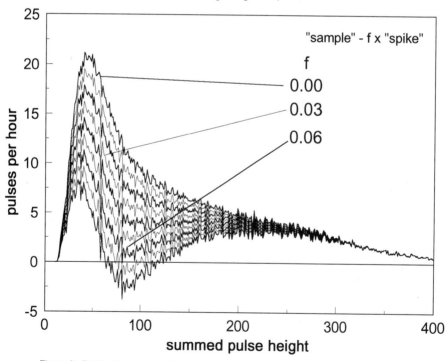

Figure 3: Residual spectra resulting from the subtraction of a fraction (from 0.0 to 0.7 in steps of 0.1) of the figure 2 spectrum from the figure 1 spectrum.

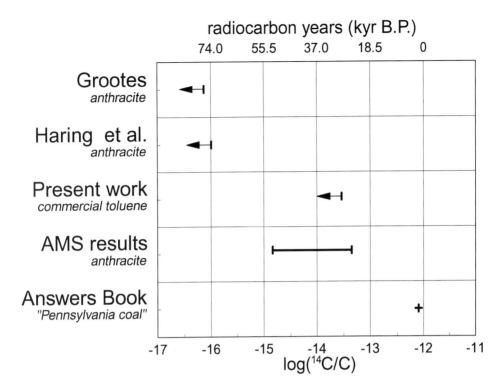

Figure 4: Various measurements on samples of interest to the present paper. Arrows indicate an upper limit of ^{14}C concentration.

range of reported AMS results. It is not clear whether we are seeing actual ^{14}C signal (indigenous or contamination) or indistinguishable background events in our spectrometer at the present time. The only way to assess this is to make improvements to the spectrometer (to reduce known background sources and thereby increase the spectrometer's sensitivity) and repeat the experiment. At the present time there are a number of suitable improvements to the spectrometer which we anticipate can be made with modest expenditure of time and money. For example, as mentioned above, no effort has been made to eliminate cosmic ray background events thus far; we plan to pursue anti-coincidence schemes and/or possibilities for locating the experiment deep underground, in addition to other improvements, as resources permit.

ACKNOWLEDGEMENTS

I am indebted to a number of individuals for their sponsorship of this research. Steve Grieshaber donated the copper pipe, Dr. Charles I. Choi's financial aid made possible the purchase of the lead shielding, and Steve Low's group at Hewlette Packard donated the digital oscilloscope and computers. The Smith-Walker Foundation, through the kind efforts of Mrs. Pam McCall, provided financial assistance, as did numerous other individuals through designated donations to the ICR Radiocarbon Lab.

BIBLIOGRAPHY

[1]   Gerald E. Aardsma, <u>Radiocarbon and the Genesis Flood</u>, 1991, Institute for Creation Research, San Diego, 73-74.

[2]   R. H. Brown, **The upper limit of C-14 age?**, Origins, **15:1**(1988) 39-43.

[3]   P. M. Grootes, **Carbon-14 time scale extended: comparison of chronologies**, Science **200**(1978) 11-15.

[4]   D. M. Gurfinkel, **An assessment of laboratory contamination at the Isotrace radiocarbon facility**, Radiocarbon **29:3**(1987) 335-346.

[5]   Ken Ham, Andrew Snelling, and Carl Wieland, The Answers Book, 1990, Master Books, Colorado, 77-75.

[6]   A. Haring, A. E. de Vries, and H. de Vries, **Radiocarbon dating up to 70,000 years by isotopic enrichment**, Science **128**(1958) 472-473.

[7]   David C. Lowe, **Problems associated with the use of coal as a source of ^{14}C-free background material**, Radiocarbon **31:2**(1989) 117-120.

[8]   Fred H. Schmidt, David R. Balsey, and Donald D. Leach, **Early expectations of AMS: greater ages and tiny fractions. One failure? - one success**, Nuclear Instruments and Methods in Physics Research **B29**(1987) 97-99.

[9]   Milton A. Trautman and Eric H. Willis, **Isotopes, Inc. radiocarbon measurements V**, Radiocarbon **8**(1966) 161-203 [sample #s I-1149 & I-1150, page 200].

[10]   A. P. Vinogradov, A. L. Devirts, E. I. Dobkina, and N. G. Markova, **Radiocarbon dating in the Vernadsky Institute I-IV**, Radiocarbon **8**(1966) 292-323 [sample # Mo-334, page 319].

[11]   J. S. Vogel, D. E. Nelson, and J. R. Southon, **^{14}C background levels in an accelerator mass spectrometry system**, Radiocarbon **29:3**(1987) 323-333.

[12]   Robert L. Whitelaw, **Time, life and history in the light of 15,000 radiocarbon dates**, Creation Research Society Quarterly **7:1**(1970) 56-71,83.

THE EXODUS HAPPENED 2450 B.C.

GERALD E. AARDSMA, Ph.D.
Institute for Creation Research
10946 Woodside Avenue N.
Santee, California 92071

KEYWORDS: Biblical chronology, date of Exodus, date of Flood

ABSTRACT

The Exodus of the Israelites was immediately preceded by an outpouring of God's power in judgement upon Egypt. This judgement took the form of a series of devastating national disasters. By the time it was over the crops and herds of Egypt had been decimated, the firstborn sons were dead, the pharaoh and his army had been destroyed, the slave labor (i.e. Israelites) had gone, and they had carried away all the wealth of the land with them. The obvious implication of these Biblical facts is that the nation of Egypt must have suffered a most severe setback, if not complete hiatus, as a result of the Exodus.

Such a pronounced setback should be an easy thing to locate in the standard, secular history of Egypt. However, nothing remotely resembling the Biblical Exodus is discernable in the secular history of Egypt anywhere near the traditional Biblical date for this event (i.e., 1450 B.C.). In fact, roughly the *opposite* of what one would expect of the Exodus is observed at this date; this was a period of unprecedented prosperity and power for Egypt.

Interestingly, a full millennium before this traditional date (i.e., at about 2450 B.C.) Egypt's secular history fits the Biblical description of the Exodus extremely well. This suggests the possibility that traditional Biblical chronology may have accidently lost 1000 years between the Exodus and the commencement of the Israelite monarchical period. This suggestion is found to work out very well when explored in depth, allowing much secular historical and archaeological data to be harmonized with the Biblical record from Abraham to Samuel for the first time.

This discovery raises the minimum age of the earth from 6000 to 7000 years, and the minimum elapsed time from the Flood to the present from roughly 4300 years to 5300 years. This additional millennium significantly impacts the time scale of such post-Flood dynamical processes as the development of a post-Flood ice age, dispersion of animal life and man over the globe, growth of radiocarbon in the atmosphere and oceans, etc.

PROLEGOMENON

In a perceptive invited paper for the December 1986 issue of the Creation Research Society Quarterly, Erich A. von Fange [6, page 97] wrote:

> "Creationists ought to encourage the responsible study of chronological problems. The final answers are not as yet in for this immensely complicated problem of dating the ancient world. To a large extent we must play a waiting game and hope that in future excavations some incontrovertible synchronism will be found that will put at rest the present uncertainty about dating the Exodus and other issues. One conclusion seems safe. No sioe or faction has yet to come up with a satisfactory solution to dating the Biblical world before 1000 B.C. ..."

---

*
Though this work has been supported in part by the Institute for Creation Research, the views which are expressed by this paper are those of the author and do not represent any officially endorsed ICR position.

I discovered a radically new possible solution to this well-worn problem of how to date "the Biblical world before 1000 B.C." in the summer of 1990. Following extensive critical investigations of this solution -- of an archaeological, historical, and Biblical sort -- I have come to believe that it is the correct solution. If I am correct, we need play von Fange's waiting game no longer.

Indeed, I am now questioning why we ever supposed we needed to play this game in the first place. It now seems to me that the "incontrovertible synchronism" which von Fange suggested might solve the problem has existed for at least the last eight decades. I refer here to the Exodus. It now seems to me that anyone who was familiar with the Biblical account of the Exodus and also the secular history of Egypt (no doubt there are many here whose education in science, like mine, has not served to familiarize them with this fascinating history), and who was prepared to take both seriously, could not fail to see that the collapse of the Old Kingdom of Egypt, as recorded in secular history, and the Exodus event, as recorded in the pages of Scripture, must, in fact, coincide.

INTRODUCTION

This small paper is a defense of the claim, expressed by its title, that the Exodus of the Israelites from Egypt happened *ca.* 2450 B.C., at the end of the Old Kingdom of Egypt, as opposed to the traditional view that this historic event should be dated to *ca.* 1450 B.C., during the New Kingdom. I have briefly discussed this assertion previously within the much broader context of Biblical chronology from Abraham to Samuel [2]. There I elaborated the hypothesis that traditional Biblical chronology has accidentally dropped out a full millennium between Solomon and the Exodus, and showed how Biblical history in the period before Samuel immediately finds many supporting evidences from secular history and archaeology when this lost millennium is restored.

In the present paper I focus on the Exodus alone. My thesis here is that what we know about the Exodus from the Bible and what we know about the history of Egypt from secular sources is sufficient to establish 1. that 1450 B.C. cannot possibly be the correct date for the Exodus, and 2. that 2450 B.C. must surely be the correct date. I will argue that the only point in Egyptian history which can possibly accommodate a truly *Biblical* Exodus is at the end of the Old Kingdom, and that the proper date for the end of the Old Kingdom is *ca.* 2450 B.C.

(I feel it is unnecessary to explicitly address the alternative view, unique to the more recent decades of the Christian era, that the Exodus should be dated to *ca.* 1210 B.C., as this view implicitly denies a literal, plain sense, approach to the interpretation of Scripture, and it seems unlikely that many who adhere to such an approach would be found at a conference such as this. Notice, however, that it is implicitly denied by the second part of my thesis above. For the same reason it seems unnecessary to discuss the current "mainstream" view, that the Exodus is a theological story only, for which one should not expect to find any real-life evidence.)

The date of the Exodus is a major landmark in the chronology of the Old Testament. It constitutes a major link in the chain of Biblical numbers which must be used to compute the date of any Biblical event prior to the Exodus, such as the Tower of Babel or the Flood. Thus, the date of the Exodus is quite important to Biblical chronology.

Biblical chronology is, in turn, important to scientific creationists. Chronology *is* the backbone of history. Obviously, we need to get our chronology right if our current efforts to build a Biblically sound, quantitatively defensible model of earth history from the Flood to the present are to succeed.

WHAT THE BIBLE DEMANDS

It seems to me that there are several parallels between the way many conservative Christians treat the Biblical Exodus account and the way the Biblical Flood account is often treated. In both cases there is a tendency to completely overlook what the natural outworking of such events would be in the real world.

In the case of the Flood, for example, it is generally acknowledged by conservative Christians that the Flood really happened, and that it accomplished God's purpose of judging the world. But, often, that's where thinking stops. Only when it is explicitly pointed out that a global Flood would, for example, necessarily bring about much erosion and deposition of sediments do many Christians begin to recognize this fact and wonder where these sediments are to be found.

So it is with the Exodus. It is generally acknowledged that it really happened, and that it accomplished God's purpose of setting the Israelites free from Egypt, but that's where thinking tends to stop. I suggest that just as surely as we can assert that the global Flood must have left behind large sedimentary layers, we can also assert that the supernatural outpouring of God's power which accompanied the Exodus must have crushed the nation of Egypt, and must have done so to such an extent that this singular event could not possibly be hid from the historian's eye. There is every reason to suppose that the Exodus should provide an easily discerned point of reference in the secular history of Egypt, facilitating synchronization of the secular and sacred histories.

The only way I know to bring this point home is to ask the reader to imagine what the outcome would be if the plagues which God inflicted upon Egypt at the time of the Exodus were to be inflicted upon the United States of America today. This is not a perfect analogy, of course. In particular, the global ties and rapid global communication and transport which exist today give the U.S. a potential resilience not parallelled in the case of ancient Egypt. But I think it is adequate, nonetheless, to open our eyes to the utter ruin which the Exodus must have entailed for Egypt.

We begin by imagining that all of the rivers, lakes, and reservoirs in the U.S. are turned to blood (for this is how the plagues which preceded the Exodus began) so that their water is useless for drinking and irrigation, and all their fish die. There is no water to drink, and none for the crops, and people are scrambling everywhere to put in wells. (In some portions of the U.S. there is enough natural rainfall to offset the felt impact of such a disaster. This would not be the case in Egypt which has a desert climate and is completely dependent upon the waters of the Nile for drinking and irrigation.)

Seven days later there is a national epidemic of frogs. Frogs everywhere -- in the houses, in the beds, in the ovens, in the factories, in the schools -- everywhere. These die off (miraculously) and are heaped in stinking piles all over the country. Nothing like this frog epidemic has ever been seen before, and it takes a toll on the nation's self-confidence. But this is no sooner over than a new epidemic breaks out. This time it is gnats (or lice) -- everywhere. In your hair, in your eyes, in your mouth. Prior to this the country's scientists (analog of the Egyptian magicians) felt they could handle the situation; now they throw up their hands in despair and acknowledge that the supernatural hand of God is at work.

But it gets worse. On the heels of the gnats come great swarms of insects, in such numbers that the land is laid waste by them. And when this plague is lifted, then another is on the way. Overnight, all of the pastured livestock die -- the cows and the steer, the sheep and the horses. And then come boils -- boils on everybody and so severe that people can't even stand. And then, continual thunder and lightening accompanied by hail over the entire country. Hail such as has never been seen before. It shatters all the trees, and strikes down every man and animal not safely indoors, and the crops ready to be harvested are ruined. The *entire country* is officially declared a disaster area by its top officials.

But there is more to come. Following a brief respite, come swarms of locusts. There are so many locusts that the surface of the ground cannot even be seen. They eat every green thing which remains in the land until the ground and the trees are stripped bare. And then, three days of total darkness -- not an ordinary darkness, rather one which is so black it can be felt, so oppressive that nobody dares even to rise from their place.

And then comes the death of the first-born of all yet living -- mankind and cattle. In the middle of the night great wailing is heard from one end of the land to the other, for not a house has escaped the visitation of the angel of death.

(Now it is customary for us, as we read the Exodus account, to identify with the Israelite slaves. Accordingly, at this point in the narrative we begin to feel pretty good, because we feel the long ordeal is over and we're on our way to better things. But, in this analysis, we are seeking to assess the probable impact of these events on *Egypt*, so we must take up the point of view of the Egyptians -- as the Israelites jubilantly walk away.)

The analogy gets a little difficult at this point, but let us do the best we can with it. The Bible tells us that when the Israelites left Egypt they "plundered the Egyptians". That is, they took most of the wealth of the land (silver, gold and clothing) with them. In modern terms, this seems roughly equivalent to the sudden loss of everyone's lifetime savings.

But, of course, it was not just the savings which were lost at this point, it was also the Israelites themselves. They were the slaves who provided the manpower to keep everything going. In modern terms, we will have to imagine that suddenly all the machinery across the nation vanishes -- all the tractors and combines, the dishwashers and clothes-washers, the factory machinery and the turbines which generate our electricity, the automobiles and railway engines, etc.

Finally, of course, we need to add to this list, after a break of just a few days, the sudden destruction of the country's choicest troops together with its political leadership.

What would such a scenario mean to the U.S. today? How would we cope if within a relatively short period of time all the waters were polluted, all the agricultural products were destroyed, the land stripped bare of vegetation, all the machinery gone, much of the money taken from the country, a large fraction of the population dead, the military destroyed, and the president dead? Is it reasonable to suppose that when it was all over one would hardly even suspect that anything had happened at all? Surely Egypt was more completely ruined than any war or single natural disaster could ever hope to accomplish. I submit that such a ruination would necessarily leave an indelible signature upon any civilization.

11

The following appear to be legitimate inferences from the Biblical account:

1. After the Exodus the land of Egypt must have experienced severe food shortage and probably famine.
2. An abrupt decrease in the wealth and prosperity of the nation of Egypt must have accompanied the Exodus.
3. Political turmoil and loss of centralized authority would almost certainly result from the Exodus. Confidence in the pharaonic rule must have been shattered. The ability of the pharaonic court to enforce its rule must have been severely set back by the loss of the pharaoh and "the choicest of his officers" in the Red Sea.
4. It would take years for Egypt to recover from this disaster. The infrastructure of the whole civilization had been shattered. It could not be rebuilt overnight.
5. Whatever international ties Egypt may have had would be impossible to maintain in the midst of the general debacle. Whatever degree of prominence Egypt may have had in the international scene before the Exodus would be lost following the Exodus. We would expect the nation to fall into relative obscurity for a significant period of time. (Note that the complete absence of Egypt from the Biblical record during the Wilderness Wandering, Conquest, and subsequent centuries of the Period of the Judges supports this inference.)

HISTORY OF EGYPT

The outpouring of God's supernatural power in the plagues of Egypt at the time of the Exodus was a unique affair. We would not expect to discover more than one such event in the secular history of Egypt. But we would also not expect such a singular occurrence to be difficult to spot, providing that at least the rough outline of the secular history of Egypt were known.

In fact, the rough outline (and more) *is* known of the history of Egypt, and has been for some time now. It is summarized in modern textbooks and histories along the following lines:

1. The Predynastic Period
    (Political unification of Upper and Lower Egypt and origin of the pharaonic system of government. Dynasties I and II).
2. The Old Kingdom
    (Very prosperous and stable. Most advanced civilization in the world at that time. Pyramids built. Dynasties III - VI.)
3. The First Intermediate Period
    (Country in chaos. Political turmoil. Social upheaval. International obscurity. Dynasties VII - XI.)
4. The Middle Kingdom
    (Things back under control. Classic period of Egyptian civilization. Prosperous, secure, expansionistic. International heavyweight. Dynasties XI - XII.)
5. The Second Intermediate Period
    (Central power subject to crisis. Civilization stable. Eventual peaceful "invasion"; Hyksos take over. Dynasties XIII - XVII.)
6. The New Kingdom
    (Hyksos expelled. Empire established to Euphrates. Period of Egypt's most widespread influence and control. Dynasties XVIII - XX.)

This outline extends from the origin of Egyptian civilization up to the time of the first kings of Israel. Thus, it must encompass the Exodus. In panoramic outline we have three periods of power and prosperity, separated by two periods of reduced fortune.

THE CASE AGAINST 1450 B.C.

The traditional 1450 B.C. date has the misfortune of placing the Exodus in an extended period of uninterrupted strength and prosperity in the New Kingdom. This period begins with the great warrior-pharaoh Tuthmosis III, and comes to its full bloom under Amenophis III, roughly 100 years later. The absolute starting and ending dates of this period are uncertain within a possible time interval of about 25 years, but in all chronologies by reputable scholars that I am aware of, 1450 B.C. -- the traditional Exodus date -- falls about 30 to 50 years into this century-long period of prosperity and power. Thus, we have considerable reason to be confident that this period of prosperity truly does encompass the traditional Exodus date, or perhaps, with much less probability, the traditional Exodus date might immediately precede this period of prosperity. But there is no sign of the Exodus anywhere during this period, and such a period of general prosperity is not what we would expect to see either immediately following the Exodus, or for a long time thereafter.

The founding warrior-pharaoh of this prosperous period for Egypt was Tuthmosis III. He conquered everything worthwhile and within striking distance of Egypt, establishing a vast Egyptian empire in the process. His empire extended into Mesopotamia (he received tribute from Babylon, for example) and included the whole of Palestine and Syria.

Most chronologies place 1450 B.C. in the latter half of the reign of Tuthmosis III. If we look more closely at these years we find only that, having completed no less than sixteen successful international campaigns, Tuthmosis III had things so completely under control he was actually able to take it easy for awhile. Nicolas Grimal, formerly a researcher at the French Institute of Oriental Antiquity in Cairo and presently Professor of Egyptology at the Sorbonne University in Paris, in a recent book, summarizes the state of affairs in the latter years of the reign of Tuthmosis III as follows:

> "The last years of Tuthmosis III's reign were more peaceful: Egyptian supremacy was, for the time being, recognized in the Near East and relations with the Aegean region were cordial." [4, page 216]

The next pharaoh, Amenophis II, could hardly hope to compete with the scintillating career of his father, but there is no sign that the general prosperity of the nation waned during his reign.

> "His [i.e., Tuthmosis III's] successor, Aakheperure Amenophis II, is remembered as a far less intellectual ruler, but he was still able to preserve the prosperity and power of Egypt." [4, page 218]

The prosperity persisted through the next pharaoh, Tuthmosis IV, and came to its full flowering under Amenophis III.

> "The rule of Amenophis III was marked by peace: the only act of war was a preventative campaign waged in the fifth year of his reign. Apart from this, the relations with the Near East during his reign bear witness to the burgeoning influence of Egypt in Asia and the Mediterranean region." [4, page 222]

> "When Amenophis III died he took with him an Egypt of political and religious certainties, a state that had regained strength and respect both at home and abroad." [4, page 225]

I submit that a more unlikely historical setting for the Exodus can probably not be found in the entire history of Egypt! There is no evidence of national disaster, economic crisis, political turmoil, or social chaos anywhere in this period of time -- only the opposite is seen. It is impossible to fit a truly *Biblical* Exodus into this period of Egypt's history. It seems to me preposterous to suppose that an event of the magnitude of the Biblical Exodus could have slipped through the cracks of history at this point somehow, or that the Egyptians somehow managed to hide the true nature of the times. It seems equally preposterous to suppose that Joshua should have conquered part of this mighty empire in Palestine, with never the slightest hint of resistance from Egypt in either the secular or the sacred histories. The Biblical Exodus simply does not belong to this period of Egypt's history.

WHERE THE EXODUS DOES BELONG

From the panoramic outline of Egyptian history given above it is clear that there are only two possible locations for the Exodus. It must either coincide with the onset of the First Intermediate Period or with that of the Second Intermediate Period. If we look a little more closely at these two periods it rapidly becomes clear that the First Intermediate Period suits the Biblical Exodus account extremely well, while the Second Intermediate Period does not suit it at all.

The collapse of the Old Kingdom and onset of the First Intermediate Period was sudden and very thorough, affecting all levels of society.

> "The Old Kingdom ended with a period of great confusion." [4, page 89]

> "It was the collapse of the whole society, and Egypt itself had become a world in turmoil, exposed to the horrors of chaos which was always waiting for the moment when the personification of the divine being -- the pharaoh -- neglected his duties or simply disappeared." [4, page 138]

> "No evidence has survived of the maintenance of links with the outside world that had been established in the Old Kingdom: the trade through Syria-Palestine with Byblos and the eastern Mediterranean seems to have stopped, and the exploitation of mines in the Sinai peninsula also seems to have been abandoned." [4, page 139]

By way of contrast, the onset of the Second Intermediate Period was gradual, and seems only to have impacted the throne.

> "Moreover, there is nothing to support the suggestion of an outbreak of violence like that at the end of the Old Kingdom: during the century and a half leading up to the appearance of the Hyksos rulers in Egypt,

the country does not seem to have collapsed in any way, either within or outside its frontiers. There is instead a feeling that it was only the central power that was subject to crisis, whereas the stability of the civilization as a whole remained constant." [4, page 171]

The First Intermediate Period is clearly the one of interest. Its onset shows all the characteristics one would expect to see as the natural result of the Biblical Exodus. No other period in Egypt's history is suitable to the Exodus, for no other period shows simultaneously the: 1. sudden onset of chaos at all levels of Egyptian society with accompanying famine and anarchy, 2. severe loss of centralized power and authority, 3. complete eclipse of Egypt's international prestige and influence, and 4. centuries-long struggle to regain what had so suddenly and completely been lost.

(Previously [2], I have shown that this recognition leads to the mandatory identification of Pepy II, who reigned for more than ninety years, with the pharaoh whose daughter raised Moses and from whom Moses fled, and his successor, Merenre II, whose reign lasted one year only, with the pharaoh of the Exodus. I have shown that both of these assignments suit the Biblical narrative extremely well. These historical details, and others, confirm the conclusion which we have arrived at here by a more panoramic approach, that the Exodus occurred at the end of the Old Kingdom.)

DATING THE END OF THE OLD KINGDOM

If the Exodus occurred at the end of the Old Kingdom of Egypt, then we can date the Exodus by simply dating the end of the Old Kingdom. The date of the end of the Old Kingdom has already been calculated any number of times by various scholars. However, their answers do not all agree, so it is necessary to review a little of the work in this area.

The well-known Egyptian scholar, James Henry Breasted, professor of Egyptology and Oriental History at the University of Chicago at the beginning of this century, placed this date at ca. 2475 B.C. back in 1914. His assigned uncertainty is summarized by the words "we may err possibly as much as a century either way" [3, page 25]. It should be noted that Breasted's computation was based upon historical data alone; radiocarbon dating would not be invented for over another 40 years. Breasted defended the sound historical basis for his chronology as follows:

> "The reader will have observed that this system of chronology is based upon the contemporary monuments and lists dating not later than 1200 B.C." [3, page 26]

More recent historical scholarship has tended to move this date about 300 years toward more recent times, with typical figures in the range 2160 - 2200 B.C. The major portion of the disagreement between Breasted and these more recent computations is, not surprisingly, due to the confusion of the First Intermediate Period and the paucity of historical sources dealing with it.

It is possible, on the basis of modern radiocarbon measurements, to determine which of these two approaches is more nearly correct. However, before proceeding along these lines, I would like to point out that it is already apparent at this stage that we cannot hope to redate the end of the Old Kingdom to 1450 B.C. (in an effort to harmonize secular history with traditional Biblical chronology at this one point). Reputable chronological scholarship, based upon the secular historical data alone, seems to demand a date for the fall of the Old Kingdom somewhere between the extremes of 2575 and 2100 B.C. Note that 1450 B.C., the traditional Biblical date for the Exodus, is 650 years removed from the extreme end of this time interval. This is very much outside the range of any actual chronological uncertainties.

(I have shown previously [2] that the traditional Biblical chronological expectation of a 1450 B.C. date for the Exodus is founded entirely upon a single number found only in one verse of Scripture (specifically, 1 Kings 6:1). This number is at odds with other chronological information in the Bible, and there is much cause to suppose that it has suffered the loss of its leading digit in the process of copying at some remote time in the past. Though such copy errors are rare in Scripture, other examples of similar problems can be unambiguously demonstrated, and the existence of such problems is universally acknowledged by conservative Bible scholars. Thus, not only is there no possibility of dating the end of the Old Kingdom to 1450 B.C., there is also no pressing Biblical motivation to warrant doing so.)

The advent of physical dating methods (most notably radiocarbon) has provided a means of independently checking historically derived dates. I have previously suggested [1] one way in which radiocarbon data might be harmonized with a global Flood model of earth history. One important result of this work was the conclusion that modern, tree-ring calibrated radiocarbon dates should be regarded as reliable and accurate for at least the duration of the historic period (i.e., the last 5,000 years). As this interval of confidence includes the entire duration of the Old Kingdom, it seems appropriate to utilize the results of radiocarbon to help settle this chronological question.

As it turns out, in fact, the application of radiocarbon to Old Kingdom monuments [5] has unambiguously supported Breasted's chronology (discussed above) and refuted the more recent dates for the collapse of the Old Kingdom put forward by modern historical scholars. This does two things. First, it provides *independent* confirmation of the general soundness of the historical dating procedure. Second, by taking all of the presently available extra-Biblical data into consideration, it strongly urges the conclusion that the collapse of the Old Kingdom of Egypt should be dated to within about 150 years of 2450 B.C.

CONCLUSION

We have seen that it is impossible to accommodate a truly *Biblical* Exodus within the known history of Egypt at the traditional Biblical date of *ca.* 1450 B.C. We have also seen that the only place in the history of Egypt where the *Biblical* Exodus can possibly be accommodated is at the end of the Old Kingdom. Finally, we have seen that the end of the Old Kingdom, and, hence, the Exodus, should be dated to within about 150 years of 2450 B.C.

In this paper I have not dealt with the Biblical chronology issues raised by this redating of the Exodus, but I have done so previously elsewhere [2]. When these are taken into consideration and the Biblical chronological data given its rightful place, it is possible to reduce the uncertainty in the date of the Exodus considerably compared to what the secular chronological data by itself allows. The best current estimate of the date of the Exodus which one then arrives at is 2447 B.C., with an uncertainty of about plus or minus five years.

This new date for the Exodus immediately implies that all Biblical dates earlier than the Exodus must also be moved back 1,000 years [7]. Of particular interest to the present conference is the conclusion that the traditional Biblical dates for the Flood (which are calculated assuming there are no gaps in the Genesis 11 genealogy) must be moved back a full millennium. This means that the minimum elapsed time from the Flood to the present should be raised from its traditional value of roughly 4,300 years (2300 B.C.) to 5,300 years (3300 B.C.). This additional millennium obviously significantly impacts the time scale during which post-Flood processes can develop.

REFERENCES

[1]   Gerald E. Aardsma, Radiocarbon and the Genesis Flood, 1991, Institute for Creation Research, San Diego.

[2]   Gerald E. Aardsma, A New Approach to the Chronology of Biblical History from Abraham to Samuel, 1993, Institute for Creation Research, San Diego.

[3]   James Henry Breasted, A History of the Ancient Egyptians, 1908, Charles Scribner's Sons, New York.

[4]   Nicolas Grimal, A History of Ancient Egypt, 1992, Blackwell Publishers, Cambridge, Massachusetts.

[5]   Herbert Haas, James Devine, Robert Wenke, Mark Lehner, Willy Wolfli, and George Bonani, **Radiocarbon chronology and the historical calendar in Egypt,** in Chronologies in the Near East: Relative Chronologies and Absolute Chronology 16,000 - 4,000 B.P., Olivier Aurenche, Jacques Evin, and Francis Hours, editors, 1987, B.A.R., 5, Centremead, Osney Mead, Oxford OX2 0DQ, England.

[6]   Erich A. von Fange, **A review of problems confronting Biblical archaeology,** Creation Research Society Quarterly, **23:3**(1986) 93-99.

[7]   The broad scope of effects which this revision to traditional Biblical chronology entails is discussed in my ICR monograph A New Approach to the Chronology of Biblical History from Abraham to Samuel [2]. This monograph has recently been severely criticized by Dr. Bryant Wood of the Associates for Biblical Research (ABR) in the ABR journal Bible and Spade [**6:4**(1993)97-114]. I have been denied opportunity to publish a response to Dr. Wood in Bible and Spade, but am happy to make my reply, **Response to Dr. Wood,** available to any who request it.

PREVENTING OUT-OF-WEDLOCK, TEEN-AGE PREGNANCY: CURRENT PRACTICE VERSUS THE EXPERIMENTAL SOCIAL PSYCHOLOGY RESEARCH BASE

PAUL D. ACKERMAN, Ph.D.
DEPARTMENT OF PSYCHOLOGY
WICHITA STATE UNIVERSITY
WICHITA, KANSAS 67260-0034

KEYWORDS:

Social Psychology, Teen-age Pregnancy, Attribution Ambiguity, Deindividuation, Excitation Transfer, Scientific Creationism, Social Facilitation, Social Impact

ABSTRACT

This paper expands the range of scientific-creationist thought to include experimental social psychology. It examines experimental research relevant to the crisis of out-of-wedlock, teen-age pregnancy in the U.S.A. The author follows the model set forth by creationists in the physical and biological sciences who have defended the Genesis record of creation over and against the claims of Darwinist evolution. As creationists have exposed Darwinism for its philosophical bias and scientific weakness, this paper examines current approaches to the teen-pregnancy crisis showing how they reflect humanist/evolutionist philosophy rather than sound experimental science. This paper shows that many sex education activities and initiatives, ostensibly aimed at reducing risky teen sexual activity, will increase it. The experimental social psychology research base is consistent with biblical principles of public and individual morality. Regarding the teen-pregnancy epidemic, the scientific evidence is consistent with biblical standards based on parental supervision, discipline and clear moral guidelines. Those who hope to see their children and grandchildren raised under the guidance of biblical values need to become informed in order to counter present-day trends.

INTRODUCTION

In Western societies, powerful currents of thought and political effort seek to depose the remaining vestiges of biblically based, Judeo-Christian values [4, p.21-25] [5] [22]. These forces are close to achieving a radical, centrally controlled transformation of Western societies and their major institutions. Those involved in this mission of societal transformation draw justification from evolution-based declarations by prominent natural and social scientists. For example, the respected psychologist Raymond Cattell has written that "science must be the source of religious values" [6, p.13]. He calls for a "One World" order with a central world research organization. Cattell envisions "a world organized richly with nerves conveying information to a research center acting in an advisory capacity to a highly differentiated array of national experiments" [6, p.11]. Christian, creationist scholars opposing these trends have focused on the natural sciences and Darwinist theory. These scholars have shown that the scientific evidence contradicts the theory of evolution, and, therefore, evolutionism is unfit as a warrant for cultural transformation. As creationist scholars and scientists critically examine research in the natural sciences, there is a corresponding need for creationist scholars to examine research in the social sciences and claims that these disciplines provide scientific evidence mandating cultural change.

In this vein, the present paper considers the social problem of out-of-wedlock, teen-age pregnancy. The way in which our society, guided by prominent psychologists and health care professionals, is approaching this problem exemplifies our drift away from the biblical world-view. Current approaches to the teen-pregnancy epidemic run counter to practices indicated by experimental social psychology research. On the contrary, experimental research in social psychology supports traditional, Judeo-Christian approaches based on clear moral guidelines and disciplinary structure.

Current experts want to curtail parental control over sex-education, birth control and abortion [13] [14] [23, chap.7]. They want to remove messages about teen sexuality that conflict with their own, especially messages stressing abstinence and moral absolutes [11] [23, p.239-240]. Persons who hope to raise their children under the guidance of biblically-based, moral values should be interested in an analysis that calls into question the scientific validity of current trends.

THE TEEN-PREGNANCY EPIDEMIC AND CURRENT "SOLUTIONS"

The problem of out-of-wedlock teen pregnancy is epidemic. Each year more than one million teen-age pregnancies occur, which translates into a ratio of roughly one pregnancy per every 10 teen-age girls [23]. For the two million girls turning fourteen each year, approximately forty percent will become pregnant during their teen-age years. The variables associated with teen pregnancy include poverty, low educational attainment, weak parental involvement, poor parent-child communication, low family involvement in religious activities, low teen involvement in religious activities, low aspirations and expectations for achievement coupled with a high value for independence, and strong peer-group influence [23, p.213-214].

In combating the epidemic, prominent psychologists recommend intensive social intervention programs focusing on feelings, choices, and insight. They also recommend readily available contraception. There are no influential social scientists calling for biblical moral guidance, structured traditional academic programs, and abstinence from premarital sex. The assumption underlying current thinking has been succinctly stated by Schinke and colleagues, "Given easy, low-cost access to sex education and contraceptive services, young men and women will become responsible and self-regulating in their reproductive behavior, and the number of unanticipated adolescent pregnancies will drop" [19, p.82].

Contraception is an invariant feature of currently recommended approaches. The 1984 National Research Council study panel on adolescent pregnancy and childbearing stated that "contraception is currently the surest strategy for achieving pregnancy prevention" [quoted in 23, p.211]. Furstenberg and Brooks-Gunn have complained about the currently low level of contraceptive use among U.S. adolescents and the "mixed messages" about contraception they receive [10, p.313]. Many health experts are saying that it is crucial for explicit education and counseling in contraceptive use to begin in late childhood or early teen years. Zabin, Kantner, and Zelnick state that "teenagers are being reached too late."

> Since *young* adolescents are the least likely to utilize contraception, and since the relative risk of pregnancy in the early months of intercourse is highest for nonusers, it is the young adolescent who runs the greatest risk of conceiving shortly after initiating intercourse . . . We now know that programs will fall short of their goals if they do not reach teenagers early. [25, p.222, emphasis in original].

The fundamental conflict between Christian and secular approaches to the teen-pregnancy epidemic comes into focus when we examine the relationship between teen sexual activity, contraceptive use, and teen pregnancy. According to the best available evidence, the incidence of sexual intercourse among teens has increased dramatically over the past 50 years. Specifically, data from the 1930s, 1940s, and 1950s show that about 7 percent of white females had sex by the age of 16. Data from the 1970s reveal a dramatic increase in teen sexual activity with 28 percent of unmarried 15-19 year-old females reporting that they had experienced intercourse. By 1980, data showed a rate of 46 percent, and by 1988 a rate of 50 percent for unmarried 15-19 year-old females [26, p.16-17]. Over the past 50 years there has also been a sharp increase in pregnancy rates for teen-agers. However, although the teen pregnancy rate has increased overall, it has not increased for sexually active teen-agers who use contraceptives. In other words, total teen pregnancy is increasing because more teens are having sex. Contraceptives are effective, however, in that fewer sexually active teens become pregnant. From this evidence, current experts argue that contraceptives will be effective in controlling the teen pregnancy epidemic if only we can increase their availability. For the secularist, the teen pregnancy problem is pragmatic, and since teen sexual activity is desirable or at least inevitable, public policy must involve widely available birth control for young adolescents. From the Christian standpoint, however, there is more to the issue than the pragmatic of pregnancy prevention. Teen pregnancy is one component of an extensive moral and public health crisis which more widely available birth control would only exacerbate.

Some experts hold that sexual abstinence for older children and teens is not healthy. Among the chief proponents of this position is Catherine Chillman, Professor Emerita of the School of Social Welfare, University of Wisconsin-Milwaukee. Chillman sees sexual activity as a "central and positive part of the total well-being of young people from the ages of about 10 to 20 years." [7, p.123] For Chillman, the "sexually healthy adolescent" should take pride and pleasure in his or her developing body, and accept sexual desires as natural and to be acted on within the limits of reasonable "reality constraints." She does not recommend purely recreational sex because it "tends to trivialize the depth and meaning of the exceptional intimacy and potential involvement of the total self through intercourse." [7, p.124] Heterosexual and homosexual forms of intercourse are equally valid for Chillman.

As of 1993, social planning experts recommend an approach to sex education called Comprehensive Sexuality Education [16]. This approach provides detailed information about sex, birth control, homosexuality, and "multicultural" values. For example, children at ages 5-8 are taught what masturbation is, how to do it, and that it should be done in a private place. In the 9-12 age range, children are taught that sexual intercourse brings pleasure, homosexual relationships are as fulfilling as heterosexual ones, and legal abortions are safe. Between the ages of 12 and 15, children are taught that people should use contraception during sexual intercourse unless they wish to have a baby, homosexual couples behave sexually in many of the same ways as heterosexual couples, and masturbation, either alone or with a partner, is one way to enjoy sex. Finally, at ages 15-18, teen-agers are taught the most satisfying way to have sex is with a partner and that sexual behaviors shared by partners include sharing erotic writings or pictures, bathing or showering together, and oral, vaginal, or anal intercourse.

FREUDIAN THEORETICAL BASIS OF CONTEMPORARY APPROACHES

In the main, one can trace the theoretical roots of contemporary sex education policy and programs such as Comprehensive Sexuality Education to the psychodynamic school of psychology founded by Sigmund Freud. Catherine Chillman, for example, draws heavily from the psychoanalytic tradition for her views. She cites the Freudian defense mechanisms of repression and denial as part of her basis for viewing abstention from sexual activity in the teen years as unhealthy and problematic [7, p.124]. Central to all of the psychologies that have grown out of the Freudian school are the concepts of catharsis and ventilation.

> People's emotions are similar to steam locomotives. If you build a fire in the boiler of a locomotive, keep raising the steam pressure and let it sit on the track, sooner or later something will blow. However, if you take it and spin the wheels and toot the whistle, the steam pressure can be kept at a safe level. [17, p.83].

Sadly but predictably our society's policy of encouraging teen-age sexual "wheel spinning and whistle tooting" has transported a generation of teens far down the tracks of dangerous sexual immorality, STDs, and out-of-wedlock pregnancies. Historian Lawrence Stone has succinctly expressed the Freudian theoretical base underlying expert approaches to sex education,

> If one follows Freudian theory, this [sexual denial among adolescents] could lead to neuroses of the kind that so regularly shattered the calm of Oxford and Cambridge colleges at this period [1500-1800]: it could help to explain the high level of group aggression, which lay behind the extraordinary expansionist violence of western nation states at this time. [20, p.120]

This is indeed a remarkable explanation of the cause of British colonialism! According to the Freudian school, biblically based restrictions on premarital sex for young men and women gave rise to high levels of neurotic aggressiveness which led England to go forth conquering the far reaches of the globe.

Despite the grip the Freudian hypothesis of an abstinence-aggressiveness link has had in forging "expert" approaches to sex education, the data from over 100 societies shows no evidence that sexual frustration, inferred from the prohibition of heterosexual intercourse, leads to aggression [20, p.120]. What the cross cultural data do show is that cultures that are tolerant of adolescent sexuality have higher frequencies of adultery. This finding is gender specific. Cultures that are tolerant of male adolescent sexual promiscuity have higher frequencies of male adultery. Cultures that are tolerant of female adolescent promiscuity have higher frequencies of female adultery [20, p.109]. Schlegel concludes that a period of adolescent promiscuity "establishes habits that are hard to break and lead to discontent and boredom with one partner" [20, p.109].

A few experts today are knowledgeable enough of the experimental social psychology literature to have rejected Freud and his ideas of ventilation and catharsis. Yet they are pessimistic about the possibility of returning to an approach involving morality and traditional academics.

> It is unlikely that an earlier morality could be reinstituted, even if that were deemed desirable. A sensible course of action in a world in which young adolescent mothers and their children are highly disadvantaged and sexually transmitted diseases are a serious threat to health and even life would be to educate our young people to be responsible about their sexual freedom and to induce them to take precautions against pregnancy and disease. [20, p.132]

In summary, the sex education experts and specialists of our day believe as follows: To insure healthy, productive, free citizens for the future, we must accelerate the psychological and social-emotional development of children and teen-agers. We must also accelerate the independence of children and teen-agers from their parents. Parental control over children and teens needs to diminish. Independent choices by teen-agers need to increase. Society needs to encourage teen-agers in their normal rebelliousness and struggle against the boundaries parents and middle-class traditions place on them. Applied to the teen pregnancy issue, this philosophy says that teens should be encouraged to decide for themselves when they will become sexually active. (Usually it is not healthy to remain sexually inactive past the mid-teens.) Parental boundaries, traditional values and taboos are not healthy. Early education in responsible choice and contraceptive use speeding teen-agers to independent maturity, wisdom, and responsibility is desirable. Whatever the program specifics, it is taken as axiomatic that to reduce pregnancy in children and teen-agers, one must talk *more* with them about sexual intercourse, contraception, and reproduction. As I shall now show, the opposite is true. To reduce teen pregnancy we should talk *less* about sex and *more* about academic subjects such as mathematics, literature and history.

EXPERIMENTAL SOCIAL PSYCHOLOGY AND THE TEEN-PREGNANCY CRISIS

From a Christian standpoint, there are many moral and practical difficulties with the above stated consensus. It is certainly biblically problematic. It is also problematic in light of experimental social psychology documenting the range of factors that can influence conduct. We attempt to protect our children from the hazards of sexual misconduct by intellectual persuasion and education. Meanwhile, we ignore dangerous settings and temptations that guarantee sexual activity, pregnancy, and venereal disease. Many public efforts ostensibly aimed at reducing risky teen sexual behavior, based on our best and most current social science research, will increase it. Yet the experts of the contemporary consensus appear oblivious to these factors, and one finds that the professional literature addressing teen-age pregnancy contains no reference to relevant experimental social psychology research.

What causes teen-agers to engage in risky sexual activities? Intercourse in unmarried teens occurs in intimate social settings where male and female teen-age couples are alone and unsupervised. It is encouraged by activities that lessen social inhibitions, modesty, and moral restraints. The problem of pregnancy among unmarried teen-agers is only one aspect of a larger moral and social context. Today, young people face dangers not only from unwanted pregnancies but also from drugs, gangs, and guns. Also, they face dangers from sexually transmitted diseases such as herpes, syphilis, and AIDS. Since teen-pregnancy ramifications extend beyond the mechanics of conception, the best approach for addressing the crisis is one that reduces the amount of premarital sexual intercourse by teen-agers. Based on experimental social psychology research, the best approach to reducing the incidence of sexual intercourse among teens and preteens is one that provides clear and consistent moral guidelines for behavior but also: (a) removes elements conducive to sexually irresponsible behavior in the social environments of teen-agers; (b) promotes constructive and beneficial activities incompatible with irresponsible sexual involvement; and (c) provides attractive alternate goals and concerns that compete with romance and social life. Regarding hazardous social situations and factors that promote risky sexual behavior in teens, the social psychology research literature contains much that is relevant. I will give four examples.

Emotional Arousal and Social Context

Every parent knows that raising children gets more difficult after they wake up in the morning. Manageability dissipates quickly as they pass from drowsy to wide awake. Scientific research has refined this common knowledge by exploring the effects of arousal on behavior [24] [18] [27] [1]. Research shows that as persons become aroused through intense activity or emotion, simple and automatic actions requiring little thought are facilitated [1] [27]. The facilitated actions differ depending on the situation. High arousal prepares a person for actions that are relevant and dominant in the situation at hand. At a funeral, it increases the likelihood that a person will cry; at a sporting event, it increases the likelihood of cheering and euphoria; if one observes a cruel injustice, it increases the likelihood of outrage and angry attack. On the other hand, high arousal makes actions that are counter to the "flow" of a situation, and that require care and forethought, more difficult. At a funeral or sporting event, high arousal makes it difficult for a person to plan for the future. In summary, research on the effects of arousal on social behavior shows that *moderate* levels of arousal are optimum for planning, learning and performing complex mental activities and behaviors. High levels of arousal, on the other hand, facilitate simple, emotional behaviors consistent with the setting.

With this understanding of arousal effects, consider the typical high school dance. According to the research, if high arousal is activated in a social situation with clear sexual overtones, sexual behavior as an emotionally dominant action will be facilitated. Simultaneously, clear and reasoned thinking, inhibitions, shyness, and moral restraints will be undermined. There are four factors that interact to produce conditions favorable to sexual intercourse, (a) sexually suggestive external stimulation; (b) sex related emotions and attitudes; (c) sex related beliefs and expectancies; and (d) sexual fantasy and imagination. Under current practices, high school dances include all these elements coupled with high arousal produced by strenuous dancing to loud, rhythmic rock music. The meaning of the social situation is directed toward sexual expression by the coital messages in the lyrics and dance movements. Thus, saying, "Yes," becomes the dominant, facilitated response; saying, "No," through a consideration of the moral issues, dangers and long term consequences, becomes more unlikely. That high frequencies of risky sexual behavior follow such functions is not surprising to one familiar with the experimental social psychology literature.

Self-Awareness Versus Mob Mentality

> Have you ever been at a party with flashing strobe lights and music so loud that you could feel the room vibrate? If so, did it seem that you were somehow merging with the pulsating crowd around you and your individual identity was slipping away? [3, p.502].

Reduced awareness of oneself as an individual leads to a sense of emersion in the social setting, a sense of anonymity and a loss of personal identity [9] [15] [28]. As with emotional arousal, a loss of personal individuality or identity can greatly increase the likelihood of risky teen-age sexual activity. In laboratory experiments, researchers reduce individual awareness, for example, by having subjects wear masks or hoods, or by putting them in darkened rooms. By contrast, experimenters heighten subjects' sense of identity and individuality by giving them name tags, or by having them perform tasks in front of mirrors. Research has shown that reducing a person's awareness of his or her individuality and identity causes a loosening of normal constraints against deviant behavior. Heightened awareness of one's identity and individuality, on the other hand, reinforces normal inhibitions about wrong doing. A research team led by Edward Diener [8] displayed this phenomenon with 1352 children trick-or-treating. Twenty-seven homes scattered throughout the city of Seattle were prepared for the experiment. When children arrived, an adult greeted them warmly and invited them to "take one of the candies." The adult then left the room. Hidden observers noted that of those children who were alone and had been asked their names and where they lived, only 8 percent transgressed by taking extra candy. However, for children in groups who were allowed to remain anonymous, 80 percent transgressed by taking extra candy.

For social activities such as teen dances, research shows that reduced self-awareness leads to (a) weakened restraints against impulsive behavior, (b) increased sensitivity to immediate cues and current emotional states, (c) inability to monitor and regulate behavior, (d) less concern about what others think, and (e) less ability to plan and think about the future [9]. How is obliviousness to self-identity fostered in the school dance? According to the research, the social-situation factors that cause reduced self-awareness are (a) anonymity, (b) high levels of arousal, (c) focus on external events, and (d) close group unity. Intense stimulation from the rock music of the typical high school dance would reduce personal identity.   Darkening the room or using strobe lights would further reduce it. Crowded social situations are conducive to a loss of individuality.

In the light of research, one can consider how to structure teen dances to promote actions that are safe and responsible. It would be better if they were modeled along the lines of a debutante ball. The debutante ball is a rite of passage into the adult world of responsibility and opportunity rather than an escape into bestial passion. It emphasizes manners, etiquette, and adult values. A scientifically sound school dance would create an environment that heightens individual sense rather the obliterating it. Thus, teen dances should be occasions for parents with camcorders to record the event in the manner of weddings and birthday parties. This practice would add adult supervision to the occasion and remind teens of their family identities, relationships and responsibilities. The dance arena would be brightly lit to accommodate taping by parents mingling through the dance floor. Announcements of names for door-prizes between dance sets could serve as "individuating" reminders that each teen is a person with an identity apart from the group.

Situations That Mask Intimacy Motives

Sometimes we do things for which the motives behind our actions are obvious. At other times, it is unclear what our motives might be. Research on settings that provide a protective cloak for one's motives has important implications for reducing risky sexual activity in teens. [21] Consider a setting that affords one teen-ager an opportunity to initiate an immoral proposal to another teen under the cover of circumstances that suggest the immoral proposal might not be serious. Such an ambiguous setting protects the initiating teen from embarrassment if the improper overture is rejected. If a person makes an indecent proposal under circumstances that clearly show his or her desire for what is proposed, a negative outcome is embarrassing. To make an indecent proposal under clear and unambiguous circumstances is to make oneself vulnerable.   However, if the circumstances are ambiguous, and it is not clear whether the proposal is serious, the initiator is protected from embarrassment. If the target responds positively, then the initiator can acknowledge serious intent and move matters forward. If, on the other hand, the target rejects the proposal, the initiator can retreat under the protective cover, "I was only joking."

The power of ambiguous circumstances to influence a male's willingness to approach an attractive female stranger was shown in a laboratory study by W. M. Bernstein and colleagues [2]. Male college students were asked to choose between two rooms where movies would be shown. Each room contained two adjacent chairs. One room was empty of people, and the other had a lone, attractive female sitting in one chair. When male college students could watch a movie seated next to the attractive female, only 25 percent chose to do so when attraction to her was transparent because the *same* movie was showing in both rooms. When the experimenters scheduled *different* movies for the rooms, the males' behavior was markedly different. *Different* movies in the two rooms provided a protective cloak to hide the males' attraction, and sitting beside her could be due to a preference for the movie being shown in that room. With this cloak of ambiguous circumstances, 75 percent of the men choose the room that allowed them to sit beside the woman.

One can readily see the implications of such research for conducting sex-education classes and teen-agers' social functions. Co-educational classes involving discussion and demonstration of birth control techniques can provide an ambiguous cloak for sexual overtures. It is easy to imagine a teen couple walking out of a sex education class where the technique of condom use had been demonstrated. The boy casually asks the girl if she would join him for some "homework." If she is offended, his line is, "I was only joking, don't you have a sense of humor?" If she is not offended, then some barriers to promiscuity -- shyness, modesty, and fear of rejection -- have been breached, and the likelihood of sexual intercourse is increased. Many practices in sex education classes could have a potent effect in undermining and circumventing healthy shyness and modesty. Consequently, human sexuality education for children and young teens should not be co-educational. Explicit discussions of sex, values, contraception, etc.

should be conducted one-on-one with a parent or school official of the same sex.

Social Influence

Researchers have studied how personal views are influenced as individuals and groups interact with one another. Much of what we know about such "social impact" has been described by the research and theoretical writing of Bibb Latané [12]. As we would expect, the impact of one person's views upon another becomes greater as the *status* and *prestige* of the former increases. The *number* of persons whose views are impacting and being impacted by social influence attempts is also critical. A group of people expressing a view will have more impact than a single individual. Surprisingly, the number of persons who are the targets of influence is also important. A person will have more impact on another's views if he or she addresses the person alone rather than as part of a group. Finally, the *similarity* and *proximity* of persons or groups expressing views are important. An influential person who is more similar to us, or closer to us in time and space, will have more impact than one who is dissimilar or distant. In an educational context, the social impact of a teacher is reduced as the size of the class increases.

It is unsettling to sketch the implications of social impact theory for the epidemic of teen sexual promiscuity. Consider status and prestige as affecting a teacher's influence in the classroom. In our society, admired and prestigious stars and public figures extol free and casual sex. By contrast, those who counsel biblical standards and values are ridiculed. Recall the public derision heaped on then vice-president Dan Quale when he made comments critical of the Murphey Brown television program. In this show, the lead character, an unmarried professional woman played by Candice Bergen, sought a man who would impregnate her so she could have a child to raise. Relative to popular stars such as Candice Bergen, a teacher who promotes traditional standards of moral conduct operates at a status and prestige deficit. The class rebel, on the other hand, has a prestige advantage since he or she espouses values in line with those of attractive stars and public figures. Also, with similarity and proximity, the teacher is at a disadvantage in the classroom. He or she is a "distant" figure in terms of age, interests and lifestyle, while the class rebel is a friend at close physical and psychological range. The issue of numbers is also significant. In a typical classroom the influence of the teacher is "diffused" over many students. On the basis of our knowledge about social influence, it is straightforward to derive guidelines about how to deal with sexuality and reproductive issues in the public schools. As stated above, a parent, teacher, or health official should handle such issues in one-on-one, same-gender settings. This would maximize the impact of the value message that young people need to hear. The one-on-one setting is maximal in terms of the number and physical proximity factors. It also maximizes the impact of the status differential between the adult and teen. For reasons of similarity and social influence, same-gender discussions are important. Also, same-gender settings allow discussion of sexuality issues without violating modesty and personal privacy.

CONCLUSION

Considering the experimental social psychology research base, the outlines of a sound approach to teen sexuality issues are not hard to imagine. Activities incompatible with sexual intimacy should be encouraged. Shyness and modesty should be protected. Educational and social activities should maximize parental/adult social values and minimize the influence of daring, attractive, but destructive rebelliousness. Among the teen activities that are most incompatible with irresponsible dating and sexual activity are commitment to education, a career, and homemaking, and involvement with parents, church groups, and civic organizations. The role of creation scientists in this and similar issues is also straightforward. It is obvious that the core element of the creation science movement has been the argument of compatibility between the Genesis record and genuine empirical science. The major focus of our work should remain the historical reliability of Genesis in the light of physical and biological science. It is also relevant, however, in the context of the social and health sciences, to show that social science evidence is compatible with and supportive of biblical principles of public and individual morality.

REFERENCES

[1]   J.B. Allen, D.T. Kenrick, D.E. Linder, & M.A. McCall, **Arousal and attraction: A response-facilitation alternative to misattribution and negative-reinforcement models**. Journal of Personality and Social-Psychology, 57:2 (1989) 261-270.

[2]   W.M. Bernstein, B.O. Stephenson, M.J. Snyder, & R.A. Wicklund, **Causal ambiguity and heterosexual affiliation**. Journal of Experimental Social Psychology, 19 (1983) 78-92.

[3]   S.S. Brehm & S.M. Kassin, Social Psychology, 2nd ed., 1993, Houghton Mifflin Company, Boston.

[4]   E. Buehrer, **Terminal vision**, Creation Social Science & Humanities Quarterly, 11:4 (1989) 21-25.

[5]   F. Capra, The Turning Point, 1982, Bantam Books, New York.

[6]   R.B. Cattell, **Evolutionary ethics, eugenics and the social sciences: the Beyondist solution**, The Mankind

Quarterly 19:4 (June, 1979); reprint #15 by The International Association for the Advancement of Ethnology and Eugenics, Inc., P.O. Box 3495, Grand Central Station, New York, NY 10017.

[7]   C.S. Chillman, **Promoting Healthy Adolescent Sexuality**, Family Relations, 39 (1990) 123-131.

[8]   E. Diener, S.C. Fraser, A.L. Beaman, & R.T. Kelem, **Effects of deindividuation variables on stealing among Halloween trick-or-treaters**. Journal of Personality and Social Psychology, 33 (1976) 178-183.

[9]   E. Diener, **Deindividuation, self-awareness, and disinhibition**. Journal of Personality and Social Psychology, 37 (1979) 1160-1171.

[10]   F.F. Furstenberg Jr. & J. Brooks-Gunn, **Teenage childbearing: Causes, consequences, and remedies.** In L. H. Aiken & D. Mechanic (Eds.), Applications of social science to clinical medicine and health policy, 1986, Rutgers University Press, New Brunswick, NJ, 307-334.

[11]   E.F. Jones, J.D. Forrest, N. Goldman, S.K. Henshaw, R. Lincoln, J.I. Rosoff, C.F. Westoff, & D.Wulf, **Teenage pregnancy in developed countries: Determinants and policy implications**, Family Planning Perspectives, 17:2 (1985) 53-63.

[12]   B. Latanè, **The psychology of social impact**. American Psychologist, 36 (1981) 343-356.

[13]   W. Marsiglio, & F.L. Mott, **The impact of sex education on sexual activity, contraceptive use, and premarital pregnancy among Americal teenagers**, Family Planning Perspectives, 18:4 (1986) 151-162.

[14]   National Research Council, Risking the future: Adolescent sexuality, pregnancy, and childbearing, Vol 1, 1987, National Academy Press, Washington, DC.

[15]   S. Prentice-Dunn, **Perspectives on research classics: Two routes to collective violence**. Contempory Social Psychology, 14:4 (1990) 217-218.

[16]   **Preaching abstinence as hearts grow fonder**, The Wichita Eagle, June 20, 1993, 1-2D.

[17]   R.C. Proctor, & W.M. Eckerd, *Toot-Toot* **or spectator sports. Psychological and therapeutic implications**. American Journal of Sports Medicine, 4 (1976) 78-83.

[18]   S. Schachter, & J. Singer, **Cognitive, social, and physiological determinints of the emotional state**. Psychological Review, 69 (1962) 379-399.

[19]   S.P. Schinke, L.D. Gilchrist, & R.W. Small. **Preventing unwanted adolescent Pregnancy: A Cognitive-behavioral approach**, American Journal of Orthopsychiatry. 49:1 (1979) 81-88

[20]   A. Schlegel & H. Barry III, **Adolescent Sexuality**, in Adolescence: An Anthropological Inquiry, 1991, The Free Press, New York.

[21]   M.L Snyder, & R.A. Wicklund, **Attribute ambiguity**. In J.H. Harvey, W. Ickes, & R.F. Kidd (Eds.), New directions in attribution research Vol 3, 1981, Erlbaum, Hillsdale, NJ, 197-221.

[22]   P. VanderVelde & K. Hyung-Chan, (Eds), Global Mandate: Pedagogy for Peace. 1985, Bellweather Press, Bellingham, WA, [Center for Global and Peace Education, School of Education, Western Washington University, Bellingham, WA 98225].

[23]   R.A. Winett, A.C. King, & D.G. Altman, Health Psychology and Public Health: An Integrative Approach, 1989, Pergamon Press, New York.

[24]   R.M. Yerkes, & J.D. Dodson, **The relation of strength of stimulus to rapidity of habit formation**. Journal of Comparative Neurology and Psychology, 18 (1908) 459-482.

[25]   L.S. Zabin, J.F. Kantner, & M. Zelnick, **The risk of adolescent pregnancy in the first months of intercourse**. Family planning perspectives 11:4 (1979) 215-226.

[26]   L.S. Zabin & S.C. Hayward, Adolescent sexual behavior and childbearing, 1993, SAGE Publications, Inc., Newbury Park, CA..

[27]   R.B. Zajonc, **Social facilitation**. Science, 149 (1965) 269-274.

[28]   P.G. Zimbardo, **The human choice: Individuation, reason, and order versus deindividuation, impulse, and chaos**. In W.J. Arnold & D. Levine (Eds.), <u>Nebraska Symposium on Motivation: 1969</u>, Vol 17, 1970, University of Nebraska Press, Lincoln, 237-307.

CATASTROPHIC FLUVIAL DEPOSITION
AT THE
ASPHALT SEEPS OF RANCHO LA BREA, CALIFORNIA

JEREMY AULDANEY
BIBLE SCIENCE ASSOCIATION OF RIVERSIDE
AND ANOMANOLOGY NEWSLETTER
2885 CALLE SAUSALITO
RIVERSIDE, CA 92503-6305

KEYWORDS

Vertebrate Paleontology, Sedimentology, Catastrophism, Fluvial Deposition - Pleistocene Fossils, La Brea Tar Pits, Asphalt Seeps, Flood Geology, Post Flood Catastrophism

ABSTRACT

The Rancho La Brea asphalt seeps of Los Angeles, California is the site of the richest and most diverse assemblage of Pleistocene mammal fossils in the world. The conventional mechanism for the formation of this deposit has herbivorous mammals getting stuck in pools of asphalt one at a time. Carnivores and scavengers were then attracted to the captive herbivore, to become trapped in asphalt themselves in large numbers. This is assumed to have occurred more or less continuously over the last 38,000 years.

Sedimentological and paleontological evidence calls for another interpretation. There is evidence that asphalt did trap some animals - mainly small mammals, small birds, reptiles, and insects in more recent times. Rancho La Brea lacks the evidence expected at a trap site. However, evidence of rapid deposition of the sediments in which the fossils are found argues that most of the animals - especially the larger Pleistocene extinct species - were actually deposited by flash flood events, which in turn attracted scavengers which may have become stuck in the asphalt and buried in subsequent floods on the Los Angeles / Orange County floodplain. Earthquake disruption and liquefaction may also have been factors which accelerated entombment of some of these animals. Evidence further indicates that deposition was not continuous, but a series of rapid catastrophic pulses. Finally, the slow seepage of asphalt through faults in the older underlying marine strata resulted in the remarkable preservation of these fossils.

This deposition is here re-interpreted to be the result of local catastrophism during the waning geologic catastrophism of the post-Flood period. This corresponds with the postFlood climatic cooling which led to what is commonly called the Ice Age.

INTRODUCTION

The Rancho La Brea fossil beds are located in Hancock Park, in downtown Los Angeles, California at an altitude of 165 to 175 Feet above sea level on the Hollywood alluvial fan, which stretches from the Santa Monica Mountains 3.54 Km to the northwest to the Pacific ocean 14 Km southwest of the pits [26, p.7-8]. The La Brea site was known for thousands of years by local Indians up to the present time as a source of asphalt for water proofing, hafting knives, cement for repairing implements, and securing ceremonial decorations [9, p.2]. The discovery of Clovis points and atlatals used to kill big game such as mammoths indicates a long history [26, p.23]. The first white man to take notice of the asphalt was Gaspar de Portola who noted it in his diary of the expedition of 1769-1770 on August 3, 1769 [26, p.2].

Original Appearance of the "PITS"

Before modern mining-by the white man started in the late 1800s the "pits" were hard asphalt mounds which looked like tar volcanos with crater-shaped vents several meters in diameter giving off explosive eruptions of large quantities of methane gas and asphalt flows. These flows ran down the mounds and in hot weather formed thin sheets only a few centimeters thick which hardened into layers. When work first started to mine the asphalt, the hard oxidized asphalt cap had to be dynamited to expose the soft liquid [17, p.178].

The Discovery of Bones

During the course of these mining operations, bones were found in the hard matrix. These were believed to be the common bones of modern cows and horses [29, p.174-175] stuck in the asphalt. These bones were thrown aside as a worthless nuisance. The discovery that these were ancient fossils of buffalo and horses was made when the owner of the property, Major Henry Hancock found a large canine tooth larger than anything he had ever seen which came from a saber-toothed cat and gave it to Professor William Denton of the Boston Society of Natural History in 1875 [26, p.3-4].

There was no further interest in these fossils until thirty years later, when geologist W. W. Orcutt re-discovered their importance when he examined the La Brea property to determine the possibility of developing the property for the production of petroleum. He discovered that several of the bones he had collected on his visit were extinct species. He immediately got permission to continue collecting bones and from 1901 to 1906 Orcutt obtained a good representative collection of typical species found at the site. This collection attracted the attention of Dr. John C. Merriam, a professor at the University of California at Berkeley, later to become president of the Carnegie Institute where he continued to fund the La Brea excavations through the work of one of his favorite students, Chester Stock. Stock became one of the most important and knowledgeable mammalian paleontologists in the United States. He also became a world expert on the La Brea site, having conducted extensive research resulting in over 25 technical papers, as well as the classic reference book Rancho La Brea: A Record of Pleistocene Life In California, sold for many decades at the Los Angeles Museum of Natural History's bookstore [26, p. xv-xiv; 18].

The Amazing Collection of Fossils

Through the work of these scientists about 10-thousand individual animals have been recovered from the asphalt [25, p.24]. The estimated total fossils recovered so far comes to 2-million bones, 100-thousand insects, 40-thousand mollusks, and uncounted microscopic plant and animal remains. There are about 600 different kinds of plant and animal species reported so far [26, p.1].

Origin of Trap Model

The interpretation of this site as a trap is found for the first time in the journal of Jose Longinos Martinez in 1792, where he states that birds and rabbits get stuck in the asphalt [8, p.114]. Then again in 1865, state geologist J. D. Whitney says he saw the bones of cattle and birds which had become entangled in what had become hardened asphalt [29, p.174-175]. Then after the discovery that these were the bones of extinct animals, John C. Merriam extended this uniformitarian explanation, claiming La Brea was an asphalt trap going back thousands of years into the Pleistocene. This theory met the expectations of Darwinian theory and it appeared to fit the observed data, so it has become dogma to the present time [19].

Trap Model Questioned

Starting immediately with the indepth research by Chester Stock and many others, evidence has accumulated which causes the researchers to question the trap model. This paper is a review of some of that evidence, and proposes a new interpretation of La Brea which is more consistent with our current level of knowledge, as well as the Biblical creation model of earth history.

THE STRATIGRAPHY OF LA BREA

The La Brea deposits are among the most superficial of deposits of the Los Angeles / Orange County Basin. Although wells have not penetrated the entire thickness of the basin sediments, it is thought that they lie atop the granodiorites and biotite-quartz diorite granites which characterize the northern margin of the Southern California batholith (see Figure 1) [33]. The origin of the batholith is conventionally assigned to the Jurassic.

The 5 to 9 Km [18] of sediments overlying the igneous bedrock are dominantly marine strata and are given stratigraphic assignment based upon contained benthic foraminifera [6; 24]. Beginning at the nonconformity above the igneous bedrock (see Figure 1) there is unidentified sediment believed to be the Sespe Formation (Lower Miocene), then (in succession) the Topanga Formation (Middle Miocene), and the Puente Formation (Upper Middle to Upper Miocene) [15]. The huge biomass of marine organisms in the Puente Formation (one of the largest in the world, producing one of the largest oil deposits) is thought to have been responsible for producing most of the petroleum in the Los Angeles / Orange County Basin syncline and surrounding areas [14, p.197; 6, p.136]. This includes the Old Salt Lake Oil Field less than a mile north of the La Brea mammal site. Atop the Puente Formation (see Figure 1) are the Repetto (Lower Pliocene) and Pico Formations (Upper Pliocene to Lower Pleistocene) [15; 21]. As the region's sediments were being deformed by faulting and tilting of the underlying rock, the Pico sediments were grading from deep-water marine turbidite sandstones, through mudstones into shallow marine coarse-grained clastics [32, p.228]. Apparently the Santa Monica Mountains were being elevated at this time, resulting in a regressive sequence of lithologies. Overlying the Pico Formation (see Figure 1), the Palos Verdes formation [15; 21] (with lateral equivalents in the Times Point Silt, La Habra, and San Pedro Formations [32, p.227]) continues this trend. The lower part of the Palos Verdes Formation (informally called member A) is composed of marine clastics which grade into more terrestrial alluvial deposits [26, p.7]. The attitude and relationships of the older underlying marine shales, sandstones, and oil sand indicate a period of upthrusting, folding, then erosion; Followed by the deposit of the terrestrial alluvial fan, made up of sand, clay, and gravel containing terrestrial material and fossils. This terrestrial material was being laid down on top of an erosional unconformity between it and the underlying marine rock as the upheaval waned, upwarping only the lowermost layers, leaving most of the mammal bonebeds in an essentially horizontal strata (see Figure 2).

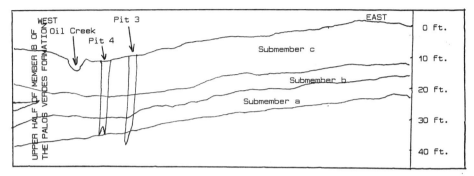

Figure 1. *A cross section of the fossiliferous strata at Rancho La Brea, along an east-west direction across Hancock Park. From Shaw and Quinn (1986) [27, p.8].*

PALOS VERDES $\dfrac{mbr\ B}{mbr\ A}$
122m (400ft)
PICO
305m to 915m (1,000ft to 3,000ft)
PEPETTO
5,490m (18,000ft)
PUENTE
2,380m (7,800ft)
TOPANGA GROUP
640m (2,100ft)
SESPE
365m (1,200ft)

Figure 2. Generalized stratigraphic chart of the Los Angeles basin from Blake [6, p. 139]

The fossils of La Brea are found in distinct bonebeds in the upper half of member B of the Palos Verdes Sand formation [26, p.12]. Marine member A and the lower half of member B of the Palos Verdes Sand formation have been conventionally assigned to the Sagamonian Interglacial period (100,000 y.b.p.) based upon foraminifera and nonoplankton assemblages [27; 30; 26, p.7]. In the bonebeds, radiocarbon dates range from 38,000 years b.p. to 11,000 (with a very few exceptions) [17; 26, p.9]. Conventional dating thus argues for a hiatus in deposition of somewhere on the order of 60,000 years within the Palos Verdes formation. At the La Brea site, the sediments of the bonebeds of upper member B are coarse angular to fine clastics of the Hollywood alluvial fan. The absence of marine organisms and the presence of terrestrial land animals and fresh-water mollusks argues that the deposits are terrestrial. The structure of the fan and the lithology of contained clasts indicates that the source rock of the Hollywood alluvial fan is outwash material whose parent rock is found in Benedict, Coldwater, and other nearby canyons northwest of the pits in the Santa Monica Mountains. The Palos Verdes Sand Formation thins from its exposures in the Santa Monica Mountains to its deposit on the coast [31]. In excess of 58 meters thick in places at the foothills of the Santa Monica Mountains, the Palos Verdes Formation has thinned to 42.7 m by the time it has gotten to the La Brea site 3.54 Km distant [26, p.12]. It is important to note that the Hollywood alluvial fan is no longer a depositional surface, but an area of erosion. The fan is currently being dissected and eroded in a dendritic pattern by rivers and streams [26, p.7]. This plus the coarse nature of the sediments indicate that substantially larger volumes of water than are experienced today were responsible for the deposition of the sediments of La Brea and other mammal sites in the Los Angeles area.

Oil, apparently derived from the organic material of the Puente formation (see Figure 1) seeped to the surface in various localities from Cape Mendocino to Los Angeles - a distance of 724 Km - from a layer of this oil bearing marine shale averaging 610 m thick. This shale outcrops and has produced asphalt seeps at McKittrick, Maracapa, the marine cliffs in Santa Barbara, Carpinteria, and at La Brea [29, pp.174-175; 19, p.20]. At La Brea, the petroleum seeped to the surface through faults produced during Pleistocene deposition. The residue of this oil upon evaporation produces asphalt. In the specific case of La Brea in Hancock Park, the clustered alignment of asphalt seeps along a northwest-southeast trend throughout the length of the park indicates seepage along the sub-surface fault discovered along Sixth Street bordering the north side of the park [26, p.8; 2]. The remarkable preservation of the fossils at La Brea is due to asphalt impregnation. The same assemblage of fossils can be found at many sites around the world, although usually not as well preserved. The unique preservation of the La Brea fossils have made them a standard for comparison. Any assemblage of fossil mammals similar to that at La Brea is conventionally considered to have been deposited in the same period of time (the 'Rancholabrean Land Mammal Age') as those at La Brea -- namely Late Pleistocene (38,000 to 11,000 y.b.p.).

In Hancock Park the bonebeds are in the upper 9 m of member B. The uppermost 9 m of member B has been informally divided into three bonebed submembers (see Figure 2) [26, p.8]. The lowermost is bonebed a, which is 3.5 m thick. Overlying this is bonebed b at 2.1 m thick, and finally atop this is bonebed c, comprising the uppermost 3.4 m of the Palos Verdes Sand formation in Hancock Park. Individual asphalt pits in the park can be restricted to one of these bonebeds or cross-cut into several of them. Since asphalt has actually caused a considerable amount of post-depositional transport of bone material, bones found in asphalt pits are often not in situ and bones from different levels in the bonebeds may be mixed together. Most of the radiocarbon ages have been determined on bones extracted from large asphalt pits. Yet, even with the mixing, the radiocarbon ages are confined to three periods of time (38,000 to 19,300 years b.p.; 15,700 to 11,000 years b.p.; and 10,000 years b.p. to the present [17]) and roughly three stratigraphic levels. Those levels may represent the three bonebeds a, b, and c, possibly indicating three periods of deposition.

Bonebeds a and b are apparently those which have produced the distinctive Pleistocene 'Rancholabrean' mammal association. The Holocene deposits of bonebed c appear to be qualitatively different. With the exception of cases where mixing has brought up material from lower bonebeds, those characteristics which distinguish bonebed c from the underlying bonebeds a and b include:

(1)   a more superficial position (above 3.4 m depth) [17].
(2)   a distinctive matrix, with a substantially lighter color [11, p.44-47; 17; 27, p.16].
(3)   exclusively Holocene (post-10,000 y.b.p.) radiocarbon dates -- which are known **ONLY** from level c deposits (e.g. the human skeleton at 9,000 +/- 80 y.b.p. [5] and an atlatal foreshaft at 4,450 y.b.p. [27]
(4)   more 'pit wear' (inter-stratigraphic abrasion due to post-depositional transport within asphalt pits)
(5)   weathering due to subaerial exposure
(6)   toothmarks from scavengers, which have **ONLY** been reported from level c deposits and never identified with Pleistocene carnivores or scavengers [26, p.19].
(7)   human bones and artifacts [26, p.10] -- which again are known **ONLY** from level c deposits (e.g. a single human skeleton and three atlatals).
(8)   a fauna with a smaller average body size [26, p.10; 11, p.46-47; 25, p.16].
(9)   a lower percentage of extinct species [11, p.44; 25, p.16].
(10)   typical Pleistocene mammals being absent or rare [11, p.44].

THE TRAP MODEL

Most people, after observing the sticky tar in pools, then the asphalt-impregnated bones of mammals, have drawn the conclusion that these are obviously the remains of animals which got stuck in asphalt. The anomalously high percentage of carnivores lends weight to this hypothesis. Of the 10-thousand animals recorded in field reports over the size of a weasel, 10% are herbivores and 90% are carnivores [26, p.177]. In a natural environment the ratio would be the opposite because it takes many herbivores to support a few carnivores. To explain the ratio, researchers suggested that herbivores got stuck in the asphalt, attracting large numbers of unwary carnivores and/or scavengers, who also became stuck. This hypothesis, which seems to explain the large predator/prey ratio, was called the "death trap of the ages" model.

Evidence Against Trap Model

(1)   An Asphalt Trap Is Not Needed

McKittrick is another asphalt site above the town of McKittrick west of Bakersfield in the oil Fields of Kern County, California - which is identical to La Brea in many ways [22]. This fact is important because, if McKittrick is fluvial and not a trap as most experts confirm, then La Brea could have formed in a similar manner. McKittrick has the same assemblage of animals, it is in the same horizon, and is dated very similar to La Brea. La Brea is dated by Carbon-14 as 11 to 38-thousand y.b.p.; to McKittrick's 10 to 38-thousand years b.p. [26, P-9; 22].

John R. Schultz, an expert on asphalt sites, concludes that McKittrick was not a trap site because the tar seeps to the surface in thin sheets only about 2-centimeters thick, much too thin to trap anything but very small animals and insects [22]. This was also true at La Brea before asphalt mining destroyed the strata and created the pits and pools [9, p.14; 17, p.178]. According to Marcus and Berger this prejudiced early researchers at La Brea to incorrectly interpret it as a trap site [17, p.178].

Additionally, the author has a coyote skull (*Canis latrans*) from Cherokee County, Iowa (see Figure 3) which is identical to coyote skulls found in the La Brea pits. It even has a bituminous coating which may have helped preserve it without petrification by mineralization. The difference is that it did not come from an asphalt seep. It came from a typical fluvial Pleistocene sand deposit, which has some post-depositional asphalt impregnation. Thus, it is at least possible to create a deposit like La Brea **WITHOUT** a trap mechanism.

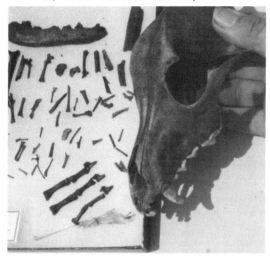

Figure 3. *Fossil bones of rodents, birds, and a fox jaw from the McKittrick asphalt seeps. The finger bones of a large rodent are twice the size of a modern squirrel. See the modern squirrels hand in the lower right corner for comparison.*

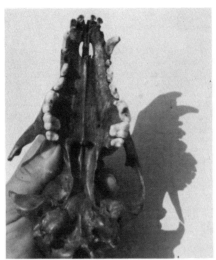

Figure 4. *Fossil coyote skull with bituminous coating From a Pleistocene fluvial deposit in Cherokee County, Iowa. Dorsal view A, ventral view B. Notice the tooth wear. It is identical to those found at La Brea and McKittrick.*

(2) Some Mammals at La Brea Definitely Were Not Trapped

The first blow to the "death trap of the ages" hypothesis which attracted the attention of La Brea researchers was in 1968 when they excavated a massive, arenaceous blue-clay enclosing grey quartz sand and gravel lenses with occasional asphalt pockets and seeps on the western margin of Hancock Park along Ogden Drive. Here they encountered isolated bones, including part of a saber-toothed (*Smilodon fatalis*) skull in sediment which contained **NO** asphalt when it was deposited. G.D. Woodard states that this, "...supports the conclusion that many bones throughout Rancho La Brea were deposited, and in all likelihood concentrated into pockets, by such fluvial agencies" [30, p.66]. Asphalt in such sedimentary pockets is a later intrusion, as indicated by higher asphalt concentration in the lower portions of the pockets [23]. The most important researcher, Chester Stock writes, "...some (animal remains) may have been transported considerable distances; such fluvial accumulations were secondarily impregnated by asphalt" [26, p.14]. This conclusion is shared by other researchers [8; 20; 23].

Again in 1975, while excavating at the east end of Hancock Park, for the foundation of the George C. Page Museum, a tongue-shaped sedimentary body was discovered which contained fully and partially articulated skeletons and associated skeletal parts. It was found 1.5 meters below ground; and was 10 meters long, 3 meters wide, and 0.4 meter thick. It was deposited in sharp basal contact with a massive claystone below, and overlain with silty claystone. This deposit was unusual because unlike all the "pit" deposits:

(1)   It was not funnel shaped with apex down (believed to have been created by the manner of excavation).

(2)   Many of the bones were not disarticulated [13, p.71].

(3)   It was poorly impregnated with asphalt [23, p.79].

Scott [23, p.79] argues that entrapment was **NOT** indicated in this particular deposit, but that asphalt impregnation was post-depositional. Thus at least some of the La Brea fossils were **NOT** captured by means of the trap mechanism.

(3) Evidence of Fluvial Deposition

Scott E. Miller states that as far as the asphalt trap model is concerned, "recent studies... indicate that such 'death traps' had only a minor role in the accumulation of fossils". He continues that the stratigraphy in the pits and Carbon-14 dating indicate fossils were deposited at sites of discontinuous active asphalt seeps during accumulation of alluvium. This was because, it was discovered during the course of excavation of undisturbed fossil bonebeds, stratification was noted which would not be found in pools of asphalt. And it was further recorded that these stratified layers continued on into non-fossiliferous, non-asphaltic sediment surrounding the pits [20, p.92-93].

All this evidence indicates that most of the animals in the asphalt deposits could have been buried by the fluvial processes which created other sedimentary fossil mammal sites. It may be that only a small percentage of the fossil material was trapped in asphalt, and the few animals that were, were buried by alluvial processes [17, p.177-178; 2] identical to other typical sedimentary fluvial deposits. These other fluvial mammal sites have these characteristics:

(1) They contain identical species of animals, such as Camp Cady, Yermo, the Calico Mountains in and near the dry Pleistocene Lake Manix Basin [12, p.94].

(2) The fossils are in the same strata and horizon.

(3) They are also in nearby areas in strata connected to the strata at La Brea, arched over the Dominguez Hills 19 Km to the south of La Brea, in the Palos Verdes Hills, and San Pedro [26, p.7].

(4) No Age or Health Bias

Dr. John C. Merriam predicted (based on the assumed trap model) in 1911, that the greatest number of animals in the tar pits would be the old and the young (i.e. the weak, diseased, and inexperienced) [19, p.209]. Since then, bone growth, tooth growth, and tooth wear studies by G. J. Miller indicate that all ages of saber-toothed (*Smilodon fatalis*) cat were present, and are consistent with the age frequency distribution found for living populations of African lion today [17, p.178]. All ages, as well as weak, and strong, are also found among the horses of La Brea [23, p.79]. Scott states that those individuals younger than six months comprise only 10% to 15% of the general population, which is normal for a herd of horses [23, p.79]. Such non-selective assemblages argue against asphalt entrapment and for catastrophic burial [1, p.122].

(5) No Fossils In Pure Asphalt

If La Brea was a trap site one might expect many of the bones to be found in pure asphalt and not just in hard sediments with asphalt between the grains. At La Brea very few bones were found in pure asphalt alone - and these were not in situ. All reports show that most or perhaps all of the bones were entombed in hard asphalt impregnated sand, gravel, or clay. Also, the greatest concentrations of bones occurred in sediments containing the highest concentrations of clasts of fluvial origin [30, p.56].

(6) Lack of Footprints

There is a mammoth trap site deposit at Hot Springs, South Dakota, where erosion of limestone produced a karst feature (a sink hole). A herd of Pleistocene mammoths ([*Mammuthus columbi*] identical to the species found at La Brea) fell into this hole alive to be mired in quicksand, trampled, then buried by incoming fluvial sediment. Tracks found in several levels of the sediment indicate the animals were alive at the time of entrapment [1, p.118]. If Rancho La Brea's mammoths, bison, horses, etc., "were captured in shallow surface sheets of viscus asphalt" as John M. Harris tells us, "rather than in large pools or 'Pits'" [9, p.10], fossil ichnites would be expected to be found on the underlying hardening asphalt or clay, but **NONE** are reported.

(7) Lack of Green-Bone Spiral Fractures

At the Hot Springs site there are many leg bones with green-bone spiral fractures, caused by torsional stress on living bone, as the animals tried to twist their feet out of the sticky mud. At the Page Museum they allow testing of the viscosity of asphalt by trying to pull a rod out of a container of asphalt. Asphalt is much stronger than mud. This being a case, there should be more green-bone spiral fractures at La Brea than at the Hot Springs site - and yet there are no reported cases of this kind of fracture at all.

(8) No Evidence of Trampling

Also at the Hot Springs site there is evidence of trampling - of crushed and broken bones. No such evidence has been reported at La Brea.

(9) Molluscs, etc.

Present were the shells of freshwater clams (*Anodonta californiensis, Pisidium casertanum, P. compressum, Musculium lacustre, and M. partumeium*) and snails (*Valvata humeralis, Pyrgulopsis californiensis, Fossaria modicella, F. parva, F. (Bakerilymnea) cubernsis, F. (B.) sonomaensis, F. (B.) bulimooides, F. (B.) cockerelli, Stagnicola elodes, S. proxima, Physella concolon, Gyraulus circumstriatus, G. parvus, Planorbella tenuis, and Menetus, opercularis*).

Since it is unlikely that such organisms could live in asphalt seeps, their presence here, as well as, the fluvial sites, such as Camp Cady in the Mojave Desert, argue that the asphalt impregnated the matrix **AFTER** deposition [12, p.94; 26, p.85]. Furthermore, since these shellfish are the kind carried into the area by freshwater rivers, and they surround the bones in the La Brea seeps, the bones may have been deposited in the same manner.

LA BREA IS A POST-FLOOD DEPOSIT

Like all Pleistocene fossil sites, La Brea was deposited in the waning catastrophism (after shocks) during the resettling period after the Flood.

Evidence:

(1) Pleistocene sites are usually only partly lithified or are unconsolidated sand and gravel laid down by glacial or fluvial processes near or on the surface.

(2) Pleistocene bones are seldom replaced by volcanic (usually silicon) mineralization. They are usually preserved as original bone under conditions of reduced decomposition in ice, caves, bogs lacking oxygen, surrounded by clay, or in asphalt.

(3) Pleistocene animals, plants, and insects are usually identical or very similar to living organisms; often still living around the fossil site or a little farther north (due to changes in weather patterns) [26, p.25].

(4) Pleistocene animals are commonly found in limestone caves or karst features. Since vast limestone deposits were formed during the Flood under submarine conditions, and caves can only form in aerial conditions, by flowing ground water above the water table; then any bones of animals entering these caves had to have been deposited after the Flood.

(5) Biblical and archaeological evidence indicates that only post-Flood or paleolithic (incorrectly called 'cave men' because of art found in French caves and ape skulls found in caves in Peking both of which were sites of industry not habitation) began with a lithic industry, because of a lack of more advanced technology; caused by their being scattered throughout the earth from Babel, according to the Bible. These paleolithic men are often associated with Pleistocene animals; drawing pictures of them on cave walls, carved on mammoth bones, left atlatl projectile points in the bones of mammoths, etc.

CREATION MODEL AT LA BREA

The evidence is overwhelmingly in favor of locally catastrophic fluvial flood plane deposition of all the sediments and most of the fossils at Rancho La Brea and at other asphalt sites. It appears that these animals were living during a stressful period of earth history - that of the immediate post-Flood era. Huge volcanoes erupting world-wide during the Flood, continued after it was over. Earthquakes upthrust mountain ranges, and torrential rains during what is called the paluvial period flooded inland areas during the cooling period (the sky was filled with volcanic dust for many years) leading to the so called, "Ice Age". This was the aftermath, or reshaping, rebalancing, and settling period of the global cataclysm called the Flood of Noah [4, p.134; 7, p.206].

The area around La Brea during this period is described by geologist Stephen Harris:

The more earth scientists learn about the physical evidence left by large earthquakes and volcanic eruptions during the recent geologic past, the clearer it becomes that such events are an integral part of the western scene [10, p.6].

Harris goes on specifically describing what happens during a huge earthquake resulting in volcanic eruptions. He says that sandy ground with a high water table turns into liquid sand geysers which erupt out of the ground [10, p.10]. It is interesting to note that Rancho La Brea is made of sand with a high water table, which could produce the liquefaction that turns the ground into rolling, gushing watery mush which can trap and bury living organisms suddenly.

Other Rancholabrean fossil sites like Camp Cady in the Mojave Desert have **ALL** the animals found at La Brea, except there is no asphalt, and there the herbivorous camels (rare at La Brea) are in the majority. Perhaps, during severe storm events in the post-Flood hard times, herbivorous animals sought food and safety on higher ground [12, p.97]. The carnivores, on the other hand, being mostly scavengers, sought an easy meal on the lower floodplanes, where the dead were washed down in the torrents.

Resent Reports Confirm these Conclusions

At this time, one of the most recent reports on research at La Brea and related asphalt sites (July 23, 1993) confirm the conclusions found in this research. The examination of thousands of jaws from several asphalt sites indicates that the teeth of Dire wolf, coyote, sabertoothed cat, and the American lion were fractured while they were still alive three times as much as equivalent carnivores today [28, p.456].

The researchers Blaire Van Valkenburgh and Fritz Hertel conclude that:

> It suggests that times were tough for these Pleistocene species; prey must have been difficult to acquire or retain. Prey availability may have been low, at least seasonally, forcing predators to fully consume their prey. Alternatively, predator densities might have been relatively high, resulting in intense competition over kills" [28, p.459] (NOTE: This would explain the high carnivore ratio).

The catastrophic aftermath of the Great Flood of Noah no doubt created catastrophic aftershocks for hundreds of years due to the resettling of the land after the upheaval, requiring rebalancing of the earth. This resettling is still going on today under Los Angeles, as well as, elsewhere around the world - resulting in earthquakes and volcanic eruptions with decreasing severity. That is, until the end times - when it will once again be like those days.

High Carnivore Ratio Explained

The fossil record shows a bias for concentrations of herbivorous animal tracks in lake, delta and costal planes; and for the tracks of carnivorous animals in floodplain depositional environments [17, p.126].

CONCLUSION

The evidence at La Brea indicates that the Pleistocene assemblage was deposited during stressful times, during a period of geologic upheaval and massive flooding.

The asphalt was the result of impregnation after and during the deposition of sedimentary strata, which resulted in the amazingly well preserved fossil bone and other organisms which would otherwise have been destroyed by acid ground water. The asphalt did trap some animals. However, they are mostly recent Holocene victims, consisting of small mammals, small birds, reptiles, and insects.

The evidence supports the conclusion that Rancho La Brea was a site of post-Flood waning local catastrophism only a few thousand years ago (possibly 5-thousand years as indicated in the Bible) where surficial deposits collected the remains of local flood victims, deposited on top of huge marine deposits formed during the Noachian Flood which collected in a sink hole created by the incline forming the Los Angeles/Orange County basin.

BIBLIOGRAPHY

[1]   L.D. Agenbroad, **Hot Springs, South Dakota: Entrapment and Tephanomy of Columbian Mammoth**, Quaternary Extinctions, P.S. Martin et al, Editors, 1984, University of Arizona, Tucson, pp. 113-127.

[2]   W.A. Akerstein, **Entrapping Pools or Flowing Streams at Rancho La Brea? Both!**, Abstract, Annual Meeting California Academy of Sciences, No. 1, 1991.

[3]   R. Arnold, **The Los Angeles Oil District, Southern California**, Bulletin of the United States Geological Survey, Professional Paper 309, (1907) pp.138-202.

[4]   J. Auldaney, **Asteroids and Their Connection to the Flood**, Proceedings of the 1992 Twin-Cities Creation Conference, The Genesis Institute, Minneapolis, MN (1992) pp. 133-136.

[5]   R.R. Berger, et al, **New Radiocarbon Dates Based on Bone Collagen of California Paleooindians**, Contributions of the University Archaeology Research Facility, Dept. of Anthropology, Berkeley 12 (1971) pp. 43-49.

[6]   G.H. Blake, **Review of the Neogene Biostratigraphy and Stratigraphy of the Los Angeles Basin and Implications for Basin Evolution**, Active Margin Basins, K.T. Biddle, Editor 1991, American Association of Petroleum Geologists, Tulsa, Oklahoma, Vol. 52, pp. 135-184.

[7]   H. Coffin, **Origin By Design**, Review and Herald Publishing Association, Washington, DC., 1983.

[8]   J.T. Doyen, et al, **Review of Pleistocene Darkling Ground Beetles of the California Asphalt Deposits (Coleoptera: Tenebrionidae, Zopheridae)**, Pan Pacific Entomologist, Vol. 56, No. 1 (1980), pp. 1-10.

[9]   J.M. Harris, et al, **Treasures of the Tar Pits**, Los Angeles Natural History Museum, Science Series, No. 31, 1985.

[10]   S.L. Harris, **Agents of Chaos**, Mountain Press Publishing Company, Missoula, Montana, 1990.

[11]   H. Howard, **The Avifauna Associated with Human Remains at Rancho La Brea, California**, Contributions to Paleontology, Carnegie Institute of Washington, 1939.

[12]   G. T. Jefferson, **The Camp Cady Local Fauna: Stratigraphy Paleontology of the Lake Manix Basin, in Inland Southern California: The Last 70 Million Years**, San Bernardino County Museum Association Quarterly, Vol. 38, Nos. 3 & 4 (1991), pp. 93-99.

[13]   G. T. Jefferson, et al, **New Articulated Vertebrate Remains from Rancho La Brea**, Current Research in the Pleistocene, J. I. Mead, Editor, A Peopling of the Americas Publication: Center for the Study of the First Americans, University of Main at Orono, Vol. 3 (1986), pp. 70-71.

[14]   A.W.A. Jeffrey, **Geochemistry of Los Angeles Basin Oil and Gas Systems**, Active Margin Basins, K.T. Biddle, Editor, 1991, American Association of Petroleum Geologists, Tulsa, Oklahoma, Vol. 52, pp. 197-220.

[15]   R.M. Kleinpell, **Miocene Stratigraphy of California**, American Association of Petroleum Geologists, Tulsa, Oklahoma, 1938.

[16]   M. Lockley, et al, **The Paleoenvironmental Context, Preservation and Paleoecological Significance of Dinosaur Tracksites in the Western USA**, In Dinosaur Tracks and Traces, Cambridge University Press, (1989) 121-134.

[17]   L.F. Marcus, et al, **The Significance of Radiocarbon Dates for Rancho La Brea, in Quaternary Extinctions: A Prehistoric Revolution**, P.S. Martin, et al, Editors, 1984, University of Arizona Press, Tucson, pp. 159-183.

[18]   T.H McCulloh, **Gravity Variations and the Geology of the Los Angeles Basin of California**, United States Geological Survey Professional Paper 400-B (1960), pp. B320-B325.

[19]   J.C. Merriam, **The Fauna of Rancho La Brea: Part I Occurrence**, 1911, Memoires of the University of California, Berkeley Press, Vol. 1, No. 2.

[20]   S.E. Miller, **Late Quaternary Insects of Rancho La Brea and McKittrick, California**, 1983, Quaternary Research, Vol. 20, pp. 90-104.

[21]   M.L. Nateland, **Pleistocene and Pliocene Stratigraphy of Southern California at Los Angeles**, 1952, (Unpublished Ph.D. dissertation), University of California at Los Angeles, 350 pages.

[22]   J.R. Schultz, **A Late Quaternary Mammal Fauna From the Tar Seeps of McKittrick, California**, 1938, Carnegie Institute of Washington Publications, Vol. 487, pp. 118-161.

[23]   E. Scott, **Skeletal Remains of Equus from the Page Museum Salvage, Rancho La Brea: A Preliminary Report**, 1989, Current Research In the Pleistocene, Vol 6, 78-81.

[24]   P.B. Smith, **Foraminifera of the Montery Shale and Puente Formation, Santa Ana Mountains and San Juan Capistrano Area, California**, 1960, Geological Survey Professional Paper 294-M, pp. 463-495, Plates 57-59.

[25]   C. Stock, **Rancho La Brea: A Record of Life in California**, Sixth Edition, 1956, Los Angeles Museum of Natural History, Science Series No. 20, Paleontology No. 11.

[26]   C. Stock, et al, **Rancho La Brea: A Record of Life in California**, Seventh Edition, 1992, Los Angeles Museum of Natural History, Science Series No. 37.

[27]   V.W. Valentine, et al, **Marine Fossils at Rancho La Brea**, Science, Vol. 169, (1970), pp. 277-278.

[28]   B.V. Valkenburgh, et al, **Tough Times at La Brea: Tooth Breakage in Large Carnivores of the Late Pleistocene**, Science, Vol. 261 (July 23, 1993), pp. 456-459.

[29]   J.D. Whitney, **Report an the General Geology of the Los Angeles Region**, 1865, Geological Survey, Vol. 1, pp. 174-175.

[30]   G.O. Woodard, et al, **Rancho La Brea Fossil Deposits: A Re-evaluation From Stratigraphic and Geological Evidences**, Journal of Paleontology, Vol. 47, No. 1, (1973), pp. 54-69.

[31]   W.P. Woodring, et al, **Geology and Paleontology of Palos Verdes Hills California**, 1946, United States Geological Survey, Professional Paper No. 207, pp. 1-145.

[32]   R.S. Yeats, et al, **Stratigraphic Controls of Oil Fields in the Los Angeles Basin in Active Margin Basins**, K.T. Biddle, Editor, 1991, American Association of Petroleum Geologists, Tulsa, Oklahoma, Vol. 52, pp. 221-238.

[33]   R.F. Yerks, et al, **Geology of the Los Angeles Basin, California An Introduction**, 1965, United States Geological Survey, Professional Paper 420-A, pp. Al-A57.

THE PRE-FLOOD/FLOOD BOUNDARY:
AS DEFINED IN GRAND CANYON, ARIZONA
AND EASTERN MOJAVE DESERT, CALIFORNIA

by

Steven A. Austin
Institute for Creation Research
Box 2667
El Cajon, CA 92021

Kurt P. Wise
Bryan College
Box 7585
Dayton, TN 37321-7000

KEYWORDS
Flood Model, Pre-Flood/Flood Boundary, Sedimentation, Sedimentary Rocks, Strata, Stratigraphy, Time, Tectonics, Erosion, Paleontology, Fossils, Discontinuity, Unconformity, Southwestern United States, Grand Canyon, Mojave Desert, Precambrian, Cambrian, Paleozoic, Megasequence, Continental Margin, Ocean Floor, Submarine Megaslide, Gravitational Collapse, Megabreccia, Megaclast, Diamictite

ABSTRACT
The singular events which occurred at the initiation of the Flood should have produced a geologic signature with at least five characteristics: 1) A mechanical-erosional discontinuity (ED) identified by regional structural analysis -- probably the most significant unconformity in any given area; 2) A time or age discontinuity (AD) identified by coarse sediments above the erosional unconformity containing lithified fragments of various sedimentary units found below the unconformity; 3) A tectonic discontinuity (TD), found at the erosional unconformity, distinguished by substantial regional tectonic disruption, especially at pre-Flood continental margins; 4) A sedimentary discontinuity (SD) consisting of a thick, fining-upward, clastic-to-chemical strata megasequence of regional to inter-regional extent defined at its base by a significant onlap unconformity; 5) A paleontological discontinuity (PD) marked by an increase in abundance of fossils and the first appearance of abundant plant, animal, and/or fungal fossils.

In Grand Canyon of Arizona one of the most significant regional unconformities (ED) is found at or near the top of the Chuar Group. Associated with the unconformity is the Sixtymile Formation -- a tectonic-sedimentary unit dominated by breccia with large clasts (TD) from the formations below it (AD). The Sixtymile Formation occurs at the bottom of a thick, regionally extensive series of strata called the Sauk Sequence, consisting of the fining-upward clastics, capped by carbonates (SD). Only low-abundance microfossils are known below the unconformity, whereas undisputed animal fossils occur only above the Sixtymile Formation, and there in great abundance (PD). We believe, therefore, that the Sixtymile Formation is the oldest preserved Flood deposit in Grand Canyon of Arizona.

In the eastern Mojave Desert region of California, the Kingston Peak Formation is a very thick, regionally extensive clastic unit containing gigantic breccia clasts (TD) from the formations below it (AD). Associated with the formation is one of the region's most prominent unconformities (ED). The Kingston Peak Formation is also the lowermost of a very thick, regionally extensive, transgressive, fining-upward, clastic-to-carbonate megasequence (SD) known as the Sauk Sequence. Only low-abundance microfossils are known from the Kingston Peak Formation and below, whereas common animal fossils are only found in rocks above the formation (PD). We believe, therefore, that the Kingston Peak Formation signals the beginning of the Flood in the Mojave region of California and should be correlated with the Sixtymile Formation of Grand Canyon of Arizona.

INTRODUCTION
Broad, theoretical studies are common in creationist geology [e.g. 34,29,44]. Theoretical studies are important, but they need to be substantially buttressed with empirical studies. In the process of applying theoretical concepts to actual data, poor theories can be rejected and better theories can be improved. The creationist literature has too few empirical studies to test the proposed theories. A general example of this phenomenon arises with the definition of the pre-Flood/Flood boundary in the stratigraphic column. As reviewed by [2], a number of (theoretical) pre-Flood/Flood boundary definitions have been introduced in creationist literature. Each definition fails when applied to actual stratigraphic sequences. Some of the

definitions are too ill-defined to be applicable to any geologic section; others, though successful in many localities, fail to define the boundary everywhere.

Revisions and additions to the previous criteria are proposed by [2]. This paper will review those criteria, discuss their applicability to the strata in Mojave Desert, California and Grand Canyon, Arizona, and, finally, propose the potential applicability of these criteria worldwide.

SUGGESTED PRE-FLOOD/FLOOD BOUNDARY CRITERIA

According to [2] the pre-Flood/Flood boundary should be associated with five geologic discontinuities. The five criteria are briefly summarized as follows:

1. *A Mechanical-erosional Discontinuity (ED)*. Energized by global tectonic activity, the early Flood waters may have caused some of the most substantial mechanical erosion in earth history. As a result, when seeking the pre-Flood/Flood boundary in a particular stratigraphic section, regional structural analysis should be undertaken to identify the most significant regional, mechanical-erosional unconformities. The pre-Flood/Flood boundary is likely to correspond to the most substantial (or one of the most substantial) of these unconformities.

2. *A Time or Age Discontinuity (AD)*. At any moment in the Flood, pre-Flood sediments will have had more than two orders of magnitude more time for lithification than any sediments formed earlier in the Flood. Among flood-generated conglomerates, those containing clasts of pre-Flood sediments would then be expected to be more common, thicker, of broader areal extent, and/or coarser than those containing clasts of Flood-generated sediments. Because later Flood deposition would bury pre-Flood source rocks, conglomerates with pre-Flood clasts are more likely to have been produced very early in Flood deposition in a given area. As a result, when seeking the pre-Flood/Flood boundary in a particular stratigraphic section, one should identify the conglomerates with clasts of underlying sedimentary units. Those conglomeratic units associated with the dominant mechanical-erosional unconformities in a region are likely candidates for the oldest preserved deposits of the Flood in that section.

3. *A Tectonic Discontinuity (TD)*. The unparalleled magnitude of tectonism in the first moments of the Flood should leave a distinctive tectonic signature in many places across the planet. Furthermore, the rapid plate motion suggested by Austin *et al.*'s Flood model [3] may leave the early Flood tectonism uniquely associated with few volcanics. As a result, when seeking the pre-Flood/Flood boundary in a particular stratigraphic section, one should search for evidences of tectonic disturbance in the region (e.g. rapid changes in sedimentary thickness, conglomerates, breccias, megaclasts, megaslides, and detachment faulting). The dominant mechanical-erosional unconformities of a region which are associated with the greatest amount of tectonic disturbance are likely candidates for the pre-Flood/Flood boundary in that region.

4. *A Sedimentary Discontinuity (SD)*. As the waters deepened at any given locality, earliest Flood erosion gave way to deposition. Waning energies would be expected to drop a megasequence of fining-upward clastics capped by chemical sediments (TST to HST in sequence stratigraphic terms). Given the unparalleled energies and the global extent of these early Flood waters, regional studies should reveal a transgressive megasequence as the largest such sequence in the stratigraphic column, and should contain sedimentary units identifiable regionally to inter-regionally. As a result, when seeking the pre-Flood/Flood boundary in a particular stratigraphic section, one should identify sedimentary sequences on a local and regional scale. The dominant, fining-upward, transgressive, clastic-to-chemical sedimentary megasequence sitting atop a dominant, mechanical-erosional onlap unconformity is likely to represent the first sediments of the Flood in that region.

5. *A Paleontological Discontinuity (PD)*. Under normal taphonomic conditions, probability of fossilization is proportional to rate of sedimentation. Compared to the rapid deposition during the Flood. The slow deposition in the pre-Flood world would have made fossilization of plant, animal and fungal remains unlikely. Also, it is very likely that the initial erosion of the Flood destroyed or reworked virtually all of the fossils which were present in pre-Flood sediments. Consequently, below the pre-Flood/Flood boundary, sediments capable of preserving fossils might, at best, contain only traces of the most abundant and easily fossilized life forms -- bacterial, algal, and protist fossils -- and probably in very low abundance. Plant, animal and fungal fossils might be expected to be found in high abundance only above the pre-Flood/Flood boundary. As a result, when seeking the pre-Flood/Flood boundary in a particular stratigraphic section, one should study the regional paleontology and note the abundance and taxonomic composition of fossils in each of the units. The dominant mechanical-erosional unconformity which has

at most uncommon fossils below and abundant plant, animal, and fungal fossils only above, is likely to represent the initial erosional event of the Flood in that region.

Rather than relying upon one criterion, the greatest strength of this analysis comes when all the criteria are used simultaneously on a particular stratigraphic section. This means that defining the pre-Flood/Flood boundary only becomes possible with a stratigraphic, structural and paleontological analysis of the region in which the section is found. The dominant, regionally defined, mechanical, erosional unconformity a) underlying the clastic unit which incorporates the highest proportion of lithified clasts from below the boundary, b) associated with the greatest amount of tectonic disturbance, c) directly underlying the most dominant clastic-to-chemical sedimentary megasequence with regionally deposited sediments, and d) underlain by low-abundance fossils of microorganisms, and overlain by high-abundance fossils of macroorganisms, can be confidently defined as the pre-Flood/Flood boundary in that region. If the geology of a region does not permit the use of any one or more of these criteria, the strength of the conclusion is lessened. If a boundary is well established in one region, correlation with other regions nearby should add strength to tentative boundary identifications in nearby areas.

APPLIED PRE-FLOOD/FLOOD BOUNDARY CRITERIA
Grand Canyon
At least 13,600 feet of Precambrian [14,17] and 4,000 feet of Paleozoic [1] strata are found in Grand Canyon. Most inter-formational contacts are gradational, intertonguing, or, at worst, paraconformable [1]. Of the ten boundaries with direct evidence of mechanical erosion, seven are not likely to have cut any more than 500 feet into underlying formations [2]. The three remaining unconformities occur in association with the Precambrian and Cambrian strata of Figure 1. In Grand Canyon the sub-Unkar Group unconformity (Figure 1) has less than 150 feet of local relief [17]. The actual depth of erosion must have been at least an order of magnitude greater. On the sub-Sixtymile unconformity, up to 230 feet of erosion is indicated by lithologic studies [11,14]. The limited exposure of the Sixtymile Formation (invisible at the scale of Figure 1), and the great thickness of the underlying Kwagunt Formation, make determination of actual depth of erosion impossible. The sub-Tapeats unconformity ("The Great Unconformity" of Figure 1) is observed to have up to 300 feet of local relief [1]. It also locally cross-cuts every sedimentary formation of the underlying 13,600 feet of Precambrian strata, and even the crystalline basement below. The most significant, direct, regional evidence of mechanical erosion in Grand Canyon is associated with The Great Unconformity. It is also possible that the sub-Sixtymile and the sub-Unkar unconformities could have been associated with comparable mechanical erosion.

In the entire Grand Canyon sequence there are just four stratigraphic horizons associated with significant evidence of a time discontinuity. The sub-Unkar unconformity separates high-temperature-generated metamorphic and igneous rocks below from sedimentary rocks above. The crystalline granitic rocks seem to have had time to cool before the unconformity was formed and subsequent deposition began. At the base of the Surprise Canyon Formation is a pebble-to-cobble, locally boulder, conglomerate with clasts of chert and limestone from the Redwall Limestone below it [4]. The breccia of the Sixtymile Formation contains clasts of the underlying Kwagunt Formation of the Chuar Group, some of which are 130 feet in length [11,14]. The base of the Tapeats Sandstone locally contains clasts eroded from the Shinumo Quartzite (a formation of the Unkar Group) which are up to 15 feet in diameter [1]. The dominant mechanical-erosional unconformities associated with the most substantial evidence of time discontinuity are the sub-Unkar, sub-Sixtymile, and the sub-Tapeats unconformities.

Thus far, evidence of four tectonic intervals can be found in the Grand Canyon sequence: a) at least 200 feet of fault displacement during deposition of the Shinumo Quartzite to account for convolute bedding [1] and variations in formation thickness [36]; b) at least 650 feet of fault displacement during deposition of the Nankoweap Formation to explain depositional features [14]; c) approximately 2,300 feet of fault displacement during the Cretaceous to explain the folding and faulting of pre-Cretaceous formations [36]; and d) up to 20,000 feet [36] of fault displacement after the deposition of the Chuar Group sediments to account for deformation of all Unkar and Chuar formations (Grand Canyon Supergroup in Figure 1), and possibly to explain the breccias and large (130 foot) clasts of the Sixtymile Formation [11,12]. It may be that the uppermost Precambrian event also generated many of the major faults in Grand Canyon, including those utilized in the Cretaceous tectonic event. The most profound tectonic discontinuity in the Grand Canyon strata sequence is associated with the sub-Sixtymile and/or the sub-Tapeats unconformities.

Most of the unconformities of Grand Canyon lack a complete fining-upward megasequence. Above the sub-Unkar nonconformity is found the Bass Limestone and the Hakatai Shale. Above the Hakatai/Shinumo

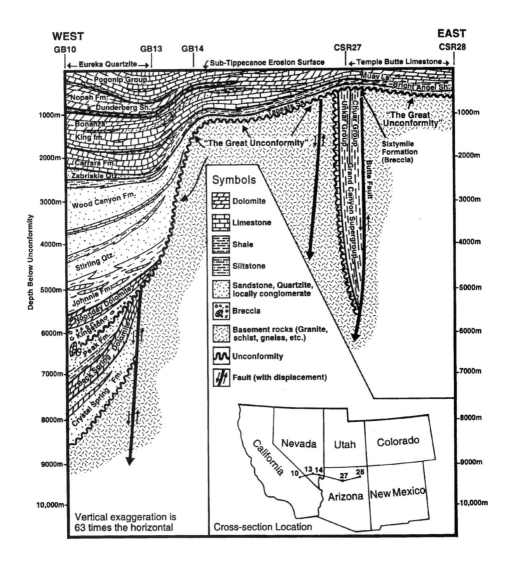

Figure 1. Paleogeologic cross-section of the southwestern United States showing the stratigraphic relationships of the uppermost Precambrian and the lowest Paleozoic strata. The cross-section indicates the original continuity of strata of the Sauk Sequence (e.g., the unconformity-bounded Kingston Peak Formation through Pogonip Group). The Sauk Sequence is separated from the pre-Sauk strata by an onlap unconformity of regional extent (The Great Unconformity). The pre-Sauk strata sequence in the eastern Mojave Desert (California) is the Crystal Spring and Beck Spring Formations, and some of the lower beds of the Kingston Peak Formations. The pre-Sauk strata sequence in Grand Canyon (Arizona) is the Grand Canyon Supergroup (the formations of the Unkar through Chuar Groups). The cross-section shows the sub-Tippecanoe erosion surface at the top as a level datum, and the diagram, therefore, emphasizes the enormous topographic relief on the sub-Sauk onlap unconformity (The Great Unconformity). Cross-cutting, faulting, tilting, and megaclasts in the diagram provide evidence of tremendous tectonic disruption of pre-Sauk rocks beneath the unconformity. [The diagram was created primarily from generalized COSUNA strata columns published by the American Association of Petroleum Geologists.]

unconformity is the fining-upward sequence of Shinumo Quartzite and Dox Formation. Above the Unkar/Nankoweap unconformity are the clastics of the Nankoweap Formation, and above the Nankoweap/Chuar unconformity are the fine clastics and carbonates of the Galeros and Kwagunt Formations. Above the sub-Sixtymile unconformity, however, are the very coarse breccias of the Sixtymile Formation, followed by the Tapeats Sandstone, the Bright Angel Shale, the silty carbonates of the Muav Formation, and the thin-bedded carbonates of the unclassified dolomites. This fining-upward, clastic-to-carbonate megasequence (Figure 1) in the western Grand Canyon is over 2,000 feet thick, and its base represents a sedimentary discontinuity associated with the sub-Sixtymile unconformity where it is exposed and The Great Unconformity elsewhere. That fining-upward sequence has been referred to as the Sauk Sequence on the North American continent. The sequence sits on an onlap unconformity of continental scale.

The paleontology of the Unkar Group includes possible stromatolites [16,17], and possible cyanophyte microfossils [16]. Fossils of the Chuar Group include possible stromatolites [15,17], *Chuaria*, a probable algae [15,16,17], microscopic acritarchs [17], melanocyrillids [6], and probable cyanophytes [16,32]. In the upper Tapeats Sandstone, several types of trace fossils [24], evidence animal life. Typical Lower Paleozoic fossils are found in abundance in the Bright Angel Shale and above [24]. The paleontological discontinuity of abundance occurs somewhere between the base of the Sixtymile Formation and the base of the Bright Angel Shale. The micro-/macro- fossil discontinuity is somewhere between the base of the Sixtymile Formation and the middle Tapeats Sandstone. Thus, the sub-Sixtymile unconformity and/or The Great Unconformity is associated with the paleontological discontinuity of abundance and micro-/macro-fossil transition.

When all five pre-Flood/Flood boundary criteria are simultaneously applied to the Grand Canyon stratigraphic sequence, the pre-Flood/Flood boundary is most likely to correspond to the sub-Sixtymile unconformity. This identifies the Sixtymile Formation as the earliest Flood deposit in Grand Canyon. In Grand Canyon the sub-Sixtymile unconformity is beneath the most substantial fining-upward megasequence (the Sauk Sequence), is directly associated with the most substantial tectonic disruption, is located within the zone of paleontological discontinuity of abundance and micro-/macro-fossil transition, is associated with the most substantial time discontinuity, and is closely related to the greatest mechanical-erosional discontinuity in the sequence.

Mojave Desert
The eastern Mojave Desert contains nearly 20,000 feet of Precambrian [27,32], and about 23,000 feet of Paleozoic [30] sediments. The Upper Precambrian to Lower Paleozoic strata are shown in Figure 1. Only four Lower Paleozoic or Precambrian inter-formational boundaries have substantial evidence of mechanical erosion: a) The nonconformity below the Pahrump Group (Crystal Spring, Beck Spring, and Kingston Peak formations in Figure 1) cuts an unknown distance into crystalline rocks. Yet, because each of the three Pahrump Group formations (up to a total of 20,000 feet thickness) lies somewhere on crystalline basement [2], it is likely that the unconformity surface has many thousands of feet of relief [22]; b) The base of the Kingston Peak Formation is locally conformable with the underlying Beck Spring Dolomite [22,25,27]. Elsewhere, it crosscuts all the 7,000 or so feet of underlying sediments and an undetermined distance into the underlying crystalline rocks [22,25,27]; c) The mid-Kingston Peak unconformity has an observed relief of more than 115 m in 600 m lateral distance [25,26]. Enclosed clasts of pre-Pahrump gneiss [25,26] imply it may cut through all of the nearly 8,500 feet of sediment stratigraphically below it; and d) Although the Noonday is occasionally conformable with the upper Kingston Peak Formation [25,27], it is usually an unconformity [25,26,27,32] with up to 300 m of observed relief [7]. It also crosscuts all the 10,000 or so feet of the Pahrump Group beneath as well as an unknown distance into the crystalline rocks below [25,26]. Any one of these unconformities -- that below the Pahrump Group and those within, below, and above the Kingston Peak Formation -- vie for the most substantial mechanical-erosional discontinuities in this section.

In Precambrian and Paleozoic strata of Mojave Desert, three substantial boulder conglomerates or breccias occur -- each containing clasts of all underlying formations: a) a conglomerate at the base of the Crystal Spring Formation [21]; b) a thick series of conglomerates and breccias in the Kingston Peak Formation [7,20,22,25,26,27,37,39,43]; and c) a conglomerate or breccia in the basal portion of the Noonday Dolomite [45,46]. Localized fault-associated lithification might account for some clasts -- for example, Kingston Peak and Noonday Dolomite clasts reported from the upper Kingston Peak [26] and the basal Noonday formations [7,46]. In contrast, the regionally distributed, thick deposits of the Kingston Peak Formation could not be entirely due to fault-associated lithification. The most substantial time discontinuities are associated with the Kingston Peak and sub-Pahrump unconformities.

Abrupt lateral changes in the thickness of the Kingston Peak Formation, and the vertical relief of the unconformity associated with it, are best explained by syndepositional faulting [25,26,27,7]. Megaclasts of lower formations up to 1,600 m long in the Kingston Peak Formation [27,38,40,41,43] and up to 15 m long in the basal Noonday Dolomite [7,46] also argue for syndepositional tectonism [43]. The best evidence of pre-Cenozoic tectonic discontinuity is associated with the deposition of the Kingston Peak Formation and earliest Noonday Dolomite.

Separating crystalline from sedimentary rocks, the sub-Pahrump nonconformity represents a sedimentary discontinuity. The Crystal Spring Formation above that nonconformity is, broadly speaking, a fining-upward (conglomerate-sandstone-shale), clastic sequence. It is capped by a cherty dolomite [21] and the Beck Spring Dolomite. The breccia-dominated Kingston Peak Formation can similarly be seen as the lowermost and coarsest clastic unit in another regionally distributed [31,38] megasequence. This sequence (the Sauk Sequence) is terminated at its top by the carbonate-dominated Bonanza King Formation, Nopah Formation, and Pogonip Group (Figure 1). Whereas the Crystal Spring/Beck Spring megasequence is up to 6,500 feet thick [27], the Kingston-to-Pogonip megasequence exceeds 30,000 feet thickness in the western Mojave region [27,30,32]. According to [38] the Kingston Peak Formation and correlatives are the oldest deposits which are distributed in a manner similar to the Lower Paleozoic sediments. This would be expected if the Kingston Peak Formation is the lowest part of the same megasequence.

Stromatolites and microfossils are known from every formation from the Crystal Spring Formation through the Johnnie Formation [2]. Macrofossils of Tommotian affinity have been reported from the Johnnie [15] and the Stirling [32]. From the lower Wood Canyon Formation, Ediacaran [19], pteropod [10], and trace fossils [10,33] are known. From the upper Wood Canyon upward, Lower Cambrian invertebrates are found in high abundance [10,28,31,37]. The paleontological discontinuity in abundance appears to occur somewhere within the middle Wood Canyon Formation. With only one possible microfossil found between the sub-Noonday unconformity and the upper Johnnie Formation (in the lower Johnnie Formation [32]), and only a few reports of microfossils in the Kingston Peak Formation [20,32], preservability of body fossils has not been well demonstrated in that zone. As a result, the paleontological micro-/macro-fossil discontinuity can only be said to lie somewhere between the basal Kingston Peak and upper Johnnie Formations. Any of the unconformities associated with the Kingston Peak Formation would be within this micro-/macro- fossil discontinuity.

Combining all five pre-Flood/Flood boundary criteria, an intra-Kingston Peak unconformity is the most likely location for the pre-Flood/Flood boundary in the Mojave region. This would identify the Kingston Peak Formation as containing the oldest preserved sediments of the Flood in this area. The intra-Kingston Peak unconformity is associated with a profound time discontinuity, lies directly below the most substantial evidence of tectonic activity, and occurs at the base of the most substantial fining-upward megasequence. It is also one of the most significant mechanical-erosional unconformities in the region, and lies below the paleontological discontinuity of abundance and somewhere within the range of the micro-/macro- fossil transition.

Grand Canyon/Mojave Correlation
Several correlations between Grand Canyon and the eastern Mojave strengthen the proposed equivalence of the Kingston Peak and Sixtymile Formations (see Figure 1): a) Both stratigraphic columns are nonconformably lying atop gneisses, schists and granitic intrusives; b) Two diabase sills in the Crystal Spring Formation of Mojave are positionally and mineralogically similar to two diabase sills in the Bass Limestone of Grand Canyon [43]; c) Microfossils found in the Pahrump Group of Mojave are similar to microfossils found in the Chuar Group of Grand Canyon [32], especially the vasiform melanocyrillids in the Kwagunt Formation of Grand Canyon and the Beck Spring Dolomite of Mojave [6,18]; d) Stromatolites similar to *Baicalia* and *Stratifera* are found in both the Galeros Formation of Grand Canyon [15] and the Beck Spring Dolomite of Mojave [23]; e) The Sixtymile and Kingston Peak Formations both contain very coarse breccias with very large clasts of local provenance [43]; f) Similar marine invertebrate fossils are found in the Paleozoic rocks (e.g. *Cruziana* in the Tapeats Sandstone and Bright Angel Shale of Grand Canyon and the Wood Canyon Formation and Zabriski Quartzite of Mojave [33]; *Olenellus* and *Glossopleura* trilobites in the Bright Angel Shale of Grand Canyon, and upper Wood Canyon and Carrara Formations of Mojave [28,31]); and g) The Tapeats Sandstone of Grand Canyon is equivalent lithostratigraphically to the Wood Canyon Formation of Mojave [13].

CONCLUSION AND DISCUSSION
It has been common to assign the pre-Flood/Flood boundary to the Precambrian/Cambrian boundary. In the eastern Mojave, where the Precambrian/Cambrian boundary is gradational and unassociated with

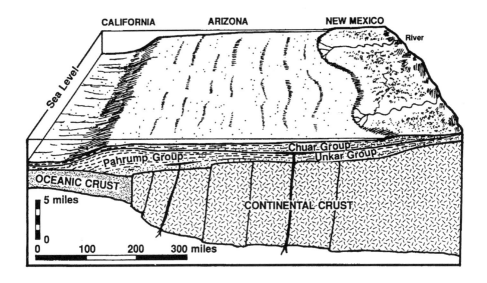

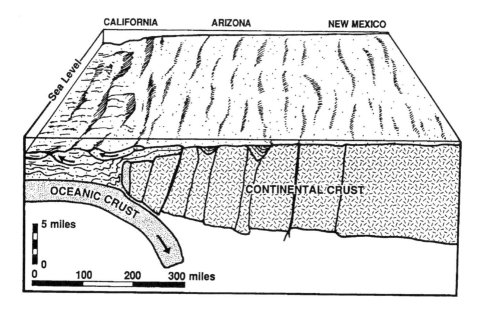

Figure 2. A tectonic-sedimentary model for the beginning of the Flood in the southwestern United States.

Top diagram: The continental margin the day before the Flood began suggesting how the ocean deepened westward. Thick pre-Flood sediments had accumulated on the continental margin.

Bottom diagram: Early in the Flood the continental margin was deformed in response to oceanic crust subduction. The oceanic crust in California was subducted causing the continental crust to be flexed, allowing Flood waters to invade the continent. The upper continental crust especially was in tension creating listric faults, rotated upper-crustal blocks (e.g., Grand Canyon Supergroup), and gravitational collapse of the sedimentary strata on the continental margin (e.g., the Kingston Peak Formation). The Kingston Peak and Sixtymile Formations are evidence of the initiation of the enormous tectonic event. With the invasion of the ocean, strata of the Sauk Sequence (Figure 1) were deposited over the disrupted continental margin.

43

an unconformity, these definitions fail to produce an unambiguous pre-Flood/Flood boundary. In contrast, the five criteria of [2] successfully identify a boundary in this sequence. We suggest the five pre-Flood/Flood boundary criteria of [2] will be sufficient to define the pre-Flood/Flood boundary worldwide.

Traditionally interpreted as a glacial deposit, we suggest that the Kingston Peak Formation be re-evaluated as a submarine landslide deposit. First, Cambrian paleomagnetics [28], Wood Canyon archaeocyathids [28,37], Kingston Peak oncolites [32], oolites [42], and carbonates [22,25,27,42] suggest a low-latitude, warm water, position for this area during the deposition of the Kingston Peak Formation. This is an improbable glacial environment. Second, faceted and striated boulders and possibly the lonestones claimed from the Kingston Peak Formation [22,25,27] can be produced in conditions of catastrophic mass movement [9,35]. Third, pillow lavas [22,25,27] and ripple marks throughout the formation [25,39] indicate subaqueous deposition. Fourth, dish structures, inverse- to normal- graded beds, turbidites, flame structures, and convolute lamination indicate not just subaqueous, but also rapid deposition [9,25,27,39,41,43]. We believe that these features of the Kingston Peak Formation can be better explained as a submarine landslide deposit than as a glacial deposit.

The Kingston Peak Formation is only one of many Upper Precambrian diamictites thought to be glaciogenic. Commonly associated with low-latitude indicators [25,26,35], these deposits may also have to be re-evaluated as non-glaciogenic. Being coarse conglomerates, they automatically represent a time discontinuity and substantial mechanical erosion. If a clastic sequence is above them, they are likely to define the base of a coarsening upward megasequence. Commonly deposited during tectonic disturbances [25,35], they seem to be associated with tectonic discontinuities. Typically found immediately below sediments containing Ediacaran organisms, they are likely to be associated with the micro-/macro-fossil paleontological discontinuity as well. We suspect upon re-evaluation that most of the Upper Precambrian diamictites will likely be understood to represent the first Flood sediments wherever they are found.

Based upon the sediments deposited atop the sub-Pahrump nonconformity in eastern Mojave [2,33], the easternmost portion of Mojave near the California/Nevada border was the location of a substantial change in the dip of basement rocks. We suggest that the change in dip may represent the shelf break on the pre-Flood cratonic margin -- with pre-Flood, basaltic ocean floor somewhere to the west, and pre-Flood shallow, continental shelf to the east (Figure 2, top diagram). We believe that the Kingston Peak Formation, which is only found to the west, and, thus, down the slope of this break, represents lithified shelf material which was disrupted and collapsed down that slope (Figure 2, bottom diagram). Olistostromes, turbidites, as well as common slump folds and soft-sediment deformation [43] seem to argue for rapid deposition by gravitational slumping on a sloping continental margin. Our proposal is that the disruption of pre-Flood sedimentary rocks occurred due to violent earthquake activity -- probably that associated with the initiation of ocean plate subduction (see [3]) (Figure 2, bottom diagram). If this is so, we would expect to see the same phenomenon along most of the world's pre-Flood cratonic margin. If we are to interpret such strata as submarine megaslide deposits, then the linearity of Upper Precambrian diamictites of western North America [25,38] may define the edge of the pre-Flood craton. We would suggest that worldwide application of the five criteria of [2] should permit an improvement in our understanding of pre-Flood geology and geography and earliest Flood dynamics.

REFERENCES

[1]   S. A. Austin, **Interpreting strata of Grand Canyon** and **A creationist view of Grand Canyon strata**, Grand Canyon: Monument to Catastrophe, S. A. Austin, editor, 1994, Institute for Creation Research, El Cajon, CA, 21-82.

[2]   S. A. Austin, and K. P. Wise, Defining the Pre-Flood/Flood Boundary within Strata of the Southwestern United States, in preparation, ICR Technical Monograph, Institute for Creation Research, Santee, CA.

[3]   S. A. Austin, J. R. Baumgardner, D. R. Humphreys, A. A. Snelling, L. Vardiman, and K. P. Wise, **Catastrophic plate tectonics: A global flood model of earth history**, this volume, 1994.

[4]   S. S. Beus, **Redwall Limestone and Surprise Canyon Formation**, in [5], 1990, 119-145.

[5]   S. S. Beus, and M. Morales, editors, Grand Canyon Geology, 1990, Oxford University, New York, NY, 518 p.

[6]   B. Bloeser, *Melanocyrillium*, **a new genus of structurally complex Late Proterozoic microfossils from the Kwagunt Formation (Chuar Group), Grand Canyon, Arizona**, Journal of Paleontology **59**:3(1985) 741-765.

[7]   P. E. Cloud, Jr., G. R. Licari, L. A. Wright, and B. W. Troxel, **Proterozoic eucaryotes from Eastern California**, Proceedings of the National Academy of Sciences **62**:3(1969) 623-630.

[8]   J. D. Cooper, and C. H. Stevens, editors, Paleozoic Paleogeography of the Western United States -- II, 1991, Pacific Section Society for Economic and Petroleum Geology, **67**.

[9]   J. C. Crowell, **Climatic significance of sedimentary deposits containing dispersed megaclasts**, in Problems in Paleoclimatology, 1963, A. E. M. Nairn, editor, Interscience, New York, NY, 86-99.

[10]   P. Diehl, **Stratigraphy and sedimentology of the Wood Canyon Formation, Death Valley area, California**, California Division of Mines and Geology Special Report **106**(1976) 51-62.

[11]   D. P. Elston, **Late Precambrian Sixtymile Formation and orogeny at the top of the Grand Canyon Supergroup, Northern Arizona**, United States Geological Survey Professional Paper **1092**(1979) 1-20.

[12]   D. P. Elston, and E. H. McKee, **Age and correlation of the Late Proterozoic Grand Canyon Disturbance, Northern Arizona**, Geological Society of America Bulletin **87**(1982) 1763-1772, referenced by [5]).

[13]   C. M. Fedo, and A. R. Prave, **Extensive Cambrian braidplain sedimentation: Insights from the southwestern U.S.A. cordillera**, in [8], 1991, 227-235.

[14]   T. D. Ford, **Grand Canyon Supergroup: Nankoweap Formation, Chuar Group, and Sixtymile Formation**, in [5], 1990, 49-70.

[15]   T. D. Ford, and W. J. Breed, **The problematical Precambrian fossil** *Chuaria*, Palaeontology **16**:3(1973) 535-550.

[16]   T. D. Ford, and W. J. Breed, **The younger Precambrian fossils of the Grand Canyon**, in W. J. Breed, and E. Roat, editors, Geology of the Grand Canyon, Museum of Northern Arizona, Flagstaff, AZ, 186 p., 1976, 34-40.

[17]   J. D. Hendricks, and G. M. Stevenson, **Grand Canyon Supergroup: Unkar Group**, in [5], 1990, 29-47.

[18]   R. J. Horodyski, **A new occurrence of the vase-shaped fossil Melanocyrillium and new data on this relatively complex Late Precambrian fossil** [abstract], Geological Society of America Abstracts with Programs **19**:7(1987) 707.

[19]   R. J. Horodyski, **Late Proterozoic megafossils from southern Nevada** [abstract], Geological Society of America Abstracts with Programs **23**:5(1991) A163.

[20]   R. J. Horodyski, and C. Mankiewicz, **Possible Late Proterozoic skeletal algae from the Pahrump Group, Kingston Range, Southeastern California**, American Journal of Science **290A**(1990) 149-169.

[21]   C. B. Hunt, and D. R. Mabey, **Stratigraphy and structure, Death Valley, California**, United States Geological Survey Professional Paper **494-A**(1966) 1-162.

[22]   T. C. Labotka, and A. L. Albee, **Late Precambrian depositional environment of the Pahrump Group, Panamint Mountains, California**, California Division of Mines and Geology Special Report **129**(1977) 93-100.

[23]   M. L. Marian, and R. H. Osborne, **Petrology, petrochemistry, and stromatolites of the Middle**

to **Late Proterozoic Beck Spring Dolomite, eastern Mojave Desert, California**, Canadian Journal of Earth Science **29**(1992) 2595-2609.

[24]   L. T. Middleton, and D. K. Elliott, **Tonto Group**, in [5], 1990, 83-106.

[25]   J. M. G. Miller, **Glacial and syntectonic sedimentation: The Upper Proterozoic Kingston Peak Formation, southern Panamint Range, eastern California**, Geological Society of America Bulletin **96**(1985) 1537-1553.

[26]   J. M. G. Miller, **Paleotectonic and stratigraphic implications of the Kingston Peak-Noonday contact in the Panamint Range, eastern California**, Journal of Geology **95**(1987) 75-85.

[27]   J. M. G. Miller, L. A. Wright, and B. W. Troxel, **The Late Precambrian Kingston Peak Formation, Death Valley region, California**, in Earth's Pre-Pleistocene Glacial Record, M. J. Hambrey, and W. B. Harland, editors, 1981, Cambridge University, New York, NY, 1004 p., 77-748.

[28]   J. F. Mount, D. L. Hunt, L. R. Greene, and J. Dienger, **Depositional systems, biostratigraphy and sequence stratigraphy of Lower Cambrian grand cycles, southwestern Great Basin**, in [8], 1991, 209-229.

[29]   B. C. Nelson, The Deluge Story in Stone: a History of the Flood Theory of Geology, 1931, Augsburgh, 190 p.

[30]   R. M. Norris, and R. W. Webb, Geology of California Second edition, 1990, Wiley, New York, NY, 541 p.

[31]   A. R. Palmer, **The Cambrian of the Great Basin and adjacent areas, western United States**, in Cambrian of the World, C. H. Holland, editor, 1971, Wiley-Interscience, New York, NY, 76 p., 1-78.

[32]   D. Pierce, and P. E. Cloud, Jr., **New microbial fossils from ~1.3 billion-year-old rocks of eastern California**, Geomicrobiology Journal **1:3**(1979) 295-309.

[33]   A. R. Prave, C. M. Fedo, and J. D. Cooper, **Lower Cambrian depositional and sequence stratigraphic framework of the Death Valley and Eastern Mojave Desert regions**, Geological Excursions in Southern California and Mexico (Guidebook: 1991 Annual Meeting, Geological Society of America), M. J. Walawender, and B. B. Hanan, editors, 1991, San Diego State University, San Diego, CA, 515 p., 147-170.

[34]   G. M. Price, The New Geology, 1923, Pacific Press, Mountain View, CA, 726 p.

[35]   L. J. G. Schermerhorn, **Late Precambrian mixtites: Glacial and/or nonglacial?**, American Journal of Science **274**(1974) 673-824.

[36]   J. W. Sears, **Geologic structure of the Grand Canyon Supergroup**, in [5], 1990, 71-82.

[37]   J. H. Stewart, **Upper Precambrian and Lower Cambrian strata in the southern Great Basin, California and Nevada**, United States Geological Survey Professional Paper **620**(1970) 1-206.

[38]   J. H. Stewart, **Latest Proterozoic and Cambrian rocks of the western United States -- an overview**, in [8], 1991, 13-38.

[39]   B. W. Troxel, **Sedimentary rocks of Late Precambrian and Cambrian age in the southern Salt Spring Hills, southeastern Death Valley, California**, California Division of Mines and Geology Special Report **92**(1967) 33-41.

[40]   B. W. Troxel, M. A. McMackin, and J. P. Calzia, **Comment and reply on 'Late Precambrian tectonism in the Kingston Range, southern California'**, Geology **15:3**(1987) 274-275.

[41]   B. W. Troxel, L. A. Wright, E. G. Williams, and M. R. McMackin, **Provenance of the Late**

Precambrian Kingston Peak Formation, southeastern Death Valley region, California [abstract], Geological Society of America Abstracts with Programs **17:6**(1985) 414.

[42]   M. E. Tucker, **Formerly aragonitic limestones associated with tillites in the Late Proterozoic of Death Valley, California**, Journal of Sedimentary Petrology **56:6**(1986) 818-830.

[43]   J. D. Walker, D. W. Klepacki, and B. C. Burchfield, **Late Precambrian tectonism in the Kingston Range, southern California**, Geology **14**(1986) 15-18.

[44]   J. C. Whitcomb, Jr., and H. M. Morris, The Genesis Flood: The Biblical Record and its Scientific Implications, 1961, Presbyterian and Reformed, Philadelphia, PA, 518 p.

[45]   E. G. Williams, L. A. Wright, and B. W. Troxel, **The Noonday Dolomite and equivalent stratigraphic units, southern Death Valley region, California**, California Division of Mines and Geology Special Paper **106**(1956) 45-50.

[46]   L. A. Wright, E. G. Williams and B. W. Troxel, **Type section of the newly-named Proterozoic Ibex Formation, the basinal equivalent of the Noonday Dolomite, Death Valley Region, California**, in Geology of the Northern Half of the Confidence Hills 15-minute Quadrangle, Death Valley Region, Eastern California: The Area of the Amargosa Chaos (California Division of Mines and Geology Map Sheet 34), L. A. Wright, and B. W. Troxel, editors, 1984, 25-31.

COMPUTER MODELING OF THE LARGE-SCALE TECTONICS
ASSOCIATED WITH THE GENESIS FLOOD

JOHN R. BAUMGARDNER, Ph.D.
1965 Camino Redondo
Los Alamos, NM 87544

KEYWORDS

Genesis Flood, geological catastrophism, runaway subduction, mantle dynamics, plate tectonics

ABSTRACT

Any comprehensive model for earth history consistent with the data from the Scriptures must account for the massive tectonic changes associated with the Genesis Flood. These tectonic changes include significant vertical motions of the continental surfaces to allow for the deposition of up to many thousands of meters of fossil-bearing sediments, lateral displacements of the continental blocks themselves by thousands of kilometers, formation of all of the present day ocean floor basement rocks by igneous processes, and isostatic adjustments after the catastrophe that produced today's Himalayas, Alps, Rockies, and Andes. This paper uses 3-D numerical modeling in spherical geometry of the earth's mantle and lithosphere to demonstrate that rapid plate tectonics driven by runaway subduction of the pre-Flood ocean floor is able to account for this unique pattern of large-scale tectonic change and to do so within the Biblical time frame.

INTRODUCTION

Many diverse mechanisms have been put forward to explain the dramatic and rapid geological changes connected with the Genesis Flood [6,7,13,14]. This event is here conceived to have generated the portion of the geological record beginning with the initial abrupt fossil appearance of multicellular organisms and including all of the so-called Paleozoic and Mesozoic eras and the lower part of the Cenozoic. In other words, the Flood is understood, in terms of normal usage of the words in the Genesis account, to be a global catastrophe that destroyed all the non-aquatic air-breathing life on the earth except for that preserved in the ark. Since the Scriptures indicate no large-scale destruction of life between the time of creation and the Flood, it logically follows that the initial abrupt appearance of multicellular fossils in the rock record must represent the onset of this cataclysm. The huge amount of energy required to accomplish such a vast amount of geological work so quickly together with the amazing order evident in the stratigraphic record and the smooth pattern seafloor spreading and continental drift documented in today's ocean floor obviously impose severe limitations on candidate mechanisms.

What constraints might one use to discriminate among possible mechanisms for the Flood? One is the pattern of downwarping and uplift of the earth's surface that produced the observed patterns of sedimentation. Broadly speaking, it is possible to divide the continental regions of today's earth into three general categories according to the type and amount of sedimentary cover. Cratonic shield areas such as the Canadian Shield, the African Shield, and the Scandinavian Shield, represent regions mostly barren of Phanerozoic, or fossil-bearing, sediment. Surface rocks are instead pre-Phanerozoic crystalline rocks, frequently displaying strong metamorphism and often deeply eroded. Cratonic platform areas, a second category, represent broad regions of continental surface with generally extensive and uniform Phanerozoic sedimentary deposits commonly a few kilometers in thickness. The third category includes Phanerozoic tectonic belts which frequently contain huge thicknesses of sediments-- often up to tens of kilometers--usually with strong compressive deformations, evidence of large vertical displacements, and vast amounts of volcanism and metamorphism. These zones are mostly located along the margins of cratonic shield or platform regions and usually contain high mountains.

These three categories, in the context of the Flood, respectively represent broadly uplifted and eroded areas, broadly downwarped areas that accumulated moderate thicknesses of sediment, and localized belts where downwarping and deformation were extreme and where huge thicknesses of sediment accumulated. The evidence indicates that when the forces responsible for the extreme downwarping in these tectonic belts abated, high mountains appeared as the deep, narrow, sediment-filled trenches rebounded isostatically. The sedimentary patterns therefore suggest that transient processes, almost certainly operating in the earth's mantle, caused dynamical subsidence and uplift within craton interiors and intense localized downwarping at craton edges. In the context of the Flood, these observational data speak of large and rapid vertical motions of the earth's surface. Such vertical motions represent distinctive patterns of internal stress and mechanical work that must be accounted for by any successful mechanism.

A second major geological constraint concerns the large lateral displacements of the cratonic blocks that also occurred during the Flood. From a stress distribution standpoint this requirement of translating continental blocks by thousands of kilometers in a short period of time severely constrains candidate mechanisms because it involves the solid-state deformation of rock in the mantle below. That craton interiors display so little Phanerozoic deformation despite the fact the cratons traversed such vast distances so rapidly means that stress levels within the cratons never approached the fracture or yield limits and that the forces responsible for moving these huge bodies of rock were diffuse and relatively uniform over the area of the block. Mechanisms that move the plates by applying forces at their edges cannot produce this general absence of deformation in the craton interiors. The only conceivable mechanisms able to move plates so far and so rapidly with hardly any internal deformation are those that involve large scale flow in the earth's mantle and that apply relatively mild and uniform tractions on the base of the plates. This constraint as well as the previous one both point to catastrophic overturning of the mantle driven by gravitational potential energy in large volumes of cold rock at the earth's surface and/or in the upper mantle and assisted by a runaway instability resulting from a temperature and stress dependent deformation law for silicate rock.

The thrust of this paper is to report advances in numerical modeling of such a mechanism for the Flood. Results from this effort have been presented in papers at the two previous ICC meetings in 1986 and 1990 [4,5]. In the 1990 paper it was shown how subducting ocean floor along the Pangean margins leads to a pulling apart of the supercontinent in a manner generally consistent with the pattern of seafloor spreading recorded in the rocks of today's ocean floor [16]. This paper describes a number of improvements in the model. One is the use of a much more detailed reference state for the earth that includes compressibility and phase changes. Another is the addition of depth variation in the mantle's viscosity structure that provides for a low viscosity upper mantle and a higher viscosity lower mantle. Another is a much improved plate treatment that includes the oceans. The plates are now tracked using a highly accurate particle-in-cell method. Dynamic surface topography and sea level are now also computed as part of a time dependent calculation. This yields maps of the continental flooding that occurs in response to the mantle's internal dynamics. In addition there are several numerical improvements that allow larger time steps and provide increased accuracy.

MATHEMATICAL FORMULATION

The earth's mantle in the numerical model is treated as an irrotational, infinite Prandtl number, anelastic Newtonian fluid within a spherical shell with isothermal, undeformable, traction-free boundaries. Under these conditions the following equations describe the local fluid behavior:

$$0 = -\nabla (p - p_r) + (\rho - \rho_r)\,\mathbf{g} + \nabla \cdot \tau \tag{1}$$

$$0 = \nabla \cdot (\rho\,\mathbf{u}) \tag{2}$$

$$\partial T/\partial t = -\nabla \cdot (T\,\mathbf{u}) - (\gamma - 1)\,T\,\nabla \cdot \mathbf{u} + [\nabla \cdot (k\,\nabla T) + \tau : \nabla \mathbf{u} + H]/\rho_r c_v \tag{3}$$

where
$$\tau = \mu\,[\nabla \mathbf{u} + (\nabla \mathbf{u})^T - 2\,\mathbf{I}\,(\nabla \cdot \mathbf{u})/3] \tag{4}$$

and
$$\rho = \rho_r + \rho_r(p - p_r)/K - \alpha(T - T_r). \tag{5}$$

Here p denotes pressure, ρ density, $\mathbf{g}$ gravitational acceleration, τ deviatoric stress, $\mathbf{u}$ fluid velocity, T absolute temperature, γ the Grueneisen parameter, k thermal conductivity, H volume heat production rate, c_v specific heat at constant volume, K the isothermal bulk modulus, and α the volume coefficient of thermal expansion. The quantities p_r, ρ_r, and T_r are, respectively, the radially varying pressure, density, and temperature of the reference state used for the mantle. $\mathbf{I}$ is the identity tensor. The superscript T in (4) denotes the tensor transpose.

Equation (1) expresses the conservation of momentum in the infinite Prandtl number limit. In this limit, the deformational term is so large that the inertial terms (as well as the rotational terms) may be completely ignored. The resulting equation (1) then represents the balance among forces arising from pressure gradients, buoyancy, and deformation. Equation (2) expresses the conservation of mass under the anelastic approximation. The anelastic approximation ignores the partial derivative of density with respect to time in the dynamics and thereby eliminates fast local density oscillations. It allows the computational time step to be dictated by the much slower deformational dynamics. Equation (3) expresses the conservation of energy in terms of absolute temperature. It includes effects of transport of heat by the flowing material, compressional heating and expansion cooling, thermal conduction, shear or deformational heating, and local volume (e.g., radiogenic) heating.

The expression for the deviatoric stress given by equation (4) assumes a viscosity μ that is dependent on the radial temperature and pressure distribution but independent of the strain rate. The stress therefore is linear with respect to velocity and represents the customary description for the deformation of a Newtonian fluid. This rheological law applies to the type of deformation in solids known as diffusion creep that is believed to occur in the mantle under conditions of extremely small strain rate. Equation (5) represents density variations as linearly proportional to pressure and temperature variations relative to a reference state. The compressible reference state is chosen to match observational data for the earth to a high degree of precision. It includes the density jumps associated with mineralogical phase changes. In the numerical model the set of equations (1)-(5) is solved for each grid point in the computational domain during each time step.

THE REFERENCE STATE

Equations (1)-(5) represent conservation of momentum, mass, and energy in terms of the local velocity, pressure, and temperature. The material properties such as thermal conductivity and specific heat may also vary with position. A much better approach than simply assuming constant values for these quantities is to rely on a reference model that provides these material properties as well as reference values for the temperature, pressure, and density as a function of depth through the mantle. Substantial effort has been invested over the last several decades to use seismic and other geophysical observations to formulate radial seismic earth models [8]. Such models typically provide density and compressional and shear wave speeds as a function of depth. It is possible, however, to construct more comprehensive earth models that give the full suite of thermodynamic quantities by using an equation of state together with estimates for material properties of silicate minerals obtained from experimental measurements. A desirable attribute of the more comprehensive models is that they reproduce the density profile of the seismic models.

The reference model used here is based on an equation of state that represents the density and temperature dependence of pressure as two independent functions, that is, $p(\rho, T) = p_1(\rho) + p_2(T)$. The Morse equation of state [2], derived from an atomic potential model of a crystalline lattice, is employed for the density dependence and given as follows:

$$p_1(\rho) = [3K_0/(K_0' - 1)] \, (\rho/\rho_0)^{2/3} \, E \, (E - 1) \tag{6}$$

where
$$E = \exp\{ (K_0' - 1) \, [1 - (\rho/\rho_0)^{-1/3}] \}$$

Here ρ_0 is the uncompressed zero-temperature density, K_0 is the uncompressed zero-temperature isothermal bulk modulus, and K_0' is the derivative of K_0 with respect to pressure. These three material parameters specify the pressure-density relationship for a given mineral assemblage. By choosing appropriate values for the upper mantle, the transition zone between 410 and 660 km depth, and the lower mantle, one can match the density profile given by the seismic models quite closely. The values used for these quantities versus depth are given below.

Depth Range (km)	ρ_0 (kg/m^3)	K_0 (Pa)	K_0'
0-410	3425	1.4×10^{11}	5.00
410-510	3695	1.6×10^{11}	4.00
510-660	3725	1.6×10^{11}	4.00
660-2890	4220	2.6×10^{11}	3.85

The thermal component assumed for the equation of state is simply $p_2(T) = \alpha KT$, where α is the thermal expansivity and K is the isothermal bulk modulus. Using standard thermodynamic relationships together with experimentally obtained estimates for quantities such as the specific heat and Grueneisen parameter, one can integrate the equation of state with depth through the mantle, starting at the earth's surface, and obtain a consistent set of thermodynamic quantities as a function of depth. Because the gravitational acceleration and the radial density distribution depend on each other, it is necessary to iterate the calculation to obtain a state that is in hydrostatic balance as well as in thermodynamic equilibrium. Depth profiles for ρ_r, T_r, p_r, g, K, α, γ, and c_v resulting from such a calculation are displayed in Fig. 1. Temperatures chosen for the top and bottom boundaries were 300 K and 2300 K, respectively. Also shown in Fig. 1 are profiles for the thermal conductivity and dynamic shear viscosity. The thermal conductivity is assumed constant with depth except in the bottom portion of the lower mantle where it is assumed to increase by about a factor of three because of the elevated temperatures.

Depth variation in the dynamic shear viscosity is modeled using a temperature and pressure dependent relationship of the form [10]

$$\mu = \mu_0 \exp[-(E^* + p_r V^*)/RT_r] \tag{7}$$

where μ_0 is a depth independent reference viscosity, E^* is an activation energy, V^* is an activation volume, and R is the universal gas constant. As in the case for the parameters of the Morse equation of state, separate values for E^* and V^* for the upper mantle, transition zone, and lower mantle are assumed. These are as follows:

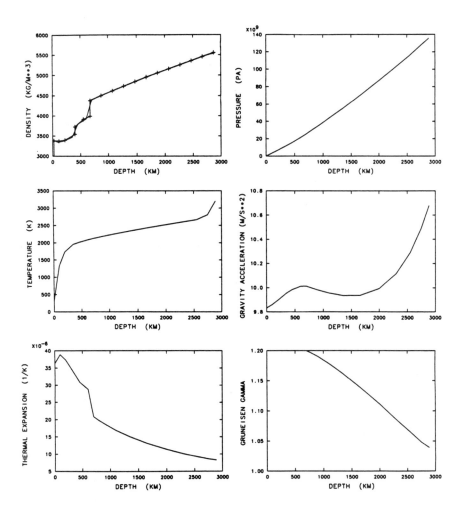

Figure 1 Radial profiles of density, pressure, temperature, gravitational acceleration, thermal expansivity, Grueneisen gamma, isothermal bulk modulus, isovolume specific heat, base 10 log of dynamic viscosity, and thermal conductivity for the earth reference state. Crosses and dotted line on density profile is the density for the Preliminary Reference Earth Model (PREM) of Dweiwonski and Anderson [8].

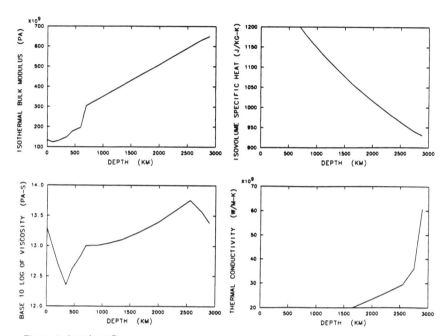

Figure 1 (continued)

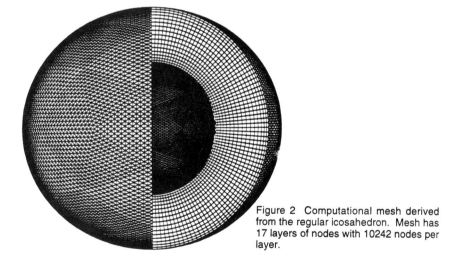

Figure 2 Computational mesh derived from the regular icosahedron. Mesh has 17 layers of nodes with 10242 nodes per layer.

Depth Range (km)	E* (kJ/mole)	V* (m^3/mole)
0-410	500	10.0×10^{-6}
410-660	555	6.0×10^{-6}
660-2890	640	2.6×10^{-6}

Due to limitations in the numerical algorithms, the extremely large viscosities that arise in the cold upper boundary layer of the mantle are clipped to a maximum value of $2\mu_o$ and the values of E* and V* are scaled by a factor of 0.7 relative to those given above. The resulting profile showing the depth variation of μ is displayed in Fig. 1.

PHASE CHANGES

The jumps in the density profile at 410 and 660 km, respectively, (Fig. 1) correspond in pressure and temperature to the transitions observed experimentally between olivine and spinel and between spinel and perovskite silicate structures. In a dynamical calculation in which silicate material is transported through these depths and undergoes these phase changes, two effects need to be taken into account. One is the latent heat released or absorbed and the other is the deflection of the phase boundary upward or downward. The latent heat may be accounted for by locally adding or removing heat through the volume heating term in equation (3) proportional to the vertical flux of material through the transition depth. The latent heat per unit mass is obtained from the Clapeyron equation which expresses that in a phase transition ΔH = (dp/dT) T ΔV, where ΔH is the enthalpy change, or latent heat, and ΔV is the change in specific volume. The Clapeyron slope (dp/dT) is a quantity that can be determined experimentally for a given transition. The deflection in the location of a phase boundary occurs because the pressure, and therefore the depth, at which the phase change occurs depends on the temperature. The effect of such a deflection enters as a contribution to the buoyancy term in equation (1). A downward deflection represents positive buoyancy because the lighter phase now occupies volume normally occupied by the denser phase. The Clapeyron slope is also a constant of proportionality in the boundary deflection Δh = -(dp/dT) $\Delta T/\rho g$ that arises from a deviation ΔT from the reference temperature. The values for the Clapeyron slope used here are 1×10^6 Pa/K for the 410 km transition and -4×10^6 Pa/K for the 660 km transition. Note that the exothermic 410 km transition leads to a positive or upward deflection for a cold slab and hence increased negative buoyancy, while the endothermic 660 km transition leads to a downward deflection and reduced negative buoyancy. The 660 km transition therefore acts to inhibit buoyancy driven flow while the 410 km transition acts to enhance it.

NUMERICAL APPROACH

The set of equations (1)-(5) is solved in a discrete manner on a mesh constructed from the regular icosahedron [2,3]. The mesh used in the calculations (Fig. 2) has 10242 nodes in each of 17 radial layers for a total of 174,114 nodes. There are 160 nodes around the equator which implies a horizontal spatial resolution of 250 km at the earth's surface. Nonuniform spacing of nodes in the radial direction assists in resolving the boundary layers.

The calculational procedure on each time step is first to apply a two-level conjugate gradient algorithm [17] to compute the velocity and pressure fields simultaneously from Eq. (1) and (2). This task involves solving 4n simultaneous equations for 3n velocity unknowns and n pressure unknowns, where n is the total number of nodes in the mesh. Key to the procedure is an iterative multigrid solver [2] formulated in terms of a finite element representation of the continuum equations. The outstanding rate of convergence in the multigrid solver is responsible for the method's overall high efficiency. Special piecewise linear spherical finite element basis functions provide second-order spatial accuracy [2,3]. The temperature field is updated according to Eq. (3) with a forward-in-time finite difference interpolated donor cell advection method.

Tectonic plates at the earth's surface are included in this framework by finding the unique Euler rotation vector ω for each plate such that the net torque ψ resulting from the surface stress field acting over the area of the plate is zero. The surface velocity field corresponding to this piecewise constant set of rigid plate rotations is then applied as a surface velocity boundary condition when solving equation (1). An iterative method is employed to determine the rotation vectors on each time step. For a given interior velocity field u and an estimate of ω for a given plate, small perturbations in ω about the x-, y-, and z-axes are made to compute torque sensitivities $\partial\psi/\partial\omega$. The current estimate for ω is improved by subtracting a correction $\Delta\omega$ proportional to $\psi/(\partial\psi/\partial\omega)$ in a manner that drives ψ to zero.

Because of the need for very accurate treatment of plate boundaries, a Lagrangian particle-in-cell method is used to define the plates themselves and to track their motion. Four particles per node have been found adequate to provide a sufficiently accurate plate representation. Piecewise linear basis functions are used to map particle data to the mesh nodes. The particles are moved in a Lagrangian manner at each time step using the same piecewise linear basis functions to interpolate the nodal velocities to the particles. The advantage of this particle method is extremely low numerical diffusion and hence the ability to minimize the smearing of the plate edges. When oceanic plate begins to overlap another plate, the ocean plates particles in the overlap zone are destroyed to model the disappearance of ocean plate beneath the surface. When two plates diverge, new oceanic plate is created by generating new particles. The plate identity of a new particle depends on the correlation of its velocity with the velocities of the plates on either side of the gap.

TREATMENT OF THE RUNAWAY INSTABILITY

A companion paper describes the consequences of using power law rheology [10,11] instead of the simpler Newtonian creep law in a model that also includes phase transitions. The result is to dramatically increase the potential for episodes of catastrophic avalanches [12,15,19,20] of cold material from the upper mantle into the lower mantle. Numerical calculations that include such physics require high spatial resolution and a robust scheme for treating strong lateral variations in the effective shear viscosity. Although this is currently feasible in two dimensions, computational costs are still prohibitive in three dimensions. An approach used to work around these limitations has been referred to as the Newtonian analog method. In this approach the effects of a nonlinear stress-dependent rheology are partially accounted for by simply using a Newtonian deformation law and reducing the value of the viscosity. Although this approach is far from satisfying, it is the best that can be done from a numerical modeling standpoint at this time. The results from such a strategy should therefore be understood as merely suggestive of what the more accurate treatment would provide. A further consideration is that spatial resolution currently still restricts the realism even of 3-D global Newtonian calculations. Some degree of scaling of parameters is usually necessary for such 3-D calculations to be stable from a numerical standpoint. One choice for reducing the steepness of the spatial gradients and thereby achieving the required numerical stability is to retain the desired value of Newtonian viscosity but to scale the thermal conductivity and the radiogenic heat production rate to values larger than those estimated for the real earth. This has the effect of lowering the overall convective vigor of the system as measured by the Rayleigh number $Ra = \alpha g \rho^2 c_v H d^5 / \mu_0 k^2$ where d is the depth of the mantle. The strategy then for mimicking the effects of power law rheology in a Newtonian 3-D model with limited spatial resolution is to select a reference viscosity μ_0 that yields appropriate velocities and to scale the thermal conductivity k and radiogenic heat production H by the amount necessary to yield a Rayleigh number low enough to be consistent with the available spatial resolution. For the calculation described below, a reference viscosity μ_0 of 1×10^{13} Pa-s, a thermal conductivity of 2×10^{10} W m^{-1}K^{-1}, and a radiogenic heat production rate of 0.02 W/m^3 are used.

INITIAL CONDITIONS

At a given instant in time the system of equations (1)-(5) can be solved given only the temperature distribution and boundary conditions. The only time dependent boundary condition is the plate configuration. Therefore to initialize a calculation one needs only an initial temperature distribution and plate configuration. The calculation shown below assumes an extremely simple initial temperature field related to an initial plate configuration that represents a late Paleozoic/early Mesozoic reconstruction of the supercontinent Pangea (Fig. 3a). This initial state is chosen because plate motions since this point in earth history are tightly constrained by observational data in today's ocean floors. The realism of the calculation in some sense can thus be tested against these observational constraints. Furthermore, geological evidence is strong that Gondwanaland--the southern portion of Pangea that included South America, Africa, India, Australia, and Antarctica--was intact throughout the Paleozoic era and that North America, Europe, and Africa also were not far apart during the Paleozoic. Therefore, the actual pre-Flood continent distribution may not have been much different from this Pangean configuration. The plate boundaries in the Pacific hemisphere are chosen to resemble the present ones. This implies the Pacific spreading ridges have not migrated significantly since pre-Flood times. The individual continental blocks represent the present continental areas mapped to their estimated Pangean locations. Initially the North American, Greenland, and Eurasian blocks are constrained to have a common rotation vector. Similarly, the Gondwana blocks initially rotate as a single unit. Later in the course of the calculation, these composite blocks are allowed to break into constituent parts with their own rigid motions.

The initial temperature distribution consists of the reference state temperatures on which is superimposed a set of slablike perturbations designed to represent incipient circum-Pangea subduction. The perturbations have an amplitude of -400 K, a depth extent of 400 km, and a width that corresponds to a single finite element basis function (about 250 km). They lie along the Pangean margin adjacent to South America, North America, and the Pacific and Tethyan coasts of Asia and along an arc in the ocean from southeast Asia, through what is now Indonesia and Australia as shown in Fig. 3a. Fig. 3b provides a cross sectional view through the earth in the plane of the equator and reveals the modest depth extent of the perturbations. Although they occupy but a tiny fraction of the total volume of the mantle, these small perturbations are sufficient to initiate a pattern of motions in the mantle that move the surface plates by thousands of kilometers. The process, of course, is driven by the gravitational potential energy existing in the cold upper boundary at the beginning of the calculation.

RESULTS

Starting with these initial conditions, the numerical model is advanced in time by solving the momentum, mass, and energy conservation equations at every mesh point on each time step. Tractions on the base of the surface plates produced by flow in the mantle below causes the plates to move and their geometry to change. Fig. 4 contains a sequence of snapshots at times of 10, 30, 50, and 70 days showing the locations of the continental blocks and the velocities and temperatures at a depth of 100 km. A notable feature in the velocity fields of Fig. 4 is the motion of the nonsubducting continental blocks toward the adjacent zones of downwelling flow. This

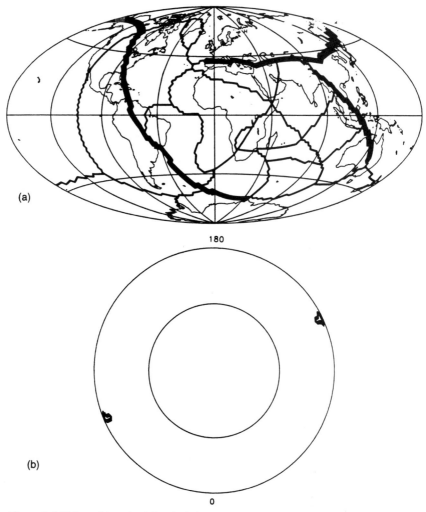

(a)

180

(b)

0

Figure 3 Initial conditions for 3-D calculation. (a) Initial plate boundaries represent present continents mapped to their approximate Pangean locations. Heavy lines represent thermal anomaly 400 K colder than reference temperature and one cell (about 250 km) in width. (b) Cross section through equatorial plane viewed from the north pole displaying deviations from the reference temperature. Temperature perturbations representing incipient subduction have a depth extent of 400 km.

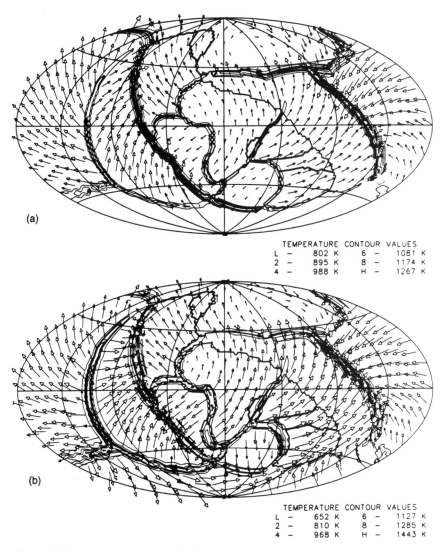

Figure 4 Temperature contours, velocities, and continent boundaries at 100 km depth at times of (a) 10 days, (b) 30 days, (c) 50 days, and (d) 70 days. Velocity magnitude is proportional to arrow length. Peak velocities at this depth are (a) 0.37 m/s, (b) 0.59 m/s, (c) 1.04 m/s, and (d) 0.98 m/s.

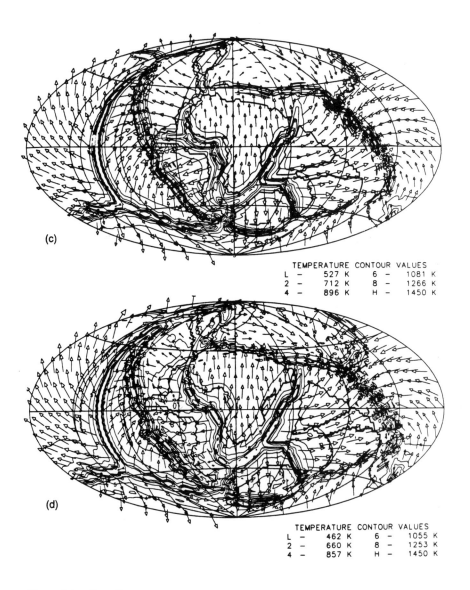

(c)

TEMPERATURE CONTOUR VALUES
L –   527 K   6 –   1081 K
2 –   712 K   8 –   1266 K
4 –   896 K   H –   1450 K

(d)

TEMPERATURE CONTOUR VALUES
L –   462 K   6 –   1055 K
2 –   660 K   8 –   1253 K
4 –   857 K   H –   1450 K

Figure 4 (continued)

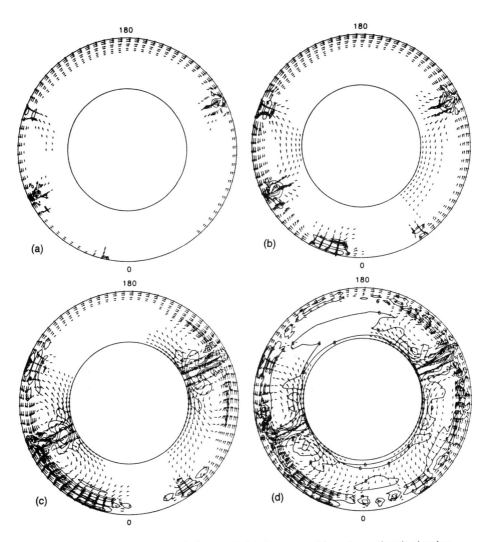

Figure 5 Cross sections through the equatorial plane viewed from the north pole showing velocities and contours of temperature deviation from the reference temperature at (a) 10 days, (b) 30 days, (c) 50 days, and (d) 70 days. The contour numbered 1 equals -400 K, the contour numbered 9 equals 400 K, and the contour interval is 100 K. Velocity magnitude is proportional to arrow length. Peak velocities are (a) 0.66 m/s, (b) 1.14 m/s, (c) 2.35 m/s, and (d) 2.57 m/s.

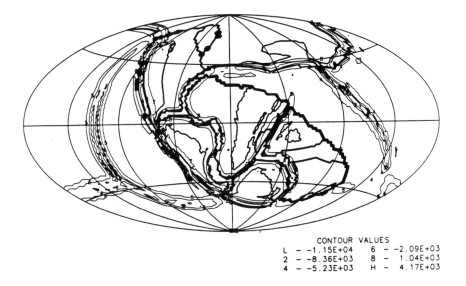

```
              CONTOUR VALUES
     L  - -1.15E+04    6  - -2.09E+03
     2  - -8.36E+03    8  -  1.04E+03
     4  - -5.23E+03    H  -  4.17E+03
```

Figure 6 Contours of surface topography in meters relative to local sea level at a time of 30 days. Heavier contour indicates sea level. Note that regions near divergent plate margins are elevated and continental areas adjacent to subduction zones are flooded.

motion is primarily a consequence of the drag exerted on a nonsubducting block by the material below it as this material moves toward the downwelling zone. Such a general pattern of flow is evident in the cross-sectional slices of Fig 5. The translation of the nonsubducting blocks in this manner leads to a backward, or oceanward, migration of the zones of the downwelling. This oceanward translation of the continental blocks as well as the subduction zones therefore acts to pull the supercontinent apart. This behavior is a basic fluid mechanical result and not the consequence of any special initial conditions or unusual geometrical specifications other than the asymmetrical downwelling at the edges of nonsubducting portions of the surface. That the continental blocks move apart without colliding and overrunning one another, on the other hand, depends in a sensitive way on the initial distribution of thermal perturbations, the shapes of the blocks, and timing of their breakup. A moderate amount of trial and error was involved in finding the special set of conditions that leads to the results shown in Fig. 4 and 5.

An important output from the calculations is the height of the surface relative to sea level. Fig. 6 shows global topography relative to sea level at a time of 30 days. Several features are noteworthy. One is the broad belt of depression and flooding of the continental surface adjacent to subduction zones, as evident, for example, along the western margins of North and South America. This depression of the surface is mostly due to the stresses produced by the cold slab of lithosphere sinking into the mantle below these regions. Narrow trenches several kilometers in depth lie inside these zones. A second feature is the elevation of the topography above the oceanic spreading ridges. This effect is so strong that some portions of the ridge are above sea level. Since the volume occupied by the ridges displaces sea water, a result is to raise the global sea level and to flood significant portions of the continent interiors. A third effect is the elevation of continent areas flanking zones of continental rifting. This is a consequence of the intrusion of a significant volume of hot buoyant rock from deeper in the mantle beneath these zones. This produces a belt of mountains several kilometers high on either side of the rift zone between North America and Africa, for example. It is worth emphasizing that the topography dynamically changes with time and that Fig. 6 is but a snapshot. It illustrates, however, that what is occurring in the mantle below has a strong and complex effect on the height relative to sea level of a given point at the earth's surface. Although this calculation is crude and merely illustrative, it shows that this mechanism produces the general type of vertical surface motions required to create key aspects of the global stratigraphic record. It produces broad scale continental flooding; it creates belts of thick sediments at the edges of cratons; it uplifts portions of the continents where broad scale erosion and scouring would be expected to occur.

CONCLUSIONS

This calculation illustrates that with relatively modest initial perturbations, gravitational potential energy stored in the earth's upper thermal boundary layer drives an overturning of the mantle that pulls the Pangean supercontinent apart, moves the continental blocks by thousands of kilometers, elevates much of the newly formed seafloor above sea level, floods essential all of the continental surface, and produces dramatic downwarpings of the continent margins that lie adjacent to zones of subduction.

The key to the short time scale is the phenomenon of power-law creep that, for parameter values measured experimentally and for strain rates observed in the calculation, yields more than eight orders of magnitude reduction in effective viscosity relative to a condition of zero strain rate. Indeed maximum strain rates implied by the calculated velocities are on the order of 10^{-4} s^{-1} --precisely in the range for which laboratory measurements have been made [10,11]. As discussed in more detail in the companion paper, the combination of the effect of the endothermic phase transition at 660 km depth to act as a barrier to vertical flow [12,15,19,20] with the tendency of thermal runaway of regions of cold material from the upper thermal boundary layer, makes a sudden catastrophic avalanche event a genuine possibility. Thermal runaway behavior is a direct consequence of the positive feedback associated with viscous heating and temperature dependent rheology [1,9] and amplified by an extreme sensitivity to strain rate. A notable outcome of the recent high resolution mapping of the surface of Venus by the Magellan spacecraft is the conclusion that there was a tectonic catastrophe on Venus that completely resurfaced the planet in a brief span of time [18]. This event in terms of radiometric time, accounting for the uncertainties in the cratering rate estimates, coincides almost precisely with the Flood event on earth. A mechanism internal to Venus was almost certainly the cause of that catastrophe. It is reasonable to suspect that simultaneous catastrophes on both the earth and Venus likely were due to the same phenomenon of runaway avalanche in their silicate mantles.

This mechanism of runaway subduction then appears to satisfy most of the critical requirements imposed by the observational data to successfully account for the Biblical Flood. It leads to a generally correct pattern of large scale tectonic change; it produces flooding of the continents; it causes broad uplifts and downwarpings of craton interiors with intense downwarpings at portions of craton margins to yield the types of sediment distributions observed. It also transports huge volumes of marine sediments to craton edges as ocean floor, in conveyor belt fashion, plunges into the mantle and most of the sediment is scraped off and left behind. It plausibly leads to intense global rain as hot magma erupted in zones of plate divergence, in direct contact with ocean water, creates bubbles of high pressure steam that emerge from the ocean, rise rapidly through the atmosphere, radiate their heat to space, and precipitate their water as rain. That no air-breathing life could survive such a catastrophe and that most marine life also perished is readily believable. Finally, numerical modeling appears to be the most practical means for reconstructing a comprehensive picture of such an event and for creating a conceptual framework into which the geological observational data can be correctly integrated and understood. This calculation, it is hoped, is a modest step in that direction.

61

REFERENCES

[1] O. L. Anderson and P. C. Perkins, **Runaway Temperatures in the Asthenosphere Resulting from Viscous Heating**, Journal of Geophysical Research, 79(1974), pp. 2136-2138.

[2] J. R. Baumgardner, **A Three-Dimensional Finite Element Model for Mantle Convection**, Ph.D. thesis, 1983, UCLA.

[3] J. R. Baumgardner and P. O. Frederickson, **Icosahedral Discretization of the Two-Sphere**, SIAM Journal of Numerical Analysis, 22(1985), pp. 1107-1115.

[4] J. R. Baumgardner, **Numerical Simulation of the Large-Scale Tectonic Changes Accompanying the Flood**, Proceedings of the International Conference on Creationism, R. E. Walsh, et al, Editors, 1987, Creation Science Fellowship, Inc., Pittsburgh, PA, Vol. II, pp. 17-28.

[5] J. R. Baumgardner, **3-D Finite Element Simulation of the Global Tectonic Changes Accompanying Noah's Flood**, Proceedings of the Second International Conference on Creationism, R. E. Walsh and C. L. Brooks, Editors, 1991, Creation Science Fellowship, Inc., Pittsburgh, PA, Vol. II, pp. 35-45.

[6] W. T. Brown, Jr., In the Beginning, 1989, Center for Scientific Creation, Phoenix.

[7] J. C. Dillow, The Waters Above, 1981, Moody Press, Chicago.

[8] A. M. Dziewonski and D. L. Anderson, **Preliminary Reference Earth Model**, Physics of Earth and Planetary Interiors, 25(1981), pp. 297-356.

[9] I. J. Gruntfest, **Thermal Feedback in Liquid Flow; Plane Shear at Constant Stress**, Transactions of the Society of Rheology, 8(1963), pp. 195-207.

[10] S. H. Kirby, **Rheology of the Lithosphere,** Reviews of Geophysics and Space Physics, 21(1983), pp. 1458-1487.

[11] S. H. Kirby and A. K. Kronenberg, **Rheology of the Lithosphere: Selected Topics**, Reviews of Geophysics and Space Physics, 25(1987), pp. 1219-1244.

[12] P. Machetel and P. Weber, **Intermittent Layered Convection in a Model Mantle with an Endothermic Phase Change at 670 km**, Nature, 350(1991), pp. 55-57.

[13] G. R. Morton, **The Flood on an Expanding Earth**, Creation Research Society Quarterly, 19(1983), pp. 219-224.

[14] D. W. Patton, The Biblical Flood and the Ice Epoch, 1966, Pacific Meridian Publishing, Seattle.

[15] W. R. Peltier and L. P. Solheim, **Mantle Phase Transitions and Layered Chaotic Convection**, Geophysical Research Letters, 19(1992), pp. 321-324.

[16] Proceedings of the Ocean Drilling Program

[17] A. Ramage and A. J. Wathen, **Iterative Solution Techniques for Finite Element Discretisations of Fluid Flow Problems**, Copper Mountain Conference on Iterative Methods Proceedings, Vol. 1., 1992.

[18] R. G. Strom, G. G. Schaber, and D. D. Dawson, **The Global Resurfacing of Venus**, Journal of Geophysical Research, 99(1994), pp. 10899-10926.

[19] P. J. Tackley, D. J. Stevenson, G. A. Glatzmaier, and G. Schubert, **Effects of an Endothermic Phase Transition at 670 km Depth on Spherical Mantle Convection**, Nature, 361(1993), pp. 699-704.

[20] S. A. Weinstein, **Catastrophic Overturn of the Earth's Mantle Driven by Multiple Phase Changes and Internal Heat Generation**, Geophysical Research Letters, 20(1993), pp. 101-104.

RUNAWAY SUBDUCTION AS THE DRIVING MECHANISM
FOR THE GENESIS FLOOD

JOHN R. BAUMGARDNER, Ph.D.
1965 Camino Redondo
Los Alamos, NM 87544

KEYWORDS

Runaway subduction, Genesis flood, power-law creep, thermal runaway, catastrophic plate tectonics

ABSTRACT

Experimental investigation of the solid state deformation properties of silicates at high temperatures has revealed that the deformation rate depends on the stress to a power of about 3 to 5 as well as strongly on the temperature. This highly nonlinear behavior leads to the potential of thermal runaway of the mantle's cold upper boundary layer as it peels away from the surface and sinks through the hot mantle. The additional fact that the mineral phase changes that occur at 660 km depth act as a barrier to convective flow and lead to a tendency for large episodic avalanche events compounds the potential for catastrophic dynamics. Two-dimensional finite element calculations are presented that attempt to model these strongly nonlinear phenomena. It is proposed that such a runaway episode was responsible for the Flood described in Genesis and resulted in massive global tectonic change at the earth's surface.

INTRODUCTION

The only event in Scripture since creation capable of the mass destruction of living organisms evident in the fossil record is the Genesis Flood. A critical issue in any model for earth history that accepts the Bible as accurate and true is what was the mechanism for this catastrophe that so transformed the face of the earth in such a brief span of time. The correct answer is crucial to understanding the Flood itself and for interpreting the geological record in a coherent and valid manner. It is therefore a key element in any comprehensive model of origins from a creationist perspective. Ideas proposed as candidate mechanisms over the past century include collapse of a water vapor canopy [5], near collision of a large comet with the earth [12], rapid earth expansion [11], and violent rupture of the crust by pressurized subterranean water [4]. There are serious difficulties with each of these ideas.

Another possibility is that of runaway subduction of the pre-Flood ocean lithosphere [2,3]. A compelling logical argument in favor of this mechanism is the fact that there is presently no ocean floor on the earth that predates the deposition of the fossiliferous strata. In other words all the basalt that comprises the upper five kilometers or so of today's igneous ocean crust has cooled from the molten state since sometime after the Flood cataclysm began. The age to today's seafloor relative to the fossil record is based on two decades of deep sea drilling and cataloging of fossils in the sediments overlying the basalt basement by the Deep Sea Drilling Program as well as radiometric dating of the basalts themselves [14]. Presumably, there were oceans and ocean floor before the Flood. If this pre-Flood seafloor did not subduct into the mantle, what was its fate? Where are these rocks today? On the other hand, if the pre-Flood seafloor did subduct, it must have done so very rapidly--within the year of the Flood. In regard to the fate of the pre-Flood seafloor, there is strong observational support in global seismic tomography models for cold, dense material near the base of the lower mantle in a belt surrounding the present Pacific ocean [16]. Such a spatial pattern is consistent with subduction of large areas of seafloor at the edges of a continent configuration commonly known as Pangea.

There are good physical reasons for believing that subduction can occur in a catastrophic fashion because of the potential for thermal runaway in silicate rock. This mechanism was first proposed by Gruntfest [6] in 1963 and was considered by several in the geophysics community in the early 1970's [1]. Previous ICC papers [2,3] have discussed the process by which a large cold, relatively more dense, volume of rock in the mantle generates deformational heating in an envelope surrounding it, which in turn reduces the viscosity in the envelope because of the sensitivity of the viscosity to temperature. This decrease in viscosity in turn allows the deformation rate in the envelope to increase, which leads to more intense deformational heating, and finally, because of the positive feedback, results in a sinking rate orders of magnitude higher than would occur otherwise. It was pointed out that thermal diffusion, or conduction of heat out of the zone of high deformation, competes with this tendency toward thermal runaway. It was argued there is a threshold beyond which the deformational heating is strong enough to overwhelm the thermal diffusion, and some effort was made to characterize this threshold.

The important new aspect addressed in this paper is the dependence of the viscosity on the deformation rate itself. Although this deformation rate dependence of viscosity has been observed experimentally in the laboratory for several decades, the difficulty of treating it in numerical models has deterred most investigators from exploring many of its implications. Results reported in the previous ICC papers did not include this highly nonlinear phenomenon. Significant improvements in the numerical techniques that permit large variations in viscosity over small distances in the computational domain, however, now make such calculations practical. The result of including this behavior in the analysis of the thermal runaway mechanism is to discover a much stronger tendency for instability in the earth's mantle. Moreover, deformation rates orders of magnitude higher than before throughout large volumes of the mantle now can be credibly accounted for in terms of this more realistic deformation law. This piece of physics therefore represents a major advance in understanding how a global tectonic catastrophe could transform the face of the earth on a time scale of a few weeks in the manner that Genesis describes Noah's Flood.

Recent papers by several different investigators [10,13,18,19] have also shown that the mineral phase changes which occur as the pressure in the mantle increases with depth also leads to episodic dynamics. The spinel to perovskite plus magnesiowustite transition at about 660 km depth is endothermic and acts as a barrier to flow at this interface between the upper and lower mantle. It therefore tends to trap cold material from the mantle's upper boundary layer as it peels away from the surface and sinks. Numerical studies show that, with this phase transition present, flow in the mantle becomes very episodic in character and punctuated with brief avalanche events that dump the cold material that has accumulated in the upper mantle into the lower mantle. The episodic behavior occurs *without* the inclusion of the physics that leads to thermal runaway. This paper argues that when temperature and strain rate dependence of the rheology is included, the time scale for these catastrophic episodes is further reduced by orders of magnitude. In this light, the Flood of the Bible with its accompanying tectonic expressions is a phenomenon that is seems to be leaping out of the recent numerical simulations.

MATHEMATICAL FORMULATION

In this numerical model the silicate mantle is treated as an infinite Prandtl number, anelastic fluid within a domain with isothermal, undeformable, traction-free boundaries. Under these approximations the following equations describe the local fluid behavior:

$$0 = -\nabla (p - p_r) + (\rho - \rho_r)\, \mathbf{g} + \nabla \cdot \tau \tag{1}$$

$$0 = \nabla \cdot (\rho\, \mathbf{u}) \tag{2}$$

$$\partial T/\partial t = -\nabla \cdot (T\, \mathbf{u}) - (\gamma - 1)\, T\, \nabla \cdot \mathbf{u} + [\nabla \cdot (k \nabla T) + \tau : \nabla\, \mathbf{u} + H]/\rho_r c_v \tag{3}$$

where

$$\tau = \mu\, [\nabla\, \mathbf{u} + (\nabla\, \mathbf{u})^T - 2\, \mathbf{I}\, (\nabla \cdot \mathbf{u})/3] \tag{4}$$

and

$$\rho = \rho_r + \rho_r (p - p_r)/K - \alpha (T - T_r). \tag{5}$$

Here p denotes pressure, ρ density, $\mathbf{g}$ gravitational acceleration, τ deviatoric stress, $\mathbf{u}$ fluid velocity, T absolute temperature, γ the Grueneisen parameter, k thermal conductivity, H volume heat production rate, c_v specific heat at constant volume, μ dynamic shear viscosity, K the isothermal bulk modulus, and α the volume coefficient of thermal expansion. The quantities p_r, ρ_r, and T_r are, respectively, the pressure, density, and temperature of the reference state. $\mathbf{I}$ is the identity tensor. The superscript T in (4) denotes the tensor transpose.

Equation (1) expresses the conservation of momentum in the infinite Prandtl number limit. In this limit, the deformational term is so large that the inertial terms normally needed to describe less viscous fluids may be completely ignored. The resulting equation (1) then represents the balance among forces arising from pressure gradients, buoyancy, and deformation. Equation (2) expresses the conservation of mass under the anelastic approximation. The anelastic approximation ignores the partial derivative of density with respect to time in the dynamics and thereby eliminates fast local density oscillations. It allows the computational time step to be dictated by the much slower deformational dynamics. Equation (3) expresses the conservation of energy in terms of absolute temperature. It includes effects of transport of heat by the flowing material, compressional heating and expansion cooling, thermal conduction, shear or deformational heating, and local volume (e.g., radiogenic) heating.

The expression for the deviatoric stress given by equation (4) assumes the dynamic shear viscosity μ depends on temperature, pressure, and strain rate. The stress therefore is nonlinear with respect to velocity, and the rheological description is non-Newtonian. This formulation is appropriate for the deformation regime in solids known as power-law creep to be discussed below. Equation (5) represents density variations as linearly proportional to pressure and temperature variations relative to a simple reference state of uniform density, pressure and temperature. Parameter values used are $\rho_r = 3400$ kg m^{-3}, $p_r = 0$, $T_r = 1600$ K, $g = 10$ m/s, $\gamma = 1$, k $= 4$ W m^{-1}K^{-1}, H $= 1.7 \times 10^{-8}$ W m^{-3}, $c_v = 1000$ J kg^{-1}K^{-1}, and K $= 1 \times 10^{12}$ Pa.

POWER-LAW CREEP

Laboratory experiments to characterize the high temperature solid state deformation properties of silicates have been carried out by many investigators over the last three decades [8,9]. These experiments have established that, for temperatures above about sixty percent of the melting temperature and strain rates down to the smallest achievable in the laboratory, silicate materials such as olivine deform according to a relationship of the form [8]

$$\dot{\varepsilon} = A \, \sigma^n \exp[-(E^* + pV^*)/RT] \qquad (6)$$

where $\dot{\varepsilon}$ is the strain rate, A a material constant, σ the differential stress, n a dimensionless constant on the order of 3 to 5, E^* an activation energy, p is pressure, V^* an activation volume, R the universal gas constant, and T absolute temperature. This relationship implies that at constant temperature and pressure the deformation rate increases dramatically more rapidly than the stress. Because the strain rate increases as the stress to some power greater than one, this type of deformation is known as power-law creep. This relationship may also be expressed in terms of an effective viscosity $\mu = 0.5\sigma/\dot{\varepsilon}$ that depends on the strain rate $\dot{\varepsilon}$ as [9, 17, p. 291]

$$\mu = B \, \dot{\varepsilon}^{-q} \exp[(E^* + pV^*)/nRT] \qquad (7)$$

where $B = 0.5A^{-1/n}$ and $q = 1 - 1/n$. A value for n of 3.5, appropriate for the mineral olivine [8,9], yields a q of 0.714. This means that the effective viscosity μ decreases strongly as the strain rate $\dot{\varepsilon}$ increases. A tenfold increase in the strain rate, for example, yields an effective viscosity, at fixed temperature and pressure, a factor of 5.2 smaller! For a 10^{10} increase in strain rate, the effective viscosity decreases by more than a factor of 10^7. The effect is even more pronounced for larger values of n.

Fig. 1 is a deformation mechanism map for olivine that shows the region in stress-temperature space where power-law creep is observed. Note that there exists a boundary between the power-law creep regime and that of diffusional creep. Because the strain rates for diffusional creep are so small--too small in fact to be realized in laboratory experiments--this boundary is poorly constrained. Kirby [8, p. 1461] states that the boundary may in actuality be substantially to the left of where he has drawn it. In any case at a given temperature there is a threshold value for the strain rate at which point one crosses from the diffusional regime--where the strain rate depends linearly on the stress--into the power-law regime. From Fig. 1 this threshold is on the order of 10^{-17} to 10^{-14} s^{-1} for temperatures about 60% of the melting temperature and shear stresses on the order of 1 MPa.

Power-law creep is included in the numerical model simply by using the effective viscosity given by (7) in (4), where the scalar strain rate $\dot{\varepsilon}$ is obtained by taking the square root of the second invariant of the rate of strain tensor $\mathbf{d} = (\nabla\mathbf{u} + \nabla\mathbf{u}^T)/2$. To remove the singularity in (7) for zero strain rate and to model explicitly the transition between diffusion creep and power-law creep, a minimum or threshold strain rate $\dot{\varepsilon}_0$ is incorporated into the formulation. For regions in the domain where the strain rate $\dot{\varepsilon}$ exceeds $\dot{\varepsilon}_0$, equation (7) applies. Otherwise the viscosity is strain rate independent. The parameter B is specified in terms of a reference viscosity μ_0 at reference temperature T_r and zero strain rate as $B = \mu_0/\{\dot{\varepsilon}_0^{-q} \exp[(E^* + pV^*)/nRT_r]\}$. To model the viscosity contrast between the upper mantle and lower mantle, the reference viscosity is allowed to vary with depth and increase in a linear fashion by a factor of 50 between 400 and 700 km. For purposes of numerical stability the threshold strain rate $\dot{\varepsilon}_0$ is assumed to vary as $1/\mu_0$.

PHASE CHANGES

The jumps in seismic quantities observed at depths of about 410 km and 660 km in the earth closely match phase transitions observed in laboratory experiments at similar temperatures and pressures for olivine to spinel and from spinel to perovskite silicate structures, respectively. These phase transitions that occur as the pressure increases and the crystal structures assume more compact configurations almost certainly play a critical role in the mantle's dynamical behavior. In a calculation in which silicate material is transported through these depths and undergoes these phase changes, two effects need to be taken into account. One is the latent heat released or absorbed and the other is the deflection of the phase boundary upward or downward. The latent heat may be accounted for by adding or removing heat through the volume heating term in equation (3) proportional to the vertical flux of material through the transition depth. The latent heat per unit mass is obtained from the Clapeyron equation which expresses that in a phase transition $\Delta H = (dp/dT) \, T \, \Delta V$, where ΔH is the enthalpy change, or latent heat, and ΔV is the change in specific volume. The Clapeyron slope (dp/dT) is a quantity that can be determined experimentally for a given transition. The deflection in the location of a phase boundary occurs because the pressure, and therefore the depth, at which the phase change occurs depends on the temperature. The effect of such a deflection enters as a contribution to the buoyancy term in equation (1). A downward deflection represents positive buoyancy because the lighter phase now occupies volume normally occupied by the denser phase. The Clapeyron slope is also a constant of proportionality in the boundary deflection $\Delta h = -(dp/dT) \, \Delta T/\rho g$ that arises from a deviation ΔT from the reference temperature. The values for the Clapeyron slope used here are 1×10^6 Pa/K for the 410 km transition and -2×10^6 Pa/K for the 660 km transition. Note that the exothermic 410 km transition leads to a positive or upward deflection for a cold slab and hence increased

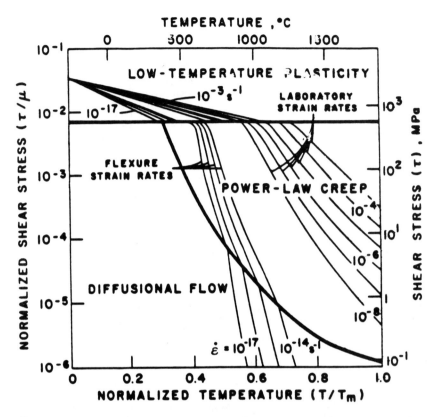

Figure 1 Deformation map for olivine with a 1 mm grain size. Shear strain rates $\dot{\varepsilon}$ (in s^{-1}) are contoured over shear stress τ normalized by shear modulus μ and absolute temperature T normalized by temperature of melting T_m. (From Kirby, [8])

negative buoyancy, while the endothermic 660 km transition leads to a downward deflection and reduced negative buoyancy. The 660 km transition therefore acts to inhibit buoyancy driven flow while the 410 km transition acts to enhance it.

NUMERICAL APPROACH

The set of equations (1)-(5) is solved in a discrete manner on a uniform rectangular mesh with velocities located at the mesh nodes and temperatures, pressures, and densities at cell centers. Piecewise linear finite elements are used to represent the velocity field, while the cell centered variables are treated as piecewise constant over the cells. The calculational procedure on each time step is first to apply a two-level conjugate gradient algorithm [15] to compute the velocity and pressure fields simultaneously from Eq. (1) and (2). This task involves solving $3n$ simultaneous equations for $2n$ velocity unknowns and n pressure unknowns, where n is the total number of nodes in the mesh. Key to the procedure is an iterative multigrid solver that employs an approximate inverse with a 25-point stencil. This large stencil for the approximate inverse enables the method to handle large variations in viscosity in a stable fashion. The outstanding rate of convergence in the multigrid solver is responsible for the method's overall high efficiency. The piecewise linear finite element basis functions provide second-order spatial accuracy. The temperature field is updated according to Eq. (3) with a forward-in-time finite difference van Leer limited advection method.

RESULTS

Two calculations will now be described that illustrate the effects of power law creep on the stability of a sinking slab. The two calculations are identical except for the value of the strain rate threshold above which power law creep occurs. In the first case, the threshold $\dot{\varepsilon}_0$ in the upper 400 km is 3×10^{-13} s^{-1} which is sufficiently large that no power law creep occurs anywhere in the domain. In the second case, the threshold is 6.5×10^{-14} s^{-1}, about a factor of five smaller. In this case runaway eventually takes place. These calculations are performed in a rectangular domain 2890 km high and 1280 km wide on a mesh with 64 x 64 cells of uniform size. The viscosity μ_0 at zero strain rate and 1600 K increases in a simple linear fashion by a factor 50 between 400 km and 700 km depth to represent the stiffer rheology of the earth's lower mantle compared with the upper mantle. The phase changes at 410 km and 660 km depth are both included. The endothermic phase transition at 660 km as well as the higher intrinsic viscosity below this depth both act to inhibit flow from above. The calculations are initialized with a uniform temperature of 1600 K except for a slablike anomaly 100 km wide extending from the top to a depth of 400 km with a central temperature of 1000 K and a thermal boundary layer at the top such that the temperature in the topmost layer of cells is initially 1000 K. The upper boundary temperature is fixed at 700 K and the bottom at 1600 K.

Fig. 2 shows four snapshots in time spaced roughly 6×10^6 years apart of the calculation with the larger strain rate threshold. Plots of temperature and effective viscosity are displayed with velocities superimposed. Note that the initial maximum velocity drops by a factor of two as the slab encounters increasing resistance from the higher viscosity and 660 km phase change. The colder material tends to accumulate and thicken in width in the depth range between 400 and 700 km. When sufficient thickening of the zone of cold material has occurred, it begins to penetrate slowly into the region below 700 km.

Fig. 3 shows the effects of a strain rate threshold $\dot{\varepsilon}_0$ sufficiently low that power law creep is occurring in a significant portion of the problem domain. The first three snapshots in time for this case resemble those for the previous case. The main difference are regions of reduced effective viscosity in the region below 700 km evident in the first and third snapshots due to the power-law rheology. A major change is observed, however, in the fourth snapshot with an increase in peak velocity and a notable reduction in effective viscosity below the head of the developing cold plume. In the fifth snapshot the peak velocity has increased by another 80% and there is more than a factor of ten reduction in the effective viscosity ahead of the plume. Also displayed in this snapshot is the viscous heating rate that shows intense heating surrounding the plume. In the sixth snapshot, the head of the cold plume is preceded by a belt of high temperature, the velocity has almost doubled again, the effective viscosities near the plume have dropped even further, and the heating rate adjacent to the plume has more than doubled. Shortly after this point in the calculation, runaway occurs and the computation crashes.

DISCUSSION

What do these calculations have to say about the mantle and the Flood? First of all, power-law rheology dramatically enhances the potential for thermal runaway. Numerical calculations are not really necessary to reach this conclusion. Equation (7) indicates an increase in the deformation rate leads to a reduction in the effective viscosity and reinforces the reduction in viscosity an increase in temperature provides. These effects work together in a potent way. An exciting further consequence of the power-law rheology is that high velocities and strain rates can now occur throughout the mantle. A hint of this can be inferred from the last two snapshots in Fig. 3. Large and increasing velocities are not just associated with the sinking plume itself but are observed throughout the domain. The remaining horizontal sections of the initial cold upper boundary layer, for example, are also moving at much higher speeds.

In interpreting these numerical experiments it is important to realize that one is attempting to explore numerically a physically unstable process. Customary numerical difficulties associated with strong gradients in the computed

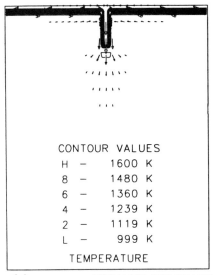
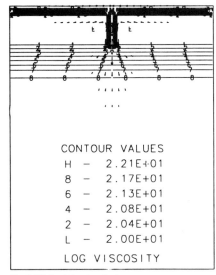

```
CONTOUR VALUES            CONTOUR VALUES
 H  -    1600 K            H  -   2.21E+01
 8  -    1480 K            8  -   2.17E+01
 6  -    1360 K            6  -   2.13E+01
 4  -    1239 K            4  -   2.08E+01
 2  -    1119 K            2  -   2.04E+01
 L  -     999 K            L  -   2.00E+01
    TEMPERATURE               LOG VISCOSITY
```

(a)   MAXIMUM VELOCITY = 9.233E+00 CM/YR

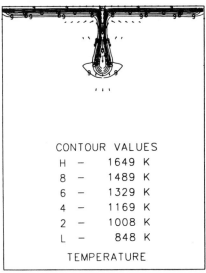
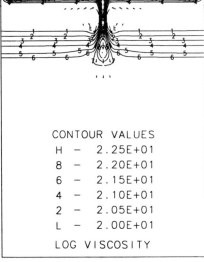

```
CONTOUR VALUES            CONTOUR VALUES
 H  -    1649 K            H  -   2.25E+01
 8  -    1489 K            8  -   2.20E+01
 6  -    1329 K            6  -   2.15E+01
 4  -    1169 K            4  -   2.10E+01
 2  -    1008 K            2  -   2.05E+01
 L  -     848 K            L  -   2.00E+01
    TEMPERATURE               LOG VISCOSITY
```

(b)   MAXIMUM VELOCITY = 4.462E+00 CM/YR

Figure 2 Numerical calculation of viscous slab sinking into viscous medium with temperature and strain rate dependent rheology. Reference viscosity is 10^{20} Pa s at 1600 K and zero strain rate in the upper 400 km and increases linearly with depth between 400 and 700 km by a factor of 50. Strain rate threshold for power law creep is 3 x 10^{-13} s^{-1}. Slab initially is 100 km wide and 400 km high. Snapshots are at (a) 0.002, (b) 6.3, (c)13.6, and (d) 20.1 x 10^6 yr. Stain rates never become large enough for power law creep to occur.

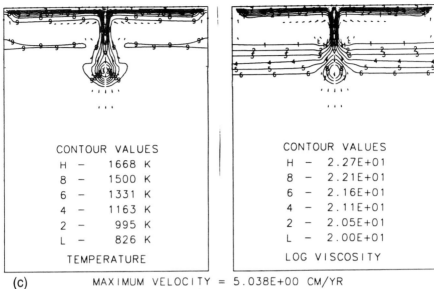

CONTOUR VALUES

H	–	1668 K
8	–	1500 K
6	–	1331 K
4	–	1163 K
2	–	995 K
L	–	826 K

TEMPERATURE

CONTOUR VALUES

H	–	2.27E+01
8	–	2.21E+01
6	–	2.16E+01
4	–	2.11E+01
2	–	2.05E+01
L	–	2.00E+01

LOG VISCOSITY

(c)   MAXIMUM VELOCITY = 5.038E+00 CM/YR

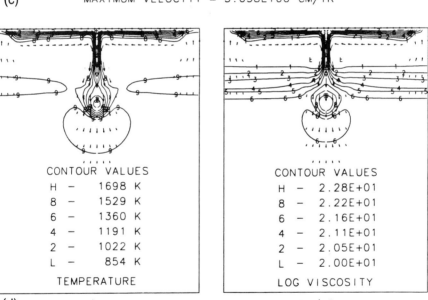

CONTOUR VALUES

H	–	1698 K
8	–	1529 K
6	–	1360 K
4	–	1191 K
2	–	1022 K
L	–	854 K

TEMPERATURE

CONTOUR VALUES

H	–	2.28E+01
8	–	2.22E+01
6	–	2.16E+01
4	–	2.11E+01
2	–	2.05E+01
L	–	2.00E+01

LOG VISCOSITY

(d)   MAXIMUM VELOCITY = 6.106E+00 CM/YR

Figure 2 (continued)

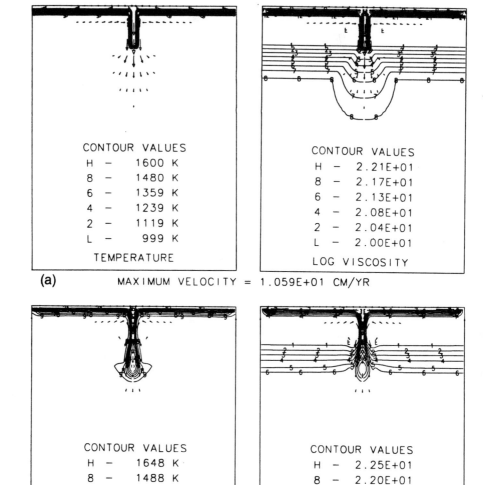

(a)   MAXIMUM VELOCITY = 1.059E+01 CM/YR

(b)   MAXIMUM VELOCITY = 4.567E+00 CM/YR

Figure 3 Same as Figure 2 except strain rate threshold is 6.5 x 10^{-14} s^{-1}. Snapshots are at (a) 0.001, (b) 6.2, (c) 13.4, (d) 18.9, (e) 22.6, and (f) 24.3 x 10^6 yr. Sinking plume runs away shortly after final snapshot.

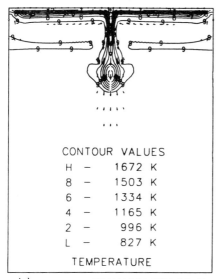
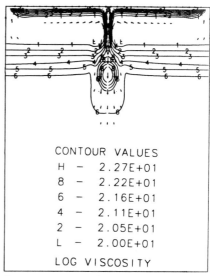

CONTOUR VALUES

H	–	1672 K
8	–	1503 K
6	–	1334 K
4	–	1165 K
2	–	996 K
L	–	827 K

TEMPERATURE

CONTOUR VALUES

H	–	2.27E+01
8	–	2.22E+01
6	–	2.16E+01
4	–	2.11E+01
2	–	2.05E+01
L	–	2.00E+01

LOG VISCOSITY

(c)   MAXIMUM VELOCITY = 5.416E+00 CM/YR

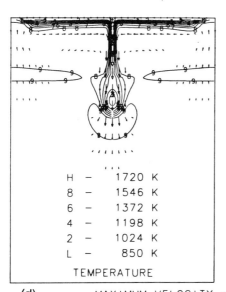
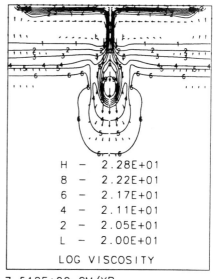

H	–	1720 K
8	–	1546 K
6	–	1372 K
4	–	1198 K
2	–	1024 K
L	–	850 K

TEMPERATURE

H	–	2.28E+01
8	–	2.22E+01
6	–	2.17E+01
4	–	2.11E+01
2	–	2.05E+01
L	–	2.00E+01

LOG VISCOSITY

(d)   MAXIMUM VELOCITY = 7.518E+00 CM/YR

Figure 3 (continued)

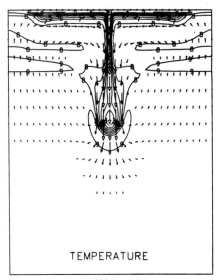

TEMPERATURE

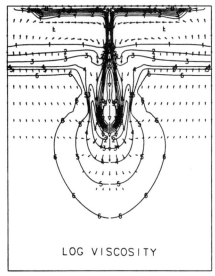

LOG VISCOSITY

MAXIMUM VELOCITY = 1.336E+01 CM/YR

CONTOUR VALUES

H	–	1759 K	H	–	2.27E+01
8	–	1579 K	8	–	2.22E+01
6	–	1399 K	6	–	2.16E+01
4	–	1219 K	4	–	2.11E+01
2	–	1040 K	2	–	2.05E+01
L	–	860 K	L	–	2.00E+01

TEMPERATURE   LOG VISCOSITY

H	–	1.60E-06
8	–	1.28E-06
6	–	9.63E-07
4	–	6.42E-07
2	–	3.21E-07
L	–	1.18E-12

SHEAR HEATING RATE
W/M3

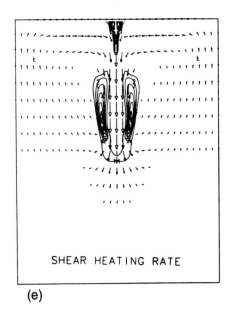

SHEAR HEATING RATE

(e)

Figure 3 (continued)

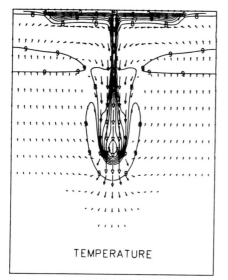

TEMPERATURE

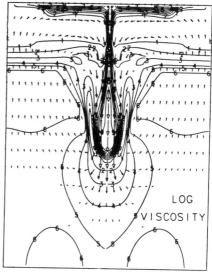

LOG
VISCOSITY

MAXIMUM VELOCITY = 2.566E+01 CM/YR

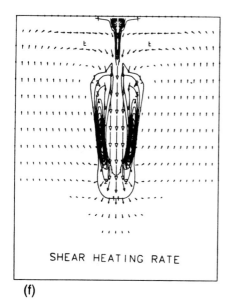

SHEAR HEATING RATE

CONTOUR VALUES

H	–	1730 K	H	–	2.27E+01
8	–	1556 K	8	–	2.22E+01
6	–	1382 K	6	–	2.16E+01
4	–	1208 K	4	–	2.11E+01
2	–	1034 K	2	–	2.05E+01
L	–	861 K	L	–	1.99E+01

TEMPERATURE   LOG VISCOSITY

H	–	2.59E−06
8	–	2.07E−06
6	–	1.55E−06
4	–	1.04E−06
2	–	5.18E−07
L	–	4.63E−12

SHEAR HEATING RATE
W/M3

(f)

Figure 3 (continued)

quantities are compounded when such a physical instability occurs. The strategy is to explore the region of parameter space nearby but not too close to where the instability actually lives. The calculation of Fig. 3 therefore does not reveal the true strength of the instability relative to the situation of a moderately lower value for the threshold strain rate. It is also useful to point out how various quantities scale relative to one another. The velocities are inversely proportional to the reference viscosity. A tenfold reduction in the reference viscosity gives ten times higher velocities. Similarly, the threshold strain rate for runaway behavior is inversely proportional to the reference viscosity since strain rate is proportional to velocity. So reducing the reference viscosity by a factor of ten yields a threshold strain rate for runaway ten times larger. This neglects the diminished influence of thermal diffusion at the higher velocities.

How do the parameters used in these calculations compare with those estimated for the earth? The values used for g, γ, k, H, ρ_r, c_v, T_r, and α in eq. (1)-(5) are all reasonable to within +/-30% for the simplified reference state that is employed. The values used for the Clapeyron slopes for the phase transitions are two to three times too small and so the effects of the phase changes are underrepresented. The most important parameters are the reference viscosity and the threshold strain rate for power-law creep. The reference viscosity leads to velocities prior to runaway that are in accord with current observed plate velocities of a few centimeters per year. The threshold strain rates used are within the power-law creep region for olivine as given by Kirby (Fig. 1). A large uncertainty is the extrapolation of the creep behavior of olivine to the minerals of the lower mantle for which there is essentially no experimental data. The issue is not whether power-law creep occurs in these minerals but what the stress range is in which it occurs. It is likely the threshold strain rate is not many orders of magnitude different from olivine. These calculations therefore seem relevant to the earth as we observe it today.

One difficulty in making a connection between these calculations and the Flood is their time scale. Some 2×10^7 years is needed before the instability occurs in the second calculation. Most of this time is involved with the accumulation of a large blob of cold, dense material at the barrier created by the phase transition at 660 km depth. This time span disappears when the initial condition consists of a large belt of cold material already trapped above this phase transition in the pre-Flood mantle. A relatively small amount of additional negative buoyancy in such a belt can then trigger runaway. One means for providing a quick pulse of negative buoyancy is by the sudden conversion to spinel of olivine in a metastable state that resides at depths below the usual transition depth of about 410 km. Such metastability can arise because the changes in volume and structure associated with a phase transition do not necessarily occur spontaneously as transition conditions are reached, especially if the material is cold. Some means of nucleation of seed crystals of the new phase is generally required. If such nucleation does not happen, then substantial amounts of the less dense phase can survive to depths much greater than what the assumption of a spontaneous transition would imply. Indeed, there is observational evidence for significant amounts of metastable olivine in the slab currently beneath Japan [7]. A shock wave passing through such a volume of metastable material can initiate the nucleation and cause a sudden conversion to the denser phase. Present day deep focus earthquakes likely represent manifestations of such a process on a small scale. In the context of the Flood, it is conceivable that an extraterrestrial impact of modest size could have triggered a sudden conversion of metastable material to the denser phase and the resulting earthquakes then propagated in a self-sustaining manner to convert the metastable material throughout much of the upper mantle to the denser spinel phase, which in turn initiated the runaway avalanche of upper mantle rock into the lower mantle. It is also conceivable that a single large earthquake generated by causes internal to the earth could have been the event that caused a sudden conversion of the metastable material and then the runaway avalanche.

CONCLUSIONS

Rapid sinking through the mantle of portions of the mantle's cold upper boundary facilitated by the process of thermal runaway appears to be a genuine possibility for the earth. A highly nonlinear deformation law for silicate minerals at conditions of high temperature known as power-law creep, documented by decades of experimental effort, in which the effective viscosity decreases strongly with the deformation rate, makes thermal runaway almost a certainty for a significant suite of conditions. This deformation law also makes possible strain rates consistent with large scale tectonic change within the Biblical time frame for the Flood. Mineralogical phase changes combined with the viscosity contrast between upper and lower mantle conspire to provide the setting in which a sudden triggering of a runaway avalanche of material trapped in the upper mantle into the lower mantle can occur. Calculations by other investigators that include the endothermic phase transition, but not temperature or strain rate dependent viscosity, also display the tendency for episodic avalanche events [10,13,18,19]. Such an episode of catastrophic runaway is here presented as the mechanism responsible for Noah's Flood.

REFERENCES

[1]   O. L. Anderson and P. C. Perkins, **Runaway Temperatures in the Asthenosphere Resulting from Viscous Heating**, Journal of Geophysical Research, 79(1974), pp. 2136-2138.

[2]   J. R. Baumgardner, **Numerical Simulation of the Large-Scale Tectonic Changes Accompanying the Flood**, Proceedings of the International Conference on Creationism, R. E. Walsh, et al, Editors, 1987, Creation Science Fellowship, Inc., Pittsburgh, PA, Vol. II, pp. 17-28.

[3]   J. R. Baumgardner, **3-D Finite Element Simulation of the Global Tectonic Changes Accompanying Noah's Flood**, Proceedings of the Second International Conference on Creationism, R. E. Walsh and C. L. Brooks, Editors, 1991, Creation Science Fellowship, Inc., Pittsburgh, PA, Vol. II, pp. 35-45.

[4]   W. T. Brown, Jr., In the Beginning, 1989, Center for Scientific Creation, Phoenix.

[5]   J. C. Dillow, The Waters Above, 1981, Moody Press, Chicago.

[6]   I. J. Gruntfest, **Thermal Feedback in Liquid Flow; Plane Shear at Constant Stress**, Transactions of the Society of Rheology, 8(1963), pp. 195-207.

[7]   T. Iidaka and D. Suetsugu, **Seismological Evidence for Metastable Olivine Inside a Subducting Slab**, Nature, 356(1992), pp. 593-595.

[8]   S. H. Kirby, **Rheology of the Lithosphere,** Reviews of Geophysics and Space Physics, 21(1983), pp. 1458-1487.

[9]   S. H. Kirby and A. K. Kronenberg, **Rheology of the Lithosphere: Selected Topics**, Reviews of Geophysics and Space Physics, 25(1987), pp. 1219-1244.

[10] P. Machetel and P. Weber, **Intermittent Layered Convection in a Model Mantle with an Endothermic Phase Change at 670 km**, Nature, 350(1991), pp. 55-57.

[11] G. R. Morton, **The Flood on an Expanding Earth**, Creation Research Society Quarterly, 19(1983), pp. 219-224.

[12] D. W. Patton, The Biblical Flood and the Ice Epoch, 1966, Pacific Meridian Publishing, Seattle.

[13] W. R. Peltier and L. P. Solheim, **Mantle Phase Transitions and Layered Chaotic Convection**, Geophysical Research Letters, 19(1992), pp. 321-324.

[14] Proceedings of the Ocean Drilling Program

[15] A. Ramage and A. J. Wathen, **Iterative Solution Techniques for Finite Element Discretisations of Fluid Flow Problems**, Copper Mountain Conference on Iterative Methods Proceedings, Vol. 1., 1992.

[16] M. A. Richards and D. C. Engebretson, **Large-Scale Mantle Convection and the History of Subduction**, Nature, 355(1992), pp. 437-440.

[17] F. D. Stacey, Physics of the Earth, 2nd ed., 1977, John Wiley & Sons, New York.

[18] P. J. Tackley, D. J. Stevenson, G. A. Glatzmaier, and G. Schubert, **Effects of an Endothermic Phase Transition at 670 km Depth on Spherical Mantle Convection**, Nature, 361(1993), pp. 699-704.

[19] S. A. Weinstein, **Catastrophic Overturn of the Earth's Mantle Driven by Multiple Phase Changes and Internal Heat Generation**, Geophysical Research Letters, 20(1993), pp. 101-104.

PATTERNS OF OCEAN CIRCULATION OVER THE CONTINENTS DURING NOAH'S FLOOD

JOHN R. BAUMGARDNER, Ph.D.
1965 Camino Redondo
Los Alamos, NM 87544

DANIEL W. BARNETTE, Ph.D.
1704 Sadler, N.E.
Albuquerque, NM 87112

KEYWORDS

Genesis Flood, ocean currents, sediment transport, sedimentation patterns, shallow water equations

ABSTRACT

This paper presents results from a set of numerical experiments that explore the patterns of ocean circulation that arise when the earth's continental surface is mostly flooded. The calculations employ a code that solves the 2-D shallow water equations on a rotating sphere with surface topography. Several continental configurations are considered, including that of a single Pangean-like supercontinent. A surprising yet persistent feature in these calculations is the appearance of high velocity currents generated and sustained by the earth's rotation above the flooded continents. Water velocities in the deeper ocean by contrast are much smaller in magnitude. The patterns typically include strong cyclonic gyres at high latitudes with water velocities on the order of 40-80 m/s. The gyres tend to be compressed against the western continental margins and produce strong equatorward currents parallel to the western coastlines. The calculations argue that strong currents spontaneously arise over flooded continents. They suggest that accurate observational data on the current directions in the Paleozoic and Mesozoic rocks coupled with careful numerical modeling could be extremely fruitful in understanding the origin of much of the earth's sedimentary record.

INTRODUCTION

A central question in understanding the Flood catastrophe is what was the hydraulic mechanism that was able to transport millions of cubic kilometers of sediment, to distribute most of it in widely dispersed layers--in many cases hundreds to thousands of kilometers in horizontal extent, and to accomplish such a vast amount of geological work in only a few months time. Clark and Voss [1] have suggested that resonant lunar tides might qualify as the primary mechanism. Such tides, if they were to occur with sufficient amplitude in the presence of the continents, could indeed erode and transport huge volumes of sediment and deposit the sediment in laterally extensive layers. A major difficulty with this idea is that the resonance condition for a smooth earth without continents is a water depth of about 8000 m [1,4]. This represents about three times the volume of water currently in the world's oceans. Resonance, however, can occur at higher spatial harmonics and smaller water depths. For a smooth earth the critical water depth for the next higher harmonic is about 2000 m [1,4], much closer to the amount of water currently at the earth's surface. But the strength of the resonance of this mode is much smaller than that of the fundamental mode. It is not clear if the effects of bottom friction and other sources of dissipation are small enough for a resonant tide in this higher mode to arise even on a smooth earth, much less for an earth with realistic topography. Detailed numerical calculations are still needed to resolve these uncertainties.

In the process of exploring the possibility of a more localized tidal resonance in the large bay on the eastern side of the Pangean supercontinent known as the Tethys Sea, an entirely different mechanism was identified. It was found that the Coriolis force arising from the earth's rotation produces strong currents on top of the flooded continents independent of any tidal forcing. These currents form closed paths that generally have the same sense of rotation as the jet streams in the atmosphere, that is, cyclonic, or counterclockwise in the northern hemisphere and clockwise in the southern hemisphere. They are stronger above a continent localized to higher latitudes where the Coriolis force is stronger that for the same continent at lower latitudes. For continental flooding depths up to several hundred meters, these currents typically achieve speeds of several tens of meters per second, which is sufficiently strong to reduce the water depth to zero in much of the region enclosed by the cyclonic patterns of flow. Such speeds are easily adequate to erode by cavitation processes [3] and transport huge volume of relatively coarse clastic sediment for large distances.

This paper describes a set of numerical experiments using a code that solves the shallow water equations on the sphere to explore the necessary conditions and dynamical characteristics of these currents. This work is seen as only a beginning effort to understand this phenomenon. It should be emphasized here that tidal effects in general would add to rather than compete with the flow produced by such currents. These Coriolis force driven currents then are almost certainly only one of several factors responsible for the large scale sedimentation patterns during the Flood.

MATHEMATICAL FORMULATION

The shallow water equations describe the behavior of a shallow homogeneous incompressible and invicid fluid layer. On a rotating sphere these equations may be expressed [8, p. 213]

$$d\mathbf{u}/dt = -f \mathbf{k} \times \mathbf{u} - g \nabla h \tag{1}$$

and

$$dh^*/dt = -h^* \nabla \cdot \mathbf{u}, \tag{2}$$

where $\mathbf{u}$ is horizontal velocity (on the sphere), f is the Coriolis parameter (equal to $2\Omega \sin \theta$ for rotation rate Ω and latitude θ), $\mathbf{k}$ is the outward radial unit vector, g is gravitational acceleration, h is the height of the free surface above some spherical reference surface, and h^* is the depth of the fluid. If h_t denotes topography on the sphere, then $h = h^* + h_t$. The d/dt operator is the material or substantial or co-moving time rate of change of an individual parcel of fluid. The ∇ operator is the spherical horizontal gradient operator and the $\nabla \cdot$ operator is the spherical horizontal divergence operator. These simple equations are appropriate when the depth of the fluid is small compared with the important horizontal length scales. This criterion is satisfied for the problem at hand where the water depths are typically less than four kilometers while the horizontal dimensions of ocean basins and continents are measured in thousands of kilometers. Also note that the fluid density does not appear in these equations. This means that to the degree the approximations apply, the same equations describe flow in both the atmosphere and oceans.

These equations are solved in discrete fashion on a mesh constructed from the regular icosahedron as shown in Fig. 1. The mesh has 40962 nodes and the spacing between nodes is about 125 km. A separate spherical coordinate system is defined at each node such that the equator of the system passes through the node and the local longitude and latitude axes are aligned with the global east and north directions. This approach has the advantage that the coordinates are almost Cartesian and only two (tangential) velocity components are needed. A semi-Lagrangian formulation [7] of equations (1) and (2) is used which involves computing the trajectories during the time step that end at each node. Values for h and $\mathbf{u}$ at the beginning of the time step at the starting point of each trajectory are found by interpolating from the known nodal values at the beginning of the time step. Changes in h and $\mathbf{u}$ along the trajectory are computed using (1) and (2). This Lagrangian-like method eliminates most of the numerical diffusion that is associated with Eulerian schemes. Second-order accurate interpolation is used to find the starting point values of the trajectories. This formulation using the icosahedral mesh has been carefully validated using the suite of test problems developed by Williamson et al. [8].

RESULTS

A small set of problems was investigated to explore some of the conditions under which a coherent pattern of strong currents arises on top of a flooded continent. Fig. 2 is a sequence of snapshots from a calculation initialized with a Pangean-like distribution of continent of uniform height flooded to a depth of 500 m. The ocean depth is also taken to be a uniform value of 3980 such that the total water volume equals that in the present oceans and ice caps. The initial velocity field is everywhere zero. Fig. 2 (a) displays the initial height of the water above the bottom topography. Frames (b)-(g) in Fig. 2 show the development of the pattern of flow with time at 10 day intervals. Two closed circulations, one in the northern hemisphere and one in the southern, emerge from the initial state. The sense of rotation of these circulations is cyclonic, which implies low pressure or reduced surface height inside the circulations. By a time of 30 days the currents are so strong that the water depth has decreased to zero over portions of the continental surface inside circulating flows. The current velocities continue to increase to peak values of about 87 m/s until the 50 day snapshot after which time there is no significant change in the peak velocity. The patterns show prominent wavelike structure in the latitude zone between 20° and 50°. In the atmosphere such features are known as planetary waves. They occur because of the variation of the Coriolis parameter with latitude and are also referred to as Rossby waves [5, p.93-95].

The effect of increasing the depth of flooding to a value of 1000 m is shown in Fig. 3. In this case the time dependence of the pattern is much stronger, the peak velocities are somewhat lower at about 78 m/s, and the reduction of the surface height inside the regions of cyclonic flow is approaching 1000 m. Snapshots at 80 and 90 days reveal how dramatically the flow pattern varies with time. Usually there is more than one cyclonic gyre in a given hemisphere. Fig. 4. shows the effect of increasing the depth of continental flooding further to 1500 m. Under these circumstances the peak velocities are reduced by almost a factor of two to about 40 m/s and the peak drawdown of the surface inside the cyclonic gyres is only about 500 m. The time variation of the pattern is still strong and the number of gyres is somewhat larger. Well-defined anticyclonic gyres are also evident. This latter case suggests that when the static water depth over the continent exceeds 1000 m, the strength of these currents begins to diminish significantly.

The calculations described thus far all used the same Pangean-like continent. To determine what role the special geometry of this continent might be playing in producing the observed patterns of flow, several cases were run with simpler continental geometries. Fig. 5 shows the results from a configuration consisting of a circular continent 50°

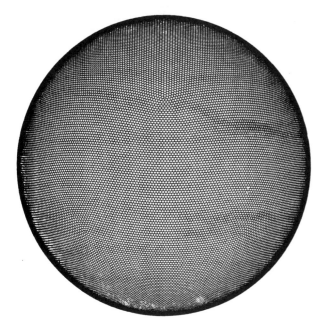

Figure 1 Computational mesh constructed from icosahedron. Mesh has 40962 nodes. Nodes are located at centers of hexagonal cells. Node spacing is about 125 km.

(a)

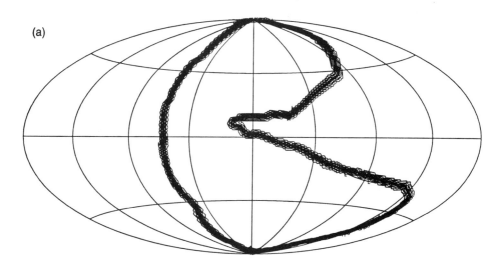

Figure 2 Snapshots from solution of the shallow water equations for a bottom topography corresponding to a Pangean-like continent initially flooded to a depth of 500 meters. Initial water depth contours are shown in (a) with the minimum contour equal to 500 m and the maximum contour equal to 3980 m. The initial velocities are everywhere zero. Frames (b)-(g) show the solution at 10-day intervals.

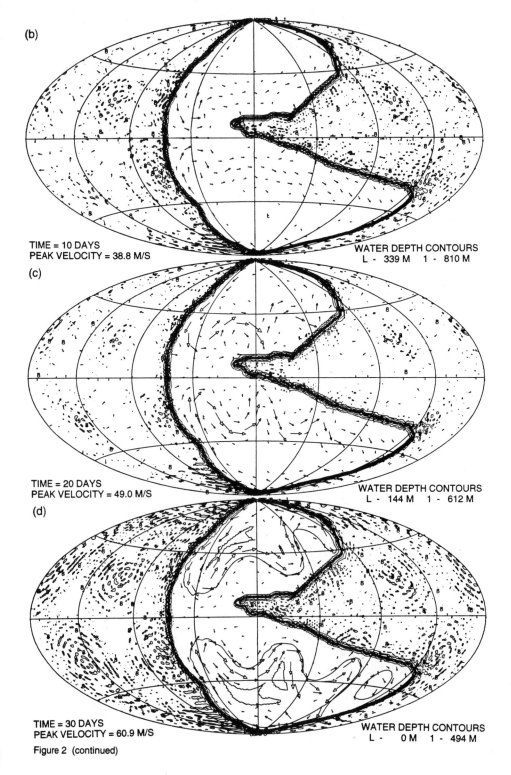

(b)

TIME = 10 DAYS
PEAK VELOCITY = 38.8 M/S

WATER DEPTH CONTOURS
L - 339 M   1 - 810 M

(c)

TIME = 20 DAYS
PEAK VELOCITY = 49.0 M/S

WATER DEPTH CONTOURS
L - 144 M   1 - 612 M

(d)

TIME = 30 DAYS
PEAK VELOCITY = 60.9 M/S

WATER DEPTH CONTOURS
L -   0 M   1 - 494 M

Figure 2 (continued)

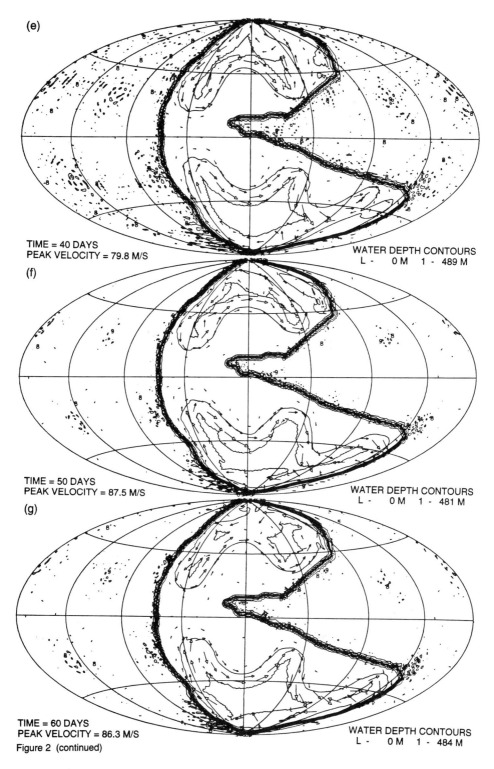

(e)

TIME = 40 DAYS
PEAK VELOCITY = 79.8 M/S

WATER DEPTH CONTOURS
L - 0 M   1 - 489 M

(f)

TIME = 50 DAYS
PEAK VELOCITY = 87.5 M/S

WATER DEPTH CONTOURS
L - 0 M   1 - 481 M

(g)

TIME = 60 DAYS
PEAK VELOCITY = 86.3 M/S

Figure 2 (continued)

WATER DEPTH CONTOURS
L - 0 M   1 - 484 M

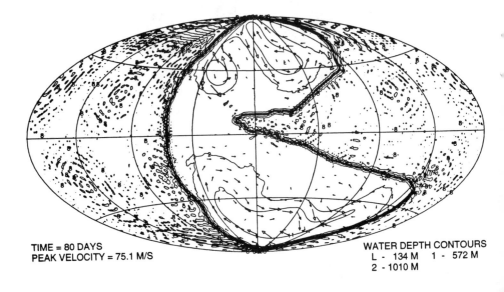

TIME = 80 DAYS
PEAK VELOCITY = 75.1 M/S

WATER DEPTH CONTOURS
L - 134 M   1 - 572 M
2 - 1010 M

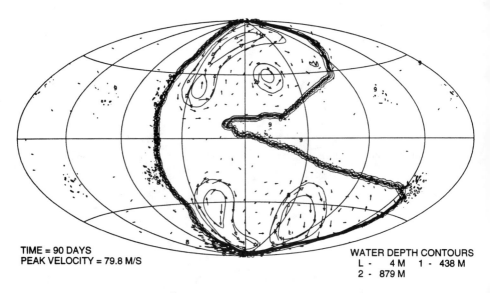

TIME = 90 DAYS
PEAK VELOCITY = 79.8 M/S

WATER DEPTH CONTOURS
L - 4 M   1 - 438 M
2 - 879 M

Figure 3 Snapshots at 80 days (a) and 90 days (b) from calculation identical to that of Fig. 2 except initial water depth over the continent is 1000 m and over oceanic regions is 3680 m. Solution displays strong time variation.

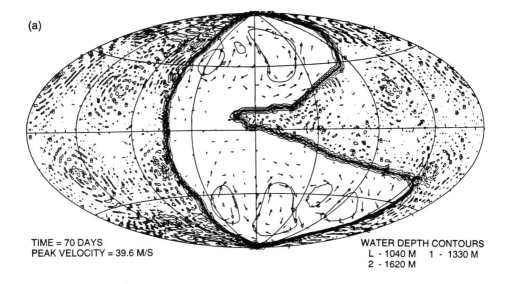

(a)

TIME = 70 DAYS
PEAK VELOCITY = 39.6 M/S

WATER DEPTH CONTOURS
L - 1040 M   1 - 1330 M
2 - 1620 M

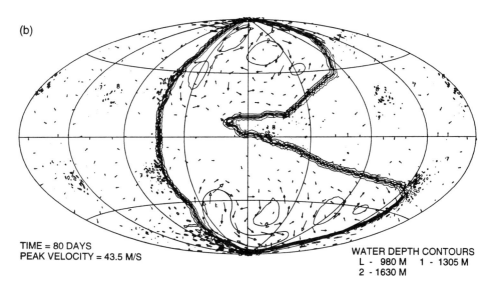

(b)

TIME = 80 DAYS
PEAK VELOCITY = 43.5 M/S

WATER DEPTH CONTOURS
L - 980 M   1 - 1305 M
2 - 1630 M

Figure 4 Snapshots at 70 days (a) and 80 days (b) from calculation identical to that of Fig. 2 except initial water depth over the continent is 1500 m and over oceanic regions is 3380 m. Solution displays moderate time variation.

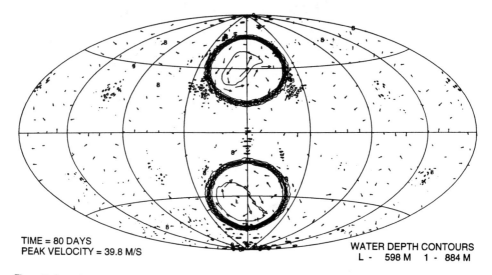

TIME = 80 DAYS
PEAK VELOCITY = 39.8 M/S

WATER DEPTH CONTOURS
L - 598 M   1 - 884 M

Figure 5 Snapshot at a time of 80 days from a solution of the shallow water equations with a bottom topography consisting of a circular continent 5560 km in diameter centered at 45 degrees latitude in each hemisphere and initially flooded to a depth of 1000 meters. Initial water depth in the oceanic areas is 3000 m.

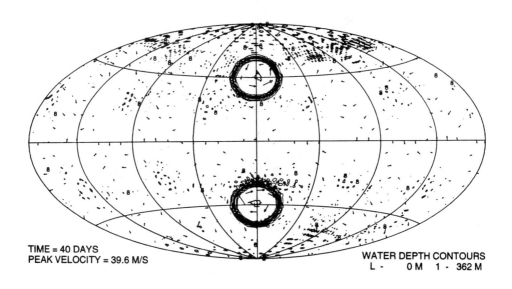

TIME = 40 DAYS
PEAK VELOCITY = 39.6 M/S

WATER DEPTH CONTOURS
L - 0 M   1 - 362 M

Figure 6 Snapshot at 40 days for a case identical to that of Fig. 5 except the continent diameter is 3330 km and the initial flooding depth is 250 m.

(5560 km) in diameter centered at 45° latitude in each hemisphere. The depth of flooding is 1000 m. The snapshot at 80 days shows single cyclonic gyres on each continent with peak velocities of about 40 m/s and reductions in surface height of about 400 m. Moderate time dependence is present. When these continents are moved to points centered at 60° latitude, the character of the solution remains the same but the strength of the flow increases to yield peak velocities of about 55 m/s and a maximum reduction in the surface height of about 1000 m. On the other hand, when the circular continents are moved such that they are centered at 30° latitude, the peak velocity falls to about 37 m/s and the maximum reduction in surface height is only about 200 m. These results reflect the fact that the magnitude of the Coriolis parameter increases with the sine of the latitude. Calculations using circular continents are thus found to yield the same general behavior as observed for the Pangean-like continent.

Another issue that was addressed was the minimum horizontal dimension for a continental region required to obtain the strong gyre-like flow. Fig. 6 displays results for a configuration consisting of a circular continent 30° (3330 km) in diameter centered at 45° latitude in each hemisphere. The depth of flooding is 250 m. The snapshot at 40 days shows nicely developed gyres on each continent with a peak velocity of about 40 m/s. The identical case except for a continent diameter of 20° (2220 km), however, fails to produce any such feature. From these relatively small number of tests, it is inferred that there is a minimum critical dimension on the order of 2500 km below which this phenomenon does not occur.

DISCUSSION

The tendency for strong cyclonic gyres to form above flooded continents, particularly at the higher latitudes, appears to be a robust characteristic of the earth's ocean. Physically, these patterns of flow arise because of the earth's rotation and are influenced by the fact that the Coriolis parameter varies with latitude and that transport of absolute vorticity is a strongly nonlinear process. The absolute vorticity is defined as $\zeta + f$, where $\zeta =$ curl $\mathbf{u}$ is the fluid vorticity in the shallow water limit and f is the Coriolis parameter. To good approximation the transport of absolute vorticity is described by the vorticity equation [5, p. 95]

$$d(\zeta + f)/dt = - (\zeta + f)\nabla \cdot \mathbf{u} \tag{3}$$

For the situation of constant water depth, the velocity divergence $\nabla \cdot \mathbf{u}$ is zero. Equation (3) in this case requires a parcel of fluid moving equatorward have its vorticity ζ increase since f decreases with decreasing latitude, while the opposite holds for a poleward moving parcel. Thus there is transfer of vorticity from the earth's rotation to the fluid and vice versa. Because absolute vorticity itself depends on the local fluid velocity $\mathbf{u}$ through ζ, the right hand side of (3) is seen to be nonlinear in terms of velocity, and the dynamics associated with the vorticity therefore are highly nonlinear. Equation (3) can also be expressed as the conservation of potential vorticity, which is defined as $(\zeta+f)/h^*$, where h^* is water depth [5, p. 96]. Since potential vorticity is inversely proportional to h^*, the nonlinear dynamics are accentuated where the water is shallow. This suggests why high velocity currents arise in the shallower depths above the continents and not in the regions of deep ocean. For such strongly nonlinear problems, physical reasoning can only take one so far, and numerical simulation is generally the most practical means for obtaining deeper understanding of the system dynamics.

Calculations described above suggest there exists a minimum diameter for the strong gyres on the order of 2500 km. This seems to account for the absence of such features today since the present continental shelves are much narrower than this minimum scale length. On the other hand, the sedimentary record indicates there have been several major, apparently global, transgressions of the ocean over the continents since the beginning of the Cambrian period. In the case of North America, Sloss [6] has described six such major transgressions. The basal formation of the second transgression that occurred during the Ordovician is composed of extremely pure quartz sand and known as the St. Peter Sandstone [2, pp. 221-225]. It is readily identified and covered a large fraction of North America. The continental areas flooded by epeiric sea during such major transgressions easily exceed the 2500 km dimension. It is difficult then to imagine how strong currents such as observed in the numerical experiments did not arise and play a major role in development of the sedimentary record. Given the fact that catastrophic cavitation occurs for water velocities generally above 30 m/s [3], one would also expect severe and rapid erosion to be associated with any major transgression of the continents by the ocean. These phenomena relating to very fundamental aspects of sedimentary geology, to the authors' knowledge, have never before been considered or addressed in the scientific literature.

CONCLUSIONS

Numerical solution of the shallow water equations on a rotating sphere with parameters appropriate to the earth and flooded continental topography yields closed patterns of flow with velocities of 40 to 80 m/s and length scales typically 2500-5000 km above the flooded continental regions. Such currents would be expected to arise in the context of a global Flood as described in Scripture when "all the high mountains everywhere under the heavens were covered" with water (Gen. 7:19). The ability of such currents, combined with cavitation, to erode huge volumes of rock and also to transport the resulting sediment and distribute it over extensive areas in a short span of time not only helps to satisfy the Biblical time constraints for the Flood but also appears to be able, in a general sense, to account for the continent-scale extent of many Paleozoic and Mesozoic sedimentary formations as well as evidence in many of these rocks for high energy water transport. Clearly, calculations with more detailed and realistic topography that is allowed to change with time are the next step in this research program. If such calculations prove to be able to reproduce some of the primary features of the sedimentary record, then confidence that the Phanerozoic portion of geological history is indeed a consequence of Noah's Flood should spread substantially beyond its present bounds.

REFERENCES

[1] M. E. Clark and H. D. Voss, **Resonance and Sedimentary Layering in the Context of a Global Flood**, Proceedings of the Second International Conference on Creationism, R. E. Walsh and C. L. Brooks, Editors, 1991, Creation Science Fellowship, Inc., Pittsburgh, PA, Vol. 2, pp. 53-63.

[2] R. M. Dott, Jr. and R. L. Batten, Evolution of the Earth, 2nd Ed., 1976, McGraw-Hill, New York.

[3] E. W. Holroyd, **Cavitation Processes During Catastrophic Floods**, Proceedings of the Second International Conference on Creationism, R. E. Walsh and C. L. Brooks, Editors, 1991, Creation Science Fellowship, Inc., Pittsburgh, PA, Vol. 2, pp. 101-113.

[4] S. S. Hough, **On the Application of Harmonic Analysis to the Dynamical Theory of the Tides**, Philosophical Transactions of the Royal Society, 119(1897), pp. 139-185.

[5] J. T. Houghton, The Physics of Atmospheres, 1977, Cambridge University Press, Cambridge.

[6] L. L. Sloss, **Sequences in the Cratonic Interior of North America**, Geological Society of America Bulletin, 74(1963), pp. 93-114.

[7] A. Staniforth and J, Cote, **Semi-Lagrangian Integration Schemes for Atmospheric Models--A Review**, Monthly Weather Review, 119(1991), pp. 2206-2223.

[8] D. L. Williamson, J. B. Drake, J. J. Hack, R. Jakob, and P. N. Swatztrauber, **A Standard Test Set for Numerical Approximations to the Shallow Water Equations in Spherical Geometry**, Journal of Computational Physics, 102:1(1992), pp. 211-224.

MAGNETIC MONOPOLES AND GRAND UNIFICATION THEORY

JERRY BERGMAN, PH.D.
ARCHBOLD, OHIO

KEYWORDS

Magnetic Monopoles, Grand Unification Theory, Big Bang Cosmology, Physical Evolution.

ABSTRACT

The theory of magnetic monopoles and its importance for Big Bang Cosmology and Grand Unification Theory are reviewed. Although indications existed that Blas Cabrera detected evidence of magnetic monopoles at Stanford in 1982, all efforts to replicate his research have so far failed. Currently no valid explanation exists as to why this important plank in Big Bang Cosmology has not been experimentally verified in spite of over a decade of sophisticated experiments. This area is a major "missing link" which argues against the evolution of matter and the four forces, and also the current big bang world view. The history of the efforts to detect magnetic monopoles are reviewed, and the reasons behind their need for big bang cosmology was discussed.

INTRODUCTION

The origin of life is postulated by the modern science establishment to have occurred by evolutionary naturalism from hypothetical "simple" one organelle animals to the complex 100-trillion-celled human beings in about 3.5 billion years. Likewise in physics, naturalism postulates that a single force and very few or even one elementary particle have developed into all of the enormous complexity existing all around us [25]. The four forces which are observed today-gravity, the strong and weak nuclear forces, and electromagnetism--are all hypothesized to have developed from one single force due to the dissipation of the heat and pressure caused by the big bang expansion. This theory is called the *grand unification theory* (GUT).

A super heavy magnetic monopole is inextricably linked to the GUT theory and thus "any true GUT necessarily implies magnetic monopoles that formed very early in the universe's history" [14, p.84]. In Taubes words, the GUT theory "positively demanded the existence of monopoles" [32, p.48]. Von Baeyer puts it as follows: "GUTs have unequivocally predicted the existence of monopoles" [33, p.3]. For this reason:

> Most hypothetical particles, such as quarks, wimps, winos and technipions, may be loved by their mothers but are easy for the rest of us to shrug off. Given that magnetic monopoles *must* exist according to theories unifying the four fundamental forces--grand unified theories, or GUTS--they are less easy to ignore [12, p.706, emphasis mine].

The GUT theory postulates that when the symmetry of the original unified force was lost, it was broken into at least four separate, disparate forces:

In the late 1970s, the Soviet theorist Sasha Polyakov (now at Princeton) proved that creation of these exotic particles *must* occur whenever any unified force breaks down to the electromagnetic force (as well as other forces). Just as the GUTs breakdown was producing baryons and generating a tiny excess of matter, therefore, it should also have created a comparable number of these ultraheavy particles, over a million billion times more massive than a proton, which possess the magnetic characteristics of a single north or south pole [27, p.162].

For this reason, although "physicists have been intrigued by magnetic monopoles for more than a century, interest in them has risen to new heights in the past decade" [33, p.2]. Their confirmation would "be the discovery of the century" because the "quest has high theoretical stakes for particle physics and cosmologists" [30; 31, p.625; 1; 2; 26; 8, p.118; 9]. Since magnetic monopoles are hypothesized to be a stable particle, if big bang evolution occurred, many would still be existing today. The number of magnetic monopoles estimated to exist varies, depending on the theory. In Krauss' words, when the "GUT symmetry breaks down into the separate strong and 'electro weak' theories, many monopoles should be produced. So many, in fact, that they would easily close the universe today [by gravity collapse]. The problem becomes not one of how to produce a single monopole, but rather how to get rid of so many" [22, p.246]. Preskill argued in 1979 that in the universe there should be one per proton, others conclude that as few as one per 10^{15} protons exist [8, p.116]. At one time huge numbers were postulated by many researchers -- as many as to account for "most of the mass of the universe--but now that no evidence of them has been produced, estimates have been drastically lowered [33, p.3].

Much of the work on magnetic monopoles is connected with the development of grand unification theories. The big bang theory hypothesizes that, although the strong and weak forces and electromagnetism all have very different strengths and properties at cold temperatures, they converge as temperatures and pressures approach the enormous levels hypothesized to have existed in the early micro-seconds of the big bang. All three were melted together as a single force in the intense heat that existed then until cooling separated them. Grard 't Hooft of the University of Utrecht and Alexander M. Polyakov of the Landau Institute for Theoretical Physics near Moscow, "demonstrated not only that a monopole solution of the classical equations governing these theories existed, but that any unified theory that breaks down to the standard model at low energies must result in magnetic monopoles" [22, p.245]. Their theory "demands" heavy monopoles to describe three of the four known forces of nature.

A super heavy monopole ($>10^{16}$ GeV/c^2) is crucial to the GUT theory because events that have been confirmed to occur in particle accelerators reveal some of the details that must have occurred in early big bang evolution had it occurred [3, p.839]. Magnetic monopoles themselves probably cannot be produced in a particle accelerator because about ten-trillion times the energy released from the current most powerful accelerators is required--the now defunct superconducting super collider would have produced only 10^4 GeV Although it is now estimated that, given the validity of GUT theory, pressure levels speculated to exist in a black hole provide enough force.

The theory received an enormous boost when Sheldon Glashow, Stephen Weinberg, and Abdus Salam reportedly achieved "unification" of the weak nuclear and electromagnetic force (called electroweak force), a feat for which they shared the Nobel Prize in physics. The next step in proving the GUT theory is a unification theory that includes the electroweak and the nuclear or color force [5].

The Theory of Magnetic Monopoles

A magnetic monopole is a particle with a charge system that has only one magnetic pole as opposed to the normal two, often called north and south poles. The theory requires that they have a large charge and therefore a rapidly moving monopole would ionize atoms far more rapidly than electrons. This property is the basis of many detectors set up to measure them. The magnetic field poles are the source of the magnetic field just as electrons and protons are the source of the electrical field [15]. A magnetic monopole is comparable to an electron which has only one unit of charge (a negative charge) or a proton which carries the other charge (a positive unit), each which is 1.6 x 10^{-19} coulomb. The isolation of "electric poles but not magnetic ones is a fundamental distinction between electricity and magnetism" [8, p.106]. Monopoles are theorized to be a concentrated point of enormous mass, about a million-billion times more massive than a proton and about one ten-trillionth of its size [27, p.162]. Krauss estimates that monopoles weigh as much as 10^{16} times the proton, or about one-billionth of a gram [22, p.245]. The heaviest particles so far discovered, the W$^+$, W$^-$ and Z^0 particles, are only about thirty to one-hundred times more massive than a proton (and a proton is about 1,800 times more massive than an electron). A large mass is predicted because particles produced in the early big bang would come from the enormous energy existing then, and the more energy used to produce a particle, the more massive it becomes [12].

The original speculation about the existence of magnetic monopoles is based on our understanding of electricity, specifically electric dipoles [33]. If a metal bar that is positively charged on one half and negatively charged on the other was cut in half, one half would have an excess of positive charges and the other half a negative charge excess. At the atomic level, protons carry the positive charge, electrons the negative. Observation reveals that if a magnet is cut in half, each of the two new magnets always has both a north and a south pole. This process can continue until the magnet is separated into its elementary spins consisting of the protons, neutrons and electrons-- and each *complete* atom functions as a magnetic dipole. A magnetic monopole is where a single particle functions as either a north or south pole.

In classical and later in quantum electrodynamics, "magnetism has been described as a byproduct of the motion of an electric charge" [15, p.674]. A magnetic field can, the monopole theory predicts, arise not only from an electric current, but also from the presence of a magnetic monopole. In 1931, physicist Paul Adrien Maurice Dirac noted that the theory of quantum mechanics indicated that the existence of a single magnetic monopole would both restore complete symmetry between electric and magnetic charges as required in Maxwell's equation, and would also help explain how electric charges existed in integer multiples of a fundamental charge [11; 22, p.245]. In his words, "the mathematics led inexorably to the monopole" [25, p.287]. The electric charge of an electron is exactly equal and opposite to that of a proton--and this consistency persuasively argues that all electrical charges exist as separate units (thus excluding quarks which exist as ±1/3, ±2/3) and are integer multiples of the basic electron charge.

Quantum mechanics and relativity also predict the magnetic monopole force [26]. Since every particle of matter, including the magnetic monopole, must have an antimatter counterpart," an antimonopole could be *either* north or south polarity in contrast to a dipole magnet, which has both north and south in a single unit [8, p.108]. When a monopole collides with a dipole of the opposite pole, an estimated one megawatt is released--an incredible amount of energy for such a small particle. Because of its huge mass, though, magnetic monopole cosmic rays would normally travel right through the earth because "its interactions with light atoms would not be sufficiently strong to impede its motion" [22, p.245]. It would, in Krauss' words, "be like trying to stop a Mack truck by throwing popcorn at it."

Detection Systems

To detect monopoles, Cabrera used a superconducting quantum interference device (SQUBD) ring connected to a low noise sensor which monitors the persistent current in the ring [20, p.835]. Magnetic monopoles must effect electric fields as they pass by them and if a monopole passes through the SQUIID loop, a DC surge of current will occur. The minimal Dirac charge monopole passing through the loop is determined by Gauss's theorem, or $4\pi g/L$ which is $4.4.xlO^{-15}/L$ for each monopole [17]. The signature of a monopole's passage through an isolate loop should be a current change of an integral multiple of $2\phi_0$ where $\phi_0 = hc/2e$ [17, p.338]. Cabrera's monopole signature was expected to produce a current transition equivalent to a flux change of $8\phi_0$ [17, p.339]. This produces a small magnetic field that is difficult to detect partly because of interference, thus a magnetic sensitivity one million times above the earth's one gauss (10^{-4} tesla) magnetic field is necessary. After the monopole has left the ring region, the current change is sustained in a SQUID system [20, p.835].

If a substance that could harbor magnetic monopoles is repeatedly passed through the SQUDD loop, the current it induces would increase incrementally, allowing detection of even single monopoles. This principle, discovered by Michael Faraday, forms the basis of all generators and alternators when a magnet is moved up or down inside a coil of wire, it induces an electric field in it. The same effect would also occur if cosmic ray monopoles passed through the detector. A SQUID unit is incredibly sensitive to magnetic fields, and can detect the hypothesized magnetic molecules moving at a wide variety of velocifies--a necessary feature since the velocity that cosmic ray monopoles travel is estimated at one-one-thousandth of the speed of light [12, p.706]. Superconductivity detectors also must incorporate superconducting shields to attenuate ambient magnetic fields [20, p.835]. Cabrera's newer shield is a lead sheeting 0.8 mm thick which surrounds the detector at a radius of 25 cm, with yet another shield around it [4; 20, p.835].

The IBM detector has "six independent planar detector coils, each connected to its own SQUID to differentiate between true and spurious signals" [3, p.839]. A magnetic monopole, according to the theory, will excite two and only two of the six coils, but other cosmic ray types will excite all six coils. Cabrera's unit functions as follows: an electric current injected into the ring can circle "forever" due to its superconductivity, thus an electrical surge caused by a monopole would persist and can easily be detected [4]. Measuring the magnitute of the current can "enable us to deduce the strength of the monopole long after the particle had disappeared into the laboratory floor" [33, p.4]. Usually niobium-titanium ribbon is used because it Kold Welds very effectively, reducing the likelihood of weld flaws, a major problem in making super-conducting magnets. When a cosmic ray or other magnetic monopole source travels through the loop, its field will interact with the loop current, creating a turbulence that effects the total superconductor loop current level.

Another detection method is the use of a photographic emulsion plate which chemically changes in response to electrically charged particles. A monopole would in theory be easy to detect because it ionizes atoms 10,000 times more effectively than electrons, thus would produce a track thousands of times darker [8, p.108]. On the Earth, they are theorized to have been pulled toward the Earth's center due to their density, the north monopoles collecting near the south geomagnetic pole, and the south near the north geomagnetic pole. The reversal of the earth's magnetic field would cause them to migrate to opposite poles, causing annihilation of those that come too close together during their migration. Research has also indicated other detectors are feasible [13].

The History of the Search

The half-century search for magnetic monopoles has involved evaluating virtually every conceivable possible source, including moon rock, the bottom of sea beds, the upper atmosphere, iron ore, flakes of mica, and the debris from high-energy particle collisions. All of these efforts have failed to find any confirming evidence [31, p.625]. On St. Valentine's Day in 1982, Blas Cabrera of Stanford in a carefully designed experiment produced the best candidate yet-but in spite of "an enormous increase in collection time and area for such detectors," his experiment has never been successfully duplicated and was later formally retracted [15, p.675; 33; 4; 5]. Cabrera concluded that his monopole coordinates were due to "mutual interference between SQUID'S, coupled through adjacent pick-up coils" and "none have occurred since we carefully adjusted the rf excitation frequency for each SQUID to avoid mutual resonances" [20, p.836-837]. All of the other putative candidates have now been ruled out [7, p.463; 18, p.463].

The Stanford detector had, as of 1990, 6,482 hours with "no candidate events" and would have seen 2,000 events by now had Cabrera's single event been real [12, p.706]. The IBM-BNL detector has as of 1990 logged 13,410 hours without experiencing a single candidate event. Researchers have also attempted to detect evidence for monopoles among both terrestrial and extraterrestrial iron atoms and the byproduct of collisions between cosmic rays atmospheric atoms, especially nitrogen, oxygen and carbon.

The most recent effort to find monopoles have not been small. One of the most ambitious projects is the Monopole, Astrophysics and Cosmic Ray Observatory (MACRO) at Italy's Gran Sasso National Laboratory, about sixty miles east of Rome [34, p.219]. This huge 20-million dollar monopole detector is 2,000 times larger than Cabrera's unit--it stretches nearly the length of a football field--and lies beneath the Apennine mountain range [30, p.625]. The approximately 15,000M^2 5m thick detector consists of alternating layers of concrete and iron to screen out unwanted particles, plus tons of clear mineral oil. In the mineral oil are fluorescent compounds which, if struck by passing monopoles, causes a trail of decaying protons which produce photons, and these discernible flashes of light are picked up by liquid scintillation counters [25, p.297]. Two other detectors are also used, one in which the monopoles cause a burst of ionized helium in plastic streamer tubes, and another which consists of a trail of cracks in plastic called a *track etch detector* [31, p.625]. The redundancy is designed to insure that spurious detections can be factored out of the data. If magnetic monopoles exist, the researchers feel that this project they has an excellent chance of finding them within five years. So far, none have been detected, prompting Von Baeyer to state the search has produced "overwhelming negative evidence" for monopoles [33, p.3].

Many physicists today are now pesimistic that evidence will ever be found because, in spite of the best designed experiments and over sixty years of searching, no clear evidence that the hypothesized super heavy monopoles exist has ever been uncovered. Even if they consisted of a relatively small percent of the particles in the universe, they would still play a significant part in physics, ranging from influencing the galaxy's magnetic fields to the interior of neutron stars. Under certain conditions, monopoles are theorized to destroy protons, releasing much energy. Consequently, they are hypothesized to play a pivotal role in detemiining the temperature of both stellar and planetary cores.

Monopoles and the Big Bang

Monopoles are theorized to have formed specifically during the second stage of the big bang, at about 10^{-35} seconds after the start of the cosmic egg's expansion [3, p.839]. The first stage produced the original cosmic egg that is theorized to have came into existence then, or had already existed. This atom sized super hot microcosmos then cooled from its high of 10^{27}K, forming monopoles at the time of the GUT spontaneous-symmetry breaking [3, p.839]. Continued expansion caused continued cooling, reaching a critical value which resulted in a second explosion that occurred as a result of a phase change from gas to liquid, a process which releases enormous energy. Specifically, the space-time fabric is hypothesized to have liquefied at this time, releasing energy which caused the reheating phase, and consequently "inflated" the universe by about 10^{50} times. Called the **inflationary model**, this view concludes that this expansion stage is still occurring. The inflationary model is a modified big bang theory, and certain aspects of it compete with the standard big bang scenario. The theory's leading proponent and inspiration was NUT's Allen Guth.

According to this model, the early phase transitions that occurred with symmetry breaking produced a number of effects, "foremost among them the *magnetic nonopole*" [29, p.123-124]. A third expansion was then produced from a second phase change, this time from liquid to solid, again releasing enormous amounts of energy. This energy is theorized to have produced the range of subatomic particles existing today. This model predicts that the number of monopoles produced depends exponentially on the reheating energy existing at this time [20].

Since monopoles are hypothesized to be very massive, they could be produced only at extremely high energies. It was during the grand-unification phase of the big bang, shortly after Planck time, about 10^{-35} seconds after the big bang began, that their development is theorized to have occur-red. Topological defects concluded to have formed between different regions of spacetime would produce the magnetic monopoles [32]. Specifically, the energy in the universe per unit area dropped after the symmetry broke and the monopoles and anti-monopoles would have annihilated each other, leaving behind those monopoles that "failed to find a partner" [29, p.124].

The magnetic monopoles are also theorized to account for "anywhere between three percent and one-hundred percent of the dark matter in the universe, depending upon how many we find and how heavy they are" [31, p.625]. This should help explain the "large" amount of "invisible and so far inexplicable-mass" [31, p.625]. Magnetic monopoles would be a perfect candidate-they contain a huge amount of mass, and it is theorized that huge numbers of them existed, at least early in the universe's evolution. Cabrera noted that the missing mass density estimate of 0.05 solar masses per cubic parsec "is in good agreement with the halo mass estimates extrapolated back to our local galactic radius" and assuming the entire hidden mass "is made up of monopoles of mass 10^{16} GeV/C^2 with isotropic velocities of over 3OOkm/sec, as suggested from grand unification theories, the number passing through the earth's surface would be 4×10^{-10} cm^{-2} sec^{-1} sr^{-1} which would result in 1.5 events per year" through Cabrera's relatively small detector loop.

CONCLUSIONS: THE IMPLICATIONS OF THE LACK OF MAGNETIC MONOPOLES

The theory has major implications for both big bang cosmology and the theories of how elementary particles came into existence. Huge numbers of magnetic monopoles must exist, but there must be far fewer magnetic monopoles than baryons, otherwise they would have dominated the universe's mass, triggering its collapse eons ago [27, p.162]. Both the inflationary universe and the GUT theory postulates magnetic molecules existing "in great profusion" and that "the universe should have been *swarming* with them, in fact, but not a single one had every been observed. Not one" [27, p.1-2]. The fact that these massive particles which "could help cosmologists out of their own theoretical bind" have not been discovered is a major missing link in the hypothetical evolution of both forces and particles and also of the universe [31, p.625]. This has forced a drastic revision of our cosmological theories, and has not been an easy task since many theories depended heavily on their existence:

> The great appeal of magnetic monopoles is that their existence would both explain why electric charge is quantized and provide clues about the structure of the Universe moments after the Big Bang. Furthermore, whole classes of theories in particle physics work only if they exist. All of which explains why two groups, one from Stanford and the other a collaboration between IBM and Brookhaven national Laboratory, have spent the past three years searching for these elusive objects--without success--and look forward to doing so for years to come [12, p.706].

The debate is to the extent that many cosmologists are now reworking their theories to account for the nonexistence of monopoles. This development illustrates the major problems in existing cosmological theories and illustrates how much is pure speculation:

> The big bang of creation would have been the only event hot enough (almost 10^{10} degrees Kelvin) to generate such particles. Both north and south magnetic monopoles would have been formed, and a small fraction of them would have recombined, annihilating each other. Most of the superheavy monopoles would have escaped an early death, however, and there is no reason to think they would not have survived to the present. It is unclear where the monopoles would have collected as the universe evolved, but then it is also unclear how the universe evolved from the big bang into the galactic structures we see today [8, p.115].

A common response to the lack of monopoles is to modify the inflationary hypothesis to conclude that "only a few monopoles can be created" and consequently the grand total is relatively small so that "unless we happen to be incredibly lucky, we can never expect to see one, no matter how long we search" [27, p.170]. Although they are now hypothesized to be rare--partly because of the negative experimental results has forced reevaluation of existing theory--they are so critical that theory cannot now account for their nonexistence today. Postulating fewer of them is speculation, as presently no evidence whatsoever exists for them even though many researchers have concluded magnetic monopoles must exist for our cosmological and GUT theories to be valid [10, p.472]. The number is a secondary issue; only one monopole need be proved to confirm the basic theory and their existence, a step we have not yet achieved [33, p.31]. Some physics have even began to develop new theories about "the nature of charged particles [which] may be used to interpret the apparent absence of magnetic monopoles" [35, p.414]. Unfortunately, the nondiscovery of magnetic monopoles is not solved so easily, especially since "the theory of inflation [itself is] ... still a hypothesis" [27, p.179]. Furthermore, disconfirmation of one aspect of the theory is generally not sufficient in order to produce a scientific revolution and the debate still involves the most basic aspects of magnetic monopole theory [6, 19, 10, 16, 17].

The theory of inflation also requires the "existence of dark matter" a view which is also not confirmed yet [23, 28]. Ironically, magnetic monopoles "were probably the first exotic cold dark matter candidates to be directly sought in a laboratory, although, "the possibility that monopoles actually make up the dark matter of the universe has subsided somewhat since the development of inflationary cosmologies" [22, p.274]. The GUT theory also has not been supported by other research such as the lack of evidence for proton decay [21]. The lack of monopoles and other problems has caused some researchers to question the validity of the GUT theory. The magnetic monopole research may turn out to be a major hole that contributes to the collapse of evolutionary naturalism. It is part of the growing evidence that the whole universe cannot be understood from the naturalism world view [24]. In conclusion, we believe we cannot improve on Groom's words:

> Over the past three years, in a search of unprecedented scale and intensity, theoretical and experimental physicists from many specialties have quested for the legendary relic magnetic monopole, a particle required in the context of a very general class of grand unified theories. Occasional rumors to the contrary, there is at this point not one shred of evidence for its existence.... We must regretfully conclude that the massive magnetic monopole is not only endangered, but very likely extinct. We hope for nothing more than to be proven wrong by future experiments [17, p.368-364].

REFERENCES

[1]   I. Adawi, **Magnetic Charges in Special Relativity**, American Journal of Physics, May, 59(5)410-413, 1991.

[2]   J.W. Barrett, **The Asymmetric Monopole and Non-Newtonian Forces**, Nature, Sept. 14, 34(6238):131-132. 1989.

[3]   S. Bermon, C.C. Chi, C.C. Tsuei, J.R. Rosen, P. Chaudhari and M.W. McElftrsh, **New Limit Set on Cosmic-Ray Monopole Flux by a Large Area Superconducting Magnetic-Induction Detector**, February 19, Physical Review Letters, 64(8), 1990.

[4]   B. Cabrera, **First Results From a Superconducting Detector For Magnetic Monopoles**, Physics Review Letters, May 17, 48:1378, 1982.

[5]   ...., **Magnetic Monopoles**, McGraw Hill Encyclopedia of Science and Technology, 10:298-301, McGraw Hill, New York, NY, 1992.

[6]   A.D. Caplin, M. Hardiman, M. Koratzinos, and J. Schouten, **The Observation of an Unexplained Event From a Magnetic Monopole**, Nature, Jan. 29, 321:402-406, 1986.

[7]   ...., M. Hardiman, J.L. Schouten, **Observation of An Unexplained Event From a Magnetic Monopole Detector**, Nature, Jan. 29, 359:463, 1987.

[8]   R.A. Carrigan, W. Peter Trower (eds), **Superheavy Magnetic Monopoles**, Scientific American, April, 246(4):106-119, 1982.

[9]   ...., **Magnetic Monopoles**, Plenum, New York, NY, 1983.

[10]   F.S. Crawford, **A Response to A. Horzela, E. Kapuscik, and C.A. Uzes' Comment on 'Magnetic Monopoles, Galilean Invariance and Maxwell's Equations**, American Journal of Physics, May 61(5):472-473, 1993.

[11]   P.A.M. Dirac, Proceedings of the Royal Society of London, Ser A 133, pp. 60-72, 1931.

[12]   H.J. Frisch, **Quest for Magnetic Monopoles**, Nature, April 19, 344(6268):706-707, 1990.

[13]   W. Gesang. et al, **Receiving and Scattering Characteristics of an Imaged Monopole Beneath a Lossy Sheet**, IEEE Transactions on Antennas and Propagation, March 41(3):287-295, 1993.

[14]   J. Gliedman, **Blas Cabrera**, OMNI, September 6:81-136, 1984.

[15]   A.S. Goldhaber, **Magnetic Monopoles**, Encyclopedia of Physics, 2nd Ed., Ed. by Rita Lemer and George L. Trigg, New York: VCH Pub.

[16]   .... and W. Peter Trower, **Resource Letter MM-1: Magnetic Monopoles**, American Journal of Physics, May, 58 (5):429-440, 1990.

[17]   D.E. Groom, **In Search of a Supermassive Magnetic Monopole**, Physics Reports, 140(6):325-373, 1986.

[18]   C.N. Guy, **Comment on Observation of an Unexplained Event From a Magnetic Monopole Detector**, Nature, 325:463, 1987.

[19]   A. Horzela, Edward Kapuscik and Charles A. Uzes, **Comment on 'Magnetic Monopoles, Galilean Invariance, and Maxwell's Equations'** by F. S. Crawford, American Journal of Physics, May 61(5)471-473), 1993.

[20]   M.E. Huber, B. Cabrera, M.A. Taber, and R.D. Gardner, **Limit on the Flux of Cosmic-Ray Magnetic Monopoles from Operation of an Eight-Loop Superconducting Detector**, Physics Review Letters 64(8):835-838, 1990.

[21]   L.W. Jones, **Magnetic Monopoles**, 1984 Yearbook of Science and the Future, Encyclopedia Britannica, Inc., Chicago, IL, pp.364-369, 1983.

[22]   L.M. Krauss, **The Fifth Essence: The Search for Dark Matter in the Universe**, Basic Books Publishers, New York, NY, 1989.

[23]   D. Lindley, **Cold Dark matter Makes an Exit**, <u>Nature</u>, Jan. 3, 349:14, 1991.

[24]   ...., **The End of Physics: The Myth of a Unified Theory**, Basic Books Publishers, New York, NY, 1993.

[25]   H. Pagels, **Perfect Symmetry: The Search For the Beginning of Time**, Simon and Schuster, New York, NY, 1985.

[26]   W. Rindler, **Relativity and Electromagnetism: The Force on a Magnetic Monopole**, <u>American Journal of Physics</u>, Nov., 57(11): 993-994, 1989.

[27]   M. Riordan and David N. Schramm with Forward by Stephen W. Hawking, **The Shadows of Creation: Dark Matter and the Structure of the Universe**, W.H. Freeman and Company, New York, NY, 1991.

[28]   W. Saunders et al., **The Density Field of the Local Universe**, <u>Nature</u>, Jan. 3, 349:32-38, 1991.

[29]   J. Silk, **The Big Bang**, Revised and Updated Version, W.H. Freeman and Company, New York, NY, 1989.

[30]   J.L. Stone. (Ed.), Monopole '83, Plenum Press, New York, NY, 1984.

[31]   R. Stone, **A Trap to Snare a Monopole**, <u>Science</u>, Aug. 9, 253(5020):625, 1991.

[32]   G. Taubes, **The Case of the Missing Magnetism**, <u>Discover</u>, January 12(l):4849, 1991.

[33]   H.C. Von Baeyer, **Dead Ringer**, <u>The Sciences</u>, July-August, 30(4):2-4, 1990.

[34]   P. Young, **Hunting Down the Magnetic Monopole**, <u>Science News</u>, Oct. 5, 140(14):219, 1991.

[35]   W.B. Zeleny, **Symmetry in Electrodynamics: A Classical Approach to Magnetic Monopoles**, <u>American Journal of Physics</u>, May 59(5):412-416, 1991.

AN UPDATE ON THE COURTS, ACADEMIC FREEDOM AND CREATIONISTS: THE PELOZA JOHNSON, AND BISHOP CASES

JERRY BERGMAN, PH.D.
ARCHBOLD, OHIO

KEYWORDS

Academic freedom, teaching of creation, freedom of religion and speech, creation and the courts.

ABSTRACT

A review of the Peloza, Johnson, Bishop, and other cases involving creationists educators terminated or censored due to their objections to naturalistic evolution illustrates the current trend for the courts to rule against educators who are labeled not only creationists, but also Christians. These examples illustrate that the law and past Supreme Court rulings are commonly misapplied, abused, or judges openly prevaricate about the conclusions of current and previous cases. The focus on this review is on tying these cases together and outlining current trends.

INTRODUCTION

Since the 1987 supreme court creationism ruling, courts have in all of the important court cases, including Webster, Peloza, Johnson and Bishop, resoundingly ruled against creationists. These cases were all well documented religious discrimination cases in which the court, in essence, ruled that only the atheistic position of origins can legally be presented in public schools. This conclusion is well documented in the cases themselves, as well as those which were recently argued before the Supreme Court, which vividly reveal that its justices perceive the concerns discussed here.

The Bishop Case

Philip Bishop is an associate professor of physiology at the University of Alabama, director of the university's human performance laboratory. An 11th U.S. Circuit Court of Appeals three-judge panel upheld a 1987 demand by the university that he not mention his religious beliefs in or outside of class. He had began each class with a two-minute discussion of how his "personal religious bias" colored his perspective of physiology, namely that a study of physiology provided evidence for intelligent design, not naturalism [30, 15, p.2]. Bishop also included an optional unit titled *Evidence of God in Human Physiology* taught on his own time which the court "also ordered him to stop" [9, p.A23; 6, p.55].

The University endeavored to stop Bishop and *only* Bishop from mentioning, even briefly, his personal world view in the classroom, which he did to "help students in understanding and evaluating" his classroom presentations [4, p.7]. His brief argued that suppressing only certain philosophical perspectives would be intellectually dishonest. If only those with an atheistic or agnostic world view could freely express their views, students may learn the erroneous opinion that all professors share this world view. McFarland characterized the case as follows:

> The university administration ordered Dr. Bishop to discontinue his classroom speech as well as his optional on-campus-talk. No other faculty and no other topic have been similarly curtailed. Dr. Bishop obtained a federal court order protecting his free speech and academic freedom, but it was overruled in a disastrous opinion by the U.S. Court of Appeals, the 11th Court. The Court held that public university professors have no constitutional right of academic freedom and that their right of free speech in the lecture hall is subject to absolute control (censorship) by the University administration [15, p.2].

The U.S. Supreme Court rejected the petition for *centiorari*, thus the case ended.

Robert Boston, a spokesman for *Americans United For Separation of Church and State* noted that he believed this was the first time "a Federal Court had applied the secondary-school ruling to a public university," and that courts in the past have viewed college students as "more mature and better able to judge" whether a professor's statements implied institutional endorsement of religion [9, p.A23]. *Americans United* are well known for their opposition to any open support for theism in public schools, and generally advocate the presentation of only non-theistic views in schools.

The Bishop case was about the college's right to restrict "occasional in-class comments and an optional out-of-class lecture," that mentioned "the professor's personal views on the subject of his academic expertise." The Amici Curiae in this case,

> reveals that the problem presented here is reoccurring on campuses throughout the nation.... We are shocked at the breadth of speech rendered vulnerable by the court of appeals' decision.... the decision ... [gives] universities broad power to censor any comments that might 'produce more apprehension than comfort in students' (Pet. App. A1O). This view is completely anethetical to the premise underlying higher education--that students grow intellectually from confronting new or disturbing ideas, not from avoiding them..... [and the] petitioner was reprimanded for his expressions solely because of the religious viewpoint presented in it ... such discrimination is, unfortunately, typical. Religiously committed academics in public universities across the country face resistance when they attempt, however briefly, to discuss or even disclose their ideological perspective in the course of their teaching or scholarship [4, p.5-6].

Another concern in this case was the university's attempt to apply derogatory labels to the Bishop's view of origins, degrading them as "Bible belt" and therefore "inappropriate" at the university. Specifically Professor Westerfield said Bishop's beliefs "hurt the reputation" of the university [17, p.2]. The Bishop brief argued that the school officials "proceeded on the mistaken assumption that religious discussion must be 'kept out of the classroom' entirely, on account of the establishment clause" and that the establishment clause forbids not only open government endorsement of religion--but by government employees acting *as individuals*. The university argued that allowing professors to present their own views in class implies that the university endorses them, i.e., the university endorses "everything it does not censor" [4, p.10]. Bishop argued that occasional expressions of personal belief at a public university "cannot be construed as bearing the university's imprimatur, and thus are protected under the First Amendment when they are nondisruptive and noncoercive" [4, p.9]. It was "undisputed that petitioner covered the course material fully and that he was a well-regarded and successful teacher" [4, p.15].

The Bishop appeal stressed that the university restricted Dr. Bishop's speech "solely because of its religious content" and that "speech presenting a religious perspective is entitled to the same non-discriminatory treatment as other forms of speech" [4, p.13]. Contrary to extensive case law and the Constitution, the court of appeals' decision authorized "virtually limitless censorship of in-class or classroom-related speech by professors" if it can be construed as "religious," or even "religiously motivated" even "if the views expressed are clearly identified as personal"[4, p.9]. Strictly applied, it would be inappropriate for a professor to state that he is Jewish, goes to church, or believes in God [24]. Yet the same professor is allowed to state that he does not believe in God, and can lecture against "religious" values or beliefs [31, 12, 14].

The court of appeals ruled that the university had a "legitimate interest" in preventing religious bias" from "infecting" the students "because expression of a religious viewpoint 'no matter how carefully presented ... engenders anxiety in students... [4, p.15]. To suppress speech on these grounds is ludicrous--it would be close to impossible for instructors to teach courses in the behavioral sciences, political science, or philosophy if this rule were consistently applied. As Bishop's attorney argued "discomfort, anger, anxiety on the part of a student or two cannot authorize suppression of a viewpoint" [4, p.15]. The whole point of free speech laws is to protect speech specifically in cases where it engenders dispute, disagreement, discomfort, anger or anxiety. Speech that does not generate these emotions is never suppressed, and thus protection is not of concern [8].

The court of appeals recognized this, concluding the university *can* "restrict speech that falls short of an establishment violation" (Pet. App. A22). In other words, the court can convict one of a crime even if it rules the person did not commit the crime! This position is totally irreconcilable with the our total freedom of speech history . Although the courts have held that schools may restrict student or teacher speech which "substantially interferes" or clearly impinges upon "the rights of others" (Tinker, Supra 393 U.S. At. 509) the court's past rulings have required *overwhelming evidence* that such major effects have occurred, and not merely indications that such *may* have occurred, as they ruled in this case. This decision signifies a new trend: if there is even a *hint* of endorsement of theism, all other considerations, including the First Amendment, must be suppressed.

The university even alleged that expressing religious views--no matter how carefully presented--may cause students to accept a similar belief and change their beliefs (Pet. App. A22). Of course, *one of the very purposes of education is to change students' beliefs* -- the definition of learning is *behavior change*. In this case, the direction students' beliefs may change is likely the court's actual concern--if it is toward the direction of religious disbelief and atheism, the professor is usually supported [18].

A good example of this is a study by Cornell Professor of biological sciences, William B. Provine. He first presents the theistic side, then for the remainder of the quarter endeavors to demolish the arguments for theism. He noted that at the beginning of his course, about 75% of the students were either creationists or believed in "purpose in evolution," i.e., believe that God directed evolution. Provine proudly notes that the percentage of theists dropped to 50% by the end of the course--this compares to about 95% in society as a whole [23, p.63]. He is obviously enormously successful in influencing his students to move toward the atheistic world view--and is very open about his success--yet the university and courts have not interfered even though he has openly "expressed his religious viewpoint" which the court ruled Bishop could not do.

Peloza v. Capistrano Unified School District

A good example of the prevarication of courts is the Peloza case, a Mission Viejo biology teacher. Peloza was not teaching, or even arguing for the right to teach, any form of creationism, but rather was endeavoring to help students think critically about atheistic evolution in general [21]. His complaint argued only that it is improper for the school district to *require* him to teach atheistic evolution *as fact*, and his request was only for permission to critique evolution as a teacher would any other theory. As a result of this request, he was removed from biology classes and forced to teach physical education where the subject of biological origins would be less likely to surface [19,25]. District Judge David W. Williams concluded without a hearing that to "teach" creationism (a term he never defined) is "illegal," relying upon the Supreme Court case, *Edwards vs. Aguillard* which in fact stated that *to teach creation-science is legal*:

> It is equally clear that requiring schools to teach creation science with evolution does not advance academic freedom. The Act *does not grant teachers a flexibility that they did not already possess to supplant the present science curriculum* with the presentation of theories, besides evolution, about the origin of life.... The Act provides Louisiana school teachers with no new authority (No. 85-1513, Je 19, 1987, p.8, emphasis mine).

Judge Williams concluded that Peloza had no basis for claiming the school officials violated his rights by ordering him to follow the state-mandated science curriculum [31, p.658]. His decision gives free rein to the California Public School to force teachers to indoctrinate in naturalistic evolution, and that no higher intelligence was involved in this process. The decision precludes theistic evolution and requires "officially embraced atheism as its state religion" [33, p.2].

The case began on September 30, 1991 when Peloza filed a lawsuit against the San Juan Capistrano Unified School District for alleged civil rights violations. Peloza claimed that the school district was in violation of the establishment clause by requiring him to teach atheistic evolution as fact which "unlawfully establishes the religion of secular humanism and atheistic naturalism" [33, p.1]. Peloza also asked the court to declare that "he had the right to discuss his personal beliefs, including religious matters, with students during non-instructional time at the high school, such as during lunch, class-breaks, and before and after school hours" [33, p.1]. The Judge Williams ruling of January 16, 1992 forbid Peloza from discussing his personal beliefs *anytime, anywhere*, on school property, and that Peloza must teach only evolutionary naturalism.

The media characterized Peloza as endeavoring to teach creationism and also commonly quoted the judge's statement that Peloza was a "loose cannon" [31, p.658, 26, p.1]. This irresponsible comment hardly describes someone who simply wishes to talk about his personal beliefs with students during his free time--a right that atheistic and agnostic instructors have. Further, Peloza was not quibbling with the requirement that he teach evolution, only with teaching cc evolution as fact" [33, p.1].

The school district filed a motion endeavoring to be reimbursed for "attorney's fees," a motion granted by Judge Williams on April 14 for the whopping amount of $32,633.49. Peloza's attorney eloquently argued that this award can only be interpreted as punishment for Peloza endeavoring to defend his right to discuss his religious beliefs with students during his own time.

Ironically, even though he was required to teach evolution as fact, the California State Board of Education policy prohibits this: "science is limited by its tools--observable facts and testable hypotheses ... nothing in science or in any other field of knowledge shall be taught dogmatically. A dogma is a system of beliefs that is not subject to scientific tests and refutation." Hartwig and Nelson [7, p.v] describe this framework as "a political document aimed at marginalizing and disenfranchising those who disagree with the authors' philosophical and scientific viewpoint; namely, Darwinistic naturalism." Ironically, the framework itself proclaims that "science is never dogmatic; it is pragmatic--always subject to adjustment in the light of solid new observations ... or new, strong explanations of nature ..." [7, p.18]. If students question evolution, the framework suggests that they respond as follows:

at times some students may insist that certain conclusions of science cannot be true because of certain religious or philosophical beliefs that they hold.... It is appropriate for the teacher to express in this regard, 'I understand that you may have personal reservations about accepting this scientific evidence, but it is scientific knowledge about which there is no reasonable doubt among scientists in their field, and it is my responsibility to teach it because it is part of our common intellectual heritage [7, p.20].

The major problem that all of these cases involve is:

Prejudice ... because the leaders of science see themselves as locked in a desperate battle against religious fundamentalists, a label which they tend to apply broadly to anyone who believes in a Creator who plays an active role in worldly affairs. These fundamentalists are seen as a threat to liberal freedom, and especially as a threat to public support for scientific research. As the creation myth of scientific naturalism, Darwinism plays an indispensable ideological role in the war against fundamentalism. For that reason, the scientific organizations are devoted to protecting Darwinism rather than testing it, and the rules of scientific investigation have been shaped to help them succeed [10, p.153].

A major problem in this controversy is that key terms as creation and evolution are rarely defined, thus one hardly knows for certain what these cases were discussing, although one can infer this by reviewing the entire decision. Evolution, for example, can be defined simply as any biological change, such as the process of breeding the 200 modern dog types from a basic dog kind. On the other hand, evolution is more commonly defined as a naturalistic process in which life changes by natural law and chance into a different--and often better--form. The word literally means to *roll out*, such as rolling out a scroll to reveal more information. What is often insisted upon in the California Framework is not simply evolution, but naturalism or atheistic evolution as discussed by Provine above.

The Byron Johnson Case

Dr. Byron R. Johnson was an assistant professor of criminology at Memphis State University from 1986 until 1991 when his contract was terminated (*Johnson v. Carpenter et al.*, No. 91-2075, at 4-8, W.D. Tenn. Jan. 25, 1991). The background of the case is as follows:

Beginning in 1987, Dr. Johnson was instrumental in organizing a Christian Faculty/Staff Fellowship at Memphis State. He did not, however, discuss his religious beliefs in class. Although Dr. Johnson published more and received higher teaching evaluations than any other assistant professor in his department, he received substantially smaller salary increases from 1988 through 1990 than other department members, and was eventually terminated. During discussions with Dr. Johnson, university officials told him he "did not fit in" and that "given his philosophical leanings, he should consider teaching at some smaller religious affiliated school." Dr. Johnson has sued the university in Federal District Court under Federal Civil rights laws ... and that lawsuit is now in pretrial discovery [4, p.4].

As of this writing, this case is still in the courts.

Center Moriches School District v. Lamb's Chapel Church

The anti-religious bias of certain segments of American society was vividly reflected in an exchange between the Supreme Court Justices and the Lamb's Chapel attorneys. The church had requested school space to show a film series by child psychologist Dr. James Dobson after school hours. The school censored the entire meeting because of the film's alleged "religious" content. When Justice White questioned why the school objected, school attorney John Hoefling stated the film had religious overtones and would "move toward entanglement" of government and religion, adding that, "It was too close to proselytizing" [16, p.1].

The case is so blatant an example of discrimination that even the *American Civil Liberties Union and Americans for Separation of Church and State* filed an amicus brief *in favor* of Lamb's Chapel, concluding that allowing the group to show the film is "unlikely to be perceived as a government endorsement of religion" [16, p.1]. The Chapel's brief concluded that since only non-school hours are involved, showing the film was denied "not because of the 'subject' it wanted to discuss-- 'the protecting and strengthening of family relationships'" -- but because it discussed that subject *from a religious perspective*.

Taking Justice Brennan's ruling that "once the government permits discussion of certain subject matter, it may not impose restrictions that discriminate among viewpoints on those subjects," justice Thomas asked the school's attorney, "what if there was to be a debate between a religious voter versus an atheist on the family?" [16, p.19]. Hoefling responded that the debate would be prohibited because an openly religious person is involved. Thomas then queried, "What if there were ten atheists debating one minister so the minister could not dominate the situation?" Hoefling indicated that this too would be disallowed because the religious world view--and only the religious world view--is to be totally excluded from the public schools [16, p.19].

Lamb's Church attorney Jay Sekulow concluded that this position openly favors the nonreligious and discriminates against religious persons--and the Supreme Court agreed in their ruling. Justice O'Connor even asked if it was "neutral" to prohibit "only persons with a religious perspective"--while allowing the other side to present their views, asking, "But are anti-religious perspectives permitted?" Hoefling replied, "Yes" adding that the *only* view which was disallowed was that which is traditionally labeled religious. Sekulow then summarized the exchange in the august court, stating atheists, agnostics, and communists can be heard, only religious people are censored, and "only one side of the debate can be heard" [16, p.19].

Justice Scalia also perceptively noted the hypocrisy of this, stating that it was widely accepted that "a lack of religious institutions" would result in more social deviancy. In view of the dramatic crime increase--the United States now has the highest crime rate of any nation--Scalia asked, "How is this new regime working? Has it worked very well?" The audience vividly got the point--a society that has banished religious values from public life does not seem to have worked [16, p.19].

Academia Is Not Consistent Banishing Religion From Public Colleges

Although those advocating the creationists world view normally face censorship, much inconsistency exists in the handling of these cases:

> Dr. Henry F. Schaefer, III, is a chaired professor of chemistry at the University of Georgia and a multiple Nobel Prize nominee. During... 1987-88, Dr. Schaefer accepted the invitation of a student religious group to present five or six one-hour lectures on campus concerning science and Christianity. The lectures were strictly optional and unrelated to any course.... A dozen or more faculty members complained to administrators about a university employee discussing a religious topic on campus. However, on advice of counsel, university officials took no action against Dr. Schaefer. Instead, they simply requested that any advertisements state that his lectures were not university-sponsored and were not required for any course. Dr. Schaefer complied. In addition, during the first class meeting of each of his courses, Dr. Schaefer makes a fifteen-second statement disclosing his religious faith and the fact that it frames his analysis of and approach to science [4, p.2].

Often threats are made but not followed through, as in the case of Dr. Clinton H. Graves who:

> has for almost 40 years been a professor of plant pathology at Mississippi State University. Spurred by a recommendation at a faculty training seminar, Dr. Graves began a practice of introducing himself to his students at the beginning of a semester by ... distributing a one-page biographical sketch summarizing his own education, scholarship, and personal interests. At the bottom of this resume, among his personal interests, Dr. Graves typically stated simply that he was committed: to the lordship of Jesus Christ." In addition, he made occasional brief, non-proselytizing comments to students in class concerning his religious beliefs and their relation to issues in plant biology.

> In 1985, Dr. Graves received a letter from the American Civil Liberties Union of Mississippi demanding that he take steps to "remedy" the "possibility that you are introducing significant religious content into your regular classroom proceedings." ... Dr. Graves responded in writing that he ... was "not required to cease being what I am, a Christian, the moment I walk on campus." The ACLU never pursued the matter, nor did it seek to remedy any intimidation or other damage its letter might have caused Dr. Graves [4, pp.3-4].

The cases cited above are instructive as to how creationists now prevail in court. The courts have increasingly ruled against attempts to prevent sectarian religious ideas in the classroom in such as way that they are perceived as indoctrination, not education. If it is perceived that the instructor is functioning as an advocate for theism, and not objectively presenting the theist as well as the atheistic side, the likelihood of prevailing in the courts is less. Secondly, it is imperative to present the case in such a way that one can obtain, as Lamb's Chapel case did, groups such as the ALCU on one's side. Creationists must be aware of the law, and insure that their actions are within it, and this must be effectively documented by affidavits from students, and tape recordings of one's lectures that show one is endeavoring to present information, and not indoctrinate. Although it was clear in all of the cases evaluated here that the person was disliked *because* of his religious belief's, these suggestions will go a long way toward achieving at least a fair hearing should those who are opposed to theism attempt to challenge the integrity of a person who holds to a non-evolutionary naturalism world view.

Marsden argues that American culture in the past decade has advocated the merits of diversity, and the problem of intolerance of religious professors can be dealt with by "a broader conception of pluralism and diversity" [13, p.12]. He notes that, "even in state schools there should be room for at least reviewing one's perspective in the classroom in the name of truth in advertising" and that "institutions that claim to serve the whole public and be internally diverse should be challenged to apply the principle of diversity by openly allowing responsible religious perspectives in the classroom." If not, Marsden concludes, catalogs should state honestly that "the school welcomes diverse perspectives, except, of course religious perspectives." Or where their catalogs or job ads talk about discrimination they "should have a sentence that reads; 'we do discriminate on the basis of religion'" [13, p.12].

CONCLUSIONS

Court rulings in cases involving creationists have been blatantly discriminatory and unconstitutional to the extreme. Indications exist that the Supreme Court is aware of this and may try to correct this problem. In the earlier cases involving creationists, the courts typically presented false reasons for dismissal or discrimination, such as incompetence or the erroneous claim that the faculty member falsified documents or other allegations which were clearly used to cover up the real reason, religious discrimination. The recent cases have been blatant about the termination reasons; consequently it is easier to litigate the actual issues in court. Cases are now fought openly on freedom of speech and First Amendment grounds: University of Chicago law professor Mike McConnell stated of the Bishop case, "This is principally a free speech case. It was litigated as a free speech case; it was decided as a free speech case" [17]. According to attorney Sam Erickson, "the practical impact [of these recent case decisions] is that universities will have to monitor *all* of the lectures, opinions, and off-the-cuff remarks of their faculty to determine whether there has been *anything* that smacks of religion. Nothing could be more repressive" [6, p.55]. In the Bishop case, Dr. Ray Mellichamp, a tenured faculty at the University of Alabama for twenty-three years, stated

> Here's [Bishop], who is a good teacher, doing a good job of research, and he makes one comment in class, that a student complains about, and the university goes into orbit. It has been a complete puzzle to me ... why they ever appealed the decision from the district court--it just doesn't make sense [17, p.1].

In all of these cases, it is not alleged that the teacher was anything less than fully competent: Peloza was acknowledged as an excellent teacher, and was a runner-up for biology teacher of the year [11]. Bishop openly labeled his beliefs as his personal bias, and no one has alleged that he engaged in prayer, Bible reading, or lectured on religious topics--the only concern was occasional comments which never exceeded a few minutes each semester [3]. According to Bishop, "the university had to scratch around to find two students who complained" and one of those later agreed to testify on Bishop's side [17, p.2].

Schools are no longer afraid to press the real issue, which is the instructor's personal religious beliefs and fear that the professor may influence students toward accepting, or positively evaluating, those beliefs. Conversely, no such fear is held in the case of professors who have expressed atheistic, Marxist, or ideas which are considered heretical by the scientific community [27]. Even if blatantly unpopular views are expressed in class, the courts have strictly defended the professor's academic freedom. Only in the case of creationists have they not prevailed in the courts. A search of published academic freedom cases by this writer found no exceptions to this generalization. As Johnson noted, "In the long run it will be hard for the authorities to say you can advocate all kinds of controversial opinions in the classroom, but not on this one subject" [17, p .2].

REFERENCES

[1]   J. Bergman, **The Criterion**, Onesimus Publishing, Richfield, MN, 1987.

[2]   ...., **Censorship in Secular Science: The Mims Case**, Perspectives on Science and Christian Faith, March, 45(1):37-45, 1993.

[3]   Bishop, Philip, Letter to Jerry Bergman, Oct. 25, 1991.

[4]   P. A. Bishop v. O.H. Delchamps, Jr., et al., Brief submitted to the Supreme Court of the Unitied States, October Term, 1991.

[5]   Christian Legal Society, **CLS in the Supreme Court**, Center Updates column, Briefly, Sept. 1992:2.

[6]   M. Hartwig, **Christian Professor Loses Free-Speech Case**, Academic Freedom column, Moody Monthly, June 24, 1991:55.

[7]   M. Hartwig and P.A. Nelson, **Invitation to Conflict: A Retrospective Look at the California Science Framework**, Access Research Network, Colorado Springs, CO, 1992.

[8]   K. Hudson, (Ed.), **Christian Biology Teacher John Peloza Loses First Round**, Education Newsline, April-May, 1992.

[9]   S. Jaschik, **Academic Freedom Could Be Limited By Court Ruling: U.S. Appeals Panel Opposed Action By U. of Alabama Against Professor**, The Chronicle of Higher Education, Apr. 17, 1991:A23.

[10]   P. Johnson, **Darwin on Trial**, Regnery Gateway, Washington, DC, 1991.

[11]   D.C. Larsen, J. Wetheimer, Rutan & Tucker, John E. Peloza vs. Capistrano Unified School District, Board of Trustees of the Capistrano Unified School District ... Memorandum of Points an Authorities in Opposition to Defendants' Motion to Dismiss January 6, 1992.

[12]   E.J. Larsen, **Trial and Error, The American Controversy Over Creation and Evolution**, Oxford University Press, New York, NY, 1985.

[13]   G.J. Marsden, **Religious Professors Are the Last Taboo**, The Wall Street Journal, Dec., 22, 1993.

[14]   S.T. McFarland, Letter to Jerry Bergman, Aug. 1, 1991.

[15]   ...., **Free Speech and Academic Censorship**, On the Front Lines column, Briefly, Christian Legal Society, Apr. 1992:2.

[16]   M. McManus, **Time For Common Sense on Church-State Issues**, Lodi News Sentinel, Feb. 27, 1993.

[17]   J. Meyers (Ed.), **U.S. Supreme Court Denies Review of Bishop: Academic Freedom Stumbles in Wake of 11th Circuit Court Ruling**, The Real Issue, 11(3) Oct. 1992.

[18]   ...., **Experts Respond to the Recent Restrictions on Faculty Freedoms: 11th Circuit Court Ruling Sparks Debate on Freedom of Expression**, The Real Issue, II (4) Dec. 1992a.

[19]   K. Nahigian, **Evolutionists vs. Creationists**, The Sacramento Union, Sat., March 21, 1992.

[20]   National and International Religion Report, The University of Alabama...., 6(5):3, July 13, 1992.

[21]   J. Peloza, **Teacher Stands Up Against Censorship: John Peloza Fights To Teach Good Science**, Education Newsline, May/June, 1991.

[22]   P.A. Bishop -vs- O.H. Delchamps Jr. et al, No. 91-286 in the Supreme Court of the U.S., October term 1991.

[23]   W.R. Provine, **Response to Johnson Review**, Creation-Evolution, Issue No.32, Summer, 1993, pp.62-63.

[24]   R.W. Robinson, **The Preachy Professor**, Letter to Editor, Perspective column, Liberty, Sept-Oct. 1991, p.28.

[25] Rutan, Tucker, David C. Larsen, Jeffrey Wertheimer, John E. Peloza vs. Capistrano Unified School District, Board of Trustees of the Capistrano Unified School District ... Memorandum of Points an Authorities in Support of Defendant's Motion to Dismiss, Dec., 16, 1991.

[26] E.C. Scott, **Peloza Lawsuit Dismissed by Federal Judge; Called "Loose Cannon" by Judge.** BASIS, Vol. 11, No. 3, March 1992.

[27] P. Smith, **Killing the Spirit: Higher Education in America**, Viking, New York, NY, 1990.

[28] U.S. District Court, John E. Peloza v. Capistrano Unified School District, et al., Memorandum No. CV 91-5268-DWW (Bx), Jan 16, 1992.

[29] U.S. District Court, John E. Peloza v. Capistrano Unified School District, et al., Order Granting Attorneys' Fees and Costs to Prevailing Party, No. CV 91-5268-DWW (Bx), Apr. 14, 1992.

[30] Wolf, Larry W., **The Preachy Professor**, Letter to Editor, Perspective column, Liberty, Nov-Dec. 1991, p.30.

[31] J.E. Wood, Jr., **Notes on Church-States Affairs**, Journal of Church and State, Autumn, Vol. 34(4), 1992.

[32] C. Zal, **Summary of the John Peloza Case**, Unpublished manuscript, 1992.

[33] ......, John E. Peloza vs. Capistrano Unified School District, Board of Trustees of the Capistrano Unified School Distfict... Opening Brief For Appellant Case No. 92-552228 Appeal.

[34] ......, John E. Peloza vs. Capistrano Unified School District, Board of Trustees of the Capistrano Unified School District ... Memorandum of Points an Authorities in Opposition To Defendants' Motion for Attorneys' Fees, April 6, 1992.

[35] ......, John E. Peloza vs. Capistrano Unified School District, Board of Trustees of the Capistrano Unified School District...Memorandum of Points an Authorities in Opposition to Defendants' Motion to Dismiss January 6, 1992.

EXPERIMENTS ON STRATIFICATION

GUY BERTHAULT
28, BOULEVARD THEIRS
78250 MEULAN, FRANCE

KEYWORDS: Superposition, Strata, Laminae, Stratigraphy, Bedding planes.

ABSTRACT

The principle of superposition requires that superposed strata in sedimentary rocks form from successive layers of sediments. The principle of continuity asserts that each layer has the same age at any point. These principles apply a relative chronology to superposed strata. The correlation between strata and time allowed Charles Lyell to establish the first geologic column in 1830.

From his examination of sediments in the Gulf of Naples in Italy a century ago, Johannes Walther, one of the founders of sedimentology, formulated his law of correlation of facies: "As with biotopes it is a basic statement of far-reaching significance that only those facies areas can be superposed primarily which can be observed beside each other at the present time" [3]. Walther's law, which gave rise to the modern sequential analysis of facies, is not in agreement with the principles of superposition and continuity. His law, as well as the observations of the Bijou-Creek deposits, suggested that the contradiction might be due to the belief that superposed strata are the same as successive layers.

The author's first experiments on lamination and those performed at the Colorado State University in large flumes showed that stratification under a continuous supply of heterogeneous sand particles can result from: segregation for lamination, non-uniform flow for graded beds, and desiccation for bedding plane partings.

In the flume experiments superposed strata were always distinct from successive layers, and neither the principle of superposition nor the principle of continuity applied to the strata.

Due to the mechanical nature of segregation and the presence of sediments and non-uniform flow in oceans and rivers being the same factors producing strata formation in the flume, the experimental results might have some application to the genesis of stratified rocks.

As the experiments cast doubt upon the use of the principles of superposition and continuity for interpreting the origin of sedimentary rocks, it would perhaps be preferable to follow the modern approach of sequential analysis, although on a larger scale. Such an approach should necessarily take into account the present series of experiments.

INTRODUCTION

Stratification is the general term for layering in rocks. A stratum is a single layer of homogeneous or gradational lithology deposited parallel to the original dip of the formation. It is separated from adjacent strata or cross-strata by surfaces of erosion, non-deposition, or abrupt change in character. A stratum includes bed and lamination which carry definite thickness connotations [1].

The principle of superposition states that layers having been deposited one upon the other, each layer superposed upon another is younger than the one underneath it [2].

The principle of continuity states that each layer has the same age at any point [2].

It follows from the above two principles that superposed strata are successive layers with each layer having the same age at any point. A relative chronology is thus attributed to superposed strata.

The correlation between strata and time allowed Charles Lyell to construct the first geologic column in 1830.

SEDIMENTOLOGICAL DATA

(1) Johannes Walther's law of the correlation of facies

At the time of the pioneering of stratigraphy, little was known about sediments. It was not until 1875, with the sea-floor core sampling of the "Challenger" vessel that sedimentology started to develop. It was the observations made by German sedimentologist Johannes Walther [3] of the littoral sediments in the Gulf of Naples that provided further data. He noted that, as one moved out from the coast to the open sea, the characteristics or facies of the sediments on the sea bottom changed. From a vertical boring, he observed that the succession of facies was identical to the superposition of facies. Walther's explanation was simple. Gradually, the gulf was filled in by fluvial, marine, detrital, chemical and organogenetic sediments. The sea floor thus spread laterally towards the open sea. This movement is called "progradation" (see Figure 1).

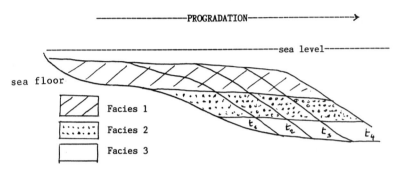

Figure 1. *Progradation.*

The facies 1, 2 and 3 prograde together toward the open sea at t1, t2, t3, t4 (t = time), and superpose each other.

The 'differentiation' of facies arises in two ways. First from the sedimentary particles undergoing a sorting process due to the action of the waves, tides and currents, whereby the larger particles care deposited near the shore and the smaller ones farther away. Second, the progressive substitution of the terriginous sediments, from the coast to the sea, by organic deposits. These latter sediments originate from benthic species at specific depths and migrating species of plankton giving rise to chemical deposits and organodetrital sediments at various levels and distances from the shore.

Walther formulated his observations on the correlation of facies into the following law:

> As with biotopes, it is a basic statement of far-reaching significance, that only those facies areas can be superposed primarily which can be observed beside each other at the present time.

Since Walther's time, sedimentologists of his school have sought an explanation for the superposition of facies in ancient sedimentary ocean basins. Being unable to observe sedimentation following the major transgressions and regressions of the past, they adopted a reasoning, based upon contemporary coastal transgressions and regressions caused by tropical hurricanes. Referring again to Figure 1, if the sea level falls abruptly at each of the times t1, t2, t3, and t4, then the level of the sediments will fall in the same way. The result is shown in Figure 2 below.

It can be seen from Figures 1-4 that superposed facies in a sequence, deposited at the same time, do not follow either the principle of superposition or the principle of continuity. These facies, however, can be composed of superposed strata. It follows that the two principles cannot apply to such strata. Consequently, such strata are not successive layers nor do they have the same age at any point.

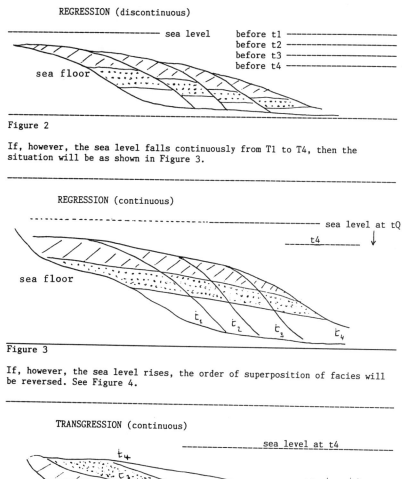

REGRESSION (discontinuous)

———————————————— sea level
sea floor

before t1 ——————————— ↓
before t2 ——————————— ↓
before t3 ——————————— ↓
before t4 ——————————— ↓

Figure 2

If, however, the sea level falls continuously from T1 to T4, then the situation will be as shown in Figure 3.

REGRESSION (continuous)

———————————— sea level at tQ

sea floor

t_1 t_2 t_3 t_4

Figure 3

If, however, the sea level rises, the order of superposition of facies will be reversed. See Figure 4.

TRANSGRESSION (continuous)

———————————— sea level at t4

t_4

t_3

t_2

sea level at t0

t_1

Figure 4

Figure 2. Discontinuous regression.
Figure 3. Continuous regression.
Figure 4. Continuous transgression.

(2)   BIJOU-CREEK Flood - field data source

The 1965 Bijou-Creek flood in Colorado, after forty-eight hours of rain, produced a deposit of sediment twelve feet in thickness in some places. After the water had receded, E.D. McKee, Crosby and Berryhill studied the site [4]. They dug trenches in the sediment in order to examine their structure and texture. They found that 90-95% of the sediment consisted of horizontal laminated strata. The external vertical face of the sediments deposited on the original bank, perpendicular to the river bed, showed strata separated by virtually horizontal cracks resembling bedding plane partings found in rocks (see photo-figure below).

105

Figure 5. *1965 Bijou Creek sediment deposit.*

As the flood only lasted forty-eight hours, it seemed that the cracks were caused by desiccation of the sediments after the water had receded.

EXPERIMENTS ON STRATIFICATION

The study of the facies sequences and cracks in the Bijou-Creek deposits gave rise to questions which were addressed by an attempt to reproduce similar deposits in the laboratory.

(1)   First series of experiments on lamination

The object of the experiments was to study lamination in continuous sedimentation in the air, in still water and water subject to a current. Up until these experiments, lamination had been interpreted as a superposition of successive layers.

Samples of laminated friable rock were crumbled to reduce them to the original particles of varying diameter that made up the rock. The particles were sorted by sieving, and the largest particles were colored. They were then remixed with the noncolored particles and allowed to flow continuously in recipients, first in the air, then in water. The experiment was repeated in a small flume in which water was circulated. The results were summarized in the abstract of the 1986 report [5]:

> These sedimentation experiments have been conducted in still water with a continuous supply of heterogranular material. A deposit is obtained giving the illusion of successive beds or laminae. These laminae are the result of a spontaneous, periodic and continuous grading process, which takes place immediately following the deposit of the heterogranular mixture. The thickness of the laminae appears to be independent of the speed of sedimentation but increases with extreme differences in the size of the particles in the mixture. Where an horizontal current is involved, thin laminated superposed layers developing laterally in the direction of the current are observed.

Figure 6. *Laminations resulting from flowing of dry sediments.*[5]

Figure 7. *Laminations resulting from flowing in water.*[5]

Figure 8. *The thickness of laminae is independent of the speed of sedimentation.*[5]

Figure 9. *The thickness increases with wide difference in the size of the particles.*[5]

Similar experiments were conducted at the 'Institut de Mecanique des fluides' in Marseilles (France). The results were summarized in the abstract of the 1988 report [6]:

> The experiments demonstrate that in still water, continuous depositing of heterogranular sediments give rise to laminae which disappear progressively as the height of the fall of particles into water, and apparently their size, increase. Laminae follow the slope of the upper part of the deposit. In running water, many closely related types of lamination appear in the deposit, even superimposed.

(2) Experiments in collaboration with Colorado State University

The project terminated by two series of experiments at the University of Colorado, the first from 1988 to 1990, and the second during 1993.

The results of the first series were summarized in the abstract of the 1993 report [7]:

> Superposed strata in sedimentary rocks are believed to have been formed by successive layers of sediments deposited periodically with interruptions of sedimentation. This experimental study examines possible stratification of heterogeneous sand mixtures under continuous (non-periodic and non-interrupted) sedimentation. The three primary aspects of stratification are considered: lamination, graded beds, and joints. The experiments on segregation of eleven heterogeneous mixtures of sand size quartz, limestone and coal demonstrate that through lateral motion of a sand mixture, the fine particles fall between the interstices of the rolling coarse particles. Coarse particles gradually roll on top of fines and microscale sorting is obtained. Microscale segregation similar to lamination is observed on plane surfaces, as well as under continuous settling in columns filled with either air or water. The formation of graded-beds is examined in a laboratory flume under steady flow and a continuous supply of heterogeneous sand particles. Under steady uniform flow, the velocity decrease caused by a tailgate induces the formation of a stratum of coarse sand particles and two strata of laminated fine particles. Over time, a thick stratum of coarse particles thus progresses downstream between two strata of laminated fine particles, continuously prograding upward and downstream. Laboratory experiments on the desiccation of natural sands also show

preferential fracturing, or joints, of crusty deposits at the interface between strata of coarse and fine particles.

Rather than successive sedimentary layers, these experiments demonstrate that stratification under a continuous supply of heterogeneous sand particles results from: segregation for lamination, non-uniform flow for graded-beds, and desiccation for joints. Superposed strata are not necessarily identical to successive layers.

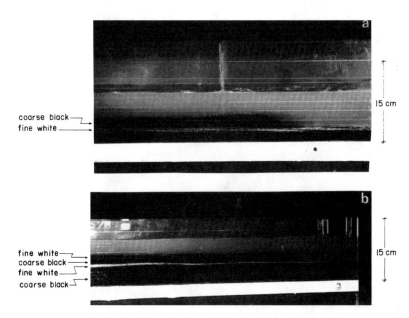

Figure 10a. *Example of graded-beds with first tailgate.*[5]
Figure 10b. *Example of graded-beds with second tailgate*[5]

Figure 11a. *Typical cross-sectional view of deposit.*[5]
Figure 11b. *Typical longitudinal view of deposit (flow from right to left).*[5]

The second series was summarized under the title "Fundamental experiments on stratification" in the 1993 report [8].

"Laboratory experiments cover three aspects of stratification:

SEGREGATION. The kinetic energy of spherical particles rolling on a plane surface at a constant velocity increases with particle mass and particle size. Particle segregation results from lateral motion of an heterogeneous mixture.

LAMINATION. Clear lamination forms from repetitive segregation in air, under water, or under vacuum. Particle lamination essentially depends on the mechanical interaction between particles of different size, density and shape.

GRADED BEDDING. A large laboratory flume measuring 20m long and 1.30m wide recirculates 30 cubic meters of water and 8 tons of an heterogeneous sand mixture. A continuous supply of coarse sands and fine sands is maintained under steady discharge. During et typical delta experiment, the coarse-grained for-set slope propagates in the downstream direction and covers the fine-grained bottom-set slope downstream between two consecutive times. A stratum defines preferential accumulation of coarse or fine particles. The formation of -a delta in the laboratory demonstrates that sediment layers are not identical to strata. Isochrons correspond to the interface between successive layers, and not the interface between strata. The chronological formation of the sedimentary deposit is therefore correlated to layers, not strata.

During the experiments, superposed strata formed under continuous settling. They were not younger than the underlying strata nor older than the overlying strata. The strata were not the same age at all points."

CONCLUSIONS

The experiments could provide a new model for explaining the formation of stratified rocks. Strata developed in the experiments wherever a non-uniform flow of water was present. The current sorted the sediments into graded beds. It appears, therefore, from the various parameters used in the experiments that the mechanism for stratification depends upon non-uniform flow of water and supply of sediment.

Due to the mechanical nature of segregation and the presence of sediments and non-uniform flow in oceans and rivers being the same elements producing strata in the flume, the experimental results might have some application to the genesis of stratified rocks.

As the experiments challenge the use of the principles of superposition and continuity as it basis for relative stratigraphic chronology, there is a need to reconstitute, as far as is possible, the true genesis of sedimentary basins. The hydraulic conditions originating the basins could perhaps la determined from the study of stratified rocks, sedimentological observations and the experiments in sedimentology.

An approach of this kind already exists in the form of sequential analysis derived from the works of Walther. It is a field that needs to be developed. The experimental fact that a continuous supply of sediment produces stratified deposits should dissipate the illusion that superposed strata result from an intermittent succession of layers taking millions of years to deposit.

My view as a Christian is that the enormous sedimentary basins covering the earth could have resulted from the Great Flood.

REFERENCES

[1]   E.D. McKee and Gordon W. Weir, **Terminology for Stratification and Cross-Stratification in Sedimentary Rocks**, Bulletin of the Geological Society of America, 1964, pp. 381-390.

[2]   Jean Aubouin, **Précis de Geologie**, Tome 2, p. 227, 1966.

[3]   Walther Johannes, 1885, **Die Gesteinbildende Kalkalgen des Golfes von Neapel und die Entstehung Strukturloser. Kalke**, Geol. Ges. Zeitschr. Deutsch., V. 37 pp. 329-357., 1893-1894, "Einleitung in die Geologie als Historische Wissenschaft: Jena, Verlag, Gustav Fischer, 3 vols.

[4]   E.D. McKee, **Flood Deposits, Bijou-Creek, Colorado**, 1965, Journal of Sedimentary Petrology, 37.3, 1967, pp. 820-851.

[5]   G. Berthault, **Experiments of Lamination**, C.R. Acad. Sc., Paris T., 303, Serie 22 17-1986.

[6]   G. Berthault, **Sedimentation of a Heterogranular mixture. Experimental lamination in still and runing water,** C.R. Acad. Sc., Paris T., 306, Serie II, pp. 717-724, 1988.

[7]   P. Julien, Y. Lan, G. Gerthault, **Experiments on stratification of hetereogeneous sand mixtures,** Bull. Soc. Geologique France, 1993, T. 164., 5, pp. 649-660.

[8]   P. Julien, G. Berthault, **Fundamental experiments on stratification**, Livre des résumés (ASF, Paris, 19.368 pp.191-192 du 4em Congrés de l'Association des Sedementologists Français, Lille, France, 17-19, November 1993, (video cassette under the same title presented with the paper at the Congress).

PARTICLE INTERACTION ANALYSIS
OF SOLAR FORMATION AND STABILIZATION

EDWARD A. BOUDREAUX, PH.D.
DEPARTMENT OF CHEMISTRY
UNIVERSITY OF NEW ORLEANS
NEW ORLEANS, LA 70148

ABSTRACT

The evolution of the solar interior is analyzed from a classical, independent, particle interaction model. In this model, it is presumed that the plasma has attained an organized state of development, thus reaching a condition of static equilibrium. Henceforth, the ionized particles remain at essentially fixed distances of interaction.

Most current standard solar parameters, as well as standard data pertinent to the associated atomic particles, have been utilized. All associated energy quantities are computed within the frame-work of the model, employing conventional techniques. The possibly of "strong force" interactions between charged particles separated at nuclear distances, is also considered.

It is shown that the total repulsive energy exceeds all other stabilizing factors, including the gravitational potential energy. A proposal regarding the deficiency in detecting solar neutrinos is also presented.

INTRODUCTION

According to the Big Bang scenario, the sun (or any other star) is formed by the condensation of hydrogen into an ion-plasma. The pertinent process involved is the nuclear fusion reaction of

$^1_1H^+$ (hereafter designated p^+) producing $^4_2He^{2+}$ (hereafter designated α^{2+}) in the presence of the ionized element (e^-) to preserve electrical neutrality. The charges on the protons and alpha particles are explicitly specifies as p^+ and α^{2+} respectively, so as to emphasize the nature of the charge interactions involved in the specific electrostatic computations. Although electrons are not explicitly involved in the nuclear reactions, they are, nonetheless, products of the initial processes and are thus regarded as non-negligible entities involved in the sum total of electrostatic interactions. Hence the reason for their explicit inclusion in equations (1a) through (1e).

$$2p^+ + 2e^- \rightarrow 2n^0 - 1.56 MeV \tag{1a}$$

$$2p^+ + 2n^0 + 2e^- \rightarrow 2^2_1H^+ + 2e^- + 2\nu + 4.46 MeV \tag{1b}$$

$$2^2_1H^+ + 2p^+ + 4e^- \rightarrow 2^3_2He^{2+} + 4e^- + 10.98 MeV \tag{1c}$$

$$2^3_2He^{2+} + 4e^- \rightarrow \alpha^{2+} + 2p^+ + 4e^- + 12.85 MeV \tag{1d}$$

these may be combined to yield the overall process

$$4p^+ + 4e^- \rightarrow \alpha^{2+} + 2e^- + 2\nu + 26.73 MeV \tag{1e}$$

The issue at hand is to examine the energetics of this process via an independent particle interaction model. The interactions of p^+ and e^- will be considered first, followed by an analysis of the collective p^+, e^- and α^{2+} interactions. The question is whether or not either the p^+, e^-, or the p^+ e^- and α^{2+} can be condensed into an ion plasma with particle interaction distances derived from known data, to produce the equilibrium conditions necessary for the stability of the sun or any other star.

111

COMPUTATIONAL PROCEDURE AND RESULTS

In order to simplify the treatment of this problem into something that is manageable, we will employ a *frozen ion-plasma* model, in which it is presumed the plasma has attained an organized state of development, maintained in static equilibrium. Thus the interparticulate interactions take place at essentially fixed distances. This removes the complexities and associated uncertainties of a dynamical model and should be an adequate approximation for providing at least the relative magnitudes of the pertinent interactions. The required information regarding chemical composition and physical parameters of the sun are presented in Table 1, as obtained from various sources [9,10,4,13,8,7]. These data are given primarily for the interior region of the sun, which is least subject to any significant fluctuations. Also based on the Cosmion model, the solar interior contains (on the average) 79.1 per cent of the total mass [8]. Cox, Guzik and Raby (1990) developed a solar model in which weakly interacting, massive particles, called "cosmions", reduce the opacity by about 10^{-3} within a central region one tenth of the solar radius, which also results in a reduced temperature of the isothermal core [7]. This model specifies a metallicity of 0.02, an initial He mass fraction of 0.277 and a mixing-length/pressure-scale-height ratio of 2.015, achieving an evolutionary stage of development to attain $1L\odot$ and $1R\odot$ in a time period of 4.6 Gyr (billion years) [7].

It is usual to express the total energy, E_T, in term of the total potential energy, E_p, by making use of the virial theorem, upon assuming that the ion-plasma has attained equilibrium.

This theorem state that the total average kinetic energy, E_k, is expressible in terms of the displacement forces of all particles in the system, as follows:

$$2\bar{E}_k = -\sum_i \bar{s}_i \bar{F}_{si} \qquad (2)$$

where s_i is the set of generalized coordinates (x,y,z) for all i particles, and F_{si} is the S component of force acting upon the ith particles. The total potential energy, E_p, is given by:

$$\sum_i s_i \left(-\frac{\partial V_i}{\partial s_i} \right) = E_p \qquad (3)$$

Since the total energy is $E_T = E_k + E_p$ and Eq (2) is the negative of Eq (3), we have the result:

$$\begin{aligned} 2\bar{E}_k &= -\bar{E}_p \\ E_T &= -\bar{E}_k = \tfrac{1}{2}\,\bar{E}_p \end{aligned} \qquad (4)$$

Thus, for all the initial particles to be stabilized in a unified ion-plasma, the total energy of the plasma must be equal to half the average potential energy of all particles in equilibrium.

For a primitive sun in its state of development at 4.6 Gyr of evolution, the appropriate data relating to its interior has been taken to be that reported by Cox and Coworkers [7]. The statistical mean values are presented in Table 1.

TABLE 1	
Elemental Composition and physical Data for the Sun [9,10,4,13,8,7].	
ELEMENT	**PERCENT**
H	78
He	20
O,C,Ne	1.7
All Others	0.3

<table>
<tr><th colspan="2" align="center">PHYSICAL DATA</th></tr>
<tr><td colspan="2" align="center">

$M_\odot$ (total mass) = 1.989 x 10^{33}g
$R_\odot$ (total radius) = 6.960 x 10^{10}cm
R (interior region):   Intermediate Zone = 0.60 $R_\odot$
                 Core   = 0.25 $R_\odot$

$\bar{H}$ (interior magnetic field): $10^2 \leq \bar{H} \leq 10^4$ gauss (est.)

</td></tr>
<tr><td colspan="2" align="center">Current Mean Statistical Data for the Solar Interior [7,8]</td></tr>
<tr><td align="center">Current Sun</td><td align="center">Primitive Sun</td></tr>
<tr><td>Age = 4.6 Gyr[a]
Cosmion Model:
Cox, Guzik and Raby, 1990 [8]</td><td>Age = 0.0 Gyr[a]
Standard Model:
Cox, Guzik and Kidman, 1989 [7]</td></tr>
<tr><td>$\bar{M}$(g)   = 1.574 x 10^{33}</td><td>7.718 x 10^{34}</td></tr>
<tr><td>$\bar{R}$(cm)   = 6.047 x 10^{10}</td><td>6.093 x 10^{10}</td></tr>
<tr><td>$\bar{\rho}$(g/cm^3)   = 103.0</td><td>81.44</td></tr>
<tr><td>$\bar{T}$(K)   = 1.00 x 10^7</td><td>1.37 x 10^7</td></tr>
<tr><td>$\bar{V}(\bar{\rho})$(cm^3)[b]   = 1.528 x 10^{31}</td><td>9.477 x 10^{32}</td></tr>
<tr><td>$\bar{V}(\bar{R})$(cm^3)[c]   = 9.262 x 10^{32}</td><td>9.477 x 10^{32}</td></tr>
<tr><td>$\bar{P}$(dynes/cm^2)   = 1.463 x 10^{17}</td><td>9.213 x 10^{16}</td></tr>
</table>

[a] Gyr = 10^9 yr.
[b] Derived from the mean density.
[c] Derived from the mean radius.

We will now proceed to the evaluation of various interactions involving the particles contained within the volume element of this system, i.e., electrostatic interactions (columbic and magnetic), gravitational, pressure-volume, effects, and the possibility of "strong force" interactions.

In treating the interionic coulombic interaction, the electrostatic energy of a fixed i^{th} in a "sea" of other mobile ions, is evaluated from statistical mechanics [11]. The pertinent expression is:

$$E(el)_i = \frac{(Z_ie_i)^2}{2\,\epsilon\,r_i}\left(1 - \frac{\kappa\,r_i}{1 + \kappa a}\right) \qquad (5)$$

Z_ie_i = the electrostatic charge of the ith ion, ϵ = the dielectric constant, r_i = the radius of the ith ion, a = distance of closest approach of mobile j ions to the ith ion (a = $r_i + r_j$), dependent only on the ion radii. For any ion, i or j, κ_{ij}^2, the Boltzman distribution of the ionic strength of the medium, is most conveniently expressed in the form

$$\kappa_{ij} = 2\left[\left(\frac{\pi}{\epsilon kT}\right)\sum_{ij}(Ze)_{ij}^2(N_{ij}/V)\right]^{\frac{1}{2}}$$ (6)

where k = Boltzman's constant. T = mean absolute temperature (see Table 1), (N_{ij}/V) the number density of ions pertinent to the appropriate volume element.

If the potential is repulsive, as in the case of p^+/p^+, α^{2+}/α^{2+}, and e^-/e^- interactions, at a = short distances, equation (5) becomes:

$$E_R(i) = \frac{(Z_i e_i)^2}{2 \epsilon r_i}\left(1 - \frac{\kappa r_i}{1 + \kappa a}\right)\exp(-2a)$$ (7)

It can be shown that E_R is independent of ϵ [11].

The attractive coulombic interactions are evaluated from the following expression for a charged sphere-lattice model derived by Chiu [5,11], which is a close approximation to a Madelung lattice sum per electron

$$E_A(i) = -\frac{9}{10}\frac{Z_i^{\frac{2}{3}}e^2}{r_e}$$ (8)

where Z is the absolute charge of the positively ionized particle and r_e is the effective radius of a sphere replacing

the volume element per electron, given by $\left(\frac{3}{4\pi Ne/V}\right)^{\frac{1}{2}}$. In this approximation, the closest distance of approach

between oppositely charged particles has been assumed for all interactions.

Magnetic interactions are also possible since p^+ and e^- have magnetic moments of 8.806 x 10^{-18} MeV/gauss and 5.789 x 10^{-15} MeV/gauss, respectively. The potential expression for the magnetic stabilization energy per particle is:

$$E_m(i) = -(\mu(i)\,\bar{H})$$ (9)

where μ is the particle magnetic moment and $\bar{H}$ the effective magnetic field of the solar interior (see Table 1). The classic gravitational potential energy is provided by the standard expression:

$$E_G = -\frac{3}{5}\frac{G\bar{M}^2}{\bar{R}}$$ (10)

where the gravitational constant, G = 6.670 x 10^{-8} dynecm^2/g^2, $\bar{M}$ and $\bar{R}$ are respectively the mean mass and radius of the solar interior.

There is also another effect to consider due to comprehensive e^- pressure on the positively charged ion sphere. It is later shown that this effect is given by:

$$E_{pV} = \frac{F\,\bar{V}}{4\pi\,\bar{R}^2}$$ (11)

where F is the effective force applied to the ion-sphere surface, $\bar{R}$ and $\bar{V}$ are the mean radius and volume of the solar interior, respectively.

The final effect is that due possibly to Strong Force interaction, because of the close distance of separation between charged particles. This could be a very significant factor for p^+/p^+ and possibly α^{2+}/α^{2+} interactions, which will be treated in detail at the appropriate place later in this paper.

PRIMITIVE SUN

For a sun in its earliest stages of mature development, the pertinent physical data are those listed in Table 1. Assuming that the hydrogen would have condensed into a constant density sphere having the reported

characteristic of the solar interior, the mean volume would have been $\bar{V}$ = 9.477 x 10^{32}cm^3 (see table 1).

114

Coulomb Interactions

The repulsive energies for p^+/p^+ and e^-/e^- interactions are computed from equation (7) using data presented in Table 2.

TABLE 2 Coulombic Interaction Data for Solar Ion-Plasma							
Particle	r $f_m = 10^{-13}$ (cm)	m $(g \times 10^{-24})$	Primitive		Current		μ $(\times 10^{-15})$ (MeV / Gauss)
			N $(\times 10^{58})$	$N/\bar{V}$ (part/cm^3 $\times 10^{25}$)	N $(\times 10^{56})$	$N/\bar{V}$ (part/cm^3 $\times 10^{25}$)	
e^-	2.818	0.0009	4.612	4.867	8.280	5.419	5.789
p^+	1.034	1.6725	4.612	4.867	7.338	4.802	0.008806
α^{2+}	2.160	6.6883	-----	-----	0.471	0.308	-----

[a]N and $\bar{V}$ are derived from Table 1.

The result for E_R (p^+/p^+) = 2.344 x 10^{58} MeV and for E_R (e^-/e^-) = 6.665 x 10^{57} MeV. Thus, the total E_r = 3.011 x 10^{58} MeV.

As far as the p^+/e^- Coulombic attractive interactions are concerned, according to equation (8), the required value of r_e = 1.699 x 10^{-9}cm. However, at a mean temperature of 1.37 x 10^7K, the energy available is 86.84 times that required to fully ionize the electron from the H atom, and 21.70 times the energy required to fullyionize the two electrons from He. At the energy of ionization for H (13.6 eV), the closest distance that the electron can be to the proton is given by $n^2 a_H$, where n is the principal quantum number of the highest orbital from which the e^- is ionized and a_H = 0.5295 x 10^{-8}cm. From the electronic spectral tables of Moore [12], the highest quantum level to which the H electron is excited at the ionization limit, has n = 49. Hence the closest e^-p^+ distance for which ionization is maintained, is $(49)^2$ (0.5295 x 10^{-8}cm) = 1.271 x 10^{-5}cm. However, so as not to minimize the effects of coulombic attraction, the value of r_e = 1.699 x 10^{-9}cm is adopted. Thus the computed upper limit is $E_A(p^+/e^-)$ ≤ -3.518 x 10^{42}MeV.

It is important to realize that because of energy conditions, constraints are placed on the minimum p^+e^- distance of approach (ex. ~ 10^{-5}cm via H spectral data), which is 10^8 times greater than the closest p^+p^+ and e^-e^- distances (~ 10^{-13}cm). Thus it would appear that the solar interior structure may conform to a central p^+ "sphere" cluster, with an outer spherical segment composed of clustered e^-, situated at a relatively large distance ($\Delta r \approx 10^4$ or 10^8cm) from the central p^+ "sphere". This does not appear to be unreasonable, as the total volume occupied by the e^- and p^+ in the solar interior is 4.534 x 10^{21}cm^3. The volume of the primitive solar interior (from Table 1) is 9.477 x 10^{32}cm^3, which is 2.09 x 10^{11} times greater than the total particle volume. The p^+ "sphere" volume is 2.135 x 10^{20}cm^3, with a radius of 3.708 x 10^6cm, while the mean radius of the solar interior is $\bar{R}$ = 6.093 x 10^{10}cm (Table 1). Thus, the height of the spherical segment containing the e^- layer is $\approx 10^7$cm. The void between the p^+ "sphere" and the e^- "spherical segment" would be 6.091 x 10^{10}cm high, very close to the mean radius of the solar interior itself. See Figure 1.

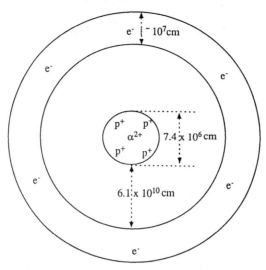

Figure 1. *Proposed Particle Structure of the Sun*

PV Compression

Because of what has been proposed above regarding the structure of the solar interior, it is interesting to consider the magnitude of PV compression from the e⁻ layer directedagainst the p⁺ "sphere".

The total average kinetic energy, $\overline{KE}$ of the solar interior is given in terms of the average

pressure $\overline{P}$ and average volume $\overline{V}$, by $\overline{KE} = \frac{3}{2}\overline{P}\,\overline{V} = 1.310 \times 10^{50}$ ergs for the primitive sun. Since the

contribution for the electrons should be about 1800 times that of the protons, hence

$$\overline{KE}(e^-) + \overline{KE}(p^+) = 1.310 \times 10^{50}$$
$$1800\overline{KE}(p^+) + \overline{KE}(p^+) = 1.31 \times 10^{50}$$
$$\overline{KE}(p^+) = 7.274 \times 10^{46} \text{ ergs}$$
$$\overline{KE}(e^-) = 1.309 \times 10^{50} \text{ ergs}$$

The force that the e⁻ layer exerts on the p⁺ "sphere" is:

$$F(e^-) = 1.309 \times 10^{50} \text{ergs}/2\pi R(p^+),$$

where R(p⁺) is the radius of the p⁺ "sphere" given above. Thus $F(e^-) = 5.618 \times 10^{42}$ ergs/cm, and the pressure is

$$5.618 \times 10^{42}/4\pi R_{(p^+)}^2 = P(e^-) = 3.252 \times 10^{28} \text{ dynes/cm}^2$$

Hence, the work done on the p⁺ "sphere" is − P(e⁻) and from the value of V(p⁺) given above, P(e⁻) • V(p⁺) = −6.942 x 10⁴⁸ ergs = −4.333 x 10⁵⁴ MeV. While this is substantially greater than the attractive coulombic energy, it is of significantly lower magnitude than the total repulsive energy.

Magnetic Interactions

According to equation (9), the total magnetic coupling of p⁺ and e⁻ with the magnetic field of the solar interior is

$E_m = -(\mu_p^+ N_p^+ + \mu_e^- N_e^-)\,\overline{H}$. From the data in Table 2, E_m is in the range −2.674 x 10⁴⁶ - 2.674 x 10⁴⁸ MeV,

depending on the value of $\overline{H}$ (see Table 1).

Gravitational Potential Energy

It is usually anticipated that the solar gravitational potential will swamp all other interactions. When the data for the

116

solar interior in Table 1 is substituted into equation (10), $E_G = -2.442 \times 10^{57}$ MeV. This does not offset the maximum repulsive energy computed in Section 1 above, however.

A complete listing of all energy contributions for both the primitive and current sun will be provided in Table 3, after a comparable set of energy data are evaluated for the current sun. There is also the very important question as to what might be the possibility of strong force involvement at such close interparticle distances. This shall be treated subsequent to the evaluation of all classical interactions for the current sun.

CURRENT SUN

Using the data from Table 1, the current masses of H and He in the solar interior are 1.207×10^{33} and 3.148×10^{32}, respectively. This translates into $7.3 \times 10^{56} p^+$, $4.7 \times 10^{55}\ \alpha^{2+}$ and $8.3 \times 10^{56}\ e^-$.

Coulomb Interaction

Utilizing the data in Table 2 and equation (7), the repulsive energies are found to be $E_R(p^+/p^+) = 2.645 \times 10^{56}$ MeV, $E_R(\alpha^{2+}/\alpha^{2+} = 5.448 \times 10^{55}$ MeV and $E_R(e^-/e^-) = 1.875 \times 10^{56}$ MeV.

The attractive interactions involve $e^-/p^+)$ and e^-/α^{2+}. From equation (8), $E_A(e^-/p^+) \leq -5.799 \times 10^{52}$ MeV, $E_A(e^-/\alpha 2+) \leq -5.910 \times 10^{51}$ MeV. Here again, the appropriate value of $r_e = 1.640 \times 10^{-9}$ cm, as determined from the data in Table 2.

PV Compressison

From Table 1, $\frac{3}{2}\ \overline{PV} = 2.032 \times 10^{50}$ ergs, which yields $\cdot \overline{KE}(e^-) = 2.032 \times 10^{50}$ *ergs*. The radius of the $p^+ \alpha^{2+}$ "sphere" is 1.087×10^6 cm. The force exerted upon the sphere by the outer band of e^- is $F(e-) = 2.974 \times 10^{43}$ ergs/cm, and the corresponding pressure is $P(e^-) = 7.248 \times 10^{29}$ dynes/cm^2.

Finally, the PV work done on the $p^+ \alpha^{2+}$ "sphere" from equation (11), is -2.437×10^{54} MeV.

Magnetic Interactions

From equation (9) and the appropriate data in Table 2, $E_M(p^+ + e^-)$ is in the range -4.800×10^{44} to -4.800×10^{46} MeV, depending on the value of $\overline{H}$ employed (see Table 1).

Gravitational Potential Energy

Upon substituting data from Table 1 into equation (10), $E_G = -1.024 \times 10^{54}$ MeV.
It is interesting to note that the total repulsive potential energy is 494.6 times greater than than the gravitational potential energy for the primitive solar interior. A listing of all energy contributions for both the primitive and current solar interiors in presented in Table 3.

<table>
<tr><td colspan="3" align="center">TABLE 3
Solar Interior Energy Parameters</td></tr>
<tr><td rowspan="2" align="center">Energy Term (1)</td><td colspan="2" align="center">Solar Interior Model (2)</td></tr>
<tr><td align="center">Primitive</td><td align="center">Current</td></tr>
<tr><td align="center">E_R</td><td align="center">3.011×10^{58}</td><td align="center">5.065×10^{56}</td></tr>
<tr><td align="center">E_A</td><td align="center">$\leq -3.518 \times 10^{42}$</td><td align="center">$\leq -6.390 \times 10^{52}$</td></tr>
<tr><td align="center">$E(PV)$</td><td align="center">-4.333×10^{54}</td><td align="center">-2.437×10^{54}</td></tr>
<tr><td align="center">E_M</td><td align="center">-2.674×10^{48} (max)</td><td align="center">-4.800×10^{46} (max)</td></tr>
<tr><td align="center">E_G</td><td align="center">-2.433×10^{57}</td><td align="center">-1.024×10^{54}</td></tr>
<tr><td align="center">$\overline{KE}$</td><td align="center">8.179×10^{55}</td><td align="center">1.269×10^{56}</td></tr>
</table>

(1) All values in MeV.
(2) See Table 1.

STRONG FORCE INTERACTIONS

Since the inter-proton distance is of the dimensions associated with that in an atomic nucleus, it is important to attain an assessment of this effect for our p+ ion-plasma. The simplest model of a measured p+p+ interaction is that present in the nucleus of a $^3_2$He atom. However, this also has a neutron (n°) in addition to the two p^+. Thus the total interactions are $2(p^+n^o)$ plus p^+p^+. Hence, we must first obtain a value for the p^+n^o interaction. The only measured case availableis $^2_1$H atom. Using the following charge radii reported for the pertinent particles

[6]: $R(^2_1H)=2.80fm$, $R_{(p+)} = 1.034$ fm, $R(n^o) \approx 0.45$ fm. Summing the diameters, $d_{(p+)}$ of the p^+ and $d(n^o)$, of the n^o, gives 2.97 fm. The diameter of $^4_1$He = 5.60 fm. Thus the p^+n^o separation = (5.60-2.97) = 2.63 fm. The

binding energy of $^2_1$H is 2.22 MeV [14] and since only the strong-force p^+n^o interaction is involved, this is the magnitude of the strong-force pairing energy, E_{SFP}, between p^+ and n^o. Of course, the magnitude of this will change with increasing numbers of nucleons in heavier nuclei, but except for even-odd relationships and nuclear surface effects, the strong-force interactions are essentially additive. We may express the binding energy of ^3_2H as:

$$E_B = 2E_B(p^+n^o)+E_B(p^+p^+) = 7.72 \ MeV \text{ [11].} \tag{12}$$

hence $E_B(p^+p^+) = (7.72-4.44) = 3.28$ MeV, and R (^3_2He) = 2,38 fm (ave.)[6]. For this case, the strong-force pairing energy is:

$$E_{SFP} = E_B(p^+p^+) + E_c(p^+p^+) \tag{13}$$

where E_c is the coulomb energy, which may be evaluated from the following expresion [3]:

$$E_c= \frac{3}{5} \frac{Z^2e^2}{R}\left[1-5\left(\frac{3}{16\pi Z}\right)^{\frac{2}{3}}\right] - \frac{27}{16} \frac{Z^2e^2}{k_F^2R^3} \tag{14}$$

for which $k_F = (\pi^2 Z \rho_{(o)})^{1/3}$ and $\rho_{(o)} = 0.170$ Z/A. Thus E_c = 4.32 MeV and E_{SFP} = 7.60 MeV. The determination of the interproton distance is complicated by the fact that the n° binds the two p^+ at a shorter distance than if it were

not involved. If we consider R (^3_2He) , the radius with the finite proton size, $R_{(p+)}$, removed (see Ref. 10), the p^+p^+

separation will be related to the following two factors 1) $R^*(^3_2He) - R_p$. and 2) $R(n^o)$. The latter factor is added to the first and the average of these two effects should yield a reasonable expression for the p^+p^+ separation, $r(p^+p^+)$

$$r(p^+p^+) \sim \frac{1}{2}\left[R^*(^3_2He) - R_{(p+)}+ R_{(n\,o)}\right] \tag{15}$$

$$= \frac{1}{2} [1.34 - 1.034 + 0.45] \ fm$$

$$= 0.38 \ fm.$$

The strong force pairing potential may be expressed as:

$$V_{SFP} = -\frac{Z^2e^2}{R} e^{-bR} \tag{16}$$

where "b" is an empirical parameter ranging from –27 to 45 (x10^{13}) depending on the value of R. V_{SFP} has its maximum value at R = 0.8 fm, "b" = 19.5 x 10 ^{13}, and goes to zero for R ≤ 0.35 f_m, "b" < –27 x 10^{13}, and for R ≥ 4 f_m, "b" ≥ 45.

Although the E_{SFP} varies substantially over a relatively small difference in $r(p^+p^+)$, the total binding energy increases regularly with the number of nucleons [14]. However, we have no way of knowing how this might behave outside the domains of atomic nuclei, A typical binding energy curve is presented in Figure 2, which shows that the binding

118

energy per nucleon, $E_{B/A}$, increases abruptly up to about 20 p^+ + 20 n^o = A = 40. It then reaches a maximum saturation limit in the range of (26-28) p^+ + 20 n^o = A, but decreases smoothly out to A ≈ 240. All elements having higher mass numbers are highly unstable, and are non-existent if $E_{B/A}$ ≤ 7 MeV, for A > 240. Hence, it is highly questionable as to whether or not the typical nuclear strong-force factors even apply to a body as massive as the sun. However, if they do, then we can expect a direct proportion of E_{SFP} to its volume element of distribution. Thus

for the single p^+p^+ pair in ^3_2He, the 7.6 MeV = E_{SFP} is over a volume element of 56.47 x 10^{-39} cm³, but for the 4.61 x 10^{58} p^+p^+ pairs in the solar interior, the distribution of E_{SFP} is over a volume of 9.48 x 10^{32} cm³. Now when the proportionalities between E_B and A in Figure 2 are applied linearly to the relative increases in nuclear volumes for nuclides, 50 ≤ A ≤ 240, then E_{SFP} = −4.76 x 10^{12} MeV relative to the primitive solar interior.

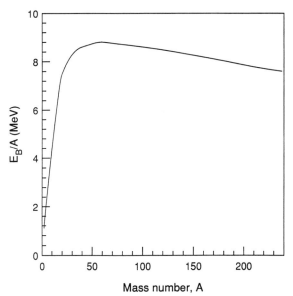

Figure 2. *Variation of binding energy per nucleon, EB/A, with atomic mass number, A.*

In the case of the current solar interior, E_{SPF} may arise form p^+p^+, $p^+\alpha^{2+}$ and $\alpha^{2+}\alpha^{2+}$ strong force pairing. A rational value for E_{SFP} (p^+p^+) has already been derived above. We now proceed to a derivation of E_{SFP} ($\alpha^{2+}\alpha^{2+}$) and E_{SFP} (α^+p^+). The following nuclear process is will documented [15].

$$^8_4Be \text{------} 2\alpha^{2+} + 0.0919 MeV \tag{17}$$

which provides the energy for decoupling two α^{2+}. This represents the difference between E_{SFP} and E_c for the two

entities, at the separation distance in the ^8_4Be nucleus, as given by:

$$r(\alpha^{2+}\alpha^{2+}) \approx 2 \left[R'(^8_4Be) - 2R'(\alpha^{2+}) \right] \tag{18}$$

where $R'(^8_4Be)$ and $R'(\alpha^{2+})$ are effective nuclear radii determined from one ^8_4Be nuclear volume and two α^{2+}

nuclear volumes, respectively. However, the ^8_4Be nuclear charge radius is not listed in ref. [6], but may be

interpolated from the comparisons of charge radii for ^6_3Li, ^7_3Li and $^{10}_5B$, $^{11}_5B$, relative to ^9_4Be, ^8_4Be. The difference

between the radii of the higher and lower mass numbered isotopes of Li and B, is an average value of 0.07 for [6].

Thus we may estimate the effective nuclear radius of ^8_4Be, ie. $R'(^8_4Be)$ as follows

$$R'(^8_4Be) \approx R(^9_4Be) + 0.07fm = 3.12fm + 0.07fm = 3.19 \ fm \tag{19}$$

Since $R'(\alpha^{2+})$ = 2.72 fm, substitution into equation (18) gives r(α^{2+}) = 0.94 fm.

Recalling that $E_{SFP}(\alpha^{2+}\alpha^{2+}) = 0.0919 - E_c(\alpha^{2+}\alpha^{2+})$(MeV), we now calculate $E_c(\alpha^{2+}\alpha^{2+})$ from Eq (14), with $\rho_{(o)} = 0.085$ and $k_F = 1.832$, which gives $E_c(\alpha^{2+}\alpha^{2+}) = 14.74$ MeV. Thus $E_{SFP}(\alpha^{2+}\alpha^{2+}) = 14.83$ MeV at $r(\alpha^{2+}\alpha^{2+}) = 0.94$ fm, and using Eq (16), it is found that the $E_{SDP}(\alpha^{2+}\alpha^{2+})$ is reduced from 42 MeV at 0.94 fm to 3.5 MeV at 2.24 fm, which is nearly a 92% decrease. On applying the energy density proportionality presented above, it is found that the effective $E_{SFP} = -4.55 \times 10^{13}$ MeV over a volume of 9.26×10^{32} cm^3.

We can reasonably estimate that the $E_{SFP}(p^+\alpha^{2+})$ - the average of that for p^+p^+ and $\alpha^{2+}\alpha^{2+}$, respectively, which gives the value -2.51×10^{13}. Hence, if we add the E_{SFP} for all particles, the total $E_{SFP} = -7.54 \times 10^{13}$ MeV. This again is not sufficient to overcome the repulsive energy.

CONCLUSION

The details of an independent particle interaction model have been presented for both the H$^+$ ion-plasma model of a primitive sun and H$^+$/He^{2+} ion-plasma model based on the currently reported composition of the sun. In both cases, it is found that the inter-ion repulsive energy exceeds all other stabilizing energy contributions of the system.

An expression of the total energy in terms of Eq (4) from the Virial Theorem yields the obvious conclusion that neither the primitive nor the current particle structure of the solar interior conforms to this theorem. Admittedly, this treatment is approximate, but should, nonetheless, not be in error by orders of magnitude. Thus, it would appear that the a priori assumption that the Virial Theorem is necessarily satisfied in solar energetics, is not justified on the basis of this analysis. However, since the solar structure is obviously stabilized, there must be some other explanation. Either unjustified constraints must be placed on the factors employed in this analysis, or the assumption that strong force stabilization decreases in proportion to the volume element over which it operates (as implied from the nuclear binding energy curve in Fig. 2, is erroneous.

Could it be that the twenty-odd years of attempts to detect solar neutrinos, having provided substantially fewer neutrinos than predicted by equation (1e), has something to do with the findings of this report? Of themselves, such results have called the solar H$^+$ fusion model into question: nonetheless, the proposal of Bahcall and Bethe [1] requiring a conversion of massless electron neutrinos, v_e, to neutrinos of "another flavor" v_x, having small mass, cannot be ignored and does indeed appear to be vindicated as more careful experimentation progresses.

It is tempting to speculate on this matter in terms of the solar, particle-structure proposed here. Well known electron-neutrino processes include:

$$e^- + v_\mu \rightarrow v_e + \mu^-$$
$$\mu^- \rightarrow e^- + v_\mu + \rightarrow e^- + \gamma$$

Recall the proposed distribution of the outer band of e$^-$ about the p^+,α^{2+} core of the solar interior. A collision of a v_e emanating from this core with an e$^-$ will occur with an availability of 0.380 MeV per e$^-$ (see Section B.1 and B.2 above). It was reported that the upper limits to the kinetic energies of v_e and v_μ were ≤ 200 eV and $\leq 3 \times 10^6$ eV, respectively [16,2] but the currently accepted mass-energy equivalents are < 18eV and < 0.25 MeV, respectively. Thus if the v_e acquired a substantial portion of instantaneous energy to mass transfer, then a neutrino of flavor v_x with mass ≤ 0.380 MeV/c^2, will appear to be produced nonadiabatically. The corresponding reaction scenario is:

$$e^- + v_e \rightarrow v_x + X^-$$

$$X^- \xrightarrow{\text{(very fast)}} e^- + v_x + v_e \rightarrow e^- + \gamma$$

where X$^-$ is some unstable (admittedly hypothetical) X-type meson undergoing very rapid decay. The net result is that the majority of v_e produced initially are converted to v_x, which are annihilated back to the electrons.

This simplistic proposal is in accord with the predictions made from the eloquent quantitative treatments of Bahcall and others [17].

REFERENCES

[1]   J. N. Bahcall and H. A. Bethe, **A solution of the solar neutrino problem**, Physical Review Letters 65 (1990) 2233-2235.

[2]   J. Bernstein, M. Ruderman and G. Feinberg, **Electromagnetic properties of the neutrino**, Physical Review 132 (1963) 1227-1233.

[3]   A. Bohn and B. R. Mottelson, Nuclear Structure, Volume 1, 1969, pp 144-152, W. A. Benjamin, Inc. New York.

[4]   J. C. Brandt and P. W. Hodge, Solar System Astrophysics, 1964, McGraw Hill, New York.

[5]   H.-Y. Chiu, Stellar Physics, Volume 1, 1968, pp 148-152, Blaisdell Pub. Co., Boston, Massachusetts.

[6]   H. R. Collard, L. R. Elton and R. H. Hofstadter, Nuclear Radii, Volume 2, 1967, Landolt-Bornstein New Series, K. H. Hellwege, editor, New York.

[7]   A. N. Cox, J. A. Geizik and R. G. Kidman, **Oscillations of solar models with internal element diffusion**, Astrophysical Journal 342 (1989) 1187-1206.

[8]   A. N. Cox, J. A. Guzik and S. Raby, **Oscillations of condensed-out iron and cosmion solar models**, Astrophysical Journal 353 (1990) 698-711.

[9]   A. N. Cox, W. C. Livingston and M. S. Matthews, Solar Interior and Atmosphere, 1991, University of Arizona Press, Arizona.

[10] E. G. Gibson, The Quiet Sun, 1974, NASA SP-303, Washington, D.C.

[11] D. A. McQuarrie, Statistical Mechanics, 1976, Chapter 15, pp 326-356, Harper & Row Pub., New York.

[12] C. E. Moore, Atomic Energy Levels, Volume 1, 1949, pp 1-7, National Bureau of Standards, Washington, D.C.

[13] F. A. Stacey, Physics of the Earth, 1969, John Wiley & Sons Pub., New York.

[14] A. H. Wapstra and K. Bos, Atomic Data and nuclear tables, Volume 19, 1977, pp 117-214, National Bureau of Standards, Washington, D.C.

[15] A. H. Wapstra and K. Bos, ibid. pp. 215-274.

[16] C.S. Wu, The weak interaction, in Theoretical Physics in the Twentieth Century, M. Fierza and V. F. Weisskopf, editors, 1990, Interscience Publishers, Inc., New York.

[17] See reference [1] and other references cited therein.

MIXING LINES --
Considerations Regarding their Use
in Creationist Interpretation of Radioisotope Age Data

ROBERT H. BROWN, Ph. D.
12420 Birch St., Yucaipa, CA 92399

KEYWORDS

Creation Account exegesis, Earth age, isochron, meteorite age, mixing line, model age, radioisotope age, radiometric dating.

ABSTRACT

Radioisotope daughter/parent ratios may be interpreted on the basis of a model for daughter accumulation, an isochron diagram, or a mixing line. Each of these interpretive treatments is evaluated for its constraint on resolution of apparent disagreement between radiometric age and the chronological specifications in the Pentateuch. A mixing-line interpretation gives no direct specification regarding time, and consequently avoids conflict between Biblical specifications and radioisotope data for minerals associated with fossils and geologic features that were formed after the beginning of Creation Week.

However, a mixing line places limits on the model age for the source material components that are required for mixing to form these minerals. Consequently, when a mixing line interpretation is used for radioisotope data associated with geologic features and fossils formed during and following the Flood, i.e., within the last 5500 years, there remains a need for a corresponding treatment of the model age limits indicated by the mixing line. Treatment of radioisotope model ages for inorganic material from a short-chronology (young earth) creationist viewpoint will be determined by the interpretor's exegesis of Genesis 1:1,2,8-10. One viewpoint constrains the terms *heaven* and *earth*, as used in connection with the Creation Account, within the definitions given in Genesis 1:8-10; and allows model ages to have a relationship with time between an uspecified primordial creation and the creation episode described in Genesis. Another viewpoint infers the entire physical universe, or at least the Solar System, to be designated by these terms; and requires radioisotope model age relationships to be design features expressed at or subsequent to the beginning of the Genesis One Creation Week.

INTRODUCTION

One of the greatest challenges in the development of a credible scientific Biblical creationism is the need for models that provide compatibility of the chronological data in the Pentateuch and scientific evidence that has chronological significance, giving proper recognition to each source of data. Unfortunately, many well-meaning attempts to establish such compatibility and maintain a direct grammatical-historical exegesis of the Pentateuch have fostered disrespect for Biblical creationism within the scientific community at large, and have failed to reduce the influence of unrestricted historical-critical exegesis among Christians and Jews.

Creationist apologists have suggested that a mixing-line interpretation of inorganic radioisotope data would provide an academically sound treatment from a Biblical short-chronology perspective. See [9] and [10], e.g. A mixing-line interpretation has been used to resolve difficulties over radiometric ages inconsistent with the conventional geologic time scale, as noted in [1], [2], [8], [11], [3], [13], [12], and [6, pp. 141-153], e.g., and has promise for similar success in resolution of difficulties with respect to a Biblically-based time scale. The purpose of this treatment is to critically examine the mixing-line concept and its significance to scientific Biblical creationism.

For an efficient development of this treatment, I will first clarify three concepts: radioisotope model age, radioisotope isochron, and mixing line. These concepts are then used in an analysis of a mixing-line interpretation of radioisotope data.

MODEL AGE

A radioisotope daughter/parent model age requires two measurements and is based on three assumptions. The measurements are the concentration of a radioactive parent, and the associated concentration of a stable daughter. The three necessary assumptions are:

1. Isolation from exchange of both parent and daughter with the sample environment throughout the time indicated by the measurements.

2. Rate of transformation of parent into daughter is constant throughout the time indicated, and equal to the presently-measured value of this rate.

3. The concentration of daughter in the sample at the beginning of the indicated time span. This is usually assumed to be equal to the concentration of daughter isotope in material that gives no evidence of having been associated with the parent element.

Using subscript o to indicate initial values of parent and daughter, p_o and d_o, with values at any subsequent time indicated by p and d, $d - d_o = p_o - p$. Representing the half-life for spontaneous transmutation of parent into daughter by $T_{1/2}$, $p = p_o e^{-(\ln 2)t/T_{1/2}}$. From combination of these two relationships $d = d_o + p[e^{(\ln 2)t/T_{1/2}} - 1]$, which can be used to calculate t from a pair of values for d and p.

$$t = (T_{1/2}/\ln 2) \ln[1 + (d - d_o)/p] \qquad [1]$$

ISOCHRON AGE

Figure 1 is a sample isochron taken from [4, p. 149]. In this figure the relative concentration of daughter [87]Sr is plotted against the relative concentration of parent [87]Rb in a suite of gneiss samples from Isua, West Greenland. An isochron plot requires several measurements of radioactive parent and stable daughter concentration in related specimens that have varying concentrations of the parent isotope. If a plot of daughter concentration against parent concentration can be satisfactorily represented by a straight line, as in Figure 1, this line has been called an isochron because it appears to provide evidence for equal time of daughter accumulation in each sample.

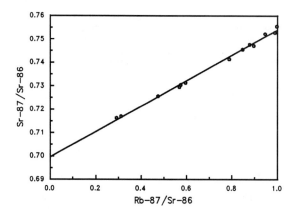

FIGURE I. Linear-array plot of daughter [87]Sr plotted against parent [87]Rb for gneisses from Isua, West Greenland. [Replotted from Dalrymple (1991), p. 149.] If interpreted to be an "isochron", the sloping line indicates an age of 3.6 billion years.

124

Because the daughter concentration d_o corresponds to zero parent concentration, the slope of an isochron line, designated by m, is equal to $(d-d_o)/p$, and the time span indicated by an isochron plot is obtained from Equ. [1] as

$$t = (T_{1/2}/\ln2)\ \ln(1 + m) . \tag{2}$$

An isochron determination has several advantages over a model age.

1. It represents an average of several independent determinations of apparent daughter increase in proportion to parent concentration.

2. It may provide freedom from the need for an estimate of the initial daughter concentration (The initial daughter concentration is assumed to be specified by the y-intercept.)

3. The linearity of the plot provides supporting evidence for the assumption of isolation from exchange with the sample environment.

For more detailed treatment of model age and isochron age see [6, pp. 141-153], or [4, Chapter 3].

MIXING LINES

To develop the concept of a mixing line, consider two sources of material, A and B, each having characteristics p and q. A portion from A is mixed with a portion from B to form the material from which sample S (see Figure 2) is obtained. The fraction f of S is obtained from A, and the fraction (1–f) is obtained from B. On a plot of q against p the coordinates of A and B are q_a,p_a and q_b,p_b, respectively. The coordinates of S are $[fq_a + (1-f)q_b]$ and $[fp_a + (1-f)p_b]$.

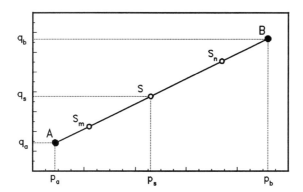

FIGURE 2. Mixing coordinates for samples S with fraction f from source A and fraction (1–f) from source B, each with characteristics p and q.

Incomplete mixing of material from A and B will produce samples of varying mixing fraction f. For two samples S_m and S_n with mixing fractions f_m and f_n the q-axis (ordinate) increment will be $[f_n q_a + (1-f_n)q_b] - [f_m q_a + (1-f_m)q_b] = (f_m - f_n)(q_b - q_a)$, providing mixing does not influence q_a and q_b in any other way than by dilution.

Similarly, the p-axis (abscissa) increment will be $(f_m - f_n)(p_b - p_a)$.

The ratio of these increments is independent of f, and specifies a straight line of slope $(q_b - q_a)/(p_b - p_a)$ for a plot of S on the p,q plane. The ordinate intercept for this line, q_o, is given by $(q_a - q_o)/(p_a - 0) = (q_b - q_a)/(p_b - p_a)$, or $q_o = q_a - p_a(q_b - q_a)/(p_b - p_a)$.

Accordingly a two-component mixing-line equation in p,q coordinates may be written

$$q = (q_a p_b - q_b p_a)/(p_b - p_a) + p[(q_b - q_a)/(p_b - p_a)], \qquad [3]$$

with the subscripts designating characteristics of the source material.

MIXING-LINE OR ISOCHRON?

The p,q characteristics for a mixing-line plot can be the concentrations of a radioactive parent and its stable daughter, the same as for an isochron plot. How can one be certain that a linear plot of daughter concentration versus radioactive parent concentration is an isochron rather than a mixing-line? A linear plot may indicate partial melting, rather than simple mixing. A decision between these possibilities will be determined largely by the perspective of the individual making the judgement. If the slope of the line does not correspond with an age that can be fitted into the conventional geologic time scale, reports in the professional literature usually resort to a mixing-line interpretation. See [1], [7], [3], [13], [12], [6, pp. 145-147], e.g.. Choice for a mixing-line interpretation is made also when the ordinate intercept (initial daughter concentration d_0) is outside the range of values for minerals that have no indication of association with the parent element.

It must be emphasized that the slope of a mixing line does not have time significance. The time at which mixing occurred must be inferred from other considerations. As stated by Zheng, "... an observed isochron does not certainly define a valid age information for a geological system, ..." [12, p. 14]. "A negative slope ... can be yielded by a mixing where the Rb/Sr ratio of high $^{87}Sr/^{86}Sr$ component is less than that in the low $^{87}Sr/^{86}Sr$ end-member. This situation has been observed for minerals ... in the Eifel, F.R.G. ..." [12, pp. 10,11].

Figure 4 is a plot of a negative slope mixing line for the Newer Volcanics in Victoria, Australia. The data for Figure 4 are taken from Table 1 and Figure 3 of reference [5].

MIXING-LINE INTERPRETATION FROM THE PERSPECTIVE OF BIBLICAL CREATIONISM

If uniformitarian scientists can comfortably resort to a mixing-line interpretation when an isochron interpretation gives an age inconsistent with the geologic time scale, there should be equal freedom to choose a mixing-line interpretation for data which give an isochron interpretation that contradicts a Biblically-based time frame.

For a closer analysis of mixing-line interpretation as it may be used in Biblical creationism modeling, consider Figure 3. This figure represents seven distinct samples S_1 to S_7 from an incomplete mixture of material from two sources A and B. Each sample S_n corresponds to a mixing fraction f_n, as used in the development of Equation 3. S_1 <u>could</u> represent source A, with $f_1 = 1$; and S_7 <u>could</u> represent source B, with $f_7 = 0$. All that the data indicate for certain is either that S_1 and S_7 represent the sources A and B, or that the mixing line at those locations points toward p and d values which represent the sources.

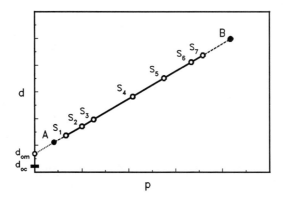

FIGURE 3. Mixing line for a suite of samples S_n (n = 1-7) formed by varying degrees of incomplete mixing of material from sources A and B, each with characteristics p (radioisotope parent) and d (daughter).

There is associated with the p and d values for S_1 a model age T_m (Equation 1) based on d_{om}, the value for d_o given by the ordinate intercept of the extended mixing line. If the p and d values for the source A were known, they would specify a model age T_c based on d_{oc}, the primordial daughter concentration conventionally assumed for model age calculations. T_m will be $<$, $=$, or $>$ T_c for source A, depending on whether d_{om} is $>$, $=$, or $<$ d_{oc}. The same comparisons apply to a T_m based on S_7 and a T_c for source B, but the difference between the two model ages will be less with respect to source B than with respect to source A; i.e., a mixing-line-based model age estimate derived from the upper terminus of a mixing line will be closer to the conventional model age for source B, than a similar estimate derived from the lower terminus will be to the conventional model age for source A.

For a horizontal mixing line $T_m = 0$, but the relationship between T_c and T_m is the same as for a line with positive slope.

For a negative-slope mixing line T_m is negative and has no significance with respect to real time, but the associated T_c values for the sources can be positive, zero, or negative. A model age interpretation of the data extremes represented in Figure 4 specifies for T_c a Rb-Sr age $\geq$ 3.10 Gy for source A, and $\leq$ 1.36 Gy for source B.

The two sources assumed in a simple mixing-line treatment of a radioisotope data set may have the same model age characteristic. Mixing of source materials that have differing concentrations of a specific daughter/parent ratio (a common radioisotope model age characteristic) can produce a range of incompletely mixed specimens which plot on a mixing line (pseudoisochron) that has no time significance as to when the mixing occurred. Such specimens have been described as samples from a heterogeneous source that has a characteristic inherited model age. The inherited age concept recognizes that a radioisotope age may be a characteristic of material, without providing an indication of the time at which that material was placed in its present association with a geological formation or a fossil.

The mixing-line considerations outlined above are illustrated by plutons in the central Idaho area of the Clearwater River South Fork [7]. Conventional geological considerations place the age of these formations in the vicinity of 80 million years. Since they are present-surface features of our planet, the record in Genesis places their origin during or following the late stages of the Flood, and restricts their real-time age to less than 6000 years (most probably less than 5500 years). The 1640 m.y. Rb-Sr isochron obtained from these formations is accounted for in [7] by proposed mixing of melted wall rocks with rising magma at the time of pluton formation. Exposed Precambrian wall rocks in the area have isochron and model ages in the range between 1500 m.y. and 1800 m.y. Various suggestions for the interpretation/explanation of these model ages, or any radioisotope model age in excess of 10,000 years, may be found in the creationist literature.

Most coordinated daughter-parent sample sets probably represent initial mixing followed by daughter buildup from radioactive decay of the parent. A major concern is the degree to which the slope of a linear-array plot represents radioactive decay rather than mixing. After the mixing that initially formed the sample suite, the daughter concentration in each unit will increase with time by the amount that the parent concentration is reduced. This change will rotate the plot counterclockwise about d_{om} as the center point, effectively adding an isochron to the initial mixing line. The resulting line interpreted as an isochron will indicate a greater time lapse than has occurred since the initial mixing. Interpreted as a mixing line it will not indicate either the time of initial formation or the additional time since formation. An illustration of such rotation is given in Figure 3a of [3].

It is important to emphasize that a mixing-line interpretation provides no direct indication of the length of time mineral specimens have been in existence, or in the association with which they are found (a geological formation or a fossil, e.g.). But a mixing-line interpretation does provide an indication of, and sets limits on, the radioisotope model age of the components that were partially mixed to form the suite of samples which define the mixing line. Thus the mixing-line interpretation gives freedom to fit fossils and geological features into a Biblical time frame, into what creationists often refer to as a young-earth short chronology; but it does not remove the challenge for an explanation of radioisotope model ages associated with primary inorganic material.

Within the constraints of a conservative grammatical-historical exegesis of the Bible there are two categories of approach for dealing with this challenge.

The first category is presumption that universally one or more of the three conditions necessary for the establishment of a radioisotope model age has/have not been met. One can assume that present-day observations of radioisotope decay provide no basis for estimating daughter-isotope accumulation in the past, i.e., that there have been multiple-order-of-magnitude changes in the factors which determine nuclear stability (half-life). And one can assume that the daughter/parent ratios indicated by mixing line termini are features of God's design, and have no more relationship to real time than does mixing line slope. According to this assumption isotope ratios essentially are features of initial creation, and may or may not have been modified by mixing and isotope separation processes since the creation of elementary matter.

In the second category the indications associated with mixing line termini are considered to be evidence outside the restrictions of chronological data in the Bible. For this approach to be effective, interpretation of Genesis 1:1 to 2;4a must be constrained within the definitions given in Genesis 1;8-10, and not based on modern designations of the terms *heaven* and *earth*. On this basis the model age implications associated with a mixing line can be related to time between a primordial creation of "the foundations of the earth" (Job 38:4; Psalm 102:25; Isaiah 48:13; 51:13,16; Zechariah 12:1), and the subsequent creation of "the earth" (Genesis 1:9,10).

Both of these categories are represented among "young earth" Biblical creationists, and there is no prospect for achievement of unanimity. Adherents to straightforward grammatical-historical exegesis of the Bible can have Christian unity in diversity of approach to radioisotope age challenges, each holding the approach which best secures his/her confidence in the historical witness of the Bible, and which is most effective in reaching those with whom he/she wishes to share that confidence.

CONCLUSIONS

A mixing-line interpretation of a related set of radioisotope daughter/parent ratios for a group of specimens removes any time significance of this data for the source of those specimens (associated fossil or geologic formation). But a mixing-line interpretation requires an explanation for the isotope ratios indicated by the mixing line terminii. An interpreter is free to hypothesize the time of mixture according to his viewpoint, but is constrained by the implications of the model ages indicated for the mixture components, whatever relationship there may be between those model ages and real time.

A Biblical creationist can propose that mixture was created at the beginning of Creation Week, occurred in the modification of the planet's surface on Day Three of Creation Week (Genesis 1:9), or occurred in connection with the crustal breakup and reformation associated with the Flood (Genesis 7,8) and its aftermath. If only one radioisotope age determination is available, or there is insufficient data for delineation of a mixing line, the model age established by one determination may be classified as a characteristic of emplacement material, rather than an indication of the time at which the material was placed in association with a geological formation or a fossil. [For example, 250 m.y. Rb-Sr age for fresh sediment on the floor of Ross Sea, Antarctica. (See Proceedings of the First International Conference on Creationism, Vol. II, p. 36.)]

Options for "young earth" explanations of radioisotope model ages, whether from single daughter/parent isotope ratio determinations, or indicated by termini of a mixing line, include: (1) consideration of model ages as having no time significance, on the basis of presumption that in no case has the requirements of the essential assumptions been met; (2) considering the isotope ratios on which model ages are based to be essentially design features exhibited at the time of creation, and mixtures of the initial ratios; but not determined in large measure by radioisotope decay; and (3) associating model ages exceeding the range of Biblical chronology with material derived from a primordial creation that preceeded the creation of *heaven*, *earth* and *sea* as defined in Genesis 1:8-10. The effectiveness of each of these options in the establishment and the retention of confidence in a grammatical-historical exegesis of the Bible is the paramount concern. There can be Christian unity in diversity, without controversy as to which option is "correct".

ACKNOWLEDGMENT

The author regrets that unnamed reviewers cannot be credited for their contributions to the development of this manuscript.

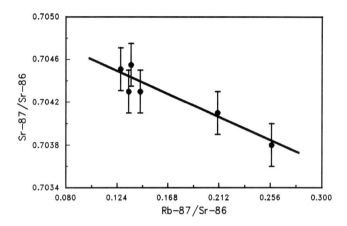

FIGURE 4. $^{87}Sr/^{86}Sr$ vs $^{87}Rb/^{86}Sr$ for Newer Volcanics in Victoria, Australia. Error bars designate the 95% confidence interval. Linear regression line is $0.7051 - 0.00490(^{87}Rb/^{86}Sr)$.

APPENDIX A

Excess, and presumably radiogenic, ^{26}Mg in certain mineral inclusions (Ca-Al-rich chondrules) of the carbonaceous chondrite classification of meteorites may be accounted for from either an isochron or a mixing-line viewpoint [11]. The excess ^{26}Mg over the concentration characteristic of minerals for which there is no indication of prior association with aluminum, plots on a straight line against the aluminum with which it is associated. The plot is against ^{27}Al, since aluminum from natural sources is monoisotopic. As would be expected on the basis of its 740,000 year half-life, ^{26}Al, the parent of ^{26}Mg, exists at present only in relatively insignificant quantities where it can be continually produced by nuclear reactions with cosmic ray particles. Accordingly the pseudoisochron of ^{26}Mg against ^{27}Al is actually a correlation line that indicates the initial $^{26}Al/^{27}Al$ ratio, rather than time since meteoroid formation or creation. The absence of ^{26}Al in these meteorites suggests that they, or the materials of which they are composed, have been in existence more than five million years ($10T_{1/2} = 7.3$ m.y.).

A two-component mixing-line interpretation places no restraint on the time the meteorite has been in existence, and allows the ^{26}Mg to either come from mature aluminum in a component of material from which the meteoroid was formed, or be a design feature expressed in a recent creation of meteoroids.

BIBLIOGRAPHY

[1] Bell, Keith, and J. L. Powell, **Strontium isotopic studies of alkalic rocks: The potassium-rich lavas of the Birunga and Toro-Ankola regions, East and Central Equatorial Africa,** Journal of Petrology **10:Part 3** (1969) 536-572.

[2] Cattell, A., T. E. Krogh, and N. T. Arndt, **Conflicting Sm-Nd whole rock and U-Pb zircon ages for Archean lavas from Newton Township, Abitibi Belt, Ontario,** Earth and Planetary Science Letters **70**(1984) 280-290.

[3] Christoph, G., **Isochron or mixing line?,** in Isotopes in Nature, Proceedings of the Fourth Working Meeting of the Academy of Sciences of the GDR, Wand, Ulrich, and Gerhard Strauch, editors, 1987, Central Institute of Isotope and Radiation Research, Leipzig.

[4] Dalrymple, G. Brent, The Age of the Earth, 1991, Stanford University Press, Stanford, California.

[5] Dasch, E. Julius, and David H. Green, **Strontium isotope geochemistry of lherzolite inclusions and host basaltic rocks, Victoria, Australia,** American Journal of Science **275**(1975) 461-469. [Figure 3 in this reference is incorrectly captioned.]

[6] Faure, Gunter, Principles of Isotope Geology, 2nd ed., 1986, John Wiley and Sons, New York.

[7] Fleck, R. J., and R. E. Criss, **Strontium and oxygen isotopic variations in Mesozoic and Tertiary plutons of Central Idaho,** Contributions to Mineralogy and Petrology, **90**(1985) 291-308.

[8] Gray, C. M., **An isotope mixing model for the origin of granitic rocks in southeastern Australia,** Earth and Planetary Science Letters, **70**(1984) 47-60.

[9] Overn, William M., **The truth about radiometric dating,** in Proceedings of the First International Conference on Creationism, Volume I 101-104, 1986, Creation Science Fellowship, 362 Ashland Ave., Pittsburgh, PA.

[10] Overn, William M., and Russell T. Arndts, **Radiometric dating - an unconvincing art,** in Proceedings of the First International Conference on Creationism, Volume II 167-171, Walsh, Robert E., et al., editors, 1986, Creation Science Fellowship, 362 Ashland Ave., Pittsburgh, PA.

[11] Nakamura, Noboru, **Is so-called Al-Mg isochron for a meteorite CAI a two component mixing line?,** Geochemical Journal, **19**(1985) 223-227.

[12] Zheng, Y.-F., **Influences of the nature of the initial Rb-Sr system on isochron validity,** Chemical Geology (Isotope Geoscience Section), **80**(1989) 1-16.

[13] Zhenwei, Qin, **Mix-isochron and its significance in isotopic chronology,** Scientia Sinica (Series B), **31:1**(1988) 96-108.

A BIBLICAL/CREATION MODEL AND RESPONSE
FOR ENVIRONMENTAL DIFFICULTIES

MARK W. CADWALLADER, M.S.
RT 13 BOX 1684F
CONROE, TEXAS 77303

KEYWORDS

environmental decay, entropy, ecosystem, curse of death, primitive cultures, ecopantheism, cleanliness laws, modern philosophy, stewardship

ABSTRACT

We seem unable to halt ecological deterioration. It's almost as if "a curse devours the earth", Isaiah 24:6. How extensive is this curse? What are its implications? Is there hope?

Environmental decay confirms the Biblical model of original creation followed by a fallen world under the curse of death. This model parallels the scientific law of entropy, of increasing disorder not increasing order as evolutionists would argue. This paper explains the Biblical confirmation of what we observe taking place in the environment today, considers historical microcosms as well, and sets forth the biblical response to environmental difficulties.

Much of the environmental movement has adopted "ecopantheism" as its conceptual model for environmental problems. This paper exposes the flaws of a pantheistic explanation and points out that the Biblical/Creation model is a better one for what we observe. Man's fundamental rebellion against God is brought to light, hidden as it may be behind a facade of science and sophistication.

INTRODUCTION

In the more than twenty years since the first Earth Day, environmental problems have become more widespread and complicated. In spite of voluminous anti-pollution laws, environmental troubles are extensive, complex, and urgent. Chemical waste, radioactive waste, deforestation, non-point source water pollution, ground water pollution, infectious waste, acid rain, and extinctions of many plants and animal species throughout the world, are some of the environmental problems corrupting the order and variety in the creation. In addition, the apparent destruction of earth's protective ozone layer and global warming due to increasing concentrations of pollutant gases, are frustrating concerns, barely anticipated twenty years ago.

We take metals, oil, and mineral salts from the ground, agricultural materials from the land, oxygen from the air, and water from rivers, and combine the various components to produce clothing, cars, antibiotics, fertilizers, pesticides, and vitamins. But in each process, waste by-products and energy are released. After the products themselves have been used or served their lifetime, they also become waste. We try to recover by-products and minimize waste, but the fact is that waste must ultimately be deposited in the environment. We have no magic box into which we can put the waste and make it disappear. This is a curse on our creative productivity.

It's easy to contaminate. It's difficult to clean up. It's easy to destroy complex order. It's very difficult to produce and restore complex order. And as we manipulate the environment, we destroy much more order and complexity than we are able to build.

Scientists understand a universal law of decay which they call the Second Law of Thermodynamics. This law is essentially a mathematical statement that all natural change proceeds toward increased disorder, randomness, and chaos. The scientific term for disorder and randomness is "entropy", usually assigned the variable "S" in engineering equations. Complex systems without outside input naturally become less complex. Ordered systems, without outside design and energy, spread or dissipate to increased disorder. The principle of the Second Law of Thermodynamics can be stated as "entropy always increases" for any closed system.

$$\Delta S > 0$$

It is the most experimentally verified fundamental principle in all of science.

The Bible in fact says that "a curse devours the earth", Isaiah 24:6, because its inhabitants have "broken the everlasting covenant", Isaiah 24:5. Holy Scripture tells us that the creation is enslaved to death because of sin. When man first sinned against God, God had to curse his creation. "Cursed is the ground because of you,...for you are dust and to dust you shall return," Gen 3:17, 19. This curse is the curse of death; which is fundamentally the curse of decay. Decay in living things is simply gradual death. People age as more body cells die than are replaced. And eventually people die when their organs are no longer able to sustain the body because they lack sufficient new cells. Our lives end when the original complexity of our interdependent body parts has been corrupted by illness or injury, or has decayed beyond repair. In like manner, decay in the environment is the disintegration of the original complexity of the earth's interdependent ecology. The curse of death is a curse of decay affecting all created things and the whole world in general.

ENVIRONMENTAL DECAY

The answer to air pollution was claimed to be catalytic converters on tailpipes and scrubbers on smokestacks. We have pursued this strategy at great cost for over 20 years. Yet cities plagued by smog have continued to suffer difficulties. And to make matters worse, air pollution problems are becoming more extensive, spreading out into traditionally smog-free rural areas in accordance with increasing entropy per the Second Law of Thermodynamics. For the first time since measurements began, for example, excessive ozone levels were recorded in 1988 in rural Maine and northern New York State [11].

Smog and haze now cloud many scenic vistas at national parks and other areas of natural beauty. The control of localized problems has seen a measure of success, but air pollution problems have actually spread, and have in fact become a more pervasive problem worldwide. Evidence is also growing that air pollution - primarily ozone and acid deposition - is causing extensive damage to vegetation, both crops and forests.

In the opinion of many scientists, air pollution now threatens the entire atmosphere of the earth with both global warming and stratospheric ozone destruction. By manufacturing millions of tons of certain very useful chlorinated compounds we have contributed to the erosion and destruction of ozone in the upper atmosphere where it is essential for shielding the earth from harmful radiation. It is widely estimated that two to five percent (overall) of the global stratospheric ozone shield has disappeared, with much higher rates of depletion near the earth's poles.

The frustrating thing is that we are polluting the lower atmosphere and damaging life on earth by creating excessive ozone (a key component of smog), while polluting the upper atmosphere and damaging life on earth by destroying stratospheric ozone. And we can't very easily collect and ship the ozone down here to the stratosphere (25 miles up) where it's needed. It is spread all over the place. The 2nd Law of Thermodynamics, the ubiquitous curse of the spread of disorder, thwarts the efforts of mankind.

If we solve one problem, it tends to generate a set of more complex problems. This is part of the curse. For instance, we have applied our talents to solving the problems of food shortages. But our present high agricultural productivity (much of it the result of the "Green Revolution") is dependent on the inherently unstable practice of continuously planting a single high yield crop, simplifying the local environment to one or two species. These genetically specialized plants are often more pest-susceptible. And reducing the numbers of species to a single crop eliminates natural checks on the pest population. Modern agriculture therefore depends heavily on chemical control of nutrients and pests. Yet the curse on man's efforts to improve his situation is revealed by this statistic from the American Chemical Society. Overall crop losses to pests have nearly doubled from the 1940's, in spite of a ten-fold increase in the application of insecticides [10, p.183]. Pesticides not only kill pests, but they kill other animals which in the "food web" (formerly the food chain) control the pests to some degree, making the genetically specialized crop even more dependent on pesticides.

When the automobile was first produced it was viewed as a solution to pollution. Millions of horses in towns and cities were more responsible for filth and stench in the streets. Yet today we know that the automobile has contributed heavily to more far reaching and troubling problems - smog, greenhouse gases, acid rain, noise, mounds of used car tires, abandoned cars, and huge oil spills all over the world. Yet for people at the beginning of the twentieth century the very form of such pollution, let alone its extensive spread and magnitude, were not even imagined. How ironic it is that what was once a solution to pollution has become one of the principle causes of pollution. Decay to increased disorder in ways we cannot even anticipate, also exemplifies a curse on our efforts.

Many plant and animal species are vanishing due to deforestation, desertification, habitat loss, pollution, intensive agriculture, poaching, encroachment of foreign species and other pressures. With fewer species, the complexity of ecosystems decays. Going from complex to less complex is another definition of entropy, the general decay from order to disorder.

Small components can be critically important to entire systems because each part, no matter how small, has some function. Indeed, as it turned out in 1986, "For want of an 'o-ring', the <u>Challenger</u> was lost." A space shuttle <u>Challenger</u> and crew were tragically lost during lift-off because a very small component of the complex system (a little gasket in the fuel system of the space shuttle was malfunctional).

The organisms and physical parts of an ecological system (ecosystem) are bound together by a maze of interactions. One simple example of these interactions is the classic food chain, in which living things depend on one another because of what they eat. Another is the very important nitrogen cycle, in which human protein ultimately depends on nitrogen's exchange with the atmosphere, through nitrogen-fixing bacteria and plant roots.

Biologists admit that there are certain species, called keystone species, on which it is quite clear the integrity of a whole ecosystem depends. If certain of these key species die, then whole environments are placed in jeopardy. In fact, every species depends on many others, often in such complex ways that it is impossible to foresee where any one extinction may ultimately lead.

For example, suppose we select three tree species which we will grow exclusively. For each of the three tree species, what are the bird species which eat most of its insect pests? What are the insect and bird species which pollinate most of its flowers? What are the animal species which spread most of its seeds? What are the insects and microorganisms which help decompose fallen leaves and needles and produce the soil enzymes to maintain soil fertility? On what other species do each of these birds, insects, animals, and microorganisms depend? They will depend in some way on the "unnecessary" tree species we decide to eliminate.

The interdependent natural ecosystems of the earth are similar to the interdependent parts of other created things such as the human body. If one body part is hurt, the whole body suffers. When a person's digestive system is upset, for example, his whole body functions less efficiently. Overall performance potential is reduced because of the suffering of one component of the body.

A similar situation occurs with the different interconnected parts of earth's ecosystems. Although redundant subsystems of design permit both ecosystems and the body to continue to function after absorbing a certain amount of abuse, the fact is that performance potential of the whole is degraded because of the hurt parts. The total system is not at its peak. The original order and complexity has decayed. In the words of Scripture, "The earth mourns and withers, the world fades and withers,..." (Isaiah 24:4).

Environmental literature makes much use of the analogy of the earth as a living system. Popular interpretations of a "living earth", which indicate "Mother Earth" as creator are totally unwarranted, however. Such interpretations are called "ecopantheism". In any case, the mutual dependence of the parts of earth's ecosystems no more proves that the earth is a goddess creator than does the fact that an insect spending its entire life in a single tree prove that the tree created it.

ENVIRONMENTAL DECAY IN PRIMITIVE CULTURES

The problem of environmental decay is a problem not just limited to modern mankind. Modern technology and increased populations may make the problems more complicated and more widespread. But contrary to popular opinion, pollution and destruction of the environment is not a new phenomenon in human history. The rate of environmental degradation has simply accelerated because of increased human activity, and increased production of goods and services. Yet many early civilizations have become victims of environmental decay which they helped to accelerate.

Early civilizations in the southwestern United States, Easter Island, Central America, southern Greece, the Indus River Valley, and the Tigris-Euphrates River Valley, among others, appear to have been aided in their collapse by environmental degradation. Climatic changes, both prior to and post environmental decay, also appear to have played a role in these civilization's demise.

Easter Island tells a sad story of environmental decay. Archaeological evidence shows that Polynesian settlement occurred on this remote island about 400 A.D. The settlers cut down trees to plant crops, build canoes for fishing, and provide logs for transporting and erecting the famous giant stone statues. The land was fertile, the sea teemed with fish, and their culture flourished. But looking at the record left by pollen deposits, scientists have constructed the following scenario. Deforestation set in by 800 A.D. and was essentially complete by 1200 A.D. There was no more forest to build canoes for fishing, and many birds no longer nested on the island. The abundant bird eggs had been a very important food source for the islanders. Deforestation caused soil erosion, reducing crop yields and silting the local waters. This led to fish declines in the surrounding estuaries. Fewer fish, eggs, and crops led to food shortages. Then hunger led to warfare and eventually caused the whole civilization to collapse. By the time European explorers arrived in the 18th century, the few people that remained had no consistent memory of the culture which produced the great stone statues. Today, Easter Island remains treeless and largely unsettled; much less life-supporting than it was formerly. Easter Island is a decayed remnant of what it once was [8, 19:4, p.38].

A tale of irreversible environmental decay is also told by the remains of pack rat nests in Chaco Canyon, New Mexico. Chaco Canyon was populated by the Anasazi Indians, builders of the famous cliff dwellings of the southwest. The numerous cliff dwellings of this bustling ancient civilization have been abandoned for hundreds of years. They are a mystery even to the neighboring modern Indian tribes of the southwestern United States. But by looking at old pack rat nests in the cliffs, and examining their hoarded remains, archaeologists have discovered considerable evidence of deforestation. The materials hoarded by the pack rats changed dramatically.

Prior to 1,000 years ago there was pinyon-juniper woodland in the Chaco Canyon, but for the past 1,000 years it has been gone. The evidence implies a civilization using up local woodlands for fuel and building projects, with subsequent erosion destroying the top soil and converting their irrigation channels into useless arroyos. The environment then could not sustain agriculture [8].

The ancient Sumerian, Babylonian, and Syrian civilizations once thrived in the area watered by the Tigris and Euphrates Rivers (Mesopotamia). Early records report that the area was once very fertile and teeming with game [6, p.59]. At one time the early civilizations harvested two crops of grain per year, grazing sheep between crops on the land [3, p.70f]. But after having been subjected to deforestation, hillside farming, and overgrazing (along with climate change), much of the area is now desert. In fact erosion problems are known to have been a headache for the Babylonians who kept whole armies of slaves busy removing the silt load from irrigation canals. Clearing the forests in the headwaters of the rivers gave rise to torrential flooding. Agriculture became much less productive with topsoil gone. Irrigation canals filled in as did the river mouth. Silt reaching the Persian Gulf has filled it in for miles so that cities which were once harbors are now many miles inland. Ur, for example, the original hometown of Abraham, was at one time a seaport. But today archaeology has shown it to be 150 miles from the sea with its buildings buried under 25 feet of silt [5, p.87].

THE EXPLANATION OF MODERN PHILOSOPHY

There is in fact a fundamental futility to life on earth because of the curse of entropy, the curse of decay. This fundamental futility has been recognized by philosophers as well as scientists. Reason, accurately applied, exposes the cruelty and futility of this present world. And reason alone is not able to give answers to ultimate questions. Reason apart from God leads to despair. Futility and despair are the consequences of living in a world relentlessly decaying, and thoroughly infected by sin and pain.

The Biblical book of Ecclesiastes is wise King Solomon's record of his experiment to test the full measure of what life "under the sun" has to offer, i.e., what life has to offer from the human perspective. Ecclesiastes reports the results of a diligent quest for purpose, meaning, and satisfaction in human life. The conclusion that he comes to is that life is futile and perplexing. "Vanity of vanities! All is vanity," Ecclesiastes 1:2. All is futile proud emptiness except to fear God, and keep His commandments", Ecclesiastes 12:13. All earthly goals and ambitions when pursued as ends in themselves lead to frustration.

Because of this observed futility, nihilist and existentialist philosophers say that truth is not objective. The logic is that since life is fundamentally futile, all is absurd. Rather than turn to God in the midst of futility, they use futility to define all reality and say simply that the most important thing is willful activity on the part of man. People under this philosophy should abandon the role of rational spectator and simply act. Why try to make sense of absurdity? Just have a plan and do it. Such philosophers are left arguing that it does not matter what the action is, the point is simply to act. Of course this justifies behavior of any kind; rational or irrational, kind or cruel, just or unjust. These are Godless philosophies which desire to escape accountability to our Creator. Much of popular philosophy and psychology have their roots in nihilism and existentialism. These modern philosophies have largely been responsible for the current substitution of politically correct amoral terms for behaviors which previously had a moral connotation [2, p.139]. (e.g., "sin" has become "dysfunction" and "adultery" has become an "affair".)

Nihilist/existentialist philosophers, like Solomon, have been realistic enough to grasp the futility of life in this world. But, unlike Solomon, they have not been wise enough and have been too proud to admit their responsibility to God in the face of death and a futile existence. Nihilism and existentialism go to great lengths to justify our natural inclination to sin. The philosophy becomes intellectual justification to vent natural self-centered behavior.

THE PANTHEISTIC EXPLANATION

Instead of turning to God in the face of environmental decay, mankind reveals his bias by making the interpretation of pantheism. Pantheism, according to C.S. Lewis, is the permanent natural bent of the human mind left to itself. A pantheistic view of a "living earth system" (Mother Earth), which is simultaneously creation and creator, has become commonplace among environmentalists. Environmental problems are often being interpreted in terms of "ecopantheism", being blended right in with the general pantheism of modern "New Age" thinking. The assumed creative powers of the earth, worked out presumably through evolution, are personified as a goddess, Gaia, the ancient Greek goddess of the earth.

British scientist, James Lovelock, chief proponent of the Gaia thesis, tries to explain the earth's unique properties among celestial bodies (e.g., why there is so much oxygen in the atmosphere) by invoking Gaia. He attaches a divine quality to the earth. Gaia, like the Hindu deity Brahman, is both creator and creation. If we don't see ourselves as one with nature, Gaia will destroy us. Lovelock writes in his recent book, "The Ages of Gaia", "if we see the world as a living organism of which we are a part - not the owner, nor the tenant, not even a passenger - we could have a long time ahead of us and our species might survive for its 'allotted span'" [9, p.236]. Notice, in this view, mankind is part of the living organism of the earth. He is not the steward, as the Bible tells us. Man is part of the goddess, Gaia. We just need to realize that. We just need to get in tune with what's natural; with what's really inside us. And then the hope is that our species will continue for a time. Under this view, the creation is divine, nature is the ultimate standard, and pantheism is the interpretation. This is no different from cultures which appeased volcano gods with human sacrifice to try to avoid destruction.

Such conclusions indicate an irrational bias against the truth of God. Like other religions and philosophies, ecopantheist environmentalists recognize a fundamental problem, but they fail to turn to God, even though the position is fundamentally hopeless. (At best the human species may continue if we don't upset Gaia, while individuals will of course die.) Mankind tries to dodge his accountability to God, makes Nature the standard, and justifies doing whatever is "natural". The predisposition toward pantheism in the environmental movement demonstrates, as C.S. Lewis said, that pantheism is indeed the natural bent of the rebellious human mind.

It is true that the complex natural ecosystems of the earth are linked together by many intricate interactions. However, popular interpretations of the linked ecosystems of earth as proof of "ecopantheism" are uncalled for. As with all machines, interdependency in the different parts of created things only reveals their complexity. It does not say that they made themselves.

In general rebellion against God's holy standard, pantheists say that moral principles are not absolute. They are simply lower level distinctions that work better in this world. But on the top level everything merges into one. Ultimately there is no difference between good and evil since good and evil, kindness and cruelty, pleasure and pain, are all found in Mother Nature. Pantheism absorbs good and bad into one cosmic being. Like nihilism and existentialism, pantheism must also come to the conclusion that truth is fundamentally absurd. There are no transcendent absolutes beyond the futility and meaninglessness of nature. Right and wrong, true and false disappear leaving a haze of nothing. Indeed, "nothingness" is the goal of eastern meditation. Hindu gurus (manifestations of Brahman) who really apply what they teach, walk around or sit in a trance of "nothingness".

No wonder eastern cultures did not come up with the scientific method and the scientific revolution. With nature as the ultimate reality, people are led to the final conclusion that absolute principles do not exist, whether they be principles of right and wrong or principles of the physical creation. Disorder coexists with order, and this is the ultimate standard. There is only confusion, chaos, and nothingness. The Biblical model, on the other hand, says that nature and the universe are not eternal. They are not a deity in themselves. God created nature, and He is the ultimate standard. "In the beginning God created the heavens and the earth", Gen 1:1. In the beginning an ordered intelligence established order in His creation. Having become enslaved to corruption, the creation has been subjected to futility through the curse of death; with, however, the promise that through God's plan of redemption in Jesus Christ the creation will be ultimately set free from its slavery into freedom and glory and life eternal.

THE BIBLICAL MODEL AND THE SCIENTIFIC OBSERVATIONS

The scientific facts reveal that disorder naturally increases. The amount of available or usable energy in the Universe is decreasing because the energy powering the Universe is being degraded, becoming less available. The Universe is running down under the law of entropy. P.W. Atkins, professor of physical chemistry at Oxford University, writes at the conclusion of his book, The Second Law,"...the deep structure of change is decay. At root, there is only corruption, and the unstemmable tide of chaos" [1, 200].

Consider an article of clothing. As it is used, it becomes threadbare and worn out. The garment loses its "newness" as it deteriorates in compliance with the Second Law. Though it is cleaned and restored it cannot maintain its original condition. Old clothes are easily distinguished from new ones. Colors fade. The fibers lose their strength and resiliency as the chemical bonds in the polymer chains of the fibers break apart. And the fabric structure (how those fibers are assembled together) unwinds and loses its organization [13]. These decay processes march on with relentless determination. Eventually the garment reaches a state of maximum disorder when it has degenerated into dust. Indeed, the fundamental principles of textile decay represent both the increasing micro and macro-molecular disorganization which governs all varieties of decay according to the Second Law of Thermodynamics. The Bible proves its grasp on truth because it has said long before thermodynamics was even a word, that the whole of creation is locked in the grip of decay:

Of old Thou didst found the earth; and the heavens are the work of Thy hands. Even they will perish, but Thou dost endure. And all of them will wear out like a garment; like clothing Thou wilt change them, and they will changed, Psalm 102:25-26.

...the earth will wear out like a garment, And its inhabitants will die in like manner, But My salvation shall be forever, And My righteousness shall not wane, Isaiah 51:6.

Fundamental decay and corruption are basic to Biblical doctrines. Traditional Christianity and Judaism have always taught that we live in a fallen world because of sin. The world is under a curse of death; separated from God's eternal life-sustaining support. Therefore, the whole of creation is headed toward a complete change. "Heaven and earth shall pass away," (Matt 24:35, Mark 13:31, Luke 21:33). Other scriptures mention the world withering and passing away (e.g., Isaiah 24:4, 1 John 2:17, 1 Cor 7:31). Romans 8:20 and 21 says:

For the creation was subjected to futility, not of its own will, but because of Him who subjected it, in hope that the creation itself also will be set free from its slavery to corruption into the freedom of the glory of the children of God, Rom 8.

Another translation of the original language puts verse 21 this way: "...in hope that the creation will be set free from its bondage to decay..." NIV.

Notice once again that the creation is "subjected to futility"; that it is "enslaved to corruption" or in "bondage to decay". What a parallel to Professor Atkins' statement of the Second Law of Thermodynamics ("...the deep structure of change is decay. At root there is only corruption..."). The fact that we live in a fallen world is a fundamental Biblical doctrine. Scientific understanding of the Second Law of Thermodynamics and its far reaching authority over even the very root structure of matter and energy did not come until the 19th and 20th centuries. Yet it's conclusions have been a basic Biblical doctrine for years.

Corruption of the environment is a symptom of the curse of death which is here because of sin. The Bible connects these three things (environmental decay, sin, curse on the world) quite specifically.

The earth is also polluted by its inhabitants, for they transgressed law, violated the statues, broke the everlasting covenant. Therefore, a curse devours the earth, and those who live in it are held guilty, Isaiah 24:5,6.

Sin and environmental decay are connected elsewhere in the Bible. For example: "There is swearing, deception, murder, stealing, and adultery. They employ violence so that bloodshed follows bloodshed. Therefore the land mourns, and everyone who lives in it languishes along with the beasts of the field and the birds of the sky; and also the fish of the sea disappear," Hosea 4:2,3.

The prophetic truth of Holy Scripture is uncanny. The Bible tells it like it is, cutting right to the heart of the matter. The environment is in decay (under the curse of death) because of sin, just as the whole world and the people in it are under the curse of death because of sin. Sin between two persons separates them. And since God is the Author and Sustainer of life, sin against God has separated us from life. The consequences of sin in society, of people living according to their own lusts, not according to what God wants, are broken relationships, people hurting and abusing others, strife, crime, war, etc. The potential order and beauty of human society becomes twisted and contaminated. Apart from the restraint of government and the grace and truth of God, society naturally degenerates toward disorder and chaos.

This is why a world fallen in sin must come under the "curse" manifested as the Second Law of Thermodynamics. Individual people doing what they want at the expense of others leads to cruelty, chaos, and disorder in society. Chaotic and disordered society cannot be maintained by an ordered creation. Corrupted mankind cannot be supported by an incorruptible creation. Justice cannot allow that.

Now this I say, brethren, that flesh and blood cannot inherit the kingdom of God; nor does corruption inherit incorruption, 1 Cor 15:50 NKJV.

The creation presses toward increasing disorder because human beings are fundamentally disordered in their motivations. God who has perfect integrity and therefore requires justice, has had to curse the physical creation, "subject it to futility" (Rom 8:20), as a result of man's sin. An incorruptible Creator of life cannot eternally give life-support to a corrupted creation. If He did, He would not be incorruptible.

In completion of our salvation, God will purify and transform this world in the same way that he will transform mortal bodies to imperishable resurrection bodies. There will be a change of scientific principle in the behavior of our physical bodies just as there was with Christ's resurrected body, yet there will be continuity with the mortal body just as there was with Christ's resurrected body. Similar change with continuity will take place in the creation as a whole [4].

> But according to His promise we are looking for a new heavens and a new earth, in which righteousness dwells, 2 Pet 3:13 (also Isaiah 65:17).

The creation will become a place "in which righteousness dwells"; or to use the terminology of 1 Cor 15:50 a place where "corruption" is replaced by "incorruption". This means that the current operation of the Second Law of Thermodynamics, the law of increasing entropy, decay, and "corruption" per Professor Atkins, will be at least modified if not radically changed. Until then, however, we must contend with the steady progress of entropy.

Increasing entropy means that the "public services" which the earth provides become less efficient. The ability of the earth to supply the oxygen we breathe, absorb the carbon dioxide we exhale, decompose our sewage, maintain the fertility of our soil, provide our food and medicines, and maintain a moderate climate wears down as the ability of the earth to support a vast array of species wears down. The species of plants and animals that we need in turn depend on other species.

Problems of ecosystem dependency are made more urgent because of the other issues of environmental decay taking place simultaneously. As climate patterns change and more harmful radiation penetrates the atmosphere because of a thinning ozone layer, environmental upsets will have greater impact. And the diminishing ability of earth to sustain life will accelerate.

The prophetic words of Isaiah sound the warning:

Lift up your eyes to the sky, then look to the earth beneath; for the sky will vanish like smoke, And the earth will wear out like a garment, And its inhabitants will die in like manner..., Isaiah 51:6.

The depth of truth in this scripture is particularly evident in the present day due to the global magnitude of the two most pressing environmental issues in the minds of environmental thinkers. In the booklet "The Crucial Decade: The 1990's and the Global Environmental Challenge", the observation is made that "the two principal threats to the global environment are large-scale atmospheric deterioration and biological impoverishment" [14]. How "coincidental" that the two threats Isaiah says to notice are that "the sky will vanish like smoke, and the earth will wear out like a garment". The sky is literally disappearing like smoke because the all-important protective ozone shield which caps the earth's atmosphere is growing thinner. In addition, the ability of the earth to sustain life is arguably wearing out ("like a garment"). Many different species inhabiting the earth are dying off, dissipating "in like manner" to smoke in their concentration on the earth.

Prophesying that "the sky will vanish like smoke" in a time when people didn't understand what the sky was composed of, would take an incredible imagination. What prophet would stick his neck out so far in prophesying something so incredible? The fact that the ozone shield is dissipating and allowing more harmful cosmic radiation to break through, and that the earth is "wearing out like a garment" in terms of integrity of the ecosystem "fabric", is one of many testimonies that the Bible is the revelation of God speaking through His committed servants as they were moved by the Holy Spirit. This is in fact what the Bible claims about Holy Scripture (1 Tim 3:16; 2 Pet 1:21).

Sin and the spread of decay are also related in many subtle and provocative ways throughout Scripture.

For example, the Second Law of Thermodynamics applied to the chemistry of solutions predicts the spread and dispersion of particles through fluids, and indeed, through everything. Sugar, salt, tea, and coffee spread in a cup of water to their greatest possible degree of disorder. So do pollution and infection. Pollution has spread to cover the entire globe. Traces of DDT for instance can be found in Antarctica and other places where it has never been used. Infection spreads through dispersion of microscopic pathogens, bacteria, and viruses. Pollution and infection both bring decay and death.

Likewise, sin is spread through the introduction of small amounts, to bring decay and death. The Bible says, "Do you not know that a little leaven leavens the whole lump of dough?," 1 Cor 5:6, Gal 5:9, Hos 7:4. (Leaven in Scripture is symbolic of sin.) And elsewhere, "Do not be deceived, bad company corrupts good morals," 1 Cor 15:33. Parents intuitively understand this as they encourage their children to associate with a good crowd of friends, not with the rebellious crowd. Parents intuitively know that sin spreads like disease, pollution, and decay in general.

Sin has brought forth death (e.g., Rom 5:12). And infection is a death process, while pollution promotes infection or itself causes death (cancer, etc.). Viruses and bacteria kill body cells. Death finally triumphs as deteriorated immune systems, and body cells are no longer able to cope with the virus, bacteria, cancer, etc.

The analogy extends further. The Bible says throughout that we are to avoid and resist sin or it will spread unchecked ("flee" temptation 1 Cor 6:18, 1 Tim 6:11, and "resist" the devil James 4:6). Similarly, pollution and disease must be contained and fought or they will spread unchecked. Our immune systems carry on some of this battle, protecting our bodies from disease. A large part of the battle against the spread of disease is also fought by, in effect, "fleeing filth", just as we are to fight sin by "fleeing temptation". Therefore, modern society places great emphasis on city sanitary systems, personal hygiene, and avoidance of infectious agents in combating the spread of disease.

The Bible has an incredible understanding of cleanliness as it relates to the spread of germs and the potential to accumulate bacteria, viruses, pathogens, etc. The Levitical Laws of the Jewish people specifically prohibit contact with body fluids and blood products, classifying them as "unclean" (Lev 15). The wisdom of these laws is especially relevant today in the face of horrible communicable diseases such as AIDS and hepatitis B - transmitted by body fluids. Fluids issuing from the body spread disease if the person is infected.

Scripture makes the analogy with sin, speaking of it as being "unclean". The Bible makes a powerful connection between washing away germs and pollution, and washing ourselves free of sin. It talks about sin as being "unclean". The analogy is so effective because the spread and effects of infection, pollution, and sin are so similar. The Jewish priests had to wash themselves and their clothes before they made atonement for sin (Lev 8:6, Num 8:6,7). They had to be clean. As the priests approached the altar in the Tabernacle of God, they had to wash their hands and feet in the special basin for washing (the laver) (Ex 40:30-32). When the High Priest made his annual entry into the holiest part of the Jewish Temple (the Holy of Holies) to atone for his and the people's sins committed in ignorance (Heb 9:7) he had to be completely clean.

The concept of "washing" to become spiritually clean is also carried over to the New Testament. For example, "Not by works of righteousness which we have done, but according to His mercy He saved us, through the washing of regeneration and renewing of the Holy Spirit," Titus 3:5.

The Bible is accurate both in dealing with 1) the physical relationship between cleanliness, body fluids, and the risk of infection, and 2) the ceremonial analogy between contamination and spread of sin, and contamination and spread of disease and pollution ("uncleanness"). To be holy is by definition to be free from sin, just as to be clean is by definition to be free from filth and germs.

Sin must be cleaned out in the same sense that pollution and infections are cleaned out. This is the whole purpose of disciplining children and administering justice to criminals. "Stripes that wound scour away evil", Prov 20:30. "Scouring", not only applies to cleaning out dirt and germs but also to cleaning out sin. The Bible tells us that sin in the heart of man (a fundamental rejection of the authority of and our responsibility to God) is the root, the cause of our present cursed existence.

Man is a rebel at heart, according to the Biblical Model. We do not reject our Designer and Creator out of any true rationality. We reject Him out of pure and simple rebellion. People are not rationally motivated to disbelieve in God. In fact all rational arguments when argued as far as they can be argued, point to God. The clearest and most straightforward reasoning points to God. People deny God out of pride and rebellion, and then try to develop rationale to justify their unbelief. The nihilist philosopher Friederich Nietzsche admitted this: "We deny God as God. And whenever you tell me I must obey God, pride comes over my soul. A little man stands up and says, 'Don't tell me I must believe in God'. If you could prove this God of the Christians to us, I would believe him all the less." [7, p.627] Indeed, as the prophet Hosea put it, "Their drink is rebellion...", Hosea 4:18. The Bible says that there is something at root wrong with the heart of man. This is why we observe entropy, futility, and evil in nature, the fallen creation.

The Biblical Model fits what science observes. Other religions may speak in terms of "cycles" of reincarnation, but they have not grasped the curse of decay, claiming that the creation itself is eternal. The fundamental tendency of events underlying cycles (a model based on the seasons) actually proceeds toward increasing randomness, chaos, and corruption. The underlying observed phenomenon is the 2nd Law of Thermodynamics; "...the deep structure of change is decay..." [1, p.200].

ENVIRONMENTAL DECAY AND CREATIONISM

The law of entropy and the observation of environmental decay as part of entropic change takes us back to a definite starting point, a definite beginning as the Bible teaches. The Universe cannot have always been winding down and be eternal. Modern cosmologies which hypothesize cycles of entropy and reverse-entropy in a creation which is eternal are pure conjecture, not science, and still leave unaccounted the need for intelligent design. This drive to eliminate the need for our creator and dispute the straightforward conclusion of Scripture exposes our rebellion and confirms again the Biblical Model and explanation of mankind as rebels at heart.

In the face of evolutionary theory, the short term nature of environmental collapses in early societies and the ascendance of environmental problems and environmental decay in modern society is quite significant. The earth wears out rather quickly, especially in the presence of human activity. Consider the experience in the "new world" of the Americas. Environmental decay has been our experience after just 200 years. The "new country" - clean, virgin, majestic - has, in many ways, become an "old country" of hazy skies, polluted waters, eroded soils, cut forests, etc.

If a "living earth" created itself through evolution, then it would indeed be both creation and creator. It would be the Goddess, Gaia. And we, as part of this living earth would be part of a cosmic "god". Even though we felt separate, we would really be connected in "Brahman" (using the terminology of Hinduism). We would need to "realize" it. Evolution believed provides intellectual justification for pantheism in general, and for ecopantheism in particular. Evolution is the foundation for resurgent pantheism in western culture. Creation believed, on the other hand, provides the basis for separating pantheistic mythology from true religion and true science.

Evolutionary science tries to make chaos itself the creator. To do so is to make the observed lack of purpose and order the driving force in life, rather than the consequence of man's sin estranging him from the Author of purpose and order. The overwhelming evidence of decay of the established order in the universe, together with environmental decay, points, in the most clear and straightforward reasoning, to two fundamental things: 1) some initial creation of complex order by a transcendent Creator, and 2) something having gone wrong with the initial created order. Rather than admit these quite logical and straightforward conclusions, "scientific" mankind concocts the fable that somehow decay and disorder itself produced incredible order and complexity - a conclusion for which no genuine evidence is available.

CONCLUSION: THE HOPE AND VIEW OF CHRISTIANITY

We are all captives of sin and decay (death) but the Bible says we can be set free unto eternal life, and we can expect a renovated creation free from the curse of decay (2 Pet 3:13) through the grace of God in Jesus Christ.

In love, God did for us, at great suffering and sacrifice to Himself, what we could not do. He paid the penalty of sin for us, in our place, the guiltless for the guilty. God has reached in to deliver us from our futile, painful existence, made ugly by sin, and given us real hope.

Some secular commentators have blamed ecological crises on the Judeo-Christian tradition [15, p.155]. Other secular thinkers realize that man's tendency to abuse earth's resources instead of exercising stewardship stems from non-Christian behavior and philosophy [12]. Greek philosophy declared man both the master and owner of nature. The influential philosopher Descartes also proclaimed the social value of striving to master and possess nature. The Biblical view, however, is that man is master of nature, but does not own or possess it. He must manage it with an accountability to God, the Owner. Atheist humanism, undergirded by the theory of evolution, declares that man, at the top of the evolutionary ladder, ought to subdue nature in an on-going survival of the fittest (the "might makes right" argument). Communist societies based on atheist principles, have left records of terrible environmental exploitation, unbalanced by conservation. Horrible pollution problems in Eastern Europe and the ex-Soviet Union were revealed through the late 1980's and early 1990's as these countries came out of communist rule. Societies based on Biblical traditions have struck a better balance between exploiting and conserving nature, between manipulating and protecting it. The National Park System of the United States, for example, has been a model for other countries seeking to conserve natural resources and natural beauty.

Justification for abusing and overexploiting the earth because God gave man "dominion" over nature is a misapplication of the Scriptures. "Thou madest him to have dominion over the works of Thy hands; Thou hast put all things under his feet: All sheep and oxen, yea, and the beasts of the field; ..."(Psalm 8:6,7 KJV). The meaning of the Hebrew word "mashal", translated "dominion" in Psalm 8:6 of the King James Version of the Bible, means to have responsible rule over the creation. The term does not justify irresponsible abuse because it means to "reign with authority as a governor" (a delegated authority with responsibility to higher authority) [16, p.132].

God is the Owner of His creation. "The earth is the Lord's, and all it contains, the world and those who dwell in it" (Psalm 24:1). We use God's creation, and then we pass on, unable to take anything with us. While we are on the earth, we are managing the Lord's property as tenant farmers. We have been entrusted with it. As King David said at the end of his career, "Thine, O Lord, is the greatness and the power and the glory and the victory and the majesty, indeed everything that is in the heavens and the earth; Thine is the dominion, O Lord, ...For we are sojourners before Thee, and tenants, as all our fathers were; our days on earth are like a shadow..." (1 Chronicles 29:11,15). The creation was entrusted to man to take care of. We are temporary stewards of it. The owner is God. Indeed, mankind's initial duty was to take care of the Lord's garden (Genesis 2:15). We are the tenant farmers, and our responsibility is to take care of the farm.

The concept of being restored to Adam's original responsibility as caretaker of the Lord's garden takes on greater force when we realize that through Christ we have been reconciled to God and led to a restored sonship much like Adam's status before his fall into sin. Romans 5:12-21 presents Christ as the second Adam who reversed the fall of man and justified us before God, restoring our relationship to Him. Christians, more than others, as restored children of God, should all the more consider themselves as tenants and stewards of God's property just as Adam was caretaker of the Lord's garden. It should be considered part of the Christian ethic, therefore, to wisely manage and conserve natural resources, to enhance the beauty and order of God's creation, to be a good steward of God's created order.

Yet the Christian should realize that Salvation is past, present, and future. The root structure of the creation is yet to be transformed, even as Christ's resurrected body was transformed (a change with continuity) and as our bodies will be similarly transformed (2 Pet 3:13, Phil 3:20,21). Romans 8:20-23 says it this way,

For the creation was subjected to futility, not of its own will, but because of Him who subjected it, in hope that the creation itself also will be set free from its bondage to decay into the freedom of the glory of the children of God. For we know that the whole creation groans and suffers the pains of childbirth together until now. And not only this, but also we ourselves, having the first fruits of the Spirit, even we ourselves groan within ourselves, waiting eagerly our adoption as sons, the redemption of our body."

At some future time, God will set the creation free from its "bondage to decay" which includes bondage to our present mortal bodies. Until then, the creation is hobbled by increasing entropy.

Due to the curse of decay, environmental problems cannot be stopped completely; therefore, they should be dealt with realistically. Legislation requiring the impossible (absolutely zero environmental degradation) is misguided. And well intentioned local citizen groups, have tied up the courts trying to block viable waste containment projects because they do not understand the futility of implementing perfect solutions in an imperfect world.

The irreversibility of entropy is a point missed by many modern environmentalists. We cannot avoid some environmental decay. Yet many environmentalists adopt the thinking that by becoming "one with Mother Nature" we can stop the problems. The truth is that the creation is distinct from God. God owns it and can do what He wants with it. Man is simply God's steward, God's tenant farmer, responsible to take care, as best he can, of all of God's resources. This understanding leads to a proper analysis of the situation.

REFERENCES

[1]   P.W. Atkins, **The Second Law**, Scientific Books, Inc., New York, 1984.

[2]   A. Bloom, **The Closing of the American Mind: How Higher Education has Failed Democracy and Impoverished the Souls of Today's Students**, Simon & Schuster, New York, NY, 1987.

[3]   R.F. Dasman, **Environmental Conservation**, Wiley and Company, New York, 1968.

[4]   C.B. DeWitt, **The Environment and the Christian**, Chpt 3, R.C. Van Leeuwen, Baker Book House, Grand Rapids, MI, 1991.

[5]   H. Halley, **Halley's Bible Handbook**, Zondervan Publishing House, Grand Rapids, MI, 1965.

[6]   E. Hyams, **Soil and Civilization**, Thames and Hudson, London, 1952.

[7]   W. Kaufman, **The Portable Nietzsche**, Viking Press, New York, NY, 1968.

[8]   Kiefer, M., **Fall of the Garden of Eden**, International Wildlife, Vol 19, No 4, National Wildlife Federation, July-August 1989.

[9]   J.E. Lovelock, **The Ages of Gaia - A Biography of our Living Earth**, W.W. Norton, New York, NY, 1988, p.236.

[10]   Marco, G.J., et al, **Silent Spring Revisited**, American Chemical Society, Washington D.C., 1987, p.183.

[11]   **Environmental Quality Index**, National Wildlife, National Wildlife Federation, Feb-March 1989.

[12]   J. Passmore, **Man's Responsibility for Nature**, London, 1974.

[13]   L. Rebenfeld, **Chemical and Physical Structure of Fibers in Relation to the Durability of Geotextiles**, Durability and Aging of Geosynthetics Conference Proceedings, Geosynthetics Research Institute, Philadelphia, PA, 1988.

[14]   J.G. Speth, **The Crucial Decade: The 1990's and the Global Environmental Challenge**, World Resources Institute, 1989, Forward.

[15]   L. White, **The Historic Roots of Our Ecologic Crisis**, Science, March 1969, p.155.

[16]   W. Wilson, **Wilson's Old Testament Word Studies**, MacDonald Publishing Co., McLean, VA, p.132.

ARE THE FUNDAMENTAL "CONSTANTS" OF PHYSICS REALLY VARIABLES?

EUGENE F. CHAFFIN, PH.D.
BLUEFIELD COLLEGE
BLUEFIELD, VA 24605

KEYWORDS

Constants, Aberration, Light, Halos, Nuclear

ABSTRACT

The equations of physics contain "constants" such as the speed of light, the value of the charge of the electron or proton, the gravitational coupling constant, the weak coupling constant, the strong coupling constant, Planck's constant, and elementary particle masses. Non-trivial variations in these quantities would not just involve a change of scale caused by a redefinition of units, but would involve the variation with time of certain dimensionless ratios of these so-called "constants." I will examine the theoretical basis for possible variations in these dimensionless ratios and relate experimental and observational results to place limits on these variations. In particular, I will examine the tunnelling theory of alpha decay and relate it to the possible variation of weak and strong interaction strengths, showing that decay rates may vary without significantly changing the radii of radiohalos. Also, I will examine the data of James Bradley taken in 1727-1747 on the aberration of light from the star gamma Draconis and show that there are extra solar and lunar influences on the nutation of the earth's axis which Bradley unfortunately left out. This suggests that the speed of light in 1727 was the same as it is today. The results will also be related to the author's study of the Roemer method for determining the speed of light [7].

INTRODUCTION

The equations of physics contain fundamental "constants." Present day physics cannot derive the values of these quantities starting from first principles, but must rely on experimental measurements. Due to the inductive nature of the reasoning which must be used in science, it is difficult to reach firm conclusions about which "constants" are truly constant. They may be constant in present day experiments but may undergo episodic variations due to the passage of a "wormhole" near to the solar system as described by Hawking [14], a phase transition of the universe as described by Crone and Sher [8], Sher [20], or Suzuki [22], or other catastrophic events which could be described as a direct intervention of God.

In general, it is necessary to formulate theories in order to have a consistent framework in which to interpret the results of experiments. For example, Canuto, Adams, Hsieh, and Tsiang [6] showed that variation of Newton's gravitational constant, G, could lead to the radius of the earth's orbit either increasing, decreasing, or remaining the same, depending on which theory was operative. This is due to the possibility of extra terms contributing to the relevant equations of motion which would be absent if G were a constant. The reasons for including these extra terms can often be quite compelling.

Bekenstein [1,2] has pointed out, on the basis of some comments of R.H. Dicke [9,10], that only the variation of dimensionless combinations of "constants" is physically meaningful. The form of physical laws should not change just because we change unit systems. It is possible to propose definitions of our units which cause some constants to vary with time. For instance, if the meter were defined in terms of the distance of the earth to the sun, then it would change with time due to the elliptical nature of the earth's orbit. But that would be a trivial variation which we do not want to be concerned with here. Hence, one should always check to see that the time variation that is examined may be reduced to a variation of a dimensionless ratio such as the fine structure constant, e^2/hc, the ratio of the mass of the electron to the mass of the proton, etc. As Bekenstein pointed out, modern scientific journals are full of errors in interpretation of the data which could have been avoided if these dimensionless ratios were used.

In the first part of this work, I will examine the effects of a possible variation of the nuclear force on the rates of radioactive decay. I will allow variation of the ratio of the depth of the nuclear potential felt by an alpha particle to the energy that the alpha particle has at infinity. As relevant experimental data we have the radii of the radioactive halos produced by minute inclusions in precambrian rocks [4,13]. I will show that standard nuclear theory allows the radii of the halos to remain the same while the radius of the nucleus and the decay constant change. Since the size of the nucleus, compared to that of the atom, is like a baseball at the center of a major league ball park, then for most practical purposes it could change size without significantly affecting atomic structure. This is because the nuclear force is short ranged and the Coulomb force is not changed by this hypothesized variation. I then also present results of a computer program showing how much the decay "constant" changes for a given change in nuclear potential. The program also shows that the expectation value of the square of the radius of the alpha particle decreases as the depth of the nuclear potential increases, in the same way that the nuclear size decreases. This makes this whole scenario plausible, but it does not prove that any changes ever occurred.

Secondly, I present some calculations to examine Bradley's data taken in the 1700's on the aberration of starlight. Bradley [3] was a pioneer in that he had to analyze his data in the era before anyone else. He showed that the stars such as gamma Draconis varied in position as the direction of the Earth's velocity changed through the year. The amount depended on the ratio of the earth's velocity to the speed of light. The value of the speed of light he obtained compared favorably with that inferred from Roemer's measurements of some forty years earlier [7]. But Bradley left out some terms for the nutation of the earth's axis. He included the largest terms due to the Moon, but left out the second order terms due to the Moon and also the terms due to the Sun [18]. Hence, the value of the speed of light inferred from his data needs to be freshly analyzed. I have written some computer programs to do that, and will present the preliminary results.

ALPHA DECAY AND THE STRENGTH OF THE NUCLEAR FORCE

One of the best treatments of the tunnelling theory of alpha decay is by Preston [19]. In fact, his theory has become the only accurate method for treating the emission of the alpha particle with non-zero angular momentum. Experimental nuclear physics uses his approach for the calculation of "hindrance factors," which measure the probability of alpha decay to an excited state rather than the ground state of the daughter nucleus. Preston's approach starts by treating the energy of the alpha particle as a complex number. The imaginary part of the energy allows the wavefunction to represent the decay of the nucleus by emission of the alpha particle. Otherwise, a real value for the energy represents a stationary state which does not decay by alpha emission. Preston derived two simultaneous equations relating four variables. The four variables are the alpha particle energy at infinite distance from the nucleus, the radius of the nucleus, the depth of the potential well for the alpha particle, and the decay constant. Thus, on the basis of the theory, knowledge of any two of the four variables is enough to algebraically determine the other two. The equations are intractable (the solutions cannot be written out explicitly), and require iteration using a method such as Newton-Raphson iteration to solve them. But a BASIC program on a microcomputer can easily perform this task; the program requires less than forty lines of code.

Unfortunately, Preston's model is not realistic since acceptable answers are obtained only by assuming that the depth parameter, V_o, of the nuclear potential well is a positive number. This is physically unrealistic since the nuclear potential is not repulsive. A remedy for this situation was proposed by Pierronne and Marquez [17]. In this approach the potential is divided into an interior and an exterior region, with the interior being a square well of constant depth V_o and the external region being a Coulomb potential (See Figures 1,2). The parameter V_o represents the strength of the nuclear force felt by the alpha particle. The solutions for the radial wavefunctions are standard Coulomb wavefunctions on the exterior and spherical Bessel functions in the interior. Matching the real and imaginary parts of the logarithmic derivatives at the boundary gives the equations which we need for a more realistic version of Preston's method. If we also adopt the Taylor series approximations that Pierronne and Marquez made, we then obtain an algorithmic procedure which is almost as simple as Preston's approach. The main difference is that we need to be able to calculate the Coulomb wavefunctions. Fortunately, Froberg [12] did most of the work for us, publishing the expansions of the Coulomb wave functions and their derivatives. The method which he called the Riccati method converges for the region of parameter space with which we are concerned here. Hence, I wrote a Fortran program incorporating subroutines to calculate the Coulomb wavefunctions and the spherical Bessel functions needed. The algorithm accepts as input from the keyboard the depth, V_o, of the alpha particle potential well, the decay energy, E_a, of the nucleus (which is the combined kinetic energies of the alpha particle and the recoil nucleus), the atomic mass number, A, of the daughter nucleus, and the proton number, Z, of the daughter nucleus. Thus, Preston would have input the values of about -50 MeV, 4.31 MeV, 234, and 90 for the decay of Uranium-238 by emission of an alpha particle (Z = 2, A = 4). Using an initial guess for the radius of the nucleus, taken as the radius for which the square well stops and the Coulomb potential begins, the algorithm iterates until the real part of the logarithmic derivative, which is Pierronne and Marquez's X function, matches for the interior and exterior solutions. It then uses the Pierronne and Marquez equations to calculate the "width," which is the decay constant times Planck's constant over two pi. Output includes the decay constant and the radius of the nucleus. If we set the imaginary part of the energy equal to zero, the wavefunction of the alpha particle can be used to calculate the expectation value of the radial coordinate of the alpha particle. The program also reports this value.

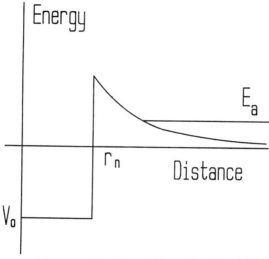

Figure 1. *A graph of the potential energy of the alpha particle as a function of distance. For radial distance less than r_n, the alpha particle is inside the nucleus and the potential energy is represetned by a constant negative value V_0. Since the nuclear force is short ranged, the potential energy may be represented by the Coulomb repulsion outside the nucleus. This is the curve starting at r_n and dropping off to zero for larger radii. The peak at r_n is called the Coulomb barrier. Since the alpha particle reaches infinity with a kinetic energy, E_a, less than the height of the Coulomb barrier, the tunneling theory of quantum mechanics is applied.*

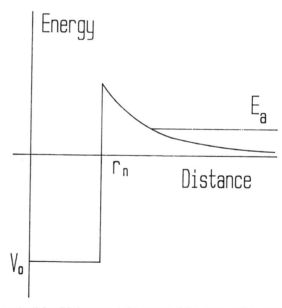

Figure 2. *If the depth of the potential well is increased, the energy of the alpha particle may be held the same with only a slight change in nuclear radius.*

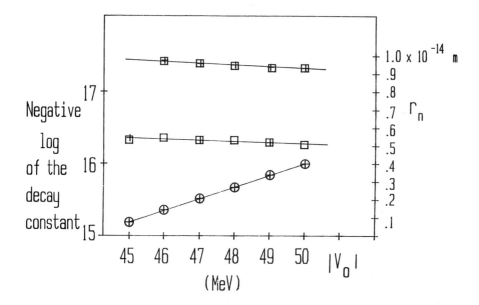

Figure 3. *The results of the computer calculations as a function of the depth, V_0, of the potential well. The lines represent lines of constant decay energy. The line drawn with circles for points is the negative of the logarithm of the decay constant versus V_0. It thus shows that a change of V_0 from 45 to 50 MeV changes the decay constant, and hence also the half life, by about one power decay constant. The lines drawn with squares for points represent the radius of the nucleus. The other line is the square root of the expectation value of the square of the radius, obtained by putting the imaginary part of the energy equal to zero. Roughly speaking, it is the most probable radius of the alpha particle before emission. Both radius estimates decrease slowly as the potential well gets deeper.*

The results are presented graphically in Figure 3. The decay energy is held constant and various values of the depth, V_0, of the nuclear potential well are used to find the radius and decay constant. The graphs show how much the radius of the nucleus must decrease in order to keep the decay energy, and hence the radius of experimentally measured radioactive halos, constant.

For a given change in depth of the potential well, there is also a corresponding change in the decay constant. One should keep in mind that only a small change in decay constant may lead to a vast change in branching ratios between alpha decay, beta-minus decay, beta-plus decay, and/or electron capture decay of some nuclei. Also shown in Figure 2 is the square root of the expectation value of the square of the alpha particle radius. As expected, this also decreases as the potential well gets deeper.

This exercise shows that the radii of the radioactive halos studied by Gentry can be held constant while still changing the decay constant. But other nuclear properties would also change. This work provides a quantitative basis, a first step, for investigating what limits these other nuclear properties may place on the variation of the nuclear force strength.

USING BRADLEY'S DATA TO FIND THE SPEED OF LIGHT IN 1727

In the early 1700's the distances to the stars were not known accurately; the only reasonable estimates were based on the assumption of equal brightnesses. One way to find the distance to a star was to measure the parallax, which is the difference in position which it appears to have due to the finite size of the earth's orbit. Unsuccessful attempts had been made to measure the parallaxes of stars; the parallax angle is much smaller (less than one tenth of one second of arc) than the aberration of light, nutation, and precession angles. These effects had to be analyzed first and separated out before Bessel finally succeeded in measuring the parallax of 61 Cygni in 1837 to 1838. The aberration of light refers to the change in angle at which a telescope must be pointed in order to see a star at different times of the year, due to the relative magnitudes of the speed of light and the speed of the earth in its orbit (Figure 4). Stewart [21] has given a good introductory review of this subject.

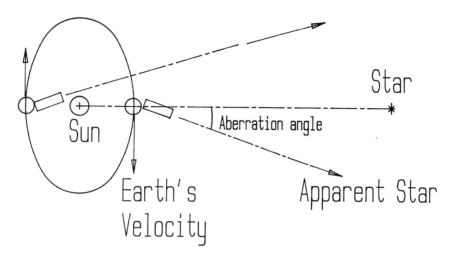

Figure 4. *Since the Earth has a non-zero velocity in its orbit, seen here obliquely, a telescope on earth must be tilted at an angle in order to see the light from a star. Six months later the telescope must be tilted in the opposite direction. The angle of tilt is the aberration angle.*

As reported in reference [3], Bradley found a useful analogy while taking a sailboat ride on the Thames river. He noticed that the direction of a pennant flying from the mast of the ship depended on both the velocity of the boat and the momentary wind velocity. In the same way, the direction in which the telescope must be pointed in order to see a star depended on both the direction of motion of the earth as well as the direction of motion of the light from the star. Bradley and Samuel Molyneux were able to make accurate observations with two telescopes, one mounted to a chimney in Wanstead, England and the other in Kew.

In reference [3] Bradley's data for gamma Draconis and other stars are given as well as his writings on how the data are to be analyzed and interpreted. We shall see that Bradley correctly interpreted the results, but that higher order terms in the nutation were left out. This means that the last two decimal places of his results for the declination correction in seconds of arc cannot be trusted unless a more detailed analysis is made. The term "nutation" refers to a fluctuating motion of the Earth's axis of spin about the smooth precessional path. Bradley's observations of 1727-1747 were sufficient to show that the main component of nutation has a period of just over 18.6 years, and were due to the changes in the Moon's orbit which occur with the same period.

I have written a computer program to analyze Bradley's data more exactly. The reason was to see if the speed of light inferred from his data for the 1700s was different from the modern value [7]. The program incorporates orbital elements and other orientation parameters computed for the Earth for the year 1727 using the programs BRETAG.BAS and ORB.BAS described in reference [7]. The Julian dates for the first 70 of Bradley's observations of gamma Draconis were computed and inserted as data into the program. It is important to note that, in Britain, the day after September 2, 1752 was September 14, 1752 due to the decision to conform to the Gregorian calendar which had already been adopted in most European nations over 150 years earlier. Except for the first observation, Bradley did not record the exact hour and minute of observation. But the technique was to observe when the star was at the zenith, so that these times can be computed in retrospect. The Julian date of the first observation was JD2352075.3 and the 70th was JD2352432.3.

The program incorporates the right ascension and declination of gamma Draconis for the ecliptic and equinox of 1950.0, and uses that data to calculate the position for 1727. Following the same approach as in references [7] and [23], the program calculates the heliocentric equatorial coordinates and velocity components of the Earth for each date in the data set. Using the trigonometric equations given in the Explanatory Supplement [11, p. 47], the corrections due to aberration for right ascension and declination are calculated and added to the 1950.0 values. But Bradley's data are recorded with respect to the equinox and ecliptic of 1727, so that a further transformation is needed. A subroutine was written to perform this transformation using the procedure outlined by Cambell [5, pp. 47-53] but with the values of the numerical data updated using Lieske, Lederle, Fricke, and Morando [15].

Next, the correction for nutation must be computed. As noted in [3, pp. lxvii, 28], Bradley took the distance of a star's right ascension from the place of the Moon's ascending node, which he entered in a column called "argument of nutation." Then he multiplied 9 seconds of arc times the sine of this quantity to get the number which he entered in the column labelled "nutation." Plummer [18, p. 305] derived a more exact equation, including the nutation caused by the Sun and additional Lunar contributions. Using revised data provided by Mathews and Shapiro [16],

I incorporated Plummer's procedure into my computer program. This gives the correction to the declination due to nutation.

The program next reads in as data Bradley's values for the position of gamma Draconis on each of the 70 dates. These were recorded in [3] in terms of the number of seconds of arc south of 38° 25' declination (which should be 51° 35' since Bradley used a reverse coordinate system from modern conventions). To these values the program then adds the corrections for aberration, nutation, and precession. Plummer [18, p.307] derived a correction for precession. This correction changes slowly with time and is small enough that it does not play a major role in these calculations. In any case, Bradley had included his estimates of this quantity. It is not necessary to include a correction for diurnal aberration [11, p. 49], since the stars were on the zenith when Bradley observed them. We have already noted that parallax corrections are too small compared to the accuracy of Bradley's data.

The program produces a number which should, theoretically be the same for each of the 70 dates. In practice the standard deviation was found to be 0.863 with a mean of 79.736 seconds of arc (south of 51°35' declination). As we have noted, Bradley ignored certain terms in the nutation correction. So to match the data, he had to assume a larger value for the speed of light. In this way, he obtained a mean of 79.826 and a standard deviation of 0.851. Since my program successfully calculates the mean position of gamma Draconis without assuming a different speed of light, and does so with about the same standard deviation as Bradley's calculations, this seems to show that the speed of light in 1727 was not significantly larger than today's value. However, one can run my program for other values of the speed of light to try to find the minimum standard deviation. It is found that the minimum standard deviation is 0.801 with a mean of 79.603. Figure 5 shows the results graphically. The "aberration amplitude" plotted on the x-axis is the angle of aberration which a star in the pole of the ecliptic would have if the eccentricity of the earth's orbit were zero and the earth had a mean daily motion of one degree per day. It is inversely proportional to the speed of light. The minumum on Figure 5 would correspond to a speed of light 2.4% larger than the modern value. But the difference in the standard deviations, 0.863 minus 0.801 is 0.062, is not large enough to draw firm conclusions (See Figure 5). Bradley's data are not accurate enough and there are higher order terms in the nutation that would have to be included in order to attach significance to this difference. I conclude that Bradley's data are consistent with the modern value for the speed of light.

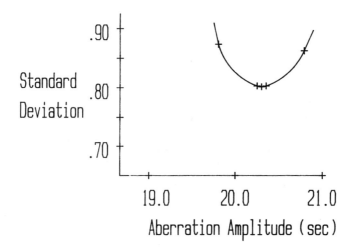

Figure 5. *When all the necessary factors are included in the computer calculations, the seventy points have deviations from the mean value. The standard deviation is plotted here as a function of the assumed amplitude for the aberration of light. The minimum occurs for a value of 20.3 seconds of arc, only 2.4% different from the value of the speed of light. But the curve is shallow enough compared to the accuracy of Bradley's data that the data consistent with the modern value of the speed of light.*

CONCLUSION

This study shows that radioactive halo radii can remain the same even if the strength of the nuclear force were to change, but the half life for alpha decay would change. Further study is needed to try to find nuclear data, preserved in nature, which would contradict this hypothesis. We are concerned here with episodic changes, changes beginning at a certain point in time and ending after a short interval, not with changes in nuclear strength which are extrapolated indefinitely into the past. Hence, excess decay heat inside the Earth is not a concern of this hypothesis since nuclear decay rates would have been the same order of magnitude before this episode of change.

The study also shows that, according to data collected by Bradley in 1727-1728, the speed of light was not significantly different from the modern value. This does not contradict the alpha decay results, since theories are possible in which dimensionless ratios containing the strength of the nuclear force are not dependent on other dimensionless ratios involving the speed of light, such as the fine structure constant, e^2/hc.

BIBLIOGRAPHY

[1]   J.D. Bekenstein, **Astronomical consequences and tests of relativistic theories of variable rest masses**, Comments on Astrophysics **8**:4(1979) 89-96.

[2]   J.D. Bekenstein, **Fine-structure constant: is it really a constant?** Physical Review **D25**(1982) 1527-1539.

[3]   J. Bradley, Miscellaneous works and correspondence of James Bradley, Stephen Peter Rigaud, editor, Johnson Reprint, New York.

[4]   R.H. Brown, **Radiohalo evidence regarding change in natural process rates**, Creation Research Society Quarterly **27**(1990) 100-102.

[5]   W.W. Cambell, The elements of practical astronomy, 2nd ed., 1926, The MacMillan Company, New York.

[6]   V. Canuto, P.J. Adams, S.-H. Hsieh, and E. Tsiang, **Scale-covariant theory of gravitation and astrophysical applications**, Physical Review **D16**(1977) 1643-1663.

[7]   E.F. Chaffin, **A determination of the speed of light in the seventeenth century**, Creation Research Society Quarterly **29**(1992) 115-120.

[8]   M.M. Crone and M. Sher, **The environmental impact of vacuum decay**, American Journal of Physics **59**(1991) 27-32.

[9]   R.H. Dicke, The theoretical significance of experimental relativity, 1965, Gordon and Breach, New York.

[10]   R.H. Dicke, **Mach's principle and invariance under transformation of units**, Physical Review **125**(1962) 2163-2167.

[11]   Explanatory Supplement to the Astronomical Ephemeris and Nautical Almanac, 1961, Her Majesty's Stationery Office, London.

[12]   Carl-Erik Froberg, Numerical treatment of Coulomb wave functions, Reviews of Modern Physics **27**(1955) 399-411.

[13]   R.V. Gentry, **Critique of "radiohalo evidence regarding change in natural process rates**, Creation Research Society Quarterly **27**(1990) 103-105.

[14]   S.W. Hawking, **Baby Universes II**, Modern Physics Letters **A5**(1990) 453-466.

[15]   J.H. Lieske, T. Lederle, W. Fricke and B. Morando, **Expressions for the precession quantities based upon the IAU(1976) system of astronomical constants**, Astronomy and Astrophysics **58**(1977) 1-16.

[16]   P.M. Mathews and I.I. Shapiro, **Nutations of the earth**, Annual Reviews of Earth and Planetary Science 20(1992) 469-500.

[17]   M. Pierronne and L. Marquez, **On the complex energy eigenvalue theory of alpha decay**, Zeitschrift fuer Physik **A286**(1978) 19-25.

[18]   H.C. Plummer, An introductory treatise on dynamical astronomy, 1960, Dover, New York.

[19]   M.A. Preston, **The theory of alpha-radioactivity**, Physical Review **71**(1947) 865-877.

[20]   M. Sher, **Comment on "Slightly massive photon,"** Physical Review **D39**(1989) 3513-3514.

[21]   A.B. Stewart, **The discovery of stellar aberration**, Scientific American, 210:3(1964) 100-108.

[22]   M. Suzuki, **Slightly massive photon**, Physical Review **D38**(1988) 1534-1550.

[23]   D. Tattersfield, Orbits for amateurs with a microcomputer, 1981, John Wiley and Sons, New York.

TOWARD AN UNDERSTANDING OF THE TIDAL FLUID MECHANICS ASSOCIATED WITH THE GENESIS FLOOD

M.E.CLARK and H.D.VOSS

GENESIS RESEARCH LABORATORY, 2020 ZUPPKE DRIVE, URBANA, IL 61801

KEYWORDS

Tidal Fluid Mechanics, Genesis Flood, Global Ocean, Sedimentary Sequences, Computer Simulation, Numerical Analysis, Resonance.

ABSTRACT

Tidal fluid mechanics associated with a global ocean are investigated using numerical analysis and computer simulation. Tidal waves, with their shallow water wave characteristics, are shown to be perfect candidates for the role of sediment transport and deposition associated with the buildup of thick sequences of sedimentary strata. The global ocean in the tidal context is shown to be near resonance which, if present, would augment the load-carrying ability of the tidal waves. Pertinent variables of fluid friction, ocean depth, and bottom relief are studied to ascertain their role in the tidal action in a global ocean.

INTRODUCTION

Even though many sedimentary strata sequences are now tilted and folded, it is still the most reasonable inference that the great bulk of these sequences were originally laid down horizontally. Because the main geometric characteristic of free-surface water is its horizontality, it easily follows that water action was responsible in forming the sequences. A second important characteristic of these sequences is the conformity of successive strata. Although this characteristic has been used to infer excessive age, it is possible to interpret the strata and their contents as having been laid down within hours of each other, resulting in a relatively short period of time for the construction of the whole sequence.

The flood of Genesis must be considered global if it is to be used to explain extensive crustal features. The questions then center around the fluid mechanics of a global ocean. What will a global ocean do? What would be the influences on such a large uninterrupted body of water? Fluid bodies can be moved by one or more of three mechanisms: pressure gradients, gravitational attraction, and boundary movements. Of these three, gravitational attraction presents itself as the primary mover of a global ocean. Newton's universal law of gravitational attraction requires that the water in that global ocean respond to the bodies neighboring the ocean. The closest most dominant neighbor would have been the large land mass beneath the ocean. This attraction is vertically downward and is responsible for the horizontal water surface. The second closest most dominant neighbor would have been the moon. The sun, although larger, is farther away and has less than half the lunar influence. The gravitational attraction of the earth-moon-sun system causes the tides. In this paper, only the influence of the lunar tides on the global ocean will be investigated.

As the earth rotates under the moon, the water, being easily moved by the lunar attraction, tends to move up toward the moon forming a tidal bulge. Due to centrifugal effects of the earth-moon system (rotating about the system's mass center located within the earth), a second, nearly equal, bulge is generated on the opposite side of the earth. The moon is relatively stationary in the earth-moon system, revolving about the earth only once a month. Since the tidal bulge stays under the moon, it moves like a wave when the observer is stationed on the earth. Hence, it is said that there is a semi-diurnal tidal wave circumnavigating the earth. The wavelength is half the circumference of the earth at any particular latitude. The amplitude of the wave is its crucial feature and the focal point of this paper.

One possible mechanism for the formation of the great bulk of strata sequences in the earth's crust is the wave action of the tides in the global flood of Genesis. The tidal waves in the oceans today range from 1 or 2 meters to more than 15 meters, depending on many factors. It should be noted that today's oceans differ greatly from the global ocean associated with the Genesis Flood. That ocean, most significantly, had no boundaries to interrupt the action of the tidal waves. Today's tidal waves operate in restricted basins of various sizes, some very large. But the tidal action is discontinuous, being stifled by the continental boundaries which form the basins. The continuity of the wave action in the global flood would have been especially beneficial in increasing the load-carrying capacity of the tidal waves by augmenting their amplitude. Large wave amplitude is desirable because the ability of the wave to envelop, transport, and deposit large sediment loads is enhanced by the associated larger velocity fields. A second, perhaps crucial, feature connected with the continuity of the wave action is the possibility that it would have been instrumental in developing resonance in the tidal action. Any cyclic system can develop the large amplitudes associated with resonance if certain criteria are met. In the global ocean context, equality of the free and forced wave speeds is necessary [1]. The free wave speed, associated with the speed with which a disturbance would propagate in the ocean, is dependent on the ocean depth; the forced wave speed, associated with the relative speed of the tidal bulge, is dependent on the rate of rotation of the earth.

A global ocean with bottom relief subjected to variable earth/moon gravitational forces is a complex system for which there are many (and, in some situations, unknown) governing parameters. To understand the fluid mechanics associated with it requires use of the relevant fluid dynamic relations, the principles of numerical analysis, and appropriate computers to evaluate the resulting mathematics. Using these tools, the fluid mechanic events associated with the Genesis Flood can be reproduced and studied. Thus, the immediate goals of this paper are to learn more about global ocean fluid mechanics and to determine the best parameters to use to calculate global ocean characteristics. An ultimate goal of this project is to use such results to analyze the sequences of sedimentary strata generated by the global ocean described in Genesis.

GOVERNING BASIC FLUID MECHANIC EQUATIONS

The most appropriate simulation of a global ocean would be constructed using a three-dimensional spherical-coordinate model with the governing equations fitted to that geometry. A textbook listing of the radial, longitudinal, and latitudinal momentum equations and continuity equation for incompressible flow for the spherical-coordinate system would show many, many terms. In 1775, Laplace was able to tailor these equations specifically for the tidal problem [6]. His simplified equations, shown in Fig.1, are called the Laplace Tidal Equations (LTE). Since any solution in his day had to be analytical, it was necessary to simplify the LTE in all possible ways. He was able to eliminate the radial momentum equation by assuming the hydrostatic pressure condition in the radial direction in conjunction with the shallow water wave condition (i.e., no variation in velocity in the radial (vertical) direction). He also eliminated the viscous terms.

Present day solutions by numerical methods allow a more rigorous solution to be considered; accordingly, the equation set used to obtain solutions in this paper essentially restored the friction terms to the LTE. These modified LTE forms, shown in Fig.2, are due to Estes [2], from whom the computer code used in the calculations was obtained. The friction terms used by Estes were proposed by Zahel [9]. As these equations

$$\frac{\partial u}{\partial t} - 2\omega v \sin\phi = \frac{-g}{R\cos\phi}\frac{\partial}{\partial\lambda}(\xi_*) + F_\lambda \qquad \text{Eastward Direction}$$

$$\frac{\partial v}{\partial t} - 2\omega u \sin\phi = \frac{-g}{R}\frac{\partial}{\partial\phi}(\xi_*) + F_\phi \qquad \text{Northward Direction}$$

$$\frac{\partial\xi}{\partial t} = -\frac{1}{R\cos\phi}\left[\frac{\partial}{\partial\lambda}(Hu) + \frac{\partial}{\partial\phi}(Hv\cos\phi)\right] \qquad \text{Conservation of Mass}$$

Hydrostatic equation $p = \rho g\xi$ applies in radial direction $\therefore$ u and v are independent of r

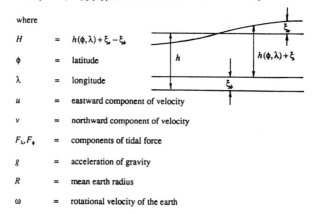

where

H	=	$h(\phi,\lambda) + \xi - \xi_*$
ϕ	=	latitude
λ	=	longitude
u	=	eastward component of velocity
v	=	northward component of velocity
F_λ, F_ϕ	=	components of tidal force
g	=	acceleration of gravity
R	=	mean earth radius
ω	=	rotational velocity of the earth

Fig.1. Laplace Tidal Equations - Shallow Water Equations on a Sphere.

$$\frac{\partial u}{\partial t} - 2\omega v \sin\phi = \frac{(1+k_L-h_L)}{R\cos\phi}\frac{\partial\Gamma}{\partial\lambda} - \frac{g}{R\cos\phi}\frac{\partial\xi}{\partial\lambda} - C_r\frac{\sqrt{u^2+v^2}}{H}u + C_{hv}\Delta u$$

$$\frac{\partial v}{\partial t} + 2\omega u \sin\phi = \frac{(1+k_L-h_L)}{R}\frac{\partial\Gamma}{\partial\phi} - \frac{g}{R}\frac{\partial\xi}{\partial\phi} - C_r\frac{\sqrt{u^2+v^2}}{H}v + C_{hv}\Delta v$$

$$\frac{\partial\xi}{\partial t} + \frac{1}{R\cos\phi}\left[\frac{\partial}{\partial\lambda}(Hu) + \frac{\partial}{\partial\phi}(Hv\cos\phi)\right] = 0$$

where

Γ = tidal potential

k_L, h_L = Love numbers

C_r = coefficient of friction (Zahel)

C_{hv} = horizontal eddy viscosity (Zahel)

Δ = horizontal Laplacian $= (1/R^2\cos^2\phi)\,\partial^2/\partial\lambda^2 + (1/R^2)\,\partial^2/\partial\phi^2$

Fig.2. Modified Laplace Tidal Equations.

stand, they cannot be solved analytically for any global ocean problem. In order to achieve such solutions, these partial differential equations will be converted to partial difference equations.

Water waves are primarily categorized by the depth to wave length ratio into deep, intermediate, and shallow water waves. In his classic book, Stoker [8] has said "It might seem incredible at first sight that the shallow water theory could possibly be accurate for the oceans, since depths of five miles or more occur. However, it is the depth in relation to the wave length of the motions under consideration which is relevant. . . . the tidal motions in the water result in waves having wave lengths of hundreds of miles; the depth-wave length ratio is thus quite small and the shallow water theory should be amply accurate to describe the tides." The shallow water wave characteristic so welcome in the context of sediment transport and deposition is the nearly uniform velocity profile with depth. Hence, this feature makes the tides a perfect candidate for the role of developing thick sequences of sedimentary strata. The surface velocity that is generated by the tides is also present and of equal magnitude at the bottom to move the sediment.

NUMERICAL ANALYSIS

The success of a finite-difference numerical analysis stems from the ability to cast the temporal and spacial derivatives found in the governing equations into temporal and spacial difference form. The time and space steps are made small enough so that the solutions of the difference equations approach the solutions of the differential equations. If there are no known solutions to the full differential equations, the schemes are matured on simpler problems where solutions by other means are available. As can be seen in the mesh sketches in Fig.3, the space domain is subdivided into many small parts, and all governing equations are solved for each mesh. Estes used the Hansen grid [3] where both the eastward and northward velocity components and the tidal elevation are computed at staggered mesh points.

Special boundary conditions need to be imposed on all coast lines. Even though a global ocean is the goal, the meshes at the higher latitudes become so small (the circumference at these high latitudes decreases while the number of meshes remains constant) that excessively small time steps are required to keep the computations stable. To avoid small time steps (and large computer times), an appropriate coastal boundary is placed at high latitude. The coastal boundary conditions are represented in the Hansen grid by horizontal and vertical lines which pass through points denoting velocity components. In this paper, the coastal boundaries are limited to horizontal lines which follow a given limiting latitude (see Fig.3). These horizontal lines pass through V (northward velocity) grid points; at these points, the vanishing perpendicular velocity requirement forces the V-velocity component on the coast to be zero at all times.

The finite-difference forms of Estes' equations are given in Fig.4. Now there are many more terms to be calculated. The time domain must be traversed slowly enough to keep the computations stable. The form of the equations is called 'explicit' because the equations need only to be solved once at each time step in contrast to the implicit form where an iterative solution meeting some closure criterion is necessary. The terms in the equations which drive the solution are associated with the components of the tidal force F_λ and F_ϕ. These expressions are written at the bottom of Fig.4 for the semi-diurnal lunar (species III) tide. A graphical depiction of the spacial variation of these forcing functions at a given time (12 minutes into the tidal period) is given in Fig.5. The F_λ variation, as a function of latitude limit, is shown in the middle row of sur-

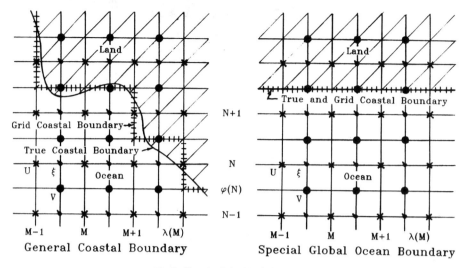

Fig.3. Sketch of the Mesh System.

face plots and the F_ϕ variation in the top row. A coefficient which contained the time step was eliminated prior to plotting so as to be able to compare the forcing function for various parameter sets; the mesh spacing (in the form of the $\Delta\lambda/2$ and $\Delta\phi/2$) was retained in the plots. As an aid to understanding the surface plots in Fig.5 (and all subsequent surface plots), an orientation sketch is shown in Fig.6.

To indicate the effect of the position of the horizontal coastal boundary at the high latitudes, a series of calculations were made at an ocean depth of 7938 m, using a parameter set consisting of a 3 deg mesh and a 1 min time step (3d,1m). The calculations were started with the limits of -87 and +87 deg latitude (note that, when the limit is set at 87 deg, the first calculations are made one mesh lower, i.e., at 84 deg) but they were found to be unstable, undoubtedly because of the small mesh size at this latitude. The next smaller limit (-84,+84) was calculated successfully with this parameter set. Additional smaller limits down to -72,+72 by 3 deg increments were also calculated. The surface plots of the tidal surface during the fifth tidal period for selected latitude limits in this sequence are shown in the bottom row of Fig.5. The maximum tidal amplitude during this period decreased with decrease in latitude limit (2.740 m, 2.717 m, 2.663 m, 2.532 m, and 2.265 m for latitude limits from 84 deg to 72 deg, respectively). Graphically, it is obvious that the tidal amplitude varies considerably more along the coastal boundary at the lower latitude limits. The unstable situation at the 87 deg latitude limit was re-investigated by reducing the time step from 1 min to 0.5 min. The calculations were then stable, and the results at the left of Fig.5 were obtained. Clearly, this representation creates the least variation at the upper latitude limit. The main, although not necessarily the only, reason for this increase in tidal variation along the coastal boundaries as the limiting latitude is decreased is to be found in the way in which the forcing functions are imposed. The forcing functions are simply truncated at the limit (see the upper two rows in Fig.5). Clearly, the coastal variation is reduced as the poles are approached. As previously stated, however, the computer effort becomes excessive for small meshes. Therefore, a set of parameters is always sought by which a suitable compromise can be achieved.

HOUGH'S PREDICTIONS

The 1897 work of Hough [5] served as a starting point in this investigation of tidal action in a flat-bottom, global ocean context. Hough solved the LTE using semi-analytical, series-solution methods. He calculated the ratios of the tidal height to the equilibrium height for various flat-bottomed global ocean depths. The term 'resonance' was not used but the term 'critical depths' was. He said "We see, then, that though, when the period of forced oscillation differs from that of one of the types of free oscillation by as little as a minute, the forced tide may be nearly 250 times as great as the corresponding equilibrium tide. . . . The critical depths for which the lunar tides become infinite are found to be 26,044 ft and 6,448 ft. Consequently, this phenomenon will occur if the depth of the ocean be between 29,182 and 26,044 ft or between 7,375 and 6,448 ft." Here then, Hough, with spherical governing equations but without friction, was able to show resonant conditions at reasonable ocean depths. Since Hough's work had goals similar to those of this paper (the assessment of situations where large tidal amplitudes occur on a completely flooded, flat-bottomed ocean), it was decided to repeat Hough's calculations using numerical analysis.

$$\xi(\phi,\lambda,t) = \xi(N,M,t_{n+1}) = \xi(N,M,t_n) +$$

Conservation of Mass

$$\frac{\Delta t}{R\cos[\phi(N)]}\left\{\frac{\frac{1}{2}[h(N,M)+h(N,M-1)+\xi(N,M,t_n)+\xi(N,M-1,t_n)]u(N,M,t_{n+1})}{\Delta\lambda}\right.$$

$$-\frac{\frac{1}{2}[h(N,M+1)+h(N,M)+\xi(N,M+1,t_n)+\xi(N,M,t_n)]u(N,M+1,t_{n+1})}{\Delta\lambda}$$

$$+\frac{\frac{1}{2}[h(N,M)+h(N-1,M)+\xi(N,M,t_n)+\xi(N-1,M,t_n)]v(N,M,t_{n+1})}{\Delta\lambda/\cos\left[\phi(N)-\frac{\Delta\phi}{2}\right]}$$

$$\left.-\frac{\frac{1}{2}[h(N+1,M)+h(N,M)+\xi(N+1,M,t_n)+\xi(N,M,t_n)]v(N+1,M,t_{n+1})}{\Delta\phi/\cos\left[\phi(N+1)-\frac{\Delta\phi}{2}\right]}\right\}$$

$$u(\phi,\lambda,t) = u(N,M,t_{n+1}) =$$

Eastward Momentum

$$\left\{1-\frac{C_r\Delta t\sqrt{u(N,M,t_n)^2+\frac{1}{16}[v(N,M-1,t_n)+v(N,M,t)+v(N+1,M-1,t_n)+v(N+1,M,t_n)]^2}}{\frac{1}{2}[h(N,M)+h(N,M-1)+\xi(N,M,t_n)+\xi(N,M-1,t_n)]}\right\}$$

$$\cdot\, u(N,M,t_n)+2\omega\Delta t\sin[\phi(N)]$$

$$\cdot\frac{1}{4}[v(N,M-1,t_n)+v(N,M,t_n)+v(N+1,M-1,t_n)+v(N+1,M,t_n)]$$

$$+C_{h\nu}\Delta t\left\{\frac{u(N,M-1,t_n)+u(N,M+1,t_n)-2u(N,M,t_n)}{[R\cos[\phi(N)]\Delta\lambda]^2}\right.$$

$$\left.+\frac{u(N+1,M,t_n)+u(N-1,M,t_n)-2u(N,M,t_n)}{R\Delta\phi^2}\right\}-\frac{g\Delta t}{R\cos[\phi(N)]}\frac{\xi(N,M,t_n)-\xi(N,M-1,t_n)}{\Delta\lambda}+F_\lambda\Delta t$$

$$v(\phi,\lambda,t) = v(N,M,t_n) =$$

Northward Momentum

$$=\left\{1-\frac{C_r\Delta t\sqrt{v(N,M,t_n)^2+\frac{1}{16}[u(N-1,M,t_n)+u(N-1,M+1,t_n)+u(N,M+1,t_n)+u(N,M,t_n)]^2}}{\frac{1}{2}[h(N,M)+h(N-1,M)+\xi(N,M,t_n)+\xi(N-1,M,t_n)]}\right\}$$

$$\cdot\, v(N,M,t_n)-2\omega\Delta t\sin\left[\phi(N)-\frac{\Delta\phi}{2}\right]$$

$$\cdot\frac{1}{4}[u(N-1,M,t_n)+u(N-1,M+1,t_n)+u(N,M+1,t_n)+u(N,M,t_n)]$$

$$+C_{h\nu}\Delta t\left\{\frac{v(N,M-1,t_n)+v(N,M+1,t_n)-2v(N,M,t_n)}{\left[R\cos\left(\phi(N)-\frac{\Delta\phi}{2}\right)\Delta\lambda\right]^2}\right.$$

$$\left.+\frac{v(N+1,M,t_n)+v(N-1,M,t_n)-2v(N,M,t_n)}{R\Delta\phi^2}\right\}$$

$$-\frac{g\Delta t}{R}\left\{\frac{\xi(N,M,t_n)-\xi(N-1,M,t_n)}{\Delta\phi}\right\}+F_\phi\Delta t$$

where

$$F_\lambda = \frac{g}{R\cos\phi}\frac{\partial\bar{\xi}}{\partial\lambda}$$

SPECIES III:

$$F_\phi = \frac{g}{R}\frac{\partial\bar{\xi}}{\partial\phi}$$

$$\left\{\begin{array}{l}F_\lambda = -\frac{CgK}{R}\cos[\phi(N)]\sin\left[2\left(\lambda(M)-\frac{\Delta\lambda}{2}\right)+\sigma t_n\right]\\[2mm]F_\phi = -\frac{CgK}{2R}\sin\left[2\left(\phi(N)-\frac{\Delta\phi}{2}\right)\right]\cos[2\lambda(M)+\sigma t_n]\end{array}\right.$$

$$K = \frac{3}{2}\left(\frac{M_{moon}}{M_{earth}}\right)\left(\frac{R_{earth}}{R_{moon}}\right)^3$$

R_{moon} = mean lunar distance

σ = tidal constituent frequency

Fig.4. Explicit Finite-Difference Forms of the Modified Laplace Tidal Equations.

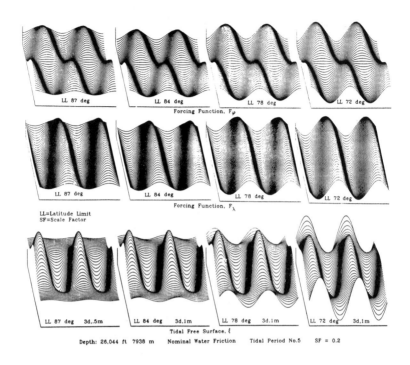

Fig.5. Top: Forcing Functions F_λ and F_ϕ. Bottom: Tidal Free Surface Plots Showing Effect of Latitude Limit.

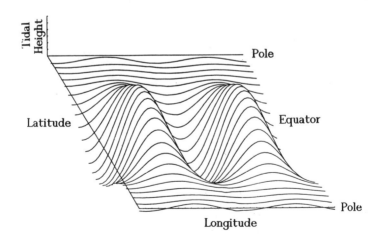

Fig.6. Orientation and Definition Sketch for a Typical Free Surface Plot.

NUMERICAL RESULTS

Hough's Upper Critical Depth. The first calculations used Hough's upper critical depth of 7938 m (26,044 ft). A 6d,6m parameter set was used. To match Hough's inviscid condition, the friction coefficient, C_r, and the coefficient of lateral turbulent viscosity, C_{hv}, (see Fig.2) for water were arbitrarily divided by 800. Hereafter, it is dubbed NWF/800 where NWF stands for nominal water friction. These and all subsequent calculations were started at time zero with the initial conditions of zero tidal amplitude and zero velocity components for all meshes. At tidal period intervals (approximately 750 min), output files were updated. One file contained the tidal amplitude at all meshes and the maximum tidal amplitude in that field. After a number of tidal periods, the program was stopped and the results perused. Sufficient data were retained so that the program could be restarted. These period maximums are shown in Fig.7 in the curve labeled NWF/800. After one dwell (near 16,000 min), the curve quickly ascends off-scale in a dramatic show of resonance. To show evidence of computational stability, a sequence of smooth surface plots of tidal amplitude are shown at the top in Fig.8.

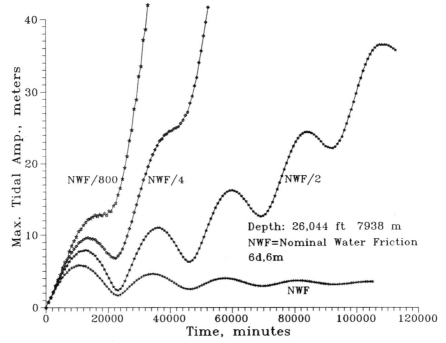

Fig.7. Maximum Tidal Amplitude as a Function of Time for Hough's Upper Critical Depth.

Using the same parameter set, viscous situations NWF/4, NWF/2, and NWF were also calculated. The maximum tidal amplitude variations with time are also shown in Fig.7, and a sequence of surface plots for NWF/2 is shown at the bottom of Fig.8. Only the NWF case was overdamped which led to a steady-state tidal amplitude of some 3 m. The other less viscous cases were underdamped and resonance resulted.

The 6-deg mesh subdivision produces some 27 latitude lines and 60 longitude lines on the globe, a somewhat coarse subdivision. The 6-min time step allows some 125 subdivisions of the tidal period, a somewhat rapid stepping in time. The calculations remained stable and smooth as seen by the surface plots, a fact that could be attributed to the absence of variability in the bottom relief and the relegation of the straight coastal boundaries to the high latitudes. There is, however, a question as to whether the calculations are producing the correct answer.

To more closely approach the mathematical concept of a derivative, the space or time steps or both can be reduced. Replacing the 6d,6m set with a 6d,2m set requires 3 times the computational effort. For the inviscid case, this change results in the maximum amplitude-time plot of Fig.9 and the surface plots shown in the middle of Fig.8. The ocean is underdamped, resonance still occurs, but it takes longer to develop. Several oscillations occur before the amplitudes become excessive. A third parameter set (4d,2m) was used for the inviscid case. Now the computational effort is over 6 times that of the original set. The result in Fig.9 is nearly the same as the 6d,2m result, having essentially the same oscillation frequency and magnitude.

157

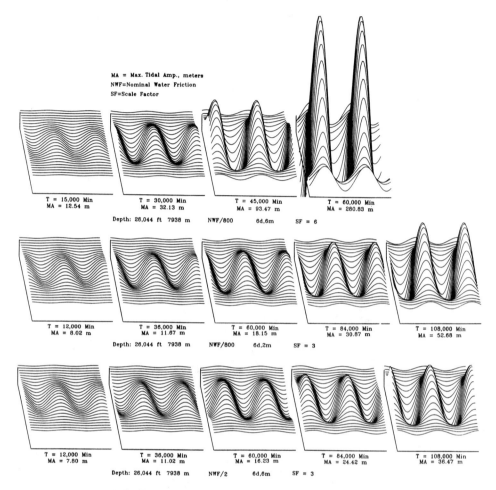

MA = Max. Tidal Amp., meters
NWF=Nominal Water Friction
SF=Scale Factor

T = 15,000 Min
MA = 12.54 m

T = 30,000 Min
MA = 32.13 m

T = 45,000 Min
MA = 93.47 m

T = 60,000 Min
MA = 260.83 m

Depth: 26,044 ft 7938 m   NWF/800   6d,6m   SF = 6

T = 12,000 Min
MA = 8.02 m

T = 36,000 Min
MA = 11.67 m

T = 60,000 Min
MA = 18.15 m

T = 84,000 Min
MA = 30.87 m

T = 108,000 Min
MA = 52.68 m

Depth: 26,044 ft 7938 m   NWF/800   6d,2m   SF = 3

T = 12,000 Min
MA = 7.80 m

T = 36,000 Min
MA = 11.02 m

T = 60,000 Min
MA = 16.23 m

T = 84,000 Min
MA = 24.42 m

T = 108,000 Min
MA = 36.47 m

Depth: 26,044 ft 7938 m   NWF/2   6d,6m   SF = 3

Fig.8. Tidal Free Surface Plots for Hough's Upper Critical Depth.

One more comparison at Hough's upper critical depth was made. The NWF case was calculated using three different parameter sets and the results are compared in Fig.10. While the 6d,6m set shows a highly oscillating result, both the 4d,2m and the 3d,1m sets give essentially the same steady-state amplitude of about 3 m after only one large and several smaller oscillations. From these results, it would seem justified to conclude that the 3d,1m set should be used to obtain accurate results from Estes' code.

Hough's Lower Critical Depth. Turning to Hough's lower critical depth of 1965 m (6,448 ft), a similar pattern of calculations was followed. In Fig.11, the NWF/800 case, calculated using the 6d,6m set, shows a series of small oscillations for the first 12,000 min and then a continuous upward sweep to resonance. Viscous situations of NWF/8, NWF/4, NWF/2, and NWF were also calculated with this set and the results plotted in Fig.11. Of these cases, only the NWF/8 case was underdamped and resonated; the rest were overdamped and went toward steady-state. The surface plots at selected times for the inviscid case are shown at the top of Fig.12. In contrast to the two-peak plots of Fig.8, additional tidal bulges and peaks occur away from the equator. Furthermore, the maximum tidal amplitude is not always located at the equator. As with the upper critical depth, a 6d,2m parameter set was used to calculate comparison results for the inviscid case. The results are included in Fig.11 and 12. The maximum amplitude curve, similar to the upper critical depth case, showed a resonance which took longer to develop. The times chosen to plot the surface configuration were those which had nearly identical maximum tidal amplitudes in the 6d,6m plots in the top row. It is seen that the two sets of plots are nearly identical in appearance.

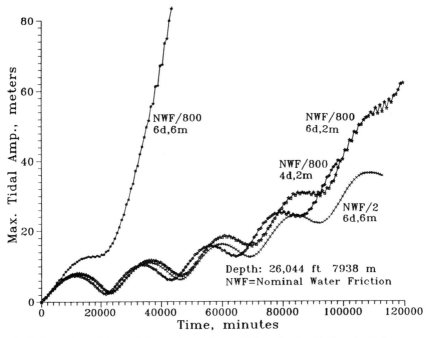

Fig.9. Comparison of the Variation of the Maximum Tidal Amplitude with Time for Various Computational Situations for Hough's Upper Critical Depth.

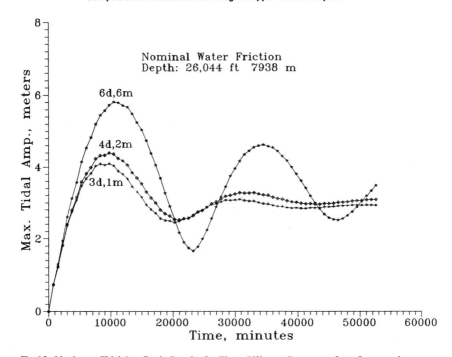

Fig.10. Maximum Tidal Amplitude Results for Three Different Parameter Sets Compared. Hough's Upper Critical Depth with Nominal Water Friction.

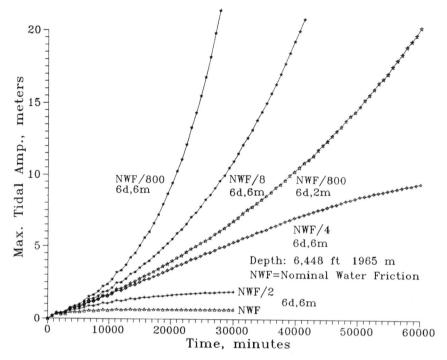

Fig.11. Maximum Tidal Amplitude as a Function of Time for Hough's Lower Critical Depth.

A Non-Critical Depth. Thus far, Hough's 1897 semi-analytical methods for calculating global ocean reson-ances seem to be vindicated. It was thought to be of interest to see what would happen with a non-critical depth. Accordingly, a depth halfway between the two critical depths was used with the 6d,6m set for the inviscid case. The results are shown in the top curve in Fig.13 using the time scale at the bottom. At first glance, the saw-toothed character of the plot and the increasing size of the teeth would indicate that the solution was becoming unstable. On closer examination, however, evidence for a stable solution was found using the surface plots and the maximum tidal heights between the tidal period times. The tidal amplitudes for 6d,6m are increasing rapidly toward resonance after 40,000 min. The surface plots at four times during the tidal period starting at 60,000 min are shown in the bottom row of Fig.12. These plots show no evi-dence of numerical instability. The original maximum amplitude-time curves in Fig.13 were plotted using only the values output at intervals of the tidal period. For a 750-min period and a 6-min time step, there are 125 maximum amplitudes at times intermediate between those plotted. Furthermore, because of the peculiar manner in which the tidal surface is configured at this depth, the location of the maximum ampli-tude can shift back and forth between equator and somewhere near mid-latitude. To show some of these intervening data, the 6-min amplitude-time plot was expanded using the time scale at the top of Fig.13. Both equator and mid-latitude maximums are plotted. The curves show a smooth variation with time and also show the maximum amplitude sometimes at the equator and sometimes at mid-latitude. The surface plots corresponding to this expanded time scale are shown at the bottom of Fig.12. The tidal bulge at the equator waxes and wanes very dramatically during this sequence while there is a much smaller variation at the mid-latitudes. Furthermore, there seems to be a difference in period between these two oscillations.

Additional 6-deg calculations at 4 and 2 min and NWF/800 were also made and are plotted in Fig.13. Both of these calculations were stable and both eventually indicated a slow rise toward resonance. The differ-ence in the character of the tidal action in this case as contrasted with the two Hough critical depths is striking. The causes for the difference are, as yet, inexplicable.

A General Depth-Effect Study. The three depths studied thus far were special depths selected in relation to the work of Hough. A need was felt to develop a more general picture of the effect of depth on the config-uration and amplitude of the tidal surface on a flat-bottomed global ocean. To develop the most realistic and accurate results, the NWF case and the 3d,1m set were selected along with latitude limits of -84, +84 deg.

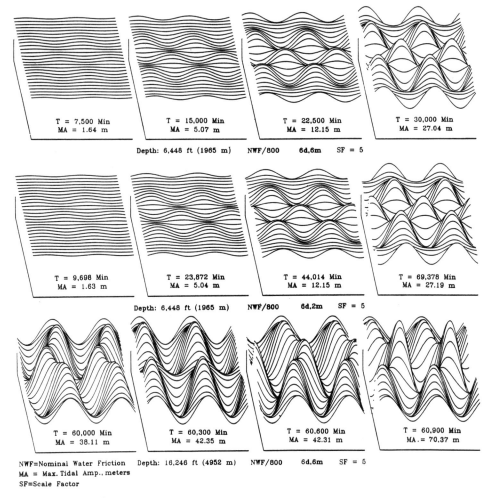

Fig.12. Top: Tidal Free Surface Plots for Hough's Lower Critical Depth.

Bottom: Tidal Free Surface Plots for an Intermediate Depth.

Initially, depths of 1,000, 3,000, 5,000, 7,000, and 9,000 meters were calculated. When results at these depths were plotted, additional depths were needed to plot a definitive curve. Accordingly, many additional depths were added especially near the depths of greatest interest, 2,000 and 7,000 meters. Once a depth was selected for inclusion in the set, the program was run using that depth until the largest maximum tidal amplitude had been determined. In some instances, only a few tidal periods were needed; in others, many. Fig.14 shows the maximum tidal amplitude as a function of depth of ocean. Two features stand out in this figure: A resonant-like peak at a depth of 7,140 m and a cusp near 2,000 m. It cannot be said that a resonance occurs when the maximum amplitude is only 9 m, but the characteristics of the curve in this vicinity have all the attributes of a resonant peak. The nearness of this peak to Hough's inviscid depth of 7,938 m is striking and possibly significant. Of course, the NWF values for the friction coefficients were responsible for the peak magnitude being only 9 m. As the position of the curve near 2,000 m was being determined, it was suspected that, due to parallelism with Hough's results, there would be a second, smaller peak there. In the end, only the cusp or change in slope of the curve could be deciphered.

To help in understanding these occurrences, the amplitude-time relations for most of the depths are shown in Fig.15. There is a distinct change in character of these curves as the depth changes: Near the overall peak at 7,140 m, the ocean seems to be critically damped; the curve bends over and gradually reaches the peak without ever oscillating. For the deeper oceans (8000 m and 9000 m) and for the shallower oceans

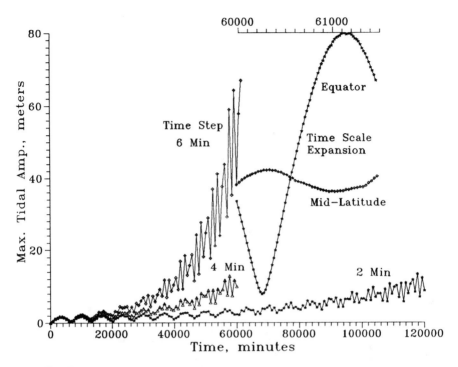

Fig. 13. Maximum Tidal Amplitude as a Function of Time for an Intermediate Depth.

(6,000 m and below), all of the curves oscillate. For some, the first oscillation contains the maximum tidal amplitude; for others, the largest amplitude occurs after 5 or 6 oscillations. For those cases below 2,000 m, the oscillations are not nearly as uniform in magnitude as those with depths 2,000 m and above.

Additional understanding of the tidal actions in this set of depths is gained from the surface plot. As can be seen in Fig.16, there are significant changes in the surface configuration with depth. For the larger depths (top row), the two major tidal bulges which are present are established right from the start of the calculations. It looks as though the F_λ forcing function on the U-velocity is dominating this tidal action since two distinct bulges also appear in Fig.3 for F_λ. For the smaller depths, the dominance of F_λ seems to have been replaced by strong contributions from both F_λ and F_ϕ since the global surfaces have patterns with several extra bulges. One pair near the equator dominates in most cases and one or two on either side of that pair occur near mid-latitude. To add to the complexity, there seems to be a difference in periods of these bulges. For the most part, temporal sequences of surface plots show that the tidal bulges straddling the equator make the largest excursions in amplitude; those at mid-latitudes vary much less.

Bottom Relief. The purpose of the foregoing flat-bottom ocean results has been to learn about the basic fluid mechanics of a global ocean in its simplest context and to determine the most appropriate approach to the numerical analysis from the standpoint of calculational parameters. However, it is not likely that the global ocean of Genesis had a flat bottom. What bottom relief that ocean did have originally is not readily known. Estes' computer code, however, is capable of setting any desired bottom relief and of placing the land and ocean boundaries in any desired position.

To start, the simplest bottom relief to program (a mid-longitude pole-to-pole ridge) was used. A 6d,6m set with NWF gave the results shown in Fig.17 for Hough's upper critical depth (7938 m, 26,044 ft). The relief sketches in the figure are approximately to scale horizontally but exaggerated vertically. The ridge is 40 deg long at the base. The one-half and three-quarters ridge depths show moderate increases in tide heights. When the ridge was barely submerged, a considerable increase in tidal amplitude (in excess of 10 m) was obtained. In all cases, the tidal action was overdamped with all curves moving towards steady-state.

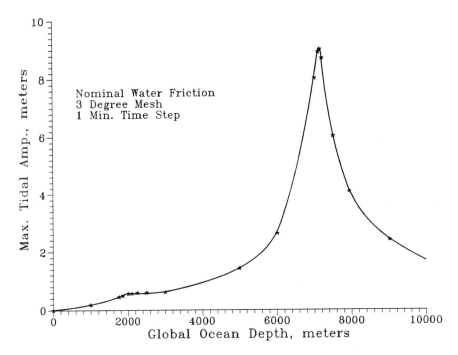

Fig.14. Maximum Tidal Amplitude as a Function of Depth.

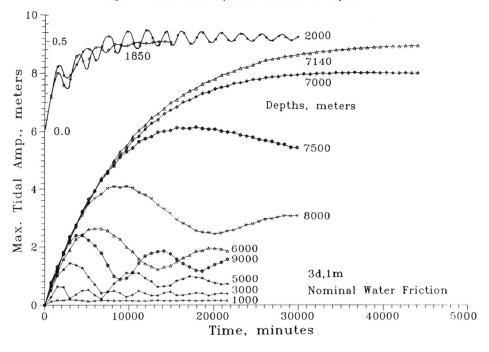

Fig.15. Maximum Tidal Amplitude as a Function of Time for the General Depth-Effect Study.

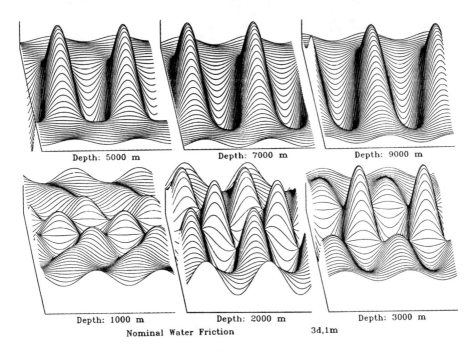

Depth: 5000 m   Depth: 7000 m   Depth: 9000 m

Depth: 1000 m   Depth: 2000 m   Depth: 3000 m

Nominal Water Friction   3d,1m

Fig.16. Surface Configuration as a Function of Depth.

A second case of bottom relief, one where there is a smooth continual variation in depth, was calculated using a sinusoidal pattern (varying with longitude; invariant with latitude). A D/A ratio (amplitude of sine wave to depth of ocean) of four was selected along with NWF and two parameter sets (6d,3m and 3d,1m) for Hough's upper critical depth of 7938 m (26,044 ft). The data were first analyzed (Fig.18) using the maximum surface amplitude which was outputted at tidal period intervals (750 minutes). Except for the drooping of the 6d,6m curve after 40,000 minutes, the two curves show essentially the same result. These results are, in general, similar to those calculated for similar depths for a flat-bottom ocean (cp Fig.10). Of course, there are many more data than those shown in Fig.18, and the results take on added meaning (and possibly greater sedimentary transport significance) when a closer look is given these intervening data.

In the Fig.18 insert, the tidal amplitudes during the last tidal period (from 58,227 min to 58,934 min) for the 3d,1m set are plotted on an expanded time scale. Here, a considerable variation in amplitude is evident. It is a situation similar to that already encountered in Fig.13 with the Hough intermediate depth where it was found that the equatorial tidal bulge was oscillating freely during the tidal period. Now, however, the action is global; the free surface of the whole ocean is pulsing up and down each period. This action can be seen in the sequence of surface plots for this time span in Fig.19. To help in understanding the action, both the actual surfaces and their negative images are given since in some cases the significant part of the plot has disappeared from view. At the start of the sequence, the tidal bulges are for the most part not seen (but seen well in the image). As time progresses, these bulges appear, maximize, and again disappear. An overall lowering of the free surface is seen during the first half of the period and then a gradual recovery during the last half. This variation is a manifestation of the principle of mass conservation: With a fixed amount of water in the ocean throughout the calculations, it should follow that, when the water bulges up near the equator and mid-latitudes, this water must come from the regions of the poles so the elevations there will be lowered. The opposite situation occurs when a negative bulge occurs near the equator.

Some complex interaction takes place between the water moving in relation to the sinusoidal bottom relief and the forcing of the water by the complex (essentially sinusoidal) lunar forcing functions. The tidal ampli-tudes are seen to have ordinary magnitudes in these two cases. The additional period by period pulsing of the whole ocean is a new phenomenon. Additional wave action of this kind has not been considered in the development of the sedimentary strata sequences. These pilot calculations indicate the need for additional work to determine the general surface and subsurface occurrences in the general context of bottom relief. Other non-sinusoidal variations would be more apropos. Most beneficial would be some sort of Pangean bottom relief to see how such a configuration would effect the tidal dynamics.

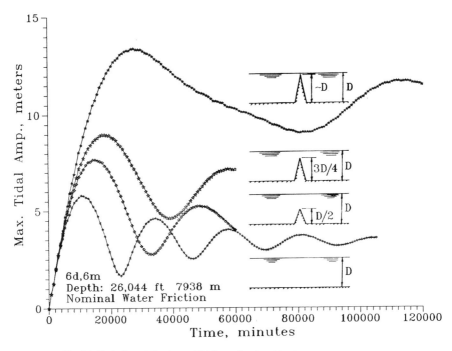

Fig.17. Variation of Maximum Tidal Amplitude with Time for a Pole to Pole Mid-Longitude Ridge of Various Heights. Hough's Upper Critical Depth.

DISCUSSION

The numerical analyses described in the preceding section were made in an attempt to answer the question "What will a no-boundary global ocean do when subjected to the lunar attraction forces?" Knowing the fluid mechanics for that situation will better enable us to understand the relation between the water action in the Genesis Flood and the sedimentary strata sequences that resulted from it. The greater the tidal action the greater would be the amount of work that could be done with the sediments. From the huge volume of sedimentary rock extant on the earth, it must be postulated that the responsible mechanism was of broad scope and great power. The phenomenon of resonance has been put forth as one means of increasing the ability of the tides to do the work. In the calculations, the global ocean resonated only when the fluid friction was reduced. Situations producing reduced friction (like increased temperature) could be postulated. It is also possible that a better representation of the frictional terms in the governing equations would allow resonance with nominal water friction to occur. Several different formulations have been found in the literature [4,7]. Considerably more computer effort would be required if Schweiderski's friction equations were used but the more accurate representation of the bottom friction might be well worth that effort.

Because the global ocean context offers extensive distances over which the fluid variables change very slowly, the numerical analyses were relatively free of instability problems. The 6-deg mesh spacing did produce results that oscillated more than results from the 3-deg spacing. The oscillations in the tidal amplitude with time could be the natural dynamic response of the system or the result of the initial conditions that were used. The method used to start a given computer run was somewhat artificial. In the real world, it would be like having a quiescent global ocean without the presence of the moon and then instantaneously placing the moon (and its force system) in its position. The initial conditions used could also be looked at as suddenly disturbing a quiescent global ocean with a strike from a giant drum-stick, the drumhead (ocean surface) reverberating from the strike; the reverberations eventually dying out with time.

While it was deemed necessary to spend the time understanding the flat-bottomed ocean before moving on to the more realistic ocean with bottom relief, the real Genesis Flood simulation must contain a rather complex bottom relief. The simple representations of relief considered in this paper showed that a Pandora's box is opened when the depth is allowed to vary. The sinusoidal bottom relief results revealed the entirely new phenomenon of whole ocean pulsation in each tidal period. This calculation, made with Hough's upper critical depth, produced a very complex situation. If this calculation were repeated with his lower critical depth, there would possibly be increased interaction with the closer bottom. Many additional simulations must be made before our understanding of the Genesis Flood fluid mechanics is anywhere near complete.

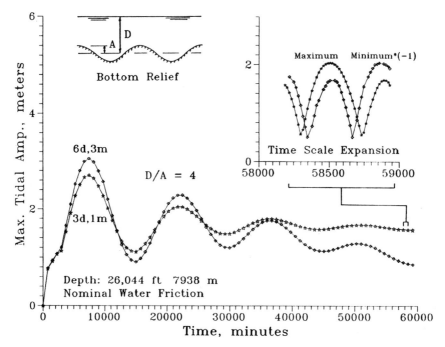

Fig.18. Maximum Tidal Amplitude as a Function of Time for Sinusoidal Bottom Relief.

Hough's Upper Critical Depth.

CONCLUSIONS

On the basis of the numerical studies of global ocean tidal mechanics reported in this paper, the following conclusions can be drawn: Even though the interaction between the moon and a completely flooded planet earth is multifaceted and complex, this action follows the basic laws of mechanics and, hence, can be analyzed and at least partially understood using computer simulation principles. The action of the tides on a global ocean would have been powerful, omnipresent, and recurring, causing dynamism and cyclicity throughout the ocean depth (because of the shallow water wave characteristics). It could have been a potent determinate in what happened in the sedimentary processes.

In the numerical analysis, there are preferred parameter sets (mesh size, time step) which maximize the fidelity of the results and minimize computer effort; progress towards the proper selection of these sets has been made in the situations studied herein. Tidal amplitude closely correlates with bottom surface velocity in the shallow water wave category. It was selected as the critical variable to be studied when the ultimate aim is to establish a correlation between the fluid mechanics of the global ocean and the sedimentary strata sequences which resulted from the water action in that ocean. Resonance would have augmented the tidal amplitudes which, in turn, would have augmented the velocity fields, especially near the bottom where sediment transport and deposition would have occurred. Herein, resonance has been shown to occur but only when reduced friction was employed in the calculations. It is hoped that a better representation of this crucial friction variable can be programmed into the code which could alter the resonance results. Ocean depth is also a critical variable whose role in the tidal action has been illucidated in this analysis. A start has been made on understanding the variation in tidal action caused by bottom relief. The additional pulsing of the tidal free surface, occurring within a tidal period and being directly attributable to the bottom relief, is the type of event that can only be discovered by computer simulation. Other phenomena, which could dramatically effect the sedimentary processes, could also be uncovered by future studies of this nature.

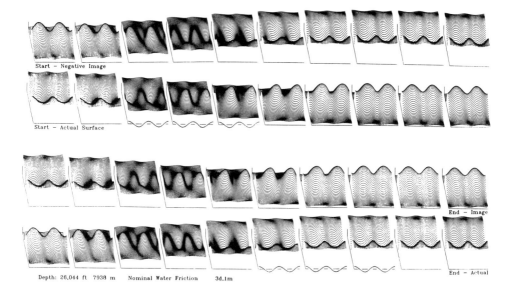

Start – Negative Image

Start – Actual Surface

End – Image

End – Actual

Depth: 26,044 ft 7938 m   Nominal Water Friction   3d,1m

Fig.19. Temporal Sequence of Tidal Free Surface Plots During One Tidal Period.

Sinusoidal Bottom Relief and Hough's Upper Critical Depth.

BIBLIOGRAPHY

[1]   G.H.Darwin, The Tides and Kindred Phenomena in the Solar System, 1911, 3rd Ed. Houghton and Mifflin, Boston.

[2]   R.H.Estes, A Computer Software System for the Generation of Global Ocean Tides Including Self-gravitation and Crustal Loading Effects, 1977, Goddard Space Flight Center, Rept. No. X-920-77-82.

[3]   W.Hansen, Hydrodynamical Methods Applied to Oceanography Problems, Symp. Math. Hydrodyn., Methods of Physical Oceanography, Hamburg (1961) 25-34.

[4]   A.D.Heathershaw, The Turbulent Structure of the Bottom Boundary Layer in a Tidal Current, Geophysical J. Royal Astron. Society, 58:3 (1979) 395-430.

[5]   S.S.Hough, On the Application of Harmonic Analysis to the Dynamical Theory of the Tides. Part I. On Laplace's "Oscillations of the First Species" and on the Dynamics of Ocean Currents, Phil. Trans. Royal Society CLXXXIX (1897) 201-257. Part II, On the General Integration of Laplace's Dynamical Equations. Phil. Trans. Royal Society, CXIX (1897) 139-185.

[6]   P.S.Laplace, Mechanique Celeste, 1799, Livre 4, c. i.

[7]   E.W.Schwiderski, Ocean Tides, Part I: Global Ocean Tidal Equations, Marine Geodesy 3 (1979) 161-217.

[8]   J.J.Stoker, Water Waves, 1957, Interscience Publishers, Inc., New York.

[9]   W.Zahel, The Diurnal K₁Tide in the World Ocean - A Numerical Investigation, Pure and Applied Geophysics (1974) 1819-1826.

DO BIRDS OF PREY DEMONSTRATE STABILITY OF SPECIES?

G. RICHARD CULP, D.O.
2260N-1100W
SHIPSHEWANA, IN 46565

KEYWORDS

Birds of Prey; Biogeography; Isolation; Kind; Baramin

ABSTRACT

The native American eagles, hawks, and owls have been carefully studied with regard to their geographic distribution. The majority have transoceanic counterparts which are variously called transoceanic, circumpolar, circumboreal, circumpolar/circumboreal and cosmopolitan.

Particular attention has been given to Cooper's, sharp-shinned and Eurasian sparrow hawks, and the sea eagles. Evolutionists [17] have claimed that evolution is promoted by isolation and a rigorous climate. The birds of prey, however, give evidence of wide distribution rather than isolation, many circumhabiting the globe. They survive well under extreme conditions, demonstrating stability of kinds or baramins, with no significant evolutionary change. They give evidence of a young earth and recent intercontinental migration.

INTRODUCTION

Birds of prey always have held a certain fascination for man. The Ancient Egyptians produced many likenesses of the Egyptian vulture, and the sculptured likeness of the golden eagle was held aloft on a rod before every Roman legion, typifying the striking power and alleged invincibility of their armies.

The powerful wings of the birds of prey enable them to be among the most distinguished of the bird families. The bird enthusiast watches with admiration as he observes, high in the air, the soaring of the great eagles and vultures, the eagles and hawks swiftly riding the air currents from one end of a canyon to the other, the peregrine falcon plunging through the air like a cannon ball toward its prey, or the kestrel hovering in midair while he locates his prey among the grasses. It is a pleasure to study them; the popularity of hawk-watching at Hawk Mountain in Pennsylvania testifies to this fact.

Since my youth I have studied birds in the field in this country, and later also in Canada, Central America and Europe, photographing many in aviaries in Switzerland, Belgium, Holland, England and the United States. [5] Some from other sources also are used in this presentation. For the sake of brevity, I have not included the vultures and condors in this study.

THE EAGLES

The golden eagle *(Aquila chrysaetos)* is a very large eagle, with uniformly brown body, and golden yellow or golden brown head and neck. I have observed this species in the Catskill Mountains soaring swiftly across a broad valley, soaring above Crater Lake in Oregon, and on occasion sitting quietly on a telephone pole in Idaho. Surprisingly, one strain is larger than the bald eagle, having a length of 75-100 cm. and a wingspread up to 225 cm. It is circumpolar in distribution (i.e., it is found in the treeless tundra all the way around the Northern Hemisphere in the arctic). It is also circumboreal in that it is found circumhabitating the earth in the boreal ("northern") forest in the far north, south of the tundra. Both of these species are sometimes found far to the South also.

The bald eagle *(Haliaeetus leucocephalus)* is an impressive, large eagle with snow-white head and tail. Its speed and agility in the air are phenomenal. This is often demonstrated by its plunging toward a flying osprey which has a fish in its talons, causing the latter to drop its prey, only to have the eagle swoop down and catch the fish in midair in its sharp claws. I have observed it flying low over a lake in Michigan's Upper Peninsula, flying down the

169

Mississippi River between Iowa and Illinois, soaring over the Willamette River, feeding on carrion in an open field in Oregon, soaring over Sherburne Lake in Glacier National Park, and riding along on the air current in Wyoming in a small group of its kind. It is found all across North America and in Northeastern Siberia, seeming therefore to be almost distinctly North American.

A second look at the eagles gives pause for reflection, however. A very similar variety, the white-tailed sea eagle *(Haliaeetus albicilla)* ranges from Greenland and western Europe, across to mountainous Eastern Siberia, South to Africa and Madagascar, and East to the Solomon Islands. It is the same size as the bald eagle, with the same yellow beak and white tail, lacking only the white head [6, p.55]. However, two other kinds of white-tailed eagles have pure white heads, the African fish eagle [4, vol. 1, pp.312-315], which has white feathers down on the back and belly also, and the white-bellied sea eagle of Australia [11 p.12], which is white in the head, belly, and much of the undersurface of the wings. They also have similar habits and diet--fish, birds, mammals and carrion [8,11]. Austin and Singer [1, p.81] includes the bald eagle among the whitetailed sea eagles, stating that "they are all of similar aspect, and vary mainly in their possession of a white head or tail". It is probable that these are all races of one kind," and should be considered of the same kind or baramin with a circumboreal distribution.

THE OSPREY

Where no eagles are found, the osprey *(Pandion haliaetus)* is usually the largest bird of prey, dwarfing the larger hawks by its size. This magnificent bird, appearing mostly white from the ground as it soars above, is most efficient in its plunging into the surface of water after fish. While returning to land to eat its catch, it shifts its hold to carry the fish head-first to reduce wind resistance. It is found over much of the earth's land surface and is thus cosmopolitan. [2, p.24].

THE HAWKS (Accipiters, Buteos, and Circuses)

Accipiters-The True Hawks

The accipiters have short, broad wings rounded at the tip. The goshawk *(Accipiter gentilis)* is considerably larger than a crow, with pale gray barred breast, darker gray back, and a white eye stripe. Like all North American accipiter's, it has red eyes. The young of the goshawk and that of Cooper's hawk are very similar [13, p.60]. At this stage, the breast of the latter is marked with gray rather than rusty horizontal bands. The goshawk is circumpolar in distribution. A red species *(Erythroetriorchis radiatus)* is found in Australia [8, p.368].

The Cooper's hawk *(A. cooperii)* and the sharp-shinned hawk *(A. striatus)* show many striking similarities. The plumage is essentially identical, with the same field marks in the head and body [7, p.105], with blue-gray back and rusty striped breast. The two are sometimes found migrating together [12, p.74], apparently more often than with other hawks. They are also much the same in habits. Terres [18, p.485] indicates that the sharp-shinned hawk, "like Cooper's hawk is sometimes seen flying over its woodland home just above the trees with steady beat of wings, then a short glide. It usually does not live in the same woods with competitive Cooper's" and both -are capable of mating before shedding immature feathers. Mumford and Keller [12, p.72] have observed that the sharp-shinned hawk's habits are similar to those of the larger Cooper's hawk, in that it spends considerable time perching quietly in dense cover watching for small birds on which it preys. The calls of each are also similar, the Cooper's hawk calling "kek-kek-kek", the sharp-shinned hawk calling "kew-kew-kew". The main morphological difference is in size, the Cooper's being 39.5 cm. long and the sharp-shinned 26.5 cm. long. The slightly forked tail of the sharp-shinned contrasts with the slightly rounded tail of the Cooper's. However, there is significant variation in size within each kind. "A large female sharp-shinned is about the same size as a small male Cooper's hawk." [7, p.105]. Furthermore, the closely related Eurasian sparrow hawk *(A. nisus)* is intermediate in size, ranging from 28 cm. to 38 cm. in length. It is also intermediate in its call, sometimes calling "kek-kek" and at other times "kew-kew-kew [8, p.368]. Both Cooper's and sharp-shinned occasionally swoop down on unprotected chickens. These are the true "chicken hawks," although they also consume large quantities of vermin and insects. They have been victims of much of the farmers' determined shooting of the birds, but they are largely beneficial to us in their habits.

The sharp-shinned and the European sparrow hawk share many similar features. They have essentially the same markings and plumage coloration.We have indicated also that the size of the European sparrow hawk is intermediate between the sizes of the sharp-shinned and Cooper's hawks, and that the European's call utilizes that of both the American hawks. Johnsgard [10, pp.168-169] has drawn many parallels between the sharp-shinned and the European sparrow hawk: e.g., the similar short duration of fledgling/nesting period. Both are capable of breeding while the plumage is still immature in some Cases (18% in male; 15% in female). He concludes that the European counterpart is very closely related to the sharp-shin [10, p.167]. Harwood [9, p.129] likewise concludes that the two are close cousins.

The Cooper's hawk and European sparrow hawk also have striking similarities. The final weaning period is short, due to sudden termination of feeding privilege [10, p.72]. Like the sharp-shin it shares virtually the same markings and color of plumage with the European sparrow hawk. The same is true in their having similar calls, early cessation of fledgling state, and early breeding [10, p.72].

It is apparent that these birds are so similar that they should probably be considered as variants within the same kind. Brown and Amadon conclude that these birds, along with Gundlach's hawk in Cuba *(A. gundlachi)* "belong to the same super species" [2, p. 175], which in this case would render them circumboreal in distribution. A case could be made also for the close relationship of these hawks with the goshawk, which also could be recognized as one of the same kind.

Thus far we find no evidence of interbreeding among these three types, either from field observations or breeding experiments. However, the concept of nonviability being the most dependable factor in separating two organisms into separate species is now questioned by many biologists [4, p.111]. For an example, the leopard frog *(Rana pipiens)* interbreeds with *Rana palustris* in New Hampshire, but produces defective intraspecific offspring in distant states and none with southern Florida frogs. *R. pipiens* from Costa Rica highlands produces fertile offspring with those in New Hampshire, but not with those in Florida! Evolutionists claim that the Northern and Florida frogs are different species.

However, it is axiomatic that if A equals B, and B equals C, A must be equal to C, as seen in the rules of geometry. Further, there is no sharp line that can be drawn in this series to differentiate geographically adjacent races from one another anywhere along the line. Scherer [16, p.1,3] states that the biospecies concept based on fertilization is not as objective as its proponents claim, and that there are insufficient data for wide application of its claims. The taxonomist and paleontologist must depend on morphological similarities for classification, "for the fossil record is almost nowhere sufficient for the direct application of species-delimiting criteria." However, he uses the broader term "basic type" (similar to our use of "baramin" as the original created kind). The use of the term species for variants within each kind can be arbitrary and based on relatively slight variations. He notes also the differences in any tendency for interspecific hybrids: e.g., it is low in the Accipetrinae/Buteonidae (hawks and buteos) and frequent in the Anatidae (waterfowl). This method of dividing species promoted by Mayr, et al. is therefore a very controversial one.

Buteos

The rough-legged hawk *(Buteo lagopes)*, the rough-legged buzzard of Europe, has a widespread circumboreal distribution. The red-tailed hawk *(Buteo jamaicensis)* is considered by some to be identical to the red-tailed buzzard of South America. Grzimek [8, p.369] states that "the red-tailed buzzard is hardly distinguishable from the light phase of the red-tailed hawk. In winter it wanders as far as Guiana, where it meets red-tailed hawks there."

Circuses

The marsh hawk or harder *(Circus cyaneus)* which occurs in most of North America is identical to the hen harder of Eurasia. They are slender with slim, slightly angled wings, long tails and long bodies, and are circumboreal.

THE FALCONS AND KITES

These birds rightly are associated with speed and deftness of flight. They have long, pointed wings, and long tails. Most famous of these is the peregrine falcon *(Falco peregrinus)*, which is endangered over much of its wide range. Recently it has been making a comeback through the efforts of dedicated conservationists. A World Peregrine Center has been established at Boise, Idaho for this purpose. In recent years it has begun to nest on the high ledges of buildings in large cities, where feral pigeons provide a large part of its diet. It occurs in Northern U.S. and Canada, Greenland, Eurasia, Africa, South Sea Islands, Australia and Tasmania. Brown and Amadon [2, p.24] state: "that it probably occupies a larger portion of the land surface of the globe ... than does any other bird," and is thus classified as cosmopolitan. A very large falcon, the gyrfalcon *(F. rusticolus)* occurs in the arctic and is paler than the peregrine falcon and does not have its "moustaches." It is circumpolar.

The pigeon hawk *(F. columbarius)*, the merlin of Europe, is known as the fastest bird in flight. It is circumboreal in distribution.

The American kestrel or sparrow hawk *(F. sparverius)* shares many features with the Eurasian kestrel (F. tinnunculus). In the same size range and configuration, it has a similar banded tail, hovering flight, and earthward plunge to catch its prey. The tail, however, is rufous (reddish) in the American race, and gray in the Eurasian. If they are recognized as the same species, they would be circumboreal.

The white-tailed kite *(Elanus leucurus)* is considered equivalent to the European black-winged kite. Both have white tail and breast, black shoulders, and red eyes [13, p.66; 15, p.62]. Brown and Amadon [2, p.24] claim that these, with such races as *E. scriptus* "comprise a cosmopolitan distribution."

THE OWLS

Many of the owls have a wide distribution. The largest owl in North America is the great grey owl *(Strix nebulosa)*, whose deep booming "hu-hu-hoo" can be heard at repeated intervals throughout the northern forests in both North America and Eurasia. It has large eye discs and grey horizontal stripes. Its distribution is circumpolar.

The beautiful snowy owl *(Nyctea scandiaca)* is also large and has yellow eyes. It can hunt during the day. It nests in the open on a slight elevation in the tundra where it can scrutinize the countryside. When its food supply runs low, it migrates to the northern United States. It is circumpolar in distribution.

Several medium-sized owls likewise are distributed over a large area. The boreal owl *(Aegolius funereus)* is called Richardson's or Tangmalm's owl in Eurasia. It nests in coniferous forests and mountains and is circumboreal. The northern hawk owl *(Sumia ulula)* ranges across northern North America and Eurasia. It is circumpolar/circumboreal in location. The short-eared owl *(Asio flammeus)* has scarcely any ear tufts. It sometimes hunts by day. It is circumpolar but can also be found in South America and the Oceanic Islands. The long-eared owl *(Asio otus)* is circumpolar/circumboreal. The pygmy owl *(Glaucidium gnoma)* occurs in the Western United States and Northern Eurasia and is thus transoceanic. Likewise transoceanic are the burrowing owl, saw-whet owl, ferruginous owl, barred owl, and screech owl.

The barn owl *(Tyto alba)* belongs to a different family (Tytonidae) than the owls mentioned above (Strigidae). The eye or facial discs are extremely large. It is an excellent mouser and appears almost white when seen from below. It is the farmer's friend and should not be shot under any circumstances. It is becoming endangered in some areas but is cosmopolitan. Brown and Amadon [2, p.29] indicate that it has the greatest range of any bird, including also many Polynesian islands.

In several instances owls that are now considered separate species eventually may be considered the same. The Eurasian tawny owl *(Strix aluco)* is similar to the Spotted owl *(Strix occidentalis)* in western United States. It also resembles the barred owl *(Strix varia)* which has a similar call: "hoo-hoo-hoo-hoo-hoo-hoo-aw." It is thus a potential circumboreal kind or baramin.

In plumage and size the Eurasian scops owl *(Otus scops)* is very similar to our screech owl *(O. asio)*, although their respective calls are not quite the same. Together they also would be a candidate for circumboreal status.

Several ornithologists call attention to the similarity between the eagle owl *(Bubo bubo)* of Eurasia and the American great horned owl *(Bubo virginianus)*. The main difference appears to be in size; the former averaging about 12.5 cm. taller. They both have prominent ears, streaked breast, white throat patch and a mean disposition. (Perhaps this is the origin of the expression, "Mad as a hoot owl.")

CONCLUSION

Of 36 recognized species of eagles, hawks and owls in North America, excluding hawks and owls along the Mexican border, 5 are circumpolar, 3 are circumboreal, 3 are circumpolar/circumboreal, 4 are cosmopolitan, and 4 are transoceanic. Those with at least transoceanic distribution or more total 19, or 52% of the total, which is significant. Taking the concept of grouping virtually identical or very closely parallel variants within a kind or baramin, the total number of kinds would be 33. Of these, 5 are circumpolar, 10 are circumboreal, 3 are circumpolar/circumboreal, 4 are cosmopolitan and 4 are transoceanic. Those with at least transoceanic distribution or more total 27 or 75% of the total, a most impressive figure.

Four other possible baramins are:

(1)   American and African swallow-tailed kites.
(2)   Red-tailed hawk and long legged buzzard.
(3)   Red shouldered hawk and European buzzard.
(4)   Mississippi and black kites.

If all were accepted, this would raise the total that are at least transoceanic to 86%. We recognize different races within presently recognized species, as well as those with different baramins, but in our observation they are much more similar in structure, habits, and even dietary preferences, than the races within the recognized species of *Homo sapiens*. These species and baramins mentioned demonstrate wide distribution, rather than isolation which figures so strongly in the arguments of evolutionists. Their stability of species argues for a young earth and recent intercontinental migration, with no significant evolutionary change.

REFERENCES

References Cited

[1]   O.L. Austin, *Birds of the World,* 1962, The Hamlyn Pubi. Group, Ltd., London

[2]   L.H. Brown and D. Amadon, *Eagles, Hawks and Falcons of the World,* (2 Vol.) 1968, Hamlyn Publ. Group, Ltd., Feltham, Middlesex, England

[3]   L.D. Brown and K. Newman, *The Birds of Africa,* Vol. 2, 1982, Academic Press, London, England

[4]   W.L. Bullock, **Systematics and Speciation,** *Evolution and Christian Thought Today,* (R.L. Mixter, Ed.) 1970, p.111-115, Wm. B. Erdmans, Grand Rapids, MI

[5]   G.R. Culp, **The Geographical Distribution of Plants and Animals,** *Creation Research Society Quarterly, 1988,* 22:182, Terre Haute, IN

[6]   H. Frieling, *Vas Fliegt denn da?* 1985, W. Keller and Co., Stuttgart (Germany)

[7]   W.E. Godfrey, *The Birds of Canada,* 1966, National Museum of Canada Bulletin 203, Biology Series #73, Ottawa

[8]   B. Grzimek, *Grzimek's Animal Life Encyclopedia (1* 3 Vol.), 1970, Van Nostrand, Rheinhold, New York

[9]   M. Harwood, *The View from Hawk Mountain,* 1978, Chas. Scribner's Sons, N.Y.

[10]   P.A. Johnsgard, *Hawks, Eagles, and Falcons in North America,* 1990, Smithsonian Inst. Press, Washington, D.C.

[11]   J. Love, *Return of the Sea Eagle,* 1983, Cambridge Univ. Press, Cambridge, England

[12]   R.E. Mumford and C. Keller, *Birds of Indiana,* 1984, Indiana Univ. Press, Bloomington, IN

[13]   R.T. Peterson, *A Field Guide to the Eastern Birds,* 1980, Houghton Mifflin Co., Boston

[14]   R.T. Peterson and J. Fisher, *Wild America,* 1955, Weathervane Books, N.Y.

[15]   R.T. Peterson, G. Mountfort, and P.A.D. Hollum, *A Field Guide to the Birds of Britain and Europe, 1988*

[16]   Siegfried Scherer (Ed.), **Basic Types of Life,** *Studium Integrale, 1993,* Pascal-Verlag, Berlin

[17]   G.G. Simpson, *Splendid Isolation,* 1980, Yale University Press, New Haven, CT

[18]   J. R. Terres, *The Audubon Society Book of North American Birds, 1982,* Wings Books, A. Knopf, New York

Other Sources Consulted

[19]   D. Brown, *Wilderness Europe,* 1976, Time Life Internat., Amsterdam, (Nederland)

[20]   L.K. Curry, *Europe, A Natural History,* 1964, Random House, New York

[21]   H. Garms, The Natural History of Europe, 1962, Paul Hamlyn, London

[22]   M.L. Grossner and J. Hamlet, *Birds of Prey of the World, 1964,* C.N. Potter, Inc., N.Y.

[23]   P.A.D. Hollum, *The Popular Handbook of British Birds,* 1988, H. & G. Witherly, Ltd., London

[24]   Z. Ji, *The Natural History of China,* 1990, McGraw-Hill Book Co., N.Y.

[25]   A. Kynstautas, *The Natural History of the U. S. S. R.,* 1 987, Centu ry Hutchinson, Ltd., London

[26]   J. and K. McKinnon, *Animals of Asia,* 1974, Holt, Rhinehart, and Winston, N. Y.

[27]   G. Moon, *The Birds Around Us,* 1979, William Heinemann, Ltd., Aukland, N.Z.

[28]   R. and S. Olendorrf, *An Extensive Bibliography on Falconty, Eagles, Hawks, Falcons,* 1968, Oregon State Univ., Corvallis, OR

[29]   C.S. Robbins, B. Braun, and H. Zim, *Birds of North America,* 1996, Golden Press N.Y.

[30]   Ian Wallace, *Birds of Prey of Britain and Europe,* 1983, Oxford Univ. Press, Oxford

[31]   J. Wattel, *Geographic Differentiation in the Genus Accipiter,* 1973, Published by Nuttall Ornithological Club 13:1-231

FIGURES

Figure 1. *The Bald Eagle, one of the fish Eagles comprising a kind or baramin.*

Figure 2. *The Barred owl, one of a circumboreal kind or baramin.*

DISTRIBUTION OF SUPERNOVA REMNANTS IN THE GALAXY

KEITH DAVIES, B.S.
55 BRIMWOOD BLVD #49
SCARBOROUGH, ONTARIO
CANADA M1V 1E4

KEY WORDS

SUPERNOVA; SUPERNOVA REMNANTS.

ABSTRACT

The number of Supernova Remnants (SNRs) observeable in the Galaxy is consistent with the number expected to be formed in a Universe that is 7,000 years old. The resulting problem of the "missing Supernova Remnants" is well known and is recognized by astronomers who work in this field.

INTRODUCTION

Supernova Remnants in our own Galaxy and in nearby galaxies are theoretically observable for over one million years before they merge into the inter-stellar background. This theoretical lifespan of over one million years makes a study of the age of SNRs particularly useful for a comparison between a YOUNG Universe Scenario and an OLD Universe Scenario. Since the 'rate of production' of SNRs is now reasonably well determined as being about one every 25 years in the Galaxy, there should be no more than about 280 galactic SNRs if the Universe is only 7,000 years old.

WHAT IS A SUPERNOVA REMNANT?

Strictly speaking, there are a variety of objects that could be described as being remnants of the huge cataclysmic event that we call a Supernova. We know, for example, that pulsars, neutron stars and perhaps black holes, can be formed. However, the term "Supernova Remnant," or SNR, is always taken to refer to the huge cloud of expanding stellar debris that hurtles outwards from the original explosion point at an initial velocity of upwards of 7,000 km.s^{-1} There are, in general, two main types of SNRs, the 'filled centre' type and the 'shell' type of which the Crab Nebula is a well-known example. The filled centre type of SNR is often called a plerion and is powered partly by the pulsar that energizes its central volume. Plerions comprise about 4% of observed SNRs. It is believed that plerions exhibit some of the features of shell-type when the plerions reach their later stages when they are no longer 'powered' by their central pulsar. (Ref: Lozinskaya [14]) The shell type comprise those objects distinguished by the conspicuous boundaries that are formed by the expanding cloud of stellar debris as they cause a 'snow-plow' effect through the inter-stellar medium (I.S.M.).

Most SNRs that are formed in our Galaxy are initially hidden from our view by inter-stellar dust. These dust particles are of a size that is comparable to the wave-length of visible light and so the dust strongly interferes with our observations. (Ref Zelik [22]) However, as the SNR expands it will start to produce very energetic synchrotron radiation at radio wave-lengths. Photons of these very long wave-lengths are not effected by the inter-stellar dust and most of the galactic SNRs then become easily observable at radio wave-lengths as a result of their huge energies. However, when we look at nearby galaxies such as the large Magellanic cloud and the M33 Galaxy, we are looking outwards from the plane of our Galaxy, and so the problem of the dust particles obscuring our observations at optical wave-lengths does not arise to the same extent. This means that we can readily study SNRs in these nearby galaxies with our optical telescopes as well as radio telescopes. Astronomers have made comprehensive whole-sky surveys of SNRs as well as more detailed studies on individual remnants. Catalogues have been prepared by astronomers working at observatories such as the Molonglo-Parkes in Australia; the Kitt-Peak in Arizona; the Cambridge 5 Km Array in England; the Jodrell-Bank dish in England; the Effelsburg 100m dish in Germany; the Cornell University Arecibo dish in Puerto Rico and the Very Large Array in Socorro in New Mexico. Useful catalogues are those of Green detailing 174 Galactic SNRs (Ref Green [9]) and an earlier catalogue of Milne (Ref Milne [17]).

A great deal of work has been done, particularly in the last 15 years, on analysing the various parameters of size, age, distance and radiative power of these remnants. Theoretical models have been made which trace the evolution of the remnants over the three main stages of their lifetime. Many surveys of distant galaxies have been made to find the value of τ, the average rate of occurence of Supernovae in the various types of galaxies. One of the most striking conclusions of these studies is given by the comments of a team of astronomers writing in a National Research Council hand-book. They stated, in the context of a discussion of the Galactic 'Problems of the Decade', "Where have all the remnants gone?"
(Ref National Research Council [20])

This present study provides an analysis of current research on:

1.   The value of τ, the rate of occurence of Supernovae in the Galaxy.

2.   The energy of an SNR.

3.   Observational limits.

4.   Kinematic and Radiative Models of the life history of SNRs.

5.   The detailed model of Cioffi and McKee.

The resulting data from the above is then used to make a comparison of the expected number of galactic SNRs that should be observeable under the 'Young Universe' model and the 'Old Universe' model.

It should be noted that the SNRs in nearby galaxies such as the LMC and M33 are virtually all the same distance away from us, and so we are seeing them all at the same epoch.

Therefore considerations of the time taken for light to travel to us does not effect the calculations of the statistics for the numerical density of those extra-galactic SNRs. (This subject, however, will not be pursued further in the present paper.)

THE VALUE OF τ, THE GALACTIC RATE
OF OCCURENCE OF SUPERNOVA

Supernova are initially so bright in optical wave-lengths that they can be observed in many other galaxies (as long as we look in directions other than our own Galactic plane.) In 1936 a systematic search for supernovae in other galaxies was begun by Fritz Zwicky (Ref Murdin [19] P43). He used the simple technique of photographing a field of galaxies and then comparing the photograph with a reference set of photographs. By this means he personally logged over 120 Supernova events in other galaxies. More sophisticated techniques are now being adopted through the use of computers that can make comparisons between digitally stored sequential images.

Many hundreds of thousands of galaxies have since been compared in this way in order to obtain good data on the frequencies of SN occurrences in galaxies of different types. Currently the best figures we have for the birth-rates in a galaxy similar to our own indicate one supernova event about every 25 years. (Ref Tamman [21]; Murdin [19] P46). $\therefore \tau_{Galaxy} \approx 25$ years

THE ENERGY OF AN SNR

Initial Energy

The energy contained by an SNR is quite prodigious. The initial source of this energy is the incredibly fast gravitational collapse of the pre-cursor star in about two seconds. This event produces enough neutrinos to power all the stars in our Galaxy for several years (Ref Henbest [10]) and, for a brief time, will shine with the power of 100 billion stars, thus outshining all of the stars in the galaxy that contains it. This is the reason why Supernovae can be observed in distant galaxies and enables us to obtain the value of τ for galaxies of different types.

Clearly a great deal of energy is also imparted to the huge expanding cloud of stellar 'debris.' It is estimated by most theorists that this energy is of the order of 10^{51} ergs (Ref Duric and Seaquist [8]). To give some idea of the amount that this represents, it would be sufficient to power 1,000 stars of the same radiative output as our sun for over 8 million years.

Second Stage Energy

After the relatively short freely-expanding first stage, the SNR enters the long second stage known as the adiabatic or Sedov stage. In this stage it emits ever more strongly at radio frequencies. SNRs are then very prominent objects in all galactic radio surveys as a result of their huge energies. Indeed, if our eyes were sensitive to radio wave-lengths we would be able to see several hundred of these magnificent objects with apparent sizes up to several times the diameter of the moon. Of course, the actual sizes of SNRs can be very large with diameters of old SNRs being theoretically over 300 light years across. This can be compared to our whole Solar System which is only about 8 light hours across.

These huge second stage SNRs radiate mainly at radio wave-lengths but some radiate strongly at X-Ray wave-lengths. It was once a mystery as to how an SNR such as the Crab Nebula could radiate at the very high energy synchroton X-Ray wave-lengths. Synchroton X-Ray photons are emitted by very fast relativistic electrons spiralling in a magnetic field. However, these high energy electrons have a half-life of only 2 or 3 years as given by the formula.

$t = 6 \times 10^{11} B_{\perp}^{-3/2} \nu^{-1/2}$ secs (Ref Manchester [16])
where $B_{\perp} \approx 6 \times 10^{-4}$ gauss is the component of the magnetic field perpendicular to the electron velocity and ν is the frequency $\approx 10^{18}$ Hz for X-Ray emission.

Since the Crab SNR is now 940 years old, the initial energy that produced the X-Ray Radiation would have long since been exhausted. It is thus clear that an on-going process must be powering the Crab SNR in addition to the kinetic energy it was initially given. This on-going energy source is now known to be the Crab pulsar which is situated at the centre of the Crab SNR. The pulsar is losing kinetic rotational energy at the rate of 5×10^{38} ergs s^{-1} which is almost exactly the rate required to keep the Crab radiating at its X-Ray level.

However, most SNRs do not rely on pulsars as their main source of radiative energy. The radiative energy of most second-stage SNRs is the synchroton radiation at radio wave-lengths again caused by electrons travelling in a helix around the extremely long-lived magnetic field of the SNR. The lifetime of these electrons is, however, much longer than that of those emitting X-Rays. Using the formula above, the lifetime of electrons emitting at the 1 GHz level is 31,000 years and at the 10^{8}Hz level is 170,000 years. This is one indication as to why the second-stage SNRs can radiate so strongly and for such a long time.

The total radiative energy expended per second in this second stage is of the order of 10^{37} ergs s^{-1} (Ref Cioffi and McKee [5]) and it will be shown that most galactic SNRs are easily observeable at this radiative level. At a rate of production of 10^{37} ergs it would take over 3 million years for just half of the initial energy of the SNR to be depleted - and this does not take into consideration any additional injection of energy sources such as that supplied by pulsars to the central core.

Third Stage Energy

In the second stage, the SNR loses very little thermal energy. However, when it enters the third and final stage, thermal radiation predominates. This is known as the isothermal stage and is theorized to last about one to six million years (Ref Ilovaiski and Lequeux [12] P.350). At the end of this stage the SNR is theorized to come to the end of its life-span when it either reaches equilibrium with the ambient pressure at a diameter of $D_e = 560$ parsec (pc) or collides with similar SNRs (Ref McKee and Ostriker [11]) at a diameter of $D_{ov} = 418$pc (One parsec = 3.2616 light years).

OBSERVATIONAL SELECTION EFFECTS

There are three main effects that limit our observation of SNRs at radio wave-lengths.

The first is related to the intensity of the flux density S (measured in Janskies), received from an individual SNR. (1 Jansky (J_y) = 10^{-26} Wm^{-2} Hz^{-1}) The flux density received is dependent upon the absolute Surface Brightness Σ of the SNR and also the distance d to the SNR. (Σ is measured in Wm^{-2} Hz^{-1} Sr^{-1}) The intensity falls off with the inverse square law and SNRs will not be observeable if they are so far away that their radio flux density falls off to a value which is below that at which background confusion sets in. Surveys commonly give the lowest value of S that is applicable to that particular survey. For example, the pencil-beam survey undertaken by Caswell (Ref Caswell [3]) was said to give a uniform coverage of sources greater than 3 Jy over its fairly limited region of the galactic plane.

The second and third observational limitation involve the difficulties of observing very small or extremely large SNRs respectively. These three effects are important for the conclusions of this paper and are detailed below.

1.   Flux Density Observational Limitation

Ilovaisky and Lequeux (1972, [11] P.174) claim that their table of Galactic SNRs is almost complete for all SNRs with flux densities greater than 10 Jansky.

Other surveys claim an even lower flux density limit. However, the 10Jy limit will be used in this section. This flux density limit can now be related to the Diameter (D), the Surface Brightness (Σ) and the distance of the SNR from the observer (d) as follows:

$$\Sigma_{1GHz} = 1.19 \times 10^{-19} \times S \times \theta^{-2} \qquad (1)$$

This equation is a standard astrophysical formula that relates the surface brightness to S, the flux density and the angle θ, in minutes of arc, that the SNR subtends at the observer.

$$\frac{D}{1000d} = \frac{\theta\pi}{180 \times 60} \qquad (2)$$

This is a straightforward trigonometric relationship corrected to the units I am using for D, d and θ (p.c's, kpcs and minutes of arc)

$$\Sigma = 4 \times 10^{-15} D^{-3.5} \qquad (3)$$

This is a theoretical relationship obtained by Duric and Sequist [8] They claim that this relationship agrees very well with the observed data.

$$S \geq 10 \, J_y \qquad (4)$$

These four equations are combined to give the following boundary $D_{min\,s} = 1160 \times d^{-4/3}$ which is plotted on the graph (Fig.1). This gives the minimum value of
The diameter of an SNR that is observeable at a distance of d, using the $S \geq 10Jy$ observational limitation.

2. $\theta < 2'$ Small SNR Observational Limitation

This is an observational limiting effect for very small and young SNRs particularly as it effected the Molonglo-Parkes whole sky radio survey (Ref Ilovaisky and Lequeux 1972 [11] P175).

By using the relationship $\frac{D}{1,000d} = \frac{\theta\pi}{180 \times 60}$ where D, d, and θ are in pc, kpc,
and minutes of arc respectively, we obtain $D_{min\theta} = .58d$ which gives the minimum 'D' value of a galactic SNR that is observeable to us at a distance of dkpc under the $\theta < 2'$ limitation.

3. $\theta > 5°$ Large SNR Observational Limit

Several authors refer to this effect which applies to those near-by SNRs which have a very large angular extent (e.g. Ilovaisky and Lequeux [11] P179 and Caswell [3]) Caswell states that remnants could escape detection "if they are close-by and have a large angular extent"

Ilovaisky and Lequeux (op cit) quantify the above as a "practical upper limit of about 5° diameter above which the source, unless strikingly symmetrical, would not be distinguishable from the galactic background."

Substitution in the standard trigonometric relationship of paragraph 2 above gives $D_{max\theta} = 87d$ which is also plotted on the D-d plane.

This relationship $D_{max\theta} = 87d$ provides the maximum value of D for an SNR to be observeable at a distance d under this $\theta > 5°$ observation limit.

These three limiting relationships are plotted on the D-d plane together with those 76 SNRs which have published values for d (Fig.2). These values were obtained from the catalogues of Green [9] and Ilovaisky and Lequeux [11]. The resulting plot clearly shows two striking features.

First the values of the observed SNRs fall within the three limiting effects.

Second there is a very clear 'short-fall' of older SNRs with diameters between 60pcs and 260pcs. It should also be noted that the 'D' axis is logarithmic and therefore, the short-fall of large SNRs is actually far more than is immediately apparent when viewing the plot.

The three relationships for $D_{mins\ S}$, $D_{min\ \theta}$, and $D_{max\ \theta}$ are all given as a function of d and can be used to calculate the percentage of galactic SNRs that should be observeable between any particular range of values of D (say D_1 to D_2). This important percentage value can be obtained directly from the graph (Fig.1) or can be evaluated from the various areas of (Fig.1) by simple integration. It should be noted when performing this calculation that the distance from the earth to the furthest extreme of the Galactic disc is $\approx$ 25 kpc. The range of 'd' is therefore taken as being from 0 - 25 kpc in order to encompass the whole disc of the Galaxy. Percentage results, evaluated as above, are given in the next section for each of the three main stages of the life-history of a standard SNR.

MODELS OF THE KINEMATIC AND RADIATIVE HISTORY
OF A TYPICAL 'SHELL-TYPE' SNR.

The evolutionary track over time of a typical 'shell-type' SNR has been modelled by a number of authors (e.g. Duric and Seaquist [8]; Ilovaisky and Lequeux Paper I [11]; Cox [6]; Chevalier [2]; McKee and Ostriker [18].) These models have been progressively refined to a high level of sophistication and confidence. To give one example, the onset of the second stage, or the 'blast-wave' stage, has been variously given as occuring at any time from about 60 years to about 600 years after the initial explosion. Recently the researchers Band and Liang (Ref Band and Liang [1] P69) at the Livermore National Laboratory, used a Cray supercomputer to complete several numerical simulations of this transition phase. The interactions involved during this relatively brief period are just too complex to allow for a concise and accurate Mathematical analysis. The numerical simulations, however, showed that the onset of the shock wave for a 'standard' SNR occurs at about 317 years. (A 'standard' SNR is taken by most authors as having an initial energy totalling 10^{51} ergs and as expanding into the I.S.M. with an ambient gas density $\rho = 10^{-24}$ gm. cm^{-3})

For the purpose of this paper, it is not necessary to detail all of the above models since they give broadly similar dynamic and radiative life-history tracks for a standard SNR. We will follow the detailed model of Cioffi and McKee of the University of California, Berkeley, for their accurate treatment of the important Second and Third stages. Cioffi and McKee claim to have achieved a relatively simple expression for accurate kinematics of SNR expansion and they imply an accuracy of $\leq$5% for the overall kinematics.

DETAILED KINEMATIC MODELS

First Stage of Expansion

Using a Cray computer, Band and Liang performed numerical simulations of the initial expansion of a supernova into the surrounding medium and followed the expansion towards the adiabatic blast wave stage (stage 2). They assume the expansion of a 1.4M star with initial expansion energy of 10^{51} ergs and expanding into a medium of $\rho = 10^{-24}$ gr cm^{-3} (Ref Band and Liang [1] P71). Other initial assumptions result in, for example, a range of sizes of SNRs of a given age scattered about the 'mean' of the standard SNR. However, this would not effect the overall numerical range of values of D that is being discussed in this paper. (The value of τ is by far the most important determining factor for the numerical density of galactic SNRs and this value is independent of the values of these initial assumptions.)

The results of this simulation showed that the blast wave (that signifies the end of the first stage) formed at a time of 317 years. The value of the diameter of the SNR at 317 years can be obtained from the following equation (after Duric and Seaquist (1983)

$$D(t) = 2.3\ E_o^{1/5}\ t^{2/5}\ /\rho_o$$

where E_o is the energy input from the explosion = 10^{51} ergs and ρ_o is the ambient gas density = 10^{-24}g. cm^{-3}
This gives $D_{317\ yrs}$ = 7 pc

It is now very easy to calculate the total number of Stage One SNRs that should be extant in the Galaxy. τ for the Galaxy $\approx$ 25 years, therefore there should be $\approx$ 12 First Stage SNRs.

Using the observational limitation formulae obtained in the last section, the actual number that should be observed will be 19% of 12 $\approx$ 2 observeable SNRs.

In Summary:

Total # of First Stage SNRs expected to be observed under an 'Old Universe' Scenario ≈ 2

Total # of First Stage SNRs expected to be observed under a 'Young Universe' Scenario ≈ 2

Actual # of First Stage SNRs observed with a diameter range from 0 - 7pcs ≈ 5

Second Stage of Expansion

A kinematic model for the evolution of an SNR was developed by D.F. Cioffi and C.F. McKee of the University of California, Berkeley (Ref Cioffi and McKee [5] P435.) They model the Second Stage after the classic Sedov-Taylor solution together with a 'pressure driven snow-plow' solution and with a cooling function $\propto T^2$. The authors claim that a comparison between their analytical model and a numerical solution agrees to within 20% as long as $t \leq 20t_{pds}$, where t_{pds} is the onset of the 'pressure driven snow-plow' which is calculated as being 50,000 years. This means that they claim that level of accuracy up to an SNR age of at least 1,000,000 yrs.

They found that the total luminosity of the SNR actually increases in value from about 10^{36} ergs s^{-1} at a theoretical age of 10,000 years up to about 1.9×10^{38} ergs s^{-1} at a theoretical age of 120,000 years. This increase in overall luminosity, of course, will result in the SNRs maintaining a high level of observeability throughout the Second Stage.

The diameter of the SNRs over this period of time will increase from 7pc to 104 according to the following expression of Cioffi and McKee

$$D = 14.0 * [\frac{(E_{51})^{\frac{2}{7}}}{n_0^{\frac{3}{7}} * \zeta_m^{\frac{1}{7}}}] * [\frac{4}{3} * \frac{t}{t_{pds}} - \frac{1}{3}]^{\frac{3}{10}}$$

Using the given values of Cioffi and McKee as follows: E_{51} = initial energy in units of 10^{51} erg. n_0, the hydrogen density of the interstellar medium, = 0.1cm^{-3} and ζ_m, the metallicity = 1 for cosmic abundances.

Note that this relation only applies for values of t after t_{pds}.

At the beginning of the second stage t = 317 yrs and D = 7pc.

At the end of the second stage t = 120,000 yrs and D = 104pc.

Once again using τ ≈ 25 years gives a total number of 4,800 extant, Second Stage galactic SNRs. Of these 47% will be observeable, or 2,256 as calculated by the method of the last section on observational limitations.

In summary:

Total # of Second Stage SNRs expected to be observed under an 'Old Universe' Scenario ≈ 2,256

Total # of Second Stage SNRs expected to be observed under a 7,000 year old Universe with τ=25 ≈ 268

Actual # of Second Stage SNRs observed with a diameter range from 6pc to 106pc ≈ 200

Third Stage of Expansion

Cioffi and McKee assume a $T^{-1/2}$ thermal cooling rate for their Third Stage model.

They find that the Third Stage starts at a theoretical age of 120,000 years with a diameter of 104pc and a total luminosity of 1.9×10^{38} erg s^{-1}. The third stage then continues for 1,000,000 years at which time the luminosity has dropped to 6×10^{36} erg s^{-1} when the diameter is 200pc.

Once again, using τ ≈ 25 years, we would expect a total of 35,200 Third Stage SNRs to be extant in the Galaxy of which approx 14.3% or 5,033 should be observeable.

In summary:

Total # of Third Stage SNRs expected to be observed under an 'Old Universe' Scenario $\approx$ 5,033

Total # of Third Stage SNRs expected to be observed under a '7,000 year old Universe' Scenario $\approx$ 0

Actual # of Third Stage SNRs observed with a diameter range from 104pc to 200pc $\approx$ 0

CONCLUSION

A Young Universe Model provides a very different prediction from an Old Universe Model as to the expected number of observeable SNRs and their range of diameters.

A Young Universe Model fits the data. There is a short fall, however, of over 7,000 galactic SNRs based upon the 'Old Universe Model.' A number of astronomers, in the context of trying to find solutions to the short-fall, have commented on the situation as follows:

"Major questions about these objects that should be addressed in the coming decade are: Where have all the remnants gone?". . . . .
. . . . National Research Council Astronomy Survey Committee
Ref: National Research Council [20]

"Another surprise is how rare Crab Nebula type SNRs are". . . . .
. . . . .Dr Malcolm Longair, Royal Observatory, U.K.
Ref: The New Physics

"Why have the large number of expected remnants not been detected?". . .
. . . . Clark and Caswell
Ref: Clark and Caswell [4]

"The mystery of the missing remnants". . . . .
. . . . Clark and Caswell
Ref: Clark and Caswell [4]

"There are about 340 SNRs in the L.M.C. which lie above the limit of detection of the Mills Cross (radio-telescope)...these SNRs should also be visible". . . . . Matthewson and Clarke
Ref Matthewson and Clarke [15]
(The above comment was made based upon the <u>expectation</u> of the number
of SNRs that <u>should</u> be observeable under an 'Old Universe' model. The survey actually found a total of 9 instead of the 340 that were expected)

"The final example is the SNR population of the Large Magellanic Cloud. The observations have caused considerable surprise and loss of confidence". . . . .
. . . . . Dr D. Cox
Ref: Cox [7]

Since the time of the above two quotes, more sensitive surveys have discovered a further 20 SNRs in the L.M.C. Since the L.M.C. is approximately 1/10 the size of the Galaxy, then $\tau_{LMC} \approx$ 250. Therefore, the Creationist Model would provide for a total of 24 SNRs in the LMC which again fits the data.

BIBLIOGRAPHY

[1]   Band and Liang, **Supernova Remnants and the Interstellar Medium** Colloquium Proceedings. Eds. Roger and Landecker, CUP 1988 Pg 69-72.

[2]   Chevalier 1975 Astrophysical Journal 198: 355-359

[3]   Caswell 1970 Astronomy and Astrophysics 7: P59

[4]   Clark and Caswell 1976 Monthly Notices of the Royal Astronomical Society 174: 267

[5]   Cioffi and McKee, Supernova Remnants and the Interstellar Medium Colloquium Proceedings. Eds. Roger and Landecker, CUP 1988 P437

[6]   Cox 1979 Astrophysical Journal 234: 863-875

[7]   Cox 1986 Astrophysical Journal 304: 771-779

[8]   Duric and Seaquist 1986 Astrophysical Journal 301:308-311

[9]   Green 1984 Publication of the Astronomical Society of the Pacific 103: 209-220

[10]   Henbest 1992 New Scientist 23rd February 1992 P.26

[11]   Ilovaisky and Lequeux 1972 Paper I Astronomy and Astrophysics 18: P174, 175

[12]   Ilovaisky and Lequeux 1972 Paper II Astronomy and Astrophysics 20: 347-356

[13]   Katgert and Oort 1967 Bulletin Astronomical Institute, Netherlands 19:239-245

[14]   Lozinskaya 1980 Sov. Astron. 24(4):407-412

[15]   Mattewson and Clarke 1973 Astrophysical Journal 180: 725-738

[16]   Manchester **Pulsars** W.H. Freeman and Company - 1977 P64

[17]   Milne 1970 Aust J. Physics 23: 425-444

[18]   McKee and Ostriker 1977 Astrophysical Journal 218: 148-169

[19]   Murdin 1985 **Supernovae** Cambridge University Press

[20]   National Research Council 1983 **Challenges to Astronomy and Astrophysics** working documents of the Astronomy Survey Committee P166 - Publishers - National Academy Press

[21]   Tamman 1970 Astronomy and Astrophysics 8:458

[22]   Zelic and Gaustad **Astronomy the Cosmic Perspective** - Harper and Row 1983 P322

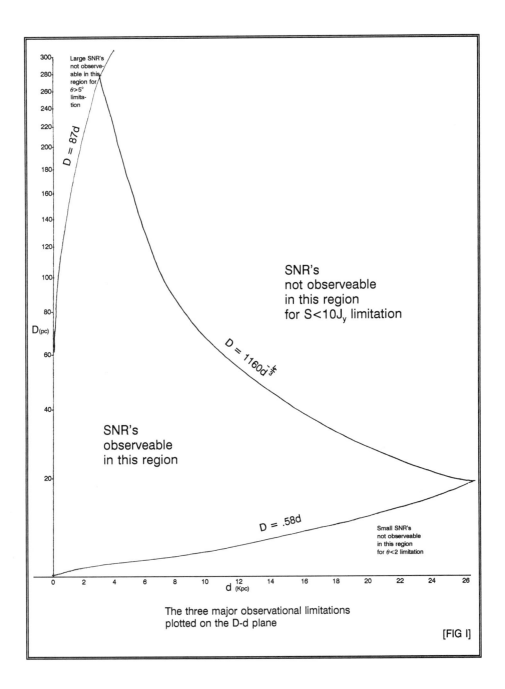

The three major observational limitations
plotted on the D-d plane

[FIG I]

183

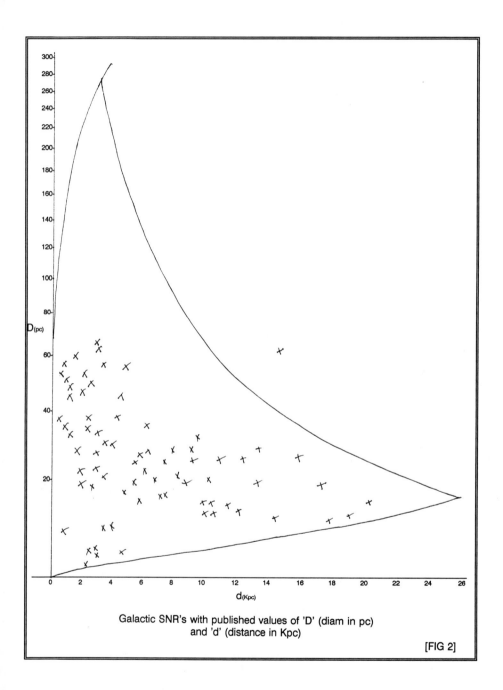

Galactic SNR's with published values of 'D' (diam in pc)
and 'd' (distance in Kpc)

[FIG 2]

A GIANT METEORITE IMPACT AND RAPID CONTINENTAL DRIFT

J. MICHAEL FISCHER, BS
1620 IRA ROAD
EFLAND, NC 27243

KEYWORDS

meteorite, impact, continental drift, plate tectonics

ABSTRACT

An alternative to plate tectonics theory is offered. It is proposed that a giant meteorite impact in what is today the Western Somali Basin sundered the protocontinent, producing the present global arrangement of landmasses and the significant topographic features in the region of the proposed impact.

INTRODUCTION

With the revival in 1961 of Alfred Wegner's ideas on continental drift, observations such as the apparent fit of landmasses together, the presence of mid-ocean ridges, the paths of transform faults across ocean basins, etc. were incorporated into the uniformitarian framework of geologic time. This framework had been devised to support evolution's requirement for vast amounts of time. Extremely slow convection hidden deep within the Earth was depicted as the mechanism that shaped the crust. The observations, the time scale, and the mechanism were combined to form the theory of plate tectonics. The positions of the continents today are presumed to be temporary, only the latest in an endless cycle of collision and division of landmasses, subduction and emergence of plates, that has been repeated in various arrangements over billions of years. Plate tectonics clearly dominates the literature of geology to the degree that it is regarded as foundational.

The creationist time scale requires that continental division occurred much more quickly than in plate tectonics theory. Because today there is no rapid continental drift (on the order of 1000 feet or more per year), creationists must regard continental separation as a fait accompli instead of as an ongoing process.

Oberbeck et al. write that "continental crustal plates are rigid and of high strength; some mechanism is required to initiate continental breakup" [44, p.15]. They have recently proposed that impacts initiated the breakup of Gondwanaland [44]. According to Hill [27], mantle plumes alone provide insufficient stress to initiate breakup. He believes they could only affect existing spreading systems. Yet even after continental breakup has been dealt with, there are questions concerning the driving mechanism of plate tectonics. Artyushkov points out that spots of hot asthenosphere, probably a result of convective upwelling, have been identified, but that this material does not spread far laterally [2]. "Convection can produce large-scale horizontal displacements of lithospheric plates only if convective cells have a large horizontal size: thousands of kilometres or more." "The distribution of inhomogeneities in the asthenosphere indicates that no convective cells of a very large horizontal scale exist in the upper mantle. This means that convective flows are unable to drive the plates for thousands of kilometres" [2, p.175].

This paper offers an alternative to plate tectonics theory: that Earth's protocontinent was rapidly sundered by a single giant meteorite impact in what is now the Western Somali Basin. Because of the scope of the theory, space allows only brief treatment of each supporting element. More detail is available from the references cited.

The Event

According to the proposed model, a giant meteorite of undetermined size, composition, and speed penetrated Earth's atmosphere unscathed [38, p.211] and struck the protocontinent at 8°S 47°E (Figure 1). The meteorite traveled on a northwest (298 degrees) to southeast (118 degrees) azimuth and impacted obliquely, probably at an angle close to 45 degrees. The bolide penetrated the crust to a depth approximately equal to its diameter [38, p.48]. Much of the ejecta was thrown out of the crater to the northeast and southwest, perpendicular to the line of travel, as is typical of oblique impacts. All continental material within the crater and along gouges to the northeast and southwest of the crater were excavated. Impact-generated tektites were carried to the upper atmosphere and beyond by a rising column of hot gas and distributed by high-altitude westerly winds to become the Australasian strewn field. Following excavation, the transient crater collapsed to form a complex crater by acoustic fluidization and "freezing" in the manner of a Bingham fluid. Wilkes Rise (8ºS 47ºE), including its moat and uplifted rim, is the roughly 200-mile-diameter central peak and ring structure, the surrounding basin is the flat interior floor, and what remains of the crater walls on the East African coast are the faulted rim. If correct, it is the largest crater on Earth, over 500 miles across.

The final form of the crater is unique (and partially disguised), however, because the shock wave from the impact overwhelmed the confining crust - first compressing, then shattering it. The amount of compression depended on the level of resistance. A small subduction zone along the Amirante Trench is a remnant of the initial pressure against the relatively narrow strip of land, composed of the Seychelles Bank, India, Australia, and Southeast Asia, which quickly yielded to the shock wave. Initial pressure against the bulk of the southern lobe of the protocontinent, composed of Africa and the Americas, had much larger consequences. The crust under Lake Victoria was downwarped, while the crust on the east and west sides of Lake Victoria was upwarped [45]. The crust fractured along what would become the East African Rift system, the largest such system in the world. Deep fracturing induced volcanism around the impact site: in Madagascar, in the island arc north of Madagascar's current position, along the East Branch of the East African Rift system, and, most dramatically, in Western India. The crust confining the impact was shattered in three places: directly in front of the oblique impact (between India and Madagascar) and northeast and southwest of the crater where ejecta had gouged the crust and thus established a natural break line.

The shock wave propagated in all directions. Africa, Madagascar, and the Seychelles Bank transmitted the pressure through themselves to the Americas, Antarctica, and India respectively, which were propelled directly away from the point of impact. Thus Africa, Madagascar and the Seychelles Bank moved very little and remain near their original positions today. The initial push-off raised low mountains on the east coasts of North and South America and the west coast of India. As has been proposed for long-runout landslides, the movement of the landmasses initiated acoustic fluidization at their bases, reducing friction to near zero and allowing them to glide across the oceanic crust without disturbing their sedimentary sequences. Prior to impact, India, Australia, and Southeast Asia formed the strip of continental crust on the east side of the southern lobe of the protocontinent (revised from [21]). The impact severed this strip where India joined Africa and forced the Horn of Africa westward about 250 miles like the closing of a lobster claw, pinching up crust and raising mountains in Ethiopia. Antarctica was pushed to the south with a counterclockwise spin, separating cleanly from Australia, Madagascar, and South Africa. Antarctica's overlap with southernmost South America began the peeling away of South America from Africa and added a slight clockwise swing to South America's movement which, like North America, was pushed away from Africa by the shock wave. The movement of India, Australia and Southeast Asia to the east, and of the Americas to the west, caused east-west extension throughout the entire region of Eastern and Central Africa and the Western Somali Basin. The East African Rift system and the north-south-aligned fractures in the Western Somali Basin are products of this extension. Southeast Asia was caught between India headed northeast and Australia headed southeast. Southeast Asia continued northeast with India, whose pull redirected Australia to the east, but in the process Australia ripped large pieces off of Southeast Asia. (The area where this happened has been designated as a large oceanic diffuse plate boundary [14]). Rolling slightly counterclockwise as it slid east, Australia peeled away the Malay Peninsula and the islands of Indonesia and the Philippines . A fluid crustal wave, which the Philippine Islands rode for several hundred miles, flowed east-northeast beyond the debris of Southeast Asia until its acoustic energy attenuated to the point where the rock regained its normal strength and "froze", forming the South Honshu Ridge and the Bonin and Mariana Trenches.

Having traveled only a short distance, the collision of India and Southeast Asia with Asia caused tremendous compressional mountain building throughout Asia east of about 70ºE. India penetrated approximately 1250 km into Asia [32] and pulled the Arabian Peninsula off of Africa. Southern India and Indochina were bent eastward by the contact with Asia with such shock that Ceylon separated from India. The collision forced all of Eurasia to rotate counterclockwise, pivoting on a point near 37ºN 75ºE. East Asia moved sharply northward leaving Japan behind, tearing open the Yellow Sea and Sea of Okhotsk, dragging Sakhalin Island and the Kamchatka Peninsula, and, in a "crack the whip" motion, spinning Alaska eastward until it collided with North America which was moving westward. Europe, which had been partially drawn out as North America pulled away from it, was forced south by the rotation of Eurasia. The resulting compression formed mountains in Southern Europe and from Turkey to Pakistan, as well as the Urals. As the Americas and Antarctica glided forward, the leading edge of their fluidized continental material gradually spread out. It eventually reached the point (because of thinning and deceleration) where acoustic energy loss exceeded gain. This led to the solidifying of the leading edge of each landmass and put a brake on forward motion. Compressional mountain building occurred behind the leading edges until each landmass slowed to the point where acoustic fluidization had ceased. Considering the similar distances that North America, South America, Australia and Antarctica travelled, braking in all four was nearly simultaneous. The crustal wave referred to earlier that "froze" south of Japan also flowed beyond Australia and "froze" to form the Tonga and

Kermadec Ridges and Trenches. The turbulence of the northern end of this section of the wave is evident between Papua New Guinea and the Tonga Islands on free air gravity maps [52].

Magma extruded during rapid sea-floor spreading quickly raised the temperature of the ocean waters rushing in to fill the gaps opened between the sundered pieces of the protocontinent. This temperature shock severely stressed the fauna and flora of the oceans [19]. Vast populations of plankton died and sank. The turbulence of in-rushing waters scoured the Western Somali Basin, and slumping from the backwash of impact-induced tsunamis [44] deposited thick sediment on the African margin. During the following months, fallout of iridium and volcanic ash and glass from the atmosphere mixed with sediment settling on the ocean floor. In contrast to the heating of the oceans, the event initiated atmospheric cooling. The injection into the upper atmosphere of particulate matter from the impact and volcanism was an important factor. However, the injection of sulfur dioxide, especially from the Deccan flood basalts, into the upper atmosphere probably had greater long-term significance. Air temperature fell dramatically and remained low for years. Hot moist air rising from the heated oceans fell as snow on the continents, building glaciers and lowering global sea level.

The sweeping landmasses and rushing waters would have reworked ocean floor sediments from the "Jurassic" up. They would subsequently have been redeposited, mixed with volcanic and other impact-related fallout. While the atmospheric and fallout phenomena persisted for months or years, according to this model the sundering of the protocontinent was completed in a matter of hours or days, in stark contrast to the pace of plate tectonics theory.

Centrality

The quality that immediately directs attention to the Western Somali Basin is its unique central position relative to the landmasses that split from the protocontinent. North America, South America, Antarctica, Australia, and India all moved directly away from this point (Figure 3). The directions of movement are clear: in each case a mid-ocean ridge lies behind the landmass, and mountain chains formed by lateral compression lie along the leading edge. In addition, to the northwest is the heart of the extensive East African Rift system, while to the northeast, by the Seychelles Bank, is the place where even plate tectonics advocates propose the massive Deccan flood basalts began to be loosed [42] [33].

Complex Craters

Simple craters form in the familiar bowl shape. On Earth, craters larger than about 2 to 4 kilometers have the characteristics of complex craters: a central peak structure, flat inner floor, and terraced rim, which slumps toward the center (Figure 4) [24]. What begins as a bowl-shaped crater quickly collapses under the force of gravity to form the complex crater. The floor under the transient crater rises, rocks under the center are uplifted, and rocks along the rim slump inward. Why this occurs is the subject of much debate, for it is apparent that the stresses related to crater collapse are far less than the strength of even loose rock debris. Terrace morphology is characteristic of the failure of plastic materials, while the central peak is essentially a hydrodynamic damped harmonic oscillator, similar to the central jet that rises from an impact in water. Yet if it remained fluid within the crater, the end result would be a flat surface. Somehow the rising jet must be suddenly "frozen" [38, p.147].

Acoustic Fluidization

A material with a plastic yield stress that flows as a fluid when applied shear stress exceeds its cohesion is called a Bingham fluid. Once shear stresses fall below its cohesion, the material quickly resolidifies [38, p.149]. Melosh contends that the Bingham fluid model describes the formation of complex craters, and has proposed that acoustic fluidization is the mechanism [38, p.154] [37]. "The basic idea behind acoustic fluidization is that rock debris subject to strong vibrations can flow like a fluid even in the absence of air or water. The vibration is transmitted as a sound wave via rock-to-rock contacts" [38, p.151]. Behind the expanding stress wave generated by the impact follows a region of random vibrations that exceed the overburden pressure. This dense acoustic energy fluidizes the debris within the crater, but is attenuated beyond the vicinity of the crater, confining the flow. Crater collapse ends when the acoustic energy has dissipated below the level of cohesion [38, p.154].

Long-runout Landslides

Avalanches typically fall a certain distance and then slide horizontally less than twice that distance [40]. However, landslides with volumes over about 100,000 cubic meters travel much farther horizontally than would be expected, as if running on a lubricated surface. The longest one measured so far, from the Nevado de Colima volcano in Mexico, ran about 25 times farther than it dropped [54]. Concerning these so-called long-runout landslides two elements are clear: the coefficient of friction (height of drop/length of runout) tends to decrease as the volume of the landslide increases [35], and the rock debris tends to keep its order, indicating a lack of turbulent flow [20]. Melosh [37] suggests that the greatly reduced internal friction in large landslides appears to have much in common with crater collapse, and has proposed that acoustic fluidization is again the active mechanism. In this case, the initial fall generates the friction that produces the acoustic energy density needed to fluidize the base of the landslide. The mass of rock over the basal layer determines both the amount of pressure applied and the degree to which the acoustic energy is contained. The larger the mass, the greater these effects. When the thickness is reduced (through spreading of the flow) to the point where acoustic radiation loss exceeds energy gained, the slide slows and then stops. Stratigraphy is undisturbed because the rocks have remained in contact with each other at all times.

I propose that the giant meteorite impact started the greatest long-runout landslide in Earth history. The shock wave provided the initial push on the sundered landmasses, equivalent to the initial fall of a typical landslide, and the slide continued virtually frictionless due to acoustic fluidization of the basal layers. Fluidization of the leading edges led to their spreading forward and thinning. Thus the point of critical energy loss was reached there first, and the result was braking and compressional mountain building along the leading edges.

Oblique Impacts

Meteorites never impact Earth precisely vertically. In fact, mathematically the most probable angle of impact is 45 degrees. Except in cases where the angle of incidence is very low, oblique impacts produce circular craters and their shock waves propagate in the same way as in vertical impacts, although they are somewhat weaker. Much of the ejecta from oblique impacts are concentrated in a "butterfly" pattern, being blown out to the sides perpendicular to the projectile's line of travel. Impacts with incident angles between 90 and 20 degrees also produce downrange jets containing the projectile and some target material [38, pp.49,101].

Tektites

Tektites are generally rounded, black, silicate glass objects resembling obsidian and range in size from less than a millimeter to chunks weighing several kilograms or more. Analysis of their composition indicates that the parent material was terrestrial sedimentary surface deposits, and that they were formed under conditions of high pressure and extremely brief but intense heating. Therefore most investigators favor a terrestrial impact origin. Areas where tektites of similar composition are found are called strewn fields. Each strewn field is thought to have been produced by a single event. Of four main strewn fields, source craters have been located for two, and an area of probable impact has been indicated for a third (North American strewn field). No source crater has been generally accepted for the Australasian strewn field. It is immense, covering one tenth of the Earth's surface (Figure 5) [22].

Hot vapor plumes rush rapidly up from high-velocity impacts. An impact that formed a large (perhaps 3 km, more likely at least 10 km) diameter crater would produce a column of hot, rising gas that would "blow out" of the upper atmosphere. Tektites within this column would be ballistically launched great distances. This apparently occurred in the cases of the Ries Crater in Germany and the Bosumtwi Crater in Ghana [38, p.212].

I propose that the impact in the Western Somali Basin, which is located on the western edge of what is estimated to be the boundary of the Australasian strewn field, is the source of the tektites in this strewn field, and that they were widely distributed by high altitude westerly winds.

Impact-generated magmatism

Jones [28] concluded that the shock wave from impacts forming craters with diameters larger than 24 km would fracture the crust all the way to the Moho. Magmatism is associated with at least three large terrestrial impact craters. Dressler [15] believes there was impact-triggered volcanism at the Manicouagan Structure in Quebec, and impact-triggered intrusive magmatism at the Sudbury Structure in Ontario. A "collar" of volcanic extrusives partially surrounds the Vredefort Dome impact structure in South Africa [34].

The volume of volcanic extrusives in the Eastern Branch of the East African Rift system, northwest of the proposed impact site, is enormous, estimated to be 500,000 cubic kilometers [29]. Models formulated from recent seismic data postulate a combination of asthenospheric upwarping with regional extension to explain the complex structure of the East African Rift system [23] [31]. Activity began with the uplift of the Kenya Dome (Figure 6), followed by continuous rifting and extrusion [26] (also in some places along the Western Branch [18]). Extension across the rift is estimated to be no more than 10 percent, so that lithospheric thinning is insufficient to account for the extensive magmatic accretion [29].

I propose that shock wave pressure against East Africa not only warped the crust at and around Lake Victoria [45], but simultaneously forced magma upward. The pull of the landmasses away from Africa to the west and east caused the regional extension.

With growing acceptance of the idea that mass extinction followed a large meteorite impact, plate tectonics theorists have tried to incorporate this catastrophe. It has been suggested that large impacts started persistent hotspots beneath them by excavating and fracturing the crust, initiating pressure relief melting and producing flood basalts similar to lunar maria. They have also been said to crack stressed lithosphere, allowing slow continental rifting to begin [1].

It has been proposed that an impact near Bombay unleashed the flood basalts of the Deccan Traps of India. India's position at the time is said to have been east of the Seychelles. The period of extrusion has been whittled down to about one million years, with a main eruptive phase of "only" about 10,000 years. The crater, however, has not been found [42] [13].

In contrast, I propose that India was adjacent to Africa and joined to the Seychelles Bank. The impact in the Western Somali Basin to the southwest rent a deep fracture at the site of a conduit structure detected near Bombay [42]. As with the Eastern Branch of the East African Rift system, shock wave pressure forced an extraordinary volume of magma up through this conduit structure in a short period of time.

The impact also induced volcanism in the Diego Basin at the northern tip of Madagascar and produced the volcanic island arc north of Madagascar (the Comoros to the Farquhar Group). This arc is concentric with the impact site.

Volcanically-induced Ice Age

The eruption of Mount Pinatubo in June 1991 had a strong cooling effect on Earth's atmosphere, the predicted maximum being 0.5 degrees Centigrade in late 1992 with temperatures returning to normal by mid-1995 [39]. Beginning in June 1783 and continuing for eight months, the eruption of the Laki crater row, Iceland, was linked to severe winters in England and the eastern United States. In the U.S., the period from December 1783 to February 1784 had an average temperature 4.8 degrees Centigrade below the 225 year average. The annual mean temperatures of 1784 and 1785 were also well below normal [51].

Volcanoes emitting large amounts of sulfur dioxide into the stratosphere cause cooling of Earth's surface temperature. Whereas volcanic ash falls out of the atmosphere before it can have a significant impact on the climate, sulfur dioxide combines with water and remains for long periods as a haze of sulfuric acid droplets. These sulfuric acid aerosols in the stratosphere absorb incoming solar radiation, warming the upper atmosphere but cooling the lower atmosphere [51].

The Laki eruption produced from 1.3 to 6.3 x 10^7 tons of sulfur dioxide and 12.3 cubic kilometers of lava [51]. By comparison, the sulfur dioxide from Mount St. Helen's was estimated at about 2.2 x 10^5 tons [5]. To a large degree, the ferrous iron (FeO) content determines the solubility of sulfur in basaltic magma [51]. The FeO content of Laki magma is 11.34% [55], Mount St. Helens magma is 4.43 to 4.78% [53], and Deccan Trap lava is 9 to 10% [49]. Considering that the volume of lava erupted at the Deccan Traps may have been over 120,000 times the volume of the Laki eruption (as much as 1,500,000 cubic kilometers [50]), the cooling effect on surface temperatures must have been staggering.

Further study is required to determine the effect of the injection of this quantity of sulfur dioxide into the stratosphere and its duration. However, it appears that the extrusion of the Deccan flood basalts could have been a key factor in initiating an ice age.

REGIONAL OVERVIEW

Only a portion of the Western Somali Basin has been studied. Paleomagnetic surveys (Figure 8) and basement sampling have been spotty. Gravity field maps made from satellite altimeter readings of the surface topography of the oceans provide a good starting picture [52] [3]. In these, the proposed crater's central peak and ring structure can be seen to center on Wilkes Rise (Figure 7).

Wilkes Rise is about 2 km high at its northern and western summits, and about 3 km high on the southern side. The highest points are 1 to 2 km below sea level [10]. It has never been geologically sampled. The moat surrounding it is roughly 200 miles in diameter [9] and contains sediment exceeding depths of 3 km in places [10]. Large amplitude magnetic anomalies are near to, and surround, Wilkes Rise (Figure 8).

The crust in the Western Somali Basin is oceanic, yet the igneous crustal thickness of 5.22 $\pm$ 0.64 km is approximately 20% thinner than what is considered normal [12]. According to Coffin and Rabinowitz [10], a high energy environment persisted there from the Middle Cretaceous through much of the Cenozoic. Intense erosion is evident in layers of the Middle Eocene through the Middle Oligocene, and a major network of canyons and channels is carved into Neogene and Quaternary deposits. A series of perhaps 4 to 6 faults have been detected north-northeast of Wilkes Rise, east of Kenya [46]. Two of these, the Dhow and VLCC, have been described as essentially north-south oriented with their scarps facing east [11].

Near the African margin is the 30 to 120 km wide Davie Ridge (or Davie Fracture Zone), which trends north-south between 19° and 9° South and rises as much as 2300 m above the sea floor. It has a west-facing scarp, apparently produced by a normal fault [41] [47]. Earthquake focal depths of up to 35 km have been observed

189

along it [6]. The Davie Fracture Zone continues north of 9º South, without the prominent ridge, to intersect the coast of Kenya. The entire feature is about 2200 km long [11] [10]. The current regional plate tectonics scenario makes the Davie Fracture Zone a relic transform fault along which Madagascar had moved south. However, Chen and Grimison write that along its entire length (2º to 18º South) "all the large to moderate-sized earthquakes have focal mechanisms of pure normal faulting with NNW trending nodal planes. ...there is no significant component of strike-slip motion" [6, p.142]. Neither has a continuous rift or system of large-scale normal faults developed [6]. There is no evidence today that the Davie Fracture Zone was ever a transform fault.

The East African Rift system has two separate branches, the Western and Eastern rift valleys. It is volcanically and seismically active, and sits upon the East African Plateau, a broad intracontinental swell. The rift valleys are made up of a series of generally asymmetric basins, each about 100 km long [17]. Seismic studies have revealed several characteristics of the system: earthquake focal mechanisms are dominated by normal faulting with horizontally oriented T-axes perpendicular to the strike of the rift valleys, i.e. in a generally east-west direction [6] [30]; the East Branch extends into oceanic lithosphere along the Davie Fracture Zone [25]; and between 10º and 20º South, a diffuse zone of extension, up to 2000 km wide, reaches from the Davie Fracture Zone west through Zambia. The westernmost part of this zone of extension lacks extensive volcanism and rift morphology, yet some of the deepest earthquakes found in Africa, nearly equal to those along the Davie Fracture Zone, have been detected there [25] [6]. Earthquake focal depths in the northern part of the East African Rift system, in the vicinity of the Afar depression in Ethiopia, are shallower than those in the southern part [30]. According to plate tectonics, upwelling along the East African Rift system began the opening of Africa and the formation of a new ocean [7, p.271]. Ebinger states that "no connection between the... Western and Kenya rifts, however, is apparent in structural, morphologic, or seismicity patterns" [17, p. 885]. Grimison and Chen [25] conclude that "a single, narrow plate boundary does not seem to exist between the Nubian and Somalian plates" [25, p.10,449]. The features appear to be expressions of broad regional extension rather than nascent continental separation.

The margins of Kenya and Tanzania are marked by severe faulting and diapirism. Landward of the Davie Fracture Zone are numerous normal faults, downthrown to the east on the Tanzanian margin and to the southeast on the Kenyan margin. The latter are apparently listric. The continental shelf is quite narrow (25 to 50 km wide), with a rather steep continental slope. There was a major sediment slide offshore Somalia and Kenya, supposedly in the mid-Tertiary. The thickness of the sediment exceeds 8 km [10].

Precambrian rocks cover approximately the central two-thirds of Madagascar, with normal faults trending north-northeast near the east coast. Volcanism is most prominent on the northern tip of the island, but narrow strips of Cretaceous volcanics line parts of the coast, primarily in the northwest (Majunga Basin), where the strip is notably concave, and on the east coast. The east coast is strikingly linear and has a narrow coastal plain. A wide band of Phanerozoic sediments covers the west and northwest coasts. These are riddled with normal faults that generally parallel the coastline [4]. The northwestern shelf of Madagascar is distinguished by the normal-fault structure of its outer ridge. A block of sialic crust lies subparallel to the shelf margin, separated from the continental bench by a deep normal-fault depression [36]. Gross sediment thickness on the conjugate margin of Madagascar exceeds 5 km. The shelf is up to 100 km wide [10]. The Mozambique Channel, separating Madagascar from Africa, averages about 400 km in width, but tapers to as little as 250 km. Boast and Nairn [4] believe, based on the geology alone, that if Madagascar moved at all it went east, and not more than 200 km.

Northeast of Madagascar lie the Amirante Arc and Trough. The arc, a 400 km-long series of banks and small islands, is bounded to the west and south by the trough, which is 600 km long and reaches depths of over 5000 m [33]. Though it is far from nonmarine sources of sediment, the trough holds sediment accumulations of over 2 km [10]. The long central portion of the trough is relatively straight and has a steep gravity gradient, while the shallower ends curve toward the east, giving the trough an overall arcuate appearance [48]. A line drawn perpendicular to the central portion of the trough and through its center passes through Wilkes Rise. Even though the Amirante region is aseismic, a reasonable interpretation of the morphology and gravity profiles of the arc and trough is that they result from a brief episode of subduction [33].

Adjacent to the Amirante Arc is the Seychelles Bank, a section of continental crust over 30 km thick. It measures about 400 x 200 km and has a nearly flat top which sits an average of 50 m below sea level. Deep saddles connect it to the Amirante Arc and the Mascarene Plateau, but in all other directions the edges of the bank drop steeply to depths exceeding 3000 m [33]. The sedimentary cover of the Seychelles Bank is up to 500 m thick, with faulted blocks of strata displaced up to 30 m from adjoining blocks [36]. Partial melting below the crust followed by intrusion apparently occurred in the western part of the bank, the end nearest the Western Somali Basin [33].

The Mascarene Plateau is a 2000 km-long arcuate series of banks extending from the Seychelles Bank to Mauritius Island. Like the Seychelles Bank, banks of the Mascarene Plateau are approximately 50 m below water, and are bounded by steep scarps that plunge to depths of over 3000 m [33]. The Chagos-Laccadive Plateau is a similar series of banks that stretches north from the island of Diego Garcia to off the west coast of India. Central portions of both plateaus are covered by carbonate bank and reef deposits up to 2 km thick. Just north of Mauritius Island lies the 450 km-long Rodrigues Ridge. This ridge intersects the Mascarene Plateau at right angles and trends toward the east. At its eastern extremity is Rodrigues Island. All of these plateaus and ridges are built on volcanic rocks [16]. I propose that these features are the product of three phenomena: first, the floor of the Mascarene Plateau region was stretched thin by the exit of India to the northeast, Australia to the east, and Antarctica to the south; second, the shallow magma below this region was forced up by the pressure of the impact, similar to what happened in East Africa; and third, concurring with Norton and Sclater [43], seafloor spreading formed the Chagos-Laccadive Plateau as the mirror image of the Mascarene Plateau.

The Northern Somali Basin is a small oceanic basin that lies between the Horn of Africa and Chain Ridge. The flat basement is one to two kilometers deeper than neighboring basement to the north or southeast. Chain Ridge can be traced south to 2º North [9]. I propose that Chain Ridge marks the original boundary of the Horn of Africa, and that the Northern Somali Basin was formed when the Horn was forced to the west by the impact.

CONCLUSION

Earth is no stranger to meteorite impacts. Approximately 130 terrestrial craters have been found so far [24], and more likely remain undiscovered. Meteorites may have encountered Earth individually or in swarms, as proposed by Clube and Napier [8, p.147-154]. With crater sizes ranging up to 140 km, and perhaps even 200 km, in diameter [24], they must have produced terrifying catastrophic events. Some are likely to have generated persistent climatic effects. Yet none are mentioned in the Bible. If the proposed giant impact caused the "dividing of the Earth" mentioned in Genesis 10:25, as seems appropriate, then it is the exception. This silence is not surprising since reports of meteorite impacts contribute nothing to the revelation of God's purpose. However, if the theory offered in this paper someday supplants plate tectonics theory in the scientific community, it will go a long way toward debunking the uniformitarian timescale and validating the creationist timescale of Earth history; and that will promote more than just good science.

REFERENCES

[1] D. Alt, J. M. Sears, D. W. Hyndman, **Terrestrial Maria: The origins of large basalt plateaus, hotspot tracks and spreading ridges**, Journal of Geology, **96:6**(1988) 647-662.

[2] E. V. Artyushkov, **The forces driving plate motions and compression of the crust in fold belts**, in Composition, Structure and Dynamics of the Lithosphere-Asthenosphere System, K. Fuchs, C. Froidevaux, editors, 1987, American Geophysical Union, Washington, D.C.

[3] G. Balmino, B. Moynot, M. Sarrailh, N. Vales, **Free air gravity anomalies over the oceans from Seasat and GEOS 3 altimeter data**, Eos, Transactions, American Geophysical Union **68:2**(1987) 17-19.

[4] J. Boast, A. E. M. Nairn, **Geology of Madagascar**, in The Ocean Basins and Margins, Volume 6: The Indian Ocean, A. E. M. Nairn, F. Stehli, editors, 1982, Plenum Press, New York.

[5] T. J. Casadevall, D. A. Johnston, D. M. Harris, W. I. Rose, Jr., L. L. Malinconico, R. E. Stoiber, T. J. Bornhorst, S. N. Williams, L. Woodruff, J. M. Thompson, **SO2 emission rates at Mount St. Helens from March 29 through December, 1980**, in U.S. Geological Survey Professional Paper 1250, P.W. Lipman, D. R. Mullineaux, editors, 1981, U.S. Government Printing Office, Washington, D.C.

[6] W.-P. Chen, N. L. Grimison, **Earthquakes associated with diffuse zones of deformation in the oceanic lithosphere: some examples**, Tectonophysics **166**(1989) 133-150.

[7] J. Chorowicz, **Dynamics of the different basin-types in the East African Rift**, Journal of African Earth Sciences **10:1/2**(1990) 271-282.

[8] V. Clube, B. Napier, The Cosmic Winter, 1990, Basil Blackwell Ltd., Oxford.

[9] J. R. Cochran, **Somali Basin, Chain Ridge, and origin of the Northern Somali Basin gravity and geoid low**, Journal of Geophysical Research, **93:B10**(1988) 11,985-12,008.

[10] M. F. Coffin, P. D. Rabinowitz, **Evolution of the conjugate East-African-Madagascan margins and the Western Somali Basin**, Special Paper 226, 1988, The Geological Society of America, Boulder.

[11] M. F. Coffin, P. D. Rabinowitz, **Reconstruction of Madagascar and Africa; evidence from the Davie Fracture Zone and Western Somali Basin**, Journal of Geophysical Research **92:B9**(1987) 9385-9406.

[12] M. F. Coffin, P. D. Rabinowitz, R. E. Houtz, **Crustal structure in the Western Somali Basin**, Geophysical Journal of the Royal Astronomical Society, **86**(1986) 331-369.

[13]   V. Courtillot, J. Besse, D. Vandamme, R. Montigny, J.-J. Jaeger, H. Cappetta, **Deccan flood basalts at the Cretaceous/Tertiary boundary?**, Earth and Planetary Science Letters 80(1986) 361-374.

[14]   C. DeMets, **Current plate motions,** Geophysical Journal International 101(1990) 425-478.

[15]   B. Dressler, **Shock metamorphic features and their zoning and orientation in the Precambrian rocks of the Manicouagan Structure, Quebec, Canada,** Tectonophysics 171(1990) 229-245.

[16]   R. A. Duncan, **The volcanic record of the Reunion hotspot,** in Proceedings of the Ocean Drilling Program, Scientific Results, Volume 115, R. A. Duncan et al, editors, 1990, Ocean Drilling Program, Texas A&M University.

[17]   C. J. Ebinger, **Tectonic development of the western branch of the East African rift system,** Geological Society of America Bulletin 101(1989) 885-903.

[18]   C. J. Ebinger, A. L. Deino, R. E. Drake, A. L. Tesha, **Chronology of volcanism and rift basin propagation: Rungwe volcanic province, East Africa,** Journal of Geophysical Research 94:B11(1989) 15,785-15,803.

[19]   C. Emiliani, E. B. Kraus, E. M. Shoemaker, **Sudden death at the end of the Mesozoic,** Earth and Planetary Science Letters 55(1981) 317-334.

[20]   T. H. Erismann, **Mechanisms of Large Landslides,** Rock Mechanics 12(1979) 15-46.

[21]   J. M. Fischer, **Dividing the Earth,** Creation Research Society Quarterly 28:4(1992) 166-169.

[22]   B. P. Glass, **Tektites and microtektites: key facts and inferences,** Tectonophysics 171(1990) 393-404.

[23]   W. V. Green, U. Achauer, R. P. Meyer, **A three-dimensional seismic image of the crust and upper mantle beneath the Kenya Rift,** Nature 354(1991) 199-203

[24]   A. F. Grieve, **Terrestrial impact: The record in the rocks,** Meteoritics 26(1991) 175-194.

[25]   N. L. Grimison, W. -P. Chen, **Earthquakes in the Davie Ridge-Madagascar region and the southern Nubian-Somalian plate boundary,** Journal of Geophysical Research 93:B9(1988) 10,439-10,450.

[26]   B. D. Hackman, T. J. Charsley, R. M. Key, A. F. Wilkinson, **The development of the East African Rift system in north-central Kenya,** Tectonophysics 184(1990) 189-211.

[27]   R. I. Hill, **Starting plumes and continental break-up,** Earth and Planetary Science Letters 104(1991) 398-416.

[28]   A. G. Jones, **Are impact-generated lower-crustal faults observable?,** Geological Survey of Canada Publication 14386, 1987.

[29]   J. A. Karson, P. C. Curtis, **Tectonic and magmatic processes in the Eastern Branch of the East African Rift and implications for magmatically active continental rifts,** Journal of African Earth Sciences 8:2/3/4(1989) 431-453.

[30]   F. Kebede, O. Kulhanek, **Recent seismicity of the East African Rift system and its implications,** Physics of the Earth and Planetary Interiors 68(1991) 259-273.

[31]   KRISP Working Group, **Large-scale variation in lithospheric structure along and across the Kenya Rift,** Nature 354(1991) 223-227.

[32]   X. Le Pichon, M. Fournier, L. Jolivet, **Kinematics, topography, shortening and extrusion in the India-Eurasia collision,** Tectonics 11:6(1992) 1085-1098.

[33]   Y. Mart, **The tectonic setting of the Seychelles, Mascarene and Amirante Plateaus in the Western Equatorial Indian Ocean,** Marine Geology 79(1988) 261-274.

[34]   J. E. J. Martini, **The nature, distribution and genesis of the coesite and stishovite associated with the pseudotachylite of the Vredefort Dome, South Africa,** Earth and Planetary Science Letters 103(1991) 285-300.

[35] A. S. McEwen, **Mobility of large rock avalanches: Evidence from Valles Marineris, Mars**, <u>Geology</u> **17**(1989) 1111-1114.

[36] V. S. Medvedev, Y. A. Pavlidis, **New geological-geomorphological data on the shelf areas of the Seychelles Islands and Madagascar**, <u>Oceanology</u> **27:6**(1987) 729-734.

[37] H. J. Melosh, **Acoustic Fluidization: A new geologic process?** <u>Journal of Geophysical Research</u> **84:B13**(1979) 7513-7520.

[38] H. J. Melosh, <u>Impact Cratering</u>, 1989, Oxford University Press, New York.

[39] P. Minnis, E. F. Harrison, L. L. Stowe, G. G. Gibson, F. M. Denn, D. R. Doelling, W. L. Smith, Jr., **Radiative climate forcing by the Mount Pinatubo eruption**, <u>Science</u>, **259**(1993) 1411-1415.

[40] R. Monastersky, **When Mountains Fall**, <u>Science News</u> **142:9**(1992) 136-138.

[41] D. Mougenot, M. Recq, P. Virlogeux, C. Lepvrier, **Seaward extension of the East African Rift**, <u>Nature</u> **321**(1986) 599-603.

[42] J. G. Negi, P. K. Agrawal, O. P. Pandey, A. P. Singh, **A possible K-T boundary bolide impact site offshore near Bombay and triggering of rapid Deccan volcanism**, <u>Physics of the Earth and Planetary Interiors</u> **76**(1993) 189-197.

[43] I. O. Norton, J. G. Sclater, **A model for the evolution of the Indian Ocean and the break-up of Gondwanaland**, <u>Journal of Geophysical Research</u> **84**(1979) 6803-6830.

[44] V. R. Oberbeck, J. R. Marshall, H. Aggarwal, **Impacts, tillites, and the breakup of Gondwanaland**, <u>Journal of Geology</u> **101**(1993) 1-19.

[45] N. M. Rach, B. R. Rosendahl, **Tectonic controls·on the Speke Gulf**, <u>Journal of African Earth Sciences</u> **8:2/3/4**(1989) 471-488.

[46] R. Schlich, F. Aubertin, J.-R. Delteil, L. Leclaire, P. Magnier, L. Montadert, P. Patriat, P.Valery, **Donnees nouvelles sur le substratum du Bassin de Somalie a partir d'un profil de sismique reflexion**, <u>Comptes Rendus Hebdomadaires des Seances de L'Academie des Sciences</u>, **Serie D:275**(1972) 1331-1334.

[47] R. A. Scrutton, **Davie Fracture Zone and the movement of Madagascar**, <u>Earth and Planetary Science Letters</u> **39**(1978) 84-88.

[48] R. A. Scrutton, W. B. Heptonstall, J. H. Peacock, **Constraints on the motion of Madagascar with respect to Africa**, <u>Marine Geology</u> **43**(1981) 1-20.

[49] G. Sen, **Possible depth of origin of primary Deccan tholeiite magma**, in <u>Deccan Flood Basalts, Memoir 10</u>, K. V. Subbarao, editor, 1988, Geological Society of India, Bangalore.

[50] Shipboard Scientific Party, **Introduction**, in <u>Proceedings of the Ocean Drilling Program, Initial Reports, Volume 115</u>, J. Backman <u>et al</u>, editors, 1988, Ocean Drilling Program, Texas A&M University.

[51] H. Sigurdsson, **Volcanic pollution and climate: The 1783 Laki eruption**, <u>Eos, Transactions, American Geophysical Union</u> **63:32**(1982) 601-602.

[52] P. W. Sloss, **Global marine gravity field map**, <u>Eos, Transactions, American Geophysical Union</u> **68:39**(1987) 770,772.

[53] D. R. Smith, W. P. Leeman, **Petrogenesis of Mount St. Helens dacitic magmas**, <u>Journal of Geophysical Research</u>, **92:B10**(1987) 10,313-10,334.

[54] G. R. Stoopes, M. F. Sheridan, **Giant debris avalanches from the Colima Volcanic Complex, Mexico: implications for long-runout landslides (>100 km) and hazard assessment**, <u>Geology</u> **20:4**(1992) 299-302.

[55] S. Thorarinsson, **The Lakagigar eruption of 1783**, <u>Bulletin Volcanologique</u>, **33**(1970) 910-927.

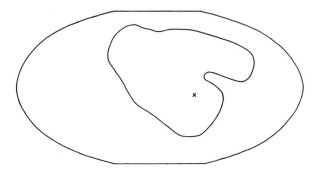

Figure 1. *Author's reconstruction of the protocontinent and proposed point of impact (X).*

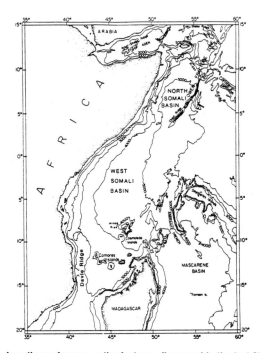

Figure 2. *Locations of some on the features discussed in the text [9,p.11,986].*

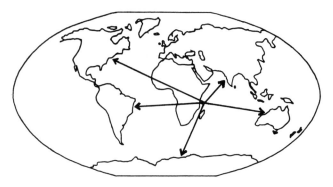

Figure 3. *Central position of the proposed impact site in relation to the directions that the continents slid.*

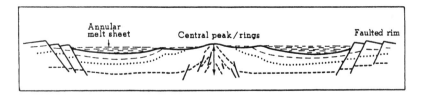

Figure 4. *Schematic cross section of a large complex crater [24,p.185].*

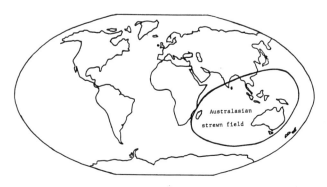

Figure 5. *Approximate boundary of the Australasian tektite strewn field [22,p.395].*

195

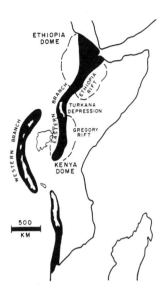

Figure 6. *Sketch map of the East African Rift system. Black shows the extent of Cenozoic rifting; white shows major rift lakes [29,p.433].*

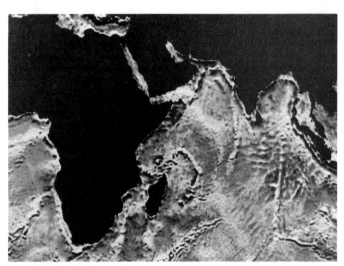

Figure 7. *SEASAT - derived gravity anomilies in the Western Indian Ocean [9,p.11,989].*

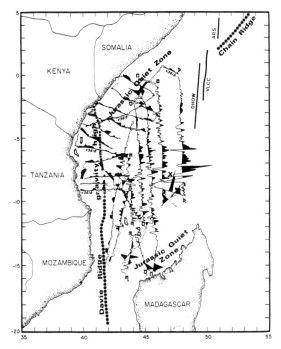

Figure 8. *Magnetic anomalies in the Wetern Somali Basin [11,p.9392]. Note Wilkes Rise (X).*

VALUES CLARIFICATION: AN EVALUATION

WARREN F. FORGAY, B. ED.
4465 SPRINGBETT DRIVE
RED DEER, ALBERTA
CANADA T4N 3N5

KEYWORDS

values clarification, progressive education, social studies, moral relativism, secular humanism.

ABSTRACT

The present paper traces the history of values clarification, showing its roots in the concept of social studies which focuses on the *process* of arriving at social values rather than the imparting of knowledge. It is shown to be alien to Christianity and Judeo-Christian tradition, and in perfect harmony with the tenets of secular humanism. Values clarification is ultimately an expression of the evolutionist/materialist understanding of reality, and particularly at odds with the biblical doctrine of Special Creation by an omniscient, omnipotent Creator.

INTRODUCTION

In a general sense, Values Clarification may be understood as a "scientific" approach to questions of values and morals. More properly, it should be recognized as a form of scientism, the belief that the *only* source of truth is that which is obtained scientifically. Values Clarification is widely used in public schools throughout Canada and the U.S. Supposedly, by using this technique, one will become almost as "objective" in determining a value as a chemist is in determining the melting point of an element.

Values Clarification is customarily recognized as beginning with a work by Raths, Harmin, and Simon, which was published in the mid-1960s [12]. An alternative approach has been developed by Dr. Lawrence Kohlberg [7, especially pp. 86-87.]; however, as his theory of morals and moral growth is based on exactly the same philosophical assumptions as is Values Clarification, it will not be examined here. Nor has his approach been as widely adopted in public schools as has Values Clarification.

WHAT IS SOCIAL STUDIES?

Values Clarification was first brought into the public schools as an improvement to their social studies programs. More recently, this approach to values has also been extended to other courses of study in many public schools, especially Sex Education and Language Arts. But to really understand Values Clarification, and why it entered by public education system, it is necessary to examine briefly the concept known commonly as Social Studies.

As the name implies, Social Studies is *the study of social problems*. Social Studies is *not* a mere general heading for the subjects of history, economics, civics, political science, and geography (though in practice it has often been that). "The ultimate goal of the social studies is to develop intelligent social actors" [1, p.13]. In social studies, "knowledge is an important component, to be used as needed when students engage in the valuing process. With this in mind, the social studies curriculum outlines major concepts and generalizations that are easily remembered, enduring, and transferable to a variety of life situations" [4, p.5].

"Concepts used in the social studies are drawn from history, geography, and the social sciences. Some social studies curricula are multi-disciplinary in that concepts from the various social disciplines remain distinct and separate. The Alberta curriculum is inter-disciplinary. Concepts from the social disciplines are integrated in such as way as to be indistinguishable as separate entities. It is our belief that man's behavior should not be compartmentalized for study" [4, p.25].

Imagine a scientist saying that scientific disciplines, such as entomology, astrophysics, and pharmacology should be "integrated in such a way as to be indistinguishable as separate entities" on the grounds that, as these disciplines are part of human behavior (which they are) they "should not be compartmentalized for study"! But based on this absurd line of reasoning, the disciplines of history and geography, for example, have practically disappeared from the Alberta school curriculum, swallowed up by what is known as "social studies."

If one wonders why students in today's public schools can graduate from high school largely ignorant of history and geography while at the same time getting high grades in "social studies," it is because progressive education theorists no longer view schooling "as purely an intellectual experience" [4, p.5]. Imparting knowledge is *not* the primary goal of "social studies." It is not the acquisition of knowledge but rather the acquisition of the valuing *process* that is the goal of the social studies. "In the decision-making process, knowledge in its various forms is essential but dependent for its existence, validity and application upon the skills used to obtain, organize and apply it, and the influence of pertinent values" [4, p.12]. More important than skills to the progressive educator is that students develop skills of a varied nature "to facilitate sound decision-making, for these are the vehicle by which knowledge is obtained" [4, p.12].

This, in a nutshell, is what is meant by the term "social studies." Once this is understood, it is easy to see Values Clarification as a logical and perhaps in some way inevitable development. For many modern educators, it is important that students adopt the Values Clarification approach to their entire lives. Much more important to them than knowledge are skills in social problem solving. This idea began long ago with such thinkers as John Dewey, who, when writing of history, for example, said, "Since the aim is not covering the ground, but knowledge of social processes used to secure social results, no attempt is made to go over the entire history, in a chronological order ... rather a series of types is taken up ... The aim is to present a variety of climatic and local conditions, to show the different sorts of obstacles and helps that people found" [2, p.419].

The Minority Report of the Alberta Royal Commission on Education for 1959 recommended that "social studies" in effect be abolished, and instead "require the course to be divided into its component elements to be taught separately with a view to giving the child a logical pattern of facts, leaving the critical thinking and evaluation to an age of maturity that is more competent to deal with it" [2 p.422]. It is certainly arguable that even high school graduates lack the maturity and knowledge base for the social studies idea of such progressivist education philosophers as Dewey and Kilpatrick. However, there has always been a great desire on the part of progressive educationists to indoctrinate (except in traditional religious catechism, which they detest), as education critic Hilda Neatby documented many years ago [11]. Indeed, they are very eager that students should adopt their ideas of "values clarification," "tolerance," "skills," "critical thinking," the "decision-making process," in short their entire Weltanschauung.

Sometimes social studies is defended on the ground that it makes students into "critical thinkers." There is little evidence for this claim (and were there no critical thinkers before social studies was invented?), but progressivist educators love to talk about "critical thinking." However,

in order to criticize something, you have to have something on which to base your criticism. Proper critical thinking presupposes having had a point of view on which to found a criticism. The progressivist appears to want only that the child develop a critical attitude without the necessary backlog of content. We are all too familiar with the common practice of having junior high school students comment on such things as the United Nations equipped with little or no knowledge of the historical, political, and economic background of the nations involved. It's a case of the little angels rushing in where even fools fear to tread.

Critical thinking as an aim in education is essential, but to the progressivist the concept operates in ignorance of an accumulation of facts. To him facts are needed only to discover the solution to a problem. Therefore, the learning experiences become a succession - and not necessarily a consecutive or logical succession - of problems. By the application of research, the necessary facts relevant to the problem are uncovered. This is followed by a process of critical thinking to appraise and resolve the problem in the light of the uncovered facts.

The essentialist ['traditionalist'] honors critical thinking as highly as the progressivist, but permits the child to indulge in it only after he has acquired and stored up a wide range of knowledge in a logical pattern upon which he will then draw to solve any number of problems. [2, p.388]

One sometimes suspects that the *real* purpose of "critical thinking," at least so far as progressivists are concerned, is to make students into cynical skeptics or agnostics, contemptuous of, for example, traditional sexual morality and religious beliefs. In fact, a good stiff course in logic, or even in logical fallacies, would certainly help make students into better, more critical thinkers, and do so without at the same time indoctrinating them in a secularist educational philosophy.

Values Clarification, then, is a child of the Social Studies. Even if at some point in the future the particular methodology known as "values clarification" is abolished, something similar to it will inevitably emerge as long as social studies and the underlying philosophy of progressivism remains part of the school curriculum. When in 1959 John S. Cormack, in his Minority Report as a member of the Royal Commission on Education, charged the public school system of Alberta with "unwarranted intrusion into the family circle" and of "driving a wedge between parent and child" [2, p.369], he was hotly denounced by the other members of the Commission in their Majority Report, who were quick to deny his charges [8, p.289]. Since then, of course, John Cormack's charges have been vindicated to a fabulous degree. Just one example of this vindication is the use of what is known as "values clarification" in the public schools. It is this particular methodology which shall now be examined.

VALUES CLARIFICATION: A DEFINITION

In briefly defining Values Clarification (VC), one can do no better than to quote the promoters of it themselves: "Very generally VC is a set of related procedures designed to engage students and teachers in the active formulation and examination of values. It does not teach a particular set of values. There is no sermonizing or moralizing. The goal is to involve students in practical experiences, making them aware of *their own* feelings, *their own* ideas, *their own* beliefs, so that the choices and decisions they make are conscious and deliberate, based on their own value system" [13, p.18].

As can be seen from this quotation, Values Clarification (VC) "is a set of related procedures," a *process*. The claim is made here (and elsewhere) [4, p.12] that VC involves "no sermonizing"; in other words, VC is objective and neutral, in and of itself. This claim is absurd on its face, for already an implicit assumption has been made, namely, that there are NO absolute values, no moral absolutes, no permanent code of ethics, unalterable by time or circumstance. If moral absolutes exist, for example, there is no need to engage in the Values Clarification process.

To the promoters of VC, therefore, values have a definition alien to the centuries-old Judeo-Christian belief. "Values are those aspects of a culture to which the groups attach a high worth of regard. The norms and sanctions in a society are expressions of its values" [1, p.204]. Such a definition of values, palpably ridiculous, is not uncommon in Values Clarification texts. "Values" defined in this way are completely subjective, individualistic, and situational. Presumably the horrific Aztec rite of human sacrifice must be regarded as a true "value" under such a definition because it was an aspect of that culture "to which they attached a high worth or regard."

In fact, in the VC scheme of things, values do not exist outside of the individual; there is no external code of morals, no external absolute standard of any kind. The emphasis instead is on process, feelings, individual choices, etc. In the final analysis, values *do not exist at all* in the VC concept; what are called "values" are really subjective opinions freely examined and chosen by the individual (and, in a larger sense, by society).

The Christian understanding of a true value is poles apart from that of Values Clarification. Christianity understands values to be absolute irrespective of times or circumstances. Being absolute, they do not depend upon a particular culture or society, and are something to be learned and lived up to, not invented or chosen smorgasbord style from any number of alternatives. This is why Christian (and many other private) schools traditionally had, for example, catechism classes to teach values, NOT a "valuing process." This has always been justified by churches on the grounds that the teachings and the values are *true*, ultimately based on revelation from God Himself, and hence not open to debate or rejection. Moral relativists, because they reject the idea that there can be any such thing as truth or moral absolutes, detest the indoctrinatory (not brainwashing) approach to values and morals. The Christian justifies the traditional approach on the ground that his values are true, and to reject truth is to commit error.

THE VALUING PROCESS

In Values Clarification there are three basic stages [12] to arriving at what is called a "value," namely, choosing, prizing, and acting. All VC educators clearly believe that one *should* engage in their VC process, that one *should* arrive at values by using their system. (Here their moral relativism and opposition to sermonizing conveniently disappears.)

Stage One: CHOOSING - First, the student is expected to identify all known alternatives, consider the consequences of each, and then make a free choice [4, p.9]. Consider carefully that in the VC scheme there are and can be no absolute values. Otherwise, they would have to be exempt from this choosing process. In the VC scheme, there is no right or wrong, good or evil. The child merely identifies all the alternatives and makes his choice. So, if a child decides to choose the homosexual lifestyle, after considering alternatives, such as heterosexual activity only within marriage, heterosexual promiscuity, abstinence, bestiality, among other choices, and has made his choice freely as an individual, he has completed the first part of the valuing process. What actual choice he makes in the VC system of thought is irrelevant; it can be neither "right" nor "wrong."

It should be emphasized here that nothing is in theory exempt from the valuing process. Since, to VC thinkers, values are merely sophisticated opinions of accepted social norms or just of individual taste, any VC social studies program will sooner or later come into conflict with at least some parents. The Alberta Social Studies Handbook states: "Each student is subject to bombardment by many, often conflicting values - from the home, the church, the peer group, the mass media. He must process these many values, accepting some, rejecting some and modifying others. His unique behavior should reflect a synthesis, resulting in a set of values that are clear, consistent and defensible in terms of the life goals of the individual as a member of society" [4, p.23].

By now it should be clear that everything taught in the home or in the church is in principle open to challenge or rejection under the VC process. The student is assumed to be completely autonomous, responsible neither to God (whose revelation and very existence is rejected or simply ignored), nor to parents. Since there is no right or wrong, each student must "decide for himself" how he shall act and what he shall believe.

Stage Two: PRIZING - Having made his choice about what to value, the student is to prize that choice by being happy with the choice and affirming it, willingly and publicly [4, p.9]. No question can ever arise as to whether or not the "value" is worth prizing, for such a question assumes that some sort of moral absolute code exists which the VC system of thought dispenses with from the outset.

Stage Three: ACTING - Having prized the value freely chosen, the student then is to act upon the choice, repeating the action consistently in some pattern of life [4]. Here there seems to be some inconsistency, for VC theorists seem to be saying at this point that the student *should* act upon the choice made, lapsing again into some form of absolutism.

All of this assumes, in fact, that VC itself is *good*, that students *should* engage in the "valuing process." It also assumes that students are by nature good (not sinful or unclean), and will not make unfortunate (VC theorists cannot in all honesty use words like "good" or "evil") choices.

It cannot be emphasized too strongly that in the VC program the concern is *not* the conclusions the students come to, but merely *how* they reach those conclusions. In this sense, what is known as "values education" in the public schools is the exact opposite to what many parents understand by the term, because for them it is precisely the conclusions the students come to, more than the "process" which is to them most important, as indeed it is.

So, in Values Clarification, what is important is not the choices the students make, but the valuing process itself. And this valuing process is never conclusive: "Values ... are explored, clarified, and assessed by the utilization of skills and in light of an ever-expanding knowledge base" [4, p.12a]. In other words, as mentioned previously, for VC theorists, values as such do not exist. What does exist is the valuing process - personal choices, judgments and feelings which, when chosen "scientifically" in accord with the VC scheme, and then prized and acted upon, become, for the individual person, his "values."

A further point needs to be made: No value not arrived at by the VC process can qualify as a true value, according to VC theorists [5, p.231-277]. Hence the Ten Commandments do not qualify as true values because they were not chosen freely from among other alternatives (they were imposed by God), nor are they often prized or acted upon, nor are they to be re-evaluated "in the light of an ever-expanding knowledge base."

VALUES CLARIFICATION IN PRACTICE

It would seem that VC must lead logically if not inevitably either to antinomianism or to arbitrary authoritarianism. Given this choice, Raths et al. choose authoritarianism, perhaps realizing instinctively that no society can be constructed or sustained on the extreme antinomian and almost anarchic individualism VC would seem to lead to. That arbitrary authoritarianism is indeed the choice of VC theorists is strikingly illustrated by the following example [12, p.115], where honesty is the value under discussion:

> Ginger: Does that mean we can decide for ourselves whether we should be honest on tests here?
> Teacher: No, that means that you can decide on the value. I personally value honesty; and although you may choose to be dishonest, I shall insist that we be honest on our test here. In other areas of your life, you may have more freedom to be dishonest, but one can't do anything any time, and in this class I shall expect honesty on tests.
> Ginger: But then how can we decide for ourselves? Aren't you telling us what to value?
> Sam: Sure, you're telling us what we should do and believe in.
> Teacher: Not exactly. I don't mean to tell you what you should value. That's up to you. But I do mean that in this class, not elsewhere necessarily, you have to be honest on tests or suffer certain consequences. I merely mean that I cannot give tests without the rule of honesty. All of you who may choose dishonesty as a value may not practice it here, that's all I'm saying. Further questions, anyone?

In other words, "you may choose to use profanity elsewhere, but not in my class," or, "all of you who choose stealing as a value may not practice it in my classroom, that's all I'm saying," or, "I don't mean to tell you what to value. If you value sexual promiscuity, that's up to you."

With such an approach to values, is it any wonder that the public schools are in the state they are in? The wonder is that things are not even worse. Of course, the VC approach is a form of moral relativism. This is why "questions should not guide toward a preconceived answer" [4, p.45]. The only thing that seems to be exempt from this moral relativism is the valuing *process* itself. In VC, there is no preconceived answer, because there is no "right" or "wrong" answer.

Moral relativism is not the only assumption underlying Values Clarification. Total atheism seems to be an accompanying trait. None of the VC theorists ever mention God, let alone base their ideas on His laws and purposes. Occasionally, the fact that some children may get certain ideas from church will be mentioned, but these ideas are treated in the same context of moral relativism as everything else. And as already noted, since values from church are not arrived at through the valuing process, the implication is that they are not real values and should be rejected. This is why VC theorists can insist that "each generation should have the right to determine its own values" [1, p.449].

"Because life is different through time and space, we cannot be certain what experiences any person will have. We therefore cannot be certain what values, what style of life, would be most suitable for any person. We do, however, have some ideas about what *processes* might be most effective for obtaining values" [12, p.28].

"It is not intended that these [VC] activities be used to determine whose values are 'right' and whose are 'wrong.' Rather, these activities are intended to help teachers and students determine the clarity, consistency and defensibility of particular values" [4, p.41].

At the same time that the moral relativists are saying students must pick their own values, they sternly insist that "tolerance" is an attitude that must be accepted without question [4, p.41]. To say that some things *should not* be tolerated is to (unconsciously perhaps) reintroduce an absolute code of ethics. However, "tolerance" is not any sort of virtue or value in and of itself; everything about it depends on just what is being tolerated.

Most people probably think that "values" education is about teaching children what is right and what is wrong. That, of course, is the one thing "values clarification" is *not* about. (The same may be said for what is passing for "moral education" in the public schools.)

THE STATE CHURCH

Values Clarification may be irreconcilable with Christianity or Orthodox Judaism, but it is in perfect harmony with Secular Humanism, the religious/philosophical world-view now dominant in the modern public education system. Humanist Manifesto II (signed by more than 200 prominent intellectuals, scientists, and educators) states that "traditional theism, especially faith in the prayer-hearing God ... is an unproved and outmoded faith" [6, p.13]. Consistent with this, God has no place in the VC scheme of things; the functional atheism of VC is so obvious that no more comment is needed. Humanist Manifesto II states that "ethics is autonomous and situational, needing no theological or ideological sanction" [6, p.17]. Consistent with this, VC teaches that values "are explored, clarified, and assessed by the utilization of skills and in the light of an ever-expanding knowledge base" [4, p.12a] Humanist Manifesto II states: "Decision-making must be decentralized to include widespread involvement of people at all levels - social, political, and economic. All persons should have a voice in developing the values and goals that determine their lives" [6, p.19]. Consistent with this, the VC program teaches that "children have to make their own choice; only then will they be apt to act according to their conviction" [4, p.45].

None of this is meant to suggest that VC theorists *consciously* plot to inculcate children in their own philosophy or religion. Most of them seem to serenely assume their own "objectivity," "neutrality," "tolerance," etc. In fact, they are just as prone to indoctrinate as anyone else; the question is really by whom and in what. (Indoctrination does not mean brainwashing or narrow-minded bigotry in its traditional sense; it simply means that certain concepts or ideas are recognized as false or true from the outset, even when they are discussed. Any philosophy with no axioms at all is merely a self-negating form of agnosticism.)

In the VC scheme there is no place for parents or for the church, whose roles are to impart to their children God-given values, morals, and revealed truths. To give just one more example of how VC works in practice, consider the following: A class of children are asked to consider the case of a boy who stole a toy from a store. The sort of question they will be asked about this will show how different the VC system of thought is from traditional values.

VC: Do you think that what the boy did was wrong? Why? Why not?
Traditional: What did the boy do that was wrong?

In VC, moral relativism is assumed from the outset; what appears to be an example of students engaged in "critical thinking" is really an example of students assuming at the outset that there is no "right" and there is no "wrong." Everything is situational and depends, not on whether or not children come to the "right" conclusion, but only that children engage in "critical thinking," i.e., the "valuing process." Of course, VC theorists like to assume that "critical thinking" is impossible without assuming also moral relativism, in this case their "valuing process." In such a way, absolute values can be excluded from the beginning.

It is becoming increasingly obvious that the public schools have in many ways attained the status of an established church. Indeed, all the things that liberals find most odious about an established religion or church apply with at least as much force to an established system of education. People who in good conscience object to the kind of philosophy underlying "public" education are nevertheless required to pay for it. Increasingly, they are coerced into sending their children to public schools (most people are too poor to pay for some sort of private school in addition to public school). Even many private schools that are allowed to exist must increasingly adhere to the public school curriculum, or its equivalent, though most private schools are started because of opposition to the public school curriculum.

David Ehrenfeld, in his critique of secular humanism, stated that in some ways humanism is not like other religions, and one example he mentions is that "there are no buildings labelled 'Church of Humanism' in your neighborhood" [3, p.4]. Strictly speaking, he is right. But in the larger sense, he may be quite wrong. The "Church of Humanism" in one's local neighborhood may very well be the local neighborhood public school. (It should be noted that some private and parochial schools have also become humanistic, usually by adopting the government's curriculum.)

PHILOSOPHICAL ROOTS

Why does VC and, indeed, social studies itself, stress process more than content? The answer to this lies in the philosophical beginnings of modern progressive education.

One of the fathers of progressive education, John Dewey, "was the first philosopher of education to make systematic use of Darwin's ideas" [14, p.252]. Progressive education may be said to be the result of applying the theory of evolution to education. Today, progressive education is so dominant that for anyone to imagine anything else has become almost impossible. Even those who consider themselves strong opponents of Dewey nevertheless accept many of his more basic ideas, perhaps without realizing it, and this would include the evolutionism that underlies progressivist educational thinking.

What progressive education has almost completely replaced is traditional education, sometimes known as essentialism. Unlike progressivism, which is based on evolution, essentialist educational philosophy is based on the concept of essences or unchanging types. As a philosophy, essentialism has its roots in the thinking of Plato and Aristotle, and was later modified to some degree by the Christian Church. It was only after evolutionary theory became widely accepted by scientists that it became the basis for education theory.

> The concepts of unchanging essences and of complete discontinuities between every eidos (type) and all others make genuine evolutionary thinking well-nigh impossible. I agree with those who claim that the essentialist philosophies of Plato and Aristotle are incompatible with evolutionary thinking. ... The assumptions of population thinking (evolution) are diametrically opposed to those of the typologists ... The ultimate conclusions of the population thinkers (evolutionists) and of the typologist are precisely the opposite. For the typologist, the type (eidos) is real and the variation an illusion, while for the populationists (evolutionists) the type (average) is an abstraction and only the variation is real. No two ways of looking at nature could be more different. [10, p.4] Nor could two ways of looking at education and values be more different.

The progressivist/evolutionist holds to the position that unchanging essences (i.e. universals, moral absolutes, things) are mere mental constructs. They do not describe reality because for the evolutionist they are all in a constant state of change. For them, reality is described only by *process*. This is why, in values clarification, the emphasis is actually on the valuing *process* and not values per se. This process is, for the progressivist, the application of evolution to the field of education. Since for him the material universe is all that exists, and since evolution applies to the entire universe, evolution must also apply to education. This also explains the strong utilitarianism in VC with its emphasis on the uses of knowledge rather than on knowledge itself. (Utilitarianism is strongly emphasized in the *Origin of Species* by Charles Darwin.)

Biologist Ernst Mayr notes that Charles Darwin lost his Christian faith after he abandoned his belief in "essences" for that of evolutionist thinking [9, p.327]. This is not surprising. The evolutionist stresses "becoming," not "being," and hence talks of "process," "change," "evolution," etc. The concept of unchanging types (essences), whether of absolute values in education or changeless types in zoology is absolutely incompatible with evolutionary thinking. It is absolutely necessary for essentialist (traditional) education.

One is hard-pressed to see how anything can be knowable if everything is mutable, as the evolutionist/progressivist asserts. However, this is a subject far too involved to be dealt with adequately here. But it should be once again stressed that the absence of moral absolutes from modern education is no mere accident. It is a logical outcome, mandated by a commitment to the basic evolutionist/materialist understanding of reality as promoted by Dewey and his modern followers. This understanding of reality is completely at odds with the Judeo-Christian understanding, which is rooted in the doctrine of Special Creation by an omniscient, omnipotent Creator.

CONCLUSION

The particular technique known as Values Clarification may be either explicit or implicit in an educational curriculum. In Alberta it was explicit from 1971 to 1982. Since then, the VC approach has become more implicit, never mentioned directly, but in its basic form assumed. And even if the particular concept of VC is rejected by public education, something similar to it, with the same philosophical assumptions or moral relativism and functional atheism will sooner or later emerge to replace it. Any attempted "reform" of such an educational system will never be anything more than superficial as long as the commitment to the underlying philosophy remains. Perhaps this is why calls for and attempted reforms of public education over the past forty and more years have never really led anywhere.

Educational theorist Jack Fraenkel strongly supports the use of VC in the schools, and praises the work of Raths, Harmin, and Simon as "provocative" [5, p.236]. Others are less impressed. Psychologist Paul Vitz stated that "the VC program should be rejected. The contradictions and incoherence of the system provide one of the shallowest and intellectually most confused systems of thought yet contrived by the human mind" [15, p.125].

The fruits of moral relativism are everywhere: rampant divorce, abortion, an explosion of sexually transmitted diseases, drug abuse, family breakdown, pornography available everywhere, and a crime rate, especially for juveniles, higher than ever. Indeed, the twentieth century has been the century of moral relativism; it is no coincidence that the twentieth century has also been by far the bloodiest in history. One cannot help thinking of a passage that summarizes the bloodiest book of the Bible, the book of Judges. At that time, too, moral relativism was rampant among a people who had turned their back on God: "In those days there was no king in Israel; every man did that which was right in his own eyes" (Judges 21:25).

ACKNOWLEDGEMENTS

This paper would not have been possible without the assistance of many individuals. I would especially like to thank the following: Miss Kathryn LaGrange of the Alberta Federation of Women United for Families, who suggested this project and encouraged me to complete it; Mr. Patrick Mealey, whose friendship and discussions with me since our days in university have been invaluable; and Mrs. Ellen G. Myers, of the Creation Social Science and Humanities Society, who suggested I submit this paper to the International Conference on Creation for consideration.

REFERENCES

[1]   J. A. Banks, Teaching Strategies for the Social Studies (Don Mills, Ont., Canada: Addison-Wesley Publishing Company, Inc., 1973).

[2]   J. S. Cormack, Minority Report of the Royal Commission on Education, 1959.

[3]   D. Ehrenfeld, The Arrogance of Humanism (New York: Oxford University Press, 1978).

[4]   Experiences in Decision Making (Province of Alberta Department of Education, January 1971, reprinted September, 1975).

[5]   J. R. Fraenkel, Helping Students Think and Value (Englewood Cliffs, NJ: Prentice-Hall, Inc., 1973).

[6]   Humanist Manifestos I and II, edited by Paul Kurtz (Buffalo, NY: Prometheus Books, 1973).

[7]   L. Kohlberg, **Stages of moral development as a basis for moral education**, in Moral Education: Interdisciplinary Approaches (University of Toronto Press, 1971).

[8]   Majority Report of the Royal Commission on Education, 1959.

[9]   E. Mayr, **Darwin and Natural Selection** in American Scientist, Vol. 65 (1977), p. 327.

[10]   E. Mayr, Populations, Species, and Evolution (Cambridge, MA: Harvard University Press, 1970).

[11]   H. Neatby, So Little For the Mind (Toronto: Clarke, Irwin & Company, Ltd., 1953).

[12]   L. E. Raths, M. Harmin, and S. B. Simon, Values and Teaching (Columbus, OH: Charles E. Merrill Books, 1966).

[13]   S. B. Simon, Leland W. Howe, and Howard Kirschenbaum, Values Clarification: A Handbook for Teachers and Students, Second Edition (New York: Hart Publishing Co., 1978).

[14]   C. O. Weber, Basic Philosophies of Education (New York: Rinehart Publishers, 1960).

[15]   P. Vitz, **Theories of Moral Education**, in Whose Values? (Ann Arbor, MI: Servant Books, 1985, Carl Horn, ed.).

APPENDIX

The ideas of the progressivist/evolutionist educators have even reached into many Christian schools, as for example with their idea of "social studies", which has replaced the separate disciplines of history, geography, and civics. John Dewey was strongly influenced by Darwin's own utilitarianism, hence it is no surprise that history, for example, which has little or no immediate utilitarian application, is deemed to have little or no intrinsic worth by progressivist educators. At most, history is regarded as perhaps being of occasional "use" to help solve a particular social problem.

But the progressivist disdain for history does not stop there. Dewey, and many of his followers, were and are atheists and materialists, denying the whole realm of spiritual values. They regard the past for the most part as pre-scientific rubbish, and the values that the past stood for as having been discredited by Modern Science and the "fact" of evolution. This is probably why "as a widespread social phenomenon, the unhistorical or anti-historical attitude is peculiar to our era. It parallels the widespread seeming indifference to the reality of the soul and the prospect of life everlasting. Quite consciously men and women uninterested in the soul may forfeit their own souls, and a people uninterested in their history may cease to have a history, or to be a people." [2, p. 19].

The crucial importance of history as opposed to "social studies" as an intellectual discipline has been noted: "Lacking a deeper knowledge of how we arrived where we stand today, lacking that deeper love of country which is nurtured by a knowledge of the past, lacking the apprehension that we all take part in a great historical continuity-why, a people so deprived will not dare much, sacrifice much, or take long views. With them, creature comforts will be everything; yet, historical consciousness wanting, in the long run they must lose their creature comforts too. At every level of instruction, from kindergarten through graduate school, the serious study of history has been declining for a half century and more. From time to time, foundations and learned societies, and newspapers and magazines, growing alarmed at the drift toward ignorance of anything not featured on television, publish surveys of the extent to which the rising generation has sunk into a Sargasso Sea of ignorance of the past." [2, p. 17].

Christopher Dawson noted that the "combination of utilitarianism and specialism is...one of the main causes of the intellectual disintegration of modern Western culture...for the Christian, the past can never be dead, as it often seems to the secularist, since we believe the past and present are united in the one Body of the Church and that the Christians of the past are still present as witnesses and helpers in the life of the Church today." [1, pp. 108, 113].

The entire progressivist way of thinking is alien to Christianity. The Christian revelation is based on numerous historic events: creation, the Fall of man, the Incarnation of Our Lord, the resurrection, the last judgment, etc. And some Christian churches place an even greater emphasis on history, as for example in dispensational Protestant theology or in the high regard for Tradition in the Roman Catholic Church. Harold Lindsell's book, The Bible in the Balance, which traces the historic decline of belief in biblical inerrancy in many supposed Bible-believing churches, is a work of history. So too is Francis Schaeffer's How Should We then Live?, subtitled The Decline of Western Thought and Culture. It is the past that is truly knowable, not the future. The progressivist educator, contemptuous of the past and knowing nothing of the future in any real sense, can only concentrate on the present, hence progressivist ideas such as "social studies" and "values clarification".

Creation is a unique moment in time- the beginning of real history. The progressivist/evolutionist, rejecting creation, can only substitute an evolutionary "history" which is really a series of endless cycles of matter throughout eternity. "Values clarification" is a logical deduction from this basic world-view. A proposed compromise, theistic evolution, not only tends to shade off into pantheism, but seems to survive as a proposal only so long as certain key terms are kept sufficiently vague.

APPENDIX REFERENCES

[1]   C. Dawson, The Crisis of Western Education (New York: Image/Doubleday Books, 1965).

[2]   R. Kirk, The Roots of the American Order Third Edition (Washington, D.C.: Regnery Gateway Publishers, 1991).

Editor's Note:

Due to reasons beyond his control, Mr. Forgay was unable to attend the Conference, and therefore did not present his paper. Because this paper was accepted into the Technical Symposium prior to these circumstances it has been included as part of the written record of the Third International Conference on Creationism.

A DIFFERENT APPROACH TO THE PROBLEM OF SCIENTIFIC KNOWLEDGE

APOSTOLOS CH. FRANGOS BA, BS
ASSOCIATION OF GREEK SCIENTISTS FOR THE SCIENTIFIC TRUTH
43 ELLANIKOU STREET
ATHENS 11635, GREECE

ABSTRACT

Recent developments in computer science (information) and in DNA as the information code of life, direct us to the consideration that the fundamental essence of all human activities is expressed information of the human mind. By the same consideration, we can also approach the fundamental issue of the ultimate substance and essence of the natural world, behind the various forms of its existence. So, the whole natural world and consequently life and its origin, is in essence information and as such, i.e. as an intellectual faculty, it is beyond the capabilities of scientific research within empirical science. This paper presents a brief analysis of this approach.

SUMMARY

Considering the developments of computer science (information) as well as the findings on the DNA function as the fundamental information code and so the essential constituent of life, we can easily regard also that the various human activities and products are in essence expressed information, i.e. products of the human intelligence function.

On the other hand, due to the fact that the scientific research of the natural world reveals, both in its construction and function, design (and as a necessary logical consequence a Designer) , it is justified to apply the same approach to the natural world. So, the essence of the natural world is information, which is expressed by the various forms of the material subjects as we see and know them. Consequently, the ultimate constituency and the real essence of the natural world is information, i.e. intellectual faculty, behind of the various appearances in the material world. These appearances (the variety of material things we see) are nothing else but expressions of information in various forms of natural world.

But the information itself, before its expression, is a mental product and as such it is beyond the capabilities of any scientific research by empirical science. What we see and investigate in the natural world is the expressions of the information and not the information itself, which is not a material substance , but an internal intellectual function and process, inaccessible to any scientific investigation by empirical science. By this approach to the problem of scientific knowledge, we can understand more clearly why matters such as the ultimate constituency and essence of the natural world, the origin and ultimate nature of life, etc, are not problems of scientific research, but rather philosophical and metaphysical issues subject to prejudice, dogmatic assumptions, or religious faith.

INTRODUCTION

It is well known that scientific knowledge, within the domain of physical empirical science, is subject to some limitations posed by various factors, i.e. the necessary presuppositions and assumptions in science, limitations in research and the nature of scientific explanations of data, depending mainly upon basic hypothesis and theories which are the explanatory framework of scientific data [4].

Especially, in the case of the origin of life and the ultimate origin of material things, as it has been shown [4], the relating hypothesis and theories are not scientific ones, but metaphysical dogmatic doctrines untestable by empirical science and hence they can not offer any scientific knowledge. It is necessary to note here that no untestable hypothesis or theory in empirical science has a philosophical or metaphysical character and consequently can not considered as a scientific hypothesis or theory (but only those that are "a priori", before any attempt to verify or falsify them). It is well known that there is an objective inability to be tested in any way not only now, but also at any time in the future, independently to the progress which would be made by discoveries of new scientific instruments and new means of investigation. The subject of such hypothesis and theories belongs to some other realm of discourse quite different from the science which we call metaphysics.

So, according to the philosophy of science, any question or answer regarding the origin of things like life, and any form of matter and energy and their ultimate cause, are excluded from the scope and capabilities of empirical science and belong to philosophy and metaphysics. But, independent of and in addition to the known inability of science to deal with such questions, there is another essential factor which illustrates why they are outside of any scientific approach. In this paper we try to explore this factor by considerations outlined in the following sections.

GENETICS - DNA - INFORMATION

We have known since the time of Pasteur that spontaneous generation of life does not occur. Biogenesis and life is not present in raw non-living matter. Developments in genetics disclosed that the main factor in living things is the DNA molecule. The DNA molecule contains the genetic code transmitting information from parents to children, from generation to generation in human beings (and in any other living thing).

From the time the program is written on the DNA there are in humans twenty-three different homologous pieces, carried by the ovum. As soon as the twenty-three chromosomes carried by the sperm encounter the twenty-three chromosomes carried by the ovum, all information necessary and sufficient to spell out all the characteristics of the new being is gathered. Inside the chromosomes is written the program and all the definitions. In fact chromosomes are, so to speak, the table of the law of each individual life.[8] But what is a DNA molecule? As it is known in human beings it is a long thread cut in twenty-three pieces. Each piece is coiled on itself very tightly to make a spiral so that finally, it looks like a little rod that we can see under the microscope that we call a chromosome. The minuteness of the language is bewildering.

Nature has used the smallest possible language to carry the information from parents to children, from generation to generation. It is very necessary because life is taking advantage of molecules, to organize the development of particles according to the needs of the new being. All the information being written must be written in the smallest language possible so that it can dictate how to manipulate particle by particle, atom by atom, molecule by molecule. Life is at the very intersection of matter, energy and information [8].

The reproduction process is a very impressive phenomenon in the sense that what is created is never merely matter, but it is also information. What is generated in any human reproduction process (stature, appearance, etc.) is not the original thing, but is the form that the genius of the maker had imprinted in the matter. The same thing is true for any reproduction whether is by photography, radio, or TV. What is printed or reproduced is the information and not merely matter which is only the support of the information, the means by which certain information is expressed. That explains how life is at all possible, because it would be impossible to reproduce matter which cannot live at all. What is reproduced and transmitted is information which will animate matter. There is no living matter. What exists is animated matter. In genetics we learn to know what animates matter, to force matter to take the form of a human being. Chromosomes are long threads of DNA containing information. A chromosome is analogous to a mini-cassette in which a symphony is recorded; the symphony of life. As when hearing the music of a symphony in a normal tape recorder, neither the musician will be reproduced, nor the notes of music, but only the movement of air which transmits the genius of the composer of the symphony, exactly the same way on the tiny "mini-cassettes" which are the chromosomes (of any living organism) have written on them the various parts of the opus - which is for a human or any living organism, a symphony. Having all the information necessary and sufficient to spell out the whole symphony of life, this symphony plays itself; that is, a new man or living creature is beginning his existence [8].

It is noteworthy that in human genetics we look at the DNA information code like the bar code used in trade of products in the market. We look at the DNA bar code and we detect every individual is different from the next one by its own bar code. So many investigations have been made that we know now that looking at the bar code with the so called Jeffrey's system the probability that you will find it identical in another person is less than one in one billion. You can take a tiny piece of DNA, one molecule taken from one cell, and you can reproduce it by the PCR technique, and when you have enough, you can make the analysis of Jeffrey's and seen once again that we have the whole demonstration of uniqueness, not only in a sample taken from the individual, but in one cell, in one nucleus of the individual.

Another important discovery is that DNA is not as dull as the "mini-cassette. Our understanding of nature is imitated by our discoveries, but there is much more yet to be discovered, in the sense that the message written on DNA is written by the changing of the various bases which come one after the other in that molecule. Some of the bases of DNA were carrying an extra little piece, a methyl (CH3) which is just hooked on it and changes the form of one of the bars of this long scale which is the DNA molecule. That is, with methylation one gene recedes, but if it is demethylated on the next division, on the next cell, then it will reappear.

The addition of the methyl group to cytosine in a DNA sequence generally causes the DNA sequence to become inactive. During DNA replication, the pattern of methylation is presented in the DNA copies. Thus, the gene will also be inactive in the new cell [13]. The basic discovery was that this is possible because this tiny change on the DNA, changes the surface of the big groove of the helix of DNA. It is inside this big groove that some molecules and proteins will hook onto different segments specific by the DNA. It is a kind of language telling the chromosome: "You have to tell this information; or do not speak this information for the moment". By this means it continues progressively; the underlining system changing so that cells do differentiate and become specialized, making a nail, hair skin, neurons, everything in an organism. The first cell of a human being knew more information than the three cell stage and the three cell stage knew more information than the morula, etc. Besides, some messenger DNA (MRNA) sequences contain a set of instruction which specify an alteration in the way the genetic code is read. This phenomenon called "recoding" may be universal and governed by diverse rules as yet undiscovered. As our understanding of genetics increases, the process is seen to be increasingly complex [14].

In the beginning fertilized egg, was not only written what is the genetic message we can read in every cell, but it was written the way it should be read from one sequence to another, exactly like in the program of a computer. That which is written in the first cell is progressively forgotten in the other cells of the body. At the end of the process when the organism has grown up it then produces it's is own reproductive cells. So, differentiation is, so to speak, prewritten in the first cell and has now an understandable physical support [8]. At the beginning of life, the genetic information and the molecular structure of the egg, the spirit and the matter, the soul and the body must-be that tightly intricate because it's a beginning of the new marvel that we call a human. The amount of information which is inside the zygote (fertilized egg) is so big that nobody can measure it and nobody can read it and no computer in the world have a storage enough just to fill the amount of data. So, one of the prime characteristics of all living organisms is the information they contain for all operational processes, although matter and energy are necessary fundamental properties of life. Matter and energy do not in themselves imply any basic differentiation between animate and inanimate systems. They are only means for expression of many various information in the natural world. We illustrate some characteristics of the DNA information code in order to underline that the genetic code necessarily has originated from a mental concept and did not arise by chance.

Information density is the amount of information in a unit volume, a measure of the efficiency of storage and transmission of information. In the simplest case when the supply of symbols consists of just two symbols which overall occur with equal frequency the information content of one of those symbols should assigned a unit of precisely 1 bit (binary digit). The highest known information density is that of the DNA molecules which comprise the genes of living cells (many genes packaged together in chromosomes). This chemical medium for storage of information is 2nm in diameter (10^9 nm is one meter) and has a 3.4nm helix pitch. This results in a volume of 1.068 x 10^{-20} cm^3 per spiral. Each spiral contains ten chemical letters (nucleotides) resulting in an information density of 9.4 x 10^{20} letters per cm^3. Since the information content of each of the 4 different nucleotides of which DNA is composed is 2 bits, the statistical information density of DNA is 1.88 x 10^{21} bits per cent, the storage capacity of DNA, the information carriers of living things is 4.5 x 10^{13} times more effective than a present day megachip (1 Mbit DRAM) [5].

It is interesting to mention that the most complex information-processing system in existence is the human being. If we take all human information processes together, i.e. conscious ones (language, information-controlled deliberate voluntary movements) and unconscious ones (information-controlled functions of the organs and other human systems) this involves the processing of 10^{24} bits daily. This astronomical and unexpressed number is greater by a factor of one million than the total human knowledge of 10^{18} bits stored in all the world's libraries [5].

Modern coded molecular biology requires a thinking concept forming instruction giving logos (i.e. a Logos full of ideas) as basis. Chaos (chance) imparts no simulated, coded instructions and develops no ideas [12]. When different kinds of chemical molecules are used to attain a uniform function or a chemical concept a plan would certainly be suspected. A concept would seem to be the work of a planning logos rather that of a non-planning logos [12].

For instance, in living organisms proteins are the basic substances and contain internally important compounds such as, enzymes, antibodies, hemoglobins, and hormones. These important substances are both organ-and species-specific. In the human body alone, there are at least 50,000 different proteins performing important functions. Their structures must be coded just as effectively as the chemical processes in the cells. It is known that all the proteins occurring in living organisms compass a total of just 20 different chemical building blocks (amino acids). The precise sequence of these individual building blocks is of exceptional significance for life and must therefore be carefully defined. This is done with the aid of genetic code. Each amino acid is coded by the well known string of three nucleotides on the DNA.

Proteins are easy to make in the laboratory, because they involve only reactions that involve a loss of energy. But producing a functional protein which is useful for an organism is an extremely difficult process [6].

To synthesize a functional protein in an organism, one kind of work is needed to make the parts joint together, another kind to make sure the parts are in the correct sequence in order to yield a specific chemical structure. A chain of amino acids hooked by random methods is not a functional protein. Biological function of proteins requires a three-dimensional morphology which depends on acquiring only left-handed amino acids (bending light to the left) only peptide bonds, in the correct sequence and with avoidance of all other organic molecules [1].

Physicochemical laws, (chaos) do not meet any of these requirements. Therefore the correct three-dimensional structure cannot develop by undirected physicochemical laws and the resulting chemical will not have any biological function. No evolutionary biologist has ever produced any quantitative proof that the designs of nature are in fact within the reach of chance [3].

Evolutionism argues that given enough time, the impossible not only becomes possible, but inevitable. But it is well known, without any exception in science, that entropy increases with time and that long time spans work the opposite for a reversible synthesis to occur and the more likely, the reverse reaction (decomposition) occurs. The greater the time elapsed, the greater should be the approach to equilibrium and it seems that this ought to take precedence in our thinking over the idea that time provides the possibility for the occurrence of the highly improbable [2].

INFORMATION IN INANIMATE MATTER

The rapid development in computer technology and generally in the new field of information science made clear and doubtless the prominent significance of information in any human activity. Especially information is expressed mainly by a set of symbols organized using a code in order to give a meaningful message. According to the Information Theory an input from an intelligent source is needed to produce information. A computer program requires an intelligent programmer and designer. For example a printed message rides upon the various kinds of alphabet, numbers, mathematical symbols, etc. Artificial languages, such as computer and transfer information constitute a mental process. So, any code in any system means that the system originated from a mental concept and it is impossible to have arisen by chance. In all sciences, in research and collecting data, in data processing, in engineering and in control engineering, in communications, in natural languages, in living cells, as we have seen, in all kind of arts, information is the main characteristic. The concept of information has become a fundamental and far-reaching, since information confronts us in everything around us. Information is the only fundamental quantity in nature beyond matter and energy, which have long been considered the two basic and universal quantities. Information can unify matter and energy.

As we have seen, the code necessary for expressing and transferring information constitutes a mental process. So, the development of computer and its interface with science and physics brought into the scene another third factor, in addition to matter and energy.

INFORMATION - THE THIRD FACTOR IN NATURE

Some consider information as one of many forms of matter and energy; it is embodied in things like computers, electrons, a brain's neural firings, and items, such as newsprint and radio waves. Others suggest that information deserves full equality with matter and energy, joining them into some sort of scientific trinity; with these three things being the fundamental ingredients of reality. Very few consider that information is more fundamental than matter and energy.

Atoms, electrons, and quarks consist ultimately of bits-binary units of information, like those that are the currency of computation in a computer [5]. The behavior of those bits and thus of the entire universe, is governed by a single programming rule. Yet through ceaseless repetition- by tirelessly taking information, it has just transformed and is transforming it further - it has generated pervasive complexity.

This programming rule is considered the cause and prime mover of everything. Such a concept opened a new area of physics, the so-called the Theory of Digital Physics [11]. In this way some scientists try to describe a new world view including great philosophical questions like; What is life? What is consciousness, thinking, memory, and how does the universe work? Trying to answer such questions it is impossible to avoid the intermixing of science with philosophy and metaphysics, since such questions are pure philosophical and metaphysical ones, to which empirical science is unable to offer any scientifically testable answers [3].

Physics is the most basic level of complexity within science. At a much higher level of complexity exists DNA, biological processes. At another level our thought processes are basically information processing. The universe can be viewed as a crystalline lattice of interacting logic units each one "deciding" zillions of times per second whether it will be off or on at the next point of time. This information, this "logic-unit" product, is the fabric of reality, the stuff of which matter and energy are made. An electron is nothing more than a pattern of information and an orbiting electron is nothing more than the pattern in motion. Indeed even this motion is in some sense illusory. The bits of information that constitute the pattern never move. There are not objects like electrons and protons and things which are themselves and nothing else. There's an information process and the bits, when they are in certain configurations, behave like the things we call the electron, or the hydrogen atom, or whatever.

INFORMATION AND ORGANIZED SYSTEMS

As we have already seen, DNA is a prominent part in the recognizing that information is a fundamental and constituent element of the natural world. DNA carries the genetic information which determines how a single cell will develop into a tree, a flower, an animal, or a man. The important and astonishing thing is that DNA, a physical substance, carries information, a non-material substance, a pure mental process and product. Human information is only one form of information. But there are also non-human forms of information. The non-random distribution of atoms and molecules in living systems, that is, the intricate organization of matter and energy which makes life possible, is itself a product of the vast store of information contained within the system itself. Disorder does not provide information of this type. Disorder could, in fact, destroy information especially high level information as in living organisms. Information is a function of organization. Disordering a system causes it to lose information. Information exists, it does not need to be understood to exist. Without this insight it becomes impossible to understand this physical universe. A book contains information whether it is read or not. The information is there, even if it is not transferred to human reader. The phenomenon we call "meaning" involves a gradient of relationships between physical information and mental interpretations [11]. Meaningful information refers to the information which can be conveyed to a receptor. Both biological and mineral systems not only contain information, but exhibit information processing capabilities as well.

So, since information and organization are intimately interrelated then

(a)   All organized structures contain information and no organized structure can exist without containing some form of information.

(b)   The addition of information to a system manifests itself by causing a system to become more organized or reorganized.

(c)   An organized system has the capacity to release or convey information, [11].

Since energy is defined as the capability to perform work, so, information can be defined as the capacity to organize a system, or to maintain it in an organized state. It becomes impossible to perform "useful" work without an input of both energy and information.

A structure or a system may be said to be organized if it exhibits order. Order is a non-random arrangement of the parts of the structure or system. Even certain forms of apparent randomness exhibit significant order, e.g. a perfect uniform distribution. For this reason the terms chaos and disorder are preferable. Analyzing the information content of a chaotic system is made more problematic by the fact that a system may only appear to be chaotic. That is, such a system actually is responding to a simple algorithm [6]. Information, like energy, is an abstract quantity. Prof. Dr. Tom Stonier [11] proposes that information, like energy, also possesses a physical reality. Structure is the product of the interaction between matter and information. Information may be considered as the more abstract quantity which, when added to matter, manifests itself as structure (organization). It should be emphasized here that information itself as a mental process and result has no material substance. Only the expression, the manifestation of information presents itself as a structure (organization). Thus the principle is that information is a property of the universe - that it comprises the "internal" structure of the universe. Tom Stonier [11] by the term "Internal" means that every time scientists define a constant, Avogadro's number, Boltzmann or Plank's Constant, etc., they have discovered another aspect of the organization of the universe. Each such discovery represents the human perception of the information contained within physical systems. The physics of information systems has a reality which is independent of human perception and which therefore transcends it. But also the mathematics of chaos has demonstrated that even apparently highly irregular patterns, may be the product of some rather simple algorithm which underlies the chaos, and algorithm is information, too.

REALITY AND INFORMATION

Since Galileo's classic experiments, physicists and engineers have described all motion in terms of distance and time. All motion involves a reorganization of the universe as such, all motion may be considered to represent an "information act'. Direction is an information term and not a form of matter or energy. The description of motion involves a statement about the changes in the information status of the system [11]. Avogadro's number, Heisenberg or Boltzmann's constant or the speed of light, all define fixed relationships or sets of relationships within the universal system which imply order within the system and in turn reflects the information contained by the system. Pauli's Exclusion Principle, so vital to the organization of matter, must reflect an information property of atomic shells. Fundamental particles themselves, may exhibit information properties. Quarks are assigned properties such as a Charm or Beauty, Up and Down which imply some relational property characteristic of systems containing information. The same may be said of electron charge. Also, distance, time, direction, velocity acceleration, represent forms of information.

INFORMATION AND ENTROPY

Any system contains information, independent of its organization. Any system either natural or man-made, contains information. The difference is the degree the quality and quantity of information it contains. The more disordered the system, the less is its information content. The second law of thermodynamics considers that for any system there exists a state of equilibrium towards which the system may change spontaneously. Such a change can occur only at the expense of the displacement of another system towards equilibrium. So, unlike heat, which may be measured precisely, entropy is not perceivable to our physical senses. Entropy is so outside the range of common experience. Entropy, in fact, is a mathematical expression describing disorder. We may disorganize a system by applying heat, as when an ice cube melts by withdrawing heat from its surroundings, or we may disorganize a system by altering its structure, as when a sugar cube is dissolved in water releasing heat to its surrounding.

The entropy of a system may be altered by altering either heat content, or the organization of the system. Either results in a change in the information content of that system. Schroedinger explained why an organism maintains its level of entropy by "sucking" order from its environment [10]. According to Stonier [11], although entropy may be increasing throughout the universe, so is information. The universe, rather than ending up as a uniform soup of particles with very low energies- the entropic death- may instead end up in a state in which all matter and energy have been converted into pure information.

The various forms of energy reflect the nature and amount of information contained within them. Also, changes in distance per unit time measure the changes in the information content of the system containing the moving particle. Space and time are organizational properties of the universe. Proof of this assertion is the General Exclusion Principle which states that no two solids may occupy the same space at the same time. Stonier [11] defines space as the internal between matter, and time, as the internal between events. Measurements of space and time establish information about the distribution and organization of matter and energy.

LIVING WITHIN INFORMATION

Our human environment is filled with devices which either convert energy into information (heat converted into mechanical energy, then into electrical energy, then into electromagnetic radiation which in turn is modulated to carry human messages), or use energy to convert information from one form to another (information transducers). Devices which convert energy into information include electronic signal generators, radios, printing press, computers, etc. A side product would be heat and the entropy of the universe would have been increased.

Not only computers, but all machines contain information. Living systems including the human brain process the most complex information known by machines. Inorganic systems, such as crystal may also be considered in terms of an information machine. The theory of cellular automata in artificial intelligence, has led some theorists [9] to suggests that the entire universe, as a gigantic information machine, processing matter, energy and information. But the energy itself in any form (including heat as a low grade form of energy) in a final analysis is a form of information. Everything in the natural world is a form of information. The difference between energy and useful work of any kind, is the quality, the quantity and the level of information which they carry.

Also, randomness is a form of information. It contains some measure of information, too. All forms of energy contain an expressed information component. Physical constants, laws and scientifically identified relationships between natural events and phenomena reflect an ordering of physical systems or events and hence information. Information is not only a product, a construct of the human mind, or a mental construct to help us understand the world we inhabit. It is also a constituent, a basic property and the ultimate constituent of the universe as real as are matter and energy. Under this perception, information itself, is beyond matter and energy, which are expressed forms of perceived information, and is the ultimate intrinsic constituent of the natural world.

CONCLUSION

On the basis of these considerations, matter and energy, any natural system (living or not), in fact, the whole universe may be considered as expressed information of various forms and levels. On the other hand, information is part of our daily experiences. Every time we talk, read, watch television, hear or look at any object, or on a piece of art, or doing anything, we express or get information. We can say that every day we are living in an immense surrounding of expressed information of various kinds and forms. All human activities, as products of mental processes, are essentially information manifested in the natural world we live. Each manifested piece of information has a meaning which is either directly comprehensible or needs an explanation and interpretation. When we see a table, a spoon, a clock, we can understand immediately what the maker pursued. But when we are looking at a piece of abstract fine art, like a painting or sculpture, we are not able directly, in most cases, to understand what the artist would like to express. In that case anyone may freely ascribe to it any meaning he prefers, unless the artist has already signified what he wanted to present and express by his piece of abstract art. The same is applicable to any natural thing, event or system. What science tries to do, is to investigate all the forms of natural things (including matter and energy) and their various forms of organization by the interpretation of the collected data, in order to find out their information content. The subject of investigation is not the information itself, but the manifested, the expressed information in the natural world, since the information itself is always inaccessible.

Information itself, as we have said, has no material substance. It is an internal intellectual function of mind quite different from any other physical or biological function prior to its expression and appearance in the natural world. Only when the information has been rendered outside the mind, when manifested in the natural world by some form (writing, orally, or by any kind of construction - natural or human), can it be approached, otherwise it is inaccessible to any other person.

There is no way or means to know the content of any unexpressed information before its appearance outside of the mind and consequently, it is beyond the capabilities of any scientific research and investigation by empirical science. So, what we see and search in the natural world, are only the expressions of information itself, which underlie natural reality, and hence it is inaccessible, as such, to scientific investigation by empirical methods.

We must emphasize that reality is not what we can see and investigate by scientific research, but what is hidden to our sensory means. What we can research and investigate is the manifestation, and expression of reality, which in fact is the pure information before any expression. Information itself is the result of a mental function, before this function appeared in the natural world in any form. These forms of expressed information are accessible to us and thus subject to scientific knowledge. Pure unexpressed information, having no material substance, is unapproachable. This is the ultimate reality behind any natural system. By this approach the problem of scientific research and knowledge can be more clearly understandable. Thus, it is apparent why matters such as the ultimate consistency, and the real essence of the natural world, the origin and the ultimate nature of life, other limitations and which existed in science [4], are not problems of any scientific research, but are transcendental, metaphysical issues, subject to dogmatic assumptions, or religious faith. Any attempt to answer these questions must be unavoidably based either on a priori untestable scientifically hypothesis and conjectural theory, or directly on a pure religious faith. In either case, we can not get any scientific knowledge.

What this concept of information offers (as not only the third fundamental quantity besides matter and energy, but as the ultimate reality), to contemporary scientific thinking, is that we may be able to define in the best possible way the boundaries between science and other realities beyond our four dimensional natural world.

REFERENCES

[1]   Kelvin L. Anderson, **New Trends in the Molecular Basis for Variation**, Creation Research Society Quarterly, Vol.26, September 1991.

[2]   H. Blum, **Time arrow and Evolution**, Princeton University Press, 1955, Princeton, NJ

[3]   M. Denton, **Evolution: A Theory in Crisis**, 1986, Adler and Adler, Bethesda, MD USA.

[4]   A. Ch. Frangos, **Some Necessary Remarks on Scientific Knowledge**, Proceedings of the Second International Conference on Creationism, 1990, Vol.1, pp.85-90, Editors: Robert E. Walsh, et al, Creation Science Fellowship, Inc., Pittsburgh, PA, USA

        _____, **The Great Delusion**, Proceedings to the First International Conference on Creationism, 1986, Vol.1 pp.49-56, Editors: Robert E. Walsh, et al, Creation Science Fellowship, Inc., Pittsburgh, PA, USA.

        _____, **The Correct Approach to Scientific Theories**, Creation Research Society Quarterly, Vol.28, June 1991.

[5]   Werner Gitt, **Information: The Third Fundamental Quantity**, Siemens Review, Germany, Vol. 56, No.6 November/ December 1989.

[6]   J. Gleick, **Chaos**, 1988, Penguin Books, New York.

[7]   David A. Kaufmann, **Functional Proteins: Chaos or Logos**, Creation Research Society Quarterly, Vol.28. September 1991. Reprinted from Kaufmann, David A., **Functional Proteins: Chaos or Logos**, Proceedings of the Second International Conference on Creationism, 1990, Vol 1., pp. 123-126, Editors: Robert E. Walsh, et al, Creation Science Fellowship, Inc., Pittsburgh, PA, USA.

[8]   Jerome Lejeune, **L' Enceinte Concentrationnaire**, 1990, Le Sarment Fayard, Libraire Artheme Fayard, France.

[9]   W. Poundstone, **The Recursive Universe**, 1985, Contemporary Books, Chicago.

[10]   E. Schrodinger, **What is Life**, 1944, Cambridge University Press, Cambridge, England.

[11]   Tom Stonier, **Information and the International Structure of the Universe**, 1990 Springer-Verlag [London] Ltd. England.

[12]   A. E. Wilder-Smith, **A Basis for a New Biology**, 1976, Telos International Eingen, Switzerland.

[13]   Jablonka, E., M. Lachmann and M. J. Lambs, **Evidence, Mechanisms and Models for the Inheritance of Acquired Characters**, 1992, Journal of Theoretical Biology, 158: 245-268,

[14]   Gesteland, R. F., R. B. Weiss and J. F. Atkins, **Recoding Reprogrammed Genetic Decoding**, 1992, Science, 257: 1640-1641.

PRESCIENCE PROPHECY: A PYRRHIC APOLOGETIC

TERRY R. GREEN
13211 FAIRVIEW
GARDEN GROVE, CALIFORNIA 92640

KEYWORDS

Prescience prophecy- prophecies of science rather than history, and so, designed and hidden insights into various facets of nature and science.

Phenomenological- describing things as they appear in nature to the average person, rather than their more literal essence, as seen in the sciences.

Nonpostulational- language and purpose in the Bible that does not address postulates or theories of a scientific nature but rather is teleologically oriented.

ABSTRACT

The worlds of science and the Bible represent two complementary sources of knowledge with different purposes, language, and methods. Linguistics is a main cause of conflict in science and Bible. Biblical language, aiming for relationship with God, is emotive and popular or the language of appearance. Science, concerned with physical and intermediate cause and effect, is precise, mechanistic and reductionistic. Scientific foreknowledge is more than just inerrancy claims and is logically classified as prescience prophecy. Yet, its innate misuse of the nature of science and Bible does not fit any biblical pattern of prophecy. A sampling of prescience prophecy shows a flawed hermeneutic which produces contradictory doctrines and a confused reliance on each generation's science.

INTRODUCTION

Our study will be primarily presuppositional rather than exegeting individual verses. Such is vital due to the perennial metamorphosis of each text which, like the blind man in a dark basement at night with the lights off, is trying to catch a black cat which isn't there. The hermeneutics of prescience will catch the cat anyway.

Science and theology are like the pair of eyes God gave us- both mutually helpful if cooperating. Bible and science bear many similarities from hermeneutics to models and language [1]. While any relation of science and Bible has its problems [74, p.129-149], there are also peculiar problems with something as basic as defining the nature and methods of science [44]; [46]. While there is a general "scientific method", such is the effect of several valid methods to establish laws [54], themselves but logical constructs subject to revision [89].

Kuhn's monumental work [44] showed every scientific method involves nonempirical or nonscientific elements. Antiquated logical positivism, as expressed by Francis Bacon, hinders both science and Bible research. The Baconian fallacy is that one can research with just the raw data or cold facts. There really are no preconceived questions, presuppositions, paradigms, prejudices, hypotheses, etc. Fischer's observation of a historian's work is also true of a scientist's: He is supposed to go a-wandering through the dark forest of the past, gathering facts like nuts and berries, until he has enough to make a general truth. Then he is to store up his general truths until he has the whole truth. This idea is doubly deficient, for it commits a historian to the pursuit of an impossible object by an impracticable method [26, p.4].

The Bible provides neither a scientific method nor a systematic cosmology. It speaks of all creation being totally dependent in its origin and existence on the will of God, Genesis 1.1ff; Acts 17.24; Romans 11.36. As one studies the origins of modern science and the history of the warfare between science and the Bible [43], he perceives that both scientist and Christian were at fault in the matter. Kuhn notes that

Scientist-historians and those who followed their lead characteristically imposed contemporary scientific categories, concepts, and standards on the past. Sometimes a specialty which they traced from antiquity had not existed as a recognized subject for study until a generation before they wrote. Nevertheless, knowing what belonged to it, they retrieved the current contents of the specialty from the past texts of a variety of heterogeneous fields, not noticing that the tradition they constructed in the process had never existed [45, p.149].

Likewise, a parallel exists today in religion. We take today's precise and empirical science and read it back into the biblical text, all the while failing to notice such "had never existed." It is not the nature of the Bible that creates this tension, most Bible-science arguments being philosophical rather than textual.

Thesis

Prescience prophecy is the teaching that the Bible, being God's word, contains many statements that are really forecasts or prophecies of then undiscovered and undiscoverable scientific truths. It is prophecy about science rather than history. If such predictions are truly in the Bible, then they are a powerful source of apologetic evidences. However, if such is not valid, it subverts faith in the Bible.

One reason for prescience prophecy's acceptance is a misunderstanding of the nature and purpose of the Bible. Some maintain that the Bible is like science's modern methods- aiming for totality in precision of empirically describing nature. Hence, the Bible is designed by God to be a touchstone for any scientific idea.

A second problem is that prescience often refers to finding a final or ultimate scientific view of the real nature of things. But scientific foreknowledge is premised on scientific knowledge. Thus to claim for Bible verses a modern scientific nature does not give them ultimacy for the simple reason that science is not nor can it ever be a total picture of reality [80, p.20-21].

Such scientism demands an interpretation of verses that must have been meaningless and absurd to the original recipients and would have tied faith into the writer's own dated science. If the Bible had been written so as to reveal and rely upon any or each generations most advanced science or philosophy such would be as strange to them as a "green cheese moon" is to us or miracles to modern man.

In short, the Bible is written in the common man's language. To ignore this simple fact directly contributes to finding fantastic prescience facts only to be rejected the next generation by an updated science and hermeneutics. If the Bible spoke in an "ultimate" language none would understand it. And if it is put in 20th century scientific language, it would be grotesque and meaningless to most people today and to all previous and subsequent generations. To go to the Bible for "proof of science, for proof of prescience, for proof of the Bible, for proof of God" is a procedure founded in a mutated hermeneutic of both science and Bible [39, p.2:624].

Linguistic Labyrinth

"And then he took the helmet off again- but it took hours and hours to get me out [of it]. I was as fast as-as lightning, you know."

"But that's a different kind of fastness," Alice objected.

The Knight shook his head, "It was all kinds of fastness with me, I can assure you!"

[Lewis Carroll, Through The Looking-Glass.]

The differences in language and purpose of both science and Bible have long been recognized [95, p.142:195-208]. From the perspective of logic or linguistics it is errant to try to force into the scriptures a special Holy Ghost "scienteese" language which is pregnant with occasional, but brilliant and revealing, insights into distant centuries of science [34, p.319]. These then are allegedly discovered by each generation as technology becomes Providence's sword to cut them open, their brilliance and inspiration shining forth.

Due to logical positivism's impact on science, religious language was considered neither true nor false but meaningless, though recent work in the philosophy of science refutes such treatment of theological language. Even in the most empirical of sciences nonempirical elements inhere [1, p.3-8]. Instead, science and the Bible are complementary, not contradictory, models [p.71-91]. Further, Kuhn historically illustrates that advocates of competing paradigms practice their disciplines in different worlds, and so will see different things looking at them from the same spot in the same direction [44, p.150].

This principle applies to both science and theology [87, p.406] and requires that we see the purpose and nature of what we study, not just "hard facts." The reductionistic and analytical methods of science are legitimate and helpful but in theology they produce not only the death of God but the death of man. A text without a context is but a pretext, and with prescience is but a physics turned philosopher. Such scientism sees the scientific method as the greatest, if not the only, path to truth and will read biblical texts this way, producing both prescience and false prophecy proofs.

Purpose

Even without any proof of prescience prophecies in the Bible some find it very difficult, in view of the doctrine of inspiration, to accept the fact that the Bible's language is not scientifically precise. To some, taking the language of the Bible as anything less than "final and absolute and perfect" is blasphemy. But the issue involves more than prescience [90].

Purpose is central to shaping the type of language we use. Several points arise here. The "Bible, in its references to nature, is concerned primarily with purpose. Pattern is related to purpose through plan. The Bible has much to say on the subject of purpose, plan, and pattern in nature" [66, p.5:294]. The Bible, in contrast to science, is theocentric or describes things, including nature, in terms of God's role. Thus all causal links are theological rather than intermediate. It is not Aristotle's efficient cause, but the formal and final causes or the plan and purpose the Bible focuses on [41, p.176]. For example, the Bible writers' primary paradigm is that of a theocentric universe rather than a geo- or helio-centric solar system.

Efforts to "scientize" the Bible have led to endless levels of distinctions which the Bible never intended for itself. Calovius' Systema Locorum Theologicorum is a good illustration of ancient scholastic distinctions of causes being applied to theology: 1) causa efficiens, 2) causa impulsiva, 3) causa instrumentalis, 4) materia creationis, 5) forma creationis, 6) fiais creationis, 7) tempus creationis, and 8) consequentia creationis [21, p.94]. Even "meaning" has twenty three definitions [64 p.186f] and "word" fragments into many specialized definitions [91, p.27]. Causation in science is not equal to purpose in theology. Even "truth" is different in logic and Bible [60; 31, p.23).

Both the respective works of McMillen and Barfield show that in the Bible there are many dietary and preventive laws that make excellent health sense and are uncorrupted by pagan concepts. Yet, the Bible was not designed to be an anthology of medical practices any more than it is to be for any other discipline. England [24, p.146], sympathetic to the possibility of a few cases of "scientific forethought" in health areas, yet wisely says that the OT "medical" practices such as not eating blood Lev. 3.17; 17.10-13; 1 Sam. 14.31-35; Ezek. 33.25] were for spiritual reasons. This was the most important element in the Bible's paradigm of redemption [35, p.191]. Being popular language, it is wrong to charge the Bible with error from ignorance in its times. Yet, since it is not written as some special ultimate language and modern medical law, it is thus also wrong to charge it elsewhere with brilliant prescientific insights, as if such were its purpose.

Second, purpose always limits a topic whether theological or scientific. If the primary purpose for the Bible's existence is to secure man's fellowship with God (1 Jn. 1.1-3), then everything within the Bible is designed from before creation to meet this goal (Eph. 1.3; 3.10f). Yet, we see that some things within the Bible are themselves limited, even for this goal. Thus, the Bible can speak of God's revealed will being spiritual, holy, good and perfect (Rom. 7.12ff) yet also being imperfect, weak and useless (Heb. 7.18f). It speaks of Christ's perfect sacrifice for sins "once for all time," (Heb. 7.26f) yet there being a lacking in it (Col. 1.24). It speaks of the Bible being the very mind and words of God (1 Cor. 2.13) yet it is in the koine or common man's Greek, with all of its limits. It speaks of Jesus as Deity (John 1.1) yet living in the flesh as human (v.14; Phil. 2.5ff) with its many limitations.

From a hermeneutical perspective, prescience is the result of a concordant view of science and Scripture, treating Bible topics as but simple points to look up as with words in a concordance. From a philosophical perspective its presupposition is that of a concordist view of Bible and science. Such appears to be but an updated version of Origen's allegorical method of interpretation. To Origen's literal, moral, spiritual and anagogical senses was added a fifth, scientific meaning [41, p.259]. Such an allegorical method capitalizes on imagination and ignorance, breeding a speculative theology reminiscent of cultic abuse of analogy, forever envisioning fantastic discoveries of modern times in the Bible text.

The Bible nowhere presents a systematized hermeneutic even of itself, much less a single "scientific method." Its very purpose is to spiritually prepare man (2 Tim. 3.16f). It is not arranged as a systematic psychology [19] a systematic history [52], a systematic cosmology [71, p.69] or a systematic theology [13, p.65-95]. We are not to bring our own modern scientific categories into the ancient texts as if these categories and doctrines are either ultimate standards or concepts the original writers were aware of. Such a Pyrrhic victory, while embellishing the Bible with glory, elevates science into a holy dogma [3, p.26]

Differences in Bible and science statements can be reconciled, but it requires careful handling of matters of both fact and faith [29. p.211-212]. Differences involve the anthropological nature of scripture where nature, God, heaven and hell are described by thought forms common to any age rather than in the dated language of each generation's scientific terminology. In no way does this accommodation affect the truth or the religious value of the passage.

That which is declared is real, but only intelligible to men through their language and in their thought form [22, p.1:34-35]. While God accommodates himself to man's understanding this "accommodatio or condescensio" refers to the method or mode of revelation, God's infiniteness incarnated in finite form, not to the quality of the revelation" [58, p.19].

Language

To classify the Bible's language as different than science's is not to limit it but to loose it for its rightful role. Without this innate self-limiting, any discipline becomes but a Humpty-Dumpty logic where words mean nothing precisely because they mean everything. Even within the broad area of "science" one cannot automatically equate the same terms from different disciplines. An elementary rule of hermeneutics is that *context* defines each word. Thus, even in strict Bible study one learns to recognize that words do not mean the same thing in different settings- as Alice experienced with the White Knight. A number of points emerge.

First, for God to reach all men of all ages He wrote the Bible so even the least educated and unscientific of men could understand it. This was by using a koine or an "overlap" language used by men of all social levels [63, p.120-125]. He did not aim at meticulous precision but phrased things as they commonly or normally are seen by man. Popular language must of necessity contain generalized numbers, imprecise quotations, and non chronological narration, but such is not error unless intended to be measured by modern scientific precision [27, p.221].

Second, this type of popular language has the value of being permanent and pervasive. Despite "all scientific advancement the world still speaks, and probably ever will continue to speak, of the sun's rising and setting" [86, p.539]. When the Bible speaks of nature, its references are simply observations of things as they appear, without being shaped by some now obsolete theory or without being explained by some as yet unintelligible, ultimate theory of the future. Furthermore, the Bible, as any discipline, develops its own uniqueness in language due to its own peculiar purpose and nature [28, p.166].

Third, the misunderstanding of Bible language may not only create prescience discoveries but may just as consistently create false prophecy proofs where the "methods of modern science are applied to Bible study: thorough analysis followed by careful synthesis" consisting of precise charting out of literalized detail [49, p.60]. It is a failure to understand or utilize the differences in the language of science and Scripture, which creates both the desire to "scientize" Scripture and the attendant problems in so doing. Scientific language is highly specialized and nonemotive, seeking to systematically classify experience under increasingly detailed categories defined by meticulously specialized vocabularies. This is all in contrast to both the purpose and language of the Bible itself. Prescience prophecy is a good example of what Nida terms "a kind of linguistic mathematics" [62, p.223].

Fourth, if the Bible has pre scientific prophecies, then it also has errant verses with false science. The same literalizing, mixing of purposes and etymologizing equally proves both prescience, false science and cultic prophecies.

For example, the Bible's nonscientific classification of the coney and the hare (Lev. 11.5,6; Deut. 14.7), and the ant (Prov. 6.6-8; 30.25), can only be non contradictory to scientific categories by recognizing the phenomenological and nonpostulational nature of Bible language. While there is "cause and effect" in the Bible, it is a very different kind than science studies. The Bible has its focus on the ultimate, not mediate, cause of a thing. Science is just the reverse of this in purpose and methodology.

This is not errancy unless one assumes some sort of scientific precision is intrinsic in the Bible's language, such being a modern categorization superimposed upon an ancient text. Further, the writers of the Bible books were not obligated to digress into a dissertation of some scientific categorization even if the popular view of the reader/hearer was errant according to science's classification]. Popular language always uses this liberty, but it is not therefore chargeable with error [50, p.9:448].

Quite often ancient etymological root meanings and modern terms are sources of prescience proofs. Such is but a radical and mutated form of what Cotterell and Turner call "etymologizing, namely anachronism; that is the explanation to etymologizing in terms of senses which only developed later" [16, p.133]. Indeed, with enough Humpty Dumpty logic and twisted hermeneutics we could ex nihilo create any type of prescience, but a foolish historian of the future may do the same with us from the same linguistic gymnastics.

The Bible clearly does not profess to anticipate later generation's scientific discoveries, historically always "ours." Rather, nature is described as it appears, not as science defines it. Wise expositors of the Scriptures, older and younger, have always recognized this [65, p.1:340].

Errancy?

Truth is like strands of a rope; each complementing the other though each strand may be distinguished. Science and Bible are like this. The Bible's phenomenological language is intended to present only a descriptive view of how things normally appear. The corollary of this is that the Bible does not speculate on the actual nature of things by giving a systematic theory of the sciences [72, p.210].

In the Bible the whole of the universe is viewed from the perspective of humans standing upon the planet earth and looking all about and above them. This is a universal practice for humans, even though it differs markedly with today's modern scientific language. Each is accurate and useful to its intended purpose [97, p.1:267].

The Bible's purpose being spiritual and not scientific, causes it to lack scientific precision, as is seen in its use of several words, phrases, or books, to describe a thing [4]. If we understood this view of Scripture we would "avoid borrowing modern scientific canons to defend the accuracy and reliability of the Bible" [37, p 9]. The Bible has its own glory and honor in its intended purpose. In this, it is all sufficient and uniquely permanent (2 Tim. 3.16f; Eph. 3.3ff; Jude 3). A true test of commitment to inerrancy is whether ones hermeneutic is tied to scientific or philosophical systems. Anytime the Bible is equated with a particular philosophy or science the Bible dies when that philosophy or science dies [8, p.268-270]. When our physics and metaphysics are married then science and theology will end up divorced [42, p.137].

While but a probability in principle, historically it is a certainty which destroys the Bible's credibility in more important areas [7, p.24:3-22]. We can always look backward in time and laugh at attempts to prove the agreement between Biblical infallibility and scientific findings [68, p.3:21-25]. But we must remember that the same thing will be done by future generations as they look back on our alleged prescience prophecies. Arguing that the tree of knowledge in Genesis 2.17 "could, in modern language, be translated as being a central computer, since knowledge is the important concept rather than the tree" [32, p.60] is a perfect example of this.

Woodbridge shows that accepting the Bible's limits on science is neither unscriptural nor recent [96, p.257-264]. The Bible was well on its way to cutting its ties with science by the second half of the seventeenth century. But, as Carson observed this uncoupling was usually followed by a shift to a liberal theological position that no longer affirmed the infallibility of Scripture [12, p.15].

Such, a shift, however, is not logically necessary. It represented a case of dethroning man's errant views of Bible and science. Scripture is written in popular language, precluding both today's precision and prescience. If it were not so written it would require one to think and see through the eyes of an ideal language framework which is not only worlds apart from the language patterns of the biblical writings but also quite foreign and elusive to our own most disciplined linguistic usage [34, p.259].

This approach does not admit of errancy in any area, but it allows the universality of the Bible to convey its perennial message. It does not contaminate but commonizes the Bible. As Jaki concludes,

> the whole history of metaphysics shows that metaphysical systems were to be discredited in the measure in which they were grafted on a particular form of physics. When the physics in question was simply a parody of physics, as a so-called "higher" physics had to be, then the force of logic asserted itself with fearful rapidity [42, p.137].

What Is Prescience?

Though eclectic in usage, the common theme of prescience is that of designed, hidden insights into future understandings of nature, indiscernible until later scientific technologies discover them. Some classify it with prophecy. Others as but natural expressions of an omniscient God. A few claim it is merely unknowable error free statements on nature. Most, however, end up with a combination of these methods, plus whatever else seems to work. One is reminded of the conversation between Alice and Humpty Dumpty:

> "You seem very clever at explaining words, Sir," said Alice. "Would you kindly tell me the meaning of the poem called Jabberwocky?"

> "I can explain all the poems that ever were invented- and a good many that haven't been invented just yet."

I have never found a lack of ability on the part of some to create meanings in prescience texts- even ones not yet thought up! Let's look at these three main positions in reverse order.

First, if prescience prophecies are only unknowable error free statements about nature then we must (1) prove such was undiscoverable to other nations; (2) prove prescience is the goal of the text; and (3) see that any such statements of prescience will only use normal language.

Second, if prescience proofs are planned and purposeful, what is their purpose but to show the Bible is from a God of prophecy? "Show us the things that are to come hereafter, that we may know that ye are gods" (Isa. 41.23) now becomes an excellent statement of what prescience is supposed to achieve- prophecy. Hence, we are lead to the only consistent position for prescience. Yet, we must remember:

(1) Accuracy of a statement of future events is not proof of inspiration or prophecy, for luck or prognostication achieve this.

(2) A close parallel to an event and a prophecy does not prove it is the fulfillment of the prophecy, prescience or otherwise. Similarity is not the same as synonymous.

(3) Whatever is allowed as proof of prescience prophecy must also be allowed as proof of historical prophecy. If etymological roots, similarity with modern words, etc. proves prescience then they also may prove false prophecy of cultists.

(4) There is a pattern to prophecy in the Bible though it may be eclectic, Hebrews 1.1. Prescience prophecy must fit into that pattern if it is to be accepted as genuine. If we claim for prescience the same honors and rights we give prophecy, then it must submit to the same qualifications and traits (51, p.147-184, 277-335).

Science's nature, our first area of concern, is such that it speaks a different language from a different purpose than the Bible. Prescience proofs are not fundamentally arguments on Bible inspiration; rather, they are statements about the nature of science and its language. Thus the Bible should not be used as either a science textbook or a prescience source book. In order to see how defective this approach is, consider applying it in the opposite manner: let us practice going to the technical, scientific journals and books and finding there the answers to the meaning and purpose of life. But is not this the very criticism which is rightly leveled at scientism's abuse of science; that it purports to be some sort of ultimate epistemology and ontology? Then by what hermeneutical process are we to justify it with the Bible toward scientific truths?

When one states that a verse is prescience prophecy, we need to ask, "Whose science?" Is it first or fifteenth or twentieth century science? All science is dated and relative, never final and exhaustive. Is one saying that a word or phrase that is used in the Bible (Hebrew, Greek, English) is identical in meaning with the same word (or word "type") used in today's science? Such no more proves prescience than pretend prophecy.

If prescience prophecy truly speaks of a deeper, hidden nature of reality, then it must speak in the scientific language of a given generation, each of which must change. If all prescience prophecy belongs to one generation then it will prove to be worthless to future generations. If it is not, then it is still cryptic and confusing as the Bible would be filled with hidden and "mixed" science from many ages. How are we to tell which proof is for which age because the relation and practice of each age is that "they all had her" (Matt. 22.28)?

Prophecy's nature is our second area of concern. With any claim of a prescience prophecy we should begin by asking "How do you know such is prophecy?"

First, prescience prophecies are said to be divinely revealed insights undiscoverable to a given generation. To so prove this point one must have an exhaustive knowledge of ancient cultures. Most prescience proofs fail here, either assuming or generalizing the ignorance of the ancients.

Second, what about the central criterion used to test other prophecies, namely, the meaning of such to contemporary hearers? Historical prophecy would be of little or no value to first century Christians if it spoke in detail about Hitler, Pope John Paul II, the Viet Nam war, etc. How much more worthless is it for ancient Hebrew saints to be told cryptically about quantum physics, Einstein's theories of relativity, and modern telecommunications? If pre scientific proofs did exist, the original hearers, the prime recipients, would be able to neither confirm nor understand it. If, as the factuality of the case would prove to be, such pre scientific proofs are stated in vague and cryptic language, then they are worthless precisely because they can mean anything. Hence, they mean nothing! With such prescience proofs one is at a loss to conjecture its real value for the many generations who perused it during the intervening millenniums [fifty-nine centuries], and may marvel still more to observe that after this long waiting it has so slight an influence on the average skeptic! The radical fallacy of all these pompous claims is the tacit assumption that the Scriptures were designed to anticipate the discoveries of science [85, p.43].

The third aspect of prescience and prophecy is their verification in the N.T. There are several NT keys to fulfilled prophecy: "This is that", Acts 2.16; time words, Daniel 2,44; parallels, Isaiah 2.2f & Micah 4.1f; and Christ, Luke 24.25ff. Yet are there any cases where a N.T. inspired writer said, "This is that..." when quoting an O.T. pre scientific prophecy in the N.T.? Never do we find even the vaguest hint of such in the N.T. It is true, that there is a wide variety of the use of prophecy in the Bible (Nicole), but we never find even one case of such prescience prophecy quoted. Why do we, however, find literally hundreds of cases in Scripture of promarturomenon (forewitnessing, Peter 1.11) about Christ yet never one single case of a prescience prophecy? It is for the simple reason that such does not exist.

For example, over twenty-five percent of the Bible is of predictive material, or prophecy [67, p.13]. Out of the 31,124 verses of the Bible 8,352 (or, 27%) of these contain predictive material. Never once in 31,124 verses does the Bible quote or allude to prescience prophecy. Such a vacuum of data hardly justifies utilization of alleged prescience proofs as strong apologetic arguments, and it weakens the use of prophecy in other areas by diluting its nature. We should expect at least one clear N.T. quotation to establish a "type" or pattern of sorts [67]. Yet, there is not a single one to be found despite a massive amount of O.T. quotations in the N.T. [59; 61]. Without exception, all purported prescience proofs are historically fulfilled a posteria, itself reflective of a defunct hermeneutic.

Finally, accepting the phenomenological and non-postulational nature of Bible descriptions frees it to be relevant for all ages. Not so if we take them as ultimate or hidden precise concepts. Without such a hermeneutical principle to guide us, prescience proofs become the proverbial enigma wrapped inside a mystery and cloaked within a riddle.

Prescience Proofs

"Reality is harsh to the feet of shadows" - [C. S. Lewis, The Great Divorce]

There are several writers who argue for and cite many alleged prescience prophecies: Barfield, Bouw, Cairney, McMillen, DeHoff, Henry Morris, Rimmer, Schnabel, Segerberg, C. R. Smith, Thompson & Jackson, and Wallace. Wallace, for example, cites five areas [92, p.22-27] and gives ten specific cases [93, p.42-46] which include such proofs "on matters of science and invention" as the telegraph and radio, modern aviation and the atomic theory.

Thompson and Jackson, while rejecting such application of prescience to inventions or technology, yet apply it to fifteen scientific discoveries [88, p.125-137]. Schnabel cites 30 cases from six categories of modern science (astronomy, physics, biology, etc.) which, he says, by a "simple, direct interpretation" [ii] of the Bible's "non-scientific terms" [iii] reveals "an amazingly accurate knowledge which will "predescribe later scientific discoveries" [iii'. Cairney claims the Bible "predicts" in "phenomenal detail and with incredible accuracy" [11, p.125] such modern discoveries. These all are but a few in the long history of failures, not only of specific cases but, of this whole approach [10; 43; 71].

Ravens & Desks

Rarely do those who cite prescience prophecies bother to develop their hermeneutical proof. Even rarer is their exegesis of the fundamental interrelation of science, language, and prophecy. If cultists were as hermeneutically negligent, we would reject their proofs a priori on the basis of viable presuppositional premises. Indeed, this same hermeneutical approach is used by religions of every nature to prove their divineness. Such a hermeneutic logically requires that we:

(1)   apply it consistently throughout the Bible, creating unavoidable contradictions.

(2)   allow it with all other religions from Nostradamus' prophecies [73, p.167] to Islam's Qur'an [9; 38] to Eastern religions like Hinduism and Buddhism [84; 98].

For example, while Plato accepted the logical possibility of a multiplicity of powerful and intelligent beings, the great Isaac Newton, also from a philosophical basis, added a new element to it, showing it is a universe, not a multiverse. Around this analogy he would build all of his science [25, p.1:674]. In more modern times, Henry Morris [55], uses such analogy to prove creation reveals "the Trinity."

Analogy is an innate part of reason in any discipline, being historically the most fruitful way of integrating science and theology [21, p.286-287]. But, Lewis Carroll's question "Why is a raven like a writing desk?" is rhetorical, pointing out anything can be compared to anything and thus similarity is not sameness [57, p.163].

Prescience prophecy commits the hermeneutical fallacy of what Lockhart termed "disconnected particulars" [48, p.176-178]. By the overextending of parallels in an analogy, as some do with parables, or by overstress on peripheral details, it forces passages to yield more than what they were meant to. Our objection is the requirement that biblical interpretation has to keep up with scientific speculation, shifting its hermeneutic and exegesis with each new theory or discovery [23, p.46].

Simply put, it is not enough to show parallels by analogy. If we claim for the Bible the glory of science we must accept what makes it so: "sharp antithesis and rigorous dichotomous divisions based on logical principles of contradiction and excluded middle [15, p. 85-86]. A raven may be like a writing desk for a good number of reasons, but scientifically such proofs are "stuff and nonsense."

Those Ignorant Ancients!

Without a doubt the very thought of an earth that spins about 1000 mph on its axis as it rushes about 70,000 mph around the sun which is 93,000,000 miles away, as it soars about 1,000,000 mph around a galaxy that is flying several million mph through an expanding universe [40, p. 56] would have been laughed at by ancient cultures. Yet a common assumption with prescience prophecy is that the ancients knew almost nothing about nature.

Prescience prophecy, based on such assumed ignorance, is just another form of arguing from silence- "I don't know they knew this so they didn't." History of science is filled with a wide spectrum of facts ancient man knew in Bible days, from medical advancement [5], the revolving of earth around the sun [36, p. 70], the Earth free floating in space [17, p. xiv] and the sizes and distances of planets in our system [47, p.72].

The reason we cite these few cases is not that any or all of them necessarily predate Bible statements, such being irrelevant. Rather, they are cited to show that awareness of them arose independent of special divine revelation. In other words, if the ancients were not nearly as unaware or ignorant in their knowledge of nature and sciences as some assume and argue they were, then many statements of biblical writers could be but expressions of common knowledge or, at least, knowable by uninspired insight. While I have elsewhere [33] examined several cases in greater detail, we will here examine only one case, focusing upon the hermeneutics and exegesis of the practice.

Daily Rotation Of The Earth

Have you ever in your life commanded the morning, and caused the dawn to know its place; that it might take hold of the ends of the earth, and the wicked be shaken out of it? It is changed like clay under the seal; and they stand forth like a garment. And from the wicked their light is withheld, and the uplifted arm is broken, [Job 38.12-15].

It is argued that "changed" connoted the meaning of to change by turning or rotating as, in the context, the signet seal rotates over the clay, changing its appearance. So, it is argued, Job speaks pre scientifically of the yet unknown fact that the sun (= ring) changes the earth (= clay) as the clay/earth rotates daily and the ring/sun is stationary. Clearly, they say, this is a prescience prophecy.

First, when the original readers heard these words what did they mean to them? Did they understand the text to be teaching a spherical rotating earth with a stationary sun or the common optical view of a natural phenomenon? England, sympathetic toward the possibility of a few prescience proofs, observes that Job 38 is one of the most greatly abused sections of nature passages in the Bible [24, p.139].

Second, notice what Job does not say. He does not say the earth rotates/revolves daily around a fixed sun (= eisegesis). He does speak of God's power to control nature (= exegesis).

Third, critical commentators disagree with this prescience view. Delitzsch [20, p.2:316] says that "the dawn is like the signet ring, which stamps a definite impress on the earth as the clay." Rawlinson adds that,

as the seal changed the clay from a dull, shapeless lump to a figured surface, so the coming of the dawn changes the earth from an indistinct mass to one diversified with form and color [75, p.7:610].

Fourth, the verses present a similitude where parts of nature (dawn and earth) are compared to or are "like" something else (a seal and changed clay). One should accept a simple, normal reading of the passage, not a forced reading of etymology. We are told that the primary meaning is to change. The secondary meaning is an imprint itself made by the seal, and the third level of meaning is rolling or rotating with a seal. Finally, the true meaning here, we are told, is the third one. Suppose we did this with heaven or hell in the Bible? This is but an example of the fallacy of etymological primacy.

Fifth, what else does this approach prove? If dawn's coming and earth being "changed as clay" prove a rotating sphere, then dawn's taking "hold of the ends of the earth" proves a nonspherical earth (flat, square or triangular?). In the first case it is specifically called a likeness or similarity ("like", "as") but in the latter (earth's "ends") no such words are used. Further, the dawn "takes hold of" earth's ends. Can we see here a "solar powered" earth rotation (and I had always believed that the winds blew on the mountains and spun it around!)? Maybe this refers to the "ghost in the atom" of quantum physics? Also, if this proves a spherical rotation, why not also panentheism, since it speaks of dawn as intelligent ("commanded" and to "know" things)?

Sixth, this passage is enmeshed in the old Ptolomaic vs. Copernician solar system model, both of which have been argued from the Bible. Martin Luther vilified Copernicus' model [94, p.1:126] but Galileo, using the same Bible, argued Joshua's command for the sun to stand still best fit the Copernician model, not the Ptolemaic one. His proof (adopting his opponent's hermeneutics) was Proverbs 8.26 ("hinges" of the earth), where "hinges" would be meaningless unless the earth turned on them [79, p.47]!

Seventh, let us grant the thesis that this verse does teach a rotating earth and stationary sun. What then is proven: prescience prophecy? Not unless all other Bible references are either silent on the matter or concur with the same paradigm, and further, that we know it took special revelation to learn it. We find neither alternative in the Bible's picture. In it the sun moves (Josh. 10.12f; Ps. 19.6f; Eccl. 1.5; Isa. 38.8) and simultaneously the earth is stationary (Ps. 18.7; 24.2; 104.5; Eccl. 1.4; Job 38.4; 2 Pet. 3.5; Rev. 6.14). What the Bible here presents (to acquiesce the point) as a rotating earth and stationary sun it elsewhere (and in a far more historical, rather than poetic, setting) presents as a moving sun and a stationary earth (Joshua 10.12f). What prescience prophecy ignores is a simple hermeneutical fact: biblical language employs an eclectic range of words and models for greater richness, not science's specialized reductionistic terminology.

If one argues that Joshua does not contradict Job here because Joshua spoke (though in a historical context) of the optical view of things, we simply reply, "Prove it." What is the hermeneutic or exegesis which differentiates the two viewpoints, and why does not Job speak optically rather than strictly empirically in his poetical section? Such remarkable homemade hermeneutics lies at the root of Henry Morris' peculiar prescience prophecies. This leads to our final point on this passage.

Eighth, while prescience prophecy often comes across as a simple "just-believe-the-Bible" approach which glorifies God (with opponents cast in quite the opposite light), it really is often rooted in an inordinate affection for science's analytical and empirical methods and is built on a faulty hermeneutic. Again, we cite the Copernican model as an historical example. It was accepted despite the fact that there were three different types of evidences that were presented against it: theological, philosophical and experiential. Since this relates to Joshua's command for the sun to stand still, it raises the issue of interfacing or correlating the hermeneutics of both theology and science [70, p.283-348; 69].

The philosophical and presuppositional basis of many "Bible-science" conflicts is illustrated here. The basis of moving from one model of creation (or parts of it) to another was based most often in the philosophical rather than the scientific or biblical realms. There were many metaphysical presuppositions inherent in the conflicts, such as whether the solar system was geocentric or heliocentric. These assumptions involved things such as the concepts of the four elements, the immutability of the heavens, the necessity of circular motion, the subtlety of the heavens and of the baser earth, the tendency for things to seek their appropriate place with reference to the heavens and earth, the centrality and immobility of the earth. Only for the latter- the centrality and immobility of the earth- could Biblical passages be marshaled... In this total picture the Biblical and strictly scientific elements were indeed meager [21, p. 23].

If Joshua's command is interpreted, not as a normal descriptive phrase but, in scientific precision, then it means that the sun itself was what was moving around the earth. But this is contradictory to the model and to empirical facts as we now know them. We may summarize the hermeneutical and philosophical problems by stating that perhaps we should argue a more sophisticated interpretation by claiming that "God stopped the sun" means that he stopped it in its motion relative to the earth. This is no longer contradictory to the Copernican system. But now the question arises: Should we adopt a simple mathematical description and a complicated, rather "unnatural" interpretation of the Bible or a more complicated mathematical description (motion in loops) and a simple "natural" interpretation of the biblical text [29, p.211-212]?

When considering the role of the critical precision of modern science and the koine (common) Greek of the N.T. days, the Christian will select a koine Bible and a critical science hermeneutic. Both are "correct" but for their respective purposes.

CONCLUSION

The Bible is God's plenary inspired book and therefore inerrant in all areas in its intended purpose. Without doubt prescience prophecy arises from a godly desire to defend God's word. Yet, to the degree that prescience prophecies are shown spurious, they will degrade the value of genuine prophecy and inerrancy. We must not throw out the baby with the bath water for "it is one thing to read modern scientific theory into ancient poetry, but it is another to exclude space-time affirmations from the book authored by the Creator of the physical universe" [30, p 13].

Leading men of science once claimed to be able to see flocks of marching sheep, tiny horses, large eared donkeys, roosters, and even humans who married and had children- all inside the seminal fluid of the respective animals. Clark observes that religious folks, not to be outdone in the field of science, used the Bible as a proof-text. Hebrews 7.9f was supposed to prove that Levi was living inside Abraham and paying tithes [14, pp. 20-24]. Indeed, the thought is father to the act, and necessity is the mother of invention.

The history of the tension between science and the Bible, especially prescience cases, reveals a pattern.

Prescience arguments, once so popular and powerful with both the public and Christians, are much like a retarded stepchild we were forced to adopt due to the necessity of circumstances. But then we politely shuffle him off into the back room because we realize he has come with more problems then he solves. To change metaphors, what began as an uneasy marriage has turned out to be an embarrassing divorce. "...your faith should not rest on the wisdom of men, but on the power of God", 1 Corinthians 2.5.

REFERENCES

[1] Ian Barbour, Myths, Models, And Paradigms: A Comparative Study In Science And Religion, 1974, Harper & Row, NY.

[2] Kenny Barfield, Why The Bible Is Number One: The World's Sacred Writings In The Light Of Science, 1988, Baker, Grand Rapids.

[3] Henri Blocker, In The Beginning: The Opening Chapters Of Genesis, 1984, InterVarsity, Downers Grove.

[4] Craig Blomberg, **The Legitimacy And Limits Of Harmonization,** Hermeneutics, Authority, And Canon, ed. D.A. Carson & John Woodbridge, 1986, Academie/ Zondervan, Grand Rapids.

[5] A.C. Bouquet, Science In The First Century: Theoretical And Applied, Everyday Life In New Testament Times, 1974, Carousel, London.

[6] Gerardus Bouw, With Every Wind Of Doctrine: Historical And Scientific Perspectives Of Geocentricity, 1984, Tychonian Society, Cleveland, Oh.

[7] John H. Brooke, **Science and the Fortunes of Natural Theology: Some Historical Perspectives,** Zygon, 24 (March 1989) 1.

[8] Colin Brown, Philosophy And The Christian Faith, 1968, Inter Varsity, Downers Grove.

[9] Maurice Bucaille, The Bible, The Qur'an And Science: The Holy Scriptures Examined In Light Of Modern Knowledge, Trans. A. Paunell & M. Bucaille, 1979, North American Trust Pub., Indianapolis.

[10] Herbert Butterfield, The Origins Of Modern Science: 1300-1800, 1965, Macmillan, N.Y.

[11] Wm. J. Cairney, **Revelatory Biology,** Evidence For Faith: Deciding The God Question, ed. John Warwick Montgomery, 1991, Probe, Dallas.

[12] D. A. Carson, **Recent Developments in the Doctrine of Scripture,** Hermeneutics, Authority, And Canon, ed. D.A. Carson & John Woodbridge, 1986, Academie/ Zondervan, Grand Rapids.

[13] ------, **Unity And Diversity In The New Testament: The Possibility Of Systematic Theology**, Scripture And Truth, ed. D.A. Carson & John Woodbridge, 1983, Academie/ Zondervan, Grand Rapids.

[14] R.E.D. Clark, Darwin: Before And After, 1967, Moody, Chicago.

[15] Morris Cohen, A Preface To Logic, 1960, N.Y.: Meridian.

[16] Peter Cotterell & Max Turner, Linguistics & Biblical Interpretation, 1989, InterVarsity, Downers Grove.

[17] Sir William Dampier, A History Of Science: And Its Relations With Philosophy And Religion, 1984, 4th ed., Cambridge U P, N.Y.

[18] George DeHoff, Why We Believe The Bible, 1966, DeHoff, Murfreesboro, Tenn.

[19] Franz Delitzsch, A System Of Biblical Psychology, 1977, Baker Grand, Rapids.

[20] ------, Commentary On The Old Testament: Job, 25 vol, 1969-1970, Eerdman , Grand Rapids.

[21] John Dillenberger, Protestant Thought And Natural Science: A Historical Interpretation, 1988, U of Notre Dame P, Notre Dame.

[22] H.L. Drumwright, Jr. **Accommodation,** Zondervan Pictorial Encyclopedia Of The Bible, 5 vols., ed. 1975, Merrill Tenney, Zondervan, Grand Rapids.

[23] D.R. Dungan, Hermeneutics, nd, Gospel Light, Delight, Ark.

[24] Don England, A Scientist Examines Faith And Evidence, 1983, Gospel Light, Delight, Ark.

[25] Frederick Ferre, **Design Argument,** Dictionary Of The History Of Ideas, 5 vols., ed. Philip Weiner, 1973-74, Charles Scribner's Sons, NY.

[26] David H. Fischer, Historians' Fallacies: Toward A Logic Of Historical Thought, 1970, Harper & Row, NY.

[27] John Frame, The Doctrine Of The Knowledge Of God, 1987, Presbyterian & Reformed Pub., Phillipsburg, N.J.

[28] ------, **God and Biblical Language: Transcendence And Immanence,** God's Inerrant Word: An International Symposium On The Trustworthiness Of Scripture, ed. John Warwick Montgomery, 1974, Bethany Fellowship, Minneapolis.

[29] Philipp Frank, **The Variety Of Reasons for the Acceptance of Scientific Theories,** Introductory Readings In The Philosophy Of Science, E.M. Klemke, et al. eds. 1980, Prometheus, Buffalo.

[30] Norman Geisler, ed., Biblical Errancy: An Analysis Of Its Philosophical Roots, 1981, Zondervan, Grand Rapids.

[31] ------, Come Let Us Reason: An Introduction To Logical Thinking, 1990, Baker, Grand Rapids.

[32] Irwin Ginsburgh, First Man, Then, Adam! 1975, Pocket, N,Y.

[33] Terry R. Green, Prescience Prophecy: A Pyrrhic Apologetic, 1988, Jabberwocky Press, Ft. Worth.

[34] Stuart Hackett, The Reconstruction Of The Christian Revelation Claim: A Philosophical And Critical Apologetic, 1984, Baker, Grand Rapids.

[35] Victor Hamilton, Theological Wordbook Of The Old Testament, 2 vols., eds. R, Laird Harris, Gleason Archer & Bruce Waltke, 1980, Moody, Chicago.

[36] Alan Hayward, Creation And Evolution: The Facts And Fallacies, 1985, Triangle/SPCK, London.

[37]   Carl F.H. Henry, Revelation And The Bible: Contemporary Evangelical Thought, ed. Carl F.H, Henry, 1974, Baker, Grand Rapids.
[38]   Perez Hoodbhoy, Islam And Science: Religious Orthodoxy And The Battle For Rationality, 1991, Zed Books, New Jersey.
[39]   Thomas Hartwell Horne, Introduction To The Scriptures, 5 vols., 1970, Baker, Grand Rapids.
[40]   Fred Hoyle, The Nature Of The Universe, 1950, Harper & Row, NY.
[41]   Charles Hummel, The Galileo Connection: Resolving Conflicts Between Science & The Bible, 1986, InterVarsity, Downers Grove.
[42]   Stanley Jaki, The Road Of Science And The Ways To God, 1980, U of Chicago P, Chicago.
[43]   E.M. Klaaren, Religious Origins Of Modern Science, 1977, Eerdman, Grand Rapids.
[44]   Thomas Kuhn, The Structure Of Scientific Revolutions, 1970, U of Chicago P, Chicago.
[45]   -------, The Essential Tension: Selected Studies In Scientific Tradition And Change, 1977, U of Chicago P, Chicago.
[46]   Imre Lakatos & Alan Musgrave, eds., Criticism And The Growth Of Knowledge, 1970, Cambridge U P, Cambridge.
[47]   Michael Lemonick, **Measuring The Earth,** July 1985, Science Digest.
[48]   Clinton Lockhart, Principles Of Interpretation, nd, Gospel Light, Delight, Ark.
[49]   George Marsden, **Dispensationalism and the Baconian Ideal,** Fundamentalism And American Culture: The Shaping Of Twentieth-Century Evangelicalism, 1870-1925, 1980, Oxford U P, NY.
[50]   John McClintock & James Strong, **Cosmology**, Cyclopedia Of Biblical, Theological, And Ecclesiastical Literature, 12 vols. 1981, Baker, Grand Rapids.
[51]   Josh McDowell, Evidence That Demands A Verdict: Historical Evidence For The Christian Faith, 1972, Campus Crusade For Christ, San Bernardino.
[52]   C.T. McIntire, ed., God, History, And Historians: Modern Christian Views Of History, 1977, Oxford U P, NY.
[53]   S.I. McMillen, None Of These Diseases, 1963, Fleming H, Revell, Old Tappan, N.J.
[54]   Henryk Mehlberg, **Types of Scientific Laws,** Philosophical Problems Of Science And Technology, ed. Alex Michalos, 1974, Allyn & Bacon, Boston.
[55]   Henry Morris, The Biblical Basis Of Modern Science, 1984, Baker, Grand Rapids.
[56]   -------, Remarkable Record Of Job, San Diego: Master, 1988.
[57]   Richard Morris, Dismantling The Universe: The Nature Of Scientific Discovery, 1984, Touchstone/Simon & Schuster, NY.
[58]   Richard Muller, Dictionary Of Latin And Greek Theological Terms: Drawn Principally From Protestant Scholastic Theology, 1985, Baker, Grand Rapids.
[59]   Roger Nicole, **New Testament Use of the Old Testament,** Revelation And The Bible, ed. Carl F.H. Henry, 1974, Baker, Grand Rapids.
[60]   -------, **The Biblical Concept of Truth,** Scripture And Truth, ed. D.A. Carson & John Woodbridge, 1983, Academie/ Zondervan, Grand Rapids.
[61]   -------, Ronald Youngblood and S, Lewis Johnson, **Quotations of the Old Testament in the New,** Hermeneutics, Inerrancy, And The Bible, eds. Earl Radmacher and Robert Preus, 1984, Academie/Zondervan, Grand Rapids.
[62]   Eugene Nida, Toward A Science Of Translating, 1964, E.J. Brill. Leiden, Netherlands.
[63]   --------, & Charles Taber, The Theory And Practice Of Translation, 1974, United Bible Societies, Leiden, Netherlands.
[64]   C.K. Ogden & A, Richards, The Meaning Of Meaning, 1936, London.
[65]   James Orr, **Science and Christian Faith,** The Fundamentals, 4 vols., ed. R.A. Torrey, 1970, Baker, Grand Rapids.
[66]   R.M. Page, **Science In The Bible**, Zondervan Pictorial Encyclopedia Of The Bible, 5 vols., 1975, Zondervan, Grand Rapids.
[67]   J. Barton Payne, Encyclopedia Of Biblical Prophecy: The Complete Guide To Scriptural Predictions And Their Fulfillment, 1973, Harper & Row, NY.
[68]   Richard Popkin, **Skepticism, Theology and the Scientific Revolution in the Seventeenth Century,** Problems In The Philosophy Of Science, ed. I. Lakatos & Alan Musgrave, 1968, Amsterdam: North Holland.
[69]   Vern Poythress, Science And Hermeneutics, 1988, Zondervan, Grand Rapids.
[70]   Earl Radmacher & Robert Preus, eds., Hermeneutics, Inerrancy, & The Bible, 1984, Zondervan, Grand Rapids.
[71]   Bernard Ramm, The Christian View Of Science And Scripture 1984, Baker, Grand Rapids.
[72]   -------, Protestant Biblical Interpretation, 1982, Zondervan, Grand Rapids.
[73]   James Randi, The Masks Of Nostradamus, 1990, Scribner's Sons, NY.
[74]   Del Ratzsch, **Christianity and the Specific Content of Science: A Typology**, Philosophy Of Science: The Natural Sciences In Christian Perspective, 1986, InterVarsity, Downers Grove.
[75]   R. Rawlinson, The Pulpit Commentary, 23 vols., 1962, Eerdmans, Grand Rapids.
[76]   Harry Rimmer, Modern Science And The Genesis Record, 1945, Eerdmans, Grand Rapids.
[77]   -------, The Harmony Of Science And Scripture, 1952, Eerdmans, Grand Rapids.
[78]   Holmes Rolston, Science & Religion: A Critical Survey, 1987, Temple UP, Philadelphia.
[79]   Bertrand Russell, The Scientific Outlook, 1959, W.W. Norton, NY.

[80]   Richard Schlegel, Inquiry Into Science: Its Domain And Limits, 1972, Doubleday, Garden City, NY.
[81]   Arnold Schnabel, Has God Spoken? 1974, Creation-Life, .San Diego.
[82]   Osborn Segerberg, , The Riddles Of Jesus & Answers Of Science: Modern Verification of His Wisdom & How it Can Help You, 1987, Regis, Kinderhook NY.
[83]   C.R. Smith, The Physician Examines The Bible, 1950, Philosophical Library, NY.
[84]   Michael Talbot, Mysticism And The New Physics, 1981, Bantam, NY.
[85]   Milton Terry, Biblical Apocalyptics, 1988 reprint, Baker, Grand Rapids.
[86]   ------, Biblical Hermeneutics, 1978, Zondervan, Grand Rapids.
[87]   Anthony Thiselton, The Two Horizons: New Testament Hermeneutics And Philosophical Description, 1980, Eerdmans, Grand Rapids.
[88]   Bert Thompson & Wayne Jackson, A Study Course In Christian Apologetics, 1991, Apologetics Press, Montgomery, Al.
[89]   Stephen Toulmin, Laws Of Nature, The Philosophy Of Science, 1965, Hutchinson's U Library.
[90]   Kern R. Trembath, Evangelical Theories Of Biblical Inspiration: A Review And Proposal, 1987, Oxford UP, NY.
[91]   Stephen Ullmann, Semantics: An Introduction To The Science Of Meaning, 1979, Barnes & Noble, .NY.
[92]   Foy Wallace, Jr., God's Prophetic Word, 1960, rev. ed. Foy Wallace, Fort Worth.
[93]   ------, The Gospel For Today: An Extended Edition Of The Certified Gospel, 1967, Foy Wallace Jr., Fort Worth.
[94]   A.D. White, A History Of The Warfare Of Science With Theology, 1932, Appleton, NY.
[95]   John Woodbridge, Does the Bible Teach Science? Bibliotheca Sacra, 142 (July-Sept, 1985).
[96]   ------, The Impact of the 'Enlightenment' on Scripture, Hermeneutics, Authority, And Canon, ed. D.A. Carson, 1986, Academie/Zondervan, Grand Rapids.
[97]   Edwin Yamauchi, Theological Wordbook Of The Old Testament, 2 vols., eds. R. Laird Harris, Gleason Archer & Bruce Waltke, 1980, Moody, Chicago.
[98]   Gary Zukav, The Dancing Wu Li Masters, 1986, Bantam, NY.

BIBLICAL NATURALISM: A TIME FOR PARADIGM CHANGE

ROBERT HARSH M.S.
439 LITTLE CREEK RD.
HARMONY, PA, 16037

ABSTRACT

The question of origins has always been an important part of the world view philosophy of humans. Most people in Western civilization used the Biblical account as the basis for their view of origins until the mid nineteenth century. From the 1850's to present there has occurred a constant decline in acceptance of the Biblical Creation view and a complementary increase in naturalistic evolution as the basis of their world view. Most educated people today have adopted the evolutionary naturalism paradigm.

Those who believe in the inspiration of the Bible face a dilemma. On the one hand, they believe that God created the universe including man, who as the most special part of creation was made in God's image. On the other hand, their formal educational training has taught them that all of the "scientific" evidence points to evolution from bacteria to man.

This dilemma is needlessly endured by millions of believers in God. Neo-Creationists must realize the need to present the alternative paradigm based on a creation model of origins in an organized and competent way.

As much of the origins puzzle as can presently be explained by the "Biblical Naturalism" model needs to be clearly identified. Those aspects of the origins puzzle that remain a mystery also need to be identified.

A necessary part of the dynamics of the shift to the biblical naturalism paradigm should be the presentation of scientific evidence for the unreliable and defective nature of evolutionary naturalism.

In this paper we will discuss what a paradigm is, define the biblical naturalism paradigm, and discuss the history of how the evolutionary naturalism paradigm came to be so universally accepted. We will present an analysis of origin science and operational science and primary cause versus secondary cause will also be explained. Finally suggestions for adoption of the biblical naturalism paradigm will be presented.

INTRODUCTION

One may question; why do so many science teachers and professional scientists believe in evolution? Is it because they have seen a great deal of empirical evidence that evolution has happened? Is it because the fossil record is so conclusive in showing gradual change from simple organisms to complex life over long periods of time? Is it even because they have given a lot of thought to investigating the pros and cons of evolution? None of these reasons correctly answers the question. The paradigm that their teachers, from grade school through graduate school taught was either Neo-Lamarckian or Neo-Darwinian evolution. Every textbook, no matter which science they studied explained concepts from a background framework of evolution. The world view that most scientists have been taught throughout their formal education has been based upon the evolutionary naturalism paradigm.

Pierre Teilhard de Chardin, although he lived before the development of the concept of paradigm described well the power and authority of the evolutionary naturalism paradigm.

"Is evolution a theory, a system, or a hypothesis? It is a general postulate to which all theories, all hypotheses, all systems must henceforth bow and which they must satisfy in order to be thinkable and true. Evolution is a light which illuminates all facts, a trajectory which all lines of thought must follow - this is what evolution is." [7]

Henry Morris communicated the importance of challenging the evolutionary naturalism paradigm. "Evolution is not merely a biological theory of little significance. It is a world view - the world view diametrically opposing the

Christian world view. Therefore, Christians ignore it or compromise with it at great peril." [21]

Evolution is not just an important scientific theory, it is much more. It is a philosophy that, because it is built upon naturalism as the source of primary and secondary origins, must leave God out.

"When a paradigm becomes established, it serves as the grand organizing principal for scientific research. This means that it defines the questions that need to be answered and the facts that need to be assembled." [14]

The topic of evolution is not studied directly by most teachers or scientists. It is not a topic they are really interested in investigating. None-the-less, with their educational background, the evolution paradigm is the framework that they use to make sense out of nature. As long as they don't look into the details they are perfectly satisfied with their understanding of nature.

"A paradigm is not merely a hypothesis, which can be discarded if it fails a single experimental test; it is a way of looking at the world, or some part of it, and scientists understand even anomalies in it's terms." [14]

How we understand nature can better be described as gestalts rather than individual observations. We often observe what we expect to see. We expect our observations of nature to fit into a pattern much as we expect the most indistinguishable piece of a jigsaw puzzle to ultimately fit logically in the puzzle. Even anomalies are expected to fit, possibly sometime in the future, when we have a more complete understanding.

EVOLUTION DOGMA

I would describe the formal education of almost all science teachers or scientists as one in which they were prescribed a pair of "rose colored evolution glasses." When, on some occasion these "evolution glasses" are removed, nature doesn't look the same and the person feels discomfort, so they put them right back on. Our friend may have been caught by one of his teachers not wearing his "evolution glasses" and was reprimanded; so in order to avoid discomfort they put them right back on. They may have attended a scientific convention where they discovered that everyone else was wearing their "rose colored evolution glasses" so they decided it would be in their best professional interest to wear theirs as well.

Perhaps they even attended a meeting at the convention where there was a discussion about a group of stupid people who didn't know enough to wear their "rose colored glasses" and naturally didn't have a very good understanding about science. Most professional scientists or science educators have been told, ever since they were young that they were smart. The last thing they want at this time in their life is to be looked upon as dumb by their colleagues.

These are some reasons why most people who work in the scientific fields believe in evolution. It is not because there is a great deal of evidence supporting evolution. It is not because most scientists have put a lot of thought into it. They believe in evolution because it is taught as dogma.

Goethe wrote, "When an erroneous hypothesis becomes entrenched and generally accepted, it is transformed into a kind of tenet that no one is allowed to question or investigate; it then becomes an evil which endures for centuries." [9] A paradigm that is held, despite mounting evidence against it may cause rational people to draw irrational conclusions, because they hold to their paradigm so tightly. "A humorous illustration is provided by the case of the deluded patient who complains to his physician, 'Doctor I'm dead.' The doctor tries to assure him otherwise, with little success, and eventually exclaims in exasperation, 'Dead men don't bleed, do they?' The patient agrees, 'No they don't.' Whereupon the doctor jabs patient the with a needle. As the blood trickles out, the patient sighs, 'OK, I was wrong! Dead men do bleed.'" [23]

The question of origins of the universe and life still occupy the human mind as they have done since the most remote antiquity. "It may be safely said that it is one the most important problems of natural history. No religious or philosophical system, no outstanding thinker ever failed to give this question serious consideration." [19]

How important is it to have a good understanding of evolution? Paul Moody, in the preface of his textbook on evolution wrote:

> Organic evolution is the greatest principle in biology. Its implications extend far beyond the confines of that science, ramifying into all phases of human life and activity. Accordingly, an understanding of evolution should be part of the intellectual equipment of all educated persons. [20]

The importance of a proper understanding of origins is explained from a Creationist's point of view.

> The matter of origins is not a peripheral issue which can be dealt with after conclusions have been reached on all other issues. This would truly be a case in point of the proverbial cart before the

horse. The matter of origins must be settled first and foremost. On this rest the foundations of everything in between. [26]

My belief is that for most Christians, who have never seriously studied the question of origins, there is much confusion. Many are convinced that the Bible teaches that God was the source of origins, but on the other hand, are also convinced that evolution must be true, because of what they have been taught in school, by television and through books. This conflict in the mind, naturally leads to doubt about either other teachings of the Bible or other teachings of science.

"The relationship between these two claimants on mankind's loyalty - science and religion - is probably the most fundamental challenge that faces the mind and spirit of human beings." [22]

Some scientists seem to have chosen an unnecessary and dangerous solution. They have chosen to check in their religious faith at the laboratory door and their science at the church door. They will eventually have to choose one over the other. If they choose the "religious' side and forget to check in their faith at the laboratory door they are sure to incur the wrath of the scientific establishment.

Ponder John Casti's ridicule of "Creationists" in general and Duane Gish in particular.

> Duane Gish holds a Ph.D. in biochemistry from the University of California at Berkeley; he is also the vice-director of the Creation Research Society and a regular participant at university debates on the merits of creation science. Since he is trained in the scientific method, especially in an experimental science like biochemistry, it's odd, to say the least, to read in his book Evolution: The Fossils Say No that 'we do not know how the Creator created, what processes He used, for He used processes which are not now operating anywhere in the natural universe . . . We cannot discover by scientific investigation anything about the creative processes used by the Creator.' With such statements, creation 'science' joins the long list of other perverse modern 'sciences', such as 'fashion science', 'dairy science', and 'educational science', all of which can be conveniently subsumed under the heading 'nonscientific science'. [4]

I have found, if a creationist is poorly educated he is attacked for his ignorance and looked down upon as a person who "doesn't know any better." If the creationist is well educated, like Dr. Gish they are portrayed as an educated person who is not really very smart. This negative attitude is well illustrated by a two paragraph reading I received recently anonymously.

> The fact that they are theories does not make them uncertain, even when various fine details are still under dispute. This is particularly true of the theory of evolution, which is under attack from people who are either ignorant of science or, worse, who allow their superstition to overcome what knowledge they might have. [27]

This is an insult to the character of creationist educators and scientists.

PARADIGM CONCEPT

Use of paradigms is a type of deductive reasoning. "If the premises of deduction are true, and our use of deduction is valid, the conclusions must be true, as surely as two plus two equals four." [6]

But what if my premises are wrong? In deductive reasoning truth is unlikely to be discovered if built upon false premises. This is the reason why one's paradigm concerning present day nature and origins in the past is so important. One's paradigm contains the set of basic premises upon which one's ability to reason is built.

"The dominant set of assumptions that underlies any branch of science is called a paradigm, a word coined by the philosopher and historian Thomas Kuhn." [5] A paradigm is a general framework into which many individual theories fit. In this vein they can be thought of as super theories.
"Paradigms govern the way scientists think, form theories, and interpret results of experiments." [5]

In this paper we will use the term, evolutionary naturalism for the paradigm that defines nature in strictly materialistic terms. Carl Sagan described the evolutionary naturalism paradigm in a nut shell. In the opening paragraph of his book, Cosmos, Sagan wrote, " The Cosmos Is All That Is Or Ever Was Or Ever Will Be." [24]

We will use the term, biblical naturalism for the paradigm that posits a supernatural Creator God, who was outside of and not a product of nature was the primary cause for all of nature. The Creator God also set the laws of nature in place. These laws of nature will be referred to as secondary cause.

It was in 1947 that the young Harvard professor, Thomas Kuhn was asked to develop a presentation on the origins of 17th century mechanics. In the course of his research Kuhn traced the subject back to the great father of the deductive method, Aristotle. Kuhn was "struck time and again by the total and complete wrong headedness of Aristotle's ideas." [4] Aristotle taught that all matter was composed of three parts: spirit, form, and the four qualities: air, earth, fire, and water. How could someone as bright and contemplative as Aristotle be so dead wrong? "Then, as Kuhn recounts it, one hot summer day the answer came to him in a flash while he was poring over ancient texts in the library: Look at the universe through Aristotle's eyes!" [4] The framework for understanding nature in Aristotle's time was not atoms, molecules and energy.

> If you adopt Aristotle's world view, one of the presuppositions is that every body seeks the location where by its nature it belongs. With this presumption, what could be more natural than to think of material bodies as having spirits, so that "heavenly" bodies of air like quality rise, while the spirit of "earthly" bodies causes them to fall? [4]

As a result of this enlightenment, Kuhn began to develop the idea that scientists work within a framework that greatly influences how they perceive nature. These views can best be described as "gestalts" which are phenomena of nature so integrated that they compose a functional unit that cannot be derived simply from summation of its parts. In other words, the whole is greater than the sum of its parts.

Kuhn borrowed the term paradigm from grammar and designated it the proper expression for the frameworks or gestalts that are guidelines for scientists as they investigate nature. In 1962 he published his hypothesis in his enormously influential book, The Structure of Scientific Revolutions.

A good analogy of a paradigm is the use of maps by explorers. In ancient times explorers had old well accepted maps which perhaps had the major landmarks such as the largest rivers, tallest mountains and best fishing lakes. As explorers using the old trusted maps would venture out and return they would come back with more information about different streams, mountain passes and better fishing lakes. Some of these new discoveries would turn out to be correct while others weren't to be trusted. As more and more explores would come back with the same discrepancies discovered in the old map there came a time when explorers would not trust their lives to the old map and would now shift their allegiance to the new one because it had better directions, especially to the best fishing lakes.

Paradigms are to scientists what maps are to explorers. Paradigms provide direction in what to explore, what to expect, and even what type of data to collect. When a new paradigm is identified it is not automatically switched over to because scientists trust their current paradigm even with its recognized faults. However just as explorers switched maps, scientists will shift to new paradigms if enough insurmountable problems are identified.

"When a paradigm becomes established, it serves as the grand organizing principle for scientific research. This means that it defines the questions that need to be answered and the facts that need to be assembled." [14]

Kuhn held that science had to be defined in terms of paradigms. He found it interesting to discover the attitude of scientists toward their paradigms. Scientists, it seems merely assume their particular paradigm is the proper framework for understanding nature. Most are neither interested in verifying any further nor attempting to falsify their paradigms. The power of paradigms should be understood. Kuhn proposed that "Science's authority ultimately resides not in a rule-governed method of inquiry where by scientific results are obtained but in the scientific community that obtains the results." [11]

The power paradigms hold helps science consolidate its activities by "preventing the energies of scientists from being dissipated by engaging in interminable disputes over basic assumptions or tackling insoluble problems." [15] Many activities are intended to prevent straying. The scientific community controls: professional training, socialization, availability of grant money, access to research facilities, and publications.

The period during which the scientific community is using the same paradigm Kuhn called "normal science." Sometimes results of experimentation are contrary to what was predicted or even allowed by the paradigm. These differences are referred to as anomalies. Occasionally so many anomalies have been observed that their sheer number becomes alarming and the scientific discipline holding that paradigm enters the crisis state. "Anomaly appears only against the background provided by the paradigm." [16]

Resolution of the crisis occurs in three ways. The anomalies get explained within the old paradigm or they are simply set aside because there is no known paradigm to answer the question. The third form of resolution is that scientists are forced "to rethink their most cherished beliefs and sometimes, toss them aside. This unsettling event is called a paradigm shift." [17]

PARADIGM SHIFT

Scientists do not take the possibility of a paradigm shift lightly. It is not like a hypothesis that may be discarded when it fails an experimental test. Kuhn saw two conditions that would allow for a paradigm shift. The old paradigm had to be in serious trouble and a new valid paradigm must already exist. "To reject one paradigm without simultaneously substituting another is to reject science itself." [16]

Sometimes those who propose a new paradigm have to pay a heavy price. In 140 A.D. the Greek Astronomer Ptolemy formulated the geocentric view in which the earth was the center of the universe, with the sun, moon, and stars revolving around the earth. Nicolaus Copernicus proved in 1580, however, that the sun rather than the earth was the center of the solar system. Copernicus was condemned as a heretic and his publication was banned. This illustrates how discomforting it is to have a paradigm challenged.

Although reluctance to change is a human trait, science cannot exist when scientists are so closed minded that they exchange truth for error. Paradigm shifts are unsettling but if truth is ignored science becomes a useless perpetuator of error.

Let's consider the individual who is both a serious student of science and also strong believer in the scientific accuracy of the Bible. Without a doubt they have been taught that the evolutionary naturalism paradigm is the proper way to understand nature. But that world view leaves out primary cause and therefore excludes God.

Some people have been satisfied with a dualistic philosophy and accept two paradigms concerning nature. For many scientists this dualistic approach is not rational and they realize a decision must be made. Although the choice is difficult my feeling is that not many reject science. The evolutionary naturalism paradigm especially as it implies the history of man has long been an effective destroyer of faith in God.

BIBLICAL NATURALISM PARADIGM

We must not allow another generation to pass without solving this dilemma! I believe a biblical naturalism paradigm is the answer. Included in this paradigm must be an understanding of the differences between operational and origins science as well as a clear understanding of primary cause and secondary cause. The rules of causality, uniformity and circumstantial evidence must be accepted as proper criteria to determine the validity of scientific hypotheses when working in the realm of origins science while empiricism and falsifiability must continue to be criteria in the realm of operational science.

For biblical naturalists there are a few central ideas that are so basic and foundational that adherents should not subject them to falsification. The two most basic are: first, God created the universe and living things and second, the Bible is understood to be God's special message to man concerning the origin and maintenance of the Universe. "The Christian sees God as the Creator and upholder of the universe. He actually expects that something about God can be obtained by an investigation of His creation."[3]

Many creationist scientists will desire to include two additional basic premises: first, the earth is thousands not millions of years old and second, the Genesis flood was a global catastrophe. Other parts of the paradigm need to be more tentative as a comprehensive creation model is developed.

The science most people are familiar with deals with regularities rather than one time events known as singularities. Regularly recurring patterns serve as a background against which theories can be falsified. Singularities, on the other hand, are not open to empirical investigation.

"The scientist will have to reconstruct the unobserved past singularity on the basis of knowledge he has from the present." [8] He must depend on the principle of uniformity. "Thus when a geologist sees a deposit in the rocks which resembles one observed to result from flooding, erosion or sedimentation in the present, he can plausibly posit a similar secondary (natural) cause for the unobserved past event." [8]

A good example of this is seen in the work of Steve Austin and Mount Saint Helens. The eruption of Mount Saint Helens was a modern day singular event that would be classified as catastrophic rather than regular. Austin observed real similarities between the sedimentation produced in a very short time at Mount Saint Helens and the sedimentation layers at the Grand Canyon. Using the criteria of uniformity and circumstantial evidence Austin made a case for the creation of the sedimentary rock layers in the Grand Canyon in a short period of time.

Original events, like for example, the origin of the universe or the origin of life are singular events and are not in the realm of empirical science. Even singularities such as macroevolution since they are not testable against any regularly recurring pattern of events must be excluded from empirical science.

Original events as well as certain unobserved secondary events are better investigated by accumulating circumstantial evidence.

> Although they are not an empirical science, never the less they function like forensic science. Just as a forensic scientist tries to make a plausible reconstruction of an unobserved (and unrepeatable) murder, so the evolutionist and creationist attempt to construct a plausible scenario of the unobserved past singularity of origin. [8]

It is possible however, to use empirical science to show that there was a beginning. We can observe such evidence as the expanding universe or entropy and deduce that the universe had to have a beginning. Our common sense tells us there had to be an original "cause" for the first living things. That cause was either natural or supernatural.

So there is what we will term "operational science" which deals with normal repeating observable events and there is "origin science" which deals with primary rather than secondary cause. Primary cause is defined as a singular event produced by a force outside the event. A simple example would be an architect designing a house to be built. A secondary cause is simply a "natural" cause that has regularity and can be empirically tested. A simple example would be a furnace that turns on (secondary cause) when the thermostat senses that the temperature has dropped to the programmed setting (primary cause).

Operational science deals with regularly repeating events, whereas origins science must be restricted to singularities. One time events dealing with origins do not necessitate <u>natural</u> cause. We are mistaken in applying uniformity philosophy to origins because origins are not in the domain of "Operational Science." Predictions or trends are foreign to singularities.

> There is a crucial difference between uniformitarianism and the principle of uniformity. Uniformitarianism assumes that all past causes will be natural ones like those observed in nature at the present. This is not a scientific assertion, but a philosophical one. That is this kind of uniformitarianism is not justified by observations of a repeated pattern of events in the present. Rather, it is a metaphysical speculation which goes well beyond the domain of operation science. Such uniformitarianism is not science but scientism. it is not scientific study of nature; it is philosophical naturalism. [8]

CAUSALITY

How then can biblical naturalists justify trying to investigate origins? Geisler and Anderson provide an excellent answer. "The basis of speculation about singular events is repeated observation of causal connection, even though the object is a single event. This is how origin science works, whether for evolution or for creation." [8] For example, if it were common for us to find that well designed machines had a knack for designing themselves and putting themselves together our general conclusion would be that design does not demand a designer. On the other hand if we observe that every single well engineered product had an engineer and builder behind it, our general conclusion would be design <u>demands</u> a designer (cause).

How important is the ability by causality argument to conclude that primary cause, the Creator, exists? "Many in the debate have come to realize that the question of the adequacy of young - earth creationism is really tangential to the main issue: can science infer a creator? If the answer to this question is no then it wouldn't really matter what else one said on behalf of any creation model - such a theory simply fails to qualify as a scientific explanation." [17]

The design we detect in present day organisms is produced by "secondary" cause in the form of their genetic code. Do we ever find an instance in nature where DNA (secondary cause) has been produced by random chemical reactions? We never have. So what should our general conclusion be? In operational science secondary cause (DNA) <u>always</u> comes from previously existing in life. But where did the first living things come from? If we could commonly observe life originating (caused) from non-life our proper general understanding would be that the first life came from non-life. However, if we observe that the law of biogenesis is never violated, what should our proper scientific conclusion be? It was a singular event and is outside of the domain of operational science. If we insist on applying the philosophy of uniformitarianism and continuity in our investigation of origins we are not practicing science but metaphysics instead.

On the basis of causal connection it is appropriate to include supernatural in science. If our common sense tells us there had to be a beginning of life and that design <u>demands</u> a designer it is proper for a believer in the biblical naturalism paradigm to include the "Supernatural" Creator in their philosophy of science.

Our uniform experience is; well designed mechanisms require an intelligent maker of the mechanism. "To posit a <u>nonintelligent natural</u> cause based on rare occurrences or minute probabilities is not science, it is luck." [8]

Origins must be excluded from the realm of operational science because, by their nature, they cannot be repeated or tested. This places origins, whether they are posited to be from natural or supernatural cause, outside the jurisdiction of empirical science.

Operational science deals with the way nature operates by natural cause, while origin science deals with how the universe came into existence and with primary rather than secondary cause. Biblical naturalists hold that primary cause is the supernatural Creator.

"The myth of objective, philosophically neutral science was spawned and spread largely because both theists and naturalists agreed that science, that is, operation science should be restricted to a study of secondary causes, which are continuously acting causes." [8]

Because nature has been observed as a pattern of regular recurrent events operational science has been married to uniformitarianism philosophy. It was a logical deduction that operational science could be used to extrapolate back in history. Secondary cause by purely naturalistic forces is all that has been allowed. If one is strictly studying operational science secondary cause should be posited but when scientists direct their interests toward singular origin type events they should defer to origin science which can and must admit "supernatural" force as primary cause. The great scientists of the 16th and 17th centuries had no problem with recognizing both operational science and origin science. They used the "biblical creationism" paradigm to help them understand nature!

Origin science naturally makes most scientists who have been trained under the reign of the evolutionary naturalism paradigm feel uncomfortable. The realm of origin science is singular non-recurring events that cannot be tested empirically and therefore cannot be falsified. Origin science "must be judged by whether a scenario satisfies the principles of causality and uniformity (analogy) and generally conforms with the accumulated circumstantial evidence in a noncontradictory way." [8] Although evolutionists do not recognize origin science they are reluctant to admit that their theories of origin of life or the universe are not falsifiable either. Because their origin hypothesis cannot be empirically tested the valid realm for evolutionary origins is also origin science rather than operational science.

BIOGENESIS VIOLATED

When we examine evolutionary views of origins by principles of causality and uniformity they come up short. In the realm of the origin of life a great secondary cause principle which has never been known to have been violated must by breached if purely naturalistic forces are posited. The law of biogenesis must be violated again and again. Do we ever see it being violated today, by purely naturalistic entities? The answer is never! On the basis of causality and uniformity this is <u>scientific</u> evidence against the validity of the evolutionary naturalism paradigm.

THERMODYNAMICS VIOLATED

The laws of thermodynamics must be violated if the naturalistic paradigm is used in the realm of origins. Entropy cannot have been in effect if purely natural forces produced the perfect engineering we observe in the solar system, Planet Earth and in living things. Ultimately we <u>always</u> observe entropy in nature. It is understood however, that during their existence living things hold entropy at bay as energy flows through the ecosystem. Living things have the ability to use energy and organize matter into usable configurations, but this only applies in the realm of operational science.

"Any attempt to limit causes of origins to purely natural (secondary) causes is misdirected historically, philosophically, and scientifically." [8]

The rejection of primary cause in origin science must be changed. If as creationists we want to understand God's revelation to man through nature we must, as a real part of our science recognize and support investigation of origins in the context of primary cause.

The great founders of modern science like Kepler, Galileo, Descartes, Harvey, Boyle and Newton all subscribed to a biblical naturalism paradigm. Their creative achievements were due in large part to their ability to bring together natural science with natural theology. "Kepler spoke of Copernican scientists as priests officiating around the altar of the Creator. Newton in turn made no secret of his pleasure that Bentley had found the <u>Principia</u> to be a storehouse of pointers toward the Maker and Creator of all." [8]

A SOLUTION

Much of the confusion on the part of scientists who are believers in God but who have received their training in the form of the naturalistic paradigm could be alleviated by recognizing the distinction between primary and secondary cause. Theistic evolution is unnecessary if one recognizes that origin science is different from operational science. Super-natural cause must be an integral part of origin science.

If one's cosmogony includes the big bang, the natural question arises, where did the matter and energy come from to make the bang? No purely materialistic paradigm can provide any answer. However the biblical naturalism paradigm, by recognizing the difference between primary and secondary cause, does provide a scientifically logical answer. Furthermore the evolutionary naturalism paradigm has no credible answer for the question; "where did living things come from"? On the other hand the biblical naturalism paradigm has an answer.

What is meant by causality in science? The principle of causality simply stated is: every event in nature has a cause. The fathers of modern science recognized God as the primary cause that originally brought about nature. They also recognized God as the "designer" of secondary causes that control the operation of nature. There could be no science without a recognition of secondary cause and there can be no real origin science without recognition of primary cause.

Discussion of primary cause has been limited, for a long time, to the areas of philosophy and religion and has been forcibly excluded from science. A recognition of the limits of operational science can help us reintroduce primary cause into science. Origin science based on causality, uniformity and circumstantial evidence can help scientists find the answers they are searching for.

UNIFORMITY

The principle of uniformity simply stated is: the present is the key to the past. If we observe an event in nature today we can use today's event to examine the past. For example, if we observe that every single complex man-made structure in existence today involved intelligent design, we can properly deduce that when we observe even more perfect engineering in nature an intelligence was involved. That intelligence may be a secondary cause like, for example, DNA for living organisms. How does a complicated life form come about today? In operational science, we would conclude; its DNA supplied by its parent or parents was the source of that intelligence. But in the realm of origins science; where did the "original" DNA come from? origins science has the answer in the form of an original Intelligence.

Where does the evolutionary naturalism paradigm stand on the question of intelligent design? Evolutionists recognize the same principle of "design demands a designer" but their paradigm completely excludes any influence of any force outside of the material world. The "internal force" which is postulated as the cause for natural phenomena is random chance. Random chance does not ever produce the kind of order we see in nature and by any logic does not require intelligence. Therefore, the evolutionary naturalism paradigm violates the teleological principle of, design demands a designer, that we clearly see in nature.

Since no one was around to observe the origin of the universe or the origin of life we must recognize the validity of employing circumstantial evidence rather than empirical evidence. Although circumstantial evidence cannot be falsified, a logical forensic case can be constructed in much the same way as a criminal investigation can reconstruct a sequence of events in the absence of eyewitnesses.

John Casti provided a list of the criteria for what constitutes valid science. This list was actually produced by Judge William Overton as a part of his ruling in the Arkansas Act 590 case.

It (science) is guided by natural law.
It has to be explanatory by reference to natural law.
It is testable against the empirical world.
It's conclusions are tentative, ie., are not
necessarily the final word.
It is falsifiable. [4]

Rather than just comparing evolution or creation to these criteria let us compare origins science and operational science to these criteria.

	Supernatural Origin	Natural Origin	Biblical Naturalism Operational	Evolutionary Naturalism Operational
Guided by natural law	No	Yes	Yes	Yes
Explained by natural law	No	Yes	Yes	Yes
Testable against empirical world	No	No	Yes	Yes
Conclusions tentative	No	Yes	Yes	Yes
Falsifiable	No	No	Yes	Yes

It is clear that Judge Overton lacked an understanding of the difference between origin science and operation science. Supernatural origin by its very definition does not rely on nor allow for any influences by natural forces. If Creation happened, the Creator was outside of and apart from the creation. However evolution also fails Overton's criteria as it applies to origins. No theory of evolution can be testable against the empirical world nor can it be falsifiable. Therefore if Judge Overton's criteria is to be followed neither the evolutionary naturalism nor biblical naturalism paradigms should be taught as science.

As anyone with an honest open mind can see the biblical naturalism paradigm meets each of the criteria as they apply to operational science. Biblical naturalism does not rely on supernatural cause.

FAILURE OF EVOLUTION

Evolution may have passed Judge overton's Criteria on three of the points that apply to natural origin, but that says nothing about whether evolutionary naturalism is a good explanation of what really happened. The evolutionary naturalism paradigm has no feasible theory for primary cause. The most popular theory of the origin of the universe, the big bang theory does not even attempt to explain where the matter and energy to "bang" came from. On the origin of life, the evolutionary naturalism paradigm is equally ineffective. Not one time in history anywhere in the world has the law of biogenesis been observed to have been violated. It should not go unnoticed that a well established "law of science" must be violated in order for the evolutionary naturalism paradigm to be valid! So, natural origin theory may be guided and explained by natural law in someone's imagination but in the real world evolutionary naturalism fails completely on these two criteria.

One thing, however, is for sure; origins as explained by the many theories of evolutionary naturalism are tentative. So the only criteria in Overton's scheme that evolution passes is really a negative for the usefulness of the evolutionary naturalism paradigm.

HISTORY

This author began his research on this paper with the hypothesis that modern day Creationists need to develop and openly acknowledge a biblical naturalism paradigm. The biblical creation paradigm, I believed, was something that a few scientists use today but have not shared it very well with other scientists. I envisioned the biblical creation paradigm to be something new. However as I did my research I soon discovered that the great founders of modern science all subscribed to that very paradigm and it was their belief in a personal rational Creator that drove these men to invent modern science.

There are those who object to "creation science" on grounds that creation entails a "supernatural cause". If the great men of science had limited themselves by ignoring a first cause Creator one wonders how much science would still be unknown today.

> For the first two-and-a-half centuries of modern science (1620-1860) most of the leading lights of science believed the universe and life gave evidence of a supernatural creator. One need only to recall names like Bacon, Kepler, Newton, Boyle, Pascal, Mendel, Agassiz, Maxwell and Kelvin - all of whom believed in a supernatural cause of the universe and life. [8]

The often heard cry from evolutionists is that the only people who believe in creation are ignorant and don't know any better. Isn't it interesting that the founders of many institutions of higher learning were creationists. "An examination of a list of the twenty universities which were established in Europe between the years 1550 AD and 1700 AD, will reveal the fact that they were all founded and maintained by some religious denomination." [1]

Kuhn wrote of Europe, "The bulk of scientific knowledge is a product of Europe in the last four centuries. No other place and time has supported that very special community from which scientific productivity comes." [16]

Why were the Greek philosophers not able to do as well as the Renaissance Europeans in inventing a workable system of science?

Jaki gave part of the answer. "The problem of the failure of ancient Greek science is largely the failure of the Greeks of old to go resolutely one step beyond the prime heavens to a prime mover absolutely superior to it."[13]

Although scientists of the 16th and 17th centuries believed in a great Creator, their emphasis was in seeking out regular patterns and ongoing operation of nature. They presupposed a Creator. But in the late 18th and early 19th centuries naturalistic science had begun to enter the domain of origin science.It was during this time that the evolutionary naturalism paradigm was being developed and materialistic nature replaced the first cause creator.

> In the latter 19th century the view became nearly universal that science is philosophically neutral and thoroughly objective. Also a new generation of scientists had arisen, one which had not only forgotten that science had a theistic base, but one which had embraced, albeit unconsciously for many, philosophical neutralism. Implicit within naturalism is the denial of a creation distinct from its creator. [25]

The evolutionary naturalism paradigm is the way many people today understand their world. Since man is by nature religious, nature and natural law have become deity. Strong evidence that this religious transition has taken place can be seen in many aspects of the "New Age" movement and with adherents to the "Gaia" philosophy.

It may be that the evolutionary naturalism paradigm did not gain its power by scientific revolution alone. Perhaps the philosophical revolution from theism to naturalism was a force even greater than any new information concerning nature. "The myth has been perpetuated that Darwin did his research as a thoroughly objective scholar. In fact, he had a viewpoint prior to doing any investigation." [25]

George Grinnell, Professor of History of Science at McMaster University wrote, "I have done a great deal of work on Darwin and can say with some assurance that Darwin also did not derive his theory from nature but rather superimposed a certain philosophical world-view on nature and then spent 20 years trying to gather the facts to make it stick." [10]

In 1874 Charles Hodge wrote the first analysis of Darwin's hypothesis and its implications. In his book What Is Darwinism? Hodge wrote that what was really at issue was whether nature was the product of intellectual process guided by God or a natural process "directed" by chance. The exclusion of design in nature is what offended Hodge the most so at the conclusion of his book Hodge wrote, "The conclusion of the whole matter is that the denial of design in nature is virtually the denial of God." [12]

Darwin's theory however continued to become accepted at a very rapid pace. In 1879 a "liberal" religious periodical, the Independent, informed its readers that the best colleges and scientific authorities were "all" teaching evolution, including the evolution of man. [18] The more conservative Observer challenged the Independent's finding by asking college presidents to disclose whether evolution was being taught. Most were reluctant to admit the truth but the Independent on further investigation found that most working naturalists in most universities did accept and teach evolution. At this time, 1880's and 1890's, the majority could best be characterized as Neo-Lamarckians rather than Darwinians. [18] It is important to notice that many theologians were not far behind in their acceptance of evolution.

In the case of Darwin's hypothesis, scientists clearly accepted it as a valid theory without much testing and did not use empirical method or falsification to prove his hypothesis was valid. What they did was to use their authority to convince the public that it was valid. "Evolutionary science became the search for confirming evidence, and the explaining away of negative evidence." [27]

When John Scopes was brought to trial in Dayton, Tennessee he was challenging the biblical creation paradigm. Many intellectuals in America in the year 1925 subscribed to the evolutionary naturalism paradigm while conservative religious people in Tennessee believed the biblical naturalism paradigm was true and had passed a law prohibiting the teaching of evolution in Tennessee's public schools. Two paradigms had come head to head. Evolutionists lost the court battle but won the popularity contest. Creationists were vilified and creation was portrayed as a simple-minded myth.

In public school education, Scopes has been portrayed as a martyr for the cause and has been compared to Copernicus and Galileo.

> To the man who pauses to think the matter through, there is no reasonable comparison. ...The

238

Ptolemaic system, which had been worked out by Ptolemy, had been regarded as the 'Scripture of astronomy' for fourteen hundred years. When Copernicus asserted that the earth rotated on its axis, in contradistinction to Ptolemy, the Roman Catholic clergy, who were the conservatives in science, charged Copernicus with heresy. The clergy were simply holding to the theory which scientists had been teaching for fourteen hundred years. When Galileo added proof to the Copernican theory with his telescope, he was handed over to the inquisition. [1]

Scopes was merely a pawn in the battle between two great paradigms. Galileo and Copernicus were great thinkers who, out of scientific honesty, believed they were compelled to present a new paradigm.

PUBLIC OPINION

It is often reported that it is only a small group of "fringe fundamentalists" who believe God created man.

This is patently not the case. In a national Gallup Survey conducted in 1982, 44 percent of Americans said that they believed God created man pretty much in his present form at one time within the last 10,000 years; 38 percent believed man has developed over millions of years from less advanced forms of life, but God guided this process, including man's creation, and 9 percent believed man has developed over millions of years from less advanced forms of life. God had no part in this process. [2]

It is interesting to hear even from a skeptic the illogical close-mindedness that the scientific establishment has against creation philosophy. Eileen Barker observed:

At one stage in my research, when I had become quite well versed in the creationist literature, I tried putting their arguments to a number of my academic colleagues. I was amazed to find that nearly every occasion we reached a point at which my friends would abandon rational or empirical argument in favor of irritated condemnation or dogmatic assertion. On one occasion a colleague ended up by exclaiming in utter exasperation, "But they're just wrong"! [2]

This shows the power of a paradigm. A paradigm once decided on is expected to go unchallenged. Even dissecting and examining parts of a paradigm are not usually welcomed. Barker's colleagues were intelligent, well-educated people. It is evident that they were also people who preferred not to examine the validity of a different explanation of nature.

One's philosophy of life and world view concerning nature is developed primarily before one enters one's adult vocation. Various experiences influence one's decisions. Family, school (elementary through college), church, reading material, television and peers are among the contributors.

As we have seen, after one decides on a paradigm there is very little interest in investigating its validity. Change is not even considered until so many unexplainable "anomalies" are discovered that make one's paradigm too ineffective. There are literally millions of people who are caught in the no-man's-land between two paradigms. These are people who believe in the Bible yet also believe in evolutionary naturalism. Their religious training and experiences have suggested evolutionary naturalism does not fit with their theology. On the other hand, their scientific side is not satisfied with creationism because of their formal and informal educational training.

FINAL SUGGESTIONS

What then can be done? We need to understand that origin science, whether based on natural causes or supernatural causes, is not in the realm of empirically based science, we have taken a giant step toward better understanding. Because origin science deals with singular rather than repeating events falsification in the usual sense is impossible. The evidence for or against these two paradigms is best evaluated by forensic science. The three evaluation criteria are: causality, uniformity and circumstantial evidence.

Evolutionary naturalism fails to answer origin science questions in an acceptable way. On the other hand, by using the three criteria, biblical naturalism is a very positive tool to investigate nature. The creation model needs to be further developed and more research needs to be done so that the biblical naturalism paradigm can become even more usable.

We, in good conscience, cannot let another generation go by without developing and promoting the biblical naturalism paradigm. As we have learned, this paradigm is not really new. It was the paradigm of choice for all of the great fathers of science in the 16th and 17th centuries. On the other hand, we need to realize that a shift from the evolutionary naturalism paradigm to the biblical naturalism paradigm will involve turmoil that is best described as, revolution. This revolution needs to start where there is the best chance of success. Churches need to teach biblical naturalism to their members. Parents need to teach it to their children. Christian elementary and secondary schools need to educate their students with this paradigm. Christian universities are the institutions which can be the most effective in teaching the biblical naturalism paradigm. Many of the students, at the very time in their lives when they are finalizing their paradigm concerning nature, find themselves in the no-man's-land between two paradigms. Too often Christian professors, who may themselves believe the biblical creationism paradigm choose to withhold influencing their students toward the proper paradigm. Many other professors are themselves caught in the no-man's-land. What are the consequences of their silence? Their college textbooks are not silent and assume the evolutionary naturalism paradigm. Students' pre-college educational background pointed them toward evolutionary naturalism. What could have become a nurturing ground for strengthening the faith of Christian students becomes a breeding ground for a faith destroying world view.

So here is a strategy I offer. I suggest that all Christian universities start offering a regular course that investigates the two paradigms in a straight forward manner. This course should be offered on one level as an elective for any non-science student and on a different level as a requirement for all science degree candidates.

Secondary science educators need to develop a curriculum for a similar course to be offered at Christian secondary schools. Finally, curriculum conducive to the educational level of the general public needs to developed and offered by Churches.

An integral part of any of these courses must be both evidence against the evolutionary naturalism paradigm and scientific support of the biblical naturalism paradigm. As we have discussed, paradigms are not easily let go of once they are personally adopted. There are however few gifts more important to pass on to our young people than the enlightenment the biblical naturalism paradigm can produce.

REFERENCES

[1]   Frank E. Allen, **Evolution In the Balances**, 1926 Revell Company, New York, 11-12, 186.

[2]   Eileen Barker, **Let There Be Light**, <u>Darwinism and Divinity</u> Ed. by John Durant, 1985, Basil Blackwell Inc. N.Y., 186, 193.

[3]   Richard Bube, **The Encounter Between Christianity and Science**, 1968, Eerdman's Pub. Comp. Grand Rapids, Mich. 68.

[4]   John Casti, **Paradigms Lost, Images of Man In The Mirror of Science**, 1989, William Morrow and Comp., Inc. N.Y. 39, 124-125.

[5]   Dan Chiras, **Environmental Science**, 1990, Benjamin/Cummings' Pub. Comp. Menlo Park, Cal., 17.

[6]   William Davis, Eldra Soleman, Linda Berg, **The World of Biology**, 1990, Saunders Coolege Publishing, Philadelphia, 29.

[7]   Pierre Teilhard de Chardin, As noted by Johnson [14], 118.

[8]   Norman Geisler and Kirby Anderson, **Origin Science**, 1987, Baker Book House, Grand Rapids, Mich. 14, 25, 30, 31, 106, 108, 109, 125-126, 128, 161.

[9]   Goethe, citation unknown.

[10]   George Grinnell, **Reexamination of the Foundations**, an interview in Pensee, May, 1972, 44 As noted in Thaxton [25] p.5.

[11]   Gary Gutting, **Paradigms and Revolutions**, 1980, University of Notre Dame Press, Notre Dame, 1.

[12]   Charles Hodge, **What Is Darwinism?**, 1984, Scribner Armstron and comp., N.Y., 173.

[13]   Stanley Jaki, **The Road of Science and the Ways of God**, 1978, Univ. of Chicago Press, Chicago, 320.

[14]   Phillip Johnson, **Darwin On Trial**, 1991, InterVarsity Press, Downers Grove, Ill., 118, 150.

[15]   M.D. King, **Reason, Tradition, and the Progressiveness of Science**, <u>Paradigms and Revolutions</u>, Ed. by Gary Gutting, 1980, University of Notre Dame Press, Notre Dame, 111.

[16]   Thomas Kuhn, **The Structure of Scientific Revolutions**, 1979, University of Chicago Press, Chicago, 65,79, 168.

[17]   Paul Nelson, **The Whole Question of Metaphysics**, 1993, Origins Research, Vol. 15, No. 1, 6.

[18]   Ronald Numbers, **Creation By Natural Law**, 1977, Univ. of Washington Press, Seattle., 106.

[19]   A.I. Oparin, **The Origin of Life**, 1953, Dover Pub., New York, 1.

[20]   Paul Moody, **Introduction to Evolution**, 1962, Harper and Row, New York, .ix.

[21]   Henry Morris, **The Long War Against God**, 1989, Baker Book House, Grand Rapids, Mich., 23.

[22]   A.R. Peacocke, **Rethinking Religious Faith In A World of Science**, Religion, <u>Science and Public Policy</u>, Edited by Frank Birtel, 1987, Crossroads Publishing Corp., N.Y., 3-4.

[23]   Holmes Rolston III, **Science and Religion**, 1987, Temple Univ. Press, Philadelphia, 11.

[24]   Carl Sagan, **Cosmos**, 1980, Random House, New York, 4.

[25]   Charles Thaxton, **The Intellectuals Speak Out About God**, Ed. by Roy Varghese, 1984, Lewis and Stanley Publishers, Dallas, 4.

[26]   Bert Thompson, **Theistic Evolution**, 1977, Lambert Book House, Shreveport, 17.

[27]   Author and source unknown.

A REMOTE SENSING SEARCH FOR EXTINCT LAKE SHORE LINES ON THE COLORADO PLATEAU

EDMOND W. HOLROYD, III, PH.D.
8905 W. 63RD AVENUE
ARVADA, CO 80004-3103

KEYWORDS

Grand Canyon, Colorado Plateau, strand line, erosion, sedimentation, lacustrine deposits, remote sensing analysis, geomorphology

ABSTRACT

The breached-dam hypothesis for the formation of the Grand Canyon needs physical evidence for the justification of extinct lakes. Digital elevation data were used for basin and proposed lake shore mapping and for cliff identification on the Colorado Plateau upstream from the Grand Canyon. Satellite images, aerial photographs, and visual searches from aircraft were used to confirm cliff locations in a search for shore line cliffs that might exhibit the missing talus phenomenon. The distributions of mapped Pliocene and Pleistocene sediments show that some may be related to the hypothesized extinct lakes. Although not proving the case for such lakes, the findings are consistent with the hypothesis.

INTRODUCTION

Inspired in part by other writers, most likely in some issue of the Bible Science Newsletter in the late 1970's, and by the basin-like appearance of the Painted Desert of Arizona in manipulations of digital elevation data, I produced a hypothetical map in December 1986 outlining a possible series of lakes that would be impounded by a plugging of the Grand Canyon. Those lakes at a surface elevation of 1700 meters above sea level were mentioned by Holroyd [8], included by Austin [1, p.78], presented by Holroyd [9, p.122], and shown in their original color and videotaped during the oral presentation of Holroyd [9] at the Second International Conference on Creationism. A different outline was independently produced and published by Brown [3, p.83] for an elevation of 5700 feet. The Austin [1] version was redrawn in Oard [10, p.41]. The suggestion has been that catastrophic breaching allowed the water from such lakes to carve most of the Grand Canyon, a hypothesis summarized by Austin [3, pp. 92-107] in a catastrophic breach.

There is little basis at this time for choosing between 1700 meters (5577 feet) and 5700 feet (1737 meters), so in this report I will illustrate the latter. The number is related to the present elevation of the pour point (PP) of the lakes at the north end of the Kaibab Plateau, near the Arizona/Utah border. The pour point is the location of the lowest elevation (apart from the Grand Canyon) through which water could spill out of the basin. That saddle is presently dry and without obvious indications of a previous stream channel. The soil is the decayed remnants of the soft, red Moenkopi siltstone. The land there could easily have been lowered by erosion since the demise of the proposed lakes. Furthermore, isostatic rebound of the regional ground after the removal of the water burden would alter former elevations.

A new illustration of the hypothetical lakes is presented in Figure 1. It differs from other versions by having the Grand Canyon (GC) artificially filled rim to rim from about the junction of the Little Colorado River to the position of Lake Mead. The terrain was then highlighted by artificial solar shading. The difference between the 1700 meter lakes and the 5700 foot lakes is shown in the white shading.

A series of articles by Williams et al. [15, 16, 17] provided an excellent review of past hypotheses on the formation of the Grand Canyon, including antecedent rivers, river capture, piping, and the breaching of dams releasing the waters of upstream lakes. Oard [10] produced studies supporting possible lakes during the Ice

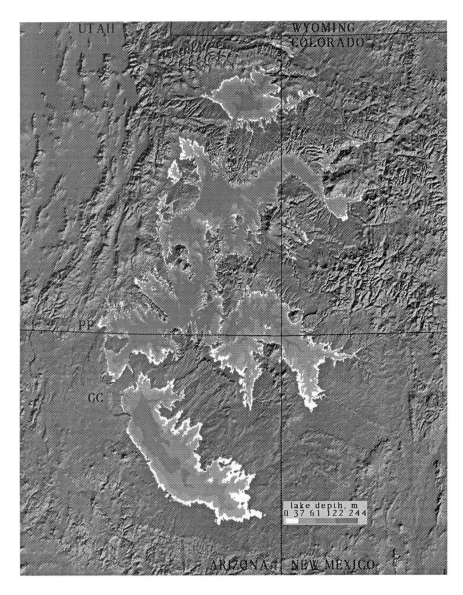

Figure 1. A view of the 5700 foot lakes that might have been impounded behind the Kaibab Uplift. The Grand Canyon has been filled in and the terrain given solar shading.

Age, but cautioned that other evidence might lead to problems with the dam-breach theory. The study that follows examined several data sources related to the dam-breach theory.

Holroyd [8, 9] suggested that the missing talus phenomenon at the bases of regional escarpments might be an indicator of shore lines of extinct lakes. The wave action at such shore line cliffs would pulverize previous talus. The present talus would have fallen since the demise of the lakes. Some of the study sites [9, Table 1] were near the pour point elevation of 1700 meters above sea level. The area and volume of a series of lakes at the 1700 meter level would be equivalent to Lake Superior. Such a possible series of lakes impounded behind the Kaibab Plateau is of importance to creationist studies. The lakes cannot coexist with the Grand Canyon. The relative youth of the angular talus boulders indicates a recent period for the demise of the lakes. If true, then the carving of the Grand Canyon must also be recent. An exact match of elevations should not be expected because of probable tectonic changes after the removal of the water overburden.

AVHRR SATELLITE VIEW

The oral presentation of Holroyd [9] included a view of the Colorado Plateau as seen in a mosaic of satellite images from the NOAA AVHRR polar-orbiting weather satellite. Figure 2 shows the AVHRR view with the 5700 foot lake shore lines superimposed. It is readily seen that the "lake" outlines surround naturally bright regions of the Colorado Plateau. The exception is along the southwest side of the southern lake where the ground is covered by black lava flows. This white enclosure is more than just a coincidence. The bright regions are low desert basins and most of the dark regions are vegetated highlands. The shading is strongly related to present elevation-controlled climate. The lowlands experience the drying effects of air subsiding from the highlands and undergoing compressional warming and relative humidity reduction. This results in much less precipitation reaching the ground in the lowlands and a higher evaporation rate there. The vegetation in the lowlands is therefore sparse. As a result the shading follows the elevations. The elevations were used to derive the "lakes" of Figure 1. This relationship does not prove that the lakes ever existed but only offers circumstantial evidence. The climatological shading and the fillable basins are both strongly related to the same elevation distributions.

AERIAL RECONNAISSANCE

Since the development of the lake hypothesis I have searched the Little Colorado and San Juan River Basins and the Uinta Basin both visually and photographically, from commercial aircraft flights and somewhat on the ground, for any shore line indications. In a similar way some Landsat satellite images of the region have been examined. While numerous suggestions have been found over several years of studies, none were clear indicators of ancient shore lines. Lake Bonneville and other lakes have left multiple and distinct strand lines (shore line carvings in hillsides) in Utah and Nevada. It is therefore of great concern for the breached-dam hypothesis that similar strand lines are not obvious throughout the Colorado Plateau.

Moderate to major cliffs are visible from high altitude. Lesser abandoned sandy beach ridges are less likely to be noticed. The Colorado Plateau has an abundance of cliffs but most seem to have little possibility of being shore line etchings. Their shapes suggest other causes for their sculpture. If lake shore lines lay against many of these cliffs, it seems only fortuitous.

Flights at low sun angle show the highlighted surface texture of the land. I noticed that there was a general tendency for the broad lowlands (basins) to have smooth surfaces while higher terrain showed erosional sculpturing. I do not have any data set whereby I can test if the demarcation between rugged and smooth terrain texture is related to the "lake" elevations, but it would be an interesting study.

The south side of the Painted Desert (Little Colorado Basin) has no shore line escarpments. The surface is the hard Kaibab limestone with sometimes a red remnant of the soft Moenkopi siltstone that was washed off elsewhere Several streams have become entrenched in the limestone. The north side of the basin is covered by Moenkopi siltstone and Chinle shales which are not capable of supporting tall cliffs. The basaltic caps on the Hopi Buttes and some exposures of the Bidahochi Formation (lacustrine and volcanic ash) do exhibit cliffs at elevations near to above the "lake" elevations being considered.

There are some cliffs within the San Juan River Basin but mostly near the highland periphery. There were no continuous topographic features that could be interpreted as a major shore line from an aerial viewpoint. The missing talus sites of Mesa Verde and Monument Valley seem like isolated occurrences compared to the rest of the basin. There are interesting escarpments on the flanks of the Chuska Mountain plateau and surrounding Defiance Uplift region but they are seemingly bent upwards with the higher terrain. Interpreting them as the sides of landslide source regions may be more reasonable.

The Uinta Basin shows some escarpments but they seem to be related more to sediment plumes from the Uinta Mountains. No good shore line remnants were noticed from the air even though the basin is filled with lacustrine deposits.

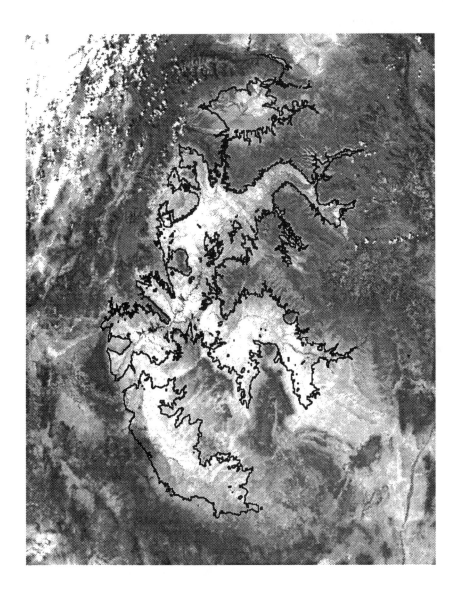

Figure 2. A view of the Colorado Plateau from the NOAA AVHRR weather satellite system. The 5700 foot "shore lines" are superimposed.

CLIFFS FROM DIGITAL ELEVATION DATA

A careful examination of some 7.5' topographic maps containing known strand lines of Lake Bonneville suggests that computer analysis of digital elevations (DEM) derived from such maps at 30 meter horizontal resolution should be able to detect the presence of those strand lines. A computer program trained on Lake Bonneville data could then be used to search the Colorado Plateau region for similar strand lines. Unfortunately, DEM data for major portions of the Colorado Plateau region (especially Arizona) are not yet available. When they are available in perhaps a decade from now, the necessary data set will cost many thousands of dollars. The present price is $7 per quadrangle, of which there are 64 in a 1-degree latitude/longitude square.

Until those data sets are available we need to use the standard topographic sets that have been available for over a decade. The data source for such elevations is the Defense Mapping Agency (DMA) analyses of 1:250,000 scale topographic maps. The data are not of the highest quality, but are complete for the entire continental United States and adjacent Mexico and Canada. They are available from a number of sources, government and commercial. Data accuracy is restricted by the contour interval of the original maps, typically 200 feet in mountainous areas. The histograms of the elevation data are full of spikes, typically at whole contour levels on the original maps. Other blemishes are discontinuities at the 1-degree latitude or longitude original map boundaries and sometimes positional errors of about a kilometer. Some parts of the data set have pits and corrugations where none exist in reality.

Following image processing notation, each location of an elevation value is called a pixel, the smallest element making up an image. The DMA data set is available in two resolutions. In the coarse set the pixel size is 30 seconds of arc, and in the fine set it is 3 seconds of arc, in both latitude and longitude. Whereas the north-south scale of each pixel is constant, there are fewer east-west meters for the northern pixels compared to the southern. The crude 30-second data set was used for Figure 1.

The missing talus phenomenon was found at cliffs that were hundreds of feet tall, at which softer shales were capped by harder sandstones. It therefore seemed appropriate to search the Colorado Plateau region for all cliffs to see if they presented any pattern, horizontally or vertically, that might be related to the hypothesized lake shore lines. No particular elevations were sought in this part of the study. The desire was to let the data nominate special elevations, if any. Digital elevation data for the entire region were examined at a resolution (3 seconds of arc) ten times finer than that used for the original lake boundary mapping.

Known regional cliffs were found from the digital terrain by computer algorithms that identified all slopes of at least 20 degrees. The value of 20 degrees obviously does not represent a real cliff. The data itself has a horizontal resolution of only about 85 meters. The vertical resolution on the maps from which the data were derived is only 61 meters (200 feet), though intermediate elevations are present in the data set. The 20 degree slope was found to be a good indicator in this data set for real cliffs that had much steeper slopes. A better computer search will be possible in the future when the 30-meter data set is complete.

The elevations, rounded to 20 meter resolution, at which such slopes were found were then recorded. River channel canyons (facing pairs of cliffs) up to a few kilometers wide that were identified by that criterion were edited out of the data set. Mountain slopes, being at much higher elevations than the potential lake shore lines, were retained but otherwise ignored. The remaining data set of steep slopes generally contained all the significant regional cliffs identified by the visual, photographic, and satellite searches.

CLIFF ANALYSES

Because the elevation data had histogram spikes at preferred values, typically 200 foot contours, ratios were made of the number of "cliff" pixels at a particular level to the total number of elevation pixels in the region of interest. Furthermore, a running mean over every three adjacent levels (20-meter) was performed to minimize the 200 foot data problem. The goal was to see if the spectrum of the ratios, plotted against elevation, would show some preferred elevations. Consistency of preferred cliff elevations could be indicative of shore line cliffs.

For convenience the watersheds upstream from the Grand Canyon were divided into five regional units (see Figure 4). They are the Little Colorado River (LC), San Juan River (SJ), Uinta Basin (UB), Upper Green River (UG), and the rest of the Green and Colorado River (CO) watersheds. Divisions were made along major basin crest lines. A watershed analysis program was used on the 30 arc-second digital elevation data to outline the sub-basins. Its only major error was in assigning the upper part of the Dolores River to the San Juan watershed. Those digital elevation data lacked the resolution to show the river passing through a major ridge northwest of Cortez, Colorado. The regional subsections were made only for summary purposes and no harm is caused by this blemish.

Figure 3 shows part of a graph of the fraction of slopes at or greater than 20 degrees (edited), detected at each elevation, and smoothed by a 20 meter running mean. The region generally has smooth flat lowlands in which cliffs are rare. The highlands have an abundance of steep mountain slopes. In between, some of the curves for each of the five regions have irregularities showing an enhanced frequency of steep slopes (cliffs) near some set of elevations.

In general, the graph shows two particular elevation bands (1.7 and 1.9 km, shaded in Figure 3) of occurrences of special elevations. The upper band is significantly higher than the 1700 meter elevation being considered in this study. An exploration of other possible lake levels showed that with the blockage of both the Grand Canyon and the pour point to the north of the Kaibab Plateau, the next pour points (three of them) would all be at about 2000 meters (6600 feet). Higher lake levels cannot be achieved with the present terrain. The 1.9 km level is appropriate to the lacustrine deposits of the Bidahochi Formation near the Arizona/New Mexico border and to erosion patterns (presented below) at Navajo Mountain. That level is found mostly in the southeastern parts (SJ) of this study. If these 20-degree "cliffs" are related to shore lines, they may indeed represent a second, higher lake level prior to the one illustrated in Figure 1.

The LC basin has a questionable ripple at 1.9 km because of the smoothness of the terrain in that basin, but that is the approximate level of the lacustrine Bidahochi Formation. The UG and CO had the largest offsets (at about the 1.7 km level) from the general curves. The 1.2 km peak on the CO curve is from Marble Canyon and may be related to the extinct Prospect Lake, dammed at Vulcans Throne after the carving of the Grand Canyon. The UB fluctuation at 1.9 km is the striped shading on the dotted curve. It overlaps the SJ curve shading.

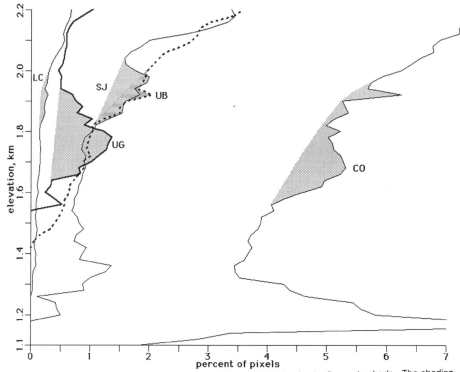

Figure 3. A part of the spectrum of cliff presence versus land elevation for the five watersheds. The shading indicates a possible enhanced presence of cliffs.

The elevations shaded in each basin were isolated from the 20-degree slope ("cliff") data. A count of the number of surviving pixels in each 10x10 pixel square provided a percentage of cliff presence at a resolution of 30" of arc, like that used for the "lake" outlines. In Figure 4 are shown the outlines of the basins used (black lines), 5700 foot lakes (gray shade), and locations having at least 5 percent cliff presence (black dots) within the special elevation bands of Figure 3.

As expected, the LC basin (south) has only a tiny scattering of special locations. The line of black dots at the northwest shore line near the GC is a fault escarpment. Except for Mesa Verde, the SJ cliffs are at the higher elevation of about 1.9 km. The CO region has a very high incidence of cliffs, especially near the shore line.

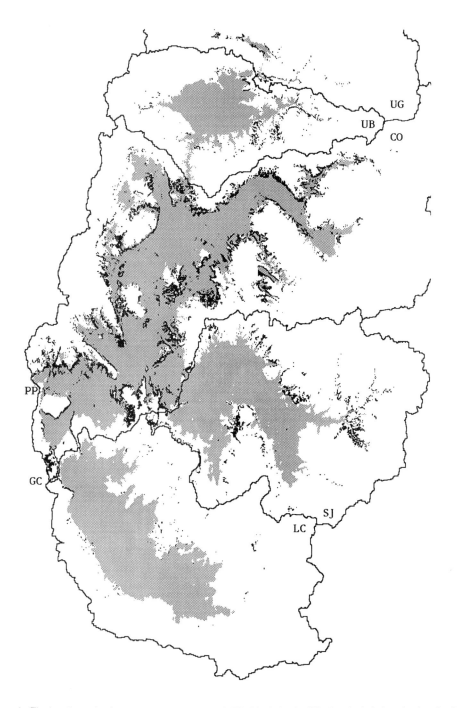

Figure 4. The locations of at least 5 percent presence of cliffs (black dots) within the shaded elevation bands of Figure 3. The basin outlines and labels are also in black and the 5700 foot lakes in gray.

249

Most of this is just caused by the general offset of the curve to higher values in Figure 3. But there are numerous regions with a clear shore line matching. The Book Cliffs at the eastern end of the northern CO shore line extend westward from Grand Junction, Colorado, to Price, Utah. In the latter region they are still present but at above 2000 meters, as if the region has been tectonically lifted. The UB region is mostly smooth, but there are some linear collections of dots in the east and west and in the north at Dinosaur National Monument (DNM). The UG cliffs are all in the DNM region and Flaming Gorge. All of the higher missing talus sites of Holroyd [9] received black marks in Figure 4. It appears that there is an abundance of other regional cliffs worth investigating with respect to the proposed shore lines.

These two digital elevation studies, presented in Figures 3 and 4 for vertical and horizontal positions, respectively, are not proof by themselves of extinct lakes. Figure 3 unexpectedly indicated two elevations to be considered. While many of the cliff positions in Figure 4 may be only coincidentally related to the possible shore line positions, some of those cliff positions should have field checks to see if there are additional indicators of strand lines.

NAVAJO MOUNTAIN

Throughout the Colorado River Basin are tall laccolith mountains that rise to above the possible lake levels being considered. It seems reasonable that if the mountains were present at the time of the lakes, then they should have remnants of a strand line in the form of cliff etchings caused by shore line wave erosion and/or small deltaic deposits at the water line. Digital elevation data at the superior 30 meter resolution were acquired for Navajo Mountain, strategically located next to the present Lake Powell and Colorado River. The data were given a "solar shading" in Figure 5 from an impossible northeast point to bring out topographic detail.

A possible shore line etching can be seen along the south side where there is a bolder pattern of alternating blacks and whites. The mountain does not flare continuously out onto the flat terrain. This is also visible in Landsat satellite image data. An oblique aerial photograph by Shelton [13] shows that there are indeed cliffs of Navajo sandstone ringing the southern base of Navajo Mountain. In that higher photographic resolution they look like sea coast promontories. The feature is more difficult to observe around the northern side of the mountain because mass wasting has destroyed most of the features at the mountain base level. The elevation of the cutting is just below 2000 meters (about 6500 feet on the 7.5' topographic map), in agreement with the 1.9 km level highlighted in Figure 3.

An examination of geologic maps of Navajo Mountain shows that Morrison strata cap the summit. Except for fluvial cuts, only older Navajo strata ring the base at about the 2000 meter level. To the west of Navajo Mountain (left side of Figure 5) an unnamed plateau is also capped by Morrison strata but at elevations almost

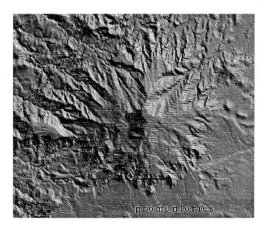

Figure 5. An artificial shading of high resolution elevation data for Navajo Mountain may indicate a shore line etching along the southern side.

entirely below the 2000 meter level. Similar but smaller Morrison remnants exist to the north in several locations and also below the 2000 meter level. The cutting away of the Morrison, Entrada, and Carmel Formations and into the more resistant Navajo Formation, completely around the mountain, is consistent with the mountain being an island in a body of water with a surface elevation lower than about 2000 meters. The Morrison remnants beyond the mountain base would have been under water and sheltered from wave action. The Morrison and intermediate strata near the mountain summit would have been higher than any wave action and also protected. The Navajo Formation would be carved by the waves into the cliffs and promontories we can still see today. The shore line evidences would then be raised nearly a few hundred feet by isostatic rebound after the demise of the lake.

Other laccoliths have not yet been examined in detail for strand lines.

SEDIMENTS

One of the difficulties of the breached dam hypothesis noted by Oard [10] was that if the lakes existed in a region of the abundant precipitation needed to keep them from simply evaporating, then there should be a variety of sediments resulting from turbid rivers entering the edges of the lakes. Such deposits have not seemed obvious to other observers. Lake Bonneville has left sediments throughout its former extent, as indicated on the geologic map of Utah [6].

The 1:500,000 scale geologic maps of Arizona, Colorado, New Mexico, and Utah [18, 14, 4, 6] and 1:1,000,000 scale geologic map of Arizona [11] were examined. Conventional geologists assign the carving of the Grand Canyon to Pliocene and Pleistocene (late Tertiary and Quaternary) times. The outlines of all Pliocene and Pleistocene sedimentary strata delineated on maps (omitting the most recent Quaternary alluvium and aeolian deposits) were transferred into the computer for comparison with the elevation data.

The elevations of all such strata are plotted in Figure 6 as cumulative curves. The figure is split into two parts for readability. The formation map notations and state abbreviations are indicated in the figures. At this writing it is not necessary to further describe their characteristics and names. Those formations that have the greater presences are in thicker lines. For comparison, the cumulative curve for regional elevation is the dotted line. Formations that exist only in a narrow elevation band are steep, such as some of those in the lower half of the figure. Those at distinct multiple elevations have some horizontal segments. Some of these recent sedimentary deposits are above the 2 km limit being considered for any lake phenomena. Some formations have a continuous distribution through that level. The best candidates for lake deposits are those whose curves are steeply climbing at elevations under 2 km. The horizontal positions of all formations having at least 10 percent presence at elevations under 2 km are plotted in Figure 7, but only up to the 2 km level.

At the south, the Bidahochi (Tsy and Tu) Formation (known to contain lacustrine components [12]) rings the eastern end of the "lake". More modern Qo (older alluvium) sediments occupy the bottom of the basin. There are a few river channel deposits in the San Juan lobe (east center) and only a few mountain-generated deposits elsewhere. The Uinta Basin (near top) is filled with recent deposits, some of which are obscured by alluvium and therefore not plotted here. A solid band of sediments seemingly unrelated to any proposed lake is at the very top of the figure. Elsewhere, within the main CO portion of the study area, there is an abundance of patchy deposits draining from the higher terrain into the periphery of the proposed "lake". They resemble deltaic deposits of small streams entering a lake but could also be alluvial fans and debris flows unrelated to any lakes. Geologic study of these sediments are needed. Figure 7 shows an abundance of deposits that are candidates for further study with respect to the lake hypothesis. Many will be shown to be unrelated to lake deposits, but some may, with further study, support the previous existence of giant lakes on the Colorado Plateau.

None of these deposits is solidly filling the basin bottoms like the Lake Bonneville sediments, with the possible exception of the Uinta Basin. The pattern elsewhere suggests that the duration of the "lake" was brief. Additional sediments, if they ever existed, were probably unconsolidated and vulnerable to sapping and a sweeping away during a catastrophic lake demise and subsequent erosion under higher precipitation rates (Oard, [10]) than today.

CONCLUSION

This study has investigated several types of data relating to the breached-dam hypothesis of the Grand Canyon. The regional topography, with its natural but dry basins, suggests the possibility of filling them with water. The missing talus phenomenon is still there to be explained, and a lake shore hypothesis is attractive. The region apparently has an abundance of cliffs at similar elevations that could also have "missing talus". Such cliffs are sometimes consistently near the proposed shore lines. There are indeed some relatively recent sediments of the same geologic age as the assumed carving of the Grand Canyon. A few of these formations are admittedly lacustrine [12]. Whether or not the rest can be related to the proposed lakes needs further study.

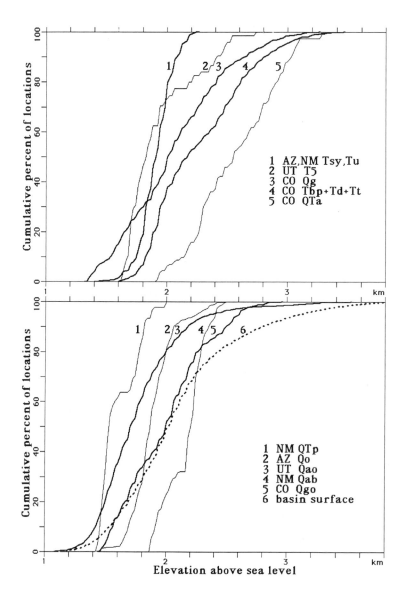

Figure 6. Cumulative distributions, against elevation, of Pliocene and Pleistocene sedimentary formations upstream from the Grand Canyon.

The major cliffs and the recent sediments are not, by themselves, indicators of extinct shore lines. The data presented here are only circumstantial evidence for the extinct lakes. More study is needed, particularly litera-ture searches and field examinations. The slope study, at the resolution used, would not have readily seen the established extinct shore lines of Lake Bonneville. That basin was different from the Colorado Basin in that the sediments never had a possibility of being swept out of the basin, and so they still cover the lowlands today. The sparseness of the recent sediments in the Colorado Basin may actually by indicative of subsequent removal rather than a negation of the lake hypothesis.

Figure 7. The locations (black) of Pliocene and Pleistocene sedimentary formations at elevations up to 2000 meters. The 5700 foot "lakes" are shaded.

ACKNOWLEDGMENTS

The image processing for this research was done on my microcomputer using the Map and Image Processing System (MIPS) software produced by MicroImages, Inc., 201 N. 8th, Suite 15, Lincoln, NE 68508-1347. Parts of this study were supported by a grant from the Creation Research Society Laboratory Project in cooperation with MicroImages, Inc. Further details related to this research are therefore expected to be submitted for publication in the Creation Research Society Quarterly. Some of the satellite images visually examined were those acquired by the Bureau of Reclamation for their normal government investigations. Digital terrain data acquired from the U.S. Geological Survey, Earth Science Information Center on 9-track tape were converted to DOS computer files on the MIPS system supervised by Dr. Tom Huber at the University of Colorado-Colorado Springs. The AVHRR image was acquired from the National Weather Service, Minneapolis.

BIBLIOGRAPHY

[1]   S. A. Austin, ed., Institute for Creation Research, Field Study Tour Guidebook, April 8 to 16, 1989, p.54 (and yearly versions thereafter).

[2]   S. A. Austin, ed., Grand Canyon Monument to Catastrophe, (1994) Institute for Creation Research, 284 pp.

[3]   W. T. Brown, In the Beginning, fifth edition (1989) Center for Creation Research, Phoenix, AZ. 122 pp.

[4]   C. H. Dane and G. O. Bachman, Geologic Map of New Mexico (1965) U. S. Geologic Survey. 1:500,000

[5]   W. K. Hamblin, **Pleistocene Volcanic Rocks of the Western Grand Canyon, Arizona**, Geology of Grand Canyon, Northern Arizona (with Colorado River Guides) Field Trip Guidebook T115/315 Chapter 23. (1989) American Geophysical Union. 190-204.

[6]   L. F. Hintze, Geologic Map of Utah (1980) Utah Geologic and Mineral Survey. 1:500,000

[7]   L. F. Hintze, Geologic History of Utah (1988) Brigham Young University Geology Studies, Special Publication 7, p. 85-89.

[8]   E. W. Holroyd, **Missing Talus**, Creation Research Society Quarterly, **24** (1987) 15-16.

[9]   E. W. Holroyd, **Missing Talus on the Colorado Plateau**, Proceedings of the Second International Conference on Creationism (1990), Vol II, pp.115-128.

[10]   M. J. Oard, **Comments on the Breached Dam Theory for the Formation of the Grand Canyon**, Creation Research Society Quarterly **30** (1993) 39-46.

[11]   S. J. Reynolds, **Geologic Map of Arizona** (1988) in J. P. Jenney and S. J. Reynolds, Geologic Evolution of Arizona, Tucson, Arizona Geological Society Digest 17 (1989). 1:1,000,000

[12]   R. Scarborough, **Cenozoic Erosion and Sedimentation in Arizona**, in J. P. Jenney and S. J. Reynolds, Geologic Evolution of Arizona, Tucson, Arizona Geological Society Digest 17 (1989), p.515-537.

[13]   J. S. Shelton, **Earth Science Slides**, W. H. Freeman and Co. (1973), Slide #416

[14]   O. Tweto, Geologic Map of Colorado (1979) U. S. Geological Survey. 1:500,000

[15]   E. L. Williams, J. R. Meyer and G. W. Wolfrom, **Erosion of the Grand Canyon of the Colorado River: Part I -- Review of antecedent river hypothesis and the postulation of large quantities of rapidly flowing water as the primary agent of erosion**, Creation Research Society Quarterly 28 (1991) 92-98.

[16]   E. L. Williams, J. R. Meyer and G. W. Wolfrom, **Erosion of the Grand Canyon of the Colorado River: Part II -- Review of river capture, piping and ancestral river hypothesis and the possible formation of vast lakes**, Creation Research Society Quarterly 28 (1992) 138-145.

[17]   E. L. Williams, J. R. Meyer and G. W. Wolfrom, **Erosion of the Grand Canyon of the Colorado River: Part III -- Review of the possible formation of basin and lakes on Colorado Plateau and different climatic conditions in the past**, Creation Research Society Quarterly 29 (1992) 18-24.

[18]   E. D. Wilson, R. T. Moore and J. R. Cooper, Geologic Map of Arizona (1969) U. S. Geologic Survey. 1:500,000

A BIBLICAL BASIS FOR CREATIONIST COSMOLOGY

D. RUSSELL HUMPHREYS, Ph.D.*
Creation Science Fellowship of New Mexico
P.O. Box 10550, Albuquerque, NM 87184

ABSTRACT
Taking Genesis 1 and other scriptures in the most straightforward possible sense leads to several conclusions of great importance for cosmology: (1) The "expanse" of Genesis chapter 1 is not the earth's atmosphere but interstellar space, (2) The "waters above the expanse" are cosmic in scale and represent a boundary for interstellar space, (3) the earth is near the center of the universe. These conclusions form the basis for a young-earth relativistic cosmology which I describe in another paper presented at this conference.

KEYWORDS
Biblical cosmology, young-earth creationism, age of universe, hermeneutics.

1. INTRODUCTION

> To him that rideth upon the heavens of heavens, which were of old — Psalm 69:33, KJV.

The Bible lays a good foundation for a young-earth relativistic cosmology. That is the main point I want to make in this paper. Contrary to impressions made by the news media, no one today can start from observed data and build up a cosmology by rigorous scientific deduction. Instead, some ideological initial assumptions are necessary, as cosmologists Stephen Hawking and George Ellis [5, p. 134] acknowledge:

> ... we are not able to make cosmological models without some admixture of ideology.

All the major cosmologies of this century, including the "big-bang" cosmologies, start with an arbitrary assumption which Hawking and Ellis call the *Copernican principle* [5, p.134]. Reduced to its essence, the Copernican principle requires matter in the universe to be *unbounded*, that is, the distribution of stars and galaxies in the cosmos can have no edges and no center. When cosmologists plug this assumption into the equations of Einstein's general theory of relativity and turn the mathematical crank, the big-bang and other famous cosmologies follow logically as a result.

In this paper I list evidence that the most straightforward understanding of the relevant scriptures gives us a cosmos which contradicts the Copernican principle. That is, the distribution of stars and galaxies in the biblical cosmos has a clearly-defined edge and a center. Moreover the earth would be, on a cosmological scale of distances, near the center. In another paper at this conference [8], I show that putting this condition of boundedness into the equations of general relativity results in a cosmos which is radically different than the conventional cosmologies. In this new picture of the cosmos, gravity and black hole physics play a central role.

In particular, an experimentally-measured general relativistic effect, called *gravitational time dilation* by some authors [10, p. 21], causes clocks (and all physical processes) to tick at different rates in different parts of the universe. (This is not the more familiar "velocity" time dilation of special relativity.) By this effect on time itself, God could have made the universe in six ordinary days as measured on earth, while still allowing time for light to travel billions of light-years to reach us by natural means. The theory also appears to explain the two other major cosmological phenomena we see: the red shifts of light from distant galaxies and the cosmic microwave background radiation. Thus, this biblical foundation appears to lead to a young-earth cosmology which is consistent with Einstein's general theory of relativity and astronomical observations. As measured by clocks on earth, the age of the universe today could be as small as the face-value biblical age of about 6000 years.

Before we examine the relevant scriptures, I want to clarify my approach to them in the next section.

2. UNDERSTANDING SCRIPTURE STRAIGHTFORWARDLY

A basic premise of modern creationism is that the Bible is an accurate message from God to man, including matters of science, and intended to be understood and used, as set forth in 2 Timothy 3:17:

> All scripture is inspired by God and profitable for teaching, for reproof, for correction, for training in righteousness; that the man of God may be adequate, equipped for every good work.

(All quotes in English are from the *New American Standard Bible*, unless otherwise indicated.) To be useful in this way, the message must be understandable, and that raises the question of how to "interpret" scripture. Scripture itself provides some guidance on that point. For example, consider Proverbs 8:8,9, where wisdom, personified as a woman, says:

> All the utterances of my mouth are in righteousness;
> There is nothing crooked or perverted in them.
> They are all *straightforward* to him who understands,
> And right to those who find knowledge.

The word "straightforward" (KJV "plain") here is from the Hebrew word נכח(*nakoach*), which one lexicon [6, p. 238] translates as "lying straight ahead ... straight, right." So the words of a wise person are characteristically straightforward. They are not "crooked or perverted," that is, they are not intended to deceive the hearer. According to Proverbs 8:22, Jehovah possesses this wisdom, and so we would expect His words to be straightforward. There may be great depth to His words, but *any deeper understandings should be encompassed within the plain, face-value meaning* of the words as they would be understood by a speaker of Hebrew or Greek in the time and place where they were first given to men. Anything else would lead to deception, which the passage says is not characteristic of wisdom.

A caution is necessary at this point. While recognizing that God is the ultimate author of the Bible, some theologians nonetheless insist that we should not look for any more meaning in scripture than its *human* intermediaries intended:

> In other words, in answer to the question, "How much scientific truth can one extract from Genesis 1?" the answer must be: "One can extract only that which the writer himself, Moses, intended to teach." [3, p. 13]

The motive of this theologian was good; he wanted to guard against the natural tendency of people to read into scripture meanings not included within the bounds of the normal meanings of the words. But good motives do not always produce good principles, and here I think the principle is clearly wrong. First of all, it is not scriptural. For example, the same Peter who wrote about the inspiration of scripture, " ... men moved by the Holy Spirit spoke from God" (2 Peter 1:21), also wrote that inspired prophets did not immediately understand fully what the Holy Spirit was moving them to say:

> As to this salvation, the prophets who prophesied of the grace that would come to you made careful search and inquiry, seeking to know what person or time the Spirit of Christ within them was indicating as He predicted the sufferings of Christ and the glories to follow — *1 Peter 1:10,11.*

If these prophets had fully understood what they were saying as they were saying it, they would not after that have had to make "careful search and inquiry, seeking to know ..." If we were to limit ourselves to the intent of the speaker or writer as he spoke or wrote, this passage says we would miss a lot of rich truth. Secondly, the principle essentially shuts us away from God and what He intended to say to us. We don't study Genesis in order to know the mind of Moses; we study to know the mind of *God*.

A straightforward approach to scripture is the only one I can think of which can yield surprising new knowledge. Without such an approach, I would tend to re-interpret any passage of scripture which did not fit into what I thought was true at the time, and scripture would lose its power to astonish me. If God intended scripture to inform us of things we would not otherwise know, then He must also have intended it to be understood straightforwardly. "Straightforward" does not mean "literal." Someone who reads straightforwardly recognizes the metaphors in scripture, while someone who reads literally will try to squeeze a metaphor into a concrete straitjacket. But when we come to a possible metaphor, we ought to try on some literal meanings for size. If we find one that seems to fit, we ought to go with that meaning as a working hypothesis until we find good reason in scripture to think otherwise.

To make these points a little clearer, imagine a young Jewish Christian of the first century who understands Greek, Hebrew, and the scriptures well. Let's call him "Timothy," since Paul's protege was like that. But let's also imagine that this Timothy knows nothing of the advanced scientific knowledge of his day, such as Aristotle's works. All that Timothy knows is from either everyday experience or careful study of scripture, which Paul says is sufficient to give us wisdom (2 Tim. 3:5). Now if scripture really is straightforward and sufficient, then the meaning Timothy derives from the words is probably the meaning that God intended everybody to get. For example, when Timothy reads in Exodus 20:11,

> For in six days the LORD made the heavens and the earth, the sea and all that is in them, and rested on the seventh day; therefore the Lord blessed the sabbath day and made it holy,

he notices that the context is that of ordinary days of the week. Not having *Scientific American* to tell him that the earth is billions of years old, Timothy is not looking for loopholes in this statement. Instead he simply concludes that scripture is saying Jehovah made the whole universe in six ordinary weekdays. My point is that if scripture is what it claims to be, then we ought to take Timothy's view of the passage and not try to twist the words into new meanings compatible with *Scientific American*'s worldview, or for that matter into anyone else's worldview.

Of all people, young-earth creationists probably take scripture the most straightforwardly. For example, see Robert Walsh's article on hermeneutics [14]. But I find that even we are prone to abandon that principle when it runs counter to some teaching or model we cherish. In this paper I intend, when presented with two or more interpretations of a passage, to apply the "Timothy test" and choose the most straightforward.

3. THE EXPANSE IS INTERSTELLAR SPACE

> *And God made the expanse, and separated the waters which were below the expanse from the waters which were above the expanse; and it was so. And God called the expanse heavens —* Genesis 1:7,8, my translation.

One question that leaps to mind when we first encounter the verses above is: What is the "expanse" (KJV "firmament")? The King James version's word appears to come from the Vulgate's word *firmamentum*, which in turn appears to stem from the Septuagint's translation, στερέωμα (*stereoma*). These three translations emphasize 3-dimensional solidity (*stereo-*) and firmness, about which I will say more in section 7. The Hebrew word is רקיע (*raqia*), meaning "extended surface" [1, p. 956]. Lexicons [2, p. 591] say it comes from the verb רקע (*raqa*), whose primary meaning is "to stamp ... stamp down ... spread out" [6, p. 347]. One 19th-century lexicon [2, p. 692], uncontaminated by 20th-century cosmology, adds to the list of the verb's meanings the interesting phrase "to expand." I will say more about that meaning in section 7. But aside from what learned commentators think, Genesis 1:14-17 gives some direct information about the expanse, which God also called "heavens":

> Then God said, let there be lights *in* the expanse of the heavens ... and let them be for lights *in* the expanse of the heavens ... and God made the two great lights ... He made the stars also. And God placed them *in* the expanse of the heavens to give light on the earth.

In this passage I have italicized the little word "in" to emphasize an important point: the sun, moon, and stars are *in* the expanse. The Hebrew for "in" here is the prefix ב (*bᵉ*), which has essentially the same range of meanings as the English word "in" [6, p. 32].

Now imagine what the Timothy of Section 2 would think about the expanse from this passage. I think everyone would agree that he would simply say the expanse is the place where the sun, moon, and stars are. Therefore, the "Timothy test" leads me to conclude the most straightforward understanding of this passage is that *the expanse is interstellar space*. Using our knowledge of the distances of heavenly bodies, that means that the waters above the expanse must now be at cosmic distances from us, billions of light-years away!

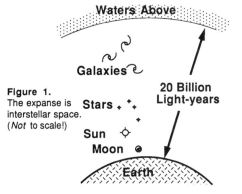

Figure 1.
The expanse is interstellar space.
(*Not* to scale!)

4. THE EXPANSE IS NOT MERELY THE ATMOSPHERE

As most creationists will recognize, the above reading of scripture conflicts with the venerable "vapor canopy" model, which holds that the expanse is merely the earth's atmosphere and that the "waters above" were a canopy of water vapor immediately above the atmosphere [3]. (Canopy theorists correctly argue that the "waters above" had to have been a large amount of water distinctly above the expanse and could not have been mere clouds in the atmosphere [3, pp. 48-58].) The canopy is supposed to have been related to the "windows of the heavens" of Genesis 7:11, and the canopy, by collapsing during the Genesis flood, is supposed to have provided some of the waters of the flood.

Advocates of the canopy model seem to have assumed without much consideration that the expanse is only the earth's atmosphere [3, p. 47]. However, two of them [15. p. 229] use an English translation of Genesis 1:20 as support for that idea:

> ... and let birds fly above the earth in the open expanse of the heavens.

The phrase "in the open expanse," used in most English translations, implies that the expanse is what birds fly in. In my early years as a creationist, I thought that was a sufficient justification for the canopy model. However, one day I discovered that the actual Hebrew phraseology is quite different. On the next page I have reproduced the last part of Genesis 1:20 from an interlinear Hebrew Bible [4, p. 1]. Read it from right to left:

הַשָּׁמָיִם:	רְקִיעַ	עַל־פְּנֵי	עַל־הָאָרֶץ	יְעוֹפֵף	וְעוֹף
the heavens	the expanse of	the face of / on	the earth / over	f ly let around	and birds

So the literal Hebrew doesn't have "in the open expanse." It doesn't even have the preposition "in." Instead it uses another preposition, עַל ('al), which means "on, over, above," but not "in" [6, p. 272]. Moreover, the word here translated "open" comes from the word פָּנֶה (paneh), whose primary meaning is "face" [6, p. 293]. I can't find "open" listed as a secondary meaning for paneh in any of my lexicons [6, p. 293] [1, p. 815] [2, p. 627]. The passage literally says "on the face of the expanse of the heavens." It is the same phraseology as in Genesis 1:2, which is correctly translated, "on the face of" the deep. In biblical usage, the "face" can be oriented in any direction, and what is "on" it need not be gravitationally above it (e.g., Exodus 34:33 and Genesis 11:28, Hebrew). Looking up into the sky, we see birds flying across it, and the passage says what they are flying in is merely at the surface of the expanse. Birds can fly up to altitudes of 25,000 feet [9, p. 785], at which point they are above two-thirds of the atoms of the atmosphere. So most of the atmosphere is merely at the surface of the expanse. Therefore the expanse itself must be something much bigger — such as interstellar space.

Figure 2. The atmosphere is only the face of the expanse.

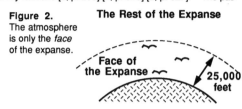

The Rest of the Expanse

Face of the Expanse

25,000 feet

Thus, the only verse allegedly justifying the identification of the atmosphere with the whole expanse really supports the idea of the expanse being interstellar space!

I also have a "prepositional" problem with the canopy model: If the expanse were really only the atmosphere, then a better preposition to use in verses 14, 15, and 17 would have been 'al, which as I mentioned means "on" or "above." Then the verses would tell us that sun, moon, and stars were "above the expanse of the heavens." But the verses don't use that preposition.

Some people say that God let the stars "appear" as if they were in the atmosphere, even though they were really above it. One problem with that view is that God did not use the word "appear" in connection with the expanse, even though in Genesis 1:9 He did use it in connection with the appearing of the dry land. However, the main problem is with the straightforwardness principle. If even you or I can think of simple ways to say the stars are above the expanse or only appeared to be in it, then why wouldn't God do so in the interest of accuracy? Perhaps He refrained from saying so because it would be inaccurate for Him to imply the expanse is merely the atmosphere.

Another biblical problem with the canopy model is Psalm 148:1-4, which mentions the "waters above":

> Praise the LORD!
> Praise the LORD from the heavens;
> Praise Him in the heights!
> Praise Him, all His angels;
>
> Praise Him, all His hosts!
> Praise Him, sun and moon;
> Praise Him, all stars of light!
> Praise Him, highest heavens,
> And the *waters that are above the heavens!*

First notice the context in which these waters appear: "heavens ... heights ... sun and moon ... stars ... highest heavens." This suggests that the waters belong 'way out there with all those other heavenly objects, not close to the earth. Next, notice the timing. The canopy model says the waters above the expanse of the heavens collapsed at the Genesis flood, but this Psalm, written after the flood, implies the waters above the heavens still exist in the present. In fact, verses 5 and 6 of the same Psalm say that the waters and the heavens are to last at least as long as the time of this physical universe endures:

> Let them praise the name of the LORD,
> For he commanded and they were created.
> He has also established them forever and ever;
> He has made a decree which will not pass away.

But if the waters are to endure "forever and ever" above the heavens, then they can't have collapsed.

A last biblical problem is with how the waters of the Genesis flood ceased:

> Also the fountains of the deep and the floodgates of the sky were closed, and the rain from the sky was restrained — *Genesis 8:2.*

Notice the account doesn't say the waters from above stopped themselves because there were none left to collapse. Instead it implies there were still some waters available, and that they had to be stopped by closing the floodgates of the sky (literally "the windows of the heavens"). In line with this, Malachi 3:10 implies that the "windows of the heavens," whatever they are, still exist. These verses do not fit very well with the concept of a collapsing vapor canopy. Thus the canopy model has considerable biblical problems. To me the most serious one is simply that the most straightforward interpretation excludes it.

5. A CANOPY IS NOT SCIENTIFICALLY NECESSARY
As a younger creationist, one of the great attractions of the canopy model for me was that its logical consequences would provide an explanation of several scientific problems for creationists. The most important of these consequences were: (1) a "greenhouse" effect to make the warm, uniform pre-flood climate indicated by the fossils; and (2) a shielding of cosmic rays to reduce carbon 14 in the pre-flood world, thus explaining "old" radiocarbon dates.

However, we now have very good scientific reasons [16] to think that the amount of carbon dioxide in the pre-flood atmosphere was many times greater than today. That would produce a strong greenhouse effect, a warm climate, and as a bonus, stimulate plant growth to produce the large amount of plant life we find in the fossils. The additional ordinary carbon in the biosphere would dilute carbon 14, so that the pre-flood $^{14}C/^{12}C$ ratio would be considerably lower due to that effect alone, thus explaining the "old" post-flood radiocarbon dates. In addition, we have evidence suggesting that the earth's magnetic field was at least ten times greater before the flood than now [6]. That would enable the geomagnetic field to be a very effective shield for cosmic rays, thus greatly reducing the production of carbon 14, making the pre-flood world a healthier place, and further explaining post-flood radiocarbon dates. Thus we have alternative scientific explanations for the main things the canopy model was supposed to explain.

For decades, creationist atmospheric scientists have put a lot of diligent work, some of it presented at these conferences, into scientifically modeling vapor canopies. I greatly respect their work, but it looks to me as if they still haven't got the problem solved. I also greatly respect the pioneers of modern scientific creationism, who in the first decades of their work developed the canopy model as part of the alternative worldview they were presenting.

However, the idea of a canopy atop the atmosphere did not come down from Sinai with Moses, engraved by the finger of God on the back side of the stone tablets. Instead, it was a human interpretation of scripture which was, for a time, the best understanding we could come up with. I think that time has passed. In spite of the large emotional investment some of us may have put into the canopy model, I suggest that now is a good time to re-evaluate the model, to see if it is worth any further effort. One thing to consider is whether other scriptures besides Genesis 1 can support the idea. If so, there need be no conflict between the cosmic-size expanse I am proposing and a vapor canopy over the pre-flood atmosphere. Lastly, if it is any comfort, my suggestion doesn't do away with a canopy of water; it simply raises it a bit higher — a cosmic canopy!

6. A BOUNDED UNIVERSE
The importance of the waters above the expanse is that they represent a boundary for the matter of the created universe. What is beyond that boundary? Take a look once more at the first two verses of Genesis:

> In the beginning God created the heavens and the earth. And the earth was formless and void, and darkness was over the surface of the deep; and the Spirit of God was moving over the surface of the waters.

The "deep" was the body of water within which God later, on day two, made the expanse, which He called "heavens" (Genesis 1:7,8). But notice that the deep has a *surface*. What is above that surface? I suggest that it is the "heavens" of Genesis 1:1. That is, on day one God made a space, called the heavens, which contained a large body of water, the deep. On day two he made the expanse, which He also called "heavens", within the waters. Thus there would be two heavens, the day-two heavens being a subset of the day-one heavens. This dual naming has a parallel in the case of the earth. Having created "the earth" as a formless body on day one (Genesis 1:1,2), God then on day three calls the dry land "earth" (Genesis 1:10). But the dry land (i.e., the continent or continents) is only a subset of the whole earth, which for example includes the seas also (Genesis 1:10). So there seem to be two meanings to the word "earth," one including the whole planet and the other limited to the dry land only. In the same way there would be two meanings to the word "heavens," the day-two heavens being the expanse, and the day-one heavens being the larger space in which the other created things exist.

Some theologians would object that Genesis 1:1 is a summary statement of all the work God would do later on in creation week, and so there would not be two heavens and two earths, but only one of each. Other theologians [11] argue strongly against that view, saying that the Hebrew phrasing favors consecutiveness from verse one to verse two. Another point is that if verse 1 is a summary of later work, then the account really begins with verse 2, leaving no statement at all about who created the matter of the earth and the deep. Thus we would no longer know for certain that God created the original matter; we would simply have an account of how He modified it. The theological consequences of that view would be major, and there would be severe inconsistences with the rest of scripture.

Thus the most straightforward view is that there are (at least) two spaces called "heavens." By this view, another scriptural name for the heavens of day one would be the "heavens of the heavens," שְׁמֵי הַשָּׁמַיִם (sh*mai ha-shamaim), which is often translated "highest heavens," as in Psalm 148:4, NAS. Although this created heavens is larger, it also is of limited extent, since Solomon said it was not big enough to contain God:

> But will God indeed dwell on earth? Behold, the heaven and heaven of heavens cannot contain thee; how much less this house that I have builded? — *1 Kings 8:27, KJV.*

This verse alone should be enough to convince most creationists that the created universe is of finite extent. A finite cosmos could still be closed and unbounded; see my other paper for the distinctions. Above I said "at least" two heavens because Paul mentions a third heavens in 2 Corinthians 12:2 :

> I know a man in Christ who fourteen years ago — whether in the body I do not know, or out of the body I do not know, God knows — such a man was caught up to the third heaven.

Let's count up heavens. Numbering outward from earth, there is the *first* heavens, interstellar space, also known as the expanse, created on day two. The earth's atmosphere, by my view, is simply the face of the expanse. Above the first heavens, out beyond the most distant galaxy, is a wall of ordinary water, of unknown thickness. Beyond the outside surface of the waters is a space which I here call the *second* heavens, also called the heavens of heavens, the heavens of day one. We know very little about the second heavens, except that it is a created thing and is of finite extent. This space could be closed and unbounded, but the matter within it is bounded. Somewhere beyond the second heavens is the *third* heavens, about which we know little. Maybe that is where God lives. Anyhow, the simple answer to the question of what is beyond the waters above is: the second heavens.

7. THE EXPANSE HAS EXPANDED

A large number of Bible verses refer to God "stretching out" or "spreading out" the heavens. Here are some:

> Who alone stretches out the heavens — *Job 9:8.*

> Stretching out heaven like a tent curtain — *Psalm 104:2.*

> Who stretches out the heavens like a curtain,
> And spreads them out like a tent to dwell in — *Isaiah 40:22.*

> He has stretched out the heavens — *Jeremiah 10:12.*

> The LORD who stretches out the heavens — *Zechariah 12:1.*

There are at least 12 other similar verses in the Old Testament. Here is a list:

2 Sam. 22:10	Job 26:7	Job 37:18	Psalm 18:9
Psalm 144:5	Isaiah 42:5	Isaiah 44:24	Isaiah 45:12
Isaiah 48:13	Isaiah 51:13	Jer. 51:15	Ezekiel 1:22

In these verses the Hebrew words translated "stretch out" come from the verb נטה (*natah*), whose primary meaning is "extend, stretch out ... spread out" [6, p. 235]. In three of the verses (2 Samuel 22:10, Psalm 18:9, and Psalm 144:5) the verb is translated by a secondary meaning, "to bow." The Hebrew words translated "spread out" come from the verbs מתח (*matach*) "spread out", טפח (*taphach*) "spread out, extend", or רקע (*raqa*) "stamp, spread out." The last verb (from Job 37:18) is related to the noun "expanse" (*raqia*) mentioned in sect. 3.

So these 17 verses use four different verbs to communicate the idea of stretching and spreading. The verses occur in a wide variety of contexts throughout the Old Testament, generally as an illustration of God's great power. The frequency, diversity, and widespread locations of these verses led me to suspect in 1985 that they were more than mere metaphor.

If there is a more literal meaning, what is it? To answer that, we must consider more precisely what the heavens are, since they are the object of the stretching. First of all, the heavens cannot be the stars, because God made the heavens on days one and two, before He made the stars on day four. Moreover, many verses, such as Nehemiah 9:6, make a distinction between the heavens and "host" of the heavens, namely the things occupying the heavens. So the word "heavens" must be roughly equivalent to our word "space."

Generally we think of space as a vacuum, an empty volume. But how can a nothingness be stretched out as if it were a *something*, like a tent curtain? To get a clue, notice how scripture speaks of other things happening to the heavens. The heavens can be *torn* (Isaiah 64:1), *worn out* like a garment (Psalm 102:25), *shaken* (Hebrews 12:26, Haggai 2:6, Isaiah 13:13), *burnt up* (2 Peter 3:12), *split apart* like a scroll when it is rolled up (Revelation 6:14), and *rolled up* like a mantle (Hebrews 1:12) or a scroll (Isaiah 34:4). It certainly sounds like space itself is a material of some sort!

Interestingly enough, there are many phenomena in modern physics which point to such a concept (such as Maxwell's displacement current and vacuum polarization), and physics even offers an explanation of why we cannot perceive this medium through which we would be moving (Dirac's electron "sea" and Pauli's exclusion principle). The physics clues suggest that such a medium would be like an elastic solid. This might explain why the words *raqia*, *stereoma*, and *firmamentum* (see section 3) all seem to have some connection with solidity and firmness:

When He made firm the skies above — *Proverbs 8:28.*

Can you, with Him, spread out the skies,
Strong as a molten [cast] mirror? — *Job 37:18.*

Notice also the references to "rolling up" the heavens like a mantle or a scroll (Hebrews 1:12 and Isaiah 34:4). This suggests that (1) there is some dimension in which space is thin, (2) space can be bent, and (3) there exists a direction it can be bent toward. Thus these verses could be hinting that a fourth spatial dimension exists, even though we can't perceive it. (Time would be a fifth dimension, dealt with separately.) Again, this idea is not foreign to modern physics. See my other paper for the ramifications in general relativity.

So if space is a material, some kind of "stuff" and not a nothingness, then it can be stretched out like a tent curtain, etc. This corresponds exactly to the picture behind the general relativistic expansion of the cosmos, where it is space itself which is being stretched out. Again, see my other paper for the physics of this phenomenon.

In summary, the verses of this section imply that God stretched out space itself at some time in the past. Now let's consider when He did this. Certainly the second day of creation is a good candidate for the starting point, because that is when He made the "expanse." But was the stretching complete at the end of the second day? There is a clue which suggests the answer is "no." The second day is the only day in which God did not comment "good" about the things he had made that day. Yet on the sixth day, God saw that *all* things He had made were very good (Genesis 1:31). The "all" would include the expanse. I suggest that He didn't call it good on the second day because the expansion wasn't complete by that time. This reasoning would correspondingly imply that the expansion stopped on or before the sixth day. (The Hebrew of 2 Samuel 22:10 and Psalm 18:9 refers to stretching the heavens (the translations usually use a secondary meaning, namely "bow"). If those passages refer to the Genesis flood, then it is possible that there was another episode of stretching during the flood. It is also possible than the expansion has been continuous from day two until now, although I consider that unlikely in the light of these verses and the above rationale.) Thus the heavens would have been complete by the time that Adam and Eve first saw them.

8. THE WATERS OF THE DEEP

And the earth was without form, and void; and darkness was on the face of the deep. And the Spirit of God was moving on the face of the waters — Genesis 1:2, KJV.

Ever since I first encountered this verse as a seven-year-old, I wondered what the "deep" in this verse was. The Hebrew word is תהום (*t*^{e}*hom*), which lexicons translate as "deep, sea, abyss ... primaeval ocean ... depth" [1, p. 1062], "primeval ocean, deep ... deeps of sea ... subterranean water" [6, p. 386]. The Septuagint translates it as the ἄβυσσος , the abyss, "the immeasurable depth" [13, p. 2]. In this section let's consider the composition of the deep.

The first clue is the last word of the verse, "waters." That word caused the seven-year-old me to think that the deep was ordinary liquid water. As grownups, however, we might wonder if the Hebrew word used here for "waters" (מים, *mayim*) could include more sophisticated useages, such as "snow," "ice," "steam," "fluid," or even "plasma."

According to three Hebrew lexicons [6, p. 193] [1, p. 565] [2, p. 694], most occurrences of this word in the Old Testament refer literally to liquid water. A few other occurrences are as part of metaphors, such as "the hearts of the people melted and became as water" (Joshua 7:5), but even in those cases the metaphors would be meaningless if the word *mayim* did not refer to ordinary water. In the few remaining cases, there are other substances in the water, such as salt or poison, but they are still essentially water. If frozen or gaseous forms of water are meant, the Bible always uses other words, as far as I have been able to find. As for the physics concept of "plasma," the words for "fire" or "flame" would be more accurate, since fire is the most common thing in everyday human experience which contains some hot plasma. In summary, *all* of the approximately 580 other uses of the word in the Old Testament refer to ordinary liquid water. Thus, according to the Timothy test, the most straightforward interpretation of Genesis 1:2 is that the deep, or at least its surface, initially consisted of ordinary water at normal densities and temperatures.

9. THE DEPTH OF THE DEEP

Then God said, "Let there be an expanse in the midst of the waters, and let it separate the waters from the waters." And God made the expanse, and separated the waters which were below the expanse from the waters which were above the expanse; and it was so — Genesis 1:6,7.

Now let's consider how big the deep was initially. Sections 3 and 4 show that the expanse is now of cosmic size, and Section 7 shows that it has expanded, so it must have started at a smaller size. In my other paper I surmise that God formed the stars from waters of the deep left behind by the expansion, so the mass of the visible universe would have been contained in the deep. A simple calculation in the other paper shows the mass is roughly 3×10^{51} kilograms. Lastly, I show evidence in the other paper that the universe is approximately spherical. So if the deep were similarly spherical (as it would be normally under the force of gravity), and if its waters were initially of ordinary density as Section 8 affirms, then a simple calculation shows that its radius had to be at least *one light-year*. I say "at least" because we also need to account for the waters above the expanse, which are of undetermined thickness.

This is surprisingly small compared to the cosmos. However, it is still huge, about 10 trillion kilometers, more than a thousand times larger than the radius of our solar system. And yet it took years for the Voyager spaceprobes, travelling at very high speeds, to reach the edge of the solar system. Imagine floating on the face of the deep and gazing down into its immense depths! "The deep" is certainly an appropriate name. Furthermore, a sphere of nothing but water is bottomless; if you plunged down to its center and kept going, you would start rising upward without ever having hit a solid bottom. So the Septuagint's word "the abyss" ("without bottom") is also a very appropriate name for the deep.

Notice that I said "how big the deep was *initially*." Strong gravitation was very likely in operation at the time of Genesis 1:2, in order to have a clearly-defined surface over a large body of liquid water in the presence of a vacuum (surface tension can't do it). The word "above" in Genesis 1:2 also hints at the existence of gravity by that time. If gravity was working normally, the gravitational force at the surface for the above mass and radius would be about 3×10^{17} (nearly a million trillion) times greater than at the earth's surface today. My other paper shows that if God let things proceed normally, these enormous gravitational forces would cause the deep to begin collapsing down toward the center.

Also, the huge gravitational forces would mean that the deep was far within a *black hole*. See my other paper for an outline of the physics of black holes. As I point out in that paper, one of the ramifications of being deep inside a black hole is that the collapse would take place very rapidly. As measured by either of the two types of clocks mentioned in my other paper, the collapse would take much less than a year, possibly a few days, to become an infinitely-small "singularity" at the center. However, the verses in the next section imply that God did not let the collapse proceed that far; you can't have a center in something infinitely small.

10. THE CENTER OF THE UNIVERSE

Since I've brought up the center of the deep several times, let's consider it more carefully. Notice the words "in the midst" in Genesis 1:6 :

> ... Let there be an expanse in the midst of the waters ...

The corresponding Hebrew word is בְתוֹךְ (*b^{e}tok*), which is the preposition בְ (*b^e*), "in," combined with the noun תוֹךְ (*tawek*) whose primary meaning is "midst, middle" [6, p. 387], "midst ... of a space or place," and with the preposition, "in the very heart and midst of" [1, p. 1063]. The middle of a sphere is its center, so the expanse must have started in the vicinity of the center. I say "in the vicinity" in order to leave some room for the approximate nature of the phrase.

Another clue is the word "below" in Genesis 1:7 :

> ... and separated the waters below the expanse from the waters which were above the expanse ...

The Hebrew translated word "below" is מתחת (*mittachath*), which consists of the preposition מִן (*min*), "from," combined with the adjective תחת (*tachath*), meaning "under, beneath" [6, p. 389]. This word, along with "above," confirms that gravity was operating. It also suggests that the center of gravity was within the waters below, providing supporting evidence for the idea that the waters below were at or near the center.

Now let's consider what the "waters below the expanse" of the heavens became:

> Then God said, "Let the waters below the heavens be gathered into one place, and let the dry land appear"; and it was so. And God called the dry land earth, and the gathering of the waters he called seas; and God saw that it was good — *Genesis 1:10.*

At this point, the waters below have become the continent(s) and seas of our own planet. Therefore during creation week, *the earth was at or near the center of the universe.* (I find nothing in the context to say that the earth was motionless with respect to the center, so it may have moved away from the center a bit since that time.)

11. TRANSFORMING THE WATERS

Section 8 has the original material of the creation being nothing but water. Yet Genesis 1:10 says that by day three dry land appeared, and dry land is obviously not water, but rather a collection of minerals containing silicon, iron, magnesium, calcium, carbon, oxygen, and many other elements. How did that happen? The apostle Peter gives us some additional insight on this point:

> ... by the word of God the heavens existed long ago and the earth was formed out of water and by water — *2 Peter 3:5.*

The word translated "formed" is the Greek participle συνεστῶσα (*sunestosa*), from the verb συνίστημι (*sunistemi*), whose primary meaning is "to place together, to set in the same place, to bring or band together" [13, p. 605]. (The KJV translation "standing" is a subsidiary meaning of the last part of the verb, ἵστημι (*histemi*); the translation does nothing with the prefix σύν (*syn*), which adds the important qualifier "together.") The American Standard 1901 translates it as "compacted." In the late 1970's this verse suggested to me that the original material God created, the deep, was pure water, which He then transformed into other materials. In my astrophysical paper I show how God could produce such transformations by simply letting the gravitational collapse take its normal course. The tremendous compression ("compaction") would raise the temperature, pressure, and density to enormous values. This would first rip the hydrogen and oxygen atoms apart into their constituent elementary particles. Then thermonuclear fusion reactions would occur, producing an intense light in the interior during the first day of creation, and generating many different atomic nuclei. The word *sunistemi* seems to me like an excellent choice of words to describe thermonuclear fusion, because it involves "putting together" or "banding together" the various elementary particles and nuclei (fusion) to make different atomic nuclei.

Here is another line of evidence for the possibility that God transformed water into the other elements of the cosmos: In the early 1980's I based a theory about the origin of planetary magnetic fields on the possibility that the earth and other bodies in the solar system were originally created as pure water. The theory has been remarkably successful, even to the point of correctly predicting the Voyager spaceprobe's measurements of the magnetic fields of the planets Uranus and Neptune [7]. The theory could not work with the present elements composing the solar system bodies, but only with water as the original material. Thus it seems that transformation — the modern word is "nucleosynthesis" — of water on day one is a distinct biblical and scientific possibility.

> In the beginning God created the heavens and the earth. And the earth was formless and void ...
> — *Genesis 1:1,2.*

If the "nucleosynthesis" scenario above is correct, then it means that at the instant of creation, the earth was merely a small region of water at the center of a much larger ball of water, the deep. That region had no distinguishing marks and was empty of any other kind of matter. This, I suggest, is the meaning of the much-discussed phrase "formless and void," or in Hebrew, ובהו תהו (*tohu wa-bohu*). In light of Sections 3 through 11, the heavens and earth God created in verse 1 consisted of: (1) a large, mostly empty space (the heavens of heavens), and (2) a ball of ordinary water more than two light-years in diameter. Item (2) contained within itself what would become (a) the waters above the expanse, (b) another heavens called the expanse and the stars within it, and (c) the earth. Thus the first verse would describe the creation of the raw materials of the whole universe, space and water.

12. EARTH STANDARD TIME
In the astrophysics paper I show that if the universe is bounded, then *gravitational time dilation* causes clocks (and all physical processes) to tick at different rates in different places. This means we must consider which set of clocks the Bible is referring to when it makes statements about time. For example, referring back to Section 2, the most straightforward understanding of Exodus 20:11 is that Jehovah made the universe in six ordinary days. But "six days" as measured by which clocks? To answer this, first notice that in Genesis 1:5 God Himself provided a definition of the word "day":

> And God called the light day, and the darkness He called night. And there was evening and there was morning, one day — *Genesis 1:5.*

It sounds like a "day" is a period of light and darkness marked off by the rotation of the earth, or in the case of day one, by the rotation of the deep. I will say more about this in the following section. Also notice God's purpose in making the heavenly bodies:

> Then God said, "Let there be lights in the expanse of the heavens to separate the day from the night, and let them be for signs, and for seasons, and for days and years; and let them be for lights in the expanse of the heavens to give light on the earth"; and it was so — *Genesis 1:14,15.*

His intention, among other things, was to give markers in the sky which would allow us to clearly measure periods of time in terms of the *earth's* rotation and the *earth's* movement around the sun, and thus he further defines "days" and "years." In other words, God quite reasonably tells us periods of time in terms of our own frame of reference, not in terms of some otherworldly frame of reference, as some authors would have it [12]. So Genesis 1, Exodus 20:11, and other passages are telling us that God made the universe in 6 days E.S.T. — Earth Standard Time.

13. DAY ONE
Now that I have laid a biblical foundation in this paper and developed a scientific blueprint in the other, let's try to re-construct the events of creation week. Many details of my reconstruction at this point are speculative and could be wrong, but it is important to spell out exactly how I am picturing these events. Keep in mind that though I write positively, this picture is always subject to revision. Also, please remember that I am not trying to deny the miraculous elements of creation; I am merely considering how God may have used some of the physical laws He Himself invented. The translations in italics from Genesis chapter 1 are my own.

In the beginning God created the heavens ... These include both the heavens of heavens (the second heavens), and also the expanse (the first heavens), as yet not defined within the deep. ... *and the earth. And the earth was without form and void* ... The earth, as I said, is a formless, undefined region within the deep, empty of inhabitant or feature.

... and darkness was on the face of the deep, and the Spirit of God was moving on the face of the waters. At the instant of creation, the deep is a sphere of liquid water more than two light-years in diameter. Electromagnetic and nuclear forces (and thus relativistic effects) are fully operational, allowing fully functioning water molecules with their constituent atoms, electrons and nuclei. The deep is rotating with respect to the Spirit of God, and probably with respect to the space within which it exists, the second heavens. There is no visible light at the surface of the deep.

The deep contains all the mass of the visible universe. Gravity is also functioning, and its great strength allows a clearly-defined interface to exist between the waters and the vacuum of the second heavens. The deep is within a black hole, whose outer boundary, called the "event horizon," is 450 million light-years further out, according to an equation in the other paper. As the other paper shows, strange and significant things happen to time near the event horizon. The intense gravity makes the deep collapse toward the center very rapidly. The rate of collapse is not limited by the speed of light (see other paper). As the deep is compressed, it becomes very hot and dense. Descending into the deep, we find that molecules, atoms, nuclei, and even elementary particles are being ripped apart.

And God said, "Let there be light," and there was light. At a certain range of depths, thermonuclear fusion reactions begin, forming heavier nuclei from lighter ones (nucleosynthesis) and liberating huge amounts of energy. An intense light illuminates the interior. As the compression continues, the fusion reactions reach a shallow enough depth to allow light to reach the surface, thus ending the darkness there. The strong gravity causes light leaving the surface to return to it, so light at the surface would be coming from all sides. The deep would have no dark side.

And God saw that the light was good, and God separated the light from the darkness. (This paragraph is the most tentative part of my reconstruction of events.) As the collapse continues, gravity becomes so strong that light can no longer reach the surface, re-darkening it. Psalm 104:2, "Covering Thyself with light as a cloak," appears to refer to day one. That suggests to me that at this point the Spirit of God, "moving [or 'hovering'] over the surface of the waters" (Genesis 1:2), becomes a light source for the surface, in the same way as He will again become a light source at a future time (Revelation 19:23, 20:5). This would give the deep a bright side and a dark side, thus dividing light from darkness and inscribing "a circle on the face of the waters, at the boundary of light and darkness" (Job 26:10, c.f. Proverbs 8:27).

And there was evening and there was morning, one day. Conservation of angular momentum causes the deep to speed up its rotation as the collapse proceeds, like a twirling ice skater speeding up as she brings in her arms. We can imagine a reference point on the surface rotating around to the dark side and continuing further around to the bright side again, marking off evening and morning. Rough calculations (see other paper) show that all of the events from the beginning instant to this point had to take place in a very short time, much less than a year. To calculate the time exactly would go beyond the frontiers of modern relativity, but I suspect that a modern clock (if it could survive) on the surface of the deep would register about 24 hours from the instant of creation to the end of day one.

14. DAYS TWO AND THREE

And God said, "Let there be an expanse in the midst of the waters, and let it separate the waters from the waters." And God made the expanse, and separated the waters which were above the expanse from the waters which were below the expanse. Possibly by direct intervention God increases the cosmological "constant" Λ (the tension of space, see other paper) to a large positive value, changing the black hole to a white hole (a black hole running in reverse, see other paper) and begins rapidly stretching out space. As I showed in the other paper, the expansion is not limited by the speed of light, even in conventional theory. God marks off a large volume, the "expanse," within the deep wherein material would be allowed to pull apart into fragments and clusters as it expanded, but He requires the "waters below" and the "waters above" to stay coherently together:

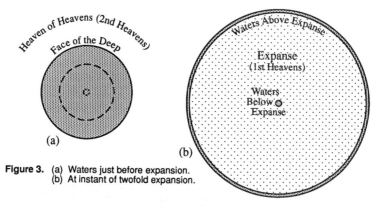

Figure 3. (a) Waters just before expansion.
(b) At instant of twofold expansion.

Normal physical processes cause cooling to proceed as rapidly as the expansion. The stretching of space causes thermal ("heat wave") electromagnetic radiation in the expanse to drop from its initial very high temperature to much lower values in direct proportion to the increase in size of the expanse. These red-shifted heat waves eventually become the cosmic microwave background radiation (see other paper). Matter beneath the expanse expands until the surface reaches ordinary temperatures, becoming liquid water underneath an atmosphere. God collects various heavier atoms beneath the surface and constructs minerals of them, laying "the foundations of the earth" (Job 38:4), i.e., its core and mantle. Gravity at the surface drops to normal values. Matter in the expanse is drawn apart into clusters of hydrogen, helium, and other atoms formed by the nucleosynthesis of the first day. The waters above the expanse stay together, becoming thinner as their surface area increases to keep the volume roughly constant. Figure 3(b) illustrates this phase of the expansion.

And God called the expanse "heavens." And there was evening and there was morning, a second day. These heavens are interstellar space, the first heavens as we count outward. The expansion continues at least until the end of the fourth day. Since God has not yet created the sun by this point, the Spirit of God continues to be the light source for the waters below the expanse.

And God said, "Let the waters under the heavens be gathered into one place, and let the dry land appear," and it was so. Rapid radioactive decay and rapid volume cooling occur as secondary effects of the rapid stretching of space (see other paper). God uses the radioactivity to heat the continental cratons and to provide power for other geologic work. Thermal expansion makes the cratons buoyant relative to the rocks below them and lifts them above the remaining waters, thus gathering the waters into ocean basins. Volume cooling (a result of the expansion, see other paper) solidifies batholiths and much of the athenosphere.

At some time during the expansion, probably on the third day, the waters above the heavens reach the event horizon and pass beyond it. The event horizon begins rapidly shrinking toward the earth (see other paper). At the same time, gravity draws together the atoms of hydrogen, helium, and other elements in each cluster left behind by the expansion. As my other paper shows, there has been plenty of time — billions of years — for that process to occur farther out, even though only days have elapsed on earth.

15. THE DAY THE UNIVERSE OPENED (DAY FOUR)
And God said, "Let there be lights in the expanse of the heavens ... to give light on the earth," and it was so. The event horizon reaches earth early in the morning of the fourth day. During that ordinary day as measured on earth, billions of years worth of physical processes take place in the distant cosmos.

And God made the two great lights ... the stars also. And God gave them in the expanse of the heavens to give light on the earth ... Early in the fourth morning, God finishes coalescing the clusters of material left behind in the expansion, and thermonuclear fusion begins in the newly-formed stars. During the fourth day the distant stars age billions of years, while their light also has billions of years to travel here. While the light from the more distant galaxies is traveling to earth, space continues to expand, stretching the wavelengths of the light and thus shifting them to the red side of the spectrum (see other paper).

And God saw all that He had made, and behold, it was very good. And there was evening and there was morning, the sixth day. God stops the expansion, reducing the cosmological constant Λ to a small positive value or zero, before the evening of the sixth day. Thus Adam and Eve, gazing up for the first time into the new night sky, can now see the Milky Way, the Andromeda galaxy, and all the other splendors in the heavens that declare the glory of God.

16. CONCLUSION
This Bible study has led us to several ideas of profound importance to cosmology:

    1. Matter in the universe is bounded.
    2. The universe has expanded.

My astrophysical paper shows that, according to the best physics and cosmological knowledge we have today, these ideas lead directly to the conclusion that our cosmos expanded out of a white hole (a black hole running in reverse). As a consequence, gravitational time dilation caused clocks (and all physical processes) both inside and outside the event horizon (the border of the white hole) to tick at vastly different rates from one another in different places. Our Bible study has brought us to several conclusions related to this matter of time:

    3. The earth is near the center of the universe.
    4. The universe is young as measured by clocks on earth.

My other paper shows that, given item 3, known physical processes explain item 4, in particular getting light from distant galaxies to us in a short time. Furthermore, the expansion would cause the proper amounts of red shift in light from those galaxies. This Bible study also leads to several other conclusions related to how God formed matter:

    5. The original matter God created was ordinary liquid water.
    6. God transformed the water into various elements by compaction.

I have suggested, but not proven, here that God did this by the simple means of creating the original waters within a black hole, allowing the resulting rapid gravitational collapse to heat the waters to the point where nucleosynthesis would occur, and finally on the second day converting the black hole to a white hole by beginning the rapid expansion of space. The high temperatures, followed by the expansion, would produce the cosmic microwave background radiation.

I have listed the above conclusions in decreasing order of their cosmological importance and biblical support. These items of vital information from the Bible, as I remarked at the beginning of this paper, lay a good foundation for a young-earth creationist cosmology. The apostle Paul has expressed my feelings about the marvelous subtlety God has shown in making all these things work together in His construction of the universe:

> O the depth of the riches both of the wisdom and knowledge of God! How unsearchable are his judgements, and his ways past finding out! — Romans 11:33 KJV.

ACKNOWLEDGEMENTS
My hearty thanks to all who have prayed for this project, to the creationist groups and individuals who gave me good biblical feedback and encouragement, to David Rodabaugh, who pointed out several supporting scriptures to me, and to my wife and children for putting up with me all these years of abstraction.

BIBLIOGRAPHY
[1]   F. Brown, The New Brown-Driver-Briggs-Gesenius Hebrew and English Lexicon, 1979, Hendrickson Publishers, Peabody, Massachusetts.

[2]   B. Davidson, The Analytical Hebrew and Chaldee Lexicon, 1970, Zondervan Publishing House, Grand Rapids. Second edition originally published in 1850 by Samuel Bagster & Sons, Ltd., London

[3]   J. C. Dillow, The Waters Above: Earth's Pre-Flood Vapor Canopy, 1981, Moody Press, Chicago.

[4]   J. Green, editor, The interlinear Hebrew/Greek English Bible, Volume I: **Genesis to Ruth**, 1979, Associated Publishers and Authors, Lafayette, Indiana.

[5]   S. W. Hawking and G. F. R. Ellis, The Large Scale Structure of Space-Time, 1973, Cambridge University Press, Cambridge.

[6]   W. L. Holladay, editor, A Concise Hebrew and Aramaic Lexicon of the Old Testament, 1971, Eerdmans Publishing Company, Grand Rapids. Based on the First, Second, and Third editions of the Koehler-Baumgartner Lexicon in Veteris Testamenti Libros.

[7   D. R Humphreys, **Good news from Neptune: the Voyager 2 magnetic measurements**, Creation Research Society Quarterly, **27:1** 1990, 15-17. Predictions of the Voyager 2 results are in **The creation of planetary magnetic fields**, Creation Research Society Quarterly, **21:4** 1984, 140-149.

[8]   D. R. Humphreys, **Progress toward a young-earth relativistic cosmology**, Proceedings of the Third International Conference on Creationism, 1994, Creation Science Fellowship, Inc., Pittsburgh.

[9]   K. D. Morrison, **Birds**, Encyclopedia Americana **3** (1969) 781-797.

[10]   W. Rindler, Essential Relativity, 1977, Revised Second Edition, Springer-Verlag, New York.

[11]   C. C. Ryrie, The Ryrie Study Bible, 1978, Moody Press, Chicago.

[12]   G. Schroeder, **The universe — 6 days and 13 billion years old**, Jerusalem Post, September 7, 1991. Schroeder has God's clocks ticking off only 6 days of time at the edge of the universe, while earth is 13 billion years old — the reverse of what the equations in my astrophysical paper say!

[13]   J. H. Thayer, Thayer's Greek-English Lexicon of the New Testament, 1889, Associated Publishers and Authors, Grand Rapids.

[14]   R. E. Walsh, **Biblical hermeneutics and creation**, in Proceedings of the International Conference on Creationism, 1987, R.E. Walsh, et al, Editors, Creation Science Fellowship, Pittsburgh, Vol. 1, pp.121-27.

[15]   J. C. Whitcomb, Jr., and H. M. Morris, The Genesis Flood, 1961, Baker Book House, Grand Rapids.

[16]   C. J. Yapp and H. Poths, **Ancient atmospheric CO_2 pressures inferred from natural goethites**, Nature **355** (23 January 1992) 342-344. The authors' result is that the partial pressure of CO_2 when the Ordovician strata were being laid down was at least 16 times greater than today.

* Dr. Humphreys is a physicist at Sandia National Laboratories, Dept. 1271, M. S. 1187, Albuquerque, NM 87185-1187. The Laboratories have not supported this work. He is also an Adjunct Professor of Geophysics and Astrophysics at the Institute for Creation Research, 10946 Woodside Ave. N., Santee, CA 92071.

PROGRESS TOWARD
A YOUNG-EARTH RELATIVISTIC COSMOLOGY

D. RUSSELL HUMPHREYS, Ph.D.*
Creation Science Fellowship of New Mexico,
P.O. Box 10550, Albuquerque, NM 87184

ABSTRACT
Another paper of mine at this conference shows evidence that the biblical cosmos has finite boundaries, and that our earth is near the center. If we put those boundary conditions into the equations of Einstein's general theory of relativity, we get an expanding cosmos in which clocks (and all physical processes) tick at different rates in different parts of the universe. The physics is that of a universe-sized "white hole" (a black hole running in reverse), with a shrinking event horizon and matter expanding out of it. At the event horizon, clocks would be momentarily stopped relative to clocks further out. At one critical moment of the expansion, the event horizon would reach the earth, and clocks there would also momentarily stop.

I propose that the critical moment arrived on earth during the fourth day of creation. During that day, billions of years would elapse in the distant sky, allowing light from galaxies to reach the earth within one ordinary day of earth's time. This theory also explains the red shifts of galaxies and the cosmic microwave background. As measured by clocks on earth, the age of the universe today could be as small as the face-value biblical age of about 6000 years.

KEYWORDS
Cosmology, general relativity, age of universe, galactic red shifts, cosmic microwave background, black holes.

1. INTRODUCTION

> *O God! I could be bounded in a nutshell, and count myself a king of infinite space, were it not that I have bad dreams* — Hamlet, Act II.

God used relativity to make a young universe! That idea, the main thesis of this paper, may seem startling to many people, some of whom may regard relativity as an invention of the devil. But I am proposing here that God invented relativity as an essential part of His universe, and that one feature of relativity in particular, called *gravitational time dilation* by some authors, enabled light from distant galaxies to get to earth in a very short time — within one ordinary day, as measured by clocks here on earth.

People having philosophical problems with relativity may be interested to know that it is possible to separate the mathematics of the theory itself from the philosophical "baggage" so often attached to it, and that a simple conceptual model can do away with the paradoxes people often object to. For example, few people know that Einstein himself came back to the idea of a luminiferous ether in 1920 [15, pp. 13, 23]. The speed of light would be constant with respect to such an ether, and then the equations of relativity would require that clocks and measuring rods moving with respect to the ether change in such a way as to always give the same number for the speed of light. I.e., objects moving through the ether would be changed by that motion. Clocks would actually slow down, measuring rods would actually shorten, and the speed of light would seem to be independent of motion [39, p.7]. By re-affirming an absolute reference frame, this view of relativity dumps the philosophical baggage and resolves the paradoxes. Section 15 briefly discusses why we might expect relativity to be in operation very early during creation week.

I hope this paper will help convince some of the doubters that relativity is not an enemy of creationism, but is instead a friend. Young-earth creationism needs friends in the area of cosmology, because up to this time, in my opinion, we have had no scientifically satisfactory explanation of the large-scale phenomena we observe in the heavens. The most important of those phenomena are:

1. **Light from distant galaxies** — We see light from galaxies which are billions of light-years away, as measured by a variety of techniques. Light travelling such great distances at today's speed would take billions of years to reach us.

2. **Galactic red shifts** — The wavelengths of light from each galaxy are shifted toward the red side of the spectrum by a factor roughly proportional to the distance of the galaxy from us. There are some exceptions, but the overall trend is very clear and must be explained.

3. **Cosmic microwave background** — The earth is immersed in a bath of low-power microwave (centimeter to millimeter wavelength) electromagnetic radiation whose spectrum is exactly like that of the thermal radiation (heat waves, black-body radiation) found within a cavity whose walls are very cold, at 2.74 Kelvin. After correction for the earth's motion through space, this radiation is very uniform, having variations with direction no greater than one part in 100,000.

All of these phenomena fit reasonably well into the "big-bang" cosmologies, and as such seem to point to a long time scale, billions of years, for the cosmos. Yet creationist scientists have found a great deal of evidence pointing to a very short time scale, much less than millions of years, for the earth and solar system. Good science requires that we try to reconcile both the young-earth data and the cosmological data, thus motivating a creationist cosmology to explain the above phenomena.

In the past, creationists have proposed several such explanations. The most prominent of these are: (*i*) the mature creation theory (light created in transit) [51, p. 369] [49, pp. 222-223] [11, pp. 88-89], (*ii*) the Moon-Spencer theory (shortcut for light) [33] [2] [7], (*iii*) the Setterfield *c*-decay theory (decrease in speed of light) [35] [16] [8], and (*iv*) the Ackridge-Barnes-Slusher theory (heating of galactic gas and dust) [2]. All of these theories seem inadequate to me. First, their proponents cite no decisive biblical support. By "decisive" I mean direct statements in the Bible which would clearly favor one theory over another; for example, statements that God created the light in transit, or made it take a shortcut, or speeded it up.

Second, none of these theories explain all three of the large-scale astronomical phenomena listed above. Theories (*i*) through (*iii*) seek mainly to explain light transit time. Theory (*iv*) seeks only to explain the cosmic microwave background. Third, each has severe scientific deficiencies. Theory (*i*) makes no scientific predictions and therefore cannot be checked. Theories (*ii*) through (*iv*) appear to many creationist scientists to have been falsified by the data, although a few remaining advocates of each theory might still disagree. Thus it appears that creationists have not yet produced a satisfactory cosmology.

To meet that need, this paper delves deeply into Einstein's general theory of relativity, going well beyond the special theory of relativity which marks the limit of most physicists' training. It will involve the strange physics of black holes, and it will be rather mathematical. The subject itself requires these things, but I will try to simplify matters as much as possible. For non-physicists I will explain the essential equations in words. For physicists without training in general relativity, I will include concepts that I found helpful as I learned the topic, but such comments may not be very helpful to the non-physicist. I ask you to please bear with me in all these esoterica, because the reward will be great — a non *ad hoc* cosmology which explains the large-scale astronomical phenomena and yet is fully consistent with a young earth.

2. BIG-BANG THEORIES ASSUME AN UNBOUNDED COSMOS

In their book *The Large Scale Structure of Space-Time*, Stephen Hawking and George Ellis [24; p.134] spell out the most fundamental assumption of the modern big-bang cosmologies:

> However we are not able to make cosmological models without some admixture of ideology. In the earliest cosmologies, man placed himself in a commanding position at the centre of the universe. Since the time of Copernicus we have been steadily demoted to a medium sized planet going round a medium sized star on the outer edge of a fairly average galaxy, which is itself simply one of a local group of galaxies. Indeed we are now so democratic that we would not claim our position in space is specially distinguished in any way. We shall, following Bondi [4], call this assumption the *Copernican principle*.

> A reasonable interpretation of this somewhat vague principle is to understand it as implying that, when viewed on a suitable scale, the universe is approximately spatially homogeneous.

By "homogeneous," Hawking and Ellis mean that all parts of the universe at any given time are essentially the same. In particular, they mean that all sections of the 3-dimensional space we live in have about the same average matter density ρ, provided that the sections are big enough to allow a good average. This same assumption is fundamental to a larger class of theories called Friedmann, or Robertson-Walker, cosmologies. These include not only the big-bang theories, but also older theories such as Einstein's static cosmos and DeSitter's empty expanding cosmos. Even Fred Hoyle's steady-state cosmology makes the same assumption — homogeneity throughout space. An older name for this "Copernican principle" is the "Cosmological principle."

Notice that Hawking and Ellis call the Copernican principle an "admixture of ideology." By this they mean that it does not come from direct observation but instead from a body of ideas that some people feel to be true. In a recent article in *Nature* [20], astrophysicist Richard Gott spells out the essential reasoning behind the principle:

> In astronomy, the Copernican principle works because, of all the places for intelligent observers to be, there are by definition only a few special places and many nonspecial places, so you are likely to be in a nonspecial place.

To clarify this reasoning further, the idea behind the Copernican principle is that we are on this planet as the result of random processes only — not because of the choice of a purposeful God — and thus it would be unlikely we are in a special place. Of course, this idea of randomness is the essence of Darwinism. Richard Gott noted this connection with evolutionary ideas to build his case that we are not in a privileged location:

> Darwin showed that, in terms of origin, we are not privileged above other species.

So the essential idea behind the Copernican principle is that of a universe ruled by randomness. Since many scientists see a great deal of purpose in nature, there is good reason to question the validity of that principle.

Supporters of the Copernican principle do not rest completely on ideology. They do point out that on a large scale, the universe appears *isotropic* from our point of view. That is, it looks pretty much the same in every direction, especially when we look at the cosmic microwave background. This observed isotropy could indeed result from homogeneity, and thus it is consistent with the Copernican principle. However, logic does not require the reverse line of reasoning — homogeneity as a result of isotropy. In this paper I will show by example that one can conceive of a universe which is isotropic from our viewpoint but not homogeneous.

I have spent some time on the Copernican principle because it has a profound effect on cosmological theory. Richard Gott underlines its importance:

> The idea that we are not located in a special spatial location has been crucial in cosmology, leading directly to the homogeneous and isotropic Friedmann cosmological models ...

You may be wondering at this point what it is about the Copernican principle, or spatial homogeneity, that makes it "crucial." To help you understand, let me spell out clearly an implication of homogeneity which often goes unstated: Homogeneity would mean that our 3-dimensional universe would have *no edges and no center!* If there were an edge or center, observers near those places would be special; they would see and measure different things than other observers, thus violating the Copernican principle.

Suppose you were able to travel instantly to any place in our 3-dimensional space. The Copernican principle says that no matter how far you might travel, you could never find a point where the average mass density ρ is much different than here. You would never encounter an end to the conventional universe of stars and galaxies. There would be no edges or boundaries. In more technical terms, matter in that sort of cosmos is required to be *unbounded*. Mathematicians call this kind of requirement a "boundary condition." Section 4 shows how this boundary condition, when applied to the equations of general relativity, results in the big-bang cosmologies. Section 3 below is an introduction for physicists to the essentials of general relativity. People less mathematically inclined can skip sections 3 and 4 without great loss of understanding.

3. BASICS OF GENERAL RELATIVITY

In 1916, eleven years after his first paper on special relativity, Albert Einstein presented his completed general theory of relativity [13]. In it he pictured space and time as being like a material which is stretched and bent by the presence of mass. Some authors resist this "geometrical" and material interpretation of space [48, p. 147] [50, p. 34], but I prefer it for two reasons: (1) it provides a heuristic picture for an otherwise very difficult subject, and (2) there are some biblical hints favoring it (see my exegetical paper at this conference). Einstein described the stretching and bending by specifying the *interval* between two events occurring at slightly different points in space and time. The interval ds is defined such that if it is a real number, it is proportional to the "natural time" or *proper time* interval $d\tau$ registered by a physical clock as it travels on a trajectory between the two events:

$$ds \equiv c \, d\tau \tag{1}$$

In the system of units I am using, the proportionality factor is the speed of light, c. (If ds is an imaginary number, i.e., if $ds^2 < 0$, then the interval is equal to i times the distance between the two events in a reference frame where they are simultaneous. Some authors define the interval with an opposite sign convention.) Einstein specified the square of the interval by means of an equation called the *metric* :

$$ds^2 = g_{\mu\nu} \, dx^\mu \, dx^\nu, \quad \mu,\nu = 0, 1, 2, 3 \tag{2}$$

The indices μ and ν run from 0 through 3, representing time and the three space dimensions respectively. The four quantities dx^μ represent the distances in time and space between the two events. For example, calling time τ and using polar coordinates (r, θ, ϕ) we might have $(dx^0, dx^1, dx^2, dx^3) = (d\tau, dr, d\theta, d\phi)$. The quantity $g_{\mu\nu}$ represents the $\mu\nu$th component of the *metric tensor*. In four dimensions, a ("second-rank") tensor is a set of 16 numbers which transform in certain ways when you change coordinate systems. Subscripted indices represent "covariant" tensors, which transform like the derivatives of a scalar function. Superscripted indices represent "contravariant" tensors, which transform like vectors. This equation has both types of tensor, with the metric tensor being in its covariant form and the distances being in their contravariant form. In his paper Einstein introduced his *summation convention*: if you see the same index repeated as both a superscript and subscript, then sum over that index. For example, this means that the right side of eq. (2) represents the sum of 16 different terms. The metric tensor $g_{\mu\nu}$ is fundamentally important in general relativity.

The major contribution in Einstein's 1916 and 1917 [12] papers was his set of 16 gravitational field equations

$$R^{\mu\nu} = \Lambda g^{\mu\nu} - \frac{8\pi G}{c^4}\left(T^{\mu\nu} - \tfrac{1}{2} g^{\mu\nu} T\right) \tag{3}$$

which govern the curvature (see section 5) of spacetime [39, p. 180]. Put very simply, these equations say that the amount of matter at a given point in spacetime determines the curvature of spacetime at that point. There is a deep similarity to the equations governing a stretched membrane with weights on it, except that here the membrane has four dimensions instead of two. The quantity $R^{\mu\nu}$ on the left side of (3) represents the $\mu\nu$th component of the *Ricci* tensor, which contains various second-order time and space derivatives of the metric tensor. The Ricci tensor is related to the curvature of spacetime [19, p. 39]. In some simple situations it reduces to the D'Alembertian operator

$$\Box \equiv \nabla^2 - \frac{1}{c^2}\frac{\partial^2}{\partial\tau^2} \equiv \frac{\partial^2}{\partial x^2} + \frac{\partial^2}{\partial y^2} + \frac{\partial^2}{\partial z^2} - \frac{1}{c^2}\frac{\partial^2}{\partial\tau^2}$$

applied to the components of the metric tensor [39, pp. 181,190]. In simple static situations, it reduces further to the Laplacian operator ∇^2 applied to the metric components.

On the right side of eq. (3), Λ is the famous "cosmological constant," which can be interpreted as being proportional to an external pressure or tension applied to the membrane of spacetime. (It does not really have to be a constant, but can depend on position or time; nevertheless, most studies keep it a constant, usually zero.) G is the Newtonian gravitational constant.

The second tensor $T^{\mu\nu}$ on the right side of eq. (3) is the *energy-momentum* tensor. It is a "source term" specifying how much mass-energy and momentum (due to non-gravitational fields) are present, causing distortions in spacetime. The third term of eq. (3) contains a scalar function T, which is simply the sum $g_{\mu\nu} T^{\mu\nu}$. The third term represents an additional mass-energy present because of the interaction of the gravitational field with the non-gravitational mass, and it, too, distorts spacetime.

4. FROM GENERAL RELATIVITY TO BIG-BANG COSMOLOGY

The usual approach in cosmology is to figure out first what form the energy-momentum tensor $T^{\mu\nu}$ should have throughout space, and then to find out what form the metric tensor $g_{\mu\nu}$ in eq. (2) must have in order to satisfy the resulting Einstein equations (3). Often cosmologists make two (reasonable) simplifying approximations: (*i*) treat the galaxies as non-interacting "dust," i.e., as if they are too far apart to interact significantly, and (*ii*) assume the galaxies are at rest with respect to space locally; i.e., their only motions are due to the expansion of space. With those approximations the only non-zero component of the energy-momentum tensor is the mass density ρ [39, p. 226]:

$$T^{00} = \rho \tag{4}$$

Here's where the Copernican principle enters the equations. The principle requires that the mass density ρ in eq. (4) be independent of the space coordinates, *throughout all available space*. Using that boundary condition, many textbooks show that the following metric [48, p. 412], usually called the *Robertson-Walker* metric, is a solution of eq. (3):

$$ds^2 = c^2 d\tau^2 - a^2\left(\frac{d\eta^2}{1 - k\,\eta^2} + \eta^2\, d\Omega^2\right) \tag{5}$$

Here η is a dimensionless radial coordinate. It is a *co-moving* coordinate, meaning the coordinate system moves with the expansion of space, as if it were a grid somehow painted onto space itself. That means for any given galaxy, η will remain the same throughout the expansion. Please note: in the Robertson-Walker metric, the origin of coordinates is completely arbitrary. It can be anywhere in our 3-dimensional space. Thus this metric is fully consistent with the Copernican principle.

The "cosmic" time τ in the Robertson-Walker metric is same as the proper time or "natural" time in eq. (1). It is the time measured by a set of clocks throughout the universe, each one riding with a galaxy as it moves with the expansion of space. These clocks can all be synchronized with one another. Later on I will introduce a distinctly different time, t, often called *Schwarzschild time*, or "coordinate" time. The difference between these two types of time measurements constitutes the essence of this paper, so stay alert for the distinctions.

The symbol a in eq. (5) is the *radius of curvature* of space and has units of distance; it depends on the cosmic time τ. (Some authors define a to be dimensionless and call it the "scale factor"; η would then have units of distance.) The radius of curvature relates the co-moving coordinate η with a radial coordinate r which is not co-moving:

$$r = a(\tau)\,\eta \tag{6}$$

The coordinate r has units of distance and is defined such that the circumference of a circle of radius r is $2\pi r$. For a particular galaxy, r increases as the radius of curvature increases, whereas η remains the same.

The symbol c in eq. (5) represents the speed of light, which is constant in the (τ, r) system for $k = 0$ or near the origin. In other coordinate systems — such as the Schwarzschild system I will introduce later — the speed of light can be c times a function of space and time and therefore not constant. In such systems c by itself does not represent the speed of light but is merely a convenient multiplying constant. (Very often general relativists use physical units such that $c = 1$.) The symbol $d\Omega$ in eq. (5) is the angle subtended, in spherical coordinates, by the two spacetime events defining the interval, so that we have:

$$d\Omega^2 \equiv d\theta^2 + \sin^2\theta \ d\phi^2$$

The constant k in the Robertson-Walker metric is very important. It can have the values 1, 0, or –1, depending on whether the space being described has, respectively, a positive, zero, or negative curvature. When $k = 1$, η has values between 0 and 1. I will try to clarify this concept of curvature in the next section.

5. CURVED SPACE AND *FIVE* DIMENSIONS

The above equations and ideas use four dimensions, one of time and three of space. They are rather mystifying to the newcomer, especially the idea that space might be curved. He asks a very natural question: "What direction could space be curved *toward*?" One of the trade secrets of general relativity is that we can answer this question if we grant admission to the idea of at least one more dimension. In particular, eq. (5) for the case of positive curvature ($k = 1$) has a rather neat geometrical interpretation: our 3-dimensional space would be merely the surface of a "hypersphere" existing in a "hyperspace" having ordinary geometric laws — except that it would have four space dimensions instead of three! Light and all physically observable matter would be confined to moving in the surface. Time would be an extra dimension, a fifth dimension, dealt with separately. To be explicit, the surface of this hypersphere would have Cartesian coordinates (w, x, y, z) such that:

$$w^2 + x^2 + y^2 + z^2 = a^2 \tag{7}$$

where a is the radius of curvature in eq. (5). Except for the extra dimension w, this is identical to the equation for a 3-dimensional sphere of radius a. Modern relativists say that the hypersphere is a "3-sphere [since its surface is 3-dimensional] embedded [existing] in a Euclidian [ordinary geometry] space of 4 [space] dimensions" [31, p. 704]. Since the radius a increases with time, we can think of the hypersphere as a four-dimensional rubber balloon being inflated. Galaxies would be like pennies pasted on the surface of the balloon; they would all be spreading apart as we inflate the balloon. Many textbooks use this example, but most of them neglect to tell the reader that the balloon has four space dimensions.

Figure 1 shows how equations (5) and (6) with $k = 1$ relate to this concept. As I mentioned before, the location of the origin (through which we put the w axis) on the surface of the hypersphere is completely arbitrary. The angle θ represents the amount of rotation around the w axis; the angle ϕ is suppressed. The figure shows three ways to specify the radial distance of a galaxy from the origin: the angle χ or the radial coordinate η (both of which are co-moving), or the radial coordinate r (which is not co-moving).

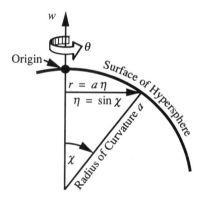

Figure 1. Positive-curvature cosmos

This hyperspherical cosmos may seem like science fiction, but it was Einstein who introduced the concept into cosmology in 1917 [12, p. 185, eq. (10)], using eq. (7) with different notation. However, he quickly performed some mathematical sleight-of-hand and swept the extra space dimension w under the rug, so that it was no longer explicit in the equations. Since then, most relativists try to regard it as a convenient mathematical fiction [29, p. 360]. Some, like John A. Wheeler [31, p. 704], even seem rather antagonistic to the possibility of the extra dimension being real:

Excursion off the sphere is physically meaningless and is forbidden. The superfluous dimension is added to help the reason in reasoning, not to help the traveler in traveling.

Possibly some of this antagonism stems from a distaste for certain 19th-century ideas, either those of the spiritualists, who seized upon hyperspace as a place for ghosts to inhabit, or those of some Christians, who imagined hyperspace as the dwelling place of God. Most likely, it stems from a desire to have the 3-dimensional universe of matter and energy be all of what exists, not merely a part of a much larger reality. Carl Sagan [42, p. 4] expressed this desire as though it were either a definition or a fact:

The cosmos is all that is or ever was or ever will be.

271

Creationists, on the other hand, need not be adverse to the possibility of a reality larger than the visible universe, particularly since there are Biblical hints of an extra dimension (see my Biblical paper). One of the difficulties, of course, is being able to visualize or imagine an extra dimension. One help in that regard is Rudy Rucker's mind-stretching little book, *The Fourth Dimension* [41]. Rucker's amusing illustrations and unabashed romps in the fields of speculation make his book an enjoyable introduction to these ideas for both lay person and scientist.

Thus far I have discussed only the case of positive curvature, $k = 1$. We can also visualize the case of zero curvature, $k = 0$, with an extra dimension. In this case, our 3-dimensional space would be the surface of a flat sheet (thin in the w direction) of rubber in a four-dimensional space. Again we glue pennies to the sheet to represent the galaxies, and we represent the expansion by stretching the sheet in the x, y, and z directions. Figures 2 and 3 illustrate the $k = 1$ and $k = 0$ cases by including the w-axis and suppressing the z-axis:

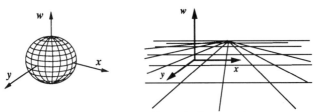

Figure 2. Positive-curvature cosmos   **Figure 3.** Zero-curvature cosmos

For the case of negative curvature, $k = -1$, we would have a saddle-shaped rubber sheet instead of a flat one. None of these universes has an edge or boundary for the matter in them. The positive-curvature universe has a finite size. If you could travel far enough in one direction (being confined to the surface of the hypersphere), you would eventually come back to your starting point. This feature makes it a *closed* cosmos. But in your travels you would never reach an edge to the stars and galaxies in it (since the matter is spread uniformly over the surface of the hypersphere), making it an *unbounded* cosmos. Thus the positive-curvature Robertson-Walker cosmos would be closed and finite, but unbounded.

The zero- and negative-curvature (flat and saddle-shaped) universes are not finite. In them, if you traveled in one direction, you could never come back to your starting point. Yet you would never encounter an edge to matter, since the matter in them extends out to infinity. These two kinds of universe would be *open* and unbounded. Thus *all Robertson-Walker (including big-bang) cosmologies have unbounded matter.*

6. MAJOR MISCONCEPTIONS ABOUT BIG-BANG THEORY

At this point we have enough background to grapple with some very common misconceptions. Most people, including most scientists, think that big-bang theorists picture a small sphere of matter exploding outward in a large, pre-existing, empty 3-dimensional space. The outer edge of the exploding matter would then be a boundary between the matter and the empty space surrounding it. But the public's picture of the big bang is wrong! In the case of the closed universe, big-bang mathematics actually says that our 3-dimensional space itself was as small as the matter. Then our 3-dimensional space expanded along with the matter. In other words, big-bang theorists imagine that in the beginning the radius a of their four-dimensional balloon was very small, but that *even then, matter was uniformly distributed along its surface*, and so matter would have no boundary in 3-dimensional space. Journalist Timothy Ferris [17] thinks that the public misconception on this point stems from the name "big bang" itself, which was originally a derogatory label the theory's opponents stuck on it:

> The term "big bang" is misleading in several respects. It implies that the expansion of the universe involved matter and energy exploding like a bomb into preexisting space. Actually the theory depicts all matter, energy, and space-time as having been bound up in the infant, high-density universe. Then, as now, all space was contained in the cosmos, even when the cosmos was smaller than an atom.

However, some of the blame for the public confusion should rest on popularizers like Ferris himself, who neglects to tell his readers that his word "space" really means the 3-dimensional space we inhabit, and who withholds from them the clarifying concept of another space dimension. Also he doesn't say that his words apply only to the positive-curvature versions of big-bang theories. For the zero- and negative-curvature (open) cases, big-bang mathematics actually says that in the beginning space and matter were infinitely large, and matter everywhere had a very high density and temperature. I.e., even at the beginning, the size and mass of the universe would be *infinite*. If in the beginning you had drawn a circle on the flat or saddle-shaped sheets, the circle would get larger as the expansion proceeded, while the density and temperature would get smaller. In other words, the open versions of the big-bang universes start infinitely large and get larger! I can understand why the popularizers are reluctant to explain these concepts to the public.

Two other misconceptions stem from the primary misconception I have mentioned above. The first is that there would be gravitational forces pointing toward the assumed center of the big bang. The second is that those assumed forces would be so strong that the initial phases of the big bang would be in a black hole (I will say much more about black holes later). But in the actual big-bang theory there is no center in 3-dimensional space for gravitational forces to point to. Every point in 3-dimensional space would have, on the average, an equal amount of matter at large distances in all directions from the point. So the overall gravitational force on each point due to the surrounding universe would be zero. (Of course the gravitational forces from nearby objects, such as our own planet, would not be zero but quite substantial.) Because of this cancellation, no large-scale pattern of gravitational forces would exist, and so a big-bang cosmos could never be in a black hole.

A fourth misconception is that no galaxy could move away from us faster than the speed of light. But many books on standard cosmology [46, pp. 148-149] point out that for every point in our 3-D space there is a "horizon" beyond which the recession velocity would exceed the speed of light, and that galaxies should exist beyond that horizon. However, at the horizon, the red shift would be infinitely large, and it would be impossible for us to see beyond it. In cosmology, matter cannot move through our 3-D space faster than the locally-measured speed of light, but *space itself* is not limited that way. (Some authors [see section 4] dislike, for philosophical reasons, this picture of space itself expanding, but they offer no alternative picture to help explain the distinctions.) For example, going back to Fig. 1, matter and light waves can only move along (or in) the surface of the hypersphere, and they cannot move faster than c with respect to the surface in their vicinity. But the surface itself can move radially outward faster than the speed of light, and according to the $k = 1$ version of big-bang theory, it is doing so right now. In fact, Alan Guth's "inflationary" version of big-bang cosmology [21] has the hypersphere, during an early phase of its expansion, increasing its radius a at 10^{20} times the speed of light!

A fifth misconception is that the red shifts of the galaxies are Doppler shifts, i.e. caused by the velocity of the galaxies away from us at the time the light starts its journey toward us. But one undergraduate textbook [23, pp. 236, 245-246] and many graduate textbooks [39, p. 213] make it clear that the red shifts are an *expansion* effect. As space is stretched out, the lengths of all electromagnetic waves passing through the space are similarly stretched out. Consequently, the *speed* of recession doesn't matter, only the *amount* of expansion that takes place as the light travels to us, whether the expansion is fast or slow. Somehow this distinction has escaped even most physicists, unless they are specialists in general relativity. I will say more about this in Section 14.

In summary, the widely accepted big-bang cosmologies have five little-known features which are very important to understand here:

1. *Matter in the universe never had any boundaries, has none now, and never will.*
2. *There is no large-scale pattern of centrally-directed gravitational forces.*
3. *The universe never was in a black hole.*
4. *Space can expand faster than the speed of light.*
5. *The red shifts are not Doppler shifts.*

It is ironic that so many enthusiastic supporters of the big bang are completely ignorant of these basic features of the theory they promote.

7. REASONS TO CONSIDER A BOUNDED COSMOS
Section 2 shows that the Copernican principle is an entirely arbitrary assumption, an "admixture of ideology" as Hawking and Ellis put it. Therefore it makes scientific sense to explore the consequences of the opposite assumption, a bounded universe. The matter in such a universe would not occupy all the available 3-dimensional space, but instead there would be empty space beyond the matter.

Another paper of mine at this conference, "A Biblical Basis for Creationist Cosmology," concludes that:

1. **The cosmos is bounded** — Interstellar space, the ordinary heavens of stars and galaxies, has a finite (though very large) size and a definite boundary. Beyond it are "the waters above the heavens," of undetermined thickness. For some unspecified distance beyond those waters there exists more space of the same sort as interstellar space, but empty of matter.

2. **The earth is near the center** — Interstellar space has a center of mass, and the earth is "near" it by cosmic standards, meaning the present distance between the earth and the center is small compared to billions of light-years.

3. **The cosmos has been expanded** — God "stretched out" interstellar space at some time in the past, probably during creation week. Space may or may not be expanding now.

4. **The cosmos is young** — God created the universe in six earth days, i.e., in six ordinary rotation periods of our particular planet.

The biblical paper offers evidence that, of all the known ways to understand the relevant scriptures, these are the most straightforward. If that is true, then it should be clear that these are not *ad hoc* assumptions, invented only recently to solve cosmological problems — because the Bible greatly predates our awareness of those problems. Thus these conclusions provide a very reasonable "admixture of ideology" to build our cosmological models upon. Conclusions 1 and 2 are the most important ones to our discussion right now. They are essentially the opposite of the Copernican principle, and so fit our scientific motivation to see what a non-Copernican cosmology would be like.

8. GRAVITY IN A BOUNDED COSMOS

Let us now see what differences boundaries make. First of all, the existence of boundaries requires the existence of a center of mass. This means that a large-scale pattern of *gravitational force* must exist throughout the cosmos, everywhere pointing toward the center of mass. If we are near the center, then the fact that the universe looks isotropic (the same in every direction) to us means that the universe must be approximately spherically symmetric. To keep things simple (they are going to get complex enough anyway) for this paper, let's assume (*i*) no overall rotation of the cosmos and (*ii*) that the mass density ρ is constant out to a radius r_0 from the center, and zero beyond that. Also, for this section only, let's ignore the effects of expansion. In that case, the large-scale gravitational force is approximately related to a Newtonian *gravitational potential* Φ [29, p. 298, 1st footnote] which depends on the radius r as follows:

$$\Phi(r) = -2\pi G \rho \left(r_0^2 - \frac{1}{3}r^2\right) \text{ for } r \leq r_0, \text{ and } \Phi(r) = -\frac{Gm}{r} \text{ for } r > r_0, \tag{7}$$

where m is the total mass of the universe,

$$m = \frac{4}{3}\pi \rho r_0^3 \tag{8}$$

(For those not familiar with this concept, gravitational potential is the energy you would need to lift one kilogram of mass from some point at radius r up to a point very far beyond radius r_0, where the gravitational force is essentially zero. It is also one-half the square of the *escape velocity* at that point, which is how fast you would have to throw the mass in order for it to escape the bounds of the universe.) Figure 4 shows how the depth of this gravitational potential "well" decreases with increasing distance r from the center. The slope of the walls of the well gives the gravitational force; the steeper the wall, the greater the force. You can think of this well as being caused by the weight of a mass upon a stretched rubber membrane. The more concentrated the mass, the deeper the well, as Figure 5 shows.

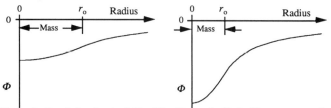

Figure 4. Gravitational potential "well." **Figure 5.** Well with more concentrated mass.

The earth, being near the center, would be near the bottom of this well, with most of the universe being at a higher (less negative) gravitational potential.

9. GRAVITY SLOWS TIME DOWN

The above differences in gravitational potential from place to place would produce differences in the rates of clocks — and all physical processes. To see this, let's consider an approximate general relativistic metric for this situation [45, p. 185]:

$$ds^2 \approx \left(1 + 2\frac{\Phi}{c^2}\right)c^2 dt^2 - \left(1 - 2\frac{\Phi}{c^2}\right)(dx^2 + dy^2 + dz^2), \tag{9}$$

where the Cartesian coordinates (x, y, z) are related to the spherical coordinates (r, θ, ϕ) in the usual way. This approximation is good when $|\Phi| \ll c^2$. Imagine the two events marking off the interval ds as being the successive ticks of a clock which is motionless in this system of coordinates. Since the two ticks take place at the same location in space, the distance differences dx, dy, and dz are all zero. Using that information plus eq. (1) in eq. (9), and taking the positive square root, gives us the following relation between the proper (or "natural") time interval $d\tau$ measured by physical clocks and the time interval dt, which is the *Schwarzschild time* (or "coordinate" time) I warned you to watch out for:

$$\boxed{d\tau \approx \left(1 + \frac{\Phi}{c^2}\right)dt} \tag{10}$$

Other authors have also derived this equation [29, pp. 248-249]. Notice that when the gravitational potential is zero, the two types of time intervals are equal, so that $d\tau = dt$. This means that Schwarzschild time t is the time measured by a clock which is not in a gravitational field. Far beyond the boundary radius r_0 of the cosmos, the gravitational potential is practically zero, so t is the time registered by very distant clocks. If we could make a set of ideal clocks throughout the universe which were not affected by gravity, we could theoretically synchronize all those clocks with one of the very distant clocks [31, pp. 597]. (One way to make such a set of gravitationally-unaffected clocks would be to let all the clocks in the set fall freely, since by Einstein's equivalence principle and also by experimental observation, free fall is equivalent to zero gravity. Another way, in theory, would be to determine the gravitational potential at every point in space and compensate the clock rates accordingly.) The synchronized set would then measure Schwarzschild time. We could think of the whole set as being "God's clock," an ideal clock completely unaffected by such mundane things as gravity. As such, Schwarzschild time makes a good standard against which we can compare the rates of less ethereal and more variable clocks.

In this light, eq. (10) says that natural, physical, clocks are indeed affected by gravity. Since the gravitational potential Φ has negative values, the equation says that wherever Φ is not zero, $d\tau$ is less than dt. I.e., clocks in a gravitational field tick slower than clocks which are not in a gravitational field. Moreover, the deeper you go into a gravitational well, the slower physical clocks tick. Although this effect is nearly unknown to the public, many authors in general relativity describe it. Here is a sampling:

> ... it follows that clocks fixed at a lower potential go slower than clocks fixed at a higher potential. This is called "gravitational time dilation" [39, p. 21].

> The rate of a clock is accordingly slower the greater is the mass of the ponderable matter in its neighbourhood [14, p. 92].

> Thus at finite distances from the masses there is a "slowing down" of the time compared with the time at infinity [29, p. 302].

> Clocks go slower in the vicinity of large masses [46, p. 27].

The second quote is by Einstein. This general-relativistic *gravitational time dilation* is not the same as the well-known "velocity" time dilation (slowdown of clocks due to motion) of special relativity. General relativity says that gravity slows down not only clocks, but also *all physical processes*: atoms, nuclei, chemical and biochemical reactions, electromagnetic waves, nerve impulses in your brain, sand in an hourglass, the watch on your arm, rotations and orbits of planets — everything! Thus we would have no direct means of observing this slowdown in our vicinity, because all of the ways we could notice or measure it are also slowed down. The slowdown is *locally* transparent to us; we cannot detect it by measurements just at one place. For example, if we were to measure the speed of light with physical clocks located near the Sun, we would get the same number as we do on earth. However, if we could do the measurements with ideal Schwarzschild clocks, we would find that the speed of light is lower near the Sun. So in general relativity, even the speed of light is affected by gravity [18, p. 23] — if we use the right clocks!

The only previous author I know of who seems to have included something like gravitational time dilation in a cosmology is Gerald L. Schroeder. His article in the *Jerusalem Post* [44] contains few scientific details, but it appears to have clocks ticking fast at the center and slow at the edge of the cosmos — just the reverse of what the equations in this section show. After submitting the first draft (8/30/93) of this article, I finally succeeded in contacting him; as far as I can tell from his reply (10/29/93), his concepts are quite different from the cosmology I am presenting here.

10. THE SLOWDOWN OF TIME — PRESENT AND PAST

Gravitational time dilation is not mere theory, however. There are ways to measure it, and it has been measured many times. Below are some samples:

1. **Deflection of electromagnetic waves** — Half of the famous deflection of light as it passes the Sun is due to gravitational slowing of the speed of light, the other half coming from the effect of gravity on space. For many years, critics of general relativity correctly pointed out that the solar eclipse measurements of the deflection of starlight were very inaccurate. But in 1975, measurements of radio waves from three quasars as the Sun passed close to them in the sky confirmed Einstein's prediction of the deflection to an accuracy of better than 1% [39, p. 22].

2. **Radar in the solar system** — In 1965, I. I. Shapiro measured the travel times of radar waves passing by the Sun and bouncing back from the planet Venus. The results confirmed the predictions of general relativity, particularly gravitational time dilation, to within 3% [46, pp. 41-45]. A few years later, the travel times of radio signals from the Mariner 6 and 7 spacecraft also confirmed the theory to about the same accuracy.

3. **Atomic clocks in airplanes** — In 1971 Joseph Hafele and and Richard Keating flew atomic clocks in eastbound and westbound airline flights, trying to measure the effect of gravitational time dilation due to the change of altitude. After correcting for velocity time dilation, they confirmed gravitational time dilation to within 10%. Four years later a team from the University of Maryland did a similar experiment, but more accurately, confirming the predicted time dilation to an accuracy of nearly 1% [46, pp. 29-35].

4. **Atomic clocks on the ground** — Wolfgang Rindler [39, p. 21] reports: "Indeed, owing to this effect [gravitational time dilation], the U.S. atomic standard clock kept since 1969 at the National Bureau of Standards at Boulder, Colorado, at an altitude of 5400 ft, gains about five microseconds per year relative to a similar clock kept at the Royal Greenwich Observatory,

England, at an altitude of only 80 ft, both clocks being intrinsically accurate to one microsecond per year."

These and other experiments make it clear that gravitational time dilation is real. However, 5 microseconds/year per mile of altitude difference does not seem like a large effect. How big would the effect be for the whole universe at present? To answer that question we need to determine the gravitational potential $\Phi(0)$ at the center of the universe. Solving eq. (8) for ρ and substituting it into eq. (7) with $r = 0$ gives us the potential at the center in terms of the total mass m and radius r_0 of the universe:

$$\Phi(0) = -\frac{3}{2} G \frac{m}{r_0} \tag{11}$$

Now we need to estimate the radius r_0 and mass density ρ of the universe. The most distant radio galaxies observed are supposed to be about 12 billion light-years away [8], according to the standard cosmological interpretation of their red shifts, so let us try $r_0 = 20$ billion light-years. The observed density of luminous matter in our cosmic neighborhood is on the order of 10^{-28} kg/m^3 [34, pp. 323-329]. Using those numbers in eq. (8) gives us an estimate for the mass of the universe:

$$m \approx 3 \times 10^{51} \text{ kg} \tag{12}$$

Using the mass and radius above in eq. (11) gives us a potential of -1.7×10^{15} m^2/s^2 at the center of the universe. Plugging that potential into eq. (10) shows that clocks at the center should presently be ticking only about 2% slower than clocks very far away. So, given the above density and size, clock rates should be about the same throughout today's universe. (Of course, if "dark matter" proves to be substantial or the size of the cosmos is much greater than 20 billion light-years, clock rates would be very different in different parts of the universe even today.)

But what about clock rates in the past? If the universe has indeed expanded, as both the biblical and scientific data indicate, then the radius r_0 of the universe was smaller in the past. That means the potential well would have been deeper than now, as eq. (11) shows and Figure 5 illustrates. In fact, eq. (11) suggests that if r_0 was about fifty times smaller, the depth of the gravitational potential well would have been about c^2. That means the escape velocity [see footnote below eq. (7)] from a point near the center would have been about the speed of light — so light from the center could not have escaped the universe! Also, using $-c^2$ for the potential in eq. (10) suggests that clocks at the center would have been stopped!

Values of potential as large as c^2 are well beyond the limits ($|\Phi| \ll c^2$) whereby equations (9) and (10) are good approximations. However, it is clear that strange things would have happened to light and time when the universe was smaller. The next section delves into those peculiarities with a more accurate metric.

11. BLACK HOLES AND WHITE HOLES
A month after Einstein published his field equations (3) with $\Lambda = 0$, Karl Schwarzschild, a German physicist serving in the Prussian army, found the first exact solution of them [30, p. 119] [29, p. 301, eq. (100.14)], a metric which describes spacetime in the vacuum surrounding a sphere of mass m :

$$ds^2 = \left(1 - \frac{r_s}{r}\right) c^2 dt^2 - \frac{dr^2}{1 - \frac{r_s}{r}} - r^2 d\Omega^2 \text{, where } r_s \equiv \frac{2 G m}{c^2} \tag{13}$$

The radial distance r is the same as in eq. (6). The time t is same as the Schwarzschild time defined in the previous section. In 1923, G. D. Birkoff [4] found that the Schwarzschild metric is valid even for contracting or expanding masses, as long as they remain spherically symmetric. The parameter r_s, called the *Schwarzschild radius*, is a critical size of great importance. Using the mass given by eq. (12), the Schwarzschild radius of the universe would be:

$$r_s = 450 \times 10^6 \text{ light-years,} \tag{14}$$

i.e., about a half-billion light-years. Remember that in the previous section we assumed the universe presently has a matter radius r_0 of 20 billion light-years. If in the past the universe were 50 times smaller, all of its matter would be inside its Schwarzschild radius. To understand what this means, we must now discuss *black holes* and *white holes*.

In the mid-1960's John Wheeler applied the term "black hole" to the idea of a collapsing star whose matter has all fallen within its Schwarzschild radius. It turns out that light or matter from such a star can never escape beyond the Schwarzschild radius. The sphere defined by the Schwarzschild radius is called the *event horizon*, because from outside it, you could never see events happening inside it. Light and matter from outside could fall into the event horizon, but nothing could ever return from it — hence the name "black hole." As more and more matter falls into a black hole, its mass increases, and so its event horizon always is moving outward. Jean-Pierre Luminet's book, *Black Holes*, recently translated into English [30], is an excellent introduction to the topic for both laymen and scientists.

There are a few misconceptions about black or white holes we should dispose of here. The first is that in them densities and tidal forces (which try to pull things apart) are always huge. But if you take the mass of eq. (12) and spread it uniformly throughout a sphere whose radius is that of eq. (14), you get a density of only 8×10^{-24} kg/m^3. Tidal forces would also be tiny. If you were to concentrate all the mass into an infinitesimal "singularity" at the very center, then the density would be infinite at that point, but zero everywhere else. Tidal forces near the singularity would be very great, but forces further out would remain small. A black hole has an event horizon long before a singularity forms, and a white hole need not have a singularity except possibly (not necessarily) at the instant of its creation. Thus forces and densities aren't necessarily large. The second misconception is that black holes are black inside. But light can and probably does exist within them. We just can't see it from outside the event horizon.

There is good astronomical evidence that black holes actually exist [30, pp. 250-252]. Astronomers have identified three objects in the sky which emit x-rays of the sort which matter falling into a black hole would emit: Cygnus X-1, LMC X-3, and A 0620-00. Each of these is a double star system, with a visible star orbiting an invisible companion. The mass of each of the companions appears to be well above 3 solar masses, the theoretical limit to the mass a compact star can have without collapsing into a black hole.

The same equations which describe a black hole also allow for the existence of an "anti-black hole" or *white hole*, the term some astrophysicists use for the idea of a black hole running in reverse. A white hole would expel matter out of its event horizon instead of pulling matter into it. Light (and matter) would leave the white hole, but no light (or matter) could go back in. As matter leaves the white hole, its mass decreases, so its event horizon would move inward. Eventually the event horizon would reach radius zero and disappear, leaving behind a widely-distributed collection of ordinary matter. The term "white hole" never really became popular, perhaps because such an object would be a source, not a "hole." Luminet suggests the poetic name "white fountain" [30, p. 165]. I like that term, but as yet it has not become familiar enough to be useful.

Matter cannot sit still inside an event horizon [29, p. 311]. In a black hole, matter *must* move inward; in a white hole, matter *must* move outward.

There is no evidence as yet that small white holes exist. However, eq. (14) suggests that the *universe* started as a white hole! This conclusion follows directly from boundedness and expansion. Such an origin is quite different from big-bang theories.

12. TIME AND THE EVENT HORIZON

Let's consider what happens to clocks near the event horizon. Again setting dr and $d\Omega$ equal to zero in eq. (13), using eq. (1), and taking the positive square root as we did in section 9, we get a relation between proper time $d\tau$ and Schwarzschild time dt:

$$d\tau = \sqrt{1 - \frac{r_s}{r}} \, dt , \quad \text{for } r > r_s \tag{15}$$

At great distances outside the event horizon, we again see that the two types of time are the same. As r decreases and gets close to the value r_s, the proper time intervals become much smaller than the Schwarzschild time intervals. Stephen Hawking [25, p. 87] tells the story of a man, say an astronaut, falling toward the event horizon of a large black hole. Here I paraphrase the story as follows:

> The astronaut is scheduled to reach the event horizon at 12:00 noon, as measured by his watch (proper time). An astronomer watching from very far away (thus being on Schwarzschild time) sees the watch tick slower and slower as the astronaut approaches the event horizon, a dark sphere blocking off a starry background. The astronomer sees the watch reach 11:57 a.m. After an hour (of Schwarzschild time) the watch reaches 11:58. After a day (of Schwarzschild time), he sees the watch reach 11:59. The astronomer never does see the watch reach 12:00. Instead he sees the motionless images of the astronaut and his watch getting redder and dimmer at the event horizon, finally fading from view completely.

Hawking didn't describe very much of what the astronaut sees, so I will take up his story:

> As the astronaut approaches the event horizon, he looks back through a telescope at the astronomer's observatory clock (Schwarzschild time) and sees it running faster and faster. He sees the astronomer moving rapidly around the observatory like a movie in fast-forward. He sees planets and stars moving very rapidly in their orbits. The whole universe far away from him is moving at a frenzied pace, aging rapidly. Yet the astronaut sees his own watch is ticking normally. Finally when the astronaut's watch (proper time) reaches 12:00 noon, he sees that the hands of the astronomer's clock are moving so fast they have become a blur. As he passes the event horizon, he feels no unusual sensations, but now he sees bright light inside the horizon. His watch reaches 12:01 and continues ticking. He looks back toward the astronomer and sees ...

To find out what the astronaut sees next, we must figure out what happens to clocks inside the event horizon. Eq. (15) does not apply when r is less than r_s. But if we consider that inside the event horizon the escape velocity must be greater than the speed of light, then we could say that the gravitational potential Φ must be more negative than $-c^2$. Eq. (10) then suggests (but does not require because of its limits of approximation) that $d\tau$ and dt might have opposite signs — the two types of clocks might *run in opposite directions!*

It appears to be another "trade secret" of general relativity, unpublicized by the adepts, that black hole theory supports this astonishing possibility. Figure 6 is adapted from a well-respected graduate textbook by John Wheeler and two colleagues, Kip Thorne and Charles Misner [31, p. 825]. It shows how the Schwarzschild time t varies as the astronaut's inward fall decreases the radius r. The arrows show the direction of increasing proper time; that is, the astronaut's watch increases its reading from point A to point B to point C. Although the Schwarzschild time goes to infinity at point B, the proper time τ does not. As the astronaut continues falling past the event horizon, the Schwarzschild time *decreases* (even while the proper time is increasing), all the way to point C. Thus, although the Schwarzschild time goes to infinity at the event horizon, the *net* amount of Schwarzschild time elapsed in going from A to C is finite. The proper time elapsed is also finite, and it is

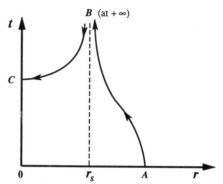

Figure 6. Astronaut falling into a black hole.

smaller than the net Schwarzschild time elapsed [31, p. 848]. Also notice that the slope of the astronaut's trajectory as it approaches C is nearly zero. This means that as measured in Schwarzschild time, the astronaut's speed is much greater than c and approaches infinity! Wheeler feels that Schwarzschild time is a bad "choice" of coordinates in this case, its "unhappy" features being shown in two ways:

> ... (1) in the fact that t goes to ∞ partway through the motion; and (2) in the fact that t thereafter decreases as τ (not shown) continues to increase.

Wheeler's word "choice" implies that Schwarzschild time is merely a matter of arbitrary theoretical taste, having no particular connection with physical measurements. However, as I pointed out in section 9 in my comments on eq. (10), Schwarzschild time has a clear physical meaning. It tells us the relation between local clocks and clocks at a distance, or between rates of physical processes and clocks unaffected by gravity. For example, it can tell us what the astronaut sees outside the event horizon when he himself is inside it:

> ... and he sees (since light can go inward through the horizon) the astronomer's clock still running so fast that the hands are a blur. As he watches, the hands of the clock slow down enough to let him see that they are moving very rapidly *counterclockwise*. The huge amount of time he saw the clock record before he crossed the event horizon is now being taken away. As the astronaut continues inward away from the event horizon, the astronomer's clock slows down toward normal speed, but it is still going backwards. The astronaut's own watch now reads 12:05. He sees the astronomer back away from the telescope and walk backwards toward the door. As far as the astronaut can see, time in the whole universe outside the event horizon is running *backwards*.

A white hole would reverse this fantastic voyage. Figure 7 shows the spacetime path of an astronaut as a white hole expels him out of its event horizon. Light and material from outside cannot move inward through the event horizon, so the astronaut cannot see the outside universe. However, an astronomer outside the event horizon would be able to see the astronaut clearly, since light and material can and do flow out of the event horizon. The arrows again show the direction of increase of proper time, from A to B to C. Again, it only takes a finite amount of proper time for the astronaut to go beyond the event horizon.

Let's say the astronaut is scheduled to cross the event horizon at 12:00 midnight by his watch. Here is his view of events:

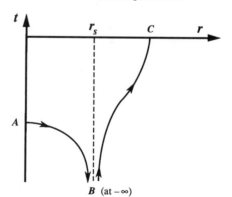

Figure 7. Astronaut expelled out of a white hole.

As the astronaut begins his journey out of the white hole, there is bright light behind him, but the event horizon looks like a black wall in front of him. As he approaches the wall he glances at his watch; it reads 11:59 p.m. A minute later, as his watch reaches 12:00 midnight, he passes through the event horizon. He feels no particular sensation, but suddenly he sees the whole starry universe outside the event horizon. He can still see the bright light coming from behind. Looking through a telescope at the astronomer's observatory clock, he sees its hands moving very rapidly

278

clockwise, and the astronomer is moving very rapidly around the observatory. Looking elsewhere, the astronaut sees the whole universe moving in fast-forward, aging very rapidly. As the astronaut gets further away from the event horizon, he sees the astronomer's clock slowing down to more normal speeds. As he arrives at the observatory, the astronomer's clock has finally slowed down to the speed of the astronaut's watch.

The astronaut tells the astronomer how fast the astronomer was aging. The astronomer has seen some strange things too, and he tells the astronaut how slowly the astronaut was aging. They argue for a while, and then finally decide that black holes and white holes do strange things to time, especially near the event horizon. But strange as such effects may seem, they are a real possibility, according to our best experimental and theoretical knowledge of physics. If the universe is bounded and has expanded, then these odd "time warps" in the past history of the cosmos are an unavoidable scientific consequence. However, creationists need not try to avoid them, because they work in our favor to allow a young universe.

13. WHAT HAPPENS INSIDE THE MATTER SPHERE
Thus, if the universe is bounded and has expanded, there was a time in its early history when all its matter was well within the event horizon, not yet having expanded to the 450 million light-years of eq. (14). During that time, the Schwarzschild metric for vacuum, eq. (13), would be valid through all the empty space between the matter and the event horizon, as well as outside it. But at some point in the expansion, the outermost matter would reach the event horizon. After that, matter would be flowing out of the event horizon, and we would expect the event horizon to start shrinking. But to properly understand what happens inside the matter's boundary, we need a different metric than eq. (13). This section will provide such a metric and explore some of its consequences.

By the time the matter reaches the event horizon, we can consider most of it as "dust," that is, the various clusters of matter are far apart enough not to be interacting significantly. Many authors on general relativity deal with the collapse of a uniform sphere of dust to become a black hole [29, pp. 316-321] [48, pp. 342-349]. The same equations apply to our situation of a uniform dustlike sphere expanding out of a white hole, except that all motions run in reverse [29, p. 320]. Therefore we can use the same metric as they derive.

The result of their work is that inside the sphere, the metric is *almost* identical to the Robertson-Walker metric, eq. (5), for $k = 1$. In the co-moving coordinate system (η, τ) of eq. (5), let's define η_0 as the co-moving radial coordinate of the sphere's edge. Then for values $\eta \le \eta_0$, eq.(5) is a valid metric. However there is one very important difference. Whereas for an unbounded Robertson-Walker cosmos, the origin can be anywhere, here the origin of coordinates *must be at the center* of the sphere and nowhere else. But seen from the center of the sphere, many phenomena will be the same as in a Robertson-Walker cosmos.

Outside the sphere, the metric has to be the same as the Schwarzschild metric, eq. (13). Therefore at the edge of the matter, at $r = r_0$ for the Schwarzschild metric and at $\eta = \eta_0$ for the Robertson-Walker metric, the two solutions must coincide. But since the two metrics use different types of coordinates, we must convert one of the metrics to the other set of coordinates. For our purposes we need the metric inside the sphere in terms of the Schwarzschild coordinates (r, t). Only two authors I know of follow that procedure, Steven Weinberg [48, pp. 345-346] and Oskar Klein [28, pp. 67-72]. Klein's interpretation of some of his mathematics is now somewhat outdated; see [29, p. 309-320] for a more recent view. But his mathematics are correct, and his exposition and notation are more suited to our needs. Unfortunately for many people, Klein's article is in German, with no published English translation that I know of. I have translated the relevant sections into English for my own convenience, and I will be happy to make the translation available to anyone who can use it [28].

As Schwarzschild did, Klein sets the cosmological constant Λ equal to zero in Einstein's equations (3). He then obtains a solution in the form of the following metric:

$$ds^2 = \beta c^2 dt^2 - \alpha dr^2 - r^2 d\Omega^2 \tag{16}$$

where α and β are functions to be specified below. Inside the sphere, for $r \le r_0$, we have:

$$\alpha = \frac{1}{1 - \dfrac{a_0 r^2}{a^3}}, \quad \text{where} \quad a_0 \equiv \sqrt{\frac{3 c^2}{8 \pi G \rho_0}} \tag{17}$$

As before, a is the radius of curvature of space, which varies with proper time τ. Under these conditions a will reach a maximum value a_0, which eq (17b) relates to the minimum matter density ρ_0 occurring at the time of maximum a. Equations (6) and (8) are also valid here, so you can use them to get ρ_0 in terms of the total mass m and η_0.

Figure 8 (on the next page) illustrates the geometry of the bounded cosmos described by equations (16) and (17), again using the extra space dimension w and suppressing the angle ϕ. As in Figure 1, the angle θ represents the amount of rotation around the w axis. The radius r_0 shows the edge of the matter distribution, also denoted by the co-moving coordinate η_0. The location of the origin cannot be moved, but must remain at the center of the matter distribution as shown. In all other ways, space inside r_0 is simply a section of the hypersphere shown in Figure 1, corresponding to the Robertson-Walker metric. Inside the sphere, the *proper distance* [48, p. 415, eq. (14.2.21)] along the surface of the hypersphere at any given proper time would be $a \chi$.

Figure 8. Geometry of bounded cosmos.

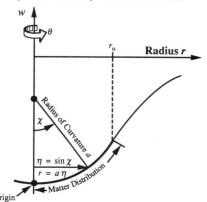

Outside of r_0, space corresponds to the Schwarzschild metric. The similarity of Figure 8 to Figure 5 is significant, but only approximate. The other coefficient of eq. (16) is related to time and therefore of more interest to us. It is:

$$\beta = \frac{\left[1 - \frac{a_0}{a}\left(1 - \frac{\left(1 - \eta_0^2\right)^{3/2}}{\left(1 - \eta^2\right)^{1/2}}\right)\right]^2}{\left(1 - \frac{a_0}{a}\eta^2\right)\left[1 - \frac{a_0}{a}\left(1 - \frac{\left(1 - \eta_0^2\right)^{1/2}}{\left(1 - \eta^2\right)^{1/2}}\right)\right]^3} \tag{18}$$

To decipher this rather formidable expression, it may help to remember that η and η_0 are the co-moving radial coordinates of, say, a galaxy and the edge of the sphere, respectively. So for a galaxy, the only variable in this equation that changes with proper time is the radius of curvature a, which is always equal to or less than a_0. Certain combinations of η and a will cause the numerator to be zero, so natural clocks would be stopped at the corresponding radii and times.

Now we need to find out how the radius of curvature a of the sphere of matter depends on proper time τ. For the case of the cosmological constant $\Lambda = 0$, many authors [27, pp. 320,321] derive $a(\tau)$ from the Einstein field equations (3). For my purposes it is easier to use $\tau(a)$:

$$\tau = \pm \frac{\tau_0}{\pi}\left[\text{Arccos}\left(2\frac{a}{a_0} - 1\right) + 2\sqrt{\frac{a}{a_0} - \left(\frac{a}{a_0}\right)^2}\right], \quad \text{where} \quad \tau_0 \equiv \frac{a_0}{c} \tag{19}$$

where I use the plus sign for a collapsing sphere and a minus sign for an expanding one.

Figure 9 shows the curve traced out by eq. (19), a cycloid. The left side of the curve shows the radius of curvature a increasing from zero at proper time $-\tau_0$ on up to its maximum value of a_0 at $\tau = 0$. If nothing intervened, the sphere would continue on to the right side of the curve, collapsing to a singularity at proper time $+\tau_0$. Thus the sphere would start as a white hole and end as a black hole.

Figure 9. Expansion and contraction of sphere

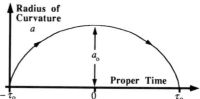

Klein calculated the Schwarzschild time t it would take for a sphere of dust to collapse from its maximum radius of curvature a_0 (at a Schwarzschild time defined as $t = 0$) to some smaller radius of curvature a. I have recalculated his expression for the reverse situation to get the time t it would take the dust sphere to expand from a radius of curvature a out to the maximum radius of curvature a_0. I have kept Klein's definition of $t = 0$ as being the time that the radius of curvature reaches its maximum, so all times before that instant are negative. Modifying Klein's nomenclature a bit, I get the following expression for the Schwarzschild time:

$$t = -t_0\left[\frac{b^3}{1 + b^2}\log\left(\frac{\zeta + b}{\zeta - b}\right) + \frac{\zeta}{1 - \zeta^2} + \left(\frac{1 + 3b^2}{1 + b^2}\right)\left(\frac{\pi}{2} - \text{Arctan }\zeta\right)\right] \tag{20}$$

The parameters t_0, ζ, and b in the above equation are defined as follows:

$$t_0 \equiv \frac{a_0}{c\sqrt{1 - \eta_0^2}}, \quad \zeta \equiv \sqrt{\frac{a_0}{a_0 - a}}\sqrt{\frac{1 - \eta_0^2}{1 - \eta^2}} - 1, \quad b \equiv \frac{\eta_0}{\sqrt{1 - \eta_0^2}}, \tag{21}$$

The normalizing parameter t_0 is a constant, has units of time, and is greater than the time it would take light to travel a distance a_0. The parameter ζ is a dimensionless variable which gets larger as the radius of curvature a increases with proper time. The parameter b is a constant. Just to refresh your memory, η is the co-moving radial coordinate and is r/a; η_0 is the value of η for the edge of the matter, namely r_0/a. Figure 10 (on the next page) plots eq. (20) with the matter radius set at $\eta_0 = 0.5$. The solid curve shows the real part of the normalized Schwarzschild time t/t_0 at the center of the universe, that is, for $\eta = 0$. The dashed curve shows t/t_0 at the edge of the matter sphere, that is, for $\eta = \eta_0 = 0.5$. Notice that as the expansion factor a/a_0 increases to roughly the value 0.25, the dashed curve goes to minus infinity and then returns, just as the curve in Figure 7. This marks the point in the expansion when the event horizon reaches the edge. A little later in the expansion, at

$a/a_0 = 0.35$, when the event horizon reaches the center, the solid curve also goes to minus infinity and returns. Inside the event horizon the Schwarzschild time also has a relatively small but non-zero imaginary component. The interpretation of an imaginary interval in section 3 (as spacelike rather than timelike) suggests that this imaginary part contributes to the stretching of space inside the event horizon.

Although the dashed and solid curves coincide at the beginning and end of the expansion, they are considerably different in between. The dashed line goes to minus infinity at a smaller value of a/a_0 than the solid line does because the event horizon reaches the edge of the matter sooner than it reaches the center.

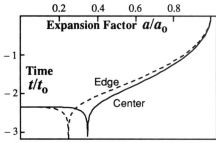

Figure 10. Schwarzschild time at two places.

After the event horizon reaches the center, the dashed curve is significantly above the solid curve until the end of the expansion. The difference between these two lines represents a large difference in Schwarzschild age. During much of the expansion, the outer parts of the universe would be older than the inner parts. At a given stage in the expansion, the age difference would be proportional to the distance from the center. Figure 11 shows how the difference in age, $t(\eta) - t(0)$, depends on the proper distance (see Figure 8). The values used in this figure are all consistent with $r_0 = 20$ billion light-years, $\eta_0 = 0.5$, and $a/a_0 = 0.4 : a_0 = 40$ billion light-years, $t_0 = 46.2$ billion years, and $a = 16$ billion light-years. The curve has different shapes at other expansion factors, but the overall age increase to billions of years at large distances exists during most of the expansion after the event horizon reaches earth.

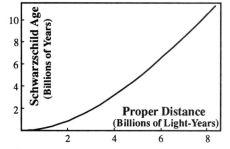

Figure 11. Age versus distance from the earth.

Except very near the event horizon, the speed of light as measured in Schwarzschild coordinates is close to c, so these large Schwarzschild ages allow time for light to cover most, if not all, the great distances to get to us during the expansion. If the expansion can take place within six days of proper time as measured on earth, then we have at least an approximate solution to the problem of seeing galaxies while standing on a young earth. Eq. (19b) shows that when the cosmological constant Λ is zero, the expansion is very slow. However, cosmologists have long known that large values of Λ, corresponding to a large tension applied to space, will enormously accelerate the expansion [32]. As I pointed out in Section 5, there is no physical law preventing an expansion much faster than the speed of light. What we really need to be specific at this point is the generalized form of equations (17) through (21) for non-zero Λ. I have made good progress on this purely mathematical problem, but as of May 30, 1994, I have not had time to complete it. The equations of this section are not a specific solution, but they imply that a solution exists, and they offer a rough outline of its basic features. Thus I think we have the main features of an answer to the light transit time problem.

14. RED SHIFTS AND THE COSMIC MICROWAVE BACKGROUND

Many authors show how the Robertson-Walker metric, eq. (5), leads to a red shift in the wavelength of electromagnetic radiation as the universe expands [48, pp. 415-418]. Since the same metric applies to our bounded cosmos with center-oriented coordinates (see beginning paragraphs of previous section), we can use the same result to specify the red shift as seen from the center:

$$\frac{\lambda_2}{\lambda_1} = \frac{a_2}{a_1} \tag{22}$$

Here λ_1 and λ_2 are, respectively, the wavelengths of the light at emission and reception; a_1 and a_2 are, respectively, the radii of curvature of the cosmos at emission and reception. Often astronomers specify red shifts in terms of a dimensionless parameter z, which is defined as $(\lambda_2 - \lambda_1)/\lambda_1$, changing eq. (22) to the form:

$$z = \frac{a_2}{a_1} - 1 \tag{23}$$

I have also derived these results from Klein's metric, eq. (16). In an expanding cosmos, a_2 is greater than a_1, so λ_2 is greater than λ_1 and the red shift parameter z is positive. Notice that these equations do not depend on velocity at all, so the effect cannot be a Doppler shift, as I explained in Section 5. Instead the effect is entirely due to the change of the radius of curvature of space while the photons are *in transit*. If you think of light as waves traveling on a sheet of rubber, these equations say that, as the sheet is stretched out, the wavelengths stretch out along with it. The equations say that the rate of expansion has nothing to do with the amount of red shift, which depends only only on the initial and final values of a. As far as the red shifts are concerned, it does not matter whether the expansion took place in 20 billion years or six days.

In 1929, Edwin Hubble found that the red shifts of light from galaxies are approximately proportional to their distance r [26]:

$$z \approx \frac{H}{c} r \qquad (24)$$

As I mentioned in section 1, there are exceptions to this, but the trend is very clear. The parameter H is called the *Hubble constant*. At present, astronomers cannot measure great distances to better than a factor of two, so they do not know the Hubble constant to better than that accuracy. But whatever the exact distances are, the cosmology I am outlining here asserts that the galaxies were indeed at those great distances when the light they emitted began its journey to us. It also asserts that the amount of expansion occurring between emission and reception was roughly the same as the standard theory claims. Thus, without doing any detailed calculations, we can say that the value of the Hubble constant given by this theory should be about the same as observed.

We now come to the third item on my list of large-scale phenomena to be explained, the cosmic microwave background radiation. Various authors have shown [49, p. 533, eq. (15.6.17)] that if when space has a radius of curvature a_1, it is filled with thermal radiation corresponding to a temperature T_1, then when space expands to a radius of curvature a_2, the same stretching effect which caused the red shift of light waves will also red-shift the heat waves, dropping the thermal radiation temperature to a value T_2 given by:

$$\frac{T_2}{T_1} = \frac{a_1}{a_2} \qquad (25)$$

Thus, if the early cosmos was filled with thermal radiation of high temperature and uniformity, then the expansion of a bounded cosmos would have the same kind of low-temperature microwave background we observe today. The next section shows that such radiation in the early cosmos would be a very reasonable result of the Genesis account.

15. RECONSTRUCTION OF SOME CREATION EVENTS
Now let's use our imaginations and try to reconstruct some of the events of the creation week from both the biblical and scientific information. At some points I will have to speculate in order to provide specific details, so please regard this reconstruction as a tentative outline of events, subject to radical revision as we learn more.

In the biblical paper I show evidence that in the first instant of creation the "deep" consisted of ordinary liquid water at normal density and temperature. This requires the existence of functioning water molecules with their constituent atoms, electrons and nuclei; in turn that requires electromagnetic and nuclear forces to be in operation. These forces (especially electromagnetism) are deeply enmeshed with relativity, and so their existence implies that relativity was operating at this time. There is also biblical evidence that gravity was operating at that instant, and if it were very strong, there would be a clearly-defined interface between the water and the presumed vacuum above it. Gravity would also shape the water into a sphere. There is biblical evidence that the sphere was slowly rotating with respect to the space within which it existed. There was no visible light at the surface of the sphere.

To contain all the mass of the visible universe, equations (8) and (12) say that the sphere would have an initial radius of at least *one light-year*. (Actually the size would have to be greater than that to account for the mass of the "waters above the heavens," but that mass is unknown.) One light-year is surprisingly small compared to the present cosmos, but it is still large enough to justify the biblical name of the sphere, "the deep." The sphere would be well within its event horizon, which according to eq. (14) would be 450 million light-years further out. Thus the universe started as either a black hole or white hole. I suggest here that it was a black hole, and that God let gravity take its course. The physics of black holes (section 11) do not permit matter in a black hole to remain motionless; it must fall inward. So unless God intervened, the sphere would collapse inward. The fall would be faster than the speed of light, as measured in Schwarzschild coordinates (remember the great speed of the astronaut as he approached point C in Fig. 6).

As the radius of the sphere shrank, the temperature, pressure, and density would rise to enormous values. Descending into the interior, we would find a depth at which molecules would be dissociated and atoms would be ionized. Further down, nuclei would be torn apart into neutrons and protons. Yet further down, even elementary particles would be ripped apart, making a dense plasma of gluons and quarks.

At a certain range of depths, thermonuclear fusion reactions would begin, forming heavier nuclei from lighter ones (nucleosynthesis) and liberating huge amounts of energy. An intense light would illuminate the interior. As the compression continued, the fusion reactions would reach a shallow enough depth to allow light to reach the surface, thus ending the darkness at that level. The strong gravity would cause light leaving the surface to return to it, so light at the surface would be coming from all sides. The sphere would have no dark side.

As the compression continued, the gravity would became so strong that light could no longer reach the surface, thus re-darkening it. The exegetical paper offers biblical evidence that the Spirit of God became a localized light source, giving the sphere a bright side and a dark side.

Meanwhile, conservation of angular momentum would have caused the sphere to speed up its rotation as the collapse proceeded. To be consistent with the Genesis account, the surface would execute a full rotation between the beginning and the end of day one. When the rotation of the sphere reached relativistically significant speeds, the Schwarzschild metric would no longer be an accurate description of the vacuum outside the sphere. Instead the more complex Kerr metric [24, pp. 161-168] would have to be used, and I haven't taken on that problem yet. As yet there is no known exact metric for the conditions inside the sphere at this point. However, because (as measured in Schwarzschild coordinates) the distance is about a light-year and the velocity of collapse is greater than c, we can say that the collapse would take less than a year of Schwarzschild time. Proper time as measured at the surface of the sphere would be less than the Schwarzschild time, and I suspect that it amounted to an ordinary day.

At some point the black hole had to become a white hole. I propose that God did this on day two by increasing the cosmological "constant" Λ to a large positive value, beginning a rapid, inflationary expansion of space. He marked off a large volume within the ball wherein material would be allowed to pull apart into fragments and clusters as it expanded, but He required the "waters below" and the "waters above" to stay coherently together, as Figure 12(a) illustrates:

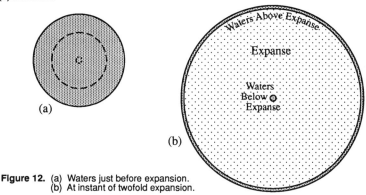

Figure 12. (a) Waters just before expansion.
(b) At instant of twofold expansion.

Cooling would proceed as rapidly as the expansion. Visible matter would cool directly by expansion, and also by losing heat to the material of space itself, according to general relativity [40, pp. 344, 355-356] [36]. Matter above and below the expanse would expand but stay dense. Matter in the expanse would be drawn apart into clusters of hydrogen and helium plasma. Figure 12(b) illustrates this phase of the expansion. At some point in the expansion, when the radius of curvature a was about a thousand times smaller than today's value, the plasma in the expanse would cool to about 3000 Kelvin, at which point the plasma would begin forming atoms and the expanse would become transparent.

At this point, thermal radiation in the expanse would be very uniform and have a blackbody spectrum, having been surrounded by optically thick walls above and below during the previous stage of expansion. According to eq. (25), the radiation temperature would now begin dropping from 3000 Kelvin to much lower values, in direct proportion to the increase in the radius of curvature a. At the end of the expansion, the radiation temperature would have dropped to the 2.76 Kelvin we see today. This explanation of the cosmic microwave background is not too different from that provided by the big bang theories, except for the boundedness and the optically thick "walls" around the expanse.

16. DAYS THREE TO SIX
The inflationary expansion of space could possibly have had second-order effects on nuclear forces and on the transport of heat from hot matter to the material of space itself [40, pp. 344, 355-356] [36]. If so, such mechanisms could explain the evidence for both rapid radioactive decay and rapid volume cooling which creationists have lately begun to notice. God could have used radioactive decay on the third day to heat the continental cratons (which today contain most of the earth's radioactive nuclei) and provide power for other geologic work, followed by volume cooling to solidify batholiths and the asthenosphere. The thermal expansion of the supercontinent would make it more buoyant with respect to the mantle rock, lifting the continent above the waters and causing them to gather in the ocean basins.

At some time during the expansion, probably on the third day, the waters above the heavens would reach the event horizon and pass beyond it. After that the event horizon would begin rapidly shrinking toward the earth. At the same time, gravity would be drawing together the atoms of hydrogen, helium, and other elements in each cluster left behind by the expansion. There would be plenty of Schwarzschild time for that process.

I suggest that the event horizon reached earth early in the morning of the fourth day. During that day of proper time on earth, according to my theory, billions of years worth of physical processes took place in the distant cosmos. I also suggest that early in the fourth morning, God finished coalescing the clusters of material left behind in the expansion and allowed thermonuclear fusion to ignite in the newly-formed stars. At this point, the stars would find themselves clustered into galaxies. As with other things in the Genesis account, the formation of stars, solar system(s?), and galaxies would be caused by a combination of natural events and direct action by God. At this point I am not trying to be specific as to which was which. During the fourth day the distant stars aged billions of years, while their light also had that much time to travel here. While the light from the most distant galaxy we have seen was traveling to us, the universe expanded by about a factor of five, stretching the light's wavelength by the same factor and giving it a red-shift parameter of about four [see eq. (23)].

My biblical paper gives reasons to think that God stopped the expansion, reducing Λ to a small positive value or zero, before the evening of the sixth day. (The biblical paper points out some evidence for another episode of expansion during the Genesis flood.) Thus Adam and Eve, gazing up for the first time into the new night sky, would be able to see the Milky Way, the Andromeda galaxy, and all the other splendors in the heavens that declare the glory of God.

17. CONCLUSION

Jean-Pierre Luminet [30, p. 161] quotes Dennis Sutton as writing that "the frontiers of science are always a bizarre mixture of new truth, reasonable hypothesis, and wild conjecture." By those criteria, then, you will probably agree that this paper is on the "frontiers of science" — or perhaps beyond! But I want to remind you that the essential hypothesis of this paper, that matter in the universe is bounded, is quite reasonable. After all, every other created thing we know of has limits, so why should we expect even the biggest thing God created to be any different?

Furthermore, the hypothesis is not something I concocted myself to generate an *ad hoc* explanation for the cosmological difficulties of young-earth creationism. Instead the idea of a bounded universe flows very naturally from the central idea of young-earth creationism: that the Bible is to be taken straightforwardly.

If the universe is bounded, the main points of this cosmology follow quite scientifically from the amount of visible matter in the universe, the evidence for its expansion, and the experimentally well-established general theory of relativity. The logical conclusion is that the universe began its existence in a black hole or a white hole. The phenomena surrounding black holes seem strange to us mainly because we are unfamiliar with them, not because they are impossible. At any rate, I did not invent the idea of such phenomena. The only thing I have done is apply the same ideas to the universe as a whole and explore some of the consequences.

At this point, I consider this paper only the outlines of a theory. As such it furnishes us with qualitative answers to the major cosmological phenomena I listed in the introduction, but it is not yet well enough developed to make detailed quantitative predictions which would observationally distinguish it from conventional theories. A large amount of work needs to be done to bring it to that point, far more than I can do alone, so I invite other creationist scientists and students to join me in this work.

There is a good possibility that developments of this theory can explain many of the anomalies encountered by the conventional theories, such as superluminal quasar jets [10], proportions of nuclei found in the cosmos [18], vestiges of rotation in the cosmos [37], numbers of galaxies at large red shifts [6], the extraordinary uniformity of the cosmic microwave background [38], the extreme brightness of the universe (10^9 photons per nucleon) [27], the cosmological constant problem [49], the flatness problem [43], and so forth.

In particular, the "quantized" distribution of galactic red shifts [3] [22], observed by various astronomers with increasing certainty over the last few decades, seems to contradict the Copernican principle and all cosmologies founded on it — including the Big Bang. But the effect seems to have a ready explanation in terms of my new non-Copernican "white hole" cosmology.

This paper covers a great deal of scientific territory unfamiliar to many readers. But the bottom line is simple: God used relativity to make a young universe.

ACKNOWLEDGEMENTS

A number of people have helped me greatly in this work. Roy Holt asked a question that made me realize the importance of the Copernican principle. John Baumgardner has encouraged me and helped untangle my thinking. James Dritt has given sensible advice and been a good editor. Gerald Schroeder's ideas [44], referred to in Section 8, though not quite correct, may have helped me solidify mine. Barry Setterfield's theory, while not correct in my eventual opinion, was a great stimulus to me. A creationist astrophysics graduate student at a major university has helped me on several mathematical problems. Many other creationist friends have prayed for this project. My heartfelt thanks go to all these people.

REFERENCES

[1] R. Ackridge, T. Barnes, and H. S. Slusher, **A recent creation explanation of the 3° K background black body radiation**, Creation Research Society Quarterly **18:3** (1981) 159-162.

[2] G. R. Akridge, **The universe is bigger than 15.71 light years**, Creation Research Society Quarterly **21:1** (1984) 18-22.

[3]   Anonymous, **Quantized redshifts: what's going on here?** Sky and Telescope   (August 1992) 28-29.

[4]   G. D. Birkoff, Relativity and Modern Physics, 1923, Harvard University Press, Cambridge, Mass.

[5]   H. Bondi, Cosmology, 1960, Cambridge University Press, London.

[6]   T. J. Broadhurst, R. S. Ellis, and K. Glazebrook, **Faint galaxies: evolution and cosmological curvature,** Nature **355** (2 January 1992) 55-58.

[7]   J. Byl, **On small curved-space models of the universe,** Creation Research Society Quarterly **25:3** (1988) 138-140.

[8]   E. F. Chaffin, **A determination of the speed of light in the seventeenth century,** Creation Research Society Quarterly **29:3** (1992) 115-120.

[9]   K. C. Chambers, G. K. Miley, and W. J. M. van Breugel, **4C 41.17: a radio galaxy at a red-shift of 3.8,** Astrophysical Journal **363:1** (1990) 21-39.

[10]   R. J. Davis, S. C. Unwin, and T. W. B. Muxlow, **Large-scale superluminal motion in the quasar 3C273,** Nature **354** (5 December 1991) 374-376.

[11]   D. B. DeYoung, Questions and Answers on Astronomy and the Bible, 1989, Baker Book House, Grand Rapids.

[12]   A. Einstein, **Cosmological considerations on the general theory of relativity,** The Principle of Relativity, 1952, Dover Publications, New York, 177-188.   Translated from **Kosmologische Betrachtungen zur allgemeinen Relativitätstheorie,** Sitzungsberichte der Preussischen Akad. d. Wissenschaften (1917) 142-152.

[13]   A. Einstein, **The foundations of the general theory of relativity,** in The Principle of Relativity, 1952, Dover Publications, New York, 111-164.   Translated from **Die Grundlage der allgemeinen Relativitätstheorie,** Annalen der Physik **49** (1916) 769.

[14]   A. Einstein, The Meaning of Relativity, 1956, Fifth Edition, Princeton University Press, Princeton.

[15]   A. Einstein, **Ether and the theory of relativity,** in Sidelights on Relativity, 1983, Dover Publications, New York, 1-25.   Translated from an address delivered on May 5, 1920 at the University of Leyden.

[16]   M. G. Evered, **The recent decrease in the velocity of light — what decrease?,** Creation Ex Nihilo Technical Journal **7:1** (1993) 93-102.

[17]   T. Ferris, **Needed: a better name for the big bang,** Sky & Telescope **86:2** (1993) 4-5.

[18]   F. Flam, **In the beginning, let there be beryllium,** Science **255** (10 January 1992) 162-163.

[19]   T. Frankel, Gravitational Curvature: An Introduction to Einstein's Theory, 1979, W. H. Freeman and Company, San Francisco.

[20]   J. R. Gott, **Implications of the Copernican principle for our future prospects,** Nature **363** (27 May 1993) 315-319.

[21]   A. H. Guth, **Inflationary universe: a possible solution to the horizon and flatness problems,** Physical Review **D 23:2** (1981) 347-356.

[22]   B. N. G. Guthrie and W. M. Napier, **Evidence for redshift periodicity in nearby field galaxies ,** Monthly Notices of the Royal Astronomical Society **253** (1991) 533-544.

[23]   E. R. Harrison, Cosmology: The Science of the Universe, 1981, Cambridge University Press, Cambridge.

[24]   S. W. Hawking and G. F. R. Ellis, The Large Scale Structure of Space-Time, 1973, Cambridge University Press, Cambridge.

[25]   S. W. Hawking, A Brief History of Time, 1988, Bantam Books, New York.

[26]   E. Hubble, **A relation between distance and radial velocity among extra-galactic nebulae,** Proceedings of the National Academy of Science **15** (1929) 168-173.

[27]   D. W. Hughes, **Considering cosmology,** Nature **353** (31 October 1991) 804-805.

[28] O. Klein, **Einige probleme der allgemeinen relativitätstheorie**, in <u>Werner Heinsenberg und die Physik unserer Zeit</u>, Fritz Bopp, Editor, 1961, Friedr. Vieweg & Sohn, Braunschweig, 58-72. In German. Partial translation, **Several problems of the theory of general relativity**, 13 pages, available from D. R. Humphreys, address on first page of this paper. Send $2.00 for cost of copying plus postage.

[29] L. D. Landau and E. M. Lifshitz, <u>The Classical Theory of Fields</u>, 1975, Fourth Revised English Edition, Pergamon Press, Oxford.

[30] J-P. Luminet, <u>Black Holes</u>, 1992, Cambridge University Press, Cambridge.

[31] C. W. Misner, K. S. Thorne, and J. A. Wheeler, <u>Gravitation</u>, 1973, W. H. Freeman and Company, New York.

[32] M. Moles, **Physically permitted cosmological models with nonzero cosmological constant**, <u>Astrophysical Journal</u> **382** (December 1 1991) 369-376.

[33] P. Moon and D. E. Spencer, **Binary stars and the velocity of light**, <u>Journal of the Optical Society of America</u> **43:8** (1953) 635-641.

[34] J. V. Narlikar, <u>Introduction to Cosmology</u>, 983, Jones and Bartlett Publishers, Boston.

[35] T. Norman and B. Setterfield, <u>The Atomic Constants, Light, and Time</u>, 1987, Technical Monograph, Flinders University, Adelaide, Australia.

[36] J. Pachner, **Nonconservation of energy during cosmic evolution**, <u>Physical Review Letters</u> **12:4** (1964) 117-118.

[37] V. F. Panov and Yu. G. Sbytov, **Accounting for Birch's observed anisotropy of the universe: cosmological rotation?**, <u>Soviet Physics JETP</u> **74:3** (1992) 411-415.

[38] R. B. Partridge, **The seeds of cosmic structure**, <u>Science</u> **257** (10 July 1992) 178-179.

[39] W. Rindler, <u>Essential Relativity</u>, 1977, Revised Second Edition, Springer-Verlag, New York.

[40] H. P. Robertson and T. W. Noonan, <u>Relativity and Cosmology</u>, 1968, W. B. Saunders Company, Philadelphia.

[41] R. Rucker, <u>The Fourth Dimension</u>, 1984, Houghton Miflin Company, Boston.

[42] C. Sagan, <u>Cosmos</u>, 1980, Random House, New York.

[43] P. Scheuer, **Weighing the universe**, <u>Nature</u> **361** (14 January 1993) 112.

[44] G. L. Schroeder, **The universe — 6 days and 13 billion years old**, <u>Jerusalem Post</u>, September 7, 1991. Schroeder's "6 days" is at the "edge of the universe," while his "13 billion years" is on the earth — exactly the reverse of what I am saying! A letter from Dr. Schroeder (10/29/93) indicates his cosmological ideas are quite different from the one I am presenting here.

[45] B. F. Schutz, <u>A First Course in General Relativity</u>, 1985, Cambridge University Press, Cambridge.

[46] R. Sexl and H. Sexl, <u>White Dwarfs—Black Holes</u>, 1979, Academic Press, New York.

[47] P. M. Steidl, <u>The Earth, the Stars, and the Bible</u>, 1979, Baker Book House, Grand Rapids.

[48] S. Weinberg, <u>Gravitation and Cosmology</u>, 1972, John Wiley & Sons, New York.

[49] S. Weinberg, **The cosmological constant problem**, <u>Reviews of Modern Physics</u> **61:1** (1989) 1-23.

[50] S. Weinberg, <u>Dreams of a Final Theory</u>, 1992, Pantheon Books, New York.

[51] J. C. Whitcomb, Jr., and H. M. Morris, <u>The Genesis Flood</u>, 1961, Baker Book House, Grand Rapids.

* Dr. Humphreys is a physicist at Sandia National Laboratories, Dept. 1271, M.S. 1187, Albuquerque, NM 87185-1187. The Laboratories have not supported this work. He is also an Adjunct Professor of Geophysics and Astrophysics at the Institute for Creation Research, 10946 Woodside Ave. N., Santee, CA 92071.

THE CANOPY, THE MOON, THE TILT OF THE EARTH'S AXIS, AND A PRE-FLOOD ICE AGE

GREG S. JORGENSEN P.ENG.
234 ENFIELD CRES.
WINNIPEG, MANITOBA
CANADA R2H 1B4

KEYWORDS

Water Vapor Canopy, Atmospheric lapse rates, Satellite Orbits, Moon Kept Perfect Month and Year, Earth's Axis of Inclination, Fast Pole Shifts, Ice Caps, Permafrost, Transient Conduction

ABSTRACT

An initial attempt is made to systematize different areas of study in that the Canopy, the moon, the tilt of the earth's axis, multiple ice ages, and geological history are all related and supported by Scriptures.

It will be argued that a vapor canopy existed around the pre-Flood earth but could not have survived the long winter periods of darkness which the poles experience today. A near zero angle of inclination would insure that the Canopy would receive continuous light over the polar regions. Symmetrical air mass movements would create the atmospheric stability required to maintain the Canopy. This paper briefly summarizes the Canopy but concentrates on the biblical and scientific evidence supporting a near zero axial tilt.

Our moon revolves about the earth at an approximate 5 degree angle of inclination to the solar ecliptic. Most of the planets satellites revolve around their planet's equator suggesting that at one time the earth may have had a 5 degree axial tilt. This reduced tilt from today's 23.5 degrees would mean colder temperatures toward the poles leading to pre-Flood polar ice caps. A possible ice age may have formed as the warm oceans of Creation Day 1 cooled.

A fast pole shift (earth roll over) is a favored mechanism, by this author, for changing the earth's axis and helps explain why the Canopy collapsed, as well as many other geological observations. It could also be responsible for destroying a perfect 360 day year where the moon kept a perfect 30 day month.

It will be argued that multiple inversions could help explain the 4500 feet of permafrost found in Yakutsk, Siberia. Calculations will show that it would take more then 50,000 years for permafrost to penetrate to this depth. It will be shown that a near zero axial tilt would decrease this time, but multiple pole inversions would deposit sediment over already frozen ground explaining the great depth of permafrost.

THE CANOPY

That the Scriptures teach of a pre-Flood water Canopy has been agreed upon by many creationists for some time. But is a pure water vapor canopy technically feasible? Would it not mix and precipitate out? What about the winter season, especially at the poles? How could the Canopy survive there? To answer these questions, a computer model was developed and first presented at the 1990 ICC Conference in Pittsburgh, see Jorgensen [17]. A number of revisions were made and presented at the 1992 Twin-Cities Creation Conference, see Jorgensen [18].

It was concluded that frozen ice caps could have existed at the poles. Sedimentary data indicates that at one time the entire planet was tropical. If the Day 1 oceans were created uniformly warm around the entire globe, they could have kept the polar regions warm enough for tropical conditions for the first few hundred years after Creation. As the poles slowly cooled could the Precambrian ice age, suggested in the literature, have formed Zumberge & Nelson [36].

The following interpretation of Genesis 1 will help in understanding the nature of the Canopy.

Day 1

God created the vacuum of space and the earth. There was a universal warm ocean and if there was no air, a pure water vapor atmosphere would be produced. There was no dry land, no light, no universe, no life. God was the "Light of the World" for the first 3 days.(Ps.84:11 and Rev.21:23). God's light was directional and produced evening and morning. The earth was rotating once every 24 hours.

Day 2

God created an oxygen-nitrogen atmosphere in between the oceans and the water vapor. The water vapor was on top of the atmosphere and produced the Canopy. For the Canopy to have received continuous light at the poles (to keep it warm) the earth could not have had any axial tilt. This is not difficult to visualize as it was the only object in the universe and all dimensions would be symmetrical to the earth's equator.

The Canopy was the water vapor atmosphere resulting from the warm oceans created on Day 1 and separated by the air atmosphere on Day 2. A 90 deg.F. initial ocean temperature would create a 50 mb. water vapor pressure (0.05 atm., 1.8 feet of liquid water, or 550 mm.). This is simply the vapor pressure over the liquid water as can be found in any steam table.

A Canopy study by Rush and Vardiman [25] also favors a relatively thin 50mb. Canopy pressure. Today's atmosphere contains less the 1 inch of water as reported by Miller & Thompson [20].

Miller & Thompson [20] define a moderate rainfall as 0.5 mm/hr and a heavy one as > 4mm/hr. For a 50mb. Canopy to rain out in 40 days and nights it would have to rain at a rate of 550 mm/40days/24hr/day= .57 mm/hr, a moderate rainfall. A global average rainfall of 1000 mm. per year falls today so over half that would have fallen in just 40 days and nights during the Flood.

Further studies are required to determine how fast the atmosphere could radiate away the heat of condensation from the Canopy. This calculation would help support the maximum rate of rainfall possible. Perhaps it would show that a thicker Canopy could not dissipate it's latent heat of condensation in 40 days. Fig.1a shows the vertical temperature profile of a 50 mb. atmosphere. Note the warm region at the air-water vapor boundary. This warm region kept the water vapor in a gaseous state and kept it from precipitating.

This model does support thicker canopies and the temperature profiles for various Canopy thicknesses are shown in Fig.1b, but note that a thicker Canopy of 175 mb. would produce equatorial temperatures of 50 to 60 deg. C. Could life exist in such climates? Perhaps one could argue that as the "Holy Spirit moved or brooded over the waters" in Genesis 1:1, He increased the natural vapor pressure to create a thicker Canopy, see Strong [30, Hebrew word #7363].

The Canopy could be compared to today's solar absorbing ozone layer at the 40-50 km. level in our atmosphere. Ozone absorbs solar radiation and warms that region of the atmosphere just as water vapor would. Ozone is produced by photochemistry which is a completely different phenomenon, nevertheless, its heat absorbing properties would create a comparable effect on the vertical temperature profile. A study of Fig.2 will show that the ozone layer is warmer because it absorbs solar radiation. A water vapor Canopy would also absorb solar radiation keeping it warm and preventing it's precipitation. Fig.2 also shows that even though the ground temperature decreases toward the poles the ozone, thus the Canopy, is actually warmer toward the poles because an absorbing layer in the atmosphere absorbs equal energy at any latitude (see Fig.3a). In addition, Fig.2 indicates that during the northern hemisphere's summer the ozone layer of the south pole is cooled due to the earth's 23.5 deg. tilt. This would mean sure death to the Canopy as it could not tolerate a 6 month period with no sunlight passing through it; it would condense and rain out.

It is important to understand that it is argued that the Canopy was pure water vapor with no air mixed in with it. This is why the tilt of the earth's axis is so critical to the Canopy theory. The Canopy would require a near zero degree of inclination to produce the symmetrical conditions required to insure its survival. It could not tolerate any violent storms which would mix it with the air below. The evidence of a near zero axial tilt is given in the section titled "The Moon" below.

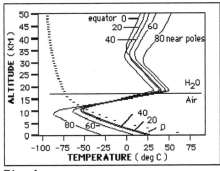

Fig. 1a PROFILE AS A FUNCTION OF LATITUDE
50 mb CANOPY Jorgensen [18]

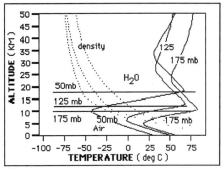

Fig. 1b PROFILE AS A FUNCTION OF CANOPY
VAPOR PRESSURE Jorgensen [18, p.40]

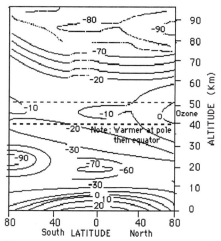

Fig. 2 Temperature Gradient in Deg C As
A Function Of Latitude & Altitude.
(From Nimbus 6 Aug 4, 1975)
Houghton [12, Fig. 12.9 p.199]

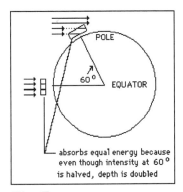

Fig. 3a Energy Absorbtion as a
Function of Latitude

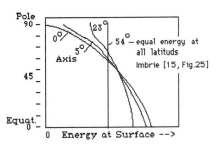

Fig. 3b Energy received at the
Poles is reduced as
inclination is reduced
Strahler [27]

Precipitation Of The Canopy

In the previous papers by Jorgensen [17] [18] it was argued that huge volcanoes from the "fountains of the deep" provided the precipitating nuclei required to condense the Canopy. As explained in Fig.4b, all ocean and atmospheric currents are reversed in a geographical pole shift and this could further help explain the destruction of the Canopy, which was a delicately balanced system requiring worldwide atmospheric stability and symmetry.

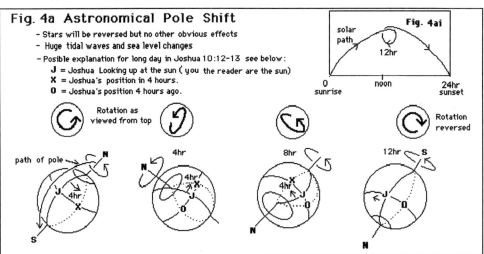

Fig. 4a Astronomical Pole Shift

- Stars will be reversed but no other obvious effects
- Huge tidal waves and sea level changes
- Posible explanation for long day in Joshua 10:12-13 see below :
  - **J** = Joshua Looking up at the sun (you the reader are the sun)
  - **X** = Joshua's position in 4 hours.
  - **0** = Joshua's position 4 hours ago.

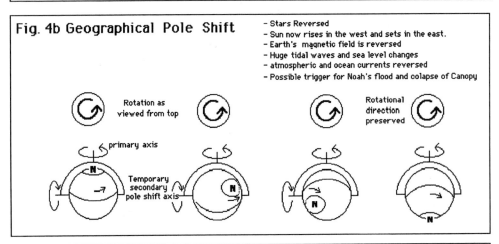

Fig. 4b Geographical Pole Shift

- Stars Reversed
- Sun now rises in the west and sets in the east.
- Earth's magnetic field is reversed
- Huge tidal waves and sea level changes
- atmospheric and ocean currents reversed
- Possible trigger for Noah's flood and colapse of Canopy

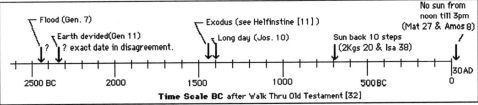

Fig. 4c **POSSIBLE BIBLICAL EVENTS ALTERING THE EARTH'S AXIS**
either by partial or complete astronomical or geographical pole shifts

PRE-FLOOD ICE AGE

The evidence of a precambrian (pre-Flood rock strata) ice age is clearly indicated in the literature and can not be ignored. Flint [6] has summarized features which indicate glaciation as follows:

(1)   Glacial diamicts or (tillites) in the strata. Electron microscope analysis   on surfaces of sand grains can indicate weight of glacier.
(2)   Fossils of low-temperature organisms.
(3)   Glacial-erosional forms, and structures created during the deformation   or stratified materials by thrust or drag of a flowing glacier.
(4)   Glacial rhythmites; dropstones.
(5)   Ice-contact stratified drift.
(6)   Outwash sediment.
(7)   Glacial loess.
(8)   Glacial-marine sediment.
(9)   Taluses, frost cracks, ice-wedge casts, patterned ground.

Most of these features have been identified in pre-cambrian rock strata indicating pre-Flood glaciers, see Flint[6] & Hambrey [9]. Molen [21] has argued that these features could also indicate gravity flows not requiring glaciation, nevertheless, they could also indicate pre-Flood glaciation as proposed below. Fig.1 shows the temperature profile with altitude for the Canopy atmosphere. Note that even though the Canopy grows slightly warmer toward the poles, the ground temperature decreases to below freezing. Fig.1 has been corrected for convection and general circulation in the atmosphere [18]. It is a common belief that the Canopy would moderate the temperatures around the globe. But Fig.1 shows that this is not the case. The general circulation of today's earth brings much energy from the equatorial regions to the poles but it is still not enough to bring temperatures above freezing. The Canopy could not tolerate the violent atmospheric storms of today, so the general circulation under the Canopy probably would not transfer as much energy to the poles as today. This would indicate pre-Flood polar ice caps. These ice caps may have formed slowly as the created warm oceans cooled. Today the deep oceans, even at the equator, are at 1 deg.C, the temperature at which sea water is the most dense [28]. This cooling period may have taken several hundred years allowing tropical climates during the early part of this period.

A near zero axial tilt would reduce the energy received at the poles as shown in Fig.3b. If the earth had a near zero tilt today, then the temperatures would be an average between the two equinoxes on March 21 and September 23. Equinoxes are the times when the sun is directly over the equator, a permanent position with a near zero tilt. It is easy to envision a cooler climate in this condition. In Minneapolis for example, there would more than likely be a permanent mild winter. Equatorial regions would be warmer as they would receive direct sunlight year-round. Exactly how warm would depend on how much cloud cover was over this region.

Guinness [7] records Yakutsk, Siberia has having 4500 feet of permafrost and as seen in Fig.5a, even at an extremely cold mean temperature it would take more than 50,000 years to penetrate to 4500 feet. Note in Fig.5b that most of the conditions ignored in the calculations will increase this time.

A large lake (8 sq.km.in area) drained near Tuktoyaktuk, N.W.T., Canada, some 150 years ago and today there is only about 35 meters of permafrost under the lake [22]. As can be seen in Fig.5a, an increase in depth by a factor of 10 increases the time by a factor of 100. With this in mind, it would take 15,000 years to reach a depth of 350 meters. If similar conditions existed at Yakutsk it would take 240,000 years to freeze to a depth of 4500 feet.

The permafrost at Yakutsk must have been frozen in layers of a few hundred meters and then buried with new sediment which would then freeze from the bottom as well as the top. Calculations show that a 500 meter layer could freeze in 1200 years under these conditions. This would indicate that the sediment was not local but was transported from the ocean floor or from some warmer climate and deposited. If this is true, there should be borehole data that shows an increase in temperature with depth and then a decrease in temperature as the relic frozen layer is reached (Fig 5d).

Geothermal gradients through the permafrost from borehole temperature data would help confirm or refute this hypothesis. The permafrost would be in a transient as opposed to a steady state condition as shown in Figs.5c & 5d. Vigdorchik [31] has found several layers of permafrost submerged under the Arctic Ocean out as far as 400 km. These layers are divided by unfrozen "talik" and have highly irregular upper and lower boundaries just as would be expected with several deposits.

Borehole temperature logs should be of great interest to Creationists as they should all be in a transient state. It takes hundreds of thousands of years for the deposits to reach equilibrium. Correlating the temperature data from the borehole should even help pinpoint dates of deposition or climate changes. This area requires further research and will be the subject of a future paper.

HEAT CONDUCTION EQUATION Williams [35] or most fundamental heat transfer texts

Rate of Heat Flow In = Rate of Heat Flow out + Rate of Change of Heat Storage

$$\frac{\partial T}{\partial t} = \alpha \frac{\partial^2 T}{\partial x^2}$$ Differential form

This differential equation can be solved for a *semiinfinite solid* to yield the following Incropera & DeWitt [16]

$$\frac{T(x,t) - T_s}{T_i - T_s} = \operatorname{erf}\left(\frac{x}{\sqrt{2\alpha t}}\right) = \operatorname{erf} w \qquad t = \frac{1}{\alpha}\left[\frac{x}{2w}\right]^2$$

Boundary Conditions	
	$T(x,0) = T_i$
	$T(0,t) = T_s$
	$T_s \neq T_i$

Where:

$T(x,t)$ = Temperature at any depth x at any time t (m,sec) 0°C at desired depth (limit of permafrost)

T_s = Mean Surface Temperature (deg C)

T_i = Mean Initial Temperature of ground before T_s imposed assumed to be geothermal gradient of 3C/100m

x = Distance from surface (m)

α = Thermal Diffusivity (m^2/sec) = $\frac{\text{conductivity}}{\text{density} \times \text{specific heat}}$

t = Time since T_s was imposed on T_i (sec.)

erf = Gaussian Error Function (see Table)

Gaussian Error Function [16, Incropera & Dewitt]

w	erf w
0.00	0.00000
0.10	0.11246
0.20	0.22270
0.30	0.32863
0.40	0.42839
0.52	0.53790
0.60	0.60386
0.72	0.69143
0.80	0.74210
0.92	0.80677
1.00	0.84270
2.00	0.99532
3.00	0.99998

RESULTS Years to build various depths of permafrost at surface temp. of -20 & -40

depth (m)	Tuktoyaktuk $\alpha = 0.18 \times 10^{-6}$		Limestone Rock $\alpha = 1.14 \times 10^{-6}$	
	-20C	-40C	-20C	-40C
10	16	10	2.6	1.6
Tuktoyaktuk 35	150			
50	400	260	64	41
100	1600	1000	260	160
500	40000	26000	6400	4100
1000	160000	100000	26000	16000
Yakutsk 1400				
1500	365000	235000	58000	37000

Thermal Diffusivity α for various materials

Clay = 1.01×10^{-6} (m^2/sec)

Granite Rock = 1.37×10^{-6}

Limestone Rock = 1.14×10^{-6}

Sandstone Rock = 1.81×10^{-6}

Ice = 0.1×10^{-6}

Soil = 0.138×10^{-6}

Soil under Frozen Lake By Tuktoyaktuk = 0.18×10^{-6}

Iron pure 23.1×10^{-6}

Aluminum pure 97.1×10^{-6}

[16, Incropera & Dewitt]

Fig. 5a Transient Heat Conduction for a **semiinfinite solid**

Items ignored in permafrost calculations	Expected effect on time
latent heat of solidification (it takes as much energy to freeze 1 lb of water as it does to cool it 144 degF)	doubles or triples the years (Williams 1989)
water movement in the permafrost region	increases the time
chemical reactions within the strata	most are exothermic so would increase the time
radioactive decay	increase the time
Geothermal heat flow from below (world average is 0.04 W/m²or enough to melt 1/5 inch of ice per year) see Strahler1976	increases the time
Increased thermal diffusivity with depth	decreases the time but diffusivity will only change slightly with depths to 1500 m
Initial ground created frozen or near zero	greatly decreases the time. How then did the fossils get into the strata ?

Fig. 5b Conditions Effecting Frost Penetration Rates.

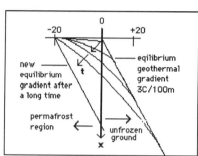

Fig. 5c Temperature isotherm development with time in response to a sudden drop in temp. of -20 toward a new equilibrium gradient.

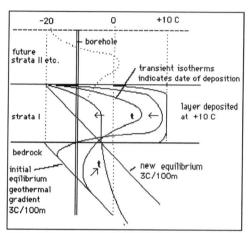

Fig. 5d Transient temperature isotherm development with deposit of unfrozen strata on top of existing permafrost

Seasons

Genesis 1:14 and 8:22 seem to indicate seasons, thus axial tilt, but in Ps.104:19 the moon is a season (same Hebrew word mo-aw-daw), Strong [29, Hebrew word #4150].

Perhaps Genesis 1:14 may be read as ... let them be for signs and wonders and for months and days, and years. The moon may have kept a perfect 30 day month. This also is in keeping with the text's important role of the moon.

Gen. 8:22 has also been cited to indicate pre-Flood seasons but here is read in the context of , from now on , ... while the earth remains ... summer and winter... Gen. 9:12 clearly indicates that the author is speaking ...for all successive generations.

It is also important to realize that even Hawaii has seasons though the summer/winter temperature variation is only a few degrees.

If Adam and Eve were to be comfortable naked in the garden there could only have been very mild seasons. Today the Tigris and Euphrates Rivers, if the location of the Garden of Eden, experiences 70 deg.F. temperature swings, see National Geographic [23]. It is doubtful that the Canopy could have moderated such a large temperature differential.

293

THE MOON

Day 4

The sun, the moon and the universe were created. (Note: earth then heavens in Gen. 2:4, Ps. 102:25, and Heb. 1:10) They were created to be a timepiece to early man. The year was made up of 360 days. Gen. 7:11 states that the Flood started on the seventeenth day of the second month. The flood prevailed until the 17 day of the seventh month which was 150 days (Gen. 8:3-4) so the months each had 30 days. A 360 day year is also suggested by Whitelaw [34] and others.

Fig.6 shows the geometry of the early sun-earth-moon system. Today the moon has an orbital period about the earth of 27.32 days. This means that the moon revolves around the earth (365.25/27.32=) 13.34 times per year. For the geometry of Fig.6 to work, the moon must revolve around the earth exactly 13 times per year. If the earth is moved closer to the sun to give a 360 day year the moon would revolve around the earth (360/27.32=) 13.18 times per year. For the moon to revolve exactly 13 times per year the earth would have to revolve around the sun in (13 x 27.32=) 355.16 days. This would mean that the earth would have to be 91.8 million miles away from the sun instead of the present 93.5 million miles.

Perhaps the forces and energy exchange involved in a close pass of a near earth-sized object slightly slowed the earth's rotation rate from 360 days per year to the 355.16 of our days required to make the moon a perfect calendar. The same or another fly-by could then have caused the earth to move to its present larger 365.25 day/year orbit. It would be interesting to calculate the energy lost in rotation and compare it with the energy gain in the larger orbit. It is also important to realize that for a rotating body there is a torque exerted on it equal to it's moment of inertia (I) times the change in rotation rate (omega/time); that is Torque = I * (delta omega/delta time), see Halliday [8]. This may be the source of the torque which toppled the earth over and is left for future research.

Note in Table 1 that the earth's moon has a low orbital eccentricity and is synchronous, suggesting that its orbit has not been altered.

Whitelaw [34] has already suggested that the earth's day has been altered to accommodate a perfect 30 day month.

The original Roman calendar was lunar. The months were based on the moon's synodic period; each month began with a new moon. It was not until 46 B.C. that Julius Caesar instigated a calendar reform, see Abell [1].

If the moon was created to circle the earth exactly 13 times per year, then the full moon marks the end of each month and the early peoples would have a perfect timepiece. One could just look up at the phase of the moon and see what day of the month it was.

Eclipses occur when the moon passes between the earth and sun along the line of nodes as shown in Fig.7. If the moon circled the earth on the solar ecliptic there would be a solar and lunar eclipse every month, but because the inclination of the moon's orbit to the ecliptic is 5 degrees, an eclipse only occurs when the sun is along or nearly along the line of nodes. There exists a geometry, for the early created system, where there would be a total solar eclipse for 7 minutes at exactly the same time every year. Perhaps this was the sign marking the end of the year for the early peoples. The same geometry may also have produce a lunar eclipse marking the middle of the year.

It is interesting to note that the 360 degree circle matches the 360 day year inferring that perhaps early man understood the earth and moon's orbital nature.

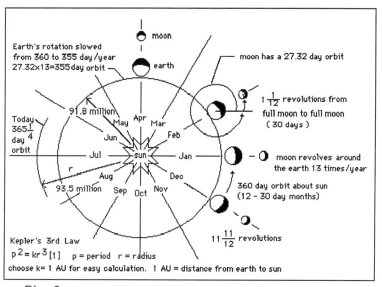

Fig. 6 Geometry for the moon to keep a perfect 30 day 12 month year.

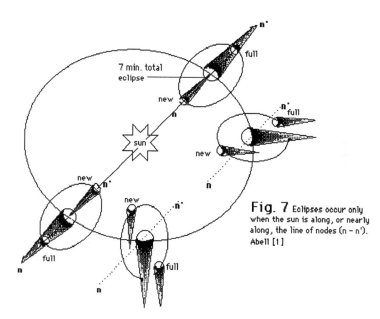

Fig. 7 Eclipses occur only when the sun is along, or nearly along, the line of nodes (n – n'). Abell [1]

THE TILT OF THE EARTH'S AXIS

As seen above, the Canopy would need symmetry and a near zero axial tilt. Table 1 shows that all the major moons of the solar system orbit about their planet's equator within a degree or two. Note that the moons that do not orbit about their planet's equator have large orbital eccentricity or have retrograde orbits which could indicate capture or some external influences.

The earth's moon orbits from 18 to 28 degrees about the earth's equator. This is not what would be expected when compared to the orbital data of all the satellites of the solar system. The moon's orbital inclination to the solar ecliptic is 5 degrees,see Abell & Morrison [1], so one might suspect that the early earth also had its equator (axial tilt) at a maximum of 5 degrees. Perhaps the Canopy could have tolerated a maximum of 5 degree angle of inclination. Figure 8 shows the calculation required to show that at a 5 degree angle of inclination any atmosphere above 24 km (80,000 feet) would receive continuous solar radiation. Note that these calculations assume that the solar rays strike the earth in a parallel fashion. Because the sun has a diameter of 108 earths, the rays will strike the poles at a very slight angle thus reducing the 24 km level of continuous light. This further supports a thin 50 mb. Canopy which would have had an 18 km. vapor to air boundary.

In 1873 J.N. Stockwell calculated the history and future of the earth's axial tilt, taking into account all known forces from the sun and planets. Simon Newcomb fit Stockwell's data into an empirical formula and published it. Newcomb's formula has been accepted for many years as the international standard, see Overn [24].

Setterfield [26] and Overn [24] have observed that earth's tilt in the past does not fit Newcomb's formula when comparing it to data gathered from various historical records. We are forced to look for other external influences to account for the discrepancies.

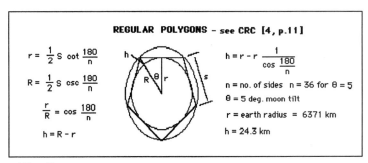

REGULAR POLYGONS – see CRC [4, p.11]

$$r = \frac{1}{2} S \cot \frac{180}{n}$$

$$R = \frac{1}{2} S \csc \frac{180}{n}$$

$$\frac{r}{R} = \cos \frac{180}{n}$$

$$h = R - r$$

$$h = r - r \frac{1}{\cos \frac{180}{n}}$$

n = no. of sides n = 36 for θ = 5

θ = 5 deg. moon tilt

r = earth radius = 6371 km

h = 24.3 km

Fig. 8   Calculating height of continuous sunlight for a 5 deg. tilt.

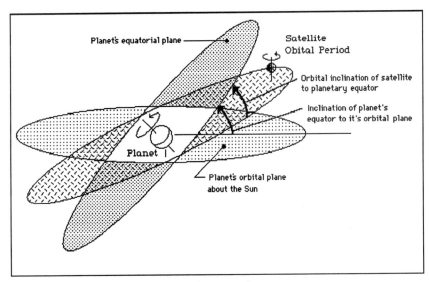

Planet's equatorial plane

Satellite
Obital Period

Orbital inclination of satellite
to planetary equator

Inclination of planet's
equator to it's orbital plane

Planet

Planet's orbital plane
about the Sun

Fig. 9 Geometry of Orbiting Satellites (see Table 1)

Planet	Inclination of Equator to Orbit (1)	Satellite	Orbital Inclination to Planetary Equator (2)	Orbital Period (days) (3)	Orbital Eccentricity (4)	Sidereal Period of Rotation (5)
Mercury	0.0					
Venus	177.3					
Earth	23.45	Moon	18.28-28.58	27.32	0.0549	S
Mars	25.19	I Phobos	1.0	0.319	0.015	S
		II Deimos	0.9-2.7	1.262	0.0005	S
Jupiter	3.12	I IO	0.04	1.769	0.004	S
		II Europa	0.47	3.55	0.009	S
		III Ganymede	0.21	7.15	0.002	S
		IV Callisto	0.51	16.69	0.007	S
		V Amalthea	0.40	0.50	0.003	S
		VI Himalia	27.63	250.60	0.158	0.4
		VII Elara	24.77	260.70	0.207	0.5
		VIII Pasiphae	145.00	735.00R	0.378	
		IX Sinope	153.00	758.00R	0.275	
		X Lysithea	29.02	259.00	0.107	
		XI Carme	164.00	692.00R	0.207	
		XII Ananke	147.00	631.00R	0.169	
		XIII Leda	26.07	239.00	0.148	
		XIV Thebe	0.80	0.67	0.015	
		XV Adrastea		0.30		
		XVI Metis		0.29		0.05
Saturn	26.73	I Mimas	1.53	0.942	0.0202	S
		II Enceladus	0.00	1.37	0.0045	S
		III Tethys	1.86	1.89	0.000	S
		IV Dione	0.02	2.74	0.002	S
		V Rhea	0.35	4.52	0.001	S
		VI Titan	0.33	15.94	0.029	S
		VII Hyperion	0.43	21.30	0.104	
		VIII Iapetus	14.72	79.33	0.028	S
		IX Phoebe	177.00	550.48R	0.163	0.4
		X Janus	0.14	0.69	0.007	S
		XI Epi-metheus	0.34	0.69	0.009	S
		XII 1980S6	0.00	2.74	0.005	
		XIII Telesto		1.89		
		XIV Calypso		1.89		
		XV Atlas	0.30	0.60	0.000	
		1980S26	0.00	0.63	0.004	
		1980S27	0.00	0.61	0.003	
Uranus (6)	97.86	I Ariel	0.30	2.52	0.0034	
		II Umbriel	0.36	4.14	0.005	
		III Titania	0.14	8.71	0.0022	
		IV Oberon	0.10	13.46	0.0008	S
		V Miranda	4.20	1.41	0.0027	
Neptune	29.56	I Triton	159.0	5.88R	< 0.01	S
		II Neried	27.6	360.2	0.75	
Pluto	118.0?	Charon	94.0	6.39		

Notes: (1)   See Fig. 9. These values from Abell, Morrison, and Wolff [1];   (2) See Fig. 9.
(3)   R = retrograde orbit (in opposite direction)
(4)   Ratio of the distance between the foci to the major axis of an elliptical orbit. A perfectly circular orbit has an orbital eccentricity of zero.
(5)   Satellite's period of rotation about itself. S indicates synchronous rotation (i.e., staellite rotates once for every revolution about the planet, making one side always face the planet.
(6)   More moons have been found around Uranus since this data, See DeYoung [5].

How Did The Earth's Axis Change?

The most intriguing mechanism for changing the earth's axis are fast pole shifts as suggested by Warlow [33]. Warlow maintains that the earth has experienced several fast pole shifts or inversions as shown in Fig.4. Warlow realized that the Earth can, in theory, be turned over in two ways: ether by moving the globe with its axis of rotation (astronomical pole shift Fig.4a), or by moving the globe about a fixed axis of rotation (geographical pole shift Fig.4b), see Huggett [13]. Astronomical pole shifts are easy enough to visualize by just turning over a globe. Geographical pole shifts are much more difficult to visualize. In a Geographical pole shift, the earth actually turns over while maintaining it's rotation as seen from space. This has the effect of actually reversing the direction of rotation. This can be demonstrated by a toy 'tippe top'.

A geographical pole shift will also produce a magnetic reversal and cause the sun to now rise in the west and set in the east. The following comments can be made regarding such inversions. Statements are quoted directly from the paper by Warlow [33].

Note:
The concept of a geographic inversion is difficult to visualize and it is suggested that a globe be used to help understand what is actually happening.

A perfect rotating sphere takes little to no energy to induce an inversion Gold 1955.

Note:
Brown [3], and later Hapgood [10], and Whitelaw [34] have all suggested that the earth could experience a fast pole shift with rapid growth of polar ice caps. The earth has an equatorial bulge but the energy required for inversion is small relative to the primary spin energy. Warlow uses a magic 'tippe top', available in most toy or science stores, to demonstrate the small external torque required for inversion. The friction between the table and the 'tippe top' is enough to invert it.

Most investigators agree on the rapidity of change. Many workers are forced to conclude that sedimentation, glaciation, climate, water temperature, polar wander, and outbursts of volcanism occurred suddenly, and often such events occurred on a worldwide scale.

An ice age would require similar energy inputs as that required to turn the earth over.

A geographic inversion would also produce a geomagnetic reversal and explains the fact that the field does not pass through a zero state.

Note:
Warlow maintains that because the earth's sense of rotation does not change during an inversion, the earth's magnetic field as observed from space does not change. But because the earth is inverted, the field, as observed by someone on the earth's surface, would appear to be inverted. A little thought and practice with a globe will prove this to be true. If Warlow is correct then we should not observe any magnetic reversals before the Flood as the first geographic inversion would have destroyed the Canopy. Also partial reversals or shifts should be observed for the times when the earth did not roll right over. Humphreys [14] has proposed that rapid up-flows of electrically conducting fluids in the earth's mantle have caused magnetic reversals. If this is correct, large forces would be required to trigger the strong convection currents required in the earth's mantle. A fast pole shift inversion could have been that trigger.

What is likely, is that a series of events occur, each varying in degree of completeness of the reversal and including minor tilts, so that the earth is left rotating about different poles between the events. These intermediate poles would then be recorded in the rock magnetism and they would show an alignment about a particular secondary axis during a limited geological period.

The inversion would take place quickly in as little as one day. The devastation caused would be less then one would at first suspect. At a uniform acceleration and deceleration there would only be 1/1000 of a 'g' force. This is hardly sufficient to spill one drop from a brim-full glass of water, but of course the effects on the oceans and other large bodies of water, and on the air masses would be considerable. The land masses too, resting on their viscous support, would show marked stress.

An earth turnover provides an explanation that accounts for the detailed behavior of the field during a reversal. Such a motion produces massive tidal waves, carrying vast quantities of debris and sediment from the ocean floors and depositing them over the land. The inevitable severe storms as the atmosphere tries to adjust to the new positioning of surface features will be augmented by ash and gas ejected by the equally inevitable volcanic activity. The continental plates themselves would be set in motion.

Note:
Baumgardner [2] requires a trigger for breaking up the oceanic lithosphere in his model. A pole inversion is an ideal mechanism.

Studies of polar wander have associated magnetic polar wander with wander of glaciated regions. Moving the earth's axis provides a better fit with the data then does the concept of plate drift alone. The glaciation in the recent ice age was not uniformly increased about the pole but is best described as a displacement of the polar cap. As the North American ice cap advanced south by 20 deg. the Siberian ice cap actually retreated by 10 degrees.

Note:
As shown by Vigdorchik [31] there is extensive submerged permafrost in the Arctic Ocean indicating ocean level changes.

A simply cooling of the earth would only extend a thin layer of permafrost uniformly around the poles. It would not yield massive glaciers. Displacement of the polar cap requires neither heating nor cooling and this is in keeping with the general evidence that the earth was not cooled overall during ice ages.

The very rapidly frozen mammoth remains would be explained by a rapid pole shift.

Note:
Helfinstine [11] has suggested that mammoth remains can be shown to have been deposited by a large tidal wave flowing northward across Siberia over the north pole into northern Europe and North America. He maintains this event can be traced to the Exodus of the Israelites from Egypt (Fig. 4c).

North American ice sheets are compatible with the concept of rapid shifts of the geographic pole and polar ice cap along the 60 deg. W. 120 deg E preferred magnetic polar wander path.

As the axis tilts the equatorial bulge will be shifted causing drastic sea level alteration. Today's difference in polar and equatorial radii is 21,500 meters (70,000 feet). In practice there is not enough sea to reach that extreme.

Catastrophic overturns observed in lake waters occur at the same periods all over the globe.

Cause Of Geographic Inversions

Warlow concludes that the meeting with another cosmic body of comparable size and in close proximity for a brief period would be required to produce an inversion. This body may have been in orbit around the sun with an earth-crossing orbit which would help explain the repeated occurrences observed (Fig.4c & Fig.10). Future research is required to detect reoccurrences at equal intervals. The most likely candidate would be a now destroyed planet which had its orbit in the asteroid belt between Mars and Jupiter (Fig.10). This would help explain the multiple geographic inversions that seem to have occurred. If the source of inversions collided with the planet Ceres producing the asteroid belt as suggested by Velikovsky then it would have to have an elliptic earth-crossing orbit as suggested by Whitelaw [34]. Today there are numerous asteroids which have an earth-crossing orbit. Huggett [13] has also suggested that geographic imbalances might just be enough to cause a pole shift.

Biblical Support For Fast Pole Shifts (Fig. 4c)

On the long day in Joshua 10:12 note that the moon stopped as well as the sun. This is just how an astronomical 12 hour pole shift would appear from the right spot on earth (Fig.4a). Fig.4ai shows the sun's path as it would appear to Joshua. An astronomical pole shift would cause the sun to appear to stop in the middle of the sky for a period of 12 hours and then set in the west. I could not get a geographical pole shift to make the sun appear to stand still. Joshua 10:13 does specifically state a whole day (inferring a 24-hour day) but this is taken to mean from sunrise to sunset. It is also interesting to note that in Joshua 10:11 great stones from the sky fell on the Amorites. Falling debris could very easily be associated with a rapid pole shift caused by a close fly-by of an extraterrestrial body.

In 2 Kings 20:9-11 and Isaiah 38:8 the sun went back 10 steps. This could indicate a partial geographic pole shift which in some parts would appear to be a west to east shift.

Amos 5:8 states that God darkens day into night and calls for waters of the sea and pours them out on the surface of the earth. This is not unlike what would occur in a fast pole shift.

Amos 8:9-10 talks about the sun going down at noon and there will be a time of mourning as for an only son. The Gospels all record that the sun was darkened from noon till 3p.m. the day Jesus was crucified in 30 AD. (Matthew

27:45,Mark 15:33,Luke 23:44-45). Matthew 27:51 also mentions that the earth shook and rocks were split. One can not argue that this was a solar eclipse as a total solar eclipse only lasts about 7 minutes. If an earth-crossing planet crossed in-between the earth and sun as shown in Fig.10 then perhaps there could have been a 3 hour total solar eclipse.

Isaiah 24:1 (King James Version) literally says the earth is turned upside down which is a polar inversion.

Job 9:6 indicates the earth has been shaken out of its place, further supporting the creation of a 360 day year.

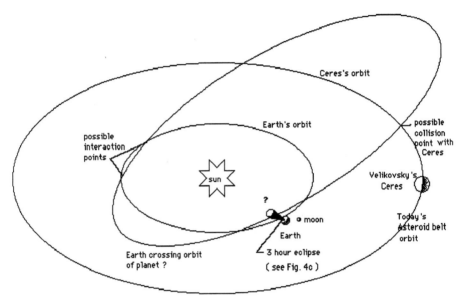

Fig. 10 Possible explanation of 3 hour eclipse in Luke 23:45 as well as source of fast pole shifts.

Other Earth History Supporting Inversions

Items are quoted directly from the Warlow [33] article.

> Plato wrote: God himself guides and helps to roll the world ... and there is a time ... when he lets go, and the world turns about and by an inherent necessity revolves in the opposite direction. Hence there occurs a great destruction of animals which extends also to the life of man.

> Herodotus the Egyptian claims that the sun had reversed its direction four times within their recorded history. The 18th dynasty tomb of Senmut has an astronomical ceiling which appears to be reversed.

> In Chinese records there is a reference to the sun setting and then rising again soon afterwards.

> In Mexican annals there is a reference to the night lasting a long time.

Note:
Velikovsky believed that two cataclysmic events occurring 3500 and 2700 years ago were documented in many historical writings, see Huggett [13]. It is interesting to note that 2700 years is in good agreement with the sun going back ten steps in Isa. 38.8 and 3500 years ago is in good agreement with Joshua's long day (Fig.4c).

CONCLUSIONS

An initial attempt has been made to systematize different areas of study in that the Canopy, the moon, the tilt of the earth's axis, multiple ice ages, and geological history are all related and supported by Scriptures.

Fast pole shifts are an intriguing mechanism in correlating the various events involved in altering the earth's axis. It is also hoped that it has been shown that there is ample evidence supporting a near zero angle of inclination for the early earth, crucial to the Canopy. Fast pole shifts provides a method for the perfect symmetry necessary for the Canopy and also provides added insight into the Canopy's destruction as all trade winds and ocean currents are reversed during a geographical pole shift.

In addition, this Canopy hypothesis also supports the Scripture's teaching that the earth was created before the sun, moon, and stars.

The fact that the moon may have been a perfect timepiece to early man is a very intriguing concept and seems to be in keeping with Genesis 1:14-19.

Finally the realization that borehole temperature gradients of the various strata may demonstrate a transient temperature profile, thus young age, is very intriguing and deserves further investigation.

BIBLIOGRAPHY

[1]   Abell, G.O. Morrison, D. & Wolff, S.C. **Exploration of the Universe**, 1987, Saunders College, Lunar orbit, p.117, Early calendars, p.109-113

[2]   Baumgardner, J.R., **3-D Finite Element Simulation of the Global Tectonic Changes Accompanying Noah's Flood**, Proceedings Second International Conference on Creationism, Editors: Robert E. Walsh, et al, Creation Science Fellowship, Inc., Pittsburgh, PA, 1991, p.35

[3]   Brown, H. A., **Popular awakening concerning the impending flood**, Published by the author., 1948.

[4]   CRC Standard Mathematical Tables, (1971), 19th Regular Polygons Formulae p.11.

[5]   DeYoung, D.B., Review Comment, 1993.

[6]   Flint, R. F., **Features Other Than Diamicts as Evidence of Ancient Glaciations, Ice Ages: Ancient and Modern**, Seel House Press, Liverpool, 1975, pp. 121-136.

[7]   Guinness Book of World Records, Bantam Books, Deepest Permafrost, 1990, p.131.

[8]   Halliday, David, & Resnick, Robert, **Fundamentals of Physics**, second ed., John Wiley & Sons Inc., New York, NY, Table 12-2, 1981, p.189.

[9]   Hambrey M. J. & Harland W. B., **Earth's Pre-Pleistocene Glacial Record**, Cambridge University Press, 1981.

[10]   Hapgood, C. H., **Earth's Shifting Crust**, New York, Pantheon Books, 1958.

[11]   Helfinstine, Robert, **Mammoth Remains: What Do They Really Indicate?**, Proceedings 1992 Twin Cities Creation Conference, Minneapolis, MN, 1992, p.14.

[12]   Houghton, J.T., **The Physics of Atmospheres**, Cambridge University Press, 1986, Fig. 12.9, p.199.

[13]   Huggett, Richard, **Catastrophism Systems of Earth History**, Edward Arnold, 1990, pp.118-124.

[14]   Humphreys, D.R., **Physical Mechanism for Reversals of the Earth's Magnetic Field During the Flood**, Proceedings Second International Conference on Creationism, Editors: Robert E. Walsh, et al, Creation Science Fellowship, Inc., Pittsburgh, PA, 1991, p.129.

[15]   Imbrie, J.& K., **Ice Ages Solving the Mystery**, Enslow Publishers, 1979, Fig. 25, p.107

[16]   Incropera, Frank P. & Dewitt, David P., **Fundamentals of Heat Transfer**, John Wiley & Sons, New York, NY, 1981, Table A.3.

[17]   Jorgensen, G.S., **A Computer Model of the Pre-Flood Atmosphere**, Proceedings Second International Conference on Creationism, Editors: Robert E. Walsh, et al, Creation Science Fellowship, Inc., Pittsburgh, PA, 1991, p.143.

[18]   Jorgensen, G.S., **Fundamental Physics of a Water Vapor Atmosphere**, Proceedings 1992 Twin Cities Creation Conference, Minneapolis, MN, 1992, p.40.

[19]   Lide, D.R., **CRC Handbook of Chemistry and Physics 73rd**, 1993, 14:26-30

[20]   Miller & Thompson, **Elements of Meteorology**, Charles E. Merrill, 1975, p43.

[21]   Molen, Mats, **Diamictites: Ice-Age Or Gravity Flows?**, Proceedings Second International Conference on Creationism, Editors: Robert E. Walsh, et al., Creation Science Fellowship, Inc., Pittsburgh, PA, 1991, p.177.

[22]   National Academy of Sciences, **Permafrost North American Contribution 2nd**, p.227.

[23]   **Atlas Of The World Fourth Edition**, National Geographic, National Geographic Society, Washington, D.C., 1975.

[24]   Overn, B., **The Tilt of Earth's Axis, and Magnetic Reversals**, Proceedings 1992 Twin Cities Creation Conference, Minneapolis, MN, 1992, p.85.

[25] Rush, D.E. & Vardiman, L., **Pre-Flood Vapor Canopy Radiative Temperature Profiles**, Proceedings Second International Conference on Creationism, Editors: Robert E. Walsh, et al, Creation Science Fellowship, Inc., Pittsburgh, PA, 1991, p.231.

[26] Setterfield, B., **The Recent Change in The Tilt of the Earth's Axis**, Science At The Crossroads: Observation or Speculation? Proceedings 1983 National Creation Conference, Onesimus Publishing, Richfield, MN, 1983, p.82.

[27] Strahler, A.N. & H. Alan, H., **Elements of Physical Geography**, John Wiley & Sons, New York, NY, 1984.

[28] Strahler, A.N., Principles of Earth Science, Harper & Row, New York, NY, 1976, p.282.

[29] Strong, J., Strong's Exhaustive Concordance of the Bible, Abingdom, Hebrew word for *seasons*, Strong's #4150, 1980.

[30] ------------, Hebrew word for *moved*, Strong's #7363

[31] Vigdorchik, Michael E., **Arctic Pleistocene History and Development of Submarine Permafrost**, Westview Press, Boulder, Colorado, Fig 3.8, Permafrost zone under the Arctic Ocean. see conclusion, 1980, p.241.

[32] Walk Thru The Old Testament, Seminar Notebook, Walk Thru the Bible Ministry, Atlanta, Georgia, Chronological Synthesis of the Old Testament, 1981.

[33] Warlow, P. **Geomagnetic Reversals?**, Journal of Physics, A:Math. Gen. Vol. 11, No. 10, Printed in Great Britain, 1978, pp.2107-2130.

[34] Whitelaw, Robert L., **The Fountains of the Deep, and the Windows of Heaven**, Science At The Crossroads: Observation or Speculation? Proceedings 1983 National Creation Conference, Onesimus Publishing, Richfield, MN, 1983, p.95.

[35] Williams, Peter J. and Michael W. Smith, **The Frozen Earth Fundamentals of Geocryology**, Cambridge University Press, eq.(4.5) p.85, effect on time of freezing 1989, p.93-94.

[36] Zumberge, J.H. & Nelson, C.A., **Elements of Physical Geology**, John Wiley & Sons, New York, NY, Precambrian Glaciation, 1976, p.318.

THE ORIGIN OF ATOMIC STRUCTURE

JOSEPH C. LUCAS
CHARLES W. LUCAS, JR. PH.D.
4511 POPPE PLACE
TEMPLE HILLS, MD 20748

KEYWORDS

ATOM, MACH'S CRITERIA, COMBINATORIAL GEOMETRY, RING MODEL, FINITE SIZE EFFECTS, MAGNETIC MOMENT, LOGIC, EVOLUTION THEORY, THEORETICAL FOUNDATION, SHELLS, PACKING MODEL

ABSTRACT

Historically the theory of evolution has always been an appendage of the theory of matter and specifically the theory of the atom. The current quantum mechanical theories of the atom represent the matter of the universe as being governed by random statistical processes. Thus they provide the necessary theoretical foundations for the theory of evolution. The theory of evolution of living things requires random processes to occur to produce mutations or changes that can be directed by certain selection principles, such as survival of the fittest.

This work identifies the false assumptions of the quantum models of the atom. It shows that these theories violate the logical principles that undergird the development of scientific theories and do not qualify as science. A new rudimentary theory of the atom based on combinatorial geometry is presented that can satisfactorily predict all the properties of the periodic table of the elements as well as explain the basis of chemical valence and bonding. This new theory of the atom is based on classical electrodynamics and represents an orderly universe governed by the laws of cause and effect. It satisfies the logical principles undergirding science, and it does not support theories of evolution.

INTRODUCTION

According to Encyclopedia Britannica's Great Books of the Western World the idea of evolution is one of the 100 great ideas of western civilization. In the two volume syntopicon for the great books[16], the history of the idea of evolution is traced from the ancient philosophers Democritus, Lucretius, Plato, and Aristotle down to Harvey, Freud, and Darwin. For 2500 years the idea or theory of evolution has been an appendage to the theory of matter.

The ancient theory of matter, called atomism, as well as the current modern theory of the atom based upon the relativisitc quantum-mechanical Dirac equation describe matter as governed by statistically random chance processes. From the beginning the theory of evolution involved the evolution of physical matter as well as living things. Both aspects require that the parent theory of matter support the existence of statistically random chance processes that will allow changes in nature over time. For living things these changes are supposedly subject to some selection principles, such as selection of the fittest, to determine the direction of evolutionary change.

The Bible represents the earth as having been created in an orderly purposeful fashion and not by random chaotic events.

> **For thus says the Lord, who created the heavens (he is God!), who formed the earth and made it (he established it, he did not create it a chaos, he formed it to be inhabited!): "I am the Lord, and there is no other. I did not speak in secret, in a land of darkness; I did not say to the offspring of Jacob, 'Seek me in chaos.' I the Lord speak the truth, I declare what is right."**
> **(Isaiah 45:18-19 RSV)**

The biblical description of the earth is in strong disagreement with the current theory of matter based upon relativistic quantum electrodynamics (QED) which describes the universe as being governed by random statistical processes or chaos.

In recent years scientists in the Judeo-Christian community have become aware of the situation. They have investigated the fundamental assumptions of relativity theory and found many of them to be false[9,14]. The logical rules upon which the scientific method has been based for thousands of years, commonly known as Mach's Critria for Scientific Propositions[17], do not allow any theories in science whose assumptions are known to be false.

Physicists Tom Barnes[1] and Charles Lucas[10,11] discovered an error had been made in electrodynamics in that the finite size and charge structure of elementary particles had been approximated by a point particle representation. They went on to show by rigorous derivation from classical electrodynamics that the equilibrium shape of finite-size elementary particles changes with velocity from spherical to ellipsoidal. Their derivations showed that the change in the shape of elementary particles at high velocity was responsible for the "so-called" relativistic effects. These include the change in the particle's electromagnetic fields at high velocity, the change of the particle's mass at high velocity, the change in the particle's binding energy at high velocity, the change in unstable particle's half-life at high velocity, as well as the general relativistic formulas for velocity and energy, i.e. $E = mc^2$.

The work of Barnes and Lucas on finite size particles was significant, especially since relativity theory assumes all particles are point-like particles. This point particle assumption is also central to the Dirac quantum theory of the atom and the nuclear quantum shell model.

The purpose of this paper is twofold. The first purpose is to identify the false assumptions of the quantum mechanical models of the atom. The second purpose is to present the foundation for a new model of the atom. Using combinatorial geometry a new rudimentary model of the atom is developed. This new model represents an orderly universe governed by the laws of cause and effect instead of random chance processes.

False Assumptions of the Quantum Model of the Atom

The first widely held quantum model of the atom was known as the Bohr model. It was a planetary model in which the electrons moved in orbits about the nucleus with specific angular momenta. The Bohr model was based upon the following postulates:[3]

o   An atom, consisting of a nucleus together with its system of electrons, possesses certain dynamical states having the property that as long as the atom remains in one of these states it does not radiate.

o   The dynamical equilibrium of the special states of the atom can be treated by ordinary mechanics; but the transitions between them can not be so treated and are not subject to explicit description.

o   When an atom makes a transition from state of energy E_1, to another, of lower energy E_2, the excess energy is emitted as radiation of a single frequency, v, related to the energy difference by Planck's relationship, $E_1 - E_2 = hv$.

o   For a single electron moving in an orbit around the nucleus, the angular momentum, L, is an integer multiple of $h/(2\pi) = \hbar$.

These postulates were deliberately designed to cover up the inadequacies of the model. For instance all electrons moving in a planetary orbit about the nucleus with a specific angular momentum should radiate electromagnetic energy continuously and eventually fall into the nucleus according to the empirical laws of electrodynamics. The first postulate says that the electron will not radiate electromagnetic radiation without any physical explanation or basis. According to Mach's Criterion for scientific theories, such an assumption is not allowable in science.

Bohr's second postulate is similar. It says that the transitions between electronic equilibrium states of the atom can not be calculated or understood using the proven laws of electrodynamics. Thus we see that Bohr's quantum model of the atom is not fully compatible with the empirical laws of electrodynamics.

After DeBroglie[4] showed that particles should possess wave properties, Schrodinger[15] combined the matter wave idea with Hamilton's formulation of Newtonian mechanics to obtain the equation for matter waves. This matter wave approach was found to be able to describe the states of matter in the atom more successfully than the Bohr model.

The Schrodinger matter wave model for the atom had the same problems with electrodynamics as the Bohr model and used similar postulates. However, it had additional problems. The form of the Hamiltonian formulation that it used is for point matter particles involving only action-at-a-distance forces. For an electron with no size the Coulomb electrical forces are infinite attempting to blow it apart. Also the real world consists of only finite-size particles involving friction and other local forces.[6,7,8]

Another philosophical problem with the Schrodinger equation had to do with the interpretation of the matter wavefunction. Normally wavefunctions are observable as in the case of water waves and sound waves. However, this matter wavefunction involves a complex number, i.e. the square root of -1, so that it can not represent a real observable quantity. Real observable quantities are always real numbers. The customary interpretation given is that the matter wavefunction is a probability amplitude. The measureable quantity is the probability density, or absolute square of the probability amplitude, and describes the probability that the electron will be found in a given region of space. Unlike other types of waves, the electrons in the matter waves are not regarded as being distributed in a cloud according to the probability distribution.

In 1928 Dirac[5] developed a relativistic version of the matter wave equation, which is now called the Dirac equation. He incorporated the magnetic moment and spin of the point electron into the matter wave equation in a more fundamental way than Schrodinger had done. The Dirac equation enabled the prediction of the existence of the positron, which was subsequently found experimentally. Despite this success, the Dirac model suffered from using exactly the same logically bad assumptions as the Schrodinger model.

In the late 1940's the theory of quantum electrodynamics was developed upon the foundation laid by Dirac much earlier. The quantum electrodynamic model of the atom is the most accurate one to date in terms of predicting the properties of the various electron energy states. However, it still has most of the same philosophical problems as the Schrodinger formulation.

Foundation for a New Model of the Atom

In 1990 Bergman[2] published the first fully successful physical model of the electron and other elementary particles. This model depicts the physical electron as a very thin ring of negative electric charge as shown in Figure 1. The charge is continuous around the ring. The ring rotates about its symmetry axis with a rim velocity approximately equal to the speed of light. The electric force of repulsion between the elements of charge in the ring is exactly balanced by the induced magnetic fields due to the current flow that causes a magnetic pinch effect. There is no radiation from the ring, because the charges occupy the entire circle of the ring continuously causing the total radiation field to vanish.[12]

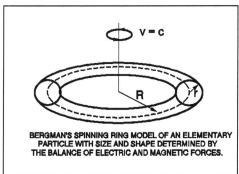

BERGMAN'S SPINNING RING MODEL OF AN ELEMENTARY
PARTICLE WITH SIZE AND SHAPE DETERMINED BY
THE BALANCE OF ELECTRIC AND MAGNETIC FORCES.

Figure 1

The essential weakness of previous models of the electron, including the Dirac model of the electron and QED models, has been that additional forces have had to be postulated ad hoc to hold the electron together against electrostatic repulsion. The Bergman model of the electron is completely stable under the action of classical electromagnetic forces alone. No strong or weak interaction forces mediated by quarks or other particles need be postulated.

The principal fundamental constant of quantum mechanics and all quantum models of elementary particles, including QED, is known as Planck's constant h. It can be determined entirely from classical electrodynamics in the Bergman model, i.e.,

$$h = e^2 \log(8R/r) / (2\pi\epsilon_o c) \tag{1}$$

where:

    h = Planck's constant
    e = charge of the electron
    c = velocity of light
    ϵ_o = dielectric constant for the vacuum
    R = radius of ring in Bergman's model
    r = half-thickness of ring in Bergman's model

Note that h depends on the size or dimensions of the internal structure of elementary particles. That structure is determined by the balance of electric and magnetic forces in the physical particle. According to the rules of logic, whenever one theory is able to derive the value of the fundamental constant of a second theory, it is automatically superior to that theory. Thus the Bergman model appears to be more fundamental than quantum mechanics and QED in which h is a fundamental constant.

The progress made by Bergman in modelling the physical electron and other elementary particles warrants a new attempt at a physical model of the atom. This is of particular interest to the Christian community, because these classical models of the atom would be consistent with a universe governed by order and purpose instead of random chance.

Previously Barnes[1] and Lucas[10,11] had shown that the principal results of relativity theory were due to changes in the shape of finite size elementary particles. In the case of the atom, the socalled "quantum effects" must be due to the finite size of the electron and its physical magnetic properties.

At the lowest level the structure of the atom is represented by the structure of the periodic table of the elements. This table may be thought of, in a physical sense, as showing how the electrons pack in layers about the nucleus.

There is a branch of geometry, called combinatorial geometry, which deals explicitly with physical problems of packing and covering. An example of this is the packing of equal sized disks in a plane about a central disk as shown in Figure 2. It is easily seen than six equal circular disks may be placed around another disk of the same size such that the central one is touched by all the others but no two overlap. In the three dimensional case, around a spherical ball it is possible to place twelve balls of equal size all touching the first one but not overlapping it or each other.

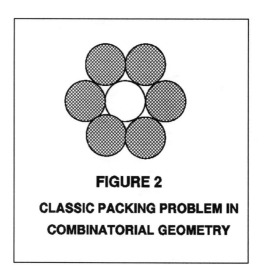

FIGURE 2

CLASSIC PACKING PROBLEM IN

COMBINATORIAL GEOMETRY

Now combinatorial geometry can also be used for the atom consisting of a central nucleus with finite size electrons packed about it in layers or shells. In this case there are some additional constraints. The balls or electrons are in the shape of a ring with a magnetic moment plus an electrical attraction to the nucleus.

From general symmetry principles it is assumed that each layer or shell must be constructed in such a way that the total magnetic moment of the filled or complete shell sums to zero. In other words the cancellation of the magnetic moments is perfectly spherical. This is equivalent to saying that all electrons in a shell or layer must lie on a great circle of the shell and that all great circles of the shell must have the same number of electrons with no net magnetic moment when the shell is filled.

The constraint above is angular in nature. A second constraint applies to the radial direction. Dipole magnets are three dimensional and tend to arrange themselves in layers such that the magnetic moment of the atom is cancelled out even in the radial direction. In order for the magnetic moments to be cancelled out in the near vicinity of the shell, a second shell of the same symmetry but opposite orientation is needed.

The electrical attraction of each negative electron shell with the positively charged nucleus decreases with increasing shell size. This leads to a third constraint on the packing. A larger shell can displace a smaller one with fewer charges providing the space it occupies is large enough to hold the larger shell. This contraint allows larger shells to displace the second shell of a pair of smaller shells.

The three constraints above will change the results of the packing from that obtained for solid spheres. These constraints will produce an infinite series of packing layers that can be compared with the shells or periods of the periodic table.

Combinatorial geometry, like Euclidean geometry, uses the method of proofs. The method that will be employed here is the method of enumeration, i.e. all cases are listed and the ones that satisfy the constraints are selected.

Consider the first shell. The first electron attracted to the nucleus can not be the first complete shell, because its magnetic moment is not zero. Also the shell can not be spherically symmetric. The smallest number of electrons to be attracted to the nucleus to make a shell that has zero magnetic moment and is spherically symmetric is two electrons as shown in Figure 3. There is one great circle with two charges symmetrically placed. The magnetic moments are alligned with the radial direction. They are perpendicular to the surface of the shell.

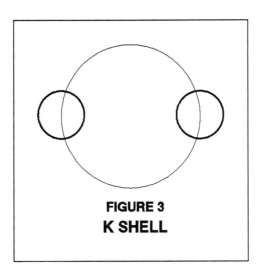

FIGURE 3
K SHELL

The orientation of the magnetic moments can be understood in terms of symmetry and balance of forces. Electrons are attracted to the positively charged nucleus by their negative charge, since opposite charges attract. They are repulsed by the nucleus according to Lenz's law and conservation of energy, by the orientation of their magnetic moments. Here, like magnetic poles repulse one another. The magnetic repulsion exactly balances the electric attraction at some value of the distance between the electron and the nucleus.

Now the second size of electron shell could have up to twelve electrons if the first shell had one electron. But, since the first shell has two electrons, the number could be even larger. What is the smallest number of electrons that could make a completely symmetric shell and have more than two electrons in it? In order to find the answer, one can attempt to construct symmetrical arrangements of 3, 4, 5, ... electrons until the next completely symmetrical shell is found. In this manner it is found to contain eight electrons as shown in Figure 4. Note that there are two symmetrical great circles. Each has four charges symmetrically placed. Any great circle drawn through any electron will always contain four electrons. The magnetic moments are alligned radially with the nucleus.

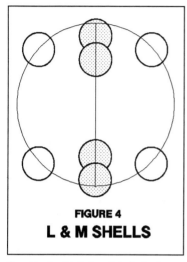

FIGURE 4
L & M SHELLS

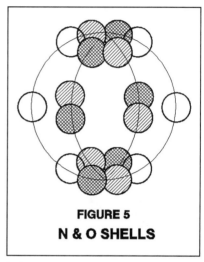

FIGURE 5
N & O SHELLS

Consider the third size of shell. Again one may construct symmetrical arrangments of 9, 10, 11, ... electrons until one the next completely symmetrical shell is found to be eighteen as shown in Figure 5. Here there are three great circles. Each has six electrons symmetrically placed. The magnetic moments are alligned radially with the nucleus.

The result for each progressive layer size can now be predicted. By inspection each successive shell consists of one more great circle. The number of electrons in each circle is exactly twice the number of great circles due to symmetry requirements. The magnetic moments of the electrons each point radially away from the nucleus for the first layer of each shell size. The magnetic moment of the electrons in the second shell of each size point inward to balance the outward pointing shell.

Thus, by enumeration one notes that the successive shell sizes that satisfy the combinatorial geometry packing constraints are:

        Shell size #1 - 1 great circle of 2 electrons (Figure 3)
        Shell size #1 - 2 great circle of 4 electrons (Figure 4)
        Shell size #1 - 3 great circle of 6 electrons (Figure 5)
        Shell size #1 - 4 great circle of 8 electrons (Figure 6)
        Shell size #1 - 5 great circle of 10 electrons

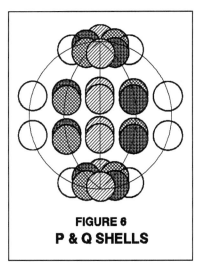

FIGURE 6
P & Q SHELLS

These are the magic numbers or sizes of the shells in the periodic table of the elements. According to constraint #2 above there are two shells of each shell size. However the first shell size is paired with the nucleus itself as its partner. Table I below summarizes the periodic table information from the use of combinatorial geometry. Note the arrows showing the opposite orientation of the magnetic moments of each shell with another.

TABLE 1
Distribution of Elements in Periodic Table Shells

# Elements	Total # Electrons in	K	L	M	N	O	P	Q shell
2	2	N-> <-2						
8	10	U-> <-2	8->					
8	18	C-> <-2	8->	<-8				
18	36	L-> <-2	8->	<-8	18->			
18	54	E-> <-2	8->	<-8	18-> <-18			
32	86	U-> <-2	8->	<-8	18-> <-18	32->		
32	118	S-> <-2	8->	<-8	18-> <-18	32-> <-32		
.								
.								
.								

Taking into account the third constraint for packing will alter the order of some of the shells in the table above to the revised form given below.

TABLE 2
Revised Distribution of Elements in Periodic Table Shells

# Elements	Total # Electrons in	K	L	M	N	O	P	Q shell
2	2	N-> <-2						
8	10	U-> <-2	8->					
8	18	C-> <-2	8-> <-8					
18	36	L-> <-2	8-> <-18	8->				
18	54	E-> <-2	8-> <-18	18-> <-8				
32	86	U-> <-2	8-> <-18	32-> <-18	8->			
32	118	S-> <-2	8-> <-18	32-> <-32	18-> <-8			
.								
.								
.								

Figure 8 shows how these numbers correlate with the structure of the periodic table.

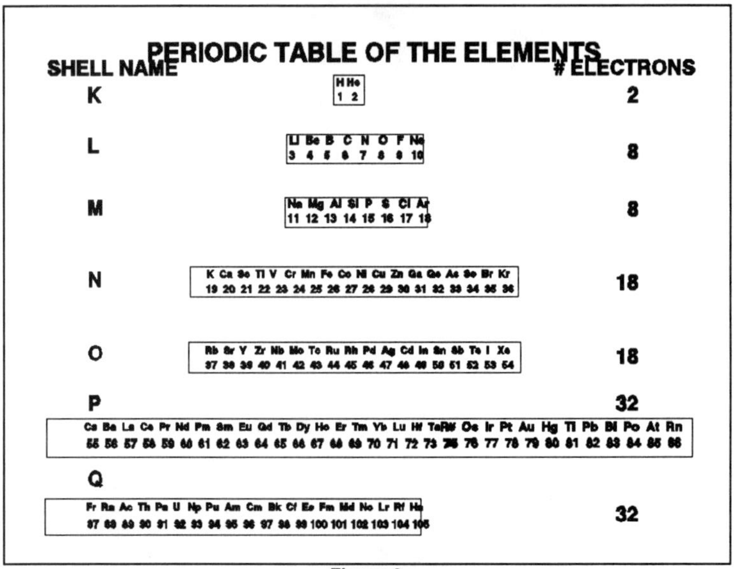

SHELL NAME PERIODIC TABLE OF THE ELEMENTS # ELECTRONS

SHELL NAME		# ELECTRONS
K	H He 1 2	2
L	Li Be B C N O F Ne 3 4 5 6 7 8 9 10	8
M	Na Mg Al Si P S Cl Ar 11 12 13 14 15 16 17 18	8
N	K Ca Sc Ti V Cr Mn Fe Co Ni Cu Zn Ga Ge As Se Br Kr 19 20 21 22 23 24 25 26 27 28 29 30 31 32 33 34 35 36	18
O	Rb Sr Y Zr Nb Mo Tc Ru Rh Pd Ag Cd In Sn Sb Te I Xe 37 38 39 40 41 42 43 44 45 46 47 48 49 50 51 52 53 54	18
P	Cs Ba La Ce Pr Nd Pm Sm Eu Gd Tb Dy Ho Er Tm Yb Lu Hf Ta W Re Os Ir Pt Au Hg Tl Pb Bi Po At Rn 55 56 57 58 59 60 61 62 63 64 65 66 67 68 69 70 71 72 73 74 75 76 77 78 79 80 81 82 83 84 85 86	32
Q	Fr Ra Ac Th Pa U Np Pu Am Cm Bk Cf Es Fm Md No Lr Rf Ha 87 88 89 90 91 92 93 94 95 96 97 98 99 100 101 102 103 104 105	32

Figure 8

Table 3 below shows empirically how the 4th shell displaces the third shell.

TABLE 3
STEP BY STEP BUILDUP OF THE FOURTH SHELL

ATOMIC SYMBOL	ATOMIC NUMBER	TOTAL NUMBER OF ELECTRONS			
		1st SHELL	2nd SHELL	3rd SHELL	4th SHELL
Ar	18	2	8	8	
K	19	2	8	8	1
Ca	20	2	8	8	2
Sc	21	2	8	9	2
Ti	22	2	8	10	2
V	23	2	8	11	2
Cr	24	2	8	13	1
Mn	25	2	8	13	2
Fe	26	2	8	14	2
Co	27	2	8	15	2
Ni	28	2	8	16	2
Cu	29	2	8	18	1
Zn	30	2	8	18	2
Ga	31	2	8	18	3
Ge	32	2	8	18	4
As	33	2	8	18	5
Se	34	2	8	18	6
Br	35	2	8	18	7
Kr	36	2	8	18	8

Magnetic Experiments on Packing

Combinatorial geometry is able to correctly predict the size of the seven shells or periods of the periodic table. However, like quantum mechanics, it predicts the size of many more periods than actually exist. This is a defect of both approaches.

This defect was removed from the combinatorial approach by performing a series of magnetic binding experiments. In a purely magnetic experiment it is not possible to completely represent the electrical forces, however an apparatus was constructed that attempted to simulate the electrical forces. The apparatus consisted of a nonmagnetic wooden board with sets of 2, 4, 6, 8, and 10 holes drilled in it in a circular symmetrical pattern that would be made by the eletron magnets in a great circle of a packing shell. The balance of electrical and magnetic forces on the electrons in the great circle is approximated in a rudimentary way by inserting pegs in the holes to hold the simple dipole ring magnets just touching in their equilibrium position. One of the magnets may be released by removing its peg. Then its binding to the rest of the configuration of magnets may be measured.

In this way it is possible to measure the relative binding force per magnet in a great circle of magnets as a function of the number of magnets in the circle. This can indicate the natural tendency of dipole magnets to group in particular configurations.

In order to represent the electron in Bergman's model as closely as possible, ceramic ring magnets were purchased from Radio Shack as shown in Figure 7. Note that the north-south poles of the magnet are oriented perpendicular to the smallest dimension of the magnet in order to be similar to Bergman's thin ring of current. Fifty magnets of equal strength were selected to perform the experiments.

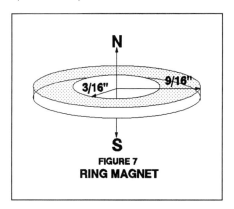

FIGURE 7
RING MAGNET

In order to eliminate the effects of friction between the magnet and the board, it was found necessary to measure the vertical force necessary to separate a magnet from the rest of the configuration. The same magnet was used for all configurations.

The results of the measurements are shown in Graph 1. Notice that odd numbers of magnets in a circle are weakly bound. Also great circles with 10 or more electron magnets are so weakly bound that they will not form shells. Thus if this data is used as a fourth constraint on the combinatorial geometry approach to the packing of electrons in shells, there will only be 7 periods in the periodic table, because the great circles of magnets in the eight and higher periods have insufficent magnetic binding to form a shell.

Also note from Graph 1 that great circles with 8 electron magnets are the most strongly bound configurations. These are too strongly bound to interact with the electrons of a neighboring atom. Thus in the outermost shell of an atom only groups of electrons smaller than eight will participate in the magnetic bond with another atom. This appears to be the origin of the chemical valence. Also this indicates that the mechanism for chemical binding of the elements is largely magnetic in agreement with long standing observations.[13]

CONCLUSIONS

The quantum theories describing matter and the atom were found to be unsatisfactory theories for science, because they incorporated many assumptions and postulates known to be in disagreement with reality. These assumptions include the use of point-particle action-at-a-distance Hamiltonian formulations of mechanics. Also the quantum theories of the atom assume that the magnetic moment and spin of particles do not have their origin in the finite size and structure of the particles. Furthermore these theories involve planetary motion of the electron about the nucleus with angular momentum I without the continuous emission of radiation that the empirical laws of electrodynamics demand. The logical rules for developing scientific theories, known as Mach's logical criteria for scientific porpositions, indicate that quantum mechanics and quantum electrodynamics(QED) are not eligible and never were eligible to be called theories in science. It is these theories that describe the universe as governed by randon statistical processes or chance in opposition to the biblical view that the universe is orderly being governed by the laws of cause and effect.

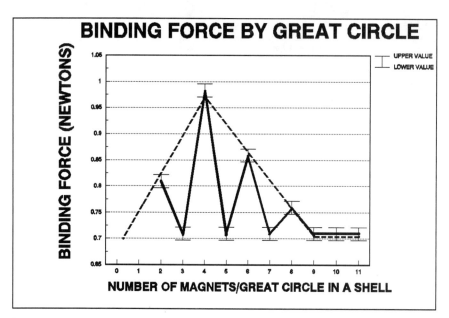

BINDING FORCE BY GREAT CIRCLE

Y-axis: **BINDING FORCE (NEWTONS)** — 0.65, 0.7, 0.75, 0.8, 0.85, 0.9, 0.95, 1, 1.05

X-axis: **NUMBER OF MAGNETS/GREAT CIRCLE IN A SHELL** — 0, 1, 2, 3, 4, 5, 6, 7, 8, 9, 10, 11

Legend: UPPER VALUE, LOWER VALUE

A rudimentary model for a new theory of the atom was developed using combinatorial geometry for finite size electrons with a physical magnetic moment that predicts all the properties of the periodic table. Using the constraints from the magnetic binding experiments for ring magnets in symmetric circular configurations, the model explains why there are only seven periods in the periodic table. The quantum theories predict an infinite series of periods.

This new model of the atom is based entirely on classical electrodynamics. It represents an orderly universe governed by the laws of cause and effect instead of random processes.

This new model of the atom incorporates in a fundamental way the finite size of the electron and its physical magnetic moment. The areas in which the quantum models err is precisely the real origin of the socalled "quantum effects". This is exactly the same sort of result found by Barnes[1] and Lucas[10,11] when they proved that the finite size of elementary particles was responsible for all the socalled "relativistic effects".

REFERENCES

* This work is based on Joseph's 1992-93 science fair project at Oxon Hill High School, Science and Technology program. For his 1993-94 science fair project he extended this work to cover the nucleus as well.

[1]   Thomas G. Barnes, Physics of the Future, 1983, Institute for Creation Research, El Cajon, CA.

[2]   David L. Bergman and J. Paul Wesley, **Spinning Charged Ring Model of Electron Yielding Anomalous Magnetic Moment**, Galilean Electrodynamics 1 no. 5(1990) 63-67.

[3]   N. Bohr, Philosophy Magazine, 26(1913) 476.

[4]   L. de Broglie, Philosophy Magazine, 47(1924) 446.

[5]   P. A. M. Dirac, The Principles of Quantum Mechanics, Fourth Edition, 1958, Clarendon Press.

[6]   R. Hofstadter, Reviews of Modern Physics 28(1956) 214.

[7]   Littauer, Schopper, and Wilson, Physical Review Letters 7(1961) 141.

[8]   Littauer, Schopper, and Wilson, Physical Review Letters 7(1961) 141.

[9]   Charles W. Lucas, Jr., Soli Deo Gloria - A Call for Reformation in Modern Science, 1985, Church Computer Services, 4511 Poppe Place, Temple Hills, MD.

[10]   Charles W. Lucas, Jr., An Electrodynamic model for Charged Elementary Particles, 1979, Church Computer Services, 4511 Poppe Place, Temple Hills, MD.

[11]   Charles W. Lucas, Jr. and Joseph C. Lucas, **Electrodynamics of Real Particles vs. Maxwell's Equations, Relativity Theory, and Quantum Mechanics**, Proceedings 1992 Twin-Cities Creation Conference held July 29 to August 1, 1992 at Northwestern College, pp. 243-252.

[12]   W. K. Panofsky and M. Phillips, Classical Electricity and Magnetism, 1962, Addison-Wesley, Reading, Massachusetts p. 370.

[13]   A. L. Parson, **A Magnetron Theory of the Structure of the Atom**, Smithsonian Miscelaneous Collections, 65 no. 11(1915).

[14]   Ruggero Maria Santilli, Il Grande Grido, Ethical Probe on Einstein's Followers in the U.S.A., 1984, Alpha Publishing, Newtonville, MA.

[15]   E. Schrodinger, Wave Mechanics, 1928, Blackie, London.

[16]   The Great Ideas - A Syntopicon of Great Books of the Western World, Volume 1, 1952, Encyclopedia Britannica, Inc., Chicago, pp. 451-467.

[17]   The International Dictionary of Physics and Electronics - Second Edition, 1961, D. Van Nostrand Co., New York, p. 699.

EVOLUTIONARY ORIGIN OF LIFE SCENARIOS:
PARADOX OF THE PLASMA MEMBRANE

RICHARD D. LUMSDEN, PH.D. AND NOEL D. FRANCIS
DIVISION OF BIOLOGICAL AND PHYSICAL SCIENCES
THE MASTER'S COLLEGE
SANTA CLARITA, CA 91322
AND
DEPARTMENT OF BIOLOGY
INSTITUTE FOR CREATION RESEARCH
SANTEE, CA 92071

KEYWORDS

abiogenesis, amphiphilicity, hydrophilicity, hydrophobicity, liposomes, membrane permeability, membrane proteins, phospholipid bilayer, plasma membrane, proteinoid, protocells, thermodynamics

ABSTRACT

The structural and functional properties of the cell surface (plasma) membrane (a.k.a. *plasmalemma*) relevant to evolutionary paradigms for biogenesis are reviewed. Such a partition would have been essential for the transition from abiotic chemistry to biochemistry, the physicochemical organization of the protocytosol, and the subsequent evolutionary differentiation of first life forms. However, an incremental evolutionary origin for the plasmalemma is gainsaid by these very requirements. The most plausible type of first membrane, a purely lipid bilayer, would have provided the necessary containment principle, but because of its demonstrable impermeability to requisite inorganic and organic molecules, the same membrane would have simultaneously precluded further development, even maintenance, of the emerging protocells. As an alternative primordial membrane model, protein microsieves are addressed and found wanting to the concentrative requirements of biologically relevant synthetic chemistry and its organization. Existing plasma membranes are composites of lipids *and* proteins, where certain of the proteins function as permeation channels and transport catalysts ("carriers" or "permeases"). However, the prospect of a selectively permeable lipoprotein membrane assembling *de novo* by purely natural processes is contraindicated not only by the egregious improbabilities but also by a number of definable physicochemical constraints. Meanwhile, to a creationist model of cell (ergo life's) origin, the integrated structural and functional complexity of extant plasma membranes provides yet further evidence of purposeful design. Not the least of this evidence would be the determinative informational principles on which membrane permeabilities are based.

INTRODUCTION

As Dutrochet [10] correctly surmised in 1824, cells are the *piece fundamentale* of organisms, i.e., the most elementary unit of structure that can manifest and sustain life. Thus, ever since Darwin [9], an explanation of the origin of cells has been incumbent on any evolutionary consideration of life's origin and subsequent diversification [35].

By definition, a cell is constructed minimally of an *endogenous* membrane (*cf.* viral envelops) enclosing a genome and the mechanisms attendant its replication. In the present, all cells originate from pre-existing cells (per Rudolph Virchow [51], *ominis cellula e cellula*). According to the creationist view, such has always been the case, the first cells having been created as units of the organisms that constituted the *baramins* (as defined by Marsh [30] and Wise [59]). The originally created kinds would of course have included prokaryotic organisms (bacteria), contemplated otherwise as the first cell type to evolve from abiotic processes, unicellular eukaryotes (protozoans, algae), and fungi, as well as multicellular plants and animals. Virchow's precept [51], articulated in 1858 as a refutation of the concept of spontaneous generation of life from non-life, remains altogether consistent with the contemporary observations of operational science. Meanwhile, the postulate of life's *abiotic* origin (Figure 1) - via spontaneous chemical formations, self-organization, and membraneous precipitation [61] - remains undemonstrated. While this is hardly disqualifying, considering its status as a one-time event in the unobservable past, it remains that as an exercise in forensics the premises are not based on a great deal of hard evidence. Indeed, for the most part the *data* from abiogenic chemistry have identified the mechanisms by which life could *not* have evolved! The thesis of chemical evolution confronts credibility when there are important - even essential - biochemical compounds for which an adequate prebiotic synthesis has not been elucidated (e.g., pyrimidine nucleosides, with the explanation that primordial nucleic acids did not contain pyrimidine bases!) or, as Stanley Miller notes [32, p. 16] "... (experimental) conditions are so forced (e.g., by use of anhdrous solvents) or ...(reactant)... concentrations are so high (e.g., 10 M formaldehyde) that the syntheses could not be expected to have occurred extensively (if at all) on the primitive earth". Then we have as "evidences" syntheses achieved only with altogether improbable reactant analogues (e.g., purine and pyrimidine phosphoroimidazolides); products frequently arising with biologically incorrect bonds (e.g., RNA polynucleotides with highly unstable 2-5 rather than 3-5 phosphodiester bonds), random (racemic) chirality, in yields of at best trace quantities, and so on. Could it be that such statements as "... the problems of the origin of life stand out as one where the greatest advances are *still to be made*" [32, p. 25, emphasis added] are no more than whistling in the cemetery where the fate of abiogenic theories is concerned? Is the idea of chemical evolution, as Yockey [60, p. 286] concludes, "latter day alchemism"? The postulate of life from non-life is nonetheless essential to the non-theistic materialist view that life - past and present - is a purely physicochemical phenomenon resulting from purely naturalistic physical processes; that the present biosphere has developed through descent with modification from a singular primordial life form; ergo that all life forms are organically related, one with nature. But if the purely physicochemical explanation fails for the beginings, can it hold for the remainder of the putative evolutionary process?

The most widely promulgated origin of life paradigms (e.g., [8, 17 - 19]) and critiques of them [6, 19, 24, 36, 39, 42, 48, 55, 56, 60] have focused predominantly on the abiotic chemistry of protein and polynucleotide formation, the development of biologically productive energy transducing mechanisms, and molecular replication. Nonetheless, for both definitional and operational reasons, the evolutionary progression from primordial molecules to cell structure and abiotic chemistry to biochemistry also requires the containment and organizational principles afforded by a membrane interposed between the physical environment and evolving protoplasm.

MEMBRANE STRUCTURE AND PROPERTIES

Abiogenesis and the requirement for a membraneous partition

Morowitz [33] has appropriately emphasized the critical role of membrane structure in abiogenesis, indeed as a step necessarily *preceding* the emergence of functional genomes and metabolic pathways. Others, e.g. Darnell [8], posit membrane structure as a *terminal* step in protocellular evolution. This school of thought derives from recognition of the permeability barrier membranes would present while serving otherwise as facillitators of organization. In the opinion of Eigen et al. [12, p. 107] "Organization into cells was surely postponed as long as possible ... transporting things across (membranes) ... are tasks accomplished today by the most refined ... processes. Achieving analogous results in a prebiotic soup must have required fundamental innovations." Yet others (e.g., de Duve [10]) are more ambivalent about the timing of this event, but all are agreed on its significance.

It is posited [10] that sooner or later evolutionary progress would have become dependent on Darwinian selection. The precipitation of a membrane sequestering a genome (or molecules with that potential) would advantage the emergence and retention of co-issuants (enzymes, etc.). This higher order of structural complexity would have contributed immeasurably to the survival and propagation of that genome in its "competition" with otherwise similarly fortuitous chemical events not so sequestered in the pre-biotic realm, where innovative products would be lost to the surroundings. And is it not of such stuff that evolution is all about?

Thermodynamic considerations

Definably living systems operate at a distance far from thermodynamic equilibrium. They are pressured by degradative physicochemical events toward the equilibrium state. This follows from the Second Law generalization that all nonequilibrium structures at temperatures >0°Kelvin (see the Third Law) are subject to thermal, ergo organizational, decay. While cellular biology can survive desiccation and ultra-cryotemperatures, it does so in a dormant state. For the most part, biological systems operate in an aqueous (intracellular) environment at temperatures normally >0°C (exceptions, if that, include some arctic, antarctic and alpine forms). Much of the abiotic synthetic chemistry touted to date requires relatively high temperatures, i.e. >150°C (significant exceptions include the polymerization of nucleotides, optimal at ca. -21°C [32, 36]), certainly where reaction rates would be concerned (e.g., thermal peptides per [18], lipids per [22]). Accordingly, most origin of life scenarios are predicated on chemical evolution in a warm aqueous mileu [33], though the simulated syntheses are more often than not best achieved with *dry* heat. Indeed, some of the currently popular versions envision a geo- or hydro-thermally hot environment (e.g., submarine vents, fumaroles, steaming limnic springs, etc.) However, high ambient temperatures would have presented some formidble problems, especially with the synthesis and stability of biopolymers [32]. Moreover, where the essential molecular components are largely water soluble or hydrophilic, their distribution in an aqueous environment tends to be, or become, homogeneous in time. Hydrolytic reaction and dispersive diffusional rates would be exacerbated by high ambient temperatures (i.e., "hot soups"). But to effect coherent systems, the tendency must be concentrative, and if coherency is to be maintained, there must be a countermechanism to diffusion. This ultimately requires a phase separation from the environment. Yet the system must remain interactive with the environment. For growth, replication and any further differentiation to ensue, the system must be able to accrete from the environment the raw materials for synthesis and the requisite energy transductive functions.

Viewed by many evolutionists as rebutting the *pro forma* creationist argument from Second Law thermodynamics [57], there is, in effect, a Fourth Law (or perhaps more accurately an additional theorem), which states that the flow of energy from a source to a sink through an intermediate system "orders" that system [17, 33]; the order so derived is equivalent to increased "complexity" in Morowitz' [33] contextual definition of the term (Figure 2). For reasons detailed elsewhere [17, 33, and references therein] its theoretical conventions are not contraindicated by Morris' [34] predictions of *disarray* consequent such energy flow. And these conventions do have pragmatic significance to the evolutionary paradigm for cell origin. It is, for example, blind physical force - ultrasonics - which converts intially multilaminate liposomes to single membrane-bound vesicles [2, 52] (Figure 6). In any case, requisite the application of "Fourth Law" thermodynamics to proto-biology, the principle of heterogeneity must be operative. Energy flow is a necessary but not a sufficient condition in and of itself for establishing anything like biological organization. Indeed, Morowitz [33, p. 83-84] adds the caveat that "This principle of complexification [per Figure 2] follows strictly from the physical chemical properties of such systems and in no way demands biological organization." He continues, however, "It seems reasonable to conclude ... that such a principle is propaedeutic to the emergence of the biosphere."

Where initial conditions are homogenously aqueous, biphasic partitioning would be accomplished by an essentially non-aqeous intervening boundary. In practical terms, this is defined as a membrane comprised of amphiphilic molecules, i.e., of both hydrophilic and hydrophobic structure.

Composition and structure of amphiphilic membranes

In present day biology, the requirement for amphiphilic membrane structure is met by phospholipids, where their fatty acid hydrocarbon "tails" establish a hydrophobic interior domain and their polar "head" groups (represented by phosphate with or without hydrophilic polar organics) interface with the adjacent water milieu:

$$O\ CH_2\ CH\ NH_2(+)COOH(-)$$
$$|$$
$$O=P\text{-}OH(-)$$
$$|$$
$$O$$
$$|$$
$$CH_2\text{-}CH\text{-}CH_2$$
$$|\quad\ \ |$$
$$O\quad O$$
$$|\quad\quad \backslash$$
$$C=O\ \ C=O$$
$$/\quad\quad\ \backslash$$
$$(CH_2)n\ (CH_2)n$$
$$|\quad\quad\ \ |$$
$$CH_3\quad CH_3$$

A phospholipid (1,2-diacyl-*sn*-glycero-3-phosphoserine)

These properties underlie the macrostructure of biomembranes as continuous lipid bilayers (Figure 3). The general concensus [8, 33] (but see [18] for exceptions) is that phospholipid bilayers, or lipoidal equivalents, also constituted the first plasma membranes. It is contended by proponents of this hypothesis that appropriate lipid precursors, including phospholipids *per se*, could have been present in an early earth "primoridal soup" [22, 33, and references therein]. It should be noted, however, that the very low water solubility of phospholipids makes the formation *de novo* of a phospholipid from water soluble precursors energetically difficult in aqueous media (experimental abiotic phospholipid synthesis involves evaporation in a hot sand or dry clay matrix, and subsequent incubation under desiccation, per Hargreaves et al. [22]). In present day cells, membranes proliferate by expansion of pre-existing membrane structure; phospholipids are synthesized in association with already extant bilayers in which the enzymology is bound or phospholipids synthesized elsewhere are incorporated therein immediately post-synthesis [4]. With very few exceptions, *omnis membrana e membrana*. Nonetheless, once formed - abiotically or otherwise - such lipids do, in fact, spontaneously form bilayered membrane structure [2, 49] (Figures 4-6).

Polypeptides, depending on their amino acid content and sequence, can be amphiphilic, a point stressed by Sidney Fox [18] in his argument for the feasibility of *protein* membranes as "first partitions". Folsome [16] has called attention to the oily film, presumably a hydrophobic polymer, that typically accompanies the formation of amino acids and oligopeptides in the Miller-type experiments. Fox [18, p. 130] asserts that his thermal protein (produced by heating amino acid mixtures to dryness) has "most of the (physical) properties of phospholipid". He moreover describes proteinoid microspheres as exhibiting "osmotic-like" swelling and shrinking, from which the existence of proteinoid membrane structure might also be inferred. Parenthetically, we note that analogous volume changes would be exhibited as well by a hygroscopic protein gel, *cf.* a semi-permeable membrane-enclosed vesicle *per se*.

The coalescence of amphiphiles into membraneous sheets is both predictable and demonstrable. For phospholipids in water, where G is the Gibbs free energy content of the system, DG for the formation of a bilayer structure is an arithmetically negative value (approximately -60 kJ/mole lipid [3] for both "free" phospholipids and those in micellar formations [30, 42]; the self-assembly of such lipids into membranes is therefore thermodynamically favored. It is also empirically observable, per the laboratory construction of liposomes (i.e., vesicles) and "black lipid membranes" (planar sheets) (Figures 4 and 6). The assembly of membrane structure per se from amphiphilic peptides is more inferential. See, nonetheless [50] and Figures 7 and 8. Fox [18] interprets electron microscope images such as Figure 7 as evidence of bilayered membrane structure (analogous to that formed by phosholipids) at the surface of proteinoid microspheres. However, for more variable-controlled systems, protein "membranes" (where such are actually formed) typically have the structure of a meshwork sieve (Figure 8), an interpretation not belied by Figure 7. There is also a porosity attendant the structure of polymeric gels (Figure 9) and even crystaline protein (Figure 10).

Absent other controlling factors, amphiphilic proteins do not form sheets but tend to a globular tertiary thence quaternary structure in an aqeous medium, with the hydrophobic sequences shielded by the hydrophilic. However, predominantly hydrophilic proteins form adsorbate layers onto planar substrates [47], as embodied in the now albeit obsolete model of biological membrane structure envisioned by Danielli and Davson [7] and Robertson [39]. Predominantly hydrophobic proteins become discrete particulate entities of membranes by insertion into their hydrophobic domains [44] per the currently accepted model of biological membranes as fluid (or "liquid crystaline") lipoprotein mosaics. There is also the potential for membrane-like protein comprised structure in sol/gel phenomena [37]. However, polymeric megamolecular gels exhibit a relatively large (micron-range) porosity and therefore relatively non-selective permeability for molecules in the size range (nanometers) of amino acids, nucleosides, sugars, etc.

Amphiphilic lipids thus remain the most plausible entities involved with "first membrane" evolution.

Membrane closure into a vesicle, an event most likely to occur when the membrane is a liquid hydrocarbon (i.e. lipid *cf.* protein-constituted), provides a tri-phasic system: exterior milieu, partition, and interior compartment. According to the evolutionary scenario, the exterior phase is the source of free energy (photonic, electromotive, and/or chemical) and the material precursors to proteins and nucleic acids; the interior becomes the sequestered microenvironment in which biologically determinative chemical reactions can occur; the partition becomes a barrier to dissipative diffusion (efflux) of reactants and products, developing thereby the critical mass for productive biochemistry. Meanwhile, the partition itself becomes a non-aqeous matrix space for the accretion of nonpolar solutes which, as detailed in Morowitz [33], could potentiate the energy transductive functions requisite to endergonic synthetic functions in the inner vesicular compartment, and possibly facilitate dehydrative condensation reactions. See also [17]. There remains the problem, however, of such membranes as barriers to accretive diffusion (influx).

Closed or open systems? The conundrum

In the formation of liposomes from initially dispersed phospholipids, the vesicles (Figure 6) demonstrably incorporate constituents of the medium into the resultant inner compartment, including, when present, proteins, nucleic acids and other molecular species of biological significance. This has had widespread biotechnological application, where liposomes have been used as delivery systems in genetic engineering, pharmacotherapy, etc. To that point, the scenario envisioned by Darnell [8] (Figure 11) is credible. However, Morowitz [33] contests the sequence of complex molecules first, then cells, from the unlikelihood that molecules needed by the biosphere (e.g., proteins, nucleic acids) would be provided by the geosphere otherwise (lithosphere, hydrosphere, atmosphere), where matter exists at the thermodynamically lowest lying combinations. He notes that whatever munificence there might be

320

forthcoming from nature is chemically parsimonious. Morowitz [33] argues persuasively that (p. 156) "... in the long run any molecules needed by the biosphere must be synthesized within the biosphere from thermodynamically low-lying input molecules"; thus (p. 154) "macromolecules (become) a consequence of evolutionary processes rather than requiring that they be prerequisite to such processes! (The) necessity of macromolecules early in the process has been a weakness of the various soup models." Yockey [60] references critically the "*myth* of the prebiotic soup", noting, e.g., that while *biologically* generated keragens (so diagnosed from their $^{12}C/^{13}C$ ratios) have been detected in the most ancient sedimentary rocks, there is no geological evidence whatsoever for *non-biologically* derived kerogens which would have preceded the emergence of the protobiont on the early Earth. In any event, the encapsulating of evolving biochemistry by a lipid bilayer presents a major stumbling block in the evolution of cells scenario. The empirically demonstrable impermeability of lipid bilayers to the hydrophilic organic and inorganic precursors (carbohydrates, amino acids, phosphate, etc.) [1, 15, 27, 40, 41, 45, 49, 53] (Figure 12) of productive biochemistry (notably protein and nucleic acid synthesis) would result in closed systems (i.e., closed to "building block" molecules), and any system in isolation (enclosed interim polymers) will decay to its lowest free-energy state (monomers, initially, and then their dissolution into simpler constitutents). This is not just a theoretical prediction, but follows the readily observed effect of 55M water (i.e. wholly aqeuous conditions) on the integrity of peptide and phosphodiester bonds, respective proteins and nucleic acids in aqeuous solution/suspension. The availability, at this stage of evolution (protocellular), of anything like the kinds of permeability modifiers discussed below (**The biological solution**), would be an altogether unrealistic assumption, though some students of this problem [10], have entertained this notion. It has also been conjectured [33], in the face of the the more realistic alternative of a purely lipoidal membrane, that the nonpolar inorganics to which purely lipid bilayers *are* permeable could serve as building matter for the abiotic assembly of polar organics within the vesicle's interior compartment. Note, however, that while lipid bilayers are permeable to the ostensible inorganic precursors to amino acids etc. (carbon dioxide, nitrogen, inorganic CN derivatives, etc.), the processes envisioned for this sort of abiotic chemistry (requiring relatively high levels of purely physical energy sources [32, 48, and references therein]) would obliterate the protocell. Requiring, on the one hand, a barrier to diffusion from within to without, which is admirably satisfied by a lipid bilayer, the same structure, on the other hand, imposes an insurmountable barrier to biochemically requisite diffusion from without to within. One way around the latter debacle would be to impose a partition structured along the lines of that shown in Figure 8, i.e. a protein microsieve, in effect a dialysis membrane which would retain macromolecules, at least, within the inner vesicular compartment. However, by observation, protein-comprised membranes of this sort are, given the large pore size, remarkably leaky and unselectively so to smaller entities such as amino acids, phosphate, etc. This property defeats the requirement for selective concentration (inside *v.* outside) of reactants, especially at the molar concentrations imperative to non-enzymatic mass action reaction rate kinetics (see, eg., net yields from artificial "soup" chemistry [17, 32, 33, 36, 48, 60 and references therein]. By the passive diffusion process (the only feasible permeation principle that could be envisioned at this stage of biogenic evolution), what "leaks in", "leaks out" with equal facility; any net movement follows the concentration differential. This would apply to permeants of either of the aforementioned protocellular membrane models. Thus, following Fick's law, the rate of flow (J) is a function of the solute diffusion (mobility) coefficient (D), membrane surface area (A), the magnitude of the concentration gradient ΔC and the distance the solute travels across the interfacial partition (x):

$$J = -DA \frac{\Delta C}{x} \qquad (1)$$

the negative sign indicating that net solute movement is in the direction of the lesser concentration in the solvent space. As a kinetic energy expression, D = w RT (where w is solute motility); for electrically charged solutes, the above function (1) expands to the Nernst-Plank equation:

$$J = -w\Delta C \left(\frac{RT}{\Delta C} \frac{\Delta C}{x} + zF \frac{\Delta \Psi}{x} \right) \qquad (2)$$

where z = the number of electrical charges (i.e., ion valence), F = Faraday's constant (96,000 coulombes/mol) and $\Delta \Psi / x$ = the charge gradient (voltage) across the membrane. The associated dissipation of energy, per the Gibbs' function, becomes

$$\Delta G = RT \ln \Delta C + z F \Delta \Psi \qquad (3)$$

where ΔG is the free energy change involved in the move of 1 mol permeant across a non-restrictive interface.

321

If, in the protocell, the internal pool concentration of amino acids, etc., were (somehow) initially higher than the external concentration, the diffusion gradient would drive *efflux* . Note, it has been estimated that standing concentrations of putative organics in the "primordial soup" could have been no higher than micromolar [32, 33, 48 and references therein]. No less an authority on this subject than Stanley Miller himself has noted [32, p. 16] that "... an amino acid concentration of ... 10^{-4}M and an adenine concentration of about ... 10^{-5}M ... can be considered as a relatively concentrated prebiotic soup."

A variety of mechanisms to thwart the permeability barrier imposed by a lipid bilayer protocell plasmalemma have been proposed. These include the intervention of aldehydes to facilitate the excursion and subsequent internal concentration of amino acids by Schiff base formation [specific references in 33]. Reasonably low environmental pH (4-5) could repress the ionization of carboxylic acid groups rendering them more compatible with a non-polar partition [33]; likewise, at extraordinarily low pH (0-1), protons could partially neutralize even inorganic phosphate [17]. But how much more permeable pH *per se* would render such solutes, given the lipophobic properties of many amino acids, etc., otherwise, is debatable. There is to be considered as well the thermodynamic barrier to the diffusion of hydrophilics across hydrophobic domains that goes beyond ionization constants, *viz.* dehydration energies [14], which applies to amino acids and other solutes. The major potential energy barrier for a non-electrolyte (non-electrolytically active) molecule moving passively according to a chemical gradient includes the necessity for the permeant to lose its water of hydration as a condition of passing the polar barrier of the lipid groups [3, 14] as well as achieving solubility in, or compatibility with, the hydrocarbon (hydrophobic) constituents of the membrane.

However passaged, solutes would have to be retained. Internal trapping of amino acids (and other organics) by non-enzymatic inorganic phosphorylation has been suggested [33] (reaction (a) below), which, in the case of amino acids would concommitantly facilitate peptide synthesis [17, 33] (reaction (b) below). However, this would require, in our estimation, unattainably high reactant concentrations (in an aqueous milieu) of pyrophosphate, where, e.g., [17]:

Amino acid + Pyrophosphate ---> Aminoacyl phosphate + Phosphate   **(a)**

Aminoacyl + Amino acid ---> Dipeptide + Phosphate   **(b)**
phosphate

Note that a system freely permeable to inorganic phosphate(s) presumably would be likewise permeable to Ca^{++}, resulting in the formation of frankly insoluble precipitates of calcium phosphate/pyrophosphate. Under such conditions, only trace quantities, at best, of pyrophosphate would be available in an aqueous milieu for the above reactions. While extant prokaryotes are known to trap permeant organics by post-transport phosphorylation [25], the complex biochemical mechanism (involving micromolar concentrations of reactant : product ratios, spacially organized enzymatically catalyzed and highly specified reaction sequences) is beyond credible expectation for an evolving protocell.

Getting around the problem of vesicle impermeability at the outset, Blobel [5] envisions the evolution of protocells from initially *inside-out* liposomal vesicles (Figure 13), a process however which fails to accommodate Morowitz's trenchant observation concerning the limited munificence of the abiotic geosphere [33]. In particular, it does not solve the problem of diffusional loss of products (or achieving sufficient reactant concentrations) in structurally "open" systems, and only begs the lipid membrane permeability problem, since this would apply once the vesicles turned right-side in. Meanwhile, the mechanism for the remarkable turn of sidedness illustrated in Blobel's model is not intuitively obvious. Its major virtue, if that, is its conjecture as to how the brute structure of gram negative bacteria (with their two membranes) (Figure 14) - putatively the evolutionarily first kinds of prokaryotes - might have developed from a "cell" initially structured of a singular membrane. A critique of that hypothesis is beyond the scope of the present paper.

The biological solution

Per deDuve [10, p. 203] "*Unless* we subscribe to special creation, we *must assume* that, where life started, local conditions were adequate to overcome the concentration problem" (emphasis added). deDuve of course is not advocating creationism, but, at this point, the reader may wonder if special creation is not the better scientific explanation afterall. An assumption forced by the thesis then used as the best *evidence* for the thesis is not inherently scientific protocol. What perforce gainsays the alternative assumption? Only one's world view? But that's not science, or so we are told, irrespective of its alleged basis. Should *ad hoc* presumptions force a *scientist* to an inescapable inference of evolutionary processes as fact?

The plasmalemma of most extant cells is of course both selectively permeable and concentrative respective the cell's biochemical and physiological requirements. Exceptions include the remarkably leaky membranes of some of the intracellular parasites (e.g., mycoplasmas, rickettsiae), on the one hand, and the insulative (electrolyte impermeable) membrane which comprises the myelin sheath of neuron axons, on the other. In addition to phospholipids, naturally occurring plasma membranes are invested to one degree or another with a variety of highly specified proteins which comprise the structure of highly selective permeant channels. (Germane to the present observations, we note that the notorious impermeability of myelin - the plasma membrane of periaxonal Schwann cells - coincides with its remarkably high lipid/low protein ratio of ca. 4-6 : 1 [52]; for plasma membranes otherwise, the lipid : protein ratio is ca. 1 : 1). These proteins take the form of more or less static pores (those, e.g., at "gap" or nexus junctions and the "porin" complexes of bacterial cell envelopes) (Figures 15 and 16) and conformationally variable channels and kinetic "carriers" (Figures 17-19). The latter, apropos of the term "permeases", are both catalytic, respective the rate kinetics of transport, and highly specific respective their solute interactions; some are vectorally specific independently of the solute concentration gradient (the phenomenon of "active transport"). Their molecular structures, ergo functional properties, are rigorously specified by genetic information *per se* and its transcription/translation *viz.* nacent protein synthesis and a variety of post-translational regulatory factors (see, e.g., the role of chaperones [13]).

To surmise that equivalent entities could have formed abiotically, *sans* informational determinants, concommitant with or prior to the first lipid bilayers in the course of protocellular evolution begs for nothing short of a miracle. de Duve [10, pp. 100-101] nonetheless offers that "The most likely (ancestral membrane) ... (would have) consisted (simultaneously) ... of lipids *and* proteins ... (the latter) **must** have included a minimum set of transport systems to maintain an adequate intracellular milieu and to mediate the necessary exchanges of matter between the cell and its environment" (emphasis added). While descriptive of the *need*, such statements do not address the *plausibility* of spontaneous occurrence or provide any *evidence* for it (*cf.* the "inescapable inference"). The bane of any theory is the *ad hoc* hypothesis - in this instance, the inexplicable simultaneous co-development of lipid membranes and selective protein permeases. When a hypothetical phenomenon is both implausible and undemonstrable, can it remain a scientific principle? Or does it become a matter of faith? The always germane theroretical constraints [57, 60] momentarily aside, there are formidible *physical* limitations that impact de Duve's account. Proteins serving as permeability modifiers must first of all be integrated into the matrix of the bilayer (Figure 20); i.e., they are integral (intrinsic) membrane proteins *cf.* extrinsic (peripheral) membrane proteins [44, 52]. Accordingly, their lipid-interfacing external surfaces must be at the outset to the largest extent hydrophobic [14]. And, empirically, so they are [20]. By observation, such water immiscible proteins tend to precipitate and denature in an aqeous environment; hence the laboratory requirement for detergents in their extraction, stabilization, etc. How, then, could such proteins originate spontaneously in an aqueous "soup"? Note, in extant cells, this problem confronting the abiogenicists is solved biologically by the mechanisms illustrated in Figures 21-23 [13, 21, 54]. While perhaps accommodated by Blobel's model (Figure 7), the flaws in reasoning for that model, discussed above, render it untenable in the first place. Otherwise, the necessary transitional conformations are not accomodated by sheerly stochastic processes [20].

Extant proteinaceous pores and permeases tend to be multi-subunit arrays with molecular weights for the polypeptides in the 10's to 100's of kilodaltons and higher [23, 40, 46], and have structurally complex colateral associations with other membrane constituents. From the engineering point of view, they are highly sophisticated machines. Conjuring the existence of simpler, i.e., smaller and less selective permeability-modifying entities analogous to present day antibiotic peptide ionophores or functionally equivalent other kinds of molecules (e.g., macrotetrolides, cyclic polyethers, trialkyltins, etc.) [14, 23, 40] is fallacious. As such initially exogenous modifiers are known, they are functionally limited to affecting the diffusional excursion across lipid bilayers of small ions (e.g., $Na+$, $K+$, $H+$, Cl^-, OH^-), ordinarily not larger ionorganics (e.g., phosphate, pyrophosphate) or organic molecules. A possible exception to this principle is the relatively small (albeit 8 kd) polypeptide component of the otherwise complex phosphate transport system in mitochondria, and perhaps ionophores like A23187 and beauverein which have a high affinity for divalent cations. Since these ionophores nonetheless operate according to the diffusional kinetcs shown in equations (1) and (2) above, the requisite co-parameter of concentrative absorption (or exclusion) is precluded (hence their physiological effect - of collapsing pre-existing gradients - as antibiotics). The net result of these kinds of modifiers, absent other principles, is equilibrium (a chemical definition of death, not life!).

When viewed independently of one another, plasmalemmal proteins integrate the cell with its environment, while the lipids, re: permeability, passively isolate. These principles are not working at cross purposes, however. Plasmalemmal lipids ensure that the selective permeability afforded by protein-specified conduits is not overridden by non-selective permeability elsewhere in the interfacial structure between interior and external compartments. This is a function that notably fails the protein-first models (i.e., passive sieves) for protocellular evolution addressed above.

Equally important to the biologically productive properties of cell surfaces are their para-investments, *viz.* the ubiquitous glycocalyx (Figure 3). Noting that phospholipid bilayers, amphiphilicity nothwithstanding, are sparingly hydrophilic at best [52], this dominantly carbohydrate-comprised (hence highly hydrophilic) structure [38, 43, 58] endows cells with their especially important characteristic of surface "wetability". For discussion, see [26, 28, 29, 58]. The glycocalyx, as a composite of highly specified peptidoglycans and glycolipids, adds yet another dimension to the functional and structural complexities challenging the evolutionary paradigms.

CONCLUSION

In sum, the inordinate complexity, demonstrable specificity, and low probability of naturally occurring plasma membranes are features daunting to current evolutionary explanations of their origin by stochastic processes. The adequacy of the more simplistic, ergo physicochemically feasible, versions contemplated for the protocell falls well short of their patent requirements. The speculation of more elaborate models at the outset defies the principle of Ockham's razor, not a trivial failing of reason, and imposes on these models an inexplicable release from a number of real physicochemical constraints. Meanwhile, the shortcomings of the most plausible evolutionary scenarios are heuristic to the conclusion drawn here from the existing data. Indeed, the most reasonable explanation for the existence of the plasma membrane, ergo cells, ergo life, is the evolutionist's anathema - deterministic, intelligent design. High complexity, high specificity, and low probability of spontaneous occurrence are the hallmarks of engineered systems, not happenstance phenomena. While he is certainly ill-disposed to the creationist view *per se*, Hubert Yockey, who is among the leading contributors to information theory in molecular biology for nearly three decades, has concluded, and we concur, that "The currently accepted ... (evolutionist origin of life) ... scenarios are untenable and the solution to the problem will not be found by continuing to flagellate these conclusions" [60, p. 289]. Conjecture, the power of imagination and rank suggestion notwithstanding, the Emperor has no clothes.

ACKNOWLEDGEMENTS

This study was facillitated by a grant from the Creation Research Society and technical support from the Institute for Creation Research. The senior author's laboratory research on membranes was supported by grants from the National Institutes of Health and the National Science Foundation during his tenure at Tulane University. The interpretations and opinions expressed in this paper remain solely those of the authors.

REFERENCES

[1]   O. Anderson, **Permeability properties of unmodified lipid bilayer membranes**, in Membrane Transport in Biology, D. Giebisch et al., editors, 1978, Springer-Verlag, New York.

[2]   A. Bangham, **Lipid bilayers and biomembranes**, Annual Reviews of Biochemistry 41 (1972) 753-805.

[3]   P. Bergethon and E. Simons, Biophysical Chemistry - Molecules to Membranes, 1990, Springer-Verlag, New York.

[4]   W. Bishop and R. Bell, **Assembly of phospholipids into cellular membranes: biosynthesis, transmembrane movement and intracellular translocation**, Annual Reviews of Cell Biology 4 (1988) 579-610.

[5]   G. Blobel, **Intracellular protein topogenesis,** Proceedings of the National Academy of Sciences USA 77 (1980) 1496-1500,

[6]   A.G. Cairnes-Smith, Genetic Takeover and the Mineral Origins of Life, 1982, Cambridge University Press, Cambridge, UK.

[7]   J. Danielli and H. Davson, **A contribution to the theory of permeability of thin films**, Journal of Cellular Physiology 5 (1935) 495-508.

[8]   J.E. Darnell, Jr., **RNA**, Scientific American 253:4 (1985) 68-78.

[9]   F. Darwin, editor, The Life and Letters of Charles Darwin, Volume 2, 1887, Appleton, New York.

[10] C. de Duve, Blueprint for a Cell: the Nature and Origin of Life, 1991, Neil Patterson, Burlington, NC.
[11] R. Dutrochet, Recherches anatomiques et physiologiques sur la structure intime des animaux et des vegetaux, 1824, Balliere, Paris.
[12] M. Eigen, W. Gardiner, P. Schuster, and P. Winkler-Oswatitsch, **The origin of genetic information**, Scientific American **244:4** (1981) 88-118.
[13] R.J. Ellis and S.M. Van der Vies, **Molecular chaperons**, Annual Reviews of Biochemistry **60** (1991) 321-347.
[14] J. Finean, R. Coleman, and R. Mitchell, Membranes and their Cellular Functions, 1978, Blackwell, London.
[15] A. Finkelstein and A. Cass, **Permeability and electrical properties of thin lipid membranes**, Journal of General Physiology **52:1, part 2** (1968) 145-173.
[16] C. Folsome, The Origin of Life: A Warm Little Pond, 1979, W.H. Freeman, San Francisco.
[17] R. Fox, Energy and the Evolution of Life, 1988, W.H. Freeman, New York.
[18] S. Fox, The Emergence of Life, 1988, Basic Books, New York.
[19] S. Fox and A. Pappelis, **Synthetic molecular evolution and protocells**, Quarterly Review of Biology **68** (1993) 79-82.
[20] L. Gierasch and J. King, editors, Protein Folding, 1990, American Association for the Advancement of Science, Washington.
[21] M. Glick, **The properties and biosynthesis of RNA associated with surface membranes of L cells**, in Biogenesis and Turnover of Membrane Molecules, J. Cook, editor, 1976, Raven Press, New York.
[22] W. Hargreaves, S. Mulvihill, and D. Deamer, **Synthesis of phospholipids and membranes in prebiotic conditions**, Nature **266** (1977) 78-80.
[23] B. Hille, Ionic Channels of Excitable Membranes, 1992, Sinauer, Sunderland, MA.
[24] G. Joyce, **RNA evolution and the origins of life**, Nature **338** (1989) 217-224.
[25] H. Kaback, **The transport of sugars across across isolated bacterial membranes**, in Current Topics in Membranes and Transport, F. Bonner and A. Kleinzeller, editors, 1970, Academic Press, New York.
[26] A. Katchalsky, **Polyelectrolytes and their biological interactions**, Biophysical Journal **4: 1, part 2** (1964) 9-41.
[27] J. Lever, **Phosphate ion transport in fibroblast plasma membrane vesicles**, Annals of the New York Academy of Sciences **341** (1980) 37-47.
[28] R.D. Lumsden, **Surface ultrastructure and cytochemistry of parasitic helminths**, Experimental Parasitology **37** (1975) 267-339.
[29] R.D. Lumsden and W.A. Murphy, **Morphological and functional aspects of the cestode body surface**, in Cellular Interactions in Symbiosis and Parasitism, C. Cook, P. Pappas and E. Rudolph, editors, 1980, The Ohio State University Press, Columbus.
[30] F.L. Marsh, Fundamental Biology, 1941, Self-published, Lincoln, NB.
[31] R.O. McCracken and R.D. Lumsden, **Structure and function of parasite surface membranes. I. Mechanisms of phlorizin inhibition of hexose transport by the cestode** Hymenolepis diminuta, Comparative Biochemistry and Physiology **50B** (1975) 153-158.
[32] S. Miller, **The prebiotic synthesis of organic compounds as a step toward the origin of life**, in Major Events in the History of Life, J.W. Schopf, editor, Jones and Bartlett, London.
[33] H. Morowitz, Beginnings of Cellular Life, 1992, Yale University Press, New Haven, CT.
[34] H. Morris, Scientific Creationism, 1985, CLP, San Diego.
[35] A.I. Oparin, [The Origin of Life on the Earth]   (in Russian), 1924, Moskovskii Rabochii, Moscow.
[36] L. Orgel, **Molecular replication**, Nature **358** (1992) 203-209.
[37] Y. Osada and S. Ross-Murphy, **Intelligent gels**, Scientific American **268:5** (1993) 82-87.
[38] J.-P. Revel and S. Ito, **The surface components of cells**, in The Specificity of Cell Surfaces, B. Davis and L. Warren, editors, 1967, Prentice-Hall, Englewood Cliffs, NJ.
[39] J.D. Robertson, **The ultrastructure of cell membranes and their derivations**, Biochemical Symposium **No. 16** (1959) 3-43.
[40] A. Schamoo, editor, Carriers and Channels in Biological Systems, 1975, The New York Academy of Sciences, New York.
[41] A. Schamoo, editor, Second International Conference on Carriers and Channels in Biological Systems - Transport Proteins, 1980, The New York Academy of Sciences, New York.
[42] R. Shapiro, Origins, A Skeptics Guide to the Creation of Life on Earth, 1986, Summit Books, New York.
[43] N. Sharon and H. Lis, **Carbohydrates in cell recognition**, Scientific American **268:1** (1993) 82-89.
[44] M. Singer and G. Nicolson, **The fluid mosaic model of the structure of cell membranes**, Science **175** (1972) 720-731.

[45]   W. Stein, **The movement of molecules across cell membranes**, Theoretical and Experimental Biology **6** (1967) 1-369.

[46]   W. Stein and W. Lieb, Transport and Diffusion Across Cell Membranes, 1986, Academic Press, Orlando.

[47]   W. Stoeckenius, **Structure of the plasma membrane - an electron-microscope study**, Circulation **26: 5, part 2** (1962) 1066-1069.

[48]   C. Thaxton, W. Bradley, and R. Olsen, The Mystery of Life's Origin: Reassessing Current Theories, 1986, Philosophical Library, New York.

[49]   H.T. Thien, **Black lipid membranes at bifaces - formation characteristics, optical and some thermodynamic properties**, Journal of General Physiology **52: 1, part 2** (1968) 125-144.

[50]   H.J.A. Trurnit, **A theory and method for the spreading of protein monolayers**, Journal of Colloid Science **15** (1960) 1-12.

[51]   R. Virchow, Die Cellularpathologie in ihrer Begrundung auf physiologie und pathologische Gewebelehre, 1858, Archiv Pathologie, Anatomie und Physiologie, Berlin.

[52]   D.F.H. Wallach, The Plasma Membrane: Dynamic Perspectives, Genetics and Pathology, 1972, Springer-Verlag, New York.

[53]   A. Walter and G. Gutknecht, **Permeability of small non-electrolytes through lipid bilayer membranes**, Journal of Membrane Biology **90** (1986) 207-217.

[54]   W. Wickner and H. Lodish, **Multiple mechanisms of insertion of proteins into and across membranes**, Science **230** (1985) 400-407.

[55]   A.E. Wilder-Smith, The Creation of Life, 1970, Shaw, Wheaton, IL.

[56]   A.E. Wilder-Smith, The Natural Sciences Know Nothing of Evolution, 1981, CLP, San Diego.

[57]   E.L. Williams, editor, Thermodynamics and the Development of Order, 1981, Creation Research Society Books, Kansas City, MO.

[58]   R. Winzler, **Carbohydrates in cell surfaces**, International Review of Cytology **29** (1970) 77-125.

[59]   K. Wise, **Baraminology: a young-earth creation biosystematic method**, in Proceedings of the Second International Conderence on Creationism, Volume II, 1990, Creation Science Fellowship, Pittsburgh, PA.

[60]   H. Yockey, Information theory and molecular biology, 1992, Cambridge University Press, Cambridge, GB.

[61]   M. Zeleny, G. Klir, and K. Hufford, **Precipitation membranes, osmotic growths and synthetic biology**, in Artificial Life, C. Langton, editor, 1989, Addison-Wesley, New York.

FIGURES

Abbreviations: AMb, ammonium molybdate; Os, osmium tetroxide; PTA, phosphotungistic acid; SEM, scanning electron micrograph; TEM, transmission electron micrograph; UAc, uranyl acetate

Figure 1.   Biogenesis as an evolutionary process. Courtesy of Dr. Harold Morowitz [33].

Figure 2.   Complexification of systems as a function of energy flow. Courtesy of Dr. Harold Morowitz [33].

Figure 3.   TEM of a plastic embedded thin section of a plasma membrane (tegument plasmalemma of *Moniliformis dubious* [27]), resolving the bilayer (here ca. 12 nm thick) and filamentous elements of the glycocalyx (arrows).

Figure 4.   TEM of a plastic embedded thin section of an artificial lipid bilayer (formed from phosphatidyl ethanolamine in n-decane per the method of [49]), fixed in lanthanum nitrate and potassium permanganate; electron opaque "lines" reflect position of polar head groups and olefin (C=C) groups which have bound the metal fixatives; the intervening hydrocarbon chains do not react with these fixatives and remain electron transparent. The thickness of this membrane is ca. 7 nm.

Figure 5.   Schematic interpretation of Figure 4.

Figure 6.   TEM of liposome vesicles formed from phosphatidylcholine per the method of [2], negatively stained with PTA.

Figure 7. Os-fixed proteinoid microspheres, TEM of plastic embedded thin section, courtesy Dr. Sydney Fox [18]. Where the plane of section becomes tangential to the surface, there is a suggestion of pores (arrows); the original interpretation [18] is otherwise that of a bilayer.

Figure 8. TEM, *en face* view of a proteinaceous (albuminoid) "membrane", prepared according to [50] and fixed in Os vapor, showing sieve-like microstructure with a pore size ranging between ca. 4 - 10 nanometers.

Figure 9. SEM of a polymeric "megamolecular" gel; the larger pores have a diameter of ca. 1 micrometer.

Figure 10. TEM of crystaline protein (catalase), AMb negative stain; electron opaque spaces between structural units (transparent) are ca. 7 - 10 nm wide.

Figure 11. Pre-biotic formation of the primordial cell according to Darnell [8]; **a**, the "soup" of abiogenically derived amino acids, nucleotides, oligo/polynucleotides and peptides; at center, amphiphilic lipids are assuming a bilayer configuration around constitutents of the soup, which includes a potential RNA-type genome; **b**, the liposomal "cell" so formed.

Figure 12. Relative permeability of a phospholipid bilayer to water and various organic and inorganic solutes (see text for references); A, H_2O; B, glycerol; C, amino acids; D, monosaccharides; E, purines and pyrimidines; F, Cl^-; G, K^+; H, Na^+; I, phosphate, Ca^{++}, and nucleotides. Note, the scale for the comparisons of permeability coefficients (ordinal values) is in *negative* orders of magnitude. The actual rate of flow across the membrane (mol/sec/cm^2) would be a function of the concentration difference (dmol/cm^3) on the two sides of the membrane multiplied by the permeability coefficient (cm/sec). For the amino acid tryptophan, e.g., at a concentration difference of 0.1 mM, its transmembrane diffusion rate would be 10^{-11} mol/sec per cm^2 of membrane surface area.

Figure 13. Pre-biotic formation of the primordial cell according to Blobel [5]. From left to right, a liposome has adsorbed already evolved ribosomes, other macromolecules (proteins and nucleic acids developed in the "soup") to its external surface; surface bound material undergoes nonrandom arranging, with the generation of a concave plane; continued involution to a "double membrane" bound semi-closed vesicle; fusion at the "orifice" produces a structure analogous to a gram-negative bacterium.

Figure 14. TEM of a thin-sectioned, gram-negative bacterium (*Escherishia coli*), showing its two membranes; courtesy Dr. Wouter van Iterson and Bacteriological Reviews.

Figure 15. TEM of protein particles with the ultrastructure of a pore isolated (by detergent extraction) from membranes of the electric organ of *Torpedo californica*, negatively stained with phosphotungstate; magnification (inset) ca. 1 million X (micrograph by J. Telford, courtesy Dr. A. Schamoo and the NYAS); these pores function as Na+ permeation channels.

Figure 16. The diagrammatic interpretation of the kind of pore shown in Figure 15; water-filled channels for the passage of ions and hydrophilic organics are formed by groupings of protein subunits.

Figure 17. TEM (courtesy Dr. John Oaks) of a cryofixed, freeze-fractured and etched microvillous "brush border" membrane preparation of the *Hymenolepis diminuta* tegument [28, 29]. This membrane is dedicated physiologically to nutrient absorption functions and accordingly contains a wide variety of transport sites for amino acids, nucleosides, sugars, etc.; note numerous particles embedded in the continous lipid matrix; original magnification is ca. 530,000X.

Figure 18. TEM of a thin section of the *H. diminuta* tegument membrane (Figure 16), cryofixed, freeze-dried, negatively stained with Os, and embedded in plastic [29]. A putative transport carrier complex in longitudinal section is demarcated at the arrows, where two subunits and the intervening aperture are resolved; a cross-sectioned carrier is seen at X; original magnification is ca. 4 million X.

Figure 19. The diagrammatic interpretation of the structure shown in Figure 18; **a**, binding of the permeant solute to an "active site" triggers a kinetic conformational change in the structure of the protein subunits opening a permeation channel to the opposite side of the membrane (**b**). See [31, 44].

Figure 20. Integral (intrinsic) protein particle within the lipid bilayer of a membrane.

Figure 21. TEM of an isolated L cell plasma membrane with adherent ribosomes [21] (courtesy Dr. Marion Glick and Raven Press); such *in vitro* preparations incorporate ^{14}C-amino acids into membrane proteins.

Figure 22. The interpretation of Figure 21.

Figure 23. An alternative mechanism, where membrane protein synthesis occurs on cytosolic ribosomes; the peptide chains are complexed with "chaperones" which provide them a configuration and surface presentation compatible with the initially aqueous mileu and facilitate their incorporation into the membrane proper. See text for references.

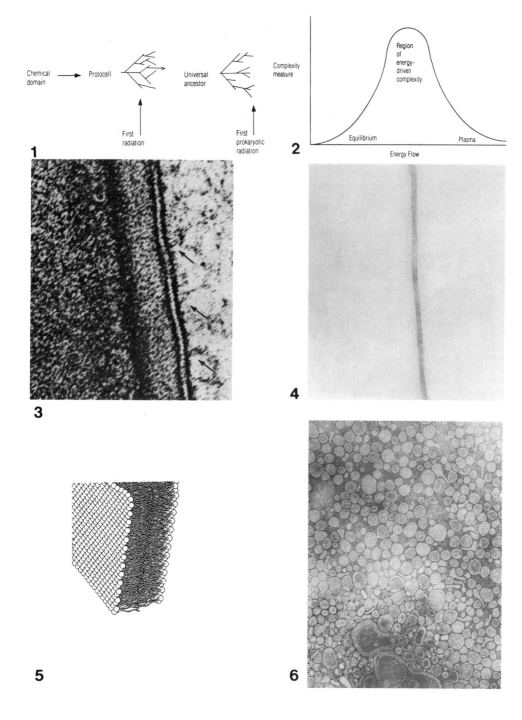

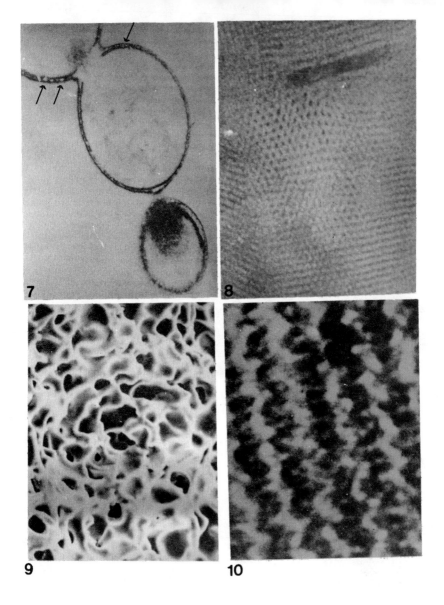

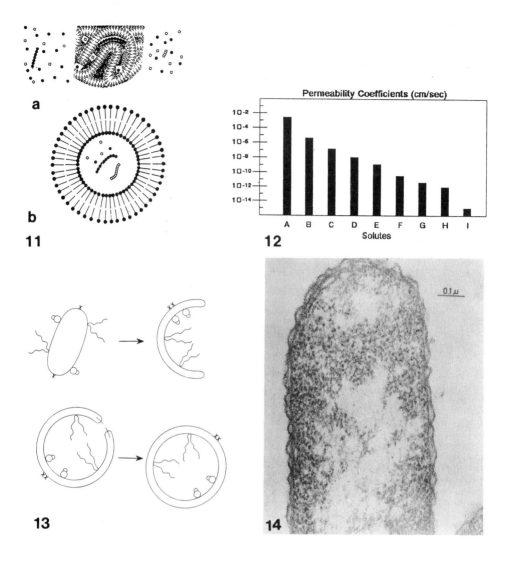

a

b

11

Permeability Coefficients (cm/sec)

10^{-2}
10^{-4}
10^{-6}
10^{-8}
10^{-10}
10^{-12}
10^{-14}

A B C D E F G H I

Solutes

12

13

$0.1\,\mu$

14

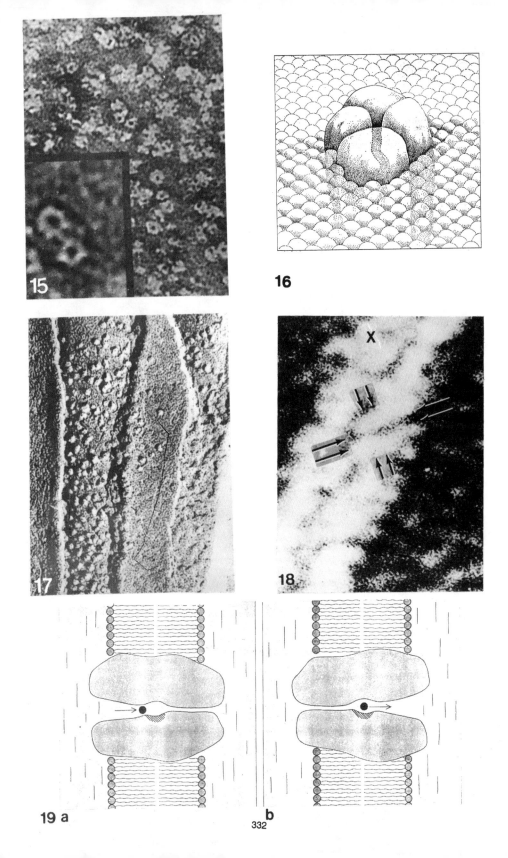

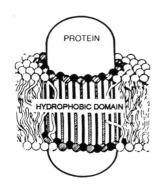

20

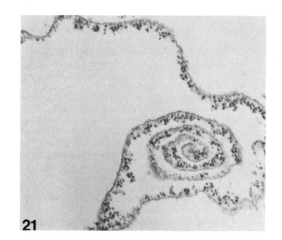

21

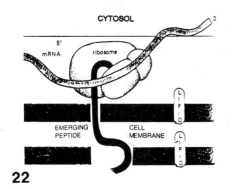

22

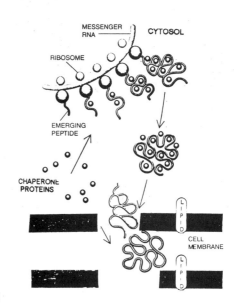

23

IMMUNE FUNCTIONS OF THE VERMIFORM APPENDIX

FRANK MAAS, M.S.
320 7TH STREET
GERVAIS, OR 97026

KEY WORDS

Mucosal immunology, gut-associated lymphoid tissues, immunocompetence, appendix (human and rabbit), appendectomy, neoplasm, vestigial organs.

ABSTRACT

The vermiform appendix is purported to be the classic example of a vestigial organ, yet for nearly a century it has been known to be a specialized organ highly infiltrated with lymphoid tissue. This lymphoid tissue may help protect against local gut infections. As the vertebrate taxonomic scale increases, the lymphoid tissue of the large bowel tends to be concentrated in a specific region of the gut: the cecal apex or vermiform appendix. The rabbit appendix has the greatest relative lymphoid development. Neonatal appendectomy in rabbits results in decreased total lymphocyte counts and lower antibody response to immune challenges relative to sham-operated controls. Appendectomy in young adult rabbits subject to whole body irradiation also depresses immunocompetence. The ultrastructure of the rabbit and human appendix mirrors that of Peyer's patches and the avian bursa of Fabricius. The appendix shares secondary functions of the avian bursa: it transports antigens from the intestinal lumen to the lamina propria; these antigens stimulate B cell proliferation, dissemination throughout the gut-associated lymphoid tissues, and differentiation into antibody secreting cells. In vitro studies indicate the human appendix contains immunocompetent B cells, T cells and natural killer cells. It is also a major site of IgA induction. Several epidemiologic studies suggest a correlation between appendectomy and cancer risk but these findings are inconclusive. Incidental appendectomy is often practiced by physicians despite the growing evidence that the appendix may be an important component of the immune system.

INTRODUCTION

Since the turn of the century it has been well documented that the human appendix is a specialized region of the gut containing considerable lymphoid tissue. Hence it has been called the "abdominal tonsil" [8]. Yet even today the appendix is probably the most commonly cited example of a vestigial organ [7]. This assertion is supported by a critique of 1991 editions of biology textbooks which were adopted by the state of Texas [31]. Textbooks selected by Texas and California typically set the national standard because of the large numbers of textbooks they purchase. In the chapters pertaining to evolution, the appendix was used as an example of a vestigial organ more than any other structure.

According to macroevolutionary theory, the appendix is a useless remnant of a large cecum which was important for digestion by hominoid ancestors [7]. This evolutionary bias has likely influenced investigators to neglect examining this organ and persuaded physicians to remove it incidentally. Specific immune functions of the human appendix have only been discovered within the last ten years. This paper reviews historical and current studies of the appendix in humans and animals. These studies are organized according to three categories: comparative anatomy of the appendix and its homologous structures, immunology of the rabbit and human appendix, and epidemiology of appendectomy and cancer.

COMPARATIVE ANATOMY

The vermiform appendix refers to a worm-like extension of the cecum also called the vermiform process of the cecum [12]. In humans and rabbits it is approximately 9 cm long. The cecum is one of the most variable digestive organs among vertebrates. Found in every vertebrate class, it ranges in size from a small pouch in man to an elongated sac twice the body length in the woolly lemur [40]. In mammals this diverticulum of the colon is located at the proximal end of the large intestine. It functions not only in fermentation of polysaccharides, but also in absorption of water and nutrients, and recycling of wastes [11]. Relatively few species have a cecum with a vermiform process. The most well known examples are the lagomorphs, great apes, and man [8]; it is also reportedly found in some monkeys and civets [46] and in the wombat [47]. The cecum in most vertebrates contains abruptly more lymphoid tissue than other sections of the colon.

Although birds do not have a vermiform appendix, they do have paired colonic ceca, some of which appear worm-like. The avian cecal lymphoid tissue is more concentrated in species with short as opposes to long ceca [8]. The small ceca of the pigeon, for example, is infiltrated with masses of lymphoid tissue especially near the junction of the colon. Regardless of length, the lymphoid tissue is more prominent in the avian ceca than in other regions of the gut. Many piscivores birds (e.g. penguins and gannets) and some carnivorous birds (e.g. hawks and eagles) allegedly have "vestigial" ceca [29]. Although these diminutive ceca do not appear to have a digestive role, they may function immunologically. Such a function should be investigated considering the high proportion of lymphoid tissue typically found in short avian ceca.

In mammals the greatest concentration of colonic lymphoid tissue lies either at the apex or the vermiform process of the cecum (if these structures are present) [8]. The cecal apex is a small sac distinguished from the body of the cecum by a slight constriction. It is found in many rodents such as mice and rats and in some carnivores as in domestic cats. In mammals possessing a cecal apex or vermiform process, nearly all the cecal lymphoid tissues is confined there. Comparative anatomy suggests that the cecal apex and vermiform appendix are homologous structures adapted for immune roles as opposed to rudimentary remnants of a longer cecum. Berry, who has performed what may be the most extensive comparative study of the vermiform appendix and its homologous structures concluded,

> The vermiform appendix of Man (sic) is not, therefore, a vestigial structure. On the contrary, it is a specialised (sic) part of the alimentary canal [8, p. 98].

If the human appendix is a useless vestige of a large cecum, then why does a rabbit have a similar appendix in addition to a large cecum? The lengthy cecum (> 30 cm) of the rabbit is an indispensable digestive organ which acts as a fermentation chamber [40]. But if the appendix is excised at birth, the developing rabbits do not appear to be handicapped nutritionally since weight gain and serum protein levels remain normal [37]. The primary function of the rabbit appendix is immunologic rather than digestive as described in the following section.

The structure and development of the human and rabbit appendix are similar. Hence the rabbit appendix has been used as a model in numerous experiments. Anatomical examinations indicate they both are well developed lymphoid organs containing numerous follicles [12,18]. The lymphoid follicles are composed of an apical dome, a germinal center in the basal nodule, and thymus dependent areas on the periphery [12]. The human and rabbit appendix are about the same length but only in the rabbit is it the largest lymphoid organ . The appendix of both typically contain fewer T than B lymphocytes. Percentages of T lymphocytes in the rabbit appendix vary from 7-40% [20]; human appendiceal T cells vary from 30-50% [25,32]. Lymphoid development begins a few days after birth and peaks in adolescence or young adulthood [3,10,12]. In humans after the age of 30, the lymphoid tissue begins to atrophy significantly [10].

IMMUNOLOGIC STUDIES

The rabbit and human appendix share secondary functions of the bursa of Fabricius, a central lymphoid organ controlling the development of B cells in peripheral lymphoid tissues of birds [5]. Although the appendix has not been shown to induce B cell differentiation from pluripotent stem cells, it does perform other functions of the bursa. It is a site of high B cell proliferation and seeding to peripheral lymphoid tissues. It may act as a B cell pool holding antibody producing precursors which upon antigenic stimulation disseminate to gut-associated lymphoid tissues (GALT) and differentiate into antibody secreting (plasma) cells.

The appendix is also anatomically similar to the avian bursa. The human and rabbit appendix, mouse Peyer's patches, and chicken bursa of Fabricius all contain a follicle-associated epithelium (FAE) which is identical in ultrastructure [13]. Tests with rabbits show that the FAE transports electron-opaque tracers from the lumen to the lamina propria. Bockman and Cooper suggested the FAE contains a pinocytotic channel through which antigens stimulate B cell proliferation and seeding throughout GALT. Most of the lymphocytes are transported by lymph from the appendix through the spleen and lymph nodes to the lamina propria throughout the gut. Many of the B cells complete their differentiation by becoming IgA secreting cells. Stimulation also occurs by macrophage processing and presentation of microbial antigens. In the germinal centers and domes, Bockman observed numerous macrophages which phagocytize bacteria from the lumen [12].

Lymphoid development of the appendix is largely dependent upon antigenic stimulation. If the appendix is ligated during neonatal development to isolate it from the intestinal contents but not the blood supply, growth of the appendiceal lymphoid follicles is significantly reduced [12]. Bockman concluded,

The appendix is a prominent example of gut associated lymphoepithelial tissue, whose function is to react to the wide variety of antigens present in the gastrointestinal tract [12, p. 271].

It is strategically located near the junction of the small and large intestines to perform such a function. It can sample the first contents of the colon and mount a specific immune response.

The appendix is one of many peripheral lymphoid organs; others include the spleen, tonsils, Peyer's patches, and lymph nodes. Does its extirpation affect immunocompetence or do other peripheral lymphoid tissues compensate for its loss? Experiments with rabbits reveals appendectomy in neonates markedly impairs immunocompetence several weeks later relative to sham-operated controls (sham surgery involves making an abdominal incision and externalizing the bowel). Antibody responses and total lymphocyte counts have been reduced significantly in five to eight week-old rabbits appendectomized at birth [3,37]. In fact neonatal appendectomy has depressed primary antibody response as much as thymectomy alone. Cell mediated responses, however, have not been affected by appendectomy as tested by delayed hypersensitivity to old tuberculin and rejection of skin homografts.

The appendix plays a significant immunologic role in young adult rabbits as well [5,38]. Recovery of antibody-forming potential after irradiation is dependent upon the appendix . Sussdorf measured the hemolysin response to sheep erythrocytes in rabbits exposed to whole or partial body irradiation in which the appendix was protected by a lead shield [42]. The antibody response was near normal in the shielded rabbits but significantly lower in the whole body irradiated animals. Nieuwenhuis et al. found a significantly greater antibody response to paratyphoid vaccine ten days after irradiation in rabbits whose appendices were left intact versus appendectomy [35]. Sussdorf and Nieuwenhuis also demonstrated regeneration of splenic lymphoid follicles (white pulp) was aided by lymphocyte migration from the appendix [35,41]. Sussdorf attributed the preserved hemolysin response in the shielded rabbits to the rapid restoration of splenic white pulp derived from the appendix. Subsequently, Ozer and Waksman found the bone marrow and appendix worked synergistically to restore splenic antibody response to sheep erythrocytes [36]. In combination the two produced 5 to 10 times more antibody than either alone or in summation. Splenic antibody response could be restored if the bone marrow was shielded during irradiation and appendiceal cells injected after radiation treatment.

With humans, no study has tested the effect of appendectomy on immunocompetence in vivo has not been documented. In vitro studies, however, do demonstrate the immunocompetence of adult appendiceal cells. Kawanishi found isolated B cells from the appendix produced mostly IgA antibodies without mitogen stimulation [25]. With stimulation, production of IgG, IgM and IgA was amplified. Suppressor T cells, if present, were not activated, but appendiceal helper T cells initiated and maintained B cell reactivity against immune challenges. Kawanishi concluded the appendix played a primary role in GALT responsiveness to foreign stimuli. He also found the appendiceal lymphocytes contained small subpopulations possessing natural killer (NK) markers and NK activity. NK cells are a subset of lymphocytes known to lyse certain tumor and virus-infected cells without specific antigenic stimulation [1]. They are the principle mediators of antibody-dependent cell-mediated cytotoxicity (ADCC). ADCC enables NK cells to increase their specificity as their target cells become coated with antibodies (IgG). These antibodies assist NK cell binding to their target which is followed by cytolysis.

Other studies indicate the human appendix is a major site of IgA induction. Benson et al. has cloned T cells from the appendix which stimulate both IgM B cell conversion to IgA (i.e. isotype switching) and IgA synthesis [6]. IgA is the major antibody found in intestinal secretions [34]. It is secreted exclusively by mucosal epithelium and is the only antibody which can be selectively transported across mucosal barriers into the gut lumen [1]. In the lumen, it helps control pathogenic microbes and infectious protozoans and tapeworms [9].

Fujihasher et al. [17] reported the appendix may be an enriched source of IgA B cells (especially IgA_2 subclass) containing abundant interleukin-6 receptors (IL-6R). Among other functions, IL-6, a T cell derived cytokine secreted in response to local inflammation, induces B cells to form plasma cells. In the appendix, human recombinant IL-6 preferentially stimulates B cells to differentiate into IgA plasma cells. They postulate the appendix may be a major source of IgA_2 B cell precursors that migrate to mucosal tissues. The appendix is the only known human lymphoid tissue with B cells expressing IL-6R endogenously unlike the spleen, tonsils or peripheral blood mononuclear cells (PBMC) which only express IL-6R when stimulated by a mitogen. Furthermore, the B cells of the appendix produce more IgA_2 in response to IL-6 than the tonsils, PBMC, and spleen [17,28].

Since human and animal studies clearly demonstrate the appendix functions immunologically, the question arises whether loss of the appendix increases susceptibility to diseases such as cancer.

EPIDEMIOLOGIC STUDIES OF APPENDECTOMY AND CANCER

Numerous epidemiologic studies have investigated an association between appendectomy and cancer [10,16,19,22,23,24,26,30,33,43,44,48]. These studies are divided in showing or failing to show a positive correlation with appendectomy and all types of cancer, especially colorectal. Epidemiologic studies often give conflicting results because of the difficulty in identifying confounding variables, selecting matched control groups, and using reliable means of data collection [27]. For instance, selecting a matched control group for diet is important since a low fiber diet has been associated with both appendicitis and colon cancer [14,16]. The strong correlation between these two diseases and the weaker association between appendectomy and colon cancer may indicate it is the low fiber intake not the appendectomy which predisposes to colon cancer. A thorough review of the literature has failed to find an appendectomy-cancer study which selected matched control groups for fiber intake.

In their book, Vestigial Organs are Fully Functional, Bergman and Howe [7] cite a 1968 study by Bierman [10] which found the incidence of leukemia, Hodgkin's disease, colon cancer, ovarian cancer and cancer in general was markedly greater in people who had appendectomies versus a control group without appendectomy. This study along with an earlier one by McVay [30] was criticized for relying on autopsy records [33]. Such records do not indicate whether the appendix was removed prior to cancer onslaught or whether it was removed during an operation for intestinal neoplasms, the latter being a common procedure. The data are unreliable since the number of appendectomies is skewed in the cancer group. Since McVay's and Bierman's study, other studies of the appendectomy-cancer association have obtained better data through hospital records or interviews. After reviewing several of these studies, an epidemiologist concluded that their results raised more questions than they answered and emphasized the need for controlled experiments in animal models,

> Clearly, further investigation into the structure and immune function of the vermiform appendix is needed. Studies assessing immune regulation and competency, pre-and post-appendectomy, in a suitable animal model are the next logical step. If appendectomy were found to affect immunocompetency adversely in animals, it would lend credence to the possibility of an appendectomy-cancer association in man particularly in view of the high incidence of neoplasia in immunosuppressed individuals [23, p. 394].

It is possible that both a low fiber diet and appendectomy contribute to the risk of colorectal cancer; the two may even have a synergistic effect. If appendectomy does impair the immune system, then examining the interaction between immunodeficiency and cancer may illuminate questions regarding an appendectomy-cancer association. Data from the Immunodeficiency Cancer Registry (ICR) established by the World Health Organization reveals children with a genetic immunodeficiency disease are a hundred times more likely to develop cancer than the average child. [15,39]. Of the cases reported in the ICR, gastrointestinal (GI) cancers were the number one neoplasm associated with selective IgA deficiency. Other studies have shown selective IgA deficiency is more frequent in GI cancer patients than normal individuals [21]. IgA deficiency is the most common primary immunodeficiency syndrome.

Elevated levels of circulating immune complexes (CIC) in the sera of cancer patients provides further evidence of the possible protective role of antibodies against neoplasia. CIC are antigen-antibody complexes which can be monitored clinically to determine the degree of tumor burden or prognosis of cancer patients [45]. IgA immune complexes have been found to be significantly higher ($p < .001$) in colon cancer patients versus normal or benign surgery controls [4]. These studies implicate IgA may bind malignant tumor antigens and help protect against cancer. The contribution of the appendix may be particularly important in protecting against GI malignancy since it may be an enriched source of IgA B cell precursors.

CONCLUSION

It is unfortunate that the appendix is still commonly considered vestigial by textbooks, instructors, and medical doctors despite the wealth of evidence to the contrary. On the positive side, the author has never found this claim made by a researcher who has published a firsthand investigation of the anatomy and/or physiology of the appendix. Rather, those who have studied this organ have described it as a specialized lymphoid structure. This lymphoid organ has distinct immune functions as well as immune functions similar to that of other peripheral lymphoid tissues such as the Peyer's patches and tonsils. Immunologic research on the appendix has lagged behind that of other lymphoid organs. The critical question remains: Does appendectomy impair the immune system? It would not be difficult to answer this question by testing immunocompetence in patients undergoing appendectomy.

Investigating the function of the appendix may not only benefit creation science but also health care. It would benefit the patient rather than a physician who considers the primary function of the appendix as financial support of his or her profession. Incidental appendectomy remains a common practice. In the United States, 36 incidental appendectomies are performed for every case of appendicitis; yet the lifetime risk of appendicitis is low (8.6% for males and 6.7% for females) and may be reduced by a high fiber diet [2,14]. One medical doctor quipped,

> The vermiform appendix, a dangling vestige of our evolutionary development, has been considered singularly devoid of any useful function, and the privilege of its amputation has rewarded many a fledgling physician for his patient pulling of retractors [33, p. 549].

Doctors who view the appendix as vestigial are reminded of the change in surgical practices regarding the criteria for performing tonsillectomy. In the 1930s, most children had their tonsils and adenoids removed [7]. Today doctors are reluctant to perform tonsillectomies unless serious infection occurs. Tonsils are believed to protect against oral infection even though the epidemiologic evidence is tenuous [27]. If appendectomy is shown to affect immunocompetence adversely, the medical profession may be more apt to consider it the "abdominal tonsil" and avoidremoving it unless it is pathologic.

REFERENCES

[1]   A.K. Abbas, A. Lichtman, and J. Pober, Cellular and Molecular Immunology, 1991, W.B. Saunders Company, Philadelphia.

[2]   D.G. Addiss, N. Shaffer, B. Fowler and R. Tauxe, **The Epidemiology of Appendicitis and Appendectomy in the United States**, American Journal of Epidemiology, 132(1990) 910-925.

[3]   K. Archer, D. Sutherland and R. Good, **The Developmental Biology of Lymphoid Tissue in the Rabbit**, Laboratory Investigations, 13(1964) 259-271.

[4]   M.W. Baseler, P. Maxim, and R. Veltri, **Circulating IgA Immune Complexes in Head and Neck Cancer, Nasopharyngeal Carcinoma, Lung Cancer, and Colon Cancer**, Cancer, 59(1987) 1727-1731.

[5]   A.D. Befus and J. Bienenstock, **The Mucosa-Associated Immune System of the Rabbit**, in Animal Models of Immunological Processes, J. Hay, editor, 1982, Academic Press, New York.

[6]   E.B. Benson and W. Strober, **Regulation of IgA Secretion by T Cell Clones Derived from the Human Gastrointestinal Tract**, Journal of Immunology, 140(1988) 1874-1882.

[7]   J. Bergman and G. Howe, "Vestigial Organs" are Fully Functional, 1990, Creation Research Society, Terre Haute, IN.

[8]   R.J. Berry, **The True Caecal Apex, or the Vermiform Appendix: its Minute and Comparative Anatomy**, Journal of Anatomy and Physiology, 40(1900) 83-100.

[9]   J. Bienenstock and A.D. Befus, **Mucosal Immunology**, Immunology, 41(1980) 249-265.

[10]   H.R. Bierman, **Human Appendix and Neoplasia**, Cancer, 21(1968) 109-118.

[11]   B. Bjornhag, **Comparative Aspects of Digestion in the Hindgut of Mammals. The Colonic Separation Mechanism (CSM) (a Review)**, Deutshe Tierarztliche Wochenschrift, 36(1987) 33-36.

[12]   D.E. Bockman, **Functional Histology of Appendix**, Archives of Histology, Japan, 46(1983) 271-292.

[13]   D.E. Bockman and M.D. Cooper, **Early Lymphoepithelial Relationships in Human Appendix**, Gastroenterology, 6(1975) 1160-1168.

[14]   D.P. Burkitt, **The Aaetiology of Aappendicitis**, British Journal of Surgery, 58(1971) 695-699.

[15]   C. Cunningham-Rundles, D. Pudifin, D. Armstrong and R. Good, **Selective IgA Deficiency and Neoplasia**, Vox Sanguinis, 38(1980) 61-67.

[16]   G.D. Friedman and B. Fireman, **Appendectomy, Appendicitis, and Large Bowel Cancer**, Cancer Research, 50(1990) 7549-7551.

[17]   K. Fujihashi, J. McGhee, C. Lue, K. Beagley, T. Taga, T. Hirano, T. Kishimoto, J. Mestechy and H. Kiyono, **Human Appendix B Cells Naturally Express Receptors for and Respond to Interleukin 6 with Selective IgA1 and IgA2 Synthesis**, Journal of Clinical Investigation, 88(1991) 248-252.

[18]   P. Gorgollon, **The Normal Human Appendix: a Light and Electron Microscopic Study**, Journal of Anatomy, 126(1978) 87-101.

[19]   O. Grobost, M. Boutron, P. Arveux, L. Bedenne, P. Chatrenet and J. Faivre, **Registre des Tumeurs Digestives, Faculte de Medecine, Dijon**, Gastroenterologic Clinique Et Biologique, 15(1991) 594-599 (English abstract).

[20]   M. Hanaoka, T. Mizumoto, and M. Takigawa, **Regulation of IgM Anti-Bovine Gammaglobulin Antibody Formation by Helper and Suppressor T Cells in Rabbits**, Cellular Immunology, 31(1977) 1-12.

[21]   L.A. Hansen, F. Bjorkander and V. Oxelius, **Selective IgA Deficiency**, in Primary and Secondary Immunodeficiency Disorders, R.K. Chandra, editor, 1983, Churchill Livingstone, N.Y., 62-84.

[22] L. Hardell and N. Bengtsson, **Epidemiological Study of Socioeconomic Factors and Clinical Findings in Hodgkin's Disease, and Reanalysis of Previous Data Regarding Chemical Exposure,** British Journal of Cancer, 48(1983) 217-225.

[23] C.P. Howson, **Appendectomy and Subsequent Cancer Risk,** Journal of Chronic Disease, 36(1983) 391-396.

[24] M. Jarebinske, B. Adanja and H. Vlajinac, **Case-Control Study of Relationship of Some Biosocial Correlates to Rectal Cancer Patients in Belgrade, Yugoslavia,** Neoplasma, 36(1989) 369-374.

[25] H. Kawanishi, **Immunocompetence of Normal Human Appendiceal Lymphoid Cells: in vitro studies,** Immunology, 60(1987) 19-28.

[26] I. Kessler, **Lymphoid Tissues in Neoplasia,** Cancer, 25(1970) 510-522.

[27] L. Mayes, R. Horwitz and A. Feinstein, **A Collection of 56 Topics with Contradictory Results in Case-Control Research,** International Journal of Epidemiology, 17(1988) 680-685.

[28] J.R. McGhee, K. Fujihashi, K. Beagley and H. Kiyono, **Role of Interleukin-6 in Human and Mouse Mucosal IgA Plasma Cell Responses,** Immunologic Research, 10 (1991) 418-422.

[29] J. McLelland, **Anatomy of the Avian Cecum,** Journal of Experimental Zoology (supplement), 3(1989) 2-9.

[30] J.R. McVay, **The Appendix in Relation to Neoplastic Disease,** Cancer, 17(1964) 929-937.

[31] G.C. Mills, M. Lancaster and W. Bradley, **Origin of Life and Evolution in Biology Textbooks--a Critique,** The American Biology Teacher, 55(1993) 78-83.

[32] T. Mizumoto, **B and T cells in the Lymphoid Tissues of Human Appendix,** International Archives of Allergy and Applied Immunology, 51(1976) 80-93.

[33] C.G. Moertel, F. Nobrega, L. Elveback and J. Wentz, **A Prospective Study of Appendectomy and Predisposition to Cancer,** Surgery, Gynecology and Obstetrics, 138(1974) 549-553.

[34] T.J. Newby, **Protective Immune Responses in the Intestinal Tract** in Local Immune Responses of the Gut, T.J. Newby and C.R. Stokes, editors, 1984, CRC Press, Inc., Boca Raton, FL.

[35] P. Nieuwenhuis, C. van Nouhuihs, J. Eggens and F. Keuning, **Germinal Centers and the Origin of the B-Cell System,** Immunology, 26(1976) 497-507.

[36] H. Ozer and B. Waksman, **Appendix and IgM Antibody Formation. IV. Synergism ofAppendix and Bone Marrow Cells in Early Antibody Response to Sheep Erythrocytes,** The Journal of Immunology, 105(1970) 791-792.

[37] D.Y. Perey, M.D.Cooper, R. Good, **The Mammalian Homologue of the Avian Bursa ofFabricius,** Surgery, 64(1968) 614-621.

[38] D.Y. Perey, and R. Good, **The Mammalian Homologue of the Avian Bursa of Fabricius,** Laboratory Investigations, 22(1970) 212-227.

[39] B.D. Spector, G. Perry III, R. Good and J. Kersey, **Immunodeficiency Diseases and Malignancy,** in Immunopathology of Lymphoreticular Neoplasms, J.J. Twoney and R. Good, editors, 1978, Plenum Medical Book Company, N.Y., 203-222.

[40] C. Stevens, Comparative Physiology of the Vertebrate Digestive System, 1988, Cambridge University Press, New York.

[41] D.H. Sussdorf, **Repopulation of the Spleen of X-Irradiated Rabbits by Tritium-Labeled Lymphoid Cells of the Shielded Appendix,** Journal of Infectious Diseases, 107(1960) 108-114.

[42] D.H. Sussdorf, **Quantitative Changes in the White and Red Pulp of the Spleen During Hemolysin Formation in X-Irradiated and Nonirradiated Rabbits,** Journal of Infectious Diseases, 105(1959) 238-252.

[43] K. Tajima and S. Tominaga, **Dietary Habits and Gastro-Intestinal Cancers: a Comparative Case-Control Study of Stomach and Large Intestinal Cancers in Nagoya, Japan**, Japanese Journal of Cancer Research, 76(1985) 705-716.

[44] J. Vobecky, J. Caro and G. Devroede, **A Case-Control Study of Risk Factors for Large Bowel Carcinoma**, Cancer, 51(1983) 1958-1963.

[45] M.L. Wasylyshyn and S. Golub, **Measurement of Immunocompetence in Cancer Patients**, in Manual of Clinical Laboratory Immunology, 3rd ed., N.R. Rose, H. Friedman and J. Fahey, editors, 1986, American Society for Microbiology, Washington, D.C., 719-722.

[46] C.K. Weichert, Anatomy of the Chordates, 3rd ed., 1965, McGraw-Hill Book Company, N.Y.

[47] R.A. Wheeler and P. Malone, **Use of the Appendix in Reconstructive Surgery: a Case Against Incidental Appendicectomy**, Brittish Journal of Surgery, 78(1991) 1283-1285.

[48] F. Yong-kang and Z. Cun-chun, **Appendectomy and Cancer, an Epidemiological Evaluation**, Chinese Medical Journal, 99(1986) 523-526.

KNEE DESIGN: IMPLICATIONS FOR CREATION VS EVOLUTION

KEVIN C. MCLEOD, M.D.
ARKANSAS BONE & JOINT CLINIC
2910 CYPRESS DRIVE
ARKADELPHIA, ARKANSAS 71923

KEY WORDS

Knee Flexion Contractor, Knee Design, Knee Evolution

ABSTRACT

This paper traces important features in human knee design that allows the unique function of plantigrade bipedalism (walking two legged on the soles of the feet). Concepts of biomechanical importance related to human gait and the problem of knee flexion contracture are discussed. Alleged hominid ancestors would have had to overcome a flexed knee stance to become efficient bipeds. Knees discovered in the fossil record, however, are fully functional. Joint replacement research has carefully followed a reproduction of the original design for a most unique joint - the human knee.

KNEE DESIGN

The human knee is an articulation of the three intra-compartmental bones - femur, tibia, and patella. The knee's unique design allows the most human feature of plantigrade bipedalism.

The distal regions of human femora show distinctive bipedal traits as described by Heiple and Lovejoy [6]. These features include a high bicondylar angle or similar to what orthopedists measure as the quadriceps angle. This angle is formed by a line through the medially inclined femoral shaft to a vertical line perpendicular to the knee joint. Illustration 1.

This angle is most important for placing the knee close to the midline of the body and produces a straight line (called the mechanical axis) between the centers of the hip, knee, and ankle. In humans the bicondylar angle is 8-10° (a range of 4-17°) with females having a slightly larger angle by virtue of a wider pelvis. Increase of this angle produces the visually recognized 'knocked' knee and a decrease of the angle is known as 'bow leg'. Other distal femoral differences include a large anterior rim on the lateral condyle, a deep patellar groove, and flattened contours on the articular surfaces of both medial and lateral condyles. Illustration 2.

The human knee does not rotate on a single axis like a wheel but acts more like a cam with a differential radial curvature. As the knee moves through flexion/extension, the instant centers of rotation also move through the distal femur forming an ellipse that closely parallels the anatomical contour of the femoral condyles. Illustration 3. Kettlekamp [8] has demonstrated that the greatest area of articular contact between the femur and tibia occurs in extension. Illustration 4. This allows for the maximum distribution of forces during any point of load bearing in knee motion.

The fully extended human knee can bear weight and remain stable with little sustained muscular action. This basically is true because in extension the articular design along with the soft tissues (especially the crucial ligaments) effect a twist upon the knee joint. The femoral condyles as viewed down the femoral shaft rotate internally while the tibial plateau rotates externally to an approximate total rotation of about 20°.

As a reemphasis, an important design feature at the distal end of the femur is the anterior enlargement of the lateral condyle. Orthopedists see this radiographically as the sulcus angle. Illustration 5. The lateral condyle helps maintain the patella, as it tracks superiorly in the femoral fossa during terminal degrees of extension. Failure of this development can be one of the causes for maltracking problems for the patella, since most subluxations or dislocations occur near knee extension.

The most distally placed quadriceps muscle called the vastus medialis obliquus is specifically oriented to assist guiding patellar motion during the terminal degrees of extension. Illustration 6. Smillie [19 p.4, 99] believes, "If complete extension of the knee joint is an attribute common only to man, then that component of the quadriceps which produces the last ten degrees of extension must surely possess the most recently acquired function and should thus show the most marked susceptibility to the effect of injury...vastus medialis is the 'key to knee'."

Human Gait

Humans alone enjoy a habitual upright posturing (orthograde meaning straight) gait that Lovejoy qualifies for hominids as striding. By convention, the human gait cycle begins at heel strike with the knee near full extension. Illustration 7. A knee stretched out near full extension allows for a full stride length and allows the trunk and head to remain erect, thus conserving energy. Early activation of the quadriceps allows weight bearing acceptance without knee collapse.

The knee nears full extension for a second time in the midstance phase when there is single limb support. During this longest phase of the gait cycle (60%, while swing phase covers the other 40%) the body weight forces are distributed over the greatest contact area between the femur and tibia. In the gait of quadrupeds such as the cat, neural reflexes are arranged to dampen quadriceps contraction at foot (paw) strike. Just the reverse is seen in biped humans when strong stimulation reaches the quadriceps to accept full body weight loads. The quantitative differences in this arrangement between cat and man are extremely large, and, as Pierro-Deseilligry [17] noted they are completely out of phase. Therefore, evolving from four limb to two limb ambulation would require a complete reversal of this neural reflex.

Perry [16] noted a dramatic increase in both quadriceps contraction forces and proximal tibial reaction forces as the knee flexion approaches 30°. Illustration 8. Perry also calculated that the maximum quadriceps strength is related to resting muscle fiber length and to the quadriceps lever arm (or moment arm). The maximum strength advantage gain can occur at knee flexion of above 60° and the least advantage is at 30°. Denham [1] found that as knee flexion angles exceeded 25°, the patellofemoral forces exceed tibiofemoral forces. Nisell [15] noted that the moment arm differences between men and women (shorter in women) give higher forces for equally extended moment magnitudes. He theorized that this factor may explain the more frequent patellofemoral osteoarthritis associated with women's knees.

Knee Flexion Contracture

In the human knee, a flexion contracture can become a dehabilitating disorder whether from congenital, developmental, or traumatic origins. The joint mechanical problems caused by an inability to extend the knee during striding can become progressive. When the knee joint is loaded in flexion, quadriceps insufficiency can develop from overstretching. This condition can lead to patella alta (superior displacement) and thereby reduce further the quadriceps lever arm. Finally this may produce instability problems and cartilage erosion as described by Sutherland [21].

Bony abnormalities accompany the flexed knee. Force distribution problems can lead to an overgrowth of the anterior tibial epiphysis which becomes an osseous block to further extension as reported by Tew [22]. Growth arrest of the posterior tibial surface can promote greater flexion contracture. Ambulation on a flexed knee (as one can appreciate by performing a duck-walk) requires a major energy expenditure. Gait progression is halting or shuffling as I observed during gait lab analysis in the Shriners' Hospital for Children in Houston, Texas. Because the stresses on the flexed knee are so significant, Perry [16] noted that contractures beyond 20° greatly compromise ambulation.

Primate and Human Ancestors

Haines [5,p.293] in his classic study of comparative anatomy on the tetrapod knee states that the most primitive type of knee found in living animals today is within the crocodiles. Yet there is a "single joint cavity for the femur, tibia and fibula, and the cruciate and collateral ligaments, the menisci and the femoro-fibular disc are all well developed." No one seems to have informed crocodiles of their primitive knees and then disallow their success in "survival" against more "advanced" species.

Dye [2] reported on a supposed tetrapod ancestor, the extinct amphibian, Eryops (fossils alleged to be 360 million years old). He shows that this creature possessed a well developed bicondylar end of the femur with a differential radius of curvature, a relatively flat tibia and a fibular articulation with the femur. Illustration 9. It appears that "kneeness" has an extremely ancient origin (if the above date were correct), and when first encountered in the fossil record knees have a fully functional form. Dye also says that there appears to be no animal model for human knees but that with further research a commonality may be uncovered in some yet unstudied small ursine (bear) type species.

Jenkins [7] studied the cineradiographic analysis of the gait in Chimpanzees. Illustration 10. At foot strike the knee is flexed 35-40°; body weight never approaches or falls forward to the knee (which would aid extension), and there is always a varus (bow leg) alignment. The bicondylar angle in chimpanzee and gorilla is 1-2° (compared to 10° for man) placing the knee outside the mechanical plumb-line seen in bipedal ambulators.

It is not this author's focus to discuss evolutionary dates or the importance of alleged hominid ancestors. However, the fossil record is supportive of human or human-like knee fossils. Leakey [11] in Africa discovered modern appearing femora which he dated to be 2.6 million years old. He classified these specimens as Homo sapiens, and his photographic evidence shows a femur with a bicondylar angle of 7-8°. Illustration 11.

Mary Leakey [9] later discovered human-like footprints, and the evidence for bipedalism was moved back to 3.6 million years.

Weaver [23, p. 593] envisions bipedal hominids running efficiently 4 million years ago and states, "Our earliest, most distinguishing characteristics were not a large brain, language, or toolmaking, but the ability to habitually walk upright."

McHenry [14] used a multivariate analysis to study the femur in early human evolution. He found the most distinguishing features of Homo femora in order of importance to be the anteroposterior diameter of the lateral condyle, femoral length, and projection of the greater trochanter.

Lovejoy and Heiple [13] reported that Australopithecus showed the highest bicondylar angle (angles of 14-15°) and was significantly larger than the mean for modern human females. Rather than being intermediate between Homo sapiens and the chimpanzee, these values are greater angles than for any known primate. This observation has led some like Reeder [18] to believe that this 'hominid' was a better biped ambulator than modern man. Illustration 12.

The 'why' of bipedalism is still a major question. Many theories have been advanced, and Leakey [10, p.77] notes, "For reasons that still leave us groping in the dark, the pressures of natural selection invented upright walking in our hominid ancestors sometime between 15 million and about 3 million years ago". Lovejoy's [12] lament seems still stark, "Why did these new features arise? It is worth stressing once again that the changes did not arise as part of an inevitable trend towards modern man, evolution does not work in a purposeful or directed manner."

Discussion

When 'knees' are first observed in the fossil record they are fully formed and functional. From one basic design all tetrapods and bipeds employ a vast variety of functions.

As noted here, the human knee extant or fossil, demonstrates design features enabling striding orthograde gait. However, in humans today, the 'atavistic' character of a knee flexion contracture is poorly functional and perpetuates its own disorder. Unlike Boule's prejudiced positioning, (an imagined hunched-over and flexed knee posture of neanderthals), modern investigators have allowed the anatomy of Homo findings to testify to efficient biped ambulation. Illustration 13. Yet Wray [25] noted that today a living primate, the pygmy chimp, appears to be a natural biped. Could these fossil findings be from nothing more than another extinct relative of the pygmy chimp? Zihlman [26] has reported her original observation on the chimplike morphology in new reconstructions of Austrolopithecus (Lucy) skeleton.

Several explanations are available if humans have always been contemporary with life on earth. If so, the fossil record predictably should yield modern human knees in allegedly ancient fossil strata. Also, since 80% of all known life forms are now extinct, it is possible that there could have been mosaic animals with biped capabilities.

In evolutionary terms some quadruped, starting out on flexed knees, required a radical set of morphological changes to make the transition to a modern plantigrade biped. Yet the fossil evidence of this transition is totally lacking and from what we know, the quadruped flexed knee would be disadvantaged for bio-mechanical reasons.

Evolutionists are looking beyond 4 million years ago for an alleged hominid who theoretically was a better biped than ourselves. These imagined pre-biped creatures would need to show evidence of a progressional change in bicondylar angles and enlargement of the lateral condylar process of the femur. And not so easily seen but just as important, they would have had quadriceps adaptions and altered neurological reflexes. The burden to uncover this first biped awaits the turning of another evolutionary spade.

Creationists say 'great design-Greater Designer', but much field research needs to be done on these fossil knee remains. No one has ever seen an australopithecine in a gait lab. Therefore, the theory of their striding behavior is conjecture. Gish's [3,p.104-113] review of the work of Zuckerman and Oxnard shows that some of the evolutionary ideas concerning Australopithecus are incorrect. One wonders if crocodiles were extinct and only known from the fossil record, would the report concerning their knee function describe a creature that we know can successfully survive in the age of mammals?

From an orthopedic perspective, we have had several decades to 'design' a better knee. Thus, in their research on total knee replacement, the manufacturers' favorite claim for a new prosthesis has been 'anatomic'. The more similar an implant is to the natural (created) part, the better its survivability and function. The best research has been forced to respect the original design.

ACKNOWLEDGEMENTS

Special appreciation goes to the ICC Reviewers who made insightful suggestions. And special consideration goes to Susan, Skye, Kassle, Cody, and Margaret Lee.

Questions for Future Study

(1) What adaptive forces would have worked (if any) to change a quadruped varus limb into a biped valgus limb?

(2) Could the adductor muscles play an important role in evolutionary terms for a more midline knee position? What osteological evidence has been investigated (i.e., the adductor tubercle on the femur, pelvic origins of the adductor muscles, etc)?

(3) Would a study of the morphology of the pygmy chimp show similarities to human knees?

(4) A review of the fossil intercondylar notch dimensions, which house the crucial ligaments, would be helpful. It is known from modern surgery that if this notch is not adequate or correctly spaced then damage can be brought to the cruciate ligaments, especially at full knee extension.

REFERENCES

[1] R. A. Denham, **Mechanics of the Knee and Problems in Reconstruction Surgery,** Journal of Bone and Joint Surgery, 60-B, 1978, p.345.

[2] S. F. Dye, **An Evoluionary Perspective of the Knee,** Journal of Bone and Joint Surgery, 69-A, 1987, pp.976-983.

[3] D. T. Gish, **Evolution, the Fossils Say No,** Creation-Life Publishers, San Diego CA, 1973, 2nd Edition.

[4] M. A. R. Freeman, **Arthritis of the Knee,** Springer-Verlag, New York, 1980.

[5] R. W. Haines, **The Tetrapod Knee Joint,** Journal of Anatomy, 76 1942 p.270-301.

[6] K. G. Heiple and C. 0. Lovejoy, **The Distal Femoral Anatomy of Australopithecines,** American Journal of Physical Anthropology, 35, 1973 p.75-84.

[7] R. A. Jenkins, **Chimpanzee Bipedalism: Lineradiographic Analysis and Implications for the Evolution Gait,** Science 178, 1972 p.877-879.

[8] D. B. Kettlecamp, **Tibiofemoral Contact Area-Determining Implications,** Journal of Bone and Joint Surgery, 54-A, 1977, p.352-353.

[9] M. Leakey, **Olduvai Gorge: Volume 3: Excavations in Beds I and 11, 1960-63,** Cambridge University Press, 1971.

[10] R. E. Leakey, **People of the Lake,** Mankind and Its Beginnings, Avon Books, The Hearst Corporation, New York, NY, 1978.

[11] R.E. Leakey, **Evidence for an Advanced Plio-Pleistocene Rominid from East Rudolph, Kenya,** Nature 242, 1973, p.447-450.

[12] C.O.Lovejoy, **The Gait of Australopithicines,** Yearbook of the Physical Anthropology 32, 1970, p.33-40.

[13]   C.O. Lovejoy and K. G. Heiple, **a Reconstruction of the Femur of Australopithecus Africans,** American Journal Physical Anthropology 32, 1970, p.33-40.

[14]   H. M. McHenry, **The Femur in Early Human Revolution,** American Journal Physical Anthropology, 49, 1978, p.473-488.

[15]   R.Nisell, **Mechanics of the Knee, ACTA Orthopedic Scandinavian,** Supplementum 216, 1985, Vol 56.

[16]   J. Perry, **Analysis of Knee Joint Forces During Flexed Knee Stance,** Journal of Bone and Joint Surgery, 57-A, 1975, p.960-967.

[17]   E. Pierro-Deseilligy, **Reflex Control in Bipedal Gait Han,** Motor Control Mechanisms in Health and Disease, Edited by J. E. Desmedt, Raven Press, New York, NY, 1983.

[18]   J. Reeder, **Missing Links,** Little, Brown and Copany, Boston, MA, 1981.

[19]   J. S. Smillie, **Injuries of the Knee Joint,** The Williams & Wilkins Company, Baltimore, MD, 1962.

[20]   C. Stringer, **In Search of the Neanderthals,** Thames and Hudson Ltd., New York, NY, 1993.

[21]   D. H. Sutherland,**The Pathomechanics of Progressive Crouch Gait in Spastic Diplegia,** Orthopedic Clinics of North America, Vol. 9, 1978, No. 1.

[22]   M. Tew, **Effect of Knee Replacement on Flexion Deformity,** Journal of Bone and Joint Surgery, 69-B, 1987, p.395-399.

[23]   K. F. Weaver, **The Search for Our Ancestors,** National Geographic, 68, No. 5, November, 1985.

[24]   B. Weissman, **Orthopedic Radiology,** W. B. Sanders Company, Philadelphia, PA, 1978.

[25]   H. Wray, **Lucy's Uncommon Forebears,** Science News, 123, 1983, p.89.

[26]   A. Zihlman, **Pygmy, Chimps, People and the Pundits,** New Scientist, November 15, 1985, p.45-46.

ILLUSTRATIONS

Bicondylar Angle Measurements

A   B

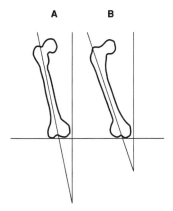

Illustration 1. *Redrawn from Lovejoy and Heiple [13], (A) showing the bicondylar angle in* Homo sapiens *and (B) showing the reconstruction for* Australopithecus. *The human femur is reduced in size for comparision. Note the greater angle for (B) (20° in his drawing and 15° for man with the actual normal value for humans at about 10○').*

347

View of Left Femoral Condyles

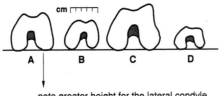

note greater height for the lateral condyle

Illustration 2. *Redrawn from Heiple and Lovejoy [6], ends of femurs. Note the greater anterior dimensions of the lateral condyle in humans to assist patellar tracking near full extension. (A)* <u>*Homo sapiens,*</u> *(B)* <u>*Australopithecus,*</u> *(C)* <u>*Homo sapiens Neanderthalensis,*</u> *and (D)* <u>*Chimpanzee.*</u>

Instant Center of Rotation

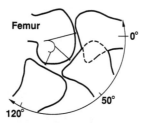

Illustration 3. *Redrawn from Freeman [4, chapter 9], the center of rotation at any one position of flexion moves along an elliptical curve within the distal femur. Notice how this ellipse closely patterns the contour of the condylar surface.*

Articular Contact Between Femur and Tibia

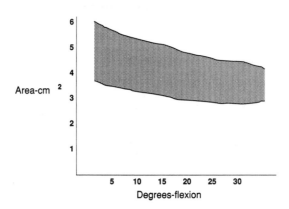

Illustration 4. *Redrawn form Kettlekamp [8], showing the greater contact area between tibia and femur in extension. The contact area is decreased by 1/2 at about 30° of flexion.*

Sulcus Angle for the Left Femur

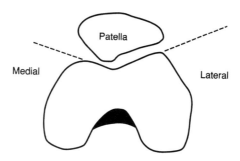

Illustration 5. *Redrawn from Weissman [24, p. 515], the sulcus angle helps determine the depth of the femoral fossa for patellar tracking. Shallow sulcus angles are related to patellar instabilities. Here the common normal angle is about 140°.*

Vastus Medialis Obliquus

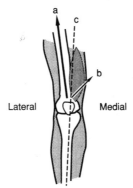

Illustration 6. *The vastus medialis obliquus (vmo), labeled (b), is developed in man to assist in terminal extension and to stabilize the patella. The major pull of the quadriceps (a) is altered by the vmo (b) to give the resultant (c) which centralizes patellar motion.*

Human Gait Cycle

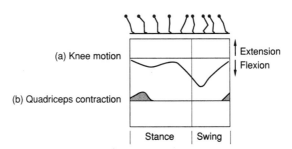

Illustration 7. *Redrawn from Pierro-Deseilligry [17], note on (a) the knee nearing extension at heel strike and in midstance. The major quadriceps action (b) occurs after heel strike to accept weight bearing and prevent knee collapse.*

Quadriceps Contraction Force and Tibial Surface Loads

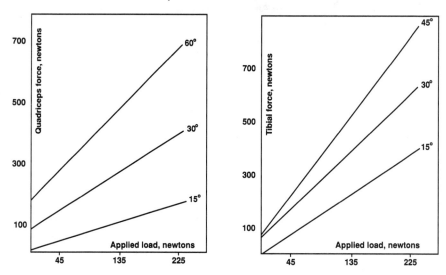

Illustration 8. *Redrawn from Perry, [16], observe the greater quadriceps force required to stabilize the knee at angles 30° or greater. Also note at these same angles the tibial surface loads double.*

Eryops Right Knee Anterior View

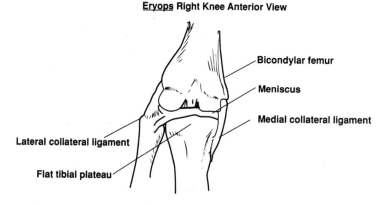

Illustration 9. *Redrawn from Dye [2], **Eryops** an alleged ancestor of all knees; yet note the classic design and form.*

The Bipedal Gait of Chimpanzee

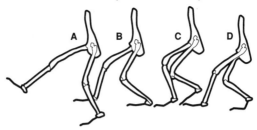

Illustration 10. *Redrawn fron Jenkins [7], the chimpanzee attempting bipedal ambulation with the knee in flexion at 35° at weight acceptance (B). Regard also the body weight never progresses anterior to the knee joint throughout the entire gait cycle. This condition places high stress if the quadriceps demanding sustained musclar action.*

East African Femur

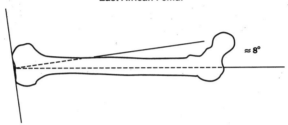

Illustration 11. *Redrawn from Leakey [11], this modern appearing femur from East Africa shows a bicondylar angle of about 8°.*

Bicondylar Angles in Primates

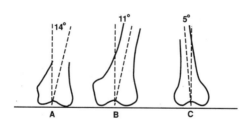

Illustration 12. *Redrawn from Lovejoy [13], measurements of bicondylar angles in (A) Australopithecus, (B) Homo sapiens, and (C) Chimpanzee. The greater angles in Australopithecus are higher than for any known living or fossil primate; therefore the australopithecines fulfil no intermediate role between humans and 'alleged' ancestors.*

The Old Stance of Neanderthal

Illustration 13. *Boules reconstruction of neanderthal with prejudiced posturing (note the knee flexion) has since been "straightened" out. This picture was redrawn from Stringer [20, p. 25].*

Editor's Note:

Illustrations redwrawn from author's sketches by ICC artist James Hilston.

MOUNTAIN BUILDING AND CONTINENTAL DRIFT

MATS MOLÉN, M.SC.
Box 3100, S-903 03
UMEÅ, SWEDEN

KEYWORDS

Mountain building, continental drift, fountains of the great deep, thixotrophy, earth history, philosophy

ABSTRACT

Philosophical constraints concerning creationist research are briefly discussed (refuting arguments like "God of the Gaps").

Earlier creationist models of continental drift and mountain building are shortly criticized. Research performed and theories forwarded by various authors are incorporated into a novel model of mountain building and continental drift based on geological data, and are also compared to Biblical interpretations.

There is geological and Biblical evidence indicating the former presence of huge subterranean water-filled caverns which became filled with sediments, i.e. geosynclines. Because the water in the geosynclines was exchanged for sediments, the underlying lithosphere became isostatically depressed and started to melt in its lower parts. The magma formed, then rose and pushed up mountains. The tectonic movements accompanying this orogenesis may have triggered continental drift. Continents may have slid on a thixotropic crystal/magma layer at the lithosphere/asthenosphere interface.

INTRODUCTION

Philosophical constraints

Christians have sometimes tried to explain observations in nature in an unfalsifiable manner, which is outside of the scientific method, and commonly not even based on interpretations of the Bible. Observations or hypotheses which have not been possible to explain by current scientific knowledge, have been saved by introducing fiat interventions from God. But, as scientific progress has produced explanations for many earlier "unexplainable" observations, God has been pushed away from reality - he was not needed - and nature has become more and more viewed as "atheistic"/naturalistic. Modern examples of "God of the Gaps" reasoning, which have been introduced to save some creationist hypotheses, are: Radioactive decay rates are proposed to have been supernaturally changed during the flood [7, 28, 35, 36], light has been proposed to be created in place from the most distant stars to the earth (which provides a philosophical problem similar to the one by Gosse, who proposed that God created the fossils in the earth strata so that it would look like the earth had a history even though it had none; [30]), it has been suggested that animals were recreated after the fall to be carnivores [26], and it has also been suggested that God helped to move the continents by changing natural laws [6, 7, 28, 35, 36].

If scientific research is to be possible, then miracles must not be invoked as soon as there are no obvious natural explanations. The only time a Bible-believing Christian may *a priori* use God in his explanations, is when the Bible clearly describes that God miraculously intervened in earth history and what He performed. Even if the meaning of many Bible verses may be debatable, a few instances are clearly miraculous and impossible to explain by current natural laws, e.g. creation of the universe and creation of different life-forms (including man). But, as the Bible may not mention in a clear way every occasion when God has intervened in earth history, some natural explanations may always prove futile.

Hence, the correct place to include God is not when we do not know how to explain an observation, but when it is obvious how something works. For example, a clock needs a watchmaker, a book an author, and the intrinsic life based on the "book of life" written in chemical language (DNA) is the work of an intelligent being. As Christians, we are not supposed to believe in a "God of the Gaps", but in the "God of the Knowledge"!

This philosophical approach is Biblically and scientifically consistent (even though it may not solve all scientific and theological problems); and will here be used when constructing a continental drift and mountain building hypothesis.

Continental drift

Throughout the 17th to the 19th centuries many different authors have suggested that the continents had drifted apart [14]. These theories were based on the configuration of the continents and/or the Bible. The current mainstream plate tectonics/convection currents continental drift theory was first proposed by Wegener, in its pristine form, at the beginning of the 20th century, and has thereafter been continually revised. However, many unsolvable problems concerning this mainstream model has made some scientists sceptical to most hypotheses of continental drift, and lead some to suggest continental drift by earth expansion [e.g. 14, 57]. A few have even suggested that continental drift was catastrophic [e.g. 16].

Many creationists have published continental drift and mountain building models [e.g. 48], but many of these models have little or no support from geophysics or geological observations. Several authors suggest that giant meteorites provided the force needed to initiate continental drift [e.g. 16, 27, 48]. Cook [19, 20] suggested that glaciers fractured the continents by brittle fracturing and made them drift apart. Brittle fracturing (spreading velocity of fractures at ca. 2 km/s) still appears to be a valid explanation. However, there are some doubts about the force which is proposed to have split the continents (e.g. geological data shows that continental drift was pre-glacial; [54]), so there must be found another mechanism of splitting the continents.

Baumgardner [7] developed a model where the complete oceanic lithosphere was replaced. Seen from the perspective of life on earth - this kind of envisioned catastrophe would actually be too large - probably nothing would survive. The heat which originated from sinking slabs of oceanic crust, from cooling lava and frictional heating (see example in Appendix 3 of this paper) is orders of magnitude too high. Also, too little consideration is given to the fact that density increases with pressure [23, pers. comm. Baumgardner], and if continental drift took place during the flood, there would be more differences in sedimentary strata, between the different continents, and between the continents and the sea (most sediments would have been deposited in the sea), than what is actually present today. However, the suggestion that oceanic lithosphere sank rather quickly to some depth, is a clear physical possibility and is incorporated in the model presented in this paper. But, in a flood model there is no need to replace the complete oceanic lithosphere, as most fossil-bearing sediments would be deposited close to the continents.

The model presented here is an attempt to compile the best data and interpretations from all continental drift and mountain building theories (i.e. I do not adhere to all interpretations proposed by the authors I refer to, but possibly only to the mechanisms/hypotheses which are referred to). As there is still no raw data available from below the earth's crust or lithosphere, except more or less questionable tectonic reflection data [21, 41], the model proposed here must be developed further in the future. Since one purpose of this paper is to try to present a possible continental drift model, little time is used to criticize the idea of continental drift itself.

EARTH HISTORY BASED ON GEOLOGICAL DATA

There are conflicting creationist models of earth history. The following are the scenarios most often proposed: 1) All of the Phanerozoic is post-flood [e.g. 56, 81]. 2) Large parts of the Phanerozoic (mainly Mesozoic and Cenozoic) is post-flood (e.g. Northtrup [64, 65] and Scheven [77, 78, 79, 80]) 3) Probably only Late Tertiary and Quaternary deposits are post-flood (the original Whitcomb and Morris 1961 hypothesis [94]).

Most scientists adhere to variations of the Scheven/Northrup (mainly in Europe) or Whitcomb and Morris (mainly in USA/Canada) hypotheses. The present paper is not concerned with details presented in these theories, and may be compatible with different interpretations. But, scientific research has to work with raw data. Hence, some fundamental geological observations are highlighted below, from Late Precambrian to Recent, which are pertinent to give a basis for the mountain building and continental drift theory presented here.

Weathering

In many Precambrian strata there are weathered horizons *in situ*, some even approaching soils (e.g. Ontario: [24, 55] and Scandinavia: [54, 55]). So-called soils in Cambrian to Tertiary strata display no extended weathering, or have been shown to be parts of transported former weathered sediments [e.g. 54]. Hence, they are not soils *in situ*. Some Middle Tertiary incipient soil horizons, exhibiting small stumps of trees, appear to have been formed *in situ* [70], and in the Quaternary there is an abundance of weathered soil horizons. So, the Precambrian-Cambrian, and to some extent, the Tertiary-Quaternary boundary, are the two greatest unconformities of Phanerozoic earth history.

Sorting/grading

The sorting displayed by most sedimentary strata indicates that they must have been deposited quickly, and for the most part uninterrupted.

The Late Precambrian terminates with a conglomerate or diamictite in many places throughout the world [52], followed by Cambrian fossiliferous sediments. In other places, the Cambrian, or other lowest lying strata (e.g. the Carboniferous of South Africa [52, 93]) starts with a conglomerate or diamictite. This may be interpreted as the initiation of a worldwide catastrophe.

Very often sediments, which according to the geological time scale have been deposited throughout millions of years, show grading. These graded strata may often (according to the geological time scale) be "interrupted" by many "millions of missing years", even though there is no physical evidence that this is the case [54].

Life communities

Fossils are, in general, sorted with the bottom-living (benthic) marine animals deepest down in the strata and the most moveable land animals at the top. This has been called ecological zonation [94]. Marine animals are often better preserved than land animals, thus indicating that the latter often floated or were rafted on the water surface while their flesh rotted (compare Coffin [17, p. 81]). Almost all fossil graveyards containing land animals carry only the bones, and usually a mix of many dismembered animal skeletons, and many graveyards contain mostly broken and shattered bones (many examples are quoted by Velikovsky [92]).

Footprints are often preserved in strata below where the bodyfossils are buried [e.g. 9, 46, 54] - thus indicating that the animals survived a while before becoming buried (e.g. Early Cambrian trilobite footprints at Lugnås, Sweden, are preserved a few meters below body fossils of trilobites which are the correct size to make the footprints; pers. comm. Jan Johansson).

Post-Paleozoic strata often are different from Paleozoic strata, indicating longer time of deposition during, what appear to be, post-flood conditions (e.g. Cretaceous biogenic chalk, compare Roth [75] and Scheven [80]). However, I do not claim that all post-Paleozoic strata are post-flood and display ecological succession.

Conclusion

The above argues a case for quick deposition of most of Paleozoic, Mesozoic and Cenozoic strata, with no or little intervening time between different strata. The evidence also shows that there was extended time periods between different strata (from maybe tens, to hundreds, to thousands of years) mainly in the Precambrian and Quaternary. Geology should therefore, to a higher degree, resort to describing local superpositions which show the environment of deposition of different areas, rather than making large geographical time correlations based on similar fossil content.

MOUNTAIN BUILDING AND GEOSYNCLINES

A model hypothesized from the Bible

According to the Bible, all the fountains of the great deep burst open at the beginning of the flood [32]. This could mean that large underground reservoirs opened up, by cracks in the overhanging ceiling (1; numbers refer to drawing), and an immense amount of water burst forth (the reservoirs may have appeared more like a network of hollows, or highly porous rock, rather than one single large reservoir - compare to discoveries of porous rock containing circulating water at depths of 11.5 km [21, 40]). As the fountains were opened, and the ceiling collapsed, the former reservoirs would turn into large troughs or depressions where sediment subsequently was deposited (2). Sediments would mainly be deposited in these depressions and at the coasts of continents, leaving the old high grounds and land areas more or less barren (i.e. many shield areas on our planet). As sediment is more dense than water, the crust/lithosphere would become depressed below the areas of deposition (2) (see Appendix 1 for details). The deepest parts of the lithosphere, below the former "fountains of the great deep", would begin to melt after becoming pressed into the asthenosphere. Also, the crust may have partly melted at the Moho (compare Rosendahl et al. [73]) and at the SIAL/SIMA boundary (i.e. compare Krauskopf [42, pp. 341-342, 430-431], Corliss [21, p. 24], and Tyler [91]). When the lithosphere melted it would become lower in density, as compared to the overlying layers. The magma thus formed would therefore move upwards, through the thick layers of sediments (3), forcing the formation of mountains (4) ([91] and Appendix 1). The rising of the magma would also cause many of the sedimentary beds to be laterally compressed, or, to slide by gravity to lower elevations and pile up upon each other and form nappes. Consequently much "crustal shortening" would take place.

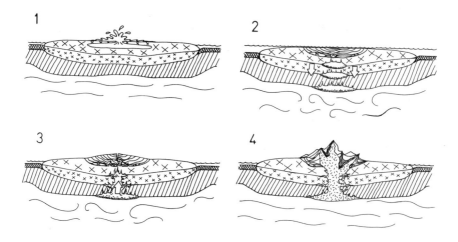

Figure 1. *Mountain building hypothesis. From above - crust (divided into upper SIAL and lower SIMA), lithosphere (diagonal lines) and asthenosphere (waved lines). (Not drawn to scale. See text for details.)*

Observed geological data

Throughout the world there are many so-called geosynclines - large hollows/troughs which have been filled with huge layers of sediment at the fringe areas of Precambrian shields. In the middle of these geosynclines magmatism and volcanism commonly has occurred - mantle plumes, diapirs and/or batholiths have risen through the earth's crust and pushed up high mountain chains. For example, the Himalayas, the Alps and most other Paleozoic to Cenozoic subaerial mountain chains were produced from large troughs which were filled with sediments. Consequently the central parts of the Alps and the Himalayas are made up of magmatic rocks, and in most other mountain chains there are abundant magmatic rocks. Many nappes have formed and, hence, "crustal shortening" has taken place (compare Carey [14]). In the Andes, the Caledonides, the Variscides, the Western United States, the Himalayas, the Mongolian Plateau, and other mountain belts, there is evidence for extensional tectonics [1, 2, 11, 22, 25, 31, 34, 38, 49, 68, 96], which would be easier explained during sliding and gravitational collapse from a high center of uplift [1, 33, 68], than from plate collision during continental drift. Furthermore, geological correlations (and paleobiogeography; e.g. the Glossopteris flora has been found far north of the Himalayas [10]) do not suggest a long isolation of India from Africa and Asia [10 and 14, p. 158-162], which may even suggest that they have been in close contact until after deposition of most of the earth's strata, and that the Himalayas, for the most part, is not a collisional orogen but a rising geosyncline.

Evidently the geosynclines and mountain chains observed on this planet show indications of having been formed in a way similar to what one would suspect from a Biblical scenario, as outlined in the preceding section. It may have taken perhaps a few hundred years for the lower lithosphere to melt enough to build up a great diapir or batholith, in a Biblical flood scenario (but of course, some mountains could have risen more quickly) (Appendix 1).

Because the energy transported to the troughs (i.e., transportation of heavy sediments to a new region, and isostatic depression) would be carried with the rising magma as heat from the mantle, there is a basis for expecting that some parts of the asthenosphere would cool down at the roots of the mountains. This could explain the deep roots of many mountains. Furthermore, because the crust was depressed below the "fountains of the great deep", larger concentrations of sediment would have been deposited here, thus giving a thicker lithosphere.

There is also much evidence in support for uplift and orogenesis while the sediments were still unconsolidated, as it is difficult or impossible to envisage bending of solid rocks, except during high heat and/or pressure leading to higher grade metamorphism. Evidently, sediments have often been contorted or squeezed without being heavily metamorphosed; for example in Scania [44] and Gotland [50] in Sweden, in California and Colorado in USA [5], where ever clastic dikes are present [74] and commonly in mountain chains. This indicates short time scales.

CONTINENTAL DRIFT - ONE MORE HYPOTHETICAL CONTRIBUTION

It may seem quite impossible to believe that great scale continental drift could have taken place during just a few thousand years, or even more impossible if it all took place during one single year (as suggested by many creationists). To open up the Atlantic, which is about 6000 km at its widest, would require a drift of 1 km/year for

3000 years in opposite directions (2x3000 km = 6000 km), i.e. a daily drift of nearly 3 m in opposite directions. The highest estimate of relative plate velocities based on the uniformitarian model is 0.38 m/year, i.e. about four orders of magnitude too slow [29]. The maximal time accepted by most creationists, between the flood and the present, is less than 10 000 years, but even 10 000 years is not much. There is, however, evidence indicating a quick continental drift, as shown below.

Hypothetical geological mechanism

At the lithosphere/asthenosphere boundary there may be a stratum of solid crystals in magma. Such material may be thixotropic, i.e. if put under differentiated pressure (i.e. shearing stress) the material will give way and behave like a fluid. If the environment is stable, a thixotropic material will behave as a solid. If huge amounts of sediments were transported and relocated on the earth's surface, unloading some areas while depositing sediments into deep troughs where the "fountains of the great deep" had been, the earth's interior would become destabilized. The vertical movements during mountain building may have fractured the lithosphere at its weakest places, close to the geosynclines where the lithosphere would be weakened, and would also have forced the plates to move horizontally, induced by gravity and horizontal pushing from the upwelling magma. (Cracks in the lithosphere may also have originated during the flood, and/or by large meteorite impacts.)

In this way a quick continental drift could have been initiated, by sliding on the thixotropic layer when becoming fluidized (idea originally from Dr. Gary Parker, pers. comm.). Initial cracking accompanied by upwelling magma, would release the tension built up in the lithosphere during mountain building, and the continents would quickly start to move. After initial acceleration the speed would slowly decrease, depending on the inertia of the continents, the oceanic crust and the lubricating thixotropic layer (Fig. 2). It may also be possible that the lithosphere was thinner closer to creation, and cooled to a much higher degree after large amounts of heat was released during and after the flood. (See Appendix 2 for more details.)

If a layer of partly melted magma is at the Moho (suggested by Rosendahl *et al.* [73]), then I would suggest that some sliding below the continents, and some initial sliding below the oceanic crust, may have taken place at this surface too.

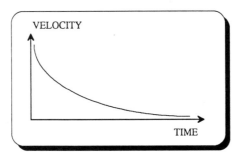

Figure 2. *Diagram showing the hypothetical velocity of movements of continents after initial rupture. (There is no scale on the diagram, since this is only presented to show the general velocity variation of the drift.)*

The drift may be separated into two periods: 1. Small scale regional continental drift during the flood, maybe 100-1000 km (impossible to know if and how much, at this stage of research). 2. Large scale world-wide post-flood continental drift (starting during the days of Peleg, see below), amounting to a (strictly hypothetical) mean of 0.278 mm/s = 0.001 km/h = 9 km/year, during ca 200 years = 1800 km. This totals to 1800 + 1800 = 3600 km (i.e. continents will drift in directions opposite to each other, but the larger mass Eurasia/Africa would of course drift with less velocity and N-S America with higher velocity). The mean drift may then have slowed down to 0.9 km/year for 500 years = 900 km, then 0.1 km/year for 1000 years = 100 km, then 0.01 km for 2000 years = 20 km. This is in total 4620 km. The above numbers may be arbitrarily changed, a little up or down, to reach the desired drift of 6000 km, for example 0.4 mm/s would mean a drift of 5050 km in 200 years. This speed is ca. four orders of magnitude lower than the highest inferred fluid velocities at the core-mantle boundary, 10 km/h (2.8 m/s), implied by changes in the magnetic field (these high velocities were doubted by Jacobs [37, p. 108], but not by Humphreys [36]). Observe that the drift decreases logarithmically and not linearly. Hence, the above hypothetical velocities show that very high drift speed is not needed in order to explain great scale post-flood continental drift.

The waves generated by the moving continents would be negligible compared to most normal tidal water (except for, of course, tsunamis generated by earthquakes that would accompany continental drift). Considering the low velocity suggested above, not much would happen just because of the drift. The water would hardly rise much above the normal seashore.

The heat production arising from the drift is elaborated on in Appendix 3.

Geological observations suggest numerous post-flood catastrophes, and many of these must have been the consequence of mountain building and/or continental drift. Examples are large consolidated (or maybe semiconsolidated) blocks of Phanerozoic sediments, some as large as 200-600 km^2 in size, which have slid many tens of kilometers [47, 72, 95], overthrusts which have been catastrophically moved [4, 64], and flood basalts in Washington (Columbia Plateau [59, 60, 61]) and India (the Deccan traps [13]). Flood basalts commonly accompany continental rifting [33], and are present at a few places on the Atlantic coast, i.e. in eastern central South America (in Brazil/Paraguay/Uruguay/Argentina), southwest Africa (Namibia), east Greenland, northern Ireland, the Atlantic just outside of the Norwegian coast and possibly the Caribbean [71]. Pieces of continents seem to have also been left behind in the oceans, during drifting [14, 21].

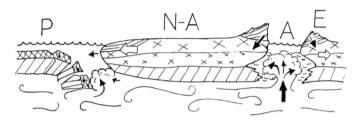

Figure 3. *Hypothetical continental drift mechanism (not drawn to scale). (See text below, Appendix 2 and Appendix 4 for details.) (P = Pacific, N-A = North America, A = Atlantic, E = Europe. Black arrows = forces. White arrows = movement of continents. Other markings as in fig. 1.)*

During continental drift the oceanic crust may have sunk more or less straight down in front of the moving continents (fig. 3; mechanism slightly similar to Baumgardner [7]; see Appendix 4) after the oceanic plates had been fractured (mechanism after Cook [20]; brittle fracture spreading velocity of ca. 2 km/s). Actually, because the oceanic lithosphere is commonly denser than the underlying asthenosphere, it would be nearly inevitable that the oceanic lithosphere sank after splitting ([15], also see Appendix 4). This may be the reason why most so-called "subducting slabs" still display down-dip tensional faulting [18]. The sinking slabs of oceanic lithosphere may even have enhanced continental drift, by creating vertical and horizontal drag in a direction away from the continents, during sinking. Almost near vertical sinking of oceanic lithosphere may also explain the occurrence of undisturbed sediments, or absence of sediments, in the oceanic trenches [e.g. 14, 87], which cannot be explained by the main stream model of subduction of oceanic lithosphere below continents.

MOUNTAIN BUILDING AND CONTINENTAL DRIFT IN A BIBLICAL PERSPECTIVE

The adjustments in the earth's lithosphere during the flood would have initiated changes in the earth's interior, but the greatest period of mountain building and continental drift may have taken place a few hundred years after the flood, at the time of Peleg (Genesis 10-11). The root of the word Peleg means to be "divided by water" [65]. There could have been a beginning of continental drift and a division of the nations at approximately the same time. This also seems to be the opinion of one of the Old Testament apochryphs - "The Book of Yashar", 7:19 [62] "... *the name of one was Peleg, for in his days the sons of men were divided, and in the latter days, the earth was divided*". This period of post-deluge catastrophes would have initiated the ice-age, by heating up the oceans and expelling large quantities of volcanic ash into the atmosphere (a similar mechanism to the one proposed by Oard [66]). Research conducted by myself [53, 54], Austin [61], Scheven [77, 79], and others, show that an ice age could not have started immediately after the flood.

The geomagnetic field reversal data as presented by Humphreys [35, Fig. 2, p. 117] may suggest that shifts in the geomagnetic polarity took place both during the flood, and later during continental drift. If the core could be destabilized once, it could well have been destabilized many times, e.g. 1) as a consequence of the onset of the flood, 2) during small scale continental drift during the flood (compare Northrup [64]), and 3) during large scale continental drift after the flood. As most Mesozoic and Cenozoic reversals have been recorded in marine strata, they may very well be post-flood (e.g. many marine Mesozoic strata are to a great part biogenic and would have needed extended time to build up). The destabilization of the upper mantle, may have "transmitted" movements to the outer core, which may have initiated the reversals of the magnetic field.

A post-flood continental drift, beginning a hundred or more years after the flood, explains recent biogeography more straightforward [51] than dispersal by the assistance of man [97].

CONCLUSIONS

The mountain building process here described fits the geological and geophysical data, even though many details need to be outlined and investigated. It is valid independently of the more speculative continental drift hypothesis.

The continental drift model may be geophysically possible, but of course, needs to be investigated more. One may wonder if some earth expansion is needed to explain all the data (e.g. that most plates seem to move away from each other [14 and 82, p. 28], but then a plausible mechanism must be found [e.g. 57].

The exact timing of continental drift may be debated. It seems probable that most is post-flood, though some mountain building and some continental drift may have occurred during the later stages of the flood.

To conclude, earth models which are based on behaviour in the interior of the earth are always to some degree hypothetical, and therefore no mountain building or continental drift theory should be accepted without provisions. Also, probably no single model will explain all continental drift and mountain building on this planet, therefore models erected by many scientists may need to be incorporated.

ACKNOWLEDGEMENTS

Helpful comments and criticism came from Dr. Harold Coffin, Peter Olsson, Dr. Sune Petterson, Krister Renard and Dr. David Tyler. Drawings were made by Rebecca Öhmark and Pavla Korostenski. The language was corrected by Myles Dean. Those mentioned here are in no way responsible for any of the conclusions in this paper. They neither endorse nor disapprove the interpretations done.

REFERENCES

[1]   Anderson, R. E. (1993) **The Newport Fault: Eocene Listric Normal Faulting, Mylonization, and Crustal Extension in Northeastern Washington and Northwestern Idaho: Discussion and Reply**, Geological Society of America Bulletin, Vol. 105, 1511-1514.

[2]   Anderson, R. E. & Barnhard, T. P. (1993) **Aspects of Three-Dimensional Strain at the Margin of the Extensional Orogeny, Virgin River Depression Area, Nevada, Utah, and Arizona**, Geological Society of America Bulletin, Vol. 105, 1019-1052.

[3]   Antoine, L. A. G. & Moyes, A. B. (1992) **Geophysical Evidence for a Causative Process for Fragmentation in Western Gondwana**, Geology, Vol. 20, 605-608.

[4]   Austin, S. A. (1984) Catastrophes in Earth History, ICR.

[5]   Austin, S. A. & Morris, J. D., **Tight Folds and Clastic Dikes as Evidence for Rapid Deposition and Deformation of Two Very Thick Stratigraphic Sequences**, Proceedings First International Conference on Creationism, Editors: Robert E. Walsh, et al, Creation Science Fellowship, Inc., Pittsburgh, PA, 1987, Vol. 2, 3-15.

[6]   Baumgardner, J. R., **Numerical Simulation of the Large-Scale Tectonic Changes Accompanying the Flood**, Proceedings First International Conference on Creationism, Editors: Robert E. Walsh, et al, Creation Science Fellowship, Inc., Pittsburgh, PA, Vol. 2, 17-30.

[7]   Baumgardner, J. R. **3-D Finite Element Simulation of the Global Tectonic Changes Accompanying Noah's Flood**, Proceedings Second International Conference on Creationism, Editors: Robert E. Walsh, et al, Creation Science Fellowship, Inc., Pittsburgh, PA, 1991, Vol. 2, 35-45.

[8]   Boulton, G. S. (1990) **Sedimentary and Sea Level Changes During Glacial Cycles and Their Control on Glacimarine Facies Architecture**, in Glacimarine Environments: Processes and Sediments, Dowdeswell, J. A. & Scourse, J. D. (Eds.), Geological Society Spec. Publ. No. 53, 15-52.

[9]   Brand, L. & Florence, J. (1982), **Stratigraphic Distribution of Vertebrate Fossil Footprints Compared with Body Fossils**, Origins, Vol. 9, 67-74.

[10]   Briggs, J. C. (1989) **The Historic Biogeography of India: Isolation or Contact?**, Systematic Zoology, Vol. 38, 322-332.

[11]   Brodie, J. & White, N. (1994) **Sedimentary Basin Inversion Caused by Igneous Underplating: Northwest European Continental Shelf**, Geology, Vol. 22, 147-150.

[12]   Brown, W. T., **The Fountains of the Great Deep**, Proceedings First International Conference on Creationism, Editors: Robert E. Walsh, et al, Creation Science Fellowship, Inc., Pittsburgh, PA, 1987, Vol. 1, 23-38.

[13]   Caldeira, K. G. & Rampino, M. R. (1990) **Deccan Volcanism, Greenhouse Warming, and the Cretaceous/Tertiary Boundary** in Sharpton, V. L. & Ward, P. D. (Eds.) Global Catastrophes in Earth History, GSA Special Paper 247, 117-123.

[14]   Carey, S. W. (1988) Theories of the Earth and Universe, Stanford University Press.

[15]   Cloos, M. (1993) **Lithospheric Buoyancy and Collisional Orogenesis: Subduction of Oceanic Plateaus, Continental Margins, Island Arcs, Spreading Ridges, and Seamounts**, Geological Society of America Bulletin, Vol. 105, 715-737.

[16]   Clube, V. & Napier, B. (1982) **Close Encounters With a Million Comets**, New Scientist, Vol. 95, 148-151.

[17]   Coffin, H. G. (1983) Origin by Design, Review and Herald Publ., Washington, 81.

[18]   Comte, D. & Suárez, G. (1994) **An Inverted Double Seismic Zone in Chile: Evidence of Phase Transformation in the Subducted Slab**, Science, Vol. 263, 212-215.

[19]   Cook, M. A. (1966), Prehistory and Earth Models, Max Parrish, London.

[20]   Cook, M. A., **How and When 'Pangea' Ruptured and the Continents Shifted**, Proceedings First International Conference on Creationism, Editors: Robert E. Walsh, et al, Creation Science Fellowship, Inc., Pittsburgh, PA, 1987, Vol. 2, 69-87.

[21]   Corliss, W. R. (1991) Inner Earth: A Search for Anomalies, The Sourcebook Project, Glen Arm.

[22]   Crouch, J. K. & Suppe, J. **Late Cenozoic Tectonic Evolution of the Los Angeles Basin and Inner California Borderland: A Model for Core Complex-Like Crustal Extension**, Geological Society of America Bulletin, Vol. 105, 1415-1434.

[23]   Dyrelius, D. & Elming, S. (1985) Bergarternas fysik, Kosmos 1985, Svenska Fysikersamfundet, 25.

[24]   Easton, R. M. (1987) **Paleozoic-Precambrian Unconformity Near Burleigh Falls, Ontario Highway 36, Ontario** in Roy, D. C. (Ed.) Northeastern Section of the Geological Society of America, Geological Society of America, 337-338.

[25]   England, P. & Houseman, G. (1989) **Extension During Continental Convergence, With Application to the Tibetan Plateau**, Journal of Geophysical Research, Vol. 94, No. B12, 17561-17579.

[26]   von Fange, E. A. (1990) Genesis and the Dinosaur, Living Word Services, Syracuse.

[27]   Fischer, J. M. (1992) **Dividing the Earth**, CRSQ, Vol. 28, 166-169.

[28]   Gentry, R. V., **Radioactive Halos: Implications for Creation**, Proceedings First International Conference on Creationism, Editors: Robert E. Walsh, et al, Creation Science Fellowship, Inc., Pittsburgh, PA, 1987, Vol. 2, 89-112.

[29]   Gordon, R. G. (1991) **Plate Tectonic Speed Limits**, Nature, Vol. 349, 16-17.

[30]   Gould, S. J. (1985) The Flamingo's Smile, W. W. Norton & Co., New York.

[31]   Harms, T. A. & Price, R. A. (1993) **The Newport Fault: Eocene Listric Normal Faulting, Mylonization, and Crustal Extension in Northeastern Washington and Northwestern Idaho: Discussion and Reply**, Geological Society of America Bulletin, Vol. 105, 1511-1514.

[32]   Hasel, G. F. (1974) **The Fountains of the Great Deep**, Origins, Vol. 1, No. 2, 67-72.

[33]   Hill, R. I., Campbell, I. H., Davies, G. F. & Griffiths, R. W. (1992) **Mantle Plumes and Continental Tectonics**, Science, Vol. 256, 186-193.

[34]   Holliger, K. & Levander, A. (1994) **Lower Crustal Reflectivity Modeled by Rheological Controls on Mafic Intrusions**, Geology, Vol. 22, 367-370.

[35]   Humphreys, D. R., **Reversals of the Earth's Magnetic Field During the Genesis Flood**, Proceedings First International Conference on Creationism, Editors: Robert E. Walsh, et al, Creation Science Fellowship, Inc., Pittsburgh, PA, Vol. 2, 113-126.

[36]   Humphreys, D. R., **Physical Mechanism for Reversals of the Earth's Magnetic Field During the Flood**, Proceedings Second International Conference on Creationism, Editors: Robert E. Walsh, et al, Creation Science Fellowship, Inc., Pittsburgh, PA, 1991, Vol. 2, 129-142.

[37]   Jacobs, J. A. (1992) Deep Interior of the Earth, Chapman & Hall, 108.

[38]   John, B. E. & Foster, D. A. (1993) **Structural and Thermal Constraints on the Initiation Angle of Detachment Faulting in the Southern Basin and Range: The Chemehuevi Mountains Case Study**, Geological Society of America Bulletin, Vol. 105, 1091-1108.

[39]   Kaye, G. W. C. & Laby, T. H. (1973) Tables of Physical and Chemical Constants, 14th ed., Longman, 55.

[40]   Kerr, R. A. (1984) **The Deepest Hole in the World**, Science, Vol. 224, 1420.

[41]   Kerr, R. A. (1991) **Coming up Short in a Crustal Quest**, Science, Vol. 254, 1456-1457.

[42]   Krauskopf, K. B. (1979) Introduction to Geochemistry, 2nd ed., McGraw-Hill, Tokyo.

[43]   Kulinich, S. (1990) **Down the Kola Well**, Geoscience Canada, Vol. 17:3, 200.

[44]   Lindström, M. (1967) **"Funnel Grabens" and Early Paleozoic Tectonism in South Sweden**, Geological Society of America Bulletin, Vol. 78, 1137-1154.

[45]   Loberg, B. (1987) Geologi, Norstedts.

[46]   Lockley, M. G., Yang, S. Y., Matsukawa, M., Fleming, F. & Lim, S. K. (1992) **The Track Record of Mesozoic Birds: Evidence and Implications**, Philosophical Transactions of the Royal Society of London, series B, Vol. 336, 113-134.

[47]   Maxwell, J. C. (1959) **Turbidite, Tectonic and Gravity Transport, Northern Appenine Mountains, Italy**, American Association of Petroleum Geologists Bulletin, Vol. 43, 2701-2719.

[48]   **Minisymposium on Orogeny** (1987), CRSQ, Vol. 24, 53-69, 125-136 (different authors).

[49]   Mpodozis, C. & Allmendinger, R. W. (1993) **Extensional Tectonics, Cretaceous Andes, Northern Chile (27°S)**, Geological Society of America Bulletin, Vol. 105, 1462-1477.

[50]   Molén, M. (1986) **Gotlands geologiska gåta (The Geologic Riddle of Gotland)**, Skapelsetro (Biblical Creation Society of Sweden), No. 1, Vol. 7, 7-23, 35.

[51]   Molén, M. (1987) **Hur kom sengångaren till Sydamerika? (How did the Tree Sloth Reach South America?)**, Skapelsetro (Biblical Creation Society of Sweden), No. 3, Vol. 8, 12-19.

[52]   Molén, M., **Diamictites: Ice-Ages or Gravity Flows?**, Proceedings Second International Conference on Creationism, Editors: Robert E. Walsh, et al, Creation Science Fellowship, Inc., Pittsburgh, PA, 1991, Vol. 2, 177-190.

[53]   Molén, M. (1990b) **Discussion**, Proceedings Second International Conference on Creationism, Editors: Robert E. Walsh, et al, Creation Science Fellowship, Inc., Pittsburgh, PA, 1991, Vol. 2, 198.

[54]   Molén, M. (1991) Vårt Ursprung? (3rd rev. ed.), Umeå FoU, 304 pp.

[55]   Molén, M. (1992) SEM-Microtextures: Attempting to Solve the Problem of the Origin of Diamictons and Diamictites, M.Sc. thesis, York University, 182 pp.

[56]   Morton, G. R., **Geologic Challenges to a Young Earth**, Proceedings First International Conference on Creationism, Editors: Robert E. Walsh, et al, Creation Science Fellowship, Inc., Pittsburgh, PA, 1987, Vol. 2, 137-146.

[57] Mundy, B. (1988) **Expanding Earth?**, Origins, Vol. 15, 53-69.

[58] Mörner, N.-A. (1979) **The Fennoscandian Uplift and Late Cenozoic Dynamics: Geological Evidence**, GeoJournal, Vol. 3, No. 3, 304-317.

[59] Nevins, S. E. (1971a) **The Mesa Basalt of the Northwestern United States**, CRSQ, Vol. 7, 222-226.

[60] Nevins, S. E. (1971b) **Stratigraphic Evidence of the Flood** in Symposium on Creation 3, Patten, D. W. (Ed.), Baker Book House, Grand Rapids, 32-65.

[61] Nevins, S. E. (1974) **Post-Flood Strata of the John Day Country, Northeastern Oregon**, CRSQ, Vol. 10, 191-204.

[62] Noah, M. M. (1972) The Book of Yashar, Hermon Press, New York.

[63] Nordling, C. & Österman, J. (1987) Physics Handbook, Studentlitteratur, Lund, 153.

[64] Northrup, B. E. (1990a) **Identifying the Noahic Flood in Historical Geology: Part One**, Proceedings Second International Conference on Creationism, Editors: Robert E. Walsh, et al, Creation Science Fellowship, Inc., Pittsburgh, PA, 1991a, Vol. 1, 173-179.

[65] Northrup, B. E., **Identifying the Noahic Flood in Historical Geology: Part Two**, Proceedings Second International Conference on Creationism, Editors: Robert E. Walsh, et al, Creation Science Fellowship, Inc., Pittsburgh, PA, 1991b, Vol. 1, 181-188.

[66] Oard, M. J., **An Ice Age Within the Biblical Time Frame**, Proceedings First International Conference on Creationism, Editors: Robert E. Walsh, et al, Creation Science Fellowship, Inc., Pittsburgh, PA, 1987, Vol. 2, 157-166.

[67] Oard, M. J. (1990) An Ice Age Caused by the Genesis Flood, ICR, El Cajon.

[68] Parsons, T., Thompson, G. A. & Sleep, N. H. (1994) **Mantle Plume Influence on the Neogene Uplift and Extension of the U.S. Western Cordillera?**, Geology, Vol. 22, 83-86.

[69] Ramberg, H. (1981) Gravity Deformation and the Earth's Crust, 2nd ed., Academic Press, 332.

[70] Retallack, G. J. (1983), **A Paleopedological Approach to the Interpretation of Terrestrial Sedimentary Rocks: The Mid-Tertiary Fossil Soils of Badlands National Park, South Dakota**, Geological Society of America Bulletin, Vol. 94, 823-840.

[71] Richards, M. A., Duncan, R. A. & Courtillot V. E. (1989) **Flood Basalts and Hot-Spot Tracks: Plume Heads and Tails**, Science, Vol. 246, 103-106.

[72] Robertson, A. H. F. (1991) **Origin and Emplacement of an Inferred Late Jurassic Subduction-Accretion Complex, Euboea, Eastern Greece**, Geological Magazine, Vol. 128, 27-41.

[73] Rosendahl, B. R., Meyers, J., Groschel, H. & Scott, D. (1992) **Nature of the Transition From Continental to Oceanic Crust and the Meaning of Reflection Moho**, Geology, Vol. 20, 721-724.

[74] Roth, A. A. (1977) **Clastic Dikes**, Origins, Vol. 4, 53-55.

[75] Roth, A. A. (1985) **Are Millions of Years Required to Produce Biogenic Sediments in the Deep Ocean**, Origins, Vol. 12, 48-56.

[76] Salda, L. D., Cingolani, C. & Varela, R. (1992) **Early Paleozoic Orogenic Belt of the Andes in Southwestern South America: Result of Laurentia-Gondwana Collision?**, Geology, Vol. 20, 617-620.

[77] Scheven, J. (1988) Mega-Sukzessionen und Klimax im Tertiär, Wort und Wissen, Band 19, Hänssler.

[78] Scheven, J., **Stasis in the Fossil Record as Confirmation of a Belief in Biblical Creation**, Proceedings Second International Conference on Creationism, Editors: Robert E. Walsh, et al, Creation Science Fellowship, Inc., Pittsburgh, PA, 1991a, Vol. 1, 197-215.

[79] Scheven, J., **The Flood/Post-Flood Boundary in the Fossil Record**, Proceedings Second International Conference on Creationism, Editors: Robert E. Walsh, et al, Creation Science Fellowship, Inc., Pittsburgh, PA, 1991b, Vol. 2, 247-266

[80] Scheven, J. (1993) **Ammonites, Mussels and Cockles**, Origins, Journal of the Biblical Creation Society, Vol. 5, No. 14, 10-17.

[81] Setterfield, B. (1993) Creation and Catastrophe, Adelaide Crusade Center.

[82] Short, N. M. & Blair, R. W. Jr. (Eds.) (1986) Geomorphology from Space, NASA, Washington DC.

[83] Stanley, S. M. (1986) Earth and Life Through Time, Freeman, 230-232.

[84] Stephansson, O. (1972) **Theoretical and Experimental Studies of Diapiric Structures on Öland**, Bulletin of the Geological Institutions, University of Upsala, New Series 3, 6:163-200.

[85] Strahler, A. N. (1971) The Earth Sciences, Harper & Row.

[86] Strahler, A. N. (1987) Science and Earth History, Prometheus Books, Buffalo.

[87] Tanner, W. F. (1973) **Deep-Sea Trenches and the Compression Assumption**, American Association of Petroleum Geologists Bulletin, Vol. 57, 2195-2206.

[88] Thompson, A. B. (1992), **Water in the Earth's Upper Mantle**, Nature, Vol. 358, 295-302.

[89] Turcotte, D. L. (1980) **Some Major Questions Concerning Mantle Convection** in Davies, P. A. & Runcorn, S. K. (Eds.) Mechanisms of Continental Drift and Plate Tectonics, Academic Press, 173-182.

[90] Twidale, C. R. (1976) Analysis of Landforms, John Wiley & Sons, Sydney.

[91] Tyler, D. J., **A Tectonically-Controlled Rock Cycle**, Proceedings Second International Conference on Creationism, Editors: Robert E. Walsh, et al, Creation Science Fellowship, Inc., Pittsburgh, PA, 1991, Vol. 2, 293-301.

[92] Velikovsky, I. (1976) Earth in Upheaval, Victor Gollancz & Sidgwick and Jackson, London, 3rd. edition.

[93] Visser, J. N. J. (1987) **The Influence of Topography on the Permo-Carboniferous Glaciation in the Karoo Basin and Adjoining Areas, Southern Africa**, in Gondwana Six: Stratigraphy, Sedimentology, and Paleontology, McKenzie, G. D. (Ed.), 123-129.

[94] Whitcomb, J. C. & Morris, H. M. (1961) The Genesis Flood, Baker Book House, Grand Rapids.

[95] Wilson, H. H. (1969) **Late Cretaceous Eugeosynclinal Sedimentation, Gravity Tectonics, and Ophiolite Emplacement in Oman Mountains, Southeast Arabia**, American Association of Petroleum Geologists Bulletin, Vol. 53, 626-671.

[96] Windley, B. F. & Allen, M. B. (1993) **Mongolian Plateau: Evidence for a Late Cenozoic Mantle Plume Under Central Asia**, Geology, Vol. 21, 295-298.

[97] Woodmorappe, J., **Causes for the Biogeographic Distribution After the Flood**, Proceedings Second International Conference on Creationism, Editors: Robert E. Walsh, et al, Creation Science Fellowship, Inc., Pittsburgh, PA, 1991, Vol. 2, 361-370.

APPENDIX 1. ORIGIN OF MOUNTAINS

(Articles referred to in the appendices, are in the main bibliography.)

1. Rising of mountains

The Pleistocene inland ice pressed the crust down to maybe 400 m (i.e. for the calculations below I will use ca. half of what was suggested by Mörner [58] and Strahler [86, p. 258]; also some of the depression may be tectonic rather than glacio-isostatic in origin). The value of 400 m conforms well with the ca. 300 m of isostatic depression suggested by Boulton [8] for a 2 km thick inland ice. The total maximum glacier thickness during the ice-age is impossible to know precisely, but I will assume a thickness of 2.6 km (which may be considered too much, compare Oard [67] and Molén [55]). If such a thick glacier would have covered 200,000 km^2, its weight would have been ca. 4.8×10^{17} kg.

If a subterranean aquifer was of the same area and volume as the above glacier, the weight of the water would be ca. 5.2×10^{17} kg. If the water was exchanged for a 3.2 km thick layer of sediment (accounting for some initial depression) the weight of the material in the depression would rise to ca. 1.41×10^{18} kg. (Assuming a density of 2.2 g/cm^3 for the sediments, computed with 30% water, and 70% minerals with an average density of 2.7 g/cm^3. The density of the upper crust is 2.7 g/cm^3, but sedimentary strata always contains some hollows, especially before compaction.)

The weight difference between the water and sediment is 8.9×10^{17} kg. If comparing this to the weight of the inland ice (which may have pushed the crust 400 m downwards), one may assume that the crust became depressed more than 600 m (i.e. closer to 700 m). The temperature rise in the crust is ca. 2.5 K per 100 m at great depth [43], which may imply that the temperature would rise ca. 15 K all around the depressed parts of the lithosphere. As the lowest part of the lithosphere is close to the melting point, it probably started to melt. (Based on interpretations of earthquake waves, approximately 1-10% of the asthenosphere is assumed to be in liquid form [45, p. 12]. In the following calculations it is assumed that the lithosphere melted.) The heat would then be transported upwards with the magma. If the geographical extent of the depressed area was 200,000 km^2, then ca. 120,000 km^3 of lithosphere would be depressed into the asthenosphere.

The above calculations of isostatic depression and temperature difference are, of course, speculative, containing many inferred factors. But they indicate that the present model may be possible.

The calculation of how quickly mountains will rise is simply made with Stokes law [91]. The magma which has lifted most mountains would be called large intrusions, i.e. batholiths or even mantle plumes, rather than diapirs. It may also be assumed that not all magma is rising as one large diapir. The below model calculation is performed only to show the rapid rising velocity.

$$V = \frac{2r^2g(p-p_0)}{9\mu}$$

V = velocity of rise of diapir (m/s)
r = radius of diapir (m)
g = gravity acceleration (m/s^2)
$p-p_0$ = density difference between diapir and surrounding rocks (kg/m^3)
μ = dynamic viscosity (Pas = Ns/m^2. 1 Pas = 10 poise.)

The following values are used for the calculations:
g = 10 m/s^2
$p-p_0$ = 50 kg/m^3 (conservatively set)
μ = 10^{12} Pas (all known magmas are $\leq 10^{12}$ Pas [69])
r = 10,000 m
Mean thickness of continental lithosphere = 125 km

If $\mu = 10^{12}$ (the same as quartz at 770 K [23]), V will be 1.11×10^{-2} m/s. At this velocity the magma would pass through the complete lithosphere in ca. 130 days. This is based on the assumptions 1) that the lower lithosphere has nearly melted, and 2) that the magma rises through many sedimentary (partly unsolidified) layers which have lower viscosity than Precambrian magmatic bedrock (i.e. 10^4-10^{18} Pas for most sedimentary strata [84]; 10^{19}-10^{21} Pas for magmatic bedrock [23]), and the well known facts that A) higher temperature reduces the dynamic viscosity, and B) water (in the newly deposited sediments, and possible also small amounts released from crystals during melting) reduces both the melting point and the viscosity [88]. A dynamic viscosity of 10^{12} Pas does not seem unjustified. Note that most rising magmas will probably not travel through continuous rocks, but fractures would be commonplace throughout (compare Cook [19, 20] and Brown [12]). Also, possible the lithosphere would partly melt at the Moho [73] and at the SIAL/SIMA boundary (i.e. compare Krauskopf [42, pp. 341-342, 430-431], Corliss [21, p. 24], and Tyler [91]), which would explain the many granitic intrusions present in mountains.

2. Melting of depressed lithosphere

The volume of a depressed "fountain" may be assumed to be ca. 120,000 km^3, with a thickness of ca. 600 m. It may further be assumed that the heat source surrounding the depressed mass is infinite, since it is the asthenosphere. The energy required to heat the rocks to melting point (or to heat the lowest parts of the lithosphere, after melting, to T = 15 K above melting point) is negligible compared to the heat required to melt silicate rock.

Heat required to melt silicate rocks is 5.6×10^9 J/m^3 [7]. Total energy required to melt 120,000 km^3 of basalt therefore is 6.72×10^{23} J. Specific heat of basalt is, $C_b = 3 \times 10^6$ J/m^3K [39]. Thermal conductivity for silicate rocks is ca., L = 3.5 W/mK [7].

As the rocks starts to melt, the conductivity and specific heat will change, but the overall heat transport will probably be near to the same order of magnitude. No values for molten silicate material has thus far been found in the available literature. (All conductivities and heat capacities are for room temperature.)

Calculations performed for 1 m^3 (1 m thick, 1 m^2 in area).

$Q = E/Area = 5.6x10^9$ J/m^2
$Q = (LC_b(T)^2t)^{1/2}$, from which follows:
$t = (5.6x10^9)^2/3.5x3x10^6x(15)^2 = 1.33x10^{10}$ s $= 421$ years

421 years is too long, but this assumes only dry heat transport through conduction. If convection is acknowledged, and water is present, a melting time of a few hundred years may be a clear possibility (e.g. compare to Krauskopf [42, pp. 341-342, 430-431] and Tyler [91]). For a 1 mm thick sheet of rock, t = 3.7 h. If the same amount of energy that melts a 1 mm thick sheet of rock, would be transported to the melting surface by convection in 3.7 h, then 600 m of rock would melt in ca. 250 years.

The total energy required to melt 600 m of rock, in the above calculation, would be stored in the asthenosphere to a depth of 75 000 m. (Calculated by the following formulae: $Q = C_bTx$, where x is the total depth from were energy is taken). If all the heat energy stored in the 75 000 m of asthenosphere would be transported upwards by convection during 250 years, than the velocity would be $9.5x10^{-6}$ m/s, i.e. a very low and reasonable velocity even for high dynamic viscosities (i.e. only ca. three orders of magnitude higher than the highest velocities calculated based on uniformitarian plate tectonic theories [29]).

APPENDIX 2. ENERGY REQUIRED TO MOVE CONTINENTS AND MECHANISM OF INITIATION OF CONTINENTAL DRIFT

A) Mass to move = total mass of all continents

Continental lithosphere, thickness: 125 km
Mean density of lithosphere: ≈ 3200 kg/m^3
(Data calculated from Strahler [86, pp. 160-163, 168-169], and Loberg [45, p. 25]).
Geographical extent of continents, including continental shelf is ca. $175x10^6$ km^2 [90, p. 24].
Total mass of continental lithosphere: $7x10^{22}$ kg

B) Energy required to move continents

Example: Accelerate all continents (m = $7x10^{22}$ kg) to an initial velocity of 1 m/s (which is probably a gross overestimation of the velocity): E = $mv^2/2 = 3.5x10^{22}$ J

C) Energy available to move continents

It may be assumed that Africa/Europe split and started to separate from N-S America because of the Appalachian/Caledonian/Variscian orogeny (compare Stanley [83]). The total energy released in this orogeny, assuming a mean uplift of only 450 m (conservatively and arbitrarily set to the same mean value as a small secondary Mesozoic uplift of the Appalachians, according to Strahler [85, p. 468]), would be on the order of $6.6x10^{21}$ J. This is based on the assumption that the total mountain chain length is 6000 km, the width is 200 km, and the height of the uplifted area is only 450 m. The density of the uplifted area is assumed to be 2700 kg/m^3, the same as the mean for normal crust.

Indirect evidence of vertical crustal movements, i.e. hot-mantle-upflow and orogeny, also exists at the triple junction of Africa, South America and Antarctica, but this data is not included in this calculation [3, 76].

Also, compare this energy release to that released by some of the larger meteorite impacts: E = 10^{21}-10^{23} J, and volcanic explosions: E = $8.4x10^{19}$ J [4, pp. 52, 81].

D) Conclusion

The energy released in the Paleozoic orogenies described above ($6.6x10^{21}$ J), is close to what is needed to accelerate all continents to 1 m/s ($3.5x10^{22}$ J). But, a velocity of 1 m/s is probably overestimated.

Thus, the entire continental drift scenario would be (copmare fig. 3): 1) The Appalachian/Caledonian/Variscian orogenies initiate large scale continental drift, by vertical and horizontal forces rising from the uplift. 2) During the initial opening of the primordial Atlantic, the continents would accelerate because of outpouring lava, and release of potential energy during gravitational rebound around the newly risen mountains. 3) Other geosynclines, and the complete thixotropic layer below the lithosphere would be destabilized, which would, at first enhance the drift. Later, especially after orogenies, the continents would decelerate and start to move similar to today.

APPENDIX 3. HEATING OF THE OCEANS DURING CONTINENTAL DRIFT

The heating of the oceans during continental drift would mainly be from two sources: 1. Heat from melted lava. 2. Frictional heat rising from the movements.

While heating from melted lava is easy to calculate, frictional heating is not. Only an approximation, comparing to frictional heat rising from a sphere which is rolled in liquid media, has been possible to conduct for this paper. It may be speculated that this process may produce heat on the same order of magnitude as a continent sliding on a thixotropic layer of magma and crystals.

1. Heating from melted lava.

It will be assumed that the Atlantic had the same mean depth as today, and that all heat from the underlying magma was instantaneously transported into the water (which of course is impossible - it would take many years). The following calculation is for one square kilometer:

Mean depth of the Atlantic: 3800 m
Volume of water: 3.8 km^3

Temperature difference between water and magma: T = 1200 K (average upper asthenosphere temperature is estimated to be ca. 1470 K [15], so a temperature difference of 1200 K is probably an overestimation).

Volume of magma = 0.1 km^3 (if it is assumed that the magma cools instantaneously down to a depth of 100 m).

Specific heat of basalt, C_b = 1.0 kJ/kgK
Specific heat of water, C_w = 4.18 kJ/kgK
Density of basalt, p_b = 3000 kg/m^3
Density of water, p_w = 1000 kg/m^3
Mass of basalt, m_b = 3.0x10^{11} kg
Mass of water, m_w = 3.8x10^{12} kg

Energy transported from basalt: E = $C_b m_b T$ = 4.41x10^{14}kJ
This energy (E) will warm the water: T_w = $E/C_w m_w$ = 27.8 K

This is a small temperature difference, which would by no means destroy life on earth or in the sea, because only water in the Atlantic would be heated and the heating would be spread over a long time period of continental drift. It would, though, help in giving moisture to rapidly growing glaciers during the ice-age (compare to Oard [66]). Similarly, any heating of water in the Pacific, rising from outpouring of lava after rapid lithospheric sinking, would stretch over a long time period (hundreds to thousands of years), and would raise the temperature even less than in the Atlantic.

2. Frictional heating.

Example: Comparing to a sphere which moves in a liquid [63].

E = -K_μVx

μ = dynamic viscosity (Pas)
V = velocity of moving continents
K = 6πr for a sphere
x = distance travelled by continent

V = 1 m/s (initial hypothetical velocity, from Appendix 2)
r = 7500 km (a sphere with the same radius as if all continents are made into one circle, including the continental shelves)
x = 100 km (hypothetical magnitude of movement with initial velocity, during brittle fracturing of continents)
μ = 10^{12} Pas (dynamic viscosity for the most viscous lava, which may be considered too high for a thixotropic material) [69]
Total volume of ocean water: 1.4x10^{18} m^3

Total frictional heating from movement of the continents:
E = 1.4x10^{25} J
This energy (E) will warm the water with: T_w = $E/C_w m_w$ = 2.4 K

Even though it is impossible to know the total friction, and the above calculation has only been performed for a sphere moving in a liquid, the temperature will probably rise very little. The values of V and μ may also be greatly overestimated.

APPENDIX 4. SINKING OF OCEANIC LITHOSPHERIC SLABS AND DEPRESSION OF LITHOSPHERE

The present model works with time scales on the order of thousands of years, but the ocean-floor must have sunk in front of the moving continents in a time period of months or years at the most. Deformational (and some frictional) heating during sinking, which reduces the viscosity, would enhance the velocity until a depth of similar density as the sinking slab would be reached.

The sinking velocity is calculated by Stokes law (compare to Appendix 1):

$$V = \frac{2r^2 g(p-p_0)}{9\mu}$$

V = velocity of sinking lithosperic slab (m/s)
r = radius of sinking slab, considered to be a sphere (m)
g = gravity acceleration (m/s^2)
$p-p_0$ = density difference between sinking slab and surrounding   rocks (kg/m^3)
μ = dynamic viscosity (Pas = Ns/m^2)

The following values are used for the calculations:
g = 10 m/s^2
$p-p_0$ = 40 kg/m^3 [15]
μ = 10^{19} Pas (see below)
r = 50,000 m (half the size of the length of the hypothetical postulated initial movement - see Appendix 3)

The value for μ, based on uniformitarian models, could be set to 10^{19} Pas for the following reasons: 1) Most estimates of the viscosity of the asthenosphere is on the order of 10^{19}-10^{22} Pas. 2) According to Dyrelius & Elming [23] there is a viscosity minimum at the asthenosphere/lithosphere boundary. 3) A value of 4x10^{18} Pas is used by Turcotte [89] while calculating mantle convection.

The sinking velocity for a slab with r = 50,000 m is 2.2x10^{-9} m/s. This value is orders of magnitude too small for the lithosphere to sink during months or years. Even a viscosity decrease caused by deformational (and frictional) heating may not be enough to achieve quick sinking slabs. But, if the upper asthenosphere was in a thixotropical state, so that the dynamic viscosity was on the order of 10^{12} Pas (similar to the most viscous lava flows [69]), would the sinking velocity be the right order of magnitude (i.e. 2.2x10^{-2} m/s which would mean that an oceanic slab would sink 125 km in ca. 60 days). This would be the right order of magnitude during the first, initial breakup of the continents. Also, a low dynamic viscosity is needed for the postulated 600 m of sinking below the geosynclines. So, the present model needs to work with a viscosity 10^7 lower than uniformitarian estimates. This is a weak part of the present model, but, if there is (or formerly was) a thixotropic layer at the lithosphere/asthenosphere boundary, then quick sinking could be accomplished by just overloading the lithosphere. At any rate, any student of earth history which believes that glaciers depressed the earth's crust during a short post-flood ice-age, must also believe that the dynamic viscosity was less than the uniformitarian postulate (e.g. compare to Oard [67, p. 176-178]).

A DETERMINATION AND ANALYSIS OF APPROPRIATE VALUES OF THE SPEED OF LIGHT TO TEST THE SETTERFIELD HYPOTHESIS

ALAN MONTGOMERY
218 MCCURDY DR.
KANATA, ON K2L 2L6
CANADA

KEYWORDS

Velocity of light, Regression Model, Sensitivity, Young earth model

ABSTRACT

The velocity of light data from four different sources are tabulated and edited to provide data sensitive enough to distinguish between a decrease in c of the size claim by Setterfield and Norman and constancy. The analysis of these values yields a time-dependent weighted regression model with significant fit and statistically significant trend. Data analyzed by time subintervals, distribution, accuracy and precision yielded results in support of the regression model. Attempts to determine an experimental or experimenter bias to account for this trend were unsuccessful. Some examples of physical evidence which might support Setterfield's hypothesis are discussed.

INTRODUCTION

In 1987 Setterfield published his monograph Atomic Constants, Light and Time[19] which raised again the question of the constancy of c. Since then there have been no less than 17 articles in the Creation Research Society Quarterly and 12 articles in the Creation Ex Nihilo Technical Journal debating this issue. Authors have used various statistical techniques including run tests, regression lines, weighted regression lines and distribution tests. One important claim made by Setterfield is that the decreasing c hypothesis explains how the transit time of light from galaxies billions of light years away takes only thousands of years. Since it would provide an alternative to well accepted scientific arguments against the credibility of biblical history and chronologies this hypothesis should be welcome among young-earth creationists. However, this has not been the case. Since this hypothesis is potentially very significant to creationist astronomy and physics, it is important to develop data and tests which are unambiguous. This paper defines a data set of c values appropriate to this purpose and analyzes this data not only for trends but also for non-physical explanations of the trends in the data.

One of the primary motivations for this analysis of the data on the velocity of light stems from a dissatisfaction with the techniques and data used in previous analyses, including my own[16]. Most analyses have used 162 or 163 data from Setterfield's tables as their basic data. If these had provided unambiguous results the matter would be settled. However, some of Setterfield's data is either non-experimental (Encyclopaedia Britannica 1771), duplicate (Cornu 1874) or regarded as unreliable (Young/Forbes 1881). This gives undue weight to some experiments and undermines the credibility of the results. Previous studies have also ignored the question of the sensitivity of the data and methods i.e. the ability of the data to detect a change of the size suggested by Setterfield. Thus, some data, which lack precise or accuracy, render the data collectively ambiguous. This study incorporates the principle of one datum to each experiment and the use of data only if it is sufficiently precise and consistent to distinguish between a constant and a decrease of the size claimed by Setterfield.

METHOD OF DATA SELECTION

Data has been drawn from four secondary sources: Setterfield[19], Froome and Essen[11], Dorsey[7] and Birge[2]. As there is agreement in these sources concerning the original published values no search of the original sources was made. The values from these four sources have been collected into a single table of 207 values (Appendix A). From these I removed duplicate values and constructed a second table of single valued independent experimental data (SVIED) which contains 158 values, one single value for every recognized experiment (S and D's removed from Appendix A). The SVIED was then analyzed for methods or data which were not acceptable because they were outliers, rejected by scientific authorities or contained anomalous and unacceptable characteristics. The remaining 119 values (SVIEAD) were subjected to a sensitivity analysis. Three additional data were eliminated by the sensitivity analysis leaving 116 data accepted for analysis (DAFA; * or M* in Appendix A). The error bars were taken from the secondary sources except for Setterfield's data where the error bars quoted in Hasofer's regression analysis [13] were used. One exception to this is the error bar for Delambre which is decidely too small and was increased to a more modest 1000 km/sec. For data which appeared in more than one source the errors were the same with two or three exceptions. The primary use of this data was in justifying the variance assumption of the weighted regression technique and secondarily in the analysis by error bar size.

Single Valued Independent Experimental Data

The data in Appendix A contains many multiple values. These may be divided into three categories. First, there are the values which have been recalculated to take into account some factor missing from the originally published value. Such original values are labelled D as defective. Mostly, these are in vacuo corrections. The second group contains values which were computed from the same original observations but with different statistical treatment. These are reworkings and are labelled M* as multiple values. These have been reduced to single values by taking the median of the various reworkings. The third category are data which were rejected by the experimenters, for example Cornu(1872), and replaced by a subsequent value from a new experiment. Typically, these new data have improved accuracy and precision. These have also been labelled D. Omitted are values which are averages of other data, including the 1771 Encyclopedia Britannica value, and values quoted from unidentified sources. These have been labelled S for secondary. In addition to removing duplicates, values were added which had previously been lumped into a single average but were experimentally different. The early aberration values from Bradley's research contains observations of different stars at 3 different observatories at different times and deserve to be recognized as separate data points. These values were calculated from Table 2 of Setterfield and Norman [19].

Unacceptable Methods And Rejected Data

Four methods contain data the majority of which is questionable: radar, quartz modulator, EMU/ESU and Kerr cell. Three radar values are in air and have not been converted to in vacuo for lack of humidity measurements. Radar waves are more sensitive to humidity than visible light so that the usual factor of 1.0002885 may be low [11,p79]. The possible range of the conversion factor is sufficient to cause the radar values to be ambiguous with respect to the hypothesis. Froome and Essen also consider these to be of poor accuracy [11,p79] and, since no humidity measurements were taken, unsuitable for conversion to in vacuo. These have been omitted. The large error bars (in comparison with the other post 1945 data) suggests they would be of little value. The quartz modulator values were considered poor by Froome and Essen. They quote Houstoun: "to say that its(minimum intensity) determination gives no feeling of aesthetic satisfaction is an understatement" [11,p84]. Neither value would survive an outlier analysis and so have been omitted. The EMU/ESU method contains 10 values from 1868 to 1883 which by simple regression line yield an anomalous 934±185 km/sec/year increase. This is clearly an experimental problem not related to any physical changes in the value of c. The magnitude of this change and the number of data is sufficient to produce a rate of increase over 188±85 km/sec/yr for the data as a whole. Exactly where this anomaly ends is difficult to tell and it must be admitted that the decision of Birge, Dorsey and Setterfield to omit all but the Dorsey 1906 datum is a necessary one. The values of the Kerr cell method are unquestionably low in comparison to post 1945 data [17]. However, no reviewer to my knowledge has been able to find errors of the size which would reconcile these results. This method was included since Birge, Dorsey and Setterfield included them in their best data.

Rejects are data whose values have been questioned by authorities because of experimental limitations or the lack of credible result. These have been labelled RJ in the Appendix A. Todd [21] in his article on solar parallax excluded both the Fizeau(1849) and Foucault(1862) values from his weighted average of c. DeBray[6] listed all the optical values prior to 1931 and selected only seven which he considered trustworthy. Fizeau(1849), Foucault(1862), Michelson(1878), Young/Forbes(1880), Newcomb(1881.8) and Cornu(1872) were among the values described as preliminary or flawed by systematic errors. Among the optical data I differ from Debray only in the use of the first and second value of the Perrotin/Prim(1900) experiments, while DeBray treats them as a single experiment. Mulligan and McDonald[17] comment extensively on the Spectral line method. Concerning the 1952 value they comment that Rank later found a systematic error which increased the total error to 15 km/sec. The Rank(1954) value was flawed by a poor wavelength which obviously affected the prior value as well. The aforementioned values are treated either as 'rejected's or as defective preliminary values replaced later by a superior datum.

An adjustment for aberration values is necessary before the data is prepared for analysis. The aberration values are calculated from the aberration angle of starlight in air. These calculated values are, thus, in air rather than in vacuo values. Since none of the sources has calculated these individually or suggested an adjustment collectively I added 95 km/sec[11,p48] to each the datum.

Outliers

For the outlier analysis data was divided into three sections: the early data up to 1890, the middle data from 1890 to 1940 and the late data from 1947 to 1967. Data were considered to be outliers if they did not fall within 3 standard deviations of the estimated value from a simple least squares linear regression. These have been labelled O in Appendix A. The laser values were omitted from analysis because atomic clocks were used as a time standard. The frequency of atomic clocks vary in direct proportion to the frequency change in light. Thus, any attempt to measure a change in the frequency of light by using atomic frequency standard is impossible. The break in values and accuracy of the late data is rather obvious and sufficient data exists to make an outlier analysis credible. There was also an obvious break between the 17th-18th century data and the more recent. However, to increase the credibility of the regression at least 25 data were included. The 1890 date provided a convenient boundary. Three of the five data labelled RJ were also determined to be outliers with the other 2 at least 2.5 standard deviations from the estimated value.

Sensitivity

Brown [3] opined that c was constant within the precision of the data. His methodology is seriously flawed [16,p141]. Humphreys [14, p42] questioned why the rate of decrease of c should decrease in direct proportion to our ability to measure it. Humphreys gave no evidence that this was true. As yet no paper has properly addressed this important issue of the sensitivity of the data. First, an estimate of the size of the change in c must be estimated for each method over the interval of time of the different methods used. The quadratic function of Hasofer [13] was used to estimate the difference in values of c at the end points of the various methods and is labelled Est. Δ c in Table 1. The ratio of this estimate to the standard deviation of the method ,which I will call the sensitivity ratio, should be normally distributed. Methods with ratios above 1.65 should be very sensitive to the hypothesized decrease, that is, there is less than a 5% likelihood that the estimated decrease would result from randomness.

The figures in Table 1 represent the sensitivity ratios for methods with 4 or more data as well as the post 1945. These are listed in order of estimated slope(Δc/yr). The EMU/ESU method has been included in the sensitivity analysis for comparison purposes. The statistic was successful in predicting the significance/insignificance of a simple linear regression line in 7 of 9 cases. Five of the six sensitive methods had simple regression line slopes which were significant at the 95% confidence level. Two of the three insensitive methods had insignificant regression lines. If the data with the two smallest ratios(insensitive data) are removed the magnitude of the slopes of their respective regression lines are decreasing significantly and in almost the same order as predicted.

The sensitivity ratio for standing wire values, .21, shows that the standing wire data has insufficient accuracy to distinguish between an empirical trend and randomness. All but the Mercier(1923) datum have been omitted as Birge, Dorsey and Setterfield all included it. The sensitivity of the Roemer data is understated due to the lack of intermediate data. This leads to an artificially high standard deviation. Extra regression lines with and without the Roemer data have been conducted for Table 2. On the other hand the decision to delete all but one of the EMU/ESU data would seem to be well justified by these results. Not only are the data insensitive to the hypothesized change but the direction and magnitude of the slope overall are anomalous.

METHOD	Est. Δ C*	Δ C /S.D.	Δ C** /yr	REGRESS'N SLOPE**	CONFID LEVEL
ROEMER	1275	.76	-9.3	-27.4	99.995%
ABERRATION	1680	3.12	-7.9	-8.0	99.995%
MIRROR	175	3.84	-3.3	-1.9	99.995%
EMU/ESU	240	.04	-4.8	188	7%
S.WIRE	87	.21	-3.1	-4.7	57%
KERR CELL	19.4	3.18	-1.6	-1.1	97.5%
INFEROMETER	2.7	2.53	-.36	-.04	55%
POST '45	4.8	2.97	-.24	-.06	96%
GEODIMETER	3.2	4.93	-.18	-.11	95%

Table 1. *Sensitivity ratios of different methods to Setterfield hypothesis*
*in km/sec **in km/sec/yr*

REGRESSION MODELS

Regression line models are based on three assumptions:

(1) The expected value of the residuals is zero i.e. $E[e_i] = 0$
(2) The variance of the errors(residuals) is constant
(3) The errors(residuals) are independent of the random variable

For a regression line to be accepted as a model (not necessarily a unique model) the residuals must be tested for these three conditions. The c data, however, does not easily lend itself to regression analysis. A simple linear regression will not take into account the varying degrees of reliability of the data. A weighted regression technique exists which weights each data with the inverse square of the error bar. This may satisfy condition 2 (homoscedasticity) but for the c data a poor fit. More importantly, this weighting procedure in the case of the c data causes a correlation between the residuals violating condition 3. The residuals are said to be autocorrelated. The standard test for autocorrelation is called the Durban-Watson test. In the case of the c data the autocorrelation stems from the time dependence of the error bars themselves. The standard technique for correction of autocorrelation is to apply an autocorrelation parameter [18,p356] to the data to smooth it prior to regression. Unfortunately, when applied to the weighted regression line for c data the residuals still fail the Durban-Watson test. Even repeated applications are ineffectual at correcting the problem.

To solve this dilemma, a different weighted regression technique will be used. Let T be the independent random variable representing time and C be the dependent random variable representing the velocity of light. The following presents a quadratic polynomial regression model:

$$C_i = a + bT_i + dT_i^2 + e_i \qquad (1)$$

where a,b,d are coefficients
C and T are random variables
and e_i is the error.

If the variance of e_i is proportional to T^2, where T is measured in years prior, the variance of e/T is constant and a regression line will be homoscedastic.

$$\sigma^2(e) = kT^2 \qquad (2)$$

where σ^2 is the statistical symbol for variance

Equation (1) is then transformed into

$$C_i/T_i = a/T_i + b + dT_i + e_i/T_i \qquad (3)$$

The variance of the errors is

$$\sigma^2(e_i/T_i) = \sigma^2(e_i)/T_i^2 = kT_i^2/T_i^2 = k \qquad (4)$$

i.e. the variance of the errors is constant.

This permits a standard simple regression to be performed on the transformed variables. Once the regression has been performed the transformation can be reversed and the appropriate coefficients will be found next to the proper power of T in equation (1) [18,p131]. The first two regressions in Table 2 were checked for autocorrelation by the Durban-Watson test. None were close to significant. These regression lines may properly be called regression models. To test for the assumed condition the data (DAFA) was divided into quintiles and the standard deviation calculated for each. A regression line was calculated for these values using the mid-point of each range for a time reference. The result showed a 2 unit per year increase (T is in time prior to 1967.5) with a coefficient of determination (r^2) of .99. Both fit and slope were significant at the 95% confidence level. Thus, the above weighted regression technique is appropriate.

Results of this regression of the data (DAFA) are recorded in Table 2. Dynamic data in the table refers to the whole set of data less the laser data which was timed using atomic rather than dynamic time. The null hypothesis is that there is no decrease in c versus the alternate hypothesis that there is. All 6 tests on the dynamic data and its major subsets showed a significant quadratic term at the 97.5% confidence level. Only the Laser values had insignificant coefficients for both the linear and the quadratic. Note that the time is calculated in years prior to 1967.5 and so positive terms mean an increase in c as one goes back in time. Other methods were also tested. In all cases at least one coefficient is significant and positive. Most of these datasets are too small for their results to be very credible in themselves. However, they are consistent with results of the larger data sets. Kerr cell, standing wire and geodimeter values also had a negative significant value.

DATA	*T COEFF'T	**CONF LEVEL	*T² COEFF'T	**CONF LEVEL
Weighted regressions Dynamic	-1.12	40	.040	99.95
Dynamic w/o Roemer	-.45	45	.031	99.95
Aberration	-5.76	14	.055	97.5
Non-aberration	-1.08	39	.067	99.95
Laser	-0.00021	7	.000025	88
Post-1945	-0.082	10	.0076	99
One-year Average	-1.14	40	.046	99.95
Simple Regression Error Bars	3.53	99		
Dynamic data less one error bar	5.40	99.5		
One-year average less one error bar	6.49	99.95		
Deleted data	98.0	99.95		

Table 2. *Regression analysis of accepted c values*

Bias

By historical accident some decades and years have more data. This is an historical bias and could led to exaggerated results. To test what bias this influence has a weighted regression was done on the data (DAFA) where values in the same year were replaced by their weighted average. This is listed under One-year Average. The significance level rose indicating this bias lowers the significance of the regression. Simple regressions were also performed on the values less their error bars, i.e. the minimum of their probable values. Since the less reliable data has larger error bars this technique lowers the value of the less reliable data more than the better data. The regression line was still positively and significantly sloped. This was still true at 1.92 times the error bar and the slope was still positive even at 2.47 times the error bar. This should not be true of a set of values representing a constant. Lastly, a simple regression was done on the deleted data. Its slope was decreasing at 98 ± 17 km/sec/yr.

Although significant quadratic relationship has been found in the accepted data and its major subsets, it cannot be assumed that this relationship is due to a physical decrease in the value of c. It has been established that this decrease is empirical and is not random.

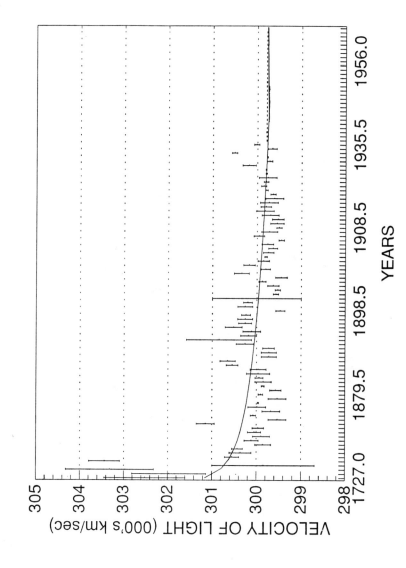

VELOCITY OF LIGHT
All Selected Data

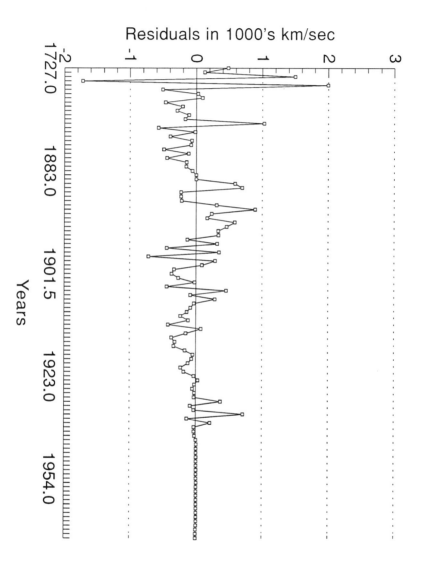

Distribution of Residuals from Regression Model

Residuals in 1000's km/sec

Years

Other possibilities must be explored as well as the physical one:

(1) Is the decrease dependent on the less reliable 18th century data?
(2) Is the decrease a product of combining methods with systematic or other errors?
(3) Is the decrease a one-sided approach to the current value of c due to experimental or experimenter bias?

To determine the answer to the first question the 18th century values were subtracted from the accepted (DAFA) data. A weighted regression was performed on the remainder. which resulted in a coefficient of T^2 significant at the 97.5% confidence level. The t test was applied to the average and was significant at the 99.9% confidence level. The removal of the 18th century data does not result in insignificant tests. Could some other data in a specific time interval be responsible for the decrease in the data. Initially a 10 year interval was chosen for analysis but too many of the cells had too little data. The interval was widened to 20 years. Even so, the 18th century data had to be grouped into a single cell and the 1940 cell was moved to 1947-67 to include the 3 extra data.

DATE	NO. DATA	AVERAGE	T VALUE	CONFIDENCE LEVEL
*1727-1967	108	300006.3	3.49	99.95%
1727-1783	6	301941.0	3.58	99.1%
1841-1860	5	300133.0	2.88	97.5%
1861-1880	10	299984.6	1.33	89%
1881-1900	22	300100.5	4.06	99.95%
1901-1920	25	299745.3	-1.09	15%
1921-1940	16	299852.7	1.10	85%
1947-1967	24	299792.9	2.29	98%

Table 3. *Analysis of accepted data by 20 years periods*
* atomic clock data excluded

The t tests for the averages of this group of cells is presented in Table 3. Laser results have been omitted. Of the 7 cells 4 have significant deviations from the accepted value of 299792.458 km/sec. This is much higher than would be expected on the basis of random chance. There were no results in the 25-75 percentile range where half the results would be expected to be. The one cell with the obviously anomalous results is the 1900-1920 era where the predominant values are by the aberration method. This suggests that the aberration values are systematically low. The distribution of aberration and non-aberration values about the accepted value was tabulated. Table 4 shows the number of values above and below the accepted value accumulated by 200 km/sec intervals and a binomial statistic and confidence level for each pair.

ACCURACY IN KM/SEC	TOTAL NON-ABERRATION ABERRATION	NUMBER ABOVE/BELOW ACCEPTED VALUE**	TOTAL	BINOMIAL STAT VALUE	CONFID LEVEL
<200	TOTAL	40/28	68	1.46	92%
	NON-ABERRATION	27/12	39	2.40	99.4%
	ABERRATION	13/16	29	-.550	29%
<400	TOTAL	49/39	88	1.07	86%
	NON-ABERRATION	29/12	41	2.65	99.6%
	ABERRATION	20/27	47	-1.02	15%
<600	TOTAL	57/39	96	1.84	96%
	NON-ABERRATION	29/12	41	2.65	99.6%
	ABERRATION	28/27	55	0.13	55.2%
<800	TOTAL	62/39	101	2.29	99%
	NON-ABERRATION	29/12	41	2.65	99.6%
	ABERRATION	33/27	60	.77	78%
ALL	TOTAL	69/39	108	2.89	99.8%
	NON-ABERRATION	31/12	43	2.90	99.8%
	ABERRATION	38/27	65	1.36	91.3%

Table 4. *Cumulative distribution of accepted c values around accepted value by 200 km/sec intervals*
** ACCEPTED VALUE=299792.458 KM/SEC

For the non-aberration values the binomial test shows significance at the 99% confidence level throughout all ranges of accuracy. The aberration values on the other hand range from 15% to 91%. Not one of the distributions are significant at the 95% confidence level. Yet from Table 2 regression results both of these subsets yield similar and significant T^2 coefficients. In addition, the number of aberration values above the accepted value prior to 1900 is 27 of 35 values whereas the after 1900 the distribution is reversed and there are only 11 of 30. The aberration values as a whole have an insignificant distribution over all ranges of accuracy but is composed of two highly different distributions pre and post 1900. It would be expected that the experimental values ought to approach the accepted value whether from above, below or both. This is true of the non-aberration values but not of the aberration values. From the above considerations it may be concluded that the aberration values are the anomalous ones, that they are decreasing at about the same rate and that they decrease to a value lower than the non-aberration values, i.e. they are systematically low. From the significance of the weighted regressions and the t-test on the post 18th century data it may be concluded that there is still a significant decrease in the values of that era and this despite the effects of a systematic error in the aberration values which reduces the value of the T^2 coefficient of the whole data below those of the corresponding aberration and non-aberration values.

The second possible explanation for the decrease in c values is that it is a product of different systematic errors in the various methods. In such cases a significant portion of the methods ought to show constancy. From the results of Table 1 it can be seen that only the EMU/ESU shows a positive slope by simple regression and of those methods which have data sensitive enough to find a decrease all but one have significant slopes. The weighted regression lines show no substantial difference. The aberration and non-aberration coefficients are both significant. The combination of these two in fact decreases the regression coefficients likely because of the systematic error in the aberration values. The omission of the Roemer data still leaves a significant weighted regression line. The post-1945 data is also significant. This leaves 15 other values representing mainly the Kerr cell and optical values. The Kerr cell values are also decreasing with time but because they are all less than the accepted value they actually decrease the size of the slope of the weighted regression model. The optical measurements have a significant linear decrease and an insignificant quadratic coefficient. There is no sign that a set of constant method(s) is(are) causing c values to be misinterpreted as a decreasing trend. In fact, certain systematic problems can be shown to be lowering the rate of decrease in the regression model.

The third possibility is harder to determine since the behaviour of the data under the assumption of a physically decreasing value of c and a decreasing value of c due to a one-sided approach to the accepted value is almost the same. The c values do contain at least one example of this kind of phenomenon. The EMU/ESU has a very steep trend in the 1868-1883 range(10 of 25 data) which is 5 times steeper than for the whole dataset. The t-test on the average of these two subsets have substantially different confidence levels(99.5% and 40%). As the experiments became more accurate a one-sided negative systematic error was obviously reduced more than all the others. After a certain point the reduction in this error was no longer significant and the values stabilized. This kind of behaviour ought to be detectable by arranging the data by error bar size and examining the results for obvious breaks in the significance.

ERROR SIZE KM/SEC	AVERAGE	NO. OF DATA	T STAT	CONFID LEVEL %	SLOPE KM/SEC/YR	CONFID LEVEL %
ALL	300006.5	108	3.49	99.9	-8.92	99.9
<<=1000	300007.7	107	3.48	99.9	-9.93	99.9
<<=500	299924.1	103	2.96	99.5	-6.48	99.9
<<=200	299882.9	99	3.14	99.5	-3.03	99.9
<<=100	299807.6	54	.64	74	-0.79	81
<<=50	299801.2	35	1.42	91	-1.21	99.9
<<=20	299795.9	31	.59	72	-1.36	99.9
<<=10	299789.9	29	-1.91	4	0.54	.1
<<=5	299793.0	23	2.43	97.5	-0.07	95
<<=2	299792.9	21	2.28	97.5	-0.08	98
<<=1	299792.6	14	2.14	97.5	-.02	94
<<=.5	299792.6	12	1.96	96	-.03	96

Table 5. Confidence levels of T test and regression slope coefficients for accepted c data by size of error bar

In Table 5, the averages and simple regression slopes for different error bars intervals are listed together with the significance of the their t-tests. If the hypothesis is that the values of c are approaching from one-side due to experimental or experimenter bias than there ought to be a break in the confidence levels. There is such a break at 100 km/sec where significance drops to 74%. However, at 5 km/sec this significance reappears and the confidence levels remains significant down to the .5 km/sec cell after which there is too little data. Furthermore, the difference in the confidence levels between the 5 and 10 km/sec group is over 93 points! This jump is caused by adding only 6 data to 23. These data contain all 4 Kerr cell values which are all below the accepted value by significant amounts. They also prevent significance in the 20 and 50 km/sec group. The 100 km/sec group contains many of the post 1900 aberration values which are systematically low and it would be anticipated that these would have considerable effect on the 100 km/sec cell. The confidence levels of the simple regression lines show an identical pattern; the only cells to show loss of significance are those affected by Kerr cell and post-1900 aberration values. The only example of one-side errors or biases which have affected the values of c to be found are the EMU/ESU values. Although others [14] have mentioned this phenomenon as an explanation for the decrease in the values of c, they have not given examples.

DISCUSSION

A major focus of this paper is to create a set of c values which is appropriate for analysis with respect to the Setterfield hypothesis. It is appropriate to examine what the inclusion of these deletions would have. The inclusion of EMU/ESU data would definitely have a significant influence on all results except the error bar analysis. This method's lack of accuracy and precision cannot justify its inclusion in this analysis. Those who would include this method will no doubt disagree with the conclusions of this analysis. Both the rejected and the outliers, if added back in would augment the size of the decrease in c. They would also increase the initial averages and slopes in the time and error bar analysis.

To ascertain what bias the deletions have as a whole a simple regression line through the deleted data was done. This yielded a 98±17 km/sec/yr decrease. The average (300157 km/sec) was above that of the DAFA data but not significantly. The regression slope is significant despite the inclusion of the EMU/ESU data. It cannot therefore be claimed that results favouring the Setterfield hypothesis are attributable to the bias in the selection of deleted data.

Regression lines have been published by a number of researchers and have played a key role in the debate [1],[4],[9],[13],[16]. It would then be appropriate to give some account of them. Norman's regression lines although significant are all unweighted as are Brown and Evered's tertiary polynomial. None of these are homoscedastic. Aardsma's and Hasofer's published weighted regression lines which are homoscedastic. Aardsma's is linear and not significant and Hasofer's is quadratic and is significant. However, but both fail the Durban-Watson statistic at the 99% confidence level i.e. the residuals of the lines are autocorrelated. In addition, some error bars in Hasofer's regression analysis have been challenged which would change the significance [10,p83]. Thus, no regression line published to date has met all three conditions for a regression line model. It may be noted in defense of Aardsma's work that he was merely constructing an weighted average rate of change. For this purpose he used the required technique. However, in my opinion he has failed to grasp the complexity and systematic errors of the data and thus the need for a broader and deeper analysis.

Several factors led me to this opinion. First, the weighting of Aardsma's line puts over 90% of the weight on 6 data points in the 1956-1967 era. The average unweighted slope in this era is less than a .03 km/sec/yr decrease. Thus there is a bias in the weights of the data towards the era with the smallest slope. In such cases, one must be wary that one's interpretations are valid beyond the small number of data which effectively determine the results. The bias can be lessened by reducing the weighting factor or reducing the number of data where the heaviest weighting occurs. The weighted one-year-average regression line in Table 2 is one such technique. Another possibility would be to regress the pre-1945 data to test whether insignificant change is restricted to the post-1945 data.

Second, the Durban-Watson test for Aardsma's regression line is significant at the 99% confidence level indicating that the residuals from this line still form a significant time dependent sequence: that is, not all the decrease in the data is reflected in the regression coefficient. Furthermore, there are major corrections which must be made to Aardsma's data. Although not stated in Setterfield's paper the EMU/ESU, standing wire and aberration methods contain 92 data for which the in vacuo adjustment has not been made. In addition, several values are duplicates and triplicates which add to the bias. These biases act together to minimize the slope and the significance of his result. Thus, his conclusions are not based on satisfactory evidence.

PREDICTIONS

The quality of a scientific hypothesis must be judged not only by its fit to empirical data but also by its predictions. The effect that a decreasing c would have on other physical constants if the frequency of light were decreasing has been presented by Norman and Setterfield[19]. They claim their analysis verifies the predictions of their hypothesis. Testing of this claim will be the subject of future research. However, there is the question whether Setterfield's distinction between atomic time and dynamic or gravitational time has long term physical effects rather than a minor temporary one. There needs to be a demonstration that over long periods the discrepancy between atomic time and gravitational time is significant. Fortunately, examples can be found.

Stars ages are calculated using atomic isotope ratios of hydrogen and helium. These ratios are interpreted as yielding ages up to billions of years. These ages are in atomic years. However, remnants of supernova stars can dated by various techniques which are dependent on its rate of expansion, a dynamic process. Their ages, according to Davies' [5] analysis of supernova remnants in our galaxy, range up to 7,000-8,000 years in gravitational time. Although age estimations are still crude it must be admitted that a wide discrepancy exists between the atomic ages of stars and gravitational age of supernova remnants and that this is not expected according to conventional theories.

Zircon crystals embedded in deep granites in the Earth's crust and studied by Gentry are dated by Uranium/Lead isotopes ratios (atomic process) to be over a billion years old. However, the rate of diffusion (dynamic process) of the helium by-product shows the radioactive decay to be 10,000 years old or less [12, p52-53]. Gentry accounts for this age discrepancy by suggesting a supernatural increase in radioactivity during brief periods prior to or during the flood. Whatever the cause, the data cannot be anticipated by the conventional view that atomic and gravitational ages are equivalent. Setterfield's hypothesis predicts what conventional scientists are forced to discount.

Another problem concerns the spiral appearance of many of the galaxies in the universe. In order for spiral galaxies to retain their shape the velocities of the stars within the arms of the spirals ought to vary in direct proportion to their radii. This is not observed. All the stars in the arms within each spiral galaxy have the approximately the same speed[20]. Thus, the stars in the outer portion of the arms, having a much longer orbit, trail farther and farther behind the inner ones as time goes on. Conversely, if one goes back in time the stars on the inner portion of the spirals would back up faster than those in the outer portion and the spiral shape would look less curved. As the astronomers look farther into space they are looking at images of galaxies whose light was emitted earlier in time which ought to appear progressively less curved or less wound-up spiral galaxies. Since the average rotation period is in the order of 200 million years there ought to be some discernable differences beyond 200 million light years. Astronomers have failed to find any such progression in their observations up to 1 billion light years [8]. This, too, is a natural consequence of the decreasing c hypothesis in that the light travel time is much lower than conventionally assumed because of the higher velocity of light in the past.

Finally, every radioactive isotope known with an atomic number less than or equal to 92 and a half-life greater than 700 million years is found naturally in the Earth's crust. With the exception of carbon-14 which is produced continually in the upper atmosphere and isotopes which are by-products of other long half-life isotopes there are no short half-life isotopes (less than 700 million years) occurring naturally in the crust [15]. If radioactive decay values were constant and the Earth were 4-5 billion years old then long half-life isotopes should still exist after 4-5 billion years but not the short half-life ones (see Table 6). This evidences agrees with the standard evolutionary geology. Setterfield's hypothesis predicts the same results as the evolutionary model but provides an alternative naturalistic explanation for this distribution, one within a short Earth history. Creationist explanations have focused heavily on individual ratios and methods. I could find no creationist papers which explain the above distribution.

Nuclide and Atomic Number	Percent Abundance in nature	Half-life Period in Years
K-40	.0117	1.3×10^9
Se-82	9.19	1.1×10^{20}
Rb-87	27.83	4.8×10^{10}
Cd-113	12.2	9×10^{15}
In-115	95.77	5.1×10^{14}
Te-130	34.49	2×10^{21}
La-138	.089	1.1×10^{11}
Nd-144	23.8	2.1×10^{15}
Sm-147	15.07	1.1×10^{11}
Sm-148	11.3	8×10^{15}
Gd-152	.20	1.1×10^{14}
Lu-176	2.6	3.6×10^{10}
Hf-174	0.16	2×10^{15}
Re-187	62.6	4×10^{10}
Pt-190	.013	6×10^{11}
Th-232	100	1.4×10^{10}
U-235	.715	7.0×10^8
U-238	99.28	4.5×10^9

Table 6. *Half-lives of naturally occurring radioactive nuclides according to McGraw-Hill Encyclopaedia of Science and Technology*

CONCLUSIONS

The above analysis has accepted the published values, reworkings and corrections as valid. This does not mean that new information has not or will not arise to change the assessment of the proper value which should be assigned to the observations. It would be entirely appropriate to reevaluate the published values in light of any new techniques or knowledge. This I leave to the physicists. My purpose here is to provide motivation and justification for such research.

From my analysis it may be reasonably concluded that:

(1)   EMU/ESU and standing wire data are too insensitive to test Setterfield's hypothesis.

(2)   Both Aberration and Kerr Cell results have systematically low values.

(3) $C(T) = 299792 + .031*(1967.5-T)^2$ is a suitable regression model for the velocity of light values in the last 250 years.

(4)   Tests of the selected data strongly support an decrease in the values of c. No evidence of experimental causes could be found for the observed decrease.

(5)   Predictive abilities of the Setterfield hypothesis make a physical interpretation of the empirical decrease not only reasonable but credible.

The regression model in this paper ought to be given priority over previously published regression lines since it is the only one which is weighted, homoscedastic and non-autocorrelated. In addition it is the only one based on one in vacuo datum per experiment. It provides the soundest grounds so far to decide the question. The various non-random distributions of the data by date, precision, accuracy, and method are too consistent and pervasive to have been caused by systematic experimental and experimenter biases. Those biases and systematic errors in the data which can be identified are not helpful in providing a non-physical explanation of the results. The prediction of a substantially divergent ages for dynamic processes proceeding from nuclear processes is a very critical test of the

Setterfield hypothesis. There exist physical examples which extend past the three hundred years of data used here. These data are compatible with Setterfield's hypothesis but unexpected from conventional physics. The agreement of statistical and physical evidences provide ample grounds for pursuing physical mechanisms to explain the decrease in the velocity of light.

ACKNOWLEDGEMENTS

I am grateful to all those who contribute their time and talents to these conferences. Their energy and commitment are admired. I would also thank Dr. Tom Goss whose professional skills in statistical analysis were not only helpful but were given freely and lovingly despite his busy schedule. Lastly, I would like to thank Lambert Dolphin for his encouragement through the trials of life as well as science.

REFERENCES

[1]   G. Aardsma, **Has the Speed of Light Decayed Recently?-paper 1**, Creation Research Society Quarterly, Vol.25:1 (1988) 36-40.

[2]   R.T.Birge, **The General Physical Constants: as of August 1941 with Details on the Velocity of Light Only**, Reports on Progress in Physics 8 (1941) 90-134

[3]   R.H.Brown, **Statistical Analysis of the Atomic Constants, Light and Time**, Creation Research Society Quarterly Vol 25:4 (1988) 91-95

[4]   R.H. Brown, **Speed of Light Statistics**, Creation Research Society Quarterly Vol 26:4 (1990) 142-143

[5]   K. Davies, **The Distribution of Supernova Remnants in the Galaxy**, Proceedings of the Third International Conference on Creationism, Editor: Robert E. Walsh, Creation Science Fellowship, Inc., Pittsburgh, PA, 1994, This Volume.

[6]   G. DeBray, **The Velocity of Light**, Nature Vol. 120 (1927) 602-604

[7]   N.E. Dorsey, **The Velocity of Light**, Transactions of the American Philosophical Society, 34 (1944) 1-110

[8]   A. Dressler, **Galaxies Long Ago and Far Away**, Sky and Telescope Vol. 85:4 (1993) 22-25

[9]   M.G. Evered, **Computer Analysis of the Historical Values of the Velocity of Light**, Creation Ex Nihilo Tech. J. Vol 5:2 (1991) 94-96

[10]   M.G. Evered, **Further Evidence Against the Theory of a Recent Decrease in c**, Creation Ex Nihilo Tech. J. Vol 6:1 (1992) 80-89

[11]   K.D. Froome and L. Essen, The Velocity of Light and Radio Waves, (1969), Academic Press, N.Y.

[12]   R.V.Gentry, **Radioactive Halos in a Radiological and Cosmological Perspective**, Proceedings of the 63rd Annual Meeting of the Pacific Division, AAAS (1984), 38-63

[13]   A.M. Hasofer, **A Regression Analysis of the Historical Light Measurements**, Creation Ex Nihilo Tech. J. Vol 4 (1991) 94-96

[14]   D.R. Humphreys, **Has the Speed of Light Decreased Recently?-paper 2**, Creation Research Society Quarterly Vol 25:1 (1988) 40-45

[15]   McGraw-Hill Encyclopaedia of Science and Technology, Sixth Ed., Vol. 15 107, McGraw-Hill, N.Y.

[16]   A.L. Montgomery, **Statistical Analysis of c and Related Atomic Constants**, Creation Research Society Quarterly Vol.26:4 (1990) 138-142

[17]   J.F.Mulligan and D.F.McDonald, **Some Recent Determinations of the Velocity of Light II**, American Journal of Science Vol. 25 (1957) 180-192

[18]   J. Neter and W. Wasserman, Applied Linear Statistical Models, 1974 , Richard D. Irwin, Homewood, IL.

[19]   T. Norman and B. Setterfield, <u>The Atomic Constants, Light and Time</u>, 1987, Invited Research Paper for Lambert Dolphin, Santa Clara, CA.

[20]   V. Rubin, **Dark Matter in Spiral Galaxies**, <u>Scientific American</u>, Vol. 248:6 (1983), 96-108

[21]   D.P. Todd, **Solar Parallax from the Velocity of Light**, <u>American Journal of Science</u>, series 3 Vol 19 (1880): 59-64

APPENDIX A

ALL DATA COMBINED

Data #	Experimenter	Date	c Value	Error Bar	Meth	Code	Comments
1	Roemer/Froome&Essen	1675.0	215,000.000	-	1	D	Of Historical Interest Only
2	Roemer/Setterfield	1675.0	307,500.000	5400	1	O	
3	Cassini	1693.0	352,000.000	18000	1	O	
4	Bradley/Busch	1727.0	303,434.000	750	2	M*	Setterfield - Table 3
5	Bradley/Newcomb(KO)	1727.0	299,289.000	1750	2	M*	Setterfield - Table 2
6	Bradley/Froome&Essen	1727.0	301,000.000	-	2	S	
7	Bradley/Auwers(KO)	1727.0	301,416.000	1070	2	M*	Setterfield - Table 2
8	Bradley(KO)	1727.0	303,430.000	750	2	M*	Setterfield - Table 2
9	Auwers(Wanstead)	1737.0	300,313.000	920	2	M*	Setterfield - Table 2
10	Busch(WO)	1737.0	304,103.000	750	2	M*	Setterfield - Table 2
11	Delambre	1738.0	303,320.000	1000	1	*	
12	Bradley/Setterfield	1740.0	300,650.000	750	2	S	Setterfield - Table 11
13	Peters(GO)	1752.0	299,406.000	1150	2	M*	Setterfield - Table 2
14	Bessel(Greenwich)	1752.0	300,093.000	1150	2	M*	Setterfield - Table 2
15	Martin	1759.0	303,440.000	350	1	*	
16	Encycl.Britannica	1771.0	302,220.000	620	1	S	Combination of previous
17	Lindenau(PO)	1783.0	300,460.000	160	2	*	
18	Struve(PO)	1841.0	300,270.000	250	2	*	
19	Folk-Struve(PO)	1841.0	300,340.000	120	2	*	
20	Lindenhager(PO)	1843.0	299,760.000	180	2	*	
21	Struve(PO)	1843.0	300,020.000	160	2	*	
22	Fizeau(Textbook)	1849.5	313,300.000	10000	3	RJ	rough approximations -
23	Fizeau(Journal)	1849.5	315,300.000	10000	3	RJ	rough approximations -
24	Fizeau	1855.0	298,000.000	5000	3	S	Original source uncertain
25	Fizeau	1855.0	305,650.000	5000	3	S	Original source uncertain
26	Weber/Kohlrausch	1856.0	310,700.000	20000	7	D	Not in vacuo
27	Weber/Kohlrausch	1856.0	310,800.000	-	7	em	
28	Nyren/Peters	1858.0	299,800.000	190	2	*	
29	Glasnapp	1861.0	300,050.000	150	1	M*	
30	Foucault	1862.8	298,000.000	500	4	RJ	Unfavourable
31	Newcomb(WO)	1864.5	299,870.000	130	2	*	
32	Glyden(PO)	1866.5	301,050.000	200	2	*	
33	Maxwell	1868.0	284,000.000	20000	7	D	not in vacuo
34	Maxwell	1868.0	284,300.000	-	7	em	
35	Nyren/Glyden(PO)	1868.0	299,440.000	200	2	*	
36	Thomson/King	1869.0	280,900.000	8300	7	em	
37	Nyren/Wagner(PO)	1870.0	299,980.000	60	2	*	
38	Cornu	1872.0	298,500.000	900	3	D	Redone 1874
39	Nyren(PO)	1873.0	299,580.000	200	2	*	
40	McKichan	1874.0	289,700.000	6800	7	em	
41	Cornu/Dorsey	1874.8	299,900.000	600	3	M*	
42	Cornu/Helmert	1874.8	299,990.000	200	3	M*	
43	Cornu	1874.8	300,400.000	800	3	M*	
44	Harvard(1844-1909)	1876.5	299,921.000	13	1	M*	
45	Sampson	1876.5	300,011.000	13	1	M*	

Data #	Experimenter	Date	c Value	Error Bar	Meth	Code	Comments
46	Michelson/Dorsey	1878.0	300,500.000	3500	4	D	Redone in 1879
47	Michelson	1878.0	300,140.000	700	4	D	Redone in 1879
48	Ayrton/Perry	1879.0	296,000.000	3000	7	D	not in vacuo
49	Ayrton/Perry	1879.0	296,100.000	-	7	em	
50	Hockin	1879.0	296,700.000	3000	7	em	
51	Rowland	1879.0	298,400.000	3400	7	em	
52	Nyren(PO)	1879.5	299,440.000	200	2	*	
53	Michelson/Dorsey	1879.5	299,900.000	200	4	M*	
54	Michelson	1879.5	299,910.000	50	4	M*	
55	Michelson/Birge	1879.5	299,990.000	200	4	M*	
56	Shida	1880.0	295,500.000	3000	7	D	not in vacuo
57	Shida	1880.0	295,600.000	-	7	em	
58	Young/Forbes	1880.0	301,382.000	2000	3	RJ	Rejected by most peers
59	Nyren(PO)	1880.5	299,480.000	130	2	*	
60	Stoletov	1881.0	299,000.000	2000	7	em	
61	Newcomb/Dorsey	1881.8	299,780.000	80	4	D	Initial values Newcomb
62	Newcomb	1881.8	299,810.000	50	4	D	Only 1882 value
63	Exner	1882.0	287,000.000	23000	7	em	
64	Newcomb	1882.7	299,860.000	30	4	*	
65	Michelson/Dorsey	1882.8	299,850.000	250	4	M*	
66	Michelson	1882.8	299,853.000	60	4	M*	
67	Thomson	1883.0	296,400.000	20000	7	em	
68	Nyren(PO)	1883.0	299,850.000	90	2	*	
69	Klemencic	1884.0	301,880.000	1500	7	D	not in vacuo
70	Klemencic	1884.0	302,000.000	-	7	em	
71	Colley	1886.0	301,500.000	6000	7	em	
72	Himstedt	1887.0	300,570.000	750	7	D	not in vacuo
73	Himstedt	1887.0	301,000.000	-	7	em	
74	Thomson et al	1888.0	292,000.000	5250	7	em	
75	Rosa	1889.0	300,000.000	800	7	D	not in vacuo
76	Rosa	1889.0	300,090.000	-	7	em	
77	W.Thomson	1889.0	300,500.000	1000	7	em	
78	Kustner(BO)	1889.5	299,870.000	260	2	*	
79	Marcuse	1889.5	299,870.000	180	2	*	
80	Doolittle(FO)	1889.5	300,460.000	130	2	*	
81	J.J.Thomson/Searle	1890.0	299,090.000	-	7	em	Froome&Essen
82	J.J.Thomson/Searle	1890.0	299,690.000	600	7	D	Not in vacuo
83	Comstock	1890.5	300,560.000	170	2	*	
84	Pellat	1891.0	300,920.000	600	7	D	not in vacuo
85	Pellat	1891.0	301,010.000	-	7	em	
86	Blondot	1891.0	302,200.000	8500	6	O	Outlier
87	Batterman(BO)	1891.5	299,630.000	170	2	*	
88	Chandler(BO)	1891.5	299,630.000	170	2	*	
89	Marcuse(BO)	1891.5	299,640.000	130	2	*	
90	Becker(SO)	1891.5	300,170.000	200	2	*	
91	Preston(HO)	1891.5	300,750.000	730	2	*	
92	Abraham	1892.0	299,220.000	-	7	em	
93	Abraham	1892.0	299,850.000	350	7	D	not in vacuo
94	Becker(SO)	1892.5	300,090.000	180	2	*	
95	Blondot	1893.0	297,200.000	5500	6	O	Outlier
96	Davidson(SFO)	1893.0	300,020.000	200	2	*	
97	Rhys/Davis(FO)	1894.5	300,430.000	190	2	*	
98	Trowbridge/Duane	1895.0	300,395.000	5600	6	s.w.	
99	Rhys/Jacob/David(FO)	1896.0	300,170.000	150	2	*	

383

Data #	Experimenter	Date	c Value	Error Bar	Meth	Code	Comments
100	Rhys/Davis(FO)	1896.5	300,170.000	170	2	*	
101	Saunders	1897.0	299,795.000	3300	6	s.w	
102	Hermuzescu	1897.0	300,100.000	300	7	D	not in vacuo
103	Grachev/Kowalski(KO)	1897.0	300,150.000	100	2	*	
104	Hermuzescu	1897.0	300,190.000	-	7	em	
105	Perot/Fabry	1898.0	299,730.000	300	7	D	not in vacuo
106	Perot/Fabry	1898.0	299,870.000	-	7	em	
107	Webster	1898.0	302,590.000	3000	7	em	
108	Grachev(KO)	1898.5	299,380.000	100	2	*	
109	Rhys/Davis(FO)	1898.5	300,170.000	170	2	*	
110	Maclean	1899.0	299,195.000	5000	6	s.w	
111	Grachev(KO)	1899.0	300,110.000	100	2	*	
112	Lodge/Glazebrook	1899.0	300,900.000	12000	7	D	not in vacuo
113	Lodge/Glazebrook	1899.0	301,000.000	-	7	em	
114	Perrotin	1900.4	299,900.000	80	3	M*	
115	Perrotin/Dorsey	1900.4	300,000.000	1000	3	M*	
116	Perrotin/Prim	1900.4	300,032.000	215	3	M*	
117	Inter.Lat.Service	1900.5	299,480.000	60	2	*	
118	Perrotin-avg	1901.4	299,880.000	50	3	S	Average of other data
119	I.L.S.	1901.5	299,440.000	60	2	*	
120	Doolittle(FO)	1901.5	299,540.000	130	2	*	
121	Perrotin	1902.4	299,860.000	80	3	M*	
122	Perrotin/Prim	1902.4	299,901.000	84	3	M*	
123	Doolittle(FO)	1903.0	299,360.000	130	2	*	
124	Ogburn(FO)	1904.5	300,250.000	170	2	*	
125	Bonsdorf(PO)	1905.0	299,710.000	100	2	*	
126	Doolittle(FO)	1905.0	300,080.000	130	2	*	
127	Doolittle(FO)	1906.0	299,760.000	130	2	*	
128	Rosa,Dorsey/F&E	1906.0	299,788.000	10	7	D	Adjusted by Birge
129	Rosa,Dorsey/Birge	1906.0	299,784.000	10	7	D	
130	Rosa,Dorsey/Dorsey	1906.0	299,803.000	30	7	*	
131	Bonsdorf(PO)	1906.5	299,650.000	120	2	*	
132	Bayswater(I.L.S.)	1907.0	299,550.000	100	2	*	
133	Doolittle(FO)	1907.0	299,670.000	130	2	*	
134	I.L.S.	1907.5	299,360.000	60	2	*	
135	Orlov	1907.5	299,860.000	120	2	*	
136	Doolittle(FO)	1908.0	299,630.000	180	2	*	
137	I.L.S.	1908.5	299,410.000	60	2	*	
138	Semenov	1908.5	299,460.000	150	2	*	
139	Doolittle(FO)	1909.0	299,440.000	130	2	*	
140	Semenov	1909.5	299,610.000	190	2	*	
141	Zemtsov	1909.5	299,730.000	200	2	*	
142	Doolittle(FO)	1910.0	299,710.000	120	2	*	
143	Numerov(PO)	1914.0	299,640.000	200	2	*	
144	Tsimmerman(PO)	1916.0	299,520.000	200	2	*	
145	Kulikov(PO)	1922.0	299,550.000	60	2	*	
146	Mercier	1923.0	299,700.000	30	6	D	not in vacuo
147	Mercier	1923.0	299,795.000	30	6	*	
148	Spencer-Jones(GO)	1923.5	299,760.000	60	2	*	
149	Michelson/Dorsey	1924.6	299,800.000	70	5	D	Adjusted by Birge
150	Michelson	1924.6	299,802.000	30	5	*	
151	Berg(PO)	1926.5	299,670.000	200	2	*	
152	Michelson	1926.5	299,796.000	15	5	M*	Adjusted by Birge
153	Michelson/Birge	1926.5	299,798.000	15	5	*	

Data #	Experimenter	Date	c Value	Error Bar	Meth	Code	Comments
154	Mittelstaedt	1928.0	299,778.000	10	8	D	Adjusted by Birge
155	Mittelstaedt/Birge	1928.0	299,786.000	10	8	*	
156	Spencer-Jones(GO)	1928.0	300,090.000	150	2	*	
157	Spencer-Jones	1930.5	299,630.000	60	2	*	
158	Pease-Pearson	1932.5	299,774.000	10	5	*	
159	Sollenberger(WO)	1933.0	300,420.000	60	2	*	
160	Romanskaya(PO)	1935.0	299,570.000	100	2	*	
161	Rabe	1935.5	299,920.000	60	2	*	
162	Anderson	1936.8	299,771.000	10	8	*	
163	Huttel	1937.0	299,768.000	10	8	D	Adjusted by Birge
164	Huttel/Birge	1937.0	299,771.000	10	8	*	
165	Anderson	1940.0	299,776.000	10	8	*	
166	Jones	1947.0	299,687.000	25	10	R	Lacks humidity
167	Smith,Franklin,Whiting	1947.0	299,695.000	50	10	R	Lacks humidity
168	Essen,Gordon-Smith	1947.0	299,792.000	3	9	*	
169	Essen,Gordon-Smith	1947.0	299,798.000	3	9	O	Outlier
170	Jones,Conford	1949.0	299,701.000	25	10	R	Lacks humidity
171	Aslakson	1949.0	299,792.400	2.4	10	D	Systematic error
172	Bergstrand	1949.0	299,796.000	2	11	*	
173	Houstoun	1950.0	299,775.000	9	18	qm	
174	McKinley	1950.0	299,780.000	70	18	qm	
175	Hansen,Bol	1950.0	299789.3000	1.2	9	D	Corrected for skin effect
176	Essen	1950.0	299,792.500	1	9	*	
177	Bergstrand	1950.0	299,793.100	0.26	11	*	
178	Hansen,Bol	1950.0	299,794.300	1.2	9	*	
179	Froome	1951.0	299,792.600	0.7	12	*	
180	Bergstrand	1951.0	299,793.100	0.4	11	*	
181	Aslakson	1951.0	299,794.200	1.9	10	*	
182	Rank,Ruth,Vander Sluis	1952.0	299,776.000	15	13	O	
183	Bergstrand	1953.0	299,792.850	0.16	11	*	
184	Rank,Shearer,Wiggans	1954.0	299,789.800	3	13	RJ	Wavelength
185	Froome	1954.0	299,792.750	0.3	12	*	
186	Florman	1954.0	299,795.100	3.1	12	*	
187	Plyler,Blaine,Connor	1955.0	299,792.000	6	13	*	
188	Scholdstrom	1955.0	299,792.400	0.4	11	*	
189	Rank,Bennett,Benett	1956.0	299,791.900	2	13	*	
190	Edge	1956.0	299,792.200	0.13	11	*	
191	Edge	1956.0	299,792.400	0.11	11	*	
192	Wadley	1956.0	299,792.700	2	14	*	
193	Wadley	1956.0	299,792.900	2	14	*	
194	Wadley	1957.0	299,792.600	1.2	14	*	
195	Froome	1958.0	299,792.500	0.1	12	*	
196	Kolibayev	1960.0	299,792.600	0.06	11	*	
197	Karolus	1966.0	299,792.440	0.2	15	*	
198	Grosse	1967.0	299,792.500	0.05	11	*	
199	Simkin et al	1967.0	299,792.560	0.11	16	*	
200	NRC,NBS	1972.0	299,792.460	0.006	17	*	Atomic clock
201	Bay,Luther,White	1972.0	299,792.462	0.018	17	*	Atomic clock
202	Evenson et al	1973.0	299,792.457	0.0011	17	*	Atomic clock
203	NRC,NBS	1973.0	299,792.458	0.002	17	*	Atomic clock
204	Blaney et al	1974.0	299,792.459	0.0008	17	*	Atomic clock
205	Woods,Shotton,Rowley	1978.0	299,792.458	0.0002	17	*	Atomic clock
206	Baird,Smith,Whitford	1979.0	299,792.458	0.0019	17	*	Atomic clock
207	NBS	1983.0	299,792.458	0.0003	17	*	Atomic clock

LEGEND:

S	- secondary data
D	- defective data
*	- accepted independent experimental data
M*	- multiple values-single experiment
R	- radar
em	- electromagnetic method
qm	- quartz modulator
s.w.	- standing wire
O	- outlier
RJ	- rejected

METHODS:

1 - Roemer, 2 - Aberration, 3 - Toothed-Wheel,
4 - Moving mirror, 5 - Rotating mirror,
6 - Standing wire, 7 - EMU/ESU, 8 - Kerr cell,
9 - Cavity resonator, 10 - Radar, 11 - Geodimeter,
12 - Inferometer, 13 - Spectral lines,
14 - Tellurometer, 15 - Modulated light,
16 - Microwave inferometer, 17 - Laser,
18 - Quartz modulator

CREATION, THE KEY TO HISTORY

ELLEN MYERS, M.A.
1429 N. HOLYOKE
WICHITA, KS 67208

KEYWORDS

Monism, prehistory, creation mandate, cyclical history, linear history, progress, determinism, chance, judgment, nations, victory at Calvary

ABSTRACT

This paper will show that what we believe about origins makes tremendous differences in our views of history. Evolutionists believe that this world is all there is (monism); biblical creationists believe that this world and time itself was created out of nothing by the personal, sovereign, transcendent God of the Bible. Evolutionist historians presuppose long aeons of "prehistory," minimizing the importance of human history as a whole; biblical creationist historians begin with man's creation in God's own image and likeness a few thousand years ago. Evolutionists are uncertain about man's historical purpose. Biblical creationists believe man's purpose is to obey God's creation mandate to be fruitful, multiply, fill the earth and have dominion over it, a mandate further charted by God's commandments and the Gospel; the key to history is how well or ill man obeys this mandate.

Ancient evolutionist paganism viewed history as recurring cycles, thereby robbing it of all meaning. For biblical creationism, history is linear from creation to Christ's Second Coming by way of the Fall, the Flood, the dispersal of the nations at Babel, the history of Israel, the Incarnation, Crucifixion and Resurrection of Jesus Christ, and the worldwide preaching of the Gospel. Modern paganism in both its materialist and pantheist "New Age" forms still believes in linear history as well though now rapidly discarding this remnant of Christian influence through "multicultural" education. It denies man's Fall and hence need for Christ as his Redeemer from sin. It believes in past upward evolutionary progress and expects change of human nature, merging of nations and one world government as history's next milestone. Evolutionist historians believe in determinism (by geography, heredity, economics, etc.) and/or chance. Biblical creationist historians believe God the Creator's will is the ultimate cause of all events, preserving man's freedom to obey or disobey God.

The biblical creation view of history is well undergirded today by the international scientific creation movement which shows that evolution cannot have happened. It is also confirmed by fulfilled biblical prophecy and by the bankruptcy of societies disregarding the creation mandate. Evolutionist educators and historians themselves have brought about the sad neglect of history study today by their reductionist, joyless theories of history as ultimately useless and meaningless. Creation based historiography has preserved consistent objective meaning and purpose for the study of history as an indispensable academic discipline. Creation based historiography recognizes the hidden role of evil supernatural spirits beginning with Satan in Eden, whose existence or evil modern evolutionists deny. Only creation based historiography joyfully promises man victory over these spirits and all adversity yesterday, today and tomorrow in Jesus Christ our Saviour (Gen. 3:15; Rom. 8:38-39; 1 Cor. 15:57).

References to St. Augustine's pivotal City of God, Herbert Butterfield's Christianity and History, Christopher Dawson's Religion and the Rise of Western Culture, R. G. Collingwood's The Idea of History, and to other contemporary historians and history textbooks round out this study.

INTRODUCTION

What we believe about origins makes tremendous differences in our views of history. Evolutionists believe that this world is all there is (monism); biblical creationists believe that this world was created out of nothing by the personal, sovereign, transcendent God of the Bible. Evolutionist historians presuppose long aeons of "pre-history" during which man slowly evolved from lower animals and primitive living to his high status today. They thus minimize the importance of human history properly speaking, and are committed to the idea of continuous progress toward a nebulous higher state, like Marx's pure communism where the state withers away, Hitler's "Thousand Year Reich" ruled by a pure Aryan superrace, or "New Age" cult hero Pierre Teilhard de Chardin's spiritual "Omega point" where the world becomes Christ.

Biblical creationist historians, on the other hand, deny evolutionist "pre-history" and begin with man's creation in God's own image and likeness a few thousand years ago, thus dealing only with true human history. They are not snared by utopian visions of progress because they believe that man fell from his original perfection as created in God's own image and desperately needs salvation and restoration in Christ. Since man was created in God's own image and likeness, he is designed to live and receive true joy exclusively from God's own life and joy: "The joy of the LORD is your strength" (Nehemiah 8:10). As C. S. Lewis says,

> What Satan put into the heads of our remote ancestors was the idea that they could ... set up on their own as if they had created themselves ... invent some sort of happiness for themselves outside God ...
>
> The reason why it can never succeed is this. ... [God] Himself is the fuel our spirits were designed to burn, or the food our spirits were designed to feed on. There is no other. ...
>
> That is the key to history. Terrific energy is expended - civilizations built up - excellent institutions devised; but each time something goes wrong. Some fatal flaw always brings the selfish and cruel people to the top and it all slides back into misery and ruin. That is what Satan has done to us humans.[8]

Ancient evolutionist paganism viewed history as recurring cycles, thereby robbing it of all meaning. For biblical Christianity history is linear from creation to Christ's Second Coming and absolutely meaningful every moment because ultimately directed by God the Creator and Sustainer, to Whom all men and nations are responsible. Modern paganism in both its materialist and pantheist "New Age" forms still believes in linear history though now also returning to ancient cyclical views.

Because evolutionists believe that this world is all there is, they have no independent, absolute standard for ethical judgment in history. They may judge on subjective grounds, or else say that events are their own justification. This robs the study of history of its instructive value. Biblical creationists have an independent, absolute standard for ethical judgment in history, namely, God's character and law revealed in the Bible. The Lord warns His people : "As the nations which the LORD destroyeth before your face, so shall ye perish; because ye would not be obedient unto the voice of the LORD your God" (Deuteronomy 8:20). Biblical creationists thus preserve the instructive value of history.

Evolutionist historians themselves have brought about the sad neglect of the study of history today by their reductionist, joyless views of history as ultimately meaningless. Only creation based historiography preserves consistent objective meaning and purpose for the study of history as an indispensable academic discipline. Creation based historiography also recognizes the role of evil supernatural spirits beginning with Satan in Eden, whose existence or evil modern evolutionists deny. Only creation based historiography joyfully promises man victory over these spirits because God as Creator is sovereign and victorious over all principalities and powers.

References to St. Augustine's pivotal *City of God*, Sir Herbert Butterfield's *Christianity and History*, R. G. Collingwood's *The Idea of History*, and to other historians and history textbooks will round out this study.

THE EVOLUTIONIST VIEW OF HISTORY

A Monistic Worldview

The evolutionist view of history is the perennial alternative and enemy of the biblical creation view. First of all, it is impersonal and *monistic*, that is, it believes that this world is all there is. The evolutionist worldview does not admit supernatural or extra-natural action in history. This is also true for idealist, "spiritual," or magical views in today's "New Age" pattern because for them physical phenomena are mere "appearances," even as ideas or non-physical phenomena are mere "appearances" for materialist thinkers. Both deny the reality of anything, spiritual or physical, above and apart from this present world here and now. For them all that exists is at bottom one; it always existed in either changing (Heraclitus) or unchanging (Plato) form or forms.

Cyclical History

Second, ancient pagans saw the history of the world and mankind as cyclical, with the same events and phases recurring forever and ever without an absolute overall beginning and end. Some spoke of each individual cycle or revolution of the great wheel of time as a "Great Year" of 36,000 ordinary years. Hindu concepts of Karma and reincarnation as well as the long time spans demanded by modern evolutionists obviously fit well into this scheme. Modern, post-Christian pagan views of evolution and history seek in part to retain the idea of linear human history inherited from Christianity, and embrace the unbiblical idea of progress from primitive to highly evolved. However, there are also modern evolutionist cyclical writers and philosophers of history such as Oswald Spengler and his

The Decline of the West, first published 1917 and 1922, or Arnold Toynbee and his *A Study of History*, which appeared in the 1930s and 40s.

Evolution and "Pre-History"

After modern Darwinian evolutionism had become well established in higher education, most historians succumbed to its postulate that millions of years of "pre-history," during which "primitive" creatures evolved from apes to men, preceded the few thousand years of recorded human history, which alone is history properly speaking. The belief of two would-be historians expressed in a recent best-seller is typical: "For tens of thousands of generations, there was no civilization. There was no written language. There was no government, no larger organization of society at all [5]."

Unfortunately many Christian historians also swallowed this myth. Thus Sir Herbert Butterfield spoke of the "personalities ... the heirs of all the ages, whom creation groaned through so many astronomical eras and such long geological epochs to produce [3]." Not only did Butterfield accept the myth of long evolutionist ages of "pre-history," he even identified them with creation! With God's creation of all things out of nothing by His Word in six days, the foundation for a sure, victorious biblical Christian view of history, thus completely corrupted in his mind, he, like "a trumpet giving an uncertain sound" (1 Cor. 14:8), could only speak gently and tentatively on behalf of God's work in history. There is a trace of this evolutionist poison even in the fine Christian historian Christopher Dawson when he wrote that "Modern scientists rightly insist on the way in which the existence of modern man is conditioned by the inheritance of his prehistoric past [6]."

History and Progress

A close corollary of belief in man's evolutionary "pre-history" is belief in man's continuing progress to ever loftier heights of knowledge, freedom and civilization. This optimistic view of history and the future was especially prevalent around the turn of the twentieth century and even bedazzled Christian historians. We see it, for example, in the great Lord Acton who intended to write a history of the progress and expansion of human freedom from antiquity to his time (he died before carrying out this project, overly ambitious as well as futile in view of history's turn shortly after his death). Historical optimism steeply declined after World War I, the first world wide war in history, and the descent into Nazi barbarism of Germany, till then one of the most highly civilized nations on the globe. The horrors of communist rule in the Soviet Union were less publicized due to the leftist leanings of the majority of Western intellectuals. The Nazis, by the way, considered their racist policies, starting with sterilization and extermination of the physically or mentally handicapped and ending with the mass genocide of Jews and gypsies, as the praiseworthy enforcement of Darwinian evolution. However, the inherent logic of man's alleged upward evolution was reformulated after World War II by the vanguard of today's "New Age" movement, among whom the apostate French Catholic priest Pierre Teilhard de Chardin (d. 1955) enjoys special veneration.

The well-known American sociologist-historian Robert Nisbet shares this idea of progress as shown in his influential *History of the Idea of Progress*. Nisbet traces the idea of progress from the ancient Greeks to the middle of the twentieth century. He believes that only a renewal of religion or of a sense of the sacred can revive the idea of progress and with it the West, and that "the fusion of science and religion achieved by Teilhard de Chardin, one based upon the inexorable progress of human knowledge into the very distant future - and with this progress, the progress also of man's spirit and his estate on earth - will hold a very prominent place in it [10]." To Nisbet, the idea of progress

> holds that mankind has advanced in the past - from some aboriginal condition of primitiveness, barbarism, or even nullity - is now advancing, and will continue to advance ... The idea ... must be thought a part of the very scheme of things in universe and society. Advance from the inferior to the superior must seem as real and certain as anything in the laws of nature [10, pp.4,5].

All this is deduced from atheistic or pantheistic evolutionism.

Nisbet maintains his defense of the idea of progress while admitting that "twentieth-century totalitarianism" and racism were founded on this idea of inexorable progress. He even writes that

> From the post-medieval disciples of Joachim, eager to hasten through sword and torch ... the arrival of the millennium, through the zealots of the Puritan Revolution, through the Jacobins in the French Revolution, down to the Lenins, Stalins, Hitlers, and Maos of the twentieth century, the most awful of persecutions, tortures, massacres, and sieges of terror have had for their justification a sense of historical development, of *necessary* historical development, every bit as galvanizing as any Crusader's sense of God needing to be avenged against the infidel [10, p.139].

Nisbet's blanket endorsement of the idea of progress, and indeed the very idea of progress itself, is questionable when appalling atrocities are condoned in its name.

History and Judgment

Since nothing exists for evolutionists apart from history/"pre-history" itself, they have no independent, absolute standard of ethics by which to judge historical human action. Instead they take the events of history itself as their "standard," saying with the famous German poet Friedrich Schiller that "world history is world judgment" ("Die Weltgeschichte ist das Weltgericht"). In Darwinist tautological fashion they believe that success in history shows who is worthiest much like "survival of the fittest" shows who is fittest. In history evaluation the evolutionist worldview, lacking God and hence God's standard of ethics, must justify mere success regardless of how it was achieved. Much like the idea of progress, itself based on evolution, it has no basis from which to condemn a Hitler or a Stalin.

Determinism, Chance and Meaning in History

Non-Christian historiography hovers between determinism and chance as directing history's course. Deterministic factors are, for example, heredity and geography, while natural catastrophes striking a particular location at a particular moment might be mere chance. Such chance events or mere "accidents of history" then contribute to the outworking of determinist fate. Examples are the proverbial saying: "For want of a nail the horse was lost, for want of the horse the battle was lost, for loss of the battle the war was lost," or British historian J. B. Bury's famous reference to the shape of Cleopatra's nose as a decisive factor in the history of Rome. A butterfly's wings fluttering in China may eventually lead to a blizzard in New England - what meteorologists today call the "butterfly effect." All chains of cause and effect may be initiated by chances no more significant than this. By the way, this ancient, perennial determinism/chance model of history well fits the "punctuated equilibrium" evolutionist model proposed by Niles Eldredge and Stephen Jay Gould; the stream of determinism is comparable to their "equilibrium," and chance is analogous to their "punctuation." Of course this means that everything called "fate" is really the result of chance, and that there is no meaning to history other than the endless interplay and conflict of impersonal forces. If this were true, then the power-hungry tyrants of history, the Stalins and Hitlers, are justified by ultimate reality.

Falsified History

Monistic, evolutionist history writing has no absolute standard of truth (the very concept of absolute truth must logically be absurd to any evolutionist aware of the epistemological void of evolutionism). Hence the temptation to falsify history in order to substantiate one's party or individual ideology is often irresistible. (Christian history writing may err, but if it deliberately falsifies the facts, it is not "Christian" in principle, for then it violates the Commandment against bearing false witness against our neighbor. This is why the Bible itself does not gloss over the sins of its heroes, like King David.) Thus we have "party" historiographies of the Nazi or Communist variety which bend or suppress historical facts. The fact that Lenin (and not Stalin) began the rule of terror in the Soviet Union was not acknowledged until the great Alexander Solzhenitsyn incontrovertibly documented it in his *Gulag Archipelago*. Another example of falsification by suppression is M. N. Pokrovsky, for years the leading Soviet historian, who remained completely silent about the crucially important religious schism between the "Old Believers" and the Russian Orthodox Church in the seventeenth century in his *History of Russia* (London: Martin Lawrence, Ltd., 1931) because Marxism does not admit religious motivation. Modern Soviet historians attempted to construct a history of the development of Russian industry in line with Karl Marx's historical stages based on economic class war, which actual Russian history does not substantiate. Of course such falsification, if and when discovered, can backfire. This writer recently translated a letter from a Russian student who requested more information about biblical creation because of his disillusionment with falsified Soviet history!

In the West, a similar example of falsification today is the suppression of the Christian motivation and faith of Christopher Columbus. Columbus is a victim of the "politically correct" anti-Christian hatred of Western culture and "white patriarchal males" currently poisoning our climate of inquiry especially at our most prestigious universities. Absurdly, the famous church father St. Augustine, a native of Hippo, North Africa, and hence presumably not white, is usually among the targets of "politically correct" racism.

An example of outright "evolutionist" history is Frederick Jackson Turner (1861-1932), author of the "frontier theory" of American history. Turner based his theory on

> the scientific "grant theory" most prominent in his own day, Charles Darwin's theory of evolution. Where Darwin had proposed an explanation for evolution in the natural world, Turner suggested that America was an ideal laboratory for the study of cultural evolution. The American frontier, he argued, returned man to a primitive state of nature. With the trappings of civilization stripped away, the upward process of evolution was re-enacted [11].

Later historians challenged or modified this theory in accordance with their own preferences. Today American frontier history is dominated by "politically correct" uncritical sympathy with American Indians, whose misdeeds are underreported. One-sided historical writing is by definition falsified.

Sometimes a prevailing false view of a certain historical period is due not so much to deliberate falsification but rather to accumulated ignorance and misinformation. In such instances evolutionists and Christian creationists may well share the same mistaken views. One example is the false idea that the French Revolution was a liberating event to which we owe many civil liberties today. In reality it was a frightening outburst of vicious hatred of Christianity, unrestrained terror, butchery of tens of thousands of innocent people, and an economic disaster for France. A number of revisionist histories of the French Revolution have been published upon its 200th anniversary in 1989. The excellent *Revolution et Christianisme*, edited by the eminent French Swiss Christian author Jean-Marc Berthoud, is the best from the biblical Christian perspective. Another related example is the false idea among both secular and Christian historians that the American Declaration of Independence was not a Christian but a deistic document, and that we hence owe our civil liberties in America to the secular Renaissance or Enlightenment. In reality the Declaration was based on biblical creation and centuries of legal development of man's creation based inalienable rights by and within the Christian Church. For full details, see the outstanding book *Defending the Declaration* by Gary T. Amos [9].

Solipsist History

Modern philosophers of history generally belong to the two main categories of post-Christian thought, materialism-atheism and idealism-pantheism. The latter is especially compatible with "New Age" theorizing. An example of it is the British philosopher of history R. G. Collingwood (d. 1943) who taught at Oxford University. We will analyze his best known, posthumously published work, *The Idea of History*, still used in college history courses today, from the biblical creation perspective.

Being an evolutionist, Collingwood could not help but be a historical relativist. He thought that there is no point in asking whether any historian is right or wrong since historians are compelled to write as they do by the circumstances of the times in which they themselves live.

Collingwood saw the historian's own present "experience" of historical facts as that which gives meaning to history and even remodels human nature. For him "the historical process is a process in which man creates for himself this or that kind of human nature by recreating in his own thought the past to which he is heir [4]." Thus for Collingwood man, not God, is man's maker by means of "recreating" history in his own mind.

Collingwood believed that "'what really happened' is only 'what the evidence obliges us to believe' [4, p.154,204]." This reductionist definition allows each historian to decide for himself what evidence he will accept as compelling on the grounds of his present historically conditioned presuppositions.

Consistent with his evolutionist, relativist process philosophy Collingwood believed that man is the product of history, and that history is in principle endless. He rejected the Enlightenment's utopian thinking because man's mind "would give rise to new moral and social and political problems, and the millennium would be as far as ever [4, p.85]." seemingly unaware of the hopeless pessimism of this evolutionist view with regard to the utility of history study. If Collingwood were right about man's mind continually operating in new and different ways, the historical record would lose not only all transcendent but also all utilitarian value or meaning.

Collingwood asserted that history "is ... the self-knowledge of the historian's own mind as the present revival and reliving of past experience [4, p.175]." If this claim is accepted, the study of history is in essence reduced to the solipsist pursuit of "historical experience" within the mind of each individual historian. A historian trying to practice his calling as defined by Collingwood could never be sure that his purported "experience of the past" is not merely his own imaginary counterfeit of the past; thus the transcendent truth value of history as an academic discipline in pursuit of true knowledge would be abandoned. The example of Collingwood shows that for the consistent modern evolutionist relativist historian history is bound to become "a tale told by an idiot, full of sound and fury, signifying nothing" (Shakespeare in *Macbeth*).

Collingwood's work may be seen as an attempt to rescue history from meaninglessness in a supposedly evolutionist, relativistic world. The meaning he hoped to establish is history as "re-creation" of the past in each historian's mind. This "meaning," however, amounts to solipsism, the black hole of ultimate meaninglessness at the end of all evolutionist process thought. Sadly other prominent modern historians such as Americans Carl Becker (1873-1945) and Charles A. Beard (1876-1948) shared Collingwood's solipsist view of history. With such opinion leaders in the field of history, it is no wonder that its study in the primary and secondary schools of the West has been watered down to "social studies" or essentially eliminated altogether. The contemptuous comments of automaker Henry Ford, made in 1916 to a *Chicago Tribune* reporter in an interview about Ford's disarmament views, "What do we care what they did 500 or 1000 years ago? ... History is more or less bunk. It's tradition. We don't want tradition. We want to live in the present, and the only history that is worth a tinker's damn is the history we make today" (*Reader's Digest*, June 1993, p. 98) could come from a "politically correct" educator or professor today. This cavalier attitude towards man's past and its lessons is suicidal but inevitable once belief in biblical creation and its personal, omnipotent, transcendent God, the key to history, is abandoned for monistic atheistic/pantheistic evolution myths.

THE BIBLICAL CREATION VIEW OF HISTORY

Is Not Monistic

The biblical Christian view holds that God is personal and transcendent, exists beyond and apart from this world here and now, precisely because this world is the product of biblical creation *ex nihilo*: God created it out of nothing, and without Him as its Creator out of nothing neither it nor history would exist at all.

Its Purpose and Meaning: the Creator's Joy

God freely created all things not out of necessity, "as though He needed anything" (Acts 17:25), but for His *joy*: "Thou hast created all things, and *for thy pleasure* they were and are created" (Revelation 4:11). Thus, God the Creator's joy is the purpose and meaning of all things whatever, and of history in particular. God was pleased with His creation when He first made it (Genesis 1:10, 12, 18, 21, 25, 31). God's creation is also meant to give joy to man, the creature made in God's own image and likeness, for "the joy of the LORD is our strength" (Nehemiah 8:10). Very few if any history books except, of course, the historical books of the Bible itself show awareness of this fundamental fact.

History is Linear; no "Pre-History"; History, "Progress," and Judgment

For the creationist there are, of course, no long ages of evolutionary "pre-history." On the basis of biblical creation fully accepted as true, and fully in conformity with science as shown today by a multitude of empirical evidences, Christian historians must not bow to any evolutionist stories of "pre-history" if they would keep faith with their Lord and honor their profession.

According to the Bible, history is linear and has a definite beginning and end. It began with creation about 6,000 years ago as shown by the biblical genealogies, and will end with our Lord's return and His final judgment of the quick and the dead (Matthew 25:31-46). He will judge our love for Him by how we have treated our fellow men, and our faithfulness to Him by how we have exercised our stewardship under Him (Matthew 24:14-30, the Parable of the Talents).

The Bible-believing Christian can never agree that the end justifies the means, or that we may do evil that good may come (Romans 3:8). Any idea of "progress" which omits, as do Nisbet and evolutionists, Creator, Fall and regeneration in Christ, is fatally flawed and doomed to failure.

From the biblical Christian perspective the idea that historical events themselves *always* constitute moral judgment is an error. C. S. Lewis rightly points to the "divine rebuffs [in Scripture] which this naive and spontaneous type of Historicism there receives; in the whole course of Jewish history, in the Book of Job, in Isaiah's suffering servant (liii), in Our Lord's answers about the disaster at Siloam (Luke xiii, 4) and the man born blind (John ix, 13). If this sort of Historicism survives, it survives in spite of Christianity [7]." How we have fulfilled our creation mandate, which is to give joy to our Lord Who created us for His joy, will thus decide whether we will "enter the joy of our Lord" (Mt. 24:21, 23) forever. Of course God's temporal judgment is pronounced upon the nations and rulers who forget Him and rebel against Him, though it may long delay and try the patience of His own obedient people (Revelation 6:10). As students of history we can and must evaluate men and nations in accordance with God's law revealed in Scripture, and this requires the utmost care in establishing the historical facts. The Christian father of history as an academic discipline, Leopold von Ranke, knew this well.

God Is Absolutely Sovereign: Neither Determinism Nor Chance

God is omnipotent and omniscient, in full control of everything, and His will is the ultimate cause of every event in history. He uses everything and everyone, even His enemies, for His purpose. This does not mean that the efficiency of secondary causes, including men's wills, thoughts and deeds, is abrogated. As the Westminster Confession so clearly states:

> God from all eternity did by the most wise and holy counsel of his own will freely and unchangeably ordain whatsoever comes to pass: yet so as thereby neither is God the author of sin, nor is violence offered to the will of creatures, nor is the liberty or contingency of second causes taken away, but rather established [12].

On the contrary, and wholly admirably and praiseworthy, God can raise up a godless Pharaoh or Nebuchadnezzar freely boasting themselves against Him to fulfill His purpose and to show His power through them. The very men who crucified our Lord fulfilled God's design (Acts 2:23-24; 3:14-18). As Dorothy L. Sayers wrote in her magnificent play *The Man Born to be King*, the prophecies are fulfilled either *in* us or *upon* us.

Because God is a person, and we are also persons created in His own image and likeness, the bane of evolutionist history, impersonal determinism and chance, are excluded from biblical creation-based history. Hence history is not an ultimately meaningless, weary, everlasting struggle of force against force but has transcendent, eternal, absolute meaning, which is to restore the Creator's and men's joy in each other. For this "joy set before Him" Christ "endured the cross, despising the shame" (Hebrews 12:2). On the contrary, each moment coming from God's hand to us, each act in history is full of meaning under God: in each moment we either turn towards Him or away from Him. Everything matters in our lives under God our Creator.

Nations in Creation and History

Nations, too, have created identities and are responsible for their actions to God their Creator. The word "nations" first occurs in the Bible in Genesis 10. Here the families of the sons of Noah are listed "after their generations, in their nations, and by these were the nations divided in the earth after the flood." Nations were in the Creator's original plan and purpose for developing mankind, and are the result of His command to our first parents and to Noah to be "fruitful and multiply, and replenish the earth" (Genesis 1:28; Genesis 9:1, 7).

Neither isolated individuals nor a one-world conglomerate of them, neither national chauvinism nor denial of separate national identities does justice to God's true created order, which is modeled after the Trinity-in-Unity of God Himself as the archetype of interpersonal and international relations. From this starting point - God Himself, in Whose image and likeness we human beings are created, as our model and pattern - and from it alone can we understand that nations are meant by our Creator to live together and to complement each other in loving harmony, yet without surrendering their respective distinct national "personalities" or created identities, even as do the Three distinct yet Triune Persons of the Godhead.

The Bible also teaches that not only individual people but nations will continue to exist in God's new heaven and new earth in eternity (Matthew 25:31-34, 41, 46; Revelation 5:9; Rev. 7:9). Consider especially Revelation 21:24, 26: "And the nations of them which are saved shall walk in the light of it: and the kings of the earth do bring their glory and honor into it. ... And they shall bring the glory and honor of the nations into it." The great Russian Christian author Fyodor Dostoevsky was right when he wrote in his notebook, "The *nation* is nothing more than the *national personality*." It could not be otherwise, for our individual created identities include our nationality.

Genesis 10 shows that nations originally arise from individual ancestors and their families. Thus God promised Abraham, "I will make of thee a great nation" (Gen.12:1-2), and also that He would make a great nation of Abraham's son Ishmael (Gen. 17:20). People from one nation may join with another, as did "mixed multitudes" with Israel on the exodus from Egypt (Exodus 12:38), Rahab of Jericho (Joshua 6:25) and Ruth of Moab (Ruth 1:16-17). The American nation (U.S.A.) which began with settlers from England is now made up of immigrants from all over the globe. While God made all nations "of one blood", He also determined their "times before appointed, and the bounds of their habitation" (Acts 17:26).

Significantly enough, a nation's awareness of its *history* is probably the most important ingredient in holding it together, as shown by the Jews, the Poles, the Swiss, and so on. Falsify or suppress a nation's history - as was done in Russia under Communism, and is being done now in America - and the survival of that nation in its created identity is endangered. Henry Ford and modern educators notwithstanding, history is not "bunk" but indispensable.

Satan and History

Secular history is generally silent about evil spirits behind events. Documented historical "occult" movements claiming them as their guides receive only minimal attention, and then as a matter of the people's *beliefs* rather than actual existence of the evil spirits in which they believe. Since Christian history begins with creation and man's fall, it accepts the actual existence and activity of Satan and his demonic hosts beneath or behind historical events.

According to the Bible satanic principalities and powers work in *all people* who disobey God (Ephesians 2:2; 6:12). Hence all atrocities ostensibly inflicted by men upon fellow men, and all vicious anti-human motives, thoughts and philosophies behind them are due ultimately to the satanic hosts. They fiercely hate God and man, the unique being created in God's own image and likeness which they want to degrade, mutilate and destroy.

Satanic violence is nothing new in history. It has marked all the great idolatrous, demon-worshiping societies of antiquity, for "the things which the gentiles sacrifice, they sacrifice to demons and not to God" (I Corinthians 10:20). In ancient Babylon Chaldean sorcerers developed charms and a spiritual poisoner's art much like voodoo. Human sacrifice was an important part of Babylonian religion. Assyrian palace walls commemorate the most horrible anti-human cruelty, especially against conquered peoples, which was also prevalent in ancient Canaan. The Aztecs practiced exceeding torture, human sacrifice, and cannibalism as part of their religion and warfare, as did the Mayans. There are many eyewitness reports of North American Indians' horrible cruelty towards strangers. Human sacrifice is reported today as part of demonic and witchcraft rituals not only in Africa but increasingly in the post-Christian West. Modern mass murder and unspeakable barbarities in this century include the Nazis (champions of Darwinian evolutionism and with important ties to the occult), the Communists, the slaughter of well over a million Armenians by the Turks during World War I, of about three million Cambodians by the communist Khmer Rouge in the 1970s, of some 500 people by communist terrorists in Angola, ushering in decades of civil war, and of 6-800,000 Serbs, often with obviously satanic methods, by the Nazi-like Croatian "Ustashi" during World War

II (which set the background for the grisly civil war in the former Yugoslavia as this is being written). Finally, since the 1970s the unprecedented abortion holocaust around the world is destroying many millions of innocent human beings and thus severely impoverishes mankind's future.

Houston Steward Chamberlain openly stated that he wrote his master work *Die Grundlagen des Neunzehnten Jahrhunderts (The Foundations of the Nineteenth Century)* while possessed by a demon. Published in 1899 (a historical period of spectacular occult revival all over Europe, especially Russia), this book profoundly influenced the Nazi movement. There is persuasive evidence that Karl Marx, the founder of Communism, turned against God and became a Satanist. The same applies to other Communist leaders including Lenin and Stalin.

There are striking similarities between individual and mass atrocities far apart in time and space. Underlying them all is the murderers' bizarre desire to strip their victims of their human identity. Because this craving is so universal and so anti-human in essence, it has a source deeper than man. Scripture teaches that this source is Satan. The bodily harm he instigates pictures what he is really after: the eternal damnation of men's souls in hell with him (Matthew 25:41; 1 Peter 5:8; Revelation 12:12). As the enemy's attacks mount, we can take courage from the fact that he has already been defeated by Christ at Calvary. Besides, he is but a creature and can never prevail over the Creator, the sovereign triune God of Scripture.

St. Augustine, Pioneer of Christian History

St. Augustine's massive and pivotal work *The City of God* was first published between 413 and 425 A.D., and has appeared in many editions and translations to our own day. Augustine affirmed that all things are ordered by God's providence. Further, throughout history there is division between God's people, the "City of God" or "City of Pilgrims," and those who reject God, the "earthly city." All human beings feel the need of social peace, but citizens of the "earthly city" feel no higher need than this. However, earthly "peace" is not man's highest goal, and citizens of the "City of Pilgrims" who seek another, heavenly country are hated and envied by the rest. The earthly city "looks for glory from men, the latter finds its highest glory in God, the witness of a good conscience. ... The one city loves its own strength shown in its powerful leaders; the other says to its God, 'I will love you, my Lord, my strength.' [2]"

The *City of God* is not about the godly pilgrims' escape or isolation from this world, but about their ordered love of God and man while in but not of this world. Troubles befall us all and are ultimately the result of sin. History is linear from creation to the last judgment. The Church will endure here and now, including through the short end time when the Devil will be unloosed and lead all nations astray to wage war on her just before our Lord's Return. The two cities are intermingled throughout history in general and even in the visible church; the Church witnesses by preaching the gospel and living faithfully and sacrificially.

Augustine's thought was so revolutionary because he began history, as does the Bible, with creation, thereby rejecting the deadening evolutionary pagan concept of cyclical history. He also "broke the mold of classical, Graeco-Roman thought by denying the classical ideal of available self-perfection. ... Without God's sacrificial intervention, this world is trapped in an endless cycle of domination and resistance, rule and revolution - all moved by the love of self and pursued by the power of death [1]." This view, of course, is echoed by C. S. Lewis's statement early in this paper about why man's earthly empire building always fails. It is the perennial unique, unchanging, creation-based Christian view of history. Later Christian thinkers elaborated it in various details but did not substantially depart from it. Examples are Johann Georg Hamann (1730-1788), who thought the Bible's history of Israel was a type for the history of other nations, or Peter Marshall and David Manuel's *The Light and the Glory* which tells how God shaped early American history and makes a fine history textbook for junior high school students today.

Augustine first gave absolute meaning and value to history by placing it within the Creator's sovereign, gracious and wise providential order. How we act out our God-given parts in this prelude for eternity determines our roles in the "main play" in God's new heaven and earth, and it has didactic value and meaning for others as well.

CONCLUSION

We have compared evolutionist and creationist ways of looking at history. We saw that the evolutionist view of history is impersonal and monistic, denying the reality of anything above and apart from this present world. It was cyclical in antiquity and is now leaning toward the cyclical view again. It postulates immense periods of "pre-history," thus robbing history proper of meaning and embracing an unbiblical idea of human "progress" from primitiveness to advanced knowledge. It has no standard for ethical evaluation of human action in history. It hovers between determinism and chance as directing history's course. It has no standard for truth and hence is open to deliberate falsification of history in addition to falsification out of ignorance. Most recently it has descended into outright solipsist history where, like the British historian R. G. Collingwood, the historian relives and recreates history within his own mind.

The creationist historian avoids all these evolutionist traps. He begins with the personal Creator, Who created all things and began history for His joy. He denies all mythical evolutionary "pre-history," thus assigning importance to history proper. He sees history as linear with definite beginning and end. He rejects any idea of "progress" omitting creation, fall and regeneration in Christ. He excludes impersonal determinism and chance and their play of "forces" in the name of the personal, sovereign Creator. He has a place for nations in history by virtue of their creation. He also recognizes the existence of Satan and evil demonic hosts behind many historical events, especially human sacrifice, violence and atrocities, but he also knows that the final victory has already been won by Christ at Calvary, a historical event.

Christian historiography with biblical creation as its starting point was introduced by St. Augustine's revolutionary *City of God* which broke with the pagan evolutionist worldview of antiquity and thus gave absolute meaning and value to history. It is unique and unchanging in principle. When it is abandoned, as it now largely is in academic circles, history as a truth-seeking, meaningful and valuable academic discipline is abandoned as well. Creation is the key to history.

REFERENCES

[1]   B. Alexander, **Burden of Conflict**, S.P.C. Journal, **17:4** (1993) 51-52.

[2]   St. Augustine, City of God, Henry Bettenson, transl., Introduction by J. O'Meara, Penguin Books, London and New York, (1972, 1984) 593.

[3]   Sir H. Butterfield, Christianity and History, Charles Scribner's Sons, New York (1950) 112.

[4]   R. G. Collingwood, The Idea of History, Press Galaxy Book, Oxford University (1956, Fourth Printing 1961) 226.

[5]   J. D. Davidson and Lord William Rees-Mogg, The Great Reckoning, Summit Books, Simon & Schuster, New York (1991) 42.

[6]   C. Dawson, The Making of Europe, 400-1000 A.D., Sheed & Ward London (1932, Cheaper Edition 1934) xxi.

[7]   C. S. Lewis, **Historicism**, in Christian Reflections, William B. Eerdmans Publishing Co., Grand Rapids, MI (1967, Reprinted January 1985) 102.

[8]   C. S. Lewis, Mere Christianity, Macmillan Publishing Co., Inc., New York (1960, Nineteenth Printing 1975) 53, 54.

[9]   Reviewed by E. Myers, Creation Social Science and Humanities Quarterly **XIV:1** (Fall 1992) 7-14.

[10]   R. Nisbet, History of the Idea of Progress, Basic Books, New York (1980) 316.

[11]   F. Stern, etc. The Varieties of History, Random House Vintage House Books Edition, New York (September 1973) 54.

[12]   **The Westminster Confession of Faith, Chapter III**, 1, quoted in R. J. Rushdoony, The Biblical Philosophy of History, Presbyterian and Reformed Publishing Company, Phillipsburg, NJ 08865 (1979) 17.

SOME QUESTIONABLE CREATIONIST AXIOMS REEXAMINED

BERNARD E. NORTHRUP, TH.D.
861 REDWOOD BLVD.
REDDING,CA 96003

ABSTRACT

In an amazing way the naturalistic geologist and the creationist tend to mistreat their major information sources concerning the order and nature of earth's earliest events. The geologist reads into the record of the rocks his own or his forerunners' presumptions about geological time even as he seeks to understand the message of the formations concerning those early events. In the same way many creationists hamper their field research by ignoring crucial areas of revelation concerning the order and the nature of those early events. Without realizing it, they frame and limit their thinking about their field research within the bounds of dogmas propounded by their creationist forerunners. As a result, scholars in both fields subject their research to an authority that is higher than the field evidence or the Biblical evidence which they study. This restricts one's research, either on the rock record or on the written record of creation, to a framework of superimposed, prior conclusions and this inevitably closes the door to accurate research.

We creationists often allow others' conclusions to shape and often to distort our own interpretation of the Biblical record or of the record of the rocks. I have a friend who has done some excellent work collating information on dinosaurs from a creationist viewpoint. He speaks with bold dogmatism on dinosaurs, but is totally unaware that his interpretative model of how and when the dinosaurs died not only ignores massive geological evidence to the contrary but gives no credence to Biblical evidence which contradicts his position. As a result, his field studies, like those of the unbelieving researcher, are distorted by a framework of questionable creationist axioms. These prevent both the record of the rocks and the Creator's own statement about earth's early events from speaking accurately for themselves. The harmony which should exist between the physical evidence (Psa. 19:1-6) and the testimony of the Word of the Creator (Psa. 19:7-8) never is achieved in detail. This research flaw which causes most creationists to attempt to explain the details of the physical, geological record only in a very general way, using nonspecific terms that never face all of the facts. This study is an attempt to draw attention to some creationist conclusions concerning the Biblical text which are both questionable and axiomatic. These play a major role in blocking the harmonization of the very real geological evidence with the true intent of the statements of the Creator's Word (Psa. 19:7-14).

Few creationists recognize that their explanation of the order of events in creation actually contradicts the Bible's own statements concerning the actual creation event series. The key axiom which actually triggers an entire series of misunderstandings relates to the timing of the creation of planet earth with reference to the rest of the universe.

Axiom # 1: THE EARTH WAS CREATED BEFORE THE SOLAR SYSTEM

It is a firmly entrenched conclusion among Biblical interpreters that Genesis 1:14-19 teaches that the sun, moon and stars were not created until the fourth day of creation. As a result, Biblical researchers postulate that a temporary sun produced the evening and morning of the first three solar days. God's Word neither teaches nor allows that presumption. This interpretative approach is the result of a serious misunderstanding of Genesis one for it is a conclusion which directly contradicts another major source of information in the Scripture concerning the order of events in creation. It directly contradicts and ignores the order of events which are set forth in Psalm 104:1-5. It also ignores the clear statement of verses 19-23 of the psalm concerning what actually happened on the fourth solar day of creation. The activity of the fourth day largely relates to the regulation of the heavenly bodies and of earth in its relationship to them. "He appointed the moon for its seasons . . . ." (The verb 'asah repeatedly is used of work done on existing material). "The sun knew its going down. It brings darkness and night comes. In it all of the beasts of the forest come forth. . . . When the sun rises, they sneak away and crouch down in their dens" (Psa. 104:20, 22). This agrees with Genesis 1:17. Here the verb nathan is similarly is used in its sense of appointment. "And God appointed them over the expanse of the (atmospheric) heavens to give light upon the earth." A parallel use of this sense in the verb nathan is observable in its use in Pharoah's appointment of Joseph over all Egypt in Genesis 41:41. There Pharaoh says to Joseph: "See, I appoint you over all the land of Egypt." It is obvious that the sense of physical transporting and placing is not present in this use. And this use is most appropriate where the sun dog and moon dog on the lower surface of the canopy are appointed their responsibilities relevant to man's time.

Most creationists do not realize that they are contradicting Genesis 1:1 by holding that earth was created *before* the sun. They hold that Earth was created either in Genesis 1:1 or in 1:1-3, while they interpret Genesis 1:14-19 as saying that the sun and moon were created on the fourth 24 hour day of creation. This "axiom" actually produces an apparent, man made contradiction in Genesis 1 itself that should be so obvious as to render the position untenable. The conclusion that the solar system comes into existence in Genesis 1:14-19 absolutely contradicts Genesis 1:1-5 and the revelational material which directly follows. First of all, Genesis 1:1 is the only place in the text of Genesis one which in any way discusses the origin of planet earth. The first verse says: "In beginning [there is no article] God created the heavens [a dual noun in Hebrew] and the earth." The translator must recognize that the compound direct objects of the verb must be considered as coming into existence together in some way. And it is crucial to note that from Genesis 1:1 onward in the chapter, earth clearly exists. Note that in verse 2 earth not only exists but already has been covered by a universal sea and shrouded in darkness. This perfectly harmonizes with the Creator's own description to Job of the earth's creation in Job 38:1-9. Earth most certainly was not created later in Genesis 1 for its rotation on its axis before a giant, distant mass which is a single, distant point, light source is required by the context. It is earth's rotation before this body in the heavens which produced the first *solar day* in verses 3-5. (Most creationists unwisely insist that these are "24 hour days," an reverse extrapolation of earth's present rotational speed into the creation week! But this assumption is axiomatic and is not specifically revealed in the text. (Shades of uniformitarianism)! What can be proven is that the rotation of the earth before a heavenly body, remarkably like the sun if not the sun itself, produced the solar days of the chapter). Therefore it should be logical to conclude from the statement of Genesis 1:1 and the evidence of the six solar days in that chapter that the solar system and possibly the entire universe had to come into existence at the same time. Is that confirmed or denied by the context? These thoughts on the subject seem to me to be worth consideration.

- Earth must exist for it to rotate before an existing light source. Earth's creation can only be described as taking place in Genesis 1:1.

- Earth must exist and begin rotating by Genesis 1:3 in order to produce the first solar day. It has become standard dogma in most creationist circles to say that earth was created *within* the first six 24 hour days of the creation week. (This seems odd, since not only the earth but the sun and moon are involved in the production of earth's days and weeks)! It is a dogma which grows out of Exodus 20:11 and 31:17 as these verses so often are translated. This will be considered in a later section.

- The "lights in the firmament of the heavens" in Genesis 1:14-19 are not the sun and moon. Of course this interpretation will trouble those who assume that ". . . the lights in the firmament of the heaven" (v. 14) are the sun and moon. But such a position is totally inconsistent with the definition of "the firmament of the heaven," that is, "the expanse of the atmospheric heavens" where the birds fly (v. 20) between the universal sea and the canopy. In no place in Genesis one does Moses redefine the rachi'a, the expanse of the atmospheric heavens so that it means "the vault of the stellar heavens" in verses 14, 15 and 17. And it is certain that the sun and moon were not placed in our "atmospheric heavens! A cardinal rule of hermeneutics is: "Interpret Scripture by Scripture." Had that rule been followed by early creationists, the untenable idea that earth was created before these heavenly bodies never would have troubled those seeking to understand the order of events in Genesis One.

- The "lights in the firmament of the heavens" simply are refracted light spots in the upper atmosphere on the lower surface of the canopy. Since the command of God directs that "lights" should be placed in the expanse of the atmospheric heavens, only one possible explanation can be given. Above the atmospheric heavens was the canopy, ". . . the waters which were above the expanse of the atmospheric heavens" (v. 7). The sun and moon, already in place in the galaxy, had been shining since their creation. The dense layer of water vapor, or most likely, ice crystal, prevented any light from reaching the surface of the earth except sufficient to distinguish day from night during the first three days. As earth was increasing its rotational velocity while approaching the 24 hour day (we assume) on the fourth day, centrifugal forces undoubtedly were acting upon the canopy. Surely these were the factor used by the Creator to elevate the canopy to its position. As it moved out above atmospheric space, it would have thinned as it occupied more and more space. I suggested long ago that the "lights" which the Creator called for "in the expanse of the atmospheric heavens" simply were the sun dog and the moon dog as the light of these heavenly bodies now shined through the thinning vapors or crystals to produce bright spots of light in the expanse of the atmospheric heavens. Adam and his descendants, by this means which had been provided by the Lord, would have regulated their day, season, month and year until Noah's sons removed the cover of the ark and looked up in amazement at the remarkable display of the heavenly bodies available after the "windows of heaven" had been opened with the collapse of the canopy. Is there any wonder that Josephus records the fact that, soon afterwards, mankind began the worship of the brilliant objects which fill the day and evening skies? This, then, would be the meaning of the phrase, "and God made two great lights, the greater light to rule the day, and the lesser light to rule the night, and the stars also" (v. 16). On the fourth day God provided man with the two major lights which are needed that he may recognize them ". . . for signs, and for seasons, and for days, and years" (v. 15). Apparently the phrase ". . .and the stars " (v. 16d) is the direct object of the infinitive in the phrase: "And God made two great lights; . . . the lesser light to rule the night and the stars," although most translations obscure this relationship of the phrase. As a result, it is easy to reach the additional illogical conclusion that the stars were created in the fourth day with the sun and moon.

- The conclusion that the sun was not created until after the creation of plant life produces another problem. Without the heat of the sun, even though that undoubtedly was widely diffused by the canopy, the seas of Genesis 1:2-9 would have been ice. Otherwise one must postulate some other source of heat. The same is true of the plants which were placed on the continent or at least in the garden on the third solar day of creation. Plant life would have been impossible unless the creationist, in order to defend his position, becomes the Creator for that day. Does not plant life require the sun to warm the soil and to produce photosynthesis?

- The setting of the "lights in the atmospheric heavens" speaks of the giving of governmental responsibility rather than physical placement. Another phrase by which the English reader easily is stumbled in trying to understand the events described as occurring on the fourth solar day is found in Genesis 1:17. "And God set them (the two great lights) in the expanse of the atmospheric heavens to give light upon the earth." The Hebrew verb which is translated "set" is the progressive form of the verb nathan. To the English reader this implies the act of moving an object and of placing it in a new location. However, the verb nathan is used in contexts of appointment to rulership in quite a different way. Its use in Genesis 41:41 is very suggestive, and indeed, instructive. There Pharaoh says to Joseph: "See, I do appoint you over all of the land of Egypt." That meaning is exceedingly appropriate here in Genesis 1:17. "Then God appointed them (the sun dog and the moon dog, bright refracted spots of light on the lower surface of the canopy) in the expanse of the atmospheric heavens to give light upon the earth."

- No light source can replace the sun as the axial point of the universe about which earth rotates in orbit. To postulate a temporary light source to produce the solar days produces a remarkably imaginative scenario that is totally unsupported by Scripture. Such an unsupportable postulate always suggests that an error is being propounded to clear up another error. Furthermore this appears to contradict Job 38:1-7. If the morning stars of verse 7 are literal, then these existed at the time that God lay the foundations of the earth. Furthermore this error requires the presence, not only of a distant light source to produce the solar day but the presence of a vast, but temporary heat source which had to keep the waters which covered the earth from Genesis 1:2-8 from freezing solid. The adoption of this assumption of a convenient heat source, apart from our sun, has serious problems. As mentioned above, this is mentioned nowhere in Scripture. No vague, phosphorescent light can possibly fill the bill. No undefined heavenly radiance provides the heavenly axis about which earth must revolve even as it begins rotating on its axis to produce the first solar day in Genesis 1:3-5. Furthermore the position contradicts another great creation concept. It directly contradicts Psalm 104:2-5 when that passage is interpreted correctly. It is plain in that passage that the first act of creation was the stretching out of the heavens like a curtain and that this took place before the casting down of the foundations of planet earth. It is inescapable that the Psalmist understood, under the guidance of the Holy Spirit, that the heavens were being spread out by the Hand of the Lord before the creation of planet earth and its subsequent covering with the preAdamic universal sea and the darkness of closely shrouding clouds as described in Genesis 1:2 and In Job 38:8-9.

- This assumption that earth existed as a solitary heavenly body contradicts every mention of the "heavens and earth" in that order. The only exception to that order in the Old Testament is Genesis 2:4. I suggest that the sense there is ". . . in the day that the Eternal Lord God worked on the earth and the heavens." That is, the material bodies have been created in

Genesis 1:1. The discussion of God's work on the earth precedes His work on the heavens for the regulating of their orbits to produce man's day, season, month and year is not described until day four.

AXIOM # 2: "IN SIX DAYS THE LORD MADE THE HEAVENS AND THE EARTH. . . ."

The concept which has dominated creation thought on the days of creation is the idea that the heavens and the earth are created within the six days of creation. To suggest otherwise is considered heresy because of the statement found in most translations: "For *in* six days the LORD made heaven and earth, the sea, and all that in them is, and rested on the seventh day. . . ." (Exo. 20:11; 31:17). The problem which makes this axiom very dubious is the fact that, first of all, it does directly contradict Genesis 1:1 and the implications of the following passage. In that text the creation of the earth is spoken in conjunction with the heavens as the one part of the double, direct object of the main verb. The Hebrew grammar of verse 2 very carefully singles out one of these two objects to discuss its condition. "But the earth, it was waste and desolate, and darkness was upon the face of the deep. . . ." (Gen. 1:2, my translation). Furthermore, if earth was not created in Genesis 1:1, then Genesis one never describes that event. Earth **must** be created in verse one, and if that is true, then the heavens are created in verse one. I therefore conclude that the Eternal created out of nothingness (bara') the heavens and the earth as the first act of creation mentioned in the chapter. This omits the detail of the creation of the angels which actually took place before the founding of the earth according to Job 38 and between the creation of the heavens and earth according to Psalm 104. This creation of the earth can only be an event which precedes the initial inception of rotation of the earth, the event which divided the creation week which followed into its 7 parts. It was the initiation of the rotation of the existing earth which provided the mechanism to divide evening and morning. Then began the six solar days described in Exodus 20:11 and 31:17. In these six solar days God did the work of preparation and of finishing the earth as an habitation for mankind and all of the creatures which preceded him in creation. This view which places the creation of the earth within the six 24 hour days obviously creates a logical problem. Remember the consistent formula by which each of the six creation days are introduced, "and God said." This formula is found in Genesis 1:3, 6, 9, 14, 20, and 24 as each day began. If the earth was not created until the first 24 hour day of creation, a day which had begun with evening and had proceeded on to morning as the earth rotated before a distant point of light, how could it cause that solar day? How could earth rotate to produce the solar day before it and the sun existed to move in the mechanics which produce the solar day described in verses 3-5? It is logically impossible for the earth to be created in the solar day which its own rotation produced!

The thesis that earth was created within the six solar days of creation also contradicts Exodus 20:11 and 31:17, the very texts used to prove the faulty thesis. But this statement is true only if the reader is studying the original Hebrew text! The problem is that the position is built upon a presupposition of the 1611 translators which required them to insert the preposition "in" in the verse. (Note that the preposition "in" is in italics, acknowledging that fact in the Authorized Version). When the insertion of this preposition was done, that act immediately required the translators to ignore the normal use of the Hebrew verb 'asah throughout the Hebrew Old Testament. In spite of the insistence of many students of English translations and some Hebrew students, the Hebrew verbs bara' and 'asah do not have the same meaning or usage. Such a view is inconsistent with a verbal plenary view of inspiration which holds that precisely the right word was used by the human author under the guidance of the Holy Spirit to convey the exact meaning intended by the Revelator. Now the Hebrew verb 'asah consistently is used of work which is performed on existing material.

The axiom that each of these days was 24 hours long also is highly unlikely. The language used to describe the fourth day of creation strongly suggests that the regulation of the day, season, month and year took place at that time. "Let there be lights in the expanse of the atmosphere to divide the day from the night; and let them be for signs, and for seasons, and for days and years. . . . And God appointed them in the expanse of the atmosphere to give light upon the earth, and to rule over the day and over the night" (Gen. 1:14, 17-18). A far more appropriate way to describe these days is to say that they are solar days. Besides, if earth existed when the first rotational day began, strongly intimated by Genesis 1:4-5, then it is highly likely that each of the first four solar days was of a different length as earth continued speeding up in its rotation until its rotational speed was regulated in the fourth day. It is inconsistent to say that the first solar day began in Genesis 1:1, especially in the light of the previous discussion of the required presence of the earth and the celestial mechanism which are spoken of in verses one and two in order for the first rotational day of creation to begin. And the evidence is in the text that these were rotational, solar days. Verse 5 closes the discussion of the first solar day with language which inescapably refers to the rotation of the earth before the center of our galaxy. "And the evening and the morning were the first day." Furthermore, the language used to describe that day requires that rotation began in that darkness shrouded scene which is described in Genesis 1:2. The expression, "the first day" means exactly that. The Hebrew expression could have been translated "day first" to emphasize this factor even more. The formula which closes the discussion of God's activities in each of these solar days follows the same pattern. It is found in verses 8, 13, 19, 23 and 31. This is evidence which we cannot ignore to maintain our pet harmonization model. Otherwise we are guilty of the same evasion of evidence which characterizes the uniformitarian who will not listen to the report concerning these events which came from the Lord of Hosts, the Creator of the universe.

Some will immediately assume that this position is being taken by the author to provide room for geological ages before the six days of creation. Absolutely not. My Catastrophe Series Harmonization Model harmonizes the physical, geological column with the five great, geological catastrophes found in Genesis and Job without modifying Biblical time in the least. My position is taken to account for the Biblical evidence and to acknowledge the impossibility of insisting that the sun, moon and earth which produced the solar days and week described in Genesis actually were created within those solar days! It also recognizes that the manner in which the problem text is translated has caused several other hermeneutical problems of interpretation for the student of creation.

AXIOM # 3: THE NOAHIC FLOOD WAS EARTH'S ONLY UNIVERSAL FLOOD

Both Job 38:8-9 and Psalm 104:6 plainly state that, immediately after its creation, the Creator covered the earth with the universal, preAdamic, universal flood. That flood covered the crust of the earth entirely through the first two solar days of creation. The common rejection of this obvious Biblical fact is an over-reaction to the error of the gap theorist who assumed that this was a judgmental flood, a universal flood which destroyed an entire, complete, previous creation. That model certainly is untenable and to be rejected as a means of harmonizing the geological record with Genesis. It does not work. But that fact is no cause for rejecting the fact that a preAdamic, universal flood actually is described in the Bible in three places. To discard that crucial fact while discarding the gap theory is "throwing the baby out with the bathwater. It results in another error that hinders creation research in the same way that the gap theory once did. In this case the fact of the reality of the preAdamic universal flood, which played such a significant role in preparing the surface of the earth for the remarkably brief event series which followed blissfully ignored. That flood was preparatory, an essential step in the preparation of the earth for the creation of plant, marine and animal and human life in the last four solar days of creation. The physical evidence found in the Archaeozoic and Proterozoic sections of the geological deposits closely parallels the Biblical evidence concerning earth's first universal flood and the uplift and drainage of the continent at the beginning of the third solar day of creation. Nothing in Genesis 7 harmonizes with that physical evidence. When the researcher finds that his harmonization model does not work, it is a sure sign that the model is faulty. This physical evidence can only be accounted for by the model which states that the Archaeozoic structures are the deposits laid down by the eruption of that first sea from within the crust of the earth as described by Job. Immediately following His description of the creation of the earth before the created (and surely unfallen) Sons of God, which all shouted for joy at the event, the Eternal then describes the eruption of that sea out of the crust of the earth. "Or who shut up the sea with doors, when it brake forth, as if it had issued out of the womb? When I made the cloud the garment thereof, and thick darkness a swaddling band for it" (Job 38:8-9).

When reexamined in this setting, Psalm 104 also remarkably parallels the Biblical evidence in Genesis 1:2-9 and in Job 38:8-9. The real significance of Psalm 104 is lost when verses 6-17 of the psalm are misapplied to the events of the Noahic flood. This is an error which is produced when the interpreter makes the mistake of "throwing the baby out with the bathwater." That is, having correctly concluded that the Gap Theory explanation of Genesis 1:1-2 as a prior creation and destruction is in error, the researcher ignores the clear teaching the text of Genesis 1:2-9, Job 38:4-10 and Psalm 104 that there really was such a flood, even if the gap theorists misinterpreted its function. These passages clearly teach that, after earth's creation, the newly created world immediately was covered by a universal flood which in some way contributed positively to scene of the six days of creation which follow. Psalm 104 is a psalm which, in a remarkable way, exults in the greatness of the Eternal Lord, the Creator, by scanning His activities in the creation week. The misapplication of the psalm to the Noahic flood long has obscured the contribution of this great creation Psalm to our appreciation of two very important events in the creation week. These Biblical events provide an explanation for the early portion of the geological record. As a result, creationists' explanations of the deposits at the Grand Canyon almost always confuse the event series which deposited the lower half of the canyon.

The Divine Author gives the order of the events of creation in Psalm 104 as follows:

(1)   Just as in Genesis 1:1 the creation of the heavens is mentioned first. After exulting in the greatness of the Creator, he says: "Oh Eternal Lord, . . . You continually are covering (a participle) Yourself with light as with a garment, stretching out [or 'having stretched out'] (a participle) the heavens like a curtain. . ." (Psa. 104:1-2). Surely there is a reason for the mentioning of this at the beginning of the discussion.

(2)   Recognizing truth not mentioned in Genesis, the writer of Psalm 104 identifies the next creative event by the Eternal as the creation of the ranks of spirit beings. He probably was drawing on truth revealed by the Creator's own speech to Job in Job 38:4-7. There the Eternal Lord plainly says that the Sons of God were present and that they all rejoiced when He laid the foundations of the earth. The Psalmist goes back before that and tells of the creation of these heavenly beings. He speaks of the Lord as ". . . making His messengers spirits, His ministers a flaming fire" (Psa. 104:4). Note that this text, with Job 38:4-7, also reveals that the angels were created even before the earth was. This strongly suggests that the book of Job probably was available to the Psalmist. Hebrews one also indicates by its

quote of Psalm 104:4 that it was the Son of God who is referred to here.

(3) According to the Psalmist, earth next was established unmoveably on its foundations. ". . .Who laid the foundations of the earth in order that it should not be moved forever" (Psa. 104:5). And that precisely agrees with Genesis 1:1. That verse has a compound direct object which follows the verb bara', "he created" and its subject, "God." The two elements which God created are "the heavens" (a dual) and "the earth." Now earth clearly exists in Genesis 1:2. There it lies covered with the first universal flood that is not removed until verse 9. It therefore is difficult for one to postulate otherwise than that the universe and the earth both were created before verse 2. Indeed, the Hebrew grammar of Genesis 1:1, with its compound object, demands that the heavens came into being either at the same time as the earth or just before it. Part of the problem which creationists have had in recognizing this has been the remarkable variety of ways that translators have mistreated Genesis 1:2. I insist that since the waw which introduces verse 2 isolates the earth from this pair of direct objects "the earth" alone, that is the second of these direct objects. The introductory conjunction must be translated adversatively as "but" and not coordinately as "and." "But the earth, it was in a state of being (a stative or state of being verb) waste and desolate, for darkness was upon the face of the deep (ocean). And the Spirit of God was moving about on the face of the waters (of that ocean)" (Gen. 1:2). For waters to cover the surface of the earth, the earth must exist in the form of a solid and not as some nebulous stream of gasses as I have heard a mislead Laurence Radiation Laboratory scientist mistakenly interpret the text. And for those waters to remain liquid, unless the crust of the earth was much warmer than would appear possible in the immediately following verses, solar radiation had to be entering the cloud cover. That cloud layer is nicely described in Job 38:8-9 as well as in Genesis 1:2.

(4) In perfect accord with Genesis 1:1-2, the Psalmist recognizes that after the creation of the earth, the next creative event described in Genesis is God's act of covering the earth with the deep as with a garment. He indicates that all of earth's mountains which then existed were covered by its waters. "You covered it with the deep as with a piece of clothing. The waters stood above the mountains" (Psa. 104:6). "Deep" here translates a Hebrew word that almost always refers to the depths of the ocean. (Cf. Genesis 1:2) The recognition of this fact, which so clearly is testified to in Genesis 1:2, does not require one to adopt the error of the gap theorists. They assume that this was a judgmental flood which destroyed a perfect creation that was complete with animals and man. This error, utterly unjustified by the teaching of Scripture, has been used to provide a very ill fitting pigeon hole into which to fit earth's teeming fossils. It is a model of explanation which totally fails to account for the physical evidence. It must achieve this if the view is correct, but it is not.

(5) The next event described by the psalmist is so catastrophic that many translations ignore and twist the obvious intent of the Psalmist's language. He actually says (in the original Hebrew text) that at the Creator's command, a great land mass abruptly was lifted out of the sea. The mountains rose up and earth's valleys were deepened. A new phenomenon, sea level, soon was established at the Creator's command. (Compare Job 38:10). At this point the researcher must avoid the error found in many "translations" which reject the grammatical subjects of the two clauses. These are "the mountains" and "the valleys." These translations erroneously make the waters the subjects and transfer the subjects to become objects. My own translation acknowledges the Psalmist's grammar and obvious intent of providing a clear interpretation of Genesis 1:9. "At Your rebuke they (the waters) fled. They hurried away at the thunder of Your voice. The mountains went up. The valleys went down to the place which You had established for them. You established a boundary which they [the waters of the newly established seas surrounding the newly exposed, single continent] should not pass over, that they should not continue to pass over the earth" (Psa. 104:7-9).

(6) Now the psalm turned in verses 10-17 to describe the drainage of the newly risen landmass, the single continent which stood above sea level for the extended period that lasted from Genesis 1:10-7:11. The psalmist speaks of newly developed streams which drain the land mass as God's wonderful provision for earth's land creatures which soon would be created in the fifth and sixth solar day of creation. "He sent the springs into the valleys which ran among the hills. These give drink to every beast of the field. The wild asses (would) quench their thirst. The fowls of the skies, which (would) sing among the branches, (would) have their dwelling places beside (the streams)" (Psa. 104:10-12).

(7) The Psalmist next meditated on God's provision of water from the heavens to provide for the vegetation which He created for the benefit of man, beast and bird. "He watered the hills from his chambers. The earth was satisfied with the fruit of Your works." The now turns to

consider the second half of the third solar day of creation and to the months following and to His purposeful provision for the continental lifeforms which would be created on the fifth and sixth solar days of creation. "He caused the grass to grow for the cattle and vegetation for the needs of man. He did this in order that man might bring forth food out of the earth and wine that makes the heart of man glad and oil which makes his face to shine and bread which strengthens the heart of man. The trees of the Eternal Lord were full of sap. There were the cedars of Lebanon which He had planted where the birds would make their nests. As for the stork, the fir trees would be her house. The high hills would be a refuge for the wild goats and the rocks for the conies." (Psa. 104:13-18). The growing of the grasses for the needs of the grazing animals obviously was an ongoing provision that continues even today.

(8)   The Psalmist then identifies the next creative act as the regulation of the sun and moon, an act which will govern the activities of all of the beings which were created on the sixth solar day. Failure to recognize the significance of the contribution of this text to our understanding of the events of the fourth solar day of creation greatly has fogged for many the explanation of the event series of the creation week. "He appointed [a participle from the same verb that is found in Genesis 1:16] the moon for seasons. The sun knew its goings. (Psa. 104:19-23). This misunderstanding of the time of the creation of the sun, moon and stars by most creationists is another of the "axioms" which is not soundly based upon the text of Genesis one itself. The cause of this misunderstanding will be discussed later.

(9)   The Psalmist then rejoices in all of the Lord's wonderful works of creation and in His wisdom for His provision of food for all of the living creatures in earth's biosphere. This included marine life which he had not mentioned previously (vv.24-30). He closes exulting in the glory and praise of the Lord, the Creator of all things (vv.31-35).

Apart from the recognition of the universal, preAdamic flood and its catastrophic retreat on the third solar day of creation as described in Psalm 104, the creationist has no explanation for the earth's oldest marine, sedimentary structures, the now fiercely distorted Archaeozoic series. It is devoid of fossils, a factor which forbids any attempt to explain these materials by the Noahic flood. Similarly, the creationist must ignore or misplace the evidence that the continentally derived, Proterozoic materials were deposited in the littoral, marine zone which surrounded a great continent. These not only contain pollen grains from mature trees (derived from the creative acts which occupied the latter part of the third day of creation in Genesis 1:11-13) but mature marine fossils (derived from the creation of the fifth day as described in Genesis 1:20-23). That evidence in itself might be adjusted somehow to fit into the Noahic flood except for the fact that the Proterozoic materials, wherever found, end in a great depositional break and never are depositionally connected with the Paleozoic materials. It is inescapable to the careful creation researcher that the Paleozoic deposits record the beginning of the Noahic flood in the ocean bottoms, its encroachment of the landmass, its stabilization after reaching universality, its early retreat stages as the wind signs of Genesis 8:1 begin to appear and finally, the oscillation signs as the retreating waters begin going and returning repeatedly on the newly exposed shorelines of the single continent (Gen. 8:3). The fact that the Proterozoic and the Paleozoic are not a single, uninterrupted deposit (as they should be if both are part of the Noahic flood) suggests that the Archaeozoic and Paleozoic deposits were deposited by two abrupt, indeed violent events in the beginning of earth's history and not by the Paleozoic, Noahic flood which universally exhibits similar fossil deposits on the continents. It requires one to recognize the possibility that the Archaeozoic and Paleozoic deposits relate to Genesis one and its catastrophic events and not to the Noahic flood. It implies that the depositional break which separates the Proterozoic deposits from the Paleozoic deposits should be identified with the more than 15 centuries which lie between these earlier geological catastrophic events and the great Noahic flood of Genesis seven and eight. This crucial harmonization clue usually is ignored in creation studies today.

But how can we explain the remarkable distortion of the Archaeozoic materials which now are almost vertically refoliated in many places? This can only be explained by recognizing that the forces which produced this preNoahic orogeny was the very catastrophically abrupt uplift of the great single continent in the very beginning of the third solar day of creation (Gen. 1:9). This event is most precisely described in Psalm 104:7-9. "At Your rebuke they (the preAdamic flood waters) fled; at the voice of Your thunder they hasted away. The mountains went up; the valleys went down to the place which You established for them. You set a bound (i.e. established sea level) that they may not pass over; that they turn not again to cover the earth." It is impossible to escape the fact that violent diastrophism is described here when one correctly reads the text in Hebrew. Those creationists demand that the passage be applied to the Noahic flood because of the last sentence should recognize the danger of over-reading Biblical evidence. What do they say about the phrase: "Who laid the foundations of the earth, that it should not be removed forever" (Psa. 104:5). By that applying that same type of interpretation which they apply to verse 9, they would contradict Revelation 20:11. That verse looks forward to the day when the earth and the heaven will flee away from the face of the Judge of the whole earth. And in reality they make verse 9 to contradict Genesis 7 when they insist upon applying this verse to the promise of Genesis 9:11 that after the Noahic flood, there never again would be a universal flood. In reality Psalm 104:9 simply refers to the establishment of sea level in the same way that Job 38:10-11 refer to the establishment of sea level after that initial period of darkness and universal sea which also is found in Genesis 1:2-8.

There is yet another factor which is ignored when one refuses to acknowledge the preAdamic, universal flood. Genesis 1:6-8 clearly indicates that in the 2nd solar day of creation (vs.6-8), the canopy is separated from the universal sea. The rachia, the expanse of the atmospheric heavens where the birds would fly on the fifth day of creation, is stretched out, and in the process divides the waters which were under the expanse, (that is, the universal sea which lay below the expanse of the atmospheric heavens) from the waters which were above the expanse . . ." (Gen. 1:7). To ignore the expanse of the atmospheric heavens and the two bodies of water which it separated leaves the creationist unable to understand what happened geologically when the great single continent of Genesis 1:9 lifted out of the sea. The testimony of the Proterozoic structures to the Creator's activities is obscured. In the same way the door is closed to his understanding the second source of the Noahic flood, the waters from above the expanse of the atmospheric heavens, the canopy. It should be obvious that the researcher must not ignore a fragment of the evidence, whether he is studying the physical record or the Biblical record of earth's early events. How can one ignore the fact that the sea universally covers the earth until that great command, the sound of the thunder of the Creator's voice, causes part of the ocean bottom to be erected above sea level? We must acknowledge that this sea which retreats from the landmass has existed, wholly covering the earth from Genesis 1:2. To do otherwise is to pay little attention to all of the extended events of the third solar day.

AXIOM # 4: IT NEVER RAINED BETWEEN CREATION AND THE NOAHIC FLOOD

Psalm 104:10-12, in a context which describes the draining of the land mass after its erection out of the sea in Genesis 1:9, says this: "He watered the hills from His chambers. The earth was satisfied with the fruit of Your works." Notice that this statement in the Psalm utterly contradicts the stedfast distortion of Genesis 2:5 so common in creation conferences today. This verse plainly says that God supplied rainfall from heaven in the days of Adam. What Genesis 2:5 actually is talking about is the time immediately before the creation of mankind. That was a time when the field plants (i.e. those outside of the garden) and the field shrubs had not yet sprouted forth. In that time between the third day creation of the special garden and the creation of mankind, it did not rain on the earth. It says nothing whatsoever about the period between Adam and the Noahic flood! Nevertheless, this idea which is very common among creationists is the result of the misinterpreting of the Hebrew word B-terem, "before" in Genesis 2:5. The word means "not yet" or "before." What the section actually is saying is that, in that time before the field plants and field shrubs had spread from the garden where they had been planted (Gen. 2:8) to the world outside of the garden, while there yet was no man to till the ground, the Eternal Lord God had not caused it to rain upon the earth. It has been very dramatic to picture the surprise of antediluvial man, having laughed at the monstrosity which Noah had been building, now that the door of the ark had been shut, to see gushing rain falling from the heavens for the first time in history. But a careful consideration of three key phrases in the verse, which ignored in the presentation of this axiom, would have prevented this interpretative blunder. The verse actually says: "Now field shrubs were not yet in the earth and field herbs had not yet sprouted forth. (This is not referring to the third day planting of the garden of Eden which already has taken place according to Genesis 2:8 when one recognizes the previous time element in the verb. See the discussion immediately below). The reason was that the Eternal Lord God had not caused it to rain upon the earth and there was no man to work the ground." The time being discussed was before Adam's creation as is obvious from the very next verse. Therefore the reference has to be to the third through the fifth solar days of creation.

AXIOM # 5: THE BIBLE CONTRADICTS ITSELF, SAYING IN GENESIS 1 THAT THE ANIMALS WERE CREATED BEFORE MAN BUT IN GENESIS 2 THAT MAN WAS CREATED BEFORE THE ANIMALS. (This axiom is held by those seeking to fault the accuracy of Genesis):

The problem here is found in translator's rendition of the syntax of Genesis 2:19. Many translations seem to indicate that after God had concluded that man was incomplete without a mate, He then ". . .formed every beast of the field, and every fowl of the air; and brought them to the man to see what he would call them. . . ." This actually is a problem which lodges in the translator's failure to grasp the fact that the context of a verb alone may indicate that the time element of a perfect or an imperfect verb can be previous past. Actually most translations occasionally render some verb forms this way. Illustrations may be found in this very context in the following passages: Genesis 2:2, "God ended His work which He had worked upon . . . ." Genesis 2:3: "God .. . rested . . . from all His work which He had worked on." Genesis 2:5: "The Eternal Lord God had not caused it to rain on the earth." Genesis 2:8b: ". . . There He placed the man whom He had formed. The previous past time of the verb also would have fit the context precisely in Genesis 2:8: Now the Eternal Lord God had planted (on day 3?) a garden. . . ." Genesis 2:9: "Now out of the ground the Eternal Lord God had made every tree to grow . . . ." This is the correct solution for Genesis 2:19. The context of Genesis 1:24-27 requires the translator to supply the English helping particle (which Hebrew does not use) so that the section reads in this way. "Then the Eternal Lord God said: Man's being alone is not good. I will make for him a counterpart. Now out of the ground the Lord God had formed every beast of the field, and every fowl of the air; and he had brought them to Adam to see what he would call them. And whatsoever Adam had called every living creature, that had become the name of it. And Adam had given names to all cattle and to the fowl of the air, and to the beast of the field; but for Adam there had not been found a counterpart for him" (Gen. 2:18-20. What is the scene being presented? In order to make the "self-satisfied old bachelor" aware of his need, to awaken his hunger for the completeness which was enjoyed by every animal pair, God brought those pairs before the man. He gave him the responsibility of naming them. This responsibility sensitized the man for the mate who was missing from his life. This strongly is suggested by the words: ". . .But for Adam there had not been found a counterpart for him." Now that the man emotionally ready for that, the Lord expresses the determination which had been part of His plan all along. "Male and female He created them" (Gen. 1:27).

Note that failure to understand the Hebrew syntax involved and failure to recognize the previous past action of the first verb, "...God had created every beast of the field and every fowl of the air," introduces a man-made contradiction into the translation through failure to observe previous context. That man-made contradiction now contradicts Gen. 1:20-27. There the order of events clearly has been established. The birds were created on the fifth day. The animals were created during the first part of the sixth day. Mankind (apparently both male and female) was created in the latter part of the sixth day. By recognizing the previous past in the first statement of Gen. 2:19, conflict disappears. By recognizing the rest of the previous perfect translations that I have suggested in Gen. 2:19 and 20, it will be seen that verses 19 and 20 give the explanation for the statement which is found in verse 18. God deliberately has brought the animals and birds pair by pair for the explicit purpose of preparing the man to recognize that something was missing from his life, that he did not have a counterpart like all of the rest of the created beings of earth.

CONCLUSION

Axioms attempt to state succinctly facts that are self evident. But when an axiom is found to contradict the evidence which it attempts to explain, it is time to revise or to discard the axiom. When the axiom seeks to explain Biblical passages and events, it is crucial that those who postulate the axiom be critical of their assumptions and lay aside those which do not work. In my study of creation over the last 43 years I have laid aside the monocatastrophic gap theory as an inadequate harmonization model. I also have been forced to lay aside the monocatastrophic Noahic flood theory and its attempt to harmonize all of geology with the Bible by that flood. It is hoped that the very controversial material contained in this presentation will help to sharpen the focus of creation studies and return them to a more thoughtful perusal of the actual evidence, whether it be Biblical or in the realm of physical geology. While Biblical evidence always must take precedence, it must never be forgotten that, properly understood, "The heavens declare the glory of God and the expanse of the atmosphere declares His handiwork" (Psa. 19:1).

SUBMARINE MASS FLOW DEPOSITION
OF PRE-PLEISTOCENE "ICE AGE" DEPOSITS

MICHAEL J. OARD, M.S.
3600 SEVENTH AVENUE SOUTH
GREAT FALLS, MONTANA, 59405

KEYWORDS

Glacial geology, pre-Pleistocene glaciation, diamictite, tillite, mass movement, gravity flow deposits, mass flow deposits, Genesis Flood.

ABSTRACT

Pre-Pleistocene "ice ages," which are based on till-like rocks, challenge the Genesis Flood as the origin of sedimentary rocks. The first postulated ancient ice age was based on a misinterpretation of a fanglomerate in England. The till-like layers exhibit several features that are contrary to recent or Pleistocene glaciation. Since 1950, mass flow has been shown to not only duplicate the till-like fabric of the rock, but also mimic many "glacial diagnostic" features. The best example of a pre-Pleistocene "ice age," the late Paleozoic Dwyka "tillite" from South Africa, will be evaluated. Submarine mass flow during the Genesis Flood is a more likely explanation for pre-Pleistocene "ice ages."

INTRODUCTION

Mainstream scientists continually challenge Flood geology and the short time scale of earth history deduced from a straightforward reading of Genesis [47]. They believe many phenomena from the rocks contradict the creation-flood model. One of these phenomena is ice ages. They maintain that each Pleistocene ice age took about 100,000 years, and there were from 15 to about 30 of them in regular succession. A model for the Pleistocene or post-Flood Ice Age, lasting about 700 years, has been developed within the creation-flood model [30-32]. The key to this vast difference in time is the catastrophe of the Genesis Flood.

Deposits from the post-Flood Ice Age cover the surface of the earth and are thin and unconsolidated. These deposits lie mostly on flat terrain and show signs of being overrun and molded by ice. However, in the hard sedimentary rocks from around the earth, layers exist that superficially resemble glacial till. These layers consist of a poorly sorted mixture of rocks of all sizes embedded in a fine-grained matrix. This mixture when unconsolidated and derived from a glacier is called till. Its lithified equivalent is called tillite. When the mixture looks like till, but its origin is uncertain, it is called a diamictite, or sometimes a mixtite. Striated and faceted stones, abraded bedrock surfaces, and rocks in varve-like sediments are noted in some of these layers of hard rock. A varve is a couplet composed of a coarse lower layer followed vertically by a fine-grained layer that was deposited in a pro-glacial lake in one year. If the period of deposition is unknown, the deposit is called a rhythmite. Other glacial-like features are cited as proof that the till-like layers represent deposits left over from ancient or pre-Pleistocene "ice ages."

Pre-Pleistocene "ice ages" cluster into four periods of geological time: 1) the mid Precambrian, 1.6 to 2.7 billion years ago; 2) the late Precambrian, 615-950 millions years ago; 3) the late Ordovician, 440 to 460 million years ago; and 4) the late Carboniferous and Permian, 270 to 340 million years ago [13].

Pre-Pleistocene ice ages, if they occurred, bring up a critical problem for creationists. These supposed ice ages occur in rocks that creationists consider Genesis Flood sediments. (Although there is disagreement among creationists, I will assume all Precambrian sedimentary rocks are Flood rocks.) How can ice ages occur within a one-year global flood? Strahler [47, p. 263], using the example of the late Paleozoic "ice age" in the Southern Hemisphere, challenges:

The Carboniferous tillites cannot be accepted by creationists as being of glacial origin for the obvious reason that the tillite formations are both overlain and underlain by fossiliferous strata, which are deposits of the Flood. During that great inundation, which lasted the better part of one year, there could have been no land ice formed by accumulation of snow.

Strahler is correct that there can be no ice age during the Genesis Flood. If these deposits really represent ancient ice ages, the Genesis Flood cannot be the explanation for these particular sedimentary rocks. If this is so, the uniformitarian time-scale is supported, which adds credence to their explanation for the remainder of the sedimentary rocks. Therefore, pre-Pleistocene "ice ages" directly confront the concept of a relatively young earth and the Genesis Flood as the origin of most sedimentary rocks.

HISTORICAL MISINTERPRETATION

The first ancient "ice age" was proposed by A.E. Ramsay in the mid 1850s. He claimed that a Permian ice age, based on angular, polished, and striated boulders, developed over portions of England [4, p. 92-94]. But scientists in England rejected Ramsay's assertion, claiming instead that he mistook a fanglomerate for glacial debris. Nevertheless, Ramsay's report spurred other scientists to look for and find a Permian "ice age" in the Southern Hemisphere. The fact that most of these "tillites" did not bother the discoverers. This problem was later solved by plate tectonics. Permian "ice age" rocks were soon discovered at many localities in the Northern Hemisphere. It almost seemed like a worldwide Permian glaciation. At the same time, "ice ages" in all the other periods of geological time were also discovered, including the three periods of the warm Mesozoic era [4].

Scientists at the time possessed only a rudimentary understanding of recent and Pleistocene glacial processes. They knew little of alternate mechanisms for forming glacial-like features. Because of the large number of pre-Pleistocene "ice ages" during the abundant warmth of geological time, many scientists became skeptical of the concept of ancient ice ages. Alternative mechanisms were discovered. Unfortunately, the concept of ancient ice ages was too engrained into the geological paradigm for much of a change in thinking. Some "tillites" were seriously challenged and rejected. Most were not. Schermerhorn [43] challenged all late Precambrian "ice ages." His careful research fell on deaf ears. Recently, Oberbeck, Marshall, and Aggarwal [35] claim that the concept of ancient ice ages has serious geological problems and that most, if not all, "tillites" are the result of debris flows caused by large meteor impacts.

CONTRARY ICE AGE FEATURES

Despite the enthusiasm of many geologists for pre-Pleistocene "ice ages," there are many features that do not compare with modern or Pleistocene glaciers [29]. One of these is that practically all "tillites" are marine, while most recent and Pleistocene glacial debris is continental. Based on the uniformitarian principle, pre-Pleistocene diamictites were originally declared continental "tillites." Increased knowledge of both ancient diamictites and modern glaciomarine sedimentation has dispelled this interpretation. Deynoux and Trompette [6, p. 1313] state: "...almost all ancient glacial deposits are marine...and deposited in geosynclinal or other unstable belts..." The most rapid paleoenvironmental revisions occurred when marine fossils were later discovered in "continental tillite."

The three-dimensional shape of "tillites" is contrary to tills from recent and Pleistocene glaciation. The largest "tillite" is one million square kilometers in the Paraná Basin of Brazil, while the second largest is 600,000 km^2 in South Africa. The remainder are much smaller. This compares to the Antarctic ice sheet, which blankets 12.5 million km^2. Pre-Pleistocene diamictites are commonly several hundred meters to several kilometers thick. The thickest is about 5,000 meters in the late Precambrian Adelaide geosyncline of Australia and in the Miocene to early Pleistocene Yakataga Formation in southern Alaska [13]. Pleistocene and recent continental tills are very thin in comparison. Pleistocene tills range from an average of about 30 meters thick near the periphery of the ancient Laurentide ice sheet to a rough average of 5 meters thick over interior Canada [11, p. 150]. Therefore, pre-Pleistocene diamictites are one hundred times thicker and cover less than one-tenth the geographical area of Pleistocene glacial debris. This lack of correspondence to recent or Pleistocene glaciation points to another mechanism, besides glacial ice, for the deposition of pre-Pleistocene diamictites.

Glaciotectonic or ice-push structures are deformed, sheared, and thrusted bedrock or basal till caused by a sliding glacier. Recognition of these features in Pleistocene glacial deposits was slow, but now glaciotectonic features are common in both Pleistocene and recent glacial debris. The shapes of these structures are sometimes distinct, such as a horseshoe-shaped hill surrounding an upflow depression. Small composite ridges, less than 100 meters high, are the most common tectonic landforms very likely pushed up by the Pleistocene ice sheets. Glaciotectonic ridges are forming today in many glaciated areas, for instance at the edge of several glaciers in Iceland.

When we turn to pre-Pleistocene diamictites, glaciotectonic structures are rarely if ever described. Flint [12, p. 125] states: "There is no obvious reason these ice-thrust structures, observed rather commonly in connection with Quaternary glaciation, should not occur in pre-Quaternary rocks." This indicates that "tillites" not only are marine, but they were also not deposited at the grounding line of a marine ice shelf. Thus, pre-Pleistocene diamictite would have to be formed almost exclusively by debris dropped from icebergs.

However, there is no indication, or at best very few claimed occurrences, of iceberg marks in pre-Pleistocene diamictites. An iceberg in shallow water will often slide, strike, or deform the bottom, usually in random fashion [48, 49, p. 248]. Iceberg drag marks are commonly observed on the ocean bottom in presently cold climates, for instance as deep as 500 meters around Antarctica [2]. They are admittedly not observed in ancient diamictites:

> Although iceberg plough and furrow marks have been widely reported from the floor of modern lakes and oceans...structures caused by the grounding and subsequent in situ decay of icebergs do not appear to have been observed in ancient sequences [49, p. 248].

Therefore, neither continental nor iceberg glaciotectonic features are observed in pre-Pleistocene diamictites. This strongly contrasts to modern and Quaternary glacial environments.

A fourth contrary feature of ancient glaciations is that many are closely associated with limestones and dolomites that indicate warm water. Dolomite especially requires a very warm environment. This association is the rule in late Precambrian "tillites." Anderson [1, p. 17] states:

> The diamictite-carbonate association is especially common in late Precambrian sequences and is, in fact, the rule rather than the exception for those rocks which have been interpreted as being of glacial-marine origin.

Frakes [13, p. 88] concurs: "Indeed, if mixtites were not known from the late Precambrian, the proportion of shelf carbonates could be taken as evidence for widespread and continuously warm climates." Very thick accumulations of carbonate rocks, measured in kilometers, predominate throughout the mid and late Precambrian, and continue into the Paleozoic.

Ice ages are not expected in the tropics at low altitude, although ice caps do top the highest mountains at present. However, the late Precambrian "ice age" faces this dilemma. Many of these "ice ages" are found near the current equator, and they are supposedly glaciomarine diamictites. No matter how the continents are rearranged by plate tectonics and paleomagnetism, many of the diamictites still fall within low paleolatitude [43, p. 674]. Frakes [13, p. 90] states: "...paleomagnetic investigations have already shown, rather startlingly, that an abundance of Late Precambrian glacial strata were deposited in relatively low paleolatitudes." The above two considerations for late Precambrian "tillites" should eliminate them as serious contenders for an "ice age."

SUBMARINE MASS FLOW

Is there another process that can account for pre-Pleistocene "ice ages"? For many years, no other process was seriously considered, so glaciation was accepted by default. In the 1950s and 1960s, earth scientists discovered that mass flow can duplicate the till-like character of diamictites. As a result, some "tillites" were reinterpreted as mass flow products, while others were seriously challenged [5, 43]. Mass flow products include at least four types, but their classification varies somewhat according to the particular author. In regard to pre-Pleistocene diamictites, debris flows and turbidity currents are the most relevant.

Debris flows manifest many important properties of pre-Pleistocene "tillites." They form a jumble of rocks of various sizes mixed within a fine-grained matrix. This fabric cannot be distinguished from glacial till. Debris flows also have the ability to transport surprisingly large boulders in laminar or non-turbulent flow [22, p. 434; 18, p. 776]. Submarine debris flows can flow long distances over nearly flat terrain. They are generated from submarine slumps or landslides on bottom slopes as low as one to three degrees [9, p. 204]. The sediments can continue traversing slopes as low as one degree or less [9, p. 189]. Therefore, submarine debris flows "freeze" on nearly flat terrain, which is one of the criteria that is sometimes employed to claim a glacial derivation for the diamictite.

A turbidity current is an underwater flow of sediment supported mainly by fluid turbulence. It usually flows swiftly down the bottom of a subaqueous slope, spreads out, and is deposited on a nearly flat bottom. A turbidity current rapidly traverses long distances. The indurated equivalent of a turbidity current deposit is called a turbidite. They likely form a significant portion of the earth's sedimentary rocks. Turbidites are most often characterized by a particular vertical sequence, which grades upward from coarse sediment, usually gravel or sand, into fine laminated silt and clay. If the turbidite lies on the ocean bottom long enough, a layer of biogenic sediments are deposited on top. The entire sequence of a turbidite is rarely found in full in the rock record. Geologists recognize two end members of turbidites with gradations between. The first is the proximal turbidite, deposited near the sediment source, and containing a thick basal layer of gravel. The second end member is the distal turbidite, deposited far from the source and containing very little coarse material. It normally alternates between a thin layer of fine sand or silt and a thin layer of clay or fine silt. This sequence can be repeated numerous times in one turbidite. Distal turbidites can mimic glacial varves, especially since each sublayer can sometimes alternate dark and light colors.

Unfortunately, this new information on mass flow did not persuade geologists to change their interpretation of most "tillites." They simply recognized that mass flow deposits are <u>common</u> within "tillites." To distinguish between a glacial or a mass flow derivation, geologists have employed three main diagnostic criteria for a tillite: 1) striated and faceted clasts, 2) abraded pavements, and 3) dropstone varvites [17, p. 17]. Varvites are assumed to be the lithified equivalent of varves. Dropstones are clasts that are larger than the layers and, therefore, are assumed to be dropped by icebergs. When any of these criteria, especially the latter two, are found in a diamictite it is almost automatically labelled a tillite. However, there is a large body of data available that shows these "diagnostic" characteristics can be formed by mass movement and tectonics.

THE LATE PALEOZOIC DWYKA "TILLITE" IN SOUTH AFRICA

The late Paleozoic "ice age" in South Africa is considered the <u>best</u> ancient glaciation [7, p. 1290]. The diamictite is called the Dwyka "tillite" and covers large areas of southern Africa (Figure 1). The Dwyka "tillite" outcrops around the Karoo Basin of South Africa and, based on numerous boreholes, is mostly continuous below the post-Dwyka sediments in the Karoo Basin. In the Kalahari Basin, the Dwyka "tillite" outcrops in the west and continues eastward underground. The Dwyka "tillite" in just the Karoo Basin occupies an area of 600,000 km^2, about the size of the state of Texas. Beautifully striated, grooved, and polished bedrock below the "tillite" are abundantly displayed in some outcrops. Not only that, what are interpreted to be special glacial marks occasionally embellish these pavements, such as chattermarks, crescentic gouges, nailhead striations, and *roches moutonnées* [60, p. 75]. U-shaped valleys, two boulder pavements, dropstone varvites, and faceted and striated clasts are also found in the Dwyka "tillite." Because of all these glacial "diagnostic" features, the evidence for a late Paleozoic glaciation in southern Africa appears impressive.

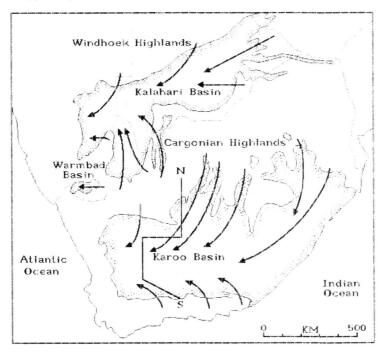

Figure 1. Map of southern Africa showing the basins that contain the Dwyka "tillite." Surrounding highlands and the flow directions of the diamictite also shown [53]. North-south line in the western Karoo Basin is cross section line for Figure 2.

The Dwyka Group in the Karoo Basin can be divided from north to south into three macrofacies: 1) the highland, 2) the valley/inlet, and 3) the southern platform (Figure 2). The most important distinctions between the northern two macrofacies are that the highland is mostly brecciated basement rock and conglomerate while the valley/inlet macrofacies is composed of mostly waterlain rocks of various sorts. These northern two macrofacies are generally thin, but of variable thickness, depending upon the relief of the Precambrian crystalline and sedimentary rocks. The diamictite fills paleovalleys and thins on ridges. The southern platform macrofacies is filled mostly with massive diamictite up to a maximum depth of 800 meters. The lower and upper boundary of the Dwyka Group slopes southward.

Because of the many striated pavements, early geologists automatically assumed the Dwyka "tillite" was a lithified continental till. By 1970, geologists realized this interpretation was based on little more than the striated pavements. Further information, mostly after 1985, has shown that the Dwyka "tillite" is mostly, if not totally, a marine diamictite with ubiquitous evidence for mass flow [15, 50, 56]. Marine microfossils have been retrieved from the interbedded mudrocks [54]. In addition, arthropod trackways and fish trails in turbidites of likely marine origin have been discovered in many outcrops of the Dwyka Group [61, p. 36]. Even the thick beds of massive diamictite in the platform macrofacies (Figure 2) are now considered the result of submarine mass flow [15]. Although Visser once believed 90% of the formation was a continental "tillite" [52], he now concludes that deposition was predominantly from a marine ice sheet. Summarizing just the geochemical data, Visser [54, p. 383] states: "All samples from the platform facies association plot in the glacial marine field, as well as all the samples, except for one, from the valley facies association..."

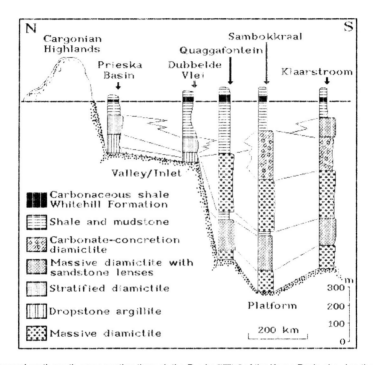

Figure 2. General north-south cross section through the Dwyka "tillite" of the Karoo Basin showing the relief of the basin floor and the lithostratigraphic units. The Whitehill Formation forms a distinctive white band that was used as a datum [53].

An unusual feature of the Dwyka "tillite" is that it thins and pinches out against basement highs; the "ice sheet" or "ice shelf" never planed down locally irregular topography. Visser [52, p. 669] writes: "In all the basins the glacial deposits either thin or pinch out against basement highs where they are overlapped by shales of the Ecca Group." Some of these high areas are tall and thin, like spires. For an "ice age" that lasted 50 million years, one would suppose that tall pinnacles would be planed down in that amount of time. Except for isolated patches in depressions, the Dwyka "tillite" also does not cover broad highlands, such as the Cargonian and Windhoek Highlands (Figure 1). These highlands are located where a thick ice sheet supposedly developed and spread out into the surrounding marine basins [53, p. 128]. One would expect substantial signs of terrestrial glacial activity on these highlands, but little or no evidence has been discovered.

These observations not only speak against a continental glaciation, but also against a marine glaciation. Debris dropped from icebergs is expected to mantle both topographic lows and <u>highs</u>. The fact that the Dwyka diamictite pinches out on basement highs is more consistent with large submarine mass flow. Submarine mass flow will deposit debris mainly in low areas. The debris will pinch out on these highs, or sometimes it will overtop higher elevation if the flow is strong enough. There are also no, or extremely few, claimed iceberg drag marks or glaciotectonic features in the Dwyka "tillite." The diamictite itself does not differ from a nonglacial diamictite from Portugal [43, p. 675,676]. Therefore, the above observations are much more in accord with a mass flow origin than a glacial origin. Here is where the glacial diagnostic criteria are invoked to claim that the Dwyka diamictite was deposited during an ancient ice age. We will examine the three main glacial criteria as applied to the Dwyka "tillite."

The first criterion is striated and faceted clasts. Facets are flattened faces on a rock due presumably to abrasion. They are rare in the Dwyka Group, but locally abundant [60, p. 75]. For instance, 50% of the rocks in a particular bouldery diamictite were striated [59, p. 40]. However, it is well known among stratigraphers that mass movement can also striate and facet rocks. Schermerhorn [44, p. 253] reports: "...nonglacial sedimentary and tectonic processes produce pseudoglacial striated and faceted clasts." Even silt and fine sand grains can striate clasts. For example silt and fine sand in an Australian mudflow scratched a little less than one-half the pebbles [62]. This mudflow deposit also resembled the texture of a nearby late Precambrian "tillite." Judson and Barks [23, p. 377] summarize evidence for macrostriations due to mass movement: "Mass movement of material has long been known as an effective process of striating rock." As for faceted clasts, Frakes [13, p. 82] considers them as even less reliable than striae as a criterion for glaciation because of their diversity of origins. The number of striated and faceted clasts varies considerably in mass movement strata, as well as in recent and Pleistocene glacial deposits. So, the occurrence of locally abundant abraded clasts in the Dwyka Formation is not a significant criterion for judging its derivation.

Dropstone varvites is a second diagnostic property used to claim the Dwyka diamictite is a tillite. This is based on the superficial resemblance of these structures to recent and Pleistocene "varves." However, this criterion has serious difficulties. One main problem is that the one-year period for each varve couplet from recent and Pleistocene rhythmites is very difficult to prove. How then can it be applied to pre-Pleistocene varve-like sediments? Although modern-day varves do form in some lakes adjacent to glaciers, they form in many non-glacial lakes as well. Moreover, recent evidence indicates that many varve-like couplets can form within one year in both glacial and nonglacial environments [33, 34]. For instance, Lambert and Hsü [24] report that 300 to 360 varve-like couplets formed in 160 years in Lake Walensee, Switzerland. The number and thickness of each couplet varied with the location, so correlation from place to place would be difficult. The extra-annual couplets likely formed by turbidity underflows caused by either melting snow or runoff into the lake after heavy rain storms. Pickrill and Irwin [38] analyzed rhythmic sediments from a deep glacier-fed lake in New Zealand. They had to depend on ^{210}Pb dating to ascertain the annual sedimentation rate, since each couplet looked similar. They found an average of three couplets per year and surmised that the extra two couplets were deposited by floods and slumps. In another instance, Wood [63] describes three varve-like couplets laid down in a new reservoir. They were formed by three peak river inflows caused by light showers within a two week period! Smith, Phillips, and Powell [45] discovered that large diurnal variation in glacial meltwater, combined with semi-diurnal tides (especially the large spring tides) form two rhythmite couplets a day in small bays of Muir Inlet!. Each couplet averages half a centimeter thick, and the sequence superficially looks like varves [25, p. 115].

As stated in the previous section, distal turbidites can mimic varves. Crowell [5, p. 1005] states: "Sandstone and mud sequences laid down by turbidity currents far removed from a glacial environment may be easily confused with varved sequences..." Therefore, turbidity currents are the likely mechanism for pre-Pleistocene varve-like sediments, which would have been deposited rapidly. In fact one of the best and most studied examples of an ancient dropstone varvite is now considered to be a turbidite [27]. This was the primary criterion for defining the mid Precambrian Gowganda "glaciation" in Ontario, Canada.

We have shown that turbidites can mimic the fine layering of dropstone "varvites." However, how do the stones become embedded within these fine layers, if they are not dropped from icebergs into real varves? It would be a happenstance to have a stone fall from an iceberg at just the right time as a turbidity current was freezing. So, the question of how the stones were emplaced determines the origin of the fine-grained layers.

Recent evidence shows that turbidity currents can emplace stones of various sizes within their fine-grained upper portion. Cobbles and boulders have been observed "floating" in the finer grained rhythmites above the turbidite traction carpet. Postma, Nemec, and Kleinspehn [39, p. 47,49] report:

> Many turbidites appear to contain floating megaclasts...Reported examples include the deposits of inferred high-density turbidity currents that contain isolated, floating megaclast up to a few decimetres or even a few metres in their longest dimension...

Pre-Pleistocene dropstones within rhythmites are small and often isolated. They rarely pierce the bed. Usually, the stone slightly depresses the bed. This simple bending is usually offered as evidence for a dropped stone. However, simple bending of beds around a stone can occur by compaction after lateral emplacement and is not diagnostic of a dropstone. Thomas and Connell [49, p. 245] state: "Thus, clasts which show either symmetric or basally asymmetric bending of laminae around them cannot be regarded as diagnostic of drop."

Comparisons with modern and inferred Pleistocene dropstones also show that stones in ancient rhythmites were likely not dropped. Glacial dropstones often cluster in mounds, caused by the overturning of debris-laden icebergs [8, 36]. Except for one possible case, no iceberg dump structure is known from any pre-Pleistocene varve-like sequence. Isolated dropstones often disrupt the bed as they strike the bottom. The amount of disruption depends upon the size, the shape, the axial orientation of the clast as it strikes the bottom, the sediment strength, and the depth of the water. Usually, the kinetic energy of falling particles reaches a maximum in a short distance. If a clast strikes vertically, it will sink into the sediment about two-thirds its length. Therefore, dropped clasts should normally rupture the sediment. From sediment cores taken from Cambridge Fjord, northern Baffin Island, Gilbert [14, p. 115] observed that small stones only slightly disturbed the sediments. But stones larger than about 8 millimeters mixed the fine sediments, obliterating the laminations. So even small stones can break the bedding. The fact that very few dropstones pierce the bedding favors lateral emplacement of the clasts.

In the Dwyka Group, "dropstone varvites" are often described, but are patchy and thin [16, p. 133]. As in other "tillites," the clasts are small and isolated [52, p. 677]. The rhythmites often display properties very unlike true varves. For instance, in northern Natal the varve colors are opposite to those of Pleistocene or recent "varves" [51]. Visser and Kingsley [58, p. 75] report that the rhythmites in the Virginia Valley display no lithological difference between the light and dark bands, except the light-colored bands are more highly indurated. Sometimes there is no grading at all within each layer [59, p. 41,42]. Therefore, rhythmites with outsized stones in the Dwyka diamictite are very likely not dropstones in ancient varves.

The many striated, grooved, and polished bedrock is the third and most significant diagnostic criterion for the Dwyka "tillite." Of all the "tillites" from around the world, the Dwyka has by far the largest number of abraded pavements. More than 100 localities, some with multiple striated pavements, are known. Abraded pavements are mostly etched on hard igneous rock in the northern and eastern Dwyka Group. However, in the southwest and east some abraded pavements are grooves within the diamictite. The best striated pavements are etched and polished on lava rocks at the Nooitgedacht farm, northwest of Kimberley, South Africa, which is now a national monument in honor of the late Paleozoic "glaciation." Visser and Loock [59, p. 38] state that 24 abraded pavements occur in just this one area.

How can a marine ice sheet can cause these abraded pavements, especially since there are few if any glaciotectonic features? This suggests another mechanism. Is mass flow up to the task? Although glaciers commonly abrade hard igneous rocks, mass movement also can striate, groove, and polish bedrock [5, p 1005; 17, p. 14; 43, p. 622]. In addition, mass movement can duplicate most, if not all, of the special features of abraded pavements. For instance, a debris flow from a flash flood striated a three square meter igneous boulder embedded solidly within alluvial gravel [21]. The resulting striae were in crossing sets, indistinguishable from "glacial" striae. Some of the striated pavements below the Dwyka "tillite" are as small as the top of this boulder. Grooves in soft sediment in the western Karoo Basin were said to be "...undoubtedly the finest examples of glacial pavements and striae yet discovered in the southwestern Cape..." [41]. However, the grooves also show delicate features that would be very difficult to preserve, if carved by an overriding ice sheet [55, p. 242]. Savage [42, p. 307] questions: "How these were protected from further ice action until buried beneath a subsequent deposit of tillite is difficult to envisage." The ice sheet likely would have torn up the soft sediments. Ice, meltwater, or further sedimentation should have obliterated the delicate features. The more valid explanation for the grooved surfaces within the Dwyka "tillite" is that a rapidly-moving debris flow carved them. After carving, the debris covered up and protected the delicate sedimentary features.

Chattermarks, crescentic gouges, and nailhead striae on the abraded pavements are actually rare [60, p. 75]. It is likely that mass movement and tectonics can duplicate such features. Crescentic cracks and nailhead striations are imprinted on a late Precambrian pavement in Brazil that Frakes [13, p. 79] insists was caused by mass flow. Oberbeck, Marshall, and Aggarwal [35, p. 11] state that, besides abraded pavements, possible nailhead striations on rocks were observed from the Ries impact crater in Germany. They also see no theoretical reason why debris flows cannot produce chattermarks and crescentic gouges. Petit [37] reports crescentic fractures, similar to glacially caused fractures, and nailhead-like striae on fault surfaces. There is no theoretical reason why mass movement cannot duplicate these features of abraded pavements. A large debris flow rapidly scoring a surface is little different from a glacier inching its way along.

Boulder beds are widely distributed within the Dwyka Formation, but only two boulder pavements are known, and they are small [57]. A boulder pavement is a layer of boulders in a diamictite in which the top has been sheared off by some moving medium. The origin of boulder pavements during the Pleistocene ice age is not well known [3]. New theories propose that they are formed by deforming glacial till below the ice, similar to a debris flow. Clark [3, p. 531] states: "Mechanics and rheologies of deforming subglacial sediment are fundamentally similar to those of debris flows." Thus, boulder pavements within pre-Pleistocene diamictites and from true glacial deposits may be formed by debris flows.

Roches moutonnées are considered a glacial diagnostic feature of abraded pavements. These are elliptical-shaped mounds or hills that have a gentle incline where the ice moved up the protuberance on the stoss side, and are usually broken or sharply sheared off on the lee side. Superb roches moutonnées are claimed at the Nooitgedacht farm near Kimberley, but, except for one, these forms are not roches moutonnées at all. Visser and Loock [59, p. 38,39] inform us:

The basement outcrops consist of polished and striated dome-like rock knobs (length:width ratio = 1) with fairly steep (up to 35°) stoss-sides and gentle leesides mostly covered by glacial debris...The glacial erosion features therefore do not comply to the definition of roche [sic] moutonnées...and can best be defined as drumlinoid complexes with a rock nucleus and a tail of glaciated debris.

The above features are not close to *roches moutonnées*. Lee-side plucking features are also rare. Since the authors are committed to the glacial hypothesis, they claimed the features are drumlinoid complexes, but they admit this interpretation is inferred [59, p. 42]. These drumlinoid complexes are likely the "drumlins" that Flint [12, p. 124] claims exist near Kimberley, South Africa. Due to the variable shape of these lava knobs, it seems more reasonable that a debris flow overran, striated, and polished them with only a slight change in their shape. It is also reasonable that a debris flow would leave debris on the downflow side of these obstructions. A glacier, on the other hand, would have either planed the knobs off or streamlined them into either *roches moutonnées* or rock drumlins.

U-shaped valleys occur in the valley/inlet macrofacies. However, these U-shaped valleys are not diagnostic either; mass movement also forms U-shaped valleys [22, p. 537-539, 565-570]. A further look at the stratigraphy of these U-shaped valleys shows they were eroded across a steep east northeastward trending paleoscarp, 300 to 500 m high, which still exists today. This is shown in the highland and valley/inlet macrofacies on Figure 2. Near the Virginia Valley in the northern Karoo Basin, the paleoscarp is 1000 meters high [58, p. 71]. The paleoscarp consists of soft Precambrian sedimentary rocks that could have been eroded rapidly by mass flow, especially if not completely consolidated. The eroded valleys started as faults [58]. Thus, mass movement could carve out U-shaped valleys rapidly by following the trend of these faults.

LARGE SUBMARINE MASS MOVEMENT DURING THE GENESIS FLOOD

We have discussed characteristics of the Dwyka diamictite that are inconsistent with the glacial interpretation but favorable to a mass movement process. Mass movement is also able to duplicate the special diagnostic features of the diamictite. Therefore, the evidence points more toward a submarine mass flow origin of the Dwyka diamictite than a glacial origin. Two other "tillites" are considered excellent examples of ancient "ice ages." These are the mid Precambrian Gowganda "glaciation" in Ontario, Canada, and the late Ordovician "ice age" in the Sahara Desert. However, the main diagnostic feature for the former, dropstone "varvites," is now considered a turbidite with embedded stones [28]. The latter "ice age" has many equivocal features that are crudely similar to features in recent glaciers and in the post-Flood ice age. However, the most significant feature is a striated and grooved surface that outcrops over hundreds of square kilometers. Rhodes Fairbridge [10, p. 271] states: "Of course, the rock pavement is the supreme criterion [for recognizing an ancient glaciation]." The problem with this feature is that the striations and grooves are in the same direction. No known glacier can striate and groove in the same direction over such a large area on soft sandstone with no glaciotectonic features. However, mass flow commonly forms parallel striations and grooves. Therefore, submarine mass flow is a much more likely explanation for the above three "tillites," as well as other "tillites" that contain fewer "diagnostic" features.

The Dwyka diamictite in the Karoo Basin alone is 600,000 km^2 in extent. The striated and grooved pavement in the Sahara Desert is parallel over hundreds of square kilometers. No modern submarine mass flow products are anywhere near this size. Based on the uniformitarian principle, present mass movement cannot account for them. Therefore the agent that caused the submarine mass flows that deposited diamictites must have operated on a scale and extent requiring at least regional catastrophic events.

The Genesis Flood provides a unique model to explain large-scale submarine mass movement. The Bible describes the Genesis Flood as a worldwide tectonic and hydrological catastrophe lasting about one year. This worldwide catastrophe would have quickly accumulated thick sediments over broad areas. Some of these sediments would either slump off unstable slopes or slide downhill from stable slopes due to tectonic accelerations, orogeny, or other processes occurring during that awesome event.

These landslides would likely travel rapidly over large distances and deposit thick diamictite. Recent subaerial landslides of large size, for some unknown reason, move rapidly and travel extraordinarily far. Melosh [27, p. 41] states:

> However, there is a class of very large landslides, or, technically, rock avalanches, that do not obey normal rules relating the total vertical drop to the distance of forward horizontal travel. These avalanches travel extraordinarily far for their vertical fall and are even capable of climbing slopes and topping ridges in their paths.

Most significantly, it is only large slides that are highly mobile [26, p. 161]. Thus, mass movements during the Flood would flow rapidly and continue moving across low slopes for large distances. No steep slope would likely be found in the immediate vicinity. Lack of a nearby steep slope is one of the main reasons why a mass flow origin for diamictites around the North Atlantic is rejected by Spencer [46, p. 216]. However, this would be expected during the Genesis Flood.

In the Dwyka diamictite, fairly large "U-shaped valleys" at the edge of the Cargonian Highlands (the valley macrofacies) could be rapidly excavated by headward erosion during mass movement, especially in soft, partially consolidated sediment. Flow directions, based mainly on directional measurements on striated bedrock, are shown on Figure 1 for southern Africa. (The flow direction in the southern portion of the Karoo Basin is questionable because it is based only on "exotic" clasts thought to originate from Antarctica.) They indicate the diamictite was sloughed off the Cargonian and Windhoek Highlands and into the basins [53, p. 128]. This is as expected from a large mass movement process in which a huge mass of sediments slides off the highlands. It also explains why diamictite is not found on the highlands, except in small basins, and pinches out against pinnacles and broad highs within the valley/inlet and platform areas.

Rapid mass movement would produce grooves and striations on the sediments below. This mechanism would account for the large-scale parallel grooves in scattered outcrops covering hundreds of square miles below the Ordovician diamictite of the central Sahara Desert [10]. Parallel grooves are normally considered a product of mass movement, but because of the large area that the grooves cover in the Sahara, geologists dismissed mass movement in favor of glaciation. Catastrophic mass movement during the Genesis Flood is the only feasible mechanism to account for them.

Striated and faceted clasts, of course, would be expected in catastrophic mass movement. Large turbidites would often be associated with these debris flows, since subaqueous debris flows sometimes change into turbidity currents [18]. The debris flows would also be a source of outsized clasts for the turbidites, and the deposit would resemble dropstone varvites. Some stones could even be dropstones, but dropped from floating logs or kelp. The Genesis Flood would explain why most, if not all, ancient "ice age" sediments are marine. There would be no trouble accounting for the presence of warmth indicators, like extensive limestones or dolomites, adjacent to diamictites.

The Genesis Flood provides an adequate mechanism for the deposition of large diamictites covering areas the size of Texas and lying on nearly flat terrain. Many glacial-like structures would be formed. The Genesis Flood very likely is the only reasonable explanation for these diamictites. Pre-Pleistocene "ice ages" need not be invoked.

ACKNOWLEDGEMENTS

I thank several creationists for their input to this paper. I especially thank Mats Molén for many fruitful discussions on the subject. I appreciate the comments of Drs. Harold Coffin, Robert Brown, and Steve Austin on an earlier manuscript. Peter Klevberg was helpful in suggesting changes to the final manuscript. I thank my son, David Oard, for drawing the figures.

REFERENCES

[1]   J.B. Anderson, **Ancient glacial-marine deposits: their spatial and temporal distribution**, in Glacial-Marine Sedimentation, B.F. Molnia, Editor, 1983, Plenum Press, New York, 3-92

[2]   P.W. Barnes and R. Lien, **Icebergs rework shelf sediments to 500m off Antarctica**, Geology, 16 (1988) 1130-1133.

[3]   P.U. Clark, **Striated clast pavements: products of deforming subglacial sediment?** Geology, 19 (1991) 530-533.

[4]   A.P. Coleman, Ice Ages Recent and Ancient, 1926, AMS Press, New York.

[5]   J.C. Crowell, **Origin of pebbly mudstones**, Geological Society of America Bulletin, 68 (1957) 993-1010.

[6]   M. Deynoux and R. Trompette, **Discussion - late Precambrian mixtites: glacial and/or nonglacial? dealing especially with the mixtites of West Africa**, American Journal of Science, 276 (1976) 1302-1315.

[7]   R.H. Dott, Jr., **Squantum "tillite," Massachusetts - evidence of glaciation of subaqueous mass movement?** Geological Society of America Bulletin, 72 (1961) 1289-1306.

[8]   J.A. Dowdeswell and E.K. Dowdeswell, **Debris in icebergs and rates of glaci-marine sedimentation observations from Spitsbergen and a simple model**, Journal of Geology, 97 (1989) 221-231.

[9]   R.W. Embley, **Anatomy of some Atlantic margin sediments slides and some comments on ages and mechanics**, in Marine Slides and Other Mass Movements, S. Saxov and J.K. Nieuwenhuis, Editors, 1982, Plenum Press, New York, 189-213.

[10]   R.W. Fairbridge, **Upper Ordovician glaciation in northwest Africa? reply**, Geological Society of America Bulletin, 82 (1971) 269-274.

[11]   R.F. Flint, Glacial and Quaternary Geology, 1971, John Wiley and Sons, New York.

[12]   R.F. Flint, **Features other than diamicts as evidence of ancient glaciations**, in Ice Ages: Ancient and Modern, A.E. Wright and F. Moseley, Editors, 1975, Seel House Press, Liverpool, 121-136.

[13]   L.A. Frakes, Climates Throughout Geological Time, 1979, Elsevier, New York.

[14]   R. Gilbert, **Rafting in glacimarine environments**, in Glacimarine Environments: Processes and Sediments, J.A. Dowdeswell and J.D. Scourse, Editors, 1990, Geological Society of London Special Publication No. 53, London, 105-120.

[15]   C.P. Gravenor and V. Von Brunn, **Aspects of late Paleozoic glacial sedimentation in parts of the Paraná Basin, Brazil, and the Karoo Basin, South Africa, with special reference to the origin of massive diamictite**, in Gondwana Six: Stratigraphy, Sedimentology, and Paleontology, G.D. McKenzie, Editor, 1987, Geophysical Monograph 41, American Geophysical Union, Washington, D.C., 103-111.

[16]   C.P. Gravenor, V. Von Brunn, and A. Dreimanis, **Nature and classification of waterlain glaciogenic sediments, exemplified by Pleistocene, late Paleozoic and late Precambrian deposits**, Earth-Science Reviews, 20 (1984) 105-166.

[17]   M.J. Hambrey and W.B. Harland, Editors, Earth's Pre-Pleistocene Glacial Record, 1981, Cambridge University Press, London.

[18]   M.A. Hampton, **The role of subaqueous debris flow in generating turbidity currents**, Journal of Sedimentary Petrology, 42 (1972) 775-793.

[19]   M.A. Hampton, **Buoyancy in debris flows**, Journal of Sedimentary Petrology, 49 (1979) 753-758.

[20]   W.B. Harland and K.N. Herod, **Glaciations through time**, in Ice Ages: Ancient and Modern, A.E. Wright and F. Moseley, Editors, 1975, Seel House Press, Liverpool, 189-216.

[21]   H.J. Harrington, **Glacial-like "striated floor" originated by debris-laden torrential water flows**, American Association of Petroleum Geologists Bulletin, 55 (1971) 1344-1347.

[22]   A.M. Johnson, Physical Process in Geology, 1970, Freeman, Cooper and Company, San Francisco.

[23]   S. Judson and R.E. Barks, **Microstriations on polished pebbles**, American Journal of Science, 259 (1961) 371-381.

[24]   A. Lambert and K.J. Hsü, **Non-annual cycles of varve-like sedimentation in Walensee, Switzerland**, Sedimentology, 26 (1979) 453-461.

[25]   N.E. Mackiewicz et al, **Interlaminated ice-proximal glacimarine sediments in Muir Inlet, Alaska**, Marine Geology, 57 (1984) 113-147.

[26]   H.J. Melosh, **Acoustic fluidization**, American Scientists, 71 (1983) 158-165.

[27]   H.J. Melosh, **The mechanics of large rock avalanches**, in Debris Flows/Avalanches: Process, Recognition, and Mitigation, J.E. Costa and G.F. Wieczorek, Editors, 1987, Reviews in Engineering Geology, Vol. VII, Geological Society of America, Boulder, 41-49.

[28]   A.D. Miall, **Sedimentation on an early Proterozoic continental margin under glacial influence: the Gowganda Formation (Huronian), Elliot Lake area, Ontario, Canada**, Sedimentology, 32 (1985) 763-788.

[29]   M. Molén, **Diamictites: ice-ages or gravity flows?** Proceedings of the Second International Conference on Creationism, R.E. Walsh, et al, Editors, 1990, Creation Science Fellowship, Inc., Pittsburgh, PA, Vol. II, pp. 177-190.

[30]   M.J. Oard, **An ice age within the Biblical time frame**, Proceedings of the First International Conference on Creationism, R.E. Walsh, et al, Editors, 1987, Creation Science Fellowship, Inc., Pittsburgh, PA, Vol II, pp. 157-166.

[31]   M.J. Oard, An Ice Age Caused by the Genesis Flood, 1990a, Institute for Creation Research, El Cajon, CA.

[32] M.J. Oard, **The evidence for only one ice age**, Proceedings of the Second International Conference on Creationism, R.E. Walsh, et al, 1990b, Creation Science Fellowship, Inc., Pittsburgh, PA, Vol II, pp. 191-200.

[33] M.J. Oard, **Varves - the first "absolute" chronology part I - historical development and the question of annual deposition**, Creation Research Society Quarterly, 29 (1992a) 72-80.

[34] M.J. Oard, **Varves - the first "absolute" chronology part II - varve correlation and the post-glacial time scale**, Creation Research Society Quarterly, 29 (1992b) 120-125.

[35] V.R. Oberbeck, J.R. Marshall, and H. Aggarwal, **Impacts, tillites, and the breakup of Gondwanaland**, Journal of Geology, 101 (1993) 1-19.

[36] A.T. Ovenshine, **Observations of iceberg rafting in Glacier Bay, Alaska, and the identification of ancient ice-rafting deposits**, Geological Society of America Bulletin, 81 (1970) 891-894.

[37] J.P. Petit, **Criteria for the sense of movement on fault surfaces in brittle rocks**, Journal of Structural Geology, 9 (1987) 597-608.

[38] R.A. Pickrill and J. Irwin, **Sedimentation in a deep glacier-fed lake--Lake Tekapo, New Zealand**, Sedimentology, 30 (1983) 63-75.

[39] G. Postma, W. Nemec, and K.L. Kleinspehn, **Large floating clasts in turbidites: a mechanism for their emplacement**, Sedimentary Geology, 58 (1988) 47-61.

[40] J.D. Rodine and A.M. Johnson, **The ability of debris, heavily freighted with coarse clastic materials, to flow on gentle slopes**, Sedimentology, 23 (1976) 213-234.

[41] I.C. Rust, **Note on a glacial pavement near Nieuwoudtville**, South African Journal of Science, 59 (1963) 12.

[42] N.M. Savage, **Soft-sediment glacial grooving of Dwyka age in South Africa**, Journal of Sedimentary Petrology, 42 (1972) 307,308.

[43] L.J.G. Schermerhorn, **Late Precambrian mixtites: glacial and/or nonglacial?** American Journal of Science, 274 (1974) 673-824.

[44] L.J.G. Schermerhorn, **Tectonic framework of late Precambrian supposed glacials**, in Ice Ages: Ancient and Modern, A.E. Wright and F. Moseley, Editors, 1975, Seel House Press, Liverpool, 241-274.

[45] N.D. Smith, A.C. Phillips, and R.D. Powell, **Tidal drawdown: a mechanism for producing cyclic sediment laminations in glaciomarine deltas**, Geology, 18 (1990) 10-13.

[46] A.M. Spencer, **Late Precambrian glaciations in the North Atlantic region**, in Ice Ages: Ancient and Modern, A.E. Wright and F. Moseley, Editors, 1975, Seel House Press, Liverpool, 217-240.

[47] A.N. Strahler, Science and Earth History - The Evolution/Creation Controversy, 1987, Prometheus Books, Buffalo.

[48] J.P.M. Syvitski et al, **Seabed investigations of the Canadian east coast and Arctic using Pisces IV**. Geoscience Canada, 10 (1983) 59-68.

[49] G.S.P. Thomas and R.J. Connell, **Iceberg drop, dump, and grounding structures from Pleistocene glacio-lacustrine sediments, Scotland**, Journal of Sedimentary Petrology, 55 (1985) 243-249.

[50] R.J. Thomas, V. von Brunn, and C.G.A. Marshall, **A tectono-sedimentary model for the Dwyka Group in southern Natal, South Africa**, South African Journal of Geology, 93 (1990) 809-817.

[51] R. Tavener-Smith and T.R. Mason, **A late Dwyka (early Permian) varvite sequence near Isandlwana, Zululand, South Africa**, Palaeogeography, Palaeoclimatology, Palaeoecology, 41 (1983) 233-249.

[52] J.N.J. Visser, **Glacial-marine sedimentation in the late Paleozoic Karoo Basin, southern Africa**, in Glacial-Marine Sedimentation, B.F. Molnia, Editor, 1983, Plenum Press, New York, 667-701.

[53]   J.N.J. Visser, **The influence of topography on the Permo-Carboniferous glaciation in the Karoo Basin and adjoining areas, southern Africa**, in Gondwana Six: Stratigraphy, Sedimentology, and Paleontology, G.D. McKenzie, Editor, 1987, Geophysical Monograph 41, American Geophysical Union, Washington, D.C., 123-129.

[54]   J.N.J. Visser, **The Permo-Carboniferous Dwyka Formation of southern Africa: deposition by a predominantly subpolar marine ice sheet**, Palaeogeography, Palaeoclimatology, Palaeoecology, 70 (1989) 377-391.

[55]   J.N.J. Visser, **Glacial bedforms at the base of the Permo-Carboniferous Dwyka Formation along the western margin of the Karoo Basin, South Africa**, Sedimentology, 37 (1990) 231-245.

[56]   J.N.J. Visser, **Sea-level changes in a back-arc-foreland transition: the late Carboniferous-Permian Karoo Basin of South Africa**, Sedimentary Geology, 83 (1993) 115-131.

[57]   J.N.J. Visser and K.J. Hall, **Boulder beds in the glaciogenic Permo-Carboniferous Dwyka Formation in South Africa**, Sedimentology, 32 (1985) 281-294.

[58]   J.N.J. Visser and C.S. Kingsley, **Upper Carboniferous glacial valley sedimentation in the Karoo Basin, Orange Free State**, Transactions Geological Society of South Africa, 85 (1982) 71-79.

[59]   J.N.J. Visser and J.C. Loock, **Sedimentary facies of the Dwyka Formation associated with the Nooitgedacht glacial pavements, Barkly West district**, Transactions of the Geological Society of South Africa, 91 (1988) 38-48.

[60]   V. Von Brunn and T. Stratten, **Late Palaeozoic tillite of the Karoo Basin of South Africa**, in Earth's Pre-Pleistocene Glacial Record, M.J. Hambrey and W.B. Harland, Editors, 1981, Cambridge University Press, London, 71-79.

[61]   V. Von Brunn and C.J. Talbot, **Formation and deformation of subglacial intrusive clastic sheets in the Dwyka Formation of northern Natal, South Africa**, Journal of Sedimentary Petrology, 56 (1986) 35-44.

[62]   E.L. Winterer and C.C. Von Der Borch, **Striated pebbles in a mud flow deposit, South Australia**, Palaeogeography, Palaeoclimatology, Palaeoecology, 5 (1968) 205-211.

[63]   A.E. Wood, **Multiple banding of sediments deposited during a single season**, American Journal of Science, 245 (1947) 304-312.

LACK OF EVIDENCE FOR HAND DOMINANCE IN THE NONHUMAN PRIMATE: DIFFICULTY FOR THE THEORY OF EVOLUTION

SUZANNE S. PALMER, PH.D.
DEPARTMENT OF PHYSICAL THERAPY
TEXAS TECH UNIVERSITY HEALTH SCIENCES CENTER
LUBBOCK, TX 79430

KEYWORDS: hand dominance, lateralization, primate brain, hand preference, brain asymmetry

ABSTRACT

Most scientists believe individual nonhuman primates can exhibit hand preference in certain manual tasks, but that there is no population-based hand dominance in prosimians, monkeys or apes like there is in the human. This paper critiques the studies attempting to find hand dominance in nonhuman primates. It also critiques a recent study seeking evidence for brain asymmetry related to hand preference in squirrel monkeys. The investigators felt their data showed that the motor cortex hemisphere contralateral to the preferred hand of squirrel monkeys had a greater number of microstimulation sites that caused forelimb muscle contractions than did the ipsilateral hemisphere. Their conclusion may have been based on faulty reasoning. Any evidence that nonhuman primates have a system homologous to that of human hand dominance (or any correlated brain asymmetry) is very weak indeed. In fact, evidence from these studies of nonhuman primates would support separate ancestries of the different types of nonhuman primates and of humans; although the evidence has not been interpreted in that manner by those who have undertaken the studies.

INTRODUCTION

Hardly any scientist would disagree with the general concept that humans are different from other primates regarding language capability and tool use. The theory that one and/or the other capability were the major factors driving brain asymmetry also has a long history [5, 17, 18]. This general theory even allows nonhuman primates to lack any particular brain asymmetry or hand dominance, and still be consistent with the theory of human origins from nonhuman primates [4], because handedness may not have appeared in the evolutionary chain until after the hominoid line leading to *Homo sapiens* branched off from the nonhuman primate line. Of course, if nonhuman primates show evidence of hand dominance similar to that of humans, this would be consistent with the evolution of man from a nonhuman primate evolutionary ancestor.

There are some investigators who maintain that so-called precursors of language, e.g. vocalizations in nonhuman primate ancestors, were related to some brain asymmetry, and that this lateralized vocalization is homologous to left-sided language centers in humans. Furthermore, these same investigators believe that motor asymmetries (viz., hand preference in particular tasks) exist in present-day prosimians, rhesus monkeys, chimpanzees, and gorillas. They interpret this to mean that they existed in nonhuman primate ancestors of *Homo sapiens* [10, 14].
Even these investigators holding to evidence for hemispheric asymmetry in nonhuman primates would agree that human language and tool use are the result of major evolutionary pressures that have selected for hemispheric asymmetry in humans in the last two million years [18], and especially in the last 30,000 years of evolution of *Homo sapiens*. [10]. These scientists hold that hand dominance in humans may be considerably different than a rudimentary hand preference in nonhuman primates, but that the two are tied in an evolutionary sense.

The controversy this paper will critique is whether hand dominance and related brain asymmetry are evident in present-day nonhuman primates. This critique will not extend into the interesting literature of language and lateralization of speech centers [12], nor into studies of whether anatomical brain asymmetries, e.g. a larger temporal planum in the left cerebral hemisphere, exist in nonhuman primates [1, 11]. The temporal planum is a region in the temporal lobe including much of Wernicke's sensory language area.

GENERAL FINDINGS

After reviewing considerable research, Bock and Marsh reached a controversial conclusion that nonhuman animals, especially primates, exhibit asymmetry or lateralization of some of their functions [4]. Early studies of chimpanzees and rhesus monkeys seemed to indicate that hand preference was a result of experience [7, 22, 23] and probably did not reflect any underlying brain asymmetry [cf. 23]. During the last 20 years a number of studies of the performance of various tasks by chimpanzees, orangutans, gorillas, and certain monkeys showed that some animals preferred using their left hand, some their right, and some did not have a preferred hand [reviewed by 5]. Some even preferred different hands in different tasks. It would seem that nonhuman primates have exhibited some evidence of right or left hand preference for a particular task, with no one preference consistent in either individual animals, a single species, or among all the different nonhuman primates studied [3, 4, 23]. Brain asymmetry and hand preference in nonhuman primates, if it exists at all, would seem to be only a rough analogue of what exists in humans. The general consensus is that handedness in nonhuman primates is not a homologue of human hand dominance in terms of evolutionary continuity [5, 9].

A few Investigators, however, have disagreed with this conclusion, as mentioned in the Introduction [6, 10, 14]. MacNeilage, Studdert-Kennedy, and Lindblom, who all have an interest in linguistics [14, cf. also 13], hypothesized that left side prehension was left behind with the advent of bipedality. They hypothesized that left handedness can be seen in present-day prosimians, and it evolved for grasping. They also hypothesized that right handedness evolved for hand manipulation, and furthermore, that right handedness for skilled hand manipulation in more complex tasks requiring bimanual coordination in nonhuman primates is a precursor of right hand dominance in humans.

Peter MacNeilage and his colleagues [14, 13] referred especially to data from stump-tailed macaques, reported by Beck and Barton in 1972 [2], and data from four female gorillas, reported by Fischer and coworkers in 1982 [8], to support their hypotheses. They provided elaborate criticisms of numerous other studies that did not support their ideas. However, commentaries by a number of scientists given at the end of the review by MacNeilage and his colleagues [14] indicate the general skepticism with which their hypotheses are viewed.

Beck and Barton [2] examined 17 different hand tasks by 10 stumptail macaques. The tasks were grouped into six subgroups: 1) simple reach, 2) complex reach, 3) expose and reach, 4) stabilize and reach, 5) manipulate and reach, and 6) stabilize and manipulate and reach. Beck and Barton arranged their data so that higher median percentages of left preferences for reaching occurred when reaching was done in combination with a bimanual complex task. For example, the median of left hand preference for simple reaching for 10 monkeys was 35%; whereas the median of left hand preference for reaching in combination with finger manipulation of a hasp container ranged from 50-100%. However, the average of median percentages of left hand preferences for all reaching tasks in 10 monkeys was only 64.7%. In contrast, Beck and Barton maintained that tasks using manipulation showed an average of the medians of right hand preference of 72.8%. (The medians ranged from 53-97% for eight tasks involving manipulation.) In other words, the data were arranged such that trends supporting their hypotheses of left-hand preference for reaching and right-hand preference for manipulation were emphasized.

The other study MacNeilage and his colleagues [14] said was consistent with their hypotheses was Fischer, Meunier, and Hunt's [8] study of four female gorillas. All four animals used their right hand to grasp food or other objects more than 80% of the time. Left hand support of a baby gorilla by the four female mothers was observed 64% of the time. This data, they said, supported the theory that right hand preference for manipulation was similar to right hand dominance in humans. In contrast to the data reported by Fischer and colleagues, another study of 10 male and female gorillas by Preilowski and Leder (referenced by MacNeilage et al. [14]) showed no interindividual hand preferences.

Several recent studies of prosimians [21], capuchins and macaques [24], and gorillas, macaques, and baboons [6] were interpreted by Fagot and Vauclair to support a so-called "nonhuman primate precursor of human hand dominance hypothesis" [6]. Like MacNeilage and coworkers [14], Fagot and Vauclair reviewed previous studies that they felt supported this hypothesis in light of their more recent data [6]. However, other scientists, viz. Hamilton and Vermeire [9], interpreted the more recent evidence [6, 21] to show that hand preference by nonhuman primates in various tasks is related to cognitive specializations that may only be coincidentally similar to those of humans. Once again, support for hand preference in nonhuman primates being continuous with human hand dominance is a very debatable interpretation.

A SPECIFIC STUDY OF MOTOR CORTEX IN MONKEYS TO LOOK AT BRAIN ASYMMETRY

A team of five investigators [15] at the University of California Medical Center in San Francisco looked for hand dominance in squirrel monkeys. They sought evidence that the motor cortex hemisphere contralateral to the dominant hand had a greater number of sites that when stimulated caused forelimb muscle contractions than did the ipsilateral hemisphere. Even if this kind of research *could* be thorough, which it cannot be, it still is not very

420

surprising that one hemisphere had a greater density of neurons projecting to forelimb muscles, and that this hemisphere was opposite to the hand used the most. (Finding stimulation sites is a somewhat hit-and-miss technique as I have experienced personally in a technically similar research project [16], even with a grid pattern like they used.) Numerous environmental enrichment studies have shown that neuronal density is related to environmental stimulation and usage [20]. Therefore, it would seem that hand preference in nonhuman primates would develop randomly, and that the motor cortex responsible for the "preferred" hand would be used more, and therefore would have a greater density of neurons projecting to hand muscles.

This study by Nudo and his coworkers [15] at the UC Medical Center at San Francisco was conducted using a modified "Kluver board" from which the monkey removed food from wells; other studies have shown that hand preference varied from task to task [reviewed by 5]. Of the six monkeys studied, four were found to have a strong left-hand preference for this task (84.35% - 99.3% preference score). One was less strongly left-handed (55.3% preference score), and one had a strong right-hand preference (86% preference score). After the investigators determined the hand-preference of the monkeys, they anesthetized the monkeys, and applied microstimuli to the right and left motor cortex hemispheres of the monkeys. The hemisphere contralateral to the preferred hand had a greater number of stimulation sites that caused hand movements. This was interpreted to mean that the hemisphere contralateral to the preferred hand had a greater density of neurons projecting to forelimb muscles.

One criticism of this study is the fact that the investigators were not blinded to the preference results as they undertook the stimulation study. Another criticism has to do with their statistics. An enormous number of different tests using the parametric analysis of variance and the Student t tests were performed using results from only five monkeys with a documented preferred hand. Parametric tests are usually not valid for a sample of only five because assumptions of normal distributions and equal variances are difficult to meet with small samples [25]. Beyond that, the major criticism of this study should be that this kind of hand preference could be thought to be similar to hand dominance in humans. This data simply showed that 4/6 squirrel monkeys had a left-hand preference for removing food from a "Kluver board". Four out of six is not even statistically significant with a nonparametric test [19]. These data also showed that contralateral brain sites with neurons projecting to hand muscles of the preferred hand used in this task were easier to find by investigators with a hit-and-miss strategy that were not blinded as to results needed to support their hypothesis. These data cannot be extrapolated to support the concept that hand preference in monkeys is an intermediate condition in an evolutionary lineage leading to hand dominance in humans.

CONCLUSIONS

Evidence of consistent hand preference exhibited by any type of prosimian, monkey or ape has not been well demonstrated, and cannot be considered homologous to the hand dominance seen in humans. Brain asymmetries correlated with hand preference have not been investigated to any great extent. There has been only one study examining motor cortex and hand preference in the squirrel monkey [15], and it provided no concrete evidence of handedness with a correlated contralateral brain asymmetry like that seen in the human. Studies of hand preference in nonhuman primates would seem to support separate ancestries of individual types of nonhuman primates, and of the human.

REFERENCES

[1]   E. Armstrong, **Evolution of the brain**, in The Human Nervous System, G. Paxinos, editor, 1990, Academic Press, San Diego.

[2]   C. H. M. Beck and R. L. Barton, **Deviation and laterality of hand preference in monkeys**, Cortex 8(1972) 339-362.

[3]   D. V. M. Bishop, Handedness and Developmental Disorder (Clinics in Developmental Medicine, No. 10), 1990, J. B. Lippincott Company, Philadelphia.

[4]   G. Bock and J. Marsh, **Final general discussion**, in Biological Asymmetry and Handedness, G. Bock and J. Marsh, editors, 1991, John Wiley and Sons, New York.

[5]   M. C. Corballis, The Lopsided Ape, 1991, Oxford University Press, New York.

[6]   J. Fagot and J. Vauclair, **Manual laterality in nonhuman primates: a distinction between handedness and manual specialization**, Psychological Bulletin 109(1991) 76-89.

[7]   G. Finch, **Chimpanzee handedness**, Science 94(1941) 117-118.

[8]   R. B. Fischer, G. F. Meunier, and P. J. Hunt, **Evidence of laterality in the lowland gorilla**, Perceptual and Motor Skills 54(1982) 1093-1094.

[9]   C. R. Hamilton and B. A. Vermeire, **Functional lateralization in monkeys**, in Cerebral Laterality:Theory and Research, F. L. Kitterle, editor, 1991, Erlbaum Associates, Publishers, Hillsdale, New Jersey.

[10]   J. B. Hellige, Hemispheric Asymmetry, What's Right and What's Left, 1993, Harvard University Press, Cambridge, Massachusetts.

[11]   M. LeMay, M. S. Bilig, and N. Geschwind, **Asymmetries of the brains and skulls of nonhuman primates**, in Primate Brain Evolution: Methods and Concepts, E. Armstrong and D. Falk, editors, 1982, Plenum Press, New York,

[12]   P. Lieberman, Uniquely Human, The Evolution of Speech, Thought and Selfless Behavior, 1991, Harvard University Press, Cambridge, Massachusetts.

[13]   P. F. MacNeilage, **The evolution of handedness in primates**, in Duality and Unity of the Brain, D. Ottoson, editor, 1987, Plenum Press, New York.

[14]   P. F. MacNeilage, M. G. Studdert-Kennedy, and B. Lindblom, **Primate handedness reconsidered**, Behavioral and Brain Sciences 10(1987) 247-301.

[15]   R. J. Nudo, W. M. Jenkins, M. M. Merzenich, T. Prejean, and R. Grenda, **Neurophysiological correlates of hand preference in primate motor cortex of adult squirrel monkeys**, The Journal of Neuroscience 12(1992) 2918-2947.

[16]   S. S. Palmer and E. E. Fetz, **Effects of single intracortical microstimuli in motor cortex on activity of identified forearm motor units in behaving monkeys**, Journal of Neurophysiology 54(1985) 1194-1212.

[17]   A. Prochaintz, How the Brain Evolved (English translation of 1989. La Construction du Cerveau), 1992, McGraw-Hill, Inc., New York.

[18]   K. D. Schick and N. Toth, Making Silent Stones Speak: Human Evolution and the Dawn of Technology, 1993, Simon and Schuster, New York.

[19]   S. Siegel, Nonparametric Statistics for the Behavioral Sciences, 1956, McGraw-Hill Book Company, New York.

[20]   S. P. Springer and G. Deutsch, Left Brain, Right Brain, 1989, W.H. Freeman and Company, New York.

[21]   J. P. Ward, **Prosimians as animal models in the study of neural lateralization**, in Cerebral Laterality: Theory and Rresearch, F. L. Kitterle, editor, 1991, Erlbaum Associates, Publishers, Hillsdale, New Jersey.

[22]   J. M. Warren, **Handedness in the rhesus monkey**, Science 118(1953) 622-623.

[23]   J. M. Warren, **Handedness and cerebral dominance in monkeys**, in Lateralization in the Nervous System, S. Harnad, R. W. Doty, J. Jaynes, L. Goldstein, and G. Krauthamer, editors, 1977, Academic Press, New York.

[24]   G. C. Westergaard, **Hand preference in the use and manufacture of tools by tufted capuchin (Cebus apella) and lion-tailed macaque (Macaca silenus) monkeys**, Journal of Comparative Psychology 105(1991) 172-176.

[25]   C. M. Woolf, Principles of Biometry, 1968, D. Van Nostrand Company, Inc., Princeton, New Jersey.

MECHANISMS FOR GENDER ROLE STASIS

C. DIANE POWELL, B.A., M.A.
1928 IDLEWILD
WICHITA, KANSAS 67216

KEYWORDS

Gender role, family structure, sex differences

ABSTRACT

Sex differences, resulting from hormonal and neurological patterns which arise during fetal development, provide the female with an advantage in verbal and social skills and the male with an advantage in visual/spatial, math and aggressiveness. In addition to the differential physiological equipping for reproduction, men and women are provided with unique motivational differences which are role-related and insure the continuance of the family. The most powerful evidence for creation is in the feature of stasis, or permanence, since what is characteristic of design is foreign and unacceptable to evolution. Because all alternatives to the family have failed both to provide for families and to do so without the "gender division of labor", the family unit has demonstrated a resistance to change not unlike that of the "living fossil".

INTRODUCTION

Key Findings from Sex Difference Research

Significant sex differences have been documented in a variety of areas, all of which may be understood by the creationist as preparation for complementary gender roles. These include differences in every major system, that is, skeletal, muscular, endocrine, metabolic and neurological [1,24,28]. The most well-established differences are a verbal advantage for females and a similar advantage for males in visual-spatial, math, and aggressiveness [1,24,28].

Baker's book [1] documents sex differences in physical stamina, physiological response to environmental stress, pain sensitivity and cognitive performance. Researchers have found a visual advantage for males and an auditory one for females [1]. For example, the female is better able to locate the source of an auditory stimulus while the male has better dynamic visual acuity. Researchers have also found differences for such basic sensory modalities as audition, vision, taste, smell, temperature, touch and pain with greater female sensitivities in most cases [1].

The basis for structural and behavioral differences lies in the process of sexual differentiation which begins prior to birth, reflected in neurological differences which are apparent soon after birth [24,40]. For example, male and female infants show an inverse relationship for tactility sensitivity and muscular strength, higher tactile/lower muscular for females and lower tactile/higher muscular for males with almost no overlap between score distributions [40, p. 18]. Adult females also show greater tactile sensitivity than males on 19 out of 20 body areas tested [28]. Female infants also show more interest in, and sensitivity for, auditory, verbal and social stimuli, while male infants demonstrate more interest in novel shapes and the manipulation of objects [28,40].

Origins Perspective

Evolutionists remain perplexed by the origin of sex since it meant that any presumably "beneficial mutations" which appeared would have had a lower probability of being passed on [2]. However, what appears to be solely disadvantageous from an evolutionary perspective acts both to conserve 'kind' and to confer survival benefits on the species through increased genetic variety, something only recently recognized by evolutionists [9,23]. They are also puzzled by the human infant who is dependent both physically and socially much longer than other primates [9,23].

According to sex difference researcher Diane Halpern, the evolution-based sociobiology "provides neither an explanation of, nor a justification for, sex differences" [24, p. 5]. In contrast, the creationist can view the features of biological and social interdependency, along with the lengthy dependency of the child, as representing the creative intentions of a faithful God, features which result in the ideal opportunity for bonding and instruction.

As pointed out by Battson, the critical discriminant between creation and evolution is "stasis" or resistance to change, since it is in fact the key difference between a system which was created and one which could have been evolved [51]. The limiting of change to within kind variation has been well-documented from research with fruit fly mutations [25]. Romer's law views biological mutations as acting to preserve the creature's basic nature, "birdness" for example, rather than acting to transform one type into another [34]. Creationists will recognize that this is in fact the role of within kind variation since mutations are inherently destructive.

Tiger suggests that cultural variations reflect such within kind variation which act to preserve innate social behavior patterns rather than to alter them, thus variation is limited while flexibility is preserved [34, p. vii]. For example, Norwegian linguist Blakar analysed gender norms as expressed in his own language and concluded that language both "reflects" and "conserves the existing sex role pattern", even to the extent that it could be said to "counteract change" [6, p. 121]. Biological continuity is represented by "living fossils", species which have provably failed to alter their basic form throughout their known history [25]. As the family has persisted worldwide despite efforts to alter it, we should regard the family as just such a "living fossil".

GENDER ROLE DESIGN

Patriarchy

Goldberg cites male dominance as a universal social pattern which results "inevitably" when hormonal-sponsored aggression, risk-taking, and spatiality interact with environmental demands such as the need for provision and protection [19]. From his observations of public gender segregation in 90 nonindustrial societies, Mackey has defined a "plowman/protector" complex as one of two such "universal constants" [34]. These patterns reflect the society's relative need for male as parent v male as "provider/protector" and are the means by which the next generation is socialized into gender-appropriate tasks [34]. While the male can in fact be both warrior and parent at the same time, since the activities are incompatible, society may not assign each to him with equal priority.

The male's greater tendency to seek authority, status, position or achievement, results in them holding the majority of the top positions in organizational hierarchies in every culture [19,32]. This is just as true in countries which have endorsed "equality" such as the Soviet Union, China, and Israel [32,40]. In spite of recent growth in the number of American women elected to political office, there are still seventeen times as many men in the U.S. Congress as women [49, p. 32]. In spite of its election of Margaret Thatcher in 1979, Great Britain has fewer women in politics now than it did in 1945 [40].

Goldberg defines aggression as the ambition, drive, and competitiveness required for success at any task, and notes that the male is more motivated to sacrifice on behalf of competitive success and dominance in personal relationships [19]. Moir and Jessel write that, in contrast, "Women won't; most of them simply are not made that way" [40, p. 162]. In discussing the male bias for competition and dominance, Moir and Jessel [40, p. 159] state that men who fail will give the excuse, "Success isn't worth the effort", while for women it appears to be more of a "self-evident truth" [40, p. 159].

Most women appear to be much less comfortable with competition. For example, women managers and leaders at a conference demonstrated a reluctance to assume leadership even though they were very capable of doing so [59]. Leadership difficulties have likewise afflicted the women's movement where traditional structure and the establishment of leadership authority was rejected [39]. Women's natural adaptability and reluctance to interact competitively with others helps to explain why those who support gender equity have been unable to make a more significant impact though social or legislative changes [11]. For example, Bunch argued that the

> problem is that in building feminist strategies around reform goals
> dependent on existing political and economic structures, feminists
> often come not only to accept the limitations of form, but also to
> defend existing institutions instead of continuing to work toward
> feminist alternatives....Longer range questions [are] put aside in the
> struggle to survive [cited in 11, p. 249].

The greatest discrepancies in wages and positions result from the greater drive of married males to achieve when compared with either single men or married women who earn similar wages given similar work histories [32, p. 142]. One of the primary reasons for the wage differential is that males typically demonstrate greater "labor force attachment" which leads to greater job-related experience and training [4]. Using actual measures of productivity, such as an hourly wage, payment by results or overtime wages, researchers were able to account for the differences between male and female pay. Similar findings applied for Stanford graduates in regard to bonuses and commissions [36, p. 38].

Bergmann accounted for 45% of the wage gap using the factors of job experience and training, noting that women significantly more often;worked part-time, took time off for illness, personal/family, placed limits on the job, or were out of the labor force or were planning to stop work [4, p. 78]. Fineman notes that the number of women working part-time has shown no tendency to decline and that having a young child is the most likely reason [15, p. 197]. The average working single mother with a child under 6 missed 10.1 days per year while a married woman with the same age child missed a full 24.8 days a year [37, p. 38]. These figures suggest remarkable motivational differences between the woman who is the "primary" wage earner and the one who is not.

Women's employment has depended upon various efforts to make work more compatible with childcare, such as, "sequencing", part-time, and the controversial "mommy track" which trades time with children for career growth [3,53]. Berg notes that women typically prefer these jobs because they are less stressful, demand less physical energy and traveling, and offer personal freedoms such as telephone access [3]. Women willingly make these choices in spite of the fact it disadvantages them economically and keeps them dependent [4,54].

Men's lower motivation to pursue occupations which are personal or child-related results in higher female employment in these areas [19]. For instance, women in law and medicine predominate in personal and child-related areas such as;OB/GYN, pediatrics and psychiatry, family law and personnel management while males predominate in the areas of academic medicine, surgery and orthopedics. More women doctors are also found in clinics and health maintenance organizations, probably due to more dependable scheduling [36, pp. 159-160]. Women lawyers most frequently work in trusts and estates, domestic relations, and tax law, all areas with more control, less litigation and more client contact.

Women lawyers surveyed were less satisfied than males with their jobs due to its adverse effect on their personal lives [15]. Mason places the blame not on "sinister cultural-conditioning" as feminists do, but on the reluctance of women to choose highly competitive positions which will "overwhelm" all of their time and energies, as they wish to preserve at least the "possibility of motherhood" [36, p. 155]. Even those who are the most successful competitively learn to hate the adversarial approach to solving human dilemmas [35].

While societies can function with little hierarchy and with a dependence on women for the major portion of food, they survive at a subsistence level because they have failed to utilize the male's aggression and organizational strengths [8,19]. While these cultures represent the social egalitarianism advocated by feminists, Chafetz writes in her analysis that

> *The apparent human desire to improve the material standard of living beyond the minimal level, which is still characteristic of most of the world's peoples, means that those technologies and forms of economic organization that produce most will tend to be adopted wherever the collectivity is able to do so [8, pp. 227-228].*

Caretaker

Mackey's second "universal constant" derives from the female's critical biological and social investment in childbearing and childcare, a feature that also frees the male to perform his provider/protector role, a role that is often not compatible with childcare. This biological and economic interdependency has been labeled the "gender division of labor". Mackey [34, p. 142] notes that the female "invariably" serves as the primary caretaker of children since, as he states, "...women do not readily assume behaviors that interfere with childrearing" [34, p. 143]. Fineman explains that it is because of their greater concern for children that women are disadvantaged economically [15]. She argues that, given reproductive realities, women would always bear the children, but if it were men who felt the greater concern, women would be able to exact from them a much higher price for their childrearing tasks [15, p. 196].

Mackey argues that by virtue of the fact that it is paid for, childcare faces an inevitable reduction of quality from what the parent can provide emotionally and socially to the child [34]. Only one of many reasons is that due to the exceptionally high turnover among childcare personnel, continuity in the primary nurturant figure is sacrificed. Because it is so labor-intensive and has strictly regulated caretaker/child ratios, the profitability of daycare is seriously limited and requires some type of subsidation of equipment/facilities such as home care or the church/school option [62].

Mackey points out that every society recorded has relied for its childcare on the "irrational system" of "emotional ties to children" and that there is no successful precedent for depending on the "rational basis" of payment [34, p. 162]. As confirmation, psychologists Bolt and Myers [7, pp. 74-79] describe the high cost of rewards, that is, extrinsic reinforcement, since it robs the individual of the enjoyment of doing something for its own sake, resulting in a reduced desire to do it without such bribery.

Family Structure

Given the intensity of the mother/child relationship, Mackey concludes that, as universal patterns, only two basic family structures are possible, either a female/child dyad or the traditional male/female/child unit [34]. Research has thoroughly supported the male's capacity to emotionally bond with his infant, as well as his ability to provide competent care [30,42,46].

Rohner noted that, universally, the voluntary presence of the father in the home is associated with the society's acceptance of children [50]. The society which does not adequately accept its children will also not grant males adequate status to elicit their cooperation in the parenting role. Rohner's other findings associate the importance of the father as caretaker with both child acceptance and paternal warmth [50], in other words, the male being accepted as a caretaker promotes the expression of paternal warmth and child acceptance. Paternal warmth is also the best preparation for father care in the next generation [30].

Taylor concludes that poverty is closely associated with the failure of fathers to provide faithful support to their families, thus the male's provider role is essential to the success of the family [58]. The male's role as secondary parent includes far more than material provision, as his contributions are essential for the healthy social, cognitive and moral development of children [30,42]. In fact, it is the absence of the father, not race or poverty, which correlates most closely with future criminality [58]. The failure to socialize males into their family roles has resulted in larger numbers of single uncommitted males who cost society in a variety of ways through significantly higher rates of social irresponsibility, social pathology, and criminality [18].

Without sufficient legal and social support for the family, the male's commitment to family will be seriously undermined [15]. These hardships have often been intensified by unrealistic assumptions made regarding equality, prompting some to label equality either a "trap" or an "illusion" [36,15]. While some feminists have expressed the realistic fear that "feminism has freed men first" [54, p. 227], others have recognized that divorce is "double-edged" and that, along with "freer abortion", may have further undermined male obligation to support women and children [29, p. 48].

Family values, that is, valuing the family, has increasingly been revealed as essential to the survival of society [61]. Taylor indicts government welfare programs which incur dependency and yet cannot transmit the essential values of self-reliance, self-control and faithfulness [58]. Regarding higher infant mortalities in the economic underclass, Thomas Sowell wrote, "The difference between married and unmarried reflects differences in attitudes, and attitude differences have consequences which can be literally fatal to infants" [quoted in 58, p. 297].

MECHANISMS WHICH PRESERVE GENDER ROLES

Biological Mechanisms

Innate behavior has been explained as the result of environmental "triggers" which release pre-programmed behavioral sequences called "fixed action patterns" [FAPs]. These have been applied by ethnologists Bowlby and Ainsworth to human attachment behavior [cited in 26]. For example, the infant demonstrates various complex behaviors such as grasping, cuddling, and staring, all behaviors to which parents respond with care and attention [22,26]. Infants even a few hours old have demonstrated a propensity to attend to the 'most human' faces, voices and eyes [26].

Research has shown that not only can inexperienced fathers provide competent care to their newborns [42], they instinctively use "caretaker speech", raising the pitch of their voices with rarely any awareness [46]. They are clearly able to bond with their infants, bonding which has been associated with their participation in later care [22,30,46]. Based on his observation of strong consistencies in paternalistic behaviors, Mackey concluded the basis for paternal behavior patterns lie in inherited behavioral tendencies which were "best viewed as biased motivational states" [34, p. 171].

Gender character likewise is supported by hormonal and neurological patterns. Restak reports that innate gender movement patterns in infants are recognizable by other infants when the subjects were cross-dressed [48]. Spiro concluded from his research that the contrasting play preferences of preschool boys for riding and climbing, and girls for fantasy, verbal and visual play should be credited to an "innate biological dimension" [cited in 28, pp. 208-209]. This pattern appears early with greater activity, risk-taking and dominance behavior even in young boys [20,28]. For example, males of every age incur higher pedestrian death rates [43]. Halpern credits biological sex differences with playing "a role in establishing and maintaining cognitive sex differences" [24, p. vii].

Social Mechanisms

Those who support gender equity are confronted by various evidences and arguments to the contrary [18,19,32,34]. A major puzzle to feminists is that women appear to "legitimate the very system that disadvantages and devalues them" [8, p. 78]. Feminist scholar Sherry Ortner has in fact warned that "female subordination" could not be altered by simply "rearranging a few tasks and roles" or even by "reordering the whole economic structure" [41, pp. 67-68]. Chafetz undertook a comprehensive analysis to determine upon what social factors gender inequity depended. She identified four primary targets for change;the gender division of labor, gender norms, superior male access to resources, and, membership in the elite [8].

Some of the most powerful factors are the "myths" that support   gender norms and the gender division of labor. These "myths" represent innate social perceptions that appear to reveal deeper truths than even observed realities do. For example, Goldberg notes that "male dominance" exists everywhere as the belief that males "should be" in control, even if, in reality, they are not [19]. This feature has been labeled "mythical dominance" by Sanday who finds it more difficult to understand than the obvious support/protection role of the male [52, p. 182]. Likewise, the male as primary provider is a similar "myth", protected at great effort by dual-income couples [5], and so critical that men who are not able to provide for their families will often leave [18, p. 59].

According to Peitchinis [44, pp. 34-37], a series of "myths" undermines the true economic significance of women's employment, as well as their commitment to it. The power of these "myths" is revealed in a review of gender-related occupational choices. For example, significantly fewer women have worked for as long as 20 years and a much higher percentage of women [26%] than men [7.8%] preferred to work part time [44]. A full 86 percent of those not working full-time were married and thus had other responsibilities, as well as not having to be self-supporting [44].

Peitchinis [44] argues that because women, as well as others, perceive the primary role of women to be the family, they underestimate their interest and competency for employment. He reports that the mandating of equal pay in Australia without adjustments in this perception has resulted in a negative impact since employers are less willing to hire women when they must be paid equally with men. Another such "myth" is the belief that women must imitate men to be successful, and that women are unable or unwilling to prepare adequately for careers [44].

In spite of the conviction of feminist parents that gender norms should be altered, they have failed to figure out how. In spite of their efforts to discourage it, feminist parents and kindergarten teachers note "chauvinistic" behavior among young boys seeking to establish their masculine identities [20,57]. Pleck recounts Pogrebin's concern that feminist parents felt more comfortable endorsing assertiveness for girls than they did sensitivity for boys. When feminist parents were asked how they were accomplishing the "non-sexist" childrearing they espoused, they "either had no response or expressed fears that any changes in traditional childrearing would make their sons homosexual" [45, p. 83].

Voluntary communal arrangements have repeatedly failed, both to function without the gender division of labor, or to provide the long-term commitment required of parenting [56]. Stacey questions the feminist belief that "equality" can be promoted and secured within the family since egalitarian relationships appear to her to be contradictory to the demands for intimacy and security required by a long-term commitment [56]. She also cites the "blurring of clearly demarcated roles and spheres" as contributing to the "instability" in modern primary relationships regardless of sexual orientation [56, p. 230].

Gender roles have likewise reasserted themselves in both in the Soviet Union and in Israel despite years of at least an outward commitment to change. The Soviet state never evidenced an ideological commitment to "equality" but only a very practical need to replace the men killed off in war and in Stalinist purges [21, p. 33]. Soviet society faced inevitable conflict when its leadership demanded that its women serve as both "producer and reproducer" [21, p. 33]. Israeli women as well experienced their lowest birthrates while the most involved in nontraditional occupations. Gender segregation of work has returned as nine out of every ten women left jobs like truckdriving for more traditional and domestic occupations, all in spite of the fact that income was irrelevant on the kibbutz [40]. These changes were motivated by the desire of Israeli women to play a larger role in their children's lives. A study of the Israeli kibbutzim using computer analyses and sociological techniques has confirmed that universal patterns have reappeared despite the commitment of their leadership to eliminate them [60].

Co-equal parenting has been offered by feminists as a strategy to alter gender norms and therefore gender inequity [13,54]. Early care that is exclusively maternal has been credited with resulting in the male's fear of female-held power since it is a reminder of his own helplessness and vulnerability. This might also be applied to women's reluctance to vest power in the hands of women [39]. Evidence cited in support of this thesis could include Coltrane's finding of greater opportunities for women in public decision-making roles whenever fathers were more involved in the routine care of their young children [10]. Sanday also reported that the more closely that fathers related to their children the more equal the society was [52]. Mackey identifies the father/child relationship as reflective of the society's demand for the male's provider/protector role [34]. These findings all reflect a "mechanism" whereby changing environmental demands result in altered socialization patterns.

427

Another better explanation locates the problem not in the intensity of the mother/child bond but in the lack of a strong father/child bond. Unless they see male role models who are strong and caring, young males often reject anything "feminine" in order to establish their own masculine identities, resulting in the "hypermasculinity" Gilder associates with social misbehavior and criminality [18]. This finding is endorsed as well by Taylor's association of father absence and future criminality [58]. Greater male involvement in childcare does have several very specific positive benefits such as greater marital intimacy and reduced gender stereotyping in children [12]. Most importantly, Pruett notes a greatly reduced rate of abuse of children by males who have been involved in the routine care of young children [46, p. 38].

Mackey notes that actual co-equal parenting is found nowhere in the world, not even among the Tchambuli, a people who, according to Margaret Mead, exhibit "role reversion" [cited in 34, p. 156]. In spite of the obvious social, moral and cognitive benefits to children of greater fathering, in his study of 16 primary-care dads, Pruett found that after two years, only half of the families continued this pattern. However, after a total of four years seven fathers still remained as the primary caretaker [46]. The Cowans found that only 20 percent of their subject couples continued this pattern after two years [12]. Besides economic realities, the "obstacles" that must be overcome in order to continue this pattern include the perception that women are better or more natural parents, an intense maternal/child bond which discourages male participation since he may fear being inadequate as a parent, as well as assorted other feedback from friends, relatives and co-workers on the "proper role" of men and women [12].

The obstacles to co-equal parenting involve not only social-economic realities like the wage differential but the gender-related preferences of men and women. Rarely suggested as an explanation for these patterns is that women themselves hold unique influence within the household/family as a result of their greater contributions and involvement [31, pp. 215, 217]. This power is especially evident as regards the father's relationship to his children, as she may act as a "gatekeeper", either supporting or thwarting his efforts to father, since she regards the house and children as her exclusive domain [22]. Citing a study by Zaslow, Pruett notes that new fathers frequently become depressed by their loss of control, resulting from a process of "freeze-out", although perhaps "freeze-in" is a more accurate label. This process is used by the mother to thwart the father's desire for direct contact with his child, thus increasing her opportunities for interaction [46, p. 30].

Feminists have recognized that women in pursuit of co-parenting and "equality" in the marketplace will first have to give up some of this "power" [13,54]. For example, Miner & Longino state,

> The role of mother and manager of the household are the two roles
> in which women's authority has not been questioned;together, they
> constitute the one area in which women have had real power and
> control. Increased paternal involvement may threaten this power
> and pre-eminence [39, p. 20].

Segal describes why it is so difficult for women to "share" parenting, commenting on the unwillingness of mothers to off-load the "labor or joys of parenting", or even the "dead of night demands for attention" [54, p. 158]. She includes the account of a mother who lost her non-biological child who spoke of gaining a "sense of power" or confidence as a result of her commitment to and care of this child, not just over a "helpless child" but in regard to other adults [54, p. 158]. Berg [3] comments on the difficulty working mothers have finding satisfactory childcare, often using as many as 4 or 5 different services on a regular basis, perhaps at least partly because they are not satisfied, or because they are reluctant to share their child's affections.

Egalitarian parenting appears to depend more on practical need than on ideological commitment. Even "egalitarian" couples studied during their transition to parenting took on increasingly specialized roles around the house compared to what they had previously, and were unable to meet their own expectations regarding "egalitarian parenting" [12]. Cowan reports that these couples

> describe the change as if it were a mysterious virus they picked up
> when they were in the hospital having their baby;they don't seem to
> view their arrangements as choices they have made [12, p. 98].

The greater male control over resources Chafetz notes derives from their innately greater dominance, something no legislation or social movement can change. In contrast, even successful women allocate less salary to themselves and spend less on expense accounts than men do [40]. The promotion of feminism has been handicapped since women who do have resources have seldom been willing to commit solely on this basis [8, p. 223].

Legislative efforts are doomed whenever they ignore innate factors like male dominance and female caretaking motivation. Women's jobs were lost when no longer 'protected' by gender stereotyping since greater numbers of men took formerly female jobs than females took male jobs [40, p. 252]. Peitchinis notes that "equal pay" in Australia has had a negative impact on women's employment [44] which would result here if "comparative worth" advocates had their way. Better pay would increase male interest in jobs which have been female-dominated, resulting in their loss to males. Chafetz fears that the higher pay comparative worth would bring would retard women's progress into other areas since it wouldn't be necessary to change fields to secure salary increases [8, p. 109].

Chafetz identified equal representation among elites as the key to establishing and maintaining gender equity [8], something that, according to all the evidence, has never occurred, and isn't likely to [19,32]. Chafetz herself admits that "equal access to the elite roles constitutes the most difficult and intractable problem in achieving gender equality" [8, p. 221]. In the first place, elites view their role as protecting the status quo and are reluctant to share power. Tokenism is fact one way of preventing the new member from establishing himself/herself as a legitimate member of the group, while still allowing their entrance.

Chafetz cites a study by Gamson of 53 challenging groups where only 2 out of 16 groups who wanted the total replacement of leadership were able to achieve any degree of success [8]. She also cites Holter's study which found that women achieve success precisely when key decision-making roles are becoming "obsolete", that is, losing skill, prestige, pay, responsibility, autonomy, and general social importance, such as, for example, on school boards and in mayoral positions as a result of the loss of autonomy to state and federal government [8]. Levin does in fact confirm this in his book [32].

Many of those women who do attain leadership positions fail to endorse feminism, women such as Indira Ghandi, Golda Meir, Margaret Thatcher, and Corazon Aquino [8, p. 221]. Several years ago, Lynn Martin while then Representative from Illinois stated,

> There isn't any politician, male or female, who likes these issues, because they're such trouble. You think anyone who got far enough to be elected to Congress is going to bring up these issues on her own? [17, p. 215].

Remarkable gains have been made for women in international leadership. Heads of state or government are up 25 from the 3 who held office twenty-five years ago [Ghandi, Meir, and Bandaranaike], there are six women prime ministers, three presidents and 300 ministers in 142 countries. However, with the exception of Bhutto in Pakistan and Mary Robinson in Ireland, these women are rarely pressuring their constituencies for women's causes or candidacies [33, p. 45].

Achieving equal representation among the elite depends upon the continuing economic need for women's services along with the potential impact of coparenting [8]. However, Chafetz admits that women are an "expendable labor force", subject to the potential for male incursion into female employment areas, depriving women of power both at home and in the marketplace. She notes that women's employment opportunities are subject to the dangers of recession or depression robbing them of any gains made. She closes her discussion with,

> The key to the consolidation of power is the continued presence of most women in the labor force and their movement in more than token numbers into the ranks of elite gatekeepers, resource and opportunity distributers, and social definition makers. It remains to be seen if this will occur [8, p. 231].

CONCLUSIONS

Despite shifts in emphasis over time, geography, and culture, universal gender patterns have persisted. This persistence depends upon a number of specific elements, elements such as the male's physical and social dominance and the female's adaptability. These translate into greater male control of resources, including membership in the elite. In addition to these, widespread "myths" regarding male as provider or female as caretaker, support the gender norms, resisting any efforts to change them. Because these "myths" reflect what each gender finds most innately satisfying they are the most profound pressure in support of traditional roles and provide an underlying foundation which supports the family structure. Legislative efforts inevitably fail when they conflict with these innate capacities and desires regarding family and work obligations.

Gender role persistence in the face of these varied challenges provides us with an even greater confidence in its having been designed since permanence is an essential quality in any design. Only when the limits of some device or structure are tested do we understand its true nature, that is, we have determined what purposes it serves and why we need it. This role persistence represents the provision of what is both useful and satisfying as well as what is essential, that is, without it, the structure fails. Flexibility can also be better recognized as an innate feature of the design, something the "coparenting" trend has explored.

Chafetz concluded that she was faced with a "discomfiting conclusion" and "an inescapable quandary" since the only way she could see for women to alter gender equity was to behave more like men and compete successfully for male power roles, even though it would mean sacrificing the feminine qualities like caring and connectedness that our culture is most in need of [8, p. 226]. However, we know that the best choices are for both men and women to exercise moral leadership as they have opportunity realizing that there are no gender restrictions when it comes to the Christ-like behavior and attitudes which God expects of each of us.

Because both men and women are equipped with unique physical and emotional strengths, it is essential that they both we held accountable for using their gifts sacrificially on behalf of the family and society rather than for the selfish exploitation of the other. In order to do so they will need to have an appreciation of the source of their unique qualities. Donald Joy discusses the contrast between patriarchy, or males dominating because they can, and biblical headship, which means men sacrificing self-interest on behalf of providing for and protecting their families [27].

The permanence of the family certainly represents to us the faithfulness of our Creator. The social nature of the individual and of the family reflects the social nature of God. That is, not only is the social unit essential to our survival but this unit itself depends on the social support of society at large. The critical nature of these functions fully justifies the biblical injunctions on behalf of commitment to family. It also represents His grace to us since despite the wickedness of man, the family remains as a means of caring for each of us, no matter what.

REFERENCES

[1]   M. A. Baker, Editor, Sex Differences in Human Performance, 1987, John Wiley and Sons, NY.

[2]   S. A. Barnett, Biology and Freedom, 1988, Cambridge University Press, Cambridge.

[3]   B. J. Berg, The Crisis of the Working Mother, 1986, Summit, NY.

[4]   B. R. Bergmann, The Economic Emergence of Women, 1986, Basic Books, NY.

[5]   C. Bird, The Two-Paycheck Marriage, 1980, Pocket Books, NY.

[6]   R. M. Blakar, **Language as a Means of Social Power,** in Studies of Language, Thought and Verbal Communication, R. Rommetveit and R. M. Blakar, Editors, 1979, Academic Press, NY.

[7]   M. Bolt and D.G. Myers, The Human Connection, 1984, IVP, Downer's Grove, IL.

[8]   J. S. Chafetz, Gender Equity, 1990, Sage, Newbury Park.

[9]   J. Cherfas and J. Gribbin, The Redundant Male, 1984, Pantheon Books, NY.

[10]   S. Coltrane, **Father-Child Relationships and the Status of Women,** American Journal of Sociology, 93:5, (March 1988) 1060-1095.

[11]   A. B. Cottrell **The Contemporary American Women's Movement,** Women and World Change, N. Black and A. B. Cottrell, Editors, 1981, Sage, Beverly Hills.

[12]   C. P. Cowan and L. C. Cowan, When Partners Become Parents, 1992, Basic Books, NY.

[13]   D. Ehrensaft, Parenting Together, 1987, The Free Press, NY.

[14]   E. U. Fierst, **Is Raging Careerism getting in the way of motherhood?,** The Wichita Eagle-Beacon, 3B (May 14, 1989).

[15]   M. A. Fineman, The Illusion of Equality, 1991, University of Chicago Press, Chicago.

[16]   M. F. Fox and S. Hesse-Biber, Women at Work, 1984, Mayfield.

[17]   B. Friedan, The Second Stage, 1981, Summit Books, New York, NY.

[18]   G. Gilder, Sexual Suicide, 1973, Quadrangle, NY.

[19]   S. Goldberg, The Inevitability of Patriarchy, 1973, William Morrow and Co., NY.

[20]   R. G. Goodenough, **Situational Stress and Sexist Behavior Among Young Children,** Beyond the Second Sex, P. R. Sanday, Editor, 1990, University of Pennsylvania Press.

[21]   F. du Plessix Gray, Soviet Women, 1989, Doubleday, New York.

[22]   M. Greenberg and N. Morris, **Engrossment,** Father and Child, S. H. Cath, A. R. Gurwitt, and J. M. Ross, Editors, 1982, Little, Brown and Co., NY.

[23]   J. C. Gutin, **Why bother?,** Discover 13:6, (1992), p.32-39.

[24]   D. F. Halpern, Sex Differences in Cognitive Abilities, 1986, Lawrence Erlbaum Associates, Hillsdale, NJ.

[25]   F. Hitching, The Neck of the Giraffe, 1982, Ticknor and Fields,London.

[26]   D.L. Holmes and F. J. Morrison, The Child, 1979, Brooks/Cole, Monterey, CA.

[27]   D. M. and R. B. Joy, Lovers-Whatever Happened to Eden?, 1987, Word, Waco, TX.

[28]   A. U. Khan and J. Cataio, Men and Women in Biological Perspective, 1984, Praeger, NY.

[29]   R. D. Klein and D. L. Steinberg, Radical Voices, 1989, Program Press, Oxford.

[30]   M. E. Lamb, The Role of the Father in Child Development, 1981, Wiley, NY.

[31]   J. Lerner and N. L. Galambos, Editors, Employed Mothers and their Children, 1991, Garland Publications, NY.

[32]   M. Levin, Feminism and Freedom, 1987, Transaction Books, New Brunswick.

[33]   E. MacFarquhar, **World Report:The War Against Women**, U.S. News and World Report, (March 28, 1994), p.42-48.

[34]   W. C. Mackey, Fathering Behaviors, 1985, Plenum Press, NY.

[35]   L. Mansnerus, **Why Women are Leaving the Law,** Working Woman, (April 1993) 64-67ff.

[36]   M. A. Mason, The Equality Trap, 1988, Simon and Schuster, NY.

[37]   E. McGrath, **Let's Make Room for Daddy,** Savvy, (June 1989) 32, p. 38-39.

[38]   D. McGuiness, **Introduction,** Sex Differences in Human Performance, M.A. Baker, Editor, 1987, John Wiley and Sons, NY.

[39]   V. Miner and H. E. Longino Competition;A Feminist Taboo?, 1987, The Feminist Press, NY.

[40]   A. Moir and D. Jessel, Brain Sex, 1991, Carol Pub, NY.

[41]   S. Ortner, **Is Female to Male as Nature is to Culture?** Woman, Culture and Society, M. Rosaldo and L. Lamphere, Editors, 1974, Stanford University Press, CA.

[42]   R. Parke, Fathers, 1981, Harvard University, Cambridge, MA.

[43]   **Pedestrian Death Rates**, Psychology Today, (January 1983) 14.

[44]   S. G. Peitchinis, Women at Work:response and discrimination, 1989, McClelland & Stewart:Toronto, Ontario.

[45]   J. H. Pleck, **Prisoner's of Manliness,** Psychology Today, (September 1981) 69-83.

[46]   K. Pruett, The Nurturing Father, 1987, Warner Books, NY.

[47]   C. Ramazanoglu, Feminism and the Contradictions of Oppression, 1989, Routledge, London.

[48]   R. M. Restak, The Infant Mind, 1986, Doubleday & Co, Garden City, NY.

[49]   P. Ries and A. J. Stone, Editors, The American Woman:1992-1993 A Status Report, 1992, W.W. Norton & Co., NY.

[50]   R. P. Rohner, The Warmth Dimension, 1986, Sage, Beverly Hills.

[51]   **Role of Natural Selection in macro-evolution theory (Battson/Wakefield dialogue)**, Origins Research, (Fall/Winter 1987), p.6-7.

[52]   P. R. Sanday, **The Bases for Male Dominance**, Female Power and Male Dominance, 1981, Cambridge University Press, Cambridge.

[53]   F. N. Schwartz with J. Zimmerman, Breaking with Tradition, 1992, Warner Books, NY.

[54]   L. Segal, Is the Future Female?, 1987, Peter Bedwick Books, NY.

[55]   S. M. Simpson, **Women Entrepreneurs,** Women at Work, J. Firth-Cozens and M. A. West, Editors, 1991, Open University Press, Bristol, PA.

[56]   J. Stacey**, Are Feminists Afraid to Leave Home?**, What is Feminism, J. Mitchell and A. Oakley, Editors, 1986, Pantheon, NY.

[57]   E. Stone, **Sons and Mothers**, Savvy (September, 1988), 116, 114.

[58]   J. Taylor, Paved With Good Intentions, 1992, Carrol and Graf Pub, Inc., NY.

[59]   S. Taylor, M. Bogandoff, D. Brown, L. Hillman, C. Kurash, J. Spain, B.Thacher and L.Weinstein, **By Women, For Women: A Group Relations Conference,** Exploring Individual and Organizational Boundaries, W. G. Laurence, Editor, 1979, John Wiley and Sons, NY.

[60]   L. Tiger and J. Sheper, Women of the Kibbutz, 1975, Harcourt, Brace, Jovanovich, NY.

[61]   B. D. Whitehead, **Dan Quayle Was Right**, The Atlantic Monthly (reprint), (April 1993).

[62]   E. Winninghoff, **Why Business Alone Cannot Solve the Childcare Crisis**, Executive Female, (Nov/Dec 1992), p.41-44.

THE BIOTIC MESSAGE — AN INTRODUCTION

WALTER JAMES ReMINE
C/O ST. PAUL SCIENCE
P.O. BOX 19600
SAINT PAUL, MN 55119

KEYWORDS

Message Theory, biologic universals, molecular sequences, fossil sequence, phylogeny, convergence, transposition, atavism, cellulose, discontinuity systematics, creation systematics, evolution.

ABSTRACT

This paper offers a tutorial introduction to Message Theory — a new theory of creation that scientifically explains the major patterns of life, while overturning the major evidences of biological evolution.

INTRODUCTION

Evolution is so well established, we are told, as to be a fact that no reasonable person could doubt. Evolutionists therefore cynically taunt the public with a question: "Why would God create a pattern that appears to be the result of evolution?" [1, p. 174] "Or is the Creator trying to trick us into believing in evolution?" [5, p. 199] Stephen Jay Gould offers a classic, "Did he create to mimic evolution and test our faith thereby?" [6, p. 123]

They are answered by a new theory of creation, called Message Theory, which shows that evolutionists do not know their own theory. Life, in fact, was intricately designed to look *unlike* evolution. Message Theory proposes that life was designed to convey a message. The central claim of the theory is as follows. Life was reasonably designed for survival, and for communicating a message that tells where life came from. The biotic message says, "Life is the product of a *single* designer — life was intentionally designed to resist all other interpretations of origin." That simple idea poses a plausible, credible motive of a designer. Life was designed as a biotic message.

Place yourself in the position of the biotic message sender, and imagine that you want to design life to look like the work of one designer. Make a list of every other conceivable interpretation of life. Be expansive and list everything you can. List Darwin's theory, Lamarck's theory, and everything else you can think of. Then ask yourself: How would you design life to resist, thwart, and defeat that list? This was the task faced by the biotic message sender. The task is not easy because evolutionary theory is extraordinarily pliable. Evolutionary theory adapts to data like fog adapts to landscape. It is really just a smorgasbord of countless possible naturalistic explanations that theorists effortlessly adapt to the data. As you will see, thwarting all those explanations is not easy. Yet life on Earth shows an elegant solution. This paper introduces the key arguments of Message Theory. Extensive documentation and arguments are given in a recent book [9].

THE MAJOR PATTERNS OF LIFE

Life's major patterns can be divided into two groups: A and B. Group A patterns are prevalent and abundant. Group B patterns are rare to non-existent.

Group A

Biologic universals (DNA, RNA, ATP, etc.)
Nested hierarchy of characters
"Convergent" character traits
Von Baer's Laws of embryology
Cladistic and phenetic patterns — as revealed by cladograms and phenograms
Sexual reproduction
An accessible, visible, substantial fossil record
A structured fossil sequence
Stasis — or non-evolution within the fossil record
Abrupt appearances of diverse life forms based on a unique new design — "adaptive radiation"

Group B

Gradual intergradations (over a large scale)
Phylogeny (over a large scale)
Intermediate and transitional forms
Transposed characters — DNA lateral transfer in multicellular organisms
Atavistic characters — Genetic throwbacks
Inheritance of acquired characters — Lamarckian inheritance
In multi-cellular animals, enzymes for efficiently digesting cellulose
Experimental demonstrations of the origin of life
Extraterrestrial life

These groups reveal something peculiar. Group B patterns are the ones that evolutionary theory would suggest should be commonplace and abundant — yet they are not. Each of these patterns is associated with specific evolutionary processes (some that are quite simple and plausible). Yet each is conspicuous by its absence. The absence of these patterns is an evolutionary enigma.

Moreover, Group A patterns (such as sexual reproduction, abrupt appearances, stasis, convergent characters, and von Baer's laws) are ones that evolutionary theory has difficulty with. Yet they are prevalent. Take the example of sexual reproduction. It is extremely widespread and its genetic mechanics are similar throughout. This feature alone does a magnificent job of unifying life. Yet the most plausible of evolutionary theories predicts that sex should not even exist. The existence and prevalence of sex is an evolutionary enigma.

Thus, the major patterns of life are precisely the reverse from what evolution would lead us to expect. This reversal is because life was intentionally fashioned to look unlike evolution. We will next examine those patterns in greater detail.

BIOLOGIC UNIVERSALS

Biologic universals are a body of evidence at the molecular level that serves to unify all life. The common examples are: DNA as the carrier of inheritance, the expression of that information as proteins by means of an RNA intermediate, the genetic code based on groups of three nucleotides, the use of left-handed amino-acids in proteins, the bi-layered phosphatide construction of cell membranes. Also, ATP (adenosine tri-phosphate), biotin, riboflavin, hemes, pyridoxin, vitamins B_{12} and K, and folic acid are used in metabolic processes everywhere. One protein called *ubiquitin* is present in all organisms, tissues, and cells studied so far, and it has an identical amino acid sequence in each case. There are many such examples, and they testify that all life came from a single common source. This construction is an ideal way to make life look like the product of one designer. If you were to unify all life — from elephants, to plants, to bacteria — then you would not give them all tusks. Bacteria do not need tusks. The ideal way to unify life is with common design at the molecular level. The pervasive unity at the biochemical level is major evidence for the biotic message.

For decades evolutionists have created the illusion that biologic universals are evidence in their favor. They maintained this illusion by artificially separating the origin of life from its subsequent evolution, as though the two are completely unrelated problems. The origin-of-life theorists were not publicizing a serious problem they were confronted with. Virtually every one of the biologic universals is too complex to have arisen directly by known processes aided by chance. So evolutionists arbitrarily got around this problem by making two untestable assumptions.

1) There are an infinitude of biochemical arrangements suitable for life and *totally unlike any known life.*
2) Many of those life forms *have existed on this planet.*

While the naturalistic origin of known life is far too improbable, evolutionists simply claimed (by assumption #1) that the origin of *some kind* of life is highly probable, and the first life forms were vastly simpler than anything known today and without any of the known biologic universals (in accordance with assumption #2). Thus, to explain away difficulties in the origin of life, evolutionists embrace assumptions which indicate that biologic universals should not exist. Evolutionists believe that life forms — totally unlike any known life — must have existed on this planet. The complete absence of such life forms is therefore evidence against evolution.

Evolutionists explain away this new problem by making another untestable assumption. They claim that the earliest life forms were inefficient, couldn't compete or were consumed, and went totally extinct. First these organisms originated and survived quite well, then they couldn't survive at all (somehow leaving only those with the biologic universals). Such claims are all too convenient. Evolutionists pretend to know the detailed survivability of life forms that exist only in their minds — organisms for which we have not the slightest evidence. Their claims are mere evolutionary storytelling, not science.

But those evolutionary stories still do not solve the problem. Nothing in evolution even hints that modern life forms should share any similarities whatever. For example, single-celled organisms have potential for the highest evolutionary speeds due to their extremely short generation time, high reproductive capacity, and because they are the most abundant organisms on earth. In addition, these organisms have had the most time to evolve. According to evolutionists, many of these living organisms shared a most recent common ancestor between one and three billion years ago, thus they are separated by two to six billion years of evolution. Assumption #1 indicates they *could have* diverged completely since it explicitly claims that an infinitude of other biological forms would be capable of life. Evolutionists ask us to believe that all life's incredible breathtaking diversity is the result of evolution, but those other life forms (those lacking the pervasive biochemical unity) were somehow excluded! Evolutionists cannot coherently make such a self-contradictory claim.

Thus, assumptions #1 and #2 each indicates that biologic universals should not exist — if evolution is true, then life forms without any of the biological universals ought to exist on this planet. Concerning the prevalence of biologic universals there can be little doubt: Message Theory is right, and evolution (if it says anything clearly on the matter) is wrong.

GRADUAL INTERGRADATIONS

If you wanted to design life to resist evolutionary interpretations, you would leave out gradual intergradations. Instead, you would design large gaps (or morphological distances) between the created life forms. How large should the gaps be? The gaps should be sufficiently large that they could not be bridged by experimental demonstrations of evolution. Life would then look like many separate, distinct, evolutionarily disconnected "kinds" of life. In addition, you would fashion the organisms so they could not interbreed between these separate groups. Life forms would then interbreed only within their own group. This would prevent hybrids from forming even the appearance of gradual intergradations between the kinds.

That pattern is precisely what we find in nature, though evolutionists avoided it. As noted by evolutionist Steven Stanley, "Since the time of Darwin, paleontologists have found themselves confronted with evidence that conflicts with gradualism, yet the message of the fossil record has been ignored." [12, p. 101]

LINEAGE AND PHYLOGENY

Lineage is identified in morphology space as a long, narrow trail of species with a void in the regions at right angles to (or orthogonal to) the lineage. This "void" or absence of certain life forms is essential. To observe a lineage, the life forms must be abundant in certain places and absent in other places. Phylogeny should be observed as clear lineages that form an identifiable tree-structure of descent.

If you wanted to design life to resist evolutionary interpretations, then you would create life without any clear lineages or phylogenies. To send the biotic message most successfully you would also try to thwart the observer's attempts at arbitrarily constructing lineages. This is accomplished by placing diversity in those places where evolutionists least want to see it: orthogonal to any presumed lineages. This places life forms into those "void" regions, thereby obstructing any attempt to impose a phylogenetic interpretation onto nature. This use of diversity thwarts lineage. By placing life forms properly, a designer can make a system of life resist the appearance of phylogeny. Life forms are like sentries standing in those void regions, guarding against the construction of lineages toward other organisms. Each sentry is guarding other life forms, and each is guarded in return by others.

As already stated, all life was intentionally knitted together (with common design) to look like the work of one designer. Thus substantial similarities between diverse organisms are not at all surprising. Many creationists, however, have been lured into the evolutionists' trap of debating whether a certain species should be classified as, for example, a reptile or a bird. That approach allows evolutionists to completely avoid the central issue, which is lineage, phylogeny, and clear-cut ancestry. Evolutionists avoid discussion of real phylogeny because they cannot find it in nature.

Instead, evolutionists distort systematics to create the illusion of phylogeny. The major methods are listed briefly here: nested supraspecific groups, paraphyletic groups, linearizing the data with a steam-roller, cladograms, phenograms, best-candidate ancestors, and so-called "convergent" characters and "lost" characters. Evolutionists use these methods to sound like they have identified phylogeny, when they have not.

Evolutionists also use the fossil sequence to create the illusion of phylogeny. Chronologically successive fossils are frequently displayed as a "lineage," even when evolutionists know the organisms could not plausibly have an ancestor-descendant relationship. [2, p. 264] Conversely, organisms are often displayed as a "lineage," even when evolutionists know the organisms do not have a proper chronologically successive fossil sequence. [4, p. 134] Evolutionists [e.g., 10, p. 223] also create illusion by claiming that no fossils are found out-of-sequence, when in fact they employ potent methods for insulating evolutionary theory from any problems with the fossil sequence.

In addition, evolutionists have re-defined and mis-used virtually every keyword of the origins debate, such as: primitive, ancestral, advanced, derived, intermediate form, transitional form, evolution, and remarkably even the words "lineage" and "phylogeny." Evolutionists now use these words without ever identifying a phylogeny, a lineage, or a single ancestor. They use the words and imagery of evolution, without supplying the evidence. All these things have been misused to create the illusion of phylogeny. Altogether it constitutes a massive program. This universal practice on their part is now material evidence that phylogeny cannot be found, quite simply, if evolutionists could have identified phylogeny, they would have.

Another way to show that large-scale phylogeny does not exist is by removing the illusions and quoting evolutionists directly. Amid their many illusions and their firm restatements of evolutionary faith, they are sometimes frank about their real inability to identify phylogeny. Boundless documentation can be provided on this point. In addition, evolutionists often disagree dramatically among themselves about proposed phylogenies, and this fact alone is substantial evidence that phylogeny cannot be found.

CONVERGENCE

Evolutionists define convergent characters as traits that, though quite similar, evolved separately from rather dis-similar ancestors. Convergent characters are abundant in nature, and evolutionists proudly point out that these are always merely similar, never identical. They claim that identical convergence would be much too improbable for evolution to explain. They thereby create the illusion that evolutionary theory has something firm to say about nature.

On the contrary, identical convergence would be trivially easy for evolutionists to "explain." In fact, evolutionists would be deeply relieved if it were abundant. To see this you must understand evolutionary theory. Darwin's is not the only theory that life was designed to resist. Life was designed to resist *all* evolutionary theories, not just Darwin's. The simplest, most powerful, most overlooked process at the evolutionary smorgasbord is transposition. A transposition process would take a character trait from one life form and transfer it to another different life form. This simple process could easily "explain" identical convergence. In my wording, if convergent character traits were identical, they would no longer be convergent — they would be transpositions. Evolutionists would simply change their story.

Convergent characters show the careful design predicted by Message Theory. They cannot be explained by common descent. They are sufficiently different that they cannot be explained by transposition. Yet they are so similar that they demand explanation. Thus they are awkward for evolutionists to explain. Convergences cannot be explained by either common descent, or by transposition. This situation cannot be the result of random chance. It requires carefully balanced design.

"Convergent" characters are also important in the biotic message for other reasons. First, these similar designs unify diverse portions of life together, subtly stitching life into a unified whole. (Often in a *visible* way that biologic universals at the biochemical level cannot do.) This helps make life look like the work of a single designer. Second, as evolutionary systematists frequently tell you, convergence thwarts their attempt to identify phylogeny. In every respect, so called "convergences" meet the goals predicted by Message Theory. That is why they are abundant.

CELLULOSE

Cellulose is the most abundant organic compound on earth. At least one-third of all vegetable matter is cellulose. It is a carbohydrate and a ready source of food. Curiously, no multicellular animals have the enzymes necessary to digest cellulose. Cows and other herbivores can use it only because their digestive system can retain it long enough for microorganisms to accomplish the digestion. Evolutionists use this situation as evidence against a designer. [11] They argue that an intelligent designer would have given herbivores — animals that eat only plants — the enzymes for efficiently digesting plants.

Evolutionists are mistaken. This situation is actually potent evidence for a designer. Plants need defenses against animals. If higher animals could efficiently devour the plant world and convert it into offspring, then those animals would prosper, but the long-term result would be catastrophic for the ecosystem. Life's designer was concerned, quite reasonably, with the overall stability of the system of life. Withholding of enzymes for efficiently digesting cellulose was a reasonable step toward providing that stability.

In addition, this situation contributes to the biotic message by being especially awkward for evolutionists to explain. A world full of cellulose, and no multicellular animals to efficiently digest it! Could natural selection fail so completely? The ability to efficiently digest cellulose would be an advantage to any animal. Why is it absent? Evolutionists ask us to believe that all life's adaptations evolved to exquisite precision; that eyesight evolved more than forty separate times; and that convergences occur commonly at morphological and molecular levels — but somehow enzymes for digesting life's most abundant food source were neither inherited by, evolved by, converged on, transposed into, nor atavistically unmasked into multicellular animals. Once again, evolution is a story both incoherent and self-contradictory. It provides no structure for understanding nature. When it predicts anything clearly, it is wrong. This is a major problem for evolutionists, and it was concealed by distorting it into an argument against creation.

TRANSPOSITION

In theory a transposition process would take a character trait from one life form and transport it (perhaps via lateral DNA transfer) to another different life form. Transposition is the simplest, most plausible, most powerful process in evolutionary theory. Yet quite likely you have never heard of it before. The *only* reason you haven't heard it trumpeted by evolutionists is because its pattern is absent. Evolutionists never have been dissuaded by their inability to sufficiently demonstrate the mechanisms of evolution. Rather, mechanisms are embraced (and renounced) wholly on the basis of pattern. (For example, the mechanisms of embryological recapitulation — terminal addition and acceleration — never were demonstrated, nonetheless these were embraced as the means to "explain" life's patterns in an evolutionary way.) If life contained a transposition pattern, evolutionists would not hesitate to invoke a transposition mechanism in their "explanations."

There are several reasons for a biotic message sender to avoid a transposition pattern, especially in multicellular organisms. First, transposition would provide a mechanism of rapid evolution. By avoiding a transposition pattern the designer defeated that evolutionary story, and simultaneously created a puzzle for evolutionists. Why isn't transposition everywhere? Why did the simplest, most powerful mechanism in evolution somehow have little effect? Why are "convergences" abundant, but transpositions rare at best? This situation is completely unexpected for evolution, especially since the universal use of DNA, RNA, and genetic code would seem to remove the major obstacle.

Second, transposition is the expected result of any ordinary designer. Designers readily take a design from one circumstance and use it in other diverse circumstances. This is usual design practice. However, life could not be usual design and also be a message. A message cannot be the usual, ordinary design, it must be distinctly different. The absence of transposition from the pattern of life is a major clue that life is intentionally different, that it is a biotic message.

Third, transposition is the expected result of *many* designers acting separately, sharing only a common technology base. For example, the key components of cars are frequently transposed into other objects (such as jets, helicopters, lawn mowers, or dish washers) by many separate human designers. By avoiding a transposition pattern, life was successfully designed to look instead like the product of a single designer.

Finally, and most importantly, the presence of a transposition pattern would allow an observer to explain away the absences of phylogeny and gradual intergradations. An observer could look at a transposition pattern and conclude that traits are transposed from many different sources, and therefore species do not have unique ancestors or phylogenies. Evolutionists are not committed to common descent, rather they are committed to "Natural" selection — they *select* whatever *natural* mechanisms they need to "explain" the data. If evolutionists saw a transposition pattern they would leap for joy. "Transposition," they would argue, "is why phylogeny and gradual intergradations are not visible." Yet life was intricately designed to look like the product of one designer, and to resist all other interpretations. For this reason a transposition pattern had to be rigorously avoided.

INTERMEDIATE FORMS

Intermediate and transitional forms ought to be identified by phylogeny. Once a clear-cut phylogeny is identified, the intermediate forms would be self-evident. Evolutionists, however, cannot identify a clear phylogeny, so they misuse the term "intermediate" by broadening it as much as possible. In their usage, an "intermediate" merely shares similarities of two different groups. To an evolutionist, an "intermediate" and a "convergent form" are virtually the same thing, the only difference is that convergence definitely cannot be explained by common descent. To evolutionists, an "intermediate" need not be an ancestor to either of the other groups, and thus can appear in any fossil sequence relative to the other groups. In this manner, evolutionists misuse the term "intermediate" in the widest, loosest, possible way, and they do this in order to find as many intermediates as possible.

Nonetheless, while using that loose definition, evolutionists themselves acknowledge that "convergent forms" are abundant and "intermediate forms" are quite rare. [3, p. 125] The patterns are reversed. The patterns that should be prevalent are rare, while those that are difficult for evolution to explain are prevalent. This reversal cannot even remotely be blamed on an incomplete fossil record, since an incompleteness would affect both forms in equal portions. This reversal can only result from design. Once again, evolutionary theory gets it wrong, and Message Theory gets it right.

THE NESTED HIERARCHY OF CHARACTERS

Any system of objects can be forced into a nested hierarchy, such as the way libraries classify books. Life, however, actually has a pattern of nested hierarchy. For example, some vertebrates are based on a tetrapod body plan; of the tetrapods, some have an amniote egg; of the amniotes, some have hair and mammary glands (mammals). There are no mammals which are not also amniotes. There are no amniotes which are not also tetrapods, etc. These are the familiar examples, and there are many more. A nested pattern is quite unique, in fact no man-made system of objects is anywhere near as nested as life.

Ever since Darwin, evolutionists claimed the nested pattern as the major evidence in their favor. They said that newly evolved characters are inherited only by descendants, not by other lineages, and this would automatically create a nested hierarchy. Niles Eldredge calls it "evolution's grand prediction." [3, p. 36] The truth is that evolutionary theory *never predicted a nested hierarchy*. Simple evolutionary processes would prevent a nested hierarchy — mechanisms such as loss, replacement, distant hybridization, anagenesis (evolution within a single lineage), transposition (lateral DNA transfer), atavism (the masking and unmasking of genetic libraries that would create "throwbacks"), or multiple separate origins of life. Evolutionary theory could easily accommodate multiple, dis-united, non-nested patterns, and evolutionists would have gladly done so. The truth is that the nested pattern was used primarily as evidence *against* a designer (not for evolution).

Message Theory now provides a direct answer. The nested pattern was utilized largely for what it is not. It is not transposition. Nested hierarchy and transposition are incompatible patterns. The nested hierarchy thwarts an observer's attempt to impose a transposition explanation onto nature. It thereby allows the absences of phylogeny and gradual intergradation to be "seen" and take on real force as evidence against evolution.

Moreover, the nested pattern unifies life's great diversity, often in a visible way, by employing features above the level of biochemicals. The possession of common biological adaptations knits all life together into one system. Hundreds of years ago, scientists like Darwin and Buffon could see life's underlying unity, even though they had no knowledge of the pervasive unity at the biochemical level. Life is united by common design, not common descent.

A nested pattern is also resistant to lost or unavailable data. It retains its structure even when most of the data is missing. Take many life forms related by a nested pattern. Randomly pluck out a hundred, and they still display a nested pattern. The nested pattern is still visible even when most of the data is absent. The life forms still share common designs, and so look like the product of one designer. Patterns of transposition and phylogeny are absent, and that looks unlike evolution. The nested pattern is thoroughly resistant to noise. It can convey the biotic message with a minimum of data. It is the only simple pattern possessing these wonderful properties.

THE ARGUMENT FROM IMPERFECTION

One of Darwin's favorite arguments was the odd, "imperfect" designs that a capable engineer would not use. His favorite examples were the peculiar reproductive structures of orchids. He said such "bad" designs are evidence that life was not fashioned by a designer, but instead has an evolutionary history. That argument is now Stephen Jay Gould's preferred line of reasoning, he calls it the "panda principle" after his favorite example, the panda's thumb. Gould says, "Odd arrangements and funny solutions are the proof of evolution."

Traditionally, creationists tried to solve this problem by showing that the basic claim is flawed, and that the designs do serve a useful purpose. They have made real headway with their efforts, particularly by overturning virtually all the so-called "vestigial" organs. However, that approach has failed to give a complete solution. There is still something "odd and curious" about these designs.

I recommend the phrase "odd and curious" for several reasons. First, it gets away from the words "perfection" and "imperfection" which led inevitably to tangential or unresolvable discussions of philosophy and religion, rather than science. Moreover, "perfect" design can only be assessed with regard to the particular design goals, and Message Theory claims substantially different design goals than most people are used to. To keep people from becoming confused I prefer the phrase "odd and curious". Second, it is like the phrase "odd and funny" which Gould uses for the very same designs, therefore we are using essentially the same terms to describe the same portion of nature. Third, the phrase is appropriate, that is, the "imperfect" designs are better viewed as "odd" (functional but unexpected from an ordinary designer) and "curious" (intended to draw attention). With that clarification of the terms

438

we can now overturn the argument from imperfection.

First, by *many* evolutionists own statements on this issue, if they had the wherewithal to create life, then they would *independently* go forth and create perfect designs. Now simply turn their statements around — they mean that a world of perfect designs could easily be viewed as the work of *many* designers who acted *independently*. Evolutionists have effectively said so. Since life was designed to look like the work of a single designer, odd and curious designs had to be used. These operate like the funny quirks and odd imperfections in someone's handwriting, they allow us to identify the work of a single handwriter, whereas articles of perfect handwriting could be viewed as the work of many separate perfect handwriters.

Second, perfect design would not look like a message. It would provide no cues that it was a message. It would look precisely like the product of an ordinary designer who had ordinary intentions. Since life was designed as a message — as the product of an unordinary designer — odd and curious designs occasionally had to be used.

Third, no matter how good or bad a design, a biotic message sender is forbidden from using the same design over and over again indiscriminately, since the biotic message places constraints on the occasions when the same design can and cannot be used. For example, the human hand is wonderfully designed, but if pandas had the same hand then it would be trivially easy for evolutionists to "explain." They would have said it was the result of transposition — nothing could be simpler. Since life was designed to resist evolutionary explanations, a transposition pattern had to be avoided — therefore odd and curious designs sometimes had to be employed. Evolutionists could not ask for a more direct (and surprising) answer.

Another example is the vertebrate eye (such as our own) which has its light-sensing cells of the retina "reversed" and pointing *away* from the light. The squid and octopus have eyes remarkably like vertebrates, except without a reversed retina. Evolutionists recently made this an issue by calling the vertebrate eye "bad" design. Creationists have already made some headway in identifying why this is good design for organisms that use and maintain their retina in brighter light. That functional approach provides a partial solution, but Message Theory provides the remainder. Evolutionists once actually tried to explain the similarities between octopus and vertebrate eyes as the result of transposition. The explanation failed precisely because of substantial differences (such as the "reversed" retina and vastly different embryology) between the two types of eyes. Message theory turns the tables on evolutionists. Not only is the vertebrate eye highly functional (perhaps optimally so), it is also designed in a way that makes evolutionary explanation difficult. Our eyes and octopus eyes are so similar as to grip our attention and demand special explanation, yet they are sufficiently different that evolutionists are left to explain them as the result of completely separate evolution and highly improbable convergence.

Odd and curious designs are not randomly distributed in life, as one would sprinkle pepper onto a dinner salad. Rather, they have a pattern that serves the purposes of the biotic message. They do that in two ways: by unifying life (to look like the work of one designer), or by resisting evolutionary explanations. The classic examples are the so-called "hips" of whales, and the so-called "hind-legs" or spurs of pythons. With considerable success, creationists have argued that these serve useful functions for anchoring muscles, etc. Nonetheless these are "odd and curious" designs in the fullest sense of the words. In these cases, the designs serve to visibly unify diverse portions of life together.

A different kind of example is the wings of three flying creatures. The bat's wing is made by lengthening the four fingers, while the pterodactyl's wing is made by lengthening only one finger (what would be our little finger), and the bird's wing is made by diminishing the hand and providing it with feathers. Evolutionists claimed this is bad engineering, and that a capable designer would not experiment with different designs but would simply use the single best design throughout. Evolutionists are mistaken. These organisms share a common body plan, that unifies them as the work of one designer. In addition, the "odd and curious" wing designs cannot be explained by common decent or by transposition. Evolutionists are left to account for the evolution of wings (and *flight!*) separately for each case. Rather than being evidence for evolution, these organisms are clean evidence for Message Theory.

Finally, as always, evolution never predicted anything about the situation. Even Gould [6, p. 122] himself claims, "perfection could be ... evolved by natural selection." Gould merely used imperfect design as evidence *against* a designer (not for evolution). Phylogeny — not imperfection — is the real evidence of evolutionary history, and Gould is acutely aware of our inability to find phylogeny in the fossil record. Gould's argument from imperfection merely misdirected our attention away from the embarrassing absence of phylogeny. That is why he emphasized the argument from imperfection so strongly.

DARWIN'S RIDDLE

Darwin noted that the same biological designs are oftentimes not used for the same purpose in different organisms, and he used that as powerful evidence against a designer. Evolutionists still employ that argument; it is one of Stephen Gould's favorites. Darwin's Riddle asks: Why would life's designer use similar designs for *different* purposes, and in other cases use different designs for the *same* purpose?

We now answer that riddle in the most direct possible way. If the same designs were used again and again, in a random and indiscriminate way, then it would have been trivially easy for evolutionists to "explain." They would say it was the result of simple transposition. On the other hand, using the same designs in a nested hierarchical pattern will unify life without supporting a transposition explanation. The nested pattern places serious constraints on the occasions when the same designs should be used, and when they must be avoided. Darwin's Riddle is solved.

EMBRYOLOGY AND VON BAER'S LAWS

Organisms that are quite different as adults, often share striking similarities when they are embryos. Darwin felt such evidence for evolution was second to none. But as always, evolutionary theory never actually predicted anything about the situation. Embryonic similarities cannot be the result of simple conservation or "holdovers" from earlier evolution, because, as Stephen Jay Gould notes, "embryonic patterns are as subject to evolutionary change as adult form." [7, p. 26] In addition, natural selection cannot explain the situation, because, as evolutionist Douglas Futuyma notes, "There are no design constraints that require sharks and humans to have similar embryos and yet develop into completely different organisms." [5, p. 225] According to evolutionists, modern sharks and humans are separated by some 400 million years of evolution, yet still share striking embryonic similarities. This situation, common throughout embryology, is actually an evolutionary problem.

Message Theory explains the situation directly. Embryonic similarities are visible to the eye, unaided by microscopes. The ancient Greeks could see these similarities, which provided powerful evidence for the unity of life. Even the Greeks, who had a pantheon of many gods, attributed the creation of all life to only one of them (in their case it was Zeus). The idea of a single creator was prevalent in civilizations around the ancient world precisely because of such evidence. I suggest that embryology was intentionally designed with this goal in mind. Embryological similarities unify life in a *widespread* way that adult organisms cannot, and in a *visible* way that biochemical universals cannot. The embryological similarities are a manifestly obvious attempt to convince the observer that life came from one designer.

Von Baer's laws describe patterns of development, and though not perfect they are our best and broadest generalizations of embryology. They indicate that life forms tend to begin development near a common point and slowly diverge away from each other, like the spokes of a wheel. There are similarities between the embryos and roughly parallel paths, but each life form tends to have its own distinctive developmental pathway. This radial spokes pattern helps convey the biotic message in two ways. (1) The separateness of life forms is awkward for evolution to explain. (2) The embryos are often sufficiently similar to look like the product of a single designer.

The visible unity of embryology is aided by a special sequence, also described in von Baer's laws. Embryos tend to develop their generalized characteristics first, followed successively by more specialized characters. Thus, the vertebrate characters tend to show up before the tetrapod characters, followed by the characters of the amniotes, then mammalian characters, etc. This trend — from generalized to specialized — I call the von Baer sequence. The von Baer sequence is ideal as a means to visibly unify life. Because of the sequence, organisms tend to look similar for as long as reasonably possible before developing their unique specializations that differentiate them from other species. In addition, the von Baer sequence is quite awkward for evolutionists to explain. Generalized and specialized characters are system patterns that *we* can see, but evolution cannot. No evolutionary process can "see" generalized characters, much less sort them into a von Baer sequence.

The theory of recapitulation was first vigorously promoted by Ernst Haeckel (who falsified his data to support his ideas). Recapitulation theory was an implicit attempt to explain von Baer's laws, and could have been devised in an armchair with no further knowledge of embryology. The explanation was never made explicit for a simple reason: The explanation falls apart when offered for inspection. To this day, evolutionists have not offered serious explanations of von Baer's laws, and despite the fact that recapitulation theory was decisively overthrown by 1920, many evolutionists still embrace some concept of recapitulation. For all its failings, they simply have no better interpretation of von Baer's laws. Taken altogether, embryology is major evidence against evolution, and for Message Theory.

MOLECULAR SEQUENCES

Proteins, DNA, and RNA, are made of long sequences of a small number of molecules, like sentences are made of sequences of letters. For twenty years, scientists have analyzed the sequences with two pattern analysis methods: cladistics and phenetics. Cladistics examines life for a nested pattern, and confirms that it is a durable, widespread pattern. The nested pattern throughout life — including the molecular level — indicates that transposition has not had a significant effect at the molecular level.

Phenetics, on the other hand, examines the pattern of 'distances' between life forms. That pattern through life — including the molecular level — shows a pattern of smooth spanning distances that evolutionists proudly display in their textbooks. Let us call it the "phenetic pattern." The pattern is so smooth that, for a while, evolutionists interpreted it as the result of an evolutionary "molecular clock." (Though the clock hypothesis has been overturned, the pattern of spanning distances is remarkably smooth nonetheless.)

To understand the phenetic pattern we must look again to evolutionary theory and one of its major mechanisms — atavism — the masking and unmasking of genetic libraries, also known as genetic throwbacks. Conceptually, the process would operate as follows. Various genetic traits become masked (somehow) and remain hidden without the organism, inherited from generation to generation. Now and then the process would unmask various combinations of ancient genetic traits into new organisms living in new environments, and this would occasionally result in the sudden appearance of "new" biological designs. In principle, the mechanism could "transpose" characters through time into distant ancestors, and could even mimic the transposition of characters between lineages. If life had a general pattern of genetic throwbacks, then evolutionists would be pleased to weave one of their stories. "The masking and unmasking of genetic libraries," they would say, "obscured phylogeny and created large morphological gaps in life's pattern." In a flash they would explain away the absences of phylogeny and gradual intergradations.

The unmasking process is a lot like lateral transposition, and for precisely the same reasons, life's designer had to pursue its undoing. This was accomplished by designing life in special ways. Take any major biological design — bats, whales, spiders, or turtles for example — and it subtly resists being explained as a genetic throwback. That pattern was carried down to the molecular level, and is neatly displayed in phenograms of the various biomolecules. For example, if an ancient hemoglobin molecule were unmasked into a modern organism, it would stick out like a sore thumb on the phenograms. The molecular phenograms would reveal an unmasking process, if it were operating.

In theory, lateral transposition would transfer characters between species of different lineages that exist at the same time, whereas the unmasking process (atavism) would transfer characters between species of the same lineage that exist at different times. The combination of the two processes could, in principle, transpose characters between any species existing at any time. These processes provide powerful evolutionary explanations, yet life was designed to defeat all those explanations simultaneously. The remarkably smooth patterns of life — visible at the morphological level and reinforced at the molecular level — reveal an incredible degree of planning, and testify that life was not substantially affected by transposition or unmasking processes. Thus they allow the absences of phylogeny and gradual intergradations to exert real force as evidence against evolution. Contrary to what evolutionists have claimed, phenograms and cladograms are not evidence for evolution. Rather, these display life's unifying design, and provide essential evidence against evolution's simplest, most plausible, most powerful processes.

THE FOSSIL RECORD AND SEQUENCE

Despite all the careful construction of life, the biotic message would have totally failed without a fossil record, or if that record were viewed as seriously incomplete. In such a case, evolutionists would be exceedingly happy. "The missing fossil record," they would declare, "contains the phylogenies and gradual intergradations expected of evolution." Traditionally, that is precisely what Darwinians tried to do.

The biotic message sender had to convince the observer that the fossil record is sufficiently complete and reliable. *The only way to accomplish that task is with a special, distinct fossil sequence.* The fossil sequence is no accident. I suggest the biotic message sender acted to ensure its abundant formation. This was essential for the success of the biotic message. The fossil sequence had to be special, a pattern that validates itself and pronounces itself "complete." A pattern that says of itself, "I am a reasonably complete pattern. You cannot just brush me aside. I must be explained!" Pause for a moment and ask yourself, What kind of pattern must that be? A pattern that validates itself?

Our fossil sequence has the necessary pattern. Its components are "abrupt appearance," and, what evolutionists call, "adaptive radiation" — the rapid appearance of a burst of diversity built upon a new innovative design. If that pattern occurred just once, then the observer might say the fossil record (and the phylogeny) just happens to be missing at the necessary time. However, the same pattern — repeated again and again — whittles that explanation down. The record cannot "just happen" to be missing data at all the necessary places. Let me describe this another way. Remember that diversity thwarts lineage — diverse organisms in the "void" regions (orthogonal to a lineage) will thwart the observer's attempts to impose a phylogeny onto nature. Previously we examined this pattern in morphology space. Now we see this same pattern is visible within the fossil sequence. In the fossil record, the time dimension runs vertically, upward through the rocks. When diverse organisms appear near the same time horizon, *they are all orthogonal to any presumed lineage,* thereby preventing the observer from identifying any phylogeny. This pattern, repeated many times throughout the record, thwarts evolutionary interpretations, while simultaneously validating itself. This fossil sequence pursues the relentless task of convincing the observer that the record is reasonably complete and reliable. In fact, that is a major success for Message Theory.

Darwinians expected the fossils to reveal phylogeny and gradual intergradations, and when the record did not comply they shouted, "Incompleteness!" The punctuationists, on the other hand, see that the fossil record cannot be brushed aside as seriously incomplete. After two centuries of close examination, the punctuationists realized the fossil record is much more complete than previously thought. So they sought to read the record more literally and explain it as it stands. They sought to explain the situation by dramatically altering evolutionary theory. Most students know that punctuated equilibria attempts to explain abrupt appearances, large gaps, stasis, and the absence of gradual intergradations. The trade secret of punctuationists is that their theory was also devised to *destroy* phylogeny. They needed to explain why phylogeny cannot be seen in the record of life. Their peculiar emphasis of speciation, species selection, and "species as individuals," arose entirely from their attempt to construct an evolutionary theory which "predicts" that clear ancestors, lineage, and phylogeny, should rarely if ever be found. Many scientists mistakenly view punctuated equilibria as virtually the same as Darwinism. In truth, the two could not be more different and still be common descent.

Darwinists and punctuationists are having a heated debate. (They unite to assure the world that evolution is a "fact" and that they are merely debating the details.) They conceal the true nature of their debate with opaque discussions of "tempo and mode." In truth, they are debating how to explain the absences of phylogeny and gradual inter-gradation. The Darwinists say these are the result of an "incomplete" fossil record. The punctuationists say the incompleteness argument does not hold up, so they try to "explain" the situation with a theory. This situation represents a major shift in evolutionary thinking and a major victory for Message Theory. This is due to the fossil sequence and its unique ability to validate the completeness of the fossil record.

EARTH IS A UNIQUE PLACE

There are some peculiar things about our planet. Earth has an abundance of fossils — on land. All around the globe, from the lowlands to the tops of mountains, there are sedimentary fossils. Most of the fossils are *marine* invertebrates. Why are they not all underwater, at the bottom of the sea? Under normal conditions, fossils rarely are formed. Even then, plate tectonics indicates that rock strata are subducted into oceanic trenches, thus wiping clean the record. Why are there fossils at all? Why are they not eroded into dust? Or only the outside layers visible, like the outside layers of an onion? Or miles beneath the surface? Why is this tremendous fossil record stacked up on land, staring at us — utterly unavoidable to anyone who looks at rocks? It is as if the evolutionists' worst nightmare had literally risen from the sea. Earth has a unique ability to *preserve and display* its fossil record. This behavior is entirely unexpected of an ordinary planet. No other planet has the capacity to form — much less preserve or display — a fossil record. Yet a fossil display was absolutely essential for the success of the biotic message. This display is another key evidence for Message Theory.

Earth also has highly improbable features that are necessary for life. It has abundant water, and an average temperature in the narrow range where water is liquid. It has a nearly circular orbit, and a distance from the sun that keeps the energy flow suitable and constant. Earth's ozone layer and magnetic field serve to shield life from harmful radiation. If the rotation rate had been slower, then daily temperature variations would swing wildly beyond the tolerance of many life forms. If the rotation rate had been ten times faster, then the crust would have been highly unstable due to centripetal forces. In addition, the tilt of the axis is ideal for making the earth habitable. If the tilt had been smaller, then more of earth would be lost to polar ice caps and equatorial deserts. If the tilt had been greater, then nighttime for large portions of the earth would be six months long, severing limiting the survival of many organisms. Other special features of earth are its mass, density, radius, chemical makeup, atmosphere, and weather system. If these features had been substantially different, then life would not survive. The earth is an extremely unique place. Its ability to support life, and its ability to preserve and display an abundant fossil record are each highly improbable. Taken together they cannot be ignored. They are our clearest indication that life's designer possessed powers at least cosmological in scope.

DISCONTINUITY SYSTEMATICS AND CREATION SYSTEMATICS

The cladistic and phenetic methods no longer supply evidence for evolution. Therefore, a new method was invented for examining the remaining key evidences of origins. [8] That method, called Discontinuity Systematics, seeks to identify the boundaries of common descent. It does that by emulating a neutral scientist who views phenetic and cladistic patterns skeptically or agnostically. In other words, Discontinuity Systematics acknowledges the phenetic and cladistic methods, and formally sets them aside, so as to focus on other patterns. Phenetics, cladistics, and Discontinuity Systematics are, like three types of film (e.g., infra-red, ultra-violet, and x-ray), for the examination of different non-overlapping patterns of life. But phenetics and cladistics no longer help evolutionists. Discontinuity systematics is now the only biosystematic method that (even in principle) could provide evidence for evolution. Evolutionists universally used systematic methods to create the illusion of phylogeny. Discontinuity

Systematics sweeps aside those illusions and examines nature for a real phylogeny. Phylogeny is a central focus of the method, and I would argue that Discontinuity Systematics is the *only* truly phylogenetic method.

With the stated exclusion of cladistics and phenetics, the method looks at all other available scientific evidences of evolutionary continuity, including fossils, and modern experimental demonstrations of variation, interbreeding and reproductive viability. The method provides: (1) a well-defined means for studying and classifying a key pattern of life, (2) terminology for conveniently communicating and debating the results, and (3) a practical means of knowledge construction and compilation.

Discontinuity Systematics is a neutral means of examining nature for a specific pattern. Message Theory then scientifically explains that pattern in a seamless fashion. The two have a clean interface. The combination of Discontinuity Systematics (a neutral observational method), and Message Theory (a scientific explanation), can rightly be called Creation Systematics. Creation Systematics (like its counterpart, Evolutionary Systematics) is not neutral or theory-free, rather it takes a definite point of view and scientifically pursues it.

The systematic method identifies a complete set of common descendants, called a holobaramin. A holobaramin is very similar to a created "kind" (a term often used by creationists), but has a more refined meaning that eliminates the notorious ambiguities of that term. In classifying organisms by their descent, Creation Systematics provides information on the content and character of the originally created life forms. It also provides the means to identify and delimit the very real biological variation that does occur in nature.

CONCLUSIONS

According to the best scientific understanding, Lamarckian inheritance is absent from life, even though some evolutionists still look for it as a major mechanism of evolution. Likewise, simple processes (such as transposition, and the masking/unmasking of genetic libraries) have failed to impact life's pattern. Large-scale phylogeny, gradual intergradations, the naturalistic origin of life, and the discovery of extraterrestrial life, each stubbornly refuses to appear. Experimental demonstrations of biological variation fall far short of spanning the countless large gaps between types of life forms. In short, the evidence for evolution is systematically missing. The patterns that ought to be prevalent are non-existent.

Conversely patterns that are awkward for evolution to explain are abundant. Examples are: "convergences," the pervasive unity of life at the biochemical level (biologic universals), sexual reproduction, von Baer's laws of embryology, abrupt appearances of substantial new biological innovations, "adaptive radiation," and stasis within the fossil record.

Evolutionists universally complain about the creationists' "two-model approach" to origins. In truth, they have no basis for complaint. Evolutionists created the two-model approach. They fostered it as a way to sell evolution, and they still use it. The evolutionists' major arguments are, and always have been, arguments against a creator (not for evolution), and in each case that approach misdirected our attention away from deep problems in evolutionary theory. The absence from multicellular animals of enzymes for efficiently digesting the world's most abundant organic compound, cellulose, is a penetrating evolutionary mystery, yet evolutionists obscured that by turning it into an argument against a creator. In the same way, evolution never predicted the nested pattern, biologic universals, convergences, the patterns of embryology or molecular sequences, or for that matter, anything else in life. Evolutionists merely used these as convenient weapons against a creator they did not understand. Then they accommodated their infinitely flexible theory to the data, and crafted the most intricate illusion in the history of science — the idea that evolutionary theory has firm structure, that it is testable, that it is scientific. Evolutionary theory is not scientific because it makes no predictions that are actually true of life. For every major pattern of life, if evolutionary theory says anything clearly whatever, then it always favors an opinion opposite from what we observe.

Message Theory professes motives for life's design that are plausible, credible, and inviting. It is a surprisingly simple theory, and simplicity is not a fault, rather it is the mark of a truly potent scientific explanation. Despite its simplicity, Message Theory is comprehensive in its ability to explain all the major patterns of life. It does this directly, without bending in incongruous ways merely to accommodate the data. It readily solves many outstanding problems in nature, and sheds new light onto matters previously overlooked. The evolutionists' major arguments — Darwin's Riddle, Gould's panda principle, the Argument from Imperfection, biologic universals, embryonic similarities, molecular sequences, the fossil sequence, and the celebrated nested pattern — are all overturned in the most direct possible way, by showing that life was intricately designed to look unlike evolution. Life is a message from one designer.

Message Theory is also very testable, that is, it is empirically vulnerable. It makes many risky predictions. If the data were different, in countless possible ways, then Message Theory would be discredited. I cannot imagine a biological theory more vulnerable — or more contrary to the claims of evolutionists — than this one. This testability is why Message Theory is scientific, and evolution is not.

REFERENCES

[1] J. Cracraft, **Systematics, Comparative Biology, and the Case against Creationism**, Scientists Confront Creationism, 1983, L. Godfrey, Editor, W. W. Norton and Company

[2] R. J. Cuffey, **Paleontologic Evidence and Organic Evolution**, Science and Creationism, A. Montagu, Editor, 1984, Oxford University Press

[3] N. Eldredge, The Monkey Business: A Scientist Looks at Creationism, 1982, Washington Square Press

[4] N. Eldredge, Macro-Evolutionary Dynamics, 1989, McGraw-Hill Publishing Co., New York

[5] D. Futuyma, Science On Trial: The Case for Evolution, 1983, Pantheon Books

[6] S. J. Gould, **Evolution as Fact and Theory**, Science and Creationism, 1984, A. Montagu, Editor, Oxford University Press

[7] S. J. Gould, **Eight (or Fewer) Little Piggies**, Natural History, January 1991

[8] W. J. ReMine, **Discontinuity Systematics: A New Methodology of Biosystematics Relevant to the Creation Model**, Proceedings Second International Conference on Creationism, 1992, Editors: Robert E. Walsh, et al, Creation Science Fellowship, Inc., Pittsburgh, PA, Vol. II.

[9] W. J. ReMine, The Biotic Message: Evolution versus Message Theory, 1993, St. Paul Science, P.O. Box 19600, Saint Paul, MN 55119

[10] S. D. Schafersman, **Fossils, Stratigraphy, and Evolution: Consideration of a Creationist Argument**, Scientists Confront Creationism, 1983, L. Godfrey, Editor, W. W. Norton and Company

[11] F. J. Sonleitner, What's Wrong with Pandas? A Closeup Look at Creationist Scholarship, Available on disk from the National Center for Science Education, Berkeley, California, in his overview of section 6, and his excursion chapters 5 and 6.

[12] S. M. Stanley, The New Evolutionary Timetable: Fossils, Genes, and the Origin of Species, 1981, Basic Books, New York

THE BIBLE AND SCIENCE:
TOWARDS A RATIONAL HARMONIZATION

JOHN MARK REYNOLDS
FELLOW
BIOLA UNIVERSITY

KEYWORDS

Reynolds, Bible, hermeneutics, creationism, exegesis.

ABSTRACT

At the Society of Christian Philosophers Midwest Regional Meeting in 1992, I proposed a new mechanism for harmonizing and interpreting the Biblical accounts in the light of scientific data and theorizing. I also presented what I believed to be sufficient reasons for rejecting methodologies proposed up to this point. This paper received a fair amount of thoughtful criticism both during and after the conference. William Hasker has been particularly cogent in his criticisms through private correspondence with the author. The methodology is modified in light of objections received during this time period, as are the arguments leading me to propose the new scheme of harmonization in the first place. All objections aside, I argue that my initial proposal is fruitful, interesting, and worthy of further study.

INTRODUCTION

There is little question that few subjects engender as much passion as the question of the proper methodology for interpreting Scripture. I will attempt to briefly present reasons for abandoning both of the most popular methods for harmonizing the truth of Scripture with that of the natural world. This is not to imply that the persons holding these beliefs are "bad" Christians or that my position is somehow more sanctified. We are discussing a group of people who take the theories of science and data of the natural world seriously. It is possible to be handle both sets of data badly without intent to do so. There is a difference between being wrong and being a willful heretic.

The arguments over the status of Scripture and scientific knowledge result from the adoption of two prominent interpretative methodologies on the part of those who try to harmonize the two. These will be labeled the "Galileo Method," and the "Story Approach." First, I will attempt to show that the "Story Approach" to Scripture contradicts certain commonly held notions about the nature of God. My next task will be a careful analysis of what I take to be the more historically important and philosophically interesting Galileo Method. This method will ultimately be rejected. I will examine a new potential approach and discuss some of its implications on the current controversy.

THE STORY APPROACH

Many evangelicals have decided that the attempt to harmonize the data and best theories of modern science is a wrong headed one. The Bible was not written to be a science text book. In fact, it contains no data of scientific interest, except accidently. These scientists have abandoned "concordism" for a different approach. Most persons following this method believe that many of the Fathers and early Church philosophers give sanction to this approach. They would reject the notion that this is a "new" interpretative mechanism. With the example of Origen firmly in mind, I am inclined to agree with them. The Bible tells ancient stories in which one may find encased the living World of God. The theological truths of Scripture are there to be mined from the mythical tales that bear them. Just as Plato's μυθος in <u>Timaeus</u> provides a mechanism to delineate his views of the human soul (for example), so too the myths of the Bible aid in developing truth. They are not "false," but literary devices. I will call this the Story Approach (SA).

What do the proponents of the Story Approach say about the relationship between the Bible and science? These persons claim that Scripture is a vehicle for the truth of God's workings with humankind. Historic and scientific accuracy is not essential to the function of that vehicle. Looking for scientific or historical data from the text is foreign to the function of the text. The text functions as a "story" to relate a message. This is why I have labeled this the Story Approach (SA) to Scripture.

This seems an implausible view given the nature of the Christian God. (I am not making the stronger claim that such a view is utterly impossible.) The Story Approach assumes that Scriptures are stories packaged to convey theological truths to scientifically simple persons. The proponent of the SA cannot keep this view of Scripture and a sufficiently robust belief in God's absolute integrity.

One early problem for the proponent of the SA is in distinguishing between science and history. The fairly conservative person must hold that the Bible describes some historical events accurately, in at least some broad manner. To pick the most obvious and important example, if the Christ is not actually risen from the dead, the heart of the gospel has lost its meaning. (This is to ignore, of course, what might loosely be described as theological "liberalism," which would, in some cases, deny any bodily resurrection. The argument with historical liberalism is beyond the scope of this paper.) It is difficult, however, to pick and choose what accounts in the Bible one will take as "serious" history and what accounts one will label as myth. One cannot simply label all those accounts that are falsifiable "myth" and all those that are not falsifiable "truth." The apologetic and argumentative circularity of such an argument is obvious.

I think that there are two general approaches, both of which are faulty. In fact, this issue is one which has rarely been addressed by those who do not read the Bible as "serious" history. How does one distinguish between the false (or mythological) and the true? The quick and easy answer is to rely on some sort of literary methodology. C.S. Lewis, for example, takes this approach in all of his writings that are on the text of the Bible[5].

The problem with this approach is that it fails to clearly eliminate certain passages that cause the chief problems to modern science. Genesis chapter one might (conceivably) be described as poetry and read as such. On the other hand, it is difficult to read the story of the Flood as anything other than an account that the writer believed. What is the literary reason for discarding this story that could not also be applied to the Gospels? In short, the literary approach is a useful one. One does not want to read the poetry of the Psalms as "history" or treat the drama of Job the same way one treats the court history of Chronicles. It does not, however, solve the problem of passages, like that dealing with the Flood, that read as history, but seem to be false.

It might be suggested that there is a literary form called "myth." The early books of the Bible might be placed in this category of "false story containing deeper truth." (There are other possible uses of the term "myth," but this is the only use that would help the proponent of SA.) I would suggest that such a notion is, however, anachronistic when applied to Genesis. If one accepts the standard (liberal) view that Genesis was completed by the mid-fifth century, such a literary form would be foreign to the text[6].

The use of myth as a literary device is found first in the Pre-Socratic philosophers and Plato. The first philosopher, Thales, flourished in Greece around 585 B.C. Plato, who clearly used this device, did not flourish until the mid-fourth century. If one assumes the standard JEPD account for the construction of Genesis, then the large parts of the text were completed long before the sixth century. The text of Genesis was, therefore, already largely in place before "myth" as a literary device, in the relevant sense, was invented. The authors of Genesis were not likely to use a literary form that was not available.

The second general approach to the text is to hold to only the minimal amount of history in the text as possible. If the facts of science contradict a particular story of Scripture, then one can abandon that particular story. The historical truth of many stories in the Bible is, after all, of only peripheral value. One could fail to believe in a flood and be a Christian, but one could hardly discard the empty tomb. It is a difference in kind. What would, after all, be lost if the story of the ark is false[7]? On the other hand, it is highly unlikely that any "facts" of science will ever come into conflict with the Jesus coming out of the tomb.

I think that the chief problem here is caused by a Hume-like consideration. The gospels ask us to believe a very improbable thing. They ask us to believe that Jesus Christ rose from the dead. This is a difficult thing to believe, to say the least. The first witnesses to this event had two major arguments for the miracle of the empty tomb. First, there was the fact of the empty tomb and the eye witness accounts of the resurrection by those still living in the community. Second, there was the putative harmony of Jesus' life with the picture of the Christ found in the Old Testament. Later generations of Christians had only the written witness of some of those early followers of Christ combined with the witness of the Old Testament. In our case, our entire rational reason, apart from our own experience, for believing that Jesus is alive must come back to these documents and Church tradition. But if God, when He has spoken in the past has not chosen to communicate with humankind in a historically reliable way, why should we suddenly believe He is doing so now? The fact that the stakes are higher here at the empty tomb should make the questing heart more skeptical, not less.

The Flood's historicity impacts geology, while the empty tomb purports to effect all of eternity. Suddenly we are asked to trust the historicity of a record and a God who has not proven trustworthy, or who has not spoken historically before. The record has seemed historical in the past, has even sounded that way (like the story of the Deluge or the court histories of the divided kingdom), only to turn out not to be history after all. Those parts of the record turned out to be pleasing and plausible myth containing spiritual truth. It seems as least plausible to demand of a putative God that He demonstrate His historical competence to leave a trustworthy record in some easy area to verify by means independent of the text. A candidate would be the description of a major cosmological event that could be scientifically verified for all eternity. How can we, using our best reason, believe His putative record of an event (that by its very nature can never be verified) if such evidence is not forthcoming? It would seem to me that either one must take all the accounts of Scripture that read like the gospels as at least containing history or one must move to the more rigorous mythological view of Scripture advocated by Bultmann.

Let me hasten to say that this argument is limited. It is not always clear that a given account is historical, as opposed to poetry or a mere "story." ("Job" is a case in point.) If we use the gospels as a bench mark for what is Biblical "history," it is difficult to see how some scientifically difficult passages like that of the Flood can be eliminated on textual grounds. (It is important to stress that I am not arguing that the gospels are "history" in the modern sense. For example, "John" may not give a chronology of the life of Christ. It would be another thing to say, as some liberal scholars do, that Jesus never said, in substance, what the gospels claim He said.) If the Flood is eliminated as scientifically false, then one is left to ask why one should suddenly begin to trust the historicity of the gospels on "faith." On the other hand, some accounts, like the account in Genesis 1, are much less clear in terms of their status. I believe my position is a "middle ground" between the two extremes.

One final comment is in order on this issue of history and Scripture. I do not believe that the "history" of Scripture can be separated from the question of its scientific accuracy. If Jesus rose from the dead in history, then some scientific facts of the matter follow. I presume that certain molecules acted differently when Jesus came to life, as opposed to when He was dead. If the Flood was historical, then certain geological consequences follow. In cosmology in particular, science is simply the tool to find a history. How can one separate the task of the historian of the earliest times from that of the cosmologist? If Scripture contains history, then it has scientific implications. Scripture is not a science or a history book in the modern sense of those terms. It does, however, seem to relate events, like the resurrection of Christ, that happened in nature. The historic fact, if such as it is, of the Resurrection has a profound set of consequences for the very notion of "law" in science, for example.

The Story Approach has a further problem, however. Even if one can determine that certain accounts in early Genesis are stories or myths on some grounds independent of the desire to "save the phenomena" of Scripture, the advocate has a severe problem. One can see this in thinking further about the actual picture of God presented by SA.

Suppose God desired to transmit the theological truth that He was the creator of the stars. He wishes to make it clear that the stars are not gods. He decides to use the vehicle of a story, because the "natives" have only a "primitive" understanding of science. This is roughly the state that the SA thinker assigns to God and those peoples who first developed the early books of the Bible. Which would be preferable: a story that was accurate scientifically (so far as it goes) or a story that was inaccurate scientifically (where it does touch on science)? In most cases, God would clearly have the choice of developing either kind of story. It seems clear that the first alternative would be preferable. Why would an omnipotent and omniscient God use a false story to convey His truth? Surely, He could have designed at least a fairly- true one to convey the same message.

Of course, it might be conceivable to imagine a situation where no scientifically accurate message (within the limits of the primitive receptor's understanding) was possible. This is not the case most of the time, however. Without believing that God's purpose was conveying scientific truth, the philosopher could wonder why the Genesis story needs to be as inaccurate as it is (when compared to modern scientific theory.) It is certainly the case that of the myths present in the ancient world some were available that were more congenial to modern evolutionary theory (for example) than the one selected by the allegedly inspired writers of Genesis. Wouldn't the selection of the most accurate myth (in the realm of science) have been preferable to a myth that was almost entirely inaccurate? It seems absurd to think that if the one myth could be modified to convey religious truth that the other could not have been changed as well.

William Hasker, a noted philosopher at Huntington College, was kind enough to respond by letter to this argument. Hasker is a philosopher of religion that I owe a great debt in my own understanding of such problems as foreknowledge and free will. His writings are a model of philosophical rigor and Christian commitment. He says his ". . . sympathies. . . basically lie in the direction of what you term the Story Approach."[2]

Hasker believes that my description of Scripture and the Story Approach are flawed in several ways. First, there is a reasonable way to understand the possibility of God's transmission of stories. Second, the "ahistorical fundamentalism" implicit in my arguments creates a brittle epistemic position. The second criticism is an important one and I will save it for the end of the paper.

Hasker says, "I think your construal of this ("God's situation") is different from the one I would endorse in important ways. Your description seems to fit the situation of, say, a scientifically literate second-grade teacher who needs to explain to her class some scientific matter (say, nuclear fusion) concerning which they are incapable of understanding an accurate explanation. Here I think your conclusion would be basically correct: she should sacrifice accuracy as needed to make herself understood by her pupils, while still staying as close as possible to what she perceives as the scientific truth of the matter."

"The situation where Genesis is concerned is, as I see it, quite different. We are not dealing with small children who, while quite immature, are growing up within a scientific culture and are at least beginning to absorb a scientific way of viewing things. I think it is of the utmost importance to recognize that the very concept of science did not exist for the Old Testament writers or their readers."[2]

Hasker believes that God used SA as the method of inspiring the human writers because that is the best that those human writers could do within their cultural framework. He concedes in further correspondence [2,2] that when speaking of the Flood, ". . . there is little if anything in the text itself to indicate that this is not a straightforward history. . . . My reason for classifying the Flood narrative as saga or legend rather than history is that (in my opinion) there cannot have been "historical memory" at the time the narrative was written, of an actual historical Flood event of the kind that is described. And my main reason for saying that is that no Flood such as is described. . . actually occurred, as is shown by geological and archaeological record."[4,3]

Hasker is to be commended for the clear insight he has into the situation at hand for the exegete. He does not try to dodge the critical issues. The Genesis text seems to demand a world wide historic flood. He has, however, managed to bring two principles to bear in order to avoid this scientific disaster (as he sees it) for the student of the Bible. First, he allows himself to translate as saga those passages that are scientifically or historically impossible given the best of modern science. This position seems dubious to me for reasons given above. Second, he believes that the historic setting of the Biblical editors themselves forbids viewing the Old Testament documents as historic. Moses (to give the author or editor of Genesis his traditional name) could not have written history, per se, because history as a concept was foreign to Moses.

God would not have addressed scientifically illiterate people in the terms of modern science. The idea of science was certainly not in the scope of the ancient Hebrew writer. If the book of Genesis was written for one small Hebrew tribe in a scientifically illiterate age, then little more would need to be said. Hasker would have proved his point. Having conceded this, however, one is forced to ask if the Bible is not only a document for one time, but a document for all time? If God is speaking merely to the particular Hebrew situation of the moment, then the Bible lacks much interest for the modern. The historical context of Scripture is interesting and illuminating, but not exhaustive. The Bible (for the orthodox believer) is a message to all humans. This is certainly the case in theology where implicit theological truths not then understood (the serpent's head prophecy to Eve is a good example) were buried in the text for later generations to more fully understand. Hasker would concede the development of theology based on these texts. The texts themselves are true in ways that go beyond the theological context of the day of the human author. Why should it not also be the case in history or science? God certainly knew who would be reading the Bible.

I believe the Bible is interested in conveying truth to all humankind at all times. One is, therefore, forced to think of the target of the Biblical message not as one individual (Hasker's hypothetical student in a second grade class), but as a composite of all the individuals in all places and times who will read the account. It should, therefore, convey that truth in a manner understandable to the ancient and to the modern. It should preserve a maximal amount of truth for both readers. This would prevent a fully "scientific" explanation (since most ages in history were non-scientific in outlook), but it would also not permit God to ignore science altogether. God would be constrained to use a story that was as near to truth as possible. The truth of the account would be restrained by the limits of the comprehension on the part of the non-scientific reader. What was the theological message of the Flood? Is it that human sin brings divine wrath and divine mercy? If so, then why tell this important theological story in an utterly false account of a world wide Flood? Why not pick a better story? The ancients surely understand the difference between a true story and a false story.

Hasker sees the Flood account as being a theologically purified version of the Babylonian account found in the Gilgamesh Epic. He agrees that it is surprising that God would work that way, but correctly points out that one should not be inclined to give God advice on how the Bible should have been written!

This seems a hopeful approach for Hasker. It has the virtue of being tied to the facts. The Gilgamesh Epic is very old, and very similar to the text of Genesis. It seem to me, however, to be inconsistent with certain divine attributes. However, I think that there is a more basic reason to reject Hasker's picture of the construction of Genesis. Put simply, it seems to me that such an image of the Flood account fails because it is too plausible in detail when compared with Near Eastern Flood myths. Creationist scientists would find the process of developing even a simple scientific theory to cover the numerous details of the Epic an even more daunting task than that faced in Genesis! The ark of Genesis is at least a plausible ship-like vessel. The boat of the Epic, a perfect square, is not even a ship in the conventional sense. The Genesis redactor, if we grant Hasker his scenario, not only cleaned up the theology of the Epic, he clearly tried in his primitive way to clean up the science and make the story more "natural." (For example, he had Noah construct a boat that looked like a boat. He allowed more time for the waters to recede.) If Hasker is right, the crucial question is, "Why?"

God could have allowed the editor of Genesis to keep all the "silly" details of the Epic in order to demonstrate that the story was just a myth. This would have been in perfect harmony with the pre-scientific views of the Hebrew writer. Better yet, the editor could have added outlandish details to the Flood epic. The water could have been full of demons and the ship could have been built out of a fig leaf. If the critical thing was the theological detail, this would not have mattered. It would have been preferable because it would have made the later reader less likely to take it as sober history. Instead, God seemed to have used the editors (or they seemed to have acted on their own) to clean up the text historically. They make the story about as historically simple and as plausible as they could. This is hard to explain on Hasker's view.

The irony is that, given conventional scientific theory, the Genesis account is about as wrong as it could be. Other stories of divine retribution without such cosmological problems were available or were shortly to be available. On the other hand, given the Flood stories of the time, it is by far the most plausible. Hasker is in an odd position. He faces a flood account in Genesis too wrong to be divine (or true), but too plausible to be a good saga. What is a person arguing for SA to do?

What then of inspiration and the human author? I would theorize that inspiration, while fixed in the historical setting of the human author, goes beyond the limitations of that author. It is important to know the historic and cultural background of the human author, but only as a key to understanding the language and ideas of the text. One cannot ignore the historic setting, one might miss important clues to linguistic understanding, but inspiration is not limited by it in terms of meaning. The historic situation of the human author is not manipulated by God in the sense of a "dictation theory." Instead, God manipulates the selection of data already in the mind of the author to assure perfect results (or results that are as perfect as possible.) Thus, the ancient had no scientific concept of God to use. We should, therefore, expect no scientific treatises in Scripture. We find none. The ancient author did have a basic concept of truth and falsehood. This happened. This did not happen. These are not modern, Greek, or even very sophisticated notions. God wished, in a colorful and brilliant manner, to express timeless truth. He did so by picking the truest accounts He could get and by telling them in the truest way (scientifically and historically) possible given the cultural limitations of the human author.

Hasker rejects this notion of divine inspiration. He does not believe that God "manipulated the biblical writers so that, unknown to themselves, they wrote words that are (at least approximately) in accord with the scientific truth of the matter. In the words of Henk Geertsma, 'God does not send people to others with a sealed envelope.'"[2] He reminds us of the importance of the truth that often persons who criticize SA speak, ". . . as if the human authorship (of Genesis) were just an incidental detail that makes no substantial difference. Literally speaking, God did not write Genesis, Moses did (with the help of whatever subsequent editors, redactors, etc.)."[3,2] He points out that, in his opinion, no "conceivable inspired text could be such that major misunderstandings could not occur, given the human propensity for error. But to minimize misunderstandings, probably local and particularized references would be kept to a minimum, leading to a blander and less interesting book. This, of course, is just not what happened."

How can Hasker consistently hold this position? Is it not clear that the passage in Isaiah, for example, dealing with the virgin birth was not at all clear to Isaiah in its full Christian context? It seems clear that Isaiah thought he was talking about Hezekiah. Did the writers of the Old Testament understand the full import of everything they said? It is clear from Paul that they did not. They saw dimly what we see fully. In the same manner, one could argue that the writers of the Old Testament did not understand the full scientific and historical context of the stories that they were inspired to use in crafting their account of the world's history. The envelope was not sealed, but there were deeper meanings to the inspired message than the writer and bearer knew. How can one make sense of the gospels' attitude toward the Old Testament without such a belief? If the theological revelation of Genesis is allowed to have progressive and deeper meanings than those originally intended by the author (within the divine economy), then why should their conveyance of historical truth be limited? The writers did not act as dictation machines for the message of God. God could inspire them; however, to select stories and wording that would inspire new levels of truth finding in future readers from a different sociological context than that of the original authors.

Hasker, and those holding the SA, cannot (ultimately) hold their view in the light of these examples without adopting a further exegetical position. Hasker sums this position up, "Your counter-examples do not move me greatly. . . : I do not consider that the New Testament use of Old Testament passages is determinative with respect to the original meaning of those passages. One reason for this is that the New Testament writers often assign meanings that the Old Testament text simply will not bear- or they cite corrupt, even unrecognizable versions of the Old Testament text. (One example is Matthew 2:23, "He shall be called a Nazarene.') What I would say in those cases, is that a new meaning was added by the New Testament writers which was not the original meaning of the passage in question. That the new meaning was added is within God's will. The new meaning is edifying, spiritually profitable, and so on, but it was not part of the original meaning of the text. Let me hasten to say that I don't claim by any means to understand everything that is going on in the New Testament's use of the Old Testament, but what I have said does define the general contours of my approach . . ."[4]

Let us concede, for the sake of argument, that Hasker is right in his description of the Biblical text. My Biblical studies training does not lead me to quarrel with any of the details or data in his argument. His conclusions are, however, not supported by the data he cites. If one agrees that New Testament writers find further meaning in the Old Testament or other writings, this does not mean (logically) that they, in the will of God, placed it there. Short of Hasker's own principle of the "sealed envelope," it seems more natural to believe that they discovered a secondary meaning that was already there. The writers themselves believed they were finding meaning in the text. The difference between adding meaning to a text and discovering new implications of the principles of a text can be made clear by looking at two examples. Paul was fond of quoting Stoic philosophers. Paul was also fond of quoting Old Testament writers. No Christian that I am aware of would argue that the poems of Cleanthes were divinely inspired. Paul uses the text for apologetic purposes. The use he makes of the text contradicts the actual purpose of the text. He gives the words a new meaning. No Stoic would be likely to agree with Pauline appropriation of Cleanthes' poem.

On the other hand, Paul often builds on meanings implicit in a text that are not found in the direct context of the passage. These were meanings and understandings that were necessarily culturally implicit at the time of the writing of the text even if the author was not aware of them or able himself to formulate them. I would suggest that though science and history as concepts would await the ancient Greeks, the implicit concepts of historical accuracy are found in the detailed genealogies of Genesis whether or not the records themselves are historically accurate [8]. Seeing proto-history or something history-like, less than the Oxford History of England, but more than the Epic of Gilgamesh is to read into the text only what was necessarily there in order for such writings to be produced. One would not go the great trouble of producing long lists that "work" mathematically without having some of these basic ideas in mind.

The best example of implicit meaning being found in a text is Paul's use of the text dealing with oxen and grain. Paul makes an argument based on the text that is not foreign to the text. Indeed, I would argue that the image of "not muzzling oxen as they tread the grain" produced the principle in the mind of Paul. Implicit in the text was the larger principle that the laborer is worthy of his or her hire. One need not even assume that Moses was aware of this deeper principle as he wrote the commandment. The larger principle, part of the Mosaic world view formed the specific command. Moses was, as author, providentially shaped to think in certain essentially correct forms and patterns.

I would argue that the New Testament interpretations of the Old Testament are implicit in the paradigms, stories, histories, and images of the Old Covenant. The first born son of a maiden was an archetype placed by God in the text, even if Isaiah intellectually would have failed to realize its full significance. Far from carrying messages in sealed envelopes the Biblical writers, like all great authors, said more than they meant.

This argument does not get one an infallible Bible in terms of history and science. It does not go as far as I might like. It does, however, prevent one from getting a Bible that has nothing to say in those areas. The big details would simply have to be right in a story like the Deluge. The Hebrews may not have been scientists or historians, but they clearly had the first concepts that would form science and history. I would argue that these concepts included a knowledge of the differences between false and true accounts, the knowledge that care needed to be taken in the transmission of information, and the understanding that knowledge of past events could be a powerful took to be used or misused. The Hebrew writers or editors were capable of writing essentially true accounts. Why would a reader believe that a truthful God help create a text that was not accurate in these areas?

The Christian god is usually held to be perfectly truthful in all his dealings. God, in the words of the Bible, "is not a man that he should lie." This attribute is taken to be a necessary feature of a morally perfect being. What would this mean? An example might clarify the issues involved.

Suppose one scientist, Hope, wants to tell another person, Aino, about a scientific experiment. Aino, a musician, is not capable of understanding all the mathematics involved in Hope's highly complex work. Is Hope deceiving Aino by giving her a rough-and-ready explanation of the experiment? I think that our intuition is that Aino has not been deceived. Aino has been given the best explanation she is capable of hearing. This intuition might be made more formal in the following manner:

*1:   It is possible that a being x is perfectly truthful, if   and only if x is as accurate as x can be in conveying information to any being y.

Notice two implications of this definition. First, this is not a sufficient definition of perfect truthfulness, it is simply a necessary condition. Second, as with our earlier example of Hope explaining the science experiment to Aino, the being x can be perfectly truthful and still be at least somewhat deceitful, if such deceit is accidental in dealing with certain sorts of not-very-knowledgeable beings.

To expect any Scripture to be accurate (fully) would be to prevent a god from speaking (meaningfully) to scientifically "primitive" peoples. A fully accurate message from an omniscient God would be very long and complex account indeed. It is doubtful that even modern society would understand it. As we have seen Hasker attempts to argue that this means God has no need to prove an account with any scientific accuracy. I have shown that this is going to far. Definition *1 does not prevent God from telling the most accurate possible story given His message and the limitations of the best possible messenger. God might be prevented from delivering the full <u>Origin of the Species</u> to early humankind, but it would also prevent him from delivering the Genesis account (assuming the truth of evolutionary theory). It is hard to imagine that the Genesis account is the most accurate possible story, even taking into account ancient language limitations. Many mythologies, including those of the Asian Indians, have been taken by scientists to harmonize more neatly with an evolutionary cosmology.

The theologically conservative person arguing for the SA believes that God is introducing new theological truth using a story. This truth is of such a profound meaning that it still retains great spiritual import thousands of years later. God is introducing this new truth through the medium of a person to whom it is "new" revelation. Yet this same God, who can devise a story to transcend culture in the case of theological truth, cannot seem to do so in the case of empirical data. He cannot, for example, devise a creation story that follows an evolutionary framework. In fact, He is forced to rely on a story that is pretty much false scientifically.

Is this at all plausible? One might claim that the scientific truth is so complex in comparison with the theological truth that the one was possible to convey to a primitive society while the other was not. This does not seem like a very hopeful objection, however. If evolution is true, it is not difficult to crudely describe it. Philosophers such as Empedocles did this in a rough-and-ready way in the ancient world around the same time as the completion of Genesis. The mechanism and details of evolutionary theory are highly complex. I am not suggesting God had to give these. But would it not be the case that a roughly evolutionary account of God's creative acts would be preferable to roughly non-evolutionary account (if evolution is true)? God was capable within the context of the ancient world of relating a coherent, roughly evolutionary account of creation. In fact, it is necessary if He is to be seen as potentially a being that is perfectly honest.

Another example will demonstrate this point. How complex is the concept of the Earth being very old? It does not seem inherently any more complex a concept than the "young earth" genealogies provided in the Biblical chronicle. The account of an "old earth" would no more have to detail the complexities of geological history, then the genealogies of the actual Old Testament have to give the science behind the aging process in order to be understandable.

If God had said through the prophet, "I made the world. I did it long ago.", there would have been no conflict with modern scientific theory. <u>In the final analysis, why would God use a story at all?</u> If the account could not be told with a (reasonably) accurate story, then why not give the theological truth and be done with it? Was this false information put there to <u>test us</u>? The whole notion begins to sound incredible.

The proponent of SA cannot argue that the purpose was literary merit. There are many beautiful evolutionary cosmological accounts in ancient literature. The Greeks certainly told some stories that harmonize (factually) much better with modern science than the Genesis account. God could have told a story like theirs, <u>but with the proper theological content</u>. If God speaks through stories, then the Bible is probably not the best candidate before the reader of a divine story.

It might be argued in the end that all of this misses the point of the SA. Scientific truth is just not, at all, the thrust of Scripture. The Scripture is no more interested in science than is J.R.R. Tolkien in <u>Lord of the Rings.</u> Tolkien created a story, a very lovely story. In doing so he conveyed certain religious truths about the actual world to some people. The scientific accuracy or inaccuracy of his story was irrelevant. To call such a story inaccurate, or less accurate, when compared to another is to miss the point of myth.

There is something odd about this argument when applied to Scripture. The proponent of SA usually believes that Scripture is, in some way, the revelation of God's word to humankind. Why is God disinterested in conveying to humankind generally accurate knowledge about the world along with "spiritual" knowledge? One can readily attribute a motivation to J.R.R. Tolkien for doing so. Creativity itself allows an unlimited variety of themes based on the score of creation. It is difficult to see why God, who is perfectly true in all His ways, should wish to do so in his primary word to Humans. A composer does not write a variation, before writing the main theme.

The God of the SA is placed in a non-falsifiable position. He tells the truth in His Word only in those areas where empirical verification is impossible. He does this for no apparent reason. He does this in language that suggests empirical content. The SA seems very unlikely.

What can the proponents of SA make of all of this? Hasker has suggested that my statement *1 is too strong. He proposes:

1':   It is possible that a being x is perfectly truthful, only if x never deliberately misleads any being y except where this is warranted by some morally overriding objective.

I do not think that *1 is in fact too strong. I am tempted to think that the phrase "morally overriding objective" in 1' is too ambiguous to be very useful. For all that, however, I believe that 1' does capture an interesting and important notion about God's nature. Since God is morally perfect (unlike humans) there is no need to fear selfishness in His objectives.

What are God's morally overriding objectives in the case of misleading the world regarding early human history? Hasker believes, in the light of Proverbs 25:2, that God does not reveal things in a full way so that humankind may have the pleasures of finding these things out.

Hasker argues that the fact that some persons are deceived by the approach taken in Scripture is not of great consequence. He says, "I would say. . . in the language of double effect, that the fact that some people are misled is 'foreseen but not intended' by God." God cannot be held responsible for our blindness and folly. God is very clear regarding the plan of salvation, an area where humans could not reason their way to truth and where error would have eternal consequences. God fulfills the requirements of 1'.

I agree that God is clearly not responsible for every off the wall reading made of the text by David Koresh or a seminary professor! In these cases of course, it is not God who deceives at all. 1' would not apply to eccentric or confused readings of difficult passages. God can also conceal an item that He does not wish us to know. The principle of double effect does apply to God.

Most of the people of faith in most places at most times misread the book of Genesis if Hasker reads it correctly. Hasker even concedes that on textual grounds alone it is impossible to tell that Genesis is not somewhat historical. On the face of it, this seems far more like a massive and harmful deception, than a misunderstanding. It does not strike one as a secondary affect of reading, but a primary one. (Of course, this assumes that Hasker knows what God intended the text to cause primarily.) Hasker has four options to explain this appearance of deception:

(A)   The text deceives and does not meet the requirements of 1'. the text is not from God or God is not perfectly truthful.
(B)   The text deceives, but the deception escapes condemnation under 1' by being compelled by serious moral objectives.
(C)   The text is from God, so the errors must not be real but imagined. The errors must be in current scientific theory or in our reading of the text.
(D)   The deception was not God's intent. The deception was the result of human failure; therefore, neither God nor the text were involved in deception.

Option A is unacceptable to Hasker as a Christian. Option B would require serious moral objectives to be served by such deceptions caused by Genesis. It is difficult to see what such objectives would be, nor does Hasker supply any (with the exception of believing that God delights in our seeking such things out for ourselves.) Option C is the traditional approach and would include the work of most creationists. Hasker rejects such "concordism." Only option D delivers God from the charge of deception, but I have already shown that D is implausible.

What would a deception look like that was not part of my moral responsibility? It would look nothing like the deception caused by Genesis. Intent alone is not enough to shift moral responsibility. It is not my fault only if you take me the wrong way (given no intent on my part to deceive) and a reasonable person would not take me the wrong way in the context of what I had to say. If I shout to you that there is a snake in the grass (knowing secretly that the snake is made of rubber), then I cannot blame you for being afraid to venture into the yard. I cannot say that the deception was not my intent and blame you for your fears. A reasonable person in your position could not know the truth from what I said. I have deceived you through my lack of clarity. My lack of bad intent does not deliver me from the responsibility not to unintentionally deceive by meeting common standards of clarity. I must speak so that my audience can reasonably be expected to understand what I am saying and not be deceived by it, otherwise such deception and the consequences of it are my moral responsibility.

One might apply the reasonable exegete standard to the Bible. Would the reasonable exegete in most places and in most times be led to fairly serious errors by the text? If she would, then the text deceives, whether the author's wish was to do so or not. A reasonable exegete is led astray by the Bible time and time again according to Hasker. The audience for Scripture, particularly the initial audience, was led to totally false conclusions about the world because of the text.

The deception and errors of the Genesis are not a secondary effect of the text. If in fact several theories of modern science are true, error is a primary result of reading the text. The false history and the bad science cannot be weeded out from the true theology. One does not blame the gardener for weeds that spring up in his garden, but it is another thing altogether if the gardener plants them there or idly watches them grow.

It seems to me that the theological truths of Scripture are inextricably linked to the story and its details that worsen this tendency to deceive. Paul, for example, in Romans makes important arguments based on the federal headship of Adam over humanity. This compounds the initial problem. Instead of letting the deception that Adam was "real man" rest or revealing it through his use of the story, Paul is inspired to repeat the story in such a way that the deception is only increased.

The SA person cannot even argue that the Biblical accounts are illuminating fiction. A novel by Dickens is not true, but it is life-like. As a result, we can treat it as true for the purpose of learning certain lessons. In so far as it is not life-like, the message of the book is weakened. (A character who acts in an improbable manner weakens the thrust of the book.) Assuming that the science and history of Genesis have been falsified leaves them more in the position of fairy stories. They are tales of things that did not happen and that more importantly could not happen in the world as it is understood by modern science.

An appeal to literary beauty would not help Hasker, either. The story "Cinderella" contains (I presume) several interesting lessons. I cannot say, however, that I take these lessons more seriously because they are, in the words of Disney, "in the sweetest story ever told." The fact that the story of Cinderella is not true weakens our attention to its moral message. It is just not the sort of thing that actually could happen, so its value as a lesson is diluted. Modern feminist writers have had a field day with this very point. Women who wait for their Prince might as well be waiting for their fairy god mother. The same can be said for the Fall and Flood accounts. They are certainly not the sort of thing that happens in our experience. They are also, if modern science is to be believed, wildly improbable.

Hasker cannot escape 1'. God does deceive people, if we believe that the science and history of Genesis are not true. Double effect cannot deliver God from this charge.

There is a further problem. Hasker has missed another important condition for perfect truthfulness. I would modify 1' to:

1": It is possible that a being x is perfectly truthful, only if x never deliberately misleads any being y except where this is warranted by some morally overriding objective z and x misleads y only to the minimum required to bring z to pass.

This addition captures the intuition that a morally overriding objective will not justify any lie, but only that lie which will achieve a moral end. For example, the person hiding Jews from the Nazis is justified in telling some lies, but not just any lie. They may only tell lies (if they wish to remain perfectly truthful) that advance their moral end. One could not, for example, tell the guard that she was a full professor of Biology at the University of Amsterdam or that the moon was made of green cheese. One would be fully justified, according to 1", in denying that there were no humans in the basement even if there were humans there in order to save lives. A person should deceive the guard only to the extent needed to safe guard human life. The person hiding the Jews should not, for example, continue their deception past the point where it is necessary. One should not over elaborate on one's deception. There is no reason to tell redundant lies.

This leaves Genesis a huge problem for the person holding to the truth of SA and 1". Genesis, if modern science is to be believed, is shot through with unnecessary false hoods. What moral end, for example, is secured by telling or including the story of the Tower of Babal that could not have been served by a much less deceptive means? If Genesis contains scientific errors, and so the SA person argues, then it contains many errors that fail to meet the requirements of 1" that such misleading be done minimally. Genesis elaborates on its myths with long genealogies that serve no function in a SA. They are not true. They do not contain moral teachings. Why are they there? They are redundant falsehoods and fail the test of 1". One could easily imagine God inspiring a person to tell a false concealing story, but in such a case it would lack redundant false detail. Hasker will have to explain why Genesis is as "wrong" as it is.

I should make one final point about my own position. I do not believe that the science or history of Genesis is hopeless. I am not totally happy with any current harmony of Genesis with the data of science. I believe there are, however, grounds for thinking that progress can be made in this area. Personally, I cannot conceive of morally sufficient grounds for God to deceive humankind about the creation event.

One final point should be made about Hasker's approach. Hasker believes that it is the place of humans (kings) to find things out that God conceals. This is Hasker's overriding moral reason for God's deception.

The problem for Hasker is that creation is not the sort of event that humans could "know" on their own. If God, for example, created with the appearance of age or history, then how could a human being ever discover this fact? The age of the cosmos has great theological and metaphysical implications and yet that is the very sort of question that science can never answer with certainty. God was the only being present at creation according to all Christians. Events like creation are not repeatable. Creation is a singular event. Why would God conceal something that by its very nature only He could know? Since this impacts humans whole image of themselves, why would He do so?

If the SA approach is valid, at best it seems to be a method of showing that the Bible probably does not contain the Word of God:

(1)   God used stories to convey theological truth.
(2)   If possible, a story that is more scientifically accurate is preferable to one that is less accurate. If it is not possible to be more accurate, an inaccurate story is acceptable to fulfill 1.

OR:

(2)   God should tell stories that deceive humans as little as possible.
(3)   It is possible to think of a simple Eastern story more accurate scientifically (given the claims of modern science), then the Genesis account.
(4)   God always acts in the best possible manner.

Therefore: The Bible is not the Word of God.

This is clearly not the intent of those who have developed the SA method. However, if each premise above is true, then SA has an unintended result. The key to the argument is premise two, which Hasker and the followers of the SA would modify or deny in important ways. At the end of the day, I have yet to hear an important modification or defense of the SA that would lead me to deny the conclusions of the argument, if the SA is the only way to go.

Why should we accept Scripture? This is a complex issue, outside the scope of this paper. I believe it must be based on more than a personal experience with God, though such experience is vital. What assurance do we have outside of ourselves and others like us, who may be deceived in the same ways, that this Bible is the very Word of God? Surely, it is important that there be some independent confirmation of the reasonable nature of our faith in Scripture. I do not believe, in the end, that Christian faith in the Bible's message lacks empirical content. The apostles pointed to an empty tomb. Modern Christians do not have the luxury. We have only a text. Can that text be trusted to tell Christians the essential truth? If it is clearly wrong in its science and history, areas where moderns have the sharpest insight, should the Bible be trusted in the much murkier areas of faith and ethics?

THE GALILEO METHOD AND THE GRAND THEORY SOLUTION

The scheme of harmonization I have labeled the "Galileo Method" was described by Galileo Galilei in his treatise The Authority of Scripture. He says, "Since the Holy Writ is true, and all truth agrees with truth, the truth of Holy Writ cannot be contrary to the truth obtained by reason and experiment. This being true, it is the business of the judicious expositor to find the true meaning of scriptural passages which must accord with the conclusions of observation and experiment, and care must be taken that the work of exposition do not fall in to foolish and ignorant hands."[1,519] Galileo then proceeds in this section to harmonize the account of the sun standing still found in the Book of Joshua with his heliocentric view of the cosmos.

This method of harmonizing Scripture with empirical data makes the interpretation of the Bible dependent of scientific fact. Roughly speaking, Galileo would have the Christian read the Bible through the lens of empirical data. This has become a common approach to the interpretation of the Bible within certain Christian circles.

This view has one basic advantage. It gives the person approaching the Bible a means to solve certain interpretative puzzles. The legendary (and somewhat mythical!) arguments over a flat or spherical earth are a case in point. Either reading could find Scriptural support. For example, the Bible speaks of the "four corners of the Earth" in Revelation 7:1. This could be interpreted poetically (as all evangelical commentators do now) or it could be interpreted literally. If interpreted literally, one could extrapolate from this reference to a rectangular Earth. On the other hand, Isaiah 40:22 which says that, "It is He who sits above the circle of the Earth. . ."[12] might be seen as textual support for a spherical Earth. This is especially true if it is read in the context of Job 26:7.

How does one decide which way to read the text? On the Galileo Method, the solution is simple. Modern science has determined that the Earth is spherical. Since Scripture is true, it must actually teach a spherical Earth. All references that seem to imply otherwise must be harmonized with the scientific data. Where science is silent, the exegete is free to pick the interpretation most natural to the text as a whole.

There are two essential problems with this methodology. First, it makes Scripture potentially non-falsifiable. Second, it frequently fails to take into account a distinction between observations and the conclusions based on observations. It is overly simplistic and too trusting of whatever scientists of an age happen to accept.

If this approach is adopted, then it is difficult to see under what conditions the Bible could be shown to be scientifically false. The persons accepting this notion are committed to the truth of the Bible when it relates to science and empirical data. There is something troubling about the fact that there is no built in limit to the amount of accommodation possible. What is meant by the statement "The Bible is true" if accommodation proceeds past a certain point? The persons holding this view would need to clarify how far they are willing to stretch language before giving up the initial premise. As the argument stands now, the Bible could theoretically be made to say the opposite of its "plain sense" and still be defended as "scientifically accurate." This is disconcerting. I read the Galileo Method as arguing the following:

(1)   The Bible is true when it describes the world.
(2)   Certain facts of Science are true about the world.
(3)   In every case, if two things are both true about the world, then they do not contradict each other.

Therefore:

(4)   The facts of science and the descriptions of the Bible do not contradict each other.
(5)   When the facts of science and the descriptions of the Bible do seem to contradict each other, then the descriptions of Scripture must be reinterpreted in light of four.

There is a two-fold problem with this argument. First, it depends on the unstated philosophical assumption that the empirical data that reaches the senses is more reliable than the human interpretation given to Scripture. This is a debatable presupposition. I am inclined, however, to grant the proponent of the Galileo Method this assumption.

The second problem with the argument is the failure to distinguish between an observation of science and a conclusion or theory of science based on the observation. The argument assumes that all scientific disagreement must be decided by changing the interpretation of Scripture. But is this plausible? Perhaps some theories of science are tenuous enough to make one wonder whether an elegant Biblical exegesis should be abandoned when they conflict. There are certain facts of experience (objects generally fall when dropped, the world is roughly spherical) that seem to be more intuitively certain than certain other human interpretations of data (certain issues of chronology, or cosmology).

The proponent of the Galileo Method appears to forget that just as Scripture is dependent on a hermeneutic for understanding, so science is dependent on an interpretive framework for comprehensibility. All the "facts" or "theories" of science do not have the same epistemic certainty.

The advocate of the Galileo Method accepts both the truth of Scripture and the reality of certain scientifically observable phenomena. He or she remembers Ockham's Razor in relation to scientific theories and chooses the simplest interpretation to fit the data. But the proponent of the Method has forgotten that as a presupposition of his or her work the Bible is also true. This assumption has equal presuppositional status within the argument. The simplest exegesis of Scripture is also to be preferred[9]. Perhaps in balancing the two theories a slightly less elegant scientific theory that preserves a remarkably elegant Biblical reading is preferable to a slightly more elegant scientific theory that produces a tortured exegesis.

In the Galileo Method argument, the truth of Scripture and the phenomena of science carry equal weight. What has been assumed is that the "facts of science" are just that, facts. In most cases, the "facts of science" are interpretations, which are more or less plausible, to explain certain phenomena. The phenomena themselves have a high degree of intuitive plausibility, but the theories have much less. It is perhaps possible, as W.V. Quine suggests, that two mutually contradictory theories could be postulated to explain the phenomena.

Theories of science are epistemologically similar to interpretations of Scripture. Both are good in so far as they explain the data at hand. It is not always a matter of some brute fact conflicting with a particular reading of Scripture but one interpretative framework confronting another. This weakens the plausibility of the conclusion of the argument.

Lines one through four of the argument form a valid argument, though one can reserve judgement on the truth or status of the individual lines. Line five, however, depends on the faulty epistemological notion that all the conflicts are between "Biblical interpretation" and "scientific facts of the matter" for its plausibility. In some cases, the conflict is between two interpretative frameworks of varying elegance and simplicity.

I would like to suggest that scientific "fact" and "theory" operate more like a continuum. There are certain brute facts about the world. These are very certain descriptions about the cosmos. An example might be, "there is a tree." These should take priority over any interpretation proposed of Scripture. If the Bible seems to say that there is not a tree over there, then (if the Bible is true) the simplest exegesis would have to be modified. An actual Biblical example might be Jesus' description of the mustard seed. He describes this seed as the "smallest" of all seeds. The most natural interpretation would be that, in fact, there were no smaller seeds than the mustard seed. Of course, science might find a smaller seed. In this case, the "fact of the matter" and an interpretation of Scripture conflict. Scripture must be reinterpreted if it is to remain "true." Another example is the prophesy that declares "a virgin" shall conceive. Contextually "virgin" is not the most natural interpretation. Further revelation in the New

Testament reveals to the reader that the obvious or natural interpretation is not always the best or "right" one.

On the other hand, some natural interpretation of Scripture based on the whole of the text might conflict with some theory of science. If there is another interpretation of the data that preserves the natural meaning of the text, it is to be preferred. I take it that evangelicals wish to preserve the most natural meaning of scripture if possible.

This model of interpretation might be based on two scales:

A. BIBLICAL KNOWLEDGE	B. SCIENTIFIC KNOWLEDGE
III. Allegorical / Mythological (possible)	III. Highly Complex Theory (possible)
II. More Complex Exegesis (plausible)	II. Fairly Complex Theory (plausible)
I. Natural Exegesis (probable)	I. Simplest Theory (probable)
Raw Data of Text	Phenomena of the Cosmos

The scale would allow for gradations between points. The object of the person harmonizing Scripture would be to get the simplest scientific theory in combination with the most natural possible exegesis. All evangelical theories of the world must include both the input from Scripture and the input from science, so that the simplest coordinated theory would be preferable. This might be called the Grand Theory (G.T.) describing and resolving conflicts around the phenomena.

The extreme end of the scale (point III) should be avoided in the G.T. if at all possible. A theory that contains a major component that is barely possible (despite the fact that the other major component is a probable explanation) is not as intuitively satisfying as a theory that contains two fairly plausible components. Hence, on the assumption that both natural and divine revelation are equally valid, one would desire as balanced a G.T. as one could get.

I do not claim that this would resolve all conflicts between science and Scripture. The question of whether a probable reading of scripture combined with a plausible scientific theory would be preferable to a probable scientific theory combined with a plausible reading of scripture is not yet resolved. For example, I would take the argument over the day-age interpretation of the Hebrew word "yom" in Genesis 1 to be such an issue[10].

It would resolve many types of conflicts between science and Scripture. A case in point is the historic controversy over the movement of the Earth. The bulk of the Bible seems to support a still Earth on the most natural reading of the text. Such a reading would be a position (I) reading. The Aristotelian theory of the cosmos was for some time a position (I) scientific theory. There was no conflict between science and Scripture: both divine Revelation and scientific theories were in the "best" positions. Following the introduction of the evidence supplied by certain late Medieval natural philosophers, the Aristotelian theory remained plausible but no longer was the most probable theory. However, on my view the Church was right in maintaining the classic unmoved earth position at that stage of the dialogue. Only when such a position became mathematically and observationally "hopeless," should the Church have abandoned it[11]. This it, in fact, did.

This theory also has the virtue of being ultimately falsifiable. Only possible interpretations of Scripture and possible scientific theories are permissible. If a Hebrew word, for example, will not bear a certain translation at all that a given scientific theory makes necessary, then Scripture will be shown to be false. If on the other hand, one should give priority to Scripture (and this issue has not been resolved by this paper), then a given scientific theory will be shown false by an absolute contradiction with the Word. My theory has the value of removing the possibility of this ultimate conflict from most attempts at harmonization.

CONCLUSION AND FINAL REFLECTIONS

My proposal places the Christian in a potentially destructive apologetic position. "Evidence that show Scripture to be mistaken will destroy the foundation of the Faith." This could happen. It is also a fact that the best current science, by which I mean the majority theories in several scientific fields, point away from the truth of the Genesis account. Since one can still be a Christian and accept something like the SA, and since the arguments against the SA are by no means the sort that "utterly defeat" the approach, why not just adopt the SA? Hasker, as usual, sums it up best. "We have the following three propositions, each enjoying significant support:

(1)   The Bible is the vehicle for God's revelation, in which we learn (among other things) about redemption from sin and the gift of eternal life.

(2)   If the Bible is the vehicle of God's revelation, then what it says when it speaks in matters of science

and history must be at least approximately correct, within the limits of the capacity of the original readers to understand.

(3)   The contemporary sciences of astronomy, cosmology, and geology are correct in the broad outlines of what they say about the history of the earth and the universe.

Each of these propositions, as I have said, enjoys significant support-- yet, when we add to them the manifest content of Scripture they cannot possibly all be true. The question, then, is: Which one should be rejected? . . ."

Hasker eloquently contends that 2 should be rejected. He points out the staggering loss in scientific terms for rejecting 3. He also points out the great spiritual loss of rejecting 1.

I do not believe that Hasker can, however, keep science and history distinct from the revelation of Scripture. My arguments have led to the conclusion that such attempts founder. Hasker's points one and two inevitably collapse in on each other leaving us to reject the totality of revelation or the modern theories of science. If this is true, then my new harmonization schema is the best candidate left on the field. Creationists must then proceed to construct better theories of science to compete with those that currently hold sway.

If, however, Hasker can sustain his separation between 1 and 2 despite my arguments to the contrary, his approach is the most prudent for Christians to take given the current state of affairs in the sciences. Prudence, however, need not hinder academic risk taking. Christians can, despite the risks involved, attempt to create an alternative scientific paradigm that will allow the theories mentioned in point three to be replaced. Such a new view would be worthwhile in avoiding the seeming conflict, a painful one for many of us, between Scripture and science. I would argue that my Scriptural harmonization scheme be used during this attempt. If such an alternative science can be developed, Hasker himself would seemingly be congenial to it. This leaves the creationist philosopher and scientist with a daunting, but exciting challenge.

ACKNOWLEDGEMENTS

I wish to acknowledge Daniel A. Reynolds for providing theological input, despite his busy work as a graduate theology student. Hope E. Reynolds and Joseph Bailey also contributed to this project in many important ways. My special thanks to Phillip Johnson whose rigorous writings have inspired my desire to seek Truth Itself. I am eternally grateful to Fieldstead and Company and Biola University for the fellowship that made this work possible. The conclusions and errors contained in this paper are, of course, my own and not necessarily those of any of the persons mentioned here.

REFERENCES

[1]   Galilei, Galileo, **The Authority of Scripture**, Outline of Great Books, Editor: Sir J.A. Hammerton, Wise and Company, New York, NY, 1937.

[2]   Hasker, William, **Letter to Author**, 9 December 1992. Used by by permission.

[3]   Hasker, William, **Letter to Author**, 21 March 1993. Used by by permission.

[4]   Hasker, William, **Letter to Author**, 21 April 1993. Used by by permission.

[5]   Lewis, C. S., **Reflections on the Psalms**.

[6]   O'Brien, J., and Major, W., **In the Beginning: Creation Myths form Ancient Mesopotamia, Israel, and Greece**, Scholars Press, New York, NY, 1982. (They cite a composition date of around 587-539 B.C.).

[7]   Review comments by Peter VanInwagen of Syracuse University on this paper.

[8]   In other words, I am not commenting on their accuracy one way or the other. If they are not accurate, the author showed by the care taken in composing such a precise list (with dates that, for example, have no patriarch but Noah living past the date of the Flood) that such historic care was lurking in the shadows at least. Such lists could not be composed without many of the basic principles of historic research being implicit in the mind of the author.

[9]   In using the terms "natural" and "simple" to describe Biblical interpretation, I am not committed to any one hermeneutic. Perhaps, a natural interpretation is one that is coherent and agreed on by all parties.

[10]   Let me be clear about my own position. For exegetical and theological reasons, I reject the "old Earth" position.

[11]   I should say that this is not a justification for the Inquisition. Rejection of a theory and the persecution of its proponents are two different things.

[12]   All scriptural references are form the New King James Version.

GOSSE AND OMPHALOS:
A DEFENSE OF AN OLD ARGUMENT

JOHN MARK REYNOLDS
FELLOW
BIOLA UNIVERSITY

KEYWORDS

Gosse, Reynolds, age of the earth, appearance of age or history, philosophy, creationism.

ABSTRACT

Philip H. Gosse presented an argument related to the age of the earth in 1857. This argument has been widely criticized by both creationists and non-creationist. Despite these wide spread attacks, many creationists make use of the "appearance of history" argument found in Gosse. Is such usage valid in the light of the many complaints of the concept? I try to formulated a clear and sound version of the Gosse arguments. I find the criticisms of Gosse unsound and the argument at least somewhat helpful to modern creationism.

INTRODUCTION

In 1857 Philip H. Gosse, an ornithologist and creationist [2, p.324], published a work entitled, <u>Omphalos: An Attempt to Untie the Geological Knot</u> [9]. This work contained an argument that has formed a part of many creationist's explanation of apparent history beyond that allowed by their interpretation of the Biblical record in the universe [7]. It has also been attacked by non-creationists as "empty" and "irrelevant."

In this paper, I will attempt to show that the omphalos argument is coherent and potentially helpful to certain attempts to reach a "creationist" [10] cosmology. In doing this, I will argue that much of creationist literature does not deal with the omphalos argument and objections to it in a respectable manner [11]. For all that, the standard objections made to the omphalos argument fail. Second, I will attempt to show that there is a good reason, apart from the argument, for some Christians to believe that the argument applies to actual history. Finally, I will suggest an opening move in creating a creationist philosophy of science that this argument suggests.

Before beginning this attempt, it is perhaps necessary to make a few "disclaimers" about the purpose of this paper. It is not an attempt to "prove" the scientific truth of creationism. I also explicitly reject the notion that "evolution" and "creation" are mutually exclusive and the only logical alternatives in origin's science. My dissertation work is on Plato's <u>Timaeus</u> which I take to be a cosmology which is neither evolutionary nor creationist. This paper will, therefore, do nothing to disprove any theory of evolution. The omphalos argument could be modified to harmonize with a desire for a "short history" evolutionary scenario. To be "helpful" to a creationist theory is not to attack an evolutionary theory. This paper is also not committed to any particular view in the debate over whether creationism is scientific [3].

GOSSE AND GOSSE HISTORY

A formal rendering of the Gosse argument as it might be used by a <u>creationist</u> (as I have described creationist) could run something like this:

(1)   God is omnipotent [8].
(2)   God created the universe at some time t1.
(3)   At the moment of creation t1, no state of affairs S existed in the actual world W such that God could not create an object O with the appearance of history [12].
(4)   Therefore: At t1 God could have strongly actualized a world with the appearance of history [13].
(5)   Therefore: (with x and n standing for any given amount of time) At t1 or t1+x the appearance of history in an object O which makes it appear that O existed at (t1 or t1+x)- n, is not equivalent to O existing at (t1 or t1+x) - n.

(6)   Therefore: Any object O that appears to have history did not necessarily exist at each moment in that history.
(7)   From 3: The universe did not exist prior to t1.
(8)   Therefore: The universe, which has an apparent history of t1-n, did not actually exist at t1-n [14].

Premises 1 and 2 are accepted by many within the Islamic, Jewish, and Christian traditions. Premise 3 is more controversial and is the crux of the attacks on the Gosse argument.

The attack on Gosse occurs on three key fronts. First, the critic asserts that Gosse has opened a Pandora's box. If Gosse is correct, then it is possible that the world was created at any moment. There are infinite numbers of possible moments of creation from which to choose [15]. Isaac Asimov claims that this makes the argument, "irrelevant, for it can neither be proved nor disproved" [1]. Robert Schadewald asserts that such an argument is empty since "an infinite number of mutually exclusive creation epochs and/or creators can be invoked." Second, it is argued that even if Gossean histories are possible, there is no good reason to reject "apparent" histories in their favor. Third, if one postulates the God of the Bible, the creation of the appearance of age is seen as being inconsistent with certain divine attributes. Since the Gossean creationist is usually within the Islamic, Jewish, or Christian tradition this is seen as a potent objection.

The standard creationist response to critics is similar to that of Henry Morris in The Biblical Basis for Modern Science. He says,

"To say that God could not create something with the appearance of age is the same as saying He could not create anything at all. Such an assertion is tantamount to atheism" [4].

Morris makes some other points, but this is the heart of his response to the critics. How adequate is it?

I believe Morris has missed the mark in his response [16]. He says:

(1)   God must create with the appearance of history (which Morris mistakenly calls the "appearance of age") to create.
(2)   To exclude the notion of appearance of age, is to therefore deny creation.
(3)   Since God must create to be God, to deny the appearance of history is equivalent to atheism.

Morris' argument flows from premise one. However, premise one is clearly false. It is not logically necessary for God to create with the appearance of history. The Gosse argument only claims that it is possible that he did so. One can imagine a possible world where, for some inscrutable divine reasons, God creates everything without the appearance of age. He could, for example, place within every object a clear token of its actual age. I am not, of course, saying God did so in the actual world, but he could have. This means that the first premise on the Morris "argument" is false. The argument, therefore, fails.

It is not clear where the argument is going in any case. The argument concludes by saying restrictions against the appearance of age lead to atheism. If the appearance of age is flawed, as the critic claims, and Morris insists on it, then it is Morris who has shown that his God cannot exist. . . not the critic. Let us, however, examine the attacks of the anticreationists to see if a better response could have been given by a Morris-style creationist.

I believe the first criticism of Gosse, that he postulates an infinite number of potential creations, misses the target. The critic believes that the Gosse-Morris style creationist is defending some particular model of creation. The Gossean argument does not prove that this model is true, since it also postulates an infinite number of other possible creations.

The Gosse argument does lead to the conclusion that it is possible that the world was created at any given time. This means that the Gossean argument does not prove some particular notion about when the universe was created. In fact, it introduces a strong element of skepticism about ever knowing when the cosmos came to be based only on the appearance of history. This may be a conclusion that the anticreationist (or anti-Gossean) dislikes, but to dislike an argument is not to refute it.

The Gosse argument does help the modern creationist. It is not as strong as the creationist might hope, but neither is it empty. The claim is made by the majority of scientists that the universe has the appearance of a history. If appearance of history is equivalent to actual existence at every point in that putative history, then creationism has been empirically falsified. But if appearance of history can be separated from actual existence, then the game is not over. The creationist will still have to show why one should not accept some particular moment of creation over another, but creation remains a possibility. If one has a Creator, then one is logically forced to admit the possibility that the moment of creation is not necessarily tied to the appearance of history.

The critic might then respond by arguing that this is, therefore, a good reason to deny the existence of a Creator.

Why open this box at all? This does not "help", however. The atheist could generate his own Gosse-type problem. How do we know that our apparent history was not generated by some evil scientist who keeps us as brains in an experimental vat? It is possible for the atheist that the appearance of history in the universe is wrong. Such arguments are exceedingly hard to refute [5].

The Gosse argument, therefore, rescues the creationists from the problem of the appearance of age to a limited extent. It prevents creationism from being falsified, it makes it possible. It does nothing, however, to make any given moment of creation more probable. This is an important limitation for creationists to keep in mind. Given the infinite number of possible creation moments now opened up, the creationist will have to show by further argument why the one postulated by his or her reading of the Bible should be selected.

The skeptic might respond that for all of Gosse's success in making a different point of creation possible, one should still accept the moment postulated by the scientific evidence. Why should a skeptic reject apparent history for any speculative Gossean history? Is not the most probable of the possible histories the one backed by the empirical data?

This second argument against the Gosse claim is an important one. It suggests that even if creation is possible, that one should still (if rational) accept the weight of evidence and go with "apparent history" over any other choice. The critic of Gosse feels that there is some advantage, and I would tend to agree, in preferring the history postulated by appearance over any of its possible competitors. This might be argued on grounds of simplicity or economy.

What if there is, however, great advantage in postulating some particular Gossean history for the universe? A rational person might decide that because of some large epistemological or ethical advantage gained by accepting certain religions postulating an "early" creation of the universe, that this was the best or most rational choice. In other words, it is plausible to think of a person having good reason to prefer some possible Gossean moment of creation on rational grounds.

What would such a person have given up? Less than might be thought. The person would still claim that rock x, for example, had the appearance of history y. She could even discuss y using standard methods of science. She could then, however, rationally state that of course this history was only a useful thought experiment, a possibility rejected because of some important advantage gained by a religious or philosophical system that postulated another logically possible moment of creation. She has denied no evidence of science or her senses. She has only denied a philosophical theory connecting that evidence with reality in a strong sense. She has done so on rational grounds.

Many critics might hold that this is not enough. They might demand any even stronger reason for postulating a Gossean history. I believe such a reason is found in the incompatibility of God's nature and the failure to create with the appearance of age. In short, for God to be what Christians claim God is, there must be an appearance of age. This sounds suspiciously like the earlier creationist argument made by Morris. In fact, given the usual insight displayed by Morris, it may have been the intent of his original comments. I am not claiming that I know what God did or must do within his sovereign will. I am fairly skeptical about such arguments. I am claiming that one standard attribute of God, namely His divine wisdom, is incompatible with the failure to create with the appearance of age.

Suppose a certain man foolishly claims to be perfectly wise. He then goes and mows his lawn. He mows his lawn using a pair of tweezers, leaving the usable lawn mower aside. He has no good reason for doing so. It would seem that this action would disqualify the man from perfect wisdom. A perfectly wise being is at least as efficient as he or she can be in order to achieve his or her ends. Put more formally:

Axiom 1:   For every being x, it is possible that x is perfectly wise if and only if x brings about every state of affairs y that in a manner z, such that x could not have brought about y in a way more efficient than z.

Axiom 2:   For all actions z and q and all states of affairs a, it is possible that an action z is more efficient than an action q if and only if z brings q to pass in the least possible amount of time.

Please note that these are necessary, but not sufficient attributes for a being to be perfectly wise or perfectly efficient.

Such constraints would of course allow for overriding reasons for behaving in "foolish" manners. The man with the tweezers might have some odd, but valid reasons for using tweezers. If the man had a good reason for cutting the lawn very slowly, his method might be justified and he might still be a candidate for perfect wisdom. On the other hand, as long as his desired end is achieved (an adequate lawn cutting in a simple case), the quickest method would the most efficient. All things being equal, the man who cuts his lawn with tweezers would not be a candidate for perfect wisdom.

Consider then the creation of the world and a perfectly wise being, God. God must act in perfectly wise manner, which means (minimally) that He must act in the most efficient manner possible. Before the creation of free will beings, all events in the universe would unfold in a regular and perfectly controlled manner. There would be no possible cosmic event that could justify the cosmos actually existing. The existence of the actual world and the unfolding of the world in the mind of God would necessarily be exactly the same. On the other hand, with the creation of free will beings the "interesting" portions of cosmic history would begin. God would need to create the world at that point. It would be far more efficient to create the world with the appearance of history, <u>even if God used evolution as a process</u>. An "old earth" is incompatible with God's perfect wisdom. It is simply a waste of time! Contrary to Morris, one can imagine a god creating with no appearance of age, just not a god who could be perfectly wise and do so. Since Morris and Gosse both believe that their God is perfectly wise, Morris and Gosse must both believe in a creation with the appearance of age.

There are no possible reasons for God actualizing the creation before the appearance of free will beings, because there is no possible action or state of affairs contrary to the will of God. Every intent and purpose of God would have been necessarily actualized in a creation without free will beings. What could there be in the state of affairs leading up to the creation of free will beings that would create a rational purpose for such actual existence of the cosmos? Let me suggest, therefore, that a Gosse history tied to the appearance of angels and humans is the natural one for a Christian who has a perfectly wise God.

Notice that this argument does not prove that the universe was created by the Gosse/Morris god. It also does not prove that the universe was created with the appearance of age. It does show that a person believing in a potentially perfect creator (like Gosse and Morris) either is forced to believe in Gossean histories or has to perform the very difficult task of finding even a potential reason for the superiority and efficiency of an actual history to a Gossean history. The Morris/Gosse believer has, therefore, an independent reason to believe in an apparent history. He has also a potential time, the creation of humans and angels, for the actualization of that history. It also leaves the critic of Morris and Gosse to wonder how she will believe in a perfectly wise God and an old earth at the same time. It places Morris in the stronger position in the midst of traditional Christian believers.

The third criticism of Gosse is an attack on premise three of the Gosse argument. It says that there is a state of affairs such that God could not create with the appearance of history. To do so, they argue would be inconsistent with the state of affairs where God is omnibenevolent at t1. To create with the appearance of evil would be to deceive. If one postulates the Jewish, Islamic, or Christian god, then such deception is inconsistent with God's character.

It is important to note that this is not (once again) a refutation of the Gosse argument. It simply argues that premise 3 of the Gosse argument is inconsistent with other beliefs of a Gosse or Morris about God. A gnostic or some other types of theist would have no problem with this objection. It does seem to prevent the argument from being used by the very persons who developed it, the creationist. If God did not choose to create with the actual age being equivalent to apparent age, then the God of Gosse and Morris cannot exist. He would be "internally inconsistent."

This argument can be responded to in two ways. First, I believe that one could be a consistent theist in the Morris-Gosse tradition and still believe in a God who deceives (in at least the one sense of deceive covered by the omphalos problem). Second, the Gosse-Morris person could argue that God did not deceive humankind. There might be sufficient evidence to make the notion of the age of the universe an uncertain one.

The notion that a good God could deceive seems at first an odd one. I believe sense can be made of it, however [17]. First, one must decide what is meant be deception. I believe most persons recognize at least two sorts of deception:

    (1)   giving false information
    (2)   withholding or obscuring some relevant information (thus allowing a person to reach a wrong conclusion).

Why would deception be wrong for God? God commands humans not to do it as part of the Ten Commandments, but that does not mean that God cannot do it. Things God forbids to humans, like taking life, are not forbidden to God. The Scripture is not clear on this issue either. "God is not a man that he should lie," but on the other hand He sends a spirit to deceive Ahab to bring about his (just) destruction.

We might generate two notions about God that are not contradictory from the Biblical evidence (which is the evidence Gosse and Morris accept):

(1) God does not deceive us to our harm.
(2) God may deceive us, if it is for our own good.

We might speculate that God does not lie in the first sense. He does not give <u>false information</u>, but he may with hold some relevant information from us if it is for our good.

God could, therefore, be trusted in what He has said. We could not, however, extrapolate beyond what He has said to speculate about the implications of what He has said with equal surety, because He may not (for good reason) have given us all the facts. Clearly some information in the hands of humans would be a very bad thing. God's obscuring certain types of knowledge (like the means to build certain types of weapons) may be the only things that allow humans to survive with free will and curiosity.

How does this relate to the Gosse problem? The critic might respond that the "apparent histories" are deceptions in the first sense. This is incorrect, however. There is no <u>necessary connection between the appearance of history and actual history.</u> God did not say that the world was created at time t1-n. The world simply appears to be that way. The Gosse argument or a modified "brain in a vat" type argument proves that <u>apparent history is inadequate to make this sort of determination without philosophical presuppositions to help choose which of the possible worlds we will choose to believe is actual.</u> In the case of a "Gosse history", the universe obscures the truth, therefore God "deceives" in the second sense.

How serious would the results of such an omphalos deception be? Schadewald says of a Christian God who creates with the appearance of history, "He creates an elaborate trap and then tortures the victims. . . who fall into it." Schadewald seems to believe that the Morris-Gosse God damns those who are mistaken about origins.

This is wrong, however. Christians do not believe that one's views about origins damn a person. I have already pointed out that Christians differ amongst themselves on this issue. The matter of origins alone will not damn a person. The issues of the time of creation do not have eternal ramifications, though they may have great temporal importance.

What could God's purpose be in obscuring this information? I can think of two possible motives. One must be careful, however, in this sort of speculation and acknowledge that though one can think of possible reasons for God's actions (or even probable ones), there is no means of actually determining if they are the real ones. It is adequate for our purposes, however, to demonstrate that there are fairly plausible motives for God's deception, even from a limited human point of view.

First, one must view the creation event from God's point of view. Up to the moment when God introduced free will agents into the universe, the actions of the universe were just those actions which God wills. There is, therefore, nothing of interest to the Divine Mind that occurs in the universe before the introduction of persons into the cosmic equation. (This, of course, assumes a Gosse-Morris theology.) There would be no reason for God to actualize pre-Adamic history, because it would be a fully determined path until the first free will agent's appearance. The universe could be created at the moment of human history <u>as if the proceeding natural history had occurred</u>, because no random or "unforeseen" events took place in it. From God's point of view, creation with appearance of age is economic.

This would not "allow" God to dispense with creation altogether, however. Once a free will agent was introduced into the cosmos (Adam), actual history becomes a necessity. God could not "predict" the outcome of the Adamic struggle with sin.

Second, from a human point of view our lack of total knowledge about origins may help to preserve our free will. If we <u>knew</u> in some strong sense that creationism was true, then only the utterly irrational could choose to reject God. We would become slaves to our knowledge. Since the Gosse-Morris God wants rational beings who freely choose to love him and, in the words of Augustine, pursue a "faith in search of understanding" some uncertainty in the area of origins might be necessary. On the other hand, even with the "apparent age of the earth" accepted as an actual age, it is still possible to come to a "saving faith." Examples were cited earlier. Therefore, this deception (in the second sense) preserves our free will and provides God economy of action without necessarily increasing the chances that humankind will reject God [18].

What am I arguing? I am suggesting deception by the Morris-Gosse God need not be inconsistent with His being all good. The God of the creationists could deceive, in the second sense, for our good. It is possible to think of some fairly plausible reasons why He would want to do so. There is no logical contradiction between an omnibenevolent God and a God who creates with apparent history.

This is different, of course, from the notion that God could just tell humans any useful lie for their won good. God must act to protect his ignorant children, but He must do so in as honest a manner as possible. He could not, for example, say that a Flood had happened when no such event took place. What would be the moral purpose served in telling outrageous lies?

The idea that God could deceive (even if limited to a second sense) may shock some theists. I would point out that God has not, even in the Bible, given humankind all the facts. Jesus spoke in parables, by his own admission, to obscure the truth. Unless God were to make humans omniscient it is difficult to see how, with all the data there is in the universe, he could fail to "deceive" (in the second sense). However, it is not necessary to accept the notion of a deceitful God to save the Gosse-Morris God from the charge of "internal inconsistency."

If Gosse and Morris were to reject any notion of God's deceiving (and perhaps there are some theological reasons I have not thought of that will force them to this position), then they still have a potential answer to the critic. The critic suggests that the universe has an apparent history. Gosse has shown that apparent history need not equal actual history. There is now some reason to be skeptical about apparent history. Before Gosse's argument, it was sufficient to accept the best apparent history to rationally determine the actual history. Small bits of contrary data could be discarded until fit into the general theory, because there was no good reason to doubt the general picture. Following Gosse, every piece of data that challenges the general apparent age of the universe should generate "Gossean skepticism" about the relationship between apparent and actual history. Conventional acceptance of the relationship between apparent history and actual history has ceased to be a matter of data but a matter of philosophy. Even all the data speaking for one age would guarantee nothing, thought it might make one data more interesting on some philosophic grounds. On the other hand, the smallest bit of hard data pointing away from that data should now make the observer ask very hard questions indeed.

The person who does not know of the Gosse argument picks the view with the most evidence. He has no reason to think the evidence could fail to say what it seems to say. Knowing (and accepting) the Gosse argument, however, would cause the investigator to examine the evidence for the age of the Earth carefully. Some small amount of irrefutable evidence for a "young earth", combined with some powerful philosophic or religious reasons for accepting such a "Gosse history" would now seem sufficient to allow the rational person to decide in favor of some model other than that suggested by the majority of "apparent history." But what does all of this have to do with the argument about God's putative deception in creating the cosmos with an omphalos?

God has not deceived us if the question is in a muddle. Given the Gosse constraint, anything less than a universal witness for one date by all the physical data would seem to leave God clear of the charge of deception. The creationist can, if he can point to non-empirical reasons to believe in a young earth and some scientific evidence for a young Earth argue that God has left the notion equivocal at worst. It is a pretty sorry deception if the planner (despite his intention to deceive and his omnipotence) leaves traces of his deception in the field of operations. Robert Gentry's work with polonium halos, if it had been successful, would have provided exactly the sort of evidence I am talking about here. In fact, it seems that Gentry's work has failed to do what he hoped, but it does provide us a model of what such evidence might look like [19]. In other words, God does not deceive if:

    (1)   He personally speaks to humankind and tells them roughly when He created the cosmos.
    (2)   He leaves powerful non-scientific reasons for accepting the message of 1.
    (3)   He leaves some traces of actual age in addition to the tricky omphalos in the physical world.
    (4)   There are plausible reasons that can be given for his creation of the world with an omphalos.

The creationist would have to argue for 1 on philosophic grounds. She would also have to reach 2 by the same methodology. It would be the job of the creationist scientist to search for 3. The creationist theologian would carry on 4. This is a research program of some magnitude. Earlier I suggested some ways several of these problems might be resolved. In any case, short of accepting some notion of a deceptive God, this would be the task before creationists.

In taking up this task, let me briefly suggest an approach to science suggested by the Gosse argument. Creationists wishing to make use of Gosse will also have this general line of reasoning open to them. Using language like that used by W.V. Quine in Word and Object in dealing with issues of philosophy of language, let me suggest that creationists begin to think of cosmological theories as being empirically underdetermined [6, p.26-30]. It seems rational to expect, given successful arguments like the Gosse argument, that two equally explanatory theories of the universe that were logically incompatible might be possible. Such theories might, for example, both equally explain the history of the world. One would postulate an ancient history and the other a recent Gossean history. Both would be logically incompatible. Only one could be right (though of course, neither might be right.) They could, therefore, co-exist forever. Neither could harm the other.

Let me stress that the fact that this construction of an alternative cosmological theory might be possible does not mean that it has been done (it has not), nor even that it can be done in a manner that would please a Morris-Gosse creationist. It might be that in some given area of science that only one theory can be constructed to answer all the data well. We simply do not know. However, it does give creationists some bare hope for their project without laboring under the necessity of falsifying evolution. One need not, I am suggesting, show evolution to be false in order to allow creationism to thrive. In fact, given the possibility that two logically incompatible theories could thrive simultaneously such an attempt is probably a waste of time. It is not, of course, a waste of time to show that modern evolutionary theory is underdetermined. Phillip Johnson has done an excellent job of doing this in his work Darwin on Trial. The important thing is to see if creationism can explain the data of science. At this point, I am sure that with sufficient accommodation of beliefs on the part of its followers that the theory of evolution will do well. If held to with sufficient tenacity almost any large scale theory can be saved, even if it is at great epistemological cost.

CONCLUSION

In summary then, we have seen that none of the attacks on the Gosse argument attempt to refute the logic of the argument. The critics only assert that the argument does not help Gosse-Morris style creationists. It does not help Gosse-Morris creationists as much as they might have hoped. It does, however, show that "appearance of history" does not immediately falsify creationism. It also sets up a research program for creationists in many fields. Gosse has provided creationists with a valuable tool. How could Gosse be defeated? It appears to me that only if it is possible to strongly refute general skeptical arguments (of which I believe the Gosse argument is a type), could one fully refute the Gosse claims. Since creationists should only use the Gosse argument to open up the possibility of their view, and since "refutations" this strong of skeptical views are hard to come by, I believe the Gosse argument will remain valuable to creationists for years to come.

ACKNOWLEDGEMENTS

I wish to thank Mary Ann White, Dorothy Ross, and Hope E. Reynolds for the invaluable time spent discussing this project. Phillip Johnson has helped form the basis for much of my thinking in areas of origins. His input and wisdom were invaluable. My sincere gratitude is also extended to Fieldstead & Company and Biola University for the fellowship which made this project possible. Any conclusions and errors are my own and not those of the brave souls listed here.

REFERENCES

[1]   Asimov, Isaac, **Armies of the Night**, Philosophy and Contemporary Issues edited by Burr and Goldinger Macmillan, New York, NY, 1984, p. 476.

[2]   Bird, W.R., The Origin of the Species Revisited, Philosophical Library, New York, NY, 1989, page 324.

[3]   The best book on this issue I have read that argues that creationism is science is Christianity and the Nature of Science by J.P. Moreland. Langdon Gilkey deals with several related issues in a readable manner (with the opposite conclusion) in the second half of his Creationism on Trial.

[4]   Morris, Henry, The Biblical Basis for Modern Science, Baker Books, Grand Rapids, MI, 1984, p. 175.

[5]   For a discussion of the "brain in the vat" problem see John L. Pollock, Contemporary Theories of Knowledge. He attempts to refute skepticism about our past. My point is not that the atheist must believe he is a brain in a vat, but that it is always going to be possible that he is one. This is not much, but it means that history and existence are not logically tied to each other.

[6]   Quine, W.V. World and Object, M.I.T. Press, Cambridge, MA, 1960, p. 26-30. Let me stress that Quine is dealing with philosophy of language and translation. The language employed here is "Quine-like." I doubt Quine would endorse such a broad application of his views here. I am confident he would reject any favorable implications for creationism.

[7]   It is important to note that not all Christians would accept this interpretation of the Bible. Many conservative Christians would reject it. See the excellent books The Fourth Day by Van Till and The Galileo Connection by Hummel for examples.

[8]   "A being x is omnipotent in a world W at a time t = df in W it is true both that (i) for every state of affairs A, if it is possible that both S(W,t) obtains and that x strongly actualizes A at t, then at t x can strongly actualize A, and (ii) there is some state of affairs which x can strongly actualize at t."

        This definition of omnipotence, which I think to be the best available, is taken from:

        Edward R. Wierenga, The Nature of God, Cornell University Press, Ithica, NY, 1989, p. 25.

[9]   It would be best if the reader understood my comments to refer to a "Gosse-like" argument. For the sake of brevity, I will label all such "Gosse-like" arguments as those of Gosse. I am not attempting to replicate the actual historic argument advanced by Gosse, but to deal with a modern argument often traced to him.

[10]   I am using the term "creationist" to refer to persons who believe in an Earth that is comparatively young, are not evolutionists, and believe in a world wide flood. I am aware that this is an imprecise characterization and that some persons label themselves "creationists" who do not hold any of these positions. I do believe, however, that the term is one that is in popular usage and is precise enough to at least label a small group of persons who would be comfortable with these notions.

[11]   In fact, I know of no creationist book that deals with the problem in a respectable manner. However, I have not read all creationist books and so limit my claim to the works cited later in this paper. I take these works to be standard expositions of the "orthodox" creationism of the sixties, seventies, and eighties.

[12]   This object O could be a person, desk, or the universe itself.

[13]   An object x has the appearance of history in a world W at a time t =df if x has any feature y that suggests the existence of x at t-n in W.

[14]   The result of t1-n would be dependent on whatever the theist held the date of creation to be and whatever scientists determined the appearance of history to be in the universe. This argument is unaffected by any actual figure suggested by either camp.

[15]   This objection was made in an unpublished letter to the author by the erudite anti-creationist Robert J. Schadewald.

[16]   Robert Schadewald let me read an unpublished paper reacting to this passage in Morris. He does an excellent job debunking this response to the Gossean critics. To be fair to Morris, it is important to note that he advances other defenses of Gosse. I would like to express my general appreciation for the work of Henry Morris, a true polymath, whose own writings continue to inspire my work.

[17]   Since this objection applies to only the Gosse-Morris god, I will assume this Christian god for the rest of the paper as being the only god under discussion.

[18]   If the Gosse argument holds, then a person would have to have more than the apparent history of the Earth in order to reject the Biblical God. If no rational reasons can be found for selecting the Gosse-Morris theology that overcomes the simplicity of merely accepting apparent history as fact, then one should reject the Gosse-Morris theology.

[19]   I am not a scientist so I cannot judge Gentry's work. I am basing my opinion on creationists and noncreationists whose opinions I trust. Of course if Gentry's work and conclusions turn out to be good, then this is all the better for creationists.

BASIC TYPES OF LIFE[1]

SIEGFRIED SCHERER, PH.D.
ARIBOSTRASSE 18,
D-85356 FREISING, GERMANY

ABSTRACT

The main conflict in the species discussion may be summarized as follows: the population geneticist is mainly interested in gene flow and, therefore, has to prefer a biospecies concept. On the other hand, the practicing taxonomist and the palaeontologist are mainly interested in similarity and, hence, have to use a morphological species concept. This conflict is fundamental and cannot easily be resolved. It is often stated that higher levels of classification are even more problematic than the species definition. Using a genetical criterion based on interspecific hybridization, it is suggested that a systematic category above the genus level may be defined rather objectively: two *organisms belong to the same basic type if (i) they are able to hybridize or (ii) they have hybridized with the same third organism.* In principle it is possible to check experimentally by artificial insemination or artificial pollination if two biparental individuals belong to the same basic type. The basic type category thus may prove to be open to empirical validation. Advantages and problems of this basic type criterion are discussed.

A general summary follows on a few basic types of the plant and animal kingdom that have been described. Based on rather limited data it appears to emerge that (i) the basic type criterion can be applied successfully in animal as well as plant taxonomy, (ii) a clear gap of overall similarity is found between different basic types, (iii) within basic types a variety of microevolutionary processes may help to understand speciation, and (iv) the distribution of characters across different species of the same basic type may be discussed under the hypothetical assumption of a large hidden variation potential harboured by a genetically complex ancestral population.

It must be emphasized that only 14 basic types have been described to date. This number is too low to provide for a reliable basis of generalization. Therefore, the basic type concept is only suggested to serve as a preliminary working hypothesis.

(I)   THE SPECIES PROBLEM

Currently, about 1.5 million species are binominally named. However, this is probably only a fraction of the total number of extant species. Estimates vary between 3-5 millions and 10-50 millions (May 1988). For four reasons, it is necessary to name the species on earth. First, only by naming is it possible for biologists to communicate on their subjects. Second, only by naming is it possible to classify. Third, only by naming is it possible to understand the mechanisms of microevolution, i.e. speciation and fourth, only by naming is it possible to protect the threatened diversity of life. Therefore, classification of organismic diversity remains one of the most important as well as most fascinating tasks of biology. (Unfortunately, there is an irritating world-wide tendency to reduce funding for such fundamental research.)

The numbers of species given above are rather unreliable estimates. In part, this is due to some uncertainty of species definitions. Very often, systematic studies, for practical reasons., cannot avoid using a morphospecies definition. The definition of the biological species (see below) is not usually applicable in field or museum studies. This causes an on-going conflict in taxonomy. Dobzhansky wrote: "The species problem is the oldest in biology" (Dobshansky 1972). Although there is a seemingly endless discussion of the species problem in the biological literature, it is still unsolved. The discussion has a long history, which is not to be summarized in this paper (see, e.g., Mayr 1982; Willmann 1985). Neither shall I present the various philosophical implications of the species definition (see, e.g., Sucker 1978; Van der Steen & Voorzanger 1986; Ereshefsky 1992).

Numerous species definitions (for review see, e.g., Hauser 1987) as well as speciation mechanisms (for review see

---

[1]This paper is reprinted from the monograph, *Basic Types of Life*, edited by Siegried Scherer, Berlin, 1993, pp.11-30.

Junker 1993a; Otte & Endler 1989), have been and are still proposed. Often, the discussion is polarized (e.g., Coyne et al. 1988), usually not free from subjective statements and not restricted to biology. As Jerry A. Coyne recently put it: "No area of evolutionary biology has been more beset by semantic and philosophical squabbles than the study of speciation. The difficulty of understanding such a slow historical process has repeatedly driven scientists out of their laboratories and into the arms of philosophy. From this union has sprung a bloated, quasi-philosophical literature about whether species exist, what they are and whether they differ from more arbitrary categories such as genera or families" (Coyne 1992a).

This paper has not been written in order to present a solution to the species problem. For reasons which are to be discussed below, a final solution probably does not exist. Instead, after a short introduction to the species discussion, a somewhat objective way to define a higher taxonomic rank than that of species and genus will be suggested.

Species concepts

Depending on the way of counting, a dozen or more different species definitions exist (Ereshefsky 1992; Lonnig 1993; Orte & Endler 1989). Hauser summarizes 15 definitions which have been proposed between 1966 and 1985 (Hauser 1987). In the author's opinion, all definitions fall into either one of four basic groups:

ecospecies, chronospecies, morphospecies and "geno"species.

Some authors suggest that the unique role of ecological niches could be used for the description of ecospecies (Simpson 1961; Turesson 1922). But what, exactly, is a particular ecological niche? Some authors feel that this species definition is open for a great deal of subjectivity (for a discussion see Mayr 1963; Willmann 1985). The chronospecies concept pays attention to the historical course of speciation (Ax 1987; Wiley 1981; Willmann 1985). Simpson suggests that a chronospecies is a phyletic lineage, evolving independently of others, with its own separate and unitary evolutionary role and tendencies. Ax and Willmann include all individuals, irrespective of morphological divergences, in one species if no split of lineages has been demonstrated. Concerning species concepts in palaeontology, Reif concludes that (i) none of the proposed concepts leads to objective criteria for the diagnosis of evolutionary species and (ii) the fossil record is almost nowhere sufficient for the direct application of species-delimiting criteria (Reif 1984).

The chronospecies is defined by criteria similar to those applicable to the morphospecies. Until 1940, the morphological species definition was most commonly accepted, but it is still used frequently. Cronquist (1978) suggests: "Species are the smallest groups that are consistently and persistently distinct and distinguishable by ordinary means". Obviously, this definition involves subjective elements, which is nicely illustrated by the definition of Ginsburg: "A given population is to be considered a species with respect to another closely related population when the degree of intergradation (overlap of the observed samples) is not more than 10 percent" (Ginsburg 1938), cited according to (Mayr 1963). Objections against this species concept have been raised repeatedly and discussed thoroughly by different authors (for a review see, e.g., Hauser 1987).

Today, genetic species concepts are most popular among biologists. The idea that gene flow is an important argument for defining species has been expressed by early biologists. Mayr defined: "Species are groups of actually or potentially interbreeding natural populations which are reproductively isolated from other such groups" (Mayr 1940). Other biologists contributed to the development of the biospecies concept as well (e.g. Dobzhansky, Huxley, Stresemann, Wright and others, for references see Mayr 1963; 1982; Willmann 1985).

Reproductive isolation of biospecies

The key issue of the biospecies concept is reproductive isolation. But what, exactly, is reproductive isolation? This is by no means a question easy to answer. In fact, one of the criticisms of the biospecies concept focuses on the definition of reproductive isolation (e.g., Cracraft 1983). The analysis of hybrid zones clearly shows that gene flow between "good species" is frequent (Barton & Hewitt 1985; 1989); the more species are closely studied, the more hybrid zones are found (e.g., Mossakowski 1990). Often, the hybrids are not only viable, but fully fertile. Nevertheless, the parental species are commonly treated as different. For example, the eastern europe fire-bellied toads *Bombina bombina* and *Bombina variegate* (Amphibia) interbreed freely in a narrow zone that extends over 1000 km. On the other hand, they differ by morphology, ecology and genetics (Szymura & Barton 1986). The straightforward solution in such cases, according to Willmann, appears to be simple: *Bombina bonibliia* and *B. variegate* should be treated as a single species (Willmann 1987). In other cases, stable hybrid zones are found but it seems that there exists a strong selection against hybrids, resulting in a substantial, though not absolute barrier to gene exchange over these tension zones (Barton & Hewitt 1989) which are considered to represent stages of speciation. To what extent is gene flow between "good species" acceptable? Strict adherents of the biospecies concept would deny any gene flow between species. Actually, in numerous cases no hybrid zone exists ("good species") but only occasionally hybridization occurs. Hence, some gene flow exists. Moreover, the hybrids sometimes display a strongly decreased fertility. Gene flow caused by these hybridization events is very minor, but is not zero: should one define one or two species? Usually, even the originators of the biospecies concept end up with two species in such cases (Barton & Hewitt 1989). However, if one would apply the biospecies concept consequently, two clearly separated species must be united even if a partially fertile hybrid is detected once in dozens of generations. This, however, would lead to a degree of lumping of species probably completely unacceptable for most taxonomists. Furthermore, biospecies recognition very often is difficult to test since it is extremely tricky to measure gene flow between populations if it occurs very rarely.

Reproductive isolation between species may comprise only certain genes.. Based on a most comprehensive study on species hybridization within the plant genera *Phaseolus, Chrysanthemum and* Pisum, Lamprecht submitted that genes exist which may be used to define species (Lamprecht 1966). He suggested to discriminate between intraspecific and interspecific genes. If the maternal genotype is AA and the paternal genotype is aa, intraspecific genes would segregate as 1 AA : 2 Aa : 1 aa or, if the maternal genotype is aa and the paternal genotype is AA, the segregation will be 1 aa : 2 aA : 1 AA. However, the segregation of interspecific genes will be 1 AA : 2 Aa : 0 aa or, if the maternal alleles are recessive, 1 aa : 2 aA : 0 AA. If AA or aa occur, these hybrids are sterile in case of interspecific genes. One interpretation of these data is that paternal alleles of interspecific genes cannot be expressed homozygotically in the maternal cytoplasm. They do not show a mendelian behaviour. Based on this observation Lamprecht defines: "All biotypes carrying the same alleles of interspecific genes belong to the same species." An advantage of such a species definition would be that it might be subject to empirical validation. An extensive discussion of this concept is given by Lonnig (1993).

It appears, therefore, that the biospecies concept does include serious problems and is not as objective as some of its proponents would suggest. Basically, it is an operational and conceptual tool to describe the process of speciation. For this purpose, no viable alternative seems to exist. This is not to say that the mechanistic basis of speciation has been unraveled. Darwin considered speciation the "mystery of mysteries", Futuyma (1983) lamented that speciation is "more thoroughly awash in unfounded and often contradictory speculation than any other single topic in evolutionary theory" and Coyne concluded that "speciation is still a little-understood area of evolution" (Coyne 1992b). Nevertheless, it seems very unlikely that speciation, which obviously is at work through different mechanisms (Coyne 1992b; Junker 1993a; Otte & Endler 1989; Zwolfer & Bush 1984), can be described adequately without using the biological species concept.

Some causes for the species conflict

What are the causes for what has been called the "species plague" (Van der Steen & Voorzanger 1986)? First, given the problems described in the previous paragraph in using the biological species concept, it has been admitted quite frankly that the biospecies concept was not developed for practical application, that is to recognize species in nature, but for theoretical reasons, i.e. to understand the role of species as natural units of microevolution (De Jong & Goodmann 1982; Willmann 1987). It is thus understandable that most practical taxonomists prefer the morphospecies concept over the biospecies concept.

The morphospecies concept, in contrast, considers only characters to describe the basic units of life. Therefore, there is a clash between these two views of species: one is based on gene flow, the other on the maintenance of a cluster of phenotypes. Sometimes, both the morphospecies and biospecies concept may lead to similar results. In these cases, reproductive isolation is coupled with morphological and, most often, genetic distance (Sperlich 1984). However, there are puzzling examples to the opposite: it was possible to demonstrate that speciation events (using the biospecies concept) can happen by changing only very few genetic characters (Coyne 1992b). In extreme cases, even single-gene speciation is possible (Orr 1991). It has been shown that sibling species, which can be almost indistinguishable morphologically, are also virtually identical alloenzymically (Johnson et al. 1986), but nevertheless provide an excellent example for "good species" which are reproductively completely isolated. Reproductive isolation may even be due to microorganisms residing in the cytoplasm of eggs, but not in sperm cells, thus causing cytoplasmic incompatibility. This results in sterility of crosses between two otherwise very closely related species (Breeuwer & Werren 1990). Another example for sterile hybrids of genetically otherwise closely related species are transposable genetic elements (P-elements), causing incompatibility when a sperm cell carrying the P-element fertilizes an egg cell without P-element (for review see Kidweel & Peterson 1991). On the other hand, morphologically quite dissimilar individuals may be nearly identical genetically (for a recent example see Ford & Gottlieb 1992).

The second reason for the conflict, therefore, may be summarized as follows: The population geneticist is mainly interested in gene flow while the taxonomist is mainly interested in the degree of similarity (i.e., differences). In order to understand speciation, similarity can be almost neglected, but for classifying organisms, similarity is one of the key issues. The biospecies concept does not allow one to decide whether two species are "closely related" while the morphospecies concept does not allow one to know whether gene flow exists. It does not seem that an easy solution to this fundamental conflict exists.

Do different disciplines need different species concepts? Perhaps a variety of views of the species is appropriate in order to describe the complexity of nature (Mishler & Donoghue 1982)? However, this would be likely to generate considerable confusion. A clear consensus is needed on what units one is talking about. In the writer's opinion, the observation that organisms form populations which may become separated, thus evolving independently, is a basic phenomenon of microevolution and, therefore, should be applied whenever possible in order to define biospecies. If no data from field studies are available (this is found in most cases), there will be no other choice than to use a morphological species concept. In case such data become available, one should give priority to species definitions based on gene flow. In doing so, over-all similarity will be excluded from the species definition but still is an important piece of information: Overall similarity, in these cases, might be used to delimit different genera. If different biospecies are readily discernible, they may be assigned to different genera. Since this latter procedure includes some subjectivity (see below), it would be desirable to have a taxonomic category available above the genus level which harbours all genera with the same overall similarity as well as the same basic genetic pattern. It would be further desirable to define such a category with some objectivity. It is suggested in the following paragraph that such a category indeed may exist.

(II)   CATEGORIES ABOVE THE SPECIES LEVEL

A review on the history of the understanding of higher categories in taxonomy can be found elsewhere (Bartlett 1940; Mayr 1982; Morton 1981; Singer 1962). Often, it is held that higher categories are completely artificial (Ax 1987; Mayr, et al. 1953; Petters 1970). However, due to some classification models, higher categories can be viewed as natural if they comprise only and all living species which descended from a single ancestral population, i.e. are monophyletic (Mayr et al. 1953; Schaefer 1976). Although there is a consensus among all authors that higher categories cannot be defined objectively, some agreement on practical rules to set these categories exist, at least among phylogenetic systematicists: higher categories (i) need to be monophyletic and (ii) should be separated by a clear gap when compared to other groups closely related. (It is not intended here to compare the cladistic, numerical and evolutionary approach to classification, for a short review see Mayr 1990.)

What is a genus?

When compared to the species discussion, only very little work has been devoted to the definition of the genus (for a detailed review see Dubois 1988). It has, for instance, been suggested that the number of species to be included in one genus should have an upper limit of 40 (Ross 1975). Mayr et al. (1953) proposed that the number of species in a genus should be inversely correlated to the morphological gap between genera. They define: "A genus is a systematic category including one species or a group of species of presumably common phylogenetic origin, which is separated from other similar units by a decided gap." According to Cain (1956), a genus is "monophyletic, but purely positional in rank, and a collection of phyletic lines.... Only comparative criteria are applicable at the level of the genus (and other higher categories)". In a discussion of the genus concept Michener concludes that "a category such as genus, as it is ordinarily used, can only be defined as a monophyletic unit of one or more species, differing in some ways from other such units" (Michener 1957). Simpson suggested that genera are "the most definite and permanent unit of modern classification, to such an extent that the genus may be considered the basic unit of practical and morphological taxonomy, although the species is the basic unit of theoretical and genetical taxonomy" (Simpson 1945). Probably, he was led by the experience that a welltrained specialist of a particular group is able to integrate a vast array of features of a group, thus developing a reliable "feeling" for relatedness. However, this feeling cannot be strictly defined, a genus "has no single, crystallized, idealized pattern or morphotype" (Simpson 1953).

Interspecific hybridization has been proposed as a criterion to define genera (Van Gelder 1977, DuBois 1988). This interesting approach will be discussed below in more detail.

What is a family?

The definition is often quite similar to that of the genus. "A family is a taxonomic category containing a single genus or a monophyletic group of genera, which is separated from other families by a decided gap. It is recommended, as in the case of the genus, that the size of the gap be in inverse ratio to the size of the family" (Mayr 1969). The family level is sometimes chosen in a way that "the gaps within the family are small enough so that the relationships are readily evident, but gaps between families are so large that the relationships can be discerned only by detailed study" (Edmunds 1962). Adaptive features have also been used for discerning families: "A family-group seems to be a group of species adapted for a broadly similar mode of life. This mode cannot be narrowly defined - it is not solely a means of food-getting, or of reproduction, or of food-type but rather a new combination of these and other adaptations" (Schaefer 1976).

Since both genus and family definitions are clearly arbitrary, Sibley et al. (1990), based on DNA-DNA hybridization, proposed a quantitative measure for defining family and genus rank within birds: they suggested using the term family if the differences in $\Delta T_{50}H$ values (these are measures of homology between DNA sequences) between individuals are not greater than 9-11 while they use the term genus if these values are lower than 2.2. However, it is unclear why these authors chose exactly those numbers and not, for instance, 14-16 for the family and 3.1 for the genus. Most probably, they calibrated their numbers by referring to preexisting taxonomic rankings. If so, this would be an example of circular reasoning, not adding any objectivity to the problem.

Interspecific hybridization

One aspect of similarity can be measured precisely these days by sequencing genes. But the information provided by gene sequences must be interpreted and may yield different classifications for different genes. More important, the most interesting differences between organisms are found in the genetic program package which leads to the formation of morphogenetic pattern during ontogeny. But this program cannot be localized in sequences of structural genes. It is also unlikely that mere sequences of various regulatory genes as such provide the basis needed in order to understand morphogenesis of an organism. It would seem that a complex interaction of a variety of regulatory genes with numerous structural genes, intimately bound to a specifically structured three-dimensional space of the zygote must be known in order to describe pattern formation during ontogeny. However, we are very far from understanding such processes and, therefore, cannot use them for classification. But it is obvious that successful hybridization is a clear indication that the species from which the germ cells are derived from are closely related. Can this important piece of information be used for classification?

Clausen et al. proposed the taxonomic categories of ecospecies, coenospecies and comparium (Clausen 1951; Clausen et al. 1939). An "ecospecies" has its own genetic system sufficiently differentiated and distinct from the genetic systems of other ecospecies to produce only hybrids with reduced fertility or viability. The ecospecies often corresponds to the species rank in common classifications. A coenospecies comprises ecospecies displaying the ability for restricted interchange of genes in spite of partial hybrid sterility. The comparium, finally, comprises coenospecies which are capable of producing sterile interspecific hybrids. There have been a number of approaches using intergeneric hybridization as an argument to lump species from different genera into one genus (Ansell 1971; Buettner-Janusch 1966; Simpson 1961; Stains 1967; Stebbins 1956). Van Gelder suggested that "species in one genus should not be capable of breeding with species in other genera" (Van Gelder 1977). In other words, if interspecific hybrids are observed (irrespective of whether they are fertile or sterile), the parental species should be included in one genus. Consequently, Van Gelder lumped 42 mammalian genera and created 17 genera instead; Stebbins (1956) suggested that it might be appropriate to merge 20 genera of Triticeae into a single genus. Probably, genus numbers would be reduced further if systematic cross-fertilization experiments were undertaken. The genus definition of Van Gelder corresponds closely to the comparium of Clausen et al. (1939). Van Gelder (1977) even wrote: "It seems to me that if the chromosomes of two taxa are compatible enough to develop a foetus to term, then the parents would seem to be more closely related than generic separation would suggest."

More recently, DuBois (1988) also suggested to use interspecific hybridization as a taxonomic criterion. He proposed that "whenever two species can give viable adult hybrids, they should be included in the same genus; if other valid criteria had led them previously to be placed into different genera, these must be merged." This approach corresponds closely to Van Gelder (1977). However, for the following reasons such a definition of a genus is probably not useful. First, the information storage capacity of biosystematic classifications is severely reduced since a variety of morphologically extremely different as well as highly similar species would be lumped together in one genus, comprising a large number of species. For instance, geese, swans and ducks would be members of the same genus (Scherer 1993b). Over-all similarity, which is the basis for most classifications, even at the species level, would be excluded as a criterion. This is highly undesirable for the practical taxonomist. Second, it would dramatically change the nomenclature currently in use and, therefore, cause tremendous confusion. These two consequences must result in the rejection of such a genus definition by most taxonomists.

The basic type criterion

Definition of basic types

A taxonomic rank termed "basic type" or "baramin" by Frank L. Marsh (1941; 1976) comprises all individuals which are able to hybridize and, therefore, appears to be related to the genus definition of Clausen, Van Gelder and Dubois discussed in the previous paragraph. Building on Clausen's, Marsh's, Van Gelder's and DuBois' work, it is submitted here that hybridization data be used by the following primary membership criterion:

Two individuals belong to the same basic type if
    (i) they are able to hybridize.

Additionally, a secondary membership criterion is proposed which greatly facilitates basic type recognition:

Two individuals belong to the same basic type if
    (ii) they have hybridized with the same third organism.

For practical reasons one may substitute the term "individual" by the term "species", although in a strict sense only individuals are able to hybridize. Note that it is neither considered to be important whether hybridization occurs in nature or in captivity, nor if it is induced by artificial insemination or artificial pollination. Note further that fertility or sterility of the hybrid is not used as a criterion of relatedness since sterility can be caused by rather minor genetic changes. In contrast, if hybridization is possible, morphogenetic programs of the parents obviously are highly similar, warranting the inclusion into one basic type.

In order to indicate basic types without confusing currently accepted taxonomic nomenclature, they will be labeled by adding the prefix *bt* to the acknowledged latin name of the group.

Advantages of the basic type definition

The basic type definition has several advantages. *First*, the criterion provides a category whose members share the same morphogenetic pattern. This has consequences for phylogenetic interpretations concerning such groups. *Second*, a wealth of interspecific hybridization data are already available (see section III of this article), which have rarely been used in classification. *Third*, if data are missing, one may introduce the experimental approach of artificial insemination or artificial pollination (Clausen et al. 1939). Therefore, this criterion is a taxonomic category which is subject to empirical validation. Fourth, this approach allows one to define the basic type taxon in much the same way as the biospecies. One of the advantages of the biological species taxon is that it can be defined without any reference to other species. Definitions of higher taxa, in contrast, "can only be relative to those of other categories, specifying relative ranks in the hierarchy and set relationships to taxa" (Simpson 1961). This limit can be overcome by the classification criterion suggested here (compare also Dubois 1988). *Fifth*, Schaefer (1976) stated correctly that, until now, it was impossible to answer the question of how a taxonomic category in one group (for instance, birds) can be made equivalent to the same category of another group (for instance, mammals or angiosperms). The criterion suggested here provides a taxonomic rank above the species level which is directly comparable within all kinds of sexually reproducing organisms. *Sixth*, the criterion proposed leaves plenty of room for using morphological similarity in defining genera. Thus, the information storage and retrieval capacity of such a classification scheme (i.e. species - genus - basic type) remains high. *Seventh*, application of this criterion does not cause major changes in nomenclature since the binominal names remain unchanged.

Problems of the basic type definition

The basic type criterion is a wholly positive one. If hybrids are known, membership is unequivocal. However, for more than 90% of the families of higher plants no intergeneric hybrids have been recorded at all. If no hybrids are known, one could use selected genera and try to breed hybrids experimentally. If one fails consistently to produce hybrids, this does not necessarily mean that the two individuals belong to different basic types. It is well known that even among members of closely related species sometimes no hybrids can be formed. In this case, one has to refer to similarity criteria in asking whether the individuals under discussion are sufficiently similar to members of a basic type which are known to be involved in hybridization. If such hybridization data are also missing, an annotation to a specific basic type is only possible by referring to taxonomic rankings currently in use.

The definition given above may, however, eventually turn out to be not entirely objective. Some of the reasons have been already mentioned when the biological species definition was discussed: there exist grades in reproductive isolation at the species level and these grades exist as well at the basic type level. The primary and secondary membership criteria use the production of offspring (hybridization) to recognize basic types. However, what does hybridization mean? There are cases where hybridization occurs and the offspring is fully viable. In other cases the offspring dies before reaching maturity; sometimes, the offspring dies shortly after birth; and in yet other cases, the development of the embryo is terminated at some stage during embryogenesis. What exactly does hybridization mean then? Is the criterion of hybridization met if, for instance, a mammalian hybrid foetus dies before birth? In order to deal with this problem, MARSH submitted the following membership criterion: "In every case where true fertilization of the egg occurs, the parents are members of the same baramin" (1941; 1976). This definition was adopted later by Scherer & Hilsberg (1982).

What does "true fertilization" mean? Certainly parthenogenesis, induced by unification of sperm cell and egg cell followed by an elimination of paternal chromosomes, should be excluded. Concerning animals, true fertilization in the sense of Marsh means: (i) recognition of sperm and egg, (ii) sperm entry, (iii) formation of haploid pronuclei, (iv) formation of a diploid nucleus, (v) activation of the zygote, (vi) doubling and separation of both maternal and paternal chromosomes and (vii) formation of the early blastomeres involving the chromosomes of both parents.

This criterion has been critically discussed by Lonnig (1993). He pointed out that during early stages of embryogenesis development including replication generally proceeds without transcription and is controlled by various cytoplasmic factors formed in the egg while it matured in the mother. According to Wolfe (1993, p.1103), "much or all (of the morphogenetic information) of early development is stored-in the egg cytoplasm, . . . early embryonic stages are under the control of maternal genes. In some organisms, such as *Drosophila*, the effects of some maternal genes are exerted through their mRNA or protein products throughout embryonic development. In others, such as mammals, the effects of maternal genes are much reduced and limited to very early embryonic stages." Only later during embryogenesis does nuclear transcription occur. What is even more important for defining 'true fertilization' is the suspicion that "the biochemistry regulating these divisions is similar, if not identical, among all the animal phyla, and that the biochemistry of cell division may be the same throughout all eucaryotes" (Gilbert 1991, p.111). Therefore, Dubois (1988, p. 42) concluded: "he fact that two species may be able to give viable hybrids until the end of the blastula stage is therefore of little genetic or phylogenetic meaning and is of little interest to the systematist."

Obviously, the definition of a basic type by using the criterion of true fertilization as given by Marsh (1941) and used later by Scherer & Hilsberg (1982) needs to be revised. Therefore, a future tertiary membership criterion could be similar to the following definition:

Two individuals belong to the same basic type if
>   *(iii) embryogenesis of a hybrid continues beyond the maternal phase, including subsequent coordinated*
>   *expression of both maternal and paternal morphogenetic genes.*

If one is going to perform test-tube hybridization between distantly related genera in order to define basic types experimentally, an appropriate tertiary membership criterion will probably be indispensable. Unfortunately, almost no comparative data are known on gene expression during early embryogenesis of closely and only distantly related species including the respective zygotes. Closer investigation of transcription during early embryogenesis in such cases eventually might reveal that some functional gene complexes are basic type specific while others are not (Lonnig 1993, p.13; compare also the idea of intra- and interspecific genes of Lamprecht 1966). Clearly, the development of a workable tertiary membership criterion is, at the best, in its initial stages.

Throughout the chapters which follow in this book, only the primary and secondary membership criteria, i.e. successful hybridization, have been used in order to delineate basic types.

(III)   APPLICATION OF BASIC TYPE TAXONOMY

In creating a classification system, one can use features of organisms which show their similarity, starting at the species level and working up the hierarchy. This was termed "upward classification by empirical grouping" (Mayr 1982). On the other hand, it is equally possible to concentrate on differences of organisms starting from higher systematic categories and working all the way down to the species level. This has been termed "downward classification by logical division" by Mayr (1982) or, more recently, "discontinuity systematics" (Wise 1992). Both strategies are useful. Classification based on interspecific hybridization, like the one based on biospecies recognition, is an "upward classification approach". First, a short review of the application of this approach is given with special reference to the papers published in this book.

The data base

It is widely believed that interspecific hybridization occurs only very rarely. However, the study of the literature reveals numerous hybrids observed in nature or derived in captivity which have often never been compiled systematically. For instance, in a recent paper it was stated that "approximately one in ten bird species is known to hybridize, and the true global incidence is likely to be much higher" (Grant & Grant 1992). Thus, from a world total of 9672 bird species, 895 species are known to have bred *in natura* with at least one other species (Panov 1989). Not only species of the same genus are involved, intergeneric hybridization in the natural habitat is also found. It is restricted to seven orders but is fairly frequent where it does occur (Grant & Grant 1992). To these hybrids, a great number of hybrids derived in captivity can be added; for instance, within the family Anatidae (approximately 150 species), well over 400 different interspecific hybrids are known (Scherer & Hilsberg 1982). In captivity, much more intergeneric hybrids occur than under natural conditions. In a few cases, check lists of all known crossings within certain groups exist, for instance for birds (Gray 1958), mammals (Gray 1972) or Poaceae (Knobloch 1968). However, many check lists are rather old and outdated. On a regular basis, new hybridization reports can be found, for instance, in the International Zoo Yearbook. It appears, therefore, that a good number of crosses are already known. These can be used immediately in order to discern basic types.

Basic types within plants and animals

An overview on the taxonomic ranks of basic types described in Scherer (1993a) can be found in Table 1. Obviously, the basic type rank depends on the author having created the systematics of that particular group. For instance, according to Wolters (1983), btAnatidae is at the family level, but could also be assigned to the subfamily level Johnsgard 1978; Scherer 1993b). Generally it appears that basic type rank is comparable with the subfamily or family level in Aves or Mammalia while it may range between tribe and family rank within plants. However, based only on a small number of 14 basic types described so far, no final statement is possible. Far more groups have to be studied, especially from other vertebrate classes, invertebrates and from other plant phyla.

Data on interspecific hybridization differ widely for the plant and animal groups investigated. For instance, within btEquidae (one genus, 6 species), from a total of 15 hybrids theoretically possible, 14 have actually been reported

(Steincadenbach 1993). In contrast, within the *bt*Accipitrinae/Buteoninae (29 genera, appr. 150 species), only seven, including two intergeneric hybrids (between *Accipiter and Buteo* and between *Buteo and Parabuteo)* are known. Interestingly, one of the intergeneric hybrids connects the two subfamilies. It is, therefore, obvious that this basic type cannot yet be defined on the basis of hybridization (Zimbelmann 1993). Although the number of intergeneric hybrids actually found will depend on the number of genera within a basic type, other parameters are also responsible for such vastly different sets of data. For instance, within *bt*Anatidae (148 species, 40 genera), which is of a similar size to the *bt*?Accipitrinae/Buteoninae, a total of more than 300 intergeneric hybrids have been observed. This difference, obviously, is due to the fact that anatids can be bred easily in captivity while birds of prey can only be bred with difficulty. If birds of prey propagate in captivity, breeders usually try to avoid any hybridization for reasons of species conservation.

From this discussion an important bias of basic type classification emerges. It is restricted to groups of organisms which are not only very well known but were kept in captivity or cultivation for some reason or the other. However, the perspective of planned hybridization, for instance by using artificial insemination or artificial pollination, should be considered carefully. First, induced by the rapid development of *in vitro* fertilization, the production of animal embryos gets easier. Second, comparatively few hybrids are necessary in order to discern a basic type. It is a general observation that species of the same genus with few exceptions will hybridize in captivity (by the way, this fact may shed some light on the "feeling" of taxonomists enabling them to assign species to a genus). Therefore, intergeneric hybrids are far more important to study than interspecific hybrids and experiments may be directed mainly to intergeneric crosses. Furthermore, it is not necessary that each intergeneric hybrid which is theoretically possible be actually achieved. The basic type definition maintains that two species are assigned to the same basic type if they are connected indirectly by hybridization. For instance, consider *bt*Cercopithecidae (9 genera, which gives 36 different intergeneric combinations). Only 9 combinations were actually reported (Hartwig-Scherer 1993) but these connect 8 from 9 genera which delimits *bt*Cercopithecidae quite clearly. As a minimum, in order to delimit a basic type, one would need to produce only (n-1) hybrids, where n is the number of genera. This task would appear to be quite feasible, at least when one is dealing with plants.

Basic types: Addition of supplementary membership criteria

Apart from a few examples, not all hybrids are available which would be necessary to discern the basic types (see table 1) unequivocally. Therefore, in order to reach a tentative basic type classification, one may wish to use additional criteria, which are provided by all levels of traditional taxonomy.

As an example, consider the genus *Miopithecus* which is not known to have hybridized with other cercopithecoids. Since it is very likely based on data from morphology, anatomy, chromosomal structure and behaviour that *Miopithecus* falls well within the range of the family, some authors have suggested abandoning the genera *Erythrocebus, Miopititecus and Allenopithecus in* order to include those species in the genus *Cercopithecus.*
On the other hand, the genera *Mandrillus and Macaca* are connected by hybridization with *Cercopithecus* but are definitively much more distant from *Cercopithcus* as is *Mlopithecus* (Hartwig-Scherer 1993). Therefore, there is little doubt that *Mlopithecus* belongs to *bt*Cercopithecidae.

Another example has been reported by Kutzelnigg (1993). According to different authors, *bt*Maloideae (including apple trees) comprises between 15-30 genera with 200-2000 species. If one decides to accept 24 genera, only 12 of them are connected by hybridization. Why should one include the other genera in the basic type? First, hybridizations have been derived mainly by chance. It is, therefore, very likely that a systematic crossbreeding programme would yield a wealth of further hybrids. Second, several hybrids have been reported between genera which are thought to be widely different according to other criteria. Third, missing hybrids often comprise genera which are thought to be closely related; some authors would rather unite them in one genus. Fourth, it is has turned out to be impossible to divide *bt*Maloideae into different subgroups without arriving at severe contradictions. So it was impossible to treat the genera involved in hybridization as a distinct subgroup, separated from the other genera. Fifth, *bt*Maloideae does show clear synapomorphies. Together, these additional criteria would suggest that all genera could tentatively be considered to belong to the same basic type.

An opposite example is provided by *Anseranas semipalmata* (Australian Magpie goose, Anseriformes). Some authors have included this species in the family Anatidae while others have created a separate monotypic family for this single species. No hybrids at all are known so far. There is an increasing number of observations based on morphology, anatomy, behaviour, biochemistry and molecular biochemistry which clearly separate *Atiseranas* from *bt*Anatidae. For instance, sequencing of hemoglobin placed *Anseranas* as distant from *bt*Anatidae as from *bt*Phasianidae (Scherer 1993b; Scherer & Sontag 1986). Therefore, it is considered to be reasonable to omit *Anseratias* from *bt*Anatidae.

A problem as yet unresolved is posed by the different avian families belonging to Galliformes (e.g. chicken, pheasants, see Kleem 1993). Usually, 250-300 species in 70-94 genera are attributed to this order and divided into 1-7 families with a total of 5-15 subfamilies. 159 hybrids are known, 28% of which connect different subfamilies. Several authors would feel that the order should be divided into three families: Phasianidae (ca. 200 species in 70 genera), Megapodiidae (12 species in 7 genera), and Cracidae (43 species in 10 genera). Within Megapodidae, no hybrids are known; within Cracidae, only two intergeneric hybrids have been reported while within Phasianidae numerous hybrids are known. It is quite likely, therefore, that *bt*Phasianidae can be postulated. The unsolved question is whether to include all three families in one basic type. There have been reports on hybrids between megapodids as well as cracids with *Gallus* (Phasianidae). However, these reports are quite old, were not reproduced and, thus, cannot be treated as sound evidence. It does not seem to be possible to divide the three families convincingly by demonstrating that each owns a clear set of synapomorphies; on the other hand, preliminary molecular data seem to indicate that Megapodidae and Cracidae are more similar to one another and somewhat distant from *bt*Phasianidae. In contrast, numerous synapomorphies exist when the order Galliformes is considered which, according to Wise (1992), would be in favour of a single basic type. As long as no more data is at hand, one would tentatively assign these three families to different basic types although it might well turn out that basic type rank is finally assigned to the order Galliformes. This is an outstanding case predetermined for experimental basic type taxonomy at the level of artificial insemination (development of embryos can be observed quite easily in bird eggs) supplemented by investigations at the molecular level.

Finally, a problematic case from the bird order Passeriformes shall be discussed. Passeriformes are considered as phylogenetically young, yet extremely diverse in terms of numerous species. Numerous hybrids are known within the finch family Fringillidae (Fehrer 1993). Two subfamilies Fringillinae and *bt*Carduelinae are often proposed. Only unreliable records on crosses between these two subfamilies are known while within the subfamilies numerous hybrids were reported. Both groups share characters but are also distinctly different with respect to others. Clear synapomorphies restricted to each group seem to be absent.

Recognizing a basic type based on hybridization

Based on the foregoing discussion, the procedure recommended for delineating a basic type may be summarized as follows:

(1) Collect all interspecific hybrids available within a particular group of organisms and produce a cross breeding matrix (or polygon), placing special emphasis on intergeneric hybrids. Check if any reliable report indicates that different groups (e.g. subfamilies or tribes) are connected by hybridization.

(2) Determine the overall range of variance which is indicated by those members of the group which are connected through hybridization. Then, check whether other species which are not involved in hybridization, would fall within the range of that variance.

(3) From these data, derive predictions on the membership of problematic species or genera and test such hypotheses by artificial hybridization.

Recognizing basic types without hybridization?

If no hybrids exist at all, one could still try to demonstrate continuity within groups or discontinuity between groups. Mentioning hybridization as the most important criterion, Wise (1992) suggested several additional membership criteria for recognizing basic types ("baramins" in his terminology). Expressed as questions which are to be answered by "YES" or "NO" these criteria are given in table 2. Wise applied his approach to the order Testudines (turtles, containing up to 16 families). No extensive record on intergeneric hybrids is known. The first result emerging from the study by Wise is that there exists a very clear phyletic discontinuity between Testudines and all other reptile orders. Turtles as a whole are united by an impressive array of synapomorphies; ancestral groups cannot be pointed out unequivocally both within extinct and extant groups. However, it was much less clear whether the turtles can be further divided. Based on limited data available, Wise arrives at the rather preliminary suggestion that the turtles may be divided into four basic types, i.e. the pleurodires, the chelonioids, the trionychids and the non-chelonioid, non-trionychid cryptodires. This suggestion can now be tested by designing suitable hybridization experiments. This approach certainly deserves extensive application by investigating numerous groups with no hybrids known.

Evolution of basic types

Macroevolution and Microevolution

Only about 14 basic types have been investigated in some detail. However, it is a general observation that the hybridization criteria would place the basic type in a taxonomic rank which has been already recognized by traditional taxonomy. Recognition of such groups has always been accompanied by pointing out that their members share clear synapomorphies and that they are clearly separated from other closely related groups. This holds for basic types at family rank as well as for basic types at the rank of tribe. In other words, there is an undisputed gap between basic types when extant organisms are compared. In the few cases investigated, these gaps seem also to be present in the fossil record of those groups, for instance for *bt*Anatidae, birds of prey or *bt*Cercopithecidae. Is it possible that, generally, no fossil links can be demonstrated which would unequivocally connect two clearly delineated basic types? However, paleontological data have yet to be related to basic type taxonomy. For instance, the fossil history of horses certainly deserves an in-depth study concerning this question (MacFadden 1993; MacFadden & Hulbert 1988). Based on the data at hand it might be expected that major discontinuities between basic types will continue to emerge at different levels of comparative biology. As a very tentative suggestion it is submitted that the term "macroevolution" be' used to describe the formation of different basic types.

In contrast, one might wish to use the term "microevolution" for processes leading to the formation of genera and species within a basic type. It is postulated that species belonging to the same basic type form a monophyletic group. This paragraph will not deal with mechanisms of speciation, which have been reviewed elsewhere (Junker 1993a), but rather with the distribution of characters throughout the members of a basic type, perhaps allowing some conclusion on the nature of the supposed ancestral population.

Nature of ancestral populations

When the results of the different papers presented in this book are reviewed, some common features emerge which are found across the different groups of animals and plants.

Hybrids of two species often have morphological or behavioural features not found in their parents. Sometimes these characters were previously unknown, but quite regularly they turn out to be similar to a third species of the same basic type (compare the membership criterion "artificial morphological discontinuity", table 2). For instance, this has been demonstrated within *bt*Anatidae (Scherer 1993b; Scherer & Hilsberg 1982), including both interspecific and intergeneric hybrids. As an extreme, it has been reported repeatedly that a hybrid between the two European species *Aythya fuligula and A. ferina* was indistinguishable from *A. affinis*, a third species from North America. Further examples were reported for *bt*Equidae (Stein-Cadenbach 1993), *bt*Estrildidae (Fehrer 1993), or *bt*Geeae (Junker 1993b). This means that the species involved in hybridization harbour an unrecognized potential of variability which is expressed upon hybridization. This potential of variation seems to be common to different species of the same basic type. A related observation concerns species within basic types which are impossible to classify. In case of *bt*Anatidae, these species are termed "aberrant types", displaying a mosaic of characters usually found in quite different tribes of the anatids. Kutzelnigg (1993) mentions monotypic genera within *bt*Maloideae: for instance, the monotypic genus *Pseudocydonia* is similar to *Cydonia,* but also *to Chaenomeles and* Pyrus. Hence, it is impossible to assign this genus to either one of these genera. A large number of such problematic species or genera are known. Interestingly, the oldest fossil remains of Anseriformes also display such a morphology: *Romanitivilla* definitively is anseriform, but has similarities to Anatini, Dendrocygnini, *Anseratias* and Anserini.

The same phenomenon has also been described for *Nycteretites* (racoon dog, *bt*Canidae). The basic type Canidae comprises three major groups: The wolf-like canids, the South American canids and the *Vulpes-like* canids. The racoon dog is similar to the wolf-like canids when its limb morphology is considered. According to its mastigory characteristics, this animal groups towards the South American canids while the over-all similarity of single copy DNA indicates that it is most closely related to the fox-like canids (Crompton 1993).

There are two potential explanations for such observations: it may be speculated that this be explained by the common ancestor already possessing a potential of variation (plesiomorphy). This does not mean that all characters of extant species were expressed in the ancestral population but that the genetic potential for such variation was hidden in the ancestral polyvalent gene pool. A hidden potential for variation suddenly becomes visible when different species or even races are hybridized; obviously, the genetic balance of a species which results in a continuous expression of species-specific features becomes disturbed upon hybridization, revealing an astonishing potential of variability. Another interpretation would be convergence (homoplasy). In that case, selective forces should exist which account for an independent origin of similar characters. Often, such selective forces are unknown (which does not necessarily mean that they do not exist).

It is found throughout the basic types described in this book that it seems impossible to construct a phylogenetic tree of all members of a particular basic type without numerous contradictions. Different characters yield different phylogenetic trees, for instance when the six species of *bt*Equidae are considered (Stein-Cadenbach 1993). This is also true for a variety of characters from other basic types, e.g. plumage pattern of anatids (Scherer 1993b) or carduelids (Fehrer 1993), the supposedly "highly reticulate evolution" within Triticeae (Junker 1993c) or a variety of characters within *bt*Maloideae (Kutzelnigg 1993). In the latter basic type, "primitive" characters are found regularly together with It advanced" characters ("heterobathmy"). However, there is no objective way in order of knowing which character is ancestral and which one is derived. Any such decisions are usually disputed. Characters, therefore, seem to form a network rather than a tree, when species of a basic type are compared.

Again, there are two potential explanations: plesiomorphy and homoplasy. Homoplasy requires mechanisms which evolve the same character independently. Such mechanisms (i.e. selective pressures) are yet to be demonstrated in each specific case. Application of the concept of plesiomorphy to such an extent which would explain the very common mosaic pattern of characters within basic types would lead to the idea of an ancestral population with an extremely high degree of polyallelism and, hence, with a large potential of variability. The evolution of different species from "complex" ancestors would scatter different characters and character combinations throughout the descendant species, the process being influenced by, e.g., size of the descendant populations, migration pattern of populations, chance effects and, finally, the action of selective forces on random character combinations. Such a process might explain the network of characters without involving unknown selective pressures.

Furthermore, it is quite well-known that speciation processes lead to specialization which means that the descendant population has lost genetic potential when compared with the ancestral population. Speciation itself would therefore appear to support the concept of ancestral populations with a large hidden potential of variation. Adler (1993) pointed out that it is possible to interpret some characters of *bt*Funariaceae in terms of a morphologically complex ancestor. The five genera of this basic type are assumed to be reduced in morphological complexity to various degrees.

(IV)   CONCLUDING REMARKS

The ideas expressed in this paper are certainly not entirely original (comp. Clausen 1951, Marsh 1976, Van Gelder 1977, DuBois 1988). In fact, they trace back to Carolus Linnaeus who, in his later writings, departed from the idea that species do not change (Landgren 1993; Mayr 1982). The basic unit of his late classification system was the genus rather than the species. He believed that these fundamental units of life, through hybridization, produced the species. Linnaeus himself did not use the category of a basic type but "...surprisingly many of the genera recognized by Linnaeus consist of well characterized groups of species, many still accepted as genera or families today" (Mayr 1982). It appears, therefore, that the genera of Linnaeus in some cases may come close to the basic types proposed in this book.

It is suggested that basic type classification is applicable to both animals and plants. This classification could comprise three main lower categories:

(i)   the biospecies concept as a means to describe biodynamical processes, i.e. speciation (comprising individuals genetically related through participation at the same gene pool);

(ii)   the genus category as a means to describe overall similarity (comprising morphologically related forms)

(iii)   the basic type category as a means to describe monophyletic, though potentially heterogenous groups (comprising morphogenetically related forms).

Basic types may be discerned experimentally by hybridization. It is now necessary to test this preliminary suggestion with as many animal and plant groups as possible. The articles which follow are only a first small step into this direction. The results available so far seem to be encouraging. Critical test cases will be provided by groups which comprise a number of closely related families or subfamilies, such as Passeriformes. However, further work could also demonstrate that the basic type criterion submitted here will not hold up when it is put to test in daily classification work of practicing taxonomists.

ACKNOWLEDGMENTS

Special thanks go to Wolf-Ekkehard Lonnig. Although not sharing all my views on taxonomy, his detailed critical discussion of the first version of this paper contributed greatly to the development of the basic type concept. Also, I received many helpful comments from Martin Adler, Reinhard Junker and Herfried Kutzelnigg.

REFERENCES

Adler M (1993) **Merkmalsausbildung und Hybridisierung bei Funariaceen (Bryophyta, Musci)**. In: Scherer S (Hg) Typen des Lebens. Berlin, S. 67-70.

Ansell WFH (1971) **Artiodactyla.** In: Meester J & Setzer HW (eds) The mammals of Africa. An identification manual. Washington, pp 1-84.

Ax P (1987) **The phylogenetic system. The systematization of organisms on the basis of their phylogenies. Chichester.**

Bartell HH (1940) **The concept of the genus.** Bull. Torrey Bot. Club 67, 349-362.

Barton NH & Hewitt GM (1985) **Analysis of hybrid zones.** Ann. Rev. Ecol. Syst. 16,113-148.

Barton NH & Hewitt GM (1989) **Adaptation, speciation and hybrid zones.** Nature 341, 497-503.

Breeuwer JAJ & Werren JH (1990) **Microorganisms associated with chromosome destruction and reproductive isolation between two distinct insect species.** Nature 346, 558-560.

Buettner-Janusch J (1966) **A problem in evolutionary systematics: Nomenclature and classification of baboons, genus Papio.** Folia Primatol. 4, 288-308.

Cain AJ (1956) **The genus in evolutionary taxonomy.** Syst. Zool. 5, 97-109.

Clausen J (1951) **Stages in the evolution of plant species.** Ithaca.

Clausen J, Keck DD & Hiesey WM (1939) **The concept of species based on experiment.** Amer. J. Bot. 28, 103-106.

Coyne JA (1992a) **Much ado about species.** Nature 357, 289-290.

Conne JA (1992b) **Genetics and speciation.** Nature 355, 511-515.

Coyne JA, Orr HA & Futuyma DJ (1988) **Do we need a new species concept?** Syst. Zool. 3 7, 190- 200.

Cracraft J (1983) **Species concepts and speciation analysis.** Current Ornithol. 1, 159-187.

Crompton N (1993) **A review of selected features of the family Canidae with reference to its fundamental taxonomic status.** In: Scherer S (Hg) Typen des Lebens. Berlin, S. 217-224.

Cronquist A (1978) **Once again: What is a species?** In: JA'Romberger (ed) Biosystematics in agriculture. Montclair, New Jersey, pp 3-20.

De Jong WW & Goodmann M (1982) **Mammalian phylogeny studied by sequence analysis of the eye lens protein a-crystallin.** Z. Saugetierkunde 47, 257-276.

Dobzhanskuy T (1972) **Species of Drosopizila.** Science 177, 664-669.

Dubois A (1988) **The genus in zoology: a contribution to the theory of evolutionary systematics.** Mem. Mus. Natn. Hist. Nat. Paris (A) 140,1-124.

Edmunds GF (1962) **The principles applied in determining the hierarchic level of the higher categories of ephemeroptera.** Syst. Zool. 11, 99-31.

Ereshefsky M (ed, 1992) **The units of selection. Essays on the nature of species.** Massachusetts.

Fehrer J (1993) **Interspecies-Kreuzungen bei cardueliden Finken und Prachtfinken.** In: Scherer S (Hg) Typen des Lebens. Berlin, pp 197-215.

Ford VS & Gottlieb LD (1992) **Bicalyx is a natural homeotic floral variant.** Nature 358, 671-673.

Futuyma DJ (1983) **Speciation.** Science 219,1059-1060.

Gilbert SF (1991) **Developmental Biology.** Sunderland, Mass.

Ginsburg I (1938) **Arithmetical definition of the species, subspecies and race concept, with a proposal for a modified nomenclature.** Zoologica 23, 253-286.

Grant PR & Grant BR (1992) **Hybridization of bird species.** Science 256,193-197.

Gray AP (1958) **Bird hybrids. A check list with bibliography.** Edinburgh.

Gray AP (1972) **Mammalian hybrids. A check list with bibliography.** Edinburgh.

Hartwig-Scherer S (1993) **Hybridisierung und Artbildung bei den Meerkatzenartigen (Primates, Cercopithecoidea).** In: Scherer S (Hg) Typen des Lebens. Berlin, pp 245-257.

Hauser CL (1987) **The debate about the biological species concept - a review.** Z. zool. Syst. Evolut. forsch. 25, 241-257.

Johnsgard PA (1978) **Ducks, swans and geese of the world.** Lincoln.

Johnson MS, Murray J & Clark B (1986) **Allozymic similarities among species of *Partula* on Moorea.** Heredity 56, 319-327.

Junker R. (1993a) **Prozesse der Artbildung** In: Scherer S (Hg) Typen des Lebens. Berlin, pp 31-45.

Junker R. (1993b) **Die Gattungen Geum (Neikenwurz), Coluria und Waldsteinia (Rosaceae, Tribus Geeae).** In: Scherer S (Hg) Typen des Lebens. Berlin, pp 95-111.

Junker R. (1993c) **Der Grundtyp der Weizenartigen (Poaceae, Tribus Triticeae).** In: Scherer S (Hg) Typen des Lebens. Berlin, pp 75-93.

Kidwell MG & Peterson KR (1991) **Evolution of transposable elements in Drosophila.** In: Warren L & Koprowski H (eds) New perspectives on evolution. New York, pp 139-154.

Klemm R (1993) **Die Huhnervogel (Galliformes): Taxonomische Aspekte unter besonderer Berilcksichtigung artiibergreifender Kreuzungen.** In: Scherer S (Hg) Typen des Lebens. Berlin, pp 159-184.

Knobloch IW (1968) **A check list of crosses in the Gramineae.** East Lansing.

Kutzelnigg H (1993) **Verwandtschaftliche Beziehungen zwischen den Gattungen und Arten der Kernobstgewachse (Rosaceae, Unterfamilie Maloideae).** In: Scherer S (Hg) Typen des Lebens. Berlin, pp 113-127.

Lamprecht H (1966) **Die Entstehung der Arten und h6heren Kategorien.** Wien.

Landgren P (1993) **On the origin of "species". The ideological roots of the speciesconcept.** IN:Scherer S (Hg) Typen des Lebens. Berlin, pp 47-64.

Lonnig WE (1993) **Artbegriff, Evolution und Schopfung.** Koln.

MacFadden BJ (1993) **Fossil horses: Systematics, paleobiology, and evolution of the family Equidae.** Cambridge.

MacFadden BJ & Hulbert RC (1988) **Explosive speciation at the base of the adaptive radiation of Miocene grazing horses.** Nature 336, 466-468.

Marsh FL (1941) **Fundamental biology.** Lincon, Nebraska.

Marsh FL (1976) **Variation and fixity in nature.** Mountain View.

May RM (1988) **How many species are there on earth?** Science 241, 1441-1448.

Mayr E (1940) **Speciation phenomena in birds.** Amer. Nat. 74, 249-278.

Mayr E (1963) **Animal species and evolution.** Cambridge, Mass.

Mayr E (1969) **Principles of systematic zoology.** New York.

Mayr E (1982) **The growth of biological thought. Diversity, evolution and inheritance.** Cambridge.

Mayr E (1990) **Die drei Schulen der Systematik.** Verh. Dtsch. Zool. Ges. 83, 263-276.

Mayr E, Linsley EG & Usinger RL (1953) **Methods and principles of systematic zoology.** New York.

Michener CD (1957) **Some bases for higher categories.** Syst. Zool. 6, 160-173.

Mishler RD & Donoghue MJ (1982) **Species concepts: A case for pluralism.** Syst. Zool. 31, 491-503.

Morton AG (1981) **History of botanical science.** London.

Mossakowski D (1990) **Hybridzonen an Artgrenzen: Regelfall oder Ausnahme in der Zoologie?** In: Streit B (ed) Evolution im Tierreich. Birkhauser, Basel. pp 201-222.

Orr HA (1991) **Is single-gene speciation possible?** Evolution 45,764-769.

Otte D & Endler J (eds, 1989) **Speciation and its consequences.** Massachusetts.

Panov EN (1989) **Natural hybridization and ethological isolation in birds.** Moscow.

Peters DS (1970) **Ober den Zusammenhang von biologischem Artbegriff und phylogenetischer Systematik.** Aufs. Reden Senckenberg, Naturf. Ges. 18,1-39.

Reif WE (1984) **Artabgrenzung und das Konzept der evolutioniren Art in der Paldontologie.** Z. Zool. Syst. Evolut. forsch. 22, 263-286.

Ross HH (1975) **Biological systematics.** Reading, Mass.

Schaeffer CW(1976) **The reality of the higher taxonomic categories.** Z. zool. Syst. Evolut.-forsch. 14, 1-10.

Scherer S (Hg, 1993a) **Typen des Lebens.** Berlin.

Scherer S (1993b) **Der Grundtyp der Entenartigen (Anatidae, Anseriformes): Biologische und paidontologische Streiflichter.** In: Scherer S (Hg) Typen des Lebens. Berlin, pp 131-158.

Scherer S & Hilsberg T (1982) **Hybridisierung und Verwandtschaftsgrade innerhalb der Anatidae: Eine evolutionstheoretische und systematische Betrachtung.** J. Ornithol. 123, 357-380.

Scherer S & Sontag C (1986) **Zur molekularen Taxonomie und Evolution der Anatidae.** Zool. Syst. Evolut.-forsch. 24,1-19.

Sibley CG & Ahlquist JE (1990) **Phylogeny and classification of birds.** New Haven.

Simpson GG (1945) **The principals of classifiation and a classification of mammals.** Bull. Amer. Mus. Nat. Hist. 85, 1-350.

Simpson GG (1953) **The major features of evolution.** New York.

Simpson GG (1961) **Principles of animal taxonomy.** New York.

Singer C (1962) **A history of biology to about the year 1900.** London.

Sperlich D (1984) **Populationsgenetische Aspekte der Artbildung.** Z. Zoo]. Syst. Evolut.-forsch. 22, 169-183.

Stains HJ (1967) **Carnivores and pinnipeds.** In: Anderson S & Knox-Jones J (eds) Recent mammals of the world. A synopsis of families. New York, pp 325-354.

Stebbins GL (1956) **Taxonomy and the evolution of genera, with special reference to the family Gramineae.** Evolution 10, 235-245.

Stein-Cadenbach H (1993) **Pferde (Equidae): Hybriden, Chromosomen und Artbildung** In: Scherer S (Hg) Typen des Lebens. Berlin, pp 225-244.

Sucker U (1978) **Philosophische Probleme der Arttheorie.** Jena.

Szymura JM & Barton NM (1986) **Genetic analysis of a hybrid zone between the fire-bellied toads, Bombina bombina and B. variegate, near Cracow in Southern Poland.** Evolution 40, 1141-1159.

Turesson G (1922) **The genotypic response of the plant species to the habitat.** Hereditas 3, 211-350.

Van Der Steen WJ & Voorzanger (1986) **Methodological problems in evolutionary biology VII. The species plague.** Acta Biotheor. 35, 205-221.

Van Gelder RG (1977) **Mammalian hybrids and generic limits.** American Museum Novitates 2635, 1-25.

Wiley EO (1981) **Phylogenetics - the theory and practice of phylogenetic systematics.** New York.

Willmann R (1985) **Die Art in Raum und Zeit. Das Artkonzept in der Biologie und Paliontologie.** Berlin.

Willmann R (1987) **Missverstandnisse um das biologische Artkonzept.** Paidont. Z. 61, 3-15.

Wise KP (l992) **Practical baraminology.** CEN Tech-n. J. 6, 122-137.

Wolfe SL (1993) **Molecular and cellular biology.** Belmont, CA.

Wolters HE (1983) **Die Vbgel Europas im System der Vogel.** Baden-Baden.

Zimbelmann F (1993) **Grundtypen bei Greifvogeln (Falconiformes).** In: Scherer S (Hg) Typen des Lebens. Berlin, p. 185-195.

Zwolfer H & Bush GL (1984) **Sympatrische und parapatrische Artbildung.** Z. zool. Syst. Evolut.forsch. 22, 211-233.

r	PLANTAE	r	ANIMALIA
sr	Embryophyta	p	Chordata
p	Bryophyta	Sp	Vertebrata
c	Musci	c	Aves
o	Funariales	o	Anseriformes
f	*bt*Funariaceae	f	*bt*Anatidae
p	Pteridophyta	f	*bt*Anhimidae*
c	Filicatae	o	Galliformes
o	Aspidiales	f	*bt*Phasianidae
f	*bt*Aspleniaceae	f	*bt*Cracidae*(?)
p	Spermatophyta	f	*bt*Megapodiidae*(?)
c	Dicotyledoneae	o	Falconiformes
SC	Rosidae	f	*bt*Cathartidae
o	Rosales	t	Accipitridae
t	Rosaceae	**sf**	*bt*Accipitrinae(?)
sf	*bt*maloideae	**sf**	*bt*Buteoninae(?)
sf	Dryadoideae	**sf**	*bt*Aegypiinae (?)
t	*bt*Geeae	f	*bt*Falconidae
c	Monocotyledoneae	o	Passeriformes
SC	Liliidae	so	Passeres
o	Poales	f	*bt*Estrildidae
f	Poaceae	f	Fringillidae
sf	Pooideae	**sf**	*bt*Carduelinae
t	*bt*Triticeae	**af**	*bt*Fringillinae(?)
		c	Mammalia
		SC	Placentalia
		o	Perissodactyla
		f	*bt*Equidae
		o	Primates
		f	*bt*Cercopithecidae
		sf	*bt*Homo

Table 1. *Taxonomical outline of plant and animal groups which have been investigated with respect to interspecific hybridization (see different authors in Scherer 1993a). Basic Types are highlighted by italics. A question-mark indicates that the assignment of Basic Type rank to this taxonomic group is uncertain.*

r = kingdom; sr = kingdom; p = phylum; sp = subphylum; c = class; sc = subclass;
o = order; so = suborder; f = family; sf = subfamily; t = tribe; bt = basic type
* assignment of Basic Type rank is based on circumstantial evidence, not primarily on hybridization data.

CRITERIA FOR COMPARING TWO GROUPS	YES	NO
Hybridization fails?	....	....
Ancestral group is uncertain?	....	....
Ancestral group is uncertain when fossils are considered?	....	....
Lineage[1] is lacking?	....	....
Lineage is lacking when fossils are considered?	....	....
Clear synapomorphies within *each* group?	....	....
Clear synapomorphies[2] when fossils are considered?	....	....
Ancestral group is younger?	....	....
Stratomorphological[3] intermediates lacking?	....	....
Artificial morphological discontinuity?[4]	....	....
Low frequency of synapomorphy when the two groups are compared with an out-group?	....	....
Molecular discontinuity?	....	....

Table 2. *Criteria to decide whether a phyletic disontinuity between any two groups of organisms exists, i.e. whether these two groups can be considered to belong to the same baramin.*

These questions are designed in order to be answered by YES or NO. If the answer to a particular question is YES, a phyletic discontinuity exists. Perhaps the two groups under discussion form two basic types. If the answer is NO, a phyletic discontinuity is lacking; in this case, the two groups may belong to the same basic type. For a more detailed discussion of the concept of discontinuity systematics please refer to Wise (1992).

[1]. A lineage is a continuous series of organisms connecting the two groups.

[2]. Synapomorphies are characters unique to all members of a particular group.

[3]. Stratomorphological intermediate is a fossil form which is morphologically intermediate between the two groups under discussion as well as stratigraphically intermediate between presumed ancestral and descendant forms.

[4]. An artificial morphological continuity would be created if a hybrid between two members of one group would bridge the gap to the other group.

REGIONAL METAMORPHISM WITHIN A CREATIONIST FRAMEWORK: WHAT GARNET COMPOSITIONS REVEAL

ANDREW A. SNELLING, Ph.D.,
Creation Science Foundation,
PO Box 6302,
Acacia Ridge D.C., Qld. 4110,
Australia.

KEYWORDS

Regional metamorphism, grade zones, garnets, compositional zoning, sedimentary precursors

ABSTRACT

The 'classical' model for regional metamorphic zones presupposes elevated temperatures and pressures due to deep burial and deformation/tectonic forces over large areas over millions of years — an apparent insurmountable hurdle for the creationist framework. One diagnostic metamorphic mineral is garnet, and variations in its composition have long been studied as an indicator of metamorphic grade conditions. Such compositional variations that have been detected between and within grains in the same rock strata are usually explained in terms of cationic fractionation with changing temperature during specific continuous reactions involving elemental distribution patterns in the rock matrix around the crystallizing garnet. Garnet compositions are also said to correlate with their metamorphic grade.

However, contrary evidence has been ignored. Compositional patterns preserved in garnets have been shown to be a reflection of compositional zoning in the original precursor minerals and sediments. Compositional variations between and within garnet grains in schists that are typical metapelites at Koongarra in the Northern Territory, Australia, support this minority viewpoint. Both homogeneous and compositionally zoned garnets, even together in the same hand specimen, display a range of compositions that would normally reflect widely different metamorphic grade and temperature conditions during their supposed growth. Thus the majority viewpoint cannot explain the formation of these garnets. It has also been demonstrated that the solid-solid transformation from a sedimentary chlorite precursor to garnet needs only low to moderate temperatures, while compositional patterns only reflect original depositional features in sedimentary environments. Thus catastrophic sedimentation, deep burial and rapid deformation/tectonics with accompanying low to moderate temperatures and pressures during, for example, a global Flood and its aftermath have potential as a model for explaining the 'classical' zones of progressive regional metamorphism.

INTRODUCTION

Of the two styles of metamorphism, contact and regional, the latter is most often used to argue against the young-earth Creation-Flood model. It is usually envisaged that sedimentary strata over areas of hundreds of square kilometres were subjected to elevated temperatures and pressures due to deep burial and deformation/tectonic forces over millions of years. The resultant mineralogical and textural transformations are said to be due to mineral reactions in the original sediments under the prevailing temperature-pressure conditions.

Often, mapping of metamorphic terrains has outlined zones of strata containing mineral assemblages that are believed to be diagnostic and confined to each zone respectively. It is assumed that these mineral assemblages reflect the metamorphic transformation conditions specific to each zone, so that by traversing across these metamorphic zones higher metamorphic grades (due to former higher temperature-pressure conditions) are progressively encountered. Amongst the metamorphic mineral assemblages diagnostic of each zone are certain minerals whose presence in the rocks is indicative of each zone, and these are called index minerals. Garnet is one of these key index minerals. Across a metamorphic terrain, the line along which garnet first appears in rocks of similar composition is called the garnet isograd ('same metamorphic grade') and represents one boundary of the garnet zone. With increasing metamorphic grade and in other zones garnet continues to be an important constituent of the mineral assemblages.

GARNET COMPOSITIONS

Variation in garnet compositions, particularly their MnO content, was for a long time used as an estimator of regional metamorphic grade. Goldschmidt [14] first noted an apparent systematic decrease in MnO content with increase in metamorphic grade, a relationship which he attributed to the incorporation of the major part of the rock MnO in the earliest formed garnet. Miyashiro [24] and Engel and Engel [11] also followed this line of thought, Miyashiro suggesting that the larger Mn^{2+} ions were readily incorporated in the garnet structure at the lower pressures, whereas at higher pressures smaller Fe^{2+} and Mg^{2+} were preferentially favoured. Thus it was proposed that a decrease in garnet MnO indicated an increase in grade of regional metamorphism. Lambert [21] produced corresponding evidence for a decrease in garnet CaO with increasing metamorphic grade. Sturt [45] demonstrated in somewhat pragmatic fashion what appeared to be a general inverse relationship between (MnO + CaO) content of garnet and overall grade of metamorphism, a scheme which was taken up and reinforced by Nandi [27].

Not all investigators, however, agreed with this line of thinking. Kretz [20] demonstrated the possible influence of co-existing minerals on the composition of another given mineral. Variation in garnet composition was seen to depend not only on pressure-temperature variation but also to changes in the compositions of the different components within its matrix as these responded to changing metamorphic grade. Albee [1], like Kretz [20] and Frost [13], examined elemental distribution coefficients in garnet-biotite pairs as possible grade indicators, but concluded that results were complex and equivocal, and suggested that metamorphic equilibrium was frequently not attained. Similarly, Evans [12] suggested caution in the interpretation of increasing garnet MgO as indicating increasingly higher pressures of metamorphism. He pointed out that the volume behaviour of Mg-Fe exchange relations between garnet and other common silicates indicates that, for given bulk compositions, the Mg-Fe ratios in garnet will decrease with pressure.

With the advent of the electron probe microanalyser it became possible to detect compositional variations even within mineral grains including garnet, where often it was found that traversing from cores to rims of grains the MnO and CaO contents decreased with a concomitant increase in FeO and MgO [15]. Hollister [16] concluded that this zoning arose by partitioning of MnO in accordance with the Rayleigh fractionation model between garnet and its matrix as the former grew. Perhaps more importantly he drew attention to the preservation of such zones, that remained unaffected by diffusion, and hence unequilibrated, throughout the later stages of the metamorphism that was presumed to have induced their growth. Concurrently, Atherton and Edmunds [5] suggested that the zoning patterns reflected changing garnet-matrix equilibrium conditions during growth and/or polyphase metamorphism, but that once formed garnet and its zones behaved as closed systems unaffected by changes in conditions at the periphery of the growing grain.

Through his own work, and that of Chinner [8] and Hutton [17], Atherton [3] drew attention to the presence of garnets of quite different compositions in rocks of similar grade, and sometimes in virtual juxtaposition. His conclusion was that the MnO content, and indeed the whole divalent cation component, of garnet was substantially a reflection of host rock composition and that any simple tie between garnet composition and metamorphic grade was unlikely. Subsequently Atherton [4] suggested that zoning and progressive changes in garnet compositions were due to changes in distribution coefficients of the divalent cations with increase in grade, and considered that 'anomalies in the sequence (were) explicable in terms of variations in the compositions of the host rock'.

Müller and Schneider [26] found that the MnO content of garnet reflected not only metamorphic grade and chemistry of the host rocks, but also their oxygen fugacity. They rejected Hollister's Rayleigh fractionation model and concluded that decrease in Mn, and concomitant increase in Fe, in garnet with increasing grade stemmed from a progressive reduction in oxygen fugacity. Hsu [18], in his investigation of phase relations in the Al-Mn-Fe-Si-O-H system, had found that the stability of the almandine end-member is strongly dependent on oxygen fugacity, and is favoured by assemblages characterised by high activity of divalent Fe. In contrast, the activity of divalent Mn is less influenced by higher oxygen fugacity. Thus Müller and Schneider [26] concluded that the observed decrease in Mn in garnet with increasing metamorphic grade is due to the buffering capacity of graphite present near nucleating garnets. With increasing grade the graphite buffer increasingly stabilises minerals dependent on low oxygen fugacity, that is, almandine is increasingly formed instead of spessartine. Müller and Schneider also noted that some of their garnets were not zoned, but exhibited inhomogeneities distributed in irregular domains throughout the garnet grains.

Miyashiro and Shido [25], in a substantially theoretical treatment, concluded that the principal factor controlling successive garnet compositions is the amount and composition of the garnet already crystallised, since the matrix will be correspondingly depleted in the oxides present in the earlier formed garnet. Also using a theoretical approach, Anderson and Buckley [2] showed that for 'reasonable diffusion coefficients and boundary conditions' observed zoning profiles in garnets could be explained quite adequately by diffusion principles: that given original homogeneities in the parent rock, the interplay of diffusion phenomena could explain variation of zoning profiles in separate grains of an individual mineral species in domains as small as that of a hand specimen.

Tracy *et al.* [47] noted that garnets from metamorphosed pelitic assemblages show, in different metamorphic zones, 'element distribution patterns that are complex functions of rock bulk composition, specific continuous reactions in which garnet is involved, P-T history of the rock, homogeneous diffusion rates with garnet, and possibly also the availability of metamorphic fluids at the various stages of garnet development'. They applied preliminary calibrations of garnet-biotite and garnet-cordierite Fe-Mg exchange reactions and several Fe-Mg-Mn continuous mineral reactions to the results of very detailed studies of zoned garnets in order to evaluate changing P-T conditions during prograde and retrograde metamorphism in central Massachusetts (USA).

Stanton [38-41], in his studies of Broken Hill (New South Wales, Australia) banded iron formations, suggested that the garnets represented *in situ* transformation of somewhat manganiferous chamositic septachlorite, and that any zoning reflected the original oolitic structure of the sedimentary chamosite. In a further study, Stanton and Williams [44] concluded that, because compositional differences occur on a fine (1-2mm) scale in garnets within a simple one-component matrix (quartz), garnet compositions must faithfully reflect original compositional variations within the chemical sediments, and not represent variations in metamorphic grade.

McAteer [23] demonstrated the presence in a garnet-mica schist of two compositionally and texturally distinct garnet types, which she attributed to a sequence of mineral reactions that proceeded with changing thermal history of the rock. Of the two types, one was coarse grained and zoned (MnO and CaO decreasing towards grain margins), while the other was fine-grained and essentially uniform in composition. Attainment of chemical equilibrium between all garnets and their rock matrix, but maintenance of disequilibrium within large garnets, appears to have been assumed.

In a review of research on compositional zoning in metamorphic minerals, Tracy [46] ignored Stanton's demonstration that the compositional zoning in garnets can only be explained in some metamorphic rocks as faithful reflections of original compositional variations within the precursor minerals and sediments, and not as a function of variations in metamorphic grade or cationic supply during crystal growth. Instead, Tracy summarised the various models already proposed — cationic fractionation particularly of Mn (resulting in variations in the supply of cations) with changing temperatures during progressive metamorphism, and reaction partitioning of cations which depends upon the exact mineralogical composition of the reservoir or matrix surrounding any one garnet grain, especially relative proportions of matrix minerals that are in direct reaction relation with a garnet grain. These models both correlate changes in garnet composition with increasing metamorphic grade, relying on mineral reactions and diffusion of cations to explain compositional zoning trends, which it is envisaged change as mineral reactions and temperatures change.

This is still the consensus viewpoint. Loomis [22], Spear [35], and Spear *et al.* [36], for example, insist that metamorphic garnets undergo a form of fractional crystallisation which involves fractionation of material into the interior of a crystallising garnet grain with consequent change in the effective bulk composition, the zoning profile preserved in the garnet being a function of the total amount of material that has fractionated. Furthermore, Spear [35] insists that because intracrystalline diffusion is so slow at these conditions, the interior of the garnet is effectively isolated from chemical equilibrium with the matrix. Spear then points to the work of Yardley [50] to insist that with increasing temperatures intracrystalline diffusion within garnet grains becomes more rapid until eventually all chemical zoning is erased. Indeed, Yardley claimed to have found that at the temperatures of staurolite and sillimanite grade metamorphism internal diffusion of cations within garnet grains is sufficient to eliminate the zoning that developed during earlier growth.

Yardley also rightly pointed out that the fractionation models for garnet zoning assume that that diffusion is negligible at lower metamorphic grades. That there is negligible cationic diffusion in garnet at lower grades is amply demonstrated in the garnets described by Olympio and Anderson [31], whose pattern of chemical zoning coincided with textural (optical) zones, clearly representing distinct presumed growth stages. Nevertheless, even where textural (optical) zones are not evident there may still be chemical zoning, as found by Tuccillo *et al.* [48]. Indeed, confusing the picture somewhat, Tuccillo *et al.* found that the chemical zoning in their garnets under study, though from a high grade metamorphic terrain, was not only preserved but was the reverse in terms of cations to that normally expected, and this they attributed to a diffusional retrograde effect.

However, the work of Stanton and Williams [44], who found marked compositional changes from one garnet to the next on a scale of 1-2mm in finely bedded banded iron formations in the high grade metamorphic terrain at Broken Hill (New South Wales, Australia), has been ignored. They found that

in view of the minuteness of the domains involved it appears evident that compositional variation cannot be attributed to variations in metamorphic pressures, temperatures or oxygen fugacities. Neither can they be attributed to variation in garnet-matrix partition functions, as most of the garnets occur in one simple matrix — quartz.

They therefore concluded

that in spite of the high (sillimanite) grade of the relevant metamorphism, any equilibration of garnet compositions, and hence any associated inter-grain metamorphic diffusion, has been restricted to a scale of less than 1mm; that garnet compositions here reflect original rock compositions on an ultra-fine scale, and have no connotations concerning metamorphic grade; that, hence, the garnets must arrive from a single precursor material, earlier suggested to be a manganiferous chamositic septachlorite; and that the between-bed variation: within-bed uniformity of garnet composition reflects an original pattern of chemical sedimentation — a pattern preserved with the utmost delicacy through a period of approximately 1800×10^6 years and a metamorphic episode of sillimanite grade. [44, p. 514]

These findings are clearly at odds with the claims of other investigators, yet Stanton [42,43] has amassed more evidence to substantiate his earlier work. To test these competing claims, therefore, a suitable area of metamorphic terrain with schists containing garnet porphyblasts was chosen for study.

THE KOONGARRA AREA

The Koongarra area is 250km east of Darwin (Northern Territory, Australia) at latitude 12°52'S and longitude 132°50'E. The regional geology has been described in detail by Needham and Stuart-Smith [30] and by Needham [28,29], while Snelling [33] describes the local Koongarra area geology.

The Archaean basement to this metamorphic terrain consists of domes of granitoids and granitic gneisses (the Nanambu Complex), the nearest outcrop being 5km to the north. Some of the lowermost overlying Lower Proterozoic metasediments were accreted to these domes during amphibolite grade regional metamorphism (estimated to represent conditions of 5-8kb and 550-630°C) at 1800-1870Ma. Multiple isoclinal recumbent folding accompanied metamorphism. The Lower Proterozoic Cahill Formation flanking the Nanambu Complex has been divided into two members. The lower member is dominated by a thick basal dolomite and passes transitionally upwards into the psammitic upper member, which is largely feldspathic schist and quartzite. The uranium mineralisation at Koongarra is associated with graphitic horizons within chloritized quartz-mica (±feldspar ±garnet) schists overlying the basal dolomite in the lower member.

Owing to the isoclinal recumbent folding of metasedimentary units of the Cahill Formation, the typical rock sequence encountered at Koongarra is probably a tectono-stratigraphy (from youngest to oldest):

— muscovite-biotite-quartz-feldspar schist (at least 180m thick)
— garnet-muscovite-biotite-quartz schist (90–100m thick)
— sulphide-rich graphite-mica-quartz schist (±garnet) (about 25m thick)
— distinctive graphite-quartz-chlorite schist marker unit (5–8m thick)
— quartz-chlorite schist (±illite, garnet, sillimanite, muscovite) (50m thick) — contains the mineralised zone

Polyphase deformation accompanied metamorphism of the original sediments, that were probably dolomite, shales and siltstones. Johnston [19] identified a D_2 event as responsible for the dominant S_2 foliation of the schist sequence, which dips at 55° to the south-east at Koongarra.

Superimposed on the primary prograde metamorphic mineral assemblages is a distinct and extensive primary alteration halo associated with the uranium mineralisation at Koongarra. This alteration extends for up to 1.5km from the ore in a direction perpendicular to the disposition of the host quartz-chlorite schist unit, because the mineralisation is essentially stratabound. The outer zone of the alteration halo is most extensively developed in the semi-pelitic schists and is manifested by the pseudomorphous replacement of biotite by chlorite, rutile and quartz, and feldspar by sericite. Metamorphic muscovite, garnet, tourmaline, magnetite, pyrite and apatite are preserved. In the inner alteration zone, less than 50m from ore, the metamorphic rock fabric is disrupted, and quartz is replaced by pervasive chlorite and phengitic mica, and garnet by chlorite. Relict metamorphic phases, mainly muscovitic mica, preserve the S_2 foliation. Coarse chlorite after biotite may also be preserved.

KOONGARRA GARNETS

Garnets are fairly common in the garnet-muscovite-biotite-quartz schist unit at Koongarra, being usually fresh and present in large quantities, often grouped, within various macroscopic layers. Within the inner alteration halo and the quartz-chlorite schist hosting the mineralisation most of the garnets have largely been pseudomorphously replaced by chlorite. Occasionally garnet remnants remain within the pseudomorphous chlorite knots, or the common boxwork textures within these pseudomorphous chlorite knots confirm that the chlorite is pseudomorphously replacing garnets.

The garnets are always porphyroblastic, and sometimes idioblastic, indicative of pre-kinematic growth. They may be up to 2cm in diameter, but most are typically about 0.5cm across. Often, the garnets also show some degree of rolling and sygmoidal traces of inclusions. These features are usually regarded as evidence for syn-kinematic growth [37]. In a few of these cases rolling is minimal and inclusion traces pass out uninterrupted into the surrounding schist. The schistosity is often draped around these garnet porphryblasts and sometimes the latter are slightly flattened. Thus the last stages of garnet growth occurred during the final stages of the D_2 deformation of the prograde metamorphic layering S_1, that is, during the development of the predominant S_2 schistosity. This, in turn, implies that garnet development and growth took place before and during the deformation of the earlier S_1 schistosity, that is, pre- and syn-kinematic to the S_2 schistosity and D_2 deformation.

Thirteen garnet-containing samples were chosen from three of the schist units — the ore-hosting quartz-chlorite schist (three samples), the sulphide-rich graphite-mica-quartz schist (five samples), and the garnet-muscovite-biotite-quartz schist (five samples). These 13 samples contained a total of 33 garnets that were all analysed using an electron probe microanalyser. Composite point analyses were made where garnets were of uniform composition, while traverses revealed compositional zoning when present. All results are listed in Snelling [32].

All the garnets are essentially almandine, the Fe^{2+} end-member, with varying amounts of spessartine (Mn^{2+}), pyrope (Mg^{2+}) and grossularite (Ca^{2+}) structural units/end-members substituting in the crystal lattices. Tucker [49] reported an analysis of a Koongarra Fe-rich garnet with an Fe_2O_3 content of 6.22%, implying that the substitution of the andradite (Fe^{3+}) end-member may be quite substantial. The compositional variations in Fe, Mn, Ca and Mg both between and within the analysed garnets were plotted in ternary diagrams, and from these

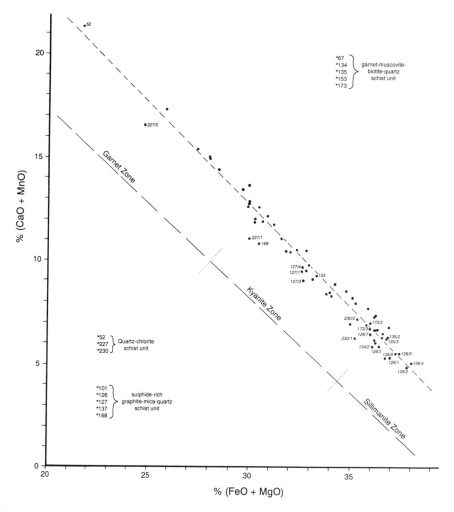

Figure 1. Plot of (CaO + MnO) vs. (FeO + MgO) variations in all analysed Koongarra garnets, after the style of Nandi [26]. His line of best fit for his data is shown, plus his boundaries between garnet compositions of each metamorphic zone. The line of best fit through the Koongarra data is shown, as are the sample/garnet numbers of all the homogeneous garnets. The analytical data are from Snelling [32].

it was determined that two principal substitutions have occurred — Mn for Fe and Mg for Ca, though the latter is very minor compared to the former. Nevertheless, these Koongarra garnets revealed the general inverse relationship between (CaO + MnO) and (FeO + MgO), which can be seen clearly in Figure 1.

Of the 33 garnets analysed, 22 had homogeneous compositions and only 11 were compositionally zoned. In the three samples from the ore-hosting quartz-chlorite schist unit five garnets were analysed and all were compositionally homogeneous, whereas in the overlying sulphide-rich graphite-mica-quartz schist unit the five selected samples contained 16 garnets, analyses of which revealed that 11 were compositionally homogeneous and the other five were compositionally zoned. Furthermore, four of the 10 samples from the two garnet-bearing schist units overlying the ore-hosting quartz-chlorite schist contain both compositionally homogeneous and zoned garnets in a ratio of six zoned to eight homogeneous, without any textural evidence to distinguish between the two. The other samples in these schist units either had all compositionally homogeneous garnets or all compositionally zoned garnets.

Traverses of point analyses across the compositionally zoned garnets enabled the compositional zoning to be quantified. The most pronounced zoning is with respect to MnO, with cores generally having higher MnO relative to rims, and as FeO substitutes for MnO, FeO follows an inverse trend (Figures 2 and 3). Zonation with respect to CaO and MgO is not pronounced, but generally CaO follows the MnO trend and MgO follows FeO. This is understandable in terms of the ionic radii for the ions involved [24]. Figure 4 shows the geochemical trends of all the analysed zoned garnets from cores to rims, the strong compositional differences following the same inverse relationship between (CaO + MnO) and (FeO + MgO) as the compositionally homogeneous garnets.

DISCUSSION

Garnets analysed in the Koongarra schists are typical of garnets from metapelites, the compositional trends between and within garnet grains being almost identical to those obtained from garnets in metapelites in metamorphic terrains in other parts of the world [26]. The (CaO + MnO) versus (FeO + MgO) plot in Figure 1 has marked on it the line of best fit and compositional subdivisions based on the typical zones of progressive regional metamorphic grade as determined by Nandi [27]. The Koongarra data are distributed along their own line of best fit and straddle the garnet, kyanite and sillimanite zones of Nandi's data.

Nandi's contention was that (CaO + MnO) content of garnets decreased with increasing metamorphic grade, as originally proposed by Sturt [45] but challenged by Bahnemann [7]. Bahnemann studied garnet compositions in granulite facies gneisses of the Messina district in the Limpopo Folded Belt of Northern Transvaal and found compositional variations which were comparable to those found by Nandi, but which scattered across the metamorphic zones of Nandi's diagram. However, Bahnemann was able to show, from earlier work on the same rocks [6,9] and by using Currie's cordierite-garnet geothermometer [10], that whatever the precise temperature-pressure conditions may have been during the formation of the garnets, they were high and uniform over much of the Messina district. Thus Bahnemann concluded that the (CaO + MnO) versus (FeO + MgO) trends on the plot reflected host rock chemistry, and that metamorphic isograds cannot be inferred from the position of points on such a line. Bahnemann nevertheless noted that his line of best fit differed slightly from that of Nandi and suggested that his own line may be characteristic for the garnets from the area he had studied.

The (CaO + MnO) versus (FeO + MgO) plots of the garnets at Koongarra (Figures 1 and 4) also define a line of best fit that differs from that of Nandi. The Koongarra schists contain some graphite, which could be an additional factor in the growth of the zoned garnets, the iron-rich rims presumably being produced by graphite buffering as the temperature of metamorphism increased. However, in four of the 13 samples there are both homogeneous and compositionally zoned garnets side-by-side. Furthermore, in one instance (sample 173) there is a compositionally zoned garnet with a core that has almost three times the (CaO + MnO) content of its rim, yet the latter's composition is very similar to the two other adjoining homogeneous garnet grains. If the presence of graphite buffering the metamorphic reactions was needed to produce the zoned garnet, then why the adjoining homogeneous garnets? A far more logical explanation is that the zonation and compositional variations are due to chemical variations in the original precursor minerals and sedimentary rocks, as suggested by Stanton [42, 43].

When Nandi produced his original plot, he used compositional data of 84 samples of garnets belonging to different grades of regionally metamorphosed pelitic rocks which he compiled from six papers in the then current literature. One of these, Sturt [45], drew on some of the same data, which comes from metamorphic terrains such as the Stavanger area of Norway, the Gosaisyo-Takanuki area of Japan, the Adirondacks of the USA, and the Moine and Dalradian of Scotland. When garnet porphyroblasts of quite different compositions from the different metamorphic terrains were plotted on a (CaO + MnO) versus (FeO + MgO) diagram Nandi found that they grouped along a line of best fit in subdivisions that reflected the different metamorphic grade zones from which they came — garnet, kyanite and sillimanite (see Figures 1 and 4). Nandi showed virtually no overlap in the compositions of garnets from different grades at the boundaries he drew across his line of best fit, yet on

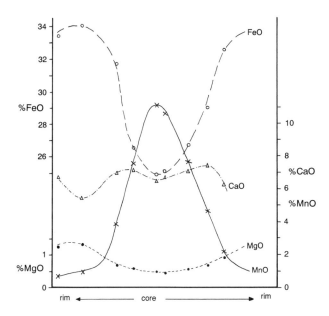

Figure 2. A line profile across a zoned garnet grain in sample 173 from the garnet-muscovite-biotite-quartz schist unit at Koongarra, showing the variations in FeO, CaO, MgO and MnO. Data from Snelling [32].

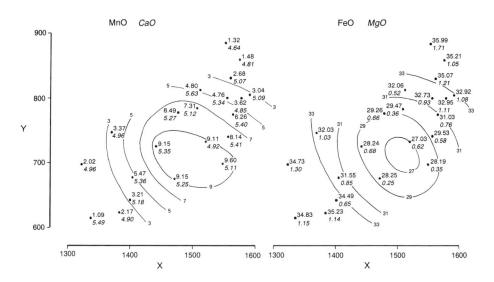

Figure 3. Plan view of a compositionally zoned garnet grain in sample 101 from the sulphide-rich graphite-mica-quartz schist unit at Koongarra showing the FeO, MgO, MnO and CaO contents at each analysed point. Compositional contours have been drawn in for FeO and MnO. The data are from Snelling [32].

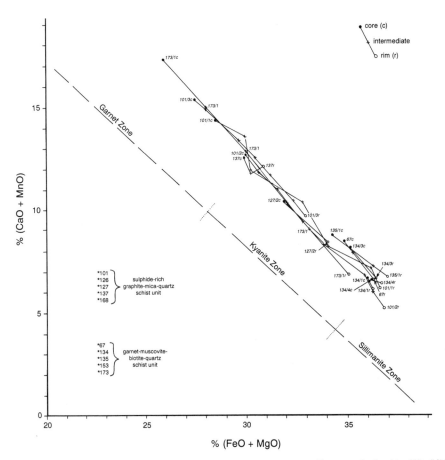

Figure 4. Plot of (CaO + MnO) vs. (FeO + MgO) variations in all analysed zoned garnets at Koongarra after the style of Nandi [26]. Again, his line of best fit for his data is shown, plus his boundaries between garnet compositions of each metamorphic zone. Core to rim compositions are plotted with lines linking them between their intermediate compositions. Sample/garnet numbers are shown. The data are from Snelling [32].

Sturt's similar plot with garnet data from the same and other metamorphic terrains there was considerable overlap of compositions between garnets from the different metamorphic grades. Furthermore, those garnets that Sturt recorded as coming from garnet grade metapelites almost exclusively plotted in Nandi's kyanite grade grouping, so the picture is far from being clear-cut as Nandi originally reported it. In other words, these data do not show that garnet compositions systematically change with increasing metamorphic grade.

As Bahnemann found in the Limpopo Folded Belt, where garnets from a number of different granulite facies host-rocks showed a wide range of composition yet reflected the same general pressure-temperature conditions of metamorphism, the data here from the Koongarra schists show widely divergent garnet compositions, even within individual grains, yet the schists are typical metapelites of a classical garnet zone within an amphibolite grade metamorphic terrain. The presence of garnet in these schists without either kyanite and/or sillimanite confirms that these schists fall within the garnet zone, although kyanite has been observed with staurolite in equivalent Cahill Formation schists to the south [30]. Nevertheless, it is inconceivable that there would be any appreciable variation in metamorphic temperature-pressure conditions over the approximate 370m of strike length and 90m of stratigraphic range from which the studied samples came. Indeed, even in the stratigraphically lowermost ore-hosting quartz-chlorite schist unit the five compositionally homogeneous garnets in the three samples at that stratigraphic level almost spanned the complete compositional range in Figure 1, from extremely high (CaO + MnO) content in the supposedly lower temperature end of the garnet zone to a lower (CaO + MnO) and high (FeO + MgO) content at the supposedly high temperature end of the kyanite zone.

Yet if any of these schist units at Koongarra should have been at a higher prograde metamorphic temperature it would have been this quartz-chlorite schist unit, because it is stratigraphically closer to the Nanambu Complex basement towards which the metamorphic grade increased, causing some of the metasediments closest to it to be accreted to it. Similarly, one of the samples from the sulphide-rich graphite-mica-quartz schist unit (sample 101) has in it a garnet whose core could be regarded as being of garnet zone composition, while its rim is supposedly indicative of the sillimanite zone.

These numerous 'anomalies' must indicate that garnet compositions are substantially a reflection of compositional domains within the precursor sediments and/or minerals, and **not** metamorphic grade. Stanton [42,43] has shown that diffusion during regional metamorphism has been restricted to relatively minute distances (<1mm) and that there is no clear, direct evidence of prograde metamorphic mineral reactions, so that metamorphic equilibrium does not appear to have been attained through even very small domains. Even though the majority of researchers maintain that compositional zoning in garnets has been due to mineral reactions and cationic fractionation, and that at higher grades the compositional zoning is homogenised by diffusion, Stanton and Williams [44] have clearly shown at Broken Hill that at the highest grades of metamorphism the compositional zoning in garnets is neither homogenised nor the result of either mineral reactions or cationic fractionation, but an accurate preservation of compositional zoning in the original precursor oolites in the precursor sediment. Nevertheless, while their conclusion is not questioned, their time-scale is, because it strains credulity to suppose that the original pattern of chemical sedimentation could have been preserved with the 'utmost delicacy' through a presumed period of 1.8 billion years.

What is equally amazing is the discovery by Stanton [43] of distinctly hydrous 'quartz' in well-bedded quartz-muscovite-biotite-almandine-spinel rocks also in the Broken Hill metamorphic terrain. He comments that it seems 'remarkable' that this silica should still retain such a notably hydrous nature after 1.8 billion years that included relatively high-grade (i.e. high temperature-pressure) metamorphism! Not only does this discovery confirm that metamorphic quartz has been produced by dehydration and transformation *in situ* of precursor silica gel and/or chert, but that the temperatures, pressures and time-scales normally postulated are not necessarily required.

Stanton [43] maintains that it has long been recognised that particular clays and zeolites derive in many instances from specific precursors. Likewise, it is self-evident and unavoidable that many metamorphosed bedded oxides (including quartz), together with carbonates and authigenic silicates such as the feldspars, have derived from sedimentary/diagenitic precursors, and the establishment thereby of this precursor derivation for at least some regional metamorphic minerals is a principle, not an hypothesis. What Stanton then proceeds to show is how this principle applies to the broader spectrum of metamorphic silicates, including almandine garnet.

He points to his earlier evidence [39,42] that almandine has derived directly from a chamositic chlorite containing very finely dispersed chemical SiO_2, and suggests that dehydration and incorporation of this silica into the chlorite structure induces *in situ* transformation to the garnet structure. Furthermore, instability induced by Mn, and perhaps small quantities of Ca, in the structure may predispose the chlorite to such transformation. Any silica in excess of the requirements of this process aggregates into small rounded particles within the garnet grain — the quartz 'inclusions' that are almost a characteristic feature of the garnets of metapelites, including the garnets at Koongarra. Stanton then supports his contention with electron microprobe analyses of several hundred chlorites, from metamorphosed stratiform sulphide deposits in Canada and Australia, and of almandine garnets immediately associated with the chlorites. These analyses plot side-by-side on ternary diagrams, graphically showing the compositional similarities of the chlorites in these original chemical sediments to the garnets in the same rock that have been produced by metamorphism. This strongly suggests that the process was one of a solid-solid transformation, with excess silica producing quartz 'inclusions'. As Stanton insists, why should these inclusions be exclusively quartz if these garnets had grown from mineral reactions within the rock matrix, because the latter contains abundant muscovite, biotite and other minerals in addition to quartz, minerals that should also have been 'included' in the growing garnet grains?

Stanton and Williams [44] have conclusively demonstrated that the compositional zones within individual garnet porphyroblasts reflect compositional zoning in precursor sedimentary mineral grains. Thus, if primary (depositional) compositional features have led to a mimicking of metamorphic grade [39,42], then it has been shown [34,42,43] that the classical zones of regional metamorphic mineral assemblages may instead reflect facies of clay and clay-chlorite mineral sedimentation, rather than variations in pressure-temperature conditions in subsequent metamorphism. Stanton [43] goes on to say that if regional metamorphic silicates do develop principally by transformation and grain growth, the problem of the elusive metamorphic reaction in the natural *milieu* is resolved. There is no destabilising of large chemical domains leading to extensive diffusion, no widespread reaction tending to new equilibria among minerals. Traditionally it has been supposed that as metamorphism progressed each rock unit passed through each successive grade, but the common lack of evidence that 'high-grade' zones have passed through all the mineral assemblages of the 'lower-grade' zones can now be accounted for. The real metamorphic grade indicators are then not the hypothetical intermineral reactions usually postulated, but the relevant precursor transformations, which may be solid-solid or in some cases gel-solid. Stanton concludes that it would be going too far to maintain that there was no such thing as a regional metamorphic mineral reaction, or that regional metamorphic equilibrium was never attained, but the role of metamorphic reactions in generating the bulk of regional metamorphic mineral matter is 'probably, quite contrary to present belief, almost vanishingly small.'

The other key factor in elucidating regional metamorphic grades, zones and mineral compositions besides precursor mineral/sediment compositions would be the temperatures of precursor transformations, rather than the temperatures of presumed 'classical' metamorphic mineral reactions. It is thus highly significant that dehydration and incorporation of silica into the chlorite structure induces *in situ* transformation to garnet at only low to moderate temperatures and pressures that are conceivable over short time-scales during catastrophic sedimentation, burial and tectonic activities. Indeed, the realization that the 'classical' zones of progressive regional metamorphism are potentially only a reflection of variations in original sedimentation, as can be demonstrated in continental shelf depositional facies today, provides creationists with a potential scientifically satisfying explanation of regional metamorphism within their time framework, which includes catastrophic sedimentation, deep burial and rapid deformation/tectonics with accompanying low to moderate temperatures and pressures during, for example, the global Flood and its aftermath [34].

CONCLUSIONS

Garnets in the amphibolite grade schists at Koongarra show wide compositional variations both within and between grains, even at the thin section scale, a pattern which is not consistent with the current consensus on the formation of metamorphic garnets. Rather than elevated temperatures and pressures being required, along with fractionational crystallization, elemental partitioning and garnet-matrix reaction partitioning, the evidence at Koongarra and in other metamorphic terrains is consistent with solid-solid transformation at moderate temperatures of precursor sedimentary chlorite, complete with compositional variations due to precursor oolites, into garnet such that the compositional variations in the precursor chlorite are preserved without redistribution via diffusion. These compositional variations in garnets contradict the 'classical' view that particular compositions represent different metamorphic grade zones, since at Koongarra the compositional variations even in single garnets span wide ranges of presumed metamorphic temperatures and grades. Thus the 'classical' explanation for progressive regional metamorphism, different grade zones being imposed on original sedimentary strata over hundreds of square kilometres due to elevated temperatures and pressures resulting from deep burial and deformation/tectonic forces over millions of years, has to be seriously questioned. A feasible alternative is that these zones represent patterns of original precursor sedimentation, such as we see on continental shelves today. Creationists may thus be able to explain regional metamorphism within their time framework on the basis of catastrophic sedimentation, deep burial and rapid deformation/tectonics, with accompanying low to moderate temperatures and pressures, during, for example, the global Flood and its aftermath.

REFERENCES

[1] A.L. Albee, **Distribution of Fe, Mg and Mn between Garnet and Biotite in Natural Mineral Assemblages**, Journal of Geology, 73 (1965) 155-164.

[2] D.E. Anderson and B.R. Buckley, **Zoning in Garnets — Diffusion Models**, Contributions to Mineralogy and Petrology, **40** (1973) 87-104.

[3] M.P. Atherton, **The Composition of Garnet in Regionally Metamorphosed Rocks**, in Controls of Metamorphism, W.S. Pitcher and G.W. Flynn, Editors, 1966, Oliver and Boyd, London, pp. 281-290.

[4] M.P. Atherton, **The Variation in Garnet, Biotite and Chlorite Composition in Medium Grade Pelitic Rocks from the Dalradian, Scotland, with Particular Reference to the Zonation in Garnet**, Contributions to Mineralogy and Petrology, 8 (1968) 347-371.

[5] M.P. Atherton and W.M. Edmunds, **An Electron Microprobe Study of Some Zoned Garnets from Metamorphic Rocks**, Earth and Planetary Science Letters, 1 (1966) 185-193.

[6] K.P. Bahnemann, **The Origin of the Singele Granite Gneiss near Messina, Northern Transvaal**, Special Publication of the Geological Society of South Africa, 3 (1973) 235-244.

[7] K.P. Bahnemann, **Garnets as Possible Indicators of Metamorphic Grade in the Limpopo Folded Belt near Messina in the Northern Transvaal**, Transactions of the Geological Society of South Africa, 78 (1975) 251-256.

[8] G.A. Chinner, **Pelitic Gneisses with Varying Ferrous/Ferric Ratios from Glen Clova, Angus, Scotland**, Journal of Petrology, 1 (1960) 178-217.

[9] G.A. Chinner and T.R. Sweatman, **A Former Association of Enstatite and Kyanite**, Mineralogical Magazine, 36 (1968) 1052-1060.

[10] K.L. Currie, **The Reaction 3 Cordierite = 2 Garnet + 4 Sillimanite + 5 Quartz as a Geological Thermometer in the Opinicon Lake Region, Ontario**, Contributions to Mineralogy and Petrology, 33 (1971) 215-226.

[11] A.E.J. Engel and C.G.Engel, **Progressive Metamorphism and Granitization of the Major Paragneiss, Northwest Adirondack Mountains, New York, Part II**, Bulletin of the Geological Society of America, 71 (1960) 1-58.

[12] B.W. Evans, **Pyrope Garnet — a Piezometer or Thermometer?**, Bulletin of the Geological Society of America, 76 (1965) 1295-1299.

[13] M.J. Frost, **Metamorphic Grade and Iron-Magnesium Distribution between Co-existing Garnet-Biotite and Garnet-Hornblende**, Geological Magazine, 99 (1962) 427-438.

[14] V.M. Goldschmidt, **Geologisch-Petrographische Studien im Hochgebirge des Südlichen Norwegen. V. Die Injektoinmetamorphose im Stavangergebiet**, Skrifter Videnskapslig Selskap, I Math.-Naturw. Kl. No. 10 (1920), Oslo.

[15] B. Harte and K.I. Henley, **Zoned Almanditic Garnets from Regionally Metamorphosed Rocks**, Nature, 210 (1966) 689-692.

[16] L.S. Hollister, **Garnet Zoning: An Interpretation Based on the Rayleigh Fractionation Model**, Science, 154 (1966) 1647-1651.

[17] C.O. Hutton, **Composition of Some Garnets in Low-Grade Schists**, Transactions of the Royal Society of New Zealand, 1 (1962) 129-133.

[18] L.C. Hsu, **Selected Phase Relationships in the System Al-Mn-Fe-Si-O-H: A Model for Garnet Equilibria**, Journal of Petrology, 9 (1968) 40-83.

[19] J.D. Johnston, **Structural Evolution of the Pine Creek Inlier and Mineralisation Therein, Northern Territory, Australia**, Ph.D. thesis (unpublished), 1984, Monash University, Melbourne, Australia.

[20] R. Kretz, **Chemical Study of Garnet, Biotite and Hornblende from Gneisses of Southwestern Quebec, with Emphasis on the Distribution of Elements in Co-existing Minerals**, Journal of Geology, 67 (1959) 371-402.

[21] R. St. J. Lambert, **The Mineralogy and Metamorphism of the Moine Schists of the Morar and Knoydart Districts of Inverness-shire**, Transactions of the Royal Society of Edinburgh, 63 (1959) 553-588.

[22] T.P. Loomis, **Metamorphism of Metapelites: Calculations of Equilibrium Assemblages and Numerical Simulations of the Crystallization of Garnet**, Journal of Metamorphic Geology, 4 (1986) 201–229.

[23] C. McAteer, **Formation of Garnets in a Rock from Mallaig**, Contributions to Mineralogy and Petrology, 55 (1976) 293-301.

[24] A. Miyashiro, **Calcium-Poor Garnet in Relation to Metamorphism**, Geochimica et Cosmochimica Acta, 4 (1953) 179-208.

[25] A. Miyashiro and F. Shido, **Progressive Compositional Change of Garnet in Metapelite**, Lithos, 6 (1973) 13-20.

[26] G. Müller and A. Schneider, **Chemistry and Genesis of Garnets in Metamorphic Rocks**, Contributions to Mineralogy and Petrology, 31 (1971) 178-200.

[27] K. Nandi, **Garnets as Indices of Progressive Regional Metamorphism**, Mineralogical Magazine, 36 (1967) 89-93.

[28] R.S. Needham, **Alligator River, Northern Territory — 1:250,000 Geological Series**, Bureau of Mineral Resources, Geology and Geophysics Australia, Explanatory Notes, 1984, SD 53-1.

[29] R.S. Needham, **Geology of the Alligator Rivers Uranium Field, Northern Territory**, Bureau of Mineral Resources, Geology and Geophysics Australia, Bulletin 224, 1988, Canberra, Australia.

[30] R.S. Needham and P.G. Stuart-Smith, **Geology of the Alligator Rivers Uranium Field**, in Uranium in the Pine Creek Geosyncline, J. Ferguson and A.B. Goleby, Editors, 1980, International Atomic Energy Agency, Vienna, pp. 233-257.

[31] J.C. Olympio and D.E. Anderson, **The Relationship between Chemical and Textural (Optical) Zoning in Metamorphic Garnets, South Morar, Scotland**, American Mineralogist, 63 (1978) 677-689.

[32] A.A. Snelling, **A Geochemical Study of the Koongarra Uranium Deposit, Northern Territory, Australia**, Ph.D. thesis (unpublished), 1980, The University of Sydney, Sydney, Australia.

[33] A.A. Snelling, **Koongarra Uranium Deposits**, in Geology of the Mineral Deposits of Australia and Papua New Guinea, F.E. Hughes, Editor, 1990, The Australasian Institute of Mining and Metallurgy, Melbourne, Australia, pp. 807-812.

(34) A.A. Snelling, **Towards a Creationist Explanation of Regional Metamorphism**, Creation Ex Nihilo Technical Journal, 8:1 (1994) 51-77.

[35] F.S. Spear, **Metamorphic Fractional Crystallization and Internal Metasomatism by Diffusional Homogenization of Zoned Garnets**, Contributions to Mineralogy and Petrology, 99 (1988) 507-517.

[36] F.S. Spear, M.J. Kohn, F.P. Florence and T. Menard, **A Model for Garnet and Plagioclase Growth in Pelitic Schists: Implications for Thermobarmoetry and P-T Path Determinations**, Journal of Metamorphic Geology, 8 (1991) 683–696.

[37] A.H. Spry, Metamorphic Textures, 1969, Pergamon, Oxford.

[38] R.L. Stanton, **Petrochemical Studies of the Ore Environment at Broken Hill, New South Wales: 1 — Constitution of the 'Banded Iron Formations'**, Transactions of the Institution of Mining and Metallurgy, London, 85 (1976) B33-B46.

[39] R.L. Stanton, **Petrochemical Studies of the Ore Environment at Broken Hill, New South Wales: 2 — Regional Metamorphism of Banded Iron Formations and Their Immediate Associates**, Transactions of the Institution of Mining and Metallurgy, London, 85 (1976) B118-B131.

[40] R.L. Stanton, **Petrochemical Studies of the Ore Environment at Broken Hill, New South Wales: 3 —**

Banded Iron Formations and Sulphide Ore Bodies, Constitutional and Genetic Ties, Transactions of the Institution of Mining and Metallurgy, London, 85 (1976) B131-B141.

[41] R.L. Stanton, **Petrochemical Studies of the Ore Environment at Broken Hill, New South Wales: 4 — Environmental Synthesis**, Transactions of the Institution of Mining and Metallurgy, London, 85 (1976) B221-B233.

[42] R.L. Stanton, **An Alternative to the Barrovian Interpretation? Evidence from Stratiform Ores**, Proceedings of the Australasian Institute of Mining and Metallurgy, 282 (1982) 11-32.

[43] R.L. Stanton, **The Precursor Principle and the Possible Significance of Stratiform Ores and Related Chemical Sediments in the Elucidation of Processes of Regional Metamorphic Mineral Formation**, Philosophical Transactions of the Royal Society of London, A328 (1989) 529-646.

[44] R.L. Stanton and K.L. Williams, **Garnet Compositions at Broken Hill, New South Wales, as Indicators of Metamorphic Processes**, Journal of Petrology, 19 (1978) 514-529.

[45] D.A. Sturt, **The Composition of Garnets from Pelitic Schists in Relation to the Grade of Regional Metamorphism**, Journal of Petrology, 3 (1962) 181-191.

[46] R.J. Tracy, **Compositional Zoning and Inclusions in Metamorphic Minerals**, in Characterization of Metamorphism through Mineral Equilibria, J.M. Ferry, Editor, 1982, Reviews in Mineralogy, 10, chapter 9, pp. 355-397, Mineralogical Society of America, Washington D.C.

[47] R.J. Tracy, P. Robinson and A.B. Thompson, **Garnet Composition and Zoning in the Determination of Temperature and Pressure of Metamorphism, Central Massachusetts**, American Mineralogist, 61 (1976) 762-775.

[48] M.E. Tuccillo, E.J. Essene and B.A. van der Pluijm, **Growth and Retrograde Zoning in Garnets from High-Grade Metapelites: Implications for Pressure-Temperature Paths**, Geology, 18 (1990) 839-842.

[49] D.C. Tucker, **Wall Rock Alteration at the Koongarra Uranium Deposit, Northern Territory**, M.Sc. thesis (unpublished), 1975, James Cook University of North Queensland, Townsville, Australia.

[50] B.W.D. Yardley, **An Empirical Study of Diffusion in Garnet**, American Mineralogist, 62 (1977) 793-800.

U-TH-PB 'DATING': AN EXAMPLE OF FALSE 'ISOCHRONS'

ANDREW A. SNELLING, Ph.D.
Creation Science Foundation,
PO Box 6302,
Acacia Ridge D.C., Qld 4110,
Australia.

KEYWORDS

Geochronology, U-Th-Pb isotopes, isochrons, uranium ore, soils

ABSTRACT

As with other isochron methods, the U-Pb isochron method has been questioned in the open literature, because often an excellent line of best fit between ratios obtained from a set of good cogenetic samples gives a resultant 'isochron' and yields a derived 'age' that has no distinct geological meaning. At Koongarra, Australia, U-Th-Pb isotopic studies of uranium ore, host rocks and soils have produced an array of false 'isochrons' that yield 'ages' that are geologically meaningless. Even a claimed near-concordant U-Pb 'age' of 862Ma on one uraninite grain is identical to a false Pb-Pb isochron 'age', but neither can be connected to any geological event. Open system behaviour of the U-Th-Pb system is clearly the norm, as is the resultant mixing of radiogenic Pb with common or background Pb, even in soils in the surrounding region. Because no geologically meaningful results can be interpreted from the U-Th-Pb data at Koongarra (three uraninite grains even yield a ^{232}Th/^{208}Pb 'age' of 0Ma), serious questions must be asked about the validity of the fundamental/foundational basis of the U-Th-Pb 'dating' method. This makes the task of creationists building their model for the geological record much easier, since claims of U-Th-Pb radiometric 'dating' having 'proven' the claimed great antiquity of the earth, its strata and fossils can be safely side-stepped.

INTRODUCTION

Radiometric dating has now been used for almost 50 years to establish 'beyond doubt' the earth's multi-billion year geological column. Although this column and its 'age' was firmly settled well before the advent of radiometric dating, the latter has been successfully used to help quantify the 'ages' of the strata and the fossils in the column, so that in many people's minds today radiometric dating has 'proved' the presumed antiquity of the earth. Of the various methods, uranium-thorium-lead (U-Th-Pb) was the first used and it is still widely employed today, particularly when zircons are present in the rocks to be dated. But the method does not always give the 'expected' results, leading to fundamental questions about its validity.

In his conclusion in a recent paper exposing shortcomings and criticising the validity of the popular rubidium-strontium (Rb-Sr) isochron method, Zheng [28, p. 14] wrote:

> ... some of the basic assumptions of the conventional Rb-Sr isochron method have to be modified and an observed isochron does not certainly define a valid age information for a geological system, even if a goodness of fit of the experimental data points is obtained in plotting ^{87}Sr/^{66}Sr vs. ^{87}Rb/^{66}Sr. This problem cannot be overlooked, especially in evaluating the numerical time scale. Similar questions can also arise in applying Sm-Nd and U-Pb isochron methods.

Amongst the concerns voiced by Zheng were the problems being found with anomalous isochrons, that is, where there is an apparent linear relationship between ^{87}Sr/^{66}Sr and ^{87}Rb/^{66}Sr ratios, even an excellent line of best fit between ratios obtained from good cogenetic samples, and yet the resultant isochron and derived 'age' have no distinct geological meaning. Zheng documented the copious reporting of this problem in the literature where various names had been given to these anomalous isochrons, such as apparent isochron, mantle isochron and pseudoisochron, secondary isochron, inherited isochron, source isochron, erupted isochron, mixing line, and mixing isochron.

Similar anomalous or false isochrons are commonly obtained from U-Th-Pb data, which is hardly surprising given the common open system behaviour of the U-Th-Pb system. Yet in the literature these problems are commonly glossed over or pushed aside, but their increasing occurrence from a variety of geological settings does seriously raise the question as to whether U-Th-Pb data ever yields any valid 'age' information. One such geological setting that yields these false U-Th-Pb isochrons is the Koongarra uranium deposit and the surrounding area (Northern Territory, Australia).

THE KOONGARRA AREA
The Koongarra area is 250km east of Darwin (Northern Territory, Australia) at latitude 12°52'S and longitude 132°50'E. The regional geology has been described in detail by Needham and Stuart-Smith [19] and by Needham [17,18], while Snelling [25] describes the Koongarra uranium deposit and the area's local geology.

The Koongarra uranium deposit occurs in a metamorphic terrain that has an Archaean basement consisting of domes of granitoids and granitic gneisses (the Nanambu Complex), the nearest outcrop being 5km to the north. Some of the lowermost overlying Lower Proterozoic metasediments were accreted to these domes during amphibolite grade regional metamorphism (estimated to represent conditions of 5-8kb and 550-630°C) at 1800-1870Ma. Multiple isoclinal recumbent folding accompanied metamorphism. The Lower Proterozoic Cahill Formation flanking the Nanambu Complex has been divided into two members. The lower member is dominated by a thick basal dolomite and passes transitionally upwards into the psammitic upper member, which is largely feldspathic schist and quartzite. The uranium mineralisation at Koongarra is associated with graphitic horizons within chloritized quartz-mica (±feldspar ±garnet) schists overlying the basal dolomite in the lower member. A 150Ma period of weathering and erosion followed metamorphism. A thick sequence of essentially flat-lying sandstones (the Middle Proterozoic Kombolgie Formation) was then deposited unconformably on the Archaean-Lower Proterozoic basement and metasediments. At Koongarra subsequent reverse faulting has juxtaposed the lower Cahill Formation schists and Kombolgie Formation sandstone.

Owing to the isoclinal recumbent folding of metasedimentary units of the Cahill Formation, the typical rock sequence encountered at Koongarra is probably a tectono-stratigraphy (from youngest to oldest):
— muscovite-biotite-quartz-feldspar schist (at least 180m thick)
— garnet-muscovite-biotite-quartz schist (90-100m thick)
— sulphide-rich graphite-mica-quartz schist (±garnet) (about 25m thick)
— distinctive graphite-quartz-chlorite schist marker unit (5-8m thick)
— quartz-chlorite schist (±illite, garnet, sillimanite, muscovite) (50m thick) — the mineralised zone
— reverse fault breccia (5-7m thick)
— sandstone of the Kombolgie Formation

Polyphase deformation accompanied metamorphism of the original sediments, that were probably dolomite, shales and siltstones. Johnston [12] identified a D_2 event as responsible for the dominant S_2 foliation of the schist sequence, which at Koongarra dips at 55° to the south-east. The dominant structural feature, however, is the reverse fault system that dips at about 60° to the south-east, sub-parallel to the dominant S_2 foliation and lithological boundaries, just below the mineralised zone.

THE URANIUM DEPOSIT
There are two discrete uranium orebodies at Koongarra, separated by a 100m wide barren zone. The main (No. 1) orebody has a strike length of 450m and persists to 100m depth. Secondary uranium mineralisation is present in the weathered schists, from below the surficial sand cover to the base of weathering at depths varying between 25 and 30m. This secondary mineralisation has been derived from decomposition and leaching of the primary mineralised zone, and forms a tongue-like fan of ore-grade material dispersed down-slope for about 80m to the south-east. The primary uranium mineralised zone in cross-section is a series of partially coalescing lenses, which together form an elongated wedge dipping at 55° to the south-east within the host quartz-chlorite schist unit, subparallel to the reverse fault. True widths average 30m at the top of the primary mineralised zone but taper out at about 100m below surface and along strike.

Superimposed on the primary prograde metamorphic mineral assemblages of the host schist units is a distinct and extensive primary alteration halo associated, and cogenetic, with the uranium mineralisation. This alteration extends for up to 1.5km from the ore in a direction perpendicular to the host quartz-chlorite schist unit, because the mineralisation is essentially stratabound. The outer zone of the alteration halo is most extensively developed in the semi-pelitic schists, and is manifested by the pseudomorphous replacement of biotite by chlorite, rutile and quartz, and feldspar by sericite. Silicification has also occurred in fault planes and within the Kombolgie Formation sandstone beneath the mineralisation, particularly adjacent to the reverse fault.

Association of this outer halo alteration with the mineralisation is demonstrated by the apparent symmetrical distribution of this alteration about the orebody. In the inner alteration zone, less than 50m from ore, the metamorphic rock fabric is disrupted, and quartz is replaced by pervasive chlorite and phengitic mica, and garnet by chlorite. Uranium mineralisation is only present where this alteration has taken place.

The primary ore consists of uraninite veins and veinlets (1-10mm thick) that cross-cut the S_2 foliation of the brecciated and hydrothermally altered quartz-chlorite schist host. Groups of uraninite veinlets are intimately intergrown with chlorite, which forms the matrix to the host breccias. Small (10-100µm) euhedral and subhedral uraninite grains are finely disseminated in the chloritic alteration adjacent to veins, but these grains may coalesce to form clusters, strings and massive uraninite. Coarse colloform and botryoidal uraninite masses and uraninite spherules with internal lacework textures have also been noted, but the bulk of the ore appears to be of the disseminated type, with thin (<0.5mm) discontinuous wisps and streaks of uraninite, and continuous strings both parallel and discordant to the foliation (S_2), and parallel to phyllosilicate (001) cleavage planes.

Associated with the ore are minor volumes (up to 5%) of sulphides, which include galena and lesser chalcopyrite, bornite and pyrite, with rare grains of native gold, clausthalite (PbSe), gersdorffite-cobaltite (NiAsS-CoAsS) and mackinawite (Fe, Ni)$_{1.1}$S. Galena is the most abundant, commonly occurring as cubes (5-10µm wide) disseminated in uraninite or gangue, and as stringers and veinlets particularly filling thin fractures within uraninite. Galena may also overgrow clausthalite, and replace pyrite and chalcopyrite. Chlorite, predominantly magnesium chlorite, is the principal gangue, and its intimate association with the uraninite indicates that the two minerals formed together.

Oxidation and alteration of uraninite within the primary ore zone has produced a variety of secondary uranium minerals, principally uranyl silicates [22]. Uraninite veins, even veins over 1cm wide, have been completely altered in situ. Within the primary ore zone this in situ replacement of uraninite is most pronounced immediately above the reverse fault breccia, and this alteration and oxidation diminish upwards stratigraphically. It is accompanied by hematite staining of the schists, the more intense hematite alteration in and near the reverse fault breccia being due to hematite replacement of chlorite. The secondary mineralisation of the dispersion fan in the weathered schist above the No. 1 orebody is characterised by uranyl phosphates found exclusively in the 'tail' of the fan. Away from the tail uranium is dispersed in the weathered schists and adsorbed onto clays and iron oxides.

The age of the uranium mineralisation is problematical. The mineralisation, however, must post-date both the Kombolgie Formation sandstone and the Koongarra reverse fault, since it occupies the breccia zones generated by the post-Kombolgie reverse faulting. The pattern of alteration which is intimately associated with the ore also crosses the reverse fault into the Kombolgie sandstone beneath the ore zone, so this again implies that the ore was formed after the reverse fault and therefore is younger than both the Kombolgie sandstone and the reverse fault. Because of these geological constraints, Page et al. [20] suggested the mineralisation was younger than 1600-1688Ma because of their determination of the timing of the Kombolgie Formation deposition to that period. Sm-Nd isotopic data obtained on Koongarra uraninites [15,16] appears to narrow down the timing of mineralisation to 1550-1650Ma. It is unclear as to when deep ground-water circulation began to cause oxidation and alteration of the primary uraninite ore at depth, but Airey et al. [1] suggest that the weathering of the primary ore to produce the secondary dispersion fan in the weathered schists above the No. 1 orebody seems to have begun only in the last 1-3Ma.

U-TH-PB DATA
'Dating' of the Primary Ore
Hills and Richards [11] isotopically analysed individual grains of uraninite and galena that had been hand-picked from drill core. Only one of the five uraninite samples gave a near-concordant 'age' of 862Ma, that is, the sample plotted almost on the standard concordia curve, and Hills and Richards [10] interpreted this as recording fresh formation of Pb-free uraninite at 870Ma. The other four uraninite samples all lie well below concordia and do not conform to any regular linear array. Hills and Richards were left with two possible interpretations. On the one hand, preferential loss of the intermediate daughter products of ^{238}U (that is, escape of radon, a gas) would cause vertical displacement of points below an episodic-loss line, but this would only produce a significant Pb isotopic effect if the loss had persisted for a very long proportion of the life of the uraninite (which is incidentally not only feasible but likely). Alternatively, they suggested that contamination by small amounts of an older (pre-900Ma) Pb could cause such a pattern as on their concordia plot, to which they added mixing lines that they postulated arose from the restoration to each uraninite sample of the galena which separated from it.

This of course assumes that the Pb in the galenas was also derived predominantly from uranium decay. They plotted their Pb ratios in all their uraninite samples on a standard ^{207}Pb/^{206}Pb diagram, and contended that the pattern of data points did not conform to a simple age interpretation. Instead, they contended that the scatter of points could be contained between two lines radiating from the diagram's origin, lines that essentially represented isochrons for uraninites and galenas from the Ranger and Nabarlek uranium deposits in the same geological region. From the positions of the Koongarra uraninites and galenas on these diagrams they claimed that the galenas contained left-over radiogenic Pb from earlier uraninites as old as 1700–1800Ma (the 'age' of the Ranger uranium mineralisation), these earlier uraninites being obliterated by the uranium having remobilised at 870Ma, the 'age' of the lone Pb-free uraninite sample.

In a separate study Carr and Dean [2] isotopically analysed whole-rock samples from the Koongarra primary ore zone. These were samples of drill core that had been crushed. Their isotopic data on four samples were plotted on a U-Pb isochron diagram and indicated a non-systematic relationship between the ^{238}U parent and the ^{206}Pb daughter. In other words, the quantities of ^{206}Pb could not simply be accounted for by radioactive decay of ^{238}U, implying open system behaviour. They also plotted their four results on a standard ^{207}Pb/^{206}Pb isochron diagram and found that these samples fell on a very poorly defined linear array whose apparent age they did not quantify.

'Dating' of Weathered Rocks and Soils

Carr and Dean [2] also isotopically analysed a further nine whole-rock samples from the weathered schist zone at Koongarra. Some of these samples were again crushed drill core, but the majority were crushed percussion drill chips. When their isotopic data were plotted on a U-Pb isochron diagram six of the nine samples plotted close to the reference 1000Ma isochron, while the other three were widely scattered. However, on the ^{207}Pb/^{206}Pb diagram all nine weathered rock samples plotted on a linear array which gave an apparent isochron 'age' of 1270 ±50Ma.

In an unrelated investigation, Dickson et al. [6,7] collected soil samples from above the mineralisation at Koongarra and from surrounding areas, and these were analysed for Pb isotopes to see if there was any Pb-isotopic dispersion halo around the mineralisation sufficiently large enough to warrant the use of Pb-isotopic analyses of soils as an exploration technique to find new uranium orebodies. The technique did in fact work, Pb-isotopic traces of the deeply buried No. 2 orebody mineralisation being found in the soils above. This mineralisation, 40m below the surface, is blind to other detection techniques.

Dickson et al. [7] found that all 113 soil samples from their two studies were highly correlated (r = 0.99986) on a standard ^{207}Pb/^{206}Pb diagram, yielding an apparent (false) isochron representing an 'age' of 1445 ±20Ma for the samples. However, most of the soil samples consisted of detritus eroded from the Middle Proterozoic Kombolgie sandstone, so because the samples from near the mineralisation gave a radiogenic Pb signature Dickson et al. interpreted the false 'isochron' as being due to mixing of radiogenic Pb from the uranium mineralisation with the common Pb from the sandstone.

DISCUSSION

Snelling [23] has already highlighted a telling omission by Hills and Richards [11]. Having included all the Pb isotopic ratios they had obtained on their five uraninite samples, they tabulated also the derived 'ages', except for those obtainable from ^{208}Pb. These Th-derived 'dates' should normally be regarded as the most reliable, since Th is less mobile in geochemical environments and therefore open system behaviour is less likely than for U. Significantly, three of the five uraninite samples therefore give, within their experimental error, a 0Ma 'age' [23]. In any case, their 'age' of 1700–1800Ma for the first generation of uranium mineralisation at Koongarra neither fits the geological criteria for an expected 1550–1600Ma 'age', nor does their 870Ma 'date' correlate with any geological event capable of remobilising U and Pb to produce the presumed second generation of uranium mineralisation.

Using Ludwig [13], standard ^{207}Pb/^{206}Pb diagrams were prepared for the uraninite, galena and whole-rock data sets, and combinations thereof, to check the regression statistics and possible derived 'isochrons' using the standard York [27] method. In each case the mean square of weighted deviates (MSWD), which tests the 'goodness of fit' of data to a line, is large to extremely large, which reflects in the derived 'ages' of 841 ±140Ma (uraninites), 1008 ±420Ma (galenas), 668 ±330Ma (whole-rocks), 818 ±150Ma (uraninites plus galenas) and 863 ±130Ma (all three data sets combined), all 'ages' being within the 95% confidence limits. It is perhaps fortuitously significant that the combination of all three data sets yields an isochron 'age' of 863 ±130Ma, almost identical to Hills' and Richards' near-concordant 'age' of 862Ma, although this was using a line-fitting routine of Ludwig [13] that assigns equal weights and zero error-correlations to each data point to avoid the mistake of weighting the points according to analytical errors when it is clear that some other cause of scatter is involved, which is clearly the case here. The normal York [27] algorithm assumes that the only cause for scatter from a straight line are the assigned errors, and for the combined data set here the amount of scatter calculated thereby yields an astronomical MSWD of 669000 and a bad line of fit that yields an isochron 'age' of 1632 ±410Ma. This 'result' may make more geological sense, but the regression statistics are such that derivation of any 'age' information from these data is totally unjustified, even though it can be rightfully argued that these samples form a cogenetic set (they are all samples of uranium ore or its components from the same primary ore zone at Koongarra).

It is not uncommon to find that 'ages' derived from standard ^{207}Pb/^{206}Pb plots are erroneous, even though the data fit well-defined linear arrays ('isochrons'). Ludwig et al. [14] found that this was due to migration of both Pb and radioactive daughters of [238]U yielding a [207]Pb/[206]Pb 'isochron' giving 'superficially attractive results which would nonetheless be seriously misleading' because the derived 'age' (in their example) was more than six times higher than the U-Pb isochron 'age'. Similarly, Cunningham *et al.* [3] obtained [207]Pb/[206]Pb isochron 'ages' up to 50 times higher than those derived from 'more reliable' U-Pb isochrons for whole-rock uranium ore samples, even though 'the apparent slight degree of scatter is almost entirely a misleading artifact'. Ironically, at Koongarra the U-Pb isochron using Ludwig [13] yields an 'age' of 857 ±149Ma (with an MSWD of 13400, tolerably large compared to that obtained with the Pb-Pb isochron), almost identical to the 'fortuitous' Pb-Pb isochron 'age' obtained using Ludwig's modified algorithm on the combined three data sets (863 ±130Ma), as well as Hills' and Richards' single near-concordant 862Ma 'age'.

Snelling and Dickson [26] demonstrated that there is significant radiometric disequilibrium in the primary ore and surrounding host rocks at Koongarra due to the redistribution of both U and its Ra decay product. That Ra mobility at depth in the primary ore zone is currently more significant than U migration was confirmed by Dickson and Snelling [8], which of course results ultimately in the redistribution of [206]Pb, the end-member of the whole [238]U decay chain. Dickson *et al.* [5,7] demonstrated that Ra is transported through the unweathered rocks in this area in the ground waters, while Davey *et al.* [4] determined the emanation rate of radon gas from the Koongarra No. 1 orebody, an ever present hazard in uranium ore mining operations. The radon gas is known to migrate along fractures and rise through the ground over considerable distances to form a halo in the air above, while radon is also transported in ground waters.

These observations alone demonstrate the open system behaviour of the U-Th-Pb system that renders meaningless any 'age' information derived. However, both Hills [9] and Snelling [21,22] have recognised that U also has migrated on a considerable scale in the primary ore zone, since supergene uraninites, often with colloform banding, are found as fracture and cavity infillings, and between quartz and gangue grain boundaries. The unit cell dimensions of these uraninites, plus this textural evidence, supports the conclusion that these uraninites have precipitated after dissolution of earlier formed uraninite and transportation in low-temperature ground waters. With such wholesale migration of U also, all attempts at 'dating' must be rendered useless, especially when whole-rock samples, in which different generations of uraninites are lumped together, are used.

In contrast to the poor-fitting linear arrays produced from the Pb-Pb data of minerals and whole-rocks from the primary ore zone, that all appear to give an apparent (false) isochron 'age' grouped around 857-863Ma, both Carr and Dean [2] and Dickson *et al.* [7] found that weathered whole-rock and soil samples produced good fitting linear arrays that would normally represent 'isochrons' that yield 'ages' of 1270Ma and 1445Ma respectively. The weathered whole-rock samples all of course come from Koongarra itself, and consist of secondary ore samples from the weathered schist zone, plus weathered schist samples that contain uranium dispersed down-slope by ground waters moving through the weathered rock. Because these whole-rock samples come from a volume of rock through which U is known to be migrating, leading to redistribution not only of U but of its decay products, it is therefore very surprising to find that these whole-rock samples define a good enough linear array to yield an 'isochron'. Even the observed scatter calculated using Ludwig [13] is much less than that associated with fitting an 'isochron' to the [207]Pb-[206]Pb data from the primary ore zone samples, which is again surprising given U migration in the weathered zone, the data from which one would expect to show considerable scatter and thus no 'age' concensus. Furthermore, it is baffling as to why the 'isochron'-derived 'age' should be so much 'older' than the 'age' of the primary ore, which of course is ultimately the source through weathering and ground-water transport of the U, decay products and the stable Pb isotopes. Perhaps the only explanation is that the 'isochron' represents the mixing of radiogenic Pb from the mineralisation with the common or background Pb in the surrounding schists.

The idea of such an 'isochron' being a mixing line was suggested by Dickson *et al.* [7]. They were however, dealing with the Pb isotopic data obtained from soil samples collected from depths of only about 30-40cm, the majority of which represented sandy soils consisting of detritus eroded from the Kombolgie sandstone. For this mixing explanation to be feasible there should be some other evidence of mobilisation of Pb in the area. Dickson *et al.* found that not only were there high [206]Pb/[204]Pb ratios in three of their soil samples from the near-surface (0-1m) zone south of the No. 1 orebody, but there was a lack of any other U-series daughter products in the same samples. This near-surface zone is inundated for approximately six months of the year as a result of the high monsoonal rainfall in this tropical area. Towards the end of the ensuing six-month dry season the water table has been known to drop in some cases more than ten metres from its wet season 'high'. This means that the top of the weathered schist zone is regularly fluctuating between wet and dry conditions, so that any trace elements such as Pb leached from the weathered ore and transported by ground water in the weathered schist zone would also be dispersed vertically up into the thin surficial sand cover on top of the weathered schist — the sandy soils that were sampled by Dickson *et al.* [6,7]. Snelling [24] found that Pb was a significant pathfinder element for uranium ore in the Koongarra environment, anomalous Pb being present in the surficial sand cover above the zone of weathered primary ore, and that there was even hydrodynamic dispersal of Pb at a depth of 0.5-1.5m. Dickson *et al.* [6] found a similarity between the isotopic ratios for Pb extracted from their soil samples by either a mild HCl-hydroxylamine (pH 1) or a strong 7M HCl-7M HNO$_3$ leach, which indicates that Pb is loosely attached to sand grain surfaces in the samples rather than tightly bound in silicate or resistate mineral lattices. This in turn suggests Pb is adsorbed from ground waters, meaning that radiogenic Pb is being added to the common or background Pb in the sand by both vertical and lateral ground-water dispersion.

However, not all of Dickson *et al.*'s soil samples came from the immediate area to the Koongarra orebodies, nor were they all the samples of Kombolgie sandstone detritus. That this mixing line explanation for the apparent 'isochron' is clearly demonstrated for these samples from the immediate Koongarra area is not in question, although it is somewhat surprising that these soil samples should give an apparent isochron 'age' somewhat higher than that obtained from the weathered schist samples beneath. Indeed, the common or background Pb in the respective samples should reflect an 'older' apparent age in the schists compared to the sandstone, due to their relative ages based on geological relationships between them. However, the apparent ages are the other way around, the sandy soils yielding an 'older' apparent age compared to that yielded by the weathered schists. Perhaps this difference is a reflection of the extent of mixing in each type of sample at their respective levels in the weathering profile. Nevertheless, what is astounding is that Dickson *et al.* [7] found that even though several of their soil samples consisted of weathered schist or basement granite (containing accessory zircon) up to 17km from the known uranium mineralisation, they still plotted on the same apparent 'isochron'. Indeed, the 'fit' is comparatively good, as indicated by the MSWD of only 964 using Ludwig [13], yet much of this observed scattered can be attributed to two samples out of the 113, one of which was subsequently known to be probably contaminated by cuttings from an adjacent drill hole [6]. If that sample is removed from the regression analysis the MSWD drops to 505, indicating that almost half of the observed scatter is due to that one data point alone. If the data point that is the next worst for fitting to the apparent 'isochron' is removed, then the MSWD drops by a further 315 to a mere 190. Yet in both cases the apparent 'isochron' or 'mixing line' still has lying on or close to it the samples from up to 17km away from the known uranium mineralisation **and** the samples that are not Kombolgie sandstone detritus. The final 'isochron' fitted to the remaining 111 samples still yields an 'age' of 1420 ±18Ma.

While Carr and Dean's nine weathered whole-rock samples are not strictly cogenetic with Dickson *et al.*'s 113 soil samples, the two sample sets are obviously related because the source of the radiogenic Pb in the majority of the soil samples from the immediate Koongarra area is the same as that in the weathered rocks. Not surprisingly, when the regression analysis was performed on Carr and Dean's nine weathered whole-rock samples using Ludwig [13], the MSWD for the observed scattered was 24100, indicating a poor fit to an 'isochron' which yielded an 'age' of 1287 ±120Ma. Yet when these nine samples were added to the 113 soil samples the MSWD dropped substantially to 1210, and not surprisingly the fitted 'isochron' yielded an 'age' of 1346 ±27Ma, an 'isochron age' intermediate between those of the two data sets being combined. However, when the two soil samples responsible for the majority of the scatter in that data set were removed the MSWD dropped to 430 and yielded an 'isochron age' of 1336 ±17Ma.

As with all the other apparent isochron 'ages' this result has no apparent geological meaning, because there is no geological event to which these 'ages' might correlate. Indeed, even in the evolutionary time-frame the weathering of the Koongarra uranium mineralisation is extremely recent, and in any case these 'ages' derived from Pb-Pb 'isochrons' from the weathered rock and soil samples are much 'older' than the supposedly more reliable U-Pb 'isochron age' of the Koongarra primary ore. But since that latter result has no apparent geological meaning, because it also cannot be correlated with any known geological event, nothing then is certain at all from any of these U-Th-Pb isotopic studies of the Koongarra ores, rocks and surrounding soils. Indeed, it is just as certain that the primary ore is 0 years old, based on three $^{232}Th/^{208}Pb$ single sample ages, as is the claim that one near-concordant result means that there was formation of Pb-free uraninite at 870Ma. After all, this postulated formation of Pb-free uraninite is supposed to have occurred in an environment where there was Pb left over from an earlier 1700-1800Ma original uranium mineralisation for which we no longer have any evidence, textural or otherwise, apart from a rather tenuous interpretation of Pb isotopic evidence that has otherwise shown itself to be devoid of any capability of providing any 'age' information.

All these results raise serious fundamental questions about the claimed validity of the U-Th-Pb 'dating' method. It may seem reasonable to regard an apparent 'isochron' as a 'mixing line' within the restricted area close to the known source of radiogenic Pb, which can be shown by independent evidence to be migrating into rocks and soils that contain common or background Pb in the immediate environs. However, it strains all credulity to suggest that a false 'isochron' through a data set derived from samples representing a variety of rock types, of significantly different evolutionary 'ages', over an area of up to 17km lateral extent from the known radiogenic Pb source, can still represent mixing! One can only conclude that all assumptions used to derive the estimates of common or background Pb, including models for the supposed evolution of the stable Pb isotopes through earth history, from their presumed commencement on the protoearth with its claimed original Pb isotope content some 4.6 billion or so years ago, cannot be valid. Equally, we cannot be sure what the U-Th-Pb system's isotopic ratios really mean, because the basic assumptions that are foundational to the interpretation of these isotopic ratios are fatally flawed. Not only has open system behaviour of these isotopes been demonstrated as the norm, but even where there is an apparent 'isochron' with an excellent 'goodness of fit' the derived 'age' is invariably geologically meaningless. Thus creationists need not be hindered in their building of the Creation-Flood young-earth model for the geological record by the many claims in the open geological literature that U-

Th-Pb radiometric 'dating' has 'proved' the presumed great antiquity of the earth, and the strata and fossils of the so-called geological column.

CONCLUSION

The concerns raised by Zheng [28] regarding U-Pb isochrons are warranted. At Koongarra a $^{207}Pb/^{206}Pb$ 'isochron' produced from 11 hand-picked uraninite and galena grains, plus four whole-rock samples, yields an 'age' of 863 Ma, the same as a near-concordant 'age' from one of the uraninite grains. Nine weathered whole-rock samples yield an 'isochron age' of 1270Ma, while 113 soil samples produce an excellent 'isochron' with an 'age' of 1445Ma. All of these 'ages' are geologically meaningless. While the apparent isochron produced by the soil samples may be identified as a mixing line, produced by the mixing of radiogenic Pb with common or background Pb in the surrounding rocks and soils, even this explanation strains credulity because the samples come from up to 17km away from known uranium mineralisation, and a few of the soil samples represent different rock types. Not only then has open system behaviour of these isotopes been demonstrated, but apparent 'isochrons' and their derived 'ages' are invariably geologically meaningless. Thus none of the assumptions used to interpret the U-Th-Pb isotopic system to yield 'ages' can be valid. If these assumptions were valid, then the $^{232}Th/^{208}Pb$ 'age' of 0Ma for three of the five uraninite samples should be taken seriously. Creationists should therefore not be intimidated by claims that U-Th-Pb radiometric 'dating' has 'proved' the presumed great antiquity of the earth, and the strata and fossils of the so-called geological column.

REFERENCES

[1]   P.L. Airey, C. Golian and D.A. Lever, **An Approach to the Mathematical Modelling of the Uranium Series Redistribution within Ore Bodies**, Topical Report AAEC/C49, 1986, Australian Atomic Energy Commission, Sydney.

[2]   G.R. Carr and J.A. Dean, **Report to AAEC on a Pb Isotopic Study of Samples from Jabiluka and Koongarra**, unpublished report, 1986, Commonwealth Scientific and Industrial Research Organisation, Division of Mineral Physics and Mineralogy, Sydney.

[3]   C.G. Cunningham, K.R. Ludwig, C.W. Naeser, E.K. Weiland, H.H. Mehnert, T.A. Steven and J.D. Rasmussen, **Geochronology of Hydrothermal Uranium Deposits and Associated Igneous Rocks in the Eastern Source Area of the Mount Belknap Volcanics, Marysvale, Utah**, Economic Geology, 77 (1982) 453-463.

[4]   D.R. Davy, A. Dudaitis and B.G. O'Brien, **Radon Survey at the Koongarra Uranium Deposit, Northern Territory**, Topical Report AAEC/E459, 1978, Australian Atomic Energy Commission, Sydney, in Koongarra Project: Draft Environmental Impact Statement, 1978, Noranda Australia Limited, Melbourne, Appendix 2.

[5]   B.L. Dickson, A.M. Giblin and A.A. Snelling, **The Source of Radium in Anomalous Accumulations near Sandstone Escarpments, Australia**, Applied Geochemistry, 2 (1987) 385-398.

[6]   B.L. Dickson, B.L. Gulson and A.A. Snelling, **Evaluation of Lead Isotopic Methods for Uranium Exploration, Koongarra Area, Northern Territory, Australia**, Journal of Geochemical Exploration, 24 (1985) 81-102.

[7]   B.L. Dickson, B.L. Gulson and A.A. Snelling, **Further Assessment of Stable Lead Isotope Measurements for Uranium Exploration, Pine Creek Geosyncline, Northern Territory, Australia**, Journal of Geochemical Exploration, 27 (1987) 63-75.

[8]   B.L. Dickson and A.A. Snelling, **Movements of Uranium and Daughter Isotopes in the Koongarra Uranium Deposit**, in Uranium in the Pine Creek Geosyncline, J. Ferguson and A.B. Goleby, Editors, 1980, International Atomic Energy Agency, Vienna, pp. 499-507.

[9]   J.H. Hills, **Lead Isotopes and the Regional Geochemistry of North Australian Uranium Deposits**, Ph.D. thesis (unpublished), 1973, Macquarie University, Sydney, Australia.

[10]   J.H. Hills and J.R. Richards, **The Age of Uranium Mineralization in Northern Australia**, Search, 3 (1972) 382-385.

[11]   J.H. Hills and J.R. Richards, **Pitchblende and Galena Ages in the Alligator Rivers Region, Northern Territory, Australia**, Mineralium Deposita, 11 (1976) 133-154.

[12]   J.D. Johnston, **Structural Evolution of the Pine Creek Inlier and Mineralisation Therein, Northern Territory, Australia**, Ph.D. thesis (unpublished), 1984, Monash University, Melbourne, Australia.

[13]   K.R. Ludwig, **ISOPLOT: A Plotting and Regression Program for Radiogenic-Isotope Data, Version 2.60**, United States Geological Survey Open-File Report 91-445, 1993, Denver, Colorado.

[14]   K.R. Ludwig, J.T. Nash and C.W. Naeser, **U-Pb Isotope Systematics and Age of Uranium Mineralisation, Midnite Mine, Washington**, Economic Geology, 76 (1981) 89-110.

[15]   R. Maas, **The Application of Sm-Nd and Rb-Sr Isotope Systematics to Ore Deposits**, Ph.D. thesis (unpublished), 1987, The Australian National University, Canberra, Australia.

[16]   R. Maas, **Nd-Sr Isotope Constraints on the Age and Origin of Unconformity-Type Uranium Deposits in the Alligator Rivers Uranium Field, Northern Territory, Australia**, Economic Geology, 84 (1989) 64-90.

[17]   R.S. Needham, **Alligator River, Northern Territory — 1:250,000 Geological Series**, Bureau of Mineral Resources, Geology and Geophysics Australia, Explanatory Notes, 1984, SD 53-1.

[18]   R.S. Needham, **Geology of the Alligator Rivers Uranium Field, Northern Territory**, Bureau of Mineral Resources, Geology and Geophysics Australia, Bulletin 224, 1988, Canberra, Australia.

[19]   R.S. Needham and P.G. Stuart-Smith, **Geology of the Alligator Rivers Uranium Field**, in Uranium in the Pine Creek Geosyncline, J. Ferguson and A.B. Goleby, Editors, 1980, International Atomic Energy Agency, Vienna, pp. 233-257.

[20]   R.W. Page, W. Compston and R.S. Needham, **Geochronology and Evolution of the Late-Archaean Basement and Proterozoic Rocks in the Alligator Rivers Uranium Field, Northern Territory, Australia**, in Uranium in the Pine Creek Geosyncline, J. Ferguson and A.B. Goleby, Editors, 1980, International Atomic Energy Agency, Vienna, pp. 13-68.

[21]   A.A. Snelling, **A Geochemical Study of the Koongarra Uranium Deposit, Northern Territory, Australia**, Ph.D. thesis (unpublished), 1980, The University of Sydney, Sydney, Australia.

[22]   A.A. Snelling, **Uraninite and its Alteration Products, Koongarra Uranium Deposit**, in Uranium in the Pine Creek Geosyncline, J. Ferguson and A.B. Goleby, Editors, 1980, International Atomic Energy Agency, Vienna, pp. 487-498.

[23]   A.A. Snelling, **The Age of Australian Uranium: A Case Study of the Koongarra Uranium Deposit**, Ex Nihilo, 4 (1981) 44-57.

[24]   A.A. Snelling, **A Soil Geochemistry Orientation Survey for Uranium at Koongarra, Northern Territory**, Journal of Geochemical Exploration, 22 (1984) 83-99.

[25]   A.A. Snelling, **Koongarra Uranium Deposits**, in Geology of the Mineral Deposits of Australia and Papua New Guinea, F.E. Hughes, Editor, 1990, The Australasian Institute of Mining and Metallurgy, Melbourne, Australia, pp. 807-812.

[26]   A.A. Snelling and B.L. Dickson, **Uranium/Daughter Equilibrium in the Koongarra Uranium Deposit, Australia**, Mineralium Deposita, 14 (1979) 109-118.

[27]   D. York, **Least-Squares Fitting of a Straight Line with Correlated Errors**, Earth and Planetary Science Letters, 5 (1969) 320-324.

[28]   Y.-F. Zheng, **Influences of the Nature of the Initial Rb-Sr System on Isochron Validity**, Chemical Geology, 80 (1989) 1-16.

THE KIDNEY: A DESIGNED SYSTEM
FOR
PLASMA HOMEOSTASIS

PATRICIA L. SPECK, DVM
RT. 1, BOX 164 B
McARTHUR, OHIO, 45651

KEYWORDS

active transport, ADH, afferent, aldosterone, brush border, capsule, concentration gradient, convoluted tubule, cortex, design, dialysis, efferent, glomerulus, hairpin loop, homeostasis, integration, juxtaglomerular apparatus, kidney, macula densa, medulla, metanephros, nephron, osmolality, permeability, purpose, reabsorption, renin, secretion, sodium cycle, symmetry, urea cycle, vasa recta

ABSTRACT

The kidney is an excellent biochemical model showing design in nature. Design implies a designer. The development of the kidney follows a very precise pattern and time schedule. The anatomy and physiology of the kidney and the entire urinary system are complex and precise. This is true when regarding the urinary system alone; and also, in studying its relationship to other systems. The urinary system is tied in with the circulatory and nervous systems in very unique fashion. Each part is carefully integrated into the whole system to form a homeostatic control network that operates efficiently in a large number of metabolic states. Each section of the urinary system is specific, yet completely dependent on other sections. Three separate mechanisms are involved in forming the end product, urine. These are filtration, reabsorption, and secretion. Filtration takes place in the glomerulus. Reabsorption and secretion occur in the tubules. The circulatory system of the kidney is unique. The capillaries in the glomerulus are more porous than capillaries elsewhere in the body. The medulla contains a specialized capillary network which forms a countercurrent mechanism along with a hairpin design. This arrangement is not found elsewhere in the body, or in any organisms except mammals and birds. This countercurrent system creates a concentration gradient which enables the production of a concentrated end product while preserving necessary ions for the body. Mechanisms within the kidney enable it to modify its function; yet function is also sensitive to hormone and neurological input. In this way, the kidney is sensitive to needs and changes throughout the entire organism. Biochemical engineers create artificial models to take the place of diseased kidneys. These models require the input of intelligence and design, yet fall short of the precision of the natural model. Therefore, I conclude that the kidney was designed by a superintelligence beyond the scope of nature.

> Ah, Sovereign Lord, You have made the heavens and the earth by Your great power
> and outstretched arm. Nothing is too hard for You. Jer. 32:17

INTRODUCTION

A designed system is an integrated, symmetrical unit which serves some purpose. Design implies a designer; someone who intelligently lays out a plan. Is the kidney the result of design or is it the result of random natural processes? The goal of biology is to ultimately explain all function in physical, mathematical, and chemical terms. We can gain a great deal of understanding by describing the anatomy, physiology, and biochemistry of the kidney; yet, to grasp how this biochemical unit came to be requires that we step outside of science and into the realm of philosophy. As a creationist I believe that the structure and function of the kidney show design, and that this was laid out by a superintelligence beyond the scope of nature. This plasma purification system is incredibly complex and precise. It consists of paired kidneys, the ureters, the bladder, and the urethra, all of which must be tied in precisely and uniquely with the circulatory system, as well as with the lymphatic and nervous systems. All of these units must be complete and functional in order to maintain chemical balance in the body and to purify the blood of toxins, drugs, and other soluble impurities.

The kidney meets these needs in a great variety of different metabolic states. It exhibits symmetry, complexity, integration, and purpose. Therefore, the kidney shows design. If any part of this extensive intricate system was not functional at the same time as all of the other parts, the whole unit could not function. For this reason, creationists believe the kidney was created by a Master Designer.

DEVELOPMENT

The urinary tract arises from three distinct embryonic tissues. The bladder and urethra arise from the uro-rectal endoderm. The kidney begins first as a pronephros, arising about the fourth week of gestation, but it quickly degenerates into a system of ducts utilized by the next stage, the mesonephros. This stage is not known to be functional in the human, although it is functional in some mammals. Some researchers are beginning to associate function with the mesonephros in the human fetus, now, too. The mesonephros develops tubules and glomeruli which degenerate into genital ducts in the male, and vestigial tissue in females. The true kidney begins to develop during the fifth week of gestation, and is functional by the eighth week. This true kidney develops from the metanephros, which consists of two parts: the metanephric diverticulum, or bud, and the metanephric mass, or blastema. The diverticulum gives rise to the ureters, renal pelvis, calyces, and collecting ducts. The blastema forms a cap over the diverticulum and differentiates into the glomerulary capsule, the proximal and distal convoluted tubules, and the intervening hairpin loops. All of this is a patent pathway and becomes patent with the collecting tubule where they meet. This system is patent from the collecting tubule to the ureters and becomes patent with the bladder, thus forming a continuous open pathway from the capsule to the external opening of the urethra. While the cells of the filtering receptacle are developing, the aorta is branching into the renal artery, which invades the kidney at the renal pelvis, where it branches and rebranches to form the supply unit-- the glomerulus, as well as the specialized system of arterioles, capillaries, and venules necessary for kidney function. The development of the filtering system shows design. A single cell, which holds all the genetic information necessary for the final product, divides again and again until some master control initiates differentiation. Differentiation includes integration with three separate embryonic tissues to form a patent pathway. Three tissues become integrated into one functional unit. Added to this complexity is further integration with the nervous system and the endocrine system for regulation. This initial level of examination gives us a sketch of a remarkable design.

ANATOMY

Looking into the anatomical layout of the kidney, even more astounding integration and complexity of design can be seen. The overall shape of the kidney is similar to a lima bean. It is covered with a tough membrane which lines the entire organ, including the sinus. The kidney is divided into three distinct parts. The outer part, called the cortex, is granular in texture due to the great number of renal tubules which comprise its structure. The renal corpuscles are located here, although they are absent from the outermost layer. Under the cortex is the medulla which looks striated to the unaided eye. This striated appearance is due to the many papillar tubules and the loops. There are no renal corpuscles in the medulla. The medulla ends in the renal papillae, which comprise the inner wall and border on the calyces. The papillae are flattened cones with tiny openings, or ducts, into which the collecting ducts empty. The papillae in turn empty into the renal pelvis. The calyces and pelvis, called the hilus, contain all of the major blood vessels, nerves, and fatty tissue. The lima bean shape, with the cortex located on the long side, and the medulla on the narrow side, creates a uniquely shaped structural unit of a wedge with the cortex forming the broad side of the wedge, and the medulla forming the narrow side. This is significant as will be seen later when considering the function of the kidney. Interestingly, the functional units are not long narrow tubes, or spheres, or cubes. They are precisely shaped like wedges, and this shape is very important to the design, because it provides the unique interrelationships between vessels and tubules necessary for the intricate job of concentrating urine.

The paired kidneys in a human weigh approximately one-half pound. In any mammal, both kidneys together weigh slightly less that one half of one percent of the total body weight. Human kidneys contain about three million nephrons, Windhager [25. p. 3]. Each nephron is 3 cm. in length, but if all the nephrons were laid out end to end, the tube would stretch for 50 miles, Prowser and Brown [18, p. 43]. This length is much more than is needed for the job of purifying the blood. There is a very large reserve of nephrons should some of them be damaged during the life of the individual.

The functional unit of the kidney is the nephron. It consists of a supply unit from the circulatory system and a collecting unit from the urinary system. These two structures are intricately intertwined with a highly specialized capillary network in order to form the urinary waste and to maintain the quality and quantity of the body fluids.

The supply system of the nephron begins with the renal artery, which gives rise to the arcuate arteries at the junction of the medulla and cortex. These arched vessels give rise to tiny afferent arterioles. Several glomeruli branch off each afferent arteriole. These glomeruli are specialized tufts of arterial capillaries which redivide many times before anastomosing within the glomeruli to form the efferent arterioles exiting from the renal corpuscle. After leaving the glomerulus, the efferent vessels again divide into a capillary network. Weiss, [24, p 820] has likened this to the portal system of the liver and calls it an arterial portal system. Some differences exist, however, since the portal system of the liver begins with a vein which breaks up into a capillary bed and finally reforms a vein; whereas, the arterial system of the glomerulus is an arteriole which breaks up into a capillary bed, then reunites into an arteriole before again forming another capillary bed. The afferent arterioles contain smooth muscle and are thicker than the efferent vessels. Adrenergic nerve fibers are located within one third of the efferent vessels and somewhat fewer in the afferent vessels, Brenner and Rector [3, p. 19]. This is an important component of the pressure control system which will be discussed later. These neural components are also important features in the structure and function of the juxtaglomerular apparatus, although renal circulation changes very little with or without nerve stimulation. Autoregulation is important in the kidney and is very efficient.

Outside of the corpuscle, in the cortex, the efferent arteries in nephrons near the capsule divide into an extensive capillary bed, the peritubular network, with no specific direction of flow. These are very thin-walled fenestrated vessels. This unique system provides an oxygen-rich blood flow with high pressure to the renal corpuscle, and an oxygen-rich but low pressure blood flow around the proximal and distal tubules, a necessary arrangement for active transport. In the corpuscles near the medulla, the efferent vessels give rise to two capillary systems. One is the peritubular network, and the other is a parallel network known as the *vasa recta*. The volume and rate of blood flow to the medulla is less than that which supplies the cortex. The oxygen tension is less, also; so the medullary cells derive much of their nutrition from glycolysis. One to two percent of the urinary blood flows through the *vasa recta*. Blood flows into the *vasa recta* without being exposed to the peritubular environment, and no solutes are contributed to the juxtanephron network. The flow is counter to the flow of the tubular solution; flowing down past the ascending loop, then up the descending loop where anastomosis with the intermediate branches of the arcuate vein occurs, ending finally with the interlobular vein. As these capillaries descend, they give off parallel branches which anastomose with the ascending vessel, forming a countercurrent pattern which is maintained among all the loops. In order to do this, adjoining nephrons share a *vasa recta*, and the loops are mirror images. The kidney capillaries have a structure that is different from capillaries elsewhere in the body. If the capillaries in the muscles, for instance, were like the capillaries in the kidneys, our muscles would be engorged with fluid and would not work properly. Imagine, too, how thick and heavy they would be. The pores in muscle capillaries occur between endothelial cells overlying a collagen-glycoprotein basement membrane; whereas, in the kidney, there are two porous layers separated by a basement membrane, which also appears to be fenestrated. The unique wedge shape of the kidney units creates a high pressure center in the glomerulus where it is needed to drive the filter system, and a low pressure system around the tubules where it enhances reabsorption. The point of the wedge is in the medulla where the osmotic gradient is the greatest. The double flow system in the medulla coupled with specific cell design creates a mechanism for concentrating urine found only in mammals and birds.

The collecting system of the nephron is composed of a glomerular capsule, a proximal convoluted tubule, a hairpin loop, and a distal convoluted tubule. The capsule is a cap of specialized cells surrounding the glomerulus. Together, this cap and the capillary tuft, or glomerulus, form the renal corpuscle. The distal convoluted tubule opens into the collecting duct. These two structures have similar function and are discussed together, although the collecting duct arises from a different embryonic tissue than does the distal tubule. The proximal convoluted tubule is a long twisted duct leading from the renal corpuscle. It winds around the cortex until it dips toward the medulla and gives rise to the hairpin loop. Some loops are short, remaining in the cortex for their entire length, while others are long and dip to various depths into the medulla. The number of nephrons with long loops and the length of the loops is correlated with the ability to concentrate urine. The greater the proportion of long loops, the greater the ability to concentrate urine. The distal convoluted tubule arises abruptly from the loop. Distal convoluted tubules are shorter and less convoluted than the proximal, and wind around the cortex near the corpuscle until they empty into the collecting duct. A specialized group of cells, called the juxta-glomerular apparatus lies between the distal tubule and the neck of the glomerulus. These cells secrete a hormone, renin, which aids in the control of the blood pressure leading into and exiting from the corpuscle.

FUNCTION

The really incredible story is a description of the kidney at work. Studying the delicate organ has not been easy. There are three distinct processes involved in urine formation: glomerular filtration, tubular reabsorption, and tubular secretion. Much of the knowledge of kidney function has come from indirect means and the study of pathological changes. Investigators injected traceable agents into rabbits or other experimental animals and studied the results. Micropuncture techniques gave proof that the glomeruli were ultrafilters. By micropuncture, scientists showed tubular reabsorption and also where in the tubules it takes place. The use of inulin and phenol red indicators aided in proving tubular secretion. Tissue cultures of embryonic and mature kidney fragments also aided in the gathering of knowledge of kidney function. Recent advancement in biochemical and histochemical research has added much to the knowledge of kidney function. The study of changes in plasma composition in relation to changes in kidney cellular morphology also gave insight into kidney function. This research is carried out by intelligent knowledgeable scientists using complex scientific instruments. The research is carefully designed so that the results can be studied in an organized fashion. Can we acknowledge our own intelligent efforts without acknowledging the Superintelligence which designed the system in the first place?

It must be remembered, too, that cells are made up of proteins and lipoproteins. Sometimes we think of cells as solid structures, like boxes or cubes. It helps clarify how the kidney works if we remember it is a network of molecules which in turn are composed of chemicals. These chemicals fit together and work together to form the united whole. This interdependence changes as we move through the nephron; so each part has a unique structure and function. Even though all of these cells originated from one cell, the master program provides immense differentiation within this organ enabling integration of function in a precise and efficient manner.

The kidneys perform an incredible function. In one day's time, they filter the equivalence of sixty times the total plasma, Berne and Levy [1, p. 752]. This system receives 20-25 percent of the blood flow of the body, Berne and Levy [1,p. 825], more than is supplied to other organs, and almost all of this blood passes through the glomeruli. The glomerular filtration rate in a 150 pound person is 180 L/day; whereas the filtration rate across other capillaries is 3 L/day, Vander and Luciano, [23, p. 428]. Plasma filtration takes place within the renal corpuscle. This structure is comprised of the glomerulus and its capsule. The cells of the capillaries and the basement membrane of the capsule are very porous. The cells of the capillary side of the cap have a completely different structure from those of the outside. The inside layer is visceral epithelium of the renal tissues and endothelium of the glomerular capillaries. In between the capillary cells and the capsule cells is a complex basement membrane. It continues around the capillary tuft and fuses with the afferent and efferent vessels as they leave the renal corpuscle. The cell body of the endothelial cells protrudes into the lumen of the capillary. The visceral epithelial cells are called podocytes, and have large central bodies with elongated primary foot processes which are largely suspended in the urinary space. Secondary foot processes are firmly adhered to the glomerular basement membrane. These epithelial cells fit together like loosely arranged puzzle pieces. The spaces between the cells form pores measuring about 40 by 140 micrometers, Berne and Levi [1, p 752]. This podocyte structure is unique to the kidney and makes its special filtering characteristics possible. Blood enters the nephron through the afferent vessel. In the renal corpuscle, 20% of the liquid constituents of the blood are filtered out. The filtrate from the glomerulus is captured within the capsular space because the outer layer of cells in the cap, the parietal epithelial layer, is composed entirely of impermeable squamous epithelium. The mesangeal cells are the fourth type of cell. They are located around the stalk formed by the afferent and efferent vessels. These cells are sensitive to angiotensin II and ADH, hormones which cause the cells to constrict. This is thought to reduce the filtration area, thereby regulating filtration.

The glomerular filter works by a pressure gradient caused by the heart beat and depends on the available area within the glomerulus. Five features of the filtering system favor high filtration. These are: the large renal blood flow, the complex shape of the podocytes, the presence of large endothelial pores, the contractile efferent arterioles which help maintain high glomerular pressure, and the high hydrostatic pressure relationship within the glomerulus. Blood pressure in the glomerulus averages 55 mg Hg. This is higher than in other capillaries of the body. The fluid within the glomerular capsule averages 15 mg Hg. Protein is present in the plasma but absent in the capsule. The osmotic pressure of the protein is 30 mg Hg. The pressure of protein and the fluid pressure of the capsule counter the blood pressure to the glomerulus. This creates a net pressure of 10 mg Hg which forces an essentially protein-free filtrate into the capsule and down the proximal tubule, Vander and Luciano. [23, p. 427]. The capillaries of the glomerulus are about 100 times more porous than other capillaries in the body. The glomerulus appears to work like a mechanical microfilter, although recent studies have shown that protein can be actively reabsorbed by the endothelial cells. Fluid travels through the endothelial pores, basement membrane, and the epithelial slit diaphragms to become an ultrafiltrate trapped by the parietal epithelium. There is a coordinated interaction among all of these distinct cells, and all must be properly structured and functional for the whole procedure to take place. Water, ions, amino acids, glucose, and other small soluble particles pass through the glomerular filter. Only the blood solids and the large protein molecules escape filtration. In the first step of kidney function, 20 percent of the total volume is removed, seemingly with very little discrimination, and no consideration of body needs! This creates a serious problem. A 170 pound person contains 40 L of water, and 3.5 L of plasma. The glomeruli filter 125 ml of plasma per minute which puts 160 L of water per day into the renal tubules. This filtrate contains 1 kg of sodium chloride, 500 Gm of sodium bicarbonate, 250 Gm of glucose, 100 Gm of free amino acids, and many other essential ions in smaller concentrations, Pitts, [17, p. 15]. The quantities filtered exceed the body stores; yet the quantities excreted are infinitesimally small. This means that tremendous amounts are reabsorbed.

Reabsorption takes place in the tubules, with about eighty-five percent occurring in the proximal tubules into which the filtrate passes after leaving the glomerulus. Solutes from the renal filtrate can pass through the proximal tubule cell membrane by osmosis, or by slipping through the junctions between the cells. Most reabsorption, however, takes place selectively by an active transport system through the cells. In contrast to the bulk flow present within the glomeruli, the flow is restricted in the tubules because no pores are present. In fact, the cells adhere to each other with tight interdiginated junctions, which form extensive processes and greatly enlarge the surface membrane on the basal side of the cells. This basolateral folding is most prominent in the first segment of the tubule and decreases in the latter segments. These junctions are sensitive to osmotic pressure changes within the cells and the intercellular spaces. These pressure changes affect transport through the intercellular junctions. The lumenal side of the proximal tubule cells consists of a dense brush border, or microvilli. Proximal tubule cells contain many mitochondria, located on the basal side. These cells also contain large vacuoles and lysosomes. Several cytomembranes, some containing ribosomes, and others being smooth walled, are present, as are numerous microtubules. The proximal tubule is divided into a highly convoluted segment and a straight segment. The cells of the first part of the convoluted segment, called S_1, are taller, more interdiginated, and have a more dense, tall brush border than the cells of the latter part of the convoluted segment and beginning of the straight segment, called S_2. Mitochondria are larger and more dense and vacuoles are more numerous in the S_1 segment. The bulk of the straight segment is called S_3. The brush border of this segment is tall and thick, but it has the fewest mitochondria. In the straight segment, the Golgi apparatus is more extensive, and the smooth-surfaced reticulum is more pronounced. The distance between microvilli increases with increased tubular flow. It is thought that this increases reabsorption, Windhager,[25, p. 71]. Even though the proximal convoluted tubule is one structure, yet it is subdivided and each section functions in a specific manner. The cells are complex and contain an enormous amount of specialized organelles. Mitochondria provide energy for the cells. Those cells having a large number of mitochondria have a high metabolic rate and many carrier proteins. These are the sites of intensive active transport. The Golgi apparatus is involved with preparing substances for secretion. Each area of the tubule has a specific design for a specific purpose.

Reabsorption mechanisms are passive or active. Passive reabsorption occurs if the substance flows out of the tubules by a concentration gradient or an electrochemical gradient. No energy is expended in passive transport, although energy is expended in establishing the necessary gradients in the first place. Active reabsorption mechanisms are complex and energy is required. $Na+$, $K+$-ATPase is present in the basolateral cell surface and activates a transcellular transport of sodium. This is highest in the first part of the tubule and decreases in the latter segments. The passive transport of water is established by the osmotic gradient created by the active transport of sodium. Urea does not permeate as readily as water, so it is at a higher concentration in the tubules, but when the concentration is high, it will passively return to the plasma. Urea is most concentrated in the collecting tubules. Here urea diffuses from the collecting tubule into the hairpin loop, thus creating a urea cycle. It is thought that retaining urea in the system in this manner creates a greater osmotic gradient than would be attainable otherwise. About half of the urea filtered is excreted. Chloride diffuses passively from the proximal tubules by the electrical gradient created by sodium. The solution in the capillaries surrounding the convoluted tubules is iso-osmotic with that in the tubules; yet the cells themselves may be hyperosmolar. This creates different electrical and ionic gradients, which enable selective retrieval of necessary ions. The carriers are specialized lipoproteins in the cell membranes to which the ions to be transported are attached. There are several carrier mechanisms. Some are specific for certain substances, whereas others carry several different substances. Sodium and glucose, for example, use the same carrier. However, glucose is carried at a fixed rate per unit of time. When more than this fixed amount is present in the filtrate, glucose is excreted in the urine. The body mechanisms that regulate glucose metabolism insure that under normal conditions the renal threshold of glucose will not be exceeded; so all the glucose in the filtrate is reabsorbed. However, in abnormal sugar metabolism, there is more glucose in the plamsa than the kidneys are capable of reabsorbing; so the excess will be excreted in the urine. Small amounts of protein filtered are reabsorbed in the proximal tubules. They are broken down into amino acids and utilized by the cells or released from within lysosomes into the tubule lumen. The permeability of the cells in the nephron to water varies along the nephron. Most of the water is reabsorbed in the proximal tubules. In humans this amounts to about 85 percent with another 5-10 percent being reabsorbed in the distal tubules. The amount reabsorbed there is regulated by antidiuretic hormone, ADH, and depends of the level of hydration. If an animal is suffering from water deprivation, the kidneys, by the action of ADH, can excrete all of the necessary substances and still maintain body homeostasis with a urine output of one pint per day, LeGrau, [10, p. 140].

The hairpin loop originates abruptly at the end of a short straight segment of the convoluted tubule. It consists of a thick descending limb, a thin descending limb, a thin ascending limb, and a thick ascending limb. The thick descending limb is similar to the last straight segment of the proximal tubule. The thin segments are found only in long loops which dip down into the medulla. Short loops remain in the cortex or dip slightly into the medulla, whereas long loops dip to varying degrees into the medulla. The number of loops is successively lessened from the medulla-cortex border to the papillae, which establishes the wedge formation. The loop has a very narrow lumen with nearly impermeable squamous cells as a border. The cells in the descending thin loops have a low permeability to sodium and chloride. a moderate permeability to urea, and a high permeability to water. No evidence for active transport has been found. The ascending thin segment is very impermeable to water, but highly permeable to sodium and chloride, and moderately permeable to urea. The thick ascending limb is the diluting limb. Sodium and chloride are reabsorbed both actively and passively and trapped within the medullary interstitium while water remains trapped within the tubule to be carried into the distal tubule located in the cortex. By enzyme action, these cells are sensitive to dietary load of protein, salt, and water. They are also sensitive to ADH levels which can be modified by diet, disease, or hormone addition. The end portion of the ascending thick limb passes very close to the junction of the afferent and efferent vessels of the glomerulus. Here, the cells become specialized *macula densa* cells. The basal portion of these cells extend between the arterioles. These cells manufacture renin in response to changes in blood pressure, salt load, tubular feedback, or nerve stimulation.

It is the haripin relationship of the loop with its accompanying capillary bed which accounts for the countercurrent mechanism. Unique arterioles known as the *vasa recta* travel downward along the ascending loop and the venous drainage travels upward along the descending loop, creating a mechanism for the transport of ions from the ascending limb to the descending limb, which in turn draws water out of the collecting tubules, thus concentrating the urine. In order to work efficiently, the hairpin arrangement and a continuous flow of solute are essential. An osmotic gradient is established from the cortex to the medulla. The solute filtered through the glomerulus is returned to the proximal tubules in such a way that the concentration of individual ions is changed; yet the solution has the same osmolality as the plasma. This holds true for the distal tubules as well. Because of the countercurrent mechanism surrounding the loop, the osmolality increases toward and into the medulla. The design of the capillary bed in the medulla slows down blood flow and helps maintain the gradient. It is based on the active reabsorption of sodium from the ascending limb. Sodium reenters the descending limb or is added to the plasma. Water is drawn out of the collecting tubule, causing the urine to become more concentrated. The presence of urea, a noncharged solute, aids in establishing an osmolal balance while preserving ions for the body. Urea and sodium cycles are established in the loop, which cause the urine to have a high concentration of urea rather than sodium.

In the distal tubule the cells change abruptly to taller cells with extensive basolateral surfaces and no brush border. As the distal tubule runs in close proximity to the renal corpuscle of its origin, the cells of the wall become narrow with nuclei that are close together. This has given rise to the name *macula densa*. ATP-ase is present and sodium and chloride are transported against a strong electro-chemical gradient. These cells respond readily to ADH levels. The distal tubule empties into the collecting duct. The water reabsorption in these cells can range from almost none to very much, depending on the level of ADH. Dilute urine can be formed if ADH is not present, and the permeability of the cells in the collecting duct to water is low. If ADH is present, the permeability to water is increased. Further water reabsorption takes place as the filtrate passes through the hypertonic environment of the medulla.

Secretion is the process of removing substances from the cellular interstitium or the capillaries and adding it to the urinary solution, or in other words, transport of solutes in the opposite direction from reabsorption. It occurs in the proximal and distal tubules. Various organic acids and bases, hydrogen and potassium ions, and complex chemicals such as penicillin are regulated in this manner. The distal tubule and collecting duct are the sites for most potassium and hydrogen secretion. The secretion of hydrogen ion is an important regulatory devise in humans, since acid-containing foods are prevalent in the diet. Removing hydrogen in this way helps prevent acidosis. Sodium and potassium transport are closely related because the electric potential of the tubules depends on sodium reabsorption. Under conditions of low dietary sodium, the potential for potassium secretion are increased as the amount of sodium is reabsorbed. The same holds true for the secretion of hydrogen. In this manner, homeostasis much more efficiently maintained in a diverse number of metabolic states.

REGULATION OF FUNCTION

The regulatory mechanism of the kidney is incredible. Blood flow through the kidney and the glomerular filter is autoregulatory. At the vascular pole of the renal corpuscle, where the afferent and efferent vessels emerge, the specialized *macula densa* cells of the distal tubule and a unique extraglomerular mesangium are in very close approximation. Renin, a powerful hormone is formed in the *macula densa*. The excretion of renin is controlled by sodium levels in the blood, blood pressure, and the stimulation of sympathetic nerves. Renin affects the entire body by causing vasoconstriction, aldosterone release, and ADH release from the pituitary. Aldosterone enhances distal tubular reabsorption of sodium, and ADH increases the permeability of the collecting duct to water and stimulates thirst. All of this creates a coordinated response to increase extracellular volume and elevate blood pressure. The peritubular network is also a stabilizing arrangement for pressure within the glomerulus. Both the afferent and the efferent vessels moderate pressure and flow within the glomerulus by exerting opposite effects of the glomerular pressure. An increase in resistance of the afferent vessel reduces pressure to the glomerulus while an increase in pressure of the efferent vessel increases pressure. The end result is that the pressure tends to be stable regardless of changes in central blood pressure. The pressure in the efferent vessel is also a regulatory mechanism on the flow and pressure within the peritubular vessels. Increasing efferent pressure decreases peritubular pressure and enhances reabsorption.

Integration of function is also an important regulatory mechanism. Each segment of the individual nephron is integrated with the other segments. Each tubule segment responds differently from every other segment to the fluid composition within them. Changes in fluid volume and composition affect the operation of other segments. The slow steady flow of fluid to the collecting duct enables the final small adjustments in urine concentration. Regional integration exists because the nephron is folded back upon itself. This enables coupling between segments not in direct contact with each other. In this way, the excretion of water and solutes are controlled independently of each other. This creates a steady state excretion of solutes despite large differences in water retention.

CONCLUSION

The kidney is indeed an incredible structure showing tremendous integration and complexity. From a very superficial examination to a detailed analysis, this design and complexity can be seen. Biologists who study this organ use highly sophisticated equipment and technology. Intelligence is necessary in order to use this equipment and technology, and to interpret findings. There are still areas of dispute in understanding and interpreting kidney function. The study of this organ continues and, as our knowledge increases, modifications in interpretation are made. Even though we are coming closer to being able to describe the organ in chemical terms, we still need to grapple with the question of how it came about in the first place. So far no one has been able to make an artificial kidney which is as efficient in function and use of space as the natural kidney.

Replacement of kidney function is an important medical consideration. People with failing kidneys must be provided with a system of plasma purification or life cannot be sustained. At the present time two methods are available to perform this service. The most prevalent one is peritoneal dialysis. The patient can be treated at home with a maximum of ambulation. This method consists of establishing two fistulas in the abdominal wall. One is used to introduce a special solution which uses the intestinal and mesenteric vessels to effect an exchange of solutes. The second provides drainage of waste solution. The peritoneal vessels are extensive and well adapted for absorption; but a limiting factor is their design. The dynamics of the kidney vessels is lacking. Autoregulation is not present either, so the patient must be monitored by his physician so that changes can be made as needed. The patient must be able to tolerate and utilize the extra fluids introduced into the abdomen. Occasionally, the fistulae will rupture, creating leakage and herniation which necessitate further intervention. The second method is hemodialysis, which must be performed with special equipment in a medical facility. Of necessity, the patient must be recumbent for this procedure. Both peritoneal dialysis and hemodialysis are inefficient and expensive. Fluid introduced into the body must be warmed to body temperature. Individual differences in metabolism must be considered. Problems can arise in creating abnormal extracellular fluid composition which must be corrected according to each patient's needs. Other problems involve the introduction of foreign substances from an external source into the closed system of the body, because both methods involve penetrating the body with needles and tubes. Changes in the structure of the blood vessels involved in the procedures create problems with absorption and exchange of solutes. Both of these methods utilize a simple filtration mechanism with solute exchange proceeding along a concentration gradient. Both require massive amounts of equipment or special solutions. Both of these methods have involved a great deal of super intelligence by human bio-engineers using extravagant intelligence-directed methods and equipment. Both of these methods involve design by human engineers who have been trying to perfect their design for several decades. No one has come up with a unit which compares with the natural kidney; yet scientists are justifiably proud of the advances they have made. How much greater is the design of the biological unit? How much more likely to have been created by the Master Designer?

BIBLIOGRAPHY

[1]   Berne, Robert, and Levy, Matthew, Physiology, C.V. Mosby Co., St. Louis, 1992, pp 745-792
[2]   Borysenke, Myrin, and Beringer, Theodore, Functional Histology, Little, Brown, and Co., Boston, 1989
[3]   Brenner and Rector, The Kidney, Third Ed., Vol. 1, Saunders, Phil., 1986
[4]   Bubel, Andreas, Microstructure and Function of the Cell, Ellis Harwood ltd., Chinchester, 1989
[5]   Crouch, James, Functional Human Anatomy, Lea and Farbinger, Phil., 1985
[6]   Edwards, N.A. and Hassell, K.A., Biochemistry and Physiology of the Cell, McGraw Hill, London. 1980
[7]   Emslie-Smith, Patterson, Scratchard, and Read, Textbook of Physiology, Blackwell Sci. Pub., Oxford, 1980
[8]   Guyton, Arthur, Textbook of Medical Physiology, W.B. Saunders, Phil., 1991
[9]   Lamb, Ingram, Johnston, and Pittman, Essentials of Physiology, Churchill Livingstone, Edinburgh, 1988
[10]   LeGrau, Marcel, Nephrology, Masson, Pub., N.Y., 1987, pp 350-354
[11]   Lloyd, C.W., Hymes, J.S., and Warn, R.M., "The Cytoskeleton; Cell Function and Organization," J. of Cell Sci. Proceedings, Cambridge, 1968
[12]   Moore, Kieth, Study Guide and Review Manual of Human Embryology, W.B. Saunders, Co., Phil., 1975
[13]   Moore, Kieth, The Developing Human, W.B. Saunders, Co. 1982
[14]   Nissenson, Allen, and Fine, Richard, Dialysys Therapy, Hanley and Belfusinc, Phil., 1986
[15]   Patten, Bradley, Human Embryology, McGraw Hill, N.Y., 1968
[16]   Patten, Fuchs, Hill, Scher, and Steiner, Textbook of Physiology, 22nd. ed., 1989
[17]   Pitts, Robert, Physiology of the Kidney and Body Fluids, 2nd. ed., Yearbook Pub., Chicago, 1972
[18]   Prowser, C. and Brown, Frank, Comparative Animal Physiology, Saunders Co., Phil., 1961
[19]   Ross, Michael, and Romwell, Lynn, Histology: a Text and Atlas, William and Wilkins, Baltimore, 1989
[20]   Rugh, Robert, Vertebrate Embryology, Harcourt and Brace, N.Y., 1964
[21]   Slack, J.M.W., From Egg to Embryo, Cambridge U. Press, Cambridge, 1983
[22]   Schmidt, Robt., and Thews, Gershard, Human Physiology, Springer Verlag, Berlin, 1989
[23]   Vander, Sherman, and Luciano, Human Physiology; The Mechanisms of Body Function, 4th ed., McGraw Hill, N.Y., 1985
[24]   Weiss, Leon, Cell and Tissue Biology, Urban and Schwartzenberg, Balt., 1992
[25]   Windhager, Erich, Handbook of Physiology, renal Function vol. 1, sec.8, Oxford Press, N.Y., 1992
[26]   Zbylut, J., Twardowski, Karl, and Ramish, Khann, Peritoneal Dialysis," Contemporary Issues in Nephrology, Vol. 22, J. Stein, ed., Churchill Livingston, N.Y., 1990, p.1.

THE ORIGIN AND HISTORY OF THE SOLAR SYSTEM

WAYNE R. SPENCER, B.S, M.S.
P.O. BOX 8164
WICHITA, KS 67208

KEYWORDS

Solar System; Catastrophism; Age

ABSTRACT

Much has been written on the origin of the solar system from evolutionary points of view. These views assume only natural processes were involved and that the solar system is billions of years in age. The currently accepted view, the Modified Nebula Hypothesis, and the Capture Theory are critiqued in the light of evidence for a young solar system. A creationist approach is proposed which allows for intelligent design, an age of less than 10,000 years, and a major solar-system-wide catastrophe in the history of our solar system. Two possibilities for such a catastrophe are examined, a destroyed planet in the asteroid region and a debris cloud passing through the solar system. This approach is more successful in explaining the solar system than the usual naturalistic origins theories.

INTRODUCTION

The evolution-based models of the origin of our solar system have experienced difficulties which have not been fully discussed in introductory astronomy textbooks. Thus there is the impression that the origin of our solar system by the collapse of a huge cloud is a completely settled issue. This gives the impression to astronomy students that long periods of time are essential, and that such nebula ideas cannot be questioned. This approach is not a good pedagogical practice considering the many limitations of solar system origins models. Also, this approach presumes a naturalistic philosophy and conveniently agrees with the relativistic values of our time. Many people trained in science incorrectly assume that this naturalistic approach is *necessary* in science.

Creationists, however, approach scientific observations with different presuppositions. To a creationist there is no a priori reason why scientists must explain things using only natural processes. Experimental science limits itself to considering only natural processes; the study of origins does not have this limitation. Supernatural processes are admissible to a creationist since he believes that a transcendent personal Creator-God was present before all else. However, most creationists would agree that supernatural processes were used primarily at the beginning. Creationists believe natural forces alone are insufficient for explaining first origins. The study of astronomy has long been very inspiring to Christian believers because it points us to the greatness of the God who made us all. The scientific implications of the creation view can be examined on their own merits, apart from the spiritual implications. But it is a tragic thing to be knowledgeable of all that the Creator-God made and yet completely miss the significance of it because of misunderstanding its origin. The study of these questions is not just facts and figures, it challenges us to consider the Creator and what His creation is revealing to us about Him.

The Creator-God is not limited merely to the familiar things we know of on Earth. There is an amazing variety in the worlds that exist in our planet's "neighborhood." Great extremes of all kinds are present, some of which indicate catastrophic events on a scale difficult for us to imagine. Close study of these worlds shows the great uniqueness of the Earth. Indeed it seems the Creator has been relatively gentle with the Earth, considering the evidence of catastrophes which have occurred elsewhere in the solar system. As Isaiah 45:18 says, "He did not create it to be empty, but formed it to be inhabited."

Three ideas have guided the author's study of the solar system: 1) that there is evidence of intelligent design, 2) that the solar system is less than 10,000 years in age, and 3) that some major catastrophe occurred in the past that affected much of the solar system in a relatively short time. Hints of such a solar-system-wide catastrophe include craters, the asteroids, planetary rings, and other observations. It is critically important in this study to pull together many different types of data. Catastrophes to be considered in this paper will be 1) an impact with a hypothetical tenth planet in the region of the asteroids, and 2) a debris cloud passing through the solar system.

Before addressing the question of a solar system catastrophe, some historical comments will be followed by a critique of two evolution-based models. It is important to briefly survey evidence for the solar system being young as well. Many processes relied on by planetary scientists require great periods of time, far more than 10,000 years. Insisting on the solar system being this young places constraints on what processes are plausible in explaining the characteristics of the various objects. A variety of facts will be related to a creation view of the history of the solar system. Assuming a young system and that there was a solar system catastrophe has advantages for explaining a number of observations. To an evolutionist the mystery is the origin of the solar system, but to a creationist who believes in an omnipotent God the mystery is its history, not so much its origin.

The History of Origins Models

In spite of some sophisticated modern modifications, the accepted model for the origin of the solar system is much like the "Nebula Hypothesis" proposed by Pierre Simon Laplace in 1796. Various criticisms arose of Laplace's hypothesis, prompting some to suggest models more catastrophic in nature. In 1917 Sir James Jeans proposed what is known as the Tidal Theory, which was the accepted view for a time. In the Tidal Theory a very massive star passes near our Sun, which had supposedly already formed by condensing from an interstellar nebula. Then the passing star causes a filament of matter to be pulled off the Sun, which would then break up into segments due to gravity. Serious problems were found with this theory as well, which even Jeans eventually conceded. The problems with the Tidal Theory led scientists in the 1930s and 40s to work on more complex approaches to the Nebula model.

Today most ideas from planetary scientists are virtually the same as ideas of the 1960s and 70s. Today solar system origins theories can be thought of as of two general classes, the Modified Nebula Models and Catastrophic Models. Modern "Nebula" ideas incorporate principles of plasma physics as well as theories on the evolution of our Sun. The Nebula models utilize the slow gradual approach in which the Sun, the planets, and all other objects condense from an interstellar nebula. The competing view to this today comes mainly from Michael Woolfson and John Dormand and is known as the Capture Theory [8]. The Capture Theory could be loosely described as the reverse of the Tidal Theory, with additional effects from a major collision of two planets.

Assumptions and Limitations of Today's Theories

Experts in planetary science have expressed concerns about the assumptions and limitations of today's theories. Modern Nebula models emphasize uniformitarianism, applied to the solar system. The Nobel prize winning astronomer Hannes Alfven makes this point very clearly [1, p.27]:

> This 'actualistic principle' which emphasizes reliance on observed phenomena, is the basis for the modern approach to the geological evolution of the Earth; 'the present is the key to the past.' This principle should also be used in the study of the solar system.

H. Reeves, writing the lead article in an important book on the origin of the solar system, calls the Nebula Model the theory with the "best fit" to the observational data. Reeves then makes the following comments [18, p.1-3].

> How much confidence can we place in this 'best fit' theory? Not very much.

> I will reconstruct the sequence of events leading to the formation of the solar system, choosing the chronological stages which seem to me to be the most likely. Even so the argument is highly speculative and some of it borders on science fiction.

If experts who have done extensive research directly related to origins make comments like this, then it is not appropriate for astronomy textbooks to treat the subject dogmatically. Textbooks are seldom written to give a balanced perspective on the various origins explanations.

Nebula models are meant to explain how a gigantic cloud in space, such as we observe, can contract and condense into our Sun, planets, over 60 moons, as well as thousands of asteroids and other small objects. Interstellar clouds are found to be rotating and possess a weak magnetic field. Some nebula models rely on the matter to come from the interstellar medium itself, rather than from a nebula. H. Reeves summarized the problems associated with forming coherent bodies from interstellar material. Three important problems are that "The clouds are too hot, too magnetic, and they rotate too rapidly" [18, p.9].

Because ideas based on uniformitarianism rely on natural processes such as gravity, gas pressure, magnetic effects, and collisions, each type of model predicts certain patterns. Standard Nebula ideas, for instance, led scientists to expect that the moons of Uranus and Neptune should not show much evidence of past geologic or tectonic activity. These moons were expected to have dull uninteresting surfaces as a result. This was due to the fact that small objects radiate heat more rapidly than larger ones and the temperatures at the time of formation would have been very cold at the distances from the Sun where Uranus and Neptune are found. Since planetary scientists assumed these moons to be very old (about 4.6 billion years), they reasoned that there should not be enough heat energy in the interiors to drive significant geological activity.

These assumptions were proven wrong as the Voyager spacecrafts discovered surprising and amazing features in the Uranian and Neptunian systems. For example, Neptune has the highest speed *retrograde* winds known-- winds which travel in a left-handed sense instead of the usual right-handed sense. ("Right-handed" means that if one points upward or northward with the right thumb, the fingers will curl in the direction of the motion or spin.) These winds reach up to 2,100 kilometers per hour and change even more rapidly than the winds of Jupiter. Furthermore, on Triton an erupting geyser was discovered ejecting material eight kilometers above the surface [11, p.179]. These features are easier to explain if the solar system is only thousands of years in age, for then primordial heat left over from creation could still be driving these processes. An even more dramatic example of the failure of the uniformitarian assumptions is the moon of Uranus known as Miranda. Two well known solar system authors made the following striking comments about Miranda [6, p. 140].

> Even the earliest pictures of Miranda were enigmatic. From a distance, it looked as though some celestial giant had painted a big white check mark on its surface, as if to say, 'Here's the answer!' Later called 'the chevron,' the immense check mark remains unexplained to this day.

I find it easier to believe in a "celestial giant" than to believe that natural processes alone are responsible for surprising features such as this. However, I prefer to call the "celestial giant" God. Miranda possesses many additional strange surface forms, such as a cliff face which is nearly 10 miles in height! These surprises were found on a moon which is only 600 miles in diameter. The solar system writers referred to above quoted a NASA scientist as saying the following about Miranda's surface [6, p.140].

> If you can imagine taking all the bizarre geologic forms in the solar system and putting them on one object, you've got it in front of you.

The usual response of planetary scientists to major surprises is to add complex and speculative processes to the basic Nebula model rather than to examine the validity of the model itself. The assumption of the system being very old comes up again and again. But assuming the solar system to be young simplifies the process of explaining various features, as will be elaborated on later in this paper.

Age of the Solar System

Since many creationists hold to the position that the solar system and universe is less than 10,000 years in age, this raises many questions about processes believed to have shaped solar system objects and their surfaces. Various processes must have happened in a much shorter time span than is generally believed. Craters, for instance, are found throughout the solar system, but are not uniformly distributed. Instead of multiple episodes of heavy bombardment separated by periods of millions of years, a young solar system would imply that somehow the many craters observed must have formed relatively quickly compared to evolutionary time scales. Certain processes assumed to be plausible by most planetary scientists would become impossible if the solar system is "young." Various types of mechanical, thermal, chemical, and radioactive processes would have a very different role in the history of our solar system from a young age interpretation. This raises many issues that creationists need to study on a technical level.

Much could be written about evidences for a young solar system. The strength of the evidence for our system being young lies in the fact that a variety of *unrelated* processes point to the same conclusion. Creationists have documented many indicators of youth for our home planet, Earth. Other processes must be brought to bear on the question of the age of the solar system as a whole. It is necessary to assemble arguments for youth from unrelated processes in different parts of the solar system.

I have calculated a rough age figure for Saturn's moon Titan of 181,000 years based on the production of ethane in Titan's atmosphere [21]. I have also studied the argument for our Moon being young based on the influx of cosmic dust from space. Some creationist writings have used outdated unrealistic numbers for the thickness of a layer of dust there would be on an old Moon. The Moon dust argument no longer seems to be valid. At the present dust influx rate, the amount of dust which would be present on a 10,000 year old Moon would be virtually immeasurable [19]. Thus, the cosmic dust influx implies some significant catastrophe occurred in the past which caused a high influx of dust in a relatively short time. Other arguments for a young solar system could be mentioned. The author is aware of such an argument related to heat dissipation in Jupiter's moon Io. If Io were 4.6 billion years in age, its orbit would have shifted farther from Jupiter than the present position [15].

The Modified Nebula Model

The Modified Nebula Model begins with a Nebula in interstellar space and attempts to explain how this cloud could contract and condense into the existing objects. Following is a description of the stages involved in the model which is the accepted view today. It must be understood that numerous variations on this have been suggested by different scientists. After looking at the Modified Nebula models, the "Capture Theory," a catastrophic model with evolutionary assumptions will be examined as well. Then catastrophic models with creationist assumptions will be mentioned.

The nebula which our solar system is believed to have formed from is frequently referred to as the "protosolar nebula." The prefix "proto" is sometimes used in reference to planets or moons as well, indicating objects that are not yet completely coherent bodies. The protosolar nebula has been assumed to have a mass of about 100,000 times the mass of our Sun and is believed to have initially been much larger than our solar system. The nebula is assumed to be initially rotating slowly and possess a weak magnetic field. Cooling of the cloud would allow it to contract due to gravity. This contraction would cause the rotation of the cloud to accelerate and the initial magnetic field would increase in intensity. Matter pulling toward the center of the cloud would form a central ball called the protosun. The combination of contraction and rotation would cause the cloud to become a disk made up of solid mineral grains (microscopic in size) and ices, with the Sun in the center. Dust and gases would surround and envelop this disk.

At this point there would be no large macroscopic rocky objects but there could be small chunks of ices. These ices would be composed of water, methane, and ammonia and would primarily form only beyond about 5 A.U. from the Sun. Most of the matter in the nebula as a whole would be hydrogen and helium, with comparatively small amounts of other elements. If the contraction merely continued as described, almost all the mass in the solar system would today be found in the Sun, as would almost all the rotational energy. However, though it is true that nearly all the mass of the solar system is in the Sun, the planets possess most of the angular momentum while the Sun spins very slowly.

To attempt to explain this, modern nebula models apply plasma physics to the contracting cloud. Scientists have attempted to explain mechanisms that can transport matter inward toward the Sun and simultaneously transfer angular momentum outward. It is assumed that before there were significant macroscopic objects, an electrical current could have flowed through the cloud, causing a "magnetic coupling" between the central mass (the protosun) and the surrounding nebula. This effect is believed to have transferred angular momentum and rotational energy from the central mass to the surrounding medium to make the planets move rapidly in their orbits compared to the spin rate of the Sun. This magnetic effect is depended on to enable the particles in the disk to accelerate to speeds such that they will follow Kepler's Laws of motion. If the tiny grains do not follow Kepler's Laws at this early stage, then the planets would not be able to travel in stable orbits after they formed.

Next the system reaches what is often referred to as an accretionary stage. The protosun would continue to heat up as it contracted until eventually nuclear reactions could begin. This marks the "birth" of our Sun. Most of the solid material would lie in the plane of the disk. It is believed this disk would separate into rings, though there is not general agreement on how this would occur. These rings would then form into planets and a similar disk to rings to object process on a smaller scale would occur to form moons.

Scientists suggest the action of turbulence and random motions could lead to grains clustering enough so that gravity could begin pulling the matter together by its own weight. It is believed that over long periods of time these grains would, by occasionally sticking together, "accrete" into larger and larger objects. These solid accreting objects would eventually reach the size of what are called "planetesimals." Planetesimals vary in shape and other characteristics and might be up to a few hundred kilometers in size. The asteroids are believed to be planetesimals which were not able to accrete into planets.

At this stage, the solar system would still be filled with much dust and gas, enough to make the whole system opaque. The young Sun would then enter a stage of its own "evolution" known as the T-Tauri stage. The result is a very intense "solar wind" of various particles and radiation emitted from the Sun. It is believed this "solar gale" would clear much of the excess gas and dust out of the system. Some astronomers also believe that electric currents would flow through this "wind" in such a way as to slow the rotation of the Sun further. Scientists have suggested that our Sun may have lost about one half of its original mass in a period of one million years during this stage. By the end of this period the solar system would be transparent and the planets, moons, and other objects would be coherent bodies but would not be layered in their interiors since gravitational accretion would not produce layered objects.

It is thought that at this point there would be very heavy bombardment by meteorites throughout the system. Meteorites, volcanic activity, and radioactive decay are believed to have caused the newly formed planets and moons to heat sufficiently so that the more dense material would sink to the center and the less dense material would move closer to the surface. This would form layered structures within the large bodies such as planets and moons. This period of many impacts is believed to have ended about four billion years ago.

Difficulties with Nebula Models

How plausible is this process? Much mathematical work has been done to attempt to give a theoretical basis for it. This technical level work sometimes looks very impressive except when one looks critically at two things, the starting assumptions built in to the calculation and the degree of fit with the observed characteristics of the solar system. Frequently it is possible to put forth impressive looking mathematical models of a small part of the process. But scientists are not always able to connect one stage to the next in a way that is physically realistic. Just as in the study of paleontology, there are "missing links." Three general types of problems will be considered here. These are 1) problems in the collapse process, 2) problems in explaining present motions of objects, and 3) problems in explaining composition relationships in the solar system.

Various problems exist in the timing of the different processes occurring during the collapse of the Nebula. One of the more perplexing problems of current interest is what is referred to the "runaway formation of Jupiter" and the other gas giant planets. Nebula collapse theories imply that nearly all hydrogen and helium would be removed from the Nebula in a time of about one million years. This means that the four gas giant planets would have to form a central core of about 10 earth masses in less than one million years. The more massive the planet, the quicker it would form by gravitational contraction. Some models show a Jupiter core forming in as little as 700,000 years, Saturn in 3.8 million years (M.Y.), Uranus in 8.4 M.Y., and Neptune in 23 M.Y. [23, p.16-17]. This is too slow because the hydrogen, helium, and other light gases would not be available long enough for a 10 earth mass core to form. Without a core of about this size, gravity would not be sufficient to complete the accretion of matter onto the body. The end result then would be that the gas giant planets would not be as large as we find them today.

Various processes would interfere with the collapse of the Nebula. The initial temperature of the nebula is a critical part of the problem and a point of controversy. Theoretical collapse models begin assuming a density of the cloud much greater than the observed densities of interstellar nebulae. Other properties of interstellar nebulae also differ from the values used in the origins calculations. The cloud must collapse a great deal, causing rotation to accelerate, magnetic field strength to increase, and temperature to increase. All three of these changes tend to stop collapse. Also, the slow rotation of the Sun coupled with the rapid motion of the planets in their orbits is not adequately explained by collapse models. The angular momentum of the protosun during collapse must be decreased by a factor of 10^4 to 10^6, and the protosun must do this in such a way as to lose only about five percent of its mass [17]. (Note that this five percent of the protosun's mass does not correspond to the mass of the planets.) Mass must somehow flow to the Sun while the material which later becomes the planets is accelerated in orbit.

Scientists have not explained how so much angular momentum could be transferred to the planets and in such a way as to leave the Sun at its present size. Hannes Alfven, who does not agree with many of the standard accepted theories, lays great emphasis on the role of magnetic fields and plasma effects to explain the angular momentum. However, most scientists generally agree that Alfven's calculations assume an unrealistically strong magnetic field at the start. Alfven has written strong criticisms of the standard Nebula models [2]. Many scientists today assume that the angular momentum problem has been long since resolved by new models. But Stuart Ross Taylor in a recent book made the comment that "The ultimate origin of the angular momentum of the solar system remains obscure [23, p. 53]."

The second class of problems with Nebula models involves various motions that exist in our solar system which do not fit the pattern implied by Nebula models. Some aspects considered to be strengths of the Nebula model are the following. All the planets orbit nearly in one plane, travelling in the same right-handed manner around the Sun (prograde direction). Most of the planets also spin in the same right-handed manner, as does the Sun. Most moons also travel around the Sun and spin in the same right-handed sense. This is said to be due to the initial spin of the original nebula.

There are striking exceptions to these regular patterns. The Sun, for instance, is tilted about 7 degrees in angle compared to the rest of the solar system. What would cause the entire disk to be tilted in relation to the central body? Also, there are six known cases of moons which orbit retrograde, opposite the direction which the planet spins. Four of these are the outermost four moons of Jupiter, one is Phoebe at Saturn, the last is Triton at Neptune. Phoebe is particularly unique since it is the only moon which orbits retrograde but that spins prograde.

In the Nebula hypothesis all rotation and orbital motion comes from the motion of the original rotating nebula. Furthermore, Venus, Uranus, and Pluto all spin retrograde. There are too many exceptions to the pattern predicted by the Nebula model. Sometimes scientists have assumed that Uranus, which is tilted 98 degrees, was at one time tilted and spinning with an orientation more like the other planets. Then something caused it to tilt over and the moons were somehow spun off of Uranus into their present orbits. Alfven makes the following comment about this scenario [2, p. 219].

In fact, to place the Uranian satellites in their present (almost coplanar circular) orbits would require all the trajectory control sophistication of modern space technology. It is unlikely that any natural phenomenon involving bodies emitted from Uranus could have achieved this result.

Another problem would include the distribution of mass across the solar system. The general approach of a cloud collapsing to form the Sun and planets should also explain the formation of moons. Again, Alfven comments [2, p.218-219].

In addition to these obvious discrepancies between the implied uniform and the actually observed distributions of mass in the solar system, the whole disc idea is tied to the theoretical concept of a contracting mass of gas which could collapse to form both the central body and the surrounding secondaries via the intermediate formation of the disc. . . . small bodies cannot be formed in this way and it is questionable whether even Jupiter is large enough to have been formed by such a collapse process.

A third general type of problem for Nebula models has to do with the composition of the planets and other objects in relation to their distance from the Sun. This subject is quite complex and much has been published about it. The study of many different radioactive isotopes has been done to discover patterns in their amounts across the solar system. According to the Nebula model, the inner planets would form at higher temperatures than the outer planets. This and other processes occurring in the cloud would determine the composition of all objects. When amounts of an element or isotope do not easily or obviously fit into the Nebula Model, it is referred to as a composition anomaly. The elaborate theory related to this is referred to as the chemical equilibrium theory. Space does not allow elaboration on these anomalies. However, I would like to suggest certain types of anomalies for creationists to study.

Attempting to explain the amounts of the many isotopes present in the planets by natural processes alone is akin to attempting to juggle perhaps 200 balls at once. Scientists have not been able to explain processes that can give the right amounts of all the constituents all at once and do so for all the planets. You just cannot keep all the balls up. One example worth study in this regard would be water contents on Venus, Earth, and Mars. Oxygen and Magnesium isotopes in meteorites have been mentioned as anomalous by various researchers. Amounts of the Noble gases on Venus, Earth, and Mars also are anomalous [13]. One NASA scientist made the following admission in an article about composition anomalies[14].

In fact, I would suggest that there is no model for the origin of our own Sun which successfully predicts all of the complex isotopic and chemical relationships observed in the comets, meteorites, and planets of our Solar System.

The Capture Theory

The modern Capture Theory represents a catastrophic evolutionary approach to the origin of the solar system. At the beginning of this scenario our Sun has formed. Then a protostar passes near our Sun, this protostar being a loosely held together ball of gas. The pull òf our Sun on the protostar severely distorts its shape and a filament of matter is pulled off of the protostar. This filament then breaks into segments, which become six large gaseous planets. In this scenario, our solar system would not possess nine planets in the beginning, but six.

A large amount of gas pulled off of the protostar supposedly becomes a cloud that surrounds our Sun after the protostar passes by. All of these six planets would initially travel in highly elliptical orbits (eccentricities estimated to be .68 to .91)[8, p.156]. It is not possible for an object that is captured into orbit to have a near circular orbit. It is believed the surrounding medium of gas would round the elliptical orbits into circular orbits such as the planets now have. This would occur due to gas drag resisting motion. Time required for this rounding is estimated to be 10^5 to 6×10^6 years.

All of the new planets thus formed would be gas and fluid in nature. The inner two of these are referred to simply as A and B. A and B would have occupied the regions in which Earth, the Asteroids, and Mars are found today. These two planets no longer exist because it is believed they collided. It is believed that our Moon and Mars were moons of planets A and B. Mercury, Venus, and Earth are believed to be fragments from the collision. Other interesting captures, orbit changes, and tidal effects are believed to have occurred as well.

Problems with The Capture Theory

The work of Dormand and Woolfson on the Capture Theory provides valuable insights into the nature of collisions and tidal interactions between objects. The idea of a filament breaking into segments seems to be exactly like the older Jeans Tidal model. Other computer studies have shown that any kind of filament drawn off of a gaseous body will either disperse into space or just fall back to the object, not condense into planets [3, p. 378]. A major problem for both the Capture Model and the Nebula Model is the evidence for a young solar system. In less than 10,000 years there would not be sufficient time for orbits to round into being nearly circular. Other problems could be mentioned such as the orientation of Uranus and its moons.

The Capture Theory tends to give much attention to certain observations about the solar system which the Nebula Model cannot explain well. The reverse may also be true. The Nebula model gives more attention to explaining the "regular" patterns in the solar system while the Capture Theory attempts to better explain retrograde orbits, composition anomalies, and the angular momentum of the Sun and planets. Our solar system is too orderly to come from something like the capture and collision processes of the Capture Theory. At the same time, our solar system contains too many surprising and varied features to fit the relationships implied by the Nebula Model. The solar system can be better understood by acknowledging there is evidence of intelligent design in the orderly regular patterns, and yet evidence of catastrophic events that have altered what was originally created.

Catastrophism in a Young Solar System

Scientists addressing solar system origins, even Nebula theorists, frequently suggest various capture and collision processes. To the author's knowledge, orbit captures have been proposed for about nine different objects in our solar system. All of these seem very unlikely in the author's opinion, except perhaps one, Neptune's moon Nereid. Nereid is the only moon or planet in our system which has a very high eccentricity, its value being .75. Pluto's eccentricity is .249. (The eccentricity measures how elongated the orbit is.) Nereid's eccentricity is consistent with it being captured into its present orbit. To have so many capture processes in one solar system, including one for every moon orbiting retrograde, is very unlikely. Captures are not possible when an orbit is circular, not that is, if orbit rounding would require millions of years. Orbit rounding, for moons, could not take place by a resisting medium because extremely long times would be required greater than the lifetime of any medium. The interaction of tides and orbits can round orbits some, but in a young solar system this probably would not be very significant in most cases. Therefore, the origin of the retrograde moons by capture represents an unrealistic application of catastrophism. Rather, the motion of these moons indicates intelligent design.

Catastrophic processes destroy order, they do not produce order, not by natural processes at least. Evidence for catastrophism must be found in irregular or random characteristics. Craters and volcanic events also can be considered catastrophism. In 1992 the author discussed evidence for design and catastrophism in our solar system [20]. Large impact sites are found on a number of objects in the solar system [20, p. 166]. A number of these were evidently caused by impacts which had a major effect on the moon or planet.

Mars, for instance, possesses two hemispheres which are quite different, the northern hemisphere is 1-2 km lower than the southern hemisphere [5, p. 64]. The northern hemisphere is quite smooth and has few craters (except in small areas). The southern hemisphere is much more heavily cratered and possesses two extremely large impact sites called Hellas and Argyre. Hellas' outer ring is 4,200 km (2,610 mi.) in diameter. Nearly on the opposite side of the planet (antipodal) is the large bulge known as the Tharsis region. Several giant volcanic mountains lie on this bulge, including Olympus Mons [22]. Massive impacts on Mars could have stimulated a great deal of volcanic activity which covered a large fraction of the surface. Surface readjustments following the impacts might explain the difference in the two hemispheres. Most planetary scientists do not believe that the Hellas impact is related to the Tharsis volcanoes because long-age assumptions lead them to conclude the two regions are of very different ages.

Craters are very important clues for us regarding the history of the solar system. They represent a record of the past. The numbers and sizes of craters show interesting relationships. Note that the largest impact sites are not craters at all but flat smooth plains surrounded by concentric rings of mountains. On icy surfaces concentric circular ridges can indicate a large impact, such as Valhalla on Jupiter's moon Callisto (outer ring 3,000 km in diameter). These smooth plains on our Moon are called Mare. These are what I refer to as super-impacts. In these impacts, extensive volcanic flows completely fill the crater, and the only visible sign of the impact are the rings of mountains around it. On the Moon the largest of these super-impact sites are found on the near side. The largest clear site such as this is the Imbrium basin, whose main rim is 1,200 km (746 mi.) in diameter; a much larger basin which *may* be an impact site is Procellarum, which is 3,200 km (1,988 mi.) [10]. The impact sites and signs of volcanism on Mars gives evidence of a very violent history for that planet. On Mars there are a number of sites which are surrounded by 4, 5, and even 6 concentric rings of mountains. The largest of these is the Elysium impact basin, whose fifth ring is 4,970 km (3,088 mi.) in diameter [12].

If the solar system is 4.6 billion years in age one would expect many objects to be saturated with craters over much or all of the surface. Crater saturation is reached when a new impact would destroy at least one other, so that the number of craters in a certain area could no longer increase. It cannot be proven that *any* object in the solar system is saturated with craters over a large part of its surface. There is evidence that even the mostly densely cratered areas on the Moon are not saturated [25]. Also, crater density is not constant over the surfaces of several bodies in the solar system.

Figure 1 graphs the total number of large impact sites found in three size ranges and in three bands of latitude for our Moon. Only the 46 largest impact sites are represented [10]. The equatorial band extends from 19.5 degrees

North to 19.5 degrees South latitude, dividing the Moon's surface into three bands of equal area. The northern and southern polar bands include all other latitudes. Figure 1 shows that there are more large impact sites around the Moon's equator (this may or may not hold true for *all* sizes of craters). There are also more large impact sites at the south pole than the north pole. The size figures indicate ranges of diameters. For instance "250" includes all the large sites from 250 to 499 kilometers.

Asymmetrical crater distribution can be explained easily by assuming the solar system is only thousands of years in age and some event caused a high rate of meteoritic bombardment in a short time. Mercury and Saturn's moon Enceladus also exhibit asymmetrical crater distribution [20, p. 166]. Saturn's moon Rhea clearly has more craters around its North pole than near its equator [16]. A former planet between the orbits of Mars and Jupiter and a cloud of debris passing through the solar system would both cause high rates of meteor bombardment for some period of years.

A question that should be asked is "what object in the solar system has the highest density of craters in a given area?" The answer does not happen to be our Moon, but seems to be the inner moons of Saturn. This is illustrated by Figure 2, which compares the density of craters for four different objects in the solar system [14, 19, 21]. Note that Figure 2 uses a logarithmic scale to compress the vertical axis. In Figure 2, Epimetheus has the highest crater density. This is a very small object and is one of the two "coorbital moons" of Saturn which exchange orbits every four years. Mimas has a crater density graph similar to Epimetheus. Moons which lie farther from Saturn show fewer craters per unit area than our own Moon.

Planetary rings and the characteristics of the asteroids also give us clues on possible catastrophes in our solar system. Scientists have argued that some planetary rings, such as at Uranus, must be less than 1,000 years in age [9]. In 1992 I suggested that there may be two classes of rings--created rings and catastrophically formed rings [20, p.164-5].

There may also be two classes of asteroids. Though many asteroids are irregular in shape, some are spherical, which should not be possible in a very old solar system, due to collisions [24]. For instance, Ceres, the largest asteroid, has an equatorial radius of 480 km and a polar radius of 453 km, making it nearly spherical [23, p. 226]. Also, large asteroids exhibit a very strange rotation pattern (See Figure 3). Apparently no one has been able to put forth a natural mechanism to explain this relationship. For asteroids larger than about 120 to 150 km in diameter, the larger the object, the *faster* it rotates [7]. This does not seem possible for objects that are collision fragments since for a given amount of angular momentum, a larger object would rotate slower. Smaller asteroids, however, show the opposite pattern.

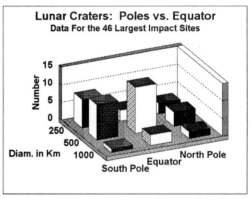

Figure 1 Number of large craters on the Moon in relation to latitude.

Two Possible Catastrophes

One possible catastrophic event which could affect the entire solar system is a former planet that existed in the region now occupied by the asteroids, between Mars and Jupiter. If a large object came from outside the solar system at high speed and struck a planet between Mars and Jupiter, what would happen? The impacting object and the planet could be deflected out of the system, leaving some debris that would scatter into various orbits within the solar system. Or, both masses might be destroyed, but in any case one would expect most of the mass to leave the solar system. Some fragments could go into orbits such as the asteroids now have. Other fragments could move off at higher speeds that could carry them to the outer solar system, for instance. After such an event, there would be collisions for some time. This impacted planet model has difficulties dealing with the rotation pattern of large asteroids.

It may be that some of the best clues on the history of our solar system come from the smallest things--such as comets and asteroids. Asteroids have varied orbital characteristics; many have elliptical orbits, but relatively few have highly elliptical orbits with eccentricity greater than 0.5. Similarly with the inclinations of their orbits: Relatively few of them have orbits inclined more than 20 degrees. This may suggest that they originate from within the ecliptic plane (the plane of the Earth's orbit), or nearly so. Asteroids seem to all orbit and spin right-handed in direction. These facts could agree well with a destroyed planet model. Comets, on the other hand, are found to travel either prograde or retrograde in their orbits. Comets also are icy objects whereas asteroids are rocky. Asteroids are today classified by their composition into 14 different types. These types have been described as either igneous (high melting point minerals), primitive (volatile lower melting point compounds), or metamorphic (volatiles removed). The igneous asteroids are found closer to the Sun while the more volatile ones are found farther from the Sun [4]. This pattern is somewhat similar to that of the planets, with the materials with higher melting and boiling points farther from the Sun.

There are certain other arguments for a possible planet breakup or collision in the asteroid region from what are called "new" comets, or "very long period comets." These are comets with very long orbital periods. From considering the orbits of these new comets, it is known that they must be on their first trip in toward the Sun. Also, the points on their orbits which are farthest from the Sun seem to cluster somewhat in certain parts of the sky. Their orbital periods also cluster about certain values, possibly indicating they could have come from a common point of origin [24, p.51-72]. This deserves further study as well and may be difficult to explain for the debris cloud model.

The "debris cloud model" would involve a cloud of solid objects passing through the solar system. Since the moons in the Saturn system have the highest crater density, perhaps that could be the region which the debris cloud first passed through. Since moons such as Enceladus and Rhea have more craters on the North poles, that could be the initial direction of approach of the debris cloud. Debris missing Saturnian objects would be scattered due to the gravitational pull of various objects into various paths. Many of these paths could take debris below the plane of the ecliptic and back up to pass through the ecliptic again "from below." By this time the debris would be in the inner solar system, having been deflected by the outer planets and perhaps Mars.

At this point could enter another assumption--that there were primordial asteroids present from creation in the asteroid region. These created

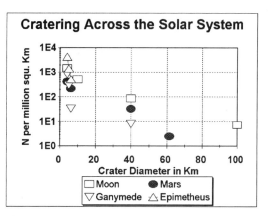

Figure 2 Number of craters per million square km area for various objects.

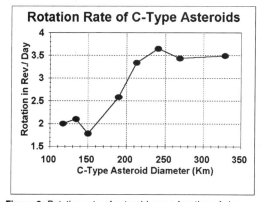

Figure 3 Rotation rate of asteroids as a function of size.

asteroids may have simply been created with the "unnatural" rotation relationship mentioned above. As the debris cloud (or a portion of it) made its second pass through the plane of the ecliptic, more collisions would result, causing some asteroids to break up and go into unstable trajectories that would cause them to later collide with our Moon, Mercury, Venus, or Mars. The objects in the debris cloud, by this scenario, would need to be large enough to be able to significantly alter the motion of asteroids they collide with. Since there are few large impact sites in the outer solar system compared to the inner solar system, I would suppose that few of the debris cloud objects would be large (such as a large asteroid or larger). After the collisions with the asteroids, asteroids and collision fragments could impact with bodies in the inner solar system over a period of years.

This debris cloud model would imply that craters in the outer solar system would show evidence of being formed in a very short time. This is exactly what the moon Enceladus at Saturn looks like. By this model, however, craters in the inner solar system would be expected to have formed over a period of years, since the asteroids and other objects put into unstable orbits would fall onto inner solar system bodies at different times. This model might explain the differences in cratering between the inner versus the outer solar systems, since the craters in the two regions would be formed by different objects, and from different directions. Neither of these catastrophic models would preclude the possibility of other unrelated impacts. Neither of these models would explain all the craters or all the varied surface features around the solar system. However, this approach seems more plausible than the current popular approach of postulating many unrelated collisions and other events over 4.6 billion years of solar system history.

CONCLUSION

Obviously these ideas are speculative. Yet a creationist approach is a valid one for unravelling the true history of our solar system. There is a need for various computer calculations to be done to simulate these type of models. There is probably not enough information available at this time to definitively judge between these two catastrophes. At this time, I find the debris cloud model the most satisfying. These two catastrophic models--the destroyed planet model and the debris cloud model--are not necessarily the only possibilities.

Though dating the time of occurrence of a major solar system catastrophe may be impossible scientifically, I suspect it would correspond in some way with God's judgement on the Earth at the time of the Noahic Flood. I say this only for theological reasons, since such catastrophes would seem to have little purpose except judgement and display of God's power. Remnants of craters of significant size are being discovered on Earth at the rate of several per year. Some have been found which would be over 100 miles in diameter. The author suspects that along with the many other atmospheric, volcanic, and tectonic activities in the Earth at that time there were also impacts from space. The author doubts that it is possible for any of the impacts discovered on Earth to have changed the earth's tilt or caused all the processes of Noah's Flood. It may be that impacts played a more significant role *after* the Flood than during the Flood year.

REFERENCES

[1]   H. Alfven, **Origin of the Solar System**, in The Origin of the Solar System, S. F. Dermott, editor, 1978, John Wiley & Sons, New York.

[2]   H. Alfven and G. Arrhenius, Structure and Evolutionary History of the Solar System, 1975, D. Reidel Publishing Co., Dordrecht, Holland and Boston, Mass.

[3]   J. F. Baugher, The Spaceage Solar System, 1988, John Wiley & Sons, New York, 203.

[4]   R. P. Binzel, M. A. Barucci, and M. Fulchignoni, **The Origins of the Asteroids**, Scientific American, **265:4**(1991), Oct., 91,93.

[5]   M. Carr, The Surface of Mars, 1981, Yale Univ. Press, New Haven and London, 64.

[6]   C. R. Chapman and D. Morrison, Cosmic Catastrophes, 1989, Plenum Press, New York, 140.

[7]   S. F. Dermott and C. D. Murray, **Asteroid Rotation Rates Depend on Diameter and Type,** Nature, **296**(April 1, 1982) 418-421.

[8]   J. R. Dormand and M. M. Woolfson, The Origin of the Solar System: The Capture Theory, (1989), Ellis Horwood Limited, Chichester, England, 156.

[9]   L. W. Esposito, **The Changing Shape of Planetary Rings**, Astronomy, **15:9**(1987), Sept., 15.

[10]   F. Horz, R. Grieve, G. Heiken, P. Spudis, & A. Binder, **Lunar Surface Processes**, Lunar Sourcebook: A User's Guide to the Moon, (1991), Cambridge University Press, Cambridge, England, 118-119.

[11]   W. J. Kaufmann, **Voyager at Neptune-A Preliminary Report**, Mercury, **18:6**(1989), Nov./Dec.

[12]   H. Kieffer, B. Jakosky, C. Snyder, M. Matthews, Mars, 1992, Univ. of Arizona Press, Tucson & London, 361.

[13]   M. B. McElroy and M. J. Prather, **Noble Gases in the Terrestrial Planets**, Nature, **293**(1981), Oct. 15, 535-539.

[14]   J. Nuth, **Small Grains of Truth**, Nature, **349**(1991), Jan. 3, 19.

[15]   J. C. Pearl and W. M. Sinton, **Hot Spots of Io**, Satellites of Jupiter, D. Morrison, editor, 1982, Univ. of Arizona Press, Tucson, Arizona, 753.

[16]   J. B. Plescia, and J. M. Boyce, **Crater Densities and Geological Histories of Rhea, Dione, Mimas, and Tethys**, Nature, **295**(1982) 285.

[17]   A. J. R. Prentice, **Towards a Modern Laplacian Theory for the Formation of the Solar System**, The Origin of the Solar System, S. F. Dermott, editor, 1978, John Wiley & Sons, New York, 116-119.

[18]   H. Reeves, **The Origin of the Solar System**, in The Origin of the Solar System, S. F. Dermott, editor, 1978, John Wiley & Sons, New York.

[19]   A. Snelling and D. Rush, **Moon Dust and the Age of the Solar System**, Ex Nihilo Technical Journal, Part I, Volume 7 (1993), 2-42.

[20]   W. R. Spencer, **Design and Catastrophism in the Solar System**, Proceedings of the 1992 Twin-Cities Creation Conference, (1992).

[21]   W. R. Spencer, **Titanic Evidence for a Young Solar System**, (1993), Unpublished paper available from Wayne Spencer, to be submitted to Creation Research Society Quarterly.

[22]   R. G. Strom, et al., **The Martian Impact Cratering Record**, Mars, H. H. Kieffer, B. M. Jakosky, C. W. Snyder, M. S. Matthews, editors, (1992), Univ. of Arizona Press, Tucson, Arizona, 384.

[23]   S. R. Taylor, Solar System Evolution: A New Perspective, 1992, Cambridge University Press.

[24]   T. C. Van Flandern, **A Former Asteroidal Planet as the Origin of Comets**, Icarus, 36(1978) 68.

[25]   A. Woronow, R. G. Strom, and M. Gurnis, **Interpreting the Cratering Record: Mercury to Ganymede to Callisto**, Satellites of Jupiter, (1982), Univ. of Arizona Press, Tucson, Arizona, 239-249.

SIR FRANCIS BACON
AND THE
GEOLOGICAL SOCIETY OF LONDON

IAN T. TAYLOR AIM
P.O. BOX 1344, STN F,
TORONTO, ON M4Y 2TL
CANADA

KEYWORDS

Francis Bacon; Scientific Method; Criticism; Evolution; Darwin; Geologic column; Royal Society; Geological Society; Freemasonry.

ABSTRACT

The historical relationship between Francis Bacon and his method of interpreting nature, the Royal Society of London and the Geological Society of London is reviewed. The Baconian method is described, its deficiencies noted and the fact that both the foundational work for geology and Darwinian evolution has slipped between the cracks of the Baconian method explained.

INTRODUCTION

There were two Bacons in the history of science, both were Englishmen, both wrote in cipher and both were concerned with the method of conducting science [20],[21]. The first was Roger Bacon, a thirteenth century scholar. His principal contribution to history was the translation of the scientific works of Aristotle from the Arabic into Latin. Roger Bacon was thus largely responsible for introducing Greek thinking into the Judeo-Christian West [5] but he also conducted many experiments and wrote briefly on the experimental method [5, 2:583]. The second was Francis Bacon, a sixteenth century scholar. However, unlike his namesake he practiced little and wrote much about experimental science. It was this Bacon, England's Lord Chancellor, who gave later generations the Baconian or Scientific method which laid the foundation for all scientific endeavor today.

The Life and Work of Francis Bacon

Francis Bacon is one of the most intriguing personalities in history and many biographers have spent years piecing together the details of this man's life. Historian James Spedding produced a seven-volume work on the life of Francis Bacon in 1861 and this has subsequently become the orthodox account. However, other researchers since that date have unearthed more material and the mystery surrounding Bacon's life and silent years have slowly been revealed. It is a remarkable story.

Princess Elizabeth Tudor came to the throne of England as Queen Elizabeth I in 1558. Within weeks of being made Queen, she arranged to have Lord Robert Dudley as her personal guard at the palace. Elizabeth soon found herself "with child", and it was arranged to have Dudley's wife, Amy Robsart, quietly murdered leaving the way clear for Elizabeth and her lover to be married in a secret ceremony within the same month. Thus, legitimized by the marriage and technically heir to the throne, the babe was born in 1561, named Francis and raised by Lord and Lady Bacon at York House in the center of London. Throughout her long reign Elizabeth encouraged her unofficial title of "The Virgin Queen", but the political climate never permitted her to acknowledge Francis as her son, and heir to the English throne [11].

This is the very stuff of historical romance and, whether we accept it or not, there does appear to be good circumstantial evidence for its support. Certainly there is more to the official biography of Francis Bacon than we have been given to believe. But this is only the beginning of the Bacon story because Elizabeth's reign was wreathed in international cloak-and-dagger spy networks and double agents with their cipher messages. The root cause of the unrest in Europe, the "Thirty-years" War, the "Hundred Years" War, the civil wars, was religion. The conflict lay between the Church of Rome and the Bible-believers, later the Protestants; each considered the other to be heretic and set about to put the good Lord's Kingdom in order by the sword and the flame. The Roman Church in particular had assumed far too much power and had become arrogant and corrupt; this would later happen to the Protestant Anglican Church. Superstitions and traditions had become entrenched as divine truth and many sincere Christian men began to regard the formal Church as the bastion of ignorance and intolerance. For example, the Church forbad dissection of cadavers, arguing that this would "spoil the resurrection", the result was a general ignorance of anatomy by the medical profession. Many intelligent Christian men therefore sought a complete Church "house-cleaning" but it was extremely dangerous to say so publicly. One such group, calling themselves "Rosicrucians" formed secretly in Germany, and Francis Bacon is known to have been very closely associated with this organization throughout his life. The early Rosicrucians sought reform of the Christian Church and had an earnest desire for genuine wisdom and knowledge through science. However, over the centuries the Rosicrucians became badly side-tracked in seeking the wisdom of the ancients, specifically the Egyptians. Historian Francis Yates documents this in detail [30].

It would be beyond the context of this paper to retrace the steps from the Rosicrucians to Freemasonry to the present political trend to one-world government. Nevertheless, there is no question that it was the genius of Francis Bacon which laid the foundation for this humanist ideal. Bacon's followers were inspired by Plato's Republic which proposed a Utopian World free from war and ruled by wise men. Plato had seen that every then-known ruling system was corrupt but he piously thought that wise men would be beyond corruption. Every republic formed since the French Revolution should be living testimony that power corrupts. Bacon was a profound writer and is best known for his Magna Instauratio which first appeared in 1605. The title is most often translated as "The Great Instauration" which tells the reader little, but occasionally the more insightful "The Great Restoration" or even "The Great Renaissance" is used. Bacon's final and unfinished work was The New Atlantis which has for its subtitle The Island of Bensalem or the Land of the Rosicrosse. Bacon died in 1626 and this work was published posthumously in that same year.

The Baconian Method of Science

Scientific enquiry, such as it was until the sixteenth century, had been based upon a Christian world-view where the Scriptures were taken as the first authority. Jones [17] has presented a very clear case to show that the Christian view at that time included the belief in the Edenic curse and the continuing Fall of Man; for this reason, the Greek writers living almost two thousand years earlier were considered to be far wiser than scholars of the Middle-Ages. Accordingly, the interpretation of Nature was based upon Scripture and the writings of the "Ancients", that is, Galen and Aristotle. Many of the explanations of these writers were simply based upon syllogisms, yet these authorities were held in esteem almost as great as the Scriptures themselves. Bacon, and other writers of that Elizabethan period, could see that this approach led to plain nonsense and he proposed turning from the past and looking to the future with an empirical approach. This was actually the turning point which led to the current belief in the "Progress of mankind" while it was done with the lofty appeal to "the betterment of man".

Francis Bacon realized at a very early age that in some areas, for example philosophy, the Greeks were very insightful but wordy arguments contributed nothing to the understanding of nature. He realized that careful observation and experiment were necessary such that the data could be received directly by the five human senses. He first published his views on this very cautiously in English in 1605 in the Magna Instauratio: here he suggested that the study of natural phenomena begin by first clearing the mind of all previous preconception. Here he was referring to the abandonment of the Greek philosophers and particularly Aristotle and, while he did not say so, Scripture would also be abandoned. As we shall see, it is humanly impossible to "clear the mind" and human reason will quickly enter the vacuum left by Scripture and the "Ancients". In was in this way that Bacon unwittingly laid the foundation for humanism. In 1620 he added the Novum Organum (New Instrument) as the second part to the Magna Instauratio. In this, he set out more specifically his proposed method of conducting scientific investigation by "Inductive reasoning". This is presented in a series of aphorisms in Book Two of Novum Organum. Finally, and in bolder terms, an expanded version of the Magna Instauratio was written in Latin and published in 1626 under the title De Augmentis Scientiarum. This was translated into English and published posthumously by Bacon's followers in 1640 under the title The Advancement of Learning.

Bacon's method for the interpretation of nature and the study of natural phenomena thus begins with the interpreter of nature first dismissing from his mind all prejudice and preconceptions; he referred to these as "idols of the mind". He then described three main steps: The first consists of a careful and methodical observation of as many facts as possible. The second step is the tabulation of all the facts into three groups, those that influence the property under investigation, those that do not and those which cause only a partial influence. The final step is a process of elimination whereby all those observations having no influence on the phenomenon under investigation are rejected. When only a single set of conditions remain, this is held to be the first approximation of the truth, or, as Bacon put it, in Aphorism 20, "the first vintage". Bacon's method of induction works by the process of elimination or, as we say today, "falsification" or "refutation". The method is just the reverse of Greek thinking which often began with a defective tradition and added observations which seemed to support it.

Bacon was sternly opposed to theorizing, yet sensibly recognized that another step was necessary which he called "Indulgence of the understanding". We would call this today "a working hypothesis". When investigating a natural process, this is simply an intuitive notion suggesting how the process might work. Ideally, experiments are then set up to try to refute or disprove the hypothesis; if the hypothesis survives the tests, it is then raised to the status of a theory. If the theory can be extended to a very wide range of phenomenon and not one observation is ever found to refute it, it then becomes a Law. Very few theories ever achieve this status. Bacon's "art of interpreting nature" was thus one of step-by-step elimination of possibilities. Automobile mechanics and television repairmen exercise this mental process daily, and never think to ascribe the cause of malfunction to malignant spirits or a curse of the gods. The scientific method has thus freed man from much superstition and scientific progress has undoubtedly been made far beyond anything Francis Bacon would have dared to hope. However, before we examine the subtle deficiencies of the Baconian method we need to see how it was promoted.

The Royal Society

After Bacon's death in 1626 his friends continued to publish his works but of particular interest is the fact that it was the Puritans who gave his work most support [17, p.87-113]. Their justification was based upon Bacon's advocacy of turning away from the "Ancients" who were recognized by the Puritans to be pagan. By 1645 a little group of like-minded individuals was meeting at Dr. Wilkin's lodgings in Wadham College, Oxford, for the purpose of laying the foundation for "all this that followed", while the University at that time had "many members of its own, who had begun a freeway of reasoning". This is the arcane language of Thomas Spratt, early president of the Royal Society in his History of the Royal Society [27, p.53]. By "all this that followed" he meant the outworking of scientific investigation according to the method set out by Francis Bacon, while those with a "Freeway of reasoning" were what would be later known as "liberal thinkers". This group, consisting mostly of intellectuals, formed themselves into what they called the "Invisible College" which met at Gresham College, London. Robert Boyle, the discoverer of the gas laws, was at this time an influential figure. The "Invisible College" finally received a Royal Charter from King Charles II in 1662 and could at this time adopt the more formal name The Royal Society of London.

The evidence for Francis Bacon's method as the actual foundation for the Royal Society of London is compelling. Not only does Dr. Spratt [26, p.35] pay deference to Bacon in this respect but Abraham Cowley acclaimed Bacon by name in an ode recited at the Royal Society referring to him as "..the Moses who led us forth from the barren wilderness to the land of experimental science ..." [27, Preface, not paginated]. Further evidence is found in Bacon's New Atlantis. This short book is a fictional account of an island state located in the North Pacific, ruled benevolently from Salomon's House by a priestly caste of Experimental Scientists divided into thirty-three secret orders. Careful reading, however, reveals that there are actually thirty-six orders, the last three being the most secret "Interpreters of Nature". Even the casual observer cannot help but note the similarity between this description and modern Freemasonry with its Solomon's Temple and thirty-three degrees, and as one descends to details the similarities go far beyond mere coincidence. Not too much digging is required to show that the early leading members of this College, and later the Royal Society, were either Rosicrucians or Freemasons. We know them by name and association: Sir Robert Boyle, Elias Ashmole, Sir Robert Moray, John Locke and later Sir Christopher Wren and possibly Sir Isaac Newton to name only a few. Joseph Glanville writing in 1665 commented that Lord Bacon's "Solomon's House in the New Atlantis was a Prophetik Scheam [sic] of the Royal Society" [27, p.xii]. Modern historians such as Alfred Dodd [11, p.1661], Sir Harold Hartley [12] and Marjery Purver [24] have restored much of the truth about the connection between Francis Bacon, the Royal Society and Freemasonry. Francis Bacon was thus regarded by the Royal Society as their Messiah who by the enlightened scientific method would lead the world into a new order based upon human rationalism rather than superstition.

The universities of England in the sixteenth century were dominated by the Anglican Church which insisted that nature be interpreted by Scripture. The Church authorities thus viewed the Royal Society with suspicion. The relationship was not helped by the fact that Roman Catholics were sometimes welcomed. The Royal Society was unconcerned with its members beliefs as long as they adhered to Christian moral principles and their concern was the genuine pursuit of knowledge. It may be appreciated then that the Royal Society tended to keep its motives secret and to adhere rigidly to Baconian principles, reporting only the facts, drawing the most conservative conclusions and never theorizing in its Proceedings. Finally, a quote from Alfred Dodd will help to bring Bacon, the Royal Society and Freemasonry into sharper focus:

> The universities had never realized that The Great Instauration was something even greater than the writing of a series of books. It was the actual establishment of groups of men that labored along certain secret lines which led to a real revival of learning and the liberalizing of Theology, culminating in the exoteric Royal society on the one hand and the esoteric Temple of Solomon [An inside nom de plume for Freemasonry] on the other. [11, p.166]

The Geological Society of London

The year was 1799 and the Republic which had dechristianized France eighteen years earlier was barely a memory in the minds of London's rising generation of society gentlemen. George Greenough was such a gentleman. At 21, independently wealthy and well educated, he and like-minded friends met regularly for dinner at the Freemason's Tavern in Great Queen Street, central London. Their consuming mutual interest was the mineral deposits of the British Isles, but this was from more than mere academic curiosity. The Industrial Revolution, then in full swing, was driven by steam and steam was generated by coal. It followed that there was a rising demand for good coal and metallurgical minerals, with great rewards for those who could find and claim them. Young Greenough organized his friends into a formal dining club limited to forty members; at fifteen shillings a head for the dinners this excluded anyone who actually worked in the mineral and coal industry. Thus, The Geological Society of London was hatched over pots of ale in the back rooms of the Freemason's Tavern in the year 1799. Its purpose was a gathering place for geological information while financial gain cannot be excluded as its motivation. Greenough was the Society's first president.

Gathering, summarizing and issuing information meant that the Geological Society required a permanent meeting place and a paid secretary. The Society found its first home in rented rooms at Somerset House just four minutes walk from Freemason's Tavern, and the first volume of the Transactions was issued to its members in 1807. Somerset House had been the home of the Royal Society since 1782 while some of its members were also members of the fledgling Geological Society. Sir Joseph Banks had been the autocratic president of the Royal Society since 1778, and also became a member of the Geological Society, one suspects, in order to keep an eye on its activities. The Royal Society made all official pronouncements on science in Britain and its president would brook no rival. Moreover, the scientific method was sacrosanct and not to be degraded by theorizing. Interestingly, the front cover of the early issues of the Geological Society Transactions contained a quote in Latin from Bacon's Novum Organum to that effect. The activities of the Geological Society were very subdued until the 1820's when several things happened which caused geology to be put on the map. Firstly, after forty-one years of iron-handed rule over the Royal Society, Sir Joseph Banks died in 1820. Five years later the Geological Society received its Royal Charter giving it almost equal status with the Royal Society whereby its members could be called "Fellows". The tension which had existed between the two Societies was now relaxed and all the leading members of the Geological Society became members of the Royal Society. Secondly, the forty-member Geological Society dining club which had always been an inner sanctum controlling the activities of the now much larger number of ordinary members, was being replaced by younger men with an urge to theorize. It was at this time, in 1823, that the young Charles Lyell became the Geological Society secretary and corresponding foreign secretary. From this point on, the Baconian restriction against theorizing began to crumble.

The Theorizing of Geology

Prior to and following the French Revolution of 1789, Paris was the center of scientific learning. Baron George Cuvier had become the head of the Museum d'Histoire Naturelle and was one of the most influential men in science. He is generally regarded as the father of comparative anatomy and paleontology. Looking at cliffs and gorges, Cuvier observed that the rock strata were of different mineral compositions, while he correctly reasoned that each mineral layer had been deposited as sediment from water. He also reasoned that the fossils within the layers were the remains of creatures which were living at the time the sediments were laid down. He observed uniform layers of sandstone lying on top of limestone which in turn lay upon layers of shale and he found it difficult to believe that so many different types of sediment had been deposited by a single flood as described in the book of Genesis. Plain common sense told him that there must have been a number of successive floods, each depositing a layer of sediment which trapped within it representatives of the plants and animals living at that particular time. Cuvier reasoned that after the flood waters receded the sediments dried out, hardened into rock and even partially eroded before a subsequent flood occurred. He identified at least twenty-eight different kinds of sedimentary rock, (e.g. limestone, slate, sandstone etc.) and proposed as many floods to account for them [7]. This was known as the "Multiple Catastrophe Theory" and, according to this approach, the Genesis Flood was simply the last of a series of floods, and occurred five or six thousand years ago. It all seemed so reasonable.

Cuvier began to promote his theory in 1795, first in French, then a little later in English and at this same time the Scotsman, James Hutton, was promoting his theory of the earth in England more boldly in terms of millions of years. Hutton had gone to Paris to study science, picked up many of the ideas which were current among the university professors and students, and then had returned to Scotland. Hutton claimed that given enough time, the natural processes we see going on today could easily explain all the geological features that were then being ascribed to catastrophes of the past, namely the Genesis Flood. Hutton's explanation was not popular in his day because it did too much violence to the Biblical account, but his idea was carried forward a generation later by Charles Lyell and the Geological Society. The multiple-flood idea was at first thought to be caused by the sea level's rising and falling, but it was realized that this would mean simultaneous world-wide flooding. The notion quickly gave way in Lyell's mind to the slow rising and falling of great areas of land, even whole continents. Lyell found evidence at the Roman temple of Serapis to support his idea that it was the land rather than the sea which had risen and fallen. In this way, the floods were local and the flora and fauna could continue to propagate, eliminating the need for Noah and his ark.

Between the years 1830 to 1840, a revolution in the study of geology took place which involved Roderick Impey Murchison, the Reverend Adam Sedgwick and, to a lesser extent, Charles Lyell. Historian paleontologist, Martin Rudwick [26], has recently documented this era in geological thinking in fine detail and shows how the Society President, Murchison, along with his friends, Sedgwick and Lyell, sought to force a fundamental change in thinking among geologists. Prior to 1830, rock strata were referred to by names corresponding to their mineral content:

528

limestone, sandstone, etc. A decade later newly-coined names such as Cambrian, Devonian, Silurian and Ordovician were commonly being used. The new names were based upon the fossils of the flora and fauna believed to have been living during successive eras of earth's history. It was presupposed that life on earth began in very elementary forms and gradually became more complex, thus the expected fossil order was ranked from simplest in the lowest and oldest strata to the most complex in the uppermost and youngest strata. They do in fact often occur this way. Differentiation among rock types was now dependent upon the fossils found in them and had little to do with their mineral content. Murchison and his collaborators had adopted both Hutton's uniformitarianism (no-catastrophe) position and William Smith's fossil-based strata identification system. Smith was employed by the Somerset Coal Company to dig canals, and he had discovered a rule-of-thumb method of knowing rock strata by the fossils found in them.

Murchison's common-sense belief was that younger strata were always deposited on top of older strata. This is the principle of superposition and the key to modern stratigraphy. For example, the distinctive formation of red sandstone in Germany was at first correlated with a similar red sandstone formation in England because both formations were always found directly on top of the coal seams. But then it was found that in England red sandstone also lay below the coal strata, while in Germany there was no red sandstone beneath what was assumed to be the same coal seam. This finding was inconsistent with the principle of superposition and the problem was solved by proposing that in England there were actually two superficially similar formations of red sandstone. The upper one became known as the "New Red Sandstone" and was believed to be the same formation as that in Germany. The lower sandstone formation in England was then named the "Old Red Sandstone". The speculative notion of great periods of time was introduced by employing the words "Old" and "New" rather than "Upper" and "Lower". This served no other purpose than to justify the preconceived idea of how the sedimentary rocks were formed. Eventually, all rock strata were directly identified with ages in earth's history and thus was constructed a theoretical scale of time now referred to as "the geologic column". This entire scheme was introduced in the early 1800's, while Lyell's part was to use his legal training to argue the case providing evidences for an old earth and arguing down any potential objection [25]. All this work prepared the way for Charles Darwin and conditioned the public mind to accept his theory of evolution offered to the world in 1859.

The Baconian Method Re-examined

Scientific investigation cannot yet be carried out without involving the human mind. Even with all the sophisticated instrumentation of today and statistical analyses of the results, the bottom line is that human nature is still involved. That is, in the initial stages someone has to decide which observations to gather and which experiments to make while in the last stage someone has to draw the final conclusions.

In his criticism of the Baconian method T. B. Macaulay, afterwards Lord Macaulay, questioned how the investigator would know when there is sufficient data, "Will ten instances do? or fifty?" [19, p.91]. The mathematician Augusta De Morgan was equally critical and pointed out that Bacon himself knew that a "thousand instances may be contradicted by the thousand and first so that no enumeration of instances, however large, is sure demonstration" [10, p.50]. This is something every investigator is aware of that every so often an anomalous result will show up for no apparent reason. However, human nature tends to "turn the blind eye" to this result even though this is dishonest. The literature shows that while most writers are supportive of the Baconian method, the few that are critical write with greater force of argument and professor of logic, W.S. Jevons [16, 2:134ff] is an example of one having great clarity of thought. In the matter of the method of induction, we find Adamson [1] slaming this hard in the Encyclopedia Britannica, the philosopher A. N. Whitehead [29, p.58ft] being highly critical while Morris R. Cohen [6, p.153ff] completely devastates the entire method. We should be reminded that these perceptive critics of the Baconian method are only those bold enough to appear in print while there is written evidence to show that they suffered a certain amount of persecution for their honesty.

The primary problem with the Baconian method was stated three centuries earlier by Roger Bacon. In his Opus Majus Roger Bacon listed the major causes of error in scientific investigation to be: Undue regard for authority, Habit, Popular prejudice and False conceit of knowledge [5, 1:3-35]. This would seem to be a remarkable insight for a thirteenth century writer, yet every word of it applies today. The Baconian problem is that it is a virtual impossibility first to clear away the "idols of the mind"; human nature does not work this way. At a very early age every human being develops a bias, a prejudice and eventually a preconceived world-view through which information from the world about us is filtered before it reaches our intellect. In practice, scientific investigation therefore begins with a theory or a hunch, sometimes based upon only one observation. Thus, the preconception or prejudice of the scientist has already formed the theory virtually before he begins the investigation and this then determines which observations will be made. This major drawback to the Baconian method is that it is an ideal to which human nature is opposed. In fact, some of the critics have even argued that no scientific discovery has yet been made using the method of induction.

A prejudiced mind is the most serious obstacle to genuine science and limits an investigation to operate within certain parameters thus rendering it a "closed system of understanding". As soon as any system closes itself this way, it is deprived of the power of self-analysis and therefore of self-criticism. A modern example is Radio-Carbon age determination. The evolutionary mindset is conditioned to believe, for example, that coal and oil deposits are millions of years old. When Willard E. Libby developed the Carbon 14 method in 1948, coal, oil and fossil bone samples were submitted to Carbon 14 analysis and for the next twenty years the ages obtained faithfully reported; in every case, they were less than 20,000 years. These were not the ages expected and students have since been led to understand that the method is not usable for artifacts older than 50,000 years. This may well be true, but it means that when artifacts are pre-judged to be older than 50,000 years, the method will not be used. The buried forest recently discovered above Canada's Arctic Circle is a case in point where, although still fresh, the wood is believed to be 45 million years old; thus, the carbon-dating method will not be applied to it [4, p.28]. The result is that an age of just a few thousand years, which the method would and does, in fact, give for the buried wood, does not then become a falsification for the currently held theory of evolution. This is typical of a closed system approach and ensures that no data contrary to the preconceived interpretation can enter the equation.

The second problem with the Baconian method stems from the first and is again related to human nature; this time the problem is pride, although in the competitive world of research grants and university politics fear plays no small part. As Roger Bacon put it, "Undue regard for authority". The Baconian method demands that a concerted effort be made to falsify any hypothesis (or "first vintage") the investigator makes. However, unlike the television repairman who works by eliminating hunches, when the scientist has a hunch he tends to call it a "theory", entertain the prospect of kudos, perhaps fame and is inclined to look for evidence to support it, not refute it. In fact, the greatest mental discipline and integrity is required to actively attempt to falsify one's own theory. Successful falsification means that the investigator is then faced with having to acknowledge that his personal "brain-child" was stillborn. After, say a decade of work, this would call for a humility of character rarely found in any of us.

A third problem, not so much with the Baconian method but rather its practitioners, is that a theory must be refutable or falsifiable in the first place in order that the Baconian method may be applied. In other words, the theory must be able to make predictions which can then be tested. Sir Karl Popper [22] is generally held to be one of the greatest living philosophers of science and has been sufficiently forthright to state:

A theory which is not refutable by any conceivable event is non-scientific. Irrefutability is not a virtue of a theory (as people often think) but a vice. [22, p.36]

Popper [23] had in mind Darwinism when he wrote this and a decade later he was more direct, "I have come to the conclusion that Darwinism is not a testable scientific theory, but a metaphysical research programme--a possible framework for testable scientific theories." [23, p.168). What he meant by this was that for a study to be "scientific" it had to be observable and repeatable while any theory had to predict events and thus be capable of refutation. Evolution, whether by Darwin's proposed mechanism or any other, fails to quality on all counts as "scientific" since events of the past can neither be observed, nor repeated. Popper was under pressure from his peers to retract this damaging statement, and in a recent interview on his ninetieth birthday he was asked again about these conclusions but he did not retract them [14, p.20). Another surprising conclusion of Sir Karl Popper concerned the term "induction". This is one of those words which are banded about often pompously while few have the temerity to ask what it means. Popper [22, p.53] gives the definition: "inference based upon many observations" and then points out that induction as a method is, in fact, a myth. As mentioned earlier, since it is a virtual impossibility to "rid the mind of idols" Popper observes that in the real world, scientific success is not based upon the rules of induction but upon luck, ingenuity and the purely deductive rules of critical argument. That is, the actual method scientists use is logico-deductive. In the worst departures from the Baconian ideal, conclusions are drawn after a single observation and the result announced as a "breakthrough"!

How the Geological Society Fell Through the Cracks in the Baconian Method

Cuvier's Multiple Catastrophe Theory, Hutton's appeal to natural processes and Lyell's promotion provided today's explanation for every geological feature; it all seemed so perfectly reasonable. Theologians struggled in vain, compromised with various theories and eventually caved in to accept evolution as the all-pervading principle of earth history. Darwin had come and gone and his theory was becoming accepted both in England and Europe, especially in Germany. In Germany, Johannes Walther was a student of Ernst Haeckel and by the 1880's had become a well-traveled and well-known professor of geology in his own right. Walther was a keen observer of nature and particularly of the sedimentary rock formations and the fossils which they contained. He wrote a three-volume German work published in 1893-4 but this has never been published in an English translation and, in fact, is not at all well known [28]. This work contained what is referred to as "Walther's Law of the Correlation of Facies" [28, 3:974]. Working in the Bay of Naples, Walther observed that as the sediments carried by the river entered the bay, they deposited from the waters in a certain order according to the decrease in the flow rate: heavy particles dropped out first while the lightest particles were carried furthest. Since this is a dynamic process proceeding in the direction of the flowing water, the heavy particles soon begin to deposit on top of the previously deposited lighter particles. See illustration. Walther expressed it as follows:

The various deposits of the same facies areas and similarly the sum of the rocks of different facies areas are formed beside each other in space, though in cross-section we see them lying on top of each other. [28, 3:979].

As Walther himself says, this has far reaching significance though unfortunately his arcane way of expressing it and lack of any diagrams has left most readers unaware of his meaning and no idea of its significance. Some work is being done today under the name "sequence stratigraphy". Guy Berthault is a French sedimentologist and recognized well the significance of Walther's work. He devised some simple experiments whereby processes of sedimentation could be observed and repeated, two fundamental requirements for real scientific investigation. His work was formally reported at the Third National Congress of Sedimentologists in France and received with loud applause from the 350 delegates present [2],[3].

In summary, Berthault's work shows that the layers of sediment seen by Cuvier were not necessarily laid down vertically like carpets one upon another. Further, the vast ages of time said to be required for this to take place are quite unnecessary. By observation, the dynamic sedimentary process operates in a horizontal manner producing neatly separated layers, one on top of the other, simultaneously. The same thing has been observed in recent natural catastrophes and, taken together, this work offers the most serious challenge to the entire concept of the geologic column. Berthault's experimental work is for the most part so simple that it would have been quite possible for Lyell and the Geological Society to have done these same experiments. However, as the record shows, they did no experiments on sediment formation at all, but adopted a theory which most appealed to human reason; then further, by sheer force and not a little back-room manipulation, declared their "science" to be the self-evident truth.

Did Darwin Follow the Baconian Method?

Both Charles Lyell and Charles Darwin behaved in the normal human way by beginning with an hypothesis based upon their preconceptions and selecting data or observations which appeared to give their support. Lyell used the Roman temple of Serapis, which has sunk below sea level in historic times then risen again, as major supporting evidence. On the other hand, they tended to ignore or rationalize away that data which did not support their ideas. All the work carried out to determine the thickness of flood deposits in the Nile delta could not give an age of more than 30,000 years, far too short a time for Lyell. He reported the work then dismissed it [18, p.26]. Darwin's primary departure from the scientific method was an overiding preconception that the Creation account was not true. In his letter of May 11th, 1863, to Asa Gray he confessed [9, 2:371]:

Personally of course, I care much about Natural Selection: but that seems to me utterly unimportant, compared to the question of Creation or Modification.

From very early in his investigations Darwin was biased toward "Modification" or, as we know it today, evolution. His theory was really based upon observations of slight changes among the living and speculations about major changes (speciation) among the dead, that is, the fossils. He lamented that there was no evidence of gradual change in the fossil record, but hoped that some might be found [8, p.280]. A moment's thought will show that since neither Darwin nor anyone else can observe events or the living creatures of the past, his interpretation had to be speculative and his theory not refutable. However, by sheer force of words in his writings, this speculation became elevated to a theory without observational support. To this day, that situation has not changed.

Darwin's second departure from the scientific method was almost sleight of hand and consisted of wordplays which allowed him to draw conclusions out of thin air. He suggested possibilities, adding one upon another, then spoke of probabilities and concluded with a virtual certainty. His description of the evolution of the eye is a classic example [8, p.186]. The rules of chance work in just the opposite direction: heaping possibilities one upon another makes an event less likely, not more probable. Science historian Gertrude Himmelfarb spotted this reversal of logic in Darwin's Origin and said he was, in effect creating a "logic of possibility" [13, p.334]. In Book One, Aphorism 125 of Novum Organum, Bacon describes the method of the "ancients", the Greeks, of which he was so critical, and his description is precisely that adopted by the Geological Society, by Darwin and hundreds of others since:

From a few examples and particulars ... they flew at once to the most general conclusions, or first principles of science; taking the truth of these as fixed and immovable [Darwin's belief in evolution], they proceeded by means of intermediate propositions to educe and prove from them the inferior conclusions; and out of these they framed the art [Darwin's Natural Selection]. After that, if any new particulars and examples repugnant to their dogmas were mooted and adduced, either they subtly molded them into their system by distinctions and explanations of their rules, or else coarsely got rid of them by exceptions, while to such particulars as were not repugnant they labored to assign causes in conformity with those their principles.

In a sense, the Geological Society of London and the Darwinian school had slipped back into "Greek science" by too quickly concluding with an hypothesis, then, using this as the Greeks had their faulty traditions, they looked for evidence to support it. Not only that, but Lyell "subtly molded" geological sciences for half a century through the Geological Society while Thomas Huxley did the same thing later for the biological sciences through the British Association. In his address given to the Philosophical Clubs of Yale and Brown Universities in 1896, William James [15] spoke on the topic of the will to believe and pointed out that in a social organism each member does his duty with a trust that the other members will simultaneously do theirs. The Geological Society or the British Association would be a classic example of such a social organism. James had something like this in mind but gave as his example a train robbery. The handful of bandits get away with the robbery because they have faith and trust in one another to do his part whereas the trainful of passengers, who may be brave enough individually, do not have that faith and trust in their fellow passengers. He concludes:

> There are then, cases where a fact cannot come at all unless a preliminary faith exists in its coming. And where faith in a fact can help create the fact, that would be an insane logic .... that faith running ahead of scientific evidence is the "lowest kind of immorality" into which a thinking being can fall. Yet such is the logic by which our scientific absolutists pretend to regulate our lives! (Emphasis in original) [15, p.25]

CONCLUSION

The Baconian method is seen to be the dream of an idealist and virtually impossible for normal human beings to achieve. This is not immediately apparent, but it is for this very reason that mankind in general, including the scientific community, has been deceived into thinking that the pronouncements of science are based upon totally objective work. The theory of evolution especially has failed to meet the Baconian ideal and long ago reached the point among those wishing the theory to be true where faith has helped to create the facts. From the time of the French Revolution the liberal spirit has tended to deny the universality of the Genesis Flood. Earth history has since been based upon observation and speculation, not experiment, while the result has been to introduce a world view which obviates the need for a Creator. Recent experimental work which should have been carried out long ago and is repeatable, observable and capable of predicting results has been confirmed by field observations. This work does indeed confirm the Genesis account of a universal flood and consequently puts into serious question the foundation laid by the Geological Society of London for today's geological sciences.

REFERENCES

[1]   Adamson, R. **Francis Bacon** in Encyclopedia Britannica. New York: The Werner Co. Ninth edition (1898) Vol. 3, p.216.

[2]   Berthault, Guy. **Sedimentation d'un melange heterogranulaire Lamination experimental en eau calme et eau courante.** Comptes Rendus Academy de Sciences Paris Vol. 306, Series 2, 21-March 1988, p.717-724.

[3]   Berthault, Guy. **Experiences sur la lamination des sediments par granoclassement periodique posterior au depot.** Comptes Rendus Academy de Sciences Paris Vol. 303, Series 2, 28-November 1988, p.1569-1574.

[4]   Basinger, James F. **Our "Tropical" Arctic.** Canadian Geoaraphic (Ottawa) Vol.106, January 1987, p.28-37.

[5]   Burke, Robert Belle. **The Opus Majus of Roger Bacon,** Philadelphia: University of Pennsylvania Press. 2 Vols. 1928.

[6]   Cohen, Morris R. **Studies in Philosophy and Science.** New York: Henry Holt. 1949.

[7]   Cuvier, G. and A. Brongniart. **Description geologique des environs de Paris.** Paris: Dufour and d'Ocagne. New edition 1882.

[8]   Darwin, Charles. On **the Origin of Species.** London: John Murray. 1859.

[9]   Darwin, Francis. **The Life and Letters of Charles Darwin.** London: John Murray. 1888.

[10]   De Morgan, Augusta. **A Budget of Paradoxes.** London: Longmans Green. 1872.

[11]   Dodd, Alfred. **Francis Bacon's Personal Life Story.** London: Rider and Co. (1949) Reprint 1986.

[12]   Hartley, Sir Harold. **The Royal Society its Origin ...** London: The Royal Society. 1960.

[13]   Himmelfarb, Gertrude. **Darwin and the Darwinian Revolution** New York: W.W.Norton. 1968.

[14]   Horgan, John. **The Intellectual Warrior.** Washington: <u>Scientific American</u> UK edition, 267(1992) p.20.

[15]   James, William. **The Will to Believe.** New York: Longmans, Green. 1919.

[16]   Jevons, William S. **Principles of Science.** London: Macmillan 2 Vols. 1874.

[17]   Jones, Richard Foster. **Ancients and Moderns.** St.Louis: Washington University. (1936) Reprint 1961.

[18]   Lyell, Charles. **The Antiquity of Man.** London: Dent and Son. (1863) Reprint 1914.

[19]   Macaulay, Thomas B. Lord Bacon. **Book review of The Works of Francis Bacon by Basil Montagu,** 1825-1834, 16 vols. Edinburgh: <u>Edinburgh Review</u> Vol. 132, July 1837, p.1-104.

[20]   Newbold, William R. **The Cipher of Roger Bacon.** Philadelphia: University of Philadelphia Press. 1928.

[21]   Owen, Orville W. **Sir Francis Bacon's Cipher Story.** Detroit: Howard Publishing 5 volumes, 1893-1895.

[22]   Popper, Sir Karl R. **Conjectures and Refutations.** New York: Basic Books. 1965.

[23]   Popper, Sir Karl R. **Unended Quest.** La Salle, IL: Open Court Publishing. 1976.

[24]   Purver, Marjery S, **The Royal Society: Concept & Creation** London: Routledge and Kegan Paul. 1967.

[25]   Rudwick, Martin **J. The Strategy of Lyell's Principles of Geology.** London: <u>Isis</u> 61 (1970) p.4-33.

[26]   Rudwick, Martin J. **The Great Devonian Controversy.** Chicago: University Press. 1985.

[27]   Spratt, Thomas. **History of the Royal Society.** St.Louis: Washington University Press Reprint. (1667) 1958.

[28]   Walther, Johannes. **Einleitung in die Geologie als historische Wissenschaft.** Jena: Verlag, Gustav Fischer. 3 Vols. 1893-1894.

[29]   Whitehead, Alfred **N. Science and the Modern World** New York: The Macmillan Co. 1925.

[30]   Yates, Francis. **The Rosicrucian Enlightenment.** London: Routledge and Kegan Paul. 1972.

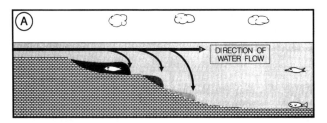

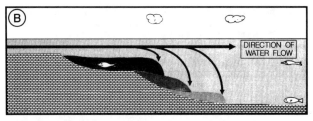

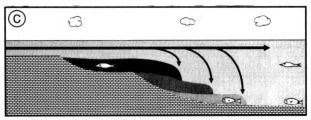

WALTHER'S LAW OF THE CORRELATION OF FACIES

Walther first observed this effect in the Bay of Naples. In **A** the velocity of River water carrying sediment decreases as it enters the Bay and the heaviest sediments drop out first while the lightest sediments are carried furthest. Note the fish trapped in its own ecological zone by the settling sediment. After a period of time, **B**, the decrease in flow velocity occurs further into the Bay. The heavier sediments now begin to fall upon the lighter sediments which had settled previously; well defined strata are beginning to form and follow the contour of the bottom. The process continues in **C**. Note another fish trapped in its own ecological zone and at a later point in time. Finding these fish as fossils and not knowing the process, it would be natural to think that the second fish (in **C**) lived in an era long before the first (in **A**).

TECTONIC CONTROLS ON SEDIMENTATION IN ROCKS FROM THE JURASSIC SERIES (YORKSHIRE, ENGLAND)

DAVID J. TYLER, PhD, MSc, BSc.
c/o P.O. Box 22, Rugby, Warwickshire, CV22 7SY, England.

ABSTRACT
One of the classic areas of British geology is reexamined using perspectives provided by the tectonically-controlled rock cycle and the Biblical record of the Flood. Field evidences are described which are highly suggestive of inter-related catastrophic processes and short time intervals. The conventional lengthy geologic timescales claimed for these rocks are challenged. The observations have a bearing on discussions relating to the position of the Flood/post-Flood boundary.

KEYWORDS

Sedimentology, Catastrophism, Diluvialism, Ecological successions, Jurassic Series, Crustal blocks, Tectonic controls, Flood/post-Flood boundary.

1. INTRODUCTION

The Jurassic rocks of England have been studied in great detail for nearly 200 years. More recently, research has intensified. Many of the workable reservoirs of oil and gas discovered in the North Sea during the past two decades lie in Middle Jurassic sandstones. The Yorkshire Coast provides exposures of all the main sequences and includes many classic localities of world renown. In general, field geologists have approached these strata from the perspective of uniformitarianism. They have attributed the sediments to a variety of depositional environments (shallow seas, estuaries, rivers and lakes) over a period of 62 million years.

An alternative conceptual model for interpreting geological phenomena has been proposed by Tyler [27], based on catastrophic rather than uniformitarian processes of erosion and deposition. Conventionally, catastrophic episodes are understood as isolated short periods of intense activity separated by long periods of quiescence. However, the tectonically controlled rock cycle provides a framework for interpreting an integrated series of related catastrophic processes - with consequent shrinking of overall timescales. The Yorkshire Coast Jurassic Series in north-east England has been reexamined from the perspective of this catastrophic conceptual model. Numerous features may be identified which have been associated with tectonic control of geologic processes [27]: abrupt transitions between sediments of different character, fault-bounded sedimentary basins, lateral persistence of both thin and thick beds, evidence of transitory occupation of environments, and characteristic features of rapid sedimentation. The field evidences can be integrated within an interpretative framework of rapidly-moving tectonic blocks to both create sedimentary basins and to control sedimentation within the basins.

This paper takes a selective view of field evidences - focusing attention on several key localities which illustrate the principles of the reinterpretation. The diversity of rock types are evidence for a geological history involving an orderly sequence of events. Certain formations can be related to modern depositional environments - but with important differences which are the subject of discussion here. It is of interest that the first serious systematic field guide to these rocks, by Young in 1822 [28], sought to interpret the observations so as to be consistent with the Biblical history of the global Flood in the days of Noah. This framework is still relevant to interpreting the British Jurassic sequences, but the conclusion of this paper is that the rocks are better interpreted as the result of post-Flood catastrophism extending over several decades.

The evidences reported here are well-known and well-documented. Field guides to the area are by Hemingway *et al.* [12], Young [30], Brumhead [8] and Rawson and Wright [22]. A technical appraisal has been published by the Yorkshire Geological Society [23], and the relevant British Geological Survey overview of the region is by Kent *et al.* [16]. An overview of the solid geology is in Figure 1. The main formations in the area are listed in Figure 2. Most of the observations reported in this paper are familiar to the writer. However, unless observations are indicated to be a personal observation [pers.obs.], reference to relevant follow-up literature is provided.

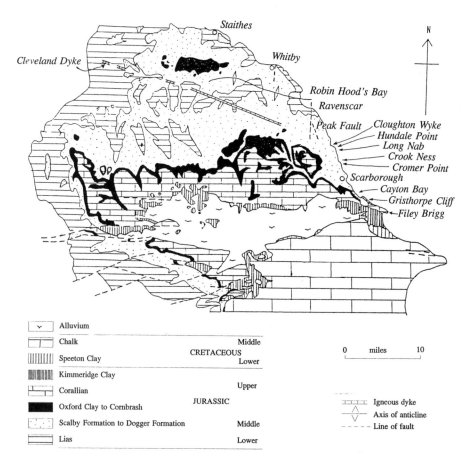

Figure 1: Solid geology of the Yorkshire Coast region
(after Brumhead [8]).

2. STRUCTURAL SETTING

The rocks under consideration in this study belong to the Jurassic Series and were deposited in a structure known as the Cleveland Basin (Figure 3). Details about the boundaries of this Basin are limited, because of the nature of the outcrop, but there are certainly fault zones to the south, where the Market Weighton Block can be recognised, and to the west, where the Basin meets the Askrigg Block. To the east is an extension of the Basin into the North Sea, known as the Sole Pit Trough. To the north are outcrops of sediments which underlie the Jurassic.

Although originally deposited in a basin, the lithified sediments have been affected by Tertiary earth movements and now form a broad antiform called the Cleveland Dome. Numerous smaller scale anticlines and synclines occur within the strata, and this has led to the same rocks being exposed repeatedly along the coast.

UPPER JURASSIC	Upper Calcareous Grit Formation Coralline Oolite Formation Lower Calcareous Grit Formation Oxford Clay Formation Kellaways Beds Formation Cornbrash Formation	
MIDDLE JURASSIC	Scalby Formation Scarborough Formation	
	Cloughton Formation	Gristhorpe Member Lebberston Member Sycarham Member Blowgill Member
	Eller Beck Formation Saltwick Formation Dogger Formation	
LOWER JURASSIC	Upper Lias	Blea Wyke Sandstone Formation	Yellow Sandstone Member Grey Sandstone Member
		Whitby Mudstone Formation	Fox Cliff Siltstone Member Peak Mudstone Member Alum Shale Member Jet Rock Member Grey Shale Member
	Middle Lias	Cleveland Ironstone Formation	
		Staithes Sandstone Formation	
	Lower Lias	Redcar Mudstone Formation	Ironstone/pyritous shales Siliceous shales Calcareous shales

Figure 2. Stratigraphic sequence exposed along the Yorkshire Coast.

The Market Weighton Block is concealed, but can be inferred from the pattern of sedimentary rocks around it. Kendall [13] and Kendall and Wroot [14] considered it an anticline, but subsequent studies did not confirm the existence of folded strata. Beds wedge out as they approach the structure, and it is more likely that they terminate in faults. Consequently, the structure is now regarded as an unfolded block that has affected sedimentation by its vertical movements [15]. Gravity anomalies show a significant low above this block, suggesting granite intrusion at depth [7,15,16].

The Askrigg Block, to the west, has been studied in much more detail. This rigid pre-Carboniferous structure has had a major effect on patterns of deposition in its immediate vicinity. The Dent Fault marks the western boundary and the Craven Fault system the southern boundary. To the north are the Teesdale and Lunedale Faults which separate the Askrigg Block from another well-documented massif, the Alston Block. Both structures are concealed but borings have been made in order to investigate their composition. The results show that both Blocks contain Caledonian granites. To the east of the Askrigg Block lies the Cleveland Basin with a faulted boundary.

For many years, the Askrigg and Alston Blocks have been recognised as actively controlling patterns of Carboniferous sedimentation by their vertical movements [16]. This paper makes the hypothesis that their influence continued into the Mesozoic and argues, furthermore, that deposition in the Cleveland Basin bears the marks of tectonic control.

Intra-basinal tectonic activity during deposition has, until recently, thought to be negligible. Those few faults that are present were widely regarded as having formed in the Tertiary. However, seismic data from within a 30 km offshore zone has led to the discovery of the Peak Trough [18], a 5 km wide graben that was active during the Jurassic. This implies that all the major faults in the Basin were capable of influencing sedimentation.

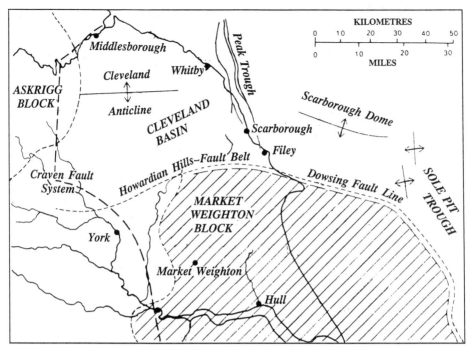

Figure 3: Major structural features associated with the Cleveland Basin
(after Kent *et. al.* [16] and Rawson & Wright [22]).

3. LOWER JURASSIC - THE LIASSIC

The Lower Liassic rocks at the base of the exposed sequence were once marine muds, but are now compressed to form dark shales. These may be examined in Robin Hood's Bay. There is no evidence of an authentic sea bed. Bivalves, for example, are not in life positions. Whereas the shells of *Pinna*, a suspension feeder, are found in life with their posterior projecting from the sediment, in the rocks, their half shells lie loose on their sides. They are often aligned [pers.obs]. Various accumulations of body fossils are observed on some bedding planes: where these contain distinctive zone fossils, they are often marked in the field guide maps. These evidences indicate that the muds and the fossils within them were reworked by currents, and that the environment was quite active. This conflicts with the conventional interpretation of a distal sea floor environment with the slow deposition of fine-grained sediments. Some have argued that the fine layering observed in the Liassic mudstones represents a broad rhythmic control of sedimentation [16]. However, it is now clear that such fine laminations may be produced by rapid, continuous processes [4,5].

North of Robin Hood's Bay are exposures of Middle Liassic sandstones and ironstones. Here, the sediments are coarser and the fauna more varied [16]. Trace fossils are common [pers.obs.]. Again, there is no evidence of an authentic sea bed. The main constraint on time is the presence of fossil traces, where organisms were able to feed and burrow during temporary lulls in sedimentation. Many of the layers in these rocks show graded bedding [pers.obs] signifying that the layers were deposited as discrete units and rapidly.

Further north still are the Upper Liassic shales. However, these are better seen at Ravenscar, Staithes and in Whitby East Cliff. As well as trace fossils, bivalves, belemnites and ammonites, these rocks have yielded spectacular saurians [3]. If it had taken thousands of years for these large marine creatures to be slowly covered by muds, they would have disintegrated and their remains, if any, would have been scattered: modern taphonomic studies suggest that sedimentation rates must be rapid to avoid the remains of dead organisms being recycled. Corroborating evidences of rapid sedimentation are numerous: accumulations of ammonites on certain bedding planes, a belemnite cutting through several centimetres of shale instead of lying flat on the surface (pers.obs.); cone-in-cone structures in one calcareous bed [pers.obs.]. (This is a phenomenon with various interpretations, but generally attributed to compression. Here, the proposal is that it is associated with rapid loading from the accumulating cover of mud).

The Peak Fault is oriented north-south and cuts the coastal cliff at Ravenscar. The Lias/Dogger junction is displaced vertically by 106 metres. In most of the area, the youngest strata of the Lower Jurassic are the Alum Shales, and these are succeeded across a marked unconformity by the Dogger Formation. At Ravenscar, however, west of the Peak Fault, the Dogger rests on the Alum Shales. East of the fault, the Dogger is separated from the Alum Shales by about 60 metres of Upper Liassic shales and sands. The Dogger itself is a different thickness on each side of the fault.

The explanation of syn-sedimentary faulting (*i.e.* deposition contemporaneous with faulting) was first suggested in 1874, and this was widely accepted by subsequent researchers [23,30]. However, it does not explain all the facts, and other scenarios have been sought [23]. Further work has established that similar Upper Liassic strata exist in small pockets in several other parts of the Cleveland Basin: namely, in the Roxby Basin, the Ralph Cross Basin and the Crosscliff Basin. It has been suggested that a combination of transcurrent and normal faulting at a much later date (during the Tertiary) could bring strata from one of these basins adjacent to strata outside it. Lateral displacements of about 8 km have been considered. This view was championed by Hemingway [12,23] and was widely accepted.

Brumhead [8] was not entirely happy with this second interpretation and suggested several arguments against it: no transcurrent faulting has been detected on any of the other faults in the Cleveland Basin; the fault breccia visible in the Peak Fault is not as severe as might be expected for transverse movements of this magnitude; and numerous points of speculation are still required for the explanation to be coherent. These arguments warrant the verdict that "no completely satisfactory analysis has been made" [8]. In addition, facies and thickness changes across the fault suggest syn-depositional movement, although these have not been easy to regonise until the structure of the Peak Fault became clear [18].

In the light of recent research, the explanation of syn-sedimentary faulting should be regarded as correct. The several small basins containing Upper Liassic sediments are referred to as "structural basins" in the literature. These must represent syn-sedimentary deformation leading to the deposition of muds and sands which, according to the section now exposed at Ravenscar, reached a thickness of at least 60 metres. The syn-sedimentary deformation may have been accompanied by syn-sedimentary faulting - as was the case with the Ravenscar deposits, which are associated with the Peak Trough. The development of local disparities in the thicknesses and character of beds on either side of the Peak Fault is by no means an intractable problem - as Figure 4 illustrates. The scenario presented does not require large transcurrent fault movements.

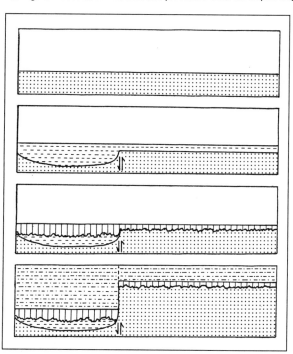

1. Deposition of the Alum Shale.

2. Localised deformation and the deposition of the Blea Wyke Formation. Early stages in the development of the Peak Trough.

3. Erosion and deposition of the Dogger Formation, which develops a different thickness on either side of the active fault zone.

4. Sedimentation continues alongside active faulting during development of the Peak Trough.

Figure 4: Proposed development of the Peak Fault

In brief, there are evidences for both syn-sedimentary and syn-sedimentary faulting deformation during the Upper Liassic. These field evidences, when understood in the context of the tectonically controlled rock cycle are associated with short timescales.

4. MIDDLE JURASSIC - THE 'DELTAIC' SERIES

The base of the Middle Jurassic is marked by the Dogger Formation: a remarkably continuous and distinctive sideritic sandstone with marine fossils. Within the basin it varies in thickness from 5m to less than 1m [16]. The lateral persistence of this thin transgressive bed does not find a ready explanation in terms of modern analogues.

Overlying the Dogger are the finer grained sediments of the Saltwick Formation as seen in Whitby East Cliff, and coarser grained sandstones which may be examined in Whitby Town and at Ravenscar. The 'Khyber Pass' mega-channels in Whitby provide a striking contrast to the well-bedded facies at East Cliff and Ravenscar [8]. The sediments are not marine: they lack marine fossils, and they contain a variety of plant remains such as *Equisetites* and also the fresh water mollusc *Unio* [16]. Modern analogues have some value here in interpreting the sedimentary structures. The mega-channels represent river bed deposits - a high energy environment which has no requirement for long periods of time. At the same stratigraphic level are finer grained sediments deposited in horizontal beds. These rocks have at least two evidences suggesting a sub-aerial environment: shrinkage cracks and several horizons of plant root development. These are interpreted here as overbank deposits, as is the case in the field guides [16,17,22]. The shrinkage cracks are considered to be mudcracks because of the association with root horizons. Whereas uniformitarian analogues for deposition require long periods of time, the evidences in the rocks do not suggest a need for anything more than a few years.

Within the overlying Cloughton Formation is the well-known Lebberston Member, or Millepore Bed. The popular name derives from the presence of a branching bryozoan in the unit, and this organism is an indicator of marine affinities. The Millepore Bed may be examined NNE of Cloughton Wyke [16,17]. It rests unconformably on shales and has 3 sub-units, none of which show any signs of in-situ accumulation [pers.obs.]. The material appears to be transported debris. Shells are generally fragmented, and the character of the bed suggests a violent and rapid deposition rather than a marine transgression lasting for an extended period. The observations are fully consistent with a tectonic control of sedimentation and relatively short timescales.

Still within the Cloughton Formation, the overlying sandstones show signs of being typical fluvio-deltaic sediments. The most interesting features of the Cloughton Formation are at least six horizons of in-situ root development [pers.obs.]. The roots have been assigned to the plant *Equisetites*, and form carbonaceous films through the sands and muds below the surface. A clear illustration is in reference 22, page 53. The lowest root bed is formed mainly in clayey muds, and measures about 2m thick [pers.obs.]. Other beds are thinner, and the roots generally pass through sands. Unlike modern horsetails, these plants did not have spreading underground rhizomes. However, other features are similar: the hollow stem, the sections of stem joined by nodes, and the tendency to have part of the stem below ground. The roots have a uniform character, suggesting that each bed is a mono-specific horizon. *Equisetites* appears to have been a pioneer species, and a single growing season would have been sufficient time to form each root bed, but time was insufficient for other species to become established. The 2m thick lowermost bed may be interpreted in the following way. Plants began to grow in an area accumulating muddy sediments. To avoid burial, the plants continued to grow upwards. The buried stems now form part of the fossilised root bed. In all six root beds observed, growth of the plants was terminated by water action - high energy currents brought in new sediment either to cover the plants or to erode the soil surface and deposit more sandy beds.

The possibility that these root beds were allochthonous was seriously considered. In the geologic record, there are many examples of polystrate plant remains which do not testify to *in situ* growth [10]. The empirical investigations of Coffin [9] are of some interest here. He has considered the way modern day *Equisetum* stems in water tend to be oriented in the upright position for many days before becoming waterlogged. However, the experiments relate to stems which were not attached to basal rhizomes, and whilst they are relevant to polystrate *Calamites* elsewhere in the Middle Jurassic sequence, they do not bear directly on the Cloughton Formation rootbeds. Coffin did argue that the surrounding palaeoecology and sediments should be examined carefully before coming to a conclusion on allochthonous or autochthonous modes of formation. This is the methodology adopted here. The downward development of roots is uniformly consistent, even with coarser sand sediments, and even when the sands show distinct signs of high energy deposition. In places the roots are seen to cross breaks in sedimentation in the beds. The roots can be traced up to stems, which may be infilled by the incoming sediment: an evidence which supports the need for an explanation which does not consider stems and roots separately. The roots permeate the rock units: they are not associated with cracks nor are they a surface phenomenon. Several beds of sand separate the units containing the root beds, an observation which argues both for the biological origin of these structures and for short timescales. The autochthonous growth interpretation was considered the only defensible option.

A further exposure of these rocks occurs further south below Gristhorpe Cliff, known as the "Gristhorpe plant bed". The rocks here contain fossilised plant parts rather than roots. The leaves of numerous plants (including Bennettitales, Ginkgoales, conifers and ferns [16]) are well preserved in mudstone. In ironstone nodules, the plant parts retain their three-dimensional form. Lack of decay may be attributed to the speed of deposition in a lacustrine environment rather than to the preservative effects of anoxic sediments.

The marine Scarborough Formation is exposed at Hundale Point (the type locality) and at Gristhorpe Cliff. Gowland and Riding have made a recent detailed analysis of the sedimentological and palaeontological data [11]. Above the root beds at Cloughton Wyke is a 1 m unit of sandstone showing soft-sediment slumping. This is associated with movement on the Peak Fault, the line of which was only a few hundred metres to the east [18,22]. This unit is thought to lie close to the base of the Scarborough Formation [11]. The rock sequence suggests submersion of the underlying non-marine deltaic sands (the upper part of the Cloughton Formation), a deepening-upward sequence of siliclastic and carbonate deposits, followed by shallowing due to a prograding sandy shore. The fossils are typically fragmented and poorly preserved, although some densely-bioturbated horizons are present. This marine transgression can be analysed into distinct phases, each having a recognisable character. The marine sediments were not swept into place as one unit, but successively. The changing character of the sediments, the fossil assemblages, the bioturbation traces and the presence of distinct boundaries between beds indicate that a depositional history over a significant period of time is necessary to explain these observations. However, none of the evidences require long timescales. If the rates of sedimentation were tectonically controlled, as is proposed here, timescales of the order of a year are adequate.

Inland, towards the top of the Scarborough Formation, *Gyrochorte* burrows are found: the *Gyrochorte* organism is thought to be "an opportunistic animal ideally suited to exploiting highly mobile substrates" [21]. The argument that the formation of these facies require high energy, shallow water, tidal beach conditions appears to be valid. If there was a tectonic control on sedimentation, there is no reason to doubt that, as well as being high energy, the strata must have accumulated rapidly.

At Hundale Point there is a major unconformity at the top of the Scarborough Formation. The spectacular cross-beds of the Moor Grit Member of the Scalby Formation outcrop here and, because the rocks are well-cemented, they form the headland. The regional picture reveals that coarse mature sands were carried into the basin by powerful rivers [16]. The current flow indicators show them to have been very disturbed [pers.obs.], suggesting high energy turbulence. Again, all this activity is suggested to be under tectonic control and relatively rapid. The Moor Grit passes up into massive quartz sandstones, well sorted by water action. These are succeeded by the famous Meander Belt deposits: the Long Nab Member of the Scalby Formation.

The Meander Belt may be examined at Crook Ness, Long Nab and Gristhorpe Cliff. In addition to the fossil meandering channels and the overbank deposits, fossil oxbow lake structures are seen at Cromer Point and Gristhorpe Cliff [16,19]. The floodplain has good examples of shrinkage cracks. These are interpreted as mudcracks because of their association with dinosaur footprints here [8,16]. Obviously, such features on bare surfaces require time: to shape the surface and to preserve the markings. However, a constraint on timescales is set by the general lack of vegetative growth over the floodplain [pers.obs.]. Other evidences of rapid sedimentation are seen. The abandoned channel at Cromer Point has been infilled by flaser-bedded sediment with rising ripples [pers.obs.] suggesting gentle but continuous sedimentation. Adjacent to Cromer Point are some point bar sediments which also show a rising ripple texture. The Cromer Plant Bed consists of coalified bed-load plant debris: some of it enclosed in sandstone, other debris wedged between cross-beds.

Livera and Leeder have reviewed sedimentological studies of these rocks [17]. They suggest that the different depositional regimes (wave-tide-fluvial) can be compared to the present day delta of the River Niger. Although there are undoubtedly elements of similarity, the modern analogue fails to account for the numerous evidences of rapid processes. The implications of these evidences in the Scalby Formation are apparent to geologists working within conventional timescales, and this has created an unresolved tension. Thus Livera and Leeder comment: "Problems arise concerning the time taken for deposition of the formation since at least 10 ammonite zones must be represented between the topmost Scarborough Formation and the overlying Cornbrash" [17]. The argument can be extended, because contacts between the Cloughton, Scarborough and Scalby Formation are all sharp and lack any evidence of significant erosion (making it difficult to introduce time gaps to the interpretation) [11].

Alexander [2] has suggested that there must be some tectonic control on the deposition of the Scalby Formation. This approach shares common ground with the views presented in this paper. However, the writer finds no evidence for long periods of time in order to form the strata with its enclosed fauna and flora. Nevertheless, it is necessary to propose a depositional history of these deposits which involves a sequence of events over a significant period of time. Modern day catastrophists have shown that particular features of the rock record can be reinterpreted in a non-uniformitarian way. For example, Oard has reviewed data related to the formation of shrinkage cracks [20] and it is clear that syneresis cracks are possible. Oard argues that it is vital for investigators to look for several corroborating lines of evidence before concluding that shrinkage cracks require a subaerial environment for formation. The evidences presented above show that for these Middle Jurassic rocks, there is a coherent picture of shallow water, non-marine deposition, with periods of subaerial exposure for plants to grow, mudcracks to form and for gentle sedimentation to occur. Whether dinosaurs walked on land or in shallow water is not an issue here: the fact that their footprints are preserved shows that preservation processes happened soon after they were formed [24]. The evidence for time is significant, but a few decades is not an unreasonable estimate.

5. UPPER JURASSIC

High Red Cliff on the southern side of Cayton Bay comprises much of the Upper Jurassic sequence. The sediments are marine, with contrasting lithologies.

Abrupt changes in the depositional environment must be postulated to explain the contrast between sandy clay (Kellaways Beds), grey uniform clay (Oxford Clay) and sandy oolitic carbonates (Corallian Beds) [16]. Such changes are more readily understood where sedimentation is tectonically controlled and rapid than where it is linked to modern analogues. A convolute bed in the Corallian is understood [18] to be induced by an earthquake shock associated with the Peak Trough.

The Corallian is best studied at Filey Brigg. This locality has some of the finest *Thalassinoides* burrows to be seen anywhere [16]. These burrows occur in both the Hambleton Oolite and the Middle Calcareous Grit. Interpreted in the light of modern analogues, these sediments represent different environments (an oolitic, sandy limestine, a limey sandstone and a sandy limestone), yet the burrowing, filter-feeding organisms were present in all three types of sediment. Moreover, the fact that these strata are intensely bioturbated by only one type of organism points to an unbalanced ecosystem. The appearance of large numbers of one species, together with colonisation of both oolite and calcareous grit sediments, suggests an abnormal and temporary situation.

6. DISCUSSION

Subsequent to the laying down of the Jurassic sediments, a notable series of events occurred. Igneous activity to the west of Scotland about 300 miles away, and particularly activity centred on the Island of Mull, led to the development of tension cracks across Scotland and Northern England [16]. The Cleveland Dyke was a major intrusion of magma across Northern England, with outcrops occurring only a few kilometres from the exposures mentioned above. Their presence is evidence that tectonic disturbances of the Earth's crust are able to affect regions far distant from their source. Vertical movements of the Cleveland Basin have produced many depositional changes, and the prime candidates for initiating these changes are the neighbouring Askrigg and Market Weighton blocks.

Any discussion of the timescales for producing these field evidences must first address questions about interpretative frameworks. The starting point chosen in this case is the pioneering work of Young [28,29]. Young was one of a number of 19th Century clerics who made themselves experts in geological science. Young differed from most, in that he adhered to short timescales of earth history and argued for the dominant role of the Genesis Flood in forming the fossiliferous strata. After a detailed description of the Yorkshire Coast field evidences, Young presented his readers with an interpretative framework, using the following arguments to prove that "the different members of our strata have been all deposited nearly about the same period".
1. All strata are affected by the same deformation and faulting processes. Wherever we look, faults pass through successive strata and are not cut off. Thus, evidence of time intervals cannot be inferred from a study of deformation.

2. There is evidence that all strata were semi-consolidated at the time of deformation. That is, rocks which are now significantly different in hardness are folded and faulted to the same extent. Consequently, if all the rocks were then semi-consolidated, it may be inferred that they did not differ markedly in age.

3. There is little evidence for long intervals of time between successive strata. Within a sequence, different beds are sometimes observed to grade into each other. Where there are distinct lines of separation, the levelness of the bedding planes is an indicator that erosive processes were minimal before the deposition of the upper beds.

Young's arguments were not accepted by his peers, primarily because of the overriding influence of Charles Lyell and the interpretative framework of uniformitarianism. Young fought a losing battle. Many years later, Kendall and Wroot [14] referred to Young in passing as "primitive". However, the three arguments for rapid deposition cannot be dismissed so easily - they are not infantile speculation but logical argument based on a close acquaintance with field evidences. Admittedly, all the points need qualifying: there is evidence for syn-sedimentary deformation, and possibly faulting; rocks experiencing creep under pressure do behave differently from rocks at the surface; there are indications of time (root horizons, sedimentary structures and trace fossils which suggest periods of non-deposition). However, none of these qualifications require us to reject Young's basic thesis that these beds were laid down over relatively short time periods.

Most contemporary geologists regard the British Jurassic as a time of placid deposition. The recent interest in neo-catastrophism has raised a few questions about timescales of deposition. Ager [1] draws attention to unusually large regional variations in thickness of a biostratigraphic zone, and also the presence of boulder beds in the Upper Jurassic in Sutherland, Scotland. However, apart from the recognition of storm deposits, few have acknowledged any role for catastrophic processes, and even fewer have moved any distance from the uniformitarian framework adopted by earlier geologists.

Berthault [6] has argued that a radical rethink is necessary on the meaning of terms like "stratum" and "layer". He has suggested that stratification can result from continuous sedimentation processes, and that this revolutionises stratigraphy. Whilst this argument has been used to promote diluvialist interpretations of the rock record, it must be tested in the field. The evidences reviewed in this paper have not been interpreted as resulting from continuous sedimentation. Footprints, bioturbated horizons, root beds, and sedimentary structures like meander beds, channels and overbank deposits, require a coherent interpretative framework: the model proposed by Berthault does not provide it.

Scheven [25] has argued a case for the Noahic Flood being the primary cause of the Palaeozoic Series of rocks. The Mesozoic and Cenozoic Series represent post-Flood catastrophism and are associated with faunal and floral mega-successions. The British Jurassic provides an instructive test case for the proposed model. The review of field evidences presented here has suggested that the Yorkshire Jurassic may be described satisfactorily as post-Flood deposits associated with transitory epi-continental seas. Contemporaneous tectonic activity resulted in the raising and lowering of crustal blocks, with consequent rapid shift of water and sediment into subsiding basins and the occurrence of syn-sedimentary deformation. Within this model, the continually changing environments had profound effects on their living inhabitants: ecological successions were characterised by rapid replacement of faunas and unbalanced ecosystems. Whilst these observations are related to a specific area, the rest of the Jurassic, and indeed the whole Mesozoic, shows a similar picture, as Scheven has indicated in a 1993 review paper [26].

Science is widely accepted to operate within large-scale interpretative frameworks, sometimes referred to as paradigms. The uniformitarian paradigm leads inevitably to a rock cycle based on present-day processes and to timescales lasting millions of years. The Diluvialist paradigm utilises a rock cycle based on catastrophic processes and timescales are consequently short [27]. Scientific work can be undertaken within both these paradigms: this paper has adopted the Diluvialist paradigm and explored the development of Jurassic Series strata deposited in the Cleveland Basin. The regional picture gives confidence that the general approach is viable and that further detailed work on specific strata will yield fruitful results. A key issue for science concerns the testing of hypotheses against data. This paper is concerned with the hypothesis that the Jurassic Series of rocks represents post-Flood depositional processes and it is concluded that, in the Cleveland Basin, the hypothesis is capable of integrating successfully numerous field evidences.

A necessary implication of the analysis presented here is that there are qualitative differences between Palaeozoic rocks (Flood deposits) and post-Palaeozoic rocks (post-Flood deposits). Differences should be apparent in studies of trace fossils (activity and escape traces vs dwelling traces); evidences of plant growth (allochthonous vs autochthonous); shrinkage cracks (subsediment syneresis cracks vs subaerial mudcracks); monospecific horizons (water sorting vs unbalanced ecosystems). Major differences should be apparent in the sedimentary basins and the smaller scale structures associated with deposition. It is the writer's judgment that such differences do exist, but documenting them is outside the scope of this paper.

7. CONCLUSIONS

(a) Different paradigms of geological interpretation exist which permit radically different interpretations to be placed on the same basic evidence. It is the work of science to test the interpretations rigorously against the data and to explore the effectiveness of different hypotheses in explaining the observations.

(b) The tectonically controlled rock cycle provides valuable assistance during field research: identifying significant and interrelated phenomena and pointing to appropriate mechanisms.

(c) The Cleveland Basin of Yorkshire provides an example of a classic area of geology with a complex geological history. Whereas all research since Young [28,29] has adhered to the uniformitarian paradigm, there are many evidences that favour an alternative interpretation based on catastrophism.

(d) The specific hypothesis that the field evidences can be explained satisfactorily by a Diluvialist model, where the Jurassic Series represents post-Flood sediments, has been explored. The results suggest that the hypothesis is viable and worthy of elaboration.

(e) This paper provides an input to discussions among Diluvialists of the positioning of the Flood/post-Flood boundary. A pre-Jurassic boundary is to be preferred.

ACKNOWLEDGEMENTS

Joachim Scheven is thanked for stimulating discussions on the field evidences, when we were co-leaders of a study week to this area in 1988. Stephen J. Robinson, Kurt P. Wise and anonymous reviewers are thanked for feedback on the draft manuscript.

REFERENCES

[1] D. Ager, The nature of the stratigraphical record, 3rd Edition, 1993, John Wiley & Sons, Chichester.

[2] J. Alexander, **Idealised flow models to predict alluvial sandstone body distribution in the Middle Jurassic Yorkshire Basin**, Marine and Petroleum Geology, 3(1986) 298-305.

[3] M.J. Benton and M.A. Taylor, **Marine reptiles from the Upper Lias (Lower Toarcian, Lower Jurassic) of the Yorkshire coast**, Proceedings of the Yorkshire Geological Society, 44:4(1984) 399-429.

[4] G. Berthault, **Experiments on lamination of sediments**, EN Technical Journal, 3(1988) 25-29.

[5] G. Berthault, **Sedimentation of a heterogranular mixture: experimental lamination in still and running water,** EN Technical Journal, 4(1990) 95-102.

[6] G. Berthault, **'Perestroika' in stratigraphy**, EN Technical Journal, 5:1(1991) 53-57.

[7] M.H.P. Bott, **The Market Weighton gravity anomaly - granite or graben?** Proceedings of the Yorkshire Geological Society, 47:1(1988) 47-53.

[8] D. Brumhead, Geology explained in the Yorkshire dales and on the Yorkshire coast, 1979, David & Charles, Newton Abbot.

[9] H.G. Coffin, **Vertical flotation of horsetails (Equisetum): geological implications.** Geological Society of America Bulletin, 82:July(1971) 2019-2022.

[10] H.G. Coffin, Origin by design, 1983, Review and Herald Publishing Association, Washington.

[11] S. Gowland and J.B. Riding, **Stratigraphy, sedimentology and palaeontology of the Scarborough Formation (Middle Jurassic) at Hundale Point, North Yorkshire**, Proceedings of the Yorkshire Geological Society, 48:4(1991) 375-392.

[12] J.E. Hemingway, V. Wilson and C.W. Wright, Geology of the Yorkshire coast, Geologists' Association Guide No. 34, Revised Edition, 1968, Benham & Company Ltd., Colchester.

[13] P.F. Kendall, **Sub-report on the concealed portion of the coalfield of Yorkshire, Derbyshire and Nottinghamshire**, in Final report of the Royal Commission on coal supplies, 1905, HMSO, London, Appendix III: 18-35.

[14] P.F. Kendall and H.E. Wroot, The geology of Yorkshire, 1924, Published by the authors, Leeds.

[15] P.E. Kent, **The Market Weighton structure**, Proceedings of the Yorkshire Geological Society, 30(1955) 197-227.

[16] P. Kent, G.D. Gaunt, and C.J. Wood, British Regional Geology: Eastern England from the Tees to The Wash, Second edition, 1980, HMSO, London.

[17] S.E. Livera and M.R. Leeder, **The Middle Jurassic Ravenscar Group ('Deltaic Series') of Yorkshire: recent sedimentological studies as demonstrated during a Field Meeting, 2-3 May 1980**, Proceedings of the Geologists' Association, 92:4(1981) 241-250.

[18] J. Milsom and P.F. Rawson, **The Peak Trough - a major control on the geology of the North Yorkshire coast**, Geological Magazine, 126(1989) 699-705.

[19] M. Nami, **An exhumed Jurassic meander belt from Yorkshire, England**, Geological Magazine, 113(1976) 47-52.

[20] M.J. Oard, **Underwater "Mudcracks"**, Creation Research Society Quarterly, 30:4(1994) 211-212.

[21] J.H. Powell, *Gyrochorte* **burrows from the Scarborough Formation (Middle Jurassic) of the Cleveland Basin, and their sedimentological setting**, Proceedings of the Yorkshire Geological Society, 49:1(1992) 41-47.

[22] P.E. Rawson and J.K. Wright, The Yorkshire coast, Geologists' Association Guide No. 34, Second Edition, 1992, The Geologists' Association.

[23] D.H. Rayner and J.E. Hemingway, The geology and mineral resources of Yorkshire, 1974, Yorkshire Geological Society.

[24] N.A. Rupke, **Prolegomena to a study of cataclysmal sedimentation**, in Why not Creation?, W.E Lammerts, Editor, 1970, Presbyterian and Reformed Publishing Co., 141-179.

[25] J. Scheven, **The Flood/Post-Flood boundary in the fossil record**, in Proceedings of the Second International Conference on Creationism, R.E. Walsh and C.L. Brooks, Editors, 1990, Creation Science Fellowship, Inc., Pittsburgh, PA, Volume II, 247-266.

[26] J. Scheven, **Ammonites, mussels and cockles**, Origins (The Journal of the Biblical Creation Society). 5:14(1993) 10-17.

[27] D.J. Tyler, **A tectonically-controlled rock cycle**, 1990, in Proceedings of the Second International Conference on Creationism, R.E. Walsh and C.L. Brooks, Editors, 1990, Creation Science Fellowship, Inc., Pittsburgh, PA, Volume II, 293-301.

[28] G. Young and J. Bird, A geological survey of the Yorkshire coast, 1822, Clark, Whitby.

[29] G. Young, A geological survey of the Yorkshire coast, 2nd Edition, 1828, Kirby, Whitby.

[30] S. Young, Geology of the Yorkshire coast, 1978, Dalesman Books.

THE GENESIS KINDS: A PERSPECTIVE FROM EMBRYOLOGY

SHEENA E.B. TYLER, PhD, BSc.
c/o PO Box 22, Rugby, Warwickshire, CV22 7SY, England.

ABSTRACT
From the days of greatest antiquity, mankind has recognised the distinctive common attributes shared by living things, and has attempted to relate these groups together by devising classification systems - the science of taxonomy or systematics. Much contemporary systematics invokes continuity in order to construct continuous transformational series. By contrast, the taxic or typological paradigm, which can be traced to the pre-Darwinian era, has gained preference over the transformational one in some secular circles [10; reviewed in 42]. This is leading to a systematics independent of evolutionary theory [4]. The types are thus considered as distinct morphological forms, sharing a common structural plan, and in which embryology is of prime concern [59]. Creationists also adopt a typological paradigm, in which the types are identified with the originally-created Genesis Kinds. The contribution of embryology to these issues is here reviewed and assessed. Particular data include hybridisation studies, egg surface structure, cleavage patterns, cell lineage and fate maps, egg capsule structure, larval ontology, sperm morphology and developmental mechanisms.

KEYWORDS
Embryology, Genesis Kinds, Developmental strategy, Cleavage patterns, Cell lineage, Fate maps, Hybridisation.

1. INTRODUCTION
For Charles Darwin embryology was of prime importance in his scheme of evolutionary change [41]. In 1859 he wrote to Hooker [21, p.60] "Embryology is to me by far the strongest single class of facts in favour of change of form." Whilst subsequent evolutionary frameworks have been modified and extended, it remains the case for evolutionists today that the origin and development of morphological diversity is ascribed to embryological processes. Evidence is thus sought for embryonic stages that reflect similarity with a common ancestor. A contrasting paradigm distinguishes distinct types in nature; for creationists, these types can be identified with the originally-created kinds. If such types indeed exist, one might expect to find type-specific characteristics of development, perhaps from even the earliest of stages. It is of interest and intrigue, therefore, to survey and compare development in a range of phyla, to discern which of these models the embryological data may in preference support.

2. BACKGROUND: ORDER IN NATURE
Two contrasting philosophical premises prevail in the search for order in nature. These premises, essentialism and nominalism, were described by Rieppel [42]. Essentialism recognises distinct types in nature. The members of each type all share a common essence. In contrast, nominalism considers the designation of types to be nominal or artificial, and that rather there is a continuous gradation of form among living things.

Essentialism has features in common with the idea of the Biblical Genesis Kinds (Genesis 1:1-27). These Kinds provided a conceptual framework for the most pre-eminent taxonomist, Linnaeus (1707-1778) [31]. Contemporary creationists have indicated the Genesis Kinds to be Basic Types of organisms, each of which may be more equivalent to the higher taxa, such as the family level, than to species. Discontinuities can be recognised between different kinds by a number of criteria e.g. morphology, molecular systematics, hybridisation [39,46,47,48,60,61]. Whilst systematists also employ at least some of these criteria and may recognise discontinuities, creationists consider the discontinuities to be ultimate and unbridgable. Biblical evidence is itself suggestive that the Genesis Kinds represent higher taxic levels than the species [28].

In contemporary literature, structuralists also recognise the essence in organisms [44]. The constancy of structural patterns is seen to result from constrained mechanisms of ontogenesis [52], with such mechanisms designated as the foundation of a taxon [59]. This contemporary renaissance of pre-Darwinian essentialist and taxic frameworks in some circles is an important development, providing stimulating ideas with which creationists can interact. Patterson [38] considered that the transformational approach is dependent on *a priori* hypotheses of transformation which are unobservable; hence, transformational pattern analysis cannot be independent from hypotheses about process. Thus, Darwin explained unity of type by unity of descent. On the other hand, the taxic approach adds the hypothesis of a subordinated, or inclusive hierarchical order [4].

Constraints on form exerted by patterns of development have become the focus of much recent interest [reviewed in 57]. If there are indeed real types in nature, a naturally following hypothesis is that members of a type may share similar mechanisms, structures and factors responsible for the generation of type-specific form [59]. Evidence for ontological manifestations of type- specific forms will now be considered.

3. TYPES: EMBRYOLOGICAL DATA

3.1 Hybridisation
The literature reveals numerous hybrids observed in nature or captivity. Often the hybrids are not only viable, but fully fertile [33]. The ability to hybridise may reflect common ontogenic pathways and mechanisms. Hybrids are well-documented in taxa such as the following:

a. Approximately one in ten bird species is known to hybridise, and the global incidence could be much higher [33]. Thus, from a world total of 9672 bird species, 895 species are known to have bred in nature with at least one other species [37]. This involves not only interspecific but intergeneric crosses. To this can be added a large number of hybrids found in captivity. Within the family Anatidae (ducks, geese and swans), for example, over 400 interspecific hybrids are known amongst the 150 or so species [46].
b. In the Equidae, out of 15 theoretically possible interspecific hybrids, 14 are known [56].
c. In the Cercopithecidae (old-world monkeys) hybridisations connect eight different genera out of the nine [22].

Thirteen potential basic types have been demarcated primarily by using hybridisation data [48]. To this list could be added the Felicidae (cats) and possibly the Ursidae (bears), Cervidae (deer-like) and a considerable number of other bird, mammal and fish taxa (S.E.B. Tyler, unpublished observations).

3.2 Egg surface topography
A variety of surface structures such as microvilli, blebs, ridges, folds, ruffles, spikes, and spines, have been observed in the eggs of certain species. The ootaxonomic significance of surface structure is particularly well documented in a number of insect orders [32]. In Gomphinid dragonflies, for example, a hexagonal reticulated surface patterning is seen [1]. Phylogenetically-distinct topographical differences have been evident in the surface architecture of amphibian, molluscan and annelid eggs [cited in 55]. For instance, in gastropod mollusc eggs such as those of *Buccinum*, *Crepidula* and *Nucella* [11], the vegetal pole is characterised by ridges of cytoplasmic outgrowths bearing microvilli. The outgrowths are arranged in a species-specific pattern. Since each of the representatives studied belong to separate families which in turn possibly may be natural types, this vegetal surface architecture may be type-specific. Similarly, the eggs of a few representatives of other phyla have also shown characteristic surface features: nemertines have a conical vegetal protuberance [23]; crustacea show surface sculpturing [40]; cnidaria possess surface microvillous spires [49].

3.3 Cleavage pattern
There are a number of notable differences in cleavage patterns, these being conspicuous between various phyla. This is demonstrated by describing a few examples.

a. *Ctenophora* [45]. The first two cleavages are of the usual meridional type (Fig. 1a). The third division is also nearly vertical and results in a curved plate of eight macromere cells (Fig. 1b). The following

Fig. 1 Ctenophores eg. *Beroïdae*

a.　　　　　　　b.　　　　　　　c.　　　　　　　d.　　　　　　　e. **a**

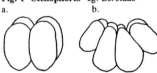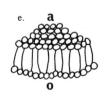

o

a = aboral　o = oral

division is latitudinal and unequal, giving rise to micromeres on the aboral, concave side of the macromere plate (Fig. 1c). The micromeres divide several times (Fig. 1d), and the macromeres produce a second set of micromeres at the oral pole (Fig. 1e).

b. *Planaria* [8]. Some in this group exhibit a typically spiral type of cleavage whilst other members show altered spiral, duet spiral, or strongly modified cleavage. Even in the typically spiral type, highly distinctive events occur. Division of the macromeres at the 32-cell stage leads to macromeres remaining at the vegetal pole, which, in spite of their name are minute (Fig. 2a). In the strongly modified cleavage of the rhabdocoels, after the first cleavage, divisions continue randomly until an irregular mass of 80-100 blastomeres is formed. In triclads, the blastomeres become isolated from one another, and are distributed among yolk cells. Yolk cells surrounding the blastomeres fuse to form a syncytium. Meanwhile some of the blastomeres transform into wandering amoeboid cells, migrating to the yolk syncitium (Fig. 2b).

c. *Mollusca* [58]. Mollusc eggs, as in a number of invertebrate phyla, exhibit spiral cleavage, in which each quartet of micromeres is rotated to the right or left of the macromeres in alternate divisions. The first two meridional divisions lead to formation of the A, B, C and D cells. In the following cleavage each of these cells, now called macromeres, divide to form a micromere at the animal pole. This process is repeated to produce further quartets of micromeres, which in turn produce further divisions (Fig. 3).

d. *Arthropoda: Insecta* [29]. Cleavage initially involves several mitotic divisions of the zygote to produce nuclei, some of which migrate to the egg periphery, where mitosis continues. Thus the cleavage nuclei are contained within a common cytoplasm, surrounded only by the egg membrane itself (Fig. 4). Gradually, the egg membrane folds inward to partition off each nucleus into a single cell. Such cells, extending around the embryo circumference, become the cellular blastoderm.

Fig. 2 Platyhelminthes: Planarians
a. *Hoploplana inquilana*   b. *Dendrocoelum lacteum*

Fig. 3 Mollusca
eg. *Crepidula fornicata*

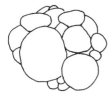  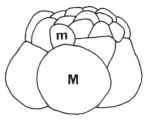

section through
45-cell stage

blastomeres (arrowed)
migrating vegetally.
e = external membrane.

sideview of 29-cell stage.
m = micromere; M = macromere

Fig. 4 Insects

**Fig.5 Echinoderms:
sea urchins**

Fig. 6 Vertebrates: mammals
a. eutherians   b. marsupials

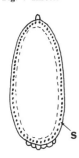  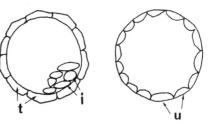

s = syncytial blastoderm

t = trophectoderm cells   u = unilamar blastocyst
i = inner cell mass cells

e. *Echinodermata* [53]. The first two divisions are meridional, and the third horizontal. In the highly characteristic 4th cleavage, the four cells of the upper, animal layer divide meridionally to form a tier of eight mesomere cells, whilst the lower layer of cells, now known as macromeres, becomes underlain with a tier of tiny micromeres (Fig. 5). In the following division, the mesomere and micromere tiers both divide horizontally, and the macromeres vertically, to produce an embryo of 32 cells arranged in 5 layers.

f. *Vertebrata: Mammalia* Eutherian mammal cleavage is strikingly different from most other patterns of embryonic cell division. During second cleavage, one blastomere divides meridionally and the other equatorially: this is rotational cleavage [20]. Alternatively, both divisions at this stage may be equatorial. Early cell divisions are asynchronous, so that odd numbers of cells are found, rather than the 2- to 4- to 8-cell stages found in other groups. At the 8-cell stage, the cells become compacted, ie. flattened. By the blastocyst stage (Fig. 6a) blastomeres have either differentiated into the trophectoderm cells which contribute the embryonic part to the placenta, or remain undifferentiated in the inner cell mass (ICM) which forms the embryo itself. It is at the blastocyst stage that implantation into the uterus occurs. In contrast, marsupial mammals (Fig. 6b) possess a unilaminar blastocyst with no ICM [50].

3.4 Cell lineage

Tracing the fates of cells through development has enabled researchers to establish homologies in different animals [6]. For example, in molluscs the first quartet of micromeres produces the pretrochal ectoderm which in turn gives rise to the head structures such as cephalic eyes, tentacles and cerebral ganglia. The second and third quartet produce the posttrochal ectoderm which includes the somatic plate from which the shell, foot and mantle cavity develop. In the cellular blastoderm of insects, dorsal cells give rise to either dorsal epidermis or an extraembryonic protective amnioserosa, while ventral cells produce the germ band, which in turn gives rise to ventral epidermis, mesoderm and the nervous system. The germ band becomes divided into consecutive metameres corresponding to the definitive body segments. Some embryologists view this uniformity of cell fates as evidence that the taxa sharing this pattern are related in some fundamental way [26]. Fate maps for representatives of 2 phyla are illustrated in Fig. 7. Each map in Fig. 8 is shown at the proposed phylotypic stage (see discussion) for each phylum, when the embryos of various taxa within the phylum may show the maximum similarity [54].

Fig. 7 Fate Maps (vertical sections)

Fig. 7a Echinoderms: sea urchins.
      Gastrula

Fig. 7b Amphibia: *Xenopus laevis*.
      Early gastrula

Key to Figs. 7,8.
Presumptive Fate regions

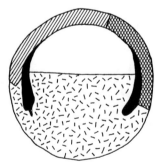

Ectoderm

Mesoderm

Endoderm

Neural

d = dorsal; v = ventral;
c = cilia; g = gut;
n = neural tube;
no = notochord;
s = stomodaeum

Fig. 8 Fate maps at phylotypic stages

Fig. 8a Annelids: eg. *Arenicola cristata*
Trochophore larva stage

Fig. 8b Cephalochordates,
eg. *Amphioxus*: elongation of notochord stage.

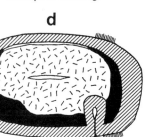

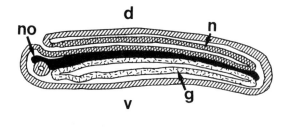

(Figs 7,8b after [5]; Fig. 8a after Okada, cited in Kume & Dan [29, p.211])

3.5 Egg capsules

There are other embryological criteria of potential taxonomic significance within particular phyla. For example, the egg capsules (spawn) of some mollusc groups are highly characteristic [43]. The Strombidae (conchs) capsules consist of long, sand-covered tubes of eggs compacted into masses (Fig. 9). The Epitoniidae (wentletraps) have clusters of capsules connected by a single thread like a necklace, and covered with sand. The planktonic egg capsules of the Littorinidae (periwinkles) vary in detail yet have in common a flattish spherical shape overlaid by concentric tiers, or a simplified version of this (Fig. 10). Most of the Naticidae (moon snails) capsules are more or less collar-shaped (Fig. 11). Both structural and behavioural characteristics may together be distinct: for example, the clustered eggs sacs of Calyptraeidae (eg. slipper limpets) are each composed of a delicate, transparent membranous wall, and a narrow stem of attachment to the underlying substrate, and all of which are brooded by the female [14] (Fig. 12); and the Eratoidae (sea buttons/false cowries) and Lamellariidae (ear shells) embed flask-shaped egg capsules within the body tissues of ascidian hosts.

Figs. 9-12 Egg capsules (after [43])

Fig. 9 Strombidae, eg. *Lambis truncata*

Fig. 10 Littorinidae A. *Nodilittorina pyramidalis*; B. *Peasiella roepstorffiana*

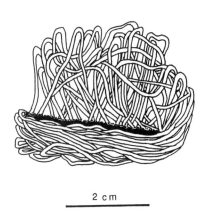

2 cm

A

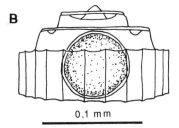

B

0.1 mm

Fig. 11 Naticidae A. *Conuber incei*;
B. *Polynices tumidus*

Fig. 12 Calyptraeidae, eg. *Crepidula fornicata*
underside of adult female, showing brooding of egg
capsules (arrowed)

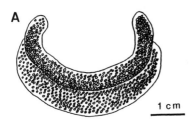

A

1 cm

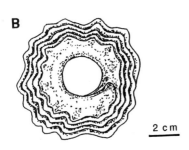

B

2 cm

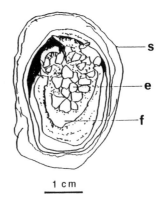

s

e

f

1 cm

e = egg capsule; f = foot; s = shell.

3.6 Protoconch characters

Certain embryological structures characteristic for a particular phylum may possess variations in
ontogenetic behaviour which may be a further aid to their demarcation as types. An example is the
mollusc protoconch (larval shell). The protoconch is secreted by an epithelium on the dorsal surface of the
embryo known as the molluscan shell field. The comparative embryology of protoconch development was
reviewed by Kniprath [30]. For example, most gastropods have helical shells. This form is produced by
an accelerated growth of the anterior and of the lateral margins of the shell field. By contrast, in
scaphopods (tusk shells), it is the lateral and posterior margins of the protoconch, preceded by similar
growth of the shell field, which grow when the lateral ones meet, a tube is thus formed.

Opinions as to the reliability of protoconch characters range from those who thought them to be highly
reliable, to those who thought them to be entirely unreliable. The opinions of the former group led to the
discrimination of genera based exclusively on protoconch characters. A reason for these opposed
opinions is that in some prosobranchs, the protoconch is uniform throughout the whole genera, whilst in
other groups there is substantial introgeneric and even intraspecific variation. Many groups do have
protoconchs with clearly uniform characters, for example, the Architectonicidae (sundial snails).

3.7 Sperm morphology

Within many invertebrate taxa, sperm ultrastructure has been used to deduce phylogenetic relationships.
For example, in a study of five families of archaeogastropods molluscs (Haliotidae, Fissurellidae,
Trochidae, Turbinidae, and Phasianellidae), it has been found possible to identify members of a family and
differentiate between families using sperm ultrastructure [24].

3.8 Developmental mechanisms

a. Cytoskeletal behaviour

The cytoskeleton is composed of microfilaments (F-actin filaments), microtubules, intermediate filaments
and their associated elements. All of these remain in place to a greater or lesser extent after detergent
extraction to remove the cell membrane, followed by washing in physiological saline containing
cytoskeletal-stabilising buffers. The elements can be distinguished in electron microscopy by their
distinctly-differing diameters.

Comprehensive data for spatio-temporal attributes of cytoskeletal elements throughout early developmental
stages is lacking in the majority of phyla, thus making comparisons difficult. However, there are
reasonable data for a few groups in the period immediately following fertilisation [reviewed in 12]. This
suggests that some organisms use predominantly microfilaments, and others predominantly microtubules

to mediate morphogenetic activities.   In annelids, the specification of the polar axis requires the initial segregation of morphogenetic plasms to both animal and vegetal regions of the egg after fertilisation: in *Tubifex* this segregation requires microfilaments whereas in *Helobdella* it requires microtubules.   At a similar stage in the nematode, *Caenorhabdites elegans*, microfilaments are required to generate asymmetry.   In several species of ascidia, the muscle-forming myoplasm is drawn down into the vegetal region by microfilaments, and then up to the prospective posterior side by microtubules.   Just after fertilisation in the amphibian, *Xenopus*, microtubules mediate the cortical rotation of cytoplasm, which determines the future dorsal axis. In the sea urchin, *Hemicentrotus pulcherrimus*, no structural polarity is apparent until after first cleavage, when cortical microtubules appear to mediate the polarisation of surface and cortical regions. In the mouse, polarity only becomes evident at the 8-cell stage, with microfilaments possibly directing the axis of cell polarity. In the mollusc, *Nassarius*, the vegetally-derived polar lobe requires microfilaments and microtubules for lobe formation and resorption respectively, by which the dorso-ventral axis is specified.

b. the cell surface

The development of form, known as morphogenesis, involves a number of cellular structures and processes. If distinct, natural types indeed exist, such structures or processes might also manifest type-specific characteristics.   At the molecular level, prime candidates for expressing morphogenetic activity at the surface are glycosylated (carbohydrate-conjugated) proteins and lipids. Their key role in morphogenesis is suggested by the following:

1. They have a potential for encoding a large amount of biological information [3,51]. A vast number of structures can be generated from a small number of saccharide units.

2. Extending outwards from the membrane surface implicates them in adhesion between cells and to the extracellular matrix.

3. A dramatic change in the developmental programme results from the application of glycosylation inhibitors.

Lectins are proteins of non-immune origin, with specific binding sites for particular oligosaccharide structures.   They therefore serve as useful probes for the detection and characterisation of surface glycosylated membrane components. For example, the lectin Concanavalin A (Con-A) has a specificity for surface glycoconjugates bearing a terminal mannose or glucosamine. In contrast to the binding of Con-A at the earliest stages of two species of mollusc eggs [12], this lectin does not bind to *Xenopus* eggs and cleavage stages [35], suggesting that either the Con-A receptor has not yet appeared or is masked at these early stages in *Xenopus* development. Particularly interesting is the contrasting behaviour of Con-A binding during gastrulation between representatives in these groups. In the amphibian *Rana* [27], but not the molluscs, a dramatic clustering of Con-A occurs. This behaviour of the Con-A receptors can be correlated with the underlying cellular rearrangements at this stage.   The difference between the Con-A binding between the two taxa thus in some way may be related to the profoundly different origins and fates of the various cells between the two groups before and after gastrulation.   The lectin-binding patterns in mollusc gastrulation can also be contrasted with the avian pattern [19], in which glucosamine residues are lost just prior to ingression. This may indicate a role of these residues in gastrulation. No loss in lectin binding was observed in molluscs at this stage [12].   The loss of binding of the lectins *Ulex europaeus* agglutinin I (UEA- I) and Con-A in mouse embryos at the compaction stage [62] contrasts with molluscs at an equivalent cell number; throughout cleavage *Nassarius* shows no UEA-I binding and Con-A binding is maintained, and binding of both lectins in *Crepidula* is maintained. The compaction stage is not evident in molluscs. Therefore the difference in binding at the equivalent cell number is consistent with the idea that there are profound differences in development at this stage between these representatives of the mollusc and mammalian taxa.

4. DISCUSSION

In some cases, the embryology of only a few representatives have been studied in characterising a phylum. In other cases, data from a number of subordinate taxa is available, which may be more closely identified with basic types. Even at the phylum level, the embryological data is sufficient for preliminary assessment of its taxonomic implications as follows.

The contemporary evolutionist view of invertebrate origins is typified by Brusca & Brusca [6], who constructed a computer-generated cladogram depicting a proposed monophyletic origin for the metazoa (Fig. 13). However, this scheme is not supported by the data outlined in Section 3, particularly concerning cleavage patterns; cell lineage and fate maps; and developmental mechanisms. Slack [53] emphasised that in a number of groups such as the molluscs, annelids, ascidians and nematodes, the key decisions of early development are made at a very early stage when there are only a few cells in the embryo. The profound significance of early development is apparent from deletion experiments: removal of individual cells from early cleavage stages in determinate embryos such as molluscs leads to loss of adult structures directly derived from these cells.   Therefore one is justified in applying early developmental criteria to phylogeny, since it appears that early development is foundational to the morphogenesis of the taxa in question. Consider then, for example, the emergence of the protostomous platyhelminth, mollusc and arthropod clade from node X on Fig. 13. How can the strikingly different cleavage patterns (Figs. 2,3,4 respectively) and cell lineages exhibited by these groups be reduced to one another? Some planarian platyhelminthes do show features of spiral cleavage in common with those of molluscs. However, in such planaria minute cells are formed at the vegetal pole (Fig. 2a), unlike in the mollusc. Moreover, other patterns are peculiar to planarian groups, namely duet spiral and modified cleavage (Fig. 2b). This can be contrasted again with the syncytial cleavage pattern in insects (Fig. 4). Regarding ctenophores, forming the outgroup at Y in Fig.13, even Brusca & Brusca [6] admit that their development is unique! In comparison of the deuterostome group described, the sea urchin (echinoderm) 32-cell stage consists of five tiers of cells (Fig. 5) resulting from a unique pattern of vertical and horizontal cleavages, and whose subsequent behaviour is peculiar to sea urchins. No such cleavage pattern or series of five tiers are evident in the ascidian embryo at such stages, neither are they seen in any mammals: in eutherian mammals, for example, early cleavage is irregular, and at the 32-cell stage rather than forming five tiers as in the sea urchin, the trophectoderm and ICM can be distinguished (Fig. 6a).

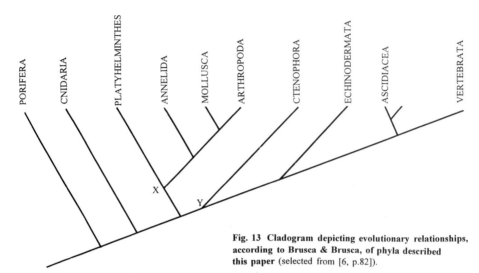

Fig. 13 Cladogram depicting evolutionary relationships, according to Brusca & Brusca, of phyla described this paper (selected from [6, p.82]).

Moreover, fundamental differences in developmental mechanisms are evident in early stages. For example, in ascidians just after fertilisation there is an extensive cytoskeletal-mediated rearrangement of egg cytoplasm, (Section 3.8a) creating distinct cytoplasmic domains unique to this group and which are crucial for later development, including muscle determination. In contrast, such rearrangements are not evident in other deuterostomes such as the echinoderms.

Davidson [9, p.365] has argued convincingly regarding different developmental strategies manifested in various taxa, as is indeed suggested above. He described how spatial patterns may be generated initially: "some embryos begin this process by intercellular interaction, and others even before there are any cells that would carry out such interactions; some rely on lineages that are autonomously committed to given functions as soon as they appear; others deal only in plastic, malleable cell fate assignments; some utilise eggs that before fertilisation are cytoskeletally organised in both axes, some in one axis only, some apparently in neither; for some types of embryos every individual has a different cell lineage, whilst for others there is a set of rigidly reproducible canonical cell lineages; and some embryos display amazing regulative capacities." Thus, he concluded [9, p.366] "the differences among the taxa in their modes of development are anything but trivial and superficial".

Other authors recognise these early differences, but merely relate them to divergence before and after the phylotypic stage stage of embryogenesis, when members of a taxon show maximum similarity, and when the body plan may be generated. Is there evidence for a common ancestry in the phylotypic stages? This has been suggested with reference to a class of genes known as the homeobox, which has been implicated in the specification of relative position within the body. A particular homeobox subset, the *Hox* gene cluster, show a comparable expression pattern in a number of phyla [reviewed in 54]. It has been suggested that the *Hox* and other genes encode relative position in the body form of all animals [54]; this pattern, or zootype, is most clearly expressed at the phylotypic stage. However, the utilisation of the phylotypic stage for hypotheses of evolutionary transformation has its problems. First, the zootype is claimed to be a system of anterior-posterior information which largely does not code for particular structures. However, a closer look at the fate maps at the phylotypic stage compared between various phyla reveals that the structural differences are profound. For example, consider annelids (Fig 8a) and cephalochordates (Fig. 8b). In the latter, even by this phylotypic stage, chordate structures such as the notochord and dorsal neural tube are apparent, whereas these are absent from annelids at or after the phylotypic stage. In the cephalopods, the notochord develops from mesodermal cells whose origin and cell lineage contrast with that of annelids. Second, developmental mechanisms, such as gastrulation, may also be profoundly different between phyla, and indeed if the phylotypic stages of two groups under comparison are at different developmental stages, it is hardly appropriate to compare their developmental mechanisms, since these are frequently stage-specific. Third, to forward the idea of evolutionary transformation during the phylotypic stage is yet again a case of superimposing it on the data. Equally, stages such as the gastrula (the phylotypic stage of some invertebrates) could be a necessary developmental stage for many phyla, just as is cleavage in all metazoa the means of attaining multicellularity! Thus similarity of stage is not necessarily suggestive of common descent: all other possible pathways may be constrained as forbidden or impossible morphologies. Fourth, interest in the phylotypic stage is primarily because, according to Hall [21, p.98] "the phylotypic stage is a search for the physical embodiment of the link between development and evolution". Thus, a developmental plasticity at this period when the basic body plan may be laid down would be open to the generation of evolutionary novelty. However, this may not be a valid claim. What exactly is meant by the laying down of the body plan? In certain phyla such as the molluscs, necessary antecedants to this stage are demonstratably present in the very earliest of stages, even in the uncleaved egg. Therefore the suggested developmental plasticity at the phylotypic stage may be constrained by earlier formative events. Fifth, caution has been urged by some authors concerning the relationship between homeotic genes and body pattern formation. These genes do not necessarily have the same role in different organisms [34], implying other factors may be important in the generation of type-specific patterns. Indeed, different genetic systems are used in arthropods and vertebrates to regulate the *Hox* complexes. The morphogenetic action for the *Hox* genes remains to be demonstrated. Therefore the sweeping assertion that the zootype - an inter-phyla common expression pattern - embodies a common ancestor, remains unjustified. This is even more the case because the molecular basis for the differences in structure and developmental mechanisms between phyla also remain to be established. It may well turn out to be that such differences cannot be reduced to any common ancestral patterns, but that they nevertheless play a central role in morphogenesis.

Another view is that genes do not so much cause or control morphogenesis; they enable it to take place. Indeed, there is a disjunction between DNA content on the one hand and morphological form on the other [15]. According to Bard [2, p.265-6], there have been few studies where the techniques of molecular genetics have been helpful in elucidating morphogenetic mechanisms. He considered that the results of such techniques have been expressed in genotypic rather than phenotypic terms, and it remains a major project for future work to translate the one into the other. Goodwin [16, p.238] added that an understanding of the sequential action of genes and their products is not a model of morphogenesis. Chemical forces, leading to standing waves of morphogens, do give spatial periodicities of the right wavelength, but these are not equivalent to the mechanical forces that generate cell/tissue shape changes during morphogenetic processes such as segmentation, gastrulation or tentacle formation. The genes may define the parameter ranges for a particular form, but the primary cause of morphogenesis may result from the transmission of stress-strain forces in the surface-cytoskeletal matrix, behaving as a visco-elastic gel. This, according to Oster [36] has the mechanical properties capable of generating form during development. Even advocates of the current "genocentric" position recognise that no genes act in isolation, each functioning within an extensive regulatory cascade [25]. The exquisite nature of regulation and processing of DNA sequences is bringing the cytoplasmic machinery responsible for this increasingly centre-stage. The genome is part of an organisation that is integral with the entire cell, and thus, according to Goodwin [15, p.35] "it is the characteristic dynamic order of the whole process that defines the unique characteristics of organismic form".

A resolution to these contrasting paradigms, or further insight into their explanatory value may be provided by the essentialist approach, which recognises distinct morphological types in nature. The development of form peculiar to each type may be the direct consequence of different strategies. It may thus turn out to be that each type manifests a unique mosaic of strategies, some of which may be evident in other types, but not the whole set [12]. The extensive hybridisation data (Section 3.1) is consistent with this idea: several hybridisation matrices have provided an objective provisional demarcation of basic types. Such hybridisations may be possible only between organisms manifesting common ontogenic pathways.

The concept of a common morphological type persists today as the *Bauplan* (*Bau*, design or type of construction; *plan*, pattern). Eldridge [13] defined the Bauplan as the common basic plan within a monophyletic taxon. Until recently, the idea of a gradual progression of structural complexity from a few simple types in the early epochs prevailed. However, the fossil fauna from the Burgess Shale (Lower to Middle Cambrian Period) contain representatives of every modern phylum except the Bryozoa [7]. Gould

[17] stated that in the 500 million years since the Burgess shale flourished, not a single new phylum, or basic anatomical design, has been added to the Burgess complement. Hall [21] asked why this is so. His solution was that the Bauplan may be protected from selection because of tightly interlocking epigenetic interactions. Thus he envisioned common networks of developmental interactions integrated with epigenetic processes preserving the basic body plans as "types".

If there are fundamental mechanisms of morphogenesis such as the generation of the primary body axis, then how are the differences between forms generated? Should there be type-specific mosaics of developmental mechanisms, then data on such mosaics need to be built up, i.e. to extend the knowledge of surface, cytoskeletal, ionic and electro-physico- chemical structure and behaviour both within and between types. A more complete picture of such mosaics may in turn provide a handle upon any more fundamental, and possibly universal, mechanisms of morphogenesis [12].

5. CONCLUSIONS

Early stages of different phyla can be distinguished by unique patterns of cleavage, cell surface characteristics and cellular morphogenetic behaviour. In addition, other embryological criteria such as sperm morphology and egg case structure show type-specific characteristics. Taken together, these data are consistent with the model that states there are types in nature which originally were created. These embryological data can be used as further criteria in the demarcation of such types. In turn the elucidation of type-specific features in early development may provide a handle upon the fundamental processes of the generation of form, which remain elusive.

7. BIBLIOGRAPHY

[1] R.J. Andrew, & D.B. Tembhare, **Surface ultrastructure of the egg chorion in the dragonfly, Ictinigomphus rapax (Rambur) (Odonata: Gomphidae)**, International Journal of Insect Morphology & Embryology, 21:4(1992) 347-350.

[2] J. Bard, **Morphogenesis**, 1990, Cambridge University Press, England.

[3] R. Bourrillon, & M. Aubery, **Cell surface glycoproteins in embryonic development**, International Review of Cytology, 116(1989) 257-338.

[4] R.H. Brady, **On the independence of systematics**, Cladistics, 1(1985) 113-126.

[5] L.W. Browder, C.A. Erickson & W.R. Jeffery, Developmental Biology, 1991, Saunders College Publishing, Philadelphia & London.

[6] R.C. Brusca, & G.J. Brusca, **Invertebrates**, 1990, Sinauer, Sunderland, Massachusetts, USA.

[7] S. Conway Morris, & H.B. Whittington, **Fossils of the Burgess shale. A national treasure in Yoho National Park, British Columbia**, Geological Survey of Canada Miscellaneous Reports 43(1985) 1-31.

[8] D.P. Costello, & C. Henley, **Spiralian development: a perspective**, American Zoologist 16(1976) 277-291.

[9] E.H. Davidson, **How embryos work: a comparative view of diverse modes of cell fate specification**, Development 108(1990) 365-389.

[10] M. Denton, Evolution: a Theory in Crisis, 1985, Addler & Addler, Bethesda, Maryland.

[11] M.R. Dohmen, & J.C.A. van der Mey, **Local surface differentiations at the vegetal pole of the eggs of Nassarius reticulatus, Buccinum undatum, and Crepidula fornicata. (Gastropoda, Prosobranchia)**, Developmental Biology 61(1977) 104-113.

[12] S.E.B. Eisaks, Cell surface studies of mollusc eggs, 1993, PhD Thesis, Manchester University, England.

[13] N. Eldredge, Macroevolutionary dynamics: species, niches and adaptive peaks, 1989, McGraw-Hill Co., New York.

[14] V. Fretter, & A. Graham, British Prosobranch Molluscs, 1962, The Ray Society, Bartholemew Press.

[15] B.C. Goodwin, **What are the causes of morphogenesis?** Bioessays, 3:1(1985) 32-36.

[16] B.C. Goodwin, **Structuralism in Biology**, Science Progress, (1990) 227-243.

[17] S.J. Gould, Wonderful life. The Burgess Shale and the nature of history, 1989, W.W. Norton & Co., New York.

[18] P.R. Grant, & B.R. Grant, **Hybridization of bird species**, Science, 256(1992) 193-197.

[19] C.M. Griffith, & E.J. Sanders, **Changes in glycoconjugate expression during early chick embryo development**, Anatomical Record, 231(1991) 238-250.

[20] B.J. Gulyas, **A reexamination of the cleavage patterns in eutherian mammalian eggs: rotation of the blastomere pairs during second cleavage in the rabbit**, Journal of Experimental Zoology, 193(1975) 235-248.

[21] B.K. Hall, Evolutionary developmental biology, 1992, Chapman & Hall, London.

[22] S. Hartwig-Scherer, **Hybridisierung und Artbildung bei den Meerkatzenartigen (Primates, Cercopithecoidea)**, in Typen Des Lebens, S. Scherer, Editor, 1993, Pascal-Verlag, Berlin, 245-257.

[23] S. Horstadius, **Nemertinae**, in Experimental Embryology of Marine and Freshwater Invertebrates, G. Reverberi, Editor, 1971, North Holland, Amsterdam.

[24] A.N. Hodgson, & G.G. Foster, **Structure of the sperm of some South African archaeogastropods (Mollusca) from the superfamilies *Haliotidea, Fissurelloidea and Trochoidea*.** Marine Biology, 113(1992) 89-97.

[25] H.R. Horvitz & I. Herskowitz, **Mechanisms of Asymmetric Cell Division: Two Bs or Not Two Bs, That Is the Question**, Cell, 68(1992) 237-255.

[26] O.M. Ivanova-Kazas, [Uniformity of cell fates.] Soviet Journal of Marine Biology, 75(1982) 275-283, Cited in [6].

[27] K.E. Johnson, & E.P. Smith, **The binding of concanavalin A to dissociated embryonic amphibian cells**, Experimental Cell Research, 101(1976) 63-70.

[28] A.R. Jones, **A general analysis of the Biblical kind (min)**, Creation Research Science Quarterly, 9:1(1972) 53-57.

[29] J. Kawana, & T. Takami, **Insecta**, in Invertebrate Embryology M. Kume & K. Dan, Editors, 1968, NOLIT Pub. Co., Belgrade, Yugoslavia, pp.405-484.

[30] E.Kniprath, **Ontogeny of the molluscan shell field**, Zoologica Scripta, 10(1981) 61-79.

[31] P. Landgren, **On the origin of "species". Ideological roots of the species concept**, in Typen des Lebens, S. Scherer, Editor, 1993, Pascal-Verlag, Berlin, 47-64.

[32] L.H. Margaritis, **Structure and physiology of eggshell**, 1985, cited in [1], pp.153-230.

[33] D. Mossakowski, **Hybridzonen an Artgrenzen: Regelfall oder Ausnahme in der Zoologie?** in Evolution im Terreich, B. Streit, Editor, 1993, Birkhauser, Basel, pp.201-222. Cited in [48].

[34] H.F. Nijhout, **Metaphors and the role of genes in development**, Bioessays, 12(1990) 441-445.

[35] D.S. O'Dell, R. Tencer, A. Monroy, & J. Brachet, **The pattern of concanavalin A-binding sites during the early development of *Xenopus laevis***, Cell Differentiation, 3(1974) 193-198.

[36] G.F. Oster, G. Odell & P. Alberch, **Mechanics, morphogenesis and evolution**, in Lectures on Mathematics in the Life Sciences G. Oster, Editor, 1980, American Mathematics Society, Providence, R.I., USA.

[37] E.N. Panov, **Natural hybridisation and ethological isolation in birds**, 1993, Nauka, Moscow. Cited in [48].

[38] C. Patterson, **Morphological characters and homology**, in Problems of phylogenetic Reconstruction, K.A. Joysey & A.E. Friday, Editors, 1982, Academic Press, New York, pp.1-74.

[39] W.J. Remine, **Discontinuity systematics: A new methodology of biosystematics relevant to the creation model**, in Proceedings of the 2nd International Conference on Creationism, R.E. Walsh & C.L. Brooks, Editors, 1990, Creation Science Fellowship, Inc., Pittsburgh, PA, Vol.2, pp.207-213.

[40] G. Reverberi, **Crustacea**, in Experimental Embryology of Marine and Freshwater Invertebrates, G. Reverberi, Editor, North Holland, Amsterdam.

[41] R.J. Richards, The meaning of evolution, 1992, University of Chicago Press, Chicago & London.

[42] O.C. Rieppel, Fundamentals of comparative biology, 1988, Birkhauser Verlag, Basel.

[43] R. Robertson, **Marine prosobranch gastropods: larval studies and systematics**, Thalassia Jugoslavia, 10(1974) 213-23

[44] A. Rosenberg, The structure of biological science, 1985, Cambridge University Press, Cambridge.

[45] C. Sardet, D. Carre, & C. Rouviere, **Reproduction and development in ctenophores**, in Experimental Embryology in Aquatic Plants and Animals, H.-J. Marthy, Editor, 1990, Plenum Press, New York.

[46] S. Scherer, & T. Hilsberg, **Hybridisation and relationships in the Anatidae - a taxonomic and evolutionary consideration**, Journal für Ornithologie, 123(1982) 357-380.

[47] S. Scherer, **On the limits of variability: evidence and speculation from morphology, genetics and molecular biology**. in Concepts in Creationism, E.H. Andrews, W. Gitt & W.J. Ouweneel), Editors, pp.219-240. Evangelical Press, Welwyn, England, pp.219-240.

[48] S. Scherer, **Basic types of life**, in Typen des Lebens, S. Scherer, Editor, 1993, Pascal-Verlag, Berlin, pp.11-30.

[49] T.E. Schroeder, **The Egg Cortex in Early Development of Sea Urchins and Starfish**, in: Developmental Biology, Vol. 2, The Cellular Basis of Morphogenesis, L.W. Browder, Editor, 1985, pp.59-97. Plenum Press, New York & London.

[50] L. Selwood, **Mechanisms underlying the development of pattern in marsupial embryos**. Current Topics in Developmental Biology, 27(1992) 175-233.

[51] N. Sharon & H. Lis, **Carbohydrates in Cell Recognition**, Scientific American, 268:1(1993) 74-81.

[52] N.H. Shubin, & P. Alberch, **A morphogenetic approach to the origin and basic organisation of the tetrapod limb**, in Evolutionary Biology, 20(1986) 319-387.

[53] J. M. Slack, From Egg to Embryo, 1991, Cambridge University Press, Cambridge.

[54] J.M.W. Slack, P.W.H. Holland, & C.F. Graham, **The zootype and the phylotypic stage**. Nature, 361(1993) 490-492.

[55] J.E. Speksnijder, M.R. Dohmen, L.G.J. Tertoolen, & de S.W. Laat, Regional differences in the lateral mobility of plasma membrane lipids in a molluscan embryo, Developmental Biology, 110(1985) 207-216.

[56] H. Stein-Cadenbach, **Hybriden, Chromosomen, und Artbildung bei Pferden (Equidae)**, in Typen des Lebens, S. Scherer, Editor, 1993, Pascal-Verlag, Berlin, 225-244.

[57] R.D.K. Thomas, & W.E. Reif, **The skeleton space: a finite set of organic designs**, Evolution, 47(1993) 341-360.

[58] N.H. Verdonk, & J.A.M. Van den Biggelaar, **Early development and the formation of the germ layers**, in The Mollusca: Volume 3. Development, N.H. Verdonk, J.A.M. Van den Biggelaar & A.S. Tompa, Editors, 1983, Academic Press, New York, pp. 91-122.

[59] G. Webster, **The relations of natural forms**, in Beyond Neo-Darwinism, M.-W. Ho & P.T. Saunders, Editors, 1984, Academic Press, London, pp.193-217.

[60] K. Wise, (1990). **Baraminology: a young-earth creation biosystematic method**, in Proceedings of the 2nd International Conference on Creationism, R.E. Walsh & C.L. Brooks, Editors, Creation Science Fellowship, Inc., Pittsburgh, PA, Vol.2, pp.345-360.

[61] K. Wise, **Practical Baraminology**, Creation Ex Nihilo Techical Journal, 6:2(1992) 122-137.

[62] I. Yotsutani, S. Niimura, & K. Ishida, **Changes in glycoconjugates on the cell surface of mouse embryos in the course of blastocyst formation: a lectin histochemistry**, Journal of Reproduction & Development, 38:1(1992) 29-33.

AN ANALYTIC YOUNG-EARTH FLOW MODEL
OF ICE SHEET FORMATION DURING THE "ICE AGE"

LARRY VARDIMAN, Ph.D.
Institute for Creation Research
10946 Woodside Avenue N.
Santee, California 92071

KEYWORDS (Flow model, Ice, Ice sheet, Ice Age, Ice cores, Climate, Glaciers, Glaciology)

ABSTRACT

Traditional interpretations of ice layers in polar regions have partially relied upon ice flow models which assume similar accumulation rates as those observed today and accumulation periods exceeding 100,000 years. If the Genesis Flood occurred less than 10,000 years ago and ice began to accumulate afterward at a high rate, decreasing to today's value, a different flow model would be needed and a completely different interpretation would result. This paper describes the development of such an analytic young-earth flow model of ice-sheet formation.

The model assumes that a sheet of ice accumulates snow on its upper surface and grows rapidly following the Flood. The accumulation rate is assumed to be ten times today's rate near the end of the Flood, decreasing to that observed today. The thickness of the ice sheet is then a function of the accumulation rate, the thinning caused by the weight of the accumulated ice, and the time since it was laid down. The thickness of the Greenland ice sheet at Camp Century and the position of annual layers are calculated as a function of time, assuming the Flood occurred 4,500 years ago. The position of ice layers are applied to the oxygen 18 record and compared to the traditional distribution of oxygen 18 versus time.

This alternative young-earth model compresses the Pleistocene record of oxygen 18 into a period of less than 500 years and expands the Holocene record into a period of about 4,000 years. This is in major contrast to the traditional model of hundreds of millennia for the pleistocene and about 10,000 years for the Holocene. If the Flood occurred 4,500 years ago, as assumed in this model, there would have been a quick "Ice Age" of less than 500 years. The oxygen 18 concentration would have decreased from a high value at the end of the Flood to a minimum 200-300 years later. It then would have increased rapidly from the minimum to the stable Holocene period in about 50 years. This latter change is in excellent agreement with the 40-year period of the Younger Dryas to the pre-boreal boundary suggested by several paleoclimatologists.

INTRODUCTION

A commonly used method for identifying the age of ice layers in an ice sheet is to calculate the age-depth relationships of the ice core by developing a mathematical model that incorporates a generally accepted flow theory and reasonable assumptions concerning the parameters that influence it. Dansgaard et al. [5] and Dansgaard et al. [6] have applied this technique to the Camp Century, Greenland core, and Lorius et al. [12,13] to the Dome C Antarctic core.

Fig. 1 shows a vertical section of an ice sheet resting on bedrock. The ice divide (a topographic feature from which ice diverges) is denoted by I-I. The ice deposited on the surface at location I is buried by succeeding snowfalls, and sinks into the ice sheet. At the same time, the layers accumulated annually become thinner by plastic deformation, as the ice flows horizontally outward from the ice divide. The core from Camp Century is shown at C-C. It contains ice formed upstream from Camp Century under similar environmental conditions. The horizontal, upper-surface velocity of the ice at Camp Century is 3.3 meters per year and, therefore, even a 15,000-year-old deep section of the ice core would originate less than 50 kilometers further inland, if it has been moving at a constant rate.

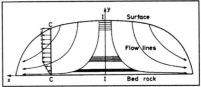

Figure 1 *Flow model of ice flowing outward from an ice divide as described by Dansgaard et al. [6].*

CLASSICAL FLOW MODELS

Several attempts have been made to develop a flow model at Camp Century. Nye [14] derived a simple relationship between the position of a layer in the ice sheet and the time since the snow fell to become ice. He assumed an infinite sheet of ice of uniform thickness with snow accumulating on its upper surface at a constant rate. He also assumed that the horizontal velocity of flow away from the ice divide was constant with depth and the ice sheet was free to slide on the bottom surface. His final result is:

$$\Delta t = -\frac{H\tau}{\lambda_H}\int_H^y\frac{dy}{y} = \frac{H\tau}{\lambda_H}\ln\frac{H}{y} \tag{1}$$

where Δt is the elapsed time since ice at a give depth fell as fresh snow (i.e., the age of a given layer), H is the total thickness of the ice sheet, τ is the accumulation period (typically one year), λ_H is the amount of snow which accumulates over the accumulation period, and y is the height above the bottom of the ice sheet.

Recognizing that Nye's model [14] was inadequate for Camp Century, particularly because of the assumption of sliding on the bottom surface, Dansgaard et al. [6] used a stress-and-strain relationship, called Glen's Law, to develop a more realistic model. The results are:

$$\Delta t = \frac{(2H-h)\tau}{2\lambda_H}\ln\frac{2H-h}{2y-h} \; ; \quad h \le y \le H \tag{2}$$

$$\Delta t = t_h + \frac{(2H-h)\tau}{2\lambda_H}\left(\frac{h}{y} - 1\right) \; ; \quad 0 < y \le h \tag{3}$$

where Δt, H, τ, and λ_H are defined in the same manner as Equation 1, h is the height above the bottom of the ice sheet at which the horizontal velocity becomes uniform with height as the ice sheet flows away from the ice divide, and t_h is the age of the ice at height, h.

This flow model can be applied to data acquired from various ice cores to estimate the age of various levels in the ice sheet. Fig. 2 shows the measured values of $\delta^{18}O$ versus depth for Camp Century, Greenland. Note the relatively uniform $\delta^{18}O$ values from the surface to approximately 1000 meters depth. Below 1000 meters, the values decrease suddenly and then slowly increase again to a depth of 1370 meters. The uniform region is typically identified as the Holocene epoch. The maximum extent of the "last Ice Age" calculated to have occurred at about 18,000 B.P. by long-age modelers, is typically identified with the "valley" at the bottom of the record.

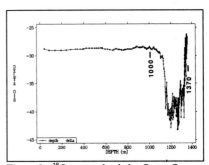

Figure 2 $\delta^{18}O$ *versus depth for Camp Century, Greenland.*

Fig. 3 shows the measured values of $\delta^{18}O$ versus the calculated values of time from Equations 2 and 3. Note how the data between 1000 and 1370 meters have been expanded dramatically in this process. In fact, the data near the bottom are stretched the most, as would be expected from the inverse y relationship in Equation 3. Markers have been placed on Figs. 2 and 3 at 1000 and 1370 meter depths to illustrate the stretching effect of the long-age time model. Time approaches infinity, as y approaches 0. The oldest ice near the bottom of the Camp Century core is estimated by Johnsen et al. [11] to be over 120,000 years old.

Other long-age time models have been developed, but most have very similar characteristics as those of Nye [14] and Dansgaard et al. [6]. Some allow the accumulation rate to vary, but only to a small degree, depending on estimated precipitation formation temperatures derived from δ^{18}O measurements. One of the most difficult problems the long-age model must explain is how more snow accumulates during an "Ice Age" when the temperature is colder. For example, see Alley et al. [2] where evidence is given that the accumulation rate of snow doubled at the end of the Younger Dryas event when the "Ice Age" was rapidly coming to an end. Colder temperatures lead to lower accumulation rates because of the Clausius-Clapeyron Equation (See Hess [9, p.46]).

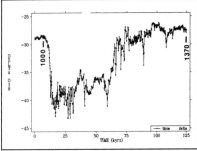

Figure 3 δ^{18}O *versus long-age model time.*

Recent cores from Greenland have been analyzed with greater precision than earlier cores using stratigraphic techniques. The primary method of estimating the age of layers is to count annual layers. Dansgaard et al. [4] claim to be able to count annual layers downward from the surface back to 14,500 years before present. Validation of these claims must wait for release of the raw data, expected in 1995.

A YOUNG-EARTH FLOW MODEL

In both of the long-age models which we have discussed above, it was assumed that new snow has been accumulating on the top of the ice sheet, at an average rate of λ_H/τ, without interruption or significant perturbation for an infinite amount of time in the past. It is this uniformitarian assumption which gives rise to the very great ages for the bottom ice (infinite age at the very bottom) which these models yield. This assumption of uninterrupted conditions similar to those observed at present is not appropriate for a Biblical, global-flood model of the past. In particular, we would expect the oldest layers of ice to post-date the Flood (i.e. have a finite age), and climatological considerations, based on the work of Oard [15,16], suggest that the annual accumulation of snow would have been much greater than the presently observed value, λ_H, in the early years following the Flood. To illustrate what can happen when assumptions which are more in line with a Flood model are used, consider the following simple flow model, discussed by Vardiman [17].

Assume that a sheet of ice of thickness, H, accumulates snow on its upper surface at a rate of λ/τ meters/year, where λ is the accumulation in meters over a time period τ in years. In this case we will not assume that the ice sheet is in mass balance, but, rather, that it grows rapidly following the Flood, and later slowly approaches the equilibrium condition observed today. This means that λ and H are functions of time, rather than being constant as the uniformitarian model requires. In fact, at the end of this derivation, λ will be assumed to be ten times the accumulation rate observed today and H will be assumed to be 0 at $t = 0$, the end of the Flood. A more complex model could be considered in the future, in which H is equal to 0 for some period after the Flood, until the temperature is cold enough for snow to begin to accumulate. The thickness of the ice sheet is then a function of the accumulation rate and the rate of thinning. The conventional long-age model developed a flow regime based on a two-dimensional assumption of incompressibility. However, in this model, I will use a linear-thinning function which is calibrated by the observed compression in the upper 4000 layers. In other words, the compression of an ice layer will be proportional to the thickness of the ice sheet.

This simple model can then be expressed as:

$$\frac{dH}{dt} = \lambda/\tau - \delta H \qquad (4)$$

where H is the thickness of the ice sheet in meters as a function of time, t is the time since the Flood in years, τ is the accumulation period in years, λ is the accumulation over the accumulation period in meters, and δ is the thinning ratio in year^{-1}. The thinning ratio is a constant and will be determined by the boundary conditions imposed on Eq. 4.

Eq. 4 says that the rate of change in the thickness of the ice sheet is the difference between the accumulation rate of snow, falling on the upper surface and the compression of the ice sheet which is linearly proportional to its thickness. This model assumes a linear thinning function which may not always be the case, particularly when the stress and strain are outside the elastic limits. Non-linear thinning may occur when the ice is melting, during massive surging, or when the underlying terrain constrains horizontal motions.

Before we can solve Eq. 4, we need to assume a functional form for λ. We have reason to believe, from our Flood model, that immediately following the Flood the oceans were warm and the continents and polar regions cold, compared to that of today as discussed by Oard [15,16] and Vardiman [17, 18]. If this was the case, the precipitation rate likely would have been much greater than that of today, and would have decreased with time. We will assume an exponentially decreasing accumulation function, which approaches today's rate in the limit. For this initial model, we will further assume that the accumulation rate at the end of the Flood was ten times that of today.

The functional form of λ described in the preceding paragraph is:

$$\lambda = \lambda_H (Ce^{-\alpha t} + 1) \tag{5}$$

where λ_H is the accumulation over a period of interest observed today, C is a constant, t is the time since the Flood, and α is the relaxation time for the decrease in accumulation since the Flood. The relaxation time will be determined by the shape of the distribution of layers to be explored shortly. Note that when $t = 0$ in Eq. 5, $\lambda = (C+1)\lambda_H$ and when $t = \infty$, $\lambda = \lambda_H$.

Combining Eqs. 4 and 5 and arranging into a standard form for solution of a linear, time-dependent differential equation gives:

$$\frac{dH}{dt} + \delta H = \frac{\lambda_H}{\tau}(Ce^{-\alpha t} + 1) \tag{6}$$

The solution to this equation is:

$$H = \frac{\lambda_H}{\tau\delta}(1 - e^{-\delta t}) + \frac{C\lambda_H}{\tau(\delta-\alpha)}(e^{-\alpha t} - e^{-\delta t}) \tag{7}$$

Note that Eq. 7 satisfies the boundary condition that $H = 0$ when $t = 0$. By applying another boundary condition, δ can be determined. Assume that $H = 1370$ meters when $t = \infty$, and $C = 9$, so that $C+1=10$ and $\lambda = \lambda_H$. Under this condition, Eq. 7 reduces to:

$$H (t = \infty) = \frac{\lambda_H}{\tau\delta} = 1370 \ m \tag{8}$$

or:

$$\delta = \frac{\lambda_H}{(1370 \ m)(\tau)} = 2.55 \times 10^{-4} \ year^{-1} \tag{9}$$

This value of the thinning function, δ, implies that the thickness of the entire ice sheet decreases by the same amount as the annual accumulation on the surface and an annual layer proportional to its thickness. This thinning function equals 8.09×10^{-12} s^{-1} when converted to standard SI units.

The thinning function is similar to a strain rate. Strain rates have been measured for ice by Higashi et al. [10] and reported in Fletcher [7, p. 189]. The strain rate in ice at -15°C under a stress of 1 bar (10^6 dynes/cm^2) exceeds 1×10^{-7} s^{-1}. This is over 4 orders of magnitude greater than the thinning function calculated above. In addition, the stress beneath a 1000-meter thick layer of ice is 88 bars, greatly exceeding the test conditions of Higashi [6]. Therefore, the calculated thinning function used in this model is much less than ice would permit under such high stress. It is likely that ice sheets could "thin" even faster than this model indicates and much faster under other hypothetical conditions. "Ice Rivers" moving at rates exceeding 1 km per year have been observed in Antarctica and it has been suggested by several investigators that ice sheets and glaciers could move laterally at high speeds if the edges are moving into deep water. The release of lateral stresses could permit the vertical thinning function to be much greater.

The rapid movement of the edges of ice sheets to form "lobes" and extensions of ice coverage tens or hundreds of kilometers away from accumulation centers is an important element of "Ice Age" research which needs investigation. Rapid accumulation of snow and ice after the Genesis Flood mixed with volcanic particulates and impurities could be a significant factor in thinning of ice sheets and lateral motions. Rapid melting during deglaciation and frequent earthquakes could cause sudden slippage at the base and rapid spreading of ice equatorward. It is conceivable that the polar oceans could have been filled with ice shelves and icebergs from ice sheets sliding rapidly into the ocean during deglaciation.

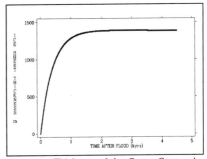

Figure 4 *Thickness of the Camp Century ice sheet as a function of time after the Flood.*

Fig. 4 shows the thickness of the Camp Century, Greenland ice sheet, H, plotted as a function of time since the Flood for a certain selection of parameters. In this case, $\lambda_H = .35$ m, $\tau = 1$ year, $\delta = 2.55 \times 10^{-4}$ year^{-1}, $\alpha = .0025$ ($1/\alpha = 400$ years), and the time since the Flood $t = 4,500$ years. Note that H starts at 0, increases rapidly, and asymptotically approaches today's thickness of 1370 meters. For larger values of α, the asymptotic approach to today's value is slower.

Fig. 4 illustrates the behavior of the entire thickness of the ice sheet, and deals primarily with the topmost layer. However, when ice cores are drilled down through the ice sheet today, we can measure the position of earlier layers which were formed and then buried. This additional information should help us develop a better estimate of the thinning function.

If we consider a given layer within the ice sheet, can we determine from this model how far it has moved downward since it was formed? If we assume that the rate of movement of an ice layer downward is proportional to the thickness of the ice sheet and the position of a layer relative to the total thickness, we obtain:

$$V_y = \frac{dy}{dt} = -\delta \frac{y}{H_0} H(t) \qquad (10)$$

where V_y is the vertical velocity of an ice layer relative to the base of the ice sheet, y is the position of a layer, δ is the thinning ratio defined earlier, H is the total thickness of the ice sheet as a function of time, and H_0 is the total thickness today.

Now, at first, one might be tempted to define the downward velocity of a layer as proportional to the thickness of ice above the layer. However, it should be noted that the weight of the entire ice sheet is responsible for the movement of a given layer, because the rate at which the ice beneath a layer thins, allowing the layer to move downward, is dependent on the total thickness. Obviously, the preferable manner of deriving V_y would be to have a complete, time-dependent flow model showing the full two-dimensional movement of ice as a function of depth. This is not easily determined, so my model will assume a simple relationship for this first effort.

Eq. 10 says that the velocity of a layer is downward following its deposition and is proportional to the total thickness of the ice sheet. However, the factor, y/H_0, causes the downward velocity to increase linearly from 0 at the bottom of the ice sheet to a maximum at the top. The bottom is assumed to be 0, because it rests on bedrock. The upper layers will subside faster, because of the accumulating compression.

Transposing Eq. 10 results in:

$$\frac{dy}{y} = -\delta \frac{H(t)}{H_0} dt \qquad (11)$$

Substituting $H(t)$ from Eq. 7 and integrating to find the change in position, y, of an ice layer over the period of time since it was laid down, gives:

$$\int_{y_i}^{y} \frac{dy}{y} = -\int_{0}^{\Delta t} \frac{\delta}{H_0} [\frac{\lambda_H}{\tau \delta}(1 - e^{-\delta \tau}) + \frac{C\lambda_H}{\tau(\delta-\alpha)}(e^{-\alpha t} - e^{-\delta \tau})]dt \tag{12}$$

where y_i is the initial position of the layer when it was deposited, y is the position of the layer as a function of time after it was deposited, and Δt is the age of the layer.

Solving for y:

$$y = y_i \, e^{-\frac{\delta}{H_0}[\frac{\lambda_H}{\tau \delta}A + \frac{9\lambda_H}{\tau(\delta-\alpha)}B]} \tag{13}$$

where:

$$A = \Delta t + \frac{1}{\delta}(e^{-\delta \Delta t} - 1)$$

$$B = -\alpha(e^{-\alpha \Delta t} - 1) + \frac{1}{\delta}(e^{-\delta \Delta t} - 1)$$

Note that Eq. 13 says that $y = y_i$ for $\Delta t = 0$. This means that the topmost layer, which is deposited today, 4,500 years after the Flood, has not yet begun to subside. Because the first layer at the end of the Flood was deposited at the position, $y_i = 0$, its position, y, will always be equal to 0. Between the Flood and today, each layer will subside a varying amount, dependent upon the total thickness of the ice sheet, its position relative to the bottom of the sheet, and the length of time from its deposition until today.

Fig. 5 shows the position of each annual layer at Camp Century as a function of time since the Flood. As the old top layer is covered by the new winter's snow, the new surface is assigned a higher vertical position. However, with time each layer subsides an amount dependent upon the time since its formation and the total depth of the ice sheet. Fig. 5 is then the height of each annual layer as a function of time after the Flood. The curve shows the greatest rate of change in layer position during the first 1,000 years after the Flood. This is due to the large change in snowfall rate immediately after the Flood. The decrease in accumulation was assumed to be exponential with a 400 year e-folding time. The top layer of the ice sheet will be precipitated at smaller increments above the preceeding layers, and will be particularly noticeable immediately after the Flood. The curve is slightly concave upward during the last 3,000 years or so. This is due to the decreasing period of time available for the ice sheet to thin, as the top of the ice sheet is approached. At the very top, the most recent layer has not had time to thin at all, and its position is the same as the thickness of the ice sheet.

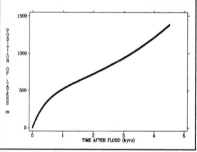

Figure 5 *Position of ice layers at Camp Century as a function of time after the Flood.*

AGE ESTIMATES OF ICE LAYERS

The curve in Fig. 5 can be used to estimate the age of the ice as a function of depth for a measured distribution of $\delta^{18}O$ versus depth, such as in Fig. 2. Unfortunately, Eq. 13, which is the basis of Fig. 5, will not allow Δt, the age of a layer, to be solved analytically. If one wishes to determine the age of a layer at a known depth, either the age must be determined graphically from Fig. 5 or a numerical analysis method must be applied to Eq. 13. The latter method was used in this work.

An iterative numerical approximation method was applied to Eq. 13 to unfold the $\delta^{18}O$ versus depth relationship for Camp Century data shown in Fig. 2 and obtain $\delta^{18}O$ versus time. The result is shown in Fig. 6. Note, that the general shape of the curve of $\delta^{18}O$ versus the young-earth model time has the same general shape as the curve of $\delta^{18}O$ versus depth shown in Fig. 2. This is in major contrast to that of the long-age model shown in Fig. 3, which compresses the data near the top of the ice sheet and dramatically stretches the data near the bottom.

If the Flood occurred 4,500 years ago, as suggested in the young-earth model, there would have been a quick "Ice Age" of about 500 years. This is in good agreement with the estimate of 500 years or so by Oard [15,16] for the formation of the Canadian ice sheets. The $\delta^{18}O$ would have decreased from a high value at the end of the Flood to a minimum about 200-300 years later. The $\delta^{18}O$ would have then increased rapidly from this minimum to the stable Holocene period over a very short time interval. This latter change is in excellent agreement with the 40 year transition period of the Younger Dryas event to the pre-boreal boundary reported by Hammer et al. [8] or even the extremely short 5-year period reported by Alley et al. [3].

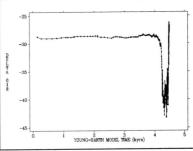

Figure 6 $\delta^{18}O$ *versus young-earth model time after the Flood for Camp Century, Greenland.*

CONCLUSIONS AND RECOMMENDATIONS

Fig. 6 is the result of assuming a relatively high precipitation rate following the Flood about 4,500 years ago. Several additional parameters were incorporated into the model, most of which were determined by given boundary conditions. However, it may be possible to derive an equally valid model with different assumptions. For example, if the Flood is assumed to have occurred 14,000 years ago, as Aardsma [1] has suggested, the model would likely assume a slightly different form.

Detailed confirmation of this model was not attempted in this report. Such an effort would require considerably more research than is reported here. The purpose of this paper is to lay the general framework of an alternative model and demonstrate that a young-earth model can be formulated. One of the next efforts needed to improve this model should be to compare the observable annual layers in the upper portion of the ice sheet with the model predictions. Adjustments will likely need to be made to the parameterization based on the degree of fit between observations and predictions. Another major effort should be the development of a non-steady-state flow model. The current one-dimensional compression model may be correct, but will likely need refinement. Finally, the model should be expanded to explain other sites on Greenland and Antarctica. Of particular interest will be the forthcoming data from the Greenland Ice Sheet Project (GISP2), previewed by Alley et al. [3].

Even with all the caveates about the current model and hopes for improvements in the future, it seems likely that Fig. 6 is closer to reality than the plot of $\delta^{18}O$ versus the long-age time model shown in Fig. 3. At the least, the young-earth model presented here is a legitimate alternative to the long-age model. It is internally consistent and capable of validation or refutation.

BIBLIOGRAPHY

[1]   G.E. Aardsma, Radiocarbon and the Genesis Flood, 1991, ICR Monograph, San Diego, 82pp.

[2]   R.B. Alley, D.A. Meese, C.A. Shuman, A.J. Gow, K.C. Taylor, P.M. Grootes, J.W.C. White, M. Ram, E.D. Waddington, P.A. Mayewski, and G.A. Zielinski, **Abrupt Increase in Greenland Snow Accumulation at the End of the Younger Dryas Event**, 1993, Nature, 362, 527-529.

[3]   R.B. Alley, C.A. Shuman, D. Meese, A.J. Gow, K. Taylor, M. Ram, E.D. Waddington, and P.A. Mayewski, **An Old, Long, Abrupt Younger Dryas Event in the GISP2 Ice Core**, 1992, Proceedings of the 1992 Fall Meeting of the American Geophysical Union, San Francisco.

[4]   W. Dansgaard, S.J. Johnsen, H.B. Clausen, D. Dahl-Jensen, N.S. Gundestrup, C.U. Hammer, C.S. Hvidberg, J.P. Steffensen, A.E. Sveinbjornsdottir, J. Jouzel, and G. Bond, **Evidence for General Instability of Past Climate from a 250-kyr Ice-Core Record**, 1993, Nature, 364, 218-220.

[5]   W. Dansgaard, S.J. Johnsen, J. Møller, and C.C. Langway, Jr., **One Thousand Centuries of Climatic Record from Camp Century on the Greenland Ice Sheet**, 1969, Science, 166, 377-381.

[6]   W. Dansgaard, S.J. Johnsen, H.B. Clausen, and C.C. Langway, Jr., **Climatic Record Revealed by the Camp Century Ice Core**, in Late Cenozoic Glacial Ages, ed., K.K. Turekian, Yale University Press, New Haven and London, 606 pp.

[7]   N.H. Fletcher, The Chemical Physics of Ice, 1970, Cambridge University Press, London, 271 pp.

[8]   C.U. Hammer, H.B. Clausen, and H. Tauber, **Ice-core Dating of the Pleistocene/Holocene Boundary Applied to a Calibration of the ^{14}C Time Scale**, 1986, Radiocarbon, 28, 284-291.

[9]   S.L. Hess, Introduction to Theoretical Meteorology, 1959, Holt, Rinehart, and Winston, New York, 362 pp.

[10]   A. Higashi, S. Koinuma, and S. Mae, **Plastic Yielding in Ice Single Crystals**, Japanese Journal of Applied Physics, 1964, 3, 610-616.

[11]   S.J. Johnsen, W. Dansgaard, H.B. Clausen, and C.C. Langway, Jr., **Oxygen Isotope Profiles through the Antarctic and Greenland Ice Sheets**, 1972, Nature, 235, 429-434.

[12]   C. Lorius, L. Merlivat, J. Jouzel, and M. Pourchet, **A 30,000-yr Isotope Climatic Record from Antarctic Ice**, 1979, Nature, 280, 644.

[13]   C. Lorius, C.J. Jouzel, C. Ritz, L. Merlivat, N.I. Barkov, Y.S. Korotkevich, and V.M. Kotlyakov, **A 150,000-year Climatic Record from Antarctic Ice, 1985**, Nature, 316, 591.

[14]   J.F. Nye, **The Motion of Ice Sheets and Glaciers**, 1959, Journal of Glaciology, 3, 493.

[15]   M.J. Oard, **An Ice Age within the Biblical Time Frame**, in Proceedings of the First International Conference on Creationism, Vol. II, 1986, R.E. Walsh, C.L. Brooks, and R.S. Crowells, eds., Creation Science Fellowship, Pittsburgh, 157-161.

[16]   M.J. Oard, An Ice Age Caused by the Genesis Flood, 1990, ICR Monograph, San Diego, 243 pp.

[17]   L. Vardiman, Ice Cores and the Age of the Earth, 1992, ICR Monograph, San Diego, 80 pp.

[18]   L. Vardiman, **A Conceptual Transition Model of the Atmospheric Global Circulation Following the Genesis Flood**, 1994, In Press, Proceedings of the Third International Conference on Creationism.

A CONCEPTUAL TRANSITION MODEL
OF THE ATMOSPHERIC GLOBAL CIRCULATION
FOLLOWING THE GENESIS FLOOD

LARRY VARDIMAN, Ph.D.
Institute for Creation Research
10946 Woodside Avenue N.
Santee, California 92071

KEYWORDS (Circulation, Atmospheric Circulation, General Circulation, Global Circulation, Hadley Circulation, Model, Conceptual Model, Wind, Storms, Hurricanes, Ice Age, Genesis Flood, Climate, Weather)

ABSTRACT

The extremely energetic events of the Genesis Flood likely would have left the oceans warmer than today and relatively uniform from top to bottom and from equator to pole. Volcanic activity during and following the Flood likely would have caused rapid cooling at the top of the atmosphere, in polar regions, and over continents. The contrast between the warm oceans and cooler continents and polar regions would have resulted in greater storminess and a more intense global atmospheric circulation than observed today. This paper describes a conceptual model of the transition in global circulation, cloudiness, and precipitation from the end of the Flood to that of today. The model will be applied specifically to the interpretation of the ice core record at Camp Century, Greenland.

INTRODUCTION

The catastrophic events of the Flood described in Genesis 6-9 are almost unimaginable. In order for man and all land-breathing animals to have been destroyed in the Flood, the entire surface of the earth would have been devastated. The layers of sedimentary rock covering most of the earth, containing millions of fossils are mute testimony to this event. Scripture says that flood waters covered the highest mountains. If this was the case, many other major geological events also occurred: mountains rose up; valleys were carved out by receding flood waters; volcanoes spewed lava and dust over vast areas; forests were buried; and earthquakes and tidal waves swept the earth. Even the continents may have been broken apart during or shortly following the Flood.

The amount of energy released during these events would have resulted in significant warming of the oceans as noted by Oard [8, p. 158], [9, pp. 23-31]. Heat released by the collapse of the waters above the earth, present before the Flood, and by magma and warm, sub-surface waters during the Flood, would have raised the average temperature of the oceans by possibly tens of degrees above that of today. Not only would the oceans have been warmer, but because of all the mixing, they probably would have been relatively uniform in temperature from top to bottom and from equator to pole. This is not true today. The oceans are colder near the poles and at the bottom as displayed in Marchuk and Sarkisyan [7, p. 171].

The Biblical description of the pre-Flood world gives the impression of a relatively warm environment, with no rain or storms. If this is true, it is likely that no ice sheets existed at the poles prior to the Flood. However, even if they were in existence before the Flood, they would have melted or have been destroyed during the Flood. Even in polar regions today, vast sedimentary rock layers exist below the ice and extend upward in isolated outcroppings called nunataks, testifying to the worldwide effects of the Flood.

Following the main deluge, many of the geologic processes did not cease abruptly, but, rather, decreased slowly in intensity and frequency, much like aftershocks following a major earthquake. Volcanoes probably continued to release dust and gases into the upper atmosphere for many years after the Flood, causing a pall over the entire earth. The observation of high concentrations of calcium, magnesium, and silicon in the lowest layers of ice cores taken from Greenland may be a reflection of these residual volcanic eruptions. This cover of volcanic dust and gases probably affected the radiation balance over the earth, causing greater cooling over continents and polar regions than we experience today.

The contrast between warm oceans and cold continents probably resulted in intense storminess along coastlines. A description of the effects of the Flood on the formation of an "Ice Age" is described by Oard [9]. He discusses, in great detail, causes of an "Ice Age"; the beginning, progression, and ending of an "Ice Age"; and evidences for a single "Ice Age", rather than many. However, Oard [9] does not treat the evidence gleaned from ice cores, which would support such an alternative model, nor does he describe, in detail, the general circulation which would likely be associated with such a model.

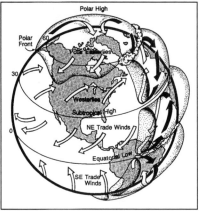

Figure 1 *The general circulation of today's atmosphere. Light arrows show air flow at the surface and dark arrows aloft.*

THE GENERAL CIRCULATION OF TODAY'S ATMOSPHERE

The general circulation of the atmosphere, as it is observed and understood today, is shown in Fig. 1. It is essentially a circulation modified by the Coriolis forces on a rotating earth as described by Lorentz [6]. The earth is observed to be in thermal equilibrium, but net radiational cooling occurs at high latitudes, near the poles, and net warming occurs in the tropics and subtropics, near the equator. To balance the thermal heat source near the equator with the heat sinks near the poles, the ocean and atmosphere transport heat from the tropics to high latitudes. This heat transfer is the driving force for weather and climate on the earth.

The circulating cells in the atmosphere nearest the equator cause air to rise over the equator and flow toward the poles, then descend near 30° latitude. In the Northern Hemisphere, air is deflected to the right of its path by the Coriolis force, so that the northeast trade winds are created as the descending air moves back toward the equator at the surface. In the rising air near the equator, clouds form, and heavy precipitation falls along a belt around the globe called the intertropical convergence zone, or the equatorial low. Near 30° latitude, where the air routinely descends, few, if any, clouds form, and desert conditions persist in a belt surrounding the earth. This region is a subtropical high.

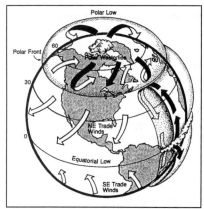

Figure 2 *The hypothetical general circulation of the atmosphere soon after the Flood. Warm oceans and large rates of radiational cooling over the poles would drive extreme convection.*

Between the subtropical high and the polar front further to the north, westerlies prevail. This region is characterized by winds blowing from the west, as surface air moves north from the subtropical high and is deflected to the right. It is also characterized by stormy weather, particularly in the winter, as storms circle the globe along the polar front.

Near the pole, air descends, as heat is removed by radiation to space. The cold air at the surface moves southward toward the polar front and is deflected to the right, forming polar easterlies. Under the polar high, relatively few clouds and little precipitation form. A typical station in central Greenland today accumulates the equivalent of one foot of water per year in the form of ice and snow. What precipitation does occur remains in a frozen state for long periods of time.

Now, how would this picture likely have been different immediately following the Flood where nonequilibrium conditions prevailed? Fig. 2 shows a two-celled Hadley circulation which may have developed during the latter stages of the Flood. The most active region in the atmosphere would likely have been near the poles. Prior to the Flood a vapor canopy has been proposed to have existed above the atmosphere creating a relatively warm, stable, uniform climate from equator to pole (See Vail [14], Whitcomb and Morris [17], Dillow [3], Vardiman [15], and Rush and Vardiman [13]).

This canopy would have collapsed during the Flood leading to greatly increased radiational cooling through the atmosphere. Maximum radiational cooling would have occurred at high levels in the atmosphere, directly over the poles. However, at the surface, the oceans would have been warm--possibly as warm as 30°C. Tremendous evaporation rates would have been present at the ocean surfaces, with condensation and freezing aloft. This situation would not only have been convectively unstable, but probably also dynamically unstable.

HURRICANE FORMATION

Figure 3 *Hurricane Gladys in the Gulf of Mexico during 1968 (NASA).*

The organization and intensification of convection in a stongly convective environment such as we have described would be very similar to the organization of a hurricane discussed by Dunn and Miller [4] and Riehl [11]. Hurricanes are one of nature's most devastating phenomena. They occur in the warm, moist environment of the tropics where convective instability is high. Fig. 3 shows an example of a hurricane -- in this case, Hurricane Gladys in the Gulf of Mexico during 1968. Hurricane Gladys filled the entire gulf with spiral rain bands from the coast of Mexico to the Florida peninsula.

Fig. 4 shows a diagram of air motions in such a hurricane relative to the spiral rain bands and the storm center. The typical hurricane contains rainbands spiraling around a central eye. The center-most rainband contains the strongest winds and heaviest precipitation. Ascending air in the main wallcloud and spiral rainbands draw moist air from the subcloud layer and exhaust it aloft. Near the surface, air converges toward the center of the hurricane to replace the air which has been removed vertically upward.

The Coriolis force causes the air to spiral inward in a counterclockwise manner, creating the characteristic spiral rain bands. The outflow aloft spirals clockwise on its way toward the edge of the hurricane and descends, drying the air aloft. Descending air typically occurs in the eye, producing clearing, cessation of precipitation, and weak winds.

Yet, even with all our knowledge about hurricanes, one of the most perplexing mysteries is the question of why hurricane formation is so rare. Although a reservoir of potential energy for hurricane formation exists over large portions of the tropical oceans for much of the year, it is seldom tapped. When conditions near the earth's surface are unusually warm and humid and conditions aloft are cool and dry, cumulus clouds will form. If a slight impulse of upward vertical motion is imparted to an air parcel under such conditions, strong convection will develop. This atmospheric condition is called, "Conditional Instability of the First Kind."

For many years, atmospheric scientists have regarded hurricanes as rare manifestations of an instability similar to that which drives cumuli. If a region of convection develops over the ocean and lasts long enough, it will result in a hurricane. Several conditions are found to be necessary. For example, the ocean temperature must be warmer than 26°C and an existing disturbance of some sort must move into the tropics which will generate convergence of boundary layer air. If these and several other conditions are met, such "organized convection" will lead to the development of a full-blown hurricane. This tendency of "organized convection" to produce hurricanes is called "Conditional Instability of the Second Kind (CISK)."

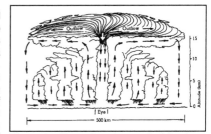

Figure 4 *Air motions in a typical hurricane relative to spiral rain bands and the storm center.*

In recent years, however, a whole new view of what causes hurricanes to form has developed. Emanuel [5] states that:

> The hurricane can be regarded as an elegant example of a natural Carnot heat engine (an idealized, reversible thermodynamic cycle that converts heat to mechanical energy). The reservoir of potential energy for hurricanes resides in the thermodynamic disequilibrium between the atmosphere and the underlying ocean. This is reflected in the fact that air immediately above the ocean is subsaturated, yielding a potential for transfer of entropy from sea to air even though the two media are usually at about the same temperture.

In this new view, called the air-sea interaction theory, the driving force behind hurricane development is not "organized convection" but, rather, the moisture transfer from the ocean surface to the subcloud layer of air which provides the fuel for the Carnot heat engine. If a sufficiently energetic disturbance (winds on the order of 10 meters/second) creates convection over a warm enough ocean (temperatures greater than 26°C through a depth of at least 60 meters) over a long enough period of time (on the order of 4 days), the circulation of a typical hurricane can become established and feed on the energy source in the ocean surface. The trick is creating the proper conditions for the subcloud layer to incorporate moisture from the ocean surface. Apparently, wind speed is the key. Emanuel [5] has shown by computer modeling that his model hurricane will not develop if maximum wind speeds are only 2 meters/second, but it will develop if they are 12 meters/second, all other conditions being appropriate.

The efficacy of air-sea interaction in providing potential energy to balance frictional dissipation depends on the rate of transfer of latent heat from the ocean to the atmosphere. This is a function of surface wind speed. Strong surface winds, which produce a rough sea surface, can greatly increase the evaporation rate. Thus, hurricane development depends on the presence of a disturbance, such as an equatorial wave, to provide the winds required to produce strong evaporation. The evaporation rate is a non-linear function of wind speed. Given a suitable initial disturbance, a feedback may occur in which an increase in inward-spiraling surface winds increases the rate of moisture transfer from the ocean. This brings the boundary layer toward saturation and increases the intensity of the convection, which further increases the inward-spiraling winds.

Despite the current limitations on the understanding of hurricane genesis, Emanuel [5] has generalized his knowledge of the dynamics and energetics of a tropical hurricane to similar phenomena outside the tropics. He believes that polar lows which occur over certain high-latitude oceans (such as the Norwegian Sea) can be explained by the same thermodynamic reasoning. These storms occur in the polar night and often wreck havoc on fishing boats and oil platforms. They form when an exceptionally deep mass of cold air flows out over relatively warm open water, creating a large air-sea thermodynamic disequilibrium. Emanuel [5] analyzed the energy potential of polar lows using the same basic equations as for tropical hurricanes and showed that moderately strong hurricane-like circulations could indeed be maintained under these circumstances. In this case, most of the total entropy difference between ocean and atmosphere results from the large temperature contrast between the two media rather than from an undersaturation of the sub-cloud layer of air.

THE GENERAL CIRCULATION AFTER THE FLOOD

An extension of this physical reasoning to a polar "hurricane" covering a large portion of the Arctic, as shown in Fig. 2, requires a larger source of energy and a longer period of development. Both of these conditions would likely be present following the Genesis Flood. The entire Arctic Ocean, North Atlantic, and North Pacific would have been warm, and not just at the surface, but throughout their depths. Any surface cooling would have resulted in immediate mixing of warmer water from below. The time required to cool the polar oceans from a uniform temperature of 30°C to temperatures observed today was calculated by Oard [8,9] to be on the order of 500 years. This is more than enough time for a hurricane-like circulation to organize itself and function for a long period. Of course, such an intense circulation might not continue to operate for the entire 500 years, if the ocean temperature dropped below certain threshold values.

In Fig. 2, the storm over the Northern Hemisphere is shown to draw warm, moist air from as far away as 45° latitude. At the surface, north of the interface between the two circulation cells, all the winds would be westerlies, feeding into the storm center near the pole. Aloft, the winds would be easterlies, as the air diverges from the storm center. At the periphery of the storm, the air would descend to make another circuit toward the pole at the surface. Less cloudiness and precipitation would have occured here, even though the oceans were warm. Near the equator, an equatorial low, similar to that of today with rising air, clouds, and precipitation would have occurred. It is likely that the intensity of the circulation would have been greater than today, however, with more precipitation.

As the polar storm continued to intensify, it is likely that it developed an eye, such as in a modern hurricane. As it intensified, the precipitation would have formed a ring around the poles which would have moved southward and expanded in size. In addition, the storm would have continued to draw warm, moist air from greater distances to the south -- even possibly south of 30° latitude, as shown in Fig. 5.

At some point, the oceans and atmosphere would have given up enough heat that the precipitation in the ring around the pole would have turned to snow. Once snow began to fall, it would have accumulated on land first (since heat capacity and transfer rates are much less on land than on water). The accumulation of snow on land would have increased the rate of cooling of the atmosphere over the continents, because of the radiational cooling of a higher albedo. The accumulation rate could have been extremely high, when the polar front was near a given location. It also could have varied somewhat as the polar front moved north and south, giving the impression of annual accumulations over shorter time periods.

Over the oceans, since vertical heat transfer is greater due to a larger heat capacity and vertical convection in the water, the atmospheric circulation could draw upon heat from greater depths and the accumulation of snow would be delayed. Since rain and melting snow produce fresh water, layers of salt-free water would have been deposited on top of normal sea water. Fresh water is less dense than salt water, so the precipitation would have tended to remain on the surface. Of course, vertical convection and storm-induced waves would have mixed fresh water with the salt water below reducing this effect somewhat. Since fresh water freezes at a warmer temperature than salt water, a layer of ice may have formed on the surface of the polar oceans before the temperature decreased to the freezing point of sea water. This layer of may have ice eventually closed off the oceans as a source of evaporation near the poles and contributed to greater cooling through the radiational effects of a greater albedo. It is likely that if such an ice layer formed, it would have developed into an ice shelf, which progressed southward from the regions of most-intense precipitation. Due to the lengthy time it probably took to remove heat from the polar oceans and the lower layers of the tropical and mid-latitude oceans, the formation of ice shelves may have been late in the "Ice Age."

Ice sheets in the Northern and Southern Hemispheres probably developed in a slightly different manner, because of a different distribution of land masses. At the North Pole, an open ocean is primarily surrounded by land masses, while at the South Pole, a large continental land mass is surrounded by extensive oceans. This may explain the problem the standard model of the "Ice Ages" has explaining the lack of correspondence between the Antarctic and Greenland ice-core records. The Antarctic ice sheet probably began to accumulate snow fairly rapidly after the Flood, relative to the Greenland ice sheet. Furthermore, the circulation around Antarctica was probably much more concentric than that around the North Pole, resulting in a more uniform accumulation.

Fig. 6 shows the global circulation at a point in time when the polar ice sheets had reached a maximum. Note that a three-celled Hadley circulation has developed, and the polar front is shown further south than is typical today. The polar front generally takes more southerly positions over the continents, because their colder temperatures combine with warm ocean temperatures to induce large standing waves in the general circulation. These standing waves tend to cause more northerly flow over the continents and more southerly flow over the oceans. The oceans are major sources of heat and moisture to the polar and continental regions. Evidence from moraines at the edge of glaciers, and sea-floor sediments beneath the edges of ice shelves reported by Ruddiman and McIntyre [12], show that in the past, an ice shelf extended south of 45° latitude in the North Atlantic. These conclusions were based on the distribution of microorganisms such as foraminifera which are temperature dependent and on ice-rafted debris. A

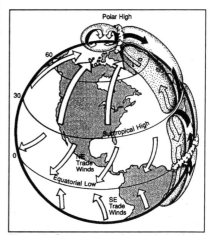

Figure 5 *Intense stage of general circulation development over the pole. This stage probably occurred within 100 years or less of the Flood. Note the development of an "eye".*

573

relatively sharp boundary of cold types of microorganisms and ice-rafted debris were found on the ocean floor as low as 45° latitude in the Atlantic Ocean.

As the oceans cooled and more of the ocean surface was covered with ice, the active precipitation zones may have moved further equatorward. The jet streams in both hemispheres probably tended to follow the edge of the ice sheets, since this was where the major north-south temperature gradient would have occurred. The massive ice sheets poleward of the polar fronts capped moisture sources, and amplified radiational cooling.

Once the oceans cooled sufficently that evaporation was reduced, melting in the summers exceeded accumulation in the winters, and the ice sheets began to recede to those observed today. Only Greenland and Antarctica retain massive ice sheets and continue to accumulate snow.

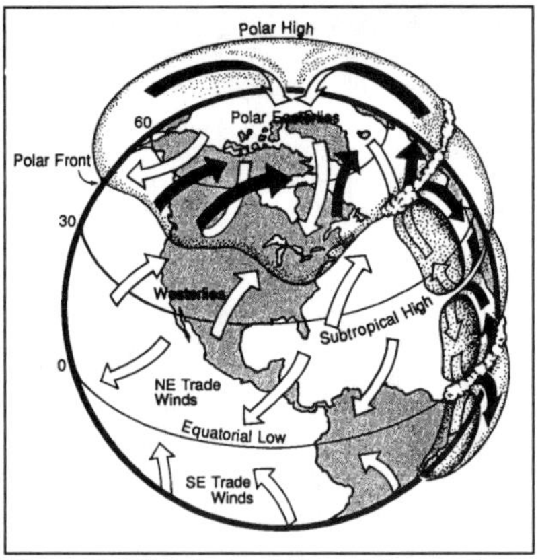

The driving mechanism for the "Ice Age" in this model was the presence of warm oceans following the Flood. The advance and retreat of the ice sheets was controlled by the

Figure 6 *Global circulation at the maximum extent of polar ice caps. This stage probably occurred 500 to 1000 years after the Flood. Note the three-celled Hadley circulation.*

time required to cool the oceans, and the distribution of snow and ice was determined by the manner in which the general circulation of the atmosphere was modulated by the temperature differences between the poles and the equator and between land and ocean.

NUMERICAL MODEL SIMULATION

In an attempt to confirm some of the ideas suggested in this paper a numerical simulation of the atmosphere was conducted with the Community Climate Model (CCM1) from the National Center for Atmospheric Research (NCAR). The model was installed on a 486 personal computer and validated with a standard simulation run for a perpetual January condition in today's atmosphere. A 600-day run was completed for validation purposes. It was found to match today's atmospheric condition well.

Uniform 30°C sea-surface temperatures were then entered into the model, oceanic ice shelves removed, and the model started again with all other initial conditions the same. A 100-day run was completed in time for this report. The conditions seem to force the model so strongly that equilibrium appears to have been achieved rapidly. However, the model will continue to be run for up to 1200 days in order to be certain. The model behaved significantly different for the warm ocean than for today's conditions.

Fig. 7 shows surface temperature for perpetual January after 100 days of simulated time. The sea-surface remains uniformly warm at 30°C, but the continents cool rapidly, in some locations to -40°C. An extreme temperature gradient is located at all continental boundaries. This temperature gradient would be expected to induce a strong thermal wind parallel to the coast lines.

Fig. 8 shows surface pressure for perpetual January after 100 days of simulated time. Relatively high pressure occurs over the warm oceans. Relatively low pressure occurs over the polar regions and continents. Pressure has not been adjusted to sea-level, so topography strongly influences the values in some locations, such as over the Himalayas in southeast Asia.

Fig. 9 shows wind speed high in the stratosphere for perpetual January after 100 days of simulated time. The wind is strongest in the northern hemisphere, as would be expected in January. The speed of the westerly jet is about 25% higher than in today's atmosphere.

Fig. 10 shows the precipitation rate at the earth's surface for perpetual January after 100 days of simulated time. The precipitation rates are extreme in the polar regions and along the continental boundaries of the northern hemisphere. Rates exceed 10 mm/day over Greenland, Antarctica, southeastern Asia, northeastern North America, northwestern Europe, and western Africa. The center of Asia and North America appear relatively dry. Of special interest is the relatively dry region from the eastern end of the Mediterranean eastward across the continent of Asia. This pattern may have been of particular value to Noah and his descendants as they left the Ark on Mt. Ararat and emigrated south and east.

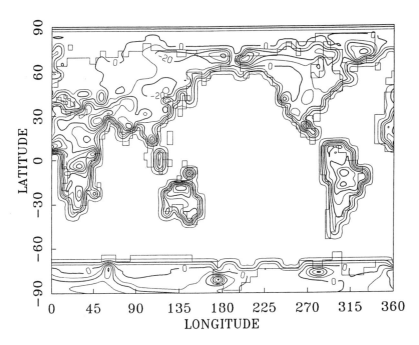

Figure 7 Surface temperature for perpetual January after 100 days of simulated time with the NCAR CCM1 model and initial uniform 30°C ocean surface temperature globally.

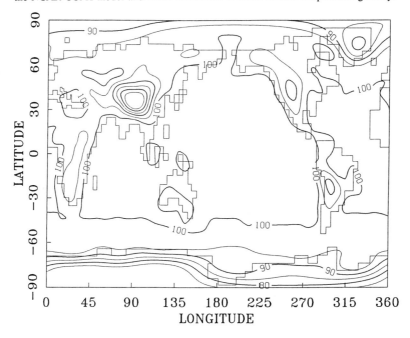

Figure 8 Surface pressure for perpetual January after 100 days of simulated time with the NCAR CCM1 model and an initial uniform 30°C ocean surface temperature globally.

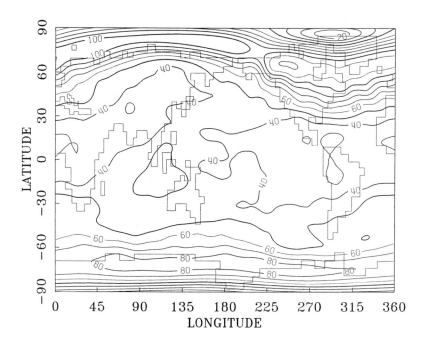

Figure 9 Stratospheric wind speed for perpetual January after 100 days of simulated time with the NCAR CCM1 model and an initial uniform 30°C ocean surface temperature globally.

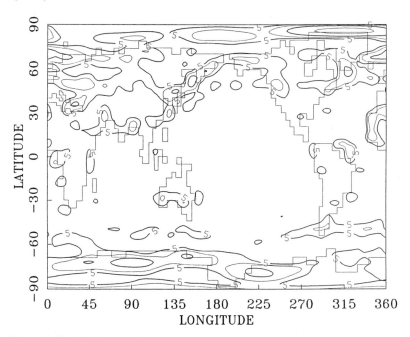

Figure 10 Precipitation rate for perpetual January after 100 days of simulated time with the NCAR CCM1 model and an initial uniform 30°C ocean surface temperature globally.

The primary purpose of this numerical simulation was to develop a young-earth, catastrophic explanation of the "Ice Age." The results offer great encouragement for the model suggested by Oard [8,9] and in this article. They also have significance for a much wider range of topics. For example, the heavy precipitation indicated by the model could be important in erosion of continents following their emergence from the oceans after the Flood, e.g. southeast Asia and western Africa. The precipitation rates are extremely high compared to those of today. The heaviest precipitation occurs in the regions of the earth necessary to explain the ice sheets and glaciers present on the earth today and in the past. A uniformly warm ocean seems to generate the necessary conditions for the rapid formation of ice sheets in polar regions.

These results should not be considered valid yet. They are very preliminary. The model must be run for a much longer period of time to insure that it has come to equilibrium. A full analysis of over a dozen variables must be explored to fully understand the three-dimensional nature of this simulation and the interplay among the variables. The topography must be modified to remove the effects of current ice sheets on Greenland and Antarctica. Simulations must be conducted for decreasing sea-surface temperatures in the polar regions. It is likely that as the sea-surface temperatures in the polar regions decreased, the precipitation rates decreased and more rain turned to snow. Seasonal changes must also be simulated.

GREENLAND ICE CORES

Given the transition in the general circulation of the atmosphere following the Flood, can some of the major features in ice cores be explained? For example, how would the trends in $\delta^{18}O$ be explained by a young-earth "Ice Age" model? Fig. 11 shows the measured values of $\delta^{18}O$ versus time for Camp Century, Greenland, according to a typical long-age time model. $\delta^{18}O$ is defined by:

$$\delta^{18}O = \frac{R - R_o}{R_o} \cdot 1000 \ \%o(per \ mil) \tag{1}$$

where R is the ratio of ^{18}O to ^{16}O in a sample of ice and R_o is the ratio of ^{18}O to ^{16}O in a reference sample, called the standard mean ocean water (SMOW).

The generally-accepted old-earth interpretation of trends in $\delta^{18}O$ with time is shown in Fig. 11. The last "Ice Age" reached its minimum temperature about 18,000 years ago after about 100,000 years of cooling. Some, as yet, unknown factor caused the "Ice Age" to end and temperatures returned to their normal interglacial values about 10,000 years ago. The increase in $\delta^{18}O$ after the minimum at 18,000 years occurred over a short period of time. This atmospheric temperature history is derived from Fig. 11 because $\delta^{18}O$ in ice is believed to be directly related to the temperature of the atmosphere from which the snow was precipitated and the old-earth time model is based on an assumption of relatively uniform snow accumulation over millions of years. For a more thorough discussion of the relationships between temperature and $\delta^{18}O$ and the use of time models, see Vardiman [16].

Fig. 12 shows the same measured values of $\delta^{18}O$ plotted against time derived from a young-earth time model. The basic assumption of this time model, discussed in detail by Vardiman [16], is that the snowfall rate was high at the end of the Flood, and decreased exponentially with time to that observed today. Note in Fig. 12 that the period of time from the Flood to the "Ice Age" temperature minimum is somewhat less than the 500 years suggested by Oard [8,9]. However, this is to be expected since it probably took a few years for the temperature to drop sufficently for snow to begin to accumulate. Recent evidence has been presented by Alley et al. [1] that the rapid change in $\delta^{18}O$ following the "Ice Age" could have occurred in as little time as 5 years. If this evidence is true, then it is likely that $\delta^{18}O$ is not dependent only on atmospheric temperature. It does not seem likely that the atmosphere, and probably the ocean, could warm by some 15°C in 5 years. It is more likely that some other factor has caused $\delta^{18}O$ to change.

Craig [2] showed that a primary factor which causes $\delta^{18}O$ in precipitation to change is the influence of formation temperature on the fractionation of the two isotopes of oxygen. However, in addition to the dependence upon formation temperature, Petit et al. [10] have reported that

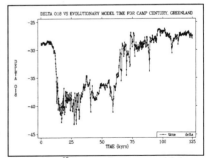

Figure 11 $\delta^{18}O$ *versus long-age model time.*

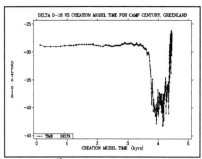

Figure 12 $\delta^{18}O$ *versus young-earth model time after the Flood for Camp Century, Greenland.*

the variation of $\delta^{18}O$ is also a function of the distance of an observation site from the source of moisture, the relative concentration of oxygen isotopes at the source of moisture, and the type of precipitation process. There are probably other factors, as well.

In a changing situation like that following the Flood where the oceans were cooling rapidly; a polar front was probably developing and moving south and then north again; and the precipitation intensity was decreasing exponentially; it is likely that all of these processes would come into play. For example, as the oceans cooled, we would expect $\delta^{18}O$ to also decrease with cooling temperatures. In addition, the warm oceans would create relatively thick, warm clouds immediately after the Flood. But, as the oceans cooled, the clouds would decrease in thickness and could become colder. This would cause $\delta^{18}O$ to decrease, as the type and intensity of the precipitation changed.

Once the snow began to accumulate over the ocean after the Flood, ice shelves probably developed, similar to those of today. The ice shelves covered sources of moisture close to the Camp Century site on Greenland. As the shelves continued to grow southward, the source region for moisture moved further away, lowering the value of $\delta^{18}O$. Precipitation over the open ocean south of the ice shelves also remained on the surface, diluting the sea water with fresh water already depleted in $\delta^{18}O$ from a previous cycle of evaporation and precipitation, thus producing a further lowering of $\delta^{18}O$. We can therefore explain the trend toward lower values of $\delta^{18}O$ for the first segment of the core from the bottom upward with our alternative conceptual model, with or without a large temperature change. But, what about the sudden change in the more recent portions of Figs. 11 and 12?

I propose that once the ocean cooled sufficiently and the ice sheets on the continents and ice shelves on the oceans stopped growing, the ice shelves began to retreat rapidly. Once the accumulation of snow decreased, the surging of ice off the continents and direct formation of shelves by precipitation on the oceans probably ceased, which led to a breakup of the shelves. As the shelves broke up, a positive radiational feedback occurred whereby the decreased albedo led to more surface heating and more destruction of the ice shelves. Ice shelves around Antarctica and in the North Sea are observed to break up very quickly in the spring today, much more rapidly than they form.

The sudden retreat of the ice shelves would cause the distance between the source and deposition site to diminish, increasing the $\delta^{18}O$ rapidly. This retreat would also be associated with less precipitation on the ocean surface beyond the ice shelves as the oceans cooled and increased mixing of surface waters because of melting of the ice, thereby increasing the $\delta^{18}O$ at the source. The cooler type of precipitation process is likely to revert somewhat to a warmer type and contibute to a slight increase in $\delta^{18}O$ as the shelves retreated. However, the change in distance between source and deposition site and change in concentration of $\delta^{18}O$ at the source alone could easily explain the increase the $\delta^{18}O$ of the snow falling at Camp Century.

CONCLUSIONS AND RECOMMENDATIONS

It seems likely that major convective activity would have occurred near the North and South poles because of warm oceans and radiational cooling aloft following the Flood. This would likely have led to the development of hurricane-like circulations over both poles which transitioned into the global circulation we observe today. The cooling near the poles would have resulted in the rapid accumulation of snow on the continents and, later, the formation of ice shelves on the polar oceans. Numerical simulation experiments with the CCM1 model show that extremely high precipitation rates occur in the polar regions and along the boundaries of the countinents of the northern hemisphere when uniformly warm sea-surface temperatures are used as input. This heavy precipitation would have produced large accumulations of snow in the polar regions. Studies from ice cores in Greenland show a slow decline in $\delta^{18}O$ with time, followed by a sudden increase at the end of the "Ice Age". These changes can be explained by fractionation of the oxygen isotopes as water is evaporated and transported from the mid-latitude oceans in the polar regions. The trends observed in ice cores are due to changes in temperature, distance from the source of evaporation, and the type of precipitation processes as the oceans cooled and the general circulation of the atmosphere responded.

It is recommended that (1) more numerical experiments be conducted on the development of hurricane-like circulations in polar regions using hurricane and global circulation models, (2) the variation of $\delta^{18}O$ in snow be quantified as a function of distance from an evaporative source and the type of precipitation process, and (3) the formation of extensive ice shelves by direct accumulation of precipitating snow be investigated.

ACKNOWLEDGEMENTS

The Climate and Global Dynamics Division of the National Center for Atmospheric Research is gratefully acknowledged for providing a copy of the Community Climate Model (CCM1) used in this study. Mr. Steve Low and his colleagues at Hewlett Packard donated the personal computer. Mr. Herman Daily donated his time and expertise to modify the model, originally designed to run on a CRAY. It now runs on a personal computer with an OS-2 operating system, albeit at about 1/100th the speed.

BIBLIOGRAPHY

[1]   R.B. Alley, C.A. Shuman, D. Meese, A.J. Gow, K. Taylor, M.Ram, E.D. Waddington, and P.A. Mayewski, **An Old, Long, Abrupt Younger Dryas Event in the GISP2 Ice Core**, Proceedings of the 1992 Fall Meeting of the American Geophysical Union, San Francisco, EOS Transactions, **73**:43(1992), 259.

[2]   H. Craig, **Isotope Variations in Meteoritic Water**, Science, **133**(1961), 1702-1703.

[3]   J.C. Dillow, The Waters Above, 1981, Moody Press, 479 pp.

[4]   G.E. Dunn and B.I. Miller, Atlantic Hurricanes, 1964, Louisiana State University Press, 377 pp.

[5]   K.E. Emanuel, **Toward a General Theory of Hurricanes**, American Scientist, **76**(1988), 371.

[6]   E.N. Lorentz, The Nature and Theory of the General Circulation, 1967, WMO Monograph, 161 pp.

[7]   G.I. Marchuk and A.S. Sarkisyan, Mathematical Modeling of Ocean Circulation, 1986, Springer-Verlag, New York.

[8]   M.J. Oard, **An Ice Age within the Biblical Time Frame**, in Proceedings of the First International Conference on Creationism, Vol. II, R.E. Walsh, C.L. Brooks, and R.S. Crowell, eds., 1986, Creation Science Fellowship, Pittsburgh, 157-161.

[9]   M.J. Oard, An Ice Age Caused by the Genesis Flood, 1990, ICR Monograph, San Diego, 243 pp.

[10]   J.R. Petit, M. Briat, and A. Roger, **Ice Age Aerosol Content from East Antarctic Ice Core Samples and Past Wind Strength**, Nature, **293**(1981), 391-394.

[11]   H. Riehl, Tropical Meteorology, 1954, McGraw-Hill Book Co, New York, 392 pp.

[12]   W.F. Ruddiman and A. McIntyre, **The Mode and Mechanism of the Last Deglaciation: Oceanic Evidence**, 1981, Quaternary Research, 16, 125-134.

[13]   D.E. Rush and L. Vardiman, **Pre-Flood Vapor Canopy Radiative Temperature Profiles**, in Proceedings of the Second International Conference on Creationism, Vol. II, R.E. Walsh and C.L. Brooks, eds. 1990, Creation Science Fellowship, Pittsburgh, 231-245.

[14]   I.N. Vail, The Deluge and its Cause, 1905, Suggestion Publishing Co.

[15]   L. Vardiman, **The Sky Has Fallen**, in Proceedings of the First International Conference on Creationism, Vol. I, R.E. Walsh, C.L. Brooks, and R.S. Crowell, eds., 1986, Creation Science Fellowship, Pittsburgh.

[16]   L. Vardiman, Ice Cores and the Age of the Earth, 1993, ICR Monograph, San Diego, 80 pp.

[17]   J.C. Whitcomb, Jr., and H.M. Morris, The Genesis Flood, 1961, Presbyterian and Reformed Publ. Co., 518 pp.

A BIBLICAL GEOLOGIC MODEL

TAS WALKER B.Eng. (Hons), Ph.D.
34 Fawkner Street
CHAPEL HILL Qld 4069
Australia

ABSTRACT

This paper describes a geologic model based on a plain reading of the Bible. A simple diagram is presented detailing the model and graphically illustrating the concepts. Each feature of the model is labelled. The terms used are consistent with the Biblical record, are in plain language intelligible to ordinary people, and are sufficiently well defined to enable ongoing discussion and evaluation within the scientific community.

Characteristics of significance to the Biblical model have been identified with a view to classifying the rocks in the field and assisting in geologic research.

The paper proposes that the model be tested against real geological sections and eventually used to reclassify geologic reference materials, such as maps, map commentaries, field guides, and handbooks, in terms of a Biblical model. It is suggested that the model, adapted to suit the needs of the audience, be widely published to help people picture the geologic concepts arising from the Biblical account, and assist scientific research.

KEYWORDS

Bible	Creation Science	Creationism
Geology	Geologic Model	Geologic Classification

1. INTRODUCTION

A geologic model is needed to help explore, classify and understand the geology of the earth.

The basis of a geologic model is a clearly defined history of the earth. Naturally any history of the earth must be an assumed history because no one alive today was present to observe what took place.

Many people believe that a plain reading of the Bible gives an accurate understanding of earth history. The basis for this belief is outside the scope of this paper, but McDowell [4] summarises many of the reasons. If the Bible is taken as accurate, then it should form the basis for an overall understanding of geology.

This paper describes a geologic model based on the belief that the Biblical record of world history is accurate.

2. THE BROAD FRAMEWORK OF THE MODEL

The Biblical history as illustrated in Figure 1 will be used as the basis for the geologic model.

For this paper the dates developed by Ussher [3, p.273-p.283], rounded to the nearest 100 years will be adopted. Ussher's chronology is based on internal evidence from the Bible itself, and is used here because it is well known. Biblical chronologies developed by others differ from Ussher depending on how the chronology was constructed and the Biblical source text used. However the differences are not large compared with non-Biblical chronologies and have no effect on the validity of the model outlined in this paper.

The creation of the earth, therefore, is taken as occurring in 4000 BC. The flood, assumed to be of world wide extent and to involve deposition of a significant portion of all sedimentary rocks, is taken as occurring in 2300 BC.

With these assumptions the creation and flood events, although of short duration, are geologically the most

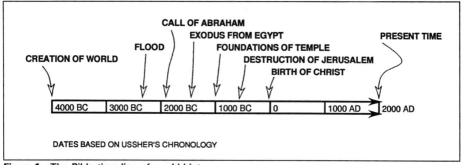

Figure 1 The Bible time-line of world history.

important times for the earth. The creation event is pre-eminent, generating a volume of roughly 1,000,000 x 10^6 cubic kilometres of material when the earth was formed. Of lesser significance was the flood event which would have involved the deposition some 300 to 700 x 10^6 cubic kilometres of material. To produce such large quantities of material in such a short time would require intense geologic processes.

By contrast, the geologic processes observed operating today are orders of magnitude less intense. If the current rates of erosion and deposition are projected over the pre-flood or the post-flood era, then the total quantity of material deposited in either era would be less than 0.05 x 10^6 cubic kilometres. Even if the rates applying during these eras were one or two orders of magnitude different from current rates, the material accumulated during these eras would still be much less than the material generated during the creation or flood event.

From a geological point of view, therefore, the history of the earth as recorded in the Bible can be divided into four parts which we will refer to as the **Creation Event**, the **Lost-World Era** (pre-flood era), the **Flood Event**, and the **New-World Era** (post-flood era). The term "Lost-World Era" refers to the time between the Creation and Flood Events. It is introduced to avoid ambiguity because the term "pre-flood" includes the Creation Event.

The important feature of the Biblical geologic model is that the intensity of geologic processes were different for each of the four parts of world history. Because geologic effects were not uniform with time, it is necessary to transform the time-scale shown in Figure 1 into a rock-scale.

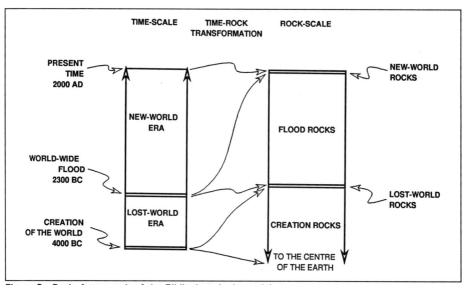

Figure 2 Basic framework of the Biblical geologic model.

The concept of time-rock transformation is illustrated in Figure 2. The time-scale is shown on the left, rotated so that the most recent time is at the top of the figure and the earliest at the bottom. The length of the time-scale reflects the durations of the events and eras.

582

To the right of the time-scale is a rock-scale with the most recent rocks at the top, and the earliest rocks at the bottom - the same way they occur in the earth. The length of the rock-scale roughly corresponds to the quantity of rock material found on the earth today.

The non-uniform effect of historical events on earth geology is indicated by the time-rock transformation. Arrows point from the Creation and Flood Events on the time scale to the rocks on the rock-scale formed during these events. Even though these events happened quickly, they were responsible for practically all the rocks on the rock-scale. The long eras, which make up virtually the whole time-scale, do not contribute much to the rock-scale. Because these eras have such little impact on the rock-scale, the exact dates of the Creation and Flood are not critical to the model.

Figure 2 represents the basic framework of the Biblical geologic model. The Biblical account is clearly set out in the figure together with the underlying concepts which relate that account to the geology of the earth.

3. DETAILED STRUCTURE OF THE MODEL

To be useful and practical, the broad framework of the model must be expanded to provide specific detail of the events and processes and their time relationships. Distinctive conditions need to be identified to correlate geologic features in the field with the model. In addition the level of detail needs to be scaled such that it bears a useful relationship with the quantity of rocks involved. As we examine the Biblical account more closely, the various processes, events, conditions and features will be defined and named.

3.1 The Creation Event

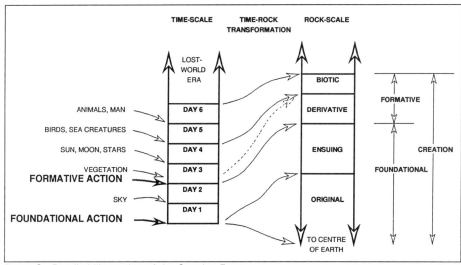

Figure 3   Detailed illustration of the Creation Event.

The Creation Event as recorded in the Bible is illustrated in Figure 3. The time-scale and corresponding rock-scale are shown together with the time-rock transformation. The earliest time is at the bottom of the figure. Details of the events on each of the six days of the Creation Event are summarised below.

Day 1 The first creative act is the most geologically significant, involving the creation of the earth on the first day [Gen 1:1-2]. Hebrews 11:3 indicates that the earth was created out of nothing. We do not know the processes involved in this action because Genesis 2:1-3 indicates that the creative process is finished, and therefore not observable today.

We will assume that the initial creative action occurred instantaneously at the beginning of the first day, and that on completion the solid sphere of the earth was in place. The form of this sphere, whether homogeneous or differentiated is not here proposed. However it is noted that this sphere was initially covered with water until dry land appeared on the third day.

As shown in Figure 3 the first creative act which founded the earth is called the **Foundational Action** and the rocks resulting from this action are called **Original** Rocks. It is envisaged that the waters would have contained additional minerals in solution, or in suspension. It is reasonable to assume that the material in solution would precipitate, and the material in suspension would settle with time. Rocks formed in this way have been termed **Ensuing** - that is rocks which quickly followed on over the next two days. These two types of rock are shown in Figure 3 and were formed during what is called the **Foundational Stage** of the Creation Event - a stage covering Day 1 and Day 2.

Day 2 The sky was created on the second day. It is not proposed that this act would produce any significant geologic effects at this time.

Wise [6, p.69] has suggested that the ocean microbiotas (plankton and other tiny sea life) were created on Day 2. The possible significance on the model is discussed under Day 5.

Day 3 On Day 3 the waters covering the earth were gathered together into one place and dry land appeared. If this gathering was brought about by movements of the solid sphere causing the overlying waters to flow over the surface, then this act would have been significant geologically.

In Figure 3 the gathering of the waters to form the ocean basins and the dry land is called the **Formative Action**. This action marks the beginning of the **Formative Stage** of the Creation Event, lasting from the beginning of Day 3 until the end of Day 6. It is reasonable to expect that material would have been eroded and redeposited as a consequence of this action. The rocks so formed are called **Derivative** because they were derived from the Ensuing and Original Rocks.

After the Formative Action the dry land produced all kinds of vegetation, seed bearing plants, and trees with fruit. Note that vegetation was created after the Foundational and Formative Actions. Although I assume that plankton and other microscopic sea life were created on Day 5, such life may have been created on Day 3. The possible significance on rock characteristics is discussed under Day 5.

Day 4 The sun, moon and stars were created on Day 4. I do not consider that these events would have produced any significant geologic effects at this time.

Day 5 All the creatures that fill the water, and the birds of the air were created on Day 5.

An interesting possibility arises in relation to the geologic significance of plankton and other tiny sea life. After they were created, some of this life may have become trapped in rocks forming in the oceans. To allow for this possibility the model includes a category designated **Biotic** for rocks formed during this period. The solid time-rock transformation arrow shown in Figure 3 assumes the tiny sea life was created on Day 5 with the other ocean life. The dotted arrow indicates the possibility that this tiny sea life was created on Day 3 with the vegetation. Whether this life was created on Day 3 or Day 5 does not affect the validity of the model.

The suggestion by Wise [6, p.69], however, that this tiny sea life was created on Day 2 would affect the form of this model. The Biotic category would need to be moved between the Ensuing and Derivative Rocks, just before the Formative Action. However this position is not proposed for the model at this stage because the Bible is silent on the matter of life being created on Day 2. Wise proposed an "aesthetic justification" for the position. Such a modification to the model should only be made if it became clear from the field that it was necessary.

Apart from the tiny sea life, it is not proposed that any other Day 5 creative actions produced significant geologic effects at this time.

Day 6 Animals and man were created on Day 6. It is not proposed that these events produced any significant geologic effects at this time.

As shown on Figure 3, the end of Day 6 marks the end of the Formative Stage of the Creation Event.

3.2 The Lost-World Era

I have called the 1700 year period between the Creation and Flood Events the **Lost-World Era**. A perfectly habitable environment existed on earth at the beginning of this era when every kind of life ever created was present.

Geologic action during the Lost-World Era may have been less intense than today. Even if the intensity were the same, not much of geologic significance would have occurred in the time available. In addition, much of what was deposited during this era may have been destroyed by the Flood. Rocks formed during this time have been called **Lost-World Rocks.** Additional classifications are not included at this stage but can be inserted if the a need is identified as the model is applied to the rocks in the field. Figure 4 shows the relationship of Lost-World Rocks with the Biblical time-scale.

3.3 The Flood Event

The Flood Event is meticulously recorded in the Bible, from which can be developed a detailed chronology. The records are tied to the age of Noah who was in his 600th year when the Flood began. The text indicates that a month consisted of 30 days [Gen 8:3-4 and 7:11]. The time-scale of the Flood Event is shown in Figure 5 with the earliest time at the bottom of the page. Full details of the chronology are as shown in Table 1. The total duration of the Flood Event is a little over one year.

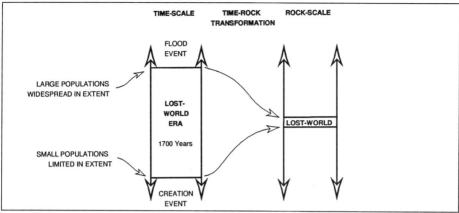

Figure 4 Detailed illustration of the Lost-World Era.

Yr	Mth	Day	Event	Duration Days	Genesis Reference
600	2	10	Noah entered the ark		7:7,10,11
600	2	17	Heavens and earth opened		7:11
600	3	27	Rain stopped	40	7:12
600	7	17	Ark rested on Ararat	110	8:3,4
600	10	1	Tops of mountains seen	74	8:5
600	11	10	Raven - did not return	40	8:6,7
600	11	18	Dove - returned	7	8:8
600	11	25	Dove - returned with leaf	7	8:10,11
600	12	2	Dove - did not return	7	8:12
601	1	1	Covering removed - ground dry	29	8:13
601	2	27	Everyone disembarked	56	8:14-16
			Total Duration of the Flood	370	

Table 1 Chronology of the Flood Event.

Geologically two stages are of significance. The first stage, during which the waters "rose and increased greatly" until the whole earth was covered [Gen 7:18], has been called the **Inundatory Stage**. The second stage during which the waters receded from the earth [Gen 8:3,5] has been designated the **Recessive Stage**.

The description "the springs of the great deep burst forth" [Gen 7:11] is taken to mean an intense world-wide geologic disturbance which initiated the Flood. This is shown on the figure as the **Eruptive Action**. Similarly the "springs of the great deep being closed" [Gen 8:2] is assumed to mean an intense world-wide disturbance which started the waters receding from the land and is called the **Abative Action**. Although these disturbances are indicated as a single act on the figure it is possible that a sequence of tectonic activity was involved lasting weeks or months.

The duration of the Inundatory Stage is not entirely clear. If the stopping of "the fountains also of the deep and the windows of heaven" [Gen 8:2 AV] occurred after 150 days [Gen 7:24] then the Inundatory Stage would have been about 150 days long and the Recessive Stage about 220 days. Alternatively, from Genesis 7:12 and 17 the duration of the Inundatory Stage can be equated to the 40 days that the "rain fell" and "the flood kept coming on the earth." In this case the Abative Action would have occurred soon after the 40 days and Genesis 8:2 would be a reference back to when "the springs of the deep and the floodgates of heaven <u>had been</u> closed" [NIV]. Therefore the Inundatory Stage could have been about 40 days long and Recessive Stage about 300 days. If the Inundatory Stage was significantly shorter than the Recessive Stage then the intensity of geological processes and the corresponding quantities of rock material deposited may well have been greater than occurred during the Recessive Stage.

Figure 5 (and Figure 7 too) is drawn assuming an Inundatory Stage a little longer than 40 days - arbitrarily shown as 60 days to allow time for the Flood to peak. Although these figures would need to be modified if the Inundatory Stage were 150 days long, the validity of the model would not be affected.

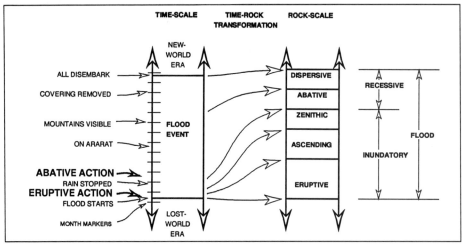

Figure 5 Detailed illustration of the Flood-Event.

As shown in Figure 5, three phases have been assigned to the Inundatory Stage, mainly to provide for the quantity of material assumed to be deposited at this time. No particular conditions are obvious from the Bible text to suggest distinctive features for each phase. Such criteria will need to be formulated as the model is applied in the field. The three phases assigned are:

Eruptive: Eruptive Rocks were formed following the Eruptive Action which involved the bursting forth of the springs of the deep [Gen 7:11], the opening of the floodgates of heaven [Gen 7:11], and rain falling on the earth [Gen 7:12].

Ascending: Ascending Rocks were formed as the rain continued and the waters rose upon the surface of the earth [Gen 7:10].

Zenithic: Zenithic Rocks were formed as the waters continued to rise to their highest point when all the earth was covered [Gen 7:20].

Two phases are designated for the Recessive Stage as indicated in Figure 5:

Abative: Abative Rocks were formed following the Abative Action when the springs of the deep [Gen 8:2], and the floodgates of heaven [Gen 8:2] closed, and after the rain ceased [Gen 8:2]. During this phase the waters covering the earth receded from the earth [Gen 8:3].

Dispersive: Dispersive Rocks were formed as the Recessive Stage continued, and the flow divided into separate water courses. The flow of water during the Dispersive Phase would steadily reduce in intensity until the land was dry [Gen 8:14].

3.4 The New-World Era

I have called the period of time since the Flood Event the **New-World Era**. Figure 6 shows the time-line for this period and the corresponding rock-line. Two phases are included:

Residual: A phase of relatively high levels of tectonic and volcanic activity as a result of residual effects from the Flood. The duration of this phase is shown arbitrarily as about 300 years but needs to be better defined by observable criteria in the rocks.

Modern: A phase of stable and relatively minor geologic processes of a similar scale of intensity as experienced today lasting approximately 4000 years.

3.5 The Model

Figure 7 shows the complete Biblical geologic model. This model is consistent with a plain reading of the Bible. The diagram illustrates the basic concepts of the Biblical model. The terms used such as era, event, action, stage, and phase are consistent with Biblical concepts. The names assigned to the events, eras, stages and phases are in plain language, faithfully portray the Biblical account, should be intelligible to ordinary people, and are sufficiently well defined to enable ongoing discussion and evaluation within the scientific community. The diagram can be customised to suit any intended audience.

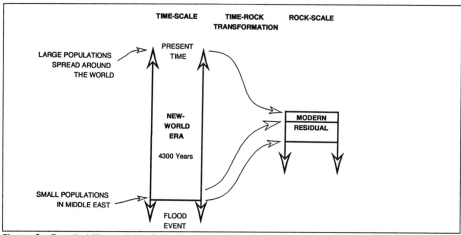

Figure 6 Detailed illustration of the New-World Era.

The concept of time-rock transformation focuses on the geologically significant processes and indicates the relative intensity of those processes. The applicability of the model is not dependent on particular mechanisms, such as a possible pre-flood vapour canopy, meteorite intervention, or plate tectonics.

The model can be used immediately for classification, mapping, and communication of the Biblical geologic concepts.

4. CLASSIFICATION CRITERIA

The Biblical model infers that geologic processes acting in the past varied in nature and intensity from time to time, and were different from what we experience today. Consequently it is anticipated that certain geologic characteristics will help classify rock formations in accordance with the model. In this section some of the characteristics of significance to the Biblical model are described. These have been identified from the detailed description of the nature and sequence of the processes which have been obtained from the Biblical account.

This list should be considered preliminary because as the model is used additional criteria will be identified. It is not intended of these criteria should be applied in isolation or without properly considering all the factors affecting the deposition and modification of a rock structure.

<u>Scale</u>   The Biblical model proposes that the intensity of action, and the geographical extent of geologic processes was different at different times in the past. The scale of a geologic structure gives an indication of the intensity and geographical extent of the process involved in forming that structure. A geologic structure can have a world-wide, continental, regional, or local scale. The scale would also reflect in the thickness of the structures. Scale is therefore expected to help classify geologic structures according to the Biblical model.

<u>Disturbance</u>   The Biblical model proposes a definite sequence for past geologic events. The major actions of great intensity which have shaped the earth are the:

*   Foundational Action
*   Formative Action
*   Eruptive Action
*   Abative Action

The Eruptive and Abative Actions probably involved tectonic activity and may have been spread over weeks or months. There would be other actions of lesser intensity occurring during the Lost-World and New-World Eras, particularly during Residual Phase of the New-World era. These however would be less significant.

The last three of these four actions would disturb structures already formed. The degree of disturbance would depend on the number and intensity of actions to which the structure was exposed. The degree of disturbance of rock structures therefore is expected to assist with their classification.

<u>Response</u>   The Biblical model proposes a definite time relationship for past geologic actions as follows:

*   Foundational to Formative Action - 2 days
*   Formative to Eruptive Action - 1700 years
*   Eruptive to Abative Action - 60 (to 150) days
*   Abative Action to present - over 4000 years.

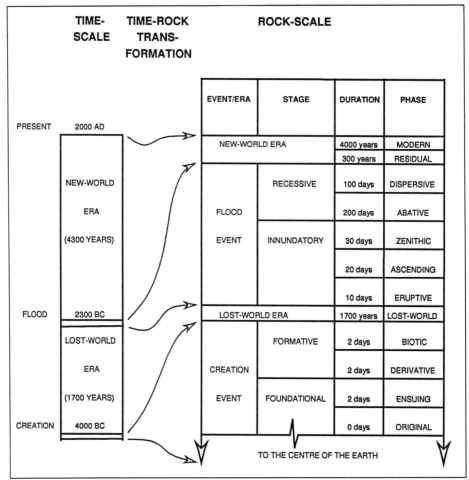

TIME-SCALE | **TIME-ROCK TRANS-FORMATION** | **ROCK-SCALE**

EVENT/ERA	STAGE	DURATION	PHASE
NEW-WORLD ERA		4000 years	MODERN
		300 years	RESIDUAL
	RECESSIVE	100 days	DISPERSIVE
FLOOD		200 days	ABATIVE
EVENT	INNUNDATORY	30 days	ZENITHIC
		20 days	ASCENDING
		10 days	ERUPTIVE
LOST-WORLD ERA		1700 years	LOST-WORLD
	FORMATIVE	2 days	BIOTIC
CREATION		2 days	DERIVATIVE
EVENT	FOUNDATIONAL	2 days	ENSUING
		0 days	ORIGINAL

TIME-SCALE:
PRESENT — 2000 AD
NEW-WORLD ERA (4300 YEARS)
FLOOD — 2300 BC
LOST-WORLD ERA (1700 YEARS)
CREATION — 4000 BC

TO THE CENTRE OF THE EARTH

Figure 7 The Biblical Geologic Model.

It is expected that the response of geologic structures to disturbances would depend on how soon they were disturbed after they were formed. Rocks may respond in a:

*   plastic manner - oozing, twisting, bending and folding.
*   brittle manner - faulting, crushing, and fracturing.

Whether a rock formation shows plastic or brittle behaviour would depend on how quickly the rock lithifies and how long before the formation is disturbed. Pressure, temperature and rate of deformation are also factors. The rate of lithification would depend on such factors as the chemical characteristics of the rock material, the temperature and pressure. Some Creation Rocks could be subject to brittle or plastic deformation, even during the Creation Event depending on the initial created state - crystalline or sediment.

Response to disturbance is therefore expected to help classify rocks.

Texture The model anticipates times when rock formations would be plastic or brittle. This, combined with the intensity of geologic action would affect the texture of geologic formations.

For example, rocks formed from soft and plastic source material would have a fine texture, no matter how intense the water flows.

However the texture of rocks formed from hard and consolidated source material would depend on the intensity of the water flows. Intense water flows on consolidated source material would result in rocks of coarse texture - conglomerates and breccias composed of sharp and angular clasts.

Clasts of soft sediments could be eroded from partially consolidated source rock. These would exhibit plastic behaviour after deposition or be rounded in shape.

Rock texture therefore is expected to be useful for classifying rocks.

Fossils Fossils indicate rapid burial of living creatures before they decompose, and before they are scavenged by other creatures. The state of preservation of the fossil would indicate how quickly the animal was buried, and whether it was subsequently disturbed. The distribution of fossils would, among other things, reflect the distribution of animals on the earth at the time of the Flood. Fossils could not occur before life was created. The requirement for rapid burial would make it more likely for fossils to form during the Flood than during the Lost-World or New-World Eras.

Fossils can be used to guide classification within the model. Fossils can also be used to correlate strata on a regional scale.

Coal It is considered that vegetation buried during the Flood produced coal. Possible mechanisms include:

* Large scale cyclic dumping of floating vegetation on shore lines by tectonically controlled hydraulic deposition [7].
* Lake deposits as observed after the explosion of Mt St Helens [1].
* Deposits in vegetation traps created by ground topology.

Coal rank and quality could indicate when burial took place, whether it was in fresh water or in salty water, how long the vegetation was floating before it was buried, and the presence of suitable catalysts [5].

Coal therefore can be used as a guide for classifying rocks.

Footprints Footprints of animals, birds and humans have often been found in rock formations. Footprints are significant for the Biblical model because the creature must be alive to make a footprint. Footprints would not be found in Creation Rocks. With the exception of the footprints of amphibians, footprints would not be found in Recessive Rocks because no land animals were alive at this time.

Footprints require special conditions for their preservation:

* The texture of the rock material must be suitable to receive the foot impression - e.g. not too wet and not too dry.
* The rock material must either be 'set' before the footprint is covered with new sediment, or covered in such a way that it does not wear away. The time elapsed, the environment, the chemical composition of the rock material, and the mode of covering are all important factors.

These conditions may make it less favourable to preserve footprints in Lost-World or New-World Rocks.

The presence of footprints can help classify rocks.

Raindrops Raindrops have been reported in rock formations. Raindrops are significant for the Biblical model because the surface must be exposed to rain. This would rule out the Foundational Rocks of the Creation Event. Also there would be some period of time during the Flood toward the end of the Inundatory Stage and the beginning of the Recessive stage when raindrops could not form because the surface was covered by water.

In addition, if as hinted in Genesis 2:5 it did not rain before the Flood then the Formative Rocks of the Creation Event and Lost-World Rocks would also be ruled out.

The presence of raindrops is expected to help classify rocks.

Natives Many countries, like Australia, have distinctive animal populations. One would not expect kangaroos, for example, to travel to Noah's Ark from Australia before the Flood, and then return to Australia from the Middle East after the Flood. (Australia, as such did not exist before the Flood.) Consequently, the kinds of animals represented in the fossil record of a country may help distinguish between Flood and New-World Rocks. Such an analysis must ensure that the fossils have been properly identified, allow for variation within created kinds, and consider the possibility of extinctions during the New-World Era.

For example, we would not expect the kinds of fossils found in Flood rocks to correlate strongly with the kinds of native animals in that country. Flood Rocks should contain fossils of some animals from other countries and lack fossils of some native animals.

On the other hand we would expect a good correlation between the kinds of fossils found in New-World Rocks and the kinds of native animals of that country.

The occurrence of native fossils should assist to classify rocks.

5. PROCESSES AND CHARACTERISTICS

We will now consider each of the different geologic phases to decide what characteristics could be expected. Such predictions would be the means by which the rocks in the field would be classified. The features discussed are not exhaustive, nor should the predictions be taken as final, because specific factors may override general expectations.

5.1 Foundational Rocks

Since the Foundational Action involved the creation of the earth, it is expected that Foundational Rocks would be of world scale and extremely thick.

Since the creative process is finished and not operating today, the nature of Original Rocks is not exactly known. We would not immediately suggest an instantaneous creation of sedimentary rocks as this would imply an inbuilt history of once having been deposited from water. Similarly, an instantaneous creation of metamorphic rocks would imply a change from some pre-existing type of rock. Instantaneous creation of crystalline rocks can be envisaged. Indeed, Gentry [2, p.35] has suggested "the Precambrian granites as primordial (or Genesis) rocks."

Original Rocks should show evidence of being subsequently disturbed by the Formative Action and Flood Event. It is possible that crystalline rocks would be hard and solid when created. Original Rocks, therefore, should show signs of being broken, faulted, and eroded by the Formative Action on Day 3 and again by the Flood Event some 1700 years later.

Ensuing Rocks were formed while the whole earth was covered with water, and should show evidence of being deposited or precipitated in a marine environment. Ensuing Rock structures should show evidence of large scale, rapid, and continuous deposition.

Ensuing Rocks should also show evidence of being subsequently disturbed by the Formative Action and Flood Event. It is likely that the Formative Action occurred while the Ensuing Rocks were still soft and pliable. Ensuing Rocks therefore should show signs of plastic deformation and erosion. Since the Flood Event occurred some 1700 years later allowing time for the sediments to lithify, Ensuing Rocks should also show signs of being broken and faulted.

Since life had not been created at the time of the Foundational Action, no trace of life should be found in Foundational Rocks.

5.2 Formative Rocks

Since the Formative Action raised the Lost-World continents from the sea, it is expected that Formative Rocks would be of continental size and thick. The scale would not be as large as the Foundational Rock structures. Formative Rocks should show signs of being deposited under intense hydraulic conditions in a marine environment, perhaps deep sea, but thicker at the margins of the Lost-World continents.

Formative Rocks would have been derived from material eroded from the Foundational Rocks, and material still dissolved and in suspension in the water over the earth. One could expect material so eroded from Original Rocks to produce conglomerates or boulders, whereas material eroded from the soft, pliable Ensuing Rocks would exhibit a fine texture. Derivative Rocks presumably would contain a far greater proportion of material eroded from the Foundational Rocks than Biotic Rocks.

Biotic Rocks would continue to form as sediments settled, but would contain a lesser proportion of material derived from Foundational Rocks. They would not show such severe hydraulic action, and their texture should be finer.

Since Formative Rocks resulted from the Formative Action, they would not be further disturbed before they consolidated. Consequently there should not be signs of plastic deformation. However Formative Rocks should show signs of being disturbed by the Flood Event. Given suitable physical conditions lithification would have ample time to occur, so fractures and faulting would be anticipated.

As the model stands Derivative Rocks would not contain any signs of life. Biotic Rocks would contain microscopic marine life, (and perhaps bacteria and stromatolites) created either on Day 3 or Day 5 and, trapped while the rocks were depositing. (If as Wise [6, p.69] suggested it was found necessary to move the Biotic Phase to Day 2, then in this case Derivative Rocks would also contain microscopic marine life.)

5.3 Lost-World Rocks

The geologic processes and depositional environments of the Lost-World Era may have been similar to the processes and environments experienced today. Therefore the quantity of material formed during the Lost-World Era would have limited area and thickness. In addition, Lost-World Rocks would have been extensively destroyed by the Flood Event. Lost-World Rocks which have survived would be limited in area and thickness and show signs of disturbance by the Flood Event.

It is possible that Lost-World Rocks may contain fossils, perhaps due to such conditions as landslides or collapsing river banks, or stromatolites.

5.4   Inundatory Rocks

The Inundatory Stage commenced with the world densely populated with people [Gen 6:1], animal life and vegetation. It involved the breaking-up of the earth's crust, immense vulcanism, the pouring out of water from under the ground, and intense rainfall. Huge sediment laden rivers scoured the earthquake shaken Lost-World continents depositing sediments in the ocean and inland basins. Water levels on the earth would have risen rapidly. The continental landform would have changed quickly due to severe erosion, deposition and tectonic movements. The oceans and seas would have mixtures of fresh and salt water, hot and cold water, and solutions and sediments of various compositions. Vegetation would have washed down the swollen rivers and floated on the oceans and lakes. Life would have been catastrophically destroyed. Some marine life would have been buried by the rivers of slurry. Air breathing animals would have been herded together on the ever decreasing land areas. In the final phases of the Inundatory Stage the crowded islands of animal life would have been overwhelmed. The corpses would have formed floating graveyards, perhaps being caught in vegetation rafts on the ocean.

It is expected that the structures formed during the Inundatory Stage would be of continental scale. These sediments would be laid unconformably over the Creation Rocks and show evidence of strong hydraulic action. The stratigraphic layers should be evident.

Inundatory Rocks would have been disturbed by subsequent tectonic action during the Inundatory and Recessive stages. The disturbance would not be as great as for Creation Rocks. Inundatory Rocks should generally exhibit a plastic response. Inundatory Rocks would also show signs of severe erosion during the Recessive Stage, the present day landforms providing a guide.

There would be abundant fossils and buried vegetation. Marine fossils should be plentiful, particularly during the early stages. Fossils of vertebrate land animals would be less abundant. Footprints could be expected because life still existed at this time. There should also be evidence of rain.

The earliest rocks in the Inundatory sequence, Eruptive Rocks, would be expected to rest unconformably on Creation Rocks. The latest in the sequence, Zenithic Rocks, would be anticipated in the central plateau regions of today's continents and to display features characteristic of the Flood zenith such as flat topped topography with relatively fine surface texture. No clear criteria are currently proposed to differentiate between Ascending Rocks and the other two phases, apart from the condition that Ascending Rocks lie in the middle. It is envisaged that distinct criteria for the top and bottom boundary of Ascending Rocks will be identified as the model is applied in the field.

5.5   Recessive Rocks

The Recessive Stage occurred as a result of crustal movements which formed the ocean basins and mountain ranges and saw the water flow off the land. It would also have been a time of vulcanism. Vegetation rafts would have continued to beach on the continents. Erosion of soft Inundatory sediments occurred during this time. The carcasses of animals would have been dumped on the continents.

Regional scale sediments would be expected during the Abative Stage as the floodwaters began to move in large sheets from the continents. Local scale sediments would be formed during the Dispersive Stage as the receding waters separated into complexes of lakes and ponds connected by flowing water courses.

Recessive sediments would exhibit less disturbance than any previous sediments. Coal buried during the Recessive Stage would probably be different from that deposited during the Inundatory Stage. This is because the extra months that the vegetation was exposed to the floodwaters would affect the rank of the coal and the level of impurities within the coal.

It is to be expected that there would be animal graveyards, particularly in Dispersive sediments. The fossils would be poorly preserved. There would be no footprints of land animals.

Today's landscapes and drainage basins would help understand where the water flowed during the Recessive Stage and the location of Recessive deposits. Abative sediments would be expected at the edges of the continents and in the basins of large inland seas. Dispersive sediments would be found in ancient lakes and water courses.

5.6   Residual Rocks

At the start of the New-World Era the land would have been freshly deposited and eroded. Continents would include many inland lakes. Vegetation debris, together with the carcasses of animals would be scattered over the land, and floating on the oceans and lakes which would also contain some living sea creatures. All other surviving animal, bird and human life would be located in the region of Mt Ararat.

With time the animal, human, fish, and bird population would multiply and spread over the earth. Vegetation would possibly start growing in situ from vegetation and seeds deposited on the land.

During the Residual Stage the water would continue to flow off the land. The scale of vulcanism, erosion and deposition of sediments would be larger than today but reduced compared the Flood Event. It is possible that ice sheets covered parts of the continents at this time. The inland seas would have gradually drained, perhaps associated with occasional breaching of lake rims. During this time changes in sea level would have produced raised and lowered beaches. Local scale structures would be expected, but not as large as Recessive structures. There would be minimal disturbance of the structures which formed.

Fossils could be formed at this time due to residual catastrophism such as landslides, breached lakes, or collapsing river banks. Fossil fragments could also be eroded from earlier sediments and redeposited.

Landscapes and drainage patterns would control the location of deposits.

5.7 Modern Rocks

The Modern Phase saw the continued geographic dispersion of animal and human life. There would be limited vulcanism, erosion and deposition of sediments.

Modern Rocks would be of limited scale, located in river courses, river deltas, desert areas, ocean basins, and inland seas. Virtually no disturbance of sediments is expected. Fossils can occasionally form when conditions are suitable. Fossil fragments can be eroded from earlier deposits.

6. CONCLUSION

Starting with the Biblical account a simple and practical geologic model has been formulated. The model has been described and labelled to facilitate scientific communication. Appropriate names and terms have been used which are compatible with the Biblical account.

The model can be represented in a diagram which graphically illustrates the concepts, and relates the Biblical record to the rocks of the earth. The diagram can be adapted to the needs of different audiences to enhance communication of the creation concepts. Frequent use of the diagram will educate people to the geologic significance of the Biblical account.

Criteria have been developed to classify rock structures. The criteria suggest directions for investigation, and they provide clues for how rock structures should be arranged. The Biblical criteria would need to be applied to the raw geologic data.

The model needs to be tested and refined by applying it a section of actual rocks in the field. In this way the validity of the model can be checked and the classification criteria can be strengthened. Ongoing work is required to tighten up the classification criteria to reduce subjectivity and make the model more useful.

Geologic resource material such as maps, explanatory reports, and handbooks need to be made available within the framework a broadly accepted Biblical model.

Confidence in the model will grow as it is applied to more geologic situations around the world. Contributions of other researchers from other continents is eagerly anticipated. It may be necessary to modify the model following wider experience in the field situation.

7. BIBLIOGRAPHY

[1]   S. Austin, **Mount St Helens: Explosive Evidence for Catastrophe!** Creation Science Foundation Video, Brisbane, 1989.

[2]   R. V. Gentry, **Creation's Tiny Mystery,** Earth Science Associates, Knoxville, 1992.

[3]   L.Hicks, **The History of the World in Christian Perspective,** Becka Book Publications, Pensacola, 1979.

[4]   J. McDowell, **Evidence that Demands a Verdict,** Here's Life Publishers, San Bernardino, 1979.

[5]   A. Snelling & J. Mackay, **Coal, Volcanism and Noah's Flood,** Creation Ex Nihilo Technical Journal, v1, p11-29, 1984.

[6]   K. P. Wise, **Some Thoughts on the Precambrian Fossil Record,** Creation Ex Nihilo Technical Journal, v6 pt1, 1992.

[7]   J. Woodmorappe, **A Diluvian Interpretation of Ancient Cyclic Sedimentation,** Creation Research Society Quarterly, v14, no4, p189-208, March 1978.

THE WORLDVIEW APPROACH TO CRITICAL THINKING

MARK E. WISNIEWSKI (MA IN EDUCATION)
7501 CAMDEN AVENUE
CLEVELAND, OHIO 44102

ABSTRACT

The material in this paper will be useful to teachers interested in presenting controversial issues in their classroom. The Worldview Approach to Critical Thinking is about teaching students the interpretive process, which involves learning critical thinking skills by the use of controversial topics. The premise of the approach is that beliefs (worldviews) are an integral part of the interpretive process. It involves three major concepts: a) the dividing of science into two major categories: Empirical and Historical, b) the effects of the worldview on interpretation, and c) how to evaluate different worldviews for their validity. Finally, an attitude of openness needs to be a part of the classroom atmosphere.

INTRODUCTION

A failing of many science courses is that they do not teach students how to interpret data; rather they teach the student what the accepted interpretation is. It is then the student's responsibility to memorize that interpretation, yet rarely are they ever exposed to any other possibilities. The supplemental material provided by this approach addresses that deficiency. The use of controversial topics is an important aspect, because it is the vehicle used to teach critical thinking skills.

The underlying premise behind the worldview approach to critical thinking is that **beliefs are an integral part of the interpretive process.**

The worldview approach not only deals with **how to** interpret but also addresses the philosophical framework underlying that process. This approach involves supplemental material that can be woven into the context of any science course, or for that matter, any course that involves the interpretation of evidence.

The approach hinges on three major concepts:

(1)   the dividing of science into two major categories: Empirical and Historical,
(2)   the effects of the worldview on **all** interpretation, and
(3)   how to evaluate different worldviews for their validity.

In addition, the teacher needs to cultivate an attitude of openness within the classroom. The plan is to take the reader through one school year and demonstrate how the three major concepts were incorporated into my physics classes. The object is to allow the reader to see how these concepts are presented within the context of my course. The material is geared for a physics course, but as was mentioned, it can be adapted to any course involving interpretation. The concepts will be introduced and defined in the same sequence that they are to my students. As appropriate, some background information will be interjected to allow the reader to share the same context that the students have when they hear the information.

The following is a brief overview of the sequence that will be covered.

(1)   Introducing and defining the concepts.
(2)   Through out the year, current and appropriate topics are examined from a worldview perspective.
(3)   There are two papers: a discovery paper, by which a student discovers his worldview; and a research paper regarding origins and the effects of the worldview on interpretation.
(4)   Sharing the instructor's worldview with the students.

After the approach has been covered student reaction, both positive and negative, will be examined.

BACKGROUND

Before getting into the meat of the material, I believe it is necessary to provide the reader with some background information. This topic needs to be removed from the ivory towers of textbook definitions and philosophical frameworks and into the real world where a person's emotions and perceptions play an essential part.

The classroom is not a sterile laboratory environment where I ring a bell and the students salivate. Rather it is an environment of human interactions. Remember Christy McAullife, the teacher who died in the shuttle explosion some years back? She is famous for the phrase, "I touch the future, I teach!" All teachers have the enormous responsibility of influencing the lives of their students. The students are not laboratory rats. They are real people and teachers need to be sensitive to their needs and perceptions.

In a similar fashion, there has been a great deal of personal and emotional involvement as this approach developed over the last twenty years. Therefore, before entering the classroom, I will provide you with some of my background experiences and observations, that in my perception, were important in the development of this approach.

INITIAL CONDITIONS

I was born in 1951 and had a middle class, Catholic upbringing; and in December of 1973, graduated from college with a Bachelor of Science in Education. My concentration was termed Comprehensive Science, which in theory, said I was qualified to teach any high school science. My first teaching assignment began in January of 1974.

I was a firm believer in evolution, not because I had examined the issue in detail; but rather, was not aware that other interpretations of the evidence existed. I was convinced that science had "proven" the FACT of evolution beyond a shadow of a doubt. At the time I was not even aware that there was a Creation - Evolution controversy.

My first teaching assignment was earth science and in line with the curriculum, in the spring of the year, I taught the students the evolutionary interpretation of the evidence. An interesting event occurred that first year. Two students came up and asked if they could have a debate between the Bible and science. In the interest of being open minded, we laid out some ground rules and had the debate. I recall sitting in the back of the room listening to the one student defend the Bible and thinking that she did not have a prayer (no pun intended) because evolution had been "proven" by science.

CHANGING WORLDVIEWS

The next year I made a decision for Christ, which was divorced from any scientific considerations. It was in the spring of the year and the evolution section of the course was coming up fast. However, deep in my heart I felt that the evolutionary ideas and my new found relationship were incompatible, but I had no idea how or in what way. I got together with an elder from my new church, who was a research scientist for NASA. We talked for several hours and the rock solid arguments that I had used for evolution over the years suddenly were riddled with holes. Unbeknownst to me I had **changed worldviews** and was now seeing the evidence from a different context. It was shortly thereafter that I became aware of the Creation-Evolution controversy. Beginning with that year I have tried a variety of methods to expose my students to more than one interpretation of the data.

DAD

For the last five or six years of my Dad's life, we would go on a two or three day trip every Easter break. Discussions would inevitably get around to Creation - Evolution. At the time I did not understand why he could not see that the creationist explanation was far superior to the evolutionists. Although several years earlier, I would have thought that the evolutionist's explanation was superior.

It was also a mystery to me how two equally qualified scientists could come up with such divergent explanations for the same evidence. I was under the impression that science could uncover definite answers that worked rather than just result in a variety of possible explanations.

Another topic would involve Biblical interpretation [4]. We would be discussing a particular verse and I would let him know what the "correct" interpretation was (my interpretation), and his standard reply was "that's just your opinion." To which I had no convincing reply.

A disturbing thought was that if the words of the Bible could be interpreted to fit any belief system [15], based on the opinion of the interpreter, then the Bible really says nothing at all. Not a comforting thought if the Bible is the authority in your life. There had to be some objective way to interpret data that would minimize opinion. Trying to find an objective way to interpret evidence was a principle factor in the development of this approach.

THE FIRST LIGHT

The first light dawned in January of 1987. In the Bible-Science Newsletter there was an interview with Charles Thaxton [1, p. 6]. In the interview he talked about dividing science into two broad categories: empirical and historical. One studied the current functioning of the natural world and the other studied the history of the natural world.

Talk about lights going off in your head. I had been through four years of college and thirteen years as a science teacher, five in earth science and eight in physics, was just finishing up my master's degree and I had never heard of such a division. NEVER! Since that time my observations have confirmed that very few people are aware of such a division. In contrast, instead of a sudden realization, discovering the worldview concept and its affect on interpretation and how to evaluate worldviews was a process that extended over the next four years.

INTO THE CLASSROOM

The '91 - '92 school year was the first time I piloted this approach in my classroom. Before I did however, I sat down with the school's administrator in charge of curriculum and laid out the procedure and rationale of what I was going to do and obtained approval.

The following are selected sections from the science philosophy of Lakewood High School:

(A) "As part of the understanding of scientific inquiry, students should learn the processes common to all fields of science." (One of those processes is the interpretation of data.)

(B) "Not only do we have a responsibility to allow students to question and search for their own answers, but also to provide them with scientific facts, inquiry and problem solving skills, and a desire to acquire new knowledge."

(C) "They must be able to collect and weigh evidence and apply this knowledge to practical situations through critical thinking in order to make their own decisions."

The Worldview Approach to Critical Thinking was tailored to fit this philosophy. An important part of this approach is that issues will be examined from multiple points of view.

If one foresees the need to deal with a controversial topic in the classroom it is a good idea to get administrative approval. In that way the administration is aware of the topic you are dealing with, Creation - Evolution in my case, and how you are presenting it in your classroom. Administrators, like most people, do not like surprises. Because the procedure involved a controversial topic, by obtaining approval ahead of time, later that first year when a parent did call the administration was supportive.

Several members of the English department were instrumental in helping to work out the mechanics of the research paper. They were also delighted that someone from another department was having the students do a research paper. They had no objections because a controversial topic was involved. A member of the Health department uses a modified version of this approach to help students understand where different values come from, and one other member of the Science department made the connection regarding the differences between empirical and historical science and has been pointing it out to his students ever since.

THE METHOD

Are you ready to get to class? Take out your notes, skip 5 lines, and put down today's date.

After the introductory material, the first topic covered is the Geocentric - Heliocentric controversy. The first week is spent teaching students about the motions of the heavenly bodies: sun, moon, stars and planets. After they get a feel for what is going on in the heavens we try to get a handle on the **why**: the cause behind the motions.

Putting yourself in the stationary frame of reference is most natural; therefore, an earth centered explanation is per-fectly reasonable. The student will get a good rundown on the Earth centered system, also called the Ptolemaic system, with it's multiple epicycles that were used to explain the retrograde motion of the planets.

The students will be introduced to Aristotelian physics. That all things on the earth are made up of four basic elements: fire, air, water and earth, and there is one set of laws that governs how things work. **All** the objects in the heavens are made up of a fifth element called quintessence. There is also a different set of laws that governs how things work in the heavens, and never the twain shall meet. In my class the boundary separating the heavens and the earth is called the, **the wall**. To the people in that day it was very real.

The purpose of this background information is to set the context for the students, to help them understand some of the bits and pieces of the worldview that was in place just before Copernicus made his debut. After the students are knowledgeable about how the heavens work, the prevailing explanations regarding why and some of the beliefs that were common at that time, Copernicus is introduced. For him to suggest a sun centered system was not just a simple change in a frame of reference. Rather, it involved rejecting common sense, direct observation, the current teaching's of philosophy and religion, and all of physical science [13, unit 2, p. 43]. Switching to sun centered meant that people would have to change their fundamental beliefs about reality. In other words they had to change worldviews. It is like an atheist becoming a fundamental Christian or vice versa. Everything you believed about reality has to be rethought.

Within the context of this controversy, the concept of a worldview is briefly introduced and how it affects one's understanding of the world. A worldview is an internal belief system about the real world - what it is, why it is and how it operates. Within a person's mind, it defines the limits of what is possible and impossible.

In "The Structure of a Scientific Revolution," Thomas Kuhn calls this changing one's belief about fundamental reality a paradigm switch [9, p. 158]. Once that switch is made, new avenues of thought are now possible. For example, before the Copernican revolution the concept of calculating the relative distances between the planets was not even a remote possibility. Even less of a possibility was that the other planets could be similar to the earth and that there might be creatures like us living on them. After the paradigm switch the preceding became valid areas of inquiry. A critical point is that even though the topic being studied, the repeating motions in the heavens, involves the current functioning of the natural world, one's belief system had an effect on the way one perceived reality.

After the introduction of Copernicus, the downfall of the Geocentric model and the rise of the Heliocentric is traced through the work of Brahe, Kepler, Galileo and Newton.

The Creation-Evolution debate is introduced as a modern day controversy within the preceding context; **but,** there are critical differences that need to be understood to fully comprehend the issues. Before examining any of the details regarding the debate, the differences between empirical and historical science are examined. To date only empirical issues have been under consideration. In other words, current functioning of the natural world, in particular the repeating motions in the heavens.

Current functioning (empirical or operational science) was the major emphasis during the formative years of modern science. Questions regarding origins (historical or origin science) were not an area of study or concern. When questions regarding the history of the natural world did begin to arise, no formal distinctions were made with respect to what was being studied and the method used; therefore, most people are under the impression that there is only one category of science, which was broadened a bit to include origins [5, p. 125]. But as will be demonstrated, the differences are significant.

EMPIRICAL SCIENCE

Empirical science involves the current functioning of the natural world. In other words, how do things work? It involves, what I call the four pillars of Empirical Science.

(1) *Direct Observation - seeing the process in action.*
   The motions of the heavenly bodies.
(2) *Repeatability - in order to understand the process you have to be able to observe it more than once.*
   The sun rises in the east, arcs across the sky and sets in the west, every day.
   There are also seasonal variations, which constitute a pattern within a pattern.
(3) *Predictability - If you understand the process, then you should be able to predict the resulting effects.*
   On any given day of the year you should be able to predict where and at what time the sun will rise.
(4) *Falsifiability - The description of the process should be stated in such a way that it can be proven false.*

The following example is used with my students. The two statements below are put on the overhead and the students are asked to decide which is scientific and which is speculation.

   (1) Life exists only on earth.   (2) Life exists in other parts of the universe.

Number two will be examined first. If one goes to Mars and finds that there is no life there, then life could be on Jupiter. If it is not on Jupiter, then it could be on Saturn or Neptune, or in the next solar system. If not in the next solar system, then maybe in the next galaxy. In other words, if you do not find it where you are presently looking, then it could always be just around the next corner. There is no way to prove it false. Statement number two is speculation. On the other hand, if one goes to some other planet and finds life there, then number one has been proven false (wrong). Statements regarding current functioning, by definition have to be very narrow and specific.

Also interpretive possibilities are limited. For example, in physics when distance time data is collected and plotted on a d-t graph and results in a straight line positive slope, that is constant velocity motion, end of discussion. In general, most scientists, regardless of their position on origins are in basic agreement regarding the current function of the natural world.

In empirical science, the word **proven**, as commonly understood, is applicable. The process in question can be experimentally observed and repeated; also the predictions can be verified. In other words, the truth or validity of the process or item in question has been established beyond doubt. Examples of **proven** theories include Newton's Laws of Motion, Laws of Electricity and Magnetism and Heat Flow. The results of basic empirical research have born much technological fruit in the areas of transportation, communication and medicine. These successes have led to the false perception that historical science can unravel the past with the same degree of accuracy. But as you will see, certainty is not a hallmark of historical science.

HISTORICAL SCIENCE

The scientist exploring the past is observing the effects and has to guess at what the process **might** have been. Many of the historical topics are singularities, one time events: the formation of the Earth, the carving of the Grand Canyon or the origin of life. These effects are singularities, which no one saw happen; therefore, there is no way of testing the actual process, whatever it may have been.

Historical science is, in a sense, like a forensic science. The investigator cannot test any of his theories against the actual crime. However, he can study a particular process under a variety of conditions and the resulting effects. If any of the studied effects match those on the victim, that would seem pretty convincing circumstantial evidence that a particular process may have been the cause. But unless the crime was observed, one cannot say for sure.

Historical science is a bit more complicated because the process in question did not happen in the present or close proximity; but happened in the unobserved past. It involves a process for which we have no experience. The formation of the earth, for example, would be analogous to a manufacturing process, like the assembly of an automobile. What we presently observe, however, is similar to the functioning and/or maintenance of the automobile after it is off the assembly line. These are two distinct phases and it is important to distinguish the differences between them. Man has access only to the functioning/maintenance processes, the manufacturing process, whatever it may have been, has yet to be observed. Therefore, any historical theories that are based on present processes involve a great deal of extrapolation. Can an actual Earth be formed under a variety of conditions in order to rule out various possibilities? Whatever erosional processes formed the Grand Canyon, no one observed it, and what has been produced in test tubes is far from alive and a great deal of intelligence has been involved in those experiments.

EXPLORING THE PAST

Extrapolation involves taking a present day process, **assume** all things remain the same, and extend that process into the past or future. In the Fall of the year, students are required to check the five day weather forecast against what actually occurs. It is no surprise when the forecast and the actual weather rarely match. The reason being the large number of unforeseen and unknown variables that cannot be taken into account in such a complex process. The further one moves from the present, the more problematic the unknowns. If the reliability of extrapolating five days into the future is questionable, then what about five months, or five years, or five million years? Will extrapolation work any better when trying to explain the past? At least with the future you can eventually check the extrapolation against what actually happens, but with the past there is no such luxury. Extrapolation has serious limits. Consequently, the initial assumptions and resulting conclusions should be critically evaluated rather than accepted without question.

Another method used to explore the past is historical records. When a historical record is used, the question of its historical and archaeological accuracy become dominant. If a particular record is found to be reliable in areas that can be verified, that is consistent with other historical sources, archeological findings and empirical facts, then that increases one's confidence that the record is factual even in areas that are beyond observable verification.

THE FOUR PILLARS

Regarding the four pillars, whatever process formed the Earth, it is beyond direct observation, thereby ruling out pillar number one. It is a singularity; therefore, it is not repeatable. Predictions, however, can be made in a certain sense. If a particular process was the cause then one would expect it to leave certain effects. Darwin predicted that there should be innumerable transitional forms in the fossil record based on his understanding of what he believed was the process. One problem is that even if the expected effects are found, since the process was never observed, one can never be sure that some other process did not produce the same effects. For example, homologous features can be explained as the result of common descent or common design. Two different

597

processes yet yielding the same effect. Convincing arguments can be made for both sides but since no one observed the process who can say for sure?

Finally, how does one write a statement about falsifiability regarding an unknown process that occurred once in the past? That raises another question, can a historical theory ever be truly falsified? In a historical theory, one is looking for broad consistencies or inconsistencies regarding the predicted effects. Because innumerable transitional forms are not found in one locality that does not falsify Darwin's theory. However, over time, as more and more localities also demonstrate an absence of the transitions, there would appear to be a definite inconsistency between the effects the theory predicts and what is actually found, thereby casting doubt on the theory. A historical theory is not "falsified" by a definite experiment or discovery like an empirical explanation. Rather, one is examining the effects and looking for consistencies or inconsistencies with regard to the theory. Consistencies strengthen the plausibility of the theory, while if the number of inconsistencies increases, then the theory needs to be modified or eliminated as new evidence comes to light. Another example is the Steady State theory regarding the origins of the universe. The theory suggests a continuous creation of matter, thereby maintaining a constant, homogenous universe in space and time. However, the observations did not match the predictions. The discovery of more and more radio sources the deeper one looked into space, which is assumed to be looking backwards into time, indicated a changing universe that is not homogenous throughout [10, p. 144-148]; therefore, the Steady State theory has fallen into disfavor.

TESTING HISTORICAL THEORIES

Historical theories **cannot be proven** in the empirical sense because the actual process or event is beyond experimental evaluation. However, disputes can be settled in a method similar to a lawyer presenting a case to a jury [17, chs. 13 & 12]. Evidence is presented along with a suggested explanation. Theories can then be evaluated in reference to their consistency with what is empirically known. For example, based on what we empirically know regarding the storage of information in systems of symbols, is DNA the product of random chance or intelligent design? The objective standard against which historical theories can be judged is our present understanding of current functioning, and how well a theory can explain observed effects and/or predict yet undiscovered effects. Historical theories **cannot be proven,** the best that can be said is that a particular theory is the most plausible. This point is critical and needs repeating, historical theories **cannot be proven,** the best that can be said is that a particular theory is the most plausible. **The key is plausibility not provability.**

In addition, the generation of a historical story is, in a sense, a chicken and egg problem. On the one hand, a person's belief about the past influences his interpretation; on the other hand, without a belief about the past he has no context that allows him to make sense of the data. Without the past as a context, a person is like one who has amnesia. He has no personal experience from which to draw; therefore, he must believe what others tell him, or he can make up his own story about what might have happened in the past.

To further emphasize the differences: Newton penned the laws of motion over 300 years ago. Those same laws are taught in physics courses all around the world. In contrast, since the discovery of dinosaurs many different theories have been suggested to explain their extinction [2, p. 117-126] and there does not seem to be an end in sight. Why does one seem unchanging and the other seems to be in a constant state of flux. Newton's laws involve current functioning while extinction theories are historical issues. Is it beginning to make sense why in some areas of science explanations never seem to change while in others the explanations are constantly changing? In historical theories, new information is always being uncovered and theories need to be adjusted or eliminated accordingly.

COMPARISON

Below are the two methods laid out side by side.

EMPIRICAL SCIENCE
Observe the process

HISTORICAL SCIENCE
Observe the effects, <u>guess</u> at the process

1. OBSERVATION
2. REPEATABLE
3. PREDICTABLE
4. FALSIFIABLE

1. GATHER EVIDENCE
2. GENERATE A <u>STORY</u> TO EXPLAIN THE EVIDENCE

TEST
EXPERIMENT

TEST
EVIDENCE / STORY
PLAUSIBILITY (consistent with
empirical knowledge)

**Studying current functioning
of the natural world**

**Studying history of the
natural world.**

As you can see, Empirical and Historical are not the same, what is studied and the methodology by which it is studied are very different. Once this distinction is recognized it becomes clear why in certain respects science can discover definite answers that work (empirical) while in other respects the best that can be accomplished is a plausible explanation of what **might** have happened (historical).

The Creation - Evolution controversy was introduced as part of the context to help students understand the critical divisions in science. Now that the divisions are understood, the controversy is reintroduced adding much more detail. The extreme positions are the emphasis. In the beginning matter, versus In the beginning God. Old earth versus young earth; uniformity of process versus global catastrophe; descent versus design. Students are made aware that shades of gray exist and in between positions are mentioned, but often times the differences between these positions can be subtle and confuse the main thrust; therefore, the emphasis is on the extremes. The extremes also help clarify **how belief and fact work together in the interpretive process.**

Take the Grand Canyon as an example. The evolutionist believing in an old universe and uniformity of process sees a canyon that formed slowly over millions of years. As supporting evidence, he will point to the present erosional rates of the Colorado river and extrapolate into the past. A creationist believing in a young universe and global catastrophe sees a canyon that is the result of a catastrophic erosional event. For supporting evidence he will point to the carving of the Little Grand Canyon that was produced by a mud flow, in one day, near Mt. St. Helens (March 19, 1982). He will envision a similar process having acted in the past.

ENTER THE WORLDVIEW

The worldview material is introduced within the context of the Creation - Evolution controversy. Notice that you have two very different scenarios to explain the Grand Canyon. What guiding principle allows one person to interpret the evidence one way and another person to interpret that same evidence so differently?

Recall what happened when Copernicus suggested a sun centered universe. Why was changing the frame of reference such a traumatic suggestion? Because it meant changing your entire belief system about reality - your worldview. As was demonstrated when discussing the Copernican revolution, one's perceptions about how the universe is **supposed** to work, influences how a person understands his world. The guiding factor is the worldview. The effects of the worldview are even greater in historical science because the actual event or process was never observed and more than one explanation is possible. In fact, the worldview affects all interpretation: scientific, religious, social and moral. The worldview is a very important part of the interpretive process.

The worldview is an internal belief system about reality. It is like a tinted pair of glasses that colors our perceptions of all of life's experiences; an internal standard against which the input received through our senses is evaluated. A worldview is not formally taught; rather, it is caught. We tend to unconsciously pick up the beliefs and values of the prevailing times and culture in which we live.

The following quote comes from a book entitled "2084: A Novel" and I think it hits the nail on the head. Dr. Larry Poland is commenting about scientific research; however, his comments have much broader applications.

> Do you really think there is any such thing as objective research? Honestly, now, have you really ever known a researcher who did not take tons of biasing baggage with him into his inquiry? Can you even postulate a person's being able to set aside all the lessons from his life experience, all of the blind socialization he has received from his culture, and all of his instinctive or learned predispositions? [12, p. 184]

This "biasing baggage" is a person's worldview.

As was already mentioned the worldview affects **ALL** interpretation, not only scientific. For example, is the Grand Canyon the result of a little bit of water and a lot of time or a lot of water and a little bit of time? How long was the Genesis DAY: 24 hours, a thousand years or an indefinite period of time? If you emerge unscathed from a terrible car accident: is the Lord's hand upon you, were you lucky or was it your karma? Is homosexuality an abomination or a viable alternative lifestyle? How you respond to any of the above is dependent upon your worldview.

The factious issues tearing apart our society are actually battles between worldviews [8, p. 35]. Debates over origins, sexual permissiveness, the breakdown of the traditional family, euthanasia, abortion, homosexual rights and the identity crisis are some of the major concerns. The student in the high school classroom rarely recognizes that all of these issues are interrelated. They are but side effects due to a changing context regarding prime reality. Dr. Francis Schaeffer, speaking about the above issues, laments that Christians "have failed to see that all of this (the factious issues) has come about due to a shift in world view - that is, through a fundamental change in the overall way people think and view the world and life as a whole" [14, p. 17]. Charles Colson recognizes the same cause and effect relationship. "Although the West is still called a "christian culture" by some, it is not. It is a distinctly post-Christian, dominated by a relativistic world-view" [3, p. 171].

The abortion controversy is a classic example. On one side, the Pro-choice people believe the fetus is just so much tissue that can be removed at the whim of the individual. The tissue is not considered to be a human being. Abortion is a basic human right, hence no crime is involved. On the other side, the Pro-life people believe the fetus is a living human being, at a very early stage of development, but no less valuable than a child or mature adult. Abortion is murder. Notice that the value and meaning of the fetus were assigned in accordance with the beliefs (worldview) of the one doing the beholding. Neither side seems to recognize that **they are examining the same item but measuring it from a different standard.**

WHAT STANDARD?

Consider the following analogy. Many years ago, before the massive increase of travel and communication there were two scientists from different countries, Dr. Aslong and Dr. Halfsize. They were both invited to attend a conference on standardizing the unit of length. Curiously, the standard of length used in both countries was called the "stadia." However, Dr. Standardlength, who organized the conference, was the only one who knew that even though the name was the same, the "stadia" from each country was a different length. Dr. Aslong's stadia was equal to our present day meter; while Dr. Halfsize's stadia was equal to only half a meter.

To make a pitch for a worldwide standard of measure, Dr. Standardlength had the two scientists independently measure his height. The results of which would be reported at the conference. Dr. Aslong reported the measurement as "2 stadia." While Dr. Halfsize reported the measurement as "4 stadia." The following conversation ensued. "Dr. Aslong, you must have made an error. We can both see that Dr. Standardlength is of average size, but your measurement makes him out to be a midget." "Not so!" replied Dr. Aslong, "I agree that Dr. Standardlength is of average height; however, your measurement makes him out to be a giant." "But Dr. Aslong," counters Dr. Halfsize, "it is so obvious that your measurement is in error. Why can't you understand that?" Dr. Aslong answers saying, "I'm just as frustrated as you are Dr. Halfsize. I agree that there is an error, but it is obvious that it is on your part." And so the conversation goes.

The problem is that they are examining the **same** item but measuring or evaluating it using different standards. As noted earlier, the same is true of the Grand Canyon, the Genesis day, emerging unscathed from a car accident or the homosexual issue.

The identity crisis is also linked to the worldview. Ultimate questions such as Who am I, Why am I here and Where am I going, all have different answers in accordance with the worldview of the one doing the answering. A biblical worldview sees man as created in the image of God. Secularism humanism understands man as having evolved from the animals and monism perceives man as being god. The diversity of answers is mindboggling?

Why do origin debates become so heated? Because they call into question the worldview of another. If it can be demonstrated that one's worldview is in error then that means that person has been living a lie and that is a hard pill to swallow.

Clearly, **a person's belief system is an integral part of the interpretative process.** In other words, evidence **DOES NOT** demand a particular interpretation; rather, a person's worldview demands the evidence be interpreted a particular way. When it comes to interpretation, the fly in the ointment is the interpreter himself, whose worldview influences the analysis.

PAST - PRESENT CONNECTION

When it comes to historical evidence the worldview provides the context for understanding the present. For example, have you ever watched a Nature special on PBS and out of the blue, the commentator begins recounting an origin scenario. He may talk about the Big Bang, common descent or natural selection. Why? He is setting a context for the listener. He is making sense of the present by grounding it in what he believes is the truth about the past. In the scriptwriter's mind it defines the limits of what is possible and impossible.

Because people have a variety of different beliefs about the past, they interpret evidence in a number of different ways. The question becomes, which past is the truth: evolution, creation, some combination or maybe endless cycles?

TRUTH

I like to use this analogy with my students. Think about your own life. From the time you were born until now there has been only one chain of events that has occurred. Each time you made a decision to follow a particular path a new link was formed; but do not lose sight of the fact that there is only one chain, not multiple chains. That chain of events is the truth about the your past. The argument can be extended to the very beginning of the universe. There has been only one course of events, not multiple courses, therefore only **one truth.**

What that means regarding worldviews is that **NOT ALL WORLDVIEWS ARE EQUALLY VALID!** The past-present connection is critical because it removes a worldview from the realm of personal opinion and connects it with the reality of what has happened and what is happening.

THE WORLDVIEW AND CRITICAL THINKING

The worldview is all encompassing, **there is NOT ONE area of interpretation that the worldview does not affect.** That being the case, it is in the student's best interest to learn to think in terms of worldviews. Very few of the students I teach are going to become scientists or engineers. However, all of them will have to come to grips with the issues facing our society and the ultimate questions. Students need to develop critical thinking skills such as analysis, synthesis, evaluation, distinguishing fact from opinion, identifying bias, judging the strength of an argument and determining the credibility of a source. The goal of worldview thinking is to help students become critical thinkers in contrast to parrots.

Recollect that for most people the worldview is caught, not taught. In other words, most people are not consciously aware of their worldview. Much like the foundation of a building, it is real, necessary but not highly visible. The result is that these internal values and beliefs are rarely ever questioned or evaluated concerning their validity.

A goal of the worldview approach is the discovering of one's worldview thereby exposing it for critical examination. Once the worldview is out in the open, another goal is to evaluate it and determine why one believes it is true in light of so many different options. Recall that the worldview is the internal standard used to assign meaning and value. Once a student understands the components that make up a worldview, he will then have the knowledge and tools to be able to discern something about the worldview of another, thereby, giving the student insight into why other people are reaching very different conclusions when examining the same evidence.

To accomplish these goals real issues need to be explored and that spells controversy. However, it is only by being exposed to foreign worldview that one begins to seriously consider his own. In the science classroom the Creation-Evolution debate provides such a vehicle.

WORLDVIEW COMPONENTS

What are the components that make up a worldview and how are they categorized? A worldview involves six components. First, because of the importance of the past-present connection one's stand regarding ultimate origins is crucial. This component forms the cornerstone upon which all the others rest. Second, what is the nature of man and how can the noble and depraved sides be explained? Third, what is death and what happens afterwards? Fourth, what is the nature of evil and suffering? Fifth, against what standard does one measure morals and ethics?

Finally, is history linear, cyclical or some combination?

One problem with worldview thinking is that if there are five billion people on the planet each having his own worldview. In that regard, worldview thinking seems a bit unmanageable. However, all worldviews have one thing in common, something is there. They differ in regards to the true nature of that something. Using ultimate nature as a guide it results in three possibilities [16, p. 17]: the fundamental essence of all things is a) matter; or b) spirit; or c) a combination of matter and spirit. Representative worldviews would be Atheistic Evolutionism, Eastern Monism and Biblical Theism respectively. Another method of categorizing worldviews is in regards to whether or not one believes in God. If one believes in God, the views can be subdivided into what type of G/god. My preference is using the ultimate nature of things.

The representative worldviews need to be defined so that everyone has the same understanding when those terms are used. A Biblical Theist begins with Scripture and interprets all data within that context. Reality has a material and spiritual component. Biblical interpretation is along fundamental, conservative guidelines. The starting point is a historical document. Atheistic Evolutionism denies a spiritual component. Impersonal, natural law is the maker of the universe and the extrapolation of present day processes is the rule. For the Eastern Monist one impersonal spiritual element constitutes all reality. "God is the cosmos. God is all that exists; nothing exists that is not God. If anything that is not God appears to exist, it is *maya*, illusion, and does not truly exist" [16, p. 140, italics in original].

When the concept of worldviews is introduced the following nine views are mentioned briefly: BIBLICAL THEISM, Deism, ATHEISTIC EVOLUTIONISM, Nihilism, Existentialism (atheistic and theistic), EASTERN MONISM, New Age and Animism. For the remainder of the year the three fundamental views, as noted above, are the predominate views under consideration and the students are given a more detailed look at each of those views as they relate to the six components that make up the framework of a worldview.

THE FUNDAMENTAL VIEWS

The following information is by no means the final word or all inclusive. Volumes have and will be written on each of these topics. One purpose is to expose the student to **the variety of responses** and their connection with the initial assumptions. As was pointed out at the conference, a way to strive for greater objectivity, than is listed below, is to obtain and document direct quotes from persons who hold the worldview being discussed. The object being to accurately represent each view under consideration.

The origin component of a worldview entails a **belief** about the initial conditions. In the beginning God, a Spirit, Who created the physical universe is a faith tenet the Biblical Theist believes because he has confidence in the credibility of a historical document. That in the beginning was a dense ball of matter before the Big Bang is a belief held by an Atheistic Evolutionist who subscribes to the backwards extrapolation of presently understood processes. Eastern thought is **radically** different from Western and entails many diverse beliefs. However, a common tenet is one of endless cycles as opposed to a distinct beginning. How one arrives at what the initial conditions may have been will vary, but the point is that what those conditions were is beyond empirical verification and accepted on faith. The initial faith assumption sets the stage for each worldview and upon that foundation everything else is built. Once the initial faith assumption is established, the other five components of a worldview are predictable if one is attempting to be consistent with the initial conditions.

The Biblical Theist believes man was created in the image of God and each human life has worth because it was reckoned so by the Creator. The noble and depraved sides of man are explainable due to the Fall. One man unselfishly risking his life for another is the Image dimly showing through, while another man involved in child pornography is a result of man's alienation from God. In contrast, the Atheistic Evolutionist believes man is fundamentally no different from all the other creatures on the planet. Man's depraved side is just a throwback of his animal ancestry and his noble side is still an enigma. The Eastern Monist believes that man is god and that noble and depraved are just two sides of the same coin.

The Biblical Theist believes death is the punishment for sin and that there was no death before the Fall. After death is judgment and heaven or hell is the final destination depending on what one has done with Jesus Christ. The Atheistic Evolutionist believes death is part of the process that brought man into existence and has always been; and when you are dead you are dead. For the Eastern Monist, death is part of the reincarnation cycle. Through this cycle of rebirths, he will eventually fuse with "ultimate reality."

To the Biblical Theist evil and suffering are intimately related to the Fall. There was a time when neither existed and there will be again, but our present situation is the result of a tragic choice. The solution is the cross. To the Atheistic Evolutionist evil is a term coined to foster superstitions and suffering is part of the selection process and has always been. The solution is the advancement of science and technology. According to the Eastern Monist there is only one ultimate reality; therefore, there are no distinctions between good and evil. Suffering is "Maya," illusion.

The Bible is the absolute, unchanging moral and ethical standard for the Biblical Theist. In contrast, the Atheistic Evolutionist believes that man is at the top of the evolutionary ladder and there is no transcendent standard; therefore, man determines the standard, which is subject to change. For the Eastern Monist, man is god, he can set his own standard and there is also no reason why it must remain fixed. The entire concepts of "right" and "wrong" are in reference to a standard. An issue plaguing society today is who has the **right** to make up that standard?

The Biblical Theist views the big picture of history as linear. Although there are internal cycles as civilizations oscillate between moral excellence and depravity. In contrast, when looking into the past or the future, the Eastern Monist perceives endless cycles. If an Atheistic Evolutionist believes in the Big Bang, the universe had a beginning, there is no particular purpose, and the working out of the natural laws will result in the heat death. On the other hand, if he believes in a oscillating universe or plasma cosmology, then endless cycles are the rule.

A key point about the above information is that it entails **beliefs** that cannot be proven in the empirical sense. How one arrives at their beliefs may entail a variety of methods: historical or religious documents, circumstantial evidence, authority figures or personal experience. Evidence that will convince one person may seem irrelevant to another. Yet each has faith that his position is true and he believes the supporting evidence is sufficient. This internal belief system (worldview) forms the context against which each of us makes sense of our world. In other words, **beliefs are an integral part of the interpretative process**. Accepting a position on faith is **NOT** intellectual suicide.

If students are to become critical thinkers, then it is important to recognize the influence of the worldview, even in a science classroom; recall that 1) empirical science is influenced by beliefs; 2) the interpretation of historical data is affected by the interpreter's world view; and 3) understanding a writer's belief structure gives the student insight into the "why" behind the explanations that appear in the text.

DECISIONS, DECISIONS, DECISIONS

Remember, based on the past - present connection not all worldviews are equally valid. Considering all of the different possibilities, how does one go about making an intelligent, evidence based, decision? Once the components of the worldview are understood then one can apply the most fundamental law of logic, the law of noncontradiction. "No two opposite statements can both be true at the same time and in the same sense" [7, p. 271]. For example, in a Biblical Theist's worldview, man cannot be an image bearer and have descended from other organisms (Gen 1:26-27; 2:7). Or in an Atheistic Evolutionary worldview, man cannot have a spiritual component that leaves the body and enters another phase of existence after death.

A worldview must also be consistent with what is empirically "known" about the physical universe and common human experience. Views that deny gravity or believe that human suffering is an illusion are inconsistent with what is empirically known. As was mentioned earlier Darwin predicted innumerable transitional forms would be found in the rocks of the earth. The absence of those transitional forms led to punctuated equilibrium theory, because gradualism was inconsistent with the data. In a like manner, the Steady State theory of the origin of the universe was abandoned because the deeper one looked into space the less homogeneous the universe became, which was inconsistent with the theory. The following example is more relevant to a high school student. If your boyfriend or girlfriend says that they love you and then you see them on a date with someone else, their actions are inconsistent with their words.

Consistency is the key. A worldview needs to be internally consistent, and externally consistent with what is empirically known about the universe. Also if an inconsistency is found one needs to determine whether or not it is apparent or real. A person should strive for the worldview with the fewest number of inconsistencies.

There are other tests. In addition, Nash [11, p. 57-63] uses the tests of practice and experience; while Geisler and Watkins [6, p. 231-241] include a fourth test called comprehensiveness along with some cautions about how not to choose a worldview. These items are very useful, but due to time constraints are not examined in detail. The law of non-contradiction is the primary focus.

100% OBJECTIVITY

Twenty years ago I set about trying to find an objective way of interpreting evidence. What I discovered was that a person's worldview is an integral part of the interpretive process. Therefore, I have concluded that one hundred percent objectivity, untainted by beliefs, does not exist. This was in conflict with the training I received at the universities, which left me with the impression that beliefs never or seldom enter into the interpretive process, especially where science is concerned. I trust that the preceding material has demonstrated the integral part that beliefs play in the interpretive process. However, one should **STRIVE** towards the goal of one hundred percent objectivity, and a very important part of that striving is a recognition of the worldview and it's far reaching effects.

OTHER TOPICS FROM A WORLDVIEW PERSPECTIVE.

The student has all the core information: the dividing of science into two major categories, how a worldview affects interpretation and how to choose among worldviews. In summary, beliefs are an integral part of the interpretive process. At this point, it is about three weeks into the school year and the core material took about one week to present. Now it is back to physics. The philosophical framework and the tools for evaluation are in place, as the year progresses, whenever a current and/or appropriate topic comes up in the news, some time will be spent examining it from a worldview perspective.

For example, one topic that was covered this year was Sex and the Worldview. December 15, 1993, was a national Aides day, and there was an all school assembly. Factual information about Aides was presented, but when it came to prevention, condoms was given about ten minutes worth of time and abstinence was mentioned in passing. It was confusing that the only sure method of prevention was passed over so casually. However, there is much more at stake. The disease is contracted primarily by sexual encounters; therefore, because of this means of transmission there are much broader consequences involved than just the prevention of a disease. It may entail the survival of society.

Sex was examined from two different worldview perspectives: Biblical Theist and Atheistic Evolutionist. Now the students have the opportunity of seeing the interpretive process in action. The emphasis, as always, was to show how and why, because of beliefs, very different conclusions are reached regarding the same item.

The stage was set by examining initial conditions: the nature of man, according to the Biblical Theist and the Atheistic Evolutionist. Next, how does each side define sex? What is it; why is it? Third, how would each side define sexual freedom and who makes up the rules regarding sexual conduct? What is the best way of preventing the spread of sexually transmitted diseases? Finally, marriage and family were investigated. Where did marriage come from? Why should there be marriage? What are the purposes of family? What, if any, are the responsibilities of being a part of a family? Is there a relationship between the health of society and the health of the family? Considering our nation, what have been some of the consequences of our changing views regarding sex? In my estimation, the discussions were fruitful and gave the students the opportunity to consider the issue from multiple perspectives.

The following are examples of some additional topics. The cover story of TIME magazine (November 8, 1993) was entitled "Cloning Humans." An additional question on the cover was "Where do we draw the line?" The June (1994) issue of National Geographic, on a page entitled "Geographica," had a column labeled, "Tyrannosaurus Sex: How Can You Tell?" Which brings up an interesting question, if you have never seen them in the flesh, how can you tell from only the bones? A good example of historical science and possible explanations. The cover story of TIME, March 14, 1994, was entitled "How Man Began? Fossil bones from the dawn of humanity are rewriting the story of evolution." Another good example of historical science and how the explanations keep changing as new information becomes available. The cover story of NEWSWEEK, June 13, 1994, was titled "The Politics of Virtue." This brings up the question of who defines the standard? The amount of time spent on any of these topics is up to the discretion of the teacher, from ten minutes to an entire period. In each case, the purpose being to show students how the worldview affects the way a person interprets the evidence, thereby helping students understand the interpretive process.

DISCOVERY PAPER

Sometime near the beginning of November the students are assigned a discovery paper. The purpose is to help (force) students to consider their positions on the six components that make up the worldview. For each of the six components the student needs to relate 1) what he believes, 2) the reasons why he believes it and 3) where he got that belief from initially. This is an opinion paper and it is stressed that the paper is graded based on the completeness of the answers, not on the content. The students are trying to discover their beliefs, not conform to any particular one. You will be amazed at the jumble of beliefs that students have tucked away in their hearts.

Once the students have had to work through these issues on their own and become familiar with the worldview components, they are now in a position to be able to discern something about the worldview of another. For example, if in the course of a conversation a person mentions things that happened in a previous life time, as casually as speaking about yesterday's dinner, it is very probable that the speaker has some New Age and/or Eastern leanings in their worldview. Or someone may profess belief in the Bible and is also convinced that an evolutionary process did occur, then that individual might be considered a progressive creationist or theistic evolutionist. Obviously, the minute bit of information in the above examples does not reveal another's worldview in all its complexity, but it will give the student some awareness regarding why a person handles issues or information a particular way. The same technique applies when reading literature or listening to a lecture.

RESEARCH PAPER

Near the beginning of the third grading period (end of January) a research paper is assigned dealing with the topic of origins. Of the six components, only origins lends itself to having an agreed upon standard, empirical knowledge, which can be used to evaluate different interpretations. The purpose of the paper is to give students the opportunity of examining a topic from two divergent points of view by putting themselves in the shoes of the one doing the interpreting.

The basic positions of the Creationist and Evolutionist are reviewed at this time.

There are six parts to the paper: introduction, the empirical evidence, the creationist interpretation, the evolutionists interpretations, the student's analysis of the evidence and an evaluation. Empirical information is material both sides agree upon. For the interpretation sections, the student answers the question that if he were an evolutionist (creationist) how could he use the empirical data to support his position? The students have to put themselves into the shoes of another. It forces them to think along guidelines that are foreign to most of them, definitely a new experience. In the analysis section, the student is free to examine the empirical evidence from his own worldview. In the last section they are asked to evaluate the validity of the learning experience.

Grading is broken down into two parts - Mechanics and Content. Mechanics is obvious. Content involves the reporting of the empirical evidence and the divergent interpretations; and how well the students support their own position. It is important that the student realize that he has free reign in the analysis section. The student is not required to conform to a particular interpretation; rather, it is how well he supports his interpretation that is critical.

Currently, the topic list from which students can choose has over fifty different items, such as, the origin of language, the wholly mammoth, homology and continental glaciers. Once the main topic has been chosen it needs to be narrowed down to one or two aspects. The student can also come up with his own topic, but it has to be a historical scientific issue.

When doing the research, the Empirical information and the Evolutionists side can readily be found in the libraries. The students are encouraged to find Creationist materials on their own; however, finding enough information is a bit difficult. Therefore, each student is supplied with a photo copy of two or three Creationist articles which must be returned when the paper is handed in.

THE INSTRUCTOR'S WORLDVIEW

A week after the research paper is assigned, my worldview is presented as an example of one that has been well thought out. The students are continually encouraged to check the consistency of their own beliefs, they have the conceptual groundwork and the tools for evaluations, they now have the opportunity to analyze the worldview of their instructor. Exposing your worldview for critical examination is helpful in pointing out blind spots that you may not be aware of. This has proven to be a valuable exercise for all involved.

ATTITUDE

The preceding involved the mechanics and rationale behind the Worldview Approach to Critical Thinking. However, there is one final element. The teacher needs to cultivate an **attitude of openness** within the classroom. There needs to be a willingness to listen to someone else's ideas without condemnation. That does not necessarily mean acceptance of the those ideas; rather, a readiness to hear the other person out. In addition, students and teachers need to be challenged to apply the evaluation tools to gain insight regarding the validity of the new and/or different ideas. The student needs to feel comfortable sharing the depths of his heart. A student will remember the attitude of the class long after he has forgotten the content material.

The above is the Worldview Approach to Critical Thinking and how I have woven the material into my physics course.

STUDENT REACTION

This year as part of their year end evaluation, the students evaluated the Discovery paper and the Research paper. Eighty-five students filled out the evaluations; the percentage break down is below. The numbers speak for themselves.

Paper	Very Helpful	Helpful	Some Good	Not Worth It
Discovery	34.5%	21.4%	32.2%	11.9%
Research	30.2%	34.9%	23.3%	11.6%

The following are some of the positive comments students made in the evaluation section of their research paper.

I think that this was a valuable means of examining a controversial topic [Origin of Language]. Being able to compare and contrast two sides of an issue and then interpreting a conclusion on my own expands [one's] intellect. We sometimes need to think about things that we never do. It exercises the brain and broadens the mind [Athena, 1st period].

Researching this topic was a rewarding way to examine both the evolutionist's side and the creationist's side on origins. It enforced the lesson that there is more than one way to look at a subject. All paths and reasons need to be examined before a judgement is made. I used to believe the evolutionists side on the origins of coal. Now after learning the creationist side my thoughts on the formation have broadened. I'm not really for one side or the other, even though they are both very influential. The creationist has a more thorough explanation however [Annie, 7th period].

I feel that both creationists and evolutionists have decent arguments for the origins of birds. I believe that this means of examining a controversial topic was pretty good. I was able to get a good solid feel for what both sides felt and the points that they wanted to get across [Scott, period 5A6A].

In general, student comments were favorable to being able to examine more than one side of an issue and give their own analysis. However, regarding the research paper there were some students who did not think the project was worth it, as the evaluation figures show, or that some part of the project was objectionable.

I also think that this assignment was inappropriate for a public school. I realize that to be fully educated that we should know about all sides, but I chose to attend a public school because at this point I also choose not to be educated in the creationist point of view [Bekki, 1st period].

Of the negative comments, Bekki's was the most articulate. Other students just made a blanket statement that they did not learn anything. Her paper was also one of the best written. This is the first time in three years that such a comment has come up. The purpose of this approach is not to teach a particular worldview or particular interpretation; rather it is to show the effect of the worldview on interpretation. Because at the extremes, these two sides (Creation - Evolution) are diametrically opposed, thereby providing an excellent example of very different interpretations of the same evidence. If the worldviews are very similar then differences in the interpretations will be subtle and not very easy for a beginner to discern. Regretfully, anytime there is a controversial topic, there is a possibility that someone will not want to have anything to do with one side or the other. But for a person to get a real feel for the full range in interpretive possibilities examining an undesired position may be necessary. However, the person is not required to believe it.

Another student anonymously wrote on the year end evaluation, regarding the discovery paper, "I object to airing my religion to the criticisms of others."   At no time was a particular worldview ever "criticized;" therefore, the comment is confusing. If it is a matter of privacy, the discovery papers were never shared with anyone. The teacher was the only one to read the papers. However, do not let a minority of negative comments detract from the numbers; most students (88%) felt the worldview papers were helpful.

At present, I have no hard data regarding the Worldview Approach as a whole. Also, I cannot say for certain that anyone has changed their worldview because of this approach. The above data, from this year's evaluations (1994), is the most objective evidence available. However, based on comments written by students in my yearbook and from individual conversations, I am more than satisfied with the impact that this approach has made. The comments have been edited, and only that information pertaining to worldviews is presented. Do not forget that these comments were written in my yearbook and were unsolicited.

This first comment is precious because Jamie was not pleased with the worldview material as we went through the year; but here are her comments at the end.

Mr. Wiz, It really has been a wonderful year, and I grudgingly admit that even the world view part of the course was enjoyable. Your gentle approach to world view did help me listen to what you said, even though at times I may have seemed angry [Jamie, 9th period].

Hey Mr. Wiz, ... Thanks for showing me there's more to life than just physics: worldview. I learned a lot about what I think and my views in your class, something I never expected from a physics class [Bridget, 1st period].

Mr. Wiz, ... You have taught me physics and many life lessons at the same time. ... I now look at things in a different perspective and I thank you for that and everything [Michaelann, period 5A6A].

Mr. Wiz, You have shown me how to find out what and why I believe in something. You have helped to show me the most important thing about school is not test grades but on what I have learned. And I have learned a lot [Carl, period 5A6A].

What more can I say?

CONCLUSION

The premise upon which the Worldview Approach to Critical Thinking is based is that **beliefs are an integral part of the interpretive process**. The three major concepts that the approach hinges on are 1) dividing of science into two categories: empirical and historical, 2) the effects of the worldview on interpretation, and 3) how to evaluate worldviews. Critical to the success of this approach is that the teacher promote an attitude of openness within the classroom. The material is supplemental and can be woven into any course that involves the interpretation of evidence. As an educator, I have found this approach to be very exciting, because it teaches students to become critical thinkers and not parrots. As the students above have indicated, they have been challenged to a) broaden their horizons, b) see the world in a new light, and c) look further than they ever have before.

REFERENCES

[1]   **An Interview with Charles Thaxton,** Bible-Science Newsletter, January 1987.

[2]   Baker, Mace, Dinosaurs, New Century Books: Redding, (1991).

[3]   Colson, Charles, The Body, Word Publishing: Dallas, (1992).

[4]   Fee, Gordon D., and Douglas Stuart, How to Read the Bible for All it's Worth, Zondervan Publishing: House: Grand Rapids, (1982).

[5]   Geisler, Norman, and J. Kerby Anderson, Origin Science: A Proposal for the Creation-Evolution Controversy, Baker Book House: Grand Rapids, (1987).

[6]   Geisler, Norman, and William D. Watkins, Perspectives: Understanding and Evaluating Today's World Views, Here's Life Publishers: San Bernardino, (1984).

[7]   Geisler, Norman, and Ron Brooks, When Skeptics Ask, Victor Books: Wheaton, (1990).

[8]   Ham Ken, The Lie: Evolution, Master Books: El Cajon , (1987).

[9]   Kuhn, Thomas S., The Structure of Scientific Revolutions, The university of Chicago Press: Chicago, (1970).

[10]   Lerner, Eric, The Big Bang Never Happened, Times Books: New York, (1991).

[11]   Nash, Ronald H., Worldviews in Conflict, Zondervan Publishing House: Grand Rapids, (1992).

[12]   Poland, Larry W., 2084: A Novel, Here's Life Publishers: San Bernardino, (1991).

[13]   Rutherford, James R., Gerald Holton and Fletcher G. Watson (Directors), The Project Physics Course, Holt, Rinehart and Winston: New York, (1970).

[14]   Schaeffer, Francis A., A Christian Manifesto, Crossway Books: Westchester, (1981).

[15]   Sire, James W., Scripture Twisting, InterVarsity Press: Downers Grove, (1980).

[16]   Sire, James W., The Universe Next Door, InterVarsity Press: Downers Grove, (1988).

[17]   Wysong, Randy L., The Creation-Evolution Controversy, Inquiry Press: Midland, (1976).

CATASTROPHIC PLATE TECTONICS:
A GLOBAL FLOOD MODEL OF EARTH HISTORY

by (in alphabetical order)

STEVEN A. AUSTIN, Ph.D.
Institute for Creation Research
P. O. Box 2667
El Cajon, CA 92021

JOHN R. BAUMGARDNER, Ph.D.
1965 Camino Redondo
Los Alamos, NM 87544

D. RUSSELL HUMPHREYS, Ph.D.
9301 Gutierrez N.E.
Albuquerque, NM 87111

ANDREW A. SNELLING, Ph.D.
Creation Science Foundation
P. O. Box 6302
Acacia Ridge D.C., Qld. 4110 AUSTRALIA

LARRY VARDIMAN, Ph.D.
Institute for Creation Research
P. O. Box 2667
El Cajon, CA 92021

KURT P. WISE, Ph.D.
Bryan College
P. O. Box 7585
Dayton, TN 37321-7000

KEYWORDS
Catastrophe, Flood Model, Plate Tectonics, Subduction, Thermal Runaway, Convection, Spreading, Fountains of the Great Deep, Windows of Heaven, Volcanoes, Earthquakes, Sediments, Precipitites, Magnetic Reversals, Isostasy, Climate, Ice Age

ABSTRACT
In 1859 Antonio Snider proposed that rapid, horizontal divergence of crustal plates occurred during Noah's Flood. Modern plate tectonics theory is now conflated with assumptions of uniformity of rate and ideas of continental 'drift'. Catastrophic plate tectonics theories, such as Snider proposed more than a century ago, appear capable of explaining a wide variety of data -- including Biblical and geologic data which the slow tectonics theories are incapable of explaining. We would like to propose a catastrophic plate tectonics theory as a framework for earth history.

Geophysically, we begin with a pre-Flood earth differentiated into core, mantle, and crust, with the crust horizontally differentiated into sialic craton and mafic ocean floor. The Flood was initiated as slabs of oceanic floor broke loose and subducted along thousands of kilometers of pre-Flood continental margins. Deformation of the mantle by these slabs raised the temperature and lowered the viscosity of the mantle in the vicinity of the slabs. A resulting thermal runaway of the slabs through the mantle led to meters-per-second mantle convection. Cool oceanic crust which descended to the core/mantle boundary induced rapid reversals of the earth's magnetic field. Large plumes originating near the core/mantle boundary expressed themselves at the surface as fissure eruptions and flood basalts. Flow induced in the mantle also produced rapid extension along linear belts throughout the sea floor and rapid horizontal displacement of continents. Upwelling magma jettisoned steam into the atmosphere causing intense global rain. Rapid emplacement of isostatically lighter mantle material raised the level of the ocean floor, displacing ocean water onto the continents. When virtually all the pre-Flood oceanic floor had been replaced with new, less-dense, less-subductable, oceanic crust, catastrophic plate motion stopped. Subsequent cooling increased the density of the new ocean floor, producing deeper ocean basins and a reservoir for post-Flood oceans.

Sedimentologically, we begin with a substantial reservoir of carbonate and clastic sediment in the pre-Flood ocean. During the Flood hot brines associated with new ocean floor added precipitites to that sediment reservoir, and warming ocean waters and degassing magmas added carbonates -- especially high magnesium carbonates. Also during the Flood, rapid plate tectonics moved pre-Flood sediments toward the continents. As ocean plates subducted near a continental margin, its bending caused upwarping of sea floor, and its drag caused downwarping of continental crust, facilitating the placement of sediment onto the continental margin. Once there, earthquake-induced sea waves with ocean-to-land movement redistributed sediment toward continental interiors. Resulting sedimentary units tend to be thick, uniform, of unknown provenance, and extend over regional, inter-regional, and even continental areas.

After the Flood, the earth experienced a substantial period of isostatic readjustment, where local to regional catastrophes with intense earthquake and volcanic activity were common. Post-Flood sedimentation continued to be rapid but was dominantly basinal on the continents. Left-over heat in the new oceans produced a significantly warmer climate just after the Flood. In the following centuries, as the earth cooled, floral and faunal changes tracked the changing climate zonation. The warmer oceans caused continental transport of moisture that led to the advance of continental glaciers and ultimately to the formation of polar ice caps.

INTRODUCTION
Early in the history of geology, it was common to appeal to the flood described in Scripture to explain the origin of most or all rocks and fossils (e.g. [100,14,126,116]). In such theories Noah's flood was typically recognized as a catastrophic event of global proportions. The earth's crust was typically pictured as dynamic and capable of rapid vertical and horizontal motions on local, regional, and global scales. However, especially with the influential works of Hutton [43,44] and then Lyell [49], Noah's flood began to play an increasingly less important role in historical geology during the nineteenth century. Theories of gradualism increased in popularity as theories of catastrophism waned. Ideas of past catastrophic geology were replaced with ideas of constancy of present gradual physical processes. Ideas of global-scale dynamics were replaced with ideas of local erosion, deposition, extrusion, and intrusion. Ideas of rapid crustal dynamics were replaced by ideas of crustal fixity -- with only imperceptibly slow vertical subsidence and uplift being possible. So complete was the success of gradualism in geology that ideas of flood geology were nowhere to be found among the English-speaking scientists of the world by 1859 [65], or rarely found at best [63].

One of the last holdouts for flood geology was a little-known work published by Antonio Snider-Pellegrini [97] -- ironically enough the same year Darwin published the *Origin of Species*. Intrigued by the reasonably good fit between land masses on either side of the Atlantic ocean, Snider proposed that the earth's crust was composed of rigid plates which had moved horizontally with respect to one another. Snider may have been the first to propose some of the main elements of modern plate tectonics theory. Snider also proposed that the horizontal divergence had been rapid and had occurred during Noah's Flood. It appears, then, that the first elaboration of plate tectonics theory was presented in the context of catastrophic flood geology. It also seems that a substantial amount of the twentieth century opposition to plate tectonics was due to the fact that geologists were, by then, firmly predisposed to believe that the earth's crust was horizontally fixed. The catastrophism school of geology was the first to propose plate tectonics; the gradualist school was the first major opponent to plate tectonics. However, by the time plate tectonics was finally accepted in the United States in the late 1960's, gradualism had become a part of plate tectonics theory as well. Rather than Snider's rapid horizontal motion on the scale of weeks or months, modern geology accepted a plate tectonics theory with horizontal motion on the scale of tens to hundreds of millions of years.

Because of the enormous explanatory and predictive success of the plate tectonics model (reviewed in [122,124]), we feel that at least some portion of plate tectonics theory should be incorporated into the creation model. It appears that taking the conventional plate tectonics model and increasing the rate of plate motion neither deprives plate tectonics theory of its explanatory and predictive success, nor does it seem to contradict any passages of Scripture. Therefore, following the example of Antonio Snider we would like to propose a model of geology which is centered about the idea of rapid, horizontal divergence of rigid crustal plates (i.e. rapid plate tectonics) during Noah's flood. We feel that this model is not only capable of the explanatory and predictive success of conventional plate tectonics, but is also capable of clarifying a number of Scriptural claims and explaining some physical data unexplained by conventional plate tectonics theory.

It is important to note, however, that our model is still in its formative stages, and is thus incomplete. What is presented here is a basic framework upon which more theory can be built. We anticipate that a substantial amount of work is still needed to explain all the salient features of this planet's rocks and fossils. Additionally, although the authors of this paper have all had some association with the Institute for Creation Research (ICR), the model presented in this paper is a composite perspective of the authors and not necessarily that of the ICR.

PRE-FLOOD GEOLOGY
Any flood model must begin by speculating on the nature of the pre-Flood world. Virtually every flood event and product is in some way or another affected by characteristics of the pre-Flood world. A partial list of Flood events determined at least in part by pre-Flood conditions would include: global dynamics of the crust (by the pre-Flood structure and nature of the earth's interior); magnetic field dynamics (by the pre-Flood nature of the magnetic field); tectonic activity and associated earthquakes (by the pre-Flood structure and dynamics of the crust); volcanic activity and emplaced igneous rocks (by the pre-Flood nature of the earth's interior); formation of clastic sediments (by the pre-Flood sediments available for redeposition and rocks available for erosion); formation of chemical sediments

(by the pre-Flood ocean chemistry); formation of fossils (by the nature of the pre-Flood biota); distribution of sediments and fossils (by the pre-Flood climate and biogeography); and the dynamics of the inundation itself (by pre-Flood topography). The more that is determined about the nature of the pre-Flood world, the more accurate and specific our flood models can be. Our initial inferences about the pre-Flood world include the following.

Pre-Flood/Flood Boundary
We agree with many previous theorists in flood geology that the pre-Flood/Flood boundary should stratigraphically lie at least as low as the Precambrian/Cambrian boundary (e.g. [100,117]). Currently there is discussion about how close [120,5] or far [94] below the Cambrian rocks this boundary should be located. For our purposes here, it is provisionally claimed that at least many of the Archaean sediments are pre-Flood in age.

Pre-Flood Earth Structure
We believe that the pre-Flood earth was differentiated into a core, mantle, and crust, very much as it is today. We conclude this for two major reasons. The first is that under any known natural conditions, core/mantle differentiation would destroy all evidence of life on earth *completely*. The current earth has a core/mantle/crust division according to the successively lower density of its components. If this differentiation had occurred by any natural means, the gravitational potential energy released by the heavier elements relocating to the earth's interior would produce enough heat to melt the earth's crust and vaporize the earth's oceans. If differentiation of the earth's elements did occur with its associated natural release of energy, it is reasoned that it most certainly occurred before the creation of organisms (at the latest Day 3 of the creation week). Secondly, even though such a differentiation could have been performed by God without the 'natural' release of gravitational potential energy, the already-differentiated earth's interior also provides a natural driving mechanism for the rapid tectonics model here described.

The earth's mantle appears to have been less viscous than it seems to be at present [6,7,8]. This is to allow for the thermal runaway instability which we believe produced the rapid plate tectonic motion we are proposing [7].

With regard to the earth's crust, we believe that there was a distinct horizontal differentiation between oceanic and continental crust, very much as there is today. First, we believe that before the Flood began, there was stable, sialic, cratonic crust. We have three major reasons for this conclusion: 1) Much Archaean sialic material exists which probably is below the pre-Flood/Flood boundary. This would indicate that sialic material was available in pre-Flood times; 2) The existence of low-density, low temperature 'keels' beneath existing cratons [45] implies that the cratons have persisted more or less in their present form since their differentiation. It also argues that little or no mantle convection has disturbed the upper mantle beneath the cratons; and 3) If the pre-Flood cratons were sialic and the pre-Flood ocean crust was mafic, then buoyancy forces would provide a natural means of supporting craton material above sea level -- thus producing dry land on the continents.

Second, we believe that the pre-Flood ocean crust was mafic -- most probably basaltic. Once again three reasons exist for this inference: 1) Pre-Flood basaltic ocean crust is suggested by ophiolites (containing pillow basalts and presumed ocean sediments) which are thought to represent pieces of ocean floor and obducted onto the continents early in the Flood; 2) If, as claimed above, the pre-Flood craton was sialic, then buoyancy forces would make a mafic pre-Flood ocean crust into a natural basin for ocean water. This would prevent ocean water from overrunning the continents; and 3) If, as claimed above, the continents were sialic, mafic material would be necessary to drive the subduction required in our flood model.

Pre-Flood Sediments
We believe that there was a significant thickness of all types of sediments already available on the earth by the time of the Flood. We have three reasons for this position: 1) Biologically optimum terrestrial and marine environments would require that at least a small amount of sediment of each type had been created in the creation week; 2) Archaean (probable pre-Flood) and Proterozoic sediments contain substantial quantities of all types of sediments; and 3) It may not be possible to derive all the Flood sediments from igneous and/or metamorphic precursors by physical and chemical processes in the course of a single, year-long Flood. We believe that substantial quantities of very fine detrital carbonate sediment existed in the pre-Flood oceans. This is deduced primarily from the fact that not enough bicarbonate can have been dissolved in the pre-Flood ocean (and/or provided by outgassing during the Flood -- see below) to have produced the Flood carbonates.

Such quantities of carbonate as we believe to have existed in the pre-Flood ocean would mean that there was a substantial buffer in the pre-Flood ocean -- perhaps contributing to a very stable pre-Flood ocean chemistry. The existence of large quantities of mature or nearly mature pre-Flood quartz sands might explain the otherwise somewhat mysterious clean, mature nature of early Paleozoic sands.

FLOOD DYNAMICS

Initiation
There has been considerable discussion -- both reasonable and fanciful -- about what event might have initiated the Flood. Considerations range from a) the direct hand of God [56-62,6-7]; b) the impact or near-miss of an

astronomical object or objects such as asteroids [102], meteorites [74], a comet [116,75], a comet or Venus [11], Venus and Mars [109], Mars [76], Mars, Ceres and Jupiter [118], another moon of earth [9], and a star [10]; c) some purely terrestrial event or events, such as fracturing of the earth's crust due to drying [14] or radioactive heat buildup [36], rapid tilting of the earth due to gyro turbulence [71] or ice sheet buildup [54], and natural collapse of rings of ice [114,103]; or d) various combinations of these ideas. We feel that the Flood was initiated as slabs of oceanic crust broke loose and subducted along thousands of kilometers of pre-Flood continental margins. We are, however, not ready at this time to speculate on what event or events might have initiated that subduction. We feel that considerable research is still needed to evaluate potential mechanisms in the light of how well they can produce global subduction.

Subduction
At the very beginning of plate motion, subducting slabs locally heated the mantle by deformation, lowering the viscosity of the mantle in the vicinity of the slabs. The lowered viscosity then allowed an increase in subduction rate, which in turn heated up the surrounding mantle even more. We believe that this led to a thermal runaway instability which allowed for meters-per-second subduction, as postulated and modeled by Baumgardner [6,7]. It is probable that this subduction occurred along thousands of kilometers of continental margin. The bending of the ocean plate beneath the continent would have produced an abrupt topographic low paralleling the continental margin, similar to the ocean trenches at the eastern, northern, and western margins of the Pacific Ocean.

Because all current ocean lithosphere seems to date from Flood or post-Flood times [88], we feel that essentially all pre-Flood ocean lithosphere was subducted in the course of the Flood. Gravitational potential energy released by the subduction of this lithosphere is on the order of 10^{28} J [6]. This alone probably provided the energy necessary to drive Flood dynamics.

The continents attached to ocean slabs would have been pulled toward subduction zones. This would produce rapid horizontal displacement of continents -- in many cases relative motion of meters per second. Collisions of continents at subduction zones are the likely mechanism for the creation of mountain fold-and-thrust-belts, such as the Appalachians, Himalayas, Caspians, and Alps. Rapid deformation, burial, and subsequent erosion of mountains possible in the Flood model might provide the only adequate explanation for the existence of high-pressure, low-temperature minerals such as coesite (e.g. [92,17,113,37,91]) in mountain cores.

Mantle-Wide Flow
As Baumgardner [6,7] assumed in order to facilitate his modelling, rapid subduction is likely to have initiated large-scale flow throughout the entire mantle of the earth. Seismic tomography studies (e.g. [28]; and as reviewed by [29]) seem to confirm that this in fact did occur in the history of the earth. In such studies velocity anomalies (interpreted as cooler temperature zones) lie along theorized paths of past subduction. These anomalies are found deep within the earth's mantle -- well below the phase transition zones thought by some to be barriers to mantle-wide subduction. In fact, the velocity anomalies seem to imply that not only did flow involve the entire depth of the mantle, but that ocean lithosphere may have dropped all the way to the core/mantle boundary.

One important consequence of mantle-wide flow would have been the transportation of cooler mantle material to the core/mantle boundary. This would have had the effect of cooling the outer core, which in turn led to strong core convection. This convection provided the conditions necessary for Humphreys' [40,42] model of rapid geomagnetic reversals in the core. As the low electrical conductivity oceanic plates subducted, they would be expected to have split up the lower mantle's high conductivity. This in turn would have lessened the mantle's attenuation of core reversals and allowed the rapid magnetic field reversals to have been expressed on the surface. Humphreys' [40,42] model not only explains magnetic reversal evidence (as reviewed in [41]) in a young-age creation time scale, but uniquely explains the low intensity of paleomagnetic and archaeomagnetic data, the erratic frequency of paleomagnetic reversals through the Phanerozoic, and, most impressively, the locally patchy distribution of sea-floor paleomagnetic anomalies [41]. It also predicted and uniquely explains the rapid reversals found imprinted in lava flows of the Northwest [21,22,2,15].

Spreading
As ocean lithosphere subducted it would have produced rapid extension along linear belts on the ocean floor tens of thousands of kilometers long. At these spreading centers upwelling mantle material would have been allowed to rise to the surface. The new, molten mantle material would have degassed its volatiles [118] and vaporized ocean water [6,7] to produce a linear geyser of superheated gases along the whole length of spreading centers. This geyser activity, which would have jettisoned gases well into the atmosphere, is, we believe, what Scripture refers to as the 'fountains of the great deep' (Genesis 7:11; 8:2). As evidenced by volatiles emitted by Mount Kilauea in Hawaii [33], the gases released would be (in order of abundance) water, carbon dioxide, sulfur dioxide, hydrogen sulfide, hydrogen fluoride, hydrogen, carbon monoxide, nitrogen, argon, and oxygen. As the gases in the upper atmosphere drifted away from the spreading centers they would have had the opportunity to cool by radiation into space. As it cooled, the water -- both that vaporized from ocean water and that released from magma -- would have condensed and fallen as an intense global rain. It is this geyser-produced rain which we believe is

primarily responsible for the rain from the 'windows of heaven' (Genesis 7:11; 8:2) which remained a source of water for up to 150 days of the Flood (Genesis 7:24-8:2).

The rapid emplacement of isostatically lighter mantle material raised the level of the ocean floor along the spreading centers. This produced a linear chain of mountains called the mid-ocean ridge (MOR) system. The now warmer and more buoyant ocean floor displaced ocean water onto the continents to produce the inundation itself.

Continental Modification
The events of the Flood would have made substantial modifications to the thickness of the pre-Flood continental crust. This would have been effected through the redistribution of sediments, the moving of ductile lower continental crust by subducting lithosphere, addition of molten material to the underside of the continental lithosphere (underplating), stretching (e.g. due to spreading), and compression (e.g. due to continental collision). These rapid changes in crustal thickness would produce isostatic disequilibrium. This would subsequently lead to large-scale isostatic adjustments with their associated earthquakes, frictional heating, and deformation. Since many of those tectonic events would have involved vertical rock motions, Tyler's [101] tectonically-controlled rock cycle might prove to be a useful tool in understanding late Flood and post-Flood tectonics.

Atmosphere
The magma at spreading centers degassed, among other things, substantial quantities of argon and helium into the earth's atmosphere. Both of these elements are produced and accumulated due to radioactive decay. However, the current quantity of helium in the atmosphere is less than that which would be expected by current rates of radioactive decay production over a four to five billion years of earth history [52,24,25,104-106], so perhaps what is currently found in the atmosphere is due to degassing of mantle material during the Flood. The same may also be found to be true about argon (see, e.g., [31]).

Flood Waters
Several sources have been suggested for the water of the Flood. Some creationists (e.g. [117,26]) have proposed that the "waters above the firmament" in the form of an upper atmosphere water canopy provided much of the rain of the Flood. However, [84,85,112] argue that if the water was held in place by forces and laws of physics with which we are currently familiar, forty feet of water is not possible in the canopy. Perhaps, they argue, the canopy could have held a maximum of only a few feet of water. This is insufficient water to contribute significantly to even forty days of rain, let alone a mountain-covering global flood. A second source suggested by [118,6,7] is condensing water from spreading center geysers. This should provide adequate water to explain up to 150 days of open 'windows of heaven'. Another substantial source of water suggested by this model is displaced ocean water [6,7]. Rapid emplacement of isostatically lighter mantle material at the spreading centers would raise the ocean bottom, displacing ocean water onto the continents. Baumgardner [7] estimates a rise of sea level of more than one kilometer from this mechanism alone.

Cooling of new ocean lithosphere at the spreading centers would be expected to heat the ocean waters throughout the Flood. This heating seems to be confirmed by a gradual increase in oxygen 18/oxygen 16 ratios from the pre-Flood/Flood boundary through the Cretaceous (e.g. [108]).

Sedimentary Production
Precipitites -- sediments precipitated directly from supersaturated brines -- would have been produced in association with horizontal divergence of ocean floor rocks. Rode [82] and Sozansky [98] have noted rock salt and anhydrite deposits in association with active sea-floor tectonics and volcanism and have proposed catastrophist models for their formation. Besides rock salt and anhydrite, hot-rock/ocean-water interactions could also explain many bedded chert deposits and fine-grained limestones.

Contributions to Flood carbonates probably came from at least four sources: a) carbon dioxide produced by degassing spreading center magmas; b) dissolved pre-Flood bicarbonate precipitated as ocean temperatures rose during the Flood (given that carbonate dissolution rates are inversely related to temperature); c) eroded and redeposited pre-Flood carbonates (a dominant pre-Flood sediment); and d) pulverized and redeposited pre-Flood shell debris. Precipitation of carbonate may explain the origin of micrite [32], so ubiquitous in Flood sediments, but of an otherwise unknown origin [78]. Until pre-Flood ocean magnesium was depleted by carbonate precipitation, high-magnesium carbonates would be expected to be frequent products of early Flood activity (see [16] for interesting data on this subject).

Sedimentary Transport
As Morton [61] points out, most Flood sediments are found on the continents and continental margins and not on the ocean floor where one might expect sediments to have ended up. Our model provides a number of mechanisms for the transportation of ocean sediments onto the continents where they are primarily found today. First, subducting plates would transport sediments toward the subduction zones and thus mostly towards the continents in a conveyor-belt fashion. Second, as the ocean plates were forced to quickly bend into the earth's interior, they would warp upward outboard of the trench. This would raise the deep sea sediments above their

typical depth, which in turn reduces the amount of work required to move sediments from the oceans onto the continents. Third, rapid plate subduction would warp the continental plate margin downward. This again would reduce the amount of energy needed to move sediments onto the continent from the ocean floor. Fourth, as more and more of the cold pre-Flood ocean lithosphere was replaced with hotter rock from below, the ocean bottom is gradually elevated. This again reduces the work required to move sediments from the oceans to the continents. Fifth, as ocean lithosphere is subducted, ocean sediments would be scraped off, allowing sediments to be accreted to and/or redeposited on the continent. Sixth, wave (e.g. tsunami) refraction on the continental shelf would tend to transport sediments shoreward. Seventh, it is possible that some amount of tidal resonance may have been achieved [18-20]. The resulting east-to-west-dominated currents would tend to transport sediments accumulated on eastern continental margins into the continental interiors. Resulting sedimentary units have abundant evidence of catastrophic deposition [1], and tend to be thick, uniform, of unknown provenance, and extending over regional, inter-regional, and even continental areas [3].

Volcanic Activity
The volcanism associated with rapid tectonics would have been of unprecedented magnitude and world-wide extent, but concentrated in particular zones and sites. At spreading centers magma would rise to fill in between plates separating at meters per second, producing a violent volcanic source tens of thousands of kilometers in length [7]. Based upon 2-dimensional experimental simulation [38,81] and 3-dimensional numerical simulation, subduction-induced mantle flow would generate mantle plumes whose mushroom heads would rise to and erupt upon the earth's surface. These plumes would be expected to produce extensive flood basalts through fissure eruptions, such as perhaps the plateau basalts of South Africa, the Deccan Traps of India, the Siberian flood basalts [80], and the Karmutsen Basalt of Alaska/Canada [73]. Correlations between plume formation and flood basalts have already been claimed (e.g. [115]). At the same time, the heating and melting of subducted sediments should have produced explosive sialic volcanism continent-ward of the subduction zone (such as is seen in the Andes Mountains of South America, the Cascade Mountains of the U.S., and the Aleutian, Japanese, Indonesian, and New Zealand Islands of the Pacific).

Earthquake Activity
The rapid bending of elastic lithosphere and rapid inter-plate shear of plates at subduction zones as well as abrupt phase transitions as subducting plates are rapidly moved downward would be expected to produce frequent, high-intensity earthquakes at the subduction zones. There is also earthquake activity associated with explosive volcanism, isostatic adjustment, continental collision, etc. This earthquake activity would facilitate thrust- and detachment- faulting by providing a) energy to aid in breaking up initially coherent rock blocks; b) an acceleration to aid in the thrusting of rock blocks; and c) vibration which reduces the frictional force resisting the motion and thrusting of rock blocks.

Termination
When virtually all the pre-Flood oceanic floor had been replaced with new, less-dense, less-subductable rock, rapid plate motion ceased. The lack of new, hot, mantle material terminated spreading-center-associated geyser activity, so the global rain ceased. This is very possibly the 150-day point in the Genesis chronology when it appears that the 'fountains of the great deep were stopped and the windows of the heaven were closed' (Genesis 8:2).

After the rapid horizontal motion stopped, cooling increased the density of the new ocean floor, producing gradually deepening oceans [7] -- eventually producing our current ocean basins. As the waters receded (the 'Great Regression') from off of the land the most superficial -- and least lithified -- continental deposits were eroded off the continents. This would leave an unconformity on the continent not reflected in ocean stratigraphy. The absence of these most superficial continental deposits may explain the absence of human as well as most mammal and angiosperm fossils in Flood sediments [123]. Sheet erosion from receding Flood waters would be expected to have planed off a substantial percentage of the earth's surface. Such planar erosion features as the Canadian shield and the Kaibab and Coconino plateaus might well be better explained by this than by any conventional erosional processes.

POST-FLOOD DYNAMICS

Flood/Post-Flood Boundary
The definition of the Flood/Post-Flood boundary in the geologic column is a subject of considerable dispute among creationists. Estimates range from the Carboniferous [86] to the Pleistocene [79,117]. For our purposes here we would like to define the Flood/post-Flood boundary at the termination of global-scale erosion and sedimentation. Based upon a qualitative assessment of geologic maps worldwide, lithotypes change from worldwide or continental in character in the Mesozoic to local or regional in the Tertiary. Therefore, we tentatively place the Flood/post-Flood boundary at approximately the Cretaceous/Tertiary (K/T) boundary. We believe further studies in stratigraphy, paleontology, paleomagnetism, and geochemistry should allow for a more precise definition of this boundary.

Post-Flood Geology

After the global effects of the Flood ended, the earth continued to experience several hundred years of residual catastrophism [7]. A cooling lithosphere is likely to have produced a pattern of decreasing incidence [68] and intensity of volcanism (such as appears to be evidenced in Cenozoic sialic volcanism in the Western United States [77]). The large changes in crustal thicknesses produced during the Flood left the earth in isostatic disequilibrium. Isostatic readjustments with their associated intense mountain uplift, earthquake, and volcanic activity would have occurred for hundreds of years after the global affects of the Flood ended (e.g. [83]). In fact, considering the current nature of the mantle, there has not been sufficient time since the end of the Flood for complete isostatic equilibrium to be attained. As a result, current geologic activity can be seen as continued isostatic readjustments to Flood events. Modern earthquake and volcanic activity is in some sense relict Flood dynamics.

Because of the frequency and intensity of residual catastrophism after the Flood, post-Flood sedimentary processes were predominantly rapid. The local nature of such catastrophism, on the other hand, restricted sedimentation to local areas, explaining the basinal nature of most Cenozoic sedimentation.

Post-Flood Climate

By the time Flood waters had settled into the post-Flood basins, they had accumulated enough heat to leave the oceans as much as 20 or more degrees centigrade warmer than today's oceans (figure 1). These warmer oceans might be expected to produce a warmer climate on earth in the immediate post-Flood times than is experienced on earth now [68]. More specifically, a rather uniform warm climate would be expected along continental margins [66-68], permitting wider latitudinal range for temperature-limited organisms [68] -- e.g. mammoths (e.g. [87]), frozen forests (e.g. [30]), and trees [121]. This avenue in turn may have facilitated post-Flood dispersion of animals [68,125]. Also expected along continental margins would be a rather high climatic gradient running from the ocean toward the continental interior [66,68]. This might explain why some Cenozoic communities near the coasts include organisms from a wider range of climatic zones than we would expect to see today -- for example, communities in the Pleistocene [35,68] and the Gingko Petrified Forest in Oregon [23].

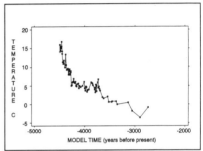

Figure 1 Cooling of polar bottom water after the Flood. From [107]. Data from [46,90].

Oard [66-68] suggested that within the first millennium following the Flood, the oceans (and earth) would have cooled as large amounts of water were evaporated off of the oceans and dropped over the cooler continental interiors. Although Oard's model needs substantial modification (e.g. to include all the Cenozoic), quantification, and testing, we feel that it is likely to prove to have considerable explanatory and predictive power. The predicted cooling [66,68] seems to be confirmed by oxygen isotope ratios in Cenozoic foraminifera of polar bottom [90,46,108] (Figure 1), polar surface, and tropical bottom waters, and may contribute to increased vertebrate body size (Cope's Law: [99]) throughout the Cenozoic. [68] suggests that the higher rates of precipitation may provide a unique explanation for a well-watered Sahara of the past [53,47,72], rapid erosion of caves, and the creation and/or maintenance of large interior continental lakes of the Cenozoic. Examples of the latter include Quaternary pluvial lakes [93,68], Lakes Hopi and Canyonlands, which may have catastrophically drained to produce Grand Canyon [13,4,70], and the extensive lake which produced the Eocene Green River deposits. We would expect floral and faunal communities to have tracked the cooling of the oceans and the corresponding cooling and drying of the continents. Such a tracking seems to explain the trend in Cenozoic plant communities to run from woodland to grassland and the corresponding trend in Cenozoic herbivores to change from browsers to grazers.

According to Oard's [67,68] model, by about five centuries after the Flood, the cooling oceans had led to the advance of continental glaciers and the formation of polar ice caps (see also [107]). Oard [68] suggests that rapid melting of the continental ice sheets (in less than a century) explains the underfitness of many modern rivers [27] and contributed to the megafaunal extinctions of the Pleistocene [12,51,48]. It may also have contributed to the production of otherwise enigmatic Pleistocene peneplains.

CONCLUSION

We believe that rapid tectonics provides a successful and innovative framework for young-age creation modeling of earth history. We feel that this model uniquely incorporates a wide variety of creationist and non-creationist thinking. It explains evidence from a wide spectrum of earth science fields -- including evidence not heretofore well explained by any other earth history models.

Predictions
This model, like many Flood models, predicts the following: a) a consistent, worldwide, initiation event in the geologic column; b) most body fossils assigned to Flood deposits were deposited allochthonously (including coal, forests, and reefs); c) most ichnofossils assigned to Flood deposits are grazing, moving, or escape evidences, and not long-term living traces; and d) sediments assigned to the Flood were deposited subaqueously without long-term unconformities between them. Since Flood models are usually tied to young-earth creationism, they also claim that it is possible on a short time scale to explain a) the cooling of plutons and ocean plate material; b) regional metamorphism (see, e.g. [95,96]); c) canyon and cave erosion; d) sediment production and accumulation (including speleothems and precipitites); e) organismal accumulation and fossilization (including coal, fossil forests, and reefs); f) fine sedimentary lamination (including varves); and g) radiometric data.

This particular model also predicts a) a lower earth viscosity in pre-Flood times; b) degassing-associated subaqueous precipitite production during the Flood; c) (possibly) east-to-west dominated current deposition during the Flood; d) (possibly) degassing-produced atmosphere argon and helium levels; e) a decrease in magnitude and frequency of geologic activity after the Flood; f) flood basalts that correlate with mantle plume events; g) a sedimentary unconformity at the Flood/post-Flood boundary on the continents not reflected in ocean sediments; h) current geologic activity is the result of relict, isostatic dynamics, not primary earth dynamics; and i) a single ice age composed of a single ice advance.

Future Research
The Flood model presented here suggests a substantial number of research projects for young-earth creationists. Besides the further elaboration and quantification of the model, the predictions listed above need to be examined. Most significantly, we still need to solve the heat problem [119,6] and the radiometric dating problem [6]. As creationists we could also use the services of a geochemist to develop a model for the origin of carbonates and precipitites during the Flood. It is also important that we re-evaluate the evidence for multiple ice ages (as begun by [39,67]) and multiple ice advances (as begun by [68,69,55]).

In addition to testing claims of the model, there are a number of other studies which could help us expand and refine the model. Successful studies on the nature of the pre-Flood world, for example, are likely to aid us in placing better parameters on our model. Events and factors postulated in the initiation of the Flood also need to be re-examined to determine which are capable of explaining the available data and the beginning of plate subduction. It is also important that we evaluate the role of extraterrestrial bombardment in the history of the earth and Flood, since it was most certainly higher during and immediately after the Flood than it is now [118,34]. The suggestion that the earth's axial tilt has changed (e.g. [64,89,71]) needs to be examined to determine validity and/or impact on earth history. It is also important that we determine how many Wilson cycles are needed to explain the data of continental motion [50,124], and thus whether more than one phase of runaway subduction is necessary. More than one cycle may be addressed by partial separation and closure during one rapid tectonics event, and/or renewed tectonic motion after cooling of ocean floor allowed for further rapid tectonics. Finally, it will also be important to determine more precisely the geologic position of the initiation and termination of the Flood around the world in order to identify the geologic data relevant to particular questions of interest.

REFERENCES
[1]   D.V. Ager, The Nature of the Stratigraphic Record, 1973, Macmillan, New York, NY.

[2]   T. Appenzeller, **A conundrum at Steens Mountain**, Science 255(1992) 31.

[3]   S.A. Austin, **Interpreting strata of Grand Canyon**, in S. A. Austin, editor, Grand Canyon: Monument to Catastrophe, 1994, Institute for Creation Research, El Cajon, CA.

[4]   S.A. Austin, **How was Grand Canyon eroded?**, in S. A. Austin, editor, Grand Canyon: Monument to Catastrophe, 1994, Institute for Creation Research, El Cajon, CA.

[5]   S.A. Austin and K.P. Wise, **The Pre-Flood/Flood boundary: As defined in Grand Canyon, Arizona, and East Mojave, California**, this volume, 1994.

[6]   J.R. Baumgardner, **Numerical simulation of the large-scale tectonic changes accompanying the Flood**, in [111], 1987, 17-30.

[7]   J.R. Baumgardner, **3-D finite element simulation of the global tectonic changes accompanying Noah's Flood**, in [110], 1990, 35-45.

[8]   J.R. Baumgardner, **The imperative of non-stationary natural law in relation to Noah's Flood**, Creation Research Society Quarterly 27:3(1990) 98-100.

[9]   H.S. Bellamy, Moons, Myths, and Man, 1936, Harper, New York, NY.

[10]   C.H. Benson, The Earth -- the Theatre of the Universe: And a Scientific and Scriptural Study of the Earth's Place and Purpose in the Divine Program, ca. 1929, Bible Institute Colportage Assoc., Chicago, IL.

[11]   C. Berlitz, The Lost Ship of Noah: In Search of the Ark at Ararat, 1987, G. P. Putnam's Sons, New York.

[12]   B. Bower, **Extinctions on ice**, Science News 132(1987) 284-5.

[13]   W.T. Brown, Jr., "In the Beginning...", 1989, Center for Scientific Creationism, Phoenix, AZ, 122 p.

[14]   T. Burnet, The Theory of the Earth: Containing an Account of the Original of the Earth and of all the Changes Which it hath Already Undergone, or is to Undergo, Until the Consumation of All Things, 1684, London [shorter version originally published in Latin, 1681].

[15]   P. Camps, M. Prévot, and R.S. Coe, **Approches quantitatives de la vitesse des impulsions géomagnétiques pendant une renversemente du champ**, Comptes Rendus des Sciences (Paris) in press.

[16]   G.V. Chillinger, **Relationship between Ca/Mg ratio and geologic age**, Bulletin of the American Association of Petroleum Geologists 40:9(1956) 2257.

[17]   C. Chopin, **Very-high-pressure metamorphism in the western Alps: implications for subduction of continental crust**, in Oxburgh, E. R., editor, Tectonic Settings of Regional Metamorphism: Proceedings of a Royal Society Discussion Meeting, 1987, Royal Society of London, London, 183-197.

[18]   M.E. Clark, and H.D. Voss, **Gravitational attraction, Noah's Flood, and sedimentary layering**, in Science at the Crossroads: Observation or Speculation?: Papers of the 1983 National Creation Conference, 1985, Bible-Science Association, Minneapolis, MN, 42-56.

[19]   M.E. Clark, and H.D. Voss, **Resonance and sedimentary layering in the context of a global flood**, in [110], 1990, 53-63.

[20]   M.E. Clark, and H.D. Voss, **Resonance on flooded planet earth**, in Proceedings of the 1992 Twin-Cities Creation Conference, 1992, Twin Cities Assoc., etc., St. Paul, MN, 30-33.

[21]   R.S. Coe and M. Prévot, **Evidence suggesting extremely rapid field variation during a geomagnetic reversal**, Earth and Planetary Science Letters 92:3/4(1989) 292-98.

[22]   R.S. Coe, M. Prévot, and P. Camps, **New results bearing on hypothesis of rapid field changes during a reversal** [abstract], Eos (1991).

[23]   H.G. Coffin, **The Gingko Petrified Forest**, Origins [of GRI] 1(1974) 101-103.

[24]   M.A. Cook, **Where is the earth's radiogenic helium**, Nature 179(1957) 213.

[25]   M.A. Cook, Prehistory and Earth Models, 1966, Max Parrish, London.

[26]   J.C. Dillow, The Waters Above: Earth's Pre-Flood Vapor Canopy, 1981, Moody, Chicago, IL.

[27]   G.H. Dury, **Discharge prediction, present and former, from channel dimensions**, Journal of Hydrology 30(1976) 219-245.

[28]   A.M. Dziewonski, **Mapping the lower mantle: Determination of lateral heterogeneity in P velocity up to degree and order 6**, Journal of Geophysical Research 89(1984) 5929-5952.

[29]   D.C. Engebretson, K.P. Kelley, H.J. Cushman, and M.A. Reynolds, **180 million years of subduction**, GSA Today 2:5(1992) 93-100.

[30]   C. Felix, **The mummified forests of the Canadian arctic**, Creation Research Society Quarterly 29:4(1993) 189-191.

[31]   D.E. Fisher, **Trapped helium and argon and the formation of the atmosphere by degassing**, Nature 256(1975) 113-114.

[32]   R.L. Folk, **Practical petrographic classification of limestones**, American Association of Petroleum Geologists Bulletin 43(1959) 8.

[33] T.M. Gerlach, and E.J. Graeber, **Volatile budget of Kilauea volcano**, <u>Nature</u> 313(1985) 273-277.

[34] L.J. Gibson, **A catastrophe with an impact**, <u>Origins [of GRI]</u> 17:1(1990) 38-47.

[35] R.W. Graham and E.L. Lundelius, Jr., **Coevolutionary disequilibrium and Pleistocene extinctions**, in [51], 1984, 223-249.

[36] J.F. Henry, **Space age astronomy confirms a recent and special creation**, in <u>Proceedings of the 1992 Twin-Cities Creation Conference</u>, 1992, Twin Cities Assoc., etc., St. Paul, MN, 88-90.

[37] K. Hsu, **Exhumation of high-pressure metamorphic rocks**, <u>Geology</u> 19(1991) 107-110.

[38] A.R. Huffman, K. McCartney, and D.E. Loper, **Hot spot initiation and flood basalts as a cause of catastrophic climate change and mass extinctions** [abstract], <u>Geological Society of America Abstracts With Programs</u> 21:7(1989) A93.

[39] W.W. Hughes, **Precambrian and Paleozoic glaciation**, <u>Origins [of GRI]</u> 6:1(1979) 49-51.

[40] D.R. Humphreys, **Reversals of the earth's magnetic field during the Genesis Flood**, in [111], 1987, 113-126.

[41] D.R. Humphreys, **Has the earth's magnetic field flipped?**, <u>Creation Research Society Quarterly</u> 25:3(1988) 130-137.

[42] D.R. Humphreys, **Physical mechanism for reversals of the earth's magnetic field during the Flood**, in [110], 1990, 129-142.

[43] J. Hutton, <u>Theory of the earth, With Proofs and Illustrations</u>, 1788, Cadell & Davies, Edinburgh, 2 volumes.

[44] J. Hutton, <u>The Theory of the Earth</u>, 1795, William Creech, Edinburgh.

[45] T.H. Jordon, **Composition and development of the continental tectosphere**, <u>Nature</u> 274(1978) 544-548.

[46] J.P. Kennett, R.E. Houtz, P.B. Andrews, A.R. Edwards, V.A. Gostin, M. Hajos, M. Hampton, D.G. Jenkins, S.V. Margolis, A.T. Ovenshine, and K. Perch-Nielson, **Site 284**, in J.P. Kennett, and R.E. Houtz, *et al.*, editors, <u>Initial Reports of the Deep Sea Drilling Project</u> 29(1975) 403-445.

[47] R.A. Kerr, **Climate since the ice began to melt**, <u>Science</u> 226(1987) 326-7.

[48] R. Lewin, **Domino effect invoked in Ice Age extinctions**, <u>Science</u> 238(1987) 1509-1510.

[49] C. Lyell, <u>Principles of Geology: Being an Attempt to Explain the Former Changes of the Earth's Surface by Reference to Causes Now in Operation</u>, 1830-1833, John Murray, London, Vol. 1 (1830); Vol. 2 (1832); Vol. 3 (1833).

[50] D.F. Mann, and K.P. Wise, **Plate tectonics: Physical and Biblical evidences** [abstract], in <u>Proceedings of the 1992 Twin-Cities Creation Conference</u>, 1992, Twin Cities Assoc., etc., St. Paul, MN.

[51] P.S. Martin and R.G. Klein, editors, <u>Quaternary Extinctions: A Prehistoric Revolution</u>, 1984, University of Arizona, Tucson, AZ.

[52] I.E. Mayne, **Terrestrial helium**, <u>Geochemica et Cosmochimica Acta</u> 9(1956) 174-182.

[53] J.F. McCauley, *et al.*, **Subsurface valley and geoarcheology of the eastern Sahara revealed by shuttle radar**, <u>Science</u> 218(1982) 1004-1020.

[54] P. McFarlane, <u>Exposure of the Principles of Modern Geology</u>, ca. 1850, Thomas Grant, Edinburgh.

[55] M. Molén, **Diamictites: Ice ages or gravity flows?**, in [110], 1990, 177-190.

[56] G.R. Morton, **Prolegomena to the study of the sediments**, <u>Creation Research Society Quarterly</u> 17:3(1980) 162-167.

[57] G.R. Morton, **Creationism and continental drift**, <u>Creation Research Society Quarterly</u> 18(1981) 42-45.

[58]   G.R. Morton, **Electrodynamics and the appearance of age**, Creation Research Society Quarterly 18(1982) 227-232.

[59]   G.R. Morton, **The Flood and an expanding earth**, Creation Research Society Quarterly 19(1983) 219-226.

[60]   G.R. Morton, **Mountain synthesis on an expanding earth**, Creation Research Society Quarterly 24(1987) 53-58.

[61]   G.R. Morton, The Geology of the Flood 1987, DMD, Dallas, TX.

[62]   G.R. Morton, **Changing constants and the cosmos**, Creation Research Society Quarterly 27:2(1990) 60-67.

[63]   B.C. Nelson, The Deluge Story in Stone: A History of the Flood Theory in Geology, 1931, Bethany, Minneapolis, MN.

[64]   R.W. Noone, Ice: The Untimate Disaster, ca. 1982, Dunwoody, GA.

[65]   R.L. Numbers, The Creationists: The Evolution of Scientific Creationism, 1992, Knopf, New York.

[66]   M.J. Oard, **A rapid post-Flood ice age**, Creation Research Society Quarterly 16:1(1979) 29-37.

[67]   M.J. Oard, **An ice age within the Biblical time frame**, in [111], 1987, 157-166.

[68]   M.J. Oard, An Ice Age Caused by the Genesis Flood, 1990, Institute for Creation Research, El Cajon, CA.

[69]   M.J. Oard, **The evidence for only one ice age**, in [110], 1990, 191-200.

[70]   M.J. Oard, **Comments on the breached dam theory for the formation of the Grand Canyon**, Creation Research Society Quarterly 30:1(1993) 39-46.

[71]   B. Overn, **The tilt of the earth's axis: Its orientation brings the new age; Its history reveals the Flood and explains the magnetic reversals**, in Proceedings of the 1992 Twin-Cities Creation Conference, 1992, Twin Cities Assoc., etc., St. Paul, MN, 83-87

[72]   H.J. Pachur, and S. Kröpelin, **Wadi Howar: Paleoclimate evidence from an extinct river system in the Southeastern Sahara**, Science 237(1987) 298-300.

[73]   B.C. Panuska, **An overlooked, world class Triassic flood basalt event** [abstract], Geological Society of America Abstracts With Programs 22:7(1990) A168.

[74]   W.S. Parks, **The role of meteorites in a creationist cosmology**, Creation Research Society Quarterly 26:4(1989) 144-146.

[75]   D.W. Patten, The Biblical Flood and the Ice Epoch: A Study in Scientific History, 1966, Pacific Meridian, Seattle, WA.

[76]   D.W. Patten, R.R. Hatch, and L.C. Steinhauer, The Long Day of Joshua and Six Other Catastrophes: A Unified Theory of Catastrophism, 1973, Pacific Meridian, Seattle, WA.

[77]   F.V. Perry, D.J. DePaolo, and W.S. Baldridge, **Isotopic evidence for a decline in crustal contributions to caldera-forming rhyolites of the Western United States during the Middle to Late Cenozoic** [abstract], Geological Society of America Abstracts With Programs 23:7(1991) A441.

[78]   F.J. Pettijohn, Sedimentary Rocks, 1975, Third edition, Harper, New York.

[79]   G.M. Price, The New Geology, 1923, Pacific Press, Mountain View, CA.

[80]   P.R. Renne, and A.R. Basu, **40Ar-39Ar Geochronologic evidence for the rapid eruption of the Siberian flood basalts at the Permian-Triassic boundary** [abstract], Geological Society of America Abstracts With Programs 23:7(1991) A395-6.

[81]   M.A. Richards, and R.A. Duncan, **Origin of flood basalts: impact, passive rifting or plume initiation?** [abstract], Geological Society of America Abstracts With Programs 21:7(1989) A93.

[82] K.P. Rode, **On the submarine volcanic origin of rock-salt deposits**, Proceedings of the Indian Academy of Science 20:B(1944) 130-142.

[83] S.H. Rugg, **Detachment faults in the southwestern United States -- Evidence for a short and catastrophic Tertiary Period**, in [110], 1990, 217-229.

[84] D.E. Rush, and L. Vardiman, **Pre-Flood vapor canopy radiative temperature profiles**, in [110], 1990, 231-245.

[85] D.E. Rush, and L. Vardiman, **Radiative equilibrium in an atmosphere with large water vapor concentrations**, Creation Research Society Quarterly 29:3(1992) 140-145.

[86] J. Scheven, **The Flood/post-Flood boundary in the fossil record**, in [110], 1990, 247-266.

[87] C.E. Schweger, et al., **Paleoecology of Beringia -- A synthesis**, in D. M. Hopkins, et al., editors, Paleoecology of Beringia, 1982, Academic, New York, 425-444.

[88] J.G. Sclater, C. Jaupart, and D. Galson, **The heat flow through oceanic and continental crust and the heat loss of the earth**, Reviews of Geophysics and Space Physics 18(1980) 269-311.

[89] B. Setterfield, **The recent change in the tilt of the earth's axis**, in Science at the Crossroads: Observation or Speculation?: Papers of the 1983 National Creation Conference, 1985, Bible-Science Association, Minneapolis, MN, 82-84.

[90] J.J. Shackleton, and J.P. Kennett, **Paleotemperature history of the Cenozoic and the initiation of Antarctic glaciation: oxygen and carbon isotope analysis in DSDP sites 277, 279, and 281**, in J. P. Kennett, and R. E. Houtz, et al., editors, Initial Reports of the Deep Sea Drilling Project 29(1975) 743-755.

[91] X. Shutong, A.I. Okay, J. Shouyuan, and A.M.C. Sengor, **Diamond from the Dabie Shan metamorphic rocks and its implication for tectonic setting**, Science 256(1992) 80-82.

[92] D.C. Smith, **Coesite in clinopyroxene in the Caledonides and its implications for geodynamics**, Nature 310(1984) 641-644.

[93] G.I. Smith, and F.A. Street-Perrott, **Pluvial lakes of the Western United States**, in H. E. Wright, Jr., editor, Late Quaternary Environments of the United States, 1983, volume 1, University of Minnesota, Minneapolis, MN, 190-212.

[94] A.A. Snelling, **Creationist geology: Where do the 'Precambrian' strata fit?**, Creation Ex Nihilo Technical Journal 5:2(1991) 154-175.

[95] A.A. Snelling, this volume, 1994.

[96] A.A. Snelling, in preparation.

[97] A. Snider-Pellegrini, La Création et ses Mystères Dévoilés, 1859 [early release, 1858], A Franck et E. Dentu, Paris.

[98] V.I. Sozansky, Geology and Genesis of Salt Formations [Russian], 1973, Izd Naukova Dumka, Kiev.

[99] S.M. Stanley, **An explanation for Cope's Rule**, Evolution 27:1(1973) 1-26.

[100] N. Steno, De solido intra solidum naturaliter contento dissertationis prodomus [Prodromus to a Dissertation on a Solid Body Naturally Contained Within a Solid], 1677, Florence.

[101] D.J. Tyler, **A tectonically-controlled rock cycle**, in [111], 1990, 293-299.

[102] D.W. Unfred, **Asteroidal impacts and the Flood-judgment**, Creation Research Society Quarterly 21:2(1984) 82-87.

[103] I.N. Vail, The Waters Above the Firmament, 1874, Barnesville, OH.

[104] L. Vardiman, **Up, up and away!: The helium escape problem**, ICR Impact Series 143(1985) i-iv.

[105] L. Vardiman, **The age of the earth's atmosphere estimated by its helium content**, in [110], 1990, 187-195.

[106] L. Vardiman, Age of the Earth's Atmosphere, 1990, Institute for Creation Research, El Cajon, CA.

[107] L. Vardiman, Ice Cores and the Age of the Earth, 1993, Institute for Creation Research, El Cajon, CA.

[108] L. Vardiman, Ocean Sediments and the Age of the Earth [ICR monograph], in preparation, Institute for Creation Research, El Cajon, CA.

[109] I. Velikovsky, Earth in Upheaval, 1955, Doubleday, New York.

[110] R.E. Walsh, and C.L. Brooks, editors, Proceedings of the Second International Conference on Creationism Held July 30 - August 4, 1990, Pittsburgh, Pennsylvania, USA, 1990, Volume 2, Creation Science Fellowship, Pittsburgh, PA, 386 p.

[111] R.E. Walsh, C.L. Brooks, and R.S. Crowell, editors, Proceedings of the First International Conference on Creationism, Held August 4-9, 1986, Pittsburgh, Pennsylvania, 1987, Volume 2, Creation Science Fellowship, Pittsburgh, PA, 253 p.

[112] T.W. Walters, **Thermodynamic analysis of a condensing vapor canopy**, Creation Research Society Quarterly 28:3(1991) 122-131.

[113] X. Wang, J.G. Liou, and H.K. Mao, **Coesite-bearing eclogite from the Dabie Mountains, central China**, Geology 17(1989) 1085-1088.

[114] S. Webb, The Creation and the Deluge, According to a New Theory; Confirming the Bible Account, Removing Most of the Difficulties Hertofore Suggested by Sceptical Philosophers, and Indicating Future Cosmological Changes Down to the Final Consummation and End of the Earth, 1854, Philadelphia, PA.

[115] S.A. Weinstein, **Catastrophic overturn of the earth's mantle driven by multiple phase changes and internal heat generation**, Geophysical Research Letters 20(1993) 101-104.

[116] W. Whiston, A New Theory of the Earth: From its Original, to the Consummation of all Things Wherein the Creation of the World in Six Days, the Universal Deluge and General Conflagration as Laid Down in the Holy Scriptures are Shewn to be Perfectly Agreeable to Reason and Philosophy, 1697, B. Tooke, London.

[117] J.C. Whitcomb, Jr., and H.M. Morris, The Genesis Flood: The Biblical Record and its Scientific Implications, 1961, Presbyterian and Reformed, Philadelphia, PA.

[118] R.L. Whitelaw, **The fountains of the great deep and the windows of heaven: A look at the canopy theory , and of a better alternative**, in Science at the Crossroads: Observation or Speculation?: Papers of the 1983 National Creation Conference, 1983, Bible-Science Association, Minneapolis, MN, 95-104.

[119] K.P. Wise, **How fast do rocks form?**, in [111], 1987, 197-203.

[120] K.P. Wise, **Some thoughts on the Precambrian fossil record**, Creation Ex Nihilo Technical Journal 6:1(1992) 67-71.

[121] K.P. Wise, **Were there really no seasons: Tree rings and climate**, Creation Ex Nihilo Technical Journal 6:2(1992) 168-172.

[122] K.P. Wise, **Creationism and plate tectonics: A re-evaluation of the evidence**, Creation Ex Nihilo Technical Journal in preparation.

[123] K.P. Wise, **Ecological Zonation and the Fossil Record**, Creation Ex Nihilo Technical Journal in prep.

[124] K.P. Wise, J.S. Stambaugh, and D. Mann, **Land's origin and Peleg's division**, Creation Ex Nihilo Technical Journal in preparation.

[125] J. Woodmorappe, **Causes for the biogeographic distribution of land vertebrates after the Flood**, in [110], 1990. 361-367.

[126] J. Woodward, An Essay Towards a Natural History of the Earth... With an Account of the Universal Deluge and of the Effects it had Upon the Earth, 1695, R. Wilkin, London.

THE BIOTA AND LOGISTICS OF NOAH'S ARK

JOHN WOODMORAPPE
M. S. GEOLOGY, B. S. GEOLOGY, B. S. BIOLOGY
6505 N. NASHVILLE #301
CHICAGO, IL 60631

KEYWORDS

Noah, Ark, Apologetics, Genesis, Flood, Vertebrate Taxonomy, Vertebrate Zoology, Vertebrate Husbandry.

ABSTRACT

This report investigates the identity and housing of approximately 16,000 animals on Noah's Ark. An evaluation of the housing, feeding, and watering requirements of these animals demonstrate the feasibility of the Ark account.

INTRODUCTION

Until the late 18th century, only a few hundred mammalian species were known [77]. Up to that time, the account of the Ark was accepted literally. No problem was seen in the housing and care of this small number of animals.

Now nearly 5000 mammalian species are known [77]. Partly because of the ever-growing number of animals discovered in the last two centuries (and needed to be accommodated on the Ark), the Ark account was gradually abandoned by most believers. For a historical survey of the rejection of the Ark account, see Browne [8, pp. 3-27].

The belief in the impossibility of the Ark spawned various compromises, such as the local flood theory. This reduced the Noachian Deluge to a glorified river flood of the Tigris-Euphrates. In recent years, the Ark account has enjoyed a renaissance of limited general attention as a result of the modern Scientific Creationist revival. This, in turn, has triggered a rather vitriolic backlash against the Ark account by anti-Creationists (notably Moore [52]).

The purpose of this work is systematically to examine the account of the Ark from the viewpoint of the feasibility of the housing of animals on the Ark. Diamond [12] has discussed the work of the 17th Century Jesuit Athanasius Kircher regarding the Ark and its logistics, and challenged modern Creationists to do the same. I have accepted the challenge.

Arguments against the Ark are basically the same, whether they are old or new, or whether they come from unbelievers, modernists, or various evangelicals (i.e. "theistic" evolutionists and semi-Creationists). Some of these arguments are examined and answered in this article. In a future monograph on the Ark, the arguments are rebutted in much more detail and comprehensiveness. The lengthy monograph is tentatively scheduled for publication by the Institute for Creation Research, probably in 1995. Owing to the space limitations of these Proceedings, only a fraction of the information to be published in the monograph can be presented here. Furthermore, only the results of some calculations, without tabulated data or supporting detail, are presented here.

THE QUESTION OF THE SUPERNATURAL

Moore [52] has alleged that the Ark account, in order to work as described in Scripture, would require so many miraculous solutions to (his imagined) insurmountable problems, that it would have been far easier for God to have transported Noah's family to heaven and just recreated a new biota on earth after the Flood. The central fallacy of his argument, solely with respect to theology, is the premise that God always prefers to work one large miracle rather than many smaller ones. Consider, for instance, the fact that God could have instantaneously teleported the Israelites into the Promised Land rather than have worked the many smaller miracles associated with the Exodus and the 40 years in the wilderness. He obviously chose not to do it this way, even though it would have been far simpler (according to Moore's thinking).

Whitcomb [75, p.19] has identified the following six areas of Divine miraculous action with regard to the Flood: 1) the divinely-revealed design of the Ark; 2) the gathering and care of the animals; 3) the uplift of oceanic waters from beneath; 4) the release of waters from above; 5) the formation of our present ocean basins; and 6) the formation of our present continents and mountain ranges. I concur with Whitcomb's analysis, except that I assume only naturalistic causes in the housing and care of animals on the Ark. The primary reason why I reject miracles not explicitly listed in Scripture (e.g. a supernaturally-induced sleep over the animals on the Ark so that they would require minimal care) is the fact that they are completely unnecessary.

ANIMALS NOT ON THE ARK

It was shown long ago [39, 76] that the Ark was not required to carry every species of Kingdom Animalia. Oblivious to this, recent critics of the Ark account (e.g. Moore [52], McGowan [46], and Futuyma [24]) continue to repeat the old canard that it did. For instance, Moore [52, p. 16] fantasizes that the Ark carried deep-sea fish. McGowan [46, p. 57], not to be outdone, puts whales and sharks on the Ark. Futuyma [24, pp. 202-3] adds to the farce by repositing all the millions of plant and animal species on to the Ark.

Fantasies and straw-men of the Ark aside, we can examine what Scripture actually says concerning the types of animal life taken on the Ark. The Hebrew terminology in the Genesis account rules out invertebrates having been taken on the Ark [39]. The same holds true for marine and amphibious vertebrates [29, pp. 86-7]. It is clear that the contents of the Ark were limited to all living and extinct land mammals, birds, and land reptiles [39].

Possibly the more terrestrial amphibians were on the Ark [39]. But since they were few in number [10, 16] and were mostly small in size [10, 35, 62], their presence on the Ark would have had a negligible effect on calculations. For this reason, they are not considered further. At the same time, it must be remembered that I have erred on the side of amphibious animals by virtue of the fact that I have included entire extant and extinct terrestrial families on the Ark, even if some of their members were amphibious. This is necessary because of the fact that many amphibious animals do not show obvious skeletal features reflecting their capability for living in water, making it virtually impossible to know for certain which extinct genera were semi-aquatic and therefore not taken on the Ark.

TAXONOMIC RANK OF ANIMALS ON THE ARK

Calculating the numbers of animals on the Ark requires not only an analysis of their taxonomic identity, but also taxonomic rank. Despite years of work by Creationists demonstrating that the Created Kind must be broader than the species, anti-Creationists (e.g. Moore [52]) continue to try to confuse the issue by insisting that the Ark had to house every *species* of animal.

It is difficult to escape the conclusion that the anti-Biblicists will stoop to any absurdity to multiply the cargo of the Ark into millions of animals in order to discredit the Ark account at any cost. To crown the fraud, the anti-Creationists (e.g. Awbrey [4] and Moore [52]) have the audacity to claim that the Creationists concocted the concept of the Created Kind as an *ad hoc* device to reduce the numbers of animals on the Ark. Clearly, the shoe is on the other foot.

The Created Kind is not some vague ethereal entity, but is well founded by Creationist scholarship. For instance, there is a wealth of evidence that, at minimum, the Created Kind is broader than the species of conventional taxonomy. Moreover, Jones [37], has showed that the *min* is a real entity and not simply that "like begets like".

Any putative difficulty in the discovery of a one-to-one correspondence between a specific taxonomic rank and the Created Kind in no way negates the concept of the Kind. It merely reflects the artificiality of human taxonomy. Gish [25] recently pointed out that he had been misrepresented by anti-Creationists, and had never suggested that the Created Kind may be as high as the order of conventional taxonomy. In his decades-long studies of turtles, Frair [22, and earlier-cited works] did suggest that the Created Kind among turtles may be as high as the order. However, the Testudines may be an atypically homogenous group, at least at the ordinal level. Furthermore, members of different families within Testudines do not freely interbreed with each other (Frair, personal communication). Following the interbreeding criteria discussed below, it follows that the Kind among turtles must be below the ordinal level.

Jones [38], largely using Scriptural evidence (e.g. the animal lists in Leviticus), demonstrated that the Created Kind is approximately equivalent to the subfamily or family, at least in the case of birds and mammals. Recently, Scherer [68] has arrived at the same conclusion, but on the basis of scientific evidence. This evidence includes numerous documented cases of interbreeding between individuals of different species and genera, as well as interbreeding with a third species or genus in situations where two species or genera do not themselves interbreed.The many instances he cites can be multiplied greatly.
For instance, Hubbs [32] has provided a large inventory of known instances of trans-specific and trans-generic breeding among fish. McAllister and Coad [44] have presented a matrix depicting all known instances of trans-generic breeding in the fish family Cichlidae. (This matrix is quite similar to the one by the Creationist Scherer [67].

The latter shows trans-generic breeding within the avian family Anatidae). Of course, there are also many more recent examples of hybridization between fish species [45, 49]. There are also many instances of trans-specific and trans-generic breeding among reptiles [5, 23, 33, 50].

Breeding among different species of birds is exceedingly common, and also occurs between genera [73]. For a bibliography of all papers providing similar examples, in just several issues of only one journal of avian biology (*Auk*), see [51]. There is a recent survey [11] of such occurrences among marsupial mammals alone. Finally, instances of hybrid zones among different species of plants and animals have recently been tabulated [28].

Of course, the above-cited examples hardly exhaust the possibilities for interbreeding between species and genera. Indeed, it is a fact that most species are named according to morphological differences between animals and not according to proven reproductive isolation (Archer [2, p. 130]):

> ...the fact that only a tiny percentage of recognized species have been tested, naturally or otherwise, for reproductive isolation from other apparently closely related forms...

Many evolutionists (e.g. Awbrey [4]) have claimed that macroevolution is simply microevolution given more time. A corollary of this is that, to be consistent and intellectually honest, since Creationists accept the fact that new species and genera can arise, then they must also accept the evolutionistic claim that new higher taxa can arise. In response to these premises, let us remember that the oft-repeated evolutionistic claim that small changes in populations add up to macroevolutionary innovations over alleged time is not proven. Moreover, the alleged evolutionary origin of families, orders, classes, phyla, and kingdoms is most certainly *not* simply the origin of new species and genera, just given more time. There is a definite, qualitative difference between the origin of new species and genera, and the supposed evolutionary origin of higher taxa. As Bullock [9, p. 90] writes:

> Most of the differences between species evolved in the diversification of species and genera, the lower categories of taxa, and are presumed to be adaptive specializations without any obvious advance in overall grade of complexity. These changes can be called *lateral radiations* (Bullock, 1991; Harvey and Pagel, 1991).

> Another kind of evolutionary change is the relatively rare increase in general complexity, such as characterizes the differences between some phyla, classes, and orders, and possibly a few families. I have already referred to these changes as *vertical grades* of complexity (italics in original).

It is interesting to note that the evolutionist Bullock not only echoes what Scientific Creationists have been saying all along, but even uses much the same vocabulary (namely lateral radiations, which is very similar to the Creationist expression: horizontal changes).

Anti-Creationists commonly raise doubts if new species and genera could arise in only the few thousand years since the Flood. In doing so, they display their ignorance of both Creationist and evolutionist research along these lines. Both Creationists [40] and evolutionists [7, pp. 442-3] have compiled numerous examples of various invertebrates and vertebrates giving rise to new species and genera in thousands of years (or much fewer). Some of these examples have subsequently been subject to detailed studies. For instance, Berry [6] has reviewed evidence of rapid speciation in mice in as short a time as a few decades, whereas Kornfield [42] has investigated the origin of reproductively-isolated species of African cichlid fishes in only 5000 years.

One consequence of the glaciation several thousand years ago is that the tropics must have undergone profound climatic changes, because belts of rainfall must have shifted considerably during glacial and interglacial intervals. As a consequence, regardless of whether one adheres to the evolutionistic or the Creationistic time scale, many species in the tropics must have arisen in only the last several thousand years. Nagel [55] has provided evidence that species of central African beetles have arisen in only 5000 years, while Moreau [53] has allowed extensive speciation among tropical birds in a comparative time period.

If, as the preponderance of evidence [38, 68] shows, the Created Kind was equivalent to the family (at least in the case of mammals and birds), then there were only about 2000 animals on the Ark [39]. In such a case it is obvious that there was no problem in housing all the animals on the commodious Ark. However, in order to make this exercise more interesting, I have been more conservative, adopting the genus as the taxonomic rank of the Created Kind. This necessitates, as shown below, approximately 16,000 animals on the Ark.

THE QUESTION OF UNKNOWN EXTINCT ANIMALS

The accommodation of undiscovered (and also undiscoverable) extinct animals on the Ark must be considered. There is no way of determining, or even intelligently guessing, the numbers and sizes of unknown animals. A number of estimates for the numbers of specific unknown types of extinct animals exist (e.g. dinosaurs [14]). However, these are all based on the assumption of the validity of organic evolution and the geologic time scale in their calculations, and thus have no meaning in the Creationist-Diluvialist paradigm.

Considering the results of calculations (not shown), there exists, once all relevant live and known extinct animals are accounted for, a significant amount of unused Ark floor space. This allows a considerable spare floor area on the Ark to account for unknown extinct animals. Of course, we must remember that there is plenty of yet additional room on the Ark by virtue of the fact that I have placed all *genera* of live and extinct land vertebrates on the Ark, when in reality there were probably only *subfamilies* or *families* of the same on the Ark.

Furthermore, the existence of unknown extinct animals is partly offset by the fact that a substantial fraction of all provisionally-accepted extinct genera, all of which are placed on the Ark in this study, are of dubious validity [10]. Indeed, since its inception, vertebrate paleontology has suffered from a proliferation of invalid generic names based on nondiagnostic material, and an exaggeration of the numbers of putatively valid generic names derived from more complete material. In recent decades, a considerable number of extinct genera have been "sunk", and this process continues today. For example, a recent study [35] has drawn several long-accepted therapsid genera into synonymy.

It is the dubious genera of large-sized animals that have the largest effect on my tabulation and calculations. For instance, for purposes of this study, I have included all 87 commonly-cited sauropod dinosaur genera as valid, and placed them on the Ark (as juveniles). Yet, according to sauropod specialist McIntosh [40, p. 345], only 12 sauropod genera can be regarded as "firmly established" and an additional 12 "fairly well established".

CLEAN ANIMALS ON THE ARK

Accounting for clean animals on the Ark is problematic for several reasons. In the first place, the concept of a clean animal at the time of Noah may not have been the same as it was millennia later with the Levitical System [43, pp. 190-191]. However, considering the perspicuity of Scripture, I will, in the absence of evidence to the contrary, provisionally assume that the concepts of clean animals were the same during the time of Noah as they were after the inception of the Law of Moses.

It is also difficult to determine whether Noah took seven individuals or seven pairs of clean animals on the Ark. Jones [39] surveyed over 40 Bible commentaries on this matter and found them about evenly divided as to whether Scripture indicates seven pairs and seven individuals.

Nor can we be certain which genera were clean (if we use the genus as the level of the Created kind, as done throughout this work). Scripture considers all reptiles unclean [63, p. 33]. Among mammals, those with cloven hooves that chew continually or chew again (not necessarily ruminate, which is a modern physiological concept) are clean (Deuteronomy 14: 4-6). Scripture specifically lists the clean mammals as consisting of approximately 13 bovid/cervid genera [38]. According to Jewish tradition (for example, Maimonides: [26, p. 49-50]), this Scriptural list is exhaustive; so no other live or extinct mammal is to be accepted as clean, even if it chews again and divides the hoof.

Thus the *simanim* (sign) of cloven hoofs and chewing again is a necessary but not necessarily sufficient condition for a land mammal to be accepted as clean [20]. For instance, the giraffe divides the hoof and chews again, but there is no clear Jewish tradition of it's being kosher [63, p. 31]. According to some other Jewish traditions [15], only domesticated animals can be clean. Pertaining to these, only a few tens of genera of mammals and birds are commonly reckoned as domesticated (for a list of these genera, see Fowler [21, p. 1067]). All these considerations rule out numerous wild and also all extinct bovid, giraffid, and cervid genera as being clean. Furthermore, if Scripture is accepted as a self-contained revelation (that is, requiring no extra-Biblical sources of information in order to be understood properly), then it also follows that only animals individually specified in Scripture as clean can be regarded as such.

As for birds, Scripture lists numerous birds which are unclean (see Jones [38] for listing along with taxonomic analysis). However, only several types of birds, belonging to a few tens of genera at most, are mentioned in the Bible as suitable for human use [63]. Again, once Scripture is its own interpreter, then these are the only birds to be accepted as clean. However, if Jewish tradition is considered, then there are only a few additional birds, not mentioned in the Bible, accepted as clean [63].

Various commentators have suggested a connection between Noah's sacrifice after the Flood (Genesis 8:20) and the identity of the clean animals, but Scripture does not indicate how many animals were sacrificed by Noah [39].

However, keeping in mind the Hebrew terminologies and usages in Scripture, we can note that Noah's sacrifice was a burnt offering (Hebrew *olah*, [64, p. 601]). This type of sacrifice, according to other examples in Scripture, is limited to bulls, sheep and goats, and birds [64, p. 601-2]. This adds further support to the limitation of clean animals to certain common animals in Bible lands. Note that this is yet another reason for eliminating from the Ark (as seven individuals or seven pairs) all extinct land vertebrates, as well as all extant land vertebrates not explicitly mentioned in Scripture as clean.

Unfortunately, even this does not allow a precise tally of the number of clean genera on the Ark because there is a notably high degree of interbreeding among genera of clean animals. This can be especially seen among genera in the families Bovidae and Cervidae [74]; genera in Galliformes (various chickens, turkeys, quail, and pheasants [1, 47]; genera in Anseriformes (i.e. many genera in Anatidae [67]; and many genera in Passeriformes (i.e. finches [66]. To further compound the uncertainty, not all genera of Anseriformes and Galliformes are accepted as clean according to certain Jewish tradition [20].

Although it is difficult to enumerate precisely how many clean genera were on the Ark, it should be obvious that there were only a few tens of clean genera at most, and they were mostly small. For this reason, calculations regarding the Ark and its logistics are relatively insensitive to the presence of the clean animals on the Ark, even if they were in seven pairs and not seven individuals. Thus the clean animals are not considered further in this report, although their minimal effect on calculations will be demonstrated in my upcoming Monograph on the Ark.

NUMBER OF ANIMALS ON THE ARK

After having determined which animals were on the Ark, I compiled and computed body-mass estimates for all the living and known extinct genera of land vertebrates. There are 85 orders of live and known extinct land vertebrates, but the distribution of their constituent genera is highly asymmetric. Merely the largest three orders (Passeriformes, Squamata, and Rodentia) contain nearly half of the 16,000 animals on the Ark. Because of this asymmetry, I followed a similar methodology employed by May [43] in his analysis of insect body sizes. I studied in great detail the body mass distributions within the several top orders which contain by far the most genera (i.e., to which the overall calculations show the greatest sensitivity), and simply assigned a characteristic value or values for body mass to each small order.

For extinct families and extinct orders, I derived body mass estimates from sources too numerous to mention here. Two of the major sources of general information on sizes (for small orders) were Carroll [10] and Potts and Behrensmeyer [58]. For extinct genera in extant reptilian and extant avian families, I simply extrapolated the total database for body weights of extant genera to the number of extinct ones.

I followed a somewhat different methodology for extinct genera in extant mammalian families. Peczkis [57] has found that 67% of mammalian genera tend to occur in the modal body-mass category of the typical mammalian family, and 90% of genera occur in the two largest weight categories of the given family. I thus extrapolated the extinct genera in extant families according to a 2:1 ratio with respect to the aforementioned body-weight categories.

I list sources only for body weights of extant genera. It is worthwhile to note that body mass estimates are available for nearly all land mammal genera [13, 56], and for most extant avian genera [18, 65].

As for extant reptiles, a compendium of body mass estimates for all or most land reptilian genera does not exist. I developed a partial one of my own, compiling estimates for a large fraction of all extant reptilian genera. For tortoises, I converted carapace sizes for various genera [19] into body masses. For squamate genera, I first utilized relatively comprehensive estimates of body masses [3,27,59,60,69,72]. I then expanded this data base by converting snout-vent lengths [17, and other less-comprehensive sources] into body mass. These snout-vent lengths were converted into body masses through the utilization of an appropriate regression [61]. The distribution of body masses obtained for many specific reptilian genera were subsequently extrapolated to the total number of extant squamate genera [16] and extinct ones [10].

To summarize, there were 7, 876 pairs of animals (that is, land-vertebrate genera) placed on the Ark, based on hundreds of sources. Because animals vary greatly in size, even to some extent individuals of the same genus, I have divided all the animals into order-of-magnitude body-mass categories. These span eight orders of magnitude of body mass, ranging in size from hummingbirds (i.e., a few grams per individual) to sauropods (up to perhaps 80 megagrams adult mass). The purpose of dividing all the animals into body-mass categories is to make possible calculations of floor-space requirements for animal housing, as well as the total mass and volume of provender and water for all the animals during a 371-day stay on the Ark.

The number of animals on the Ark, apportioned per body-mass category, in summary is as follows: 869 animals in the 1-10 gram body-mass category, 2343 at 10-100 grams, 1619 at 100 g-1 kg, 1176 at 1-10 kg, 964 at 10-100 kg, 594 at 100-1000 kgs, 258 at 1000-10,000 kgs, and 53 at 10,000-100,000 kgs.

As can be seen from the tabulation, the vast majority of the animals on the Ark were small. The median animal on the Ark was the size of a small rat, about 100 grams [30, p.70]. It is obvious that Whitcomb and Morris [76] have been overly generous to their detractors when they had suggested that the average animal on the Ark was the size of a sheep. In fact, from the tabulation, it can be seen that only about 11% of the animals on the Ark were substantially larger than sheep.

As concerning medium to large animals (that is, all animals greater than 10 kg as adults), I have represented them on the Ark as juveniles. It would not have been worth it to have represented animals smaller than 10 kg as juveniles, because the juveniles would have been near or at adult size by the time of their disembarkation from the Ark.

ARK FLOOR SPACE ALLOTMENT FOR THE ANIMALS

How much floor space should be allowed for each size category of animal on the Ark? Moore [42] has cited large floor areas, based on the claims of zoo keepers. However, the zoo is a very inappropriate and misleading analog for the housing requirements of the animals on the Ark. First of all, the zoo is a facility intended for the public display of captive animals, as well as for the relatively comfortable confinement of animals on a permanent basis. Enclosures must generally also be spacious enough for animals to breed in captivity. By contrast, the Ark represents temporary confinement of animals without their necessarily breeding during the stay on the Ark. Furthermore, the zoo represents the elective keeping of wild animals for educational, scientific, and entertainment purposes, whereas the Ark represents an extreme and emergency situation. The Ark was most certainly not a floating zoo, but a floating Flood shelter.

Indeed, during emergencies, we are not primarily concerned with either human or animal comfort, but only with physical survival through the emergency itself (i.e., think of the comfort of people confined in a fallout shelter). Since we only need consider the minimum floor space for animals to survive in reasonable health for one year, we must orient ourselves not according to modern zoos, but according to modern examples of animals kept under conditions of extreme confinement. The closest modern analogues to the Ark are not the zoo but the laboratory animal situation and the intensive livestock unit, commonly known as the factory farm [36]. In the latter, we have up to 100,000 animals, living under very crowded conditions under one roof, and cared for by a handful of people.

We might naturally suppose that there might be some analogy between the Ark and situations where modern animals are transported en masse on ships. However, such animals are at sea usually only a few days or weeks. Clearly, the duration is not comparable enough for a meaningful comparison with the year-long Ark experience.

Moore [52] has criticized Creationists [76] for suggesting that the confinement of animals on the Ark could be compared to the confinement and transport of livestock on railroad cars, because livestock are allowed to leave the cars, during railroad stops, for exercise. He is clearly clutching at straws, because the above-cited examples of intensive animal confinement (namely factory farms and laboratory-animal situations) reflect long-term intensive animal confinement, for months or years, with few or no opportunities for animals to leave their enclosures.

For purposes of estimating the minimum floor space needed for small animals on the Ark, I have used recommended floor-space areas for the housing of laboratory animals [70]. The floor areas for animals of various sizes are: 38.7 square cms for an animal under 10 grams, 110 square cms for 100 grams, 387 square cms for 350 grams, 0.28 square meters for 2-4 kg. For larger animals, I used the values for floor spacing of intensively-housed livestock, because animals must be kept tightly enclosed so that they will be forced to trample their manure through slatted floors (as opposed to lying in it). The floor areas I used (based on [34]) are: 0.56 square cms for a 50 kg animal, 1.11 square meters for a 350 kg one (juvenile of a 1000-10,000 kg adult), and 2.51 square meters for a several hundred kg (or more) animal (juvenile of a 10,000-100,000 kg sauropod dinosaur).

Throughout the calculations, I used these values as midpoints of the body-mass categories. For small to medium-sized animals (i.e., 1 gram to 100 kg), I used the arithmetical midpoint of each category (5 grams, 50 grams, 500 grams, etc.). For larger animals (i.e., 100 kg to 100 tons), I used the geometric midpoint (adults would be: 316 kg, 3160 kg, and 31,600 kg), because larger animals appear to occur at a greater frequency towards the lower category of each respective body-mass category. I used all the midpoints, multiplied by the number of animals in each body-mass category, not only to calculate floor space for housing, but also for purposes of computing the total volumes of potable water and provender for 371 days.

CALCULATIONS OF WATER AND PROVENDER FOR ANIMALS ON THE ARK

Based on the animals and their sizes quoted above, and various equations for water intake of captive animals, I estimate that the total amount of potable water on the Ark was 3.64 million liters. This comprised only 8.43% of total Ark volume, which was 43,169 cubic meters (based on a cubit of 45.72 cm).

As for food, the calculations were not as straightforward, for several reasons. First of all, there is a very large disparity between the food requirements of ectotherms (i.e., reptiles) and endotherms (mammals and birds). We do not know the thermal physiology of therapsids nor dinosaurs, both of which are extinct with no close relatives in the extant fauna. However, I have assumed that their thermal physiology was halfway between that observed in modern mammals/birds and reptiles. This assumption is consistent with the belief that therapsids possessed an intermediate thermal physiology between that usually observed in modern reptiles and modern mammals [31]. Small to medium dinosaurs could have been either ectothermic or endothermic [71]. However, sauropod dinosaurs have been treated here as ectotherms, because a recent biophysical analysis [71] has just about ruled out any possible thermal physiology for them significantly different from that of modern reptiles (scaled, of course, for size).

A further source of complication is the following: Food requirements themselves are subject to a large number of variables, such as dry matter content, digestibility, and bulk density. Based on these and still other factors, along with equations for animal food intake per given ectothermic or endothermic animal mass, I have reached the following conclusion: The total volume of food on the Ark was approximately 3-6 thousand cubic meters. This represented 6-12% of the total Ark volume. The reason for the range of values quoted reflects different combinations of feedstuffs of varying bulk density, digestibility, and moisture content.

CONCLUSION

It is obvious from this work that none of the oft- repeated criticisms of the Ark account can stand up to critical examination. Nor is a constant stream of *ad hoc* Divine miracles necessary for the Ark account to have happened exactly as the Scriptures teach. Of course, it is not surprising that the Ark account is the butt of ridicule today (note, for instance, the sarcastic cartoon of the hole-filled Ark reproduced in Moore [52] from a newspaper editorial). Fallen man does not want to be reminded of God's judgement in the past any more than he wants to be told of God's judgement in the future.

REFERENCES

[1]   V. S. Amundsen and F. W. Lorenz, **Pheasant-turkey hybrids,** Science 121: (1955) 307-8.
[2]   M. Archer, **Systematics: an enormous science rooted in instinct,** in Vertebrate Zoogeography and Evolution in Australasia, 1981, M. Archer and G. Clayton, editors, Hesperian Press, Australia.
[3]   R. M. Andrews and F. H. Pough, **Metabolism of squamate reptiles: allometric and ecological relationships,** Physiological Ecology 58: (1985) 214-231.
[4]   F. T. Awbrey, **Defining "kinds"--do Creationists apply a double standard?** Creation/Evolution 5 (1981) 1-6.
[5]   R. M. Bailey, **An intergeneric hybrid rattlesnake,** American Naturalist 76 (1942) 376-385.
[6]   B. J. Berry, **The significance of island biotas,** Biological Journal of the Linnean Society 46: (1992) 3-12.
[7]   J. C. Briggs, **Marine Zoogeography,** 1974, McGraw Hill Book Company, San Francisco.
[8]   J. Browne, **The Secular Ark,** 1983, Yale University Press.
[9]   T. H. Bullock, **How are more complex brains different,** Brain, Behavior, and Evolution 41:2 (1993) 88-96.
[10]   R. L. Carroll, **Vertebrate Paleontology and Evolution,** 1988, W. H. Freeman and Company, New York.
[11]   R. L. Close and P. S. Lowry, **Hybrids in Marsupial Research,** Australian Journal of Zoology 37: (1990) 259-267.
[12]   J. Diamond, **Voyage of the overloaded Ark,** Discover 2:2 (June 1985) 82-92.
[13]   J. Damuth, **Interspecific allometry of population density in mammals and other animals: their independence of body mass and population energy-use,** Biological Journal of the Linnean Society 31: (1987) 193-246.
[14]   P. Dodson, **Counting dinosaurs: how many kinds were there?** Proceedings of the National Academy of Sciences (USA) 87: (1990) 7608-7612.
[15]   S. H. Dresner, and S. Siegel, **The Jewish Dietary Laws,** 1959, 1966, Burning Bush Press, New York.
[16]   W. E. Duellman, **The numbers of amphibians and reptiles,** Herpetological Review 10:2 (1979) 83-84.
[17]   A. E. Dunham, D. B. Miles, and D. N. Resnick, **Life history patterns in squamate reptiles,** in Biology of the Reptilia, Vol. 16, 1988, C. Gans, editor, Alan R. Liss, Inc., New York.
[18]   J. B. Dunning, **Body masses of birds of the world,** in CRC Handbook of Avian Body Masses, J. B. Dunning, editor, 1993, CRC Press, Boca Raton, Florida.
[19]   C. H. Ernst and R. W. Barbour, **Turtles of the World,** 1989, Smithsonian Institution Press, Washington, D. C.
[20]   B. Forst, **The Laws of Kashrus,** 1993, Mesorah Publications, New York.
[21]   M. E. Fowler, **Common and scientific names of animals classed as domestic,** in Zoo and Wild Animal Medicine, 2nd Edition, M. E. Fowler, editor, 1986, W. B. Saunders and Company, Philadelphia.

[22]   W. Frair, **Original kinds and turtle phylogeny,** <u>Creation Research Society Quarterly</u> **28:1** (1991) 21-24.
[23]   F. L. Frye, **Biomedical and Surgical Aspects of Captive Reptile Husbandry,** 2 Volumes, 1991, Krieger Publishing Company, Malabar, Florida.
[24]   D. J. Futuyma, **Science on Trial,** 1983, Pantheon Books, New York.
[25]   D. T. Gish, **Creation Scientists Answer Their Critics,** 1993, Institute for Creation Research, El Cajon, California.
[26]   D. I. Grunfeld, **The Jewish Dietary Laws,** 1972, Soncino Press, London, Jerusalem.
[27]   C. Guyer and M. A. Donnelly, **Length-mass relationships among assemblages of tropical snakes in Costa Rica,** <u>Journal of Tropical Ecology</u> **6:** (1990) 65-76.
[28]   R. G. Harrison, **Hybrid zones: windows on evolutionary process,** <u>Oxford Surveys in Evolutionary Biology</u> **7:** (1990) 69-128.
[29]   G. F. Hasel, **Some issues regarding the nature and universality of the Genesis Flood narrative,** <u>Origins</u> **5:2** (1978) 83-98.
[30]   R. Hendrickson, **More Cunning than Man,** 1983, Dorset Press, New York.
[31]   W. J. Hillenius, **Late Permian origins of mammalian endothermy,** <u>Journal of Vertebrate Paleontology</u> **12:** (1992), Supplement to No. 3, p. 32A.
[32]   C. L. Hubbs, **Hybridization between fish species in nature,** <u>Systematic Zoology</u> **4:1** (1955) 1-20.
[33]   T. A. Huff, **Captive propagation of the subfamily Boinae with emphasis on the genus** *Epicrates,* in <u>Reproductive Biology and Diseases of Captive Reptiles</u>, J. B. Murphy and J. T. Collins, editors, 1980, Society for the Study of Reptiles and Amphibians, Lawrence, Kansas.
[34]   ILAR (Institute of Laboratory Animal Resources, **Guide for the care and use of laboratory animals,** NIH (National Institutes for Health) Publication Number 78-23, Bethesda, Maryland.
[35]   F. A. Jenkins and D. M. Walsh, **An early caecilian with limbs,** <u>Nature</u> **365:** (1993) 246-250.
[36]   A. Johnson, **Factory Farming,** 1991, Blackwell Scientific Publishing Company, Oxford, England.
[37]   A. J. Jones, **A general analysis of the Biblical "kind" (min),** <u>Creation Research Society Quarterly</u> **9:2** (1972a) 53-57.
[38]   A. J. Jones, **Boundaries of the min: an analysis of the Mosaic lists of clean and unclean animals,** <u>Creation Research Society Quarterly</u> **9:2** (1972b) 114-123.
[39]   A. J. Jones, **How many animals on the Ark?** <u>Creation Research Society Quarterly</u> **10:2** (1973) 102-108.
[40]   A. J. Jones, **The genetic integrity of the "kinds" (baramins): a working hypothesis,** <u>Creation Research Society Quarterly</u> **19:1** (1982) 13-18.
[41]   G. M. King and B. S. Rubidge, **A taxonomic revision of small dicynodonts with postcanine teeth,** <u>Zoological Journal of the Linnean Society</u> **107:** (1993) 131-154.
[42]   I. L. Kornfield, **Evidence for rapid speciation in African cichlid fishes,** <u>Experientia</u> **34:3** (1978) 335-336.
[43]   R. M. May, **The dynamics and diversity of insect faunas,** in <u>Diversity of Insect Faunas</u>, L. A. Mound and N. Waloff, editors, 1978, Blackwell Scientific Publishing Company, Oxford, London.
[44]   D. E. McAllister amd B. W. Coad, **A test between relationships based on phenetic and cladistic taxonomic methods,** <u>Canadian Journal of Zoology</u> **56:** (1978) 2198-2210.
[45]   M. R. McClure and J. D. McEachran, **Hybridization between** *Prionotus alatus* **and** *P. paralatus* **in the northern Gulf of Mexico (Pisces: Triglidae),** <u>Copeia</u> **1992:4** (1992) 1039-1046.
[46]   C. McGowan, **In the beginning: a scientist shows why the Creationists are wrong,** 1984, Prometheus Books, New York.
[47]   T. A McGrath, M. D. Shalter, W. Schleidt, and P. Sarvella, **Analysis of distress calls of chickenXpheasant hybrids,** <u>Nature</u> **237:** (1972) 47-8.
[48]   J. S. McIntosh, **Sauropoda,** in <u>The Dinosauria</u>, D. B. Wieshampel, P. Dodson, and H. Osmolska, editors, 1992, University of California Press.
[49]   S. Meagher and T. E. Dowling, **Hybridization between the Cyprinid fishes** *Luxilus albeolus, L. cornutus,* **and** *L. cerasinus* **with comments on the proposed hybrid origin of** *L. albeolus,* <u>Copeia</u> **1991:4** (1991) 979-991.
[50]   R. von Mertens, **Uber reptilienbastarde, IV,** <u>Senckenbergiana Biologia</u> **49:1** (1968) 1-12.
[51]   B. L. Monroe, **Ten-year index to the** *Auk* **(volumes 98-107), 1981-1990,** 1991, American Ornithologist's Union, Washington.
[52]   R. A. Moore, **The impossible voyage of Noah's Ark,** <u>Creation/Evolution</u> **11** (1983) 1-43.
[53]   R. E. Moreau, **The bird faunas of Africa and its islands,** 1966, Academic Press, New York.
[54]   H. Morris, **The Genesis Record,** 1976, Creation-Life Publishers, San Diego.
[55]   P. Nagel, **Die methode der arealsystemanalyse als beitrag zur rekonstruktion der landschaftsgenese im tropischen Africa,** <u>Geomethodica</u> **11:** (1986) 145-176.
[56]   R. M. Nowak and J. L. Paradiso, **Walker's Mammals of the World,** 1983, 4th Edition, Volume 1, John Hopkins University Press, Baltimore and London.
[57]   J. Peczkis, **Predicting body-weight distribution of mammalian genera in families and orders,** <u>Journal of Theoretical Biology</u> **132:** (1988) 509-510.
[58]   R. Potts and A. K. Behrensmeyer, **Late Cenozoic terrestrial ecosystems,** in <u>Terrestrial Ecosystems Through Time</u>, A. K. Behrensmeyer, J. D. Damuth, W. A. DiMichele, R. Potts, H.-D. Sues, and S. L. Wing, editors, 1992, University of Chicago Press, Chicago and London.
[59]   F. H. Pough, **Lizard energetics and diet,** <u>Ecology</u> **54:** (1973) 837-844.

[60]   F. H. Pough, **The relationship between body size and blood oxygen affinity in snakes,** Physiological Zoology **50:** (1977) 77-87.

[61]   F. H. Pough, **The advantages of ectothermy for tetrapods,** American Naturalist **115:1** (1980) 92-112.

[62]   F. H. Pough, **Amphibians: a rich source of biological diversity,** in Nonmammalian Animal Models for Biomedical Research, A. D. Woodhead and K. Vivirito, editors, 1989, CRC Press, Florida.

[63]   H. Rabinowitz, **Dietary Laws,** in Encyclopedia Judaica, Volume 1, 1972.

[64]   A. Rainey, **Sacrifice,** in Encyclopedia Judaica, Volume 14, 1971.

[65]   S. Ritland, **The allometry of the vertebrate eye,** 1982, University of Chicago Phd Dissertation, 4 volumes.

[66]   S. Roberts, **Bird Keeping and Bird Cages, a History,** 1973, Drake Publishers, New York

[67]   S. Scherer, **On the limits of variability,** in Concepts in Creationism, E. H. Andrews, W. Gitt, and W. J. Ouweneel, editors, 1986, Evangelical Press, Welwyn, Herts, England.

[68]   S. Scherer, **Basic types of life,** in Studium Integrale, S. Scherer, editor, 1993, Pascal-Verlag, Berlin.

[69]   R. S. Seymour, **Scaling of cardiovascular physiology in snakes,** American Zoologist **27:** (1987) 97-109.

[70]   R. C. Simmonds, **Standards: the guide for the care and use of laboratory animals,** in Handbook of Facilities Planning, Volume 2, T. Ruys, editor, 1991, Van Nostrand Reinhold, New York.

[71]   J. R. Spotila, M. P. O'Connor, P. Dodson, and F. V. Paladino, **Hot and cold running dinosaurs: body size, metabolism and migration,** Modern Geology **16:** (1991) 203-227.

[72]   R. D. Stevenson, **Body size and limits to the daily range of body temperature in terrestrial ectotherms,** American Naturalist **125:** (1985) 102-117.

[73]   L. P. Tatarinov, **Certain aspects of the theory of speciation,** Paleontological Journal **20:2** (1986) 1-8.

[74]   R. G. Van Gelder, **Mammalian hybrids and generic limits,** American Museum Novitates 2635: (1977) 1-25.

[75]   J. C. Whitcomb, **The World that Perished,** 1973, Baker Book House, Michigan.

[76]   J. C. Whitcomb and H. M. Morris, **The Genesis Flood,** 1961, Presbyterian and Reformed, New Jersey.

[77]   J. D. E. Wilson and D. M. Reeder, **Introduction,** in Mammal Species of the World, D. E. Wilson and D. M. Reeder, editors, 1993, Smithsonian Institution Press, Washington, D. C.

ARCHAEOLOGY AND CREATION SCIENCE

J. A. YOUNG
MISSIONARY TO MEXICO WITH
GOSPEL RECORDINGS, INC.
28 HANO TRAIL
FLAGSTAFF, AZ 86001

KEYWORDS

Archaeology; Arctic; Carbon-14 Dating; Chronology, Biblical; Continental Drift; Dendrochronology; Genesis 11:10-19; Ice Age; Pangaea; Uniformitarianism; Volcanism, Post-Flood.

ABSTRACT

In order to integrate Biblical creation science with the modern discipline of archaeology, creation science itself must become unified, specific, sequential, and definitive. Only then can it provide a basic geochronological framework for interpreting archaeology. This paper will explore three Biblical creationist models: a development of the post-Flood Ice Age, a treatment of continental separation, and a mathematical equation which translates carbon-14 age data into real-time equivalents. It will apply these models to uniformitarian ages of ancient cultures, using a Biblical chronology, to begin the process of re-evaluating prehistoric archaeology from the perspective of Biblical creation science.

INTRODUCTION

To develop a complete, systematic, Biblical creation science paradigm requires defining the various aspects of the general model with a view toward integrating it with other disciplines and sciences. We recognize that these disciplines have already become fairly well developed from quite a different perspective. One distinctive of Biblical Creationism is its insistence on a young earth. The present structure of prehistoric archaeology is built on a framework of long ages. In order to reinterpret archaeology from a Biblical perspective, we must radically revise conventional timescales for human cultural development and migration during the Holocene. To accomplish this, we must set forth definitive proposals regarding Biblical chronology, the relative sequence of major geological events, and causative mechanisms for the succession of those events.

The modern discipline of archaeology is the study of the remains of specific objects fashioned by human hands, from prehistoric to modern times. This study requires a careful examination of the antiquities, which is seldom controversial; and then a thoughtful interpretation of the evidence, which is often very controversial! To interpret archaeological artifacts in the light of Biblical creation science, we must first establish a reasonable chronology which both satisfies the requirements of young-earth creationists and allows sufficient time for the necessary geological and archaeological developments to occur. Within that chronology, we will see that some of the epochs or periods into which archaeologic prehistoric time has been divided are contemporary with each other. In fact, they are not epochs at all, but merely different patterns of material culture, grouped for technological convenience, some of which are successive in certain geographic localities.

UNIFORMITARIAN PREHISTORIC ARCHAEOLOGY

One's view of the past is conditioned not only from material evidence, but from the presuppositions one accepts. Meaningful arrangements of the data can only be made within the framework of some sort of conceptual model which will permit their interpretation. Standard prehistoric archaeological models are largely evolutionary in their presuppositions. However, we can take the same human artifacts that have been interpreted from an evolutionary perspective and set them forth in a Scriptural perspective. This demonstrates that accepting evolution as a world view is a choice that one makes, rather than an intellectual imperative. We can develop a new, more compressed interpretation of pre-history. We can re-think the generally-accepted chronology and develop a system that is compatible with the chronological data in Genesis. This will require a revision of some widely-accepted interpretations, but would be a significant advance in the development of a complete creation paradigm.

DISCORDANCE IN CHRONOLOGY

Since archaeology deals with man-made artifacts, the junction between creation science and archaeology is basically the immediate post-Flood environment. A Biblical creationist looking at the past four or five thousand years in archaeology, will generally be content with the findings and their proposed dating schemes, since many interpretations are supportive and illustrative of the Biblical narrative. But, moving back in the past, the closer one comes to the time of the Genesis Flood, the more discontented the creationist will be. He can co-exist reasonably happily with the Egyptologist and the Sumerologist, but will find great difficulties in relating to the observations and conclusions of the pre-historic archaeologist.

An international symposium held in La Jolla, California in January, 1993, brought together prominent Biblical archaeologists and prehistorians from Israel, England, France, Canada, and the United States. These scholars presented 31 papers covering, in chronological order, the "history of the Holy Land from 120,000 B.C. to the present" [24]. This illustrates our basic difficulty. The problem is not the raw data, the actual physical remains that are discovered, nor really with the relative sequence into which these artifacts are placed. It is simply the inflated ages assigned to early artifacts.

This is particularly obvious in the case of early villages and construction. On the face of it, any construction found anywhere in the world, must be declared "post-Flood" by a Biblical creationist, because the Deluge we postulate must have destroyed any pre-Flood buildings that existed. Therefore, as far as in-situ village sites and their associated artifacts are concerned, creationism will declare them all post-Flood. Furthermore, creationists declare the shallow Pleistocene deposits with their associated artifacts post-Flood as well. Depending on the date we assign to the Genesis Flood, then, we will find that we cannot accept a good number of the dates that evolutionary prehistoric archaeology assigns to various early discoveries.

If the only purpose of the Biblical creationist were to place the broad spectrum of prehistoric man within the larger framework of creationism, the safest position would be to rest content within the wider limits of the period between the Flood and Abraham. Simply left like this, there would be no danger of grave miscalculation. But the subject is of such interest and importance that it urges the student to attempt the risky task of placing events and cultures more exactly.

The modern discipline of archaeology is basically undergirded by four major dating methods. (There are various means, but they can fall into these classifications.) First is the historical method: actual written records supply human testimony to events and places. Second is the relative method supplied by typology and stratigraphy: younger cultures have lived on top of older cultures that were there before them. Third, archaeology has reference to certain geochronological constructs. The Alpine model, or the concept of the four Pleistocene ice ages, accommodates the entire Paleolithic [13]. And fourth is the method of radiocarbon dating, which supplies coherence and a measure of "proof" to the last stages of the model.

A Biblical creationist seeking to interpret archaeological data in a young-earth context will find it is possible to retain history and stratigraphy. He will, however, propose a different geochronological model, and re-evaluate radiocarbon ages, submitting all dates to the constraints and controls of a Biblical chronology, thus reaching a satisfying synthesis.

THE LOWER PALEOLITHIC

What, then, can we say about early evidences of human life and activity? Our creationist model does not make us think that every person born in the families of Ham, Shem, and Japheth stayed at home or settled nearby. Genesis 10, the Table of Nations, makes it quite clear that the families were rapidly dispersed; Genesis 11 tells us why. Towns, cities, kingdoms, nations, tribes, families, and lands are mentioned. We are led to predict that the evidence would show a population boom and a race towards new frontiers. If there were to be a creationist "Big Bang," this would be it. From one central point, men set out to colonize the earth.

The Lower Paleolithic of the Old Stone Age is represented by actual stone tools fashioned by human hands: African pebble tools, Western flint core bi-face and flake tools, and Eastern chopper-chopping tools. Many thousands of these have been excavated from open-air sites such as re-deposited gravel beds and deserts, and have been sorted into various tool-making traditions of standardized forms. Lacking organic material, they cannot be dated by ^{14}C methods, and so are placed into the standard prehistorical charts mainly by reference to the geochronological theories of glaciation imposed upon the particular glacial moraine, river terrace, or desert deposits involved. Therefore, we are justified in applying creationist interpretations of glaciation to this problem.

A CREATIONIST GLACIATION MODEL

If we envision gradual post-Flood glacial growth, and postulate a period of time with milder temperatures between the end of the Flood and the eventual development of a great ice sheet, we have what we need to explain the presence of the stone tools. Animals swiftly dispersed from the Ark. Shem, Ham, and Japheth, however, lingered and started their families. While some of the families stayed close to home, others did not. Intelligent, intrepid explorers fanned out from the nuclear area. As they migrated, they established campsites, made the tools they needed, and hunted and gathered their food.

We are indebted to Michael J. Oard for developing a model of the glacial epoch as a single post-Flood phenomenon. The Deluge, in Oard's model, terminated with a much warmer ocean, due to the volume of hot water added to the pre-Flood ocean from the eruptions of the "fountains of the great deep." Given an initially warm, uniform ocean temperature, the first century after the Flood would have been a century of mild but gradually cooling temperatures. Significant volcanic activity continued after the Flood, and volcanic dust and aerosols produced summer cooling over mid-and high-latitude continents. Oard suggests that the time to reach Ice-Age maximum was about 500 years, with a necessary melting time of only 100 years. (He does not say it must have melted that fast, but that it could have, and in some places did.) The range of ice depths is 500-840 meters for the Northern Hemisphere and 880-1850 meters for Antarctica. He presents evidence that a single, thinner, dynamic ice sheet that fluctuates widely at its margins can better explain the evidence than the conventional Alpine system of four ice ages with interglacial periods [21].

After a period of time of fairly moderate weather, those in northern Europe would have noticed that the animals they hunted were moving south, and it was getting colder. They would have moved south, too. An enormous sheet of ice was accumulating where they had been, and flowing a little under its weight, crushing, breaking, and plowing up everything on the surface, including their abandoned camp sites. Some rocks were ground to gravel, but hard tools of flint often remained whole. Debris and mud captured by the ice were either dropped where the ice melted, in "drift" or till, or carried off by melt water.

It is known that during and after the time of the glaciers in the higher latitudes, there was more rainfall in the lower latitudes than there is now. Even the deserts, including the Sahara, experienced pluviation, and maintained pluvial lakes and rivers for hundreds of years after the Genesis Flood. All the lakes and interior basins had higher water levels, and the world's rivers carried more water than today. So now, in the glacial gravels, or in river terrace gravels, or on the deserts, we find the stone tools that survived.

Due to the residual catastrophism of the post-Flood readjustments, with the coming of the glaciers, the weather became inclement, with cold temperatures, violent storms, and continued tectonic and volcanic activity. Storms tended to track parallel to the edge of the Laurentide ice sheet, and most moisture fell over the cold continents. Those who could find natural caves to move into, did so. Thus from the Middle Paleolithic we begin to find that generations of people called certain large and accommodating caves "home." The French Fontéchevade, and the Mount Carmel Kafzeh, are examples of stratified cave sites showing occupation by several generations. The bones of animals in the lowest layers are from animals that lived in a warm climate. Bones of animals that could stand cold weather, like the reindeer and the mammoth, are above them. The stone tool industries show a variety of mixtures of the different habits or traditions of tool-making. The caves seem to portray a variety of loosely-related cultures at about the same stage of development. [6]

GENESIS 11 SEPTUAGINT DATES

Although many scholars generally prefer the Masoretic text of the Old Testament, the Septuagint version of Genesis 11:10-19 may help us develop a more specific chronological picture of these events. Some Biblical creationist scholars have stated a preference for the Septuagint rendering of this passage, which is attested by the Samaritan Pentateuch, and used, it is thought, by New Testament authors. These scholars suspect a possible intentional corruption of the Masoretic chronology by later scribes to support apocryphal millennial theories. [9, pp. 57, 58] (It is most unfortunate that the Dead Sea Scrolls cannot help us here, for although the Septuagint, its Hebrew *Vorlage*, the proto-Masoretic, and the Samaritan Pentateuch are represented among them, chapter 11 of Genesis has not yet been identified among the fragments.) [22]

According to the Septuagint, Arphaxad was born to Shem two years after the Flood; we would expect that Cush was born to Ham soon after the Flood as well. When Arphaxad was 135 years old, Cainan was born to him. (Luke 3:36 agrees with the Septuagint in mentioning Cainan, whom the Masoretic text leaves out.) Cush likewise begat Nimrod; although we don't know just when, he was in the second generation. Nimrod could have been born as early as thirty years after the Flood, but in the Septuagint setting, 100 years after the Flood may be more consistent. When Cainan was 130 years old, Sala (or Salah) was born, now 267 years after the Flood. One hundred thirty years later, Eber (or Heber) was born, now 397 years after the Flood. Another 134 years later, Peleg (or Phaleg) was born, at 531 years after the Flood [23].

With a Hebrew sojourn in Egypt of 430 years, the data in the Septuagint place the end of the Flood at 3402 B.C., according to Dr. Robert H. Brown [8]. If we therefore postulate a date of 3402 B.C. for the Flood, then we have Peleg's birth, by the Septuagint chronology, in 2871 B.C.

In the quest for an absolute chronology, a preliminary, tentative, and suggestive harmonization model could put the Flood at about 3400 B.C. and the Babel episode at about 3275 ±50 B.C. (Nimrod may have come to what was left of Babel, or he may have started the colony there; Genesis is not conclusive.) If, say, Nimrod had been born 100 years after the Flood, a 3275 B.C. dispersion from Babel would have occurred when he was about 25 years old.

There may have been some pre-Babel migration away from the nuclear area by those who were willing to follow the Lord's will and re-settle the earth (Genesis 9:1), leaving only the rebellious to unite to prevent the dispersion. It seems unlikely that Noah or Shem participated in the Babel rebellion [17, pp. 267, 269]. In this model we would assume that families did not wait very long before they started migrating, because we presume they reached distant areas fairly soon. As will be discussed below, we will assume that a single supercontinent existed at this point (Pangaea). Nevertheless, it is a long way to South Africa. We can postulate that impenetrable jungles had not yet been re-established following the Flood, that the travelers followed animals, and that they used coastal and river routes.

HARMONIZATION CHRONOLOGY

We may therefore attempt a preliminary Biblical creationist chronology of early artifacts. We can assign some lower Paleolithic remains [2, 6, 7] to the first two centuries after the Flood when temperatures were moderate but cooling, generally keeping the relative stratigraphic and typological sequence into which they have been placed by archaeologists. Glaciation terminology is European. Standard uniformitarian dating, although not universally agreed on, is indicated in parentheses. The stratigraphic correlations of Dr. Bernard Northrup are included [20]. Our new proposed dates B.C. refer to the approximate inception of the industry in question, and are rounded, tentative, and relative:

EVENT	DATES B.C.
Disembarkation from Noah's Ark	3402
Arphaxad is born	3400
Post-Flood drainage, volcanic activity, pluviation	3400-3300
(Dr. Northrup: early Mesozoic winds, sand storms)	
First-Fourth Nile Terraces	3350-3280
(silting of Nile delta, and of Mesopotamian plain)	
Babel dispersion	3275
Cainan is born	3265
Pebble tools, choppers (south and east Africa)	3265
(potassium-argon 1.9-.5 million years BP)	
Abbevillian (Chellean) handaxe industry, Europe	3260
(Mindel glaciation: 475-435 thousand years BP)	
Fifth Nile Terrace, Abbevillian types	3255
Early Acheulian handaxe, Torralba & Ambrona, Spain	3250
(Late Mindel glaciation)	
Clactonian pebbles, choppers, flakes, No. Europe, England	3245
(Mindel-Riss interglacial: 435-230,000 BP)	
Middle Acheulian handaxe industry	3235
(Riss glaciation: 230-187,000 BP)	
Tayacian, Fontéchevade, France (similar to Clactonian)	3225
(Riss-Würm interglacial: 187-70,000 BP)	
Late Acheulian handaxe industry	3220
(Late Riss-Würm interglacial)	
Tayacian coarse flake tools, Mount Carmel	3220
(First cave deposits, France and Palestine)	
Sixth Nile Terrace (Acheulian flint)	3220
Jabrudian industry, Syria, Middle East	3220
(contemporary with Late Acheulian)	
Amudian blade and burin industry, Levant	3220
(coeval with Late Acheulian; pre-Aurignacian)	

As we approach the beginnings of written history our chronology will need to include traditional dates based, accurately or not, on written records as interpreted by archaeologists, in addition to the industries and archaeological sites for which the only dating is supplied by relating them to each other and to an assumed Alpine glacial scenario. This results in a model where we see tremendous differences in contemporaneous cultures that are developing in different geographical areas. This is not, of course, unlike what we observe even today around the world.

The inclusion of historically-based dating, as with the inclusion of the Septuagint chronology, can give us a series of controls to help in assigning prehistoric cultures to appropriate time-slots in the geochronologic picture. For example, the Mesolithic assemblages at Fayum and Merimde in Egypt, being pre-dynastic, give us a good point of tie-in between Mesolithic industries and the founding of the First Dynasty. Many Egyptologists put that at around 3100 B.C. [3] However, a number of researchers have disputed this date for good reasons [16; 17, p. 558; 27, pp. 178, 181]. As will be explained shortly, radiocarbon considerations will cause us to want to place the First Dynasty several centuries later.

Climatological notes and pollen zones in the list refer to Europe. Some Greenland Ice-core Project (GRIP) methane peaks and minima are indicated (dated by oxygen isotope) [25]. Now the developing ice sheet enters a more advanced stage:

EVENT	DATES B.C.
Levalloisian core-tool technique begins	3210
(extends through to Mousterian)	
Mousterian flint industry, Eurasia, No. Africa, Levant	3205
Neandertal (Riss through Würm, 70-32,000 BP)	
Seventh and Eighth (lowest) Nile terraces, Egypt	3200
Levalloisian-Mousterian paleoliths	
Châtelperronian (Périgordian) SW, central France	3175
(35-31,000 BP, Upper Paleolithic)	
Aurignacian flint industry, France to Palestine	3167
(pre-31,000 BP)	
Gravettian (Pèrigordian), France to Cent. Eur., Russia	3150
(28,000-20,000 BP)	
Invention of pictographic writing in Mesopotamia	3150
Sala is born	3135
Egyptian First Dynasty founded (traditional date)	3100
Solutrean, France and Spain	3058
(19,000-17,000 BP)	
Magdalenian, W. Europe and England	3015
(Würm Glaciation, 17,000-12,000 BP)	
cave art; bears, rhinoceros, mammoths	
Heber is born	3005
Lascaux, France cave painting (15,500 ± 900 BP)	2975
Oldest Dryas, pollen zone Ia; tundra, reindeer	2960
(Late Glacial, 15,000-12,500 BP)	
GLACIAL MAXIMUM REACHED	2900
GRIP methane low (12,700 BP)	2891
Peleg is born	2871

A CREATIONIST MODEL OF CONTINENTAL SEPARATION

Some creationists have proposed that continental separation occurred during the Flood, under water. They note the amazing similarity of sedimentary strata in the northeastern United States compared to those of Britain (Carboniferous coal strata and Devonian red sandstones) and the absence of these in the North Atlantic. The presence of such similar sedimentary strata seems to preclude a pre-Flood continental split. The Flood could provide a driving force to break the lithosphere into moving plates; for a short time they could overcome the viscous drag of the earth's mantle [18, 27]. A subduction of the pre-Flood ocean lithosphere during the Flood could explain the absence of Precambrian and Cambrian strata [4]. However, the lack of sedimentary Paleozoic and Mesozoic strata as well, in the bottom of the earth's great ocean basins, may indicate that the present basins with passive margins were formed after the Flood. It is worth exploring the idea that the rupture and subsequent movement of the twenty-mile-thick continental granitic crust, and the formation of most of the present ocean basins, took place after the Flood.

Dr. Northrup has discussed geological reports describing crustal movement in the Paleozoic, which he interprets as during the Flood. This expansion of the sea basins to hold the Flood runoff, is also viewed as the initiation of continental separation. The brief crustal movement quieted, only to begin again in earnest in the later Mesozoic, which he interprets as about five generations after the Flood. This is perhaps the Caledonian orogeny [19].

As the icecaps built after the Flood, the Poles became depressed by the weight of the ice. Dr. Melvin A. Cook, at the First International Conference on Creationism, presented a detailed treatment of the rupture and shifting of Pangaea due to overgrown ice caps resting in deep bowl-shaped depressions on the Poles. [12] One generally-accepted model of Pangaea puts Greenland in the Arctic Basin. Dr. Cook feels the maximum ice load was inside the boundaries of Greenland, and the primary brittle fracturing of the continental granite crust began there. A secondary fracture occurred under the southern ice cap by the combined effects of ice weight and seismicity. Ice drove into the primary crack fracture from north to south. Dr. Cook explains:

> While not considered quantitatively, the time required for most of continental drift was months or years, not megayears, based on the magnitude of the forces applied and terrestrial rheidity. Thus 'shift' is a better description than 'drift.' The splitting 'load' that initiated the breakup of Pangaea was in excess of 10^{13} tons based on at least 2000 feet average depth of the northern (ice cap) depression zone (not considering the elastic component) and a diameter of about 3000 miles. The forces responsible for continental drift were one or two orders of magnitude greater, telescoping thusly by ice driving into the fracture zones following the initiation of crack fracturing. [12, p. 70].

Sea water is very difficult to freeze and Michael Oard feels that even at the Poles the ocean would have remained ice-free until near glacial maximum, 500 years after the Flood [21, p. 165]. The idea, therefore, that with the collapse of the vapor canopy at the start of the Flood, an open Arctic Ocean would have immediately frozen over, is probably baseless. It is further negated by the proposition that juvenile or tectonic water released by the fountains of the great deep would have been hot, perhaps even 200°C. Dr. Cook's model of the rupture of Pangaea requires a thick buildup of ice over Greenland and Antarctica. One could adduce reasons explaining how this could happen during the Flood; but with at least a thousand feet of Flood water on top of Greenland, it is difficult to start freezing the North Pole then. The 2,000-foot icecap that Dr. Cook needs, seems to fit better with Michael Oard's proposal of a post-Flood glaciation.

GEOLOGICAL RESULTS OF THE DIVISION OF THE EARTH

The northeastern coast of Pangaea (which became the coast of Siberia) situated by the warm ocean, with much greater precipitation and more vegetation than at present, would have provided a good environment for cold-tolerant animals as the glaciation built up. After glacial maximum, the northern climate became colder and drier. Following the rupture of Pangaea, as Greenland moved out of the Arctic Basin, the open sea would have moved into the abyssal plain at the North Pole. Soon the new Arctic and Atlantic Oceans would have frozen over (see Job 38:30). Very strong cold fronts, with strong winds giving very cold wind chills, could have occurred. Some of the woolly mammoths near the coast of Siberia may have been quick-frozen at this time and entombed in the developing permafrost [21, p. 165]. Such strong, cold winds could perhaps have freeze-dried whatever Siberian and Canadian Arctic forests had been re-established since the Flood, desiccating the timbers and burying them in sand.

The opening of the Atlantic Basin involved hinging over the whole Aleutian Arc, a 41° dextral rotation, and a 600 mile translation of North America relative to Eurasia. Powerful seismic waves split off Australia from Antarctica perpendicular to the north-south fracture [12, pp. 73,78].

Dr. Cook proposes that ice driving into the primary crack fracture brought into effect the powerful Coriolis forces, oppositely directed rotations causing the Tethys Shear Zone: 4,000-mile fracture ridges from Mount Ararat (and the Atlas Mountains) to Panama. Later this zone was apparently rejoined by welding due to collisions when Africa drove into Eurasia. The initial stage of this collision built the Alps, Balkans, and Carpatheans. Arabia was squeezed between Africa and Asia in the continental shifting to build the Taurus, Ararat, Caucasus, and Zagros mountains. The collision of Africa with Eurasia and the squeezing of Arabia between them caused the Great African Rift Valley. Still later, when India collided with Asia to form the Himalayas, the initial 41° rotation was driven back about 6°. The weld between Africa, the Tethys Shear Zone, and Europe was broken, and the zone again separated from between Laurasia and Gondwanaland. The Earth Girdling Rift and Ridges (EGRR) occurred after both the rupture of Pangaea and its shifts, mainly following a path predetermined by compressions locked in by shock and plastic wave distortions, or in some places by prefractures [12].

SYNTHESIS OF MODELS

In this synthesis of the two models of Michael Oard and Dr. Cook, we consider that the single, rapid post-Flood Ice Age that Michael Oard proposes is the causative mechanism for the Pangaea rupture and shift that Dr. Cook proposes. However, the catastrophic events of continental division, violent mountain uplift, and vast volcanism with explosions of steam and volcanic ash, would have delayed the melting of the ice sheets. Thus the Pangaea geologic events are both preceded and followed by the Ice Age. They begin soon after the time of Ice-Age maximum, which is about 500 years after the Flood, by Oard. Interestingly, this corresponds closely to the Septuagint date of the birth of Peleg, soon after which, Genesis 10:25 and I Chronicles 1:19 tell us, "the earth was divided."

The concept of a supercontinent existing for five hundred years between the Flood and this point, gives us an opportunity to consider some Ice-Age, pre-rupture colonizing of the Americas from Europe and Africa, as there was no Atlantic Ocean to stop them. We can also consider some American colonizing after the continental shifting but during the continued Ice Age, across the Bering Strait in the time of low sea level. One single, united land mass also makes other animal and human migration easier to understand.

Returning, then, to our archaeological scenario, based on a date of c. 3400 B.C. for the Flood, we have glacial maximum reached about 2900 B.C. and Peleg being born around 2870 B.C. In the time period of 2850 ±25 B.C. we can then logically place the rupture of Pangaea, the continental shifting, continental collisions, and then the formation of the EGRR. In the period of major adjustment that follows, we find Job trying to understand Divine providence.

POLAR UPLIFT

Dr. Cook refers to work done on the global correlation of uplifts at the poles and downwarping at the equator following sudden denudation in the loss of a great ice cap [12, p. 79]. "In other words, with Canada separated from Greenland and in turn from Fennoscandia, an ice cap of appreciable depth would simply flow down hill into the Atlantic Ocean" [12, p. 69]. "The initially rapid uplifts in Fennoscandia, at first immediate to relieve the elastic component of the total depressions, ...have decayed exponentially since their beginning in a manner characteristic of sudden unloading of the crust and in no possible way related to the melting of the ice cap in place." A mathematical analysis he refers to, based on classical physics, dates the beginning of the uplifts to 2550 B.C. [12, p. 80].

We note from the Septuagint that Peleg lived a total of 339 years, from 531 to 870 years after the Flood. Returning to our postulated date of 3402 B.C. for the Flood, Peleg's lifespan would then have been from 2871 to 2532 B.C. The Bible indicates that "in his days" the earth was divided. Polar uplifts at 2550 B.C., dramatically ending the Ice Age, therefore fit comfortably into this Biblical chronology.

A French analysis of historic evidence from Egypt concludes that there was somewhat more moisture than modernly all the way into historic times, especially closer to the Mediterranean, and the contemporary condition of aridity did not set in until after 2500 B.C. [15]

Our model indicates that at the time of Ice Age maximum, adaptable people living in caves began inventing stone tools to make tools. They made various specialized blade tools, weapons, and articles of other materials, such as bone and antler, which they decorated. Art began in the Magdalenian in terms of figurines, carvings, and cave paintings. As some organic material has survived, there is the possibility of using ^{14}C tests to attempt some age determinations on these man-made artifacts.

CHRONOLOGY BY CARBON-14 AGE CONVERSION

As we consider these early organic remains, we again encounter assigned dates which to the Biblical creationist are unacceptably expanded. However, we realize that these dates are based on interpretations of ^{14}C tests, which we may legitimately question, and in fact re-work, based on our creationist assumptions. Robert Whitelaw wrote an article reviewing 32 radiocarbon papers published from 1950 to 1990. He documents how creationists have grappled with the problem of establishing a method of quantitatively reconciling radiometric dates with creationist models [28]. Most of the creationists who have worked on this are happy with a traditional Biblical date for the Flood, using a non-equilibrium method of conversion.

A mathematical conversion of radiocarbon dates has been provided by Dr. Robert H. Brown, who presented papers in the First and Second International Conferences on Creationism. He has derived a conversion formula by which a ^{14}C age may be translated into a real-time equivalent that is consistent with the chronological data given in the Bible and also with ^{14}C age data for historic events [10].

A real-time equivalent age obtained by a mathematical conversion from a ^{14}C date carries uncertainty, both from the statistical uncertainty of the initial ^{14}C determination, and also from uncertainty due to fluctuations of the biosphere ^{14}C concentration about the average concentration trend. The scenarios presented by Michael Oard and Melvin Cook, with drastic ocean and atmosphere temperature changes and global post-Flood land movements, could provide fluctuations of ^{14}C activity from a smooth exponential trend. There are difficulties in assuming that all factors influencing the level of ^{14}C in the biosphere after the Flood can be satisfactorily represented by a first-order exponential function. A simplified mathematical representation may not adequately represent the concentration at all points over the time range. Consequently, real-time conversions obtained from ^{14}C ages by a mathematical formula covering an extended time range are useful only for establishing broad features of time relationship, and in some cases may be anomalous. To fit this model, it appears that a steep slope must be maintained for a longer period of time than a smooth exponential trend set to begin at the end of the Flood would generally yield.

In Dr. Brown's judgment, the most suitable value for the date of the Flood is about 5,350 years before present, as measured from 1950, so 3400 B.C. He has found that amino acid racemization/epimerization rate constants for ^{14}C dated material are more consistent when computed with real-time age equivalents based on 5350 BP than on values a few hundred years less or greater. As much coal centers around a radiocarbon age of about 43,000 years, he associates the Flood with that value [10]. He feels that at the beginning of the Flood the biosphere had no more than about 1/100 of the present ^{14}C/^{12}C ratio. [9, p. 59]

According to his conversion, over the first ten years after the end of major Flood activity, radiocarbon age characteristics drop to about 34,000 years. By fifty years after the Flood a representative ^{14}C age is about 23,000 years. At 3050 B.C., the radiometric age is about 10,000 years before present, having decreased about 33,000 years in only 350 real-time years. This decrease represents a rapid buildup of the ^{14}C/^{12}C ratio in the biosphere during the post-Flood era. Applications of this conversion formula to a frozen musk ox, and ground sloth dung accumulation rates, demonstrate that the very steep initial slope of his equation is essentially correct [10] (See figure 1).

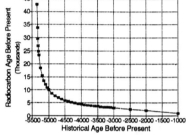

Figure 1. *Plot of real time versus radiocarbon time from equation 1.*

What factors could contribute to such a rapid buildup of the carbon-14 concentration? A higher snow accumulation rate in the past could mean that the ice-core tests in Greenland are showing us a higher rate of ^{14}C production then [14]. A major decrease in geomagnetic field strength during the Flood, with post-Flood geomagnetic reversals and subsequent fluctuations before field strength recovery, could have encouraged that higher rate of production. Furthermore, if antediluvian atmospheric CO_2 were approximately 16 times greater than at present, decreasing after the Flood through a transitional period to the present value [26], an initially dilute amount of ^{14}C would have increased in concentration relative to the decreasing amount of atmospheric carbon dioxide. CO_2 solubility increases with lower water temperature, so at the conclusion of the Flood, if the ocean water temperature were high, atmospheric CO_2 would not be as soluble as at present in the surface water. As the oceans cooled, and vegetation was reestablished, the amount of atmospheric CO_2 would be reduced. Later, during the period of colder, dryer northern air (less precipitation) in an Ice Age climate, there would be a decrease in the rate of transfer of eroded material from northern land masses into the ocean; transfer of ^{14}C to inactive sediment would decrease. The rate at which CO_2 was taken out of the atmosphere by vegetation in mid- to high-latitudes would be depressed. We could also conjecture that due to the long half-life of radiocarbon (5,730 years) which compares with the length of our chronology (nearly 5,400 years since the flood), destruction of post-Flood ^{14}C by simple radioactive decay might not noticeably impact the ^{14}C inventory for some time following the Flood, during which period the rate of accumulation would be significantly higher. These altered production, mixing, exchange, and transfer rates provide support for a rapid post-Flood buildup of the ^{14}C/^{12}C concentration, reflected in a steep slope for our exponential equation that continues through the Ice Age.

Using Dr. Brown's equation as a basis, we can proceed to make some very useful inferences. With a trial setting of radiocarbon ages being 5% older than historical ages at 4000 BP, an initial fraction of equilibrium of .011, and placing the Flood at 5350 BP, his equation is as follows [10]:

$$R_k = T_k + 8.3\{\ln[1 - 0.989e^{-2.211(5.35-T_k)}](-1)\} \tag{1}$$

where:

R_k = radiocarbon age in thousands of years
T_k = historical age in thousands of years

It yields the following results for these sample assemblages:

Lascaux Cave, France (15,500 BP ±900 BP)	5200 BP or 3250 B.C.
Zawi Chemi Shanidar (10,850 ±300 BP)	5040 BP or 3090 B.C.
Hacilar, Turkey (7,450 BP)	4770 BP or 2820 B.C.
Fayum, Egypt, pre-dynastic (6390 ±180 BP)	4610 BP or 2660 B.C.

It appears that we need a steeper slope for the lower range. An initial equilibrium fraction of .017, a setting of radiocarbon ages being 5% older than real ages at 3156 BP, and setting the equation to run from 5132 BP, yield values for these assemblages which fit this model rather well. These values have the effect of depressing the equation in order to obtain a steep slope after the Pangaea break-up. (These values in the equation also yielded the above-quoted dates B.C. in the chart, from the Châtelperronian at 35,000 radiocarbon years BP to the cave at Lascaux, France at 15,500 years BP.)

$$R_k = T_k + 8.3\{\ln[1 - 0.983e^{-1.5106(5.132-T_k)}](-1)\} \tag{2}$$

THE CHALLENGE OF DENDROCHRONOLOGY

One really serious objection to a Flood date of 3000 ±500 B.C. seems to come from the field of dendrochronology. Dr. Gerald E. Aardsma vigorously contests this date. Because of purportedly extant continuous tree-ring series containing up to 11,300 growth rings, he feels we should look at the possibility of the Flood occurring more than 10,000 years ago [1].

In the 15 years following the production of the first dendrochronological calibration curve, a bewildering number of calibration curves appeared together with statistical interpretations and compilations of the curves. Of all these, in 1990 the international radiocarbon community was recommending the 1986 curves produced by Gordon Pearson and Minze Stuiver, for the period back to 2500 B.C. This is because two high-precision laboratories, Belfast and Seattle, using different radiocarbon techniques and different tree species, had independently produced curves in agreement to within a few years for each sample of corresponding twenty tree rings. Curves extending back beyond 2500 B.C. had been produced, but lacked verification by a second laboratory [5].

Considering the claimed longer tree-ring series, we should give particular consideration to possible mismatching by dendrochronologists in an effort to accommodate uniformitarian chronological views. Ring-patterns used to compare rings from living trees to older fallen logs, and from one log to another, have a certain statistical probability of being correctly matched, but are not perfect matches because they come from different trees. As Dr. Robert Brown observes:

"A Biblical creationist developing a master dendrochronology would look for justifiable large overlaps between specimens, as a uniformitarian scientist with respect for the views of fellow scientists in other disciplines would look for minimal overlaps to develop a master chronology that would be least objectionable in professional circles" [11].

Biblical creationists also propose that unusual climatic conditions following the Flood gave rise to multiple ring growth per year in the tree-ring series, with the average number of growth rings per year decreasing after the end of the Ice Age. An atmospheric CO_2 level significantly higher than we find at present would have profound implications for the biomass accumulation rate of trees [25]. Even now, a tree under stress from drought or frost is quite capable of producing multiple ring-growth, as Dr. Walter Lammerts demonstrated experimentally in 1983 with bristlecone pine seedlings [27]. The model that we are proposing here protracts the unusual climatic conditions by nine centuries after the Flood--in fact, the earth does not really normalize and stabilize until after the polar uplift near the end of Peleg's lifespan. The polar uplift date of 2550 B.C., dramatically dumping the remaining ice-caps into the ocean, and ending the Ice Age as such, coincides remarkably well with the date of the end of the high-precision calibration curve, 2500 B.C. (as of 1986). It also roughly coincides with the establishment of our oldest bristlecone pine trees. The climatological considerations of our model could lead us to predict a number of multiple growth rings per year, with local variations, from trees growing between 3400 and 2500 B.C. (compared to wider, single-year rings in fossil pre-Flood specimens); and then a trend towards normalization of the growth patterns, reaching stability, as today, after 2500 B.C. This, combined with potential mismatches, would explain the existence of long tree-ring series.

A radiocarbon test run on material from the Egyptian tombs of Sneferu and Zoser (Djoser) gave a weighted average only 2% too old at 2650 B.C., compared to a theoretical calculated age [13]. If radiocarbon dates normalized before the trees did, it is clear why the dendrochronology series shows the radiocarbon dates as too recent in that period.

THE UPPER PALEOLITHIC AND MESOLITHIC

So it seems that, with the help of our conversion equation, we can continue assigning Upper Paleolithic and Mesolithic archaeological discoveries to this next period of time. Four-digit accuracy is not claimed but is indicated at times merely to indicate sequence:

EVENT	DATES B.C.
Peleg born; Pangaea ruptures	2871
(Dr. Northrup: late Mesozoic) [20]	
Ice drives into cracks, north to south	2870
Greenland moves out of Arctic basin; open sea moves in	2868
Late Magdalenean pollen zone Ib; park tundra, warmer	2865
(Bølling Oscillation, 12,500-12,100 BP)	
Antarctica separates from Africa and South America	2865
Australia marches north toward southeast Asia	2863
Arctic & North Atlantic Oceans freeze	2860
(Siberian coastal mammoths freeze)	
Older Dryas, pollen zone Ic; tundra, reindeer, subarctic	2855
(Late Glacial, 12,100-11,900 BP)	
Tethys Shear Zone, transverse to main crack fracture	2850
circum-global equatorial current warming	
Glacial ice begins melting (11,900 BP)	2850
(Dr. Northrup: begin Cenozoic...?) [20]	
Azilian, SW France, No. Spain, warmer	2850
(Allerød Oscillation, 11,900-10,900 BP)	
pollen zone II; park tundra to birch forest;	
giant Irish deer, elk, beaver, bear	
GRIP methane rise (11,550 BP)	2842
Africa drives into Eurasia, re-welds Tethys Shear Zone	2835
Alps, Balkans, Carpatheans built	
Arabia squeezed--Taurus, Ararat, Caucasus, Zagros built	2832
India drives into Asia, forms Himalayas,	2828
Tethys welds re-broken; 6º reverse rotation	
Younger Dryas, pollen zone III; sub-arctic, tundra to	2825
park tundra; reindeer, bison, alpine hare	
(10,900-10,300 BP)	
Zawi Chemi Shanidar, Northern Iraq; domesticated sheep	2824
(10,850 ±300 BP)	
Early Dynastic Mesopotamia	2815
Mehi, Baluchistan, Indus area in India	2815
Earth-Girdling Rift and Ridges open; ocean crust melting	2810
magnetic anomalies forming (polarity reversals)	
Pre-Boreal, pollen zone IV; birch forest,	2810
wild horse, reindeer, bison, aurochs, elk. Slow	
rise in temperature. (10,300-9700 BP)	
Maglemosian microlithic wood-working tools, No. Europe	2800
Mesolithic (9,950 BP)	

LATE MESOLITHIC, NEOLITHIC, CHALCOLITHIC

After about 10,000 radiocarbon years BP, again to retain a steeper slope of the curve, the equation needs to be re-set to yield values that are in accord with this model. Apparently the slope really doesn't start to level out until after 6,000 radiocarbon years BP. For converting radiocarbon years from ten to six thousand BP, the equilibrium fraction of .017 is retained, but the equation is re-set to run from 4770 BP with a 5% difference at 4672 BP.

$$R_k = T_k + 8.3\{\ln[1 - 0.983e^{-30.5(4.77-Tk)}](-1)\} \tag{3}$$

EVENT	DATES B.C.
Boreal, pollen zones V & VI; rising temperature, pine/birch forest to pine/hazel, start of mixed oak forest; aurochs, elk, deer, wild pig, beaver, bear, dog (9700-7500 BP)	2795
Natufian, Levant Late Mesolithic (9700-9500 BP)	2795
Lauricocha Caves, at 13,000 feet in Peruvian Andes (9450 BP)	2793
Old Cordilleran Culture, Oregon & Washington in USA (8950 BP)	2790
Jericho; Jarmo, Iraq Pre-pottery Neolithic (8700±200 BP)	2789
Nea Nikomedeia, Macedonia; ground stone axes, pottery Early Neolithic (8200±150 BP)	2785
Ayampitín, Argentina (7950 BP)	2783
Sarab, Iranian Kurdistan (7950 BP)	2783
Hassuna, Iraq (7550±250 BP)	2780
Atlantic, pollen zone VII, warm, moist; oak, elm, lime, alder; aurochs, deer, dog (7500-5000 BP)	2780
Hac1lar, Turkey; pottery (7450 BP)	2779
Fayum and Merimde Mesolithic, Egypt (6390±180 BP)	2765
Sub-Boreal, pollen zone VIII, drier; introduction of cereals and weeds of cultivation. Oak forest, grasses, heather; tame horse, deer, wild pigs, domesticated sheep, goat, ox, pig,dog (5000-2500 BP)	2755
Egyptian Pre-Dynastic Cultures: Tasian, Badarian, Amratian, Gerzean, Semainean; earliest picture of a sail	2745
First Dynasty, Egypt	2720
Egyptian trading vessels ply the Red Sea, E. Mediterranean	2640
Pharaoh Djoser (Zoser), Third Dynasty, (Traditional date) step pyramid, Sakkara	2630
Icecaps slip off Scandinavia and Canada	2555
Polar depression uplifts, equatorial downwarping	2550
Higher sea level	2550
Death of Peleg	2532

Rather than taking Dr. Brown's equation down in three discrete steps, we could obtain a fairly good fit to the data points presented in the above tables, between the radiometric ages 30,000 and 6,000 BP with

$$R = 43,000 \{1 - 1.300e^{-0.062[T/(5350 - T)]}\} \qquad (4)$$

where:

R = radiocarbon age
T = historical age

which places Fayum at 2716 B.C. (and therefore the First Dynasty somewhat later). [11] This relationship does not resort to any model for justification of the values of the constants, except for the Flood date. It is only useful where $R > 6000$, and functions badly in the $R = 0$, $T = 0$ region.

Figure 2. *Plot of real time versus radiocarbon time from equation 4.*

A better fit in this region would require second-order terms in T/(5350 - T) [11]. The model significance for such terms, if any, would need to be explored.

CONCLUSION

The attempt to integrate the creationist model of origins with the modern discipline of archaeology is a necessary and important goal. Indeed, a general, systematized model, incorporating a radical revision of the chronology of the ancient world, would unite ancient earth history, prehistory, and recorded history in one continuous and understandable sequence. It could resolve many problems that still beset the honest investigator, correlate with other dating methods such as oxygen isotope, and open new areas of research. It would be interesting to develop a computer simulation based on this scenario. Many inferences from the model presented here should prove to be testable.

The diastrophic history of the earth is not a matter of opinion. Our planet, however inscrutable the evidence, has only followed one course of development through time. Likewise, human cultural development only happened once; but it is remarkable how many imaginative but confusing interpretations have been generated in the search for that one elusive course (due in part to the complexity and fragmentary nature of the available evidence). Confusion, mixed with the apparent inability of a brief timescale to adequately encompass the scope and range of the evidence, led past thinkers to the point where a naturalistic explanation attained the place of cultural dominance. However, this paper has demonstrated that it is theoretically possible to interpret archaeological prehistory in a young-earth context. We do seem to be on the right track, and getting closer in our search for a satisfactory Biblical creationist perspective on earth history and the data base of archaeology. From this presentation perhaps others will think it a worthy goal to pursue and refine. "...God...will have all men...to come unto the knowledge of the truth." (I Timothy 2:3,4)

ACKNOWLEDGMENTS

I greatly appreciate the helpful and supportive correspondence with Dr. Robert H. Brown.

REFERENCES

[1]   G.E. Aardsma, **Tree-Ring Dating and Multiple Ring Growth per Year**, <u>Creation Research Society Quarterly</u>, 29 (1993) 187-189.

[2]   W.F. Albright, <u>The Archaeology of Palestine</u>, 1949, Richard Clay & Co., Ltd., London. Reprinted 1961), Chapter 3.

[3]   C. Aldred, <u>Akhenaten, King of Egypt</u>, 1988, Thames and Hudson, Ltd., London, 1991 ed., p. 10.

[4]   J.R. Baumgardner, **3-D Finite Element Simulation of the Global Tectonic Changes Accompanying Noah's Flood**, <u>Proceedings of the Second International Conference on Creationism</u>, R.E. Walsh, et al, Editors, 1990, Creation Science Fellowship, Inc., Pittsburgh, PA, Vol. II, p. 36.

[5]   S. Bowman, <u>Radiocarbon Dating</u>, 1990, British Museum Publications Ltd., London, pp. 45, 46, 58, 61.

[6]   R.J. Braidwood, <u>Prehistoric Men</u>, 1963, Chicago Natural History Museum, Chicago, 6th ed., pp.43-52, 68.

[7]   W. Bray, & D. Trump. The Penguin Dictionary of Archaeology, 1972, Penguin Books, Ltd., Harmondsworth, Middlesex.

[8]   R.H. Brown, **Scientific Creationism and Radiocarbon Dating**, Proceedings of the Second International Conference on Creationism, R.E. Walsh, et al, Editors, 1990, Creation Science Fellowship, Inc., Pittsburgh, PA, Vol. I, p. 45.

[9]   R.H. Brown, **Correlation of C-14 Age with the Biblical Time Scale**, Origins, 17:2 (1992).

[10] R.H. Brown, **Correlation of C-14 Age with Real Time**, Creation Research Society Quarterly, 29, (1992) 46.

[11] R.H. Brown, Personal correspondence with the author, 1993.

[12] M.A. Cook, **How and When "Pangaea" Ruptured and the Continents Shifted**, Proceedings of the First International Conference on Creationism, R.E. Walsh, et al, Editors, 1987, Creation Science Fellowship, Inc., Pittsburgh, PA, Vol. II, p. 69-87.

[13] D. Glynn, **The Origins and Growth of Archaeology**, 1968, Thomas R. Crowell Co., New York, pp. 257, 265.

[14] D.R. Humphreys, **Comment**, Proceedings of the Second International Conference on Creationism, R.E. Walsh, et al, Editors, 1990, Creation Science Fellowship, Inc., Pittsburgh, PA, Vol. I, p. 12.

[15] S.A. Huzzayin, **The Place of Egypt in Prehistory**, Memoires prèsentès al'Institut d'Egypte, XLIII (1941).

[16] P. James, et al. Centuries of Darkness, 1993, Rutgers Univ. Press, New Brunswick, N.J., Chap. 10.

[17] H.M. Morris, The Genesis Record, 1976, Baker Book House, Grand Rapids, MI, pp. 267, 269, 558.

[18] S.E. Nevins, **Continental Drift, Plate Tectonics, and the Bible**, ICR Impact Series, No. 32 (1976) p. iii.

[19] B.E. Northrup, **Identifying the Noahic Flood in Historical Geology, Part One**, Proceedings of the Second International Conference on Creationism, R.E. Walsh, et al, Editors, 1990, Creation Science Fellowship, Inc., Pittsburgh, PA, Vol. I, p. 178.

[20] B.E. Northrup, **Identifying the Noahic Flood in Historical Geology, Part Two**, Proceedings of the Second International Conference on Creationism, R.E. Walsh, et al, Editors, 1990, Creation Science Fellowship, Inc., Pittsburgh, PA, Vol. I, p. 182,183.

[21] M.J. Oard, **An Ice Age Within the Biblical Time Frame**, Proceedings of the First International Conference on Creationism, R.E. Walsh, et al, Editors, 1987, Creation Science Fellowship, Inc., Pittsburgh, PA, Vol. II, p. 157, 161,165.

[22] H. Scanlin, The Dead Sea Scrolls and Modern Translations of the Old Testament, 1993, Tyndale House, Wheaton, IL, p. 141.

[23] The Septuagint. 1970. Zondervan, Genesis 11:10-16, p. 13.

[24] Shoemaker, Michael. **International Symposium Charts the Future of Biblical Archaeology** Biblical Archaeology Review 19:3 (1993) 20.

[25] F.A. Street-Perrott, **Ancient Tropical Methane**, Nature, 366 (1993) 412.

[26] B.J. Taylor, **Carbon Dioxide in the Antediluvian Atmosphere**, Creation Research Society Quarterly, 30 (1994) 193-197.

[27] R.L. Whitelaw, **The Fountains of the Great Deep and the Windows of Heaven**, Proceedings, National Creation Conference, ,1983, Minneapolis, MN, pp. 95-104.

[28] R.L. Whitelaw, **Radiocarbon Dating After Forty Years: Do Creationists See It as Supporting the Biblical Creation and Flood?**, Creation Research Society Quarterly) 29 (1993) 170-183.